Great Events from History

The Ancient World

Prehistory - 476 C.E.

Great Events from History

The Ancient World

Prehistory - 476 C.E.

Volume 1

c. 25,000 B.C.E. - 312 B.C.E.

Editor

Mark W. Chavalas

University of Wisconsin-La Crosse

Consulting Editors

Mark S. Aldenderfer, *University of California, Santa Barbara*

Carole A. Barrett, *University of Mary*

Jeffrey W. Dippmann, *Central Washington University*

Christopher Ehret, *University of California, Los Angeles*

Katherine Anne Harper, *Loyola Marymount University*

SALEM PRESS

Pasadena, California Hackensack, New Jersey

Editor in Chief: Dawn P. Dawson
Editorial Director: Christina J. Moose
Project Editor: Rowena Wildin
Copy Editor: Leslie Ellen Jones
Assistant Editor: Andrea E. Miller
Editorial Assistant: Dana Garey
Photograph Editor: Philip Bader
Acquisitions Editor: Mark Rehn
Research Supervisor: Jeffry Jensen
Research Assistant: Desiree Dreeuws
Production Editor: Cynthia Beres
Graphics and Design: James Hutson
Layout: William Zimmerman

Cover photos: Library of Congress

∞ The paper used in these volumes conforms to the American National Standard for Permanence of Paper for Printed Library Materials, Z39.48-1992 (R1997).

Some of the essays in this work originally appeared in the following Salem Press sets: *Great Events from History* (1972-1980, edited by Frank N. Magill), *Chronology of European History: 15,000 B.C. to 1997* (1997, edited by John Powell; associate editors, E. G. Weltin, José M. Sánchez, Thomas P. Neill, and Edward P. Keleher), and *Great Events from History: North American Series, Revised Edition* (1997, edited by Frank N. Magill; associate editor, John L. Loos).

Library of Congress Cataloging-in-Publication Data

Great events from history. The ancient world, prehistory-476 C.E. / editor, Mark W. Chavalas ; consulting editors, Mark S. Aldenderfer . . . [et al.].

p. cm.

Some essays previously published in Great events from history (1972-1980), Chronology of European history, 15,000 B.C. to 1997 (1997), and Great events from history, North American series (1997).

Includes bibliographical references and indexes.

ISBN 1-58765-155-6 (set : alk. paper) — ISBN 1-58765-156-4 (v. 1 : alk. paper) — ISBN 1-58765-157-2 (v. 2 : alk. paper)

1. History, Ancient. I. Title: Ancient world, prehistory-476 C.E. II. Chavalas, Mark W. (Mark William), 1954- III. Aldenderfer, Mark S.

D65.G74 2004

930—dc22

2004001360

First Printing

PRINTED IN THE UNITED STATES OF AMERICA

Contents

25,000 - 10,001 B.C.E.

10,000 - 5001 B.C.E.

5000 - 3001 B.C.E.

3000 - 2001 B.C.E.

2000 - 1501 B.C.E.

1500 - 1001 B.C.E.

1000 - 801 B.C.E.

800 - 701 B.C.E.

700 - 601 B.C.E.

600 - 501 B.C.E.

500 - 401 B.C.E.

400 - 301 B.C.E.

PUBLISHER'S NOTE

Great Events from History is a multivolume series projected to cover from prehistory to the twenty-first century. It is a revision and expansion of the twelve-volume *Great Events from History* (1972-1980) set and also incorporates essays from the three-volume *Chronology of European History: 15,000 B.C. to 1997* (1997) and the three-volume *Great Events from History: North American Series, Revised Edition* (1997). The existing essays are enhanced by the addition of new entries covering a wider geographical area and including more women, updated bibliographies for existing entries, a new page design, a section containing maps, plus succession tables, genealogies, and numerous illustrations.

The first installment in the revised and expanded series, *Great Events from History: The Ancient World, Prehistory-476 C.E.* contains 418 essays: 289 all new essays, 94 from *Chronology of European History*, 29 from *Great Events from History: Ancient and Medieval Series*, and 6 from *Great Events from History: North American Series*. The date of 476 C.E., the Fall of Rome, was selected by the editors as the cutoff between the ancient world and the Middle Ages. The events are arranged chronologically, forming a time line, and each right-hand page contains a date-range tag so that essays can be located easily.

Nineteen maps of portions of the ancient world appear grouped together for easy reference in the front of each volume. Accompanying the essays are about 175 illustrations (mostly line art and photographs of busts, sculptures, coins, paintings, and drawings depicting the individual) and 86 maps, succession lists, genealogies, and other sidebars.

In compiling the list of contents, Salem enlisted a group of scholars who provided their knowledge on different areas of the ancient world: general editor Mark W. Chavalas, University of Wisconsin-La Crosse (Near East, Greece, Rome, and Israel), and consulting editors Mark S. Aldenderfer, University of California, Santa Barbara (South America, Mesoamerica); Carole A. Barrett, University of Mary (North America); Jeffrey W. Dippmann, Central Washington University (China); Christopher Ehret, University of California, Los Angeles (Africa); and Katherine Anne Harper, Loyola Marymount University (Central, South, and Southeast Asia).

The events—which range from "c. 25,000 B.C.E., San Peoples Create Earliest African Art" to "September 4, 476 C.E., Fall of Rome"—are grouped into one or more of the following categories: 126 on prehistory and ancient cultures; 107 on government and politics; 91 on cultural and intellectual history; 88 on religion; 80 on wars, uprisings, and civil unrest; 74 on expansion and land acquisition; 30 on science and technology; 24 on literature; 21 on philosophy; 19 on architecture; 19 on trade and commerce; 18 on agriculture; 13 on laws, acts, and legal history; 4 on health and medicine; 4 on mathematics; and 3 on historiography. The scope of this set is worldwide, with essays on events associated with one or more ancient locales: Greece (46), Rome (57), and the Mediterranean (26); Britain (5) and other parts of Europe (21); northern and southern Africa (49) as well as Egypt (21) and Alexandria (6); Asia Minor (23); Israel (22), Mesopotamia (16), Persia (15), and other parts of the Middle East (37); Central Asia (15), India (38) and South (4) and Southeast Asia (7); China (54), Japan (7), and Korea (2); Oceania (4); North America (21), South America (11), and Mesoamerica (9).

The articles in this set range from 1,000 to 1,500 words in length and follow a standard format. Each article begins with a date and title followed by ready-reference listings. A summary of the event and its significance is followed by a line giving the event's locale, with the modern place-name if it has changed, and a categorization of the type of event. A list of the major figures, if any, involved in the event follows, with their birth and death dates, a brief descriptor, and their reign dates if a ruler. In the listing of key figures and in parenthetical material within the text, the editors have used these abbreviations: "r." for "reigned," "b." for "born," "d." for "died," and "fl." for flourished. The text of each essay is divided into "Summary of Event" and "Significance" sections, so that each event is described fully and its impact analyzed. Each essay has an annotated list of suggestions for further reading and is cross-referenced to other essays within the set as well as to related essays in Salem's companion publication, *Great Lives from History: The Ancient World, Prehistory-476 C.E.* (2 vols., 2004).

At the front of both volumes appears a Keyword List of Contents, a list of essay titles arranged alphabetically by the keywords of each title. The set also features a Time Line, a Glossary, a Bibliography, a list of Web sites, and a Chronological List of Entries. The Time Line is a chronological listing of the 418 events covered by the entries in the set as well as more than 275 additional events of the ancient world, arranged by subject area. The Glossary contains definitions of selected terms used in the set, arranged alphabetically. The Bibliography lists sources for further study, arranged by subject, and the Web Sites list contains the major ancient history and other pertinent Web sites. The Chronological List of Entries lists the 418 entries in the set in chronological order. The set has four indexes with page numbers: the Category Index of Entries, a list of essays under their categories; the Geographical Index of Entries, a list of essays under their geographical area; the Personages Index, an index containing the major personages in the work; and the Subject Index.

The worldwide scope of *Great Events from History* resulted in the inclusion of many names and words that must be transliterated from languages that do not use the Roman alphabet, and in some cases, there is more than one transliterated form in use. In many cases, transliterated words in this set follow the American Library Association and Library of Congress (ALA-LC) transliteration format for that language. However, if another form of a name or word was judged to be more familiar to the general audience, it is used instead. The variants for names of essay subjects are listed in ready-reference top matter and are cross-referenced in the Subject and Personages indexes. The Pinyin transliteration is used for Chinese topics, with Wade-Giles variants provided for major names and dynasties. In a few cases, a common name that is not Pinyin has been used (for example, "Confucius"). Sanskrit words generally follow the ALA-LC transliteration rules, although again, the more familiar form of a word is used when deemed appropriate for the general reader (for example, sutra rather than *sūtra*).

Latin nomenclature uses three names: *praenomen*, *nomen* or family name, and *cognomen*. Most individuals are listed by their *nomen*, but some are listed by their common English name. For example, Marcus (*praenomen*) Tullius (*nomen*) Cicero (*cognomen*) is commonly known as Cicero. Many Roman men had at least two names, a *praenomen* and *nomen*. Roman women were given the grammatically feminine form of their father's *nomen*. For example, Cicero's daughter is Tullia. If there were two daughters, they were called Major and Minor for elder and younger. In some cases, the common English name (for example, Agrippina the Younger) has been used. In addition to the *praenomen* and *nomen*, some men had a *cognomen*. In some cases, this is the common English name of famous Romans such as Caesar, Cicero, and Scipio. A name may have more than one *cognomen*, and these are typically nicknames or titles given for military success. Notable exceptions to these basic rules are Augustus and the emperors following him. Augustus was born Gaius Octavius and by adoption became Gaius Julius Caesar Octavianus. In 27 B.C.E., he was given an honorary and quasi-religious name Augustus. All subsequent emperors took the name Caesar Augustus followed by their *praenomen*, *nomen*, and *cognomen*.

Research on the ancient world is ongoing, with contributions from historians, linguists, archaeologists, anthropologists, and other scholars supplementing and revising what is known of ancient peoples and cultures. Therefore, the dates, names, and descriptions of events in *Great Events from History* represent a consensus of generally accepted modern scholarship.

Salem Press would like to extend its appreciation to all who have been involved in the development and production of this work. Each essay was written by an academician who specializes in the area of discussion, and without their expert contribution, a project of this nature would not be possible. A full list of contributors and their affiliations appears in the front matter of this volume.

Contributors

Amy Ackerberg-Hastings
Independent Scholar

Richard Adler
University of Michigan - Dearborn

J. M. Adovasio
Mercyhurst Archaeological Institute

Mark Aldenderfer
University of California, Santa Barbara

Emily Alward
Henderson, NV District Libraries

Earl R. Andresen
University of Texas at Arlington

James A. Arieti
Hampden-Sydney College

Mary Pat Balkus
Radford University

Carl L. Bankston III
Tulane University

Maryanne Barsotti
Independent Scholar

Rozmeri Basic
University of Oklahoma

Barbara C. Beattie
Independent Scholar

Katherine B. Beem
Independent Scholar

Tanja Bekhuis
TCB Research

Milton Berman
University of Rochester

Jon L. Berquist
Chalice Press

Mellissa Betts
Independent Scholar

Sheena L. Binkley
Independent Scholar

Nicholas Birns
New School University

Jackie R. Booker
Claflin University

Erica Brindley
University of California, Santa Barbara

Ben Brose
Stanford University

David L. Browman
Washington University

Kendall W. Brown
Brigham Young University

Daniel C. Browning, Jr.
William Carey College

Jeffrey L. Buller
Mary Baldwin College

Joseph P. Byrne
Belmont University

Jack Carter
University of New Orleans

Cherie C. Castillo
University of Wisconsin—Fox Valley

James T. Chambers
Texas Christian University

Paul J. Chara, Jr.
Northwestern College

Frederick B. Chary
Indiana University Northwest

Mark W. Chavalas
University of Wisconsin—La Crosse

David Christiansen
Truman State University

Douglas Clouatre
Kennesaw State University

Carl W. Conrad
Washington University

Michael Coronel
University of Northern Colorado

Patricia Coronel
Colorado State University

M. Joseph Costelloe
Creighton University

Antonio Rafael de la Cova
Rose-Hulman Institute of Technology

David A. Crain
South Dakota State University

Thomas I. Crimando
SUNY College at Brockport

LouAnn Faris Culley
Kansas State University

John Coleman Darnell
Yale University

Frank Day
Clemson University

Rene M. Descartes
SUNY, Cobleskill

M. Casey Diana
University of Illinois at Urbana-Champaign

Jeffrey W. Dippmann
Central Washington University

William J. Dominik
University of Otago

Marjorie Donovan
Pittsburg State University

David Allen Duncan
Tennessee Wesleyan College

Jennifer Eastman
Clark University

Samuel K. Eddy
Syracuse University

K Edgington
Towson University

Candace R. Ellington
Independent Scholar

Robert P. Ellis
Independent Scholar

James D. Farmer
Virginia Commonwealth University

Randall Fegley
Pennsylvania State University

Everett Ferguson
Abilene Christian College

Chauncey E. Finch
Saint Louis University

Richard D. Fitzgerald
Onondaga Community College

Robert J. Forman
St. John's University, New York

Catherine Cymone Fourshey
Susquehanna University

John C. Fredriksen
Salem State College

C. George Fry
University of Findlay

Richard N. Frye
Harvard University

Michael J. Garcia
Arapahoe Community College

Karen K. Gould
Independent Scholar

Daniel G. Graetzer
University of Washington Medical Center

Christopher E. Guthrie
Tarleton State University

Michael Haas
Occidental College

Irwin Halfond
McKendree College

Gavin R. G. Hambly
University of Texas at Dallas

Brian Hancock
Rutgers University Libraries

Wells S. Hansen
Milton Academy

Katherine Anne Harper
Loyola Marymount University

Kevin Herbert
Washington University

Anna Dunlap Higgins
Gordon College

Carl W. Hoagstrom
Ohio Northern University

David B. Hollander
Iowa State University

John R. Holmes
Franciscan University of Steubenville

James P. Holoka
Eastern Michigan University

Leslie J. Hoppe
Catholic Theological Union

Patrick Norman Hunt
Stanford University

Mary Hurd
East Tennessee State University

Raymond Pierre Hylton
Virginia Union University

Mary Evelyn Jegen
University of Dayton

Jeffry Jensen
Independent Scholar

Bruce E. Johansen
University of Nebraska at Omaha

Edward Johnson
University of New Orleans

Yoshiko Kainuma
University of California, Los Angeles

Charles L. Kammer III
The College of Wooster

Mathew J. Kanjirathinkal
Texas A&M University—Commerce

Edward P. Keleher
Purdue University—Calumet

Leigh Husband Kimmel
Independent Scholar

Fred B. Kniffen
Louisiana State University

Gayla Koerting
University of South Dakota

Grove Koger
Boise (Idaho) Public Library

Edgar M. Krenz
Concordia Seminary

Julian Kunnie
University of Arizona

David J. Ladouceur
University of Notre Dame

Philip E. Lampe
University of the Incarnate Word

Eugene Larson
Los Angeles Pierce College

John Lewis
Ashland University

Thomas Tandy Lewis
Anoka Ramsey Community College

Huping Ling
Truman State University

Elizabeth Johnston Lipscomb
Randolph-Macon Women's College

Guoli Liu
College of Charleston

Craig Lloyd
College of Mount St. Joseph

Peter A. Lorge
Vanderbilt University

R. C. Lutz
CII Group

Colleen Manassa
Yale University

Mark J. Mangano
Lincoln Christian College & Seminary

Chogallah Maroufi
California State University, Los Angeles

Ralph W. Mathisen
University of South Carolina

T. Davina McClain
Loyola University, New Orleans

C. Thomas McCollough
W. F. Albright Institute of Archaeological Research

William P. McDonald
Tennesee Wesleyan College

Thomas McGeary
Independent Scholar

Michael J. McGrath
Georgia Southern University

Roger B. McShane
Trinity University

Ruben G. Mendoza
California State University, Monterey Bay

Hwa-Soon Choi Meyer
Seton Hall University

Elizabeth L. Meyers
Independent Scholar

Diane P. Michelfelder
Utah State University

Alice Myers
Simon's Rock College

Gary A. Olson
San Bernardino Valley College

Sara E. Orel
Truman State University

Zola M. Packman
Washington University

Robert J. Paradowski
Rochester Institute of Technology

David R. Pedler
Independent Scholar

Connie Pedoto
Miles College

George M. Pepe
Washington University

Mark Anthony Phelps
Drury University

Darryl A. Phillips
College of Charleston

Thomas C. Pleger
University of Wisconsin—Fox Valley

George R. Plitnik
Frostburg State University

Marguerite R. Plummer
Louisiana State University in Shreveport

Edmund Dickenson Potter
Independent Scholar

Luke A. Powers
Tennessee State University

Carolyn V. Prorok
Slippery Rock University

William H. Race
University of North Carolina

Steven J. Ramold
Virginia State University

Paul L. Redditt
Georgetown College

Kristofor Rico
Independent Scholar

Edward A. Riedinger
Ohio State University Libraries

Edward J. Rielly
Saint Joseph's College of Maine

Joseph J. Romano
Cabrini College

Joseph R. Rosenbloom
Washington University

Robert Rousselle
Independent Scholar

Adriane Ruggiero
Independent Scholar

Jason D. Sanchez
Tulane University

Richard Sax
Madonna University

Daniel C. Scavone
University of Southern Indiana

Raymond H. Schmandt
Saint Joseph College

Rose Secrest
Independent Scholar

Lynda Sexson
Montana State University

Evan Scott Shuey
Independent Scholar

R. Baird Shuman
University of Illinois at Urbana-Champaign

Narasingha P. Sil
Western Oregon University

Michael J. Siler
California State University, Los Angeles

Donald C. Simmons, Jr.
South Dakota Humanities Council

Michael W. Simpson
Bluefox Productions

Shumet Sishagne
Christopher Newport University

David Charles Smith
Bates College

Norris K. Smith
Washington University

Roger Smith
Independent Scholar

Sonia Sorrell
Pepperdine University

Joseph L. Spradley
Wheaton College

Steven M. Stannish
SUNY, Potsdam

August W. Staub
University of Georgia

Barry M. Stentiford
Grambling State University

Stephen A. Stertz
Mercy College

Joan C. Stevenson
Western Washington University

Leslie A. Stricker
Park University

Sally A. Struthers
Sinclair Community College

Glenn L. Swygart
Tennessee Temple University

Guillaume de Syon
Albright College

Robert D. Talbott
University of Northern Iowa

Andrius Tamulis
Cardinal Stritch University

Donathan Taylor
Hardin-Simmons University

Susan M. Taylor
Indiana University, South Bend

Cassandra Lee Tellier
Capital University

Gale M. Thompson
Delta College

Burt Thorp
University of North Dakota

Louis P. Towles
Southern Wesleyan University

Andrew G. Traver
Southeastern Louisiana University

Jiu-Hwa Lo Upshur
Eastern Michigan University

Peter L. Viscusi
Central Missouri State University

Gilmar E. Visoni
Queensboro Community College, CUNY

Meera S. Viswanathan
Brown University

Carl A. Volz
Concordia Seminary

J. A. Wahl
Saint Jerome's College

Christopher J. Ward
Ouachita Baptist University

Albert T. Watanabe
Louisiana State University

Thomas H. Watkins
Western Illinois University

J. Francis Watson
Grace Lutheran Church

Richard D. Weigel
Western Kentucky University

Winifred O. Whelan
St. Bonaventure University

Carlis C. White
Slippery Rock University

Thomas Willard
University of Arizona

Julie A. Williams
Independent Scholar

John F. Wilson
University of Hawaii—Manoa

John D. Windhausen
Saint Anselm College

Michael Witkoski
University of South Carolina

Shelley Wolbrink
Drury University

Shawn Woodyard
Independent Scholar

Richard J. Wurtz
Southern Illinois University

Susan J. Wurtzburg
University of Canterbury

Kristen L. Zacharias
Albright College

Yunqiu Zhang
North Carolina A&T State University

KEYWORD LIST OF CONTENTS

List of Maps and Tables

GREECE AND MACEDONIA

INDIA AND SOUTHEAST ASIA

ISRAEL

JAPAN

THE MEDITERRANEAN

MESOPOTAMIA, PERSIA, AND THE MIDDLE EAST

OCEANIA

Rome and the Roman Empire

The Origin of Humans, c. 4 million–100,000 years ago

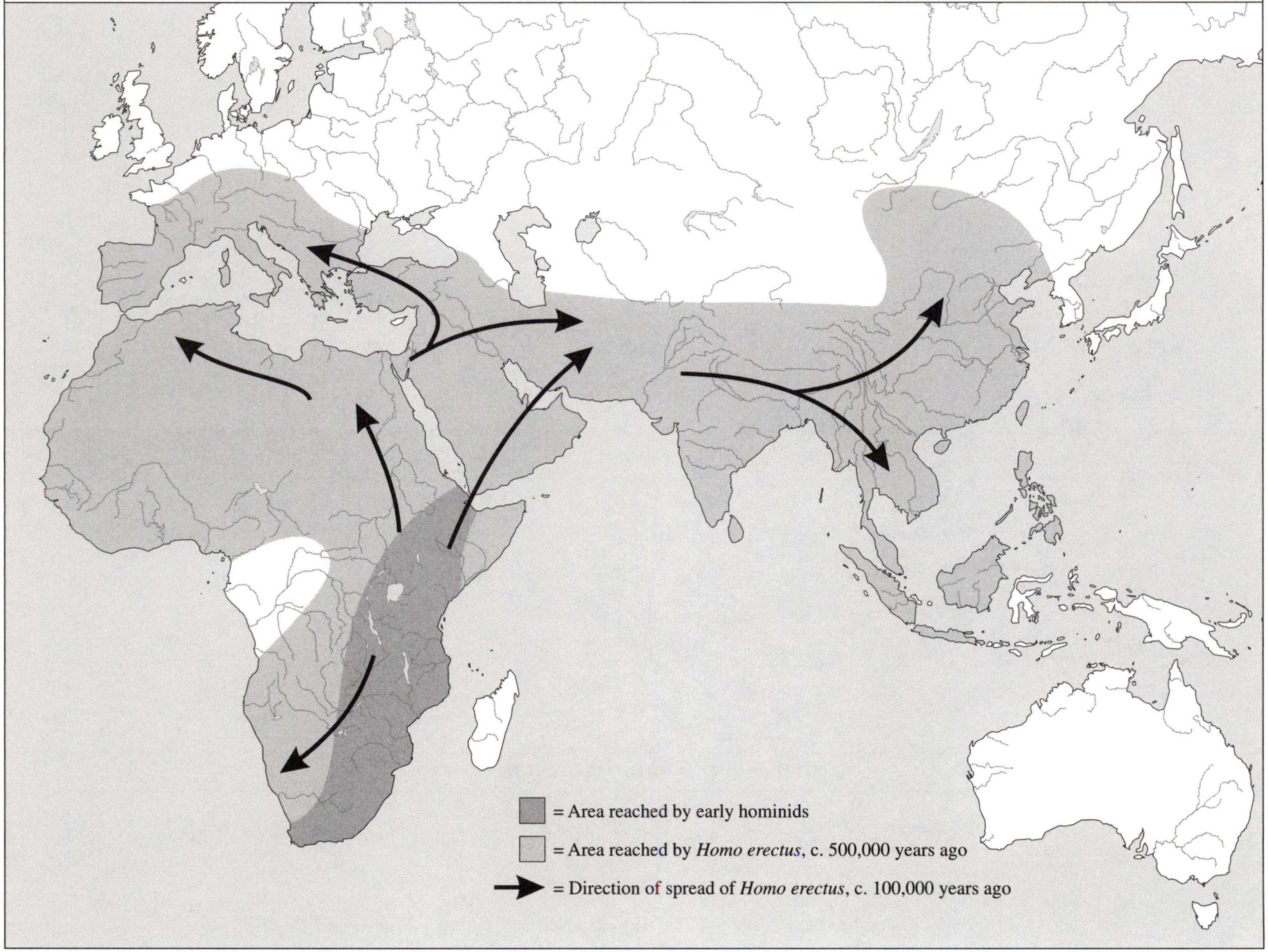

The Ancient World, c. 200-500 C.E.

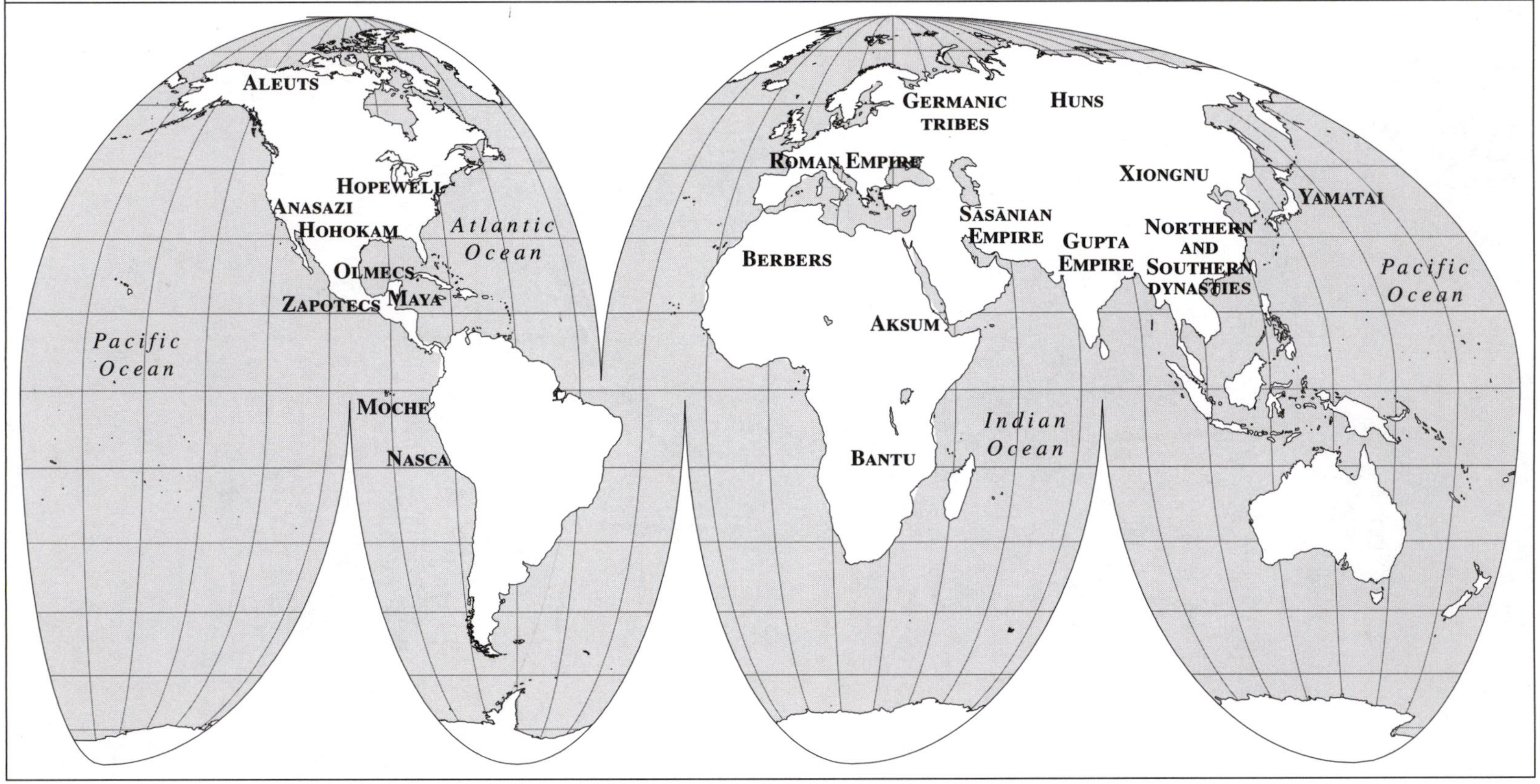

Ancient North America

• = Sites

Cultures indicated by **Bold Small Caps**

Ancient Mesoamerica

Ancient South America

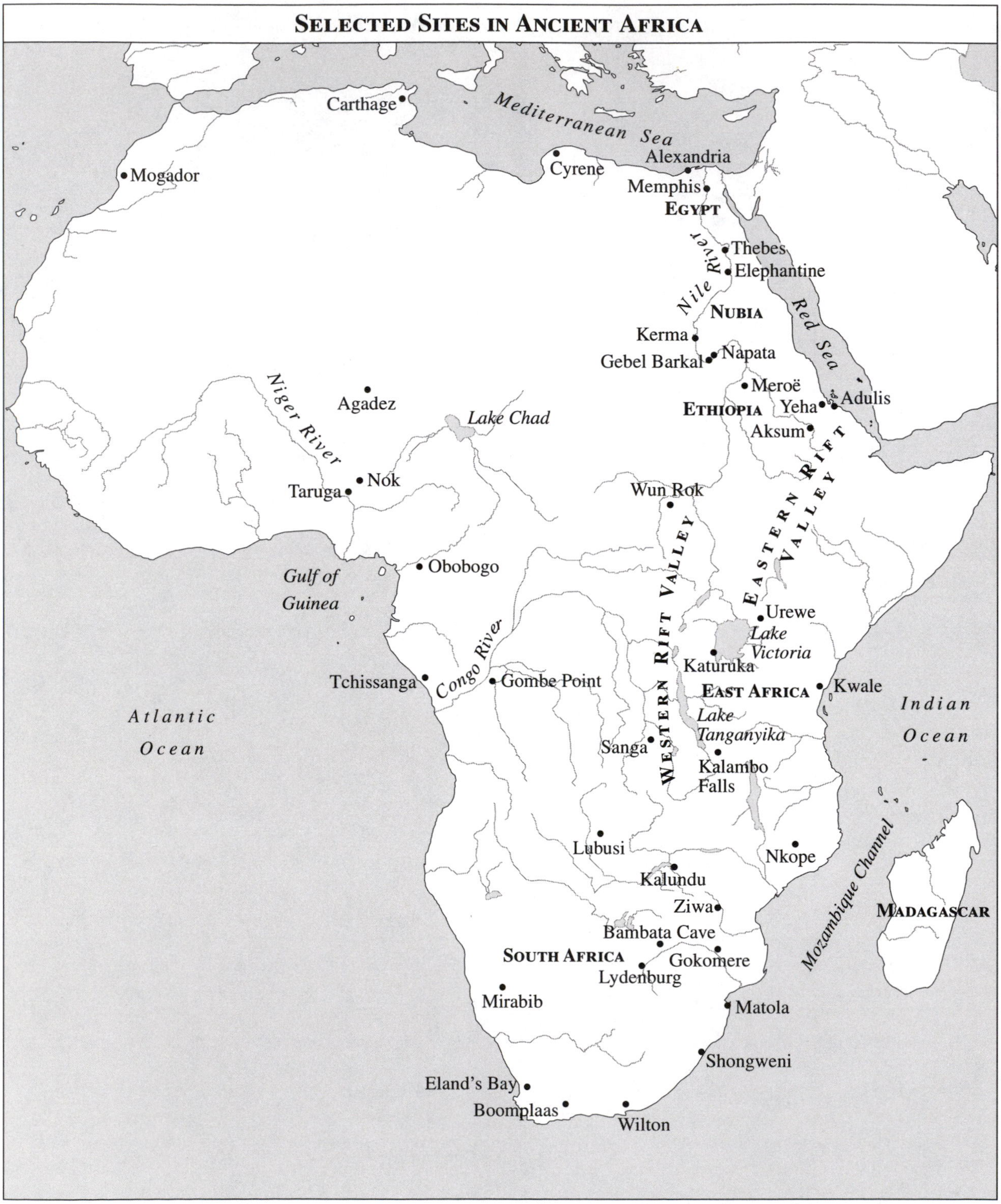
SELECTED SITES IN ANCIENT AFRICA
Carthage
Mediterranean Sea
Alexandria
Cyrene
Mogador
Memphis
EGYPT
Thebes
Elephantine
Nile River
NUBIA
Red Sea
Kerma
Napata
Gebel Barkal
Meroë
Adulis
Yeha
ETHIOPIA
Aksum
Niger River
Agadez
Lake Chad
Nok
Taruga
Wun Rok
EASTERN RIFT VALLEY
WESTERN RIFT VALLEY
Obobogo
Gulf of Guinea
Urewe
Lake Victoria
Katuruka
Congo River
Tchissanga
Gombe Point
EAST AFRICA
Kwale
Indian Ocean
Atlantic Ocean
Lake Tanganyika
Sanga
Kalambo Falls
Lubusi
Nkope
Mozambique Channel
Kalundu
Ziwa
MADAGASCAR
Bambata Cave
SOUTH AFRICA
Gokomere
Lydenburg
Mirabib
Matola
Shongweni
Eland's Bay
Boomplaas
Wilton

Old Kingdom Egypt, c. 2687-c. 2125 B.C.E.

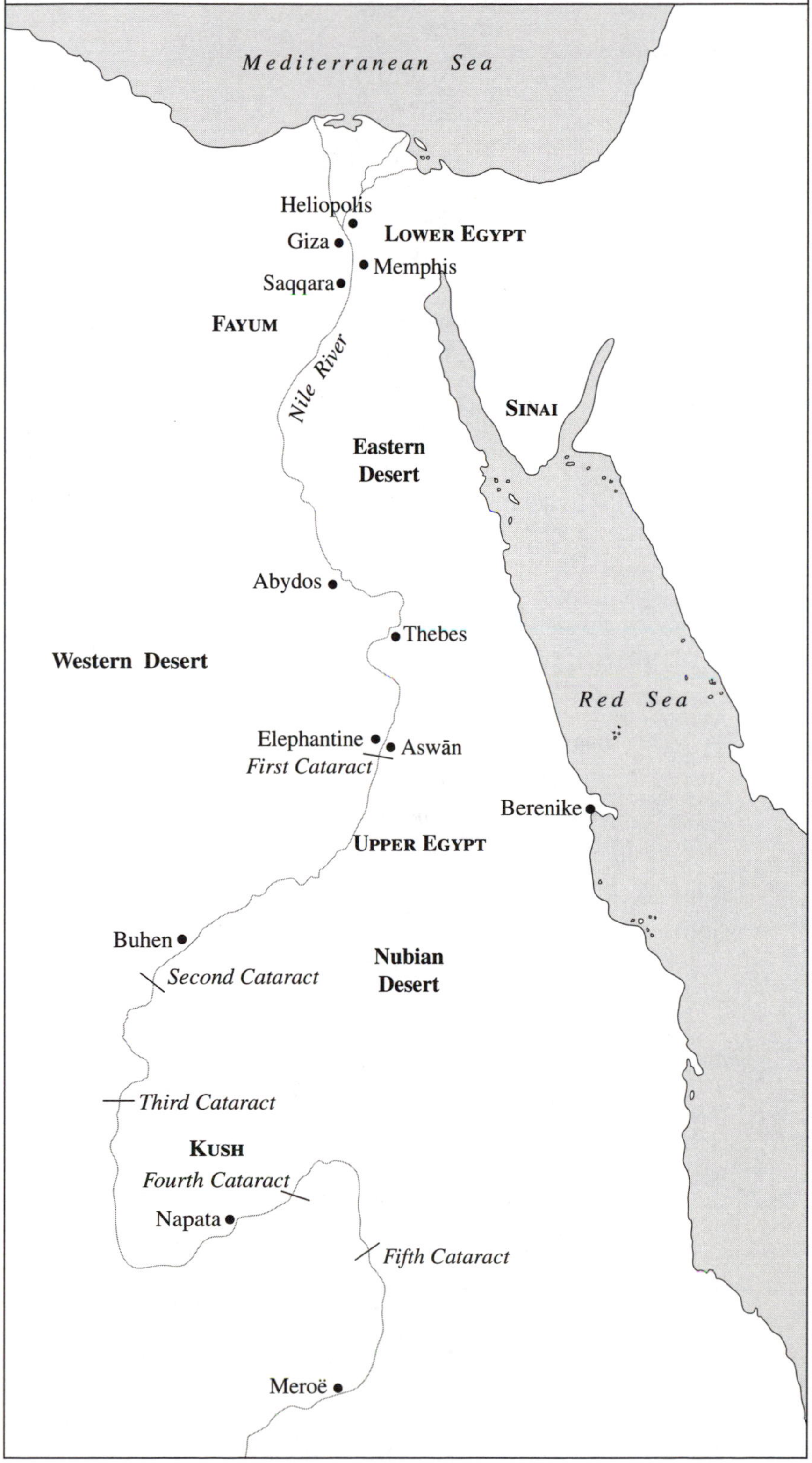

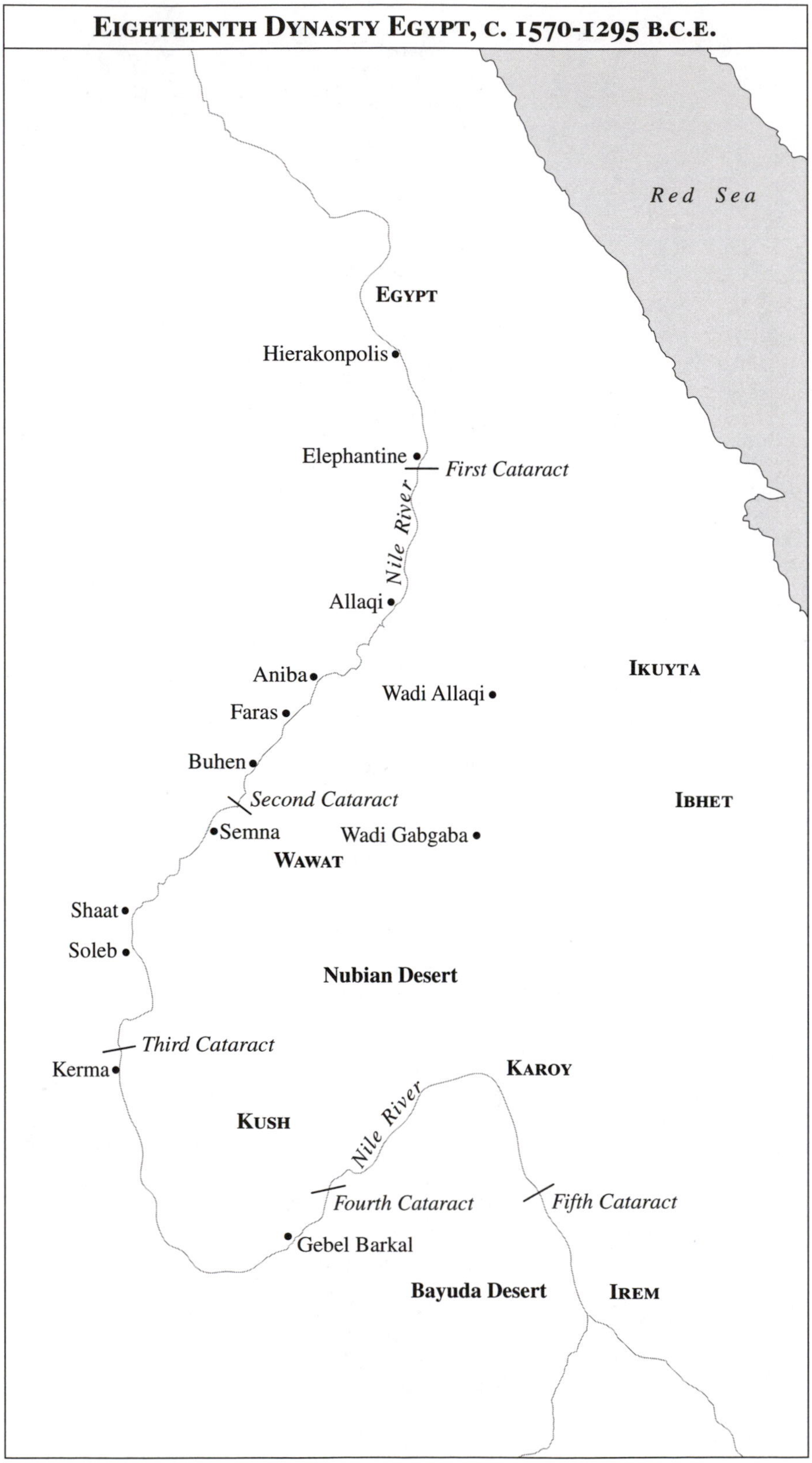
EIGHTEENTH DYNASTY EGYPT, C. 1570-1295 B.C.E.
Red Sea
EGYPT
Hierakonpolis
Elephantine
First Cataract
Nile River
Allaqi
Aniba
Wadi Allaqi
IKUYTA
Faras
Buhen
Second Cataract
IBHET
Semna
Wadi Gabgaba
WAWAT
Shaat
Soleb
Nubian Desert
Third Cataract
Kerma
KAROY
KUSH
Nile River
Fourth Cataract
Fifth Cataract
Gebel Barkal
Bayuda Desert
IREM

The Mediterranean World, 7th Century B.C.E.

Classical Greece, 5th Century B.C.E.

The Hellenistic World, 185 B.C.E.

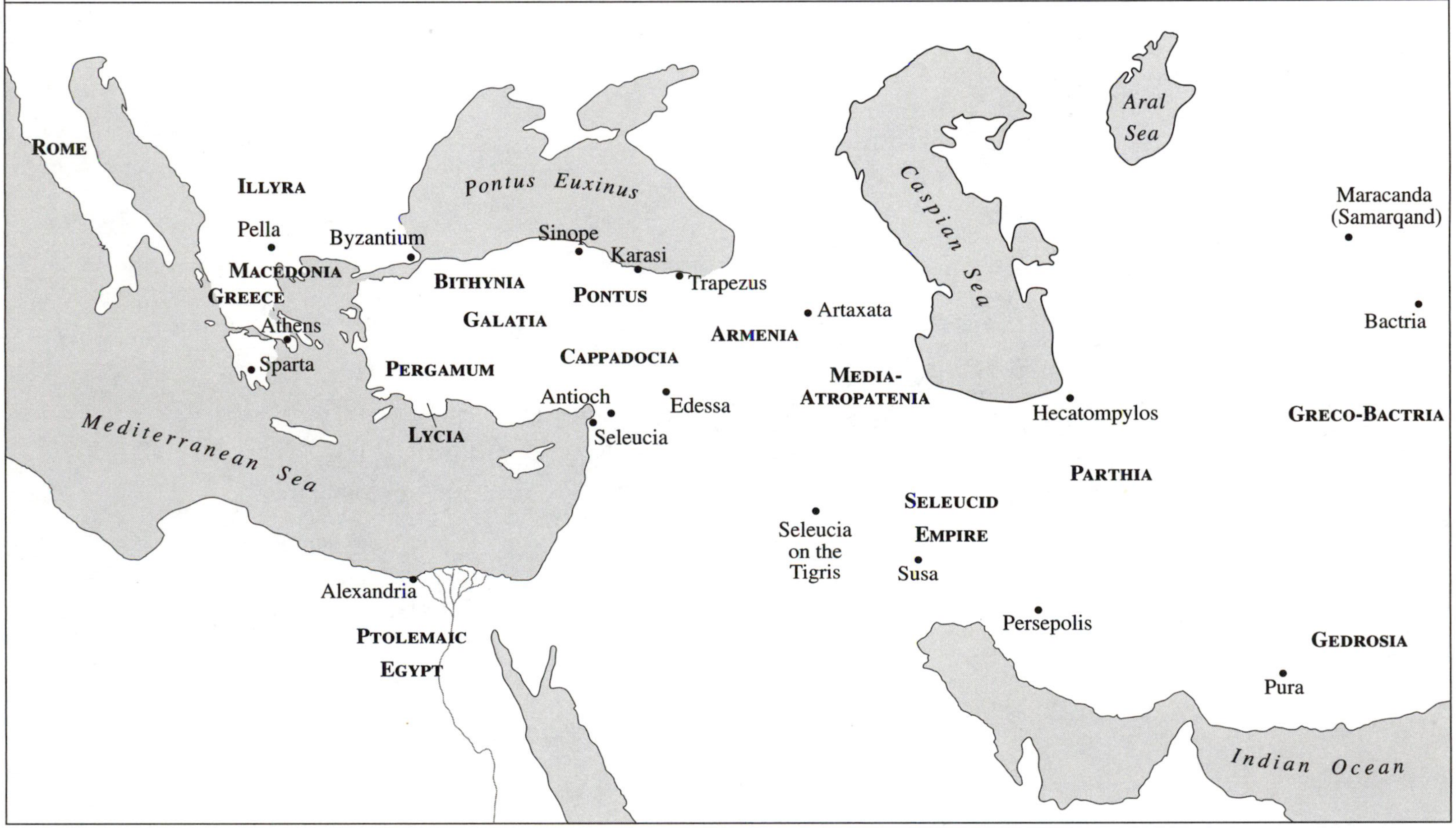

IMPERIAL ROME, C. 200 C.E.

Roman Empire, c. 400 C.E.

Sumer and Akkad, c. 4000-2000 B.C.E.

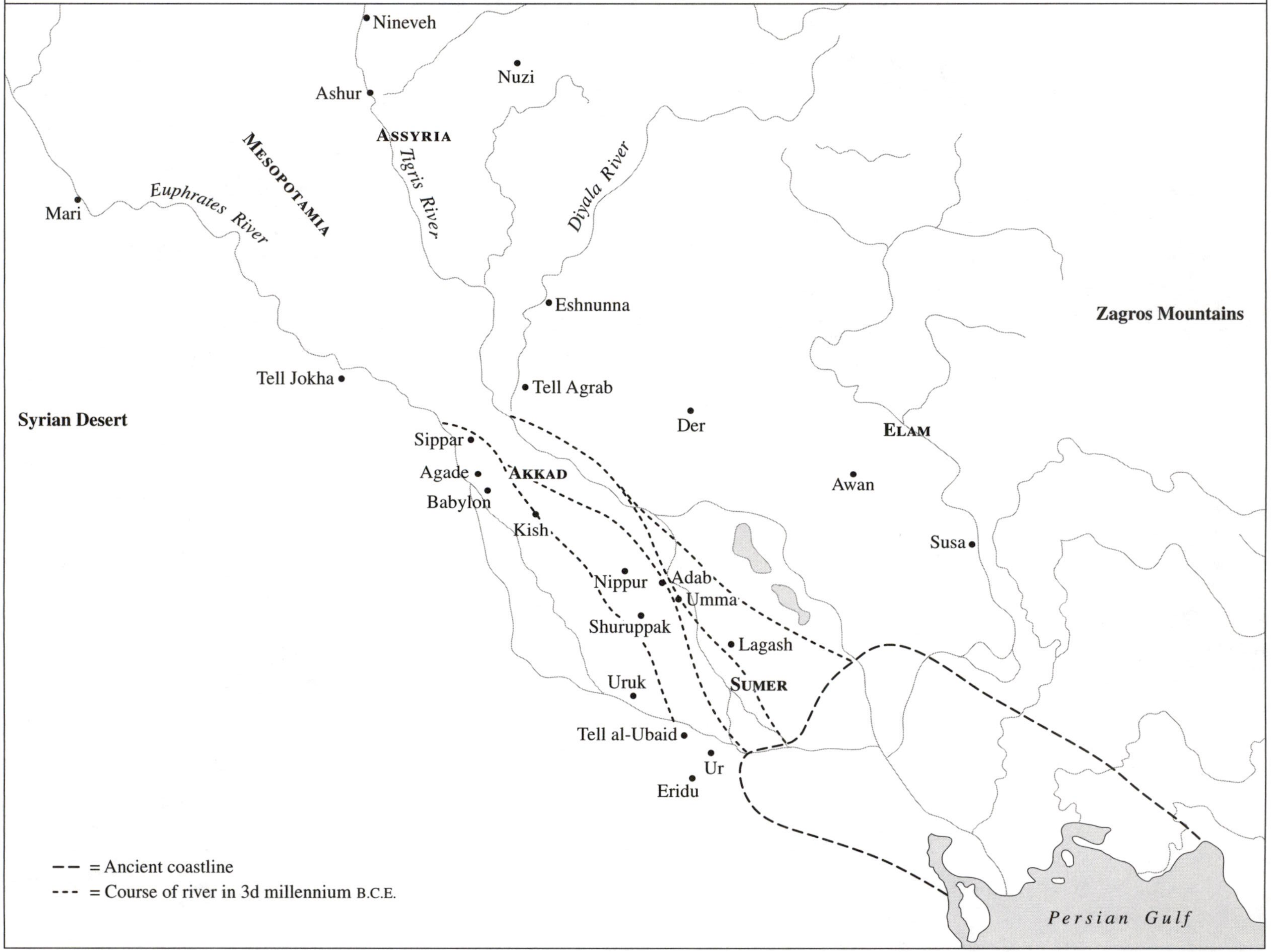

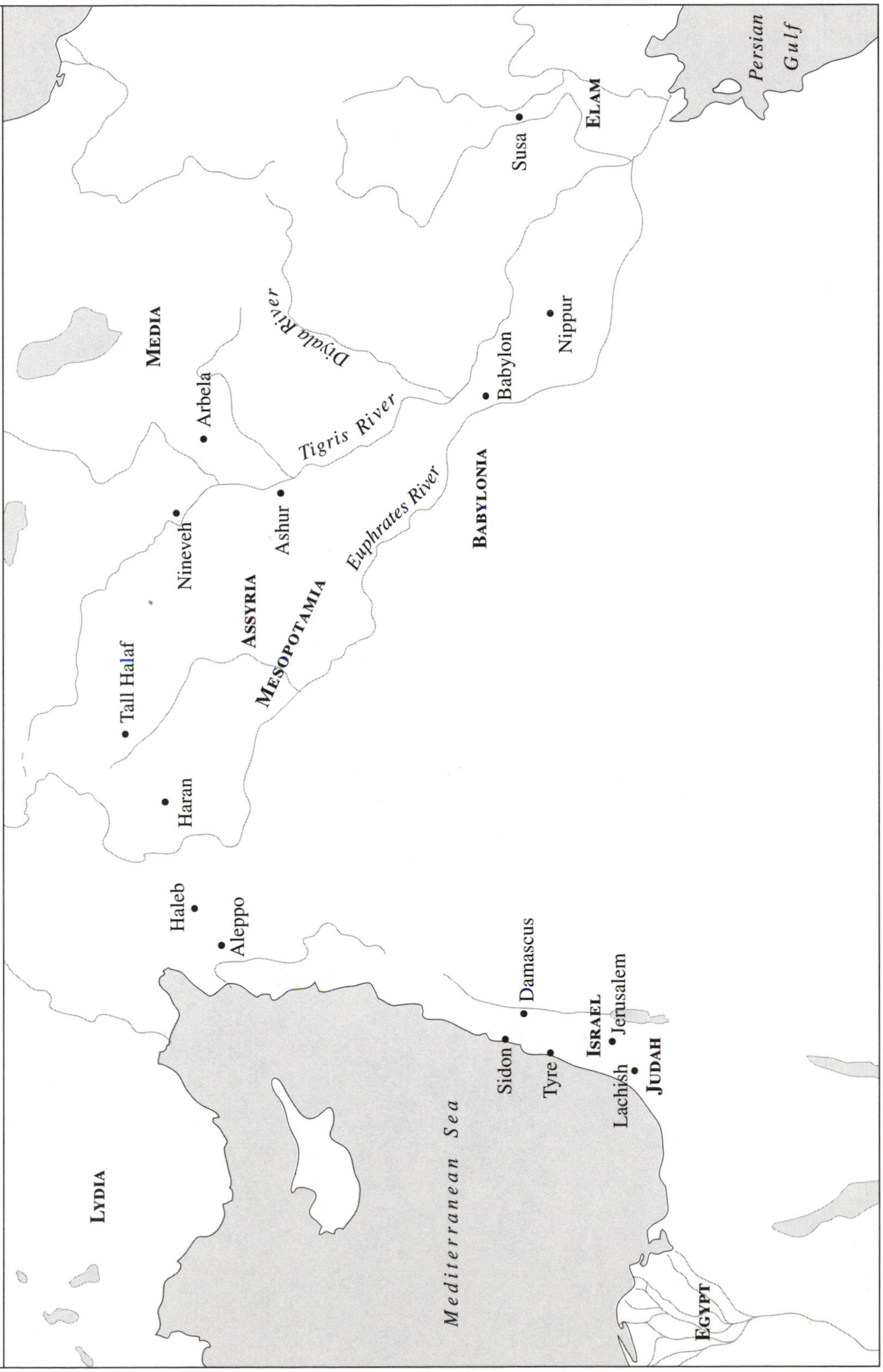

ASSYRIA AND BABYLONIA, 600-500 B.C.E.

PERSIAN EMPIRE, C. 500 B.C.E.

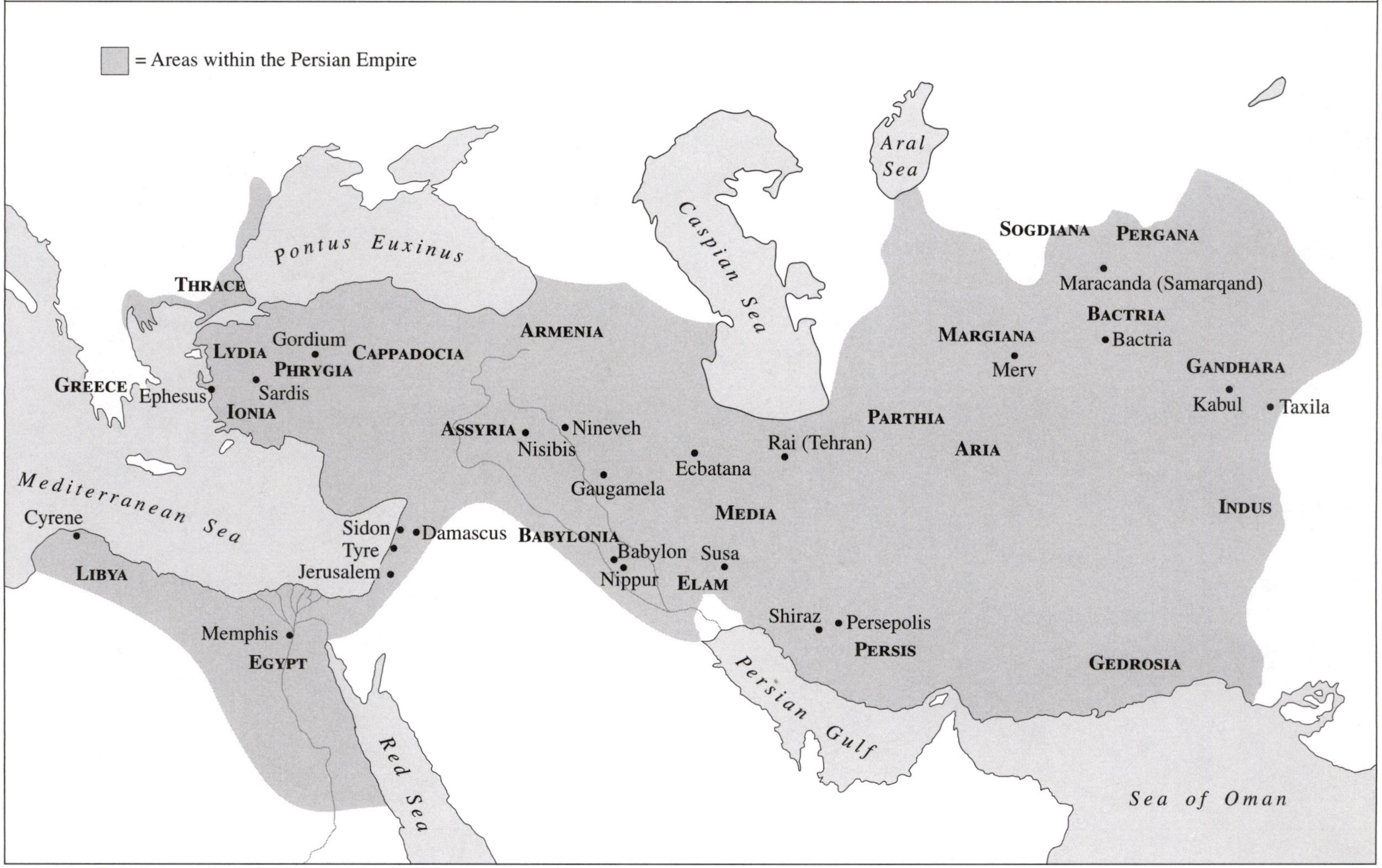

Parthian and Sāsānian Empires, c. 230 B.C.E.-500 C.E.

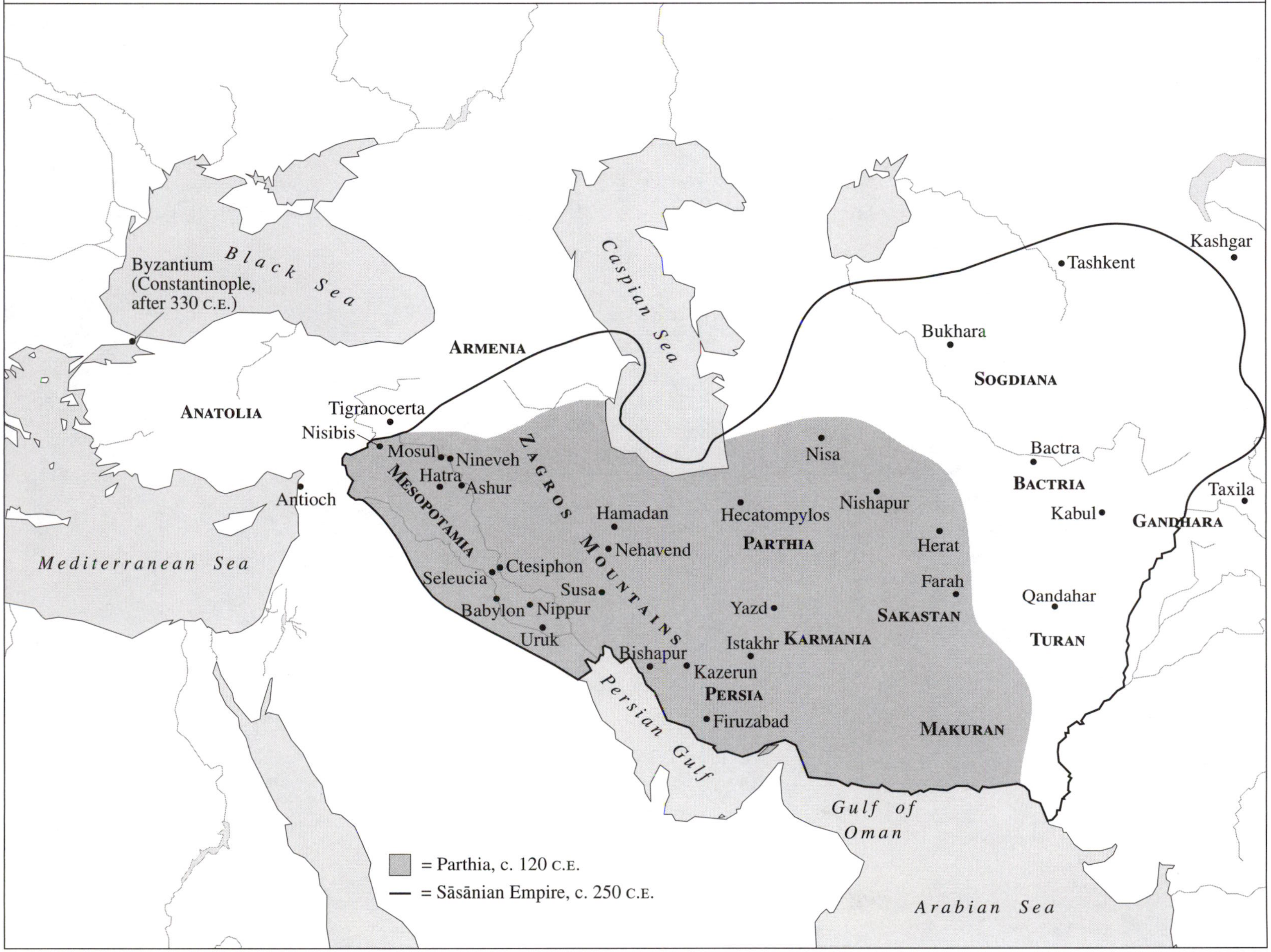

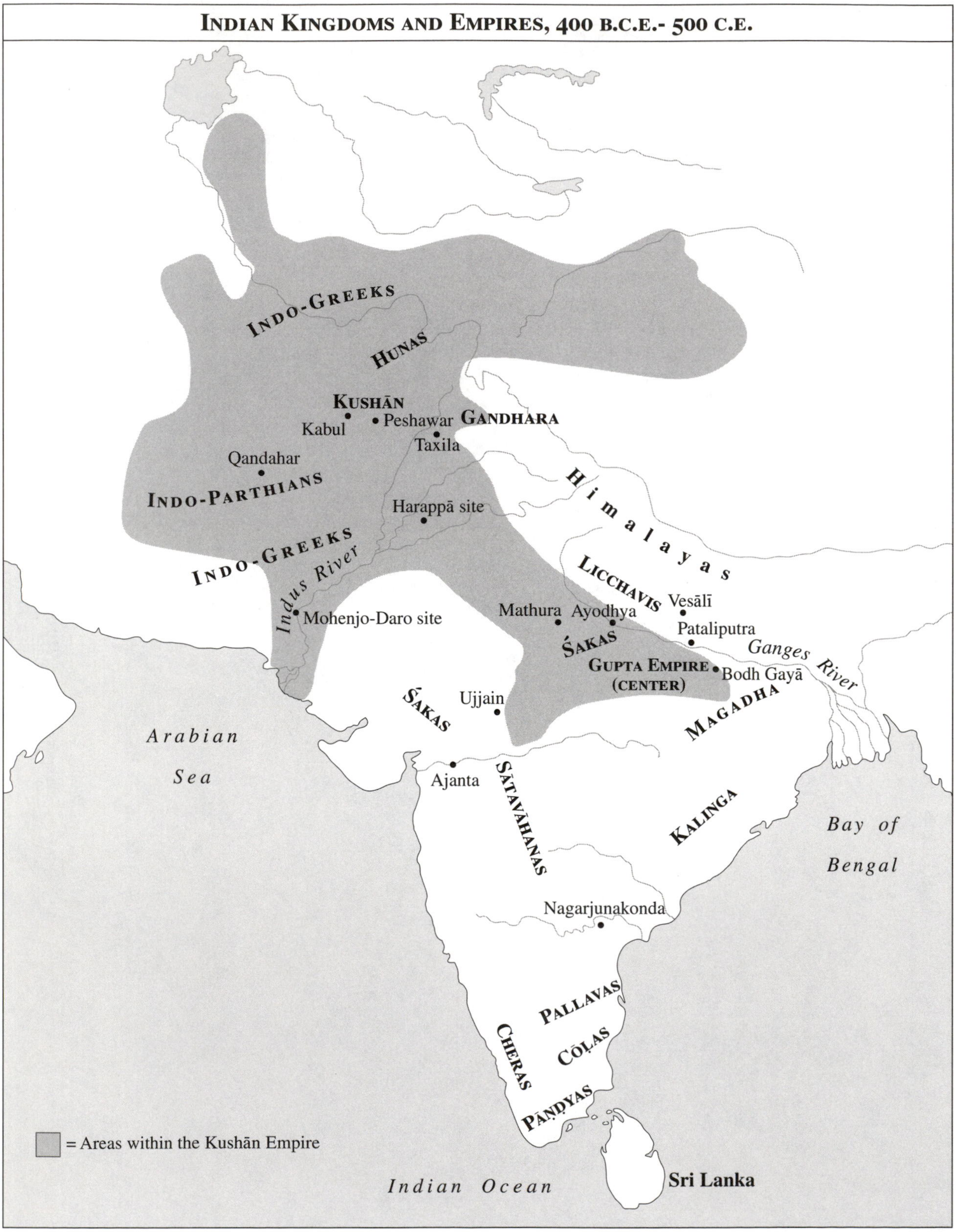
INDIAN KINGDOMS AND EMPIRES, 400 B.C.E.- 500 C.E.
INDO-GREEKS
HUNAS
KUSHĀN
Kabul
Peshawar
GANDHARA
Taxila
Qandahar
INDO-PARTHIANS
Himalayas
Harappā site
INDO-GREEKS
Indus River
LICCHAVIS
Vesālī
Mohenjo-Daro site
Mathura
Ayodhya
Pataliputra
ŚAKAS
Ganges River
GUPTA EMPIRE
(CENTER)
Bodh Gayā
ŚAKAS
Ujjain
MAGADHA
Arabian
Sea
Ajanta
SĀTAVĀHANAS
KALINGA
Bay of
Bengal
Nagarjunakonda
PALLAVAS
CHERAS
CŌḶAS
PĀṆḌYAS
= Areas within the Kushān Empire
Indian Ocean
Sri Lanka

China During the Warring States and Han Dynasty, 475 B.C.E.-220 C.E.

Great Events from History

The Ancient World

Prehistory - 476 C.E.

c. 25,000 B.C.E.

San Peoples Create Earliest African Art

More than thirty thousand examples of rock art by a people called the San have been identified in Namibia, including paintings in rock shelters and engravings on large boulders and open rock surfaces.

Locale: Namibia, Africa
Category: Prehistory and ancient cultures

Summary of Event

The San, a Khoisan-speaking people also known as the Bushmen, were a Stone Age people who inhabited southern Africa in what is now modern Namibia and Botswana. As hunter-gatherers, they lived in groups within what was most likely an egalitarian society. Today the San occupy the Kalahari Desert and have no longer have a rock art tradition, but more than thirty thousand documented examples of their ancestors' rock art have been identified in Namibia. This coastal country on the Atlantic Ocean has evidence of two basic types of rock art: paintings in rock shelters and engravings more commonly found on large boulders and open rock surfaces. Among the major sites of these images are the Apollo 11 Cave, the Brandberg monolith, Tweyfelfontein, and Piet Alberts Kopjes.

The earliest known examples of San rock art were discovered at a rock shelter known as the Apollo 11 Cave, located in the Huns Mountains of southern Namibia. There, eight painted stone fragments were excavated in organic debris. The debris associated with these fragments has been dated between approximately 27,000 and about 2,000 B.P. (before the present). This period, while not necessarily applicable to the rock paintings themselves, establishes the time in which the stones were introduced from another area. Nevertheless, these images are believed to represent the oldest art on the continent of Africa. Imagery on the stone surfaces at Apollo 11 (so called because it was excavated by Wolfgang E. Wendt in 1969, the same year in which the spacecraft of the same name landed on the Moon) represents animals painted in solid black or red, with some drawn in outline. One curious animal appears to be a composite of an antelope and a lion, while others represent single indigenous animals.

In the Namibian interior, on the edge of the Namib Desert, the granite outcropping known as Brandberg Mountain, approximately 2,600 meters (8,550 feet) high, houses approximately one thousand sites containing some fifty thousand rock art paintings. In the Tsisab Gorge in the Brandberg, archaeologists have found remarkable painted human figures dating to 2000 B.P. The figures are both standing and in motion, walking, in procession or possibly dancing. Surface detail appears on some figures possibly representing body painting or decorative ornamentation such as jewelry. Scholars have wondered about the meaning of white dots found on ankles, on knees, and in the hair. White ostrich-shell beads used in this region may be represented, or an abstract religious meaning could apply. One of these figures, the so-called White Lady (neither white nor a lady but more likely the image of a shaman), was described by its discoverer, Reinhard Maack, in 1918 as the most detailed rock painting he had ever seen.

Tweyfelfontein, in Damaraland, has more than twenty-five hundred images, predominantly engravings on sandstone boulders. This site was first recorded in 1921 and was made a national monument in 1952. It is home to both paintings and engravings, rare for a single site. Moreover, the engravings at this site are very dense.

The range of subject matter in San rock art includes animals, humans, animal tracks, and abstract shapes, with humans and animals predominant. In Namibian rock engravings, there is a ratio of 16 animals to 1 human; in rock paintings, humans dominate animals by a ratio of 2 to 1. Among animal types, the giraffe and oryx were the more frequently painted in the Brandberg. It is important to note the lack of landscape or physical settings within either painting sites or engraving sites. The compositional relationship of images to one another in any environment at any one moment in time is unclear, especially because some images are superimposed on others. In general, both humans and animals are depicted in the prime of life without injury or disease. Animals and humans were represented to be unmistakable to the viewer. Using a twisted perspective, the artists depicted the features of their subjects as they best understood them. Torsos, for example, were depicted frontally, while legs, hips, and heads were shown in profile.

Red, brown, and yellow ocher were the main colors employed. Usually pigments contained no organic carbon; most came from ground minerals. Black was acquired from manganese ores; whites from clays, calcite, or quartz; red from iron oxides. Application of pigments was intended to fill in flat areas with color to form images. While no modeling is evident, some forms are clearly distinguished by the use of outlines.

A San Peoples cave painting, copied in watercolor, hangs on the wall above a South African researcher who is copying other cave paintings. (Hulton|Archive)

SIGNIFICANCE

There has been no agreement among scholars as to the meaning or content of the large body of San rock art. Several possible reasons for these works may include documenting events, religious ceremonies, and hallucinatory or trance experiences. In addition, scholars have postulated the use of these images to teach or communicate, especially about animals and geographic resources. The controversy over the images' use is ongoing, however. Images of repeated animal tracks, for example, were once thought to be instructional, helping adults to teach children about hunting. Today scholars have called this assumption into question, wondering, for example, why so many tracks of the same animal would be engraved if their purpose was merely to identify the animal. Today's San, moreover, learn from watching other hunters, not from formal symbolic instruction. One hypothesis is that the images of the tracks really are associated with images of ancient shamans in animal form.

Questions regarding sex or gender distinctions in Namibian rock art have been addressed in the Brandberg paintings. This area appears to be distinct, especially when compared with other south African rock art, in that there is no apparent conventional division of gender roles by showing the majority of humans without any clear indication of sex, age, or status. It is significant that, at the Apollo 11 Cave for example, although a few of the images suggest different roles for women and men, the vast majority of these images suggest no distinction in gender roles.

Ethnographic studies combined with historic documentation of thousands of works of rock art currently indicate two significant facts. One dated fact is that the San peoples of Namibia were the first art-producing peoples in Africa. Second, San images reflect their surrounding animal environment as well as their ritual experiences.

—*Patricia Coronel and Michael Coronel*

FURTHER READING

Barnard, Alan. *Hunters and Herders of Southern Africa: A Comparative Ethnography of the Khoisan Peoples*. New York: Cambridge University Press, 1992. A thorough anthropological overview of the Khoisan.

Dowson, T. A. *Rock Engravings of Southern Africa*. Johannesburg, South Africa: Witwatersrand University Press, 1992. Good for numerous illustrations covering the breadth of engraved imagery.

Garlake, Peter. *Early Art and Architecture of Africa*. New

York: Oxford University Press, 2002. Chapter 2 offers an excellent overview of southern African rock art, including interpretive approaches by leading scholars.

Guenther, Mathias. *Tricksters and Trancers: Bushman Religion and Society*. Bloomington: Indiana University Press, 1999. Combines early historiography and recent ethnography to explain figurative forms that surface in Bushman rituals and religion.

Lewis-Williams, J. D. *Believing and Seeing: Symbolic Meanings in Southern San Rock Paintings*. London: Academic Press, 1981. Connects painting imagery with San beliefs and ritual practices.

SEE ALSO: c. 16,000-c. 3000 B.C.E., BaTwa Peoples Thrive in Central Africa; c. 15,500 B.C.E., Early Australians Create the Bradshaw Rock Paintings; c. 15,000 B.C.E., Early Europeans Create Lascaux Cave Paintings.

c. 18,000-c. 11,000 B.C.E.
BERING STRAIT MIGRATIONS

Using a land bridge between modern-day Siberia and Alaska, the first human beings arrived in North America and gradually moved east and south into South America, populating these two continents.

LOCALE: Beringia (now the Bering Strait, between Siberia and Alaska)
CATEGORY: Prehistory and ancient cultures

SUMMARY OF EVENT

About two million years ago, for reasons not entirely understood, earth's temperature began to fall. In the north, more snow fell in winter than melted in summer, and great sheets of ice formed on the landmasses. These glaciers went through a series of advances and retreats—sliding forward under the influence of gravity and melting back under warmer climatic conditions.

At the same time, a group of primates (monkeys, apes, and their relatives) was evolving in Africa. This group had already developed the ability to walk on their hind limbs rather than on four feet, thus freeing the forelimbs for functions other than locomotion. Climatic change had initiated a drying trend in Africa, replacing rain forests with grasslands and savannas. Several species of the two-legged primate group had successfully invaded the grassland environment and spread throughout Africa. Well into the Ice Age, late-developing species migrated north into Europe and Asia, using tools, animal skins, and fire to cope with the cold. Some members of one species, today called *Homo sapiens* (literally, wise human), eventually moved into frigid Siberian environments.

Eastern Siberia and western Alaska were not covered by glaciers, even at the height of glacial advance. Although the climate in these unglaciated regions was cold, a number of large mammal species (mammoths, mastodons, giant bison, and others) had invaded the northern environment ahead of the humans. The newcomers probably used many food sources, but they became especially skilled at hunting the large animals.

Tremendous amounts of water were required to build the continental glaciers. That water came primarily from the most abundant source of water on the planet, the oceans. As a result, each advance and retreat of the glaciers was accompanied by dramatic changes in sea level—the sea rose as glaciers melted and fell with each glacial advance. Today, only about 50 miles (80 kilometers) of water separate Siberia from Alaska across the Bering Strait. The Bering Strait is less than 200 feet (60 meters) deep, and the adjacent parts of the Chukchi and Bering seas are not much deeper. Because of this, a strip of Bering Strait and adjacent sea floor 1,000 miles (1,600 kilometers) wide became dry land whenever extensive glaciation occurred. Along with adjacent parts of Siberia and Alaska, this region is called Beringia. When the glaciers were in full retreat, the Bering Strait reformed, splitting Beringia and placing a barrier between the two continents.

The sea level rose and fell throughout glacial times, and the connection between Alaska and Siberia was established and broken repeatedly. Various land organisms crossed the bridge when it was available, but exchange between the continents was blocked when it was inundated. Mammoths, mastodons, camels, horses, and many other species of animals and plants crossed throughout the Ice Age, but humans probably did not reach northeastern Siberia until the most recent glacial advance.

In North America, the last glacier (the Wisconsin) advanced until approximately sixty thousand years ago, at which time it began a retreat called the mid-Wisconsin interglacial. Fewer than thirty thousand years ago, it began its final advance (the late Wisconsin glaciation) fol-

BERING STRAIT MIGRATIONS, C. 18,000-C. 11,000 B.C.E.

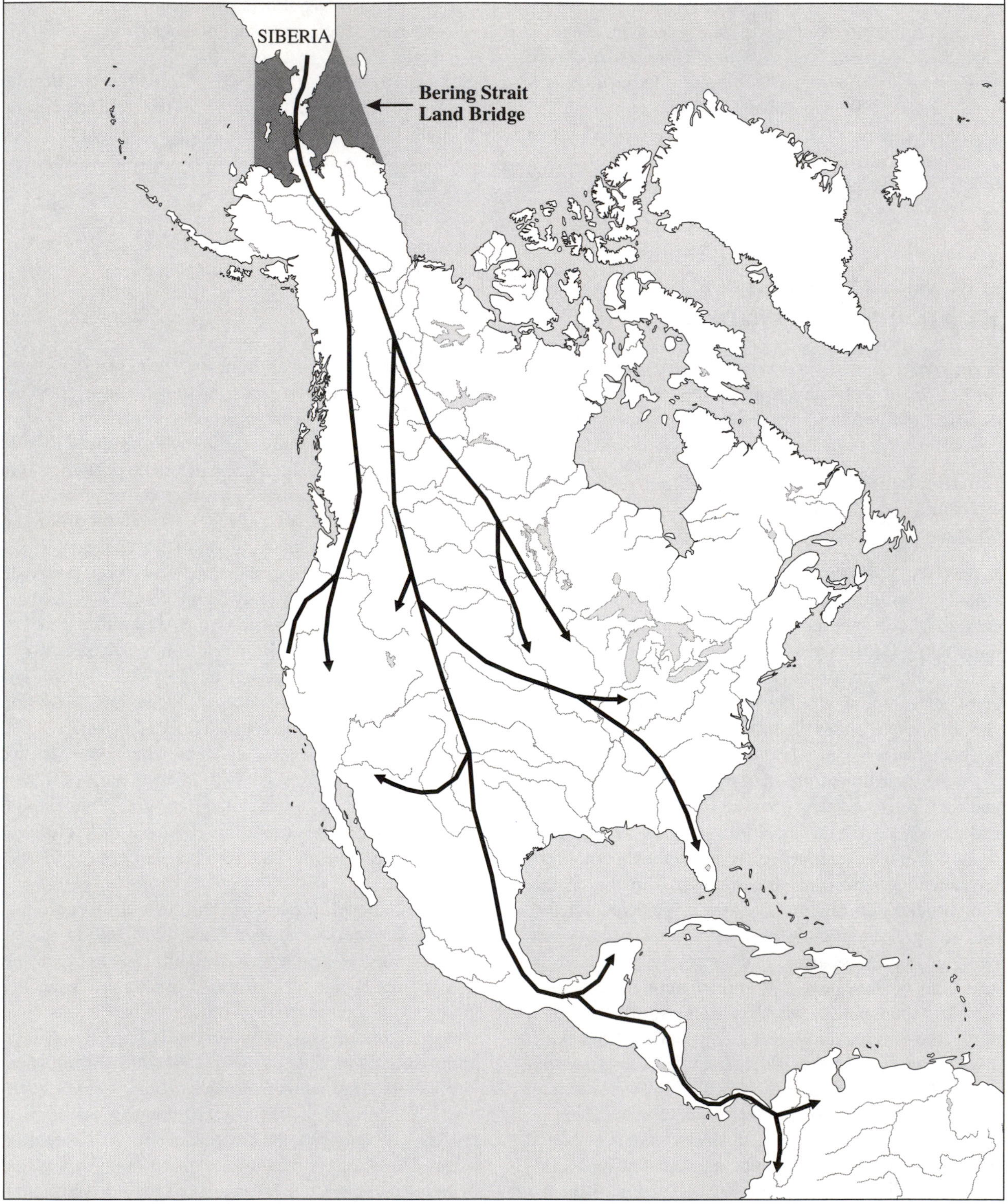

According to one theory, the first people to arrive in North America traveled over a land bridge between modern-day Siberia and Alaska. Once on the continent, they gradually spread southward and eastward.

lowed by its most recent retreat, which began eighteen thousand years ago. It was during or after the mid-Wisconsin interglacial that humans from Siberia made their way across Beringia into North America.

This migration was not a directed, purposeful movement to a new continent. It is unlikely that the first Americans had any sense of their role in history or the nature of continents. The migration probably was the simple result of growing populations expanding into new regions, perhaps drawn by the presence of herds of the large mammals they were so adept at hunting.

The populations continued to expand throughout Alaska and adjacent Canada but were restricted from much of Canada by two major glacial masses. The Laurentide ice sheet covered most of Canada and much of the northern United States, from the East Coast to the Rocky Mountains. The second mass of ice resulted from the coalescence of a number of mountain glaciers into a single glacial complex, the Cordilleran glacier located between the Rockies and the coastal mountain ranges.

During glacial advance, the two ice masses probably met and blocked the migrants' route south. However, when the glaciers melted, a corridor opened between them. The migrants moved south through Mexico and Central America, and on to the tip of South America. As the most recent glacial retreat continued, the first Americans expanded their range into all parts of Canada as well.

Anthropologists and archaeologists call these first Americans (or their immediate descendants) Paleo-Indians. Many details of relationship and pathways of descent are not known, but the Paleo-Indian culture gave rise to another widespread culture, called the Archaic, around 7000 B.C.E. Approximately two thousand years ago, the Archaic culture began to give way to the mound-building culture of eastern North America (the Adena, Hopewell, and Mississippian), the agricultural groups of the southwestern deserts (the Hohokam, Mogollon, and Anasazi), and other cultures. Some time before 1500 C.E., these prehistoric cultures gave rise to the Native American tribes that were later displaced by European settlement. Some archaeologists argue that a similar sequence of cultural replacement took place in Mexico and Central and South America, culminating in the Inca, Aztec, and Mayan civilizations decimated by the Spanish conquistadores in the 1500's.

One of the most vituperative arguments in the history of science centers on the question of when the first Americans arrived. A few students of the question argue for dates earlier than the mid-Wisconsin interglacial, and some argue for entry times more than thirty thousand years ago (during the mid-Wisconsin interglacial) or around 18,000 B.C.E., during the last glacial maximum, but many favor from 15,000 to 11,000 B.C.E.

The basis for the most popular position is the widespread occurrence of a particular type of spear point found at archaeological sites all over North America, sites determined to be between 11,500 and 10,500 years old. These sites constitute the first recognized North American Paleo-Indian culture, now called the Clovis culture because it was established on the basis of finds in Blackwater Draw near Clovis, New Mexico. Because the culture was so widespread, archaeologists assume that Native Americans must have been on the continent some time before the Clovis dates. Discoveries at sites such as Meadowcroft Rockshelter in southwestern Pennsylvania and Cactus Hill and Saltville in Virginia support the idea that other cultures preceded the Clovis culture. At these sites, archaeologists found artifacts that are very different from and are significantly older than those found at Clovis. Although many archaeologists believe that the first immigrants spread from Beringia to Tierra del Fuego and throughout both continents, the discovery of sites that appear to predate the Clovis culture in South America have caused others to believe that South America may have been populated separately, perhaps even earlier than North America.

Evidence based on Native American languages, tooth anatomy, and genetics suggests that there were at least three migrations of different Siberian peoples into North America. The first group of migrants gave rise to most Native American groups. One of the later migrant groups was ancestral to the Navajo, Apache, and some western Canadian tribes; the Eskimo (Inuit) and Aleut peoples derived from the other group. Each migration probably involved movement of many subgroups through an extended time period. Some archaeologists believe that marine travelers, along the coast or across open seas, may have contributed to the colonization as well.

Significance

Although the timing and details of the colonization of North America are unsettled, most archaeologists agree on its basic character. Northern Asiatic people crossed Beringia into North America and spread fairly rapidly throughout North and South America. These people, with possible contributions from earlier and later (and perhaps seagoing) immigrants, developed into the multitude of Native American groups present when Europeans "discovered" the continents. By the most conservative estimates, ancestors of the Native Americans who met the European explorers and colonists more than five hundred years ago had occupied the Americas for more than twelve thousand years.

—*Carl W. Hoagstrom*

FURTHER READING

Adovasio, J. M. *The First Americans: In Pursuit of Archaeology's Greatest Mystery.* New York: Random House, 2002. An examination of the first human beings to populate the Americas. Bibliography and index.

Dixon, E. James. *Bones, Boats, and Bison: Archeology and the First Colonization of Western North America.* Albuquerque: University of New Mexico Press, 1999. Dixon looks at the archaeological evidence surrounding the peopling of North and South America. Bibliography and index.

_______. *Quest for the Origins of the First Americans.* Albuquerque: University of New Mexico Press, 1993. An archaeologist discusses the first Americans in the context of his own research. Illustrations, index, bibliography.

Fagan, Brian M. *Ancient North America: The Archaeology of a Continent.* 3d ed. New York: Thames and Hudson, 2000. A consideration of the first Americans in the context of North American archaeology. Illustrations, index, bibliography.

Jablonski, Nina G., ed. *The First Americans: The Pleistocene Colonization of the New World.* Memoirs of the California Academy of Sciences, no. 27. San Francisco: California Academy of Sciences and University of California Press, 2002. A collection of papers from the fourth Wattis Symposium held in October, 1999, discussing various aspects of the peopling of the Americas. Bibliography and index.

West, Frederick Hadleigh, and Constance F. West, eds. *American Beginnings: The Prehistory and Palaeoecology of Beringia.* Chicago: University of Chicago Press, 1996. This collection of essays examines topics concerning the Bering land bridge, including excavations in the surrounding area. Bibliography and index.

SEE ALSO: c. 13,000 B.C.E., Humans Enter the South American Continent; 13,000-c. 7000 B.C.E., Paleo-Indian Culture Flourishes in North America; c. 9500-c. 9000 B.C.E., Clovis Culture Rises in New Mexico; c. 9000-c. 8000 B.C.E., Cochise Culture Thrives in American Southwest; c. 8800-c. 8500 B.C.E., Folsom People Flourish in New Mexico; c. 8000-c. 4000 B.C.E., Plano Culture Flourishes in Great Plains Area; c. 8000-c. 1000 B.C.E., Archaic Indians Adapt to Warmer Climates; c. 7700-c. 1000 B.C.E., Native Cultures Flourish on the North Pacific Coast; c. 7200 B.C.E., Kennewick Man Lives in North America.

c. 16,000-c. 3000 B.C.E.
BATWA PEOPLES THRIVE IN CENTRAL AFRICA

The BaTwa were ancient hunter-gatherer peoples of central Africa who have been believed to represent the life and culture of "primordial" humans.

LOCALE: Central Africa (present-day Rwanda, Burundi, Uganda, and the Congo Basin)
CATEGORY: Prehistory and ancient cultures

SUMMARY OF EVENT

Scholarly knowledge of BaTwa history before 3000 B.C.E. is sparse. What is known about the BaTwa ancestral communities in ancient times and even before the nineteenth century comes from the available archaeological data. The fact that hunter-gatherers utilized large territories over relatively short periods of time and may have commonly reused many tools and products, combined with the reality of decay and disintegration of material culture in humid forest climates, makes it difficult to recover historical evidence to reconstruct a consistent cultural profile for BaTwa in earlier millennia. Based on available data that have been recovered for the period 16,000-3000 B.C.E., it is evident that the BaTwa ancestral communities were hunter-gatherers who made use of Stone Age technologies. Less definitive is whether the various scattered communities categorized as BaTwa descend from a shared common language and how far back that language might be traced. The oldest proposed date for a BaTwa ancestral community is fifty thousand years ago.

Although the BaTwa are thought to have descended from ancestral BaTwa who inhabited the central regions of the African continent by about eighteen thousand years ago, in the present, not all BaTwa speak a common BaTwa language; rather, they have adopted Bantu, Central Sudanic, and even French dialects. Modern-day BaTwa are typically referred to by the derogatory term "Pygmies" and are defined not so much by their language and cultural or ethnic practices as by their lifestyle of forest-based hunting and their physiology, a noticeably short average stature that is a direct function of environment and diet.

Archaeologists have uncovered a set of microlithic stone tool technologies in the Rwanda-Burundi forest regions that indicate that the ancestral BaTwa predominantly inhabited areas around modern-day Rwanda and Burundi until about five thousand years ago. The archaeological evidence for a claim of BaTwa occupation of the areas in the northeastern Congo Basin has been analyzed and connected to the Tshitolian tradition to the west in the central Congo Basin, a connection that indicates a widespread hunting-gathering network of communities possessing a common tool tradition.

Tshitolian Stone Age technology emerged on the fringes of the equatorial forest and is distinct from the central African Savanna microlithic tradition. Tshitolian appears to be an innovation on Lupemban traditions beginning in about the thirteenth millennium B.C.E., at which point tools began to decrease in size and became, more typically, double-sided blades also known as backed blades or parallel-sided blades. In the denser forested river valleys of Zaire, Gabon, Congo, and Cameroon to the west of Rwanda and Burundi, there are high proportions of the backed blades in the archaeological record. The microlithic tools appear to have been displaced by larger tools, particularly in the savannas, where presumably a different set of economic practices was pursued and different foods consumed. Those who lived on the forest fringes could be distinguished economically and culturally from those BaTwa inhabiting the dense forests based on tool assemblages and the more abundant material culture indicative of settled agricultural communities on the forest fringes.

The BaTwa historically practiced hunting and gathering economies whereby they acquired both food for their own consumption and items to trade with neighboring agriculturalists from about the fourth millennium B.C.E. By 4000 B.C.E., the Bantu had moved into and begun to cultivate lands surrounding dense forests that happened to be inhabited by BaTwa hunter-gatherers in southern Cameroon. The proximity of these distinct communities facilitated the trading of Bantu cultivated food resources, iron, and pottery for the favored forest products—honey, forest meat, and medicinal products from forest roots and plants—acquired by BaTwa.

All that is presently known of BaTwa artistic culture through historical evidence is that the musical tradition included flutes and whistles and that dancing emphasized choreographed foot movements as opposed to focusing on bodily movements. BaTwa produced barkcloth as well as stools with woven seats. Whether such utilitarian art was produced before Bantu contact c. 3000 B.C.E. is not yet known.

The modern BaTwa are believed to be descendants of the ancient group. This BaTwa man, photographed in 1954, made his living by making earthenware. (Bettmann/Corbis)

BaTwa social, economic, political, and cultural practices are not well understood beyond the fact that they were hunter-gatherers who inhabited rain forests, and who lived in small, semisedentary or nonsedentary bands. Limited types of material culture have been reconstructed in connection with the BaTwa; there is significant evidence of hunting apparatus, but almost nothing to indicate specific cultural practices, clothing, or housing styles has been uncovered. To a great extent, these hunter-gatherers used the crossbow in hunting and employed microlithic stone tools. After 3000 B.C.E., there was also use of Bantu iron tools that the BaTwa most likely obtained through trade.

Significance

The BaTwa ancestors may have been one of the first "modern" African communities that formed in the dense forest regions of the continent fifty to eighteen thousand years ago. The ancestors of modern day BaTwa would have been primarily food collectors and may have been culturally and linguistically linked to other hunter-gatherers of the western equatorial rain forests of central Africa. The easternmost BaTwa would have inhabited forested lands of modern-day Rwanda and Burundi. The westernmost BaTwa had extensive trade relations with Bantu agriculturalists, at least since the fourth millennium B.C.E.

BaTwa ancestry is one of the great unanswered questions of African history. The various BaTwa communities are distinguished from each other in scholarly literature according to language and culture. Although they are distinguished from the Bantu, Sudanic, Cushitic, and even Khoisan language communities, BaTwa cannot necessarily be traced to a single ancestral community and may have been historically connected to one or all of the aforementioned language families. There is no strong linguistic evidence to indicate a single BaTwa ancestral language, but there is ancient technology that is common in various regions in which historical hunting and gathering territory has been identified.

Present-day hunting-gathering communities of the wider Congo Basin that are considered BaTwa are the Twa in the regions around Lake Kivu; the Gesera and Zigaba in Rwanda and Burundi; the Binga, Beku, Bongo, Jelli, Koa, Kola, Kuya, Rimba, and Yaga in the far west along the Atlantic coast; and the Aka, Efe, and Mbuti of the Ituri forest in northeastern Democratic Republic of Congo (Zaire). BaTwa are typically linked to other BaTwa because of their physical size and reliance on hunting and gathering as a central part of food acquisition. Paradoxically, Rwanda's approximately thirty thousand Twa today speak a dialect of a Bantu language, and although they are not always so petite in height that they are conspicuously different from Hutus and Tutsis, they do typically practice hunting and gathering (though not always to the exclusion of cultivation or livestock keeping). Thus, those referred to as "Pygmies," or Twa, for the past 150 years most commonly spoke a Bantu or Central Sudanic language, may have been taller than 5 feet (150 centimeters) in height, and may have combined agricultural food production practices with those of hunting and gathering.

Although the majority of BaTwa have been forced to abandon the hunting and gathering lifestyle, there is a subgroup within the Twa, referred to as the Impunyu, who have managed to sustain forest life and, in the twenty-first century, continue to live in the Nyungwe forest of Rwanda. Whether the BaTwa populations, which predate the bordering agricultural peoples, were of a common linguistic or cultural origin remains to be uncovered, but what is certain is that hunting and gathering populations have long inhabited the forests of central Africa and have practiced similar types of economies and shared a common tool technology.

The notion that "Pygmies" are relics or vestiges of the ancestral human type remains unproven and is an untenable theory. Because historical processes change all communities over time, modern-day BaTwa cannot be viewed as examples of how ancient peoples lived because they too have incorporated elements of various Bantu cultures, commercial trade, and even European languages into their lives for at least the past five millennia.

—Catherine Cymone Fourshey

FURTHER READING

Booth, Graham, et al. "Voices of the Forest." Africa National Geographic Television, Tigress Productions 2001. A documentary that presents modern-day Baka (a BaTwa group) and their lifestyle and social struggles.

Klieman, Kairn A. *The Pygmies Were Our Compass: Bantu and BaTwa in the History of West Central Africa, Early Times to c. 1900 C.E.* Portsmouth, N.H.: Heinemann, 2003. The history of Central African BaTwa of Congo and Gabon and their social and economic relationships with Bantu-speaking peoples in the forest regions.

Lewis, Jerome. *The BaTwa Pygmies of the Great Lakes Region*. London: Minority Rights Group International, 2000. This report focuses on the human rights of modern-day BaTwa descendants.

Ntibazonkiza, Raphaîl. *Au royaume des seigneurs de la lance: Une Approche historique de la question ethnique au Burundi*. Brussels: Bruxelles Droits de l'Homme, 1992-1993. Focuses on the ethnic and cultural relations among BaTwa, Hutu, and Tutsi in Rwanda and Burundi. There is some attention to the origins of the BaTwa, but this work focuses primarily on contemporary issues related to democracy. In French.

SEE ALSO: c. 25,000 B.C.E., San Peoples Create Earliest African Art; c. 10,000 B.C.E.-c. 1 C.E., Saharan Peoples Create Rock Art; c. 9000-c. 7000 B.C.E., Nilo-Saharan Peoples Produce Food and Pottery; c. 7000-c. 6000 B.C.E., Khoisan Peoples Disperse Throughout Southern Africa; c. 400 B.C.E.-c. 300 C.E., Bantu Peoples Spread Farming Across Southern Africa; 3d century B.C.E., Commercial City of Jenne Is Founded on Niger River.

c. 15,500 B.C.E.
EARLY AUSTRALIANS CREATE THE BRADSHAW ROCK PAINTINGS

Almost twenty millennia ago, members of a sophisticated hunter-gatherer culture in northwest Australia created thousands of images, known as the Bradshaw paintings, on rock walls.

LOCALE: Kimberley region of northwest Australia
CATEGORIES: Prehistory and ancient cultures; cultural and intellectual history

SUMMARY OF EVENT

The Kimberley region is in the northern section of western Australia and includes the King Leopold mountain range, from which several rivers descend to the Indian Ocean. North of the mountain range are plateaus of grassland, but land travel over the mountains remains difficult. In 1838, one of the earliest nonindigenous visitors to the area, the British explorer Sir George Grey, described the Kimberley as the roughest terrain he had ever seen. Grey discovered a group of rock paintings now described as belonging to the Wandjina period, the youngest epoch of paintings in the region. The rocks in this region are extremely ancient, more than 400 million years old, and it is believed that certain unique climatic and chemical factors preserved the paintings by embedding them in the sandstone. Grey's published drawings of these images stirred excitement in the academic world.

In 1891, explorer Joseph Bradshaw, along with his brother, was surveying the upper Price Regent River in the Kimberley area for potential grazing land. He found a "gallery" of remarkable paintings and was struck by their appearance.

> I rode out and found that the river at this place emerges through a gorge in the sandstone range . . . in the secluded chasms of these rocks were numerous aboriginal paintings which appeared to be of great antiquity . . . some of the human figures were life-size, the bodies and limbs very attenuated, and represented as having numerous tassel-shaped adornments appended to the hair, neck, waist, arms and legs . . . the figures are endowed with a strong feeling of reality and graceful movement.

During the century after the initial discovery, more than one thousand paintings were found within an area covering approximately 19,300 square miles (50,000 square kilometers), and thousands more undiscovered or undocumented galleries are believed to exist. The Bradshaw family name was given to this style and epoch of paintings, which represent some of the oldest known human artifacts.

Later expeditions, including the German Frobenius expedition of 1938, provided further documentation of the vast range of sites, and the Bradshaw rock art was eventually divided by style into four major categories: The oldest are the Tassel Figures, which portray extensive ornamentation; followed by the Sash Figures; the Elegant Action Figures, which are shown running and hunting; and the more abstract Polychrome Clothes Peg Figures, believed to be the most recent.

The precise antiquity of the paintings is unknown, and estimates reach as far back as 60,000 years. In 1996, Grahame L. Walsh, one of the most active researchers of Bradshaw art, discovered a means to establish the minimum age for some of the paintings. He found a Bradshaw painting that was partly covered by a fossilized-mud wasp nest. By using the luminescence method, scientists were able to determine the age of single grains of quartz embedded in the nest, showing that the painting underneath the nest was made at least 17,500 (±1,800) years ago. Other paintings dated using the radiocarbon method appear to be younger, but there is little doubt that a wide span of human history is represented. Traditional carbon-dating technology is problematic in the case of the Bradshaw paintings because with the passage of time, the original pigments were infused into the rock itself as petrified shades of mulberry red, impervious to rain, wind, and the curiosity of scholars.

The connection between the ancient Bradshaw paintings and the Aboriginal Australians of modern times is not clear, and the topic remains highly controversial. In some Aborigine legends, the images were painted by birds, who pecked the rocks until their beaks bled and used their tail feathers to paint with their own blood. Although Aboriginal peoples living in the immediate area have dismissed the paintings as being of little significance and of a time before theirs, other Aboriginal groups have identified them as part of their heritage and wish to restrict access to them. Although the Bradshaw paintings remain enigmatic, there are proven connections between contemporary Aboriginal cultures and later rock art styles, which are also found in other regions of Australia. Still ancient by Western standards, the newer styles have striking features of their own, including simultaneous representation of interiors and exteriors (this technique is sometimes referred to as X ray).

Walsh of the Bradshaw Foundation has suggested a possible Asian origin for the people who created the Bradshaw art. He points out that the Kimberley shoreline is only about 300 miles (480 kilometers) from Indonesia and was even closer during the last Ice Age, permitting waves of immigration. However, other than the paintings themselves, material remains of the culture that produced the images have been very sparse, so researchers have focused on the content of the pictures to gather clues about the people. For example, boomerangs are included in some of the paintings, suggesting a connection to more recent Australian cultures, but other details, such as the elaborate headgear with tassels, are very unfamiliar. Some of the animals represented in the paintings are now extinct, and this has attracted the interest of paleontologists and bio-historians.

SIGNIFICANCE

Understanding the Bradshaw art is an ongoing challenge that will require the joint efforts of scholars from many disciplines, and these activities are likely to continue for many years. Aside from the technical issues mentioned above, the sheer volume of the material is daunting; of an estimated 100,000 Bradshaw galleries distributed over 19,300 square miles (50,000 square kilometers) of rough terrain, only a handful, estimated at between 1 percent and 2 percent of the total, have been documented.

The International Rock Art Research Team (IRART), which has representatives from the United States, Canada, and Denmark as well as Australia and began its work in 1998 under the guidance of Per Michaelsen of James Cook University, has been collecting data and conducting new analyses using digital photography. Walsh, who was awarded the Thompson Medal by the Royal Geographical Society in 1990 for his many years of research on the Bradshaw paintings, continues to advocate for the preservation of the paintings, which are potentially threatened by artifact poachers and corrosion from industrial pollutants.

Most researchers agree that the Bradshaw paintings can provide valuable information about human life at the end of the last ice age. Because of the wide scope of time represented, changes in subject matter of the Bradshaws suggest human responses to significant environmental changes during the last glacial-interglacial cycle. The early Bradshaw images show abundant plant material, and the later images show more weapons, a possible response to an increasingly dry climate with dwindling food supplies.

Aside from questions about one of the earliest known human civilizations, there is strong consensus on the aesthetic value of Bradshaw art. The Bradshaw artists' use of powerful, dynamic silhouettes, especially in the Elegant Action Figures genre, has been compared to the work of the twentieth century French artist Henri Matisse, whose silhouettes of dancing human figures are especially well-loved. The elongated human figures in the ancient art from Kimberley are frequently portrayed in graceful, balanced postures that seem to be on the verge of escaping gravity. Many of these earliest depictions of human clothing show that our forebears of the last ice age, with tassels flying away from their heads, shared our desire for personal ornamentation.

—*Alice Myers*

FURTHER READING

McCarthy, Frederick. *Australian Aboriginal Rock Art.* Sydney, Australia: Australian Museum, 1958. General survey of Australian rock art and paintings. Illustrated.

Mowaljarlai, David, and Jutta Malnic. *Yorro Yorro: Aboriginal Creation and the Renewal of Nature.* Rochester, Vt.: Inner Traditions, 1993. Rock paintings and stories of the Wandjina people, the other major group in the Australian Kimberley region. Color plates, glossaries.

Walsh, Grahame L. *Australia's Greatest Rock Art.* Bathurst, N.S.W., Australia: E. J. Brill/Robert Brown, 1988. An examination of rock art by an expert in the field.

_______. *Bradshaw Art of the Kimberley.* Toowong, Qld.: Takarakka Nowan Kas, 2000. In this work, Walsh focuses on the Bradshaw paintings of the Kimberley area. Illustrations and colored maps.

_______. *Bradshaws: Ancient Rock Paintings of North-West Australia.* Carouge-Geneva: Edition Limitee, 1994. Published for the Bradshaw Foundation, this is the definitive source of information on the subject. Includes illustrations, maps, photographs, and diagrams.

SEE ALSO: c. 25,000 B.C.E., San Peoples Create Earliest African Art; c. 15,000 B.C.E., Early Europeans Create Lascaux Cave Paintings; c. 10,000 B.C.E.-c. 1 C.E., Saharan Peoples Create Rock Art; c. 3000 B.C.E., Australian Aborigines Create Wandjina Cave Paintings.

c. 15,000 B.C.E.
EARLY EUROPEANS CREATE LASCAUX CAVE PAINTINGS

Upper Paleolithic peoples, the first anatomically modern people in Europe, created paintings in the Lascaux cave, providing evidence of Magdalenian culture and demonstrating their behavioral sophistication.

LOCALE: Lascaux cave, near Montignac, Dordogne, France

CATEGORIES: Prehistory and ancient cultures; cultural and intellectual history

SUMMARY OF EVENT

The first cultural remains of anatomically and behaviorally modern people in Europe are described by archaeologists as the Upper Paleolithic and are dated to the later part of the last glaciation of the very Late Pleistocene (40,000-35,000 to 12,000-10,000 years ago). These Upper Paleolithic peoples created cave paintings, which were unknown in Europe before the appearance of anatomically modern peoples. Some of the most dramatic examples of these paintings are in Lascaux cave, discovered on September 12, 1940, by four teenage Montignac boys: Marcel Ravidat, Jacques Marsal, Simon Coencas, and Georges Agnel. At least six hundred paintings and nearly fifteen hundred engravings are in this cave system. Charcoal discovered on the floor of the cave was dated to c. 15,000 B.C.E. indicating that the paintings are at least that old.

It was Ravidat's idea to explore the cave. An elderly woman had buried a dead mule there and claimed that the hole extended to a medieval passage underground. She believed that it ended at a chateau at the base of a hill near Lascaux. The boys decided to test her assertion and had brought a lamp to light their way. They noticed the paintings and were quite excited. Soon many knew of their find, and their schoolteacher notified the priest, Abbé Henri-Édouard-Prosper Breuil, who arrived on September 21, 1940, and was the first to describe and analyze the paintings.

The first Upper Paleolithic cave paintings were discovered by a landowner, Marcelino Sanz de Sautuola, in Altamira Cave in northern Spain in 1879, but many doubted their authenticity. Further examples were discovered in southwestern France by the early 1900's, and this additional evidence reassured most doubters. The controversy resurfaced in 1952, when French literary Surrealist André Breton visited Pech-Merle and touched one of the apparently wet paintings. He was convinced it was a forgery. Breuil pointed out that the dampness of the caves prevented the paint from drying and that in many cases the pigments were overlain by whitish calcite deposits, supporting their antiquity.

The Upper Paleolithic peoples were culturally very different from the peoples they followed. The tools and artifacts left by the preceding Neanderthals were remarkably uniform and differed only in the relative proportions of the same artifact types. Tools changed very slowly over thousands of years. That pace was altered dramatically with the appearance of Upper Paleolithic peoples, who from 34,000 to 11,000 years ago left a series of tool industries known to archaeologists from older to younger as the Aurignacian, Gravettian (Perigordian), Solutrean, and Magdalenian. Each industry was distinguished by specific artifact types either rare or absent in other traditions. The Magdalenian culture, with which Lascaux cave is identified, is dated between 16,500 and 11,000 years ago and is found in France, northern Spain, Switzerland, Germany, Belgium, and southern Britain. Its most characteristic implements are composed of bone and antler, which were fashioned into points, harpoons, and other tools.

Upper Paleolithic peoples lived by hunting and gathering wild animal and plant resources. Game was abundant at this time, including woolly mammoth, reindeer, bison, horse, and saiga antelope. They were apparently more successful than the Neanderthals, because Upper Paleolithic sites are more numerous and populated more densely. Bird and fish bones in particular are more common than for older sites. There was also more contact and exchange among groups because archaeologists have found amber, finer flint, and seashells sometimes hundreds of miles from their source.

The social organization of these groups probably varied tremendously, with small family groups in the harsher environments and most likely complex, stratified societies, perhaps hereditary chiefdoms, in the richer environments. One of these resource-rich areas was the Franco-Cantabrian region (southwestern France and northern Spain), inhabited 15,000-11,000 years ago by Magdalenian peoples. More than 150 caves with late Pleistocene paintings and engravings have been located in this area. Most of them cannot be dated precisely, but representations of extinct animals such as mammoth and bison suggest Pleistocene age, and most are stylistically the same as the carved bone and antler animal figurines dated to the Magdalenian period.

Upper Paleolithic imagery has been subdivided into two kinds: wall (or parietal) art, including paintings and the more numerous engravings on rock surfaces, and portable or home art (*art mobilier*), which consists of movable artifacts such as engraved bone or antler. The term Paleolithic art has been used to describe materials that span 25,000 years in time and are found from the Iberian Peninsula to Russia. The famous, mostly stylized, Venus figurines with exaggerated buttocks and breasts are dated to the Gravettian period. Preserved images, numerous during the Upper Paleolithic, are new to the archaeological record, but what they mean in terms of human existence is in dispute.

SIGNIFICANCE

Over the years, experts have tried to determine the significance of the Upper Paleolithic cave paintings to their creators in order to understand what this art means in terms of human and cultural development. Archaeologist Margaret W. Conkey notes that the cave paintings have been interpreted in two main ways, as sympathetic hunting magic or as a sort of language or type of communication about the creators' worldview. According to the former interpretation, originally promoted by Breuil and called the foundation interpretation by Conkey, the Upper Paleolithic peoples created the animals and signs in order to guarantee future hunting success. By the 1960's, André Leroi-Gourhan and other archaeologists were criticizing this interpretation and providing alternative explanations. One difficulty with the hunting hypothesis was that the animals represented in the art were not necessarily the most common animals in these early peoples' refuse.

Leroi-Gourhan's work is described as the mythogram interpretation, because the images and their creation were seen as attempts to represent mythological structures and symbolic systems. Certain species of animals, particularly horse and bison, were more common than others and were thus assumed to have symbolic meaning. Conkey argues that this shift to describing the imagery as a sophisticated communication system is a profound statement about how Upper Paleolithic peoples were essentially mentally the same as contemporary peoples. In addition, this change to the production of wall and portable art has been observed all over the world. Thus, Conkey suggests that investigators should avoid the cultural preconceptions associated with the term "art" and try to understand the works in terms of local cultural adaptations. Unlike Western art, images are often superimposed and are usually not set off from each other or provided with a clear orienting context. Many images probably represent different times and peoples. For example, Lascaux cave exhibits a heterogeneity in style.

The discovery of other cave paintings, notably those discovered by Jean-Marie Chauvet and two friends in 1994 near Vallon-Pont-d'Arc in southeast France, has added to the debate about what these paintings meant to their creators. The Chauvet-Pont-d'Arc cave contains more than 400 paintings, including renderings of rhinoceros, lions, mammoths, horses, bison, bears, reindeer, aurochs, ibex, and stags. The inclusion of both predators and prey would seem to negate Breuil's early theory. The complexity of these paintings, believed to be about 31,000 years old and created by the Aurignacians, calls into question some of Leroi-Gourhan's theories, including his idea of a slow yet steady maturing of artistic talents during the Upper Paleolithic period that led to the Lascaux paintings created by the Magdalenians. Some experts believe that the Chauvet-Pont-d'Arc cave may have had a religious function.

—Joan C. Stevenson

FURTHER READING

Bahn, Paul G., and Jean Vertut. *Journey Through the Ice Age*. London: Weidenfeld and Nicolson, 1997. In this revision of Bahn and Vertut's *Images of the Ice Age* (1988), the authors describe where and when these images were found around the world and their many interpretations. Bibliography and index.

Bataille, Georges. *Lascaux: Or, The Birth of Art*. The Great Centuries of Painting series. Translated by Austryn Wainhouse. Lausanne: Skira, 1955. The interpretation of the cave paintings is dated, but the paintings are vividly presented. Color plates, maps, and plans.

Conkey, Margaret W., et al., eds. *Beyond Art: Pleistocene Image and Symbol*. Memoirs of the California Academy of Sciences, no. 23. San Francisco: California Academy of Sciences and University of California Press, 1997. A collection of papers presented at the second Wattis Symposium in March, 1995, on Pleistocene images and symbols. Bibliography and index.

________. "Humans as Materialists and Symbolists: Image Making in the Upper Paleolithic." In *The Origin and Evolution of Humans and Humanness*. Boston: Jones and Bartlett, 1993. Conkey presents a critique of the interpretations and advances in the studies of Upper Paleolithic imagery.

Lauber, Patricia. *Painters of the Caves*. Washington, D.C.: National Geographic Society, 1998. Focuses primarily on the 1994 discovery of the Chauvet-Pont-d'Arc cave but also examines the significance of cave art to prehistoric and modern peoples. Bibliography and index.

Leroi-Gourhan, André. *The Dawn of European Art.* Translated by Sara Champion. New York: Cambridge University Press, 1982. Leroi-Gourhan's interpretive framework is explained clearly, and there is much description including a map and pictures of Lascaux Cave.

Ruspoli, Mario. *The Cave of Lascaux: A Final Photographic Record.* London: Thames and Hudson, 1987. A photographic record of the paintings in the Lascaux cave. Illustrations, some in color, and maps.

See also: c. 15,500 B.C.E., Early Australians Create the Bradshaw Rock Paintings; c. 10,000 B.C.E.-c. 1 C.E., Saharan Peoples Create Rock Art; c. 3000 B.C.E., Australian Aborigines Create Wandjina Cave Paintings.

c. 13,000 B.C.E.
Humans Enter the South American Continent

Evidence is increasing that the human population of South America may have arrived before the population of North America and may have migrated by a route other than the Bering Strait. The issue is contentious because it raises many questions about the relationships between the various early native cultures on both continents.

Locale: South America
Category: Prehistory and ancient cultures

Summary of Event

South America generally and eastern Brazil in particular, are areas in which evidence of the oldest human inhabitants in the Western Hemisphere have been unearthed. Remains from various sites in western and southern regions also indicate that the first peoples of South America may have had several points of origin and may well have arrived before the first inhabitants of North America.

Archaeology indicates that the first peoples entered South America by around 13,000 B.C.E. They came most probably by sea, from the east, across the Atlantic Ocean. By 7000 B.C.E. there were at least three clearly defined migrant groups, with as many as a dozen related subdivisions indicated by genetic, biological, and linguistic studies. Genetic evidence indicates that the oldest skeleton ever found in South America, that of a female unearthed in eastern Brazil at the end of the twentieth century, originated in Africa. Other early sites of similar age have been found in Argentina and Chile. Estimates regarding how long people have lived in South America continue to be pushed further back in time as cave paintings, such as those depicting giant armadillos, which were extinct before the last ice age, and other remains are found. Such remains suggest the intriguing possibility that the ancestors of later humans might have first arrived in eastern Brazil as early as fifty thousand years ago.

The earliest human inhabitants of South America are not likely to have come overland from the north, as was once thought, but rather to have come by sea from other directions. Some evidence suggests that rather than a single migration by one type of people from a single place, early entry into South America could also have been accomplished by peoples from Austronesia to the south or Oceania to the west across the Pacific. Remains in southern South America suggest the possible first arrivals were aborigines who came from Australia to the southern tip of South America at Cape Verde, across the South Pacific. They would have migrated northward along the coasts after making landfall. They established the continent's first fishing encampments and villages, where the oldest known pottery made in the Americas was produced between 7500 and 5000 B.C.E.

The vegetation and climate of eastern South America are classified as typical closed-canopy rain forests with a humid tropical monsoon climate. Rainfall averages upward of 80 inches (2 meters) or more a year. The first people lived in small groups, engaged in some farming of wild plants, and hunted small game. They lived in caves or temporary thatched dwellings and did not cultivate crops. There is no indication that they used seed from any plants that originated in the north, nor that they used any plants other than those in their immediate locale.

Hundreds of distinct cultural groups eventually developed from the original people. No matter where they many have come from, each led a lifestyle unique to and appropriate for their local environment. In time these differences led to ongoing conflicts between groups. This resulted in much genetic and cultural mixing.

Studies show that by the Early Archaic period, around 7000 B.C.E., another type of peoples, originating in Eurasia, had migrated from North America and either melded with or wiped out the original people. These peoples were masters of big-game hunting and expert gatherers of vegetable foods. They followed the hunt southward in their search for more game. These peoples might have been responsible for hunting to extinction many of the larger animals of North America, such as mammoths and the ancestors of the camels. Then they headed south in search of new sources of food. They perfected slash-and-burn agriculture as they moved into the jungles and destroyed established populations, replacing them with their own cultures as they went.

Highly developed agricultural peoples eventually dominated the richer maritime and riverine environments, and they drove the hunter-gatherers inland into more marginal areas. Sometimes the hunting peoples practiced cannibalism. Whether this was done for survival or for ritual purposes is unclear. Their lifestyles remained remarkably consistent, relying on skills developed during earlier periods. Hunting; fishing; gathering fruits, nuts, and seeds; and slash-and-burn agricultural practices required each group to move periodically within their territory to new ground once a site's food growing potential was exhausted. Such groups were small, mobile, and relatively simple.

The greatest concentrations of population occurred among the agricultural cultures. In larger settlements and cities, tens of thousands of people descended from the original inhabitants lived together and developed highly abstract belief systems and intricate economies involving trade with surrounding peoples. The south and west Andes regions were home to some of the most advanced monolithic agricultural civilizations in the Americas. By 2500 B.C.E., they had tamed the camelids of the Andes: the llamas, vicuñas, and alpacas. From the end of the Archaic Transition, between 2000 B.C.E. and 1400 C.E., to the rise of the Incas, there were seven major periods, each marked by unique variations in architecture, use of textiles, and ceramics technology.

SIGNIFICANCE

The new evidence for multiple migrations into South America from several directions and points of origin over a period of several thousand years, somewhere between 29,000 and 12,000 B.C.E., complicates the traditional picture of the peopling of the Americas. Early South American cultures were more diverse than previously realized, and their existence puts a new light on the migration of Eurasian peoples from the north. These peoples did not move into an empty continent but rather encountered previous inhabitants, whom they had to conquer or assimilate.

—*Michael W. Simpson*

FURTHER READING

Fagan, B. *The Great Journey: The Peopling of Ancient America*. New York: Thames and Hudson, 1987. Reconstructs the sources and defines the distribution of peoples across the American continent.

Kolata, A. L. *Valley of the Spirits*. New York: John Wiley and Sons, 1996. A beautiful and haunting look at a south American archaeological site, interpreting its possible uses and meanings.

Masuda, S., I. Shimada, and C. Morris, eds. *Andean Ecology and Civilization*. Tokyo: University of Tokyo Press, 1985. A collection of articles that details the ways in which the early South American environments and cultures of the Andes interacted to give rise to various later highly evolved civilizations.

Moseley, M. *The Maritime Foundations of Andean Civilization*. Menlo Park, Calif.: Cummings, 1975. Focuses on evidence supporting entry into the west coast of South America from the eastern Pacific, and how the sea shaped the lives and societies of those who depended on it for their livelihoods.

Richardson, James B., III. *People of the Andes*. Washington, D.C.: Smithsonian Books, 1994. Details origins and histories of peoples of western South America.

Sorenson, J. *Pre-Columbian Contact with the Americas Across the Oceans*. Provo, Utah: Research Press, 1990. Looks at various peoples' first entry into the Americas from various directions by sea rather than overland from the north.

SEE ALSO: c. 18,000-c. 11,000 B.C.E., Bering Strait Migrations; c. 9500-c. 9000 B.C.E., Clovis Culture Rises in New Mexico; c. 8800-c. 8500 B.C.E., Folsom People Flourish in New Mexico; c. 8000 B.C.E., Permanent Settlement of the Andean Altiplano Begins; c. 7200 B.C.E., Kennewick Man Lives in North America.

c. 13,000-c. 7000 B.C.E.
Paleo-Indian Culture Flourishes in North America

The Paleo-Indians, the earliest colonists of the New World and their late Pleistocene and early Holocene descendants, originated from multiple points and displayed highly varied technology and lifestyles.

Locale: North America
Category: Prehistory and ancient cultures

Summary of Event

Originally, the term "Paleo-Indian" referred to the earliest inhabitants of the New World, especially those first recognized in the American Southwest during archaeological excavations in the 1920's and early 1930's. Largely on the basis of these and later excavations, which were conducted in New Mexico, Arizona, and sites in the Great Plains region, Paleo-Indian was defined to encompass a specific lithic (stone tool) technology signified by the distinctive "fluted" Clovis projectile point, named after a small town in New Mexico near which this type of point was found. Because Clovis points were often found in apparent association with Pleistocene big-game animals, especially mammoth, the Paleo-Indian lifeway was thought to be centered on the systematic predation of now-extinct Ice Age megafauna. By the late 1950's, the term Paleo-Indian came to include the presumed descendants of the Clovis point makers, namely the Folsom and so-called Plano complex "cultures" of the Great Plains and other groups from eastern North America, notably the Dalton complex of the American Midsouth and Southeast. Like their putative Clovis forebears, these later Paleo-Indian groups were thought to be almost exclusively big-game hunters.

By the late 1960's and early 1970's, it was widely accepted that Clovis was the New World's founding population and the direct ancestor of all other Paleo-Indian cultures in the New World. Based on numerous radiocarbon dates, mainly from western North America, Clovis appeared to date c. 9500-9000 B.C.E., with the culture's initial crossing of the Bering Strait occurring c. 500 radiocarbon years earlier. Clovis was presumed to have descended from a single founding population whose homeland was northeastern Asia, despite the absence of the distinctive Clovis points and related forms in artifact assemblages from the Arctic, Subarctic, or Siberia.

Because of the apparent synchrony between the rapid spread of Clovis and the widespread extinction of Ice Age megafauna, a causal relationship was presumed to exist between that extinction and Clovis. Hence, the understanding of Clovis was recast as a highly specialized and mobile, rapidly moving hunting culture that played a direct role in a hemisphere-wide extinction scenario. Moreover, because of its highly visible trail of apparently standardized and readily recognizable artifacts, Clovis came to be considered as a single culture with a uniform technology and associated lifeway, essentially analogous to the Magdalenian of France or the Solutrean of the Iberian Peninsula in southwestern Europe.

This characterization of Clovis culture and the timing of its arrival in the New World began to unravel in the mid- to late 1970's, however, with the discovery of sites such as Meadowcroft Rockshelter in southwestern Pennsylvania and Monte Verde in Chile. These two localities yielded artifacts that were both radically different from Clovis material culture and recovered from radiocarbon-dated contexts at least 1,000 to 2,500 radiocarbon years earlier than Clovis's presumed crossing of the Bering Strait. As Monte Verde lies outside the North American focus of this discussion, the following shall concentrate on Meadowcroft Rockshelter.

Meadowcroft Rockshelter is a deeply stratified, multicomponent site on the north bank of Cross Creek, a third-order tributary of the Ohio River, southwest of Pittsburgh, Pennsylvania. The eleven strata at Meadowcroft, which represent the longest occupational sequence in the New World, yielded a remarkable corpus of artifactual, floral, and faunal data anchored by fifty-two stratigraphically consistent radiocarbon dates. Human use of the site minimally extends from c. 12,500-12,000 B.C.E. to 1776 C.E. The earliest occupants at Meadowcroft ascribe to the Miller complex, a pioneer population of generalized hunter-gatherers with a sophisticated lithic technology based on the production of blade tools produced from polyhedral blade cores and also characterized by the manufacture of a distinctive unfluted projectile point called the Miller Lanceolate. Significantly, the extant paleoenvironmental data indicate that the site's earliest inhabitants operated in an environment not radically different from that of present times.

In addition to Meadowcroft, other pre-Clovis sites have been discovered at widely separated locations in North America, including Cactus Hill and Saltville in Virginia, Topper in South Carolina, the Nenana complex sites in Alaska, and a cluster of Chesrow complex sites in Wisconsin. All these localities are as old as or significantly older than Clovis, and none appears to be related to that entity. Significantly, the lifeways reflected at Cactus Hill and Saltville reflect the same sort of generalized hunting and gathering pattern evidenced at Meadowcroft.

Based on data from archaeological sites that are contemporaneous with and substantially older than the Clovis culture, it is now clear that the first Paleo-Indians entered the New World well before Clovis and the previously accepted arrival date of c. 10,000 B.C.E. Indeed, based on archaeological, linguistic, and mitochondrial DNA (deoxyribonucleic acid) evidence, it appears that the first Paleo-Indians may have arrived around the time of the last glacial maximum, which occurred c. 18,000 B.C.E.

Whenever they arrived, these first Americans clearly belonged to several distinct cultural traditions and may well have originated from different parts of northeastern Asia. Additionally, their percolation into the New World appears not to have been a single movement but rather a series of peopling incursions, some of which doubtless failed to survive. In addition to the traditional pedestrian route across the interior of the glacially exposed Bering Land Bridge, a combination of land and sea travel may also have occurred on the southern margin of the bridge. Thereafter, movement south could have occurred through the so-called ice-free corridor between the Cordilleran and Laurentide ice sheets as well as down the Pacific coast, again via a combination of land and sea travel.

The earliest Paleo-Indians were few in number, and hence their sites are widely scattered and difficult to identify. Although it is clear that at least some of these groups exploited big game, it appears that all groups also took a variety of smaller animals and doubtless exploited plants and aquatic resources. Hunting efficiency was enhanced by the atlatl (spear thrower), which has an ancient pedigree in the Old World, but the ultimate success of the colonization effort was due to a highly elaborated perishable technology that included plant fiber products (basketry, textiles, cordage, netting, and sandals) and items fashioned of wood, leather, and other nondurable materials. These perishable artifacts formed an integral element of the technology of the first Paleo-Indians who entered the New World. By no later than 13,000-12,500 B.C.E., at least some of these colonists were sufficiently numerous and regionally adapted to live in some permanent settlements such as Monte Verde, while others retained a much more mobile lifestyle.

By the onset of Clovis times, now more tightly fixed at c. 9200-9000 B.C.E., virtually the entire New World was populated, albeit thinly. Interestingly, most of the excavated early Paleo-Indian sites are large mammal kill or, more likely, scavenging localities. Large Clovis-era multi-seasonal campsites such as Gault in Texas, Shoop in Pennsylvania, Thunderbird and Williamson in Virginia, and Carson-Conn-Short in Tennessee attest to the rapid increase of population in later Paleo-Indian times.

By c. 8800-8500 B.C.E., Clovis in western North America had been succeeded by makers of much thinner fluted points called Folsom; in turn, these populations were followed by makers of a wide array of often delicately pressure flaked points collectively called Plano. These later Paleo-Indians were also hunter-gatherers who manifested varying degrees of mobility and subsistence strategies, which in many areas included the systematic production of both extinct (*Bison antiquus*) and modern (*Bison bison*) bison, usually via communal hunting techniques.

Despite a focus on bison, these later Paleo-Indian groups also exploited a wide array of medium-sized to small game as well as plants, waterfowl, and other non-megafaunal resources. Indeed, many of these groups led broad-spectrum foraging lifeways that were virtually identical to those of the generally later Western Archaic populations that replaced them c. 8000-7000 B.C.E.

In eastern North America, Paleo-Indians only occasionally hunted mastodon, more often focusing on a mixed diet of caribou, white-tailed deer, elk, smaller game, fish, and a broad assortment of plants. As in western North America, the Paleo-Indian period in eastern North America grades almost imperceptibly into the Eastern Archaic, which begins c. 8000-7000 B.C.E.

SIGNIFICANCE

During the Paleo-Indian period, North America underwent dynamic climatic and physiographic change, dramatic floral and faunal transformations, and the peopling of its entire extent. This latter populational transformation involved many founding groups with diverse technologies and adaptations who used several different coastal and interior routes. The Paleo-Indian lifeway was highly variable, heavily dependent on perishable technology, and dietetically broad-based, with only occasional hunting of now extinct big game. This view of Paleo-Indians represents a radical revision of earlier scholarship, which tended to focus on Clovis as the highly specialized, sole progenitor of all cultures encompassed by the time period.

—*J. M. Adovasio and David R. Pedler*

FURTHER READING

Adovasio, J. M. *The First Americans: In Pursuit of Archaeology's Greatest Mystery.* New York: Random House, 2002. An insider's look at the heated controversies surrounding the initial peopling of the New World. Bibliography and index.

Dillehay, Tom D. *The Settlement of the Americas: A New Prehistory.* New York: Basic Books, 2000. A careful examination of the colonization of the New World from the perspective of South America.

Fagan, Brian M. *Ancient North America: The Archaeology of a Continent.* 3d ed. New York: Thames and Hudson, 2000. A broad synthesis of the prehistory of North America from the first colonists to European contact. Bibliography and index.

Meltzer, David J. *Search for the First Americans.* Washington, D.C.: Smithsonian Books, 1993. A balanced study of the history of research into and major issues surrounding the first migrants into the New World.

See also: c. 18,000-c. 11,000 B.C.E., Bering Strait Migrations; c. 13,000 B.C.E., Humans Enter the South American Continent; c. 9500-c. 9000 B.C.E., Clovis Culture Rises in New Mexico; c. 9000-c. 8000 B.C.E., Cochise Culture Thrives in American Southwest; c. 8800-c. 8500 B.C.E., Folsom People Flourish in New Mexico; c. 8000-c. 4000 B.C.E., Plano Culture Flourishes in Great Plains Area; c. 7700-c. 1000 B.C.E., Native Cultures Flourish on the North Pacific Coast; c. 7200 B.C.E., Kennewick Man Lives in North America; c. 5800-c. 3700 B.C.E., Chinchorro Inhabit the Peruvian and Chilean Coasts; c. 5000 B.C.E., Aleutian Coastal Hunters Flourish.

c. 10,000-c. 300 B.C.E.
Jōmon Culture Thrives in Japan

The Jōmon culture in prehistoric Japan persisted for nearly ten thousand years and was known for its pottery, which had distinctive cord markings on the surface and was some of the earliest pottery in the world.

Locale: Japan
Categories: Prehistory and ancient cultures; cultural and intellectual history

Summary of Event

The Jōmon period, one of the better-recorded periods in prehistoric Japan, is characterized by pottery decorated with *jōmon* (cord markings). The period follows the Paleolithic or Pre-Ceramic period, and the culture meets the criteria of Mesolithic to Neolithic elsewhere in the world. During the Paleolithic stage in Japan, its inhabitants used only chipped stone tools in the hunting-gathering economy. Although the Jōmon peoples also subsisted by hunting, fishing, and gathering, the production of pottery for storing and cooking food indicates that their adaptive skills had advanced over those of the Paleolithic peoples.

Jōmon pottery is the first ceramic ware produced in Japan and among the oldest pottery in the world. The shards from Fukui cave in Nagasaki Prefecture, Kyūshū, were dated c. 10,000 B.C.E. by the carbon-14 radiocarbon dating process. The Fukui shards are largely accepted as some of the oldest Jōmon pottery and mark the beginning of the Jōmon period. Jōmon culture lasted for nearly 10,000 years, peaking around 3000 B.C.E. and continuing until around 300 B.C.E., when it was replaced by Yayoi, a more advanced culture marked by rice cultivation and the use of metal. Throughout the ten millennia, pottery making was Jōmon's essential activity, and the vessels spread from Hokkaidō to Okinawa with great emphasis on eastern Japan. The Jōmon vessels, which maintained cord-marking motifs throughout their long history, present both chronological and regional variations in their types and modes.

The chronology of the Jōmon period varies. Some posit its beginning at 12,000 B.C.E. or earlier, while some place it as late as 8000 or 6000 B.C.E. The period is, however, generally agreed to have lasted from around 10,000 to 300 B.C.E. The Jōmon period is subdivided into six phases on the basis of the pottery types. The dates, which vary by the source, are Incipient Jōmon (c. 10,500-7500); Earliest Jōmon (c. 7500-5000); Early Jōmon (c. 5000-3500); Middle Jōmon (c. 3500-2500); Late Jōmon (c. 2500-1000), and Latest Jōmon (c. 1000-300).

Jōmon pottery was made of unrefined, low-fired clay. From the Incipient to the Earliest phase, production consisted of deep bowls with round or pointed bottoms and wavy lip-zones, which were suitable for cooking or boiling food. The tapered bottom made the vessel stable when placed in the soil. The decorative patterns include markings made by pressing shells and cords into, or by rolling a thin stick on, the clay surface of the vessels. The shell marks were popular in northern Japan, but pressing or rolling patterns were more often used in western Japan.

The development taking place in the Jōmon culture becomes evident in the Earliest phase. Archaeological excavations in the late twentieth century have provided evidence that habitation took place earlier in southern Japan rather than in the northern areas. For example, in 1997, the remains of forty-six pit houses dated around 7500 B.C.E. were discovered in the Uenohara site in Kagoshima Prefecture, Kyūshū. The warm environment of this southern island is theorized to have made habitation possible earlier than it was on the main island. However, the continued climatic warming trend is believed to have encouraged people's migration to and habitation of the highland regions. During the Early and Middle Jōmon phases, increases in settlements and in lifestyle stabilization can be seen at various sites throughout Japan. In these phases, villages were established, and harvests were stored.

Jōmon culture seems to have reached its zenith in the Middle Jōmon phase. The largest Middle Jōmon site, Sannai Maruyama in Aomori Prefecture, which was uncovered in 1992, necessitated a full revision of existing views on the Jōmon period. Discoveries at this site date to around 3500-2000 B.C.E. and include large-scale pit dwellings and other buildings, graves, cylindrical earthenware, more than seven hundred clay figurines, lacquerware, an oar, and other accessories. The lacquerware and a braid made of vines are considered to date from around 3500 B.C.E. The finds include highly technical products and suggest the existence of artisans. An oar and semiprecious stones, such as amber and jade, from distant places suggest Jōmon people engaged in sailing and trading. More than five hundred buildings remain, including large pit houses with a hearth in the center, probably used for communal life. An enormous pillar-supported structure was possibly used for ceremonies. Storehouses from around 2500 B.C.E. were constructed in the raised-floor mode, which is the technique often seen in the storage buildings of the subsequent Yayoi period. The Jōmon had advanced skills in engineering and formed a cooperative society. The burial sites for children were usually located near dwellings, and adults were buried at more removed sites. In 1998, seven stone circles were discovered along a passage of graves that was a cemetery for adults. Along with clay figurines, stone circles are often found near burial grounds, suggesting a religious function.

A figurine from the latter part of the Jōmon period. (Sakamoto Photo Research Laboratory/Corbis)

The Jōmon seemed to have been engaged in the cultivation of crops to support their large settlements. Thus far, the crops have been found to include starchy yam and taro. However, research based on an analysis of pollen and DNA (deoxyribonucleic acid) strongly suggests that Jōmon people cultivated chestnut and walnut trees. The cultivation of chestnut trees is especially notable in eastern Japan and may be one of the important factors behind the greater development of Jōmon culture in that region.

A stable economy and large habitation further promoted pottery manufacture. The pottery vessels found in the Middle Jōmon sites are plentiful and highly decorated. The types and styles of vessels are extensive, as they apparently served various purposes from practical to ceremonial. The earlier cord-marking patterns were often replaced by three-dimensional designs that involved applying clay pieces to the surface of the vessel. The sculptural treatment sometimes extended to the use of zoomorphic or anthropomorphic motifs on the rim areas. A few vessel types including Katsusaka, Daigi, and Umataka are particularly noted for their decorative styles. Katsusaka pottery produced by mountain dwellers in central Japan often consists of cylindrical urns or pots featuring highly sculptural forms and decorative raised-line patterns. Daigi pottery of northern Japan features the application of thin coils shaping a swirl to the surface of the vessel, which is incised by a combed pattern; the beauty of the pottery is in the contrast of the two patterns. The most decorative and sculptural vessels can be found in Umataka pottery, found in the Hokuriku district. The flame-type pottery forms flamboyant, pierced projections that resemble leaping flames above the simple cylindrical body.

In the Middle Jōmon phase, the warming trend peaked, and a colder climate emerged. The cold forced migration to the eastern coast of Honshū, the main island. In these newer sites, the pottery is characterized by a sharp decline in decoration and an increase in the number of unpretentious vessels. The designs are relatively plain, with erased cord markings, and emphasize the form of the pots. Some vessels have spouts and hooks for hanging and thinner walls. They exhibit fine workmanship, suggesting more sophisticated methods of manufacturing and an increase in the number of potters.

The clay figurines excavated from the earlier Jōmon sites were produced continually during the later phases. The figurines, which usually take the shape of women, are often interpreted as symbols of fertility or food gathering. Some researchers believe that the mass production of female figurines indicates that the Jōmon culture was a woman-centered society. Alternatively, some researchers believe the figurines represent deities. In the Latest Jōmon phase, the figurines were created in an abstract manner, with stress often placed on the face. Examples include a figurine with a heart-shaped face in Gunma Prefecture and figurines with enormous eyes, reminiscent of snow goggles. Such figurines may represent deities by emphasizing the eyes as windows of the soul. The Jōmon population decreased remarkably during the final phase, probably because of the colder climate, contagious diseases, and a new cultural group arriving from the continent.

Significance

The Jōmon period lasted for nearly ten thousand years, and the culture developed continually, centered on its pottery. The decorative patterns of Jōmon pottery are unique. The vessels and figurines are not only the product of the Jōmon people's religious beliefs but also extraordinary art objects that are formed based on their practical needs. Discoveries in the late twentieth century and beyond reveal the Jōmon people's lifestyle to be far beyond the primitive one that earlier scholars described. A global archaeological perspective or an ecological viewpoint may further clarify the long-lasting history of the Jōmon people and their pottery.

—*Yoshiko Kainuma*

Further Reading

Fitzhugh, Ben, and Junko Habu, eds. *Beyond Foraging and Collecting: Evolutionary Change in Hunter-Gatherer Settlement Systems*. New York: Kluwer Academic/Plenum, 2002. New research on the changes in the settlements in the prehistoric period on a global scale, including the Jōmon sites. Index.

Imamura, Kenji. *Prehistoric Japan: New Perspectives on Insular East Asia*. Honolulu: University of Hawaii Press, 1996. Contains up-to-date research on the prehistoric period from an East Asian perspective. Bibliography and index.

Kenrick, Douglas M. *Jōmon of Japan: The World's Oldest Pottery*. London; New York: Kegan Paul International, 1995. A survey of stylistic variations of Jōmon pottery and figurines. Bibliography and index.

Mizoguchi, Kōji. *An Archaeological History of Japan: 30,000 B.C. to A.D. 700*. Philadelphia: University of Pennsylvania Press, 2002. A study of the prehistoric inhabitants of Japan and their self-identification through archaeological evidence and its interpretation by contemporary theory. Bibliography and index.

See also: c. 7500 B.C.E., Birth of Shintō; c. 300 B.C.E., Yayoi Period Begins.

c. 10,000 B.C.E.-c. 1 C.E.
SAHARAN PEOPLES CREATE ROCK ART

Some of the oldest African art, Saharan rock art provides visual evidence of the early environmental and cultural events that shaped this area's history.

LOCALE: Sahara, Africa
CATEGORIES: Prehistory and ancient cultures; cultural and intellectual history

SUMMARY OF EVENT

The Sahara offers some of the oldest examples of African art. Dating perhaps to the tenth millennium B.C.E., rock art is found across the vast stretch of northern Africa from the Nile Valley to sites near the Atlantic Ocean; from Morocco's Atlas Mountains to the southern foothills of the Ennedi highlands in present-day Chad. Major sites in the central Sahara include Tassili n' Ajjer, Fezzan, Tibesti, Adrar des Iforas, and Hoggar. These artworks form a visual record of events that shaped the area's history.

Rock art includes petroglyphs (engravings or carvings) and pictographs (paintings and drawings). Petroglyphs were gouged into the rock with stone tools and abrasives. Pictographs were executed by outline or flat wash using earthen-based pigments to create colors of black, red, brown, and white. Such paintings were created on walls of shallow rock shelters; engravings were produced both in rock shelters and on exposed rock surfaces.

Over hundreds of millennia, the climate of the Sahara gradually fluctuated between arid and wet periods. During such a wet period about 10,000 B.C.E., humans appeared in the area. Then a vast savannah, the Sahara supported cultural development for the next seven thousand years. This wet period came to a close when the climate shifted and ushered in an almost continuous dry era. By about 2000 B.C.E., the Sahara had transformed into desert.

Saharan rock art is not easily categorized. Representations of changing fauna, stylistic approaches, and production techniques have been used for classification. Although there is general agreement on major categories, there are differences of opinion on commencement dates and time spans. As paintings and engravings appeared in many regions across the vast expanse of northern Africa, developments occurred in different areas at different times. Rock art did not develop in a linear progression, and styles within a single area often overlapped. The establishment of a precise chronology has been further impeded by the fact that some sites are not associated with archaeological deposits or materials that would enable the use of radiometric dating.

Another source of disagreement is the interpretation of these art forms. Early works in particular reflect a rich, symbolic, perhaps spiritual, world. Depictions have been attributed to hunting magic and fertility or fecundity cults. Other images have been interpreted to be sacred beings. Original meanings are lost, and such symbolic speculations, however interesting, are based on guesswork. There have been efforts to correlate myths and legends of present groups, such as the Fulani, with rock art symbols, but scholars are unable to establish firm historical links between Saharan groups of several thousand years ago and inhabitants of the area today. There is less disagreement on the interpretation of later works, as artists turned away from the symbolic realm to address issues of daily life.

The earliest period of Saharan rock art is known as the *Bubalus*, or Large Wild Fauna, period. This style appeared sometime after 10,000 B.C.E. and continued in some areas for the next five thousand years. Its name is derived from large-scale depictions of the now extinct buffalo, *Bubalus antiquus*, which was distinguished by its long, forward-thrusting horns. These petroglyphs were formed with deeply incised, continuous outlines. It appears that they were done from direct observation, as there was demonstrated familiarity with animal anatomy and movements. Despite conventions such as the use of composite views (for example, animals often were shown in profile with horns depicted frontally), the overall style was naturalistic. Although the *Bubalus* was the primary image, works from this period also depicted other animals that inhabited the Sahara: elephant, giraffe, antelope, crocodile, rhinoceros, and hippopotamus. Humans were portrayed, but their images were small and schematic. They were shown holding boomerangs, clubs, and axes.

Many works of the *Bubalus* period appear to have a supernatural dimension. As this was a hunter-gatherer society, it is speculated that some images played a role in hunting magic, with humans seeking to gain control over animals they wished to trap or kill. Depictions of therianthropes are thought to represent supernatural beings. It has been suggested that these figures are precursors of Egyptian animal-headed deities, but no firm conclusions can be drawn. Although it frequently has been asserted that works of this period were highly developed at their first appearance, it should be noted that earliest examples of rock art might not have survived.

Overlapping the *Bubalus* period, the Round Head period occurred from c. 8000-6000 B.C.E. Dates are more reliable because use of organic pigments has enabled carbon-14 testing. The period takes its name from large paintings of human figures with featureless faces and distinct, rounded heads. Many paintings were polychromatic; red ocher, white, or black contours were employed along with rows of dots and fine lines to represent body decoration and details. This period later incorporated people with elaborate headdresses and costumes who seem to float or dance through space. It has been suggested that these figures represent supernaturally transformed dancers and provide evidence of early African masquerades. It is further speculated that other images symbolize horned "goddess," and larger "great god" figures. Some scholars believe that the horned "goddess" image is a predecessor of Hathor, the great cattle-headed deity of Egypt. Such scenes are probably imbued with sacred symbols, but as with the earlier rock art, interpretations are speculative.

The Pastoralist, or Cattle, period falls broadly within the limits of 5500-2000 B.C.E. New groups settled in the Sahara, and farming and herding replaced the hunting and foraging lifestyle. Wild animals were still depicted, but domestic stock such as sheep, goats, and especially cattle predominated in both paintings and engravings. Pastoral scenes representative of the Neolithic era generally replaced the symbolic drama of the Round Head period. Animals were smaller, and the human figure now played a more central role. Men were armed with spears or bows and arrows.

By the second millennium B.C.E., the Sahara had undergone climatic change. The new arid period left the area too dry for agriculture and herding. Many inhabitants moved southward and eastward to the plains near the Nile. After the Hyksos rule of Egypt in the seventeenth and sixteenth centuries B.C.E., metal weapons, horses, and horse-drawn chariots were introduced into the Sahara. Those who remained in the area integrated these imports into their art. The resulting styles constitute the Post-Neolithic period, which incorporates later Horse and Camel stages.

Horses were introduced to this general area during the first millennium B.C.E. Their rock art depictions were simple and schematic. Early wheeled vehicles, possibly chariots, were represented as single shafts with a horse on each side; later images depicted "flying" vehicles with teams of two to four horses driven by armed men. The extent of chariot use has yet to be determined, as they were impractical on the sand and rocks of the desert. Humans were also depicted schematically, their faceless bodies sometimes reduced to two triangles placed apex to apex. Men frequently held spears, shields, and daggers, possibly with metal blades. Representations of people riding horses and, eventually, camels replaced the "charioteer" images.

Debate exists about when camels were introduced into the Sahara. They appeared in central Saharan rock art, along with short inscriptions written in a script known as Libyco-Berber, in the last centuries before the common era. Their images were accompanied by smaller depictions of giraffes, Barbary sheep, antelopes, and ostriches. As the Sahara became more arid, camels, which were able to go for weeks without water, assumed a position of major importance. They became the primary means of desert transport and key components in the development of trans-Saharan trade. Rock art from this phase was schematic and crudely executed. No longer symbolic, it reflected the harsh reality of this desert environment as it is known in modern times.

SIGNIFICANCE

Over the millennia, inhabitants of the Sahara marked the landscape in descriptive and symbolic ways. Their art forms a visual record of environmental and cultural changes that provides important insights into the history of this area. Paintings and engravings depict modes of subsistence, development of spiritual beliefs, development of agriculture and pastoralism, and the formulation of group life. They record the results of drastic climatic change. Although desert populations migrated to the north, south, and east, rock art attests to the continued development of cross-cultural contacts and exchanges, innovations in technology, and development of trade. Saharan cultures and art forms underwent change, but it is believed that key concepts were diffused to provide the basis for artistic traditions of many surrounding groups, including the Egyptians. Study of Saharan rock art demonstrates that these North African groups, far from being simple hunter-gatherers, developed complex cultures.

—*Cassandra Lee Tellier*

FURTHER READING

Clottes, Jean. *World Rock Art*. Los Angeles: J. Paul Getty Museum, 2002. Surveys forty thousand years of rock art. Includes discussions of artistic processes, methods of dating, interpretations, and preservation. Bibliography.

Coulson, David, and Alec Campbell. *African Rock Art: Paintings and Engravings on Stone*. New York: Harry N. Abrams, 2001. A good survey of African rock art. Bibliography, index, and outstanding photography.

Perani, Judith, and Fred Smith. *The Visual Arts of Africa: Gender, Power, and Life Cycle Rituals*. Upper Saddle River, N.J.: Prentice Hall, 1998. An overall survey of African art that includes works from the Saharan area. Bibliography and index.

Visonà, Monica B., Robin Poynor, Herbert M. Cole, and Michael D. Harris. *A History of Art in Africa*. New York: Harry N. Abrams, 2001. A survey of African art that includes discussion of works from the Sahara. Bibliography and index.

SEE ALSO: c. 25,000 B.C.E., San Peoples Create Earliest African Art; c. 15,500 B.C.E., Early Australians Create the Bradshaw Rock Paintings; c. 9000-c. 7000 B.C.E., Nilo-Saharan Peoples Produce Food and Pottery; c. 6500-c. 5000 B.C.E., Nilo-Saharan Farmers Spread Cultivation and Herding.

c. 9500-c. 9000 B.C.E.

CLOVIS CULTURE RISES IN NEW MEXICO

The Clovis culture in New Mexico was one of the oldest Paleo-Indian cultures in prehistoric North America.

LOCALE: Clovis, New Mexico, and surrounding area
CATEGORY: Prehistory and ancient cultures

SUMMARY OF EVENT

The populating of North America began with a migration in which *Homo sapiens* traveled northward from Africa, Europe, and Asia, finally reaching present-day Siberia about 35,000 years ago. These hunters followed mammoths, musk oxen, and woolly rhinoceroses across Siberia, going farther north and east until they happened on a land bridge leading to the New World. Exactly when humans first crossed this bridge remains a matter of scholarly debate. Estimates range from 18,000 to 11,000 B.C.E.; however, there is convincing evidence that the migration began approximately 15,000 years ago, when this large landmass formed a subcontinent called Beringia, which extended hundreds of miles to the north and south of today's Bering Strait. Many generations lived in this area, hunting caribou, giant bison, and mammoths until planetary warming caused the glaciers to melt, raising the sea level and causing the land bridge to disappear. The migration southward probably began around 11,000 B.C.E., spreading in all directions across the continent.

All across North America, the descendants of the first people who came south from the Arctic continued a lifestyle of hunting and gathering, with only small but significant changes from one generation to the next. They wandered about, following the animal herds, taking with them only animal skins for clothing and weapons and tools made of stone and bone. Gradually, they modified and improved their tools and weapons, developing new spear points and using them in distinctive ways that defined their cultures.

One of the first cultures to be identified was the Folsom. In 1908, a cowboy named George McJunkin discovered a layer of bison bones and projectile points buried 20 feet (6 meters) deep in the bank of an arroyo near the town of Folsom, New Mexico. Later, the site became the focus of scientific attention, with scholars determining that the bison had been extinct for some ten thousand years. The Folsom points were exquisitely made, varying in length from 1 to 3 inches (2.5 to 7.7 centimeters), with a groove running up either side. Soon, these Folsom points were discovered at other sites ranging over a wide area. One such site, located in eastern New Mexico south of Folsom, revealed not only Folsom points but evidence of a second Paleo-Indian culture as well.

In 1932, along the bed of an ancient river called Blackwater Draw near the small town of Clovis, the New Mexico Highway Department dug a gravel pit, which revealed tons of extinct animal bones and flint points. Below a level of Folsom points, scientists found a main layer of mammoth bones and large lance points that were the hallmark of an older culture—the Clovis culture. These points are about 3 to 6 inches (8 to 15 centimeters) long and almost perfectly symmetrical, tapering from a broad, blunt base to a sharp point. The blade is flaked smooth on both sides to reduce resistance to its thrust, with a central channel, or flute, carved into both sides extending about one-third of the way from the base to the tip. This fluting allowed the spear point to fit snugly into the notched end of the shaft, where it was then secured with sinews. This strengthening of the link between shaft and point was a major advance in hunting technology.

Scientists believe it is possible that Clovis hunters also used the atlatl to increase the range of their spears. The atlatl is a piece of wood or bone about 2 feet (0.6 meter) long with a handle at one end and a hooked tip at the other that fits into the notched end of the spear. The hunter, holding the handle end of the atlatl, used it as an extension of his arm to hurl the spear with increased speed, range, and striking power.

While Clovis hunters killed mammoths for food, they also apparently hunted extinct types of horse, camel, and bison for their hides, which were much more desirable for making clothing. Clovis people worked the soft hides from these animals with scrapers and knives made from flint or obsidian.

SIGNIFICANCE

Although no human fossils from the Clovis culture have yet been discovered, there is abundant evidence of their excellent craft work as Clovis points have been found from coast to coast. This might represent the passing on of a new idea from one hunting group to another or it could mean a migration of the Clovis people themselves. In any case, the spread of people—or perhaps only of tool design—was very rapid, with all the points that can be dated falling within a span of one thousand years.

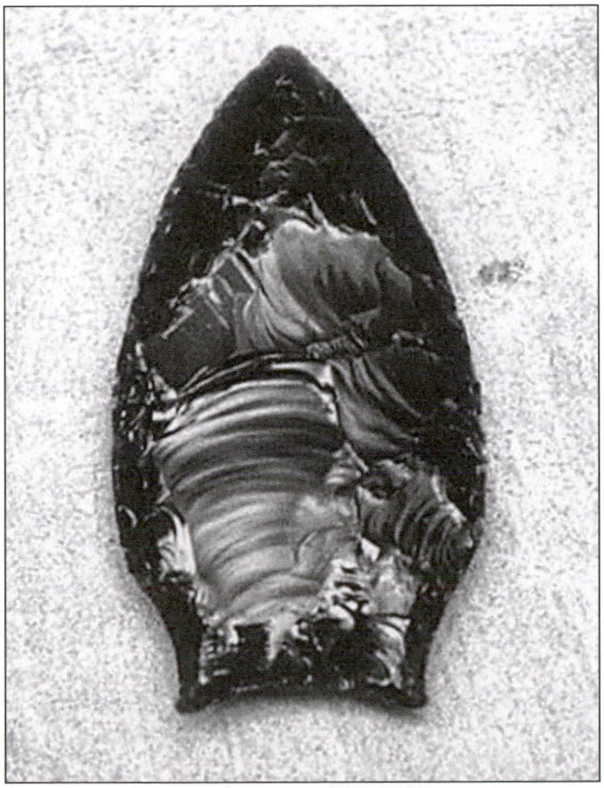

This Clovis-style fluted spear point was rendered in obsidian by Rex Watson, a modern-day stone tool maker in Oregon. (AP/Wide World Photos)

Based on site distribution and other evidence, scholars have proposed that the Paleo-Indians were not aimless wanderers but rather moved in annual circuits, based on the seasonal availability of game and edible plants and the need for winter shelter. Clovis sites tend to be located on high points with good views all around; near rivers, streams, and springs; and close to sources of good-quality stone. Indeed, evidence suggests that the Clovis people chose the stone that they worked into tools with an eye to their aesthetic qualities as well as their appropriateness for the job at hand.

In all probability, the typical Clovis group consisted of around fifty members of a single extended family. Each group interacted with neighboring bands, hunting, trading, intermarrying, and maintaining a sort of communications network, as evidenced by the distribution of similar spear points across the continent. Artifacts, however, tell little about other aspects of their life, such as their language, family relationships, spirituality, rituals, or medicines. The use of red ochre, which seems to be associated with abstract notions of birth, death, reproduction, and hunting in the Old World, may indicate similar beliefs in the New. The Clovis people also incised decorations on their implements, perhaps purely as decoration or perhaps as some sort of symbolic system.

—*LouAnn Faris Culley*

FURTHER READING

Boldurian, Anthony C., and John L. Cotter. *Clovis Revisited: New Perspectives on Paleo-Indian Adaptations from Blackwater Draw, New Mexico*. Philadelphia: University of Pennsylvania Museum, 1999. A detailed analysis of Clovis artifacts. Using both traditional and current theories and their own insights, the authors provide an extended reference to the lifeways of early humans in the Americas. Well illustrated with photos, line drawings, and schematics.

Bonnichsen, Robson, and Karen L. Turnmire, eds. *Clovis: Origins and Adaptations*. Corvallis: Oregon State University Press, 1991. A detailed discussion of the Clovis culture. Bibliography.

Frison, G. C. "Paleo-Indian Large Mammal Hunters on the Plains of North America." *Proceedings of the National Academy of Science* 95 (1998): 14,576-14,583. Discusses the evidence of hunting methods among Clovis peoples.

Hofman, Jack L. *From Clovis to Comanchero: Archeological Overview of the Southern Great Plains*. Fayetteville: Arkansas Archeological Survey, 1989. Discusses the artifacts and human settlements of the prehistoric Southwest. Bibliography.

Reid, J. Jefferson, and David E. Doyel, eds. *Emil W. Haury's Prehistory of the American Southwest*. Tucson: University of Arizona Press, 1986. Well-illustrated account of the major Paleo-Indian sites. Bibliography.

Soffer, O., and N. D. Praslov, eds. *From Kostenki to Clovis: Upper Paleo-Indian Adaptations*. New York: Plenum Press, 1993. A collection of papers presented at a congress in 1989. Focuses on documenting and comparing the archaeological evidence for Late Paleolithic life in Beringia.

Tankersley, Kenneth. *In Search of Ice Age Americans*. Layton, Utah: Gibbs Smith, 2002. Presents the history of the archaeological discoveries of Clovis culture and also discusses the controversies over whether the Clovis people were, in fact, the first humans to reach the Americas.

Taylor, R. E., C. V. Haynes, and M. Stuiver. "Clovis and Folsom Age Estimates: Stratigraphic Context and Radiocarbon Dating." *Antiquity* 70 (1996): 515-525. Revisits the question of dating the Clovis and Folsom cultures.

Waldman, Carl. *Atlas of the North American Indian*. New York: Facts on File Publications, 1985. Historical and cultural maps of the major Paleo-Indian cultures.

SEE ALSO: c. 18,000-c. 11,000 B.C.E., Bering Strait Migrations; c. 13,000 B.C.E., Humans Enter the South American Continent; c. 13,000-c. 7000 B.C.E., Paleo-Indian Culture Flourishes in North America; c. 9000-c. 8000 B.C.E., Cochise Culture Thrives in American Southwest; c. 8800-c. 8500 B.C.E., Folsom People Flourish in New Mexico; c. 8000 B.C.E., Permanent Settlement of the Andean Altiplano Begins; c. 8000-c. 1000 B.C.E., Archaic Indians Adapt to Warmer Climates; c. 2100-c. 600 B.C.E., Mogollon Culture Rises in American Southwest.

c. 9500-c. 5000 B.C.E.
SETTLEMENT ESTABLISHED AT ABU HUREYRA IN SYRIA

The large settlement at Abu Hureyra in northern Syria provided evidence of early peoples' transition from a sedentary hunting and gathering economy to one based on farming and livestock husbandry.

LOCALE: Northern Syria, east of Aleppo
CATEGORIES: Prehistory and ancient cultures; agriculture

SUMMARY OF EVENT

A portion of the large site called Abu Hureyra, 28.5 acres (11.5 hectares), was excavated in a salvage context during 1972 and 1973 by a team of British, American, and Australian archaeologists: A. M. T. Moore, G. C. Hillman, A. J. Legge, and their colleagues. Surveys suggested that the tell, or site, held promise for answering specific questions linked to the evolution of agriculture in the Euphrates Valley. Queries included the circumstances and chronology leading to domestication, the settlement pattern and construction techniques of the village, the attendant social and cultural changes, and specifics on the inhabitants such as health, ideology, and occupational specializations. The salvage excavation proved to be exceptionally rich in human burials, the remains of faunal and vegetal foods, architectural features, and artifact types.

The cultural history of ancient Abu Hureyra was the result of a long series of planned, coordinated projects. The site was originally selected about 9500 B.C.E. by hunters and gatherers who found the environment to be abundant in wild cereals, nuts, fruits, and a spectrum of fauna, particularly the gazelle, which was extensively hunted. This was a healthy population, enjoying high levels of nutrition. Presumably when yields of wild vegetal foods declined because of environmental changes about 9000 B.C.E., the population of Abu Hureyra began cultivating rye. The permanent settlement of pit houses numbered between one hundred and three hundred individuals.

Archaeological work determined that Abu Hureyra 1 (9500-8000 B.C.E.) was succeeded by an intermediate period (8000-7400 B.C.E.) that witnessed a population decline, as well as reduced wild-plant foraging. Village construction shifted to timber and reed huts. Cultigens were expanded during the intermediate period to include several varieties of wheat, barley, and lentils.

Abu Hureyra 2 (7400-5000 B.C.E.) demonstrates a cultural and technological lineage that links it to the earlier settlement. However, during three continuous occupation stages (Abu Hureyra 2A, 2B, and 2C), the inhabitants built on previous adaptations and ultimately created a productive economy dependent on domesticated species. Archaeological evidence indicates that early in Abu Hureyra 2, both sheep and goats were domesticated. By c. 7000 B.C.E., the population increased to 2,500 to 3,000 people; by c. 6000 B.C.E., the village population rose to 5,000 to 6,000 individuals. Mud-brick, multiroomed, single-family, single-story houses, up to 68 square yards (82 square meters) in area were constructed in close proximity to one another. Some houses contained colored plastered floors.

Syria was the site of many ancient cities, including Abu Hureyra and the 6,000-year-old Tell Hamoukar pictured here. (AP/Wide World Photos)

The economy of Abu Hureyra 2 focused on cereal cultivation, in addition to lentils, peas, vetches, and beans. Gazelle hunting remained important until about 6300 B.C.E., when sheep and goat husbandry, long an economic pursuit, replaced it. Pottery was developed about 7500 B.C.E. Cattle and pigs were added to the list of domesticates, the former perhaps being used to pull a primitive tillage tool, the ard. With the possible exception of cattle as draft animals, agricultural labor was most likely accomplished with hand tools, such as the digging stick.

The social organization of the community gradually became more complex as new economic and domestic challenges arose. Cooperation and coordination of large-scale gazelle hunting, village planning and construction, mud-brick manufacture, the transportation of materials, and decisions on field preparation, harvesting, and pasturing animals were prerequisites for the successful adaptation and continuity of the village.

Complex ideology in the form of ancestor worship appears to have emerged at Abu Hureyra: Burials were placed beneath the floors of houses, with special attention given to some skulls, which were separated from the skeletons. Evidence suggests a multistaged burial ceremony in which significant reverence and veneration were channeled toward the deceased.

Economic responsibility was divided along gender lines. Mass killing of gazelles was probably accomplished by male cooperation, coordinated by some form of leadership. Degenerative changes and stress on female skeletons revealed the physical problems linked to prolonged grain grinding through the use of the quern. Hence role specialization emerged in the village.

Long-term residency of families in particular dwellings suggests some form of close-knit lineage organization. This cooperative unit would have facilitated domestic craftsmanship and enhanced productive capacity and the successful maintenance of an agricultural surplus, at least a millennium earlier than other Neolithic sites in the area.

The 1972-1973 excavations yielded artifacts that mirrored the economic pursuits of the village during the forty-five hundred years of its existence. Bone, stone, and obsidian points, scrapers, grinding dishes, querns, and pestles used in milling were recovered as well as pottery.

Environmental changes that led to increased temperatures and decreased rainfall and most likely declining soil fertility caused the villagers to abandon the settlement c. 5000 B.C.E.

Significance

Abu Hureyra is without qualification one of the world's first, largest, and best-documented early farming sites. It clearly demonstrates the economic, technological, and cultural changes inherent in the shift from a hunting-and-gathering way of life to an economy based on early farming techniques.

—*Rene M. Descartes*

FURTHER READING

Harris, David R., ed. *The Origins and Spread of Agriculture and Pastoralism in Eurasia*. Washington, D.C.: Smithsonian Institution Press, 1996. A collection of twenty-nine articles on early domestication, including several that discuss Abu Hureyra. Bibliographies, index.

Hillman, G. C., P. A. Rowley-Conwy, and A. J. Legge. "On the Charred Seeds from Epipaleolithic Abu Hureyra: Food or Fuel?" *Current Anthropology* 38 (1997): 651-655. Discussion of the vegetal remains from Abu Hureyra.

Legge, A. J., and P. A. Rowley-Conwy. "Gazelle Killing in Stone Age Syria." *Scientific American* 257, no. 2 (1987): 88-95. An examination of large-scale gazelle slaughter long after agriculture emerged.

Moore, A. M. T., G. C. Hillman, and A. J. Legge. *Village on the Euphrates*. New York: Oxford University Press, 2000. Complete coverage of the 1972-1973 excavations at Abu Hureyra. Bibliography, index.

SEE ALSO: c. 6200-c. 3800 B.C.E., Ubaid Culture Thrives in Mesopotamia; c. 5500-c. 4500 B.C.E., Halafian Culture Flourishes in Northern Mesopotamia; c. 3800 B.C.E., Cities and Civic Institutions Are Invented in Mesopotamia.

c. 9000-c. 8000 B.C.E.
COCHISE CULTURE THRIVES IN AMERICAN SOUTHWEST

The Cochise culture of Arizona and New Mexico marked a significant advance in technology and lifestyle over the previous Desert culture.

LOCALE: Present-day Arizona and New Mexico
CATEGORY: Prehistory and ancient cultures

SUMMARY OF EVENT

The various prehistoric periods in the New World began and ended at different times in different locations. Moreover, most human remains and ancient artifacts have disappeared, with but a few scattered human bones, stone articles, and pottery fragments remaining. There are two principal scientific techniques for dating ancient artifacts: dendrochronology, which is the study of tree ring growth in wood samples, and radiocarbon dating, which measures the amount of the radioactive isotope carbon 14 in organic material. Both these methods, however, are subject to a certain margin of error, which increases over time. Therefore, the categories and dates that have been developed by scholarly research provide only a general structure for the study of the prehistoric cultures of the New World.

Archaeologists have proposed that the Paleo-Indian period of the Pleistocene era began evolving into the Archaic period sometime around 9000 to 8000 B.C.E., reaching its height from 5000 to 1000 B.C.E. There were five major Archaic cultures: the Old Cordilleran in the Pacific Northwest; the Old Copper culture in the Great Lakes region; the Red Paint People in New England and eastern Canada; the Desert culture in the Great Basin region of Utah, Nevada, and Arizona; and the Cochise culture, which evolved from the Desert culture and was centered in Arizona and New Mexico.

The Paleo-Indians of New Mexico and Arizona relied on big-game hunting and gathering wild fruits and grains for subsistence. When the mammoths, horses, camels, bison, and giant ground sloths that once found forage in the rich grasslands of the area disappeared because of the climatic change at the end of the Pleistocene period, the Archaic people of the Desert culture hunted smaller game such as turkey, rabbits, and deer, while continuing to harvest wild fruits and grains. In Danger Cave, one of the major sites of the Desert culture, archaeologists have found small stone points for hunting small animals as well as baskets woven from plant fiber. They also found millstones used to grind wild seeds and nuts into flour, which formed the basis for an unleavened bread that was cooked in a shallow basket placed on hot stones.

The first evidence of the Cochise culture was found in 1926 near the town of Cochise, Arizona, named for the nineteenth century chief of the Chiricahua Apaches. Carbon-14 testing dated artifacts found there to about 9000 B.C.E. Small stone points, baskets, and millstones similar to those from Danger Cave were found at this site. These millstones are called manos and metates and are similar to a mortar and pestle; the metate is a flat stone with a depression in the center, while the mano is a round grinding stone held in the hand. In early Sulphur Springs and Chiricahua phases of their development, the Cochise were not yet farmers. Several millennia later, however, at Bat Cave, a site in west-central New Mexico dating from about 3500 B.C.E., archaeologists discovered a number of corncobs, almost 1 inch (2.5 centimeters) in length, from a cultivated primitive species. This indicates that the Cochise people, in the third or San Pedro phase of their development, had acquired the concept of planting crops for food rather than relying on gathering. From the cultures to the south, in Mexico, the Cochise also learned to grow squash and beans.

At this stage, the Cochise people also began building shallow pit houses, which were pits dug into the ground and roofed over with twigs and small branches. They continued to weave baskets from willow, yucca, and agave fibers, and they began to make small, crudely shaped clay figurines and vessels, which were fired in open-pit fires. Scholars have also determined that the Cochise imported shells from the Pacific coast.

SIGNIFICANCE

As the big-game hunters of the Paleo-Indian cultures vanished along with their quarry, the Cochise people learned to hunt smaller game and, more important, began to cultivate crops. About the same time, they also began to make pottery. This introduction of agriculture and pottery into the area north of Mexico, along with the building of simple shelters, also prompted the appearance of semipermanent villages, which resulted in the creation of more complicated social patterns. One of the most significant legacies of the Cochise culture was the cultivation of corn, which not only provided a stable food supply but also often produced a surplus for trade. All these developments influenced the Southwest cultures in the Formative period (1000 B.C.E. to 1500 C.E.), the most organized and prominent of which were the Mogollon (direct descendants of the Cochise), Hohokam, and Anasazi. These three cultures, shaped by agriculture, developed a village lifestyle that led to the further development of tools, arts, and crafts, especially basketry and pottery.

—LouAnn Faris Culley

FURTHER READING

Dick, Herbert W. *Bat Cave*. Santa Fe, N.Mex.: School of American Research, 1965. Archaeological report on a significant Cochise culture site.

Griffin-Pierce, Trudy. *Native Peoples of the Southwest*. Albuquerque: University of New Mexico Press, 2000. A comprehensive account of modern Native American groups, with particular attention to ways in which they continue cultural traditions inherited from their ancient ancestors.

Jennings, Jesse D. *Danger Cave*. Reprint. Salt Lake City: University of Utah Press, 1999. The excavation report for one of the important Cochise culture sites, first published in 1957. Long renowned as a model of well-controlled archaeological excavation in difficult circumstances.

Sayles, E. R. *The Cochise Cultural Sequence in Southeastern Arizona*. Tucson: University of Arizona Press, 1983. A good survey of the culture and its archaeological remains.

Stuart, David, and Rory Gauthier. *Prehistoric New Mexico*. Albuquerque: University of New Mexico Press, 1984. A profusely illustrated account of the New Mexico Historic Preservation Program's efforts to identify and evaluate the state's prehistoric resources.

SEE ALSO: c. 18,000-c. 11,000 B.C.E., Bering Strait Migrations; c. 13,000-c. 7000 B.C.E., Paleo-Indian Culture Flourishes in North America; c. 9500-c. 9000 B.C.E., Clovis Culture Rises in New Mexico; c. 9000-c. 8000 B.C.E., Cochise Culture Thrives in American Southwest; c. 8000-c. 1000 B.C.E., Archaic Indians Adapt to Warmer Climates; c. 2100-c. 600 B.C.E., Mogollon Culture Rises in American Southwest; c. 300 B.C.E., Hohokam Culture Arises in American Southwest; 200-1250 C.E., Anasazi Civilization Flourishes in American Southwest.

c. 9000-c. 7000 B.C.E.

NILO-SAHARAN PEOPLES PRODUCE FOOD AND POTTERY

Ancient Nilo-Saharan peoples are believed to have been the producers of the first African pottery and to have initiated the African domestication of cattle and cultivation of the grain sorghum.

LOCALE: Between the Red Sea Hills and the Nile River (modern Egypt, Sudan, Eritrea, and Ethiopia)
CATEGORIES: Prehistory and ancient cultures; agriculture; cultural and intellectual history

SUMMARY OF EVENT

Nilo-Saharan peoples can be defined as those populations who inhabited territory west of the Red Sea Hills up to the Nile River region in the period 9000-7000 B.C.E. Nilo-Saharans were among the first food producers in the world. In particular they began to domesticate African wild grasses and to raise wild cattle, both of which could be sustained in the Red Sea Hills and in small pockets of the eastern Sahara. Nilo-Saharan descendants typically established seasonal patterns of herding, moving livestock between highland and lowland pastures to the east and west of the Nile, where native wild grasses were sustained in the desert steppe climate and in the hills. Some time around 10,000 B.C.E., populations were moving farther north into the dry steppe regions, where Nilo-Saharans invented the production of food by cultivating wild grains and raising cattle for meat and even dairy products. It seems, from available evidence, that the grain cultivating and cattle raising innovations of Nilo-Saharan peoples emerged partially because the new ecosystem in the expanding grasslands provided an environment distinct from the more arid parts of the southeastern Sahara. The discovery of new ideas and techniques was furthered in the new ecological context. These first agriculuralists spoke a proto-Sudanic language of the Nilo-Saharan language family. Before 10,000 B.C.E., the pre-agropastoral Nilo-Saharans collected food by hunting small- to medium-sized mammals of the grassland steppe such as hares. The practice of hunting most likely continued as a supplement in conjunction with food production for several millennia.

The Nilo-Saharans of the eleventh millennium and later centuries increasingly came into contact with Erythraian populations speaking Afrasan languages (also known as the Afro-Asiatic language family). Nilo-Saharan and Afrasan contacts between the Nile River and the Red Sea Hills extended over three millennia and resulted in a cultural exchange and interaction that produced a fertile tradition of grain cultivation. The Northern Sudanians adopted the practice of grain collecting from their Erythraian neighbors and went beyond collection to the domestication of the grains. Northern Sudanians also incorporated the grindstone into their own technological repertoire. Interestingly, the Northern Sudanians employed the grindstone in slightly different ways than their Erythraic neighbors had, in that they refined tropical African grasses such as fonio, pearl millet, and sorghum rather than the grains that their neighbors more typically utilized.

The Nilo-Saharans began to produce so-called Wavy Line pottery in quantity from about 9000 B.C.E., and it is assumed that they had attained this skill even centuries before production became widespread. This pottery is identified by the wavy line motifs used in decorating the exterior of the pots. By 9000 B.C.E., their skill in pottery had achieved a relative sophistication, and between 8000 and 6000 B.C.E., the technique began to spread to Erythraite communities to the north and east of the Nilo-Saharans. By 7000 B.C.E., Nilo-Saharan pottery skills had spread into Saharan Africa to the west as well. Thus there was an extended period of pottery dispersal out of the corridor between the Red Sea and the Nile into the regions to the north and northwest. Both Nilo-Saharan Northern Sudanians and the Afrasian Erythraites had drawn on ideas introduced by their regional neighbors and then made innovations to suit their own environmental needs and sociocultural preferences.

Through the archaeological evidence, agroecology, and geographic analysis, a history of interaction between Nilo-Saharan and Erythraic communities is evident. In the Nile-Sahara cross-zone, ancient cattle bones, potshards, and grain seeds are distributed in a manner that demonstrates to scholars that communities with distinct backgrounds came together in certain regions and shared ideas; from about 10,000 B.C.E., there was population movement that resulted in identifiable cross-cultural interaction between Nilo-Saharan and Erythraic communities in northeastern Africa. Food production began to emerge between 10,000 and 9000 B.C.E., and through Nilo-Saharan and Erythraic interactions, grain cultivation and cattle raising spread at the crossroads of the Nile and Sahara. Within the same broad time frame, pottery production emerged as an extension of the new economic lifestyle and new needs that arose within that way of life.

Significance

Wavy Line pottery is the oldest known earthenware pottery of Africa, and in terms of global history it is second only to ceramics of Japan in antiquity. Pottery's significance lies in its usefulness for innovation in cultural and everyday practices. In particular, pottery allowed for novelty and diversity of cuisine and food preparation. With pottery, people could prepare porridge, stews, soups, and sauces to be integrated as supplements into a diet of breads and roasted meats.

For settled populations, pottery also provided creative storage options not only for food, but also for fermented drinks of alcohol, medicinal brews, and herbal products. Pots could be heated to high temperatures, unlike wooden or leather holding vessels; other containers such as the vessels made from animal skins, gourds, and wood that preceded ceramic wares were less durable and less varied in size and shape than the earthenwares could be, and thus ceramics allowed more choice, diversity, and creativity.

A major significance of food production in cattle raising and grain cultivation is that it supported Nilo-Saharan population growth. As populations increasingly expanded in numbers, they often opened out into new territories, carrying the Wavy Line pottery as well as systems of food production into new regions. Population growth and expansion lead to even greater innovation and diversity in the language, culture, and lifestyle of northeastern and north central Africa.

The ancient Nilo-Saharans and their Erythraian neighbors developed lifestyles and economic systems that have served as the basis of economy and society for Sudanic and Cushitic peoples of northeastern Africa into modern times. Although there has been significant change over time, elements of the socioeconomic structures of northeastern Africa are a result of ancient Nilo-Saharan agropastoral innovators.

—Catherine Cymone Fourshey

Further Reading

Bender, M. Lionel. *The Nilo-Saharan Languages: A Comparative Essay.* Munich, Germany: Lincom Europa, 1997. A linguistic analysis of the Nilo-Saharan language family.

Ehret, Christopher. *A Historical-Comparative Reconstruction of Nilo-Saharan.* Cologne, Germany: R. Köppe Verlag, 2001. An analysis of Nilo-Saharan languages in historical context, with vocabulary, etymology, and bibliography.

_______. "Nilo-Saharans and the Saharo Sudanese Neolithic." In *The Archaeology of Africa: Foods, Metals and Towns*, edited by Thurstan Shaw et al. New York: Routledge, 1993. A discussion of Nilo-Saharan archaeology and the development of tools and food production.

Morgan, Ben. *Tropical Grasslands.* Austin, Tex.: Raintree Steck-Vaughn, 2003. An atlas textbook for secondary schools that depicts the agroecology of grass and grasslands in tropical and subtropical regions.

Welsby, Derek. "Early Pottery in the Middle Nile Valley." In *Pottery in the Making: Ceramic Traditions*, edited by Ian Freestone and David R. M. Gaimster. Washington, D.C.: Smithsonian Institution Press, 1997. A historical examination of the world's potteries. Welsby's chapter focuses on the earliest pottery of the Middle Nile Valley, Kerma, and Dongola.

See also: c. 10,000 B.C.E.-c. 1 C.E., Saharan Peoples Create Rock Art; c. 6500-c. 5000 B.C.E., Nilo-Saharan Farmers Spread Cultivation and Herding; c. 6000-c. 1000 B.C.E., Omotics Advance Farming Practices in Horn of Africa; c. 4000 B.C.E., Horse Is Domesticated; c. 2700-c. 1400 B.C.E., Gash Civilization Thrives in Africa.

c. 8800-c. 8500 B.C.E.
FOLSOM PEOPLE FLOURISH IN NEW MEXICO

The discovery of the Folsom site in New Mexico proved that North America had been populated much earlier than archaeologists had previously believed.

LOCALE: Folsom, New Mexico
CATEGORY: Prehistory and ancient cultures

SUMMARY OF EVENT

In 1908, after a prolonged dry spell, a powerful storm dumped more than 10 inches (25 centimeters) of rain on the small northeastern New Mexico town of Folsom. The town sustained substantial damage, and there was a significant amount of erosion in the vicinity. Among other effects of the storm, the local arroyos (dried-out streambeds or riverbeds) were deepened and widened.

Outside town, in Wild Horse Arroyo, George McJunkin, an African American cowboy who was foreman at the Crowfoot Ranch, found many unusually large bones protruding from the wall of the arroyo while he was inspecting the ranch's fence for storm damage. Although he was unable to identify the bones, he knew that they did not belong to any of the animals commonly found in the area, and he reasoned that they might be very old because he had found them where they would have remained deeply buried if the storm's runoff had not exposed them. McJunkin, an amateur surveyor, carefully noted and recorded the location, which he called the Bone Pit.

McJunkin tried to interest various people in his find, but no one wanted to make the long trip on horseback to the site. McJunkin died in 1922, and a few months afterward, Carl Schwachheim and Fred Howarth, both of nearby Raton, traveled to the site that McJunkin had described to them. They were sufficiently impressed by the bones they found there to contact Jesse Figgins, director of the Colorado Museum of Natural History. Figgins identified the bones as belonging to an extinct species of bison, *Bison antiquus*. In May of 1926, Figgins and Harold Cook, honorary curator of paleontology at the Colorado Museum of Natural History, began excavating at Wild Horse Arroyo.

By summer, many bison bones as well as projectile points that had belonged to spears or darts had been uncovered. When one of the Folsom points, as they came to be called, was discovered in the carcass of an extinct bison, Figgins and Cook called in numerous experts to examine the find. The consensus of the experts was that the find provided evidence that humans had lived in North America during the Ice Age, far earlier than scientists had previously believed. In later years, more such finds came to light.

Although little detailed evidence regarding the lifestyle or beliefs of the Folsom people is available, it is clear that they were nomadic hunter-gatherers whose primary prey was bison, which they killed with throwing or thrusting spears as well as atlatls, implements that enable a hunter to throw a projectile with up to 150 times the force of a hand-thrown spear. (Experiments with the carcasses of elephants, which are similar to bison in terms of skin thickness, have demonstrated the penetrating power of darts thrown with atlatls.) Most experts believe that Folsom hunters used the terrain to their advantage, driving their prey into arroyos or other natural traps to facilitate the hunt. This appears to have been the case at Wild Horse Arroyo, where the remains of a herd of approximately thirty-two bison were found.

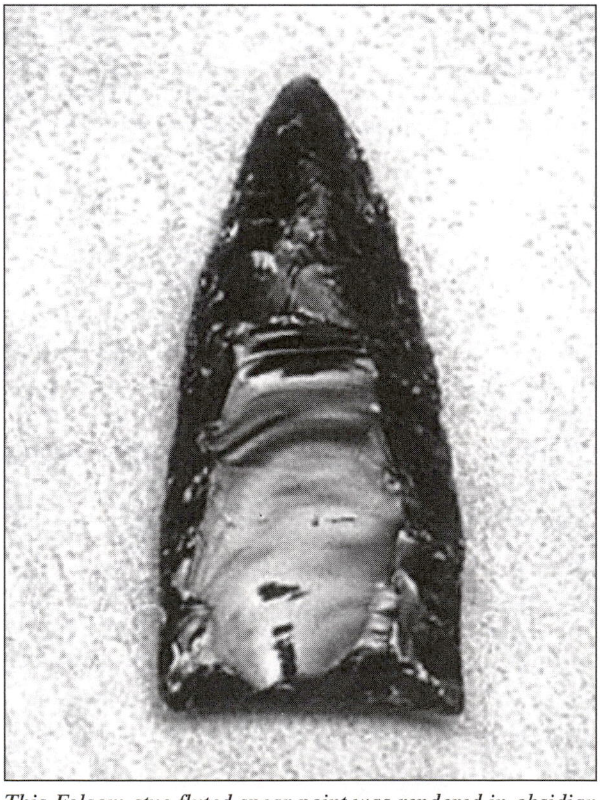

This Folsom-stye fluted spear point was rendered in obsidian by Rex Watson, a modern-day stone tool maker in Oregon. (AP/Wide World Photos)

Sometimes Folsom people processed the carcasses of their prey very carefully where the kill occurred; in other cases, such as that of Wild Horse Arroyo, the processing was less thorough, perhaps because of cold weather at the high altitude of nearly 7,000 feet (2,100 meters). Such a kill would have taken at least several days to process thoroughly.

It is clear that the makers of Folsom points were concerned with not only the efficiency of their weapons but also their aesthetic value. Folsom points are remarkably beautiful artifacts characterized by fluting (the removal of large flakes with stone implements), which is accomplished by means of a shaping process called knapping. In the case of Folsom points, the fluting covers the entire length of the points on both sides. Knapping points in this way is an extremely difficult process, and it is likely that even the best Folsom knappers broke many points while shaping them.

Folsom knappers went out of their way to obtain not only hard and practical stone but also beautiful stone with which to make points. In some cases, points were manufactured of stone too fragile to yield usable points, which leads scholars to believe that they were used for ritual purposes. Some of the approximately sixteen points found at Wild Horse Arroyo were made of varieties of stone procured hundreds of miles from the site. Although it is likely that some stone was obtained by trade, it was not uncommon for Folsom people to transport stone hundreds of miles before they knapped it.

SIGNIFICANCE

Until the discovery of the Folsom site proved that New Mexico had been populated between 10,900 and 10,000 B.C.E., it was believed that humans had not lived in North America at such an early date. Even after the Folsom discovery, some archaeologists, such as the noted Ales Hrdlicka, believed that Ice Age Americans had never existed. Later, the discovery of the Clovis site in eastern New Mexico proved that North America had been populated even before the Folsom period.

—*Shawn Woodyard*

FURTHER READING

Cordell, Linda. *Archaeology of the Southwest*. 2d ed. San Diego, Calif.: Academic Press, 1984. This book, the best overview of its subject available, contains a concise discussion of the Folsom culture.

Frison, George, and Bruce Bradley. *The Fenn Cache: Clovis Weapons and Tools*. Santa Fe, N.Mex.: One Horse Land and Cattle Company, 1999. Although this beautifully illustrated book focuses on Clovis artifacts and culture, it sheds much light on the daily life of Paleo-Indians.

Meltzer, David J., Lawrence C. Todd, and Vance T. Holiday. "The Folsom (Paleo-Indian) Type Site: Past Investigations, Current Studies." *American Antiquity* 67, no. 1 (2002). This relatively technical article, which deals with new research into the original Folsom site, provides much information that can be understood by nonspecialist readers.

Tankersley, Kenneth. *In Search of Ice Age Americans*. Layton, Utah: Gibbs Smith, 2002. An entertaining, illustrated examination of both the lives of Ice Age Americans and the history of archaeological discovery in the Southwest, this volume focuses primarily on Clovis culture but also addresses Folsom culture.

SEE ALSO: c. 18,000-c. 11,000 B.C.E., Bering Strait Migrations; c. 13,000-c. 7000 B.C.E., Paleo-Indian Culture Flourishes in North America; c. 9500-c. 9000 B.C.E., Clovis Culture Rises in New Mexico; c. 9000-c. 8000 B.C.E., Cochise Culture Thrives in American Southwest.

c. 8000 B.C.E.

PERMANENT SETTLEMENT OF THE ANDEAN ALTIPLANO BEGINS

Early peoples first established permanent settlements on the high Andean grasslands, gradually shifting from hunting and gathering to domesticating animals and plants and engaging in agriculture.

LOCALE: Central Andean high grasslands, Peru
CATEGORIES: Prehistory and ancient cultures; agriculture

SUMMARY OF EVENT

The early part of the Archaic period (8000-2000 B.C.E.) is marked by rapid change in environment and therefore in human lifeways. For the most part, the early Archaic Andean peoples were generalists, hunting and collecting, using spears, atlatls, nooses, snares, and traps to secure animals and opportunistically collecting plants available in the local setting.

Work at Lauricocha and Guitarrero caves in northern Peru indicated that these early peoples had seasonal occupations, with groups dependent on hunting deer and wild camelids (guanaco and vicuña) beginning 8000 B.C.E. In this area, researchers first noticed the virtual depopulation during the middle Archaic period, coinciding with the Hypsithermal climatic period (a warmer period that lasted from 6000 to 3500 B.C.E.), a pattern that is seen much more clearly farther south.

In central highland Peru, the sites of Pachamachay and Telarmachay were inhabited by groups of people ranging in size from fifteen to fifty members, with a norm of around twenty-five members, of relatively egalitarian status. Based on the large quantities of camelid bones found in the excavations at Pachamachay, the excavators argued for the existence of a hunting group with limited mobility by 6000 B.C.E., followed by a group of specialized, year-round, sedentary, full-time vicuña hunters from 4000 to 2000 B.C.E., with a later shift to herding of camelids and some farming of quinoa and tubers. However, reanalysis of the materials indicated a seasonal utilization, not a year-around sedentary camp.

The work at Telarmachay also produced prodigious numbers of camelid bones, but analysis indicated that the site was used only during the wet season from November to March. Telarmachay burials included a child covered with red ocher and wearing a necklace of shell beads and pendants and a woman buried with a hide-working kit, including needles, awls, knives, and scrapers. Based on these burials and evidence from other high Andean sites, archaeologists believe that, beginning in the early Archaic period, these peoples developed a ritual treatment of the dead in which the bodies were treated with red ocher, and individuals were buried with decorative items (pendants and necklaces) and productive items (sewing, hunting, and butchering tool kits).

The Telarmachay site provides the first good evidence for a shift from the mixed hunting of deer and wild camelids to a focus almost exclusively on wild camelids by 4000 B.C.E. and the first domestication of alpaca after 4000, with full-time pastoralism by 3500. Work with mitochondrial and microsatellite DNA (deoxyribonucleic acid) indicates a very high genetic similarity between the alpaca and vicuña and between the llama and guanaco. The llama and alpaca were probably not domesticated in the same region. Domestic llama remains from 2500 B.C.E. have been recovered from the south-central Andean region, and it appears that both llamas and alpacas were available to Andean herders by 3000-2500 B.C.E.

In the southern Peruvian zone, the sites at the Ayacucho caves and Asana provide additional patterns of settlement. During the early and middle Archaic period, Ayacucho caves were inhabited by larger bands that broke into smaller bands and dispersed during the dry season. Intensive utilization of guinea pigs began as early as 9000 B.C.E. in Ayacucho, with possible domestication of the animal by 3500. During the middle and late Archaic period, the cave inhabitants added llamas, alpacas, quinoa, squash, bottle gourd, chili pepper, amaranth, potato, beans, and cotton to the list of plants and animals that they used.

Asana was first used about 8000 B.C.E. by coastal groups as a temporary hide-working camp. After 7500, it was transformed into a base camp for a hunting group exploiting the high sierra and puna (basin) resources. During this early Archaic period, the residents constructed small circular residential structures, which were covered with brush and hides. The economy was based primarily on hunting deer, wild camelids, and various small mammals and collecting various wild fruits and tubers. Nearby were short-term field camps (such as stone quarries, hunting blinds, butchery sites, and plant-gathering loci). The site function changed dramatically and abruptly at 3000 B.C.E., no longer serving as a base camp for hunter-gatherers but rather as the herding residence for a single extended family, with a corral. The economy of these herders exhibited more intensive plant usage, including a domestic chenopod (quinoa), algarroba (mesquite) pods, cactus fruits, wild seed plants, and wild tubers. Asana has provided a very dynamic record of evolution of patterns, from the early transitory exploitation of mountain resources by coastal populations beginning to colonize the sierra, to permanent establishment of high sierra base camps used for several millennia, to the shift toward puna agro-pastoralism.

Quelcatani in the Titicaca basin exhibits a slightly different pattern. In this area, from 4500 to 2000 B.C.E., the rainfall was much reduced, resulting in Lake Titicaca dropping in level 380 feet (100 meters) or more, becoming a highly saline, landlocked lake with no functioning outlet, and the basin itself having a comparable greatly reduced number of animals and plants available. Quelcatani, however, was situated on a small marsh. Hunters lived in small ovoid rock houses and used the site as a short-term residential base camp until 2000 B.C.E., when there was a shift to llama herding, guinea pig raising, and the beginnings of potato, oca, ullucu, tarwi, and quinoa agriculture over the new few centuries. Cave sites here are well known for a variety of rock art, including images of deer, camelids, felines, humans hunting and herding, and various geometric patterns—some of the art drawn by earlier hunters and some by later herders.

The dry and salt punas of the south-central Andes show evidence of the Middle Archaic period depopulation. In the north Chile altiplano, paleo-lakes disappeared shortly after 6000 B.C.E. As the area became progressively drier, populations either moved down to the coast or adopted more sedentary patterns of resource use by settling close to the few perennial water bodies. From 6000 to 2000 B.C.E., only a few sites, such as Purpica 1 and Tulan 52, occur near permanent water sources. Both of these were sedentary villages of twenty to forty circular stone houses. Domestication of camelids began 2500 B.C.E., and irrigated agriculture of quinoa, potato, beans, gourds, and chili peppers developed with the large-scale reoccupation of the sierra area linked with the lake level rising, perhaps as early as 2000 B.C.E.

SIGNIFICANCE

The settlement of the high Andean grasslands, beginning in about 8000 B.C.E., led to a significant increase in their usage by human populations. During the early half of the Archaic period, these populations followed two general patterns of settlement: a high grassland edge or high sierra pattern, in which groups hunted wild camelids and deer, supplemented their food sources by collecting, and moved with the seasons between the highlands and lowland, and a central puna and altiplano pattern, in which the populations were much more sedentary. During the Archaic period, these populations expanded their subsistence resources with the addition of domestic plants and animals, further enabling the settlements to become permanent and the land to become continuously populated. A period of warmer and drier climate led to a reduction in the use of the high grasslands but not their abandonment.

—*David L. Browman*

FURTHER READING

Aldenderfer, Mark. "An Archaeological Perspective on the Human Use of Cold Montane Environments in Andean South America." *Revista de Arqueologia Americana* 17-19 (2001): 75-96. Summary of different archaeological models for the first human exploitative strategies for the high Andes, beginning at 8000 B.C.E.

Bruhns, Karen. *Ancient South America*. New York: Cambridge University Press, 1994. Major synthesis of the archaeological cultures of South America from the earliest inhabitants, placing some of the developments in the Central Andes in a wider context.

Lavallee, Daniele. *The First South Americans: The Peopling of a Continent from the Earliest Evidence to High Culture*. Translated by Paul Bahn. Salt Lake City: University of Utah Press, 2000. Archaeological review of the first colonization of South America at the end of the Pleistocene and review of the evidence for early cultural developments leading to later civilizations.

Lynch, Thomas. "The Earliest South American Lifeways." In *South America*, edited by Frank Salomon and Stuart Schwartz. Vol. 3 in *The Cambridge History of the Native Peoples of the Americas*. New York: Cambridge University Press, 1996-2000. Summary of the first colonizers of the high Andean grasslands, by one of the skeptics, with a hard look at the evidence.

MacNeish, Richard. "The Beginnings of Agriculture in Central Peru." In *Origins of Agriculture*, edited by Charles Reed. The Hague, Netherlands: Mouton, 1977. Summary of the origins of agriculture in the central highlands, by one of the pioneers in the field.

Peregrine, Peter, and Melvin Ember, eds. *South America*. Vol. 7 in *Encyclopedia of Prehistory*. New York: Kluwer Academic/Plenum, 2001. Six articles on cultural periods detail evidence relating to the Archaic period occupations of the high Andes.

SEE ALSO: c. 5800-c. 3700 B.C.E., Chinchorro Inhabit the Peruvian and Chilean Coasts; c. 2500 B.C.E., Construction of Monumental Architecture at Caral in Peru.

c. 8000-c. 4000 B.C.E.

PLANO CULTURE FLOURISHES IN GREAT PLAINS AREA

The emergence of Plano culture in the Great Plains area marked the beginning of increasing Native American population density as a result of the more suitable climatic conditions that followed the warming of the post-Wisconsin glacial period.

LOCALE: Prairie grasslands of western North America, between Texas and the western Canadian provinces
CATEGORY: Prehistory and ancient cultures

SUMMARY OF EVENT

The term "Plano" is derived from the Spanish word for plains, the region in which the Plano culture flourished after the huge ice sheets that had covered much of North America began to recede as the Wisconsin glacial period came to an end about 13,000 years ago. The effect of these climatic changes on the everyday life of the people who lived in the region is not fully understood and has been the subject of much scholarly debate. There is considerable disagreement over the proper placement of Plano culture within competing time periods. Although some scholars include Plano culture within the Paleo-Indian period, others argue that it is more suited to the beginning stage of the more contemporary Early Archaic period.

The people of the Plano cultures differed from their predecessors, the Folsom people, in a number of ways. The diversity of their use of resources was considerable and is indicated by broader subsistence patterns, including bison-based and more generalized hunter-gatherer patterns. They appear to have been much less nomadic than previous inhabitants of the region. Plano cultures also show evidence of organized hunting methods, including the herding of large numbers of bison off cliffs and into other topographic traps. Plano reliance on big-game hunting indicates that although their projectile points are found in mountainous areas, they were not frequent inhabitants of higher altitudes.

The plants and animals that inhabited the emerging grasslands of the Plano period provided a stable and readily available food supply for the people of the region, resulting in a dramatic increase in population. Caribou, in the northern plains, and bison, in the southern regions, served as year-round sources of food and clothing for the inhabitants. Evidence suggests that Plano culture may be best characterized as a collection of small, highly mobile groups whose subsistence was based on efficient utilization of available plant foods, such as sunflowers and berries, in combination with meat from large grazing mammals, fish, and small animals. Grinding tools found at Plano-era campsites indicate that grains were also part of their diet.

Anthropologists and archaeologists have divided Plano cultures into subcultures, most often based on the varied geographic and ecological locales inhabited, but all the subcultures share the distinctive method of chipping stone that produced projectile points that differed from the fluted points of earlier periods. The emergence and prolific use of projectile points corresponds with the increase of population throughout much of North America as the receding glaciers left grasslands that expanded northward in their wake.

SIGNIFICANCE

The stable and readily available food supply, in combination with the production of more effective projectile points, resulted in a dramatic increase in population and perhaps life expectancy for the people of the Plano cultures. Plano peoples served as the evolutionary precursor for Early Archaic cultures, whose tools eventually became more varied and displayed greater technological innovation than those of their predecessors.

—*Donald C. Simmons, Jr.*

FURTHER READING

Bower, John R. F., and Michal Kobusiewicz. *Comparative Study of Prehistoric Foragers in Europe and North America: Cultural Responses to the End of the Ice Age*. Lewiston, N.Y.: Edwin Mellen, 2002. A fascinating comparative look at the response of Americans and Europeans to the end of the Ice Age. Bibliography and index.

Deller, D. Brian, and Christopher J. Ellis. *An Early Paleo-Indian Site Near Parkhill, Ontario*. Seattle: University of Washington Press, 2001. Provides details and analysis of the life of Paleo-Indians who were living near the Parkhill site in southern Ontario as the great ice sheets melted and caribou began to migrate through the area. Bibliography.

Dyck, Ian G., and Richard E. Morlan. *The Sjovold Site: A River Crossing Campsite in the Northern Plains*. Hull, Quebec: Canadian Museum of Civilization, 1995. This fascinating work contains details of a site in Saskatchewan. Bibliography and index.

Fagan, Brian M. *Ancient North America: The Archaeology of a Continent*. New York: Thames and Hudson,

2000. A narrative account of what is known of the diverse cultures of ancient North America. Bibliography and index.

Frison, George C. *Prehistoric Hunters of the High Plains*. San Diego, Calif.: Academic Press, 1991. One of the most respected works about plains archaeology. Bibliography and index.

Frison, George C., and Dennis J. Stanford. *Agate Basin Site: A Record of the Paleo-Indian Occupation of the Northwestern High Plains*. New York: Academic Press, 1997. Bibliography and index.

Holliday, Vance. *Paleo-Indian Geoarchaeology of the Southern High Plains*. Austin: University of Texas Press, 1997. Provides detailed information about Paleo-Indian archaeological sites in northwestern Texas and eastern New Mexico. Southern High Plains sites are also compared with other sites across the Great Plains. Bibliography and index.

Jablonski, Nina G., ed. *The First Americans: The Pleistocene Colonizations of the New World*. Memoirs of the California Academy of Sciences, no. 27. San Francisco: California Academy of Sciences and University of California Press, 2002. A collection of papers by well-known scholars who address theories about many of the unanswered questions about the arrival of modern humans in the Americas. Bibliography and index.

Stone, Tammy. *The Prehistory of Colorado and Adjacent Areas*. Salt Lake City: University of Utah Press, 1999. Provides an interesting survey of Paleo-Indian culture in the region. Maps and illustrations. Bibliography and index.

SEE ALSO: c. 18,000-c. 11,000 B.C.E., Bering Strait Migrations; c. 13,000-c. 7000 B.C.E., Paleo-Indian Culture Flourishes in North America; c. 9500-c. 9000 B.C.E., Clovis Culture Rises in New Mexico; c. 8800-c. 8500 B.C.E., Folsom People Flourish in New Mexico; c. 8000-c. 1000 B.C.E., Archaic Indians Adapt to Warmer Climates.

c. 8000-c. 1000 B.C.E.
ARCHAIC INDIANS ADAPT TO WARMER CLIMATES

North American Archaic Indian cultures adapted to changing environments, evolving from hunter-gatherer bands into organized communities that supplemented natural food sources with cultivation, developed artwork, and formed trade networks.

LOCALE: North America
CATEGORY: Prehistory and ancient cultures

SUMMARY OF EVENT

Archaeologists identify three major Archaic cultural areas and trace their evolution through the Early (8000-5500 B.C.E.), Middle (6000-3000 B.C.E.), and Late (3000-1000 B.C.E.) Archaic periods. The Western Indian culture extended from the Pacific Ocean east to the Rocky Mountains and south into Mexico. The Plains Indians ranged from the eastern Rockies to the Red River and lower Missouri River drainage area. The Eastern Woodland culture covered the United States from the Mississippi River eastward to the Atlantic Ocean. As climate changes brought environmental change, Archaic Indians adopted new technologies and lifestyles.

By 8000 B.C.E., the western United States and northern Mexico were undergoing searing heat and drought. Lakes evaporated, forests receded, grasslands withered, large game animals migrated to more favorable climes, and the Indians of the Southwest began their evolution into what archaeologists call the Desert Archaic period. Some archaeologists think that the Desert Archaic culture originated in northern Mexico, while others point to evidence of origins in southern California, Nevada, and western Arizona.

The Early Desert Archaic people traveled continuously in small bands in their seasonal searches for food and water. They may have built brush or skin shelters at campsites, or lived in available caves and rock shelters. They spent spring and summer in the mountains, hunting deer and gathering berries, acorns, and pine nuts, then returned to lower elevations for the winter. The hunters used spears and fiber nets for hunting mule deer, mountain sheep, and rabbits. Women used sharp stones and chopping blades to chop agave and yucca stalks, and stone bowls and mortars for pulverizing large seeds and cracking nuts.

The Middle Desert Archaic period saw an easing of the drought. As a result, the people settled into village life, growing maize, squash, and other crops in addition to hunting and gathering. Between 2500 and 1000 B.C.E., the Late Desert Archaic cultures established villages consisting of pit houses, fire hearths, and roasting pits grouped around a central plaza. They sent out hunting parties to bring back game, plants, and stone for tools. As the Late Desert Archaic people prospered, they opened trade routes to the Pacific coast and Mexico. Village workers dug wells to supplement water reserves. Craftspeople made bone and shell beads. Shaman artists painted and chiseled figures and symbols on stone surfaces, probably of spiritual significance.

When the Late Desert Archaic people faced another period of drought (c. 1000 B.C.E.), they enlarged the permanent villages with more pit houses. They expanded their range of wild plant resources and agriculture, adding pumpkins, beans, amaranth, and more productive strains of corn. They created methods of preserving and storing food and maintained caches of materials for tool and trade goods. Desert Archaic people honored some but not all of their dead with grave goods, suggesting differences in social standing or material wealth.

Early Archaic sites of occupation in the Plains and Eastern Woodlands are identified by tools required in big-game hunting—chipped stone spear points and knives, atlatls (throwing spears), and bone needles for sewing animal skins. By 7000 B.C.E., the large mammoths were gone and the Early Archaic people turned to forest mammals such as deer, bear, elk, fox, opossum, raccoon, squirrel, and rabbit, supplemented by nuts and plant foods. As the nomadic bands found plant and animal species in specific locations during particular seasons, the hunter-gatherers developed permanent camp sites and a regular pattern of moving to and from hunting and gathering grounds to coincide with the availability of resources at particular places.

There is little archaeological evidence of occupation in the Plains until about 2500 B.C.E. Campsites of big-game hunters dating from 5000 B.C.E. indicate that the Plains people remained primarily hunter-gatherer bands for another two thousand years, although sites at Mummy Cave and Medicine Lodge Creek in northwestern Wyoming show evidence of prolonged seasonal residence. Cultural evidence includes tubular bone pipes, fragments of coiled basketry and vegetable-fiber netting, leather scraps, wood trimmings, and flint chips. Refuse indicates reliance on numerous types of small animals and fowl for meat until the Late Archaic period, when the bison population began to recover from the severe drought.

The efficient hunters and gatherers of the Eastern Woodland thrived throughout the Archaic period. Early Archaic hunters and gatherers occupied base camps along major waterways and utilized nearby food and tool resources. Middle Archaic Indians in the southeast developed permanent settlements and adapted technology to exploit the specialized plant and animal resources of a specific environment. Excavations at sites near rivers and lakes have produced numerous stone tools, including knives, choppers, scrapers, gouges, perforators, drills, and hammer stones, as well as corner, basal, and side-notched arrow and spear points. Recent findings at the Windover site near Titusville, Florida, include bone and barbed points, fishhooks, pins, shell adzes, cloth fragments, and wooden canoes, which indicate an established community relying on fishing and gathering for subsistence.

As southeastern forests increased, the people developed tools for building canoes, housing, and other wooden objects. Archaeological digs of base camp sites along rivers and streams have uncovered storage pits, parts of house floors, and prepared burials, confirming the transition to permanent villages. Radiocarbon samples in Louisiana have confirmed mound-building traditions in use by 3000 B.C.E.

The Late Archaic period (3000-1000 B.C.E.) in the eastern United States was marked by the transformation of economies from family and community subsistence to extended trade networks. Pottery technology flourished and dispersed through the trade networks. Excavations reveal regional specialization by ethnic cultures whose tools and practices reflect their adaptation to the changing environment. In New England, for instance, smooth, half-moon-shaped knives were used to exploit sea mammals and forest animals for furs, food, and bone tools. The use of "sweet" acorns (with little tannic acid) marks the spread of Lamoka cultural patterns along the Susquehanna River and the Atlantic slope. South Atlantic coastal cultures settled in villages and utilized saltwater oyster beds as resources. In the Northeast, the forest culture is sometimes called the Shield Archaic, for the distribution of this Algonquian-speaking culture conforms to the spread of the Canadian Shield, a horseshoe-shaped geographic area covering eastern and central Canada and a small part of the northern United States. The Shield Archaic people were direct ancestors of the Algonquian tribes of the historic period.

Cultural differences were reflected in burial traditions. Unlike the pit burials found in Maine, in Newfoundland, and on the Quebec-Labrador border, the Eastern Woodland culture established villages with cemetery mounds of stone or logs covered with earth. In the Late Archaic Midwest, the dead were either cremated or interred in flexed or extended positions.

Shell ring sites along the coasts of South Carolina, Georgia, and northern Florida, as well as the great earthen mounds of the Mississippi culture, appeared during the Late Archaic period. Kenneth Sassaman examined deposits at the Stallings Island site on the Savannah River upstream from Augusta, Georgia, and found evidence of intensive occupation for about two centuries beginning in 3000 B.C.E. Recent excavations at Mims Point in South Carolina uncovered houses of a Stallings culture community (c. 1600 B.C.E.) that were arranged in ringlike fashion around a communal plaza. A shell ring in Beaufort County contained pottery identical to the Stallings fiber-tempered pottery. Archaeologists speculate that the larger shell ring sites, like the massive earthworks at Poverty Point in Louisiana, served as regional centers for cultural ceremonies, games, and trade.

Significance

The Late Archaic period (1000 B.C.E.), marked the evolution of hunter-gatherer bands into organized sedentary communities, where subsistence depended upon agriculture and horticulture in addition to hunting and gathering. The appearance of fiber-tempered pottery in the southeastern United States and its spread northward and westward was a cultural advance that enhanced the development of widespread trade. The Desert Archaic culture spread throughout Arizona, New Mexico, western Texas, southern Utah, Colorado, northern Sonora, and Chihuahua, foreshadowing the rise of the Pueblos of the Southwest. The Eastern Archaic Indians initiated the mound-building traditions of the successive Woodland and Mississippi cultures.

—Marguerite R. Plummer

Further Reading

Fiedel, Stuart J. *Prehistory of the Americas*. 2d ed. New York: Cambridge University Press, 2002. An introductory overview of Indian life before European contact. Contains a substantial chapter on the Archaic period. Bibliography and author and subject indexes.

Jennings, Jesse D. *Ancient North Americans*. San Francisco: W. H. Freeman, 1983. A textbook of essays tracing the origin and evolution of prehistoric Native Americans.

Kehoe, Alice B. *North American Indians: A Comprehensive Account*. Englewood Cliffs, N.J.: Prentice-Hall, 1981. Traces the evolution of the first inhabitants of North America, region by region, from prehistory to the present. Contains recommended readings and sources at the end of each chapter.

Mulloy, William. "The Northern Plains." In *Archaeology of Eastern United States*, edited by J. B. Griffin. Chicago: University of Chicago Press, 1952. Interprets the evidence gleaned from sites on the Northern Plains. Bibliography.

Prufer, Olaf H., Sara E. Pedde, and Richard S. Meindl, eds. *Archaic Transitions in Ohio and Kentucky Prehistory*. Kent, Ohio: Kent State University Press, 2002. A collection of essays on the Eastern Archaic period.

See also: c. 13,000-c. 7000 B.C.E., Paleo-Indian Culture Flourishes in North America; c. 2100-c. 600 B.C.E., Mogollon Culture Rises in American Southwest; c. 1800-c. 700 B.C.E., Poverty Point Culture Builds Earthworks; c. 1000 B.C.E.-c. 900 C.E., Woodland Culture Flourishes in Northern America; c. 700 B.C.E.-c. 500 C.E., Mound Builders Rise in Ohio Valley; c. 300 B.C.E., Hohokam Culture Arises in American Southwest; 200-1250 C.E., Anasazi Civilization Flourishes in American Southwest.

c. 7700-c. 1000 B.C.E.
NATIVE CULTURES FLOURISH ON THE NORTH PACIFIC COAST

The northern Pacific coast was a fertile ground for the mixing of peoples from a number of different areas: Siberia, China, and Oceania. The linguistic differences among the various groups that currently inhabit the coastal area provide clues to the speakers' origins.

LOCALE: Yakutat Bay, Alaska, to Cape Mendicino, California
CATEGORY: Prehistory and ancient cultures

SUMMARY OF EVENT

From 7700 to 1000 B.C.E., the cultures of the northwestern coast of North America advanced, eventually rivaling those of ancient Greece, thousands of years before the rise of Western civilization. Their technologies were remarkably sophisticated and provide the oldest and most varied substantial evidence for flaked stone technological traditions in North America. More than one hundred tribes lived in the Northwest Coast culture area in prehistoric times. Their cultures and civilizations ranged from simple fishing camps to advanced and diverse population centers in which thousands of people lived and worked together, engaging their neighbors in both war and trade.

The first people to enter this area appear to have come from Siberia. The theory that the entire population of the pre-Columbian Americas descended from peoples who migrated across the Bering Land Bridge through the ice-free corridor thirteen to twenty thousand years ago has long held sway. The most current archaeological evidence is causing this theory gradually to be revised.

The peoples originating in Siberia spoke a language known as Athapaskan. The distribution of this language and its relatives across North America indicates that it indeed came from north Asia. However, the distribution of languages along the northern Pacific coast suggests a more complex migration pattern for that area. Athapaskan is spoken only the northern areas of this region, where evidence indicates that its speakers have lived in the far north since the last glacial retreat ten thousand years ago. In contrast, the first people to populate the Canadian coastline south of Alaska, in the area now known as British Columbia, spoke a completely different language known as Salish. Current evidence places the origin point for this language along the coast of northeastern China.

During the glaciation, the ocean's waters were bound up in ice that covered the earth from the North Pole to central Oregon, and retreat of the waters uncovered a coastal plain along the western edge of North America. Like the Athapaskan speakers, the Salish speakers migrated along the continental shelf from northeastern China, moving west across the north Pacific. Later, as the oceans later rose again, inundating the coastal pathway, the Salish-speaking population of North America became cut off from its Asian parent culture. Evidence indicates these peoples have lived in their coastal homelands in isolation from others for only about five thousand years, since 3000 B.C.E.

To the south of the Columbia River, now the boundary between the states of Oregon and Washington and the southern limit of Salish-speaking peoples, another group of languages called Penutian is spoken. This language family spreads from the Columbia River south, all the way down the West Coast to the Yucatan Peninsula in Central America. This southernmost member of the Penutian language family is known as Mayan. Evidence suggests that the Penutian speakers came from Oceania across the Pacific Ocean by way of Easter Island to Central America. They then followed the coastline northward until they reached the Columbia River. There are no Penutian speakers north of that boundary, although there are related tribes and languages upriver to the east, including the modern Yakima and Nez Percé.

There were many different peoples, languages, and dialects in the Northwest. Over time, a trade language called Chinook developed, which was spoken by as many as 300,000 people at the height of its use. The area's cultural and linguistic diversity can be traced to the wide variety of environments within which people settled as the glaciers withdrew. The land was unimaginably lush, and the pristine resource base was vast. The people flourished as a result of the natural abundance of their temperate zone rain-forest environment. Between 7700 and 3500 B.C.E., they developed into a wide variety of cultures populated with upward of 100,000 people.

The peoples in the far north had more complex cultures, with intricate ceremonial lives, efficient technology for food extraction, and large cedar-plank homes and oceangoing canoes. They were maritime people, drawing much of their lives from the sea. They wore elaborate clothing made of cedar bark and used the totem pole to define relationships and territory. They also practiced potlatch on a grand scale. In this ceremony, an individual gave away or destroyed a lifetime's worth of possessions in order to guarantee social and economic positions. Status and wealth were deeply connected, and giving was a practiced art.

As the people settled in the southern reaches of the region, their cultures became simpler, oriented toward the more accessible and less dangerous bays and rivers and the even richer untouched terrestrial environments. However, the ocean remained the center and source of life. The abundance of fish, shellfish, big and small forest game, and plant life provided the people with large surpluses of time in which to develop ceremony, arts, and craft work to new heights.

However, the terrain was rough and often rocky, so the environment discouraged the development of farming and animal domestication. The hardness of local stone prevented the development of advanced tool-making techniques. The difficulty of travel helped to keep the peace among most peoples, who stayed at home except for trade voyages or skirmishes over territorial boundaries. The village was the primary social unit. The people lived in solid, roomy houses in clan or kinship units. They shared their wealth among themselves and with their neighbors and were generally affluent, with highly complex societies and a high level of integration with their surroundings and interaction with their neighbors. Over time, elaborate, extensive, and widespread trade networks developed.

Significance

The Northwest Coast culture area has probably been occupied continuously since 8000 B.C.E. The many common elements in the archaeological remains on the broadest scale suggest a singular culture complex originating in the north and spreading south over several thousand years. More detailed interpretations suggest a wide variety of subtle differences from area to area within the region. These extend to canoes, housing, clothing, basketry and weaving, carvings in wood and stone, and other remains, suggesting great developmental diversity and, possibly, multiple origins. The advanced hunter-gatherers of the north Pacific Coast utilized their abundant resources to create diverse cultures that were highly civilized and comparable to later civilizations elsewhere whose growth was fueled by agriculture and animal domestication. By 1000 B.C.E., the area contained the largest number of American Indian cultures, languages, and language groups on the continent.

—*Michael W. Simpson*

Further Reading

Ames, Kenneth M., and Herbert D. G. Maschner. *Peoples of the Northwest Coast: Their Archaeology and History.* New York: Thames and Hudson, 2000. A well-illustrated introduction to the Northwest Indians. Traces the changes in lifestyle and culture from 3000 B.C.E. to the present.

Borden, Charles E. *Origins and Development of Early Northwest Coast Culture to About 3000 B.C.* Ottawa: National Museums of Canada, 1975. Reviews the evidence of cultural development along the Northwest Coast in the early period and provides a good overview of its evolution.

Cressman, Luther S. *The Sandal and the Cave: The Indians of Oregon.* Corvallis: Oregon State University

University of Oregon researchers dig the remains of a 9,500-year-old house once used by hunter-gathers from a northwestern coast culture. They believe the house to have been a teepee-like structure covered with bundles of grass, cattails, or bullrushes. (AP/Wide World Photos)

Press, 1981. An excellent documentation of the discovery of well-preserved evidence, normally subject to decay and destruction, that pushes back the dates of the earliest human habitation of the Northwest further than ever.

Dixon, E. James. *Bones, Boats, and Bison: Archaeology and the First Colonization of Western North America.* Albuquerque: University of New Mexico Press, 2000. A succinct review of the evidence for migrations from multiple locations at multiple times to the Northwest Coast. Includes figures, tables, bibliography, and index.

"The Patterns of Culture." In *Indians of the North Pacific Coast*, edited by Tom McFeat. 1966. Reprint. Seattle: University of Washington Press, 1989. One in a compilation of articles on the cultural uses and practices of many groups along the Northwest coast.

Ruby, Robert H., and John A. Brown. *A Guide to the Indian Tribes of the Pacific Northwest.* Rev. ed. Norman: University of Oklahoma Press, 1992. A classic work in the field and a must-read for anyone wishing to know the details of the many bands, tribes, and civilizations of the area from prehistoric times.

SEE ALSO: c. 18,000-c. 11,000 B.C.E., Bering Strait Migrations; c. 9500-c. 9000 B.C.E., Clovis Culture Rises in New Mexico; c. 8000-c. 1000 B.C.E., Archaic Indians Adapt to Warmer Climates; c. 7200 B.C.E., Kennewick Man Lives in North America; c. 5000 B.C.E., Aleutian Coastal Hunters Flourish.

c. 7500 B.C.E.
BIRTH OF SHINTŌ

The Shintō faith developed out of Japanese traditions, rituals, and customs intermingled with legends and myths of ancestors and heroes. Daoist, Confucian, and Buddhist influences from Korea and China and the establishment of an imperial hegemony by the Yamato clan contributed to the organization and final form of Shintō.

LOCALE: Japan
CATEGORIES: Religion; cultural and intellectual history

KEY FIGURES

Jimmu Tennō (possibly fl. third century C.E.; traditionally 711-584 B.C.E.), legendary first emperor of Japan

Himiko (third century-after 238 C.E.), queen and shaman who ruled Yamatai territory during the third century C.E.

SUMMARY OF EVENT

The origin of the Shintō faith and even the approximate date for its foundation are matters of conjecture among historians. Shintō has no recorded founder and no true set of doctrines. Even the term "Shintō" is of Chinese derivation and was not applied to the indigenous Japanese religion until centuries after Shintō practice had become rooted and established. Most scholars link it to an archaeological period known as the Jōmon, which derives its name from the rope pattern (*jōmon*) pottery found at the sites connected to this early Japanese culture. However, there is also great disagreement among scholars over the dates for the Jōmon period (c. 10,000-c. 300 B.C.E.). Some estimates place its beginning as early as 10,000 B.C.E., some as late as 2500 B.C.E., with a vast variety of speculative dates in between those years. Most scholars place the end of the Jōmon period and its supercession by the Yayoi period around 300 B.C.E. The advent of Shintō also cannot be coupled with the emergence of the Ainu, who have maintained a separate religious and cultural tradition of their own. Shintō originated as a purely ethnic religion—or group of religions—of the *Wajin* (as the Ainu labeled the ancestors of the modern Japanese).

There is even more contention over exactly when Shintō was organized into a national faith encompassing all those people who came to be classified as Japanese. The most extreme view holds that Shintō should not be considered as an organized religion at all, but rather as a conglomeration of diverse cults gradually brought together over centuries and ultimately consolidated by the government of an emerging Japanese state as a method for achieving unity.

Shintō was adapted to strengthen the pretensions of the Yamato clan as it began to extend its hegemony from its base on the northwestern coast of Honshū island, eventually claiming the imperial throne of Japan. Veneration of the emperors and empresses of the semidivine Yamato Dynasty became a significant part of Shintō practice.

By the fifth century C.E., Korean and Chinese influences on the ruling and educated classes effected a transformation of traditional Japanese societal structures and ideas. Daoist, Confucian, and Buddhist beliefs all made appreciable inroads, and some scholars suggest that Japanese consciousness of having unique religious traditions arose out of the threat that these traditions might be overwhelmed by imports from the Asian mainland.

The name Shintō comes from the Chinese *shen-dao* (*shen-tao*) and has been rather misleadingly translated as "the way of the gods." The Japanese term *kami-no-michi*, "the way of the *kami*," is a more accurate description. The concept of *kami* is not exactly the same as "god"; it is a much broader term, encompassing local spirits, animating forces in natural phenomena, and extraordinary, legendary heroes and heroines of half-human, half-divine status as well as gods in the strict sense. The idea of a code of ethics is at best vaguely expressed. The closest the Shintō religion comes to the endorsement of an abstractly ethical principle is through the concept of *makoto*, "truthfulness." Proper purification, correct ritual procedure, veneration of the *kami* and of ancestral spirits, correct deportment, and respect for tradition are all significant features of Shintō—particularly early Shintō before the inroads made by the major Asian mainland faiths.

The best-known manifestations of Shintō worship are the *torii*, which serve as entrance gates to the numerous shrines to the *kami* located all over Japan. Ritualistic cleansing by bathing or by rinsing one's mouth and the magical exorcism of one's soul by priests are considered essential to appease the *kami* and attain harmony with the elements in nature.

The various mythical accounts preserved in oral tradition seem to have been set to writing in the seventh and eighth centuries C.E., at a time when the Yamato clan was solidifying its control and when the educated classes were forging a Shintō-Confucian-Daoist-Buddhist synthesis (or at least coexistence). These sacred texts included *Kojiki* (712; *Records of Ancient Matters*, 1883) and *Nihon shoki* (compiled 720 C.E.; *Nihongi: Chronicles of Japan from the Earliest Times to A.D. 697*, 1896).

The myths center around the interrelationships between the various *kami* as they set about creating the earth out of the primeval chaos, and then the islands that form Japan itself (or the Luxuriant-Reed-Plain-Land-of-Fresh-Rice-Ears). Amaterasu, the goddess of the sun, took a particular interest in Japan and sent her descendants to live and rule there. According to the *Records of Ancient Matters*, Amaterasu's great-great-great-grandson Jimmu Tennō was the first of the Yamato Dynasty and became Japan's first emperor in 660 C.E., ruling until his death in 584 (traditional dates). However, the first known historical individual in the dynasty is a queen and priestess named Himiko, who ruled over the territory of the Yamatai during the third century C.E. What is known for certain is that after the solidification of Yamato control and the acceptance of a compromise between Asian mainland religion and philosophy and Shintōist tradition whereby these elements could act in concert with one another, the imperial Yamato family was elevated to *kami* status and, until after World War II, accepted as such by the population at large.

SIGNIFICANCE

Though its origins are clouded in uncertainty, the Shintō faith, especially achieving a flexible synthesis with Daoism, Confucianism, and Buddhism, proved to be a formative and enduring influence on Japanese civilization and on the values of the Japanese people themselves. State Shintō, which set up the emperors as demigods, played a crucial role in kindling militaristic sentiment, and the other manifestations of Shintō, such as Shrine, Domestic, and Sectarian, continue to function as cornerstones of Japanese culture and belief.

—Raymond Pierre Hylton

FURTHER READING

Breen, John, and Mark Teeuwen. *Shintō in History: Ways of the Kami*. Honolulu: University of Hawaii Press, 2000. A collection of essays that constitutes one of the most comprehensive of the recent studies on aspects of Shintō.

Kitagawa, Joseph M. *On Understanding Japanese Religion*. Princeton, N.J.: Princeton University Press, 1987. Attempts to resolve controversial issues regarding the origins and initial influence on Japanese beliefs and spirituality.

Littleton, C. Scott. *Understanding Shinto: Origins, Beliefs, Practices, Festivals, Spirits, Sacred Places*. London: Duncan Baird, 2002. A concise introduction to contemporary Shintō, written by a comparative mythologist. Discusses how the historical development of the beliefs and practices of Shintō affect the form of contemporary Japanese society.

Martin, Peter. *The Chrysanthemum Throne: A History of the Emperors of Japan*. Honolulu: University of Hawaii Press, 1997. Focuses on the imperial family as a catalyst for many Shintō practices.

Morton, W. Scott. *Japan: Its History and Culture*. New York: McGraw-Hill, 1994. Advances its own theories as to when early Shintō emerged and speculates on a later date for the Jōmon era.

Picken, Stuart D. B. *Historical Dictionary of Shintō*. Metuchen, N.J.: Scarecrow Press, 2002. Entries cover major rituals, myths, and deities, as well as the relationship between Shintō and the other Japanese religions, Shintō's relationship to Nō drama, and much else. Intended to provide a comprehensive, convenient guide to the key words and names of the Shintō tradition for researchers, students, and the general reader.

Schwade, Arcadio. *Shintō Bibliography in Western Languages*. Boston: Brill, 1997. Useful resource for further research.

Varley, H. Paul. *Japanese Culture*. Honolulu: University of Hawaii Press, 1984. Highly useful placement of Shintō into the overall Japanese cultural context. The formation of the Shintō faith is effectively brought into context of what is known about Japanese historical development, including the reign of Queen Himiko and the impact of Asian mainland ideas.

See also: c. 10,000-c. 300 B.C.E., Jōmon Culture Thrives in Japan; c. 300 B.C.E., Yayoi Period Begins; 3d century B.C.E. (traditionally 660 B.C.E.), Jimmu Tennō Becomes the First Emperor of Japan; c. mid-3d century C.E., Himiko Rules the Yamatai; c. 300-710 C.E., Kofun Period Unifies Japan; 390-430 C.E. or later, traditionally r. 270-310, Ōjin Tennō, First Historical Emperor of Japan, Reigns.

Related articles in *Great Lives from History: The Ancient World*: Jimmu Tennō; Jingū.

c. 7500 B.C.E.
East Asian Grain Cultivation Begins

The beginnings of grain cultivation in East Asia have been traced back to Neolithic village sites in the middle and lower Yangtze River regions.

Locale: Present-day Hunan and Hubei Provinces, China

Categories: Prehistory and ancient cultures; agriculture

Summary of Event

Although China's history is ancient and well documented, the origins of agriculture in this Asian cradle of civilization predate its written history by thousands of years. There are five "sacred foods" in Chinese lore: rice, millet, nuts, soybeans, and barley, all of which have been cultivated since prehistory. It is likely that their elevated status is due to both their nutritional value and the ease of long-term storage. Of these foods, domesticated rice has had the most wide-ranging effects throughout the world.

Rice chaff and husks have been found in pottery containers at Pengtoushan in the central Yangtze Valley, dated from between 9000 and 7800 B.C.E. No agricultural tools were discovered among the artifacts, and it is unclear whether this the rice was wild or cultivated. Many Asian archaeologists believe the latter is the case, based on study of plant remains from more than a hundred such early sites.

Bashidang, a site that has been carbon-dated to approximately 7540-7100 B.C.E., holds voluminous proof of rice cultivation. Like Pengtoushan, it is on the Dongting Lake plain in the middle Yangtze region. Bashidang is a stratified site with layers of rice paddies, dwellings, burials, polished stone tools, and many plant and animal remains. Its material culture traits seem directly descended from those found at Pengtoushan.

Hemudu, a lakeside village near the coast in the river's lower reaches, provides a glimpse into the spread of rice culture and the material changes that had accompanied it by 5000 B.C.E. Besides the grains, stalks, and leaves of rice, there are other food remains such as sour dates and many varieties of fish. Hemudu also had tools for digging and spreading.

Geography and climate combined to create conditions for the agricultural revolution in China. Periods of cold, dry weather alternated with warmer periods, which allowed wild grains to spread profusely. The Yangtze basin had many lakes as well as seasonal flooding, which provided both rich soil and the periodically flooded fields that are optimal for rice's growth cycle.

Most of the archaeological studies on these and other sites of early Chinese grain growing have taken place since the 1970's. Although new findings could lead to new theories, it appears that grain cultivation in the Yangtze basin predates that of other areas in Asia. It may even predate the earliest known traces of barley cultivation elsewhere, which date back to 8000 B.C.E. and were found at the Netiv Hagdud site in present-day Israel.

There is no evidence of contact between very early farmers in the Middle East and in China. Agriculture seems to have been invented independently in the two areas.

Along with rice, millet was also cultivated, as well as being grown in the Yellow River region of northern China. Millet, the grain of a number of different grasses, is hardier and thrives in a colder climate than rice, so it was a natural crop for the more northerly region to adopt. Ongoing contact between the two regions in prehistoric times is more than likely. Millet is relatively neglected today as a human food source, but its protein and vitamin content is high. Flatcakes, wine, and gruel made from millet have long been consumed in China.

Chinese mythology recognizes the importance of grain growing in several myths regarding its origin. Shen Nong (Shen Nung) is said to have been the first farmer, an agricultural god who invented the digging stick and the spade. His son Zhu is given credit for first growing millet. Another tradition tells of Zhou Qi (Chou Ch'i), who discovered how to grow edible plants as an abandoned child and in adulthood was made the official in charge of agriculture. Both versions ascribe the invention of agriculture to the need to feed a growing population. Whether or not this is historically true, the influence of population pressures is a persistent theme in Chinese history.

A modern-day farmer plants rice in a paddy, much as Asians did in ancient times. (Corbis)

Significance

Rice and millet cultivation spread from China to the rest of Asia. Japan and Korea, Taiwan, the Southeast Asian countries, and India all built cultures with an agricultural base of rice cultivation. Grain cultivation is closely linked with solidification of permanent settlements and the domestication of animals. In China as in other places, the dog was the only animal to be domesticated before the agricultural revolution. The settled life and increased food supply of an agricultural lifestyle led, in China, to the early domestication of pigs and chickens, as well as oxen, goats, sheep, and cats. Throughout the world, the agricultural revolution marked a major change in the way that society was structured and functioned; in China, the revolution was centered on rice.

—*Emily Alward*

Further Reading

Higham, Charles. "The Transition to Rice Cultivation in Southeast Asia." In *Last Hunters—First Farmers*, edited by T. Douglas Price and Anne Birgette Gebauer. Santa Fe, N.Mex.: School of American Research Press, 1995. Describes climatic sequences and ties them into the earliest rice cultivation and related phenomena.

Hughes, Meredith Sayles. *Glorious Grasses: The Grains*. Minneapolis: Lerner, 1998. Although written for a young audience, this book contains much historical detail, helpful diagrams, and illustrations.

Normile, Dennis. "Yangtze Seen as Earliest Rice Site." *Science* 275, no. 5298 (January 17, 1997): 309. Summarizes report by Chinese and Japanese archaeologists on 11,500-year-old rice-growing sites along the middle Yangtze. Also mentions a tentative report on a very early fortified town in the region.

Yan, Wen-ming. "Origins of Agriculture and Animal Husbandry in China." In *Pacific Northeast Asia in Prehistory: Hunter-Fisher-Gatherers, Farmers, and Sociopolitical Elites*, edited by C. Melvin Aikens and Song Nai Rhee. Pullman: Washington State University Press, 1992. An introduction, including legendary backgrounds and a good discussion of both wetland and Yellow River dryland millet sites.

See also: c. 9500-c. 5000 B.C.E., Settlement Established at Abu Hureyra in Syria; c. 6500-c. 5000 B.C.E., Nilo-Saharan Farmers Spread Cultivation and Herding; c. 6000-c. 1000 B.C.E., Omotics Advance Farming Practices in Horn of Africa; c. 5500-c. 4500 B.C.E., Niger-Congo Peoples Spread Agriculture in Africa.

c. 7200 B.C.E.
KENNEWICK MAN LIVES IN NORTH AMERICA

Kennewick Man is a nearly complete skeleton dating to about 9,300 years before the present that was found during 1996 in eastern Washington State. Because the skeleton resembles no known ethnic group, it has provoked major debate regarding origins of humankind in the Western Hemisphere.

LOCALE: Near Kennewick, Washington
CATEGORY: Prehistory and ancient cultures

SUMMARY OF EVENT

Kennewick Man is a 9,300-year-old, nearly complete skeleton of roughly 350 pieces found in eastern Washington State during 1996. Because the remains resemble no present-day ethnicity, a major archaeological debate ensued between Native Americans and archaeologists regarding ownership of the remains. This debate provoked the first major legal test of the Native American Graves Protection and Repatriation Act (NAGPRA, signed into federal law during 1990). The discovery of Kennewick Man's remains also sparked debate over human origins in the Americas, which may be much more complex (and much more multicultural) than has been commonly supposed.

Kennewick Man's remains were first stumbled on by two college students, twenty-one-year-old Will Thomas and twenty-year-old Dave Deacy, on July 28, 1996. The two residents of nearby West Richland, home from college for the summer, were looking for a spot on the banks of the Columbia River from which to watch the annual hydroplane races. Recent flushing from Columbia River Dams, an attempt to preserve salmon runs for commercial and Native American fishing, had disturbed the sediments and exposed the human remains that became known as Kennewick Man. James Chatters, whose company, Applied Paleoscience, routinely conducted skeletal forensics for Benton County coroner Floyd Johnson, helped police gather what eventually became a skeleton that was complete except for its sternum and a few small bones in the hands and feet.

The skeleton seemed to Chatters to have belonged to a man who was old by the standards of his time (between forty and fifty-five years of age) and about five foot nine or ten inches, tall for a human being that old. He evidently had led a rough life: He had compound fractures in at least six ribs and damage to his left shoulder, which probably caused his arm to wither. He also had a healed-over skull injury. Kennewick Man, whose dietary staple was fish, probably died of injuries sustained after a stone projectile point pierced his thigh and lodged in his pelvis. The projectile probably caused a fatal infection that may have festered for as many as six months. Kennewick Man had a long, narrow skull, a projecting nose, receding cheekbones, a high chin, and a square mandible.

As publicity about Kennewick Man spread, the Army Corps of Engineers received more than a dozen claims for the skeleton, including one from the Asatru Folks Assembly and another from Old Norse, a California-based religious organization. Amid the adamant statements of some non-Indians that they had found a long-lost "white" brother, Vine Deloria, Jr., writing in the Denver *Post*, reminded his readers that, "In September, 1997, the American Anthropological Association sent a report to the Bureau of the Census, saying one could not determine race scientifically. So much for narrow skulls and high cheek-

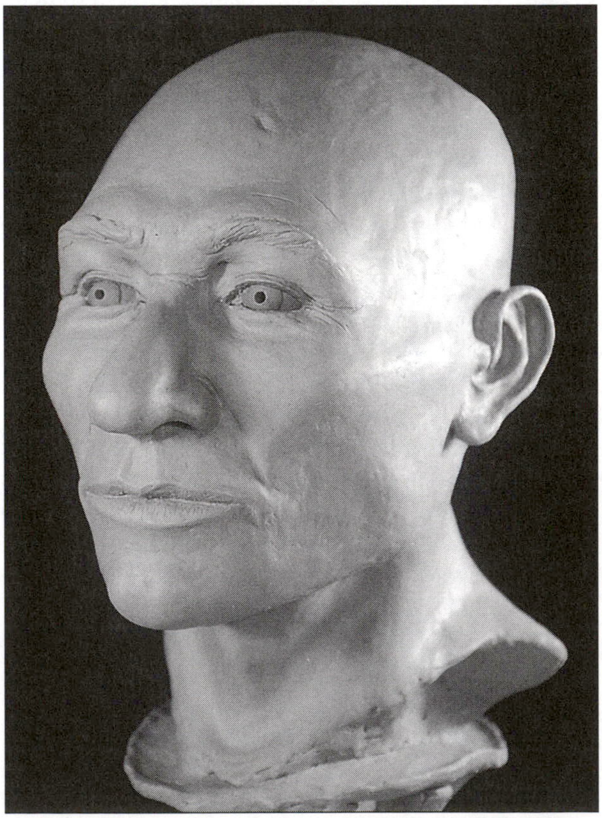

Sculptor Tom McClelland and anthropologist Jim Chatters created this clay likeness of the Kennewick Man from his skull. (AP/Wide World Photos)

bones." University of Washington anthropologist Charles Keyes agreed fundamentally with Deloria: "Race does not exist. Racism *does* exist."

Significance

A lawsuit filed against the Corps of Engineers regarding Kennewick Man by eight anthropologists represented the first major legal challenge by scientists to NAGPRA, a 1990 law that provides for the repatriation to tribes of Indian skeletons and ceremonial and mortuary artifacts. Writing to the Corps of Engineers, physical anthropologists Douglas W. Owsley of the Smithsonian Institution and Richard L. Jantz of the University of Tennessee, Knoxville, warned, "If a pattern of returning [such] remains without study develops, the loss to science will be incalculable and we will never have the data required to understand the earliest populations in America."

NAGPRA is, by and large, a reflection of Native American views on repatriation. The eight anthropologists, however, wanted to use archaeological remains for scientific study. Such explorations are opposed by a number of Native American groups including the Native Nations, who also have claimed the remains of Kennewick Man. "Native remains are not objects for scientific curiosity. They are relatives. They are grandmothers and grandfathers," said Debra Harry, coordinator of the Indigenous Peoples Coalition Against Biopiracy, in Nixon, Nevada. "When these relatives are put away . . . they're not to be disturbed by anyone . . . and the place that they rest is sacred ground."

In the case of human remains inadvertently discovered on federal land, NAGPRA regulations require the government to notify Indian nations "likely to be culturally affiliated with" the remains, tribes "which aboriginally occupied the area," and "any other Indian tribe . . . reasonably known to have a cultural relationship to" the remains in question. Kennewick Man was found within the traditional territory of the Umatilla tribes (as determined by the Indian Claims Commission). The Umatillas' claim to the land on which Kennewick Man was found is supported by a treaty signed with the United States government in 1855. The Corps of Engineers initially determined that the remains might be affiliated with the Yakima and Nez Perce as well. On August 27, the Corps notified these three tribes; Chatters informed the Colvilles himself.

During August of 2002, after more than a year of deliberation (much of it spent reading several thousand pages of documentation), U.S. District Court judge John Jelderks found for the scientists, denying the four tribes possession of Kennewick Man's remains under NAGPRA. "Allowing study is fully consistent with applicable statutes and regulations, which are clearly intended to make archaeological information available to the public through scientific research," Jelderks wrote.

Chatters, who had first handled the remains, joined the scientists in maintaining that he could support the provisions of NAGPRA and oppose returning Kennewick Man to the tribes for reburial. "I have conducted repatriations for some of the same tribes who claimed this skeleton," Chatters wrote in the *Wall Street Journal*. "I support the purpose of the law." Chatters maintained that Kennewick Man's remains were outside the scope of NAGPRA. "The act," he wrote, "was not intended to turn over all ancient skeletons to some Indian tribe, regardless of relationship. . . . The past is not a possession."

To the tribes that had sought to rebury the remains, Chatters's statement came as something of a simplification, because the point of NAGPRA is that, when human remains are concerned, the past is indeed a possession. The basic question was—and remains—how far back in time the legality of possession reaches.

In February, 2004, the Ninth United States Appeals court upheld Jelderks's decision.

—*Bruce E. Johansen*

Further reading

Chatters, James C. "Politics Aside, These Bones Belong to Everybody." *Wall Street Journal*, September 5, 2002, p. D-10. A perspective by the man who uncovered Kennewick Man's remains.

Deloria, Vine, Jr. "Balancing Science, Culture: Do Scientists Have Rights to All Finds?" Denver *Post*, November 29, 1998, p. G-1. A noted Native American scholar and activist reflects on Kennewick Man, race, and racism.

Lasswell, Mark. "The 9,400 Year Old Man: The White House Keeps Trying to Bury Him; Scientists Are Furious." *Wall Street Journal*, January 8, 1999, p. W-11. Outlines events in the Kennewick Man case to 1999.

Lemonick, Michael P. "Bones of Contention: Scientists and Native Americans Clash over a 9,300-year-old Man with Caucasoid Features." *Time*, October 14, 1996. An account of the conflict between Native Americans and scientists.

Miller, John J. "Bones of Contention: A Federal Law Stands Between Scientists and America's Prehistoric Past." *Reason* (October, 1997). A philosophical treatment of the case.

Petit, Charles W. "Rediscovering America: The New

World May Be 20,000 Years Older than Experts Thought." *U.S. News and World Report*, October 12, 1998. Kennewick Man against a broader perspective of changing views in archaeology.

Preston, Douglas. "The Lost Man." *The New Yorker*, June 16, 1997, 70-77. A detailed summary of the Kennewick Man controversy, concentrating on archaeological matters.

Slayman, Andrew L. "A Battle Over Bones." *Archaeology* 50, no. 1 (January/February, 1997): 16-23. One of the most complete treatments of the suit brought by archaeologists to allow study of Kennewick Man's remains.

SEE ALSO: c. 18,000-c. 11,000 B.C.E., Bering Strait Migrations; c. 13,000 B.C.E., Humans Enter the South American Continent.

c. 7000-c. 6000 B.C.E.
KHOISAN PEOPLES DISPERSE THROUGHOUT SOUTHERN AFRICA

The Khoisan spread from the Kalahari desert throughout southern Africa, where they adapted their hunter-gatherer lifestyle to best utilize the natural environment and became the dominant group.

LOCALE: Southern Africa
CATEGORY: Prehistory and ancient cultures

SUMMARY OF EVENT

The Khoisan people are considered one of the oldest living peoples, tracing their origins to forty thousand years ago, like other hunter-gathering peoples such as the Australian Aborigines and the Inuit people of North America. They represent the merger of two peoples, the Khoikhoi (*Khoekhoe* in the Nama language), who were herders, and the San, who were hunters. As the first peoples of Africa, they have been disparaged as "primitive," resulting in their denigration by European colonizers as "Bushmen." The Khoisan are an essentially hunter-gatherer people who have thrived for millennia in a socio-economy that relies on harmony with nature. They continue to be hunter-gatherers, refusing to be assimilated into evolving forms of technology and modernity.

Archaeological evidence drawn from sites in the Sahara indicates that animals were domesticated around seven thousand years ago. Around 4500 B.C.E., the lakes around the Sahara dried up, compelling various peoples to migrate to different parts of the African continent. Some archaeologists believe that the ancestors of the Khoisan may have migrated to the southern and western parts of Africa from central Africa because there are words used by the Khoikhoi that are found in some central African languages. Still others suggest an Asian origin for the Khoisan.

However, some scholars dismiss these theories as Eurocentric constructions and believe the Khoisan people originated in part of southern Africa. Archaeological evidence seems to support this view. Late twentieth century findings of early human activity on rocks in the Western Cape, dating back to 100,000 years ago, suggest that human settlement of southern Africa may have been earlier than commonly thought. Remains of skeletons found in Orange Free State of Azania in South Africa and at Kabwe in Zambia confirm a history of human settlement dating back at least 10,000 years, to what is referred to as the Later Stone Age. It seems probable that there were fraternal, even kinship, ties between the San and other African peoples who lived farther north.

Based on archaeological findings such as at Klasies River and Border Cave in the Cape region of South Africa, the probable ancestors of the San and the Khoikhoi were present in southern Africa 100,000 years ago. Some scholars maintain that the San were essentially a hunter-gatherer people and the Khoikhoi were herders descended from the hunter community in Botswana about 2,000 years ago because evidence of domestic animals dating back to 1,600 years ago has been found.

The Kalahari Desert in Botswana is believed to be the original place from which the Khoisan dispersed throughout southern Africa about 7000-6000 B.C.E. Because the Kalahari is an extremely dry and arid region, small bands of Khoisan people began to migrate to other regions in search of water sources and hunting grounds. The Khoisan possessed a distinctive and intimate knowledge of the natural environment because they depended on finding water in waterless zones and on gathering wild plants for food. They collected water in ostrich eggshells and tapped underground water supplies by digging holes in the sand, inserting a reed, and sucking water through the reed with a grass filter at the bottom. Such strategies enabled the Khoisan to survive in the harshest of environmental conditions, even in their migration to diverse locations from central Botswana to places in the

Khahlamba Mountains (Drakensberg) in the northern portion of Kwazulu Province in South Africa (Azania). It appears that the Khoisan opted to settle in mountainous areas thousands of years ago, before other African groups that migrated to southern Africa.

The Khoisan were skilled hunters and lived in areas in which there was abundant game. They hunted animals above and under the ground, small and large. Underground game such as the duiker, steenbok, hare, wildcat, antbear, and porcupine were hunted through traps laid in the ground or through mobile hunting, which involved the use of bows and sometimes poisoned arrows. The modern-day Khoisan believe that animals should be hunted for food and never for sport. When they use arrows, the objective is to kill rather than to wound the hunted animal so that its pain is not prolonged. Game birds were also hunted, such as guinea fowl and korhaan.

Based on the practices of the modern-day Khoisan and archaeological evidence, the Khoisan communities were collectively defined. Duties and responsibilities were shared by women and men, and food was shared by all members of the community. The Khoisan had a venerable respect for nature, including its powers and creatures. Decisions affecting the community were made in consultation with its members. Although after their subjugation by Westerners, the conditions of their existence were altered somewhat negatively, the ancient Khoisan people enjoyed nutritious diets, thriving on protein from meat and vitamins from wild plants.

SIGNIFICANCE

As the Khoisan established themselves in southern Africa and became the dominant group, they maintained a remarkable ecological balance and harmony with the natural environment, one that marked them as true environmentalists, both in history and in the present. Their ability to survive as a people in harsh environments for forty thousand years is remarkable and a valuable resource from which much can be learned about living in harmony with nature.

—*Julian Kunnie*

FURTHER READING

Bank, Andrew, ed. *The Proceedings of the Khoisan Identities and Cultural Heritage Conference*. Cape Town, South Africa: Institute for Historical Research in conjunction with Infosource, 1998. A collection of papers written by Khoisan people and others on the history, culture, art, identity, language, music, and folklore of the San people. These papers were presented at a conference held at the University of the Western Cape in July, 1997.

Boonzaier, Emile, Penny Berens, Candy Malherbe, and Andy Smith. *The Cape Herders: A History of the Khoikhoi of Southern Africa*. Athens: Ohio University Press, 1996. Provides information on archaeological findings throughout southern Africa regarding the Khoikhoi and the San. Demonstrates their presence thousands of years ago and pays particular regard to the manner in which hunters became herders.

Lee, Richard Borsay. *The !Kung San: Men, Women, and Work in a Foraging Society*. New York: Cambridge University Press, 1979. Though this work shares the limitations of any anthropological study, it offers concrete details on the science, technology, medicinal, plant, and environmental knowledge of the San people.

Lewis-Williams, David, and Thomas Dowson. *Images of Power: Understanding Bushman Rock Art*. Johannesburg, South Africa: Southern Book Publishers, 1989. This book explains the manner in which the Khoikhoi and the San became differentiated and settled in various parts of southern Africa.

Ottenberg, Simon, and Phoebe Ottenberg, eds. *Cultures and Societies of Africa*. New York: Random House, 1964. This work contains sections on the culture and life of the San people and their tenacity amid sparse environmental resources and harsh climatic conditions.

SEE ALSO: c. 300 B.C.E.-c. 100 C.E., Khoikhoi and Kwadi Adopt Pastoral Lifestyle.

c. 7000-c. 4900 B.C.E.

ÇATALHÜYÜK FLOURISHES AS CENTER OF ANATOLIAN CULTURE

The level of development at Çatalhüyük, the largest and most advanced Neolithic city yet found, indicates that the birth of civilization was not limited to the Fertile Crescent.

LOCALE: Konya (now in south-central Turkey)
CATEGORY: Prehistory and ancient cultures

SUMMARY OF EVENT

The importance of the Anatolian Neolithic world is still to be determined. Archaeologists have unearthed small Neolithic settlements dating from around 7000-6000 B.C.E. at Mersin and Tarses along the coast of eastern Cilicia and made other finds in southwestern Anatolia at Suberde and Halicar. Each of these settlements was small, ten houses or fewer, and each provides evidence of the transition of its inhabitants from food gatherers to food producers. Still, because of their size and limited evidence, these sites have introduced little to the world of Neolithic study.

Çatalhüyük, or Çatal Mound, on the south Konya Plain, however, is the largest Neolithic site discovered anywhere to date. The mound, which covers 32 acres (13 hectares), faces west on the Çarsamba River and east on Hasan Dağ. When fully excavated, it is expected to include several thousand homes, each of which is roughly 300 square feet (28 square meters) in area, if one or more adjunct storehouses are included. The walls and floors were made out of mud brick, and the walls, especially on the northern and eastern sides, were plastered. Some were embellished with painted murals of nature or animal life. Common representations included Hasan Dağ, the great mountain that the city mined for obsidian, and the horse, the deer, the ibex, the cow, and the goat. The leopard and the vulture, sacred animals, were frequently depicted, with the latter having an unusual wingspan. Archaeologists have compared the style and theme of painting to those of the cave paintings in Lascaux in southern France.

The city's dead were placed in fetal positions beneath the floor of the home of the patriarch of the family, where they were allowed to decompose. Although most homes have only a few remains, the largest concentration of dead yet unearthed in a home is sixty-four. An examination of these remains, heavily infant and female, indicate that all were remarkably healthy.

The diet, as at the other Anatolian sites, was partly vegetable—wheat, barley, lentils, and peas—and partly meat. Wild animals, which may have included the cow, provided a substantial part of the food consumed, with sheep and goats, already domesticated, also prominent. Therefore, Çatalhüyük was a food-gathering society shifting to a food-producing one.

The city on the Çarsamba River, unlike almost all Neolithic finds, including Jericho, did not have a traditional wall. Instead, like Halicar, it had houses that butted against one another with one wall of each home reinforced to produce a common exterior wall for the city. Gates and doorways were unknown, and a person entered his or her home via a short ladder through a hole in the roof placed as far as possible from the exterior city wall. All life took place in the single great room below. A fireplace for cooking and warmth was at one end, and benches and platforms were used for sitting and sleeping.

The city was not just an entity unto itself but traded with peoples on the Anatolian plain, Syria, and the Red Sea. At first, these exchanges were limited to natural materials—flint, obsidian, white marble, greenstone, calcite, and cowrie shells—but as settlements matured, so did their products. By 5400 B.C.E., for example, Çatalhüyük produced quality woodware, fine pottery, and textiles.

Around 5700 B.C.E., settlers abandoned the city on the mound. There is no evidence of fire, destruction, or health problems. People crossed the river to a new site, possibly in search of better water. People lived at Çatalhüyük B, usually called the West Mound, for another nine hundred years until the settlement was, once again, mysteriously abandoned. Thereafter, and with the exception of a minor Byzantine settlement of a much later date, the region reverted to a land of wheat fields, sheep, and goats.

Çatalhüyük remained undisturbed until the 1950's, when James Mellaart, an English archaeologist, visited the site. The excavation of a mosaic wall, the oldest of its kind in the world, on the third day convinced Mellaart that the site would revise all previous estimates of the value of Neolithic Anatolia. He initiated a dig in 1961 that lasted until 1965, when the Turks revoked his permit. Mellaart excavated more than two hundred houses, a very small part of a city that may have housed ten thousand people.

In the late 1960's and the two decades that followed, Mellaart attempted to convince Turkey to allow him to return. He failed, but his lectures at the University of

London inspired others to take up the work. In 1993, a second team, headed by Mellaart's former students Ian Holder and Louise Martin, returned to the site and continued the work until 1999. A third expedition followed in 2001.

Today, the importance of the find is unquestioned. Çatalhüyük is clearly the largest Neolithic city ever discovered, with the oldest and best-preserved mosaic walls. It is even more unusual because of its homes, with their reinforced exterior walls and the dead buried under the floors.

However, interpretation of the site's significance is not as clear cut. Mellaart and his student Holder cannot agree. Mellaart argues that Halicar and Çatalhüyük demonstrate a definitive shift from food gathering to food producing and that the city, under a priesthood or an elite group of some type, was a predecessor of Knossus on Crete. Part of Mellaart's elite theory rests on the presence of the "mother earth" fertility cult in the city. This religion, which preceded the worship of Demeter, relied on the leopard, the vulture, the horse, and the bison in its worship. Holder has serious reservations. He sees the city without a ruling elite of any kind and still heavily reliant on food gathering. Although Holder notes the presence of the fertility goddess, he is unable to find enough evidence to support Mellaart's theses of Demeter and Knossus.

Significance

The significance of Çatalhüyük relates to its size, its density of houses and people, and the quality and quantity of its artwork, which are superior to anything else produced at the same time. Even Jericho, thought to be the oldest city in the world before the discovery of Çatalhüyük, cannot compete with its Anatolian rival in these respects. The problem lies in how to tie the city with other Anatolian sites and to agree on an interpretation of all finds. Other questions must also be answered, including whether there are other similar cities, whether Çatalhüyük can be connected to any known peoples, who its trading partners were, and why it was abandoned.

—*Louis P. Towles*

Further Reading

Conolly, James. "Technical Strategies and Technical Change at Neolithic Catalhoyuk, Turkey." *Antiquity* 73 (1999): 791-800. A study of Obsidian work at Çatalhüyük.

Kunzig, Robert. "A Tale of Two Obsessed Archeologists, One Ancient City, and Nagging Doubts About Whether Science Can Ever Hope to Reveal the Past." *Discovery* (May, 1999): 84-92. The discovery of Çatalhüyük and the controversy that swirls around the interpretations of the site.

Mellaart, James. *Earliest Civilizations of the Near East*. New York: McGraw-Hill, 1965. The importance of Çatalhüyük to archaeology.

_______. "The Earliest Settlements in Western Asia From the Ninth to the End of the Fifth Millennium B.C." In *Prolegomena and Prehistory*, edited by I. E. S. Edwards, C. J. Gadd, and N. G. L. Hammond. Vol. 1 of *The Cambridge Ancient History*. 2d ed. Cambridge, England: Cambridge University Press, 1984. An analysis of Neolithic Anatolia.

See also: c. 9500-c. 5000 B.C.E., Settlement Established at Abu Hureyra in Syria; c. 3800 B.C.E., Cities and Civic Institutions Are Invented in Mesopotamia; c. 3500 B.C.E., Indus Valley Civilization Begins in South Asia.

c. 6800-c. 4900 B.C.E.
KITOI PEOPLE LIVE NEAR LAKE BAIKAL IN SIBERIA

The Kitoi culture, a hunter-fisher society, inhabited central Siberia in the late Mesolithic and early Neolithic periods before disappearing, perhaps because of harsh conditions.

LOCALE: The Lake Baikal region of Siberian Russia
CATEGORY: Prehistory and ancient cultures

SUMMARY OF EVENT

The Kitoi culture was the first of three early fisher-hunter societies that occupied the north and west regions adjacent to Lake Baikal, including the Lena and Upper Angara River valleys. This Cis-Baikal area is enveloped by three mountain ranges: the Baikal and Primorskiy to the north, and the higher Sayan range to the southwest. Kitoi settlements were centered in the permafrost-free areas of the Little Sea and Ol'khon Island and south along the west side of Lake Baikal, where the climate is roughly Continental.

A sequence of cultures first developed by scholar A. P. Okladnikov in the 1930's suggested a natural progression from the Kitoi to the Serovo to the Glazkovo societies. However, radiocarbon dating of habitation sites conducted in the late twentieth century shows little, if any, progression, as well as a significant gap between the Kitoi and their successors. The Kitoi experience dates from approximately 6800 to 4900 B.C.E., after which about seven hundred years of unexplained developments occur before the rise of the Serovo and Glazkovo civilizations.

The first sites from the Lake Baikal area—Rogatka, Ulan-Khada, Sarma, Berloga, Ludar, and Kurla—attest to the dominance of the hunting culture peculiar to the Mesolithic and early Neolithic periods. The Kitoi diet relied on the killing of red, roe, and musk deer, and moose. Smaller game such as boar and hare were also sought. Fish, including whitefish, pike, perch, and Siberian dace, were very important for their survival. Unlike the Serovo-Glazkovo peoples, the Kitoi devoted little attention to seal hunting.

The Kitoi produced new techniques and tools, such as stone-polished ceramics and slate fishhooks, adzes, and knives. Copper alloys were not yet employed. Ceramic tools appeared in the middle of the Kitoi era, and somewhat later, there is evidence of incised, geometrical motifs. The Kitoi made projectile points that may have been used for darts or arrows, but the use of bows and arrows dates from a later time. The Kitoi also produced perforators, drills, and harpoon heads. The cemetery sites that produced these artifacts also produced bones of forest animals and are located near what were probably seasonal campsites of tents. The Locomotiv cemetery in the present environs of Irkutsk dates between 5800 and 5300 B.C.E. Excavations there in the 1920's, 1950's, and 1980's uncovered more than a hundred Kitoi gravesites.

Goods in these graves may reveal belief in the afterlife. Whether the extant ornaments reveal religious symbolism can only be conjectured, as the religious values of the Kitoi are yet undetermined. Hunter-gatherers commonly associated features in the natural environment with parts of the spiritual world. Although it is believed that shamanism did not yet exist during this period, its basis can be found in similar cultures.

The variability in the size of the gravesites indicates that the Kitoi were not egalitarians. Some graves were for single individuals, and some larger sites contained a number of personal adornments and semiprecious stones such as green jade. Graves held green and white polished nephrite disks, but it is not clear that they were worn by the living. The plentiful red ocher in Kitoi graves was rarely found among the Serovo-Glazkovo gravesites. The colorful nephrite, traced to the Sayan Mountains, may indicate a trade network. Shell and antler beads and pendants from bear, deer, and boar teeth were not uncommon.

Other findings demonstrate that this culture was extremely fragile because the food supply was erratic and undependable. Attempts to master the environment were feeble and unproductive. Although there was little sharing of food among the families, making life more insecure, there was little evidence of violent contests regarding land and resources. The social experiences of the Kitoi culture were simple and primitive, nearly nonexistent. The relative scarcity of adult women seriously curtailed population growth and hampered more sophisticated social needs. Kitoi women were less healthy nutritionally than the men and also less healthy than women in the later Serovo-Glazkovo societies. The lifespan in general was exceedingly short, despite a lack of evidence indicating violence or widespread chronic or endemic diseases.

The Kitoi peoples' activities took place in a restricted geographical range. They engaged in organized foraging during the warmer seasons but over a limited land area. Consequently, subsistence problems developed in the later era, and the food supply was distributed unequally, favoring the adult males. These conditions probably explain the eventual disappearance of this civilization, as there is no evidence that external factors account for the end of the Kitoi culture. The area became completely depopulated, rather than undergoing a decline followed by a period of recovery among the survivors. Immigrant groups did not arrive in the area until seven hundred or eight hundred years later.

Significance

The cultural and even biological (cranial) discontinuity between the end of the Kitoi culture, the earliest civilization in Cis-Baikal, and the succeeding cultures of the Serovo and Glazkovo, and the distinctiveness of the Kitoi are the subjects of continued speculation and research. Scholars are especially interested in the Baikal region because of its archaeological relevance to similar cultures of hunter-gatherers in early North America, especially in Canada.

—*John D. Windhausen*

Further Reading

Asimov, M. S., et al. *Ethnic Problems of the History of Central Asia in the Early Period (Second Millenium B.C.)*. Moscow: Izd-vo Nauka, 1981. A collection of papers from a 1977 symposium attended by Soviet scholars who were pioneers in this region. Bibliography.

Christian, David. *Inner Asia from Prehistory to the Mongol Empire*. Vol. 1 in *A History of Russia, Central Asia, and Mongolia*. Oxford, England: Blackwell, 1998. An excellent summary of the work of archaeologists, although the most recent work is not included. Bibliography and index.

Edwards, I. E. S., C. J. Gadd, and N. G. L. Hammond, eds. *Prolegomena and Prehistory*. Vol. 1 in *The Cambridge Ancient History*. 2d ed. New York: Cambridge University Press, 1984. Places the region in perspective with the other civilizations of Siberia and Central Asia. Bibliography, maps and index.

Weber, Andrzej W., David W. Link, and M. Anne Katzenberg. "Hunter-Gatherer Culture Change and Continuity in the Middle Holocene of the Cis-Baikal, Siberia." *Journal of Anthropology and Archeology* 21, no. 2 (2002): 230-299. A review of Kitoi culture by the leading team of Canadian researchers. Bibliography and index.

See also: c. 5000-c. 3000 B.C.E., Kelteminar Culture Flourishes in Central Asia; c. 4000 B.C.E., Horse Is Domesticated; 1750-800 B.C.E., Andronovo Culture Rises in Central Asia; 8th century B.C.E., Scythians Drive the Cimmerians from Central Asia.

c. 6500-c. 5000 B.C.E.
Nilo-Saharan Farmers Spread Cultivation and Herding

Nilo-Saharan speakers spread the practices of cultivation and herding westward across the Sahara and the Sudan Belt into the Eastern Sahara and also eastward across the upper Nile plains; these practices led to the establishment of farmsteads and the production of cotton textiles and leather products.

Locale: Sahara and Sudan belt (across modern-day Sudan, Egypt, Chad, Niger)

Categories: Prehistory and ancient cultures; agriculture

Summary of Event

One of the most remarkable early events in the history of Africa is the shift from food consumption by way of collection to food production in farming and herding. In the long view, agricultural production and animal husbandry created new opportunities and resources that had a major impact on all aspects of society, economy, and politics throughout the continent.

One of the independent inventions of agriculture linked to animal husbandry took place between 6500 and 5000 B.C.E. among Nilo-Saharan people. The Nilo-Saharan language family includes groups as diverse as the Kanuri of Kanem-Bornu region in the central Sahel and the Luo and Maasai of eastern Africa. Before true cultivation, Nilo-Saharan speakers collected wild grains and in time added wild grass (sorghum, fonio, pearl millet) to their repertoire. Along with grain collection came important technologies such as grindstones and pottery, which the archaeological record reveals preceded the development of agriculture by as much as two millennia. Although still collectors of grasses and grains, the Nilo-Saharan communities had the apparatus necessary to stew porridge and sauces. In particular, it was the Northern Sudanic branch of Nilo-Saharan that collected grains and produced pottery by the tenth millennium B.C.E.

Archaeology indicates that by 8000 B.C.E., the Northern Sudanic communities had begun to domesticate wild cattle, an event that may mark the first production of food in all of Africa. The deliberate act of nurturing and looking after animals that would be used for human consumption had such an important impact on the control people had in sustaining their communities nutritionally that animal domestication itself constituted a revolution. Cattle keeping in fact had major demographic consequences, as it must have been at least partially responsible for greater population growth and density. Culturally, reliance on domestic cattle as a food resource reshaped how people thought about the land; they no longer looked at the use of land for food collection but rather as a place to graze cattle. Archaeological and linguistic evidence indicates that in the eighth and ninth millennia B.C.E., northern Sudanians practiced seasonally migratory cattle raising to maximize use of Sahelian grazing lands and to avoid depleting them.

One branch of descendants of the Northern Sudanians, the Saharo-Sahelians, began plant domestication in this region between 8000 and 7000 B.C.E. Much as their northern Sudanian ancestors had done before them with cattle, the Saharo-Sahelians began to intentionally sow grain seeds and nurture the plants. The combination of grain cultivation and cattle raising once again enhanced the yield of food production, which provided resources to sustain growing populations. The intensification of food production would have preceded substantial population growth. This tradition of cultivation began as a grain-seed tradition, but between 7000 and 5000 B.C.E., these cultivators incorporated gourds, calabashes, watermelons, and even nonfood crops such as cotton into their agricultural system. These burgeoning farmers, speaking languages of the Nilo-Saharan language family, spread cultivation and herding westward across the Sahara and the Sudan Belt, into the eastern Sahara and also eastward across the upper Nile plains. Particularly in the later sixth millennium B.C.E., these Sudanic farmers spread as far west as the bend of the Niger.

SIGNIFICANCE

The invention of food production through agriculture revolutionized societies at all levels. Agropastoralism fundamentally changed the way ancient people related to their environments, how they used time, and how they organized communities politically, socially, and economically.

Although cattle raising required transhumance (seasonal movement of livestock by herders), grain cultivation necessitated longer-term settlement in order to care for farm plots. The settlements of the Saharo-Sahelians can be characterized as farmsteads that were communities enclosed by thorn-bush fences to safeguard cattle, granaries, and households from predatory animals and wild vermin. The residential structures were adaptations of earlier temporary settlements. These tended to be dwellings for extended families, built on a circular floorplan, that were topped off with conical thatched roofs.

The farmstead was divided into spaces for living, cattle pens, granaries, and probably public activity. The cultivation of grain crops thus led to new social organization, new architectural styles, and the development of granaries for storage. Additionally, the Saharo-Sahelians who were cultivating more regularly began to bore water holes and wells in or near the farmstead to make water available for both human and animal needs. Cattle feeding still necessitated seasonal grazing, but the presence of well water and food stores alleviated the need for frequent movement of the entire population. These agropastoralists were increasingly seeking out permanent local resources for subsistence. What is striking about the Sudanic homestead is that the house building style shows a pattern of uniformity from the Niger Bend in the west to the Middle Nile Basin in the east.

Beyond the realm of subsistence, the development of agropastoral food production contributed also to the growth of material products such as cotton textiles and leather products. As Saharo-Sahelians experimented with cultivation of grain seeds, they also domesticated cotton. The domestication of cotton was followed by the important development of the spindle whorls made of baked clay. As early as 5000 B.C.E. cotton was being spun and woven; this is demonstrated in the Middle Nile Basin inhabited by Saharo-Sahelians by the presence of the spindle whorls used to twist and coil cotton thread. This technology spread farther west, where cotton weaving became an important domain of cultural and artistic production.

Parallel to cotton textiles emerging from agriculture, the production of leather goods emerged as a result of cattle domestication. The presence of domesticated cattle in significant numbers, particularly for human consumption, contributed to the availability of raw leather and horns for production of material objects. Horns were used for musical instruments such as trumpets for either entertainment or sounding news. The availability of new kinds of excess raw materials such as cotton, horns, and leather provided the materials that creative persons used to establish professional occupations.

Thus the important developments of food production in agriculture and cattle raising also produced cultural innovations. It is the Nilo-Saharan, Northern Sudanian, and Saharo-Sahelian legacies of agropastoral invention and elaboration that served as the foundations for the important technological and creative arts, which were widely separated temporally and geographically, spreading from ancient Egypt to Kanem-Bornu.

—*Catherine Cymone Fourshey*

FURTHER READING

Abdel-Magid, Anwar. *Plant Domestication in the Middle Nile Basin: An Archaeoethnobotanical Case Study.* New York: Oxford University Press, 1989. Focuses on archaeoethnobotany from Sudan.

Bender, Lionel M. *The Nilo-Saharan Languages: A Comparative Essay.* Munich: Lincom Europa, 1997. An in-depth analysis of the Nilo-Saharan language family.

Connah, Graham. *African Civilizations: Precolonial Cities and States in Tropical Africa, an Archaeological Perspective.* New York: Cambridge University Press, 1994. A historical account of ancient African towns that draws from archaeological data. Includes a section on ancient Egypt.

Ehret, Christopher. *The Civilizations of Africa.* Charlottesville: University of Virginia Press, 2002. A textbook survey of Africa before, during, and after the agricultural revolution.

_______. *A Historical-Comparative Reconstruction of Nilo-Saharan.* Cologne: R. Köppe Verlag, 2001. An analysis of Nilo-Saharan languages in historical context.

Shaw, Thurstan, et al., eds. *Archaeology of Africa: Food, Metals, and Towns.* New York: Routledge, 1993. This book covers a number of historical topics that influenced ancient African history from climate and geography to Iron Age tools and economies. This source draws heavily from archaeological data.

SEE ALSO: c. 10,000 B.C.E.-c. 1 C.E., Saharan Peoples Create Rock Art; c. 9000-c. 7000 B.C.E., Nilo-Saharan Peoples Produce Food and Pottery; c. 6000-c. 1000 B.C.E., Omotics Advance Farming Practices in Horn of Africa.

c. 6200-c. 3800 B.C.E.
UBAID CULTURE THRIVES IN MESOPOTAMIA

The Ubaid period, transitional between Neolithic farming cultures and early civilization, witnessed a series of economic and ideological changes that culminated in urbanism and more complex forms of social organization.

LOCALE: Greater Mesopotamia (now Iraq and parts of Syria, Iran, and Turkey)
CATEGORY: Prehistory and ancient cultures

SUMMARY OF EVENT

The term Ubaid refers to an archaeological site, a distinctive ceramic type, and a long cultural period. The site, Tell al-Ubaid, is located about 4 miles (6 kilometers) west of Ur (now Muqaiyir) along the Euphrates River in Iraq. The site was explored by the British Museum in 1919 under Harry R. Hall and during 1923-1924 by Sir Leonard Woolley. Woolley applied the term Ubaid to designate the prehistoric sequence associated with painted ceramics. In 1960, the ceramic sequence for the Ubaid period was constructed by Joan Oates, and ultimately five phases (Ubaid 0-Ubaid 4) have been recognized.

The wares of Ubaid potters enjoyed a wide distribution: They have been found from central Turkey to the highlands of Iran and southward to the Persian Gulf region. Pottery was painted and unpainted as well as impressed and incised. Examples included beakers, bowls, and jars of different sizes and shapes. Ubaid ceramics enjoyed a remarkable homogeneity in terms of style, shape, and decorative motif, while being locally manufactured. Painted Ubaid ware was fired at high temperatures and constructed of a green, red, or buff paste, with brown or black geometric designs.

As a cultural period, Ubaid marks the earliest appearance of sedentary agricultural communities on the southern Mesopotamian alluvial plain. Settlements, both on the southern alluvial plain and in northern Mesopotamia, were small. On the Diyala Plain in Iraq, villages approximating fifty to one hundred individuals were located about 6 to 12 miles (10 to 20 kilometers) apart. However, in the southern region, the rich soil and improved agricultural techniques, such as irrigation, permitted a surplus that fostered population growth. By the terminus of the Ubaid culture, the urban center of Eridu in southern Mesopotamia (site now south of An Nāsirīyah, Iraq) contained between two thousand and four thousand people.

The earliest Ubaid sites from northern Mesopotamia are quite small: Arpachiyah, east of Nineveh (near Mosul, Iraq), covered an area of about 1.5 acres (slightly over 0.5 hectare) and may have contained only one or two dwellings. Settlements seldom approached 2 acres (about 1 hectare) in size. Small population densities suggest that the northern Ubaid communities had an egalitarian, highly autonomous character. The absence of elaborate grave offerings in the Ubaid mortuary complex and the small community size suggest that complex social ranking and developed social differentiation were lacking. Any form of political hierarchy would appear to be weakly expressed, particularly during the sixth and fifth millennia B.C.E.

Archaeologists, however, have called attention to a shift that was under way by the mid-fourth millennium B.C.E., in which a structural change evolved whereby community-oriented interests and concerns were replaced with an ideological orientation on the individual level. This social change, evident in domestic architecture, early temples, and grave offerings, gradually replaced an egalitarian ideology with one rooted in social inequalities. This is particularly evident in southern Mesopotamia, where the need for centralized coordination of labor projects such as irrigation works and construction of sacred architecture gradually spread into other areas of society and culture. In northern Mesopotamia, however, the prerequisites for economic life were more variable and less dependent on collective labor.

Modern archaeological work has suggested that the Ubaid is not a single cultural entity, but rather a composite, consisting of widespread local variability. The general cultural style has been preserved in Ubaid artifacts, such as pottery and food-processing equipment, and in architecture, both domestic and sacred.

Mud brick was the basic construction material for Ubaid village architecture. Domestic units were small, with equally diminutive rooms that may have been used for storage of food, fuel, or animal fodder. Buildings were constructed on a tripartite plan that consisted of a rectangular room extending the length of the house, with smaller rooms placed along each side. The central room was secluded from the outside through the addition of flanking rooms. Floors were often coated with a gypsum plaster.

The Ubaid period witnessed the first appearance of sacred public architecture in Mesopotamia. The rectangular temples were of mud-brick construction and contained altars and other features, such as niches, which facilitated ceremonial activity. Temples appear early in the archaeological sequence (Ubaid 1, about 5500 B.C.E.) and gradually become larger.

Agriculture was diversified: Several types of wheat, barley, beans, linseed, peas, lentils, the date palm, and vegetable crops were grown. Irrigation was a necessity in southern Mesopotamia. Sheep and goats were kept, in addition to cattle. The ox-drawn plow may have been in use by the fifth millennium B.C.E. The site of Tell Abada excavated in the 1970's by the Iraqi archaeologist Sabah Jasim provided evidence that hunting (of gazelle, deer, and boar, among other wild fauna) remained important. At Tell Abada, a water-distribution system was discovered in which ceramic pipes channeled river water and water trapped in large wadis (streambeds, usually wet only during the rainy season) into the village, presumably for human use.

Craft specialization and a variety of industries flourished during the Ubaid. Pottery kilns, ranging from simple to complex in construction, have been excavated at numerous Ubaid sites. Ceramic vessels, figurines, and other ceramic artifacts reveal a high degree of ceramic specialization. The output of Ubaid ceramic production was significant. Ubaid pottery was not made on a potter's wheel but on a tournette, in which the potter's table rotated on a peg. The true potter's wheel emerged toward the end of the Ubaid sequence. In addition to ceramic workshops, the stone-tool industry produced hoes, axes, sickles, scrapers, pestles, and grinding tools for processing cereals. Weaving and basket manufacture were also important industries in Ubaid villages.

SIGNIFICANCE

The Ubaid period is positioned at the terminus of prehistory. Although certain features of civilization are lacking, such as warfare and a developed social stratification system, the Ubaid period ushered in a number of prominent civilizational processes.

Ubaid settlements reveal the gradual formalization of religion. Large, nonresidential buildings of mud brick, most likely temples, were erected on platforms of clay or imported stone. Stairs led to the top of these structures, and they may anticipate the great ziggurats of Sumer. A platform at Susa (ruins at Shūsh, Iran) that may have provided the base for a temple was 11 yards (10 meters) high, about 88 yards (80 meters) long, and 71 yards (65 meters) wide.

The gradual movement toward occupational specialization during the fifth millennium B.C.E. suggests that the family as a productive and property-controlling unit was being replaced by more formalized social institutions. The older kinship-oriented society was ultimately eclipsed by formalized managerial institutions such as the temple, which in post-Ubaid times was a powerful economic, coercive, and spiritual force.

Regional trade was active during the Ubaid period. Items that were essential to the productive economy of the village but were absent from local environments were sought after. Obsidian, limestone, natural asphalt, carnelian, and marine products from the Gulf region provide examples of desirable materials.

The precise form of leadership during the Ubaid period remains unknown. No archaeological evidence has been found attesting to great differences in political power, wealth, or prestige. By the latter stages of the Ubaid, a religious authority or a chief possibly controlled agricultural resources and coordinated labor projects. These functions may have been previously addressed through a council of village elders or a kin-oriented structure, for example, a lineage.

Small clay tokens, modeled into different shapes and found in Ubaid sites, may anticipate either a formalized record-keeping system or perhaps written accounts of business transactions. At Tell Abada, a clay proto-tablet was discovered, on which were inscribed numerous signs arranged in four lines. Jasim suggests these inscriptions may stand for numerical values and may anticipate writing for administrative and economic activity.

The Ubaid is a long and crucial archaeological sequence in which the prerequisites for an urban-based, state-level society were slowly becoming institutionalized.

—*Rene M. Descartes*

Further reading

Henrickson, Elizabeth, and Ingolf Thuesen, eds. *Upon This Foundation: The Ubaid Reconsidered*. Copenhagen: Carsten Niebuhr Institute of Ancient Near Eastern Studies, 1989. An important study consisting of seventeen papers that deal with various issues in Ubaid archaeology. Bibliography.

Jasim, Sabah Abboud. *The Ubaid Period in Iraq: Recent Excavations in the Hamrin Region*. 2 vols. Oxford, England: BAR International Series, 1985. A discussion of the excavations at Tell Abada in Iraq and a comparison with other Ubaid sites. Appendixes, bibliography.

Roaf, Michael. "Ubaid Houses and Temples." *Sumer* 43 (1984): 80-90. A discussion of Ubaid domestic and religious architecture and its defining features.

Stein, Gil, and Mitchell S. Rothman, eds. *Chiefdoms and Early States in the Near East: The Organizational Dynamics of Complexity*. Madison, Wis.: Prehistory Press, 1994. A collection of thirteen papers that deal with the Ubaid period, in addition to other political formations at the threshold of civilization. Bibliographies.

Wengrow, David. "The Changing Face of Clay: Continuity and Change in the Transition from Village to Urban Life in the Near East." *Antiquity* 72 (1998): 783-795. A discussion on the uses of clay and changing patterns of labor in Ubaid society.

See also: c. 5500-c. 4500 B.C.E., Halafian Culture Flourishes in Northern Mesopotamia; c. 4000 B.C.E., Sumerian Civilization Begins in Mesopotamia; c. 3800 B.C.E., Cities and Civic Institutions Are Invented in Mesopotamia; c. 3100 B.C.E., Sumerians Invent Writing; c. 2900-c. 2340 B.C.E., Early Dynastic Period Flourishes in Southern Mesopotamia.

c. 6000-c. 5000 B.C.E.
NIGER-CONGO RELIGION TAKES HOLD ACROSS WEST AFRICA

The Niger-Congo religion recognized three levels of spirits: ancestral spirits, territorial spirits, and, by the sixth millennium B.C.E., a creator god, suggesting an early manifestation of monotheism.

LOCALE: Western Africa and modern-day Nigeria and Cameroon
CATEGORIES: Prehistory and ancient cultures; religion

SUMMARY OF EVENT

The practice among the Niger-Congo-speaking peoples of a religious belief system that included an omnipotent god of creation can be traced back to the sixth millennium B.C.E. These ancient peoples spoke ancestral Niger-Congo languages, inhabited the woodland savanna of West Africa, and produced microlithic stone tools from the seventeenth millennium B.C.E.

Niger-Congo religious beliefs and practices centered on basic human concerns regarding the creation of the world, human origins, malevolence caused by evildoers, and protection and beneficence emanating from the spiritual (divine) sphere. From at least the sixth millennium B.C.E., Niger-Congo religious philosophy consisted of a creator god, who stood at the zenith of the religious hierarchy and was the maker of all things; various other levels of spirits; and a realm of evil. The spirits included ancestral and territorial spirits, which were both forces that had more immediate consequences for the day-to-day lives of the Niger-Congo than did the creator god. Evil was believed to be caused by human malice or ill will that was animated through curses and medicinal mixtures employed with witchcraft.

Evil was perceived by the ancient Niger-Congo peoples to be a human force caused by people's feelings of resentment, envy, greed, or the like combined with techniques of witchcraft. This faith had no devil figure, no embodiment of evil. Wicked individuals faced serious consequences for their actions, but at no time were they thought to have communed with a satanic figure. An evil person's punishment was the most extreme retribution Niger-Congo society could confer on any person: The individual was ritually forgotten by his or her society and thus unable to receive blessings, bound to roam Earth alone. In societies such as the Niger-Congo, in which belonging to a lineage through sanguine or fictive ties was crucial to religious and social existence, becoming a social outcast was a highly undesirable fate. Integral to the notion of evil was the potential for remedy through assistance from ancestors and doctor-diviners who diagnosed causes and prepared curative therapy with medicines and religious rituals. The Niger-Congo religion had no concept of a final redemption and did not focus on an afterlife. Its main focus was life itself.

According to ancient Niger-Congo religious beliefs, ancestral spirits remained part of the lineage or family line as participating members who could help or harm the kin group and therefore had to be paid due respect and be formally remembered in ceremonial acts. Because of the belief that ancestral spirits continued to play an active role and could thus have momentous impact on community welfare and well-being, these spirits were venerated and called on in times of misfortune or tragedy and for sanctions of celebrations and as sources of goodwill. Ancestor spirits were not gods, so they were not worshiped but venerated.

Niger-Congo territorial spirits were important because they inhabited or presided over specific places such as a meadow, a river, a woodland, or a particular village. They were spirits bound to a particular territory. In the minds of believers and practitioners of the Niger-Congo religion, these territorial spirits affected the outcome of events that occurred within their sphere of influence. For example, the favor of a river spirit granted safety on the water, while disfavor could cause harm. In this sense, the social and physical landscape, which included the spirit or spirits that inhabited the space, affected social life.

Religious belief and practice carried over into the social and political realm. Niger-Congo clan chiefs wielded religious power and were accountable for particular ritual responsibilities. Therefore, there was a close connection between cosmology and political power that translated into a view of the kin leader as an individual who had the power to protect the lineage. The perception that a particular individual had the ability to communicate personally or through diviner-priests with ancestral and territorial spirits meant the difference between a community accepting or rejecting a leader. One of the critical precepts of the Niger-Congo religion was the scope of human society. In this religion, the creator god and spirits of the religion were seen as being on a communal level. Religion permeated every aspect of a community's life, from economic, social, and political activities to the events of birth and death.

Although the Niger-Congo religious ideology consisted of many levels of spirits, at the zenith was a creator god, seen as the first being in the world, but one who participated little in the daily lives of the Niger-Congo people. The word for creator god varied by culture; today some Niger-Congo descendant communities call this figure Muumba, Obassi, or Choko. Regardless of the word used, this god figure was the creator of all. This concept is traced with confidence to the sixth millennium B.C.E., and its nascent origins seem to have taken root even earlier.

Niger-Congo places of worship tended to be in nature. People thought of mountains, rivers, and forests as places of deep religious significance (interestingly, the sun has never been an object of worship for these peoples). However, while Niger-Congo society worshiped in nature, they never worshiped nature itself. Mountains, trees, rivers, and other such landscape features were never prayed to but were places of worship, sites seen as somehow sacred for being connected to a specific spirit or to the creator god.

Historians' knowledge of ancient Niger-Congo religion comes from linguistic evidence, archaeological findings, and oral traditions of the Niger-Congo descendant peoples. Written literature or religious texts from ancient Niger-Congo communities are not available for analysis, as this was an oral not a literary society. By comparing vocabularies from the descendant Niger-Congo languages that spread throughout western, eastern, central, and southern Africa, it has been determined that the concept of the creator god goes back to a period before the widespread growth, expansion, and divergence of Niger-Congo peoples. Similarly, scholars have compared oral traditions across the Niger-Congo language family and have been able to reconstruct elements of prototraditions based on specific commonalities within the traditions on religious beliefs and practices.

SIGNIFICANCE

The Niger-Congo language family is one of the four language families of Africa. The Niger-Congo family includes the well-known subbranches of Mande, West Atlantic, and Benue-Kwa, which together cover approximately two-thirds of the African continent. The name Niger-Congo descends from a proto-Niger-Congo community, which would have spoken a common language and began to develop distinctive cultural and religious practices around the time of the sixteenth millennium B.C.E. Scholars have been able to reconstruct religious ideas and culture back to 16,000 B.C.E., but the concept of the creator god seems to be solidly established ten millennia later in the sixth millennium B.C.E.

The fact that Niger-Congo peoples had conceptualized a creator god, an omnipotent creator of all, together with a variety of spirits, as opposed to multiple gods, implies that there was a form of monotheism very early in religious practice in some parts of Africa. Niger-Congo religious belief portrayed a perfect world in which humankind and the creator existed in harmony. Then, a major cataclysmic event separated the creator from the people. Niger-Congo traditions indicate that humans offended God with rude behavior, such as filling his residence with dirt or smoke. Others claim humanity directly disobeyed the orders of the creator, causing a fissure. Within Niger-Congo religious philosophy, humanity's mistakes separated the creator from people's daily lives.

Significantly, the Niger-Congo concept of death was neither a trip to an afterlife nor a permanent sleep; instead, the departed became an ancestral spirit. Although his or her body had perished, the person's "divine spark" was inextinguishable. Scholars have referred to ancestral spirits as the living dead, for they were neither physically with their family nor completely absent. Ancestors could thrive only if their families made a conscious effort to remember them, particularly through consultation with them in times of crisis or for a blessing. Thus, the ancestors "survived" in the memories of their kin. This notion continues to hold salience among many Niger-Congo descendants and even influences modern-day communities.

Because the Niger-Congo peoples saw it as the family's duty to remember all ancestors and to pass this tradition on to future generations, those who regularly honored their dead were believed to receive the blessing of the ancestors. Conversely, a forgotten ancestor had the power to curse his or her family for such disrespect. Often, times of misfortune were attributed to the disregard of a family's ancestral duties. Because a neglected relative was believed to have the power to curse the family who forgot their duties, the curses of ignored ancestors were often one way the Niger-Congo peoples explained the existence of evil, crisis, and unforeseen tragedy in society.

Malicious acts could be targeted even toward those who venerated their lost loved ones. In this case, the evil manifested itself in the hatred or spite of a living being using negative energy for selfish purposes. These people were said to attack their enemies through spells, curses, and medicinal herbs.

The Niger-Congo in the sixth millennium B.C.E. were already developing complex notions of creation, gods, evil, and goodwill that incorporated elements of both divine and human actions. Although ancient Niger-Congo practices have been transformed in the past eight millennia, there are some elements of these religious beliefs that are still evident in the current practices of the descendant cultures of the Niger-Congo peoples.

—*Evan Scott Shuey*

FURTHER READING

Ehret, Christopher. *The Civilizations of Africa: A History to 1800*. Charlottesville: University Press of Virginia, 2002. An excellent source on prehistoric Africa.

Mbiti, John. *African Religions and Philosophies*. New York: Praeger, 1969. Helps explain African religion by discounting mistaken notions commonly held by Western observers.

_______. *Introduction to African Religion*. Portsmouth, N.H.: Heinemann Educational Books, 1975. A general overview of African belief systems.

Parrinder, Geoffrey, D. D. *West African Religion*. London: Epworth Press, 1961. Helps to explain and conceptualize the many different views of the various Niger-Congo descendant cultures.

SEE ALSO: c. 5500-c. 4500 B.C.E., Niger-Congo Peoples Spread Agriculture in Africa; c. 500 B.C.E.-c. 300 C.E., Socially Stratified Kingdoms Arise Around the Middle Niger River.

c. 6000-c. 1500 B.C.E.
YANGSHAO AND LONGSHAN CULTURES FLOURISH IN CHINA

Yangshao and Longshan were the first known farming cultures in what is now northern China. During their existence, settled agriculture developed, and then villages and towns were formed.

LOCALE: Yangshao, Henan Province, and Longshan, Shandong Province, China

CATEGORIES: Prehistory and ancient cultures; agriculture

SUMMARY OF EVENT

Modern humans, *Homo sapiens*, arrived in the Yellow River (Huang He) Valley no later than 50,000 B.C.E. and survived by hunting and gathering. Early agriculture in northern China began perhaps as early as 8000 B.C.E., probably as slash-and-burn gardens in the uplands of the Yellow River Valley. Solid evidence of agriculture from Neolithic sites in northern China dates to about 5500 B.C.E. Because agriculture and bronze technology had probably existed earlier in Southeast Asia, the appearance of agriculture in the Yellow River Valley most likely resulted from the diffusion of culture from Southeast Asia through southern and central China. However, millet, the staple of early agriculture in northern China, is most likely native to the area and was probably domesticated locally.

The first fully Neolithic culture identified in what is now China was first recognized in 1921 at Yangshao (Yang-shao), in Henan (Honan) Province, from where the culture takes its name. Since the initial identification of Yangshao culture, hundreds of sites have been discovered in northern China. Yangshao culture, also called the Painted Pottery culture, was once thought to be directly ancestral to Chinese culture but is now seen as one of several Neolithic cultures that gave rise to Chinese culture. Yangshao was a step in the development of culture from total dependence on hunting and gathering to dependence on settled agriculture. Yangshao culture flourished in northern China from approximately 6000 to about 1500 B.C.E., when urban civilization began to replace it and other Neolithic cultures.

Yangshao culture developed in the semiarid environment of northern China along the loess regions of the highlands of the Yellow River Valley. The presence of the loess, a fertile windblown sand that holds moisture well, allowed the development of widespread agriculture in this semiarid climate. Yangshao sites have been found along terraces on riverbanks. Yangshao settlements were usually situated in lands above the floodplain but near enough to a river to provide a stable water source. One of the most valuable of the Yangshao sites was found at Banpo (Panp'o), near the present city of Xi'an (Hsien) in the province of Shaanxi. The site, dated at around 4000 B.C.E., consists of a small village covering roughly 2.5 acres (1 hectare). The village contained forty-five houses, with some two hundred storage pits scattered thoughout the site. People from Yangshao culture villages grew millet, the main item in their diet, and raised domestic pigs, along with sheep and goats. They supplemented their diet with hunting and fishing. The Banpo site also indicated special burial grounds for the dead, with one area containing the graves of 174 adults and 76 children. Another 37 funerary urns were also present at the site. Despite their relatively more sophisticated culture over earlier hunter-gatherers, Yangshao people still depended on tools made of stone, wood, and bone. They remained ignorant of metal until around 2000 B.C.E., when bronze technology arrived from the south.

Yangshao culture is identified by its style of pottery. Yangshao pottery was made without the benefit of a potter's wheel. Instead, strips of red or gray clay were pressed into shape. Red clay pottery was decorated with symmetrical abstract designs in red or black and occasionally with fish and human faces. Yangshao people hardened their pottery in kilns. Evidence of Yangshao culture has been found along a vast belt in northern China, roughly following the course of the Yellow River and its tributaries. In the east, Yangshao culture later overlapped with another Neolithic culture called Longshan.

A painted red pottery jar from the Yangshao culture. (Christie's Images/Corbis)

Longshan culture, the next major identifiable Neolithic culture in China, was discovered in 1928 at Longshan (Lung-shan), in Shandong (Shantung) Province. Longshan culture probably arose about one thousand years after Yangshao first appeared, around 4000 B.C.E., and existed at least through 2000 B.C.E. Longshan culture, also known as Black Pottery culture, represented a transition from slash-and-burn farming in the hills to settled agriculture on the floodplains. The exact relationship between Yangshao and Longshan cultures remains uncertain, with a basic disagreement over whether Longshan represents a later development of Yangshao or a culture that developed separately.

Villages sites from Longshan culture are usually surrounded by walls made from stamped earth. Artifacts include fine pottery made with the use of wheels. At Longshan sites, researchers have identified high-temperature kilns in which Longshan people produced their gray pottery. Although Longshan people did not paint their pottery, they did decorate it with raised or grooved rings. Like the Yangshao people, Longshan people raised millet and pigs. However, evidence supports that they had domestic oxen and dogs. Also found at Longshan sites are heat-cracked animal bones, showing the widespread practice of scapulimancy, the interpretation of cracks caused by rapid heating and cooling of animal bones. This practice evolved to scratching symbols on the bones, which became the basis for a pictographic and later ideographic writing system, which evolved into the Chinese writing system in use today. Late Longshan people had learned to make silk, which would remain an exclusively Chinese skill for millennia. Evidence of early metal technology also exists, but its links to the later bronze technology found at a site in central Henan are uncertain.

Archaeological evidence uncovered near modern Zhengzhou (Chengchou) in 1957 dates from 1900 to 1600 B.C.E. The site, surrounded by earthen walls 20 feet (6 meters) high and 1 mile (1.6 kilometers) square, might be the capital city of Yangcheng in traditional histories. One large complex, interpreted as a palace, was estimated to have taken 100,000 worker-days to build. Outside the walls were two foundries for casting bronze, indicating relatively advanced metallurgical skills. Traditional Chinese histories referred to the existence of a dynasty predating the Shang (1600-1066 B.C.E.), although no physical evidence existed until the discoveries near Zhengzhou. According to legend, the Xia (Hsia; c. 2100-1600 B.C.E.) Dynasty was founded by the legendary Yu (Yü), who personified the ideal public servant. Yu was the last of five mythical pre-Xia emperors. The five were credited with the development of fire, agriculture, animal domestication, writing, calendars, and flood control. These developments actually took place over many centuries but had all been achieved by the end of the Longshan period.

The Xia might simply be the late Longshan period, when various cultures merged. Although the existence of the Xia Dynasty has never been firmly proved, the site near Zhengzhou does show the existence of centralized control in parts of the Yellow River Valley in the late Longshan period, before the rise of the Shang Dynasty, and identifiable city-based civilization. That later Chinese historians wrote of a dynasty existing before the Shang indicates some continuity of culture from prehistoric to historic times in China.

SIGNIFICANCE

Although other Neolithic cultures contributed to the origins of Chinese culture, Yangshao and Longshan cultures represent a linear development of human society in northern China from earlier hunting and gathering to fully settled agricultural societies. Longshan peoples developed many of the cornerstones of later Chinese civilization, including writing, veneration of ancestors, a tendency to build walls around towns, and the raising of animals such as pigs, which did not require pasturage or forage. Longshan later evolved into civilization in the Yellow River Valley, and late Longshan towns might be the basis for the perhaps mythological Xia Dynasty.

—*Barry M. Stentiford*

FURTHER READING

Chang, K. C. *The Archeology of Ancient China*. 4th ed. New Haven, Conn.: Yale University Press, 1987. A thorough survey of archaeological sites and findings of human activity in China in prehistoric times. Bibliography and index.

Gernet, J. *A History of Chinese Civilization*. Translated by J. R. Foster. New York: Cambridge University Press, 1995. A history of China, beginning with prehistoric times and focusing on the civilizations that developed. Bibliography and index.

Keightley, D., ed. *The Origins of Chinese Civilization*. Berkeley: University of California Press, 1983. Focuses on the period at the end of the Longshan culture, when it and other neolithic cultures contributed to the development of true civilization in the Yellow River Valley. Bibliography and index.

Murphey, Rhoads. *East Asia: A New History*. New York: Longman, 2001. Designed for use in college classes, this book provides a clear description of Yangshao and Longshan cultures, with accompanying photographs. Index and suggestions for further reading.

SEE ALSO: c. 7500 B.C.E., East Asian Grain Cultivation Begins; 2953-2838 B.C.E. traditionally, Reign of China's Legendary First Ruler, Fu Xi; c. 2600 B.C.E., Leizu Discovers Silk Making; c. 2100 B.C.E., Xia Dynasty Marks Start of Historical China; c. 1600 B.C.E., Shang Dynasty Develops Writing and Bronzework; c. 500 B.C.E., Acupuncture Develops in China.

c. 6000-c. 1000 B.C.E.
OMOTICS ADVANCE FARMING PRACTICES IN HORN OF AFRICA

Omotic peoples cultivated the ensete plant and yams and later interacted with Cushitic cattle and grain farmers to create an elaborate agricultural system that used irrigation, plowing, fertilizing, and stone-terraced mountainsides.

LOCALE: Horn of Africa (Ethiopia)
CATEGORIES: Prehistory and ancient cultures; agriculture

SUMMARY OF EVENT

Omotic populations descend from ancient southern Afrasans of northeast Africa who inhabited the southwestern region of what is now known as Ethiopia. Omotic culture began to emerge as a distinct ethnic group around 6500 B.C.E. The proto-Omotic peoples were at the forefront of a major cultural development in southern Ethiopia's highlands, where they pioneered the cultivation of the ensete plant and Ethiopian yams. By the early third millennium B.C.E., Omotic populations had initiated another set of agricultural innovations in collaboration with their Cushitic and Nilo-Saharan neighbors. Cross-cultural interactions in the southern regions of the Ethiopian highlands on the Rift Valley borders resulted in the spreading across Ethiopia's highlands of irrigation and plowing, which came into practice by 2500 B.C.E.

Historically, the Ethiopian highlands were well positioned for agricultural invention and innovation. Surrounded by the Afrasan and Nilo-Saharan populations as well as the peoples of the Mediterranean and the Arabian Peninsula, the populations of the Ethiopian highlands have been able to draw from a variety of traditions in conceiving and crafting new forms of subsistence production. This central part of the Horn of Africa has provided an unusual environment for populations, which have had to endure the climate changes that have occurred over the millennia. As climate and rainfall patterns have shifted and affected economic choices throughout the Horn of Africa, the people of the Ethiopian highlands also faced challenges but were able to maintain a varied agricultural system because of the region's high altitude, which ranges from 3,300 to 13,100 feet (1,000 to 4,000 meters), and environmental diversity.

The southern Afrasan, proto-Omotic populations first began to use uncultivated ensete (*Ensete ventricosum*) and to protect the plant in its natural habitat around 6000 B.C.E. True cultivation of ensete emerged among proto-Omotic populations between 6000 and 5000 B.C.E. because of climatic changes and increased rainfall that turned grasslands into forest in the Ethiopian highlands. Because the grains and sedges that Afrasan populations had collected for consumption became less plentiful as rainfall increased, the proto-Omotic people of the southern highlands increasingly shifted to tending the wild and abundant ensete by clearing land and cutting back forest to shelter the plant. Ensete, which thrives in high-rainfall regions, resembles the banana plant, with a fleshy stalk containing soft, pulpy tissue, but is fruitless. The pulp of the ensete trunk was dried, pounded, and used to make flour for porridge. This starchy staple was eaten with stews, vegetables, and sauces.

The Omotic populations of the sixth millennium B.C.E. inhabited the highlands bordered by Cushitic-speaking agropastoralists in the lowlands on the east, northeast, and southeast. In the west, Omotic communities shared borders with Sudanic pastoralists, particularly the East Sahelians and Nilotes of the lowlands. Between 5500 and 3500 B.C.E., Cushitic populations absorbed large segments of the Omotic population as they settled on Omotic land. The synthesis between Omotic ensete cultivation and the Cushitic farming practices of grain cultivation and livestock domestication (cattle, sheep, and goats) enhanced the economic options of lowland and highland populations.

Omotic peoples spoke languages of the Afrasan language family (also referred to as the Afroasiatic family), but lived in close proximity to Saharo-Sahelians, speakers of languages from the Nilo-Saharan language family. In this multicultural and multilingual context, there was a mixing of agricultural traditions as Nilo-Saharan farmers domesticated gourds, watermelons, and castor beans, which spread northward to Egypt and east into the Rift Valley region by 3500 B.C.E. Gourds and beans added nutritional complexity to the diet.

Between 3500 and 1000 B.C.E., Cushitic populations were involved in a series of expansions into lands inhabited by Omotics. The Agaw Cushites became established in the north and north-central highlands at some point during this period. The Agaw carried finger millet, t'eff, wheat, and barley cultivation into the southern frontier of their settlements and absorbed the existing Omotic populations. The Agaw who moved into the northern highlands dominated because grain was better suited to cultivation in the northern highlands than ensete after the climate shifted back to being arid around 2000 B.C.E.

In the far south, the Eastern Cushites moved into the eastern highlands following the path of the dry Rift Valley lands and raising livestock such as cattle and goats. The Eastern Cushites also cultivated finger millet while the Omotic populations in the bordering highlands continued to grow ensete. The Highlands Eastern Cushites emerged as a subculture of Eastern Cushites by the second millennium B.C.E. They moved into the western edges of the rift onto Omotic lands, which created more of a cultural synthesis than did the Agaw movements. The major crop in the regions settled by the Highlands Eastern Cushites continued to be ensete, and finger millet served as an important secondary staple. Not later than the second millennium B.C.E., the Highlands Eastern Cushites developed an irrigation system on the slopes of the Rift Valley that employed natural streams and gravity to create furrows to move water to cultivated lands. The creation of this system corresponds to the drying out of the climate around 2000 B.C.E. The synthesis of Omotic and Highlands Eastern Cushites peoples resulted in some communities speaking Ometo and others speaking Highlands Eastern Cushitic, but all cultivated the two primary staple crops and raised cattle. Although the cultures divided linguistically, their cultures and economies blended. The Ometo speakers were in many areas absorbed by Cushites but not completely, as after 500 B.C.E., there was a resurgence and spread of Omotic populations and culture.

SIGNIFICANCE

Life in northeastern Africa before 6000 B.C.E. was predominantly dependent on food collection. This lifestyle of searching for and gathering wild game and foodstuffs became increasingly sedentary and agrarian in nature between 6000 and 4000 B.C.E. The invention of ensete agriculture among the southernmost Afrasans located in the Ethiopian highlands was one of three independent inventions of agriculture that had occurred in Africa by 5000 B.C.E. and was the second invention that had occurred in the Horn of Africa. Although ensete cultivation began in the southern highlands with proto-Omotic cultivators, it spread into the northern and central highlands.

By 2500 B.C.E., agriculture had become increasingly intensive in nature. The Highlands Eastern Cushite agropastoralists developed a system of irrigation at about the same time that three other important agricultural techniques—terracing, fertilizing, and plowing—began to be used in the area. These techniques, used in combination, facilitated agricultural intensification, allowed for longer continuous cultivation of a plot of land without leaving it fallow, and increased yields. Stone and mud-wall terracing, which created new land on steep slopes, began to be employed in the highlands between the third and second millenniums B.C.E. Terracing also helped farmers minimize soil erosion. The plow, which had spread from the Middle East via Egypt into the highlands, was used in the regions of Ethiopia in which volcanic topsoil provided a buffer (this type of land is not typical of most other regions of Africa). The presence of the plow and of wheat and barley demonstrate the ways in which culture and economy moved across large world regions even in ancient times.

With these varied agricultural practices, the Highland Eastern Cushites were able to prepare more of the increasingly dry Rift Valley lands for cultivation. The Highland Eastern Cushites expanded their settlements the length of the valley along the highlands and carried these innovations to new regions. Neighboring populations adopted combinations of fertilizing with manure, plowing, terracing, and irrigation. By the mid-second millennium B.C.E., Omotic and Eastern Cushitic populations in both the highlands and lowlands of southern Ethiopia had incorporated these practices to varying degrees. In the lowlands, populations such as the Eastern Cushites, Proto-Oromo, and Omo of the Tana River region continued to grow grain crops and raise livestock using the new techniques of intensification. They traded their lowland products for crops and products that could not be produced in the dry lowlands, even with irrigation. Meanwhile, in the southern highlands, unlike in the north, rainfall remained at levels conducive to the cultivation of ensete.

The interactions among the populations of Omotics, lowland and highland Cushites, Nilotes, and Sudanians in northeastern Africa demonstrate how diverse and complex this region was culturally and economically in ancient times. The Ethiopian highlands was a region in which new agricultural ideas were being invented or adapted and put into practice as early as the seventh millennium B.C.E., and at the same time, it was a region from which ideas and products were diffusing to other parts of the world.

—*Catherine Cymone Fourshey*

FURTHER READING

Bender, Lionel M. *The Nilo-Saharan Languages: A Comparative Essay.* Munich, Germany: Lincom Europa, 1997. An in-depth analysis of the Nilo-Saharan language family, geared toward specialists in linguistics.

Ehret, Christopher. *The Civilizations of Africa: A History to 1800.* Charlottesville: University Press of Virginia, 2002. A textbook survey of Africa before, during, and after the agricultural revolution.

_______. *A Historical-Comparative Reconstruction of Nilo-Saharan.* Cologne, Germany: R. Köppe Verlag, 2001. An analysis of Nilo-Saharan languages in historical context.

Pankhurst, Richard. *The Ethiopians: A History.* Oxford, England: Blackwell Publishers, 2001. Covers the ancient history of Ethiopia from the era before the interactions of Abyssinia and the pharaohs of Egypt up to the modern period.

Phillipson, David W. "The Antiquity of Cultivation and Herding in Ethiopia." In *Archaeology of Africa: Food, Metals, and Towns*, edited by Thurstan Shaw et al. New York: Routledge, 1993. The book covers a number of historical topics that influenced ancient African history, from climate and geography to Iron Age tools and economies. Draws heavily from archaeological data. Phillipson's article discusses the antiquity of cultivation and herding in Ethiopia and contains maps, images, and a description of the various crops.

Ruskin, F. R., ed. *Lost Crops of Africa: Grains.* Vol. 1. Washington, D.C.: National Academy of Sciences, 1996. This excellent source on grain origins gives a detailed list and description of the crops indigenous to Africa such as t'eff, millet, and sorghum and gives a historical account of grain domestication.

Sato, Shun, and Eisei Kurimoto. "Essays in Northeast African Studies." In *Senri Ethnological Studies.*

Osaka: National Museum of Ethnology, 1996. This study covers riverbank cultivation in the Lower Omo Valley and the intensive farming system in southwestern Ethiopia. Includes a section on cultivation strategies and historical change in the Horn of Africa.

SEE ALSO: c. 9000-c. 7000 B.C.E., Nilo-Saharan Peoples Produce Food and Pottery; c. 7500 B.C.E., East Asian Grain Cultivation Begins; c. 6500-c. 5000 B.C.E., Nilo-Saharan Farmers Spread Cultivation and Herding; c. 5500-c. 4500 B.C.E., Niger-Congo Peoples Spread Agriculture in Africa.

c. 5800-c. 3700 B.C.E.
CHINCHORRO INHABIT THE PERUVIAN AND CHILEAN COASTS

The fisher folk living along the Peruvian and Chilean coasts created the world's earliest intentional mummies, two thousand years older than those of Egypt.

LOCALE: South coast of Peru and north coast of Chile
CATEGORIES: Prehistory and ancient cultures; religion

SUMMARY OF EVENT

The oldest intentionally prepared mummies in the world, which are at least two millennia older than those found in Egypt, were found on the southern coast of Peru and the northern coast of Chile. These mummies were first reported in the scientific literature in 1917 by Max Uhle, and the Chilean archaeologists have named the culture Chinchorro, after the location where Uhle first identified the remains. The Chinchorro tradition evolved from an earlier group of maritime gatherers roughly 10,000 to 8,000 years ago. The early groups had little specialized technology but were mainly generalized maritime collectors, supplementing their economies with inland plants and animals.

With the Chinchorro tradition, however, came the first true fishermen, c. 6000-5800 B.C.E., who developed fishhooks made of shell and nets and harpoons with detachable heads. They lived in villages with small circular huts of cane and matting with stone foundations and plastered clay floors. The people fished, collected shellfish, hunted sea lions, and cut up beached whales. Bone chemistry analyses indicate that roughly 90 percent of the diet was marine-based. Some of the adult mummies from phases after about 4500 B.C.E. exhibit auditory exostoses or aural osteomas, a pathological condition related to deep-sea diving, indicating yet another new marine exploitative technique.

More than 1,500 Chinchorro burials are known, although fewer than 250 elaborate mummies have been recovered. The period of intentionally modified mummification practices runs from roughly 5800 to 1700 B.C.E. There are four main varieties of the mummy preparation. The least important is the treatment of essentially naturally mummified bodies; these mummies occur as early as 7000 B.C.E., at the early end of the sequence, and again during the last few millennia, at the late end of the sequence. Early examples may have their faces painted in designs with red ocher and black manganese and may be wrapped in mats or animal skins; the very late examples are wrapped in elaborate woven woolen and cotton textiles, but otherwise little else is done except to let the hot, dry sands naturally desiccate the bodies.

Beginning at 5800 B.C.E. and persisting until 2800 B.C.E., however, is the most complex variety of artificial treatment, sometimes known as the "black mummies" because of the black manganese used to draw facial features and other designs on this class of mummies. The skin was slit open and removed in segments, then treated to arrest deterioration (early on with salt, later with other procedures). All the internal organs were removed and discarded, and the brain was extracted through the occipital hole. The body was then defleshed and disassembled, and the main muscle masses were removed by stone and shell tools. The interior of the body was then dried by means of fire embers or hot ashes; long bones may have been dried out over campfires.

After the body was thus disassembled, prepared, and dried, it was ready to be reconstructed into the mummy. The main body cavity was filled with ash and clay. Next the corpse was reinforced and stiffened with an elongated piece of wood attached along the vertebral column, and the limbs were reassembled using cane or wooden shafts for support structure. The kneecaps and elbow joints were rasped and filed down to help make the limbs rigid. The limbs were wrapped with mats of woven rushes and then tightly wrapped with cords for reinforcement. The preserved skin was adjusted and sewn back onto the whole body in patches, like a glove. To restore some appearance of life, the body was coated with a layer of clay, in a kind of modeling, and often decorated in black, with manganese-based pigments; hence the name black mummies. The face was likewise modeled in white clay and sculpted into a mask with eyes and mouth indicated by holes and incisions that were sometimes outlined in black. In some later examples, false teeth were added to the mouths. Both male and female sexual organs were often modeled in clay. The end result was a kind of sophisticated rigid vertical statue.

The "red mummies" period followed, beginning roughly 2800 B.C.E. and lasting until 2100. The preparation of the corpse was not quite as elaborate during this period. Red mummies were prepared without disarticulation (the limbs being separated from the body). They were partially eviscerated, and the body cavity was dried over coals. Incisions were made, and sticks were slid under the skin to add rigidity to the body, and then the incisions were sewn back together. The body was stuffed with ashes, soil, grass, shells, feathers, or other fill. Like the black mummies, the red mummies were covered with an exterior coat of clay to permit sculpting and painting of facial and body details, although body modeling was less detailed. As a finishing touch, wigs of human hair were often fixed on the skull.

The last major intentionally fabricated type of mummy was the mud-coated variety. This type was found from 2100 to 1700 B.C.E. The corpses were smoke-dried by fire but were not reinforced; then the body was covered with a thick layer of mud and painted, usually in the red mummies style. The mummies were often wrapped in mats or textiles. After 1700, local residents appear simply to have relied on natural desiccation in the hot sands, even though they continued to inter the dead wrapped in textiles and mats.

Because the Chinchorro mummy tradition lasted more than four thousand years, it should not be surprising that the material culture of the group changed, and the purposes for producing the mummies may have changed as well. Thus, for example, plant foods become more important after roughly 4000 B.C.E.; sites have more grinding stones, plants such as manioc and quinoa are found as offerings and in desiccated human scats (excrement), and more inland animals get added to the diet. Early mummies are associated with only mats, twined textiles, and basketry, but by later periods, woven textiles of cotton and wool are common, and "repp" (or ribbed) geometric design woolen belts are added. Headgear of later mummies sometimes includes woven turbans and "crowns" made from red, yellow, and blue tropical parrot feathers. In later periods, other animals, such as birds and dogs, are also treated with the same mummification techniques. Highland obsidian artifacts come in with the textiles. Additional ritual gear begins to occur. With the black mummies are some of the earliest examples of the South Andean hallucinogenic complex, with snuff, snuff trays, inhaling tubes, spatulas, brushes, boxes, and other ritual containers associated with the mummies.

SIGNIFICANCE

Many of the early Chinchorro mummies were children, leading some scholars to suggest the possibility of a special adoration of children, but at the early cemetery of Morro 1, the mummies recovered included forty-two children and fifty-four adults, so it is evident that adults were not being ignored. The rigidity of the mummies is thought to have been a deliberate feature to aid families in transporting their dead from site to site; it is therefore believed that the mummies were meant to be accessible to the living for an extended period of time before final disposal by interment. Some of the mummies exhibit considerable surface damage that was later repaired. There is evidence that the facial clay masks were refinished, body surfaces were repainted, and damaged body extremities were repaired. In some cases, several different types of clay have been applied in different repairs, suggesting a prolonged period of ritual use of the mummies. At some point, the mummies were finally interred, sometimes as family groups, other times apparently as individuals. Exactly when and why this final interment occurred is not yet clear. Mummification continued until the Spanish Conquest in 1519, notably by the last Incas to honor their emperors.

—David L. Browman

FURTHER READING

Arriaza, Bernardo. *Beyond Death: The Chinchorro Mummies of Ancient Chile*. Washington, D.C.: Smithsonian Institution Press, 1995. Discusses the origins, construction, and evolution of the Chinchorro mummies, with definitive details.

Lavallee, Daniele. *The First South Americans*. Salt Lake City: University of Utah Press, 2000. An overall view of the early cultures of South America that places Chinchorro in a wider context. Contains chapters on the origins and development of archaic maritime cultures along the Peruvian and Chilean coast.

Llagostera, Agustin. "Early Occupations and the Emergence of Fishermen on the Pacific Coast of South America." *Andean Past* 3 (1992): 87-111. Deals with the emergence of maritime specialization on the Peruvian and Chilean coasts in the early Holocene, establishing the context for the development of the Chinchorro mummy complex.

Núñez, Lautaro. "Archaic Adaptation on the South-Central Andean Coast." In *Pacific Latin America in Prehistory*, edited by Michael Blake. Pullman: Washington State University, 1998. Review of the Archaic period cultures of the south-central Pacific coast, detailing the beginnings of maritime specialization and reviewing the Chinchorro complex.

Rivera, Mario. "The Preceramic Chinchorro Mummy Complex of Northern Chile." In *Tombs for the Living: Andean Mortuary Practices*, edited by Tom Dillehay. Washington, D.C.: Dumbarton Oaks Research Library and Collection, 1995. Discussion of the Chinchorro peoples by an archaeologist who has devoted his lifetime to studying the people, placing the mummy activities in a wider complex.

See also: c. 13,000 B.C.E., Humans Enter the South American Continent; c. 8000 B.C.E., Permanent Settlement of the Andean Altiplano Begins.

c. 5500-c. 4500 B.C.E.
Halafian Culture Flourishes in Northern Mesopotamia

Halafian culture, transitional between farming villages and early cities, developed increasing social and technological complexity, including sophisticated ceramics, perhaps draft animal power, burial ceremonialism, and mud-brick architecture, with defensive works.

Locale: Northern Mesopotamia (now northern Iraq, northern Syria, and southern Turkey)

Categories: Prehistory and ancient cultures; agriculture; cultural and intellectual history

Summary of Event

Early twentieth century archaeological work recognized the high-quality ceramics associated with the Halafian period. Between 1911 and 1929, Max von Oppenheim worked at Tell Halaf on the Syrian-Turkish border, roughly 205 miles (330 kilometers) northeast of Aleppo, Syria. Large quantities of pottery were recovered, and several occupations of the site were exposed. The earliest settlement was a sixth millennium B.C.E. community, which provided the name for the broad cultural distribution that stretches across northern Mesopotamia. In the 1930's, Max Mallowan's excavations at Arpachiyah, a small agricultural village about 3.5 miles (6 kilometers) east of Nineveh (near Mosul, Iraq), contributed to the chronological positioning of the Halafian culture in the Mesopotamian sequence, in addition to describing the ceramic trends. Since the period of Mallowan's work, important fieldwork has been accomplished by Iraqi, British, Russian, and American archaeologists. Although considerable substantive information has been recovered on the cultural and technological aspects of the Halafian period, problems persist regarding understanding both the mechanisms responsible for the diffusion of Halafian culture and the political and social organization of this evolving agrarian economy.

Halafian agricultural villages were situated in fertile regions; however, sites were not always located in proximity to major tributaries. In most areas, annual rainfall was adequate to permit nonhydraulic farming. Halafian village sites vary in size: Domuztepe in southern Turkey is about 8 acres (20 hectares); Tell es-Sawwan in Iraq is about 26,000 square yards (about 24,000 square meters). Population numbers for Halafian villages are estimated at between thirty and two hundred individuals. During the immediate post-Halaf at the site of Domuztepe, however, the population may have approached fifteen hundred to two thousand individuals.

The Halafian agriculturalists were engaged in a mixed farming economy. At Tell es-Sawwan, rudimentary irrigation was initiated. Crops grown included wheat, barley, lentils, flax, vetch, and chickpeas. A number of wild species were also collected, including pistachio and ryegrass. Domesticated fauna included sheep, goats, cattle, and pigs. Wild faunal remains from Halafian sites suggest the importance of hunting for furs or meat. Patty Jo Watson and Steven LeBlanc, excavators of Girikihaciyan in southeastern Turkey, have suggested that cattle may have been used to pull plows, as they were kept alive longer than other domesticates. Another reason for their longevity may be tied to the development of dairy activities.

The proximity of Tell es-Sawwan to the Tigris and the fish remains recovered attest to the dietary variability of the Halafian people, which reflected their local environmental resources. Fish remains, however, are not common in Halafian sites.

Halafian cultural remains include various stone tools for processing cereals (grain grinders, pestles, and mortars), axes, mace heads, and bowls constructed from obsidian, alabaster, and sandstone. Spindle whorls, pendants, beads, zoomorphic figurines, a variety of bone and horn tools, and flint blades and scrapers suggest a tool kit consistent with expanding economic and ceremonial functions. Ovoid clay pellets discovered at different sites have been interpreted as sling missiles, perhaps used for defensive purposes.

Halafian ceramics are among the most sophisticated to be produced in prehistory. Pottery was fired evenly at about 900 degrees Fahrenheit (482 degrees Celsius), giving it a porcelain-like finish. Colors range from red to orange and black to brown. Vessels and plates used for ceremonies and special occasions were particularly spectacular in design, while others remained unpainted. The Burnt House at Arpachiyah, excavated by Mallowan in the 1930's, provided ceramic examples that established the Halaf as a period of high technical achievement. Ceramics—bowls of varied styles, jars, and plates—were produced in large quantities and bore geometric, zoomorphic, and anthropomorphic motifs. At Yarim Tepe II in Iraq, the earliest pottery kilns were excavated by a Russian expedition and dated to the fifth millennium B.C.E. Halafian culture was engaged in incipient metallurgy: Small copper artifacts, as well as copper ore, were discovered at Yarim Tepe II.

Halafian village architecture does not suggest deliberate planning. Domestic structures are circular or rectilinear. Stone foundations were used on certain, but not all, units. The use of mud brick dates to the sixth millennium B.C.E. in northern Mesopotamia and is the basic construction material. The earliest Halafian dwellings were round, slightly over one yard (one meter) in diameter, with a domed or flat roof. In the fifth millennium B.C.E., rectangular, single-story structures of varied dimensions are the usual architectural form. Houses were small: At Girikihaciyan, circular dwellings ranged from about 2.5 to about 5 yards (2.25 to 4.5 meters) in diameter. Individual rooms within rectangular structures at Yarim Tepe II were about 2 yards (1.65 meters) by slightly over 1 yard (1.2 meters) in width. Halafian buildings embraced a range of shapes and room sizes: At Tell Sabi Abyad in northern Syria, one structure was 12 yards (11 meters) long by 3.5 yards (3 meters) wide and contained long, narrow rooms. It was common to plaster floors and occasionally walls by using a gypsum-based material.

SIGNIFICANCE

Although Halafian agricultural villages convey the appearance of small mud-brick domesticate units, ovens, kilns, and granary structures, the culture approximates an intermediate stage between the small Neolithic food-producing village and the first true Mesopotamian cities. A number of evolving institutional formats attest to this: trade, craft production, property control, ideological orientation, and defense.

Regional trade, a feature of early civilization, was present in Halafian culture and is evidenced by the movement of obsidian from volcanic sources to communities that processed the raw material into a variety of products, including bowls, tools, and plaques. In addition, Halafian ceramics were distributed over northern Mesopotamia.

The use of stamping seals has an ancient lineage in Mesopotamia, including in Halafian culture. Seals of lithic (stone) material and of various shapes bore geometric motifs. These seals may reflect a developing social hierarchy that controlled certain forms of property. By late Halafian times, seals increased statistically in the archaeological record, and they probably mark an institutional transition to more complex forms of economic administration.

Halafian sites have yielded a variety of implements used in weaving: spindle whorls, bone needles, and awls. At Domuztepe, both sheep and goats were managed into advanced ages, implying that wool and hair may have been important agricultural commodities. Weaving would appear to be an element of Halafian technological development designed to meet the needs of an expanding population.

Halafian archaeological sites document the high degree of craftsmanship and technical development in stone, seals, pottery, and figurine production. Evolving social and cultural institutions are further evidenced in a complex mortuary cult. At Yarim Tepe II, burials were of numerous types: cranials, secondary, and cremations. Burial offerings of animal remains and artifacts were placed in prepared chambers. At Tell es-Sawwan, the sixth millennium B.C.E. cemetery containing four hundred graves provided evidence on a spectrum of fertility symbols and assorted offerings. D. G. Youkana, an excavator at Tell es-Sawwan, suggested that this site was the center of a mother goddess cult that stretched across northern Mesopotamia. Additionally, the economic importance of cattle may have ceremonial parallels. Artistic representations of cattle (bucranium motifs on pottery) suggests cult activity, similar to the cattle cult at

Çatalhüyük, an agricultural settlement in south-central Turkey that lasted from about the eighth to the fifth millennium B.C.E. However, cattle cult shrines have not been excavated in Halafian sites.

The presence of defensive works at Tell es-Sawwan reflects increasing patterns of social complexity. A mud-brick wall, 151 yards (138 meters) in length, and a moat reveal the inhabitants' concern for safety. Clay balls, perhaps sling missiles, were discovered in the moat.

Increasing patterns of leadership and community organization in the Halaf culture are reflected in the transport and manufacture of craft and construction materials. Cooperative labor projects are obvious in trade, agriculture, and edifices such as the Tell es-Sawwan defensive wall. However, Halafian culture lacks public architecture, occupational specialization, and elaborate social divisions based on wealth, power, and prestige.

—*Rene M. Descartes*

FURTHER READING

Campbell, Stuart. "The Halaf Period in Iraq: Old Sites and New." *Biblical Archaeologist* 55, no. 12 (1992): 182-187. A brief overview of Halafian culture, including modern trends in research.

Watson, Patty Jo, and Steven A. LeBlanc. *Girikihaciyan: A Halafian Site in Southeastern Turkey.* Monograph 33. Los Angeles: Institute of Archaeology, University of California, Los Angeles, 1990. A site report that discusses Halafian material culture and interprets a wide range of faunal and artifact finds. Bibliography.

Yaffee, Norman, and Jeffery J. Clark. *Early Stages in the Evolution of Mesopotamian Civilization: Soviet Excavations in Northern Iraq.* Tucson: University of Arizona Press, 1993. A discussion of the Soviet excavation on a number of Neolithic sites in Iraq. Bibliography, index.

Youkana, Donny George. *Tell es-Sawwan: The Architecture of the Sixth Millennium B.C.* London: NABU Publications, 1997. An examination and comparison of Halafian architecture and material culture. Bibliography.

SEE ALSO: c. 9500-c. 5000 B.C.E., Settlement Established at Abu Hureyra in Syria; c. 7000-c. 4900 B.C.E., Çatalhüyük Flourishes as Center of Anatolian Culture; c. 6200-c. 3800 B.C.E., Ubaid Culture Thrives in Mesopotamia; c. 4000 B.C.E., Sumerian Civilization Begins in Mesopotamia.

c. 5500-c. 4500 B.C.E.
NIGER-CONGO PEOPLES SPREAD AGRICULTURE IN AFRICA

Niger-Congo peoples spread both mixed agriculture and systematic agriculture and laid the foundation for advanced civilizations in West Africa.

LOCALE: Western and central Africa
CATEGORIES: Prehistory and ancient cultures; agriculture

SUMMARY OF EVENT

According to most scholars, the earliest plant domestication for food occurred around 10,000 B.C.E. in different parts of the world. This transition from food gathering to food production constituted an agricultural revolution, taking place simultaneously in various parts of the world. In Africa, this major change in food production probably took place in Egypt close to 8000 B.C.E. Cereals produced in Egypt and later transferred to the Niger-Congo region differed from the Asian grains, which required more rainfall.

About 5500 B.C.E., people living along the banks of the Niger and Congo Rivers in western and central Africa slowly transformed their lives. They transitioned from hunter-gatherers who practiced minimal agriculture along the western and southern regions of the Sahara to an expanding population of farmers who cultivated cereals, including millet and sorghum, in western and central Africa.

The Niger-Congo peoples had begun cultivating yams around 8000 B.C.E. They later domesticated okra, oil palms, blackeyed peas, and guinea fowl, using digging-stick agriculture rather than mound agriculture. In a region in which tropical rainfall softened the ground, stick agriculture predominated. Agricultural tools—an axe, hoe, and sickle—were also most likely in evidence by this time period. By about 6000 B.C.E., Niger-Congo peoples planted cowpeas, yams, cereals, and root crops, including the potato. However, as the climate in the Sahara changed and the area became drier, the food producers moved deeper into the rain-forest zones of West Africa and even to the Atlantic coast. These changes in climate forced an environmental adaptation but promoted the spread of agriculture by the Niger-Congo peoples from the fringes of the Sahara into the more tropical zones of western Africa.

Other bands of Niger-Congo peoples moved into the areas along the equatorial belt. Farmers began cultivating grain crops such as millet and sorghum. These cereals most likely arrived in the region from Egypt, the site of Africa's first food-producing economy. Millet and sorghum thrived in the tropical rain-forest region of West Africa, particularly along the banks of the Niger and Congo Rivers. This advanced agriculture laid the foundation for population growth among the Niger-Congo peoples.

The Niger-Congo population in this region is estimated to have been about 500,000 or less by 6000 B.C.E. However, because of the increased food supply stemming from organized agriculture, it rose to about one million inhabitants by 1000 B.C.E. The sustainable population, based on food production, mixed agriculture, and a higher fertility rate (which usually accompanies an improved diet), could have been even larger, perhaps 1.5 million people. In addition to a greater food supply, the Niger-Congo peoples also came to depend on mixed agriculture, producing large herds of domesticated goats, cattle, and sheep. Large herds of such animals were present in the central Sahara by 7000 B.C.E., but domesticated animals did not reach the Niger-Congo region until sometime around 5000 B.C.E. Slowly, large herds of domesticated animals spread from western and central Africa into South Africa, virtually covering the entire continent by 1000 B.C.E. Mixed agriculture, in addition to systematic agriculture, led to the population explosion among the Niger-Congo peoples.

The changing climate forced the Niger-Congo peoples even farther from the Sahara, causing more resettlement along the banks of the Niger and Congo Rivers and their tributaries. Some groups moved into central Africa, close to present-day Zaire. Wherever the Niger-Congo peoples spread, they took with them the agricultural technology necessary to spread the cultivation of cereals and other crops. The spread of systematic agriculture into new regions fostered diverse systems of food production that led to settled communities elsewhere in Africa.

Systematic agriculture entailed using hundreds and perhaps thousands of people in an organized manner to produce food. Many crops, especially millet and sorghum, were labor-intensive; that is, they required a large number of workers to produce small yields of food. However, systematic agriculture among the Niger-Congo peoples in Central and West Africa led to settled communities, far more advanced than the hunter-gatherers who preceded them.

SIGNIFICANCE

Systematic agriculture and its spread by the Niger-Congo peoples into the tropical rain forest along the western and southern Sahara laid the foundation for the powerful civilizations of Ghana, Mali, and Songhay. Niger-Congo peoples organized around agriculture became the most significant development in West Africa before the formation of the great Sudanic kingdoms.

—*Jackie R. Booker*

FURTHER READING

July, Robert W. *A History of the African People*. Prospects Heights, Ill.: Waveland Press, 1998. Chapter 1 provides background to African agriculture. Maps, bibliography, and index.

Munson, Patrick J. "Africa's Prehistoric Past." In *Africa*, edited by Phillis M. Martin and Patrick O'Meara. Bloomington: Indiana University Press, 1977. This essay gives information on crops and environmental factors in ancient African agriculture. Maps, bibliography, and index.

Oliver, Roland, and Brian M. Fagan. *Africa in the Iron Age*. New York: Cambridge University Press, 1975. Chapter 2 examines food production in ancient Africa.

Schoenbrun, David L. "We Are What We Eat: Ancient Agriculture Between the Great Lakes." *Journal of African History* 34 (1993): 1-31. This article explores food-producing communities in east Africa and examines previous works on the subject

Van Der Veen, Marijke, ed. *The Exploitation of Plant Resources in Ancient Africa*. New York: Kluwer Academic/Plenum, 1999. A series of essays on agriculture in ancient Africa. Maps and index.

SEE ALSO: c. 9000-c. 7000 B.C.E., Nilo-Saharan Peoples Produce Food and Pottery; c. 6500-c. 5000 B.C.E., Nilo-Saharan Farmers Spread Cultivation and Herding; c. 6000-c. 5000 B.C.E., Niger-Congo Religion Takes Hold Across West Africa; c. 6000-c. 1000 B.C.E., Omotics Advance Farming Practices in Horn of Africa.

c. 5000 B.C.E.

ALEUTIAN COASTAL HUNTERS FLOURISH

Hunter-gatherers from Siberia crossed the Bering Strait land bridge into Alaska, eventually establishing a culture that still thrives in what is now the Aleutian Island peninsula.

LOCALE: Alaska's Aleutian Islands
CATEGORY: Prehistory and ancient cultures

SUMMARY OF EVENT

Most archaeologists agree that between fifty thousand and thirteen thousand years ago, during the last ice age, people migrated from eastern Asia into North America via the Bering Strait land bridge. With the sea level as much as 350 feet (105 meters) lower than its current level, this causeway linked Siberia's Chukchi Peninsula and Alaska's Seward Peninsula into one massive land area now called Beringia. The earliest flow of Paleo-Siberian immigrants foraged eastward into Alaska in search of food sources such as mastodon and mammoth, eventually migrating southward into the Aleutian Islands and beyond. Alaska's present-day Inuit and Aleuts are more closely descended from a second wave of hardier, more Arctic immigrants, who reached Alaska between 6000 and 4000 B.C.E.

The population of the Aleuts (an eighteenth century Russian term, readily adopted by the Aleut peoples) is often divided into eastern, central, and western island groups, based on language differences. Studies indicate a division between the Siberian-influenced Aleut language and the earliest Eskimo languages occurring approximately 5000-4000 B.C.E. Similarities between Siberian and early Alaskan peoples extend beyond linguistics; shared physical traits also support the theory of a prehistoric eastward transcontinental migration. Both groups exhibit similar facial features: high cheekbones, low-bridged noses, a somewhat flattened face, little male facial hair, and epicanthic eyelid folds. With their straight, dark hair and minimal body hair, short stature, stocky but muscular physique, and light skin color, these two groups more closely resemble one another than they do other neighboring populations. The decorative use of labrets (wooden or ivory discs) among the Aleuts and Siberians is another indicator of Siberian influence. No longer used today, labrets were typically inserted into slits in the skin between the mouth and chin, one at each corner of the mouth.

The Aleuts lived in in Siberian-style pit houses called *barabaras* dug 4 to 6 feet (1.2 by 1.8 meters) below ground level and measuring approximately 40 by 25 feet (12 by 8 meters), covered with whalebone-and-sod roofs. Special compartments were dug into the earthen walls for sleeping, storage, and sometimes burials.

Abundant fish and wildlife provided sustenance for this hardy maritime population. In approximately 11,000 B.C.E., Alaska's minimal population was composed primarily of nomadic hunter-gatherers in search of caribou, bison, and other land animals. Distribution of archaeological artifacts suggests that these groups slowly moved deeper into Alaska for the next four thousand years until, between 7000 and 4000 B.C.E., certain changes became apparent: Hunting tools, for example, became noticeably more regional, suggesting a less nomadic existence. Within this same time period, a focus on seal, walrus, and whale emerged. Tools for hunting and processing these animals have been found in archaeological sites. Remnants of whaling harpoons with a prong at one end, unlike the toggle-head harpoons of earlier Eskimo groups, have been found in Aleutian Island sites. Essential domestic tools such as sewing needles and animal skin scrapers made of bone have also been found. One important food source was the Stellar sea lion (*Eumetopias jubatus*), which provided not only food but also other essentials: skin for boats; sinew for line, cord, and thread; blubber for oil; bone and teeth for tools, jewelry, weapons, and fishhooks; flippers for soles of boots; and other innards for various articles of clothing and storage containers.

Following a regimen of superstition and ritual, Aleut whalers hunted from one- or two-man kayaks (*baidarkas*), poisoning their prey with a harpoon dipped in a derivative of the aconite plant. As the poisoned, harpooned whale gradually died over several days, the hunter secluded himself and feigned illness, believing that the whale would follow his example, growing ill and dying. Once dead, the whale would be hauled to shore, unless it died out at sea and was lost. From an early age, young boys were taught strengthening exercises to help develop the requisite skill and strength for harpooning whales and seals while seated in a *baidarka*. Along with seals, whales, and sea otters, the sea lion made up half of the Aleut diet. Other important food sources were caribou and fish, as well as bird eggs, sea urchins, plants, and berries, which were gathered by women and children.

Limited information regarding early Russian, Siberian, and Alaskan skin boats comes from prehistoric rock carvings depicting prototypes of the *baidars* and *baidarkas* used by the Paleo-Siberians, Aleuts, and other groups in the Bering Strait vicinity. These seal-, sea lion-, and walrus-skin boats were constructed with watertight seams stitched with animal sinews, making them sturdy enough to withstand the often violent storms of the Arctic waters.

An active belief in the supernatural underlay many of the Aleuts' views on death. They treated illness with spiritualistic rituals in addition to medical methods. The deceased were handled in a number of ways, including burial in the pit-home wall compartment, mummification, interment in large wood or stone burial monuments, and elaborate burials in caves. According to this belief system, a person's spirit continued to live after death, and sometimes the deceased's body was dismembered to prevent his or her spirit from living on and doing harm to the living.

SIGNIFICANCE

The eastward advance of Asian subarctic hunter-gatherers into the Aleutian Islands spawned a similar advance into other inland areas of the North American continent, particularly Alaska's Yukon region. This systematic invasion peopled northern North America and left behind many prehistoric tools and artifacts for archaeologists to discover centuries later.

—*Cherie C. Castillo*

FURTHER READING

Coon, Carleton S. *The Hunting Peoples*. Boston: Atlantic-Little, Brown, 1971. A study of ten thousand years of hunter-gatherers, including Eskimos, Aleuts, and other Alaskan peoples.

Jochelson, Waldemar. *Archaeological Investigations in the Aleutian Islands*. Salt Lake City: University of Utah Press, 2002. A report from Jochelson's 1909-1910 expedition to Alaska. Includes photographs and drawings.

_______. *History, Anthropology, and Ethnology of the Aleut*. Salt Lake City: University of Utah Press, 2002. The report of a 1933 anthropological expedition led by Jochelson. Provides an overview of Aleut prehistory and history, as well as their social and material culture.

Johnstone, Paul. *The Sea-craft of Prehistory*. Cambridge, Mass.: Harvard University Press, 1980. Discusses worldwide prehistoric vessels, ranging from simple log rafts, to skin boats of Russia and the Arctic, to other seacraft for travel and hunting.

Langdon, Steve J. *The Native People of Alaska*. 4th ed. Anchorage, Alaska: Greatland Graphics, 2002. Thorough treatment of Alaska's five main native groups, including Aleut.

Levinson, David, ed. *Encyclopedia of World Cultures*. 10 vols. New York: Gale, 2002. This authoritative series overseen by cultural anthropologist Levinson includes a volume on North America that covers the Aleuts. Includes maps, bibliographical references, and indexes.

SEE ALSO: c. 18,000-c. 11,000 B.C.E., Bering Strait Migrations; c. 13,000-c. 7000 B.C.E., Paleo-Indian Culture Flourishes in North America; c. 7700-c. 1000 B.C.E., Native Cultures Flourish on the North Pacific Coast; c. 7200 B.C.E., Kennewick Man Lives in North America.

c. 5000-c. 3000 B.C.E.
KELTEMINAR CULTURE FLOURISHES IN CENTRAL ASIA

Kelteminar culture was the first extended settled civilization in the western part of Central Asia.

LOCALE: Central Asia south of the Aral Sea
CATEGORY: Prehistory and ancient cultures

SUMMARY OF EVENT

Kelteminar culture was discovered as the result of aerial searches in 1939 by Soviet archaeologist S. P. Tolstov. In 1946, he led an expedition to Khwarizm that produced further discoveries there. The heartland of Kelteminar was along the eastern bank of the Amu Dar'ya (Oxus) River in Khwarizm. That great river then emptied out into the Caspian Sea as well as the Aral Sea and produced a lake in Khwarizm called Lyavlyakan. The fertile region to the east and south formed part of what is today the Kyzyl Kum Desert. Nine Neolithic open-air sites have been uncovered in this region, all exhibiting the material culture that has been labeled Kelteminar. The center of this culture lay just east of the Karakalpak Autonomous Region in modern Uzbekistan. Kelteminar culture extended south of the Aral Sea throughout the now dry Akcha Dar'ya Delta and in the lower Zeravshan River areas. To the north, this culture extended into western Siberia. It was named after an abandoned canal in Khwarizm, where the initial discoveries were made.

The Kelteminar location placed it near three other civilizations of Central Asia: Afanasievo, Andronovo, and Karasuk. The valley of the lower course of the Karasuk River was historically an important area between nomadic tribes and the settled farming cultures to the south. It produced numerous ethnic peoples of Eurasia. The Kelteminar society maintained some contacts with the Anau culture, an agricultural society, to the south, about 8 miles (13 kilometers) southeast of Ashkhabad, and also with the Neolithic communities to the north in the Ural and lower Ob River regions.

Incised pottery and pottery made from shells, dating from as early as the fifth millennium B.C.E., was discovered south of the Aral Sea. Round clay pots, pointed on the bottoms, were decorated with drawings and stamped designs. Shells have also been discovered as grave goods. Grave sites reveal artifacts of flint and quartz that were inserted into wooden or bone handles. Arrowheads were abundant, but the bow had not yet been invented. Kelteminar people lived in seasonal villages composed of oval-shaped frame homes, with about 100 to 120 residents per village. Contemporary settlements from Xinjiang (Sinkiang) to eastern Mongolia were similar.

Early Kelteminar people engaged in fishing, hunting, and food gathering, maintaining few, if any, domesticated animals and doing little farming, in contrast to both the Anau and Jeitun societies to the south and east. Sickle blades have been found in this region, suggesting a trend toward a more settled existence as time progressed. In modern Turkmenistan, mixed farming appeared about 5300 B.C.E. both within and east of the Jeitun culture as far as the Hindu Kush Mountains. It is uncertain when the Kelteminar populations began to participate in this activity. Kelteminar grave sites have yielded bones of wild pigs, deer, and turtles. The people maintained herds of sheep, horses, and pigs that were often guarded by huge, half-wild dogs, *Canis familiaris matris optimae*; there are also signs of domesticated goats, sheep, oxen, pigs, and cattle. In the later stage of this society, from 4300 to 3000 B.C.E., the practice of metallurgy was developing, and barley was being supplemented by a new hybrid of wheat. South of this region fortified walls engulfed the many round houses, an indication that the inhabitants feared Kelteminar warriors, who were still recognized as nomads. This threat may have provided an impetus for the beginnings of town life.

SIGNIFICANCE

Kelteminar was the first extended settled civilization in the western part of Central Asia and was undoubtedly the first Neolithic civilization in Khwarizm. However, the process by which stock breeding arose in ancient Khwarizm remains a question. One theory is that the practice of domesticating certain animals among the fisher-hunter peoples of the steppes came from contact with the peoples to the south, but there is scant evidence to indicate a mass movement of the southern peoples northward to the Amu Dar'ya and beyond to the steppes. Oxen and cattle were of little use to the Kelteminar nomads, although some remains of these animals have been found in Kelteminar sites. Pigs were animals that bridged that divide. The dominant opinion is that the domestication of certain animals arose within Kelteminar society itself. The later stage of Kelteminar life indicates a society that was gradually developing a more settled existence in contrast to its purely nomadic existence in the fifth millennium B.C.E., although it is unknown whether this arose through contact with the Jeitun and Anau cultures.

—*John D. Windhausen*

FURTHER READING

Christian, David. *Inner Asia from Prehistory to the Mongol Empire*. Vol. 1 in *A History of Russia, Central Asia and Mongolia*. Oxford, England: Blackwell, 1998. A prominent historian analyzes and summarizes the materials in the larger context. Bibliography and index

Davis-Kimball, Jeannine, Vladimir A. Bashilov, and Leonid T. Yablonsky. *Nomads of the Eurasian Steppes in the Early Iron Age*. Berkeley, Calif.: Zinat Press, 1995. Offers analysis of Soviet studies since 1960 by various experts. Bibliography and index.

Edwards, I. E. S., et al., eds. *Prolegomena and Prehistory*. Volume 1 of *Cambridge Ancient History*. 3d ed. New York: Cambridge University Press, 1971. An older but indispensable starting point for an overview of the region. Bibliography and index.

Frye, Richard N. *The Heritage of Central Asia: From Antiquity to the Turkish Expansion*. Princeton, N.J.: Marcus Weiner, 1996. A well known scholar of Iranian history extends his analysis to the northeast. Bibliography and index.

Levine, Marsha, Yuri Rassamakin, Aleksandr Kislenko, and Nataliya Tatarintseva. *Late Prehistoric Exploitation of the Eurasian Steppe*. Cambridge, England: McDonald Institute for Archaeological Research, 1999. Since nomadic cultures leave few settled archaeological sites, this study utilizes bone analysis to discuss the lifestyle of the Kelteminar culture, among others.

SEE ALSO: c. 6800-c. 4900 B.C.E., Kitoi People Live Near Lake Baikal in Siberia; c. 4000 B.C.E., Horse Is Domesticated; 1750-800 B.C.E., Andronovo Culture Rises in Central Asia; c. 1250-c. 700 B.C.E., Karasuk Culture Flourishes on Eurasian Steppes.

c. 5000 B.C.E.-c. 1 C.E.
RED PAINT CULTURE FLOURISHES IN EASTERN NORTH AMERICA

Archaeological evidence suggests that a prehistoric culture known as the Red Paint culture existed in New England and the Canadian maritime provinces and ultimately, some say mysteriously, disappeared.

LOCALE: North America, from northern Labrador and Newfoundland, down through New England, and to the Great Lakes
CATEGORY: Prehistory and ancient cultures

SUMMARY OF EVENT

The term Red Paint culture or Red Paint people refers to a prehistoric people who existed in the Archaic period and had a tradition of burying their dead with gifts and then covering both with red ocher (iron oxide powder) pigment. The term Maritime Archaic tradition, popularized by archaeologist James A. Tuck, also appears in the archaeological literature concerning these people. As Tuck defines the term, it refers to the place, the time, and the characteristics of the culture. "Maritime" suggests the people's situation near and reliance on the coast. "Archaic" places the culture from c. 5000-3000 B.C.E. to c. 1 C.E. and defines them as a preagricultural, hunter-gatherer people who flourished in eastern North America. "Tradition" points to the fact that this culture and its distinct ways of life persisted for a significant period of time. Neither label—Red Paint people nor Maritime Archaic tradition—is accepted by all archaeologists, a fact that is indicative of the many controversies surrounding these people.

Evidence of a prehistoric culture was found throughout the nineteenth century, most often stone artifacts such as woodworking tools, knives, spearheads, and implements for fishing buried in deposits of red ocher. It was not until 1892, however, that Charles Willoughby conducted the first detailed excavations for Harvard's Peabody Museum, publishing in 1899 an account of his findings that garnered a good deal of attention. Still, it would be a decade until the next important excavations, when Warren K. Moorehead, director of the Peabody Museum in Andover, Massachusetts, conducted the first detailed archaeological digs (1912-1920's). Moorehead's findings, in particular the character of the red ocher deposits, brought about more than increased interest in the mysterious culture. Moorehead's site was clearly a burial ground; no one argued that fact. However, the graves were so old that no bones were unearthed. Even some of the stone artifacts were badly decayed. The character of the evidence led Moorehead to publish an article in the well-respected journal *American Anthropology*. This article triggered one of the earliest controversies when he identified his evidence as belonging to a prehistoric culture so old that it had nothing to do with later Algonquian peoples. At the time, theories about the prehistory of Native Americans were tending toward a separation of Native Americans and any prehistoric finds, so David T. Bushnell of the Smithsonian Institution made a rebuttal, arguing that the graves were much more recent than Moorehead had suggested and that they were indeed those of a Native American culture. Advancements in the field of archaeology, in particular radiocarbon (carbon-14) dating, resolved one aspect of this controversy by dating Moorehead's graves between c. 4000 B.C.E. and 1 C.E.

Initially, this controversial prehistoric culture was recognized through such cemetery sites as those Moorehead excavated, in particular their red-ocher-covered burial gifts. In archaeological studies, such artifacts are referred to as belonging to the Moorehead Burial tradition. Evidence of this tradition has been found from southern Maine to the Great Lakes and up into Labrador. In the late 1960's, after construction workers discovered evidence of burials on a small promontory in Port au Choix, located on the Gulf of St. Lawrence, south of the Strait of Belle Isle, archaeologist Tuck of Memorial University of Newfoundland excavated more than fifty graves. Radiocarbon dating placed this important site at c. 2400-1200 B.C.E. Buried with the dead were gifts of tools, various implements used for fishing, animal bones, carved animal effigies, and small white quartz stones, all of which were covered with the telltale red ocher, thus connecting this site to those of the Moorehead Burial tradition. Combined with other crucial discoveries, such as those at L'Anse-Amour, the excavated evidence suggests that these prehistoric peoples were present in southern Labrador by c. 5500 B.C.E. and flourishing along most of the coastlines of Labrador and Newfoundland by 2000 B.C.E. Many archaeologists believe that this more northerly culture was the ancestor of the peoples of the Moorehead Burial tradition.

The unearthed evidence to date—from sites in New England to those in the Canadian Maritime Provinces—suggests a reliance on the sea and its resources. The burial gifts in a L'Anse-Amour grave included a toggling harpoon used for seal hunting, a walrus tusk, and an assortment of fish bones. The Port au Choix excavation unearthed numerous fishhooks, harpoons, fish-bone tools, lances for hunting whale and walrus, fish spears, and tool kits that contained woodworking implements intended for watercraft. A more recent excavation at the Turner site on North Haven Island in the Penobscot Bay of Maine has unearthed barbed bone fishhooks and swordfish spears. Based on findings such as these and the evidence that such artifacts were traded, archaeologists have inferred the importance of the sea and sea travel to these peoples.

The Red Paint people's seafaring skills plus the discovery of certain similar attributes in excavations in Europe led to still another controversial theory, that the Red Paint people had European ancestors. Recent scientific methods suggest that these similarities might be an example of parallel cultural revolution rather than evidence of contact. However, archaeologists and other experts do not agree on any single theory of these people's origin—or disappearance. Some see the Red Paint culture/Maritime Archaic peoples as a distinct race that appeared and then suddenly disappeared from the coastal lands of North America. Others argue that only their unique traditions, in particular the inclusion of red ocher in burial practices, disappeared. Later archaeological studies—for example, those conducted by the Maine State Museum, various campuses of the University of Maine, and the Memorial University of Newfoundland—focus not only on burial sites but also on occupation or habitation sites, which may shed light on such issues. Because a rising sea level is slowly destroying many coastal sites, the answers to the controversies and mysteries surrounding the Red Paint people may never be resolved.

Significance

Red Paint culture/Maritime Archaic tradition sites provide glimpses into the lives of a people who flourished for thousands of years in the Archaic period of North American history. Some of these people were the first to occupy Labrador, predating the Norse expeditions of c. 1000 C.E.; others were the first to colonize the Island of Newfoundland. As is evidenced by their apparent trade activity, these people were excellent seafarers with a lively economy. The specialization and complexity of their tools suggest their craftsmanship and adaptability. Their mortuary ceremonialism provides evidence of an active intellectual and religious life. The rarity of Red Paint culture/Maritime Archaic tradition sites and the fact that this culture disappeared from the archaeological record altogether make these people's story even more compelling.

—*Anna Dunlap Higgins*

Further reading

Bourque, Bruce J. *Diversity and Complexity in Prehistoric Maritime Societies: A Gulf of Maine Perspective*. New York: Plenum Press, 1995. One of the basic resource materials for information on Maine's Native American prehistory.

Folsom, Franklin, and Mary Elting Folsom. *America's Ancient Treasures: A Guide to Archeological Sites and Museums in the United States and Canada*. 3d ed. Albuquerque: University of New Mexico Press, 1983. A good source for finding places to visit as well as information.

Sanger, David, ed. *Discovering Maine's Archaeological Heritage*. Augusta: Maine Historic Preservation Commission, 1979. Considered one of the early basic resource texts for information on Maine's Native American prehistory and still valued as an important source.

Snow, Dean R. *The Archaeology of New England*. New York: Academic Press, 1980. This work provides a basic introduction to the archaeology of Maine and comments specifically on the "myths" of New England such as the Red Paint people.

Trigger, Bruce G., and Wilcomb E. Washburn. *The Cambridge History of the Native Peoples of the Americas*. Vol. 1. New York: Cambridge University Press, 1996. An invaluable basic resource.

Tuck, James A. "An Archaic Cemetery at Port au Choix, Newfoundland." *American Antiquity* 36, no. 3 (1971): 343-358. An important early resource on the Maritime Archaic tradition by the archaeologist who excavated the Port au Choix site.

SEE ALSO: c. 13,000-c. 7000 B.C.E., Paleo-Indian Culture Flourishes in North America; c. 8000-c. 4000 B.C.E., Plano Culture Flourishes in Great Plains Area; c. 8000-c. 1000 B.C.E., Archaic Indians Adapt to Warmer Climates; c. 4000-c. 1000 B.C.E., Old Copper Complex Flourishes in North America.

c. 4000 B.C.E.
HORSE IS DOMESTICATED

People in Turkistan domesticated the horse, which became a valuable source of labor and transport in Central Asia and much of Europe and later played a crucial role in the military forces of the Greeks and Romans.

LOCALE: Turkistan (now Turkmenistan, Uzbekistan, Kyrgyzstan, Tajikistan, south Kazakhstan, western China, and northeast Afghanistan), Central Asia
CATEGORY: Prehistory and ancient cultures

SUMMARY OF EVENT

Strangely enough, the horse was among the last important animals to be tamed. Although it is not possible to pinpoint when horses were first domesticated, a reasonably close estimate can be made. As long ago as the Solutrean period of the Old Stone Age, perhaps nearly twenty thousand years ago, European wild horses were hunted so eagerly as big game that they were apparently brought to extinction in parts of Europe. There is no evidence that any efforts were then made to tame these animals despite their appearance in primitive statuary and cave paintings.

For tens of thousands of years, the homeland of the true horse was the north European plains and the western Asiatic steppes. Other forms of equids were distributed throughout the grasslands of Asia and Africa, but because there was no significant overlapping of their ranges, distinct species evolved; the hemionids, such as the onager, inhabited southwest Asia, the true asses lived in north Africa, and the zebras claimed east and south Africa.

Two types of wild horses survived in the Old World. One of these, known as Przewalski's horse, evolved in Mongolia (where wild survivors may still exist) but spread into southwest Asia and eastern European grasslands after the retreat of the last of the Pleistocene ice. Przewalski's horse is a heavily built animal with sturdy short legs; its head is large and mulish in appearance, and it stands about thirteen hands high.

The other type of horse, the tarpan, evolved in south Russia, although it was known archaeologically and historically to central Sweden and the North Sea coast. It survived in the Ukraine until the mid-nineteenth century. Generally smaller than the Mongolian wild horse, the tarpan had a stiff upright mane and a dark stripe extending from mane to tail on its mouse-gray body. It was systematically hunted to extinction by Ukrainians because wild stallions enticed domesticated mares away from the farms.

Present-day evidence strongly suggests that tarpan stock was the principal contributor to the modern domesticated horse, although some authorities consider Przewalski's horse to be the dominant strain. Because these two horse ranges overlapped in eastern Europe and Turkistan, it is possible that the modern horse is descended from a mixture of the two. Genetic studies, however, have established that Przewalski's horse has a different chromosome number (2n = 66) from all types of modern horses (2n = 64). This fact strengthens the claim for the tarpan contribution being the greater of the two. This question cannot be resolved because the tarpan is extinct and its chromosome number cannot be determined. All present-day Mongolian ponies have come from the West. There is still debate whether the heavy Western European draft horse was derived from tarpan stock or from some yet undiscovered large type of horse. A heavy-boned Pleistocene horse has been found in glacial deposits in Western Europe, but it is known neither archaeologically nor historically. Horse bones do not show any singular osteological changes concomitant with domestication as do the horns of sheep, goats, and cattle.

Although the first historical writings that mention horses as being usefully employed by humans date from about 2000 B.C.E., it seems safe to infer that the horse had already been domesticated for at least two millennia by that time. After 2000 B.C.E., there are numerous literary references to the horse in addition to various representations in statuary and paintings. An educated guess for the beginnings of horse domestication is about 4000 B.C.E.

On the basis of the distribution of the true horse six thousand years ago, it appears that the area in which domestication was first tried was Turkistan in Central Asia. Perhaps around 3000 B.C.E., small numbers of domesticated horses diffused to eastern and north-central Europe. About the same time, the same type of horse appeared in the Iranian plateau, and it appeared a little later in Bronze Age cultures of the Near East.

Significance

Since its domestication, the horse has served humankind as a means of transportation and as a source of labor, during both war and peacetime. The first application of the horse as an aid to humankind was in the dubious role of chariot puller. The chariot, developed from the two-wheeled cart originally drawn by cattle, had obvious strategic value in giving greater mobility to a single warrior. When this vehicle was introduced into Egypt by the Hyksos in 1788 B.C.E., the accompanying horses were almost certainly of Asian origin but of tarpan ancestry. They were rather large in size but delicate in head and body build and bay or black in color. These animals were the progenitors of the Nubian horse, the strain from which the Barb of Morocco was derived and whose genes may still be viable in some modern thoroughbreds, hunters, remounts, and plow horses. The chariot was in use in Greece in 1000 B.C.E. but survived in Julius Caesar's Rome mainly for ceremonial occasions and for races.

Riding astride the horse may have begun in Turkistan before 3000 B.C.E. Cavalry, an integral part of the Greek fighting force by 800 B.C.E., became a dominant force in the Roman fighting machine. Continuing through feudal times in Europe until the beginning of World War II, the development of several new breeds of horses was influenced by military needs.

As a source of labor, horses have contributed greatly to improving the quality of human life; however, many scholars believe that the horse's greatest influence on history has been in warfare. Classic events such as the Battle of Poitiers in 732 C.E. when Charles Martel defeated the Saracen invaders, and the Siege of Tenochtitlán by the Spaniards in 1521, may well have been changed by the presence of horses.

—*Fred B. Kniffen*

Further reading

Clutton-Brock, Juliet. *Horse Power: A History of the Horse and the Donkey in Human Societies.* Cambridge, Mass.: Harvard University Press, 1992. Clutton-Brock focuses on the history of horse and donkey, focusing on their roles and influence after domestication. Bibliography and index.

_______. *A Natural History of Domesticated Mammals.* 2d ed. New York: Natural History Museum and Cambridge University Press, 1999. An examination of domesticated animals, including the horse, from early times. Bibliography and index.

Edwards, Elwyn Hartley. *Horses: Their Role in the History of Man.* London: Willow Books, 1987. An examination of how horses have affected human beings throughout history. Bibliography.

Kust, Matthew J. *Man and Horse in History.* New York: Advent Books, 1983. Kust traces the history of the domestic horse and its interactions with humans. Bibliography and index.

Mason, Ian L., ed. *Evolution of Domesticated Animals.* New York: Longman, 1984. A collection of essays tracing the development of various domestic animals, including the horse. Bibliography and indexes.

See also: c. 6800-c. 4900 B.C.E., Kitoi People Live Near Lake Baikal in Siberia; c. 2000 B.C.E., Mongols Inhabit Steppes North of China; 1750-800 B.C.E., Andronovo Culture Rises in Central Asia; c. 1250-c. 700 B.C.E., Karasuk Culture Flourishes on Eurasian Steppes; c. 1000-c. 690 B.C.E., Cimmerian Culture Rises in Russia.

c. 4000 B.C.E.

SUMERIAN CIVILIZATION BEGINS IN MESOPOTAMIA

The Sumerians, building on previous societies, founded complex political, economic, social, and cultural superstructures and therefore came to be regarded as one of the world's earliest civilizations.

LOCALE: Mesopotamia (now Iraq and parts of Iran, Syria, and Turkey)

CATEGORY: Prehistory and ancient cultures

SUMMARY OF EVENT

"Mesopotamia," based on the Greek for "land between the rivers," is used to describe what many historians define as the world's earliest civilization. This civilization arose between the Tigris and Euphrates Rivers, a mess of mud, clay, and reedy swamps roughly 200 miles (320 kilometers) long and 100 miles (160 kilometers) wide (at its widest point). This area was subject to torrential rainstorms, periodic flooding, sweltering heat, and blazing sunlight. By 6000 B.C.E., the agricultural revolution brought settled Neolithic societies to the hilly north and to the mountains east of Mesopotamia, but not until a thousand years later were agricultural techniques sufficiently understood for a few adventuresome peoples to migrate into these inhospitable river plains. It would take another thousand years for the Sumerians to build on the work of previous cultures and turn a scattering of settlements into a series of thriving city-states.

In central Mesopotamia, the Samarra culture (5500-5000 B.C.E.) established agricultural settlements. Houses, built with mud and clay bricks, appear to have contained about ten rooms. Ceramic wares and grain were traded for copper (used in jewelry) and for semiprecious stones such as obsidian and turquoise. By 5000 B.C.E., a few small settlements extended into southern Mesopotamia. In northern Mesopotamia, Halafian culture (5500-4500 B.C.E.) established settlements, which took the form of a large number of tiny communities, and the Halafians engaged in extensive trade of their distinctive pottery.

The Ubaid people (named after Tell-al Ubaid in southern Mesopotamia near what would become the city of Ur and now is Muqaiyir) are generally credited with the settlement of southern Mesopotamia and the creation of more complex towns. Use of the slow wheel and unlimited access to clay resulted in the production of large amounts of greenish colored pottery decorated with brown or black geometric designs and loop handles. This distinctive pottery appears to have eclipsed that of the Samarrans and Halafians in popularity.

The Ubaid people developed irrigation and marsh-drainage techniques to allow them to practice agriculture along the Tigris and Euphrates Rivers. Without irrigation and canals, the fierce storms that struck during the spring and caused the river to flood would have made planting impossible. The rich mud of the plains produced bountiful crops of barley, lentils, and wheat. Fired clay was used to create hoes, adzes, sickles, and other tools. They raised cattle, largely as work animals; sheep for wool; and goats for their milk, which was turned into cheese. Like the Samarrans, the Ubaid people built houses made of molded sun-dried mud brick. However, unlike the Samarran settlements, Ubaid towns kept on expanding in both size and complexity. By 4500 B.C.E., towns numbering several thousand inhabitants were not uncommon. The largest of these was Eridu (site south of present-day An Nāsirīyah, Iraq), which had houses crowded together, forming narrow alleyways. Houses were built on a tripartite plan: A full-length large rectangular room was flanked with rows of smaller rooms on each side. Larger houses, apparently constructed for the upper class, contained storage facilities. Eridu also contained a large, richly decorated temple built of mud brick and supported by complicated buttresses and niches. This temple was first excavated by Sir Leonard Woolley in 1922. The simplest houses, often composed of reed, were reserved for the farmers who lived on the outskirts of Eridu.

Because mud bricks are weakened by rain, buildings in Eridu and other Ubaidan settlements lasted no longer than a generation. Each rebuilding seems to have resulted in larger buildings, general expansion of the size of the town, and much larger temples (suggesting that irrigation projects were directed by a priestly elite). Trade for precious stones extended to distant India and down into the Persian Gulf and modern-day Saudi Arabia, where a number of Ubaid trading outposts were constructed. To direct northern trade, Ubaidans constructed Tepe Gawra (discovered in 1927 by the archaeologist Ephraim Speiser, near modern Mosul, Iraq), which contained three large temples similar to the one found at Eridu. By 4300 B.C.E., when the Sumerians arrived on the Mesopotamian river plains, they catalyzed a process already in motion of producing sophisticated, ever-expanding towns with linked agricultural and trading communities.

The Sumerians, who called themselves "the black-headed peoples," spoke a monosyllabic language unrelated to any other language group. Their origins (probably India, Persia, and the area around the Caspian Sea) and relationship to any other known ethnic group have yet to be determined. The Sumerians soon dominated and eclipsed their Semitic-speaking neighbors. They introduced improved and new techniques that led to continued population growth and urbanization, resulting in what can be called the advent of civilization.

Sumerian innovations included the building of roads on which donkeys brought goods to market and canals to more efficiently irrigate fields and to facilitate the transportation of goods by boat. The Sumerians were building the infrastructure necessary for complex urban life. They invented the quick wheel for the mass production of pottery. They built channels, dikes, and reservoirs for flood control and water conservation. Considerable care was devoted to the cultivation of dates, trees that do not self-pollinate and require five years of nurturing before they produce their high-energy and vitamin-laden fruits. Evidence suggests that a priestly class might have had a role in directing economic activity and extracting tribute in return. Record keeping began in the form of clay tokens imprinted with the characteristic seals of the two parties involved in a contract. Other inscriptions probably denoted the item involved and represent pre-cuneiform writing. The shape of the token denoted the quantities involved (small cone = one, circle = ten, large cone = sixty). In this way, the Sumerians were developing mathematical systems in addition to record keeping and writing.

By 4000 B.C.E., Uruk (called Erech in the Bible and identified as Warka in modern Arabic; site northwest of modern-day Muqaiyir, Iraq) began to emerge as the major Sumerian center, a model for what would become, over the course a millennium, twelve major Sumerian city-states. The city-state appears to have resulted from the merging of two neighboring settlements, Kullaba and Eanna. The city was dedicated to the goddess of love, Inanna (later called Ishtar), and a mound temple was built

A man and a child view the ruins of Uruk, a major Sumerian center and city-state in ancient times. (Nik Wheeler/Corbis)

to honor her. Inanna had been the patron goddess of Eanna. Another temple was dedicated to the sky god Anu, the patron god of Kullaba. Both temples were based on the Ubaid style, and both were rebuilt many times, forming two of the several ziggurat temple complexes in Uruk. Security considerations also came to the fore, and work began on a wall that was to surround the city (eventually reaching 6 miles, or 9.5 kilometers, in length) and was to be surrounded by a moat for further protection. The semilegendary first king of Uruk, Gilgamesh, is credited with completing the walled fortifications.

SIGNIFICANCE

Organized human activity was able to overcome harsh environmental obstacles and exploit the agricultural potential of the fertile Mesopotamian plains, creating a population explosion in a limited geographic area. The resulting food surplus sustained increasing numbers of artisans, craftspeople, and merchants living in continually expanding urban centers. Capitalizing on developments over the previous thousand years, the Sumerians introduced new advancements, resulting in the creation of Uruk, an urban center large enough to be considered the world's first city-state. Located on the Euphrates River, Uruk was a seminal influence for the development of other Sumerian city-states such as Ur, Kish, and Lagash. Through wide-ranging trade by land and sea, the Sumerian civilization influenced the development of civilization in other Middle Eastern as well as Asian societies. Although the process of civilization was taking place in other river-based agricultural societies, Mesopotamia was transformed earlier and more extensively. Rapid population growth, urbanization, complex social stratification, and extensive trade were first experienced by the Sumerians in Mesopotamia; these steps toward civilization would be followed elsewhere. For this reason, Mesopotamia has long been regarded as the cradle of civilization.

—*Irwin Halfond*

FURTHER READING

Kramer, Samuel N. *The Sumerians*. Chicago: University of Chicago Press, 1990. An overview of the Sumerian culture in Mesopotamia.

Nemet-Nejat, Karen R. *Daily Life in Ancient Mesopotamia*. Westport, Conn.: Greenwood Press, 1998. An updated and well-organized account of daily life in ancient Mesopotamia written with the general reader in mind.

Oppenheim, A. Leo. *Ancient Mesopotamia: Portrait of a Dead Civilization*. Chicago: University of Chicago Press, 1986. A well-written and illustrated introduction to the growth of Mesopotamia based on interesting historical and archaeological data.

Pollack, Susan. *Ancient Mesopotamia*. New York: Cambridge University Press, 1999. A scholarly and well-illustrated anthropological study of life in Mesopotamia.

Postgate, J. Nicholas. *Early Mesopotamia: Society and Economy at the Dawn of History*. New York: Routledge, 1994. A readable description of city life, economic activity, and the role of kings, priests, and scribes in Mesopotamia.

Rothman, Mitchell S., ed. *Uruk, Mesopotamia, and Its Neighbors: Cross Cultural Interactions in the Era of State Formation*. Santa Fe, N.Mex.: School of American Research Press, 2001. Twelve field and theoretical archaeologists discuss the causes of urban expansion, cross-cultural influences, and life in the fifth and fourth millennia B.C.E.

SEE ALSO: c. 6200-c. 3800 B.C.E., Ubaid Culture Thrives in Mesopotamia; c. 5500-c. 4500 B.C.E., Halafian Culture Flourishes in Northern Mesopotamia; c. 3800 B.C.E., Cities and Civic Institutions Are Invented in Mesopotamia; c. 3100 B.C.E., Sumerians Invent Writing; c. 2900-c. 2340 B.C.E., Early Dynastic Period Flourishes in Southern Mesopotamia; c. 2000 B.C.E., Composition of the Gilgamesh Epic.

c. 4000-c. 1000 B.C.E.
Old Copper Complex Flourishes in North America

A series of related Archaic Indian cultures in the western Great Lakes known as the Old Copper complex mined copper to produce tools and ornaments.

Locale: Western Great Lakes of North America
Categories: Prehistory and ancient cultures; science and technology

Summary of Event

As early as the late 1800's, historians and archaeologists began to note the collection of copper tools and ornaments from plowed fields and exposed soils in areas of Wisconsin and Michigan. Some early scholars thought these artifacts were the products of lost races or cultures that preceded the North American Indians. However, as more and more were discovered and as archaeology advanced the understanding of North American prehistory, it became clear that Great Lakes Indians had developed a copper-based metal technology as early as 4000 B.C.E.

Between approximately 4000 and 1000 B.C.E., a number of Archaic tradition Indian groups in the western Great Lakes of North America mined and collected nearly pure copper in the Lake Superior Basin and adjacent areas. Archaeologists refer to these early copper-working cultures as the Old Copper complex. These early metalsmiths used hot- and cold-hammering, grinding, and polishing techniques to produce a variety of copper tools and ornaments. They used copper along with stone and bone technology to produce artifacts for survival and for trade.

Thousands of heavy copper tools have been recovered in Wisconsin, Michigan, Minnesota, and Ontario. These tools include spear points, knives, awls, harpoons, fishhooks, axes, chisels, celts, and needles. Additionally, copper ornaments have also been recovered from this region including beads, bangles, and bracelets.

In the 1940's, 1950's, and 1960's, a number of Old Copper-related cemeteries were professionally excavated in Wisconsin, the Upper Peninsula of Michigan, and on the Ottawa River in Quebec. These sites produced the first undisturbed archaeological evidence about these early peoples. The data collected from these sites and analyses of the surface-collected copper tools suggest that Old Copper complex Indians were hunter-gatherer cultures. They made a living by exploiting a wide variety of terrestrial game, migratory waterfowl, fish, and plants.

Old Copper cemeteries indicate that early in the cultural sequence, copper was used to produce primarily tools for subsistence-related tasks. Copper artifacts were also traded to cultures outside the region for materials such as marine shells from the southeastern United States and exotic flaked stone tools from the Ohio River Valley and the plains.

Early Old Copper complex sites, such as the Oconto Old Copper Cemetery in Oconto County, Wisconsin (dating to 4000-3000 B.C.E.), show evidence of a relatively egalitarian society. Analysis of the artifacts found with burials indicates that the vast majority of the artifacts were tools. Although there is evidence of trade for marine shells, most of the artifacts were probably produced from local materials. The Oconto site yielded a variety of copper, stone, bone, and shell artifacts. One of the most notable artifacts is a musical instrument or whistle made from the wing bone of a Tundra swan.

Later Old Copper complex burial sites indicate that by 1500 to 1000 B.C.E., there was a gradual increase in the manufacturing of copper jewelry and in the amount of trade inside and outside the Great Lakes region. At the Reigh site in Winnebago County, Wisconsin, archaeologists recovered graves containing copper projectile points, knives, axes, a variety of bead necklaces, and even a copper feathered headdress. Many of these objects or grave goods can be interpreted as status markers. This pattern suggests that some members of this society had differential access to trade and valuable resources. By this time, a new burial ceremonial practice emerged: the extensive use of red ocher or ground hematite to cover the dead.

By 1000 B.C.E., copper tool production was in decline. This decline is what defines the terminus of the Old Copper complex. Although some copper tools continued to be made by later cultures, many of the large socketed projectile points are not found in later periods.

Although archaeologists have excavated a number of Old Copper cemeteries, few habitation sites have been discovered. There are still a great many unanswered questions about these first metalworking native cultures of the western Great Lakes.

Significance

The Old Copper complex represents the oldest metalworking in North America. Between 4000 and 1000

B.C.E., Native American cultures of the western Great Lakes developed a complex metal-smithing technology that was used to hot and cold hammer tools and ornaments from nearly pure copper. This cultural complex also led to the development of a far-reaching trade system that connected cultures of the Great Lakes with areas as far away as the plains and the Gulf coast.

—*Thomas C. Pleger*

FURTHER READING

Birmingham, Robert A., Carol I. Mason, and James B. Stoltman, eds. *Wisconsin Archaeology*. Vol. 78. Milwaukee, Wis.: The Wisconsin Archaeological Society, 1997. Contains a chapter on each archaeological tradition recognized in Wisconsin. The Archaic tradition chapter by James B. Stoltman contains an excellent summary of the Old Copper complex.

Halsey, John R., ed. *Retrieving Michigan's Buried Past: The Archaeology of the Great Lakes State*. Bulletin 64. Bloomfield Hills, Mich.: Cranbrook Institute of Science, 1999. Contains a chapter on each archaeological tradition recognized in Michigan.

Martin, Susan R. *Wonderful Power: The Story of Ancient Copper Working in the Lake Superior Basin*. Detroit: Wayne State University Press, 1999. Outstanding summary of the history of Native American copper working in the western Great Lakes.

Martin, Susan R., and Thomas C. Pleger. "The Complex Formerly Known as a Culture: The Taxonomic Puzzle of 'Old Copper.'" In *Taming the Taxonomy: Toward a New Understanding of Great Lakes Archaeology*, edited by Ronald F. Williamson and Christopher M. Watts. Toronto: Eastend Books and the Ontario Archaeological Society, 1999. A summary of the history of research concerning the Old Copper complex and a discussion of how it should be viewed in relation to today's archaeological classification system.

Mason, Ronald J. *Great Lakes Archaeology*. New York: Academic Press, 1981. A classic work summarizing the archaeology of the Great Lakes.

Pleger, Thomas C. "Old Copper and Red Ocher Social Complexity." *Midcontinental Journal of Archaeology* 25, no. 2 (2000): 169-190. This article is a summary of a comparative analysis of burial patterns at the Oconto Old Copper Cemetery, Oconto, Wisconsin and the Riverside Red Ocher Cemetery, Menominee County, Michigan.

SEE ALSO: c. 8000-c. 4000 B.C.E., Plano Culture Flourishes in Great Plains Area; c. 8000-c. 1000 B.C.E., Archaic Indians Adapt to Warmer Climates; c. 1000 B.C.E.-c. 100 C.E., Adena Mound Builders Live in North America; c. 1000 B.C.E.-c. 900 C.E., Woodland Culture Flourishes in Northern America; c. 700 B.C.E.-c. 500 C.E., Mound Builders Rise in Ohio Valley.

c. 4000 B.C.E.-c. 100 C.E.
BAN CHIANG CULTURE FLOURISHES IN THAILAND

In the late 1960's, a series of archaeological sites was discovered near the village of Ban Chiang, in northeastern Thailand, revealing what some scientists now refer to as Thailand's cradle of civilization.

LOCALE: Khorat Plateau and the surrounding lowlands of northeastern Thailand

CATEGORIES: Prehistory and ancient cultures; cultural and intellectual history

SUMMARY OF EVENT

The Ban Chiang culture of northeastern Thailand probably emerged when early hunting and gathering people belonging to the Hoabin-hian migrated from northern Vietnam to Malaysia. The neolithic people of the Hoabin-hian are believed to be among the first people to have systematically gathered and later to have cultivated the wild forms of rice found naturally in northern Southeast Asia and southern China. Finding the Khorat Plateau and surrounding lowlands a rich environment, some Hoabin-hian remained in the area and eventually began cultivation of various wild forms of rice until several varieties were domesticated. This process allowed them to create settlements that further encouraged the development of more sophisticated material culture. The development of the Ban Chiang culture parallels that of the Shang culture of China at about the same time. A key difference, though, is that the Ban Chiang culture remained relatively peaceful and rural, while the Shang culture of China evolved into a more urbanized and aggressive culture.

The discovery of the Ban Chiang culture was accidental. Steven Young, a young student from Harvard University who was spending the summer of 1966 in Thailand studying politics, was taking a walk near the village of Ban Chiang when he tripped over a tree root and fell. Through this accident, he found a piece of pottery sticking out of the ground. It took several years to organize excavation of the 62-acre (25-hectare) mound, with archaeologists from Thailand and the United States. In the meantime, it was difficult to protect the site from looters. Despite losing an unknown number of objects, to their amazement, the archaeologists found thousands of shards of pottery, hundreds of burials, countless examples of bronze and ironwork in the form of tools and jewelry, and much evidence of agricultural activity. It is extraordinary not only that they found such a rich site for an early Southeast Asian culture but also that the culture it represented was of great sophistication. The ceramics were among the most elegant in the world, and the jewelry was of such fine quality that its creation required difficult and expensive techniques. There is evidence that advancements in metallurgy for the Ban Chiang probably had more to do with the desire to create more beautiful jewelry and implements than with the desire to create stronger materials for practical uses. This, among other evidence from the site, indicates that the Ban Chiang people were peaceful, unlike their counterparts in China and the Middle East, where metallurgy was developed primarily for making weapons and only secondarily for beautiful, functional items. Among the most famous of the Ban Chiang artifacts are its pottery, bracelets, anklets, pendants, and beads.

The Ban Chiang culture most likely declined because of incursions from the north by the Chinese as their civilization expanded during the Han Dynasty (206 B.C.E.-220 C.E.). Given the historic peacefulness of the Ban Chiang people and the extraordinary sophistication and wealth of their civilization, they would have been a prime target and would have lacked the weaponry to defend themselves against such a strong outside force.

Significance

In 1992, Ban Chiang was added to the World Heritage Site list. This places it among the most significant historic sites in the world. This significance can be measured in a number of ways. First and foremost, it provides Thailand with a well-documented illustration of its prehistoric culture. Second, the rich treasure of artifacts meant that many theories of human prehistory and the early formation of agriculture had to be rewritten. Until the discovery of Ban Chiang, most social scientists and historians could point only to the Middle East, India, and China as the places of earliest agricultural activity and metallurgy. Despite debates on the exact dating of artifacts and activity at the Ban Chiang sites, scholars have come to the conclusion that Ban Chiang ranks with the Nile Valley, Mesopotamia, Indus Valley, and the Huang He Valley as a center of innovation. It is likely that people of Ban Chiang were exposed to metallurgy by the Chinese to the north, but they went on to develop their own sophisticated techniques in production and usage of both bronze and iron. Apparently they strove for unusual coloring of the finished product; thus aesthetics played a primary role in their innovations. Moreover, they are credited with the earliest socketed tools. Finally, it is clear that Ban Chiang was connected to India, China, and the rest of Southeast Asia through trade networks. Because of its innovations in technology and aesthetics, its culture diffused outward rather than borrowing from other cultures. Thus Ban Chiang has been a major influence at least twice: once, while it was at the height of its development, and in modern times, as revelations about its culture affect current scholarship on the development of early civilizations.

—*Carolyn V. Prorok*

Further Reading

Bayard, D. "Bones of Contention: The Non Nok Tha Burials and the Chronology and Context of Early Southeast Asian Bronze." In *Ancient Chinese and Southeast Asian Bronze Cultures*, Vol. 2, edited by N. Barnard and F. Bulbeck. Taiwan: Taipei Southern Material Center, 1996. An essay examining the chronology of bronze work in Southeast Asia.

Higham, C. F. W. *The Bronze Age of Southeast Asia*. New York: Cambridge University Press, 1996. Higham examines the development of bronze work in ancient Southeast Asia.

Labbe, A. J. *Ban Chiang: Art and Prehistory of Northeastern Thailand*. Santa Ana, Calif.: Bowers Museum, 1985. An exhibition catalog showing the art of Ban Chiang.

O'Reilly, D. "From the Bronze Age to the Iron Age in Thailand: Applying the Heterarchial Approach." *Asian Perspectives* 39, nos. 1/2 (2001). A look at the development of metallurgy in Thailand.

Theunissen, R., P. Grave, and G. Bailey. "Doubts on Diffusion: Challenging the Assumed Indian Origin of Iron Age Agate and Carnelian Beads in Southeast Asia." *Archaeology in Southeast Asia* 32, no. 1

(2000): 84-105. This essay questions traditional beliefs about the origins of metallurgy in Southeast Asia.

White, J. C. *Ban Chiang: Discovery of a Lost Bronze Age*. Philadelphia: University of Pennsylvania Press, 1982. An examination of the archaeological finds at Ban Chiang and an analysis of the culture.

SEE ALSO: c. 2000 B.C.E., Mon-Khmer Migrate into Southeast Asia; Early 1st century C.E., Pyu Kingdom Develops Urban Culture; 1st century C.E., Tai Peoples Migrate into Southeast Asia; 1st century-c. 627 C.E., Kingdom of Funan Flourishes; 25 C.E., Guang Wudi Restores the Han Dynasty.

c. 3800 B.C.E.

CITIES AND CIVIC INSTITUTIONS ARE INVENTED IN MESOPOTAMIA

The Sumerians ushered in the transition between increasingly complex society and civilization by 3800 B.C.E., producing civic institutions to structure new challenges developing from city life. The earliest major world city, Uruk, became a model for the development of other Sumerian cities.

LOCALE: Mesopotamia (now Iraq and parts of Iran, Syria, and Turkey)

CATEGORY: Prehistory and ancient cultures

SUMMARY OF EVENT

Between 5500 and 4500 B.C.E., numerous small agricultural settlements arose in northern and central Mesopotamia. In southern Mesopotamia, the Ubaidans built larger and more complex towns, the largest being Eridu (site south of present-day An Nāsirīyah, Iraq). Though only several in number, the Ubaidan towns produced bountiful food supplies through organized irrigation and cultivation of land outside the town. Inside the town, merchants and craftspeople plied their trades and obtained wealth. By 4300 B.C.E., the Sumerians, a people of unknown origins, migrated to southern Mesopotamia, bringing with them advanced methods of construction and water management. Because land that uses irrigation can feed at least ten times the number of people as land dependent on rainfall (disregarding the rich fertility of southern Mesopotamian soil, which allowed for three crops per year), population growth rapidly accelerated. Within three centuries, Uruk (site northwest of modern-day Muqaiyir, Iraq), with a population of about ten thousand, emerged as the largest city in Mesopotamia. Uruk dominated Mesopotamia for the next thousand years and became a model for twelve other large Sumerian cities. The thirteen cities stretching from south to north were Eridu, Ur, Larsa, Uruk, Bad-tibira, Lagash, Umma, Adab, Nippur, Larak, Akshak, Kish, and Sippar. Around each city grew many important and linked towns.

Large numbers of people living in a small area necessitated the development of civic institutions to provide structure and organize life. In Uruk and other Sumerian cities, the priestly class first established civic institutions. Priests served as engineers, administrators, scientists, landowners, and industrialists. They also were creators of popular beliefs about why society was structured to give the temple elite so much authority. In Uruk and other Sumerian cities, the largest structure was the temple. Priests were specialists in administration, in planning city and agricultural expansion, in drafting common people to work on irrigation and other community projects such as draining swamps, in organizing and monitoring trading activities, in employing the finer craftspeople for production of the highest quality products, in directing how and when planting should take place, and in running vast temple estates. It is estimated that about a third of the land in Sumerian city-states was controlled by the temples. The temple also played a role in organizing and controlling trade and in educating new priests to play a leadership role in the future.

Located near the temple were granaries and other storage facilities and the large houses of the wealthiest citizens. More modest houses of merchants and craftspeople formed a middle ring around the temple, and the poorer houses of the working class formed a densely populated ring on the fringes of the city. The temple contained a large inner space that was apparently used for storage and as a work area by artisans, craftspeople, and those involved in providing services for the priesthood. The inside of the temple may have housed an assembly hall used for meetings of a civic nature. All Sumerian city structures were built first by placing rounded mud bricks in alternating horizontal and vertical rows, then filling the gaps with plant matter and bitumen. Heavy rains made it impossible for most structures to survive more than a generation. For the cities, this meant continued urban renewal, with each generation aspiring to build bigger structures.

Taxes were paid to the temple, usually consisting of part of the crop, to ensure the continual operation of the priesthood. All this was natural because the people believed that human beings were created as slaves for the many arbitrary and wrathful gods and were destined to feed and venerate them or suffer cataclysmic destruction. Through burnt offerings from the top of the temple (ziggurat) and proper rituals, the priesthood cast itself as the first line of defense in warding off destruction from the heavens caused by the gods' displeasure. The priests could also bring about intervention by the city's patron god and goddess. Uruk's protectors were Enlil, the god of wind and thunder, and Inanna (Ishtar), the goddess of love. There is much evidence that religious ceremonies were performed by priests and did not involve popular participation.

As a defense against destruction by more earthly forces, the position of king developed in Uruk and the other Sumerian cities. Sumerian cities tended to quarrel with each other about water rights, trading jurisdictions, and every other conceivable matter. The king (called *lugal*, or great man) lived in a great house (*egal*, or palace) second in size only to the temple. His powers appear to be justified by the temple, which cast the ruler as god's representative on Earth. In some city-states, the ruler was called lord (*en*) or governor (*ensi*). Often there was a queen (*nin*) who played a role in both civic and religious affairs. The king was in charge of building city walls to protect the city as well as commanding soldiers armed with spears, battle axes, bows, swords, and daggers. Engravings indicate that soldiers probably were trained to fight in battle formations. Kings were also in charge of four-wheeled war chariots. The Sumerians are the people credited with inventing the chariot.

One institution that helped organize urban life was the city council of elders, which usually consisted of elder heads of leading families. Priests also appear to have sat on the city council. Agreement by both the temple and city council was usually needed in the selection of the right individual to be king.

Civil institutions, both secular and religious, were needed to stimulate and control the tremendous economic activity in Uruk and other city-states. Expansion of irrigation technology and the use of the plow caused large food surpluses, and the development of the potter's wheel led to rapid production of ceramics. The use of donkeys, wheeled carts, and boats enabled production to be used for trade to obtain items needed in Uruk such as silver, copper, and timber. The lucrative nature of trade caused Uruk people to move to distant places and establish enclaves of traders and even permanent settlements. The complicated nature of commerce and trade led to recording contracts on clay tokens containing pictoforms of the contract, symbols representing numbers, and seals identifying the contracting parties. Within several centuries, the record keeping in Uruk in 3800 B.C.E. evolved into the Sumerian cuneiform system of writing. The more important clay tokens were first kept in temple archives and then in both palace and temple archives. Such records along with witnesses were used to settle business disputes in what must have been an early Sumerian version of a court system.

Significance

Scholarly debate continues about whether areas outside Uruk developed socially complex and technologically advanced societies on their own or whether Uruk was the primary influence leading to advancement of neighboring societies in what later became Iran, Syria, and Turkey. There is also debate over the degree of regulation of trade and commerce taking place in early Uruk. Yet it is clear that civil institutions and city life took root in Sumerian Mesopotamia, resulting in one of humanity's first civilizations, and that this civilization had a complex social stratification structure with heads of leading families, a powerful priesthood, and the monarch occupying the top rungs. Lack of written records and limited archaeological evidence make it difficult to analyze with more precision the specific characteristics of social life and civic institutions in the world's first cities.

—*Irwin Halfond*

Further reading

Bottero, Jean, ed. *Everyday Life in Ancient Mesopotamia*. Baltimore: The Johns Hopkins University Press, 2001. A collection of fifteen articles by major scholars on social and cultural life in early Mesopotamia.

Kramer, Samuel N. *The Sumerians*. Chicago: University of Chicago Press, 1990. An overview of the Sumerians, examining their lives and political and social organization.

Nemet-Nejat, Karen R. *Daily Life in Ancient Mesopotamia*. Westport, Conn.: Greenwood Press, 1998. An updated and well-organized account of daily life in ancient Mesopotamia written with the general reader in mind.

Oppenheim, A. Leo. *Ancient Mesopotamia: Portrait of a Dead Civilization*. Chicago: University of Chicago Press, 1986. A well-written and illustrated introduction to the growth of Mesopotamia based on interesting historical and archaeological data.

Pollack, Susan. *Ancient Mesopotamia*. New York: Cambridge University Press, 1999. A scholarly and well-illustrated anthropological study of life in Mesopotamia.

Postgate, J. Nicholas. *Early Mesopotamia: Society and Economy at the Dawn of History*. New York: Routledge, 1994. A readable description of city life, economic activity, and the roles of kings, priests, and scribes.

Rothman, Mitchell S., ed. *Uruk, Mesopotamia, and Its Neighbors: Cross Cultural Interactions in the Era of State Formation*. New York: School of American Research Press, 2001. Twelve field and theoretical archaeologists discuss the causes of urban expansion, cross-cultural influences, and life in Mesopotamia in the fifth and fourth millennium B.C.E.

Woolley, C. Leonard. *The Sumerians*. New York: Norton, 1978. An overview of the development of Sumerian civilization from one of the world's leading archaeologists.

SEE ALSO: c. 6200-c. 3800 B.C.E., Ubaid Culture Thrives in Mesopotamia; c. 5500-c. 4500 B.C.E., Halafian Culture Flourishes in Northern Mesopotamia; c. 4000 B.C.E., Sumerian Civilization Begins in Mesopotamia; c. 3100 B.C.E., Sumerians Invent Writing; c. 2900-c. 2340 B.C.E., Early Dynastic Period Flourishes in Southern Mesopotamia.

c. 3500 B.C.E.
INDUS VALLEY CIVILIZATION BEGINS IN SOUTH ASIA

The Indus Valley civilization was the first great culture of the Indian subcontinent. Contemporary with ancient Egyptian and Mesopotamian cultures, the Indus Valley, or Harappān, civilization was the largest of the world's ancient riverine civilizations.

LOCALE: Pakistan and North India
CATEGORY: Prehistory and ancient culture

SUMMARY OF EVENT

Sir John Marshall conducted the first excavation of an Indus Valley site at Mohenjo-Daro in Sind, India, in the 1920's. He uncovered one of several ancient cities located along the Indus River that were part of the Indian subcontinent's earliest civilization. The archaeological material that he uncovered provided evidence of a highly sophisticated and complex culture. Later surveys and excavations have revealed the scope of the culture that extended from Baluchistan (in Pakistan) in the west to the desert of Rajasthan in the east and from the foothills of the Himalayas in the north to the Gulf of Kutch in the south. Large cities with populations of several thousand people, small townships, and villages were linked by rivers, seaports, and overland routes. Later surveys reveal numerous settlements along the Hakra-Ghaggar Rivers that indicate that the culture was more widespread and dense than originally thought. Specialists now have a picture of an extensive, complex web of settlements that supported an economy based on agriculture, various industries, and trade.

The ancient Indus Valley culture had its roots in the Neolithic settlements of northwest Pakistan and India. The earliest settlement, Mehrgarh in Baluchistan, dated to c. 7000 B.C.E., consisted of mud huts with hearths. The occupants cultivated wheat and barley and herded cattle, sheep, and goats. Kot Diji and Amri were the early settlements in the Indus River plain. In addition to engaging in rudimentary farming practices, the inhabitants created fine painted pottery with *pipal* leaf motifs and fish designs. Many of the characteristics of the neolithic settlements persisted into the later Indus Valley culture. In the Chalcolithic phase, the smelting of raw metals led to the crafting of metal artifacts, although people continued to use stone tools. With the increasing spread of settlements in the late Chalcolithic period, a gradual shift toward urbanization is noticeable in the archaeological finds. It is important to appreciate the continuous habitation of sites and continuity in patterns of living that persisted virtually from the dawn of time well into the mature phase of Indus culture. This protohistoric phase can be dated from c. 3500 until around 2700 B.C.E., at which time, a sophisticated and complex culture can be recognized.

The mature phase of Harappān culture (c. 2700-1900 B.C.E.) gives evidence of advanced technologies, systematic standards of weights and measures, complex social organization, large cities, and writing skills. The complex culture was formulated around a number of large cities, which received many of the necessities for living from outlying feeder villages. The layout of the cities was surprisingly consistent in that they were organized on a grid system that was oriented to the cardinal directions. The larger urban centers demonstrated an astute concern for sanitation and had extensive systems of sewers and drains fashioned from terra-cotta conduits. Many houses had a separate room for bathing, with a drain connected to outside sewer lines; some houses had dustbins located against the outer walls. Also public dustbins were provided throughout the cities. Sanitation was a paramount interest.

The rather mysterious Indus culture poses many questions for archaeologists. Each of the cities had an acropolis (an area raised above the level of general habitation). Some specialists have referred to the acropolis as a citadel because some of the raised precincts have what might be called defense walls, but it is not certain if military defense was the intention of the builders. Many regard the raised sections of the city as ritual centers; however, there are no structures at any site that can be identified definitively as having a sacred function. It seems logical to assume that the bath at Mohenjo-Daro, constructed on the acropolis of tightly fitted bricks reinforced with bitumen for waterproofing, fulfilled some ritual requirements, but its function is still not clearly known. No building in any city can be identified as a palace. However, the obviously well-governed and strictly organized cities suggest a paramount authority acting as overseer. Some specialists suggest that political and religious functions were combined in the office of the rulers, who used their sacral functions to create a social distance between rulers and ruled in order to legitimize power and privilege. Although the assumption seems likely, the lack of identifiable royal structures or any physical evidence renders the theory tenuous. Generally, however, early states are societies in which rulers and ruled are distinguished in their access to basic resources and the accumulation of luxury products. The cities demonstrate a concentration of wealth but, surprisingly, do not show any accumulation or display of wealth by any one group or individual, either living or dead.

There is little in the Indus Valley cities to indicate social stratification. Certainly some domestic structures are larger than others, but overall, the plans were similar, with rooms arranged around a central courtyard. Some of the houses with many rooms may have served a dual function, providing living quarters as well as spaces for business or manufacturing. All buildings were constructed of bricks of precise and uniform measures. In fact, the bricks used in even the smallest and most remote settlements of the Indus region were of identical size and weight, a fact that points to a strong central authority. The central authority devised a system of graded weights and measuring rods that enforced uniform weights and measures. Such uniformity also indicates strong control of the labor force throughout the region.

Another important marker of the sophistication of the culture was the increasing occupational specialization. Some people were specialists in writing and engraving seals, others were employed in farming, manufacturing of various crafts, or construction. Specialization implied a certain independence in that anyone with a single livelihood must have had access to and the means by which to procure food, clothing, cooking pots, and other necessities while concentrating on his or her exclusive trade.

There can be no doubt the Indus people were endowed with an entrepreneurial spirit. The enterprising inhabitants conducted trade with other distant peoples; Indus Valley artifacts have been found in cities of the ancient Near East and in settlements along the Persian Gulf. Scholars believe that the Indus Valley may be Meluhha, a place mentioned in ancient Near Eastern records. To keep track of exchange goods, systems of counting and writing were devised. The Indus script was inscribed on thousands of steatite seals; many of the inscriptions must have established ownership and were used to mark trade goods. This writing, however, has yet to be convincingly deciphered. In addition to trading agricultural products and possibly woven fabrics, the Indus inhabitants made and traded beads and jewelry. They used raw materials from diverse sources to fashion beads and jewelry from gold, copper, ivory, cowries and conch shells, steatite, carnelian, crystal, agate, amethyst, mother of pearl, coral, onyx, turquoise, and fuchsite. Beads were made throughout the region. Goods were traded overland by caravan or across water by boats. The port city of Lothal in Gujerat was a coastal trading center that linked the riverine culture with ports around the Persian Gulf; a large building in the dock area was used as a warehouse to store products for shipment. Large buildings with platforms at Mohenjo-Daro and Harappā undoubtedly served as warehouses for grains or manufactured goods.

The religion of the Indus inhabitants is still difficult to determine. In the earlier Neolithic settlements, burials with a few grave goods were standard. In the late post-Harappān phase, the bodies were cremated and the fragments interred in burial urns. The burials of the mature Indus Valley are relatively few, and there is a noticeable lack of burial objects; therefore, that rich source of information on religious beliefs is not available. The paucity of burials and skeletons also makes identifying the racial composition of the Indus Valley very difficult, and identification of the original Indus inhabitants has yet to be determined. The initial excavators and most scholars believe that they were related to India's Dravidian populations, early inhabitants of the subcontinent who migrated southward to their present home in south India, but it is also reasonable to assume that there was some ethnic diversity, particularly in a civilization that endured for several thousand years. It is possible that a number of diverse groups, varied in cultural heritage or ethnic identity, formed the constituent units of the Indus civilization.

There are few of the usual indicators that inform about religion in the Indus Valley. A few relatively small stone sculptures, seemingly portraits of high-ranking individual men, may suggest an elite ruling class. Two slender female figures of bronze, a costly material, were found at Mohenjo-Daro; their significance or purpose is not clear. Numerous small terra-cotta figurines of mother goddesses were found in houses throughout the region; they perhaps provide evidence of some animistic religious notions centered on the female procreative capacity. Such figures were found at the earliest Neolithic levels of occupation and continued to be produced through the latest phase of the society. The steatite seals carry engraved images; most display animals familiar to the region that may function as a some sort of totemic emblem reduced to a heraldic device representing a kinship group. The most frequent image on the seals, however, is a unicorn-like creature that occurs on 66 percent of the seals. Often shown with a manger or brazier, some scholars have postulated that the animal symbolizes a mark of state authority.

In the late phase of the Indus Valley civilization (c. 1900-1750 B.C.E.), there are signs that the culture was on the wane. The cities were in the process of abandonment. Various theories concerning the desertion of the cities have included continual flooding of the rivers in the region; tectonic shifts caused by earthquakes, resulting in the drying of water resources; and invasion by outsiders, notably the Aryans. Currently, all the theories are being reevaluated. Until the Indus script is definitively deciphered, and many more sites have been excavated and evaluated, the mysteries concerning the religion and particularly the demise of the great civilization will remain unsolved.

SIGNIFICANCE

One of the world's earliest civilizations, the highly advanced and complex Indus culture prospered for millennia, seemingly as the result of a strong central authority. Through trade, the populace created a manufacturing and mercantile sphere of influence that transcended its borders. The technologies of the Indus Valley persist to the present; undoubtedly some of the social and religious customs lived on well into later historical periods.

—*Katherine Anne Harper*

FURTHER READING

Kenoyer, Jonathan Mark. *Ancient Cities of the Indus Valley Civilization*. Karachi, Pakistan: Oxford University Press and the American Institute of Pakistan Studies, 1998. An exhibition catalog that provides a detailed examination of the archaeological finds with interpretive material. Bibliography.

Possehl, Gregory L. *Harappān Civilization*. Warminster, England: ARIS and Phillips and the American Institute of Indian Studies, 1982. An excellent evaluation of the current information and theories concerning the ancient culture. Bibliography.

Ratnagar, Shereen. *Enquiries into the Political Organization of Harappān Society*. Pune: Ravish Publishers, 1991. A carefully executed study that applies comparative logic to the Indus Valley remnants. Bibliography.

SEE ALSO: c. 7000-c. 4900 B.C.E., Çatalhüyük Flourishes as Center of Anatolian Culture; c. 3800 B.C.E., Cities and Civic Institutions Are Invented in Mesopotamia; c. 1500-c. 1000 B.C.E., Aryans Appear in India.

c. 3300-c. 1500 B.C.E.

VALDIVIA CULTURE FORMS VILLAGES IN COASTAL ECUADOR

The Valdivia culture made a highly successful hunting-and-gathering adaptation to life in the tropical forest of northwestern South America, involving the formation of nucleated settlements and the construction of complex ceremonial and ritual architecture.

LOCALE: Southwestern coastal Ecuador, primarily the Guayas Basin, including the Colòniche Hills
CATEGORIES: Prehistory and ancient cultures; architecture

SUMMARY OF EVENT

For most of the twentieth century, southwestern coastal Ecuador was seen as an archaeological backwater, where little interesting had happened in the past. All of this changed in the 1960's, when American archaeologist Betty Meggers and her colleagues published their research on a series of sites in the region. Among the most startling of their claims was that the ceramics found at the earliest sites they excavated, such as Valdivia, were derived from trans-Pacific contacts with the Jōmon culture of Japan. The Valdivia ceramics, they argued, had strong stylistic affinities with the Jōmon materials and were, in their opinion, too finely made to have been the first ceramic assemblage to have developed in Ecuador. Their claim provoked controversy and led to renewed research effort into the Formative period archaeology of Ecuador.

Other controversies soon arose, the most important of them the argument that maize diffused into the Valdivia region from Mesoamerica fairly early and formed the basis of the subsistence economy. The quantities of maize found at Early Valdivia sites was always very small, less than would be expected if maize was a staple, but supporters of the argument maintained that poor preservation in the tropical forest soils explained this discrepancy.

The presence of advanced ceramics and maize at an early date led many archaeologists to assume that Valdivia was somehow a precocious culture and that it was necessarily foundational to many cultural practices seen in later time periods, not only in Ecuador, but further to the south in Peru as well.

However, the intensive archaeological work conducted in southwestern Ecuador since the 1970's has shown that, in fact, ceramics from Valdivia sites were local in origin and could not be traced to Japan and that maize, while present, was not likely to have been a subsistence staple until late in Valdivia times. In this sense, then, Valdivia was not precocious, but the research has demonstrated that Valdivia is important for different reasons and is an outstanding example of how social and political complexity can arise from a hunting-and-gathering economy.

Valdivia culture is divided into three chronological phases: Early (3300-2300 B.C.E.), Middle (2300-1850 B.C.E.), and Late (1850-1500 B.C.E.). More than one hundred sites across a range of locations and sizes are known, and among the most important sites are Valdivia, Real Alto, Loma Alta, and Punta Concepción. Most Early Valdivia sites are found on the Punta Arenas peninsula along the courses of small rivers and streams. Most are found within 6 miles (10 kilometers) of the coast, and range in size from 2-5 acres (1-2 hectares) in size. A number of domestic residences of Early Valdivia date have been excavated at Real Alto. Most were small, single-roomed, ovoid to rectangular in form, and surrounded by posts that supported mud walls and thatched roofs. Each had a central cooking hearth, and activities in and around the houses included cooking, stone-tool manufacture, and cotton spinning. There was little variability in the size of these simple houses. Burials are found near many of these houses, some accompanied by small, stone, anthropomorphic figurines.

The layout of Early Valdivia sites was either circular or U-shaped, and domestic structures surrounded a central plaza remarkably clean of artifacts and debris. The size of the population in these early villages is estimated to have ranged between 150 and 200 persons. These villages are similar in shape and size to those found among contemporary horticultural peoples in the Amazon basin. Unlike these groups, however, Early Valdivia economy was based solely on hunting terrestrial mammals and maritime resources (primarily fish) and gathering seasonal wild plants. These resources were apparently sufficient to support a sedentary population, and the data suggest that Early Valdivia was egalitarian in nature.

The first evidence for greater social complexity is found at Real Alto and dates to the Middle Valdivia period. Although smaller sites similar in form to those of Early Valdivia are still found at this time, Real Alto is large, measuring more than 30 acres (12.5 hectares) in size. Not only does the size of the entire settlement increase, but also the numbers of domestic structures within it increase. Early Valdivia houses were thought to be the residences of single nuclear families. Middle Valdivia houses were much larger and most likely housed eight to ten occupants. This signals a change in residence patterns toward extended families. However, the same range of activities took place within them. Some domestic residences at Real Alto are quite large, and this suggests that their inhabitants had larger families or greater wealth than others, or were of high rank. The form of the site changes dramatically, becoming a large rectangle or oval with its opening to the south. Domestic structures mimic this pattern. Instead of a single open plaza or courtyard surrounded by domestic structures, the site is divided by low mounds into two plazas, a small inner plaza and a larger outer plaza. Atop these mounds are constructions thought to be ceremonial in function, although they could also have served as residences.

Real Alto appears to have become a ceremonial center in Middle Valdivia times, although there continued to be a large residential population surrounding it. The size of the site and the presence of ceremonial features support an inference that differences in rank and social status had also begun to develop. The subsistence economy is largely unchanged, continuing to be based on foraging and hunting. Small quantities of maize have been found at the site, but not enough to be of any economic significance. There is evidence, however, that it had a sacred or ceremonial role and was used to make a fermented alcoholic beverage. A form of bowl commonly found at the site is thought to have been used in a ritual context to consume this beverage. By the end of Middle Valdivia times, Real Alto had become the only ceremonial center of Valdivia culture.

Significant social changes took place in Late Valdivia times. While Real Alto continued as a ceremonial center, it was no longer a residential site. Other sites in the region took on ceremonial functions through the construction of their own mound and plaza complexes, and Real Alto became one of a small set of ceremonial centers serving dispersed local populations. Settlement shifted to smaller villages and hamlets along major streams and rivers, a pattern resembling Early Valdivia. Late Valdivia culture also became more widespread in southwestern Ecuador. Maize was present in quantity, and some have argued that its cultivation enabled the shift in settlement to dispersed villages. This pattern of population dispersion continued from Late Valdivia through subsequent time periods. Hunting and gathering continued to be of importance. Long-distance trade with the Andean highlands began during this period.

SIGNIFICANCE

Although research at Valdivia culture sites had its origins in major debates about the transoceanic diffusion of ceramics and early diffusion of maize into a cultural backwater, the lessons learned go well beyond controversy. Valdivia culture represents a remarkable and successful adaptation to a tropical forest environment wherein significant social and political complexity were founded on a hunting-and-gathering lifestyle. Research has shown that Valdivia communities were sedentary and resilient and had a rich and impressive religious and ritual life. Although the details of social rank and power in Valdivia society are still known only in outline, it is clear that Valdivia culture had a significant influence on the trajectory of development of later societies in this region that is only now being explored.

—Mark Aldenderfer

FURTHER READING

Lathrap, Donald, W. Donald Collier, and H. Chandra. *Ancient Ecuador: Culture, Clay, and Creativity, 3000-300 B.C.E.* Chicago: Field Museum of Natural History, 1975. Good overview of the ancient cultures of Ecuador.

Meggers, Betty J., Clifford Evans, and Emilio Estrada. *Early Formative Period of Coastal Ecuador: The Valdivia and Machalilla Phases*. Smithsonian Institution Contribution to Anthropology 1. Washington, D.C.: Smithsonian Institution Press, 1965. Now dated, this volume provided the first systematic description of Valdivia culture. Excellent artifact illustrations.

Raymond, J. Scott, and Richard Burger, eds. *Archaeology of Formative Ecuador.* Washington, D.C.: Dumbarton Oaks, 2003. Wide-ranging summaries of topics on the Ecuadorean Formative ranging from diet and subsistence through ideology, ritual, and religion.

Staller, John. "Reassessing the Developmental and Chronological Relationships of the Formative of Coastal Ecuador." *Journal of World Prehistory* 15 (2001): 193-256. A comprehensive and authoritative examination of what is known of the Formative cultures of coastal Ecuador, including Valdivia.

SEE ALSO: c. 5800-c. 3700 B.C.E., Chinchorro Inhabit the Peruvian and Chilean Coasts; c. 2500 B.C.E., Construction of Monumental Architecture at Caral in Peru; c. 1800-c. 1500 B.C.E., Construction of El Paraíso in Peru; 700 B.C.E.-100 C.E., Paracas Culture Develops a Sophisticated Textile Tradition; 200 B.C.E.-200 C.E., Nasca Lines Drawn in Desert Near Coast of Peru.

c. 3100 B.C.E.
SUMERIANS INVENT WRITING

The Sumerians, the first peoples known to use a writing system, contributed to one of the most significant cultural breakthroughs in the history of humankind.

LOCALE: Southern Mesopotamia (now southern Iraq)
CATEGORY: Cultural and intellectual history

SUMMARY OF EVENT

The Sumerians are generally credited with practicing the first known form of writing, toward the end of the fourth millennium B.C.E. The exact date for such an invention is difficult to pinpoint because writing developed over time, and it is difficult to draw a line between rudimentary protowriting and true writing. Many scholars, pointing to tablets from the city of Uruk that date to c. 3100 B.C.E., have pegged the start of writing to that date. However, the unearthing of additional artifacts as well as new interpretations of existing facts has caused this date to come into question. Evidence now suggests that writing was in development as early as 3300 B.C.E. in Mesopotamia, Egypt, and the Indus Valley. The traditional theory that the Sumerians influenced the beginning of writing in these other areas is also being challenged by the possibility that the three cultures developed writing systems independently or that Egypt possibly was the first to develop a writing system.

The invention of writing was a reflection of humankind's ability to adapt to the changing needs of society. The Sumerians were farmers living between the Tigris and Euphrates Rivers in southern Mesopotamia. By the fourth century B.C.E., the agricultural lifestyle was in full swing. In this region, roaming hunter-gatherers had long since settled down as farmers and shepherds. As settlements grew, merchants and craftspeople grew more numerous, and these early societies became increasingly complex. With this complexity came the need to keep track of inventories, accounts, and transactions. Simple prehistoric mnemonic devices, such as tally sticks, knotted cords, and tokens, were not adequate to record the details of these more sophisticated interactions. The earliest writing, therefore, which was created to avoid ambiguity and provide permanence, was for the purpose of accountancy.

The earliest writing form was not phonetic. There was no relationship between the symbols used and the speech sounds of the language. Rather, Sumerian writing started out as a pictographic system, consisting of simplified drawings of animals and objects. The early clay tablets of Uruk contained concrete representations of such things as cattle and bags of grain along with symbols representing numbers. Over time, ideographic signs developed, which symbolized more abstract concepts relating to the original pictograms. For example, a picture of the Sun might also connote "day" or "light." This allowed for an expansion of the concepts that could be represented in written form. Further abstraction led to logographic signs, which were symbols that stood for words but had no direct pictorial connection.

The evolution of writing was also influenced by the surrounding environment and the tools used to record communications. Clay was the most abundant writing medium in Mesopotamia, and a pointed stylus made from reeds, bone, or wood was used to draw the symbols in the wet clay. Over time, scribes looked for ways to make their inscriptions more quickly and efficiently. It was somewhat awkward to pull the stylus through the quick-drying clay, and doing so left ridges along the edges of the writing. The pointed stylus was discarded in favor of a stylus with a triangular-shaped tip that could be pressed quickly into the clay. Because of this practical adaptation, by 2900 B.C.E., the style of the symbols had changed from curving lines to straight, angular, wedge-shaped markings. This marked the beginning of the writing system known as cuneiform, from the Latin word *cuneis*, meaning "wedge." The symbols also became more stylized so that they could be impressed on the clay more quickly. A benefit of using clay as a writing medium was that it could be baked and hardened to preserve it indefinitely. Thus, the newly developing system of written communication was provided even more permanence by virtue of using a nonperishable medium.

A significant advancement in the development of writing was when signs began to represent the sounds of the language. Before this, the writing symbols were purely conceptual. A symbol stood for the image it depicted or for an abstract concept related to the picture. At some point, the Sumerians hit on the idea of using pictograms to stand for sounds in the words they represented. The pictograms thus began to stand for parts or syllables of words. For example, the pictogram of a bee would be combined with the pictogram for a leaf to make the abstract word "belief." This rebus principle was a pivotal development toward a true writing system, which is defined as a system of symbols that represent the sounds of a language. As cuneiform transitioned from a pictographic to a logosyllabic system, the number of symbols decreased dramatically, from an unwieldy two thousand symbols to six hundred symbols by the end of the third millennium B.C.E.

Once cuneiform became systemized, it began to spread throughout Mesopotamia and eventually to almost all of the peoples of the ancient Near East. Because of its primary dependence on logographic signs as opposed to phonetic signs, it was easily adaptable to other languages. The Akkadians of northern Mesopotamia, the Babylonians, and Assyrians succeeded each other as the dominant powers in Mesopotamia from 2500 to 700 B.C.E. They adopted cuneiform to record their own Semitic language and over time simplified it to an increasingly syllabic system. The Elamites of Persia adapted cuneiform, creating some of their own signs for their non-Semitic language. The Eblaites and Hurrians of Syria also employed cuneiform, as did the Hittites of Asia Minor.

Although credited as the first true writing system, cuneiform never developed into a fully syllabic writing system, much less a phonetic system. It had done its job, however, of introducing the ancient world to the utility of the craft of writing, an art and invention that would eventually lead to the truly phonetic systems of today.

SIGNIFICANCE

The impact of the invention of writing on human civilization cannot be underestimated. This cultural achievement serves as the vehicle of civilization and recorded history. Writing evolved because of the needs of an increasingly urbanized society, and it became a basic and essential tool for everyday activities. The development of writing was inextricably intertwined with the increasing sophistication of society, in that it was a product of, as well as a facilitator of, human utilitarianism. It allowed the Sumerians to communicate effectively, to organize relationships, and to create permanent records of the happenings of their world.

Writing also facilitated the development of philosophic and scientific thought and consequently people's ability to understand themselves and their environment. With writing came opportunities for self-expression, the transmittal of ideas, and the recording of these thoughts, opinions, and feelings for posterity. Writing became an integral element of religion. Hymns and divination texts could be recorded and systemized, and their permanent recording added to their sanctity. In short, the beginning of writing marked the beginning of a body of literature that included accountancy, astronomical charts, legal and medical writings, philosophy, religion, and literature.

—Barbara C. Beattie

FURTHER READING

Claiborne, Robert. *The Birth of Writing*. New York: Time-Life Books, 1974. Covers the evolution of writing in the ancient world, with good coverage of writing tools and scribal arts.

Diringer, David. *Writing*. New York: Praeger, 1962. A classic text on the subject of the origins of writing.

Jean, Georges. *Writing: The Story of Alphabets and Scripts*. New York: Harry N. Abrams, 1992. Describes the evolution of writing in Mesopotamia, Egypt, and China, with chapters on the emergence of the alphabet.

Lawler, Andrew. "Writing Gets a Rewrite." *Science* 292, no. 5526 (June 29, 2001): 2418-2420. A concise discussion of the newest thoughts concerning the evolution of writing.

Robinson, Andrew. *The Story of Writing: Alphabets, Hieroglyphics, and Pictograms*. London: Thames and Hudson, 1995. Provides good coverage of protowriting, Sumerian cuneiform, Egyptian hieroglyphics, and Mayan script.

Van de Mieroop, Marc. *Cuneiform Texts and the Writing of History*. New York: Routledge, 1999. Explores how historians have gained insight into Mesopotamian history through the study of cuneiform texts.

Walker, C. B. F. *Cuneiform*. Berkeley: University of California Press, 1987. Surveys the development of cuneiform and analyzes sample texts to give insight into the structure of the script.

SEE ALSO: c. 6200-c. 3800 B.C.E., Ubaid Culture Thrives in Mesopotamia; c. 5500-c. 4500 B.C.E., Halafian Culture Flourishes in Northern Mesopotamia; c. 4000 B.C.E., Sumerian Civilization Begins in Mesopotamia; c. 3800 B.C.E., Cities and Civic Institutions Are Invented in Mesopotamia; c. 3000-c. 500 B.C.E., Elamite Empire Rises in Near East; c. 2900-c. 2340 B.C.E., Early Dynastic Period Flourishes in Southern Mesopotamia; c. 2340 B.C.E., Sumerian Uruk-Agina Makes Social and Political Reforms; c. 2334-c. 2279 B.C.E., Sargon of Akkad Establishes the Akkadian Dynasty; c. 1250 B.C.E., Transmission of the European Alphabet.

c. 3100-c. 1550 B.C.E.
Building of Stonehenge

Building the megalithic monument Stonehenge required a level of sophistication and social organization in the late Stone Age and early Bronze Age cultures of Britain comparable to any of the contemporary civilizations of the Near East.

Locale: Southern England
Categories: Prehistory and ancient cultures; religion; science and technology

Summary of Event

Stonehenge is the most important prehistoric monument in Europe, a circular stone structure built on Salisbury Plain in southern England. Although it is only one of thousands of megalithic, or large stone, structures erected in western Europe, its unique features have made it the most famous, generating centuries of speculation about who built it.

In his *History of the Kings of Britain* (1136 C.E.), Geoffrey of Monmouth attributed Stonehenge to Merlin the Magician, claiming that it held the tombs of Aurelius, Constantine, and Uther Pendragon, father of King Arthur. Royal architect Inigo Jones, commissioned by King James I in 1620 to study the matter, concluded that it was Roman. According to antiquarians John Aubrey (1666) and William Stukeley (1740), Druid priests were its source, an idea still cherished by latter-day Druid cultists. In the late twentieth century, theorists suggested that colonists from the lost continent of Atlantis or possibly extraterrestrial beings were responsible for constructing Stonehenge.

Until the 1970's, most archaeologists preferred to see Stonehenge as the result of Near Eastern influence. It was believed that civilization first arose in the Near East, later spreading advanced knowledge and skills outward to less capable peoples in a ripple effect. In 1965, Stonehenge authority R. J. C. Atkinson attributed the monument to Mycenaean Greeks, dismissing the local Britons of the period as "howling barbarians."

This diffusion theory was undermined by recalibrated radiocarbon dates, which showed that some European megalithic constructions existed as early as 4500 B.C.E. These dates helped classify such structures as the earliest stone architecture in the world. Rather than considering the megaliths to be imports, scholars turned their attention to understanding the *in situ* cultural evolution of late Stone Age farming peoples.

Farming was introduced to Britain in the Neolithic period, with wheat being grown in Wessex by 4000 B.C.E. Villages were small, organized socially as egalitarian tribes. This social organization is reflected in their burial practices, in which bones of people of all ages and sexes were placed in stone chambers, some with stone passageways. Excavated dirt from a surrounding ditch was placed over these megalithic structures, thus producing the long barrow.

Groups of barrows are associated with a larger British structure, the Causewayed Camp. These barrow enclosures were created by digging ditches with adjacent banks to the interior. Natural breaks, or causeways, in the perimeter of ditches probably served as entrances. The use of these ditches included excarnation, exposing bodies to remove flesh before interring the bones in the barrows. These structures required considerable labor to build and are believed to have served the living as well as the dead. Robin Hood's Ball, located 3 miles (5 kilometers) from the later site of Stonehenge, enclosed 2.5 acres (1 hectare) of land. It probably symbolized tribal identity and possession of the land and might have served as a community center.

A new feature appeared around 3200 B.C.E.—the henge. Similar to causewayed camps, the bank (or built structure) typically was constructed outside the ditch, with one or two entrances. Thirteen such structures include standing stones—the earliest British stone circles.

Scholars believe that after 3100 B.C.E., work began on Stonehenge by enclosing a circle 320 feet (98 meters) in diameter with a 6-foot (2-meter) bank. Stonehenge is an unusual henge in that its ditch lies outside its bank, echoing the older causewayed camp. Flanked by two stones, Stonehenge's entrance is oriented to the northeast, the direction of the summer solstice sunrise. This axis is also marked by a 16-foot-high (79-meter-high), 35-ton (32-metric-ton) Heel Stone, located 96 feet (30 meters) beyond the entrance. Just inside the bank lies a circle 284 feet (88 meters) in diameter of fifty-six Aubrey Holes. Named for antiquarian John Aubrey, these holes are evenly spaced some 16 feet (79 meters) apart, are from 2 to 4 feet (0.6 to 1.2 meters) deep, and were filled with chalk soon after being dug. Excavations revealed that some holes contained human cremations from a later date. In this form, Stonehenge was used for several centuries and then abandoned.

There is evidence that tribal societies were evolving into status-conscious chiefdoms around 2700 B.C.E.

Many theories have been advanced about the building of Stonehenge. (PhotoDisc)

Communal long barrow graves were replaced by round barrows that covered a single rich grave. Copper daggers and gold earrings have been recovered from such sites, along with fine Beaker pottery, characterized by a distinctive drinking cup without handles.

Once believed to have reflected an actual invasion of Beaker people, such barrows and grave goods now seem to reflect an emerging leadership elite who were engaging in a wider trade in flint, copper, tin, and prestige items while continuing their rich Neolithic farming traditions. New henges began to appear, three of which are located within two miles of Stonehenge itself. At Avebury to the north, ninety-eight stones are enclosed by a ditch 1 mile (1.6 kilometers) in circumference. The prodigious labor required to construct these sites reflects the growing wealth and power of a royal elite entering the Bronze Age.

New work began at Stonehenge itself around 2100 B.C.E. By building two parallel chalk banks with exterior ditches more than one-third of a mile (one-half of a kilometer) long, the new builders created an avenue leading up to the northeast entrance. Eighty bluestones, each measuring 6 feet (2 meters) in height and imported from the Preseli Mountains in Wales, were set up in two incomplete concentric circles. Researchers believe that this may have been the time when four station stones were set up on the Aubrey Circle, imposing on it a rough rectangle. In 1978, a Beaker burial was discovered in the ditch, continuing the association of enclosures with death and ritual.

Between 2000 and 1550 B.C.E., Stonehenge became truly unique. The bluestones were removed, and large sarsen (foreign) sandstone blocks were brought from Marlborough Downs some 20 miles (32 kilometers) to the north. Thirty upright blocks, weighing 25 tons (22 metric tons) each, were arranged 3.5 feet (1.1 meters) apart to form a circle 100 feet (30 meters) in diameter. These blocks were then topped by lintels, in essence creating a flat circular sidewalk elevated 16 feet (79 meters) above the ground. Inside this sarsen circle is a horseshoe-shaped arrangement of five structures, known as trilithons, with the open end of the horseshoe oriented on the northeast axis. Each trilithon was made of two upright blocks topped by a lintel; these structures include the largest stones in the monument. Bluestones were again added to the design. Sixty individual bluestones were positioned to form a circle 75 feet (23 meters) in diameter just within the sarsen circle. Nineteen bluestones placed within the trilithons formed a bluestone horseshoe.

The workmanship of these structures sets Stonehenge apart from other megalithic structures. The interior sides of all the sarsens reveal that workers pounded them smooth with stone hammers. Each lintel had two depressions on the bottom that allowed them to fit over projections on the adjacent uprights. Tongue-in-groove joints were used between the lintels that met each other over the uprights in the sarsen circle. Beveling, curvature, and the use of perspective are evident, providing a glimpse of the skills of master craftspeople who seem to have adapted the art of fine woodworking on a massive scale to shape stone. Evidence of such attention to detail, along with the innovative design of the sarsen circle, occurs in no other megalithic monument on the earth.

Later alterations of Stonehenge have been attributed to the Wessex culture of southern Britain's early Bronze Age. Dozens of their round barrows dot the surrounding ridges. In 1808, Sir Richard Colt Hoare excavated one such barrow in the Normanton group located just south of Stonehenge. Called Bush Barrow, it contained the skeleton of a tall male; with him were two bronze daggers and a bronze axe. A stone mace and a beautifully incised golden pectoral (breast ornament) found near him may have been the symbols of authority of one of the actual builders and lords of Stonehenge, a monument central to his reign.

In 1965, Harvard astronomer Gerald Hawkins claimed that Stonehenge served these people as a giant astronomical observatory. He explained that numerous stone alignments marked key positions of both the sun and the moon. Noting that the cycle of lunar eclipses occurs in a pattern of fifty-six years (nineteen plus nineteen plus eighteen), he believed that this pattern explained the purpose of the Aubrey Holes, which were used as a lunar eclipse predictor.

Archaeologists have been skeptical of these claims, questioning the precision of the alignments and the builders' possession of the required knowledge to construct such an observatory. Missing and displaced stones at the site, as well as alterations in the ground plan over the centuries, combine to make an analysis of such precision difficult. Harvard researcher Alexander Marshack has made the claim that 25,000-year-old bones found in European sites have been engraved with precise day-to-day markings of the exact positions and phase of the moon. If Marshack is correct, ancient knowledge of astronomy that could validate Hawkins's claims for Stonehenge may have been available in Europe for a very long time. Within the vast scope of human history, the science of astronomy has only recently been divorced from astrology; control over cosmology and an ability to predict eclipses would have been of great value in reinforcing the power and prestige of the lords of Wessex.

SIGNIFICANCE

Although archaeologist may never determine how Stonehenge was used—whether for religious rituals, in association with burials, or as an astronomical guide—its existence, the workmanship and design that went into its construction, show that the cultures in ancient Britain were as sophisticated and advanced as those in the Near East.

—*Gary A. Olson*

FURTHER READING

Burl, Aubrey. *Great Stone Circles: Fables, Fictions, Facts*. New Haven, Conn.: Yale University Press, 1999. Archaeologist Burl analyzes the various stories concerning about twelve megalithic monuments, including Stonehenge, often using scientific evidence to debunk myths. Bibliography and index.

Chippindale, Christopher. *Stonehenge Complete*. Rev. ed. New York: Thames and Hudson, 1994. A comprehensive overview of all facets of the topic.

Cleal, Rosamund M. J., K. E. Walker, R. Montague, et al. *Stonehenge in Its Landscape: Twentieth Century Excavations*. London: English Heritage, 1995. An archaeological report on the excavations of Stonehenge in the twentieth century. Includes maps, bibliography, and index.

Cunliffe, Barry, and Colin Renfrew, eds. *Science and Stonehenge*. New York: Oxford University Press, 1997. A collection of papers from a conference on Stonehenge organized by the Royal Society and the British Academy in cooperation with the English Heritage and held March, 1996. Bibliographical references and index

Gibson, Alex M. *Stonehenge and Timber Circles*. Charleston, S.C.: Tempus, 2000. An examination of Britain at the time of timber circles, including Stonehenge and Woodhenge. Bibliography and index.

North, John David. *Stonehenge: A New Interpretation of Prehistoric Man and the Cosmos*. New York: Free Press, 1996. North, a historian of science with an extensive background in astronomy, argues that Stonehenge was used as an astronomical observatory. Index.

Souden, David. *Stonehenge Revealed*. New York: Facts on File, 1997. An analysis of Stonehenge that contains many maps and charts and about two hundred color photographs, taken from all directions. Index.

SEE ALSO: c. 2300-c. 1800 B.C.E., Beaker People Live in Western Europe; 14th-9th centuries B.C.E., Urnfield Culture Flourishes in Northwestern Europe; c. 1100-c. 500 B.C.E., Hallstatt Culture Dominates Northern Europe.

c. 3050 B.C.E.
UNIFICATION OF LOWER AND UPPER EGYPT

The unification of Lower and Upper Egypt produced the first unified bureaucratic state in world history and also created the first theocratic nation-state in the history of ancient and modern international systems.

LOCALE: Northern and southern Egypt
CATEGORIES: Expansion and land acquisition; religion

KEY FIGURES

Menes (Narmer; c. 3100-c. 3000 B.C.E.), pharaoh and founder of the ancient Egyptian state
Hor-Aha (fl. c. 3000 B.C.E.), first warrior pharaoh of ancient Egypt, r. c. 3000-c. 2970 B.C.E.
Den (fl. c. third millennium B.C.E.), first pharaoh with the title King of Lower and Upper Egypt, r. c. mid-third millennium B.C.E.

SUMMARY OF EVENT

The Egyptian Predynastic Period (c. 3050-c. 2925) and First Dynasty (c. 2925-c. 2775) laid the foundation for a highly effective bureaucratic civilization that was based on the unification of culture, religion, land, and the state and that lasted for more than three thousand years. It is suggested that religion was the central impulse for the unification of the Egyptian nation-state, and economic maturation and cultural development continued to cement the unification. The data on the general and specific historical events—as well as the central personalities involved—that produced the conditions required for the rise and progress of a predynastic Egypt continue to develop through archaeological analysis and historical research. However, the record remains cloudy on many important questions related to the origins and conditions driving the rise and development of predynastic Egypt.

It is clear that the Predynastic Period and the First Dynasty were collectively responsible for the invention of the 365-day calendar, the Memphite theology (one of the first organized human searches for the divine intelligence underlying the universe), an advanced agricultural and industrial production system, a centralized national government, and a sophisticated commerce, trading, tax, and monetary system. The combined effect of these two periods in launching the great Egyptian civilization cannot be denied.

The predynastic founding of the Egyptian nation-state (or the uniting of Upper and Lower Egypt) by Irihor, Scorpion, and Menes in the late fourth millennium B.C.E. is shrouded in both legend and mystery. The available historical information on both the individual lives and specific historical roles of these early kings is not very revealing. In addition, the strategic political, military, economic, and cultural accomplishments of these individuals are not clear. However, some scholars suggest that they descended from or were related to a very powerful ruling family from Upper Egypt who arrived in Lower Egypt around 3050 B.C.E. and built a capital at Memphis, the midpoint between Lower and Upper Egypt. It is argued that the leaders of the ruling family used advanced political and diplomatic skills as well as superior military force to culturally unite the disparate peoples of Lower and Upper Egypt, initiating the revolutionary dynastic developments that would last for more than three millennia.

In this historical context, all that is known is that Pharaohs Irihor and Scorpion were important in both organizing and leading military forces that provided the central impulse in the uniting of Lower and Upper Egypt. However, it is Menes who was viewed by most ancient Egyptians as the true founder of the Egyptian nation-state and the first pharaoh to provide a real sense of Egyptian nationalism. Some scholars, in fact, argue that Menes, Scorpion, and Irihor were all the same king,

IMPORTANT EARLY RULERS OF EGYPT, C. 3050-C. 2775 B.C.E.

PREDYNASTIC PERIOD, C. 3050-2925

Ruler
Irihor
Scorpion
Menes (Narmer)

FIRST DYNASTY, C. 2925-C. 2775

Ruler	*Reign*
Hor-Aha ("Fighting Hawk")	c. 3000-2970
Djer (Sekhty)	c. 2970-c. 2950
Djet ("The Serpent")	2920-c. 2880
Den (Dewen)	from c. 2880
Anedjib	
Semerkhet	
Qa'a	

Note: Dynastic research is ongoing; data are approximate.

or at most two kings. Menes is the king credited with introducing Egyptians to the benefits of high civilization and high culture; initiating the idea that the pharaoh was a god and embodied the state; founding the capital city of Memphis in Middle Egypt; connecting Lower and Upper Egypt; draining the marshes that surrounded the great Nile River system, which allowed agriculture and related economic activities to flourish; and initiating extensive trading and financial links with Palestine, Lebanon, and surrounding states.

During the Archaic period (c. 3000-c. 2650 B.C.E.), the historical data indicate that Hor-Aha, the first warrior pharaoh, expertly used the strategic tools of military power, political diplomacy, and a sophisticated intelligence system to unite Lower and Upper Egypt at the turn of the third millennium B.C.E. through wars of political, economic, and cultural unification. Hor-Aha conducted extensive military campaigns against dangerous external enemies, such as Nubia in the south, as well as against internal foes, with noticeable success. He opened key trading and commercial links with Lebanon, Syria, and Mesopotamia to economically strengthen the state. However, Hor-Aha found himself constantly at odds with the feudal governors, who provided him with military contingents in exchange for land rights and material privileges. It took him a number of years to reverse this situation, finally laying the basis for an efficient national army. Even so, the pharaohs who followed Hor-Aha did not have an easy time holding together the Egyptian state. Local governors and aristocrats dominant both in the Delta region and in the south fiercely resisted the movement toward national unity and the spiritual, cultural, and economic consolidation of Egypt. In fact, the two principal regions of ancient Egypt often found themselves engaged in intermittent civil war, while at the same time opposing the rule of the pharaohs.

Hor-Aha's successor Djer (r. c. 2970-c. 2950 B.C.E.) continued the internal political, economic, cultural, and military consolidation of Egypt. He pursued an aggressive foreign military policy toward a resurgent Nubia and toward Libya in the Delta region. Pharaoh Djet (r. c. 2920-c. 2880 B.C.E.) was one of the most prominent of the pharaohs during the Archaic period; he continued the consolidation of power in Egypt while pursuing an active foreign military policy near the northern and southern borders of the country. About 2880 B.C.E., Pharaoh Den assumed the throne and was the first pharaoh to bear the title of king of Lower and Upper Egypt, presumably earned as a result of his success in finally uniting the country, as well as his successful military campaigning in the Sinai region and elsewhere on the borders of Egypt. At the end of the First Dynasty, political change and social turmoil negatively affected the rule of the last three pharaohs, Anedjib, Semerkhet, and Qa'a.

Significance

The political, economic, and cultural unification of Lower and Upper Egypt between c. 3050 and c. 2775 B.C.E. created the world's first bureaucratic (and theocratic) state. Pharaohs Menes, Hor-Aha, and Den played important roles in ancient Egypt's integration of culture, religion, land, government, and the state. The notion of the pharaoh as god was extremely long-lived and provided the justification of monarchical power down to the time of the Ptolemies. The conceptualization of Egypt as a unitary whole persisted even during times of political upheaval when the government of the area was splintered. The idea of Egyptian identity also provided the impetus for the enormously syncretic nature of Egyptian religion, with local deities incorporated into an ever-increasing pantheon while the worship of certain gods, such as Osiris, became pan-Egyptian.

—Michael J. Siler

Further Reading

Assmann, Jan. *The Mind of Egypt: History and Meaning in the Time of the Pharaohs*. Translated by Andrew Jenkins. New York: Metropolitan Books, 2002. Although dense reading, this book presents an insightful analysis of the way in which the ancient Egyptians themselves perceived their history.

Johnson, Paul. *The Civilization of Ancient Egypt*. New York: HarperCollins, 1998. A fine analysis of the civilization in ancient Egypt.

Shaw, Ian, ed. *The Oxford History of Ancient Egypt*. New York: Oxford University Press, 2003. Presents a thorough approach to the vexed question of establishing sound chronologies for early Egypt. A useful reference, intended for advanced students and knowledgeable general readers.

Wilkinson, Toby A. H. *Early Dynastic Egypt: Strategies, Society, and Security*. New York: Routledge, 2001. One of the few studies to focus specifically on the early dynastic era and the process of unifying Egypt into a nation-state.

_______. *Genesis of the Pharaohs*. New York: Thames and Hudson, 2003. Argues that the predynastic Egyptians were not primarily flood-plain farmers but seminomadic pastoralists. Wilkinson bases much of his thesis on interpretation of early Egyptian rock paintings. Illustrations.

SEE ALSO: c. 2687 B.C.E., Old Kingdom Period Begins in Egypt; c. 2575-c. 2566 B.C.E., Building of the Great Pyramid; c. 2160 B.C.E., First Intermediate Period Begins in Egypt; c. 2055 B.C.E., Middle Kingdom Period Begins in Egypt; c. 1650 B.C.E., Hyksos Create Second Intermediate Period; c. 1570 B.C.E., New Kingdom Period Begins in Egypt; From c. 1500 B.C.E., Dissemination of the Book of the Dead; c. 1338 B.C.E., Failure of Akhenaton's Cultural Revival; 1069 B.C.E., Third Intermediate Period Begins in Egypt.

RELATED ARTICLE in *Great Lives from History: The Ancient World*: Menes.

c. 3000 B.C.E.

AUSTRALIAN ABORIGINES CREATE WANDJINA CAVE PAINTINGS

Early aboriginal peoples in northwestern Australia believed that beings called Wandjina were associated with the Creation and controlled the elements, human fertility, and the maintenance of other natural species. The ritual of repainting these ancestral images on cave walls was believed to guarantee the continuation of life.

LOCALE: Northwestern Kimberley, Australia
CATEGORY: Prehistory and ancient cultures

SUMMARY OF EVENT

Rock shelter paintings created by the Worrorra, Wunambal, and Ngarinyin peoples in the northwestern part of Kimberley, Australia, are examples of how rock art established both a source of origin and a place of cultural significance for the Aborigines in this area. The Wandjina were mythic cultural heroes credited with creating the aboriginal social order during a creative period called the Dreamtime, and totemic clans identified themselves by a Wandjina hero. Legends explaining Wandjina vary according to regional lore. Wandjina have been recorded as originally inhabiting the sea and later moving onto land and eventually transforming themselves into painted images on the walls of indigenous rock shelters. Other myths indicate these beings may have been ancestors whose deeds had significance worthy of perpetual remembrance in the form of cave paintings. In either instance, it is within the rock that they continue to exist with the help of initiated male Aborigines who celebrated the spirits by performing a repainting ceremony to maintain their existence.

Like all Dreamtime spirits, the Wandjina could intervene in human lives and are credited with controlling natural phenomena, particularly the clouds, water, and lightning. They are sometimes described as "cloud spirits" and were thought to be responsible for lightning associated with the monsoon rains occurring between December and March. For this reason, Wandjina annual ceremonies were performed prior to the onset of the rainy season. A connection to water may also explain why the Aborigines believed the Wandjina related directly to fertility, since it was believed that the spirit of an unborn child existed in water pools where fish, turtles, or crocodiles containing a child's spirit might be caught, consumed, and then brought into the human cycle of life. Such animals can be found with Wandjina images on rock walls. The ritual upkeep of these sacred images is the manner in which Aborigines to this day ensure a balanced relationship with nature and maintain a historical legacy for future generations.

Painted Wandjina figures were seen by a European, the English explorer Lieutenant George Grey, for the first time in 1838. The impressive figures, reaching 6 meters or more in height, were painted standing or lying horizontally. Frontally depicted, they have round heads, circular eyes, no mouths, radiating lines or semicircular bands around the tops of their heads, and a biomorphic oval shape extending below the head in what would be the chest area. Some representations are from the chest upward; others are covered or clothed figures with arms and feet. Lines coming out from the top of the head are thought to represent feathers or perhaps lightning.

Although exact dating of the Wandjina style is difficult because ritual repainting of the images makes it impossible to identify an "original" Wandjina, most scholars believe this type of rock art to have appeared about three thousand years ago; this dating has been aided by the associated depiction of stone-tipped spears, a technology that dates to this period. Some argue that the figures may be eight thousand years old or even significantly older.

Male artists assigned to repainting the cave images commonly belong to groups thought to have descended from the Wandjina. Generations of artists have used the same pigments for each repainting. Black charcoal and red or yellow ochre are applied over a white background, enhancing the clarity of the figure. The pigments are mixed with water and applied with fingers, the hand, or a fibrous natural brush. White is applied first with the hand to create a background. Then colors are added using the artist's finger for thicker lines and a fine brush for thin lines. This repeated and sacred act of overpainting the spirits is thought by the Aborigines to supply them with a direct conduit to the primordial world, a multidimensional connection linking past, present, and future.

Contemporary southwestern migrations of the Worrorra and Ngarinyin peoples have introduced Wandjina to other areas outside northwestern Kimberley. New materials—bark, engraved shells, nuts, stone—have been explored as expressive means of propagating the sustaining power of Wandjina.

SIGNIFICANCE

The existence of the ghostlike Wandjina images in northwestern Australia has shown not only that the area was populated several thousand years ago but also that these people had a well-developed belief system. These and other rock paintings in the Kimberley region, especially the Bradshaw figures, are among the oldest in the world. The ability of human beings to invest representational art with symbolic power—here to preserve essential ancestral power through the generations—thus received early expression in these figures.

—Michael Coronel and Patricia Coronel

FURTHER READING

Capell, A. "Cave Painting Myths: Northern Kimberley." *Oceania and Linguistic Monographs* 18. Sydney: University of Sydney Press, 1972. Interpretation of 1930's and 1940's research into the linguistic and metaphysical origins of Wandjina.

Chaloupka, G. *Journey in Time: The World's Longest Continuing Art Tradition*. Sydney: University of Sydney, 1993. General conceptual information. Well illustrated.

Crawford, I. M. *The Art of the Wandjina: Aboriginal Cave Paintings in Kimberley, Western Australia*. Melbourne: Oxford University Press, 1968. Good overview of Wandjina regional variations, painting techniques, and related imagery. Numerous illustrations in both color and black and white.

Sutton, P., ed. *Dreamings: The Art of Aboriginal Australia*. New York: Viking Press, 1988. Serves to place Wandjina within the aboriginal concept of Dreamtime.

SEE ALSO: c. 25,000 B.C.E., San Peoples Create Earliest African Art; c. 15,500 B.C.E., Early Australians Create the Bradshaw Rock Paintings; c. 15,000 B.C.E., Early Europeans Create Lascaux Cave Paintings.

c. 3000 B.C.E.
CANAANITES INHABIT THE LEVANT

The Canaanites, a new culture in an already ancient land, inspired city building, metalworking, and large-scale trade with Mesopotamia and Egypt, ultimately leading to alphabetic writing and biblical religions.

LOCALE: Canaan (now in Israel, Jordan, Lebanon, and adjacent areas of southern Syria)

CATEGORIES: Prehistory and ancient cultures; trade and commerce

SUMMARY OF EVENT

Human presence and village life in the Levant go back many millennia. Excavations at Jericho reveal levels of habitation dating back to at least 8500 B.C.E. The Canaanites appeared around 3000 B.C.E., with a new way of life based on cities. There is some controversy over whether the Canaanites were invaders or a group already living in the region. They may have incorporated elements of both. Archaeologists have found their urban sites throughout the area, including 5,000-year-old stone gates at Beirut. An emerging, relatively coherent Canaanite culture was accompanied by technological advances.

Writing, which had already been invented in Mesopotamia, apparently had not reached the Levant by this time. There are no king lists or commercial records of early Canaan. Archaeological evidence can show much about material culture and city layout and sometimes can reveal the makeup of populations, but archaeologists can only make guesses regarding many matters of Canaanite social organization, based on later patterns and those in neighboring lands.

Canaanite cities, like those in Mesopotamia, had sturdy fortifications, public buildings, and some sort of water supply, which might include cisterns and irrigation measures. Presumably an administrative class and methods developed. As its early Bronze Age designation implies, this era was typified by advances in metalworking, especially useful for the production of weapons and tools. Potter's wheels came into general use, and a wide variety of ceramics were made and decorated. In agriculture, the subsistence farming and herding of earlier times changed to large-scale production, creating a surplus for trade and storage.

These events did not take place in isolation. At the same time, Egypt and Mesopotamia were inventing the building blocks of their civilizations. In Egypt, the Old Kingdom had begun, and an overall political structure was emerging. Sumeria was at the prosperous center of Mesopotamia. Because of their location, Canaanite cities and towns received influences from both directions.

Canaanites participated actively in the exchange of goods and cultural traits in the ancient Near East. Their cities flourished by trade. Almost certainly they organized some of the donkey caravans that carried cargo overland at the time; a tomb in Lachish contains bones of a domesticated donkey. Wood from the cedars of Lebanon, famous in biblical lore, was already being shipped to Egypt from the port of Byblos.

Canaanites were also involved in commercial production of food for export. At Tell es-Sa'idiyeh in the Jordan Valley, excavations revealed a large Early Bronze Age complex apparently devoted to such an enterprise. Large empty jugs were stacked in a storeroom, and charred olives, grapes, wheat, and figs were found in other rooms. Presumably a fire devastated this early factory, which seems to have made, stored, and shipped textiles along with olive oil, wine, and other foodstuffs. Much of Canaan's commerce was with Egypt, which imported its olive oil and wine in large quantities. Many trade goods also went to Syria and points east. Although more commerce probably took place with Egypt, in this era, Canaan seems to have shared more cultural traits with Mesopotamia. This may be partly because of similar climates and terrain as well as migration.

Such findings are interesting not only because they show the extent of commerce and manufacturing some five millennia ago. Also notable is the fact that Canaan, living midway between the two "cradles of civilization," was in an ideal location to benefit from the cultural diffu-

The remains of an ancient Canaanite temple and a round altar in Tel Megiddo, Israel. (Hanan Isachar/Corbis)

sion that accompanied trade and travel. After this era, a succession of incursions and conquests occurred, but successor cultures remained Canaanite in many ways. During this process two very important elements were transmuted, to form a part of future history and its cultures.

Significance

Canaanite hegemony in the Levant profoundly affected Judaism and its offspring, Christianity. The early Bronze Age era far predates the development of a Hebrew nation or the historical events of the Bible. However, the Canaanites had a complex pantheon and religion that endured through the following centuries. The religion placed much emphasis on blood sacrifices, often of children, to pacify the various deities.

When a rudimentary Jewish identity emerged, it was largely out of the Canaanite milieu and incorporated features of the religion into its own. Abraham's near-sacrifice of Isaac may represent one such remnant. Later, as the Israelites attempted to claim Canaan as their promised land, their religion came to be defined in opposition to that of Canaan. Yahweh became a sole deity, distinct from the Canaanites' high god El, and polytheism was denounced, along with the worship of idols.

The alphabet is the Canaanites' other lasting legacy. Sumerian cuneiform sign-script was invented before 3300 B.C.E. and gradually found its way to the Levant. Over time, the Canaanites transformed it into a phonetic alphabet (so called for the Phoenicians who were latter-day Canaanites). All later alphabetic writing systems, from the Greek and Roman to our own, are built on this achievement.

—*Emily Alward*

Further Reading

Albright, William Foxwell. *Yahweh and the Gods of Canaan*. London: The Athlone Press, 1968. Interesting survey of trade relations, the Canaanite pantheon, and Mesopotamian and Canaanite elements in Hebrew religion.

Fritz, Volkmar. "Israelites and Canaanites: You *Can* Tell Them Apart." *Biblical Archaeological Review* 28, no. 4 (July/August 2002): 28-31. Throws light on the differentiation between Israelite and other Canaanite residents in the early Iron Age.

Snell, Daniel C. *Life in the Ancient Near East*. New Haven, Conn.: Yale University Press, 1997. Emphasizes ties with Mesopotamia during this era.

Tubb, Jonathan N. *Canaanites*. Norman: University of Oklahoma Press, 1998. The most comprehensive study of Canaanite history and civilization written for the nonspecialist.

See also: c. 2687 B.C.E., Old Kingdom Period Begins in Egypt; c. 1280 B.C.E., Israelite Exodus from Egypt; c. 1250 B.C.E., Transmission of the European Alphabet; c. 1000 B.C.E., Establishment of the United Kingdom of Israel; c. 966 B.C.E., Building of the Temple of Jerusalem; c. 922 B.C.E., Establishment of the Kingdom of Israel.

c. 3000-c. 500 B.C.E.
Elamite Empire Rises in Near East

The empire of Elam, with its capital city at Susa, had a culture similar to that of other ancient Near Eastern civilizations, although its language was unrelated to any other. A loose federation of states, the Elamites gained and maintained their wealth largely through trade and the development of fine arts.

Locale: Elamite Empire (modern-day province of Khuzistan in southwestern Iran)

Categories: Prehistory and ancient cultures; trade and commerce

Key Figures

Peli (fl. c. 2500 B.C.E.), first king of the Awan Dynasty, r. c. twenty-sixth to twenty-fifth century B.C.E.

Untashagal (c. 1275-1240 B.C.E.), king of the Middle Elamite period, builder of the sanctuary of Tchoga Zanbil, r. c. thirteenth century B.C.E.

Summary of Event

Elam is mentioned many times in the Bible (for example, in Acts 2:9, Genesis 14:14 and 10:22, and Daniel 8:2), but rarely in the contemporary Mesopotamian sources in Sumerian and Akkadian scripts. Original clay tablets with texts containing relevant information are scarce and not fully understood because the language, Elamite, is neither Semitic nor Indo-European, and its relation to other languages is yet to be determined. Therefore, it is common practice to link the history of Elam to the chronology of other ancient Mesopotamian cultures, primar-

MAJOR DYNASTIES OF THE ELAMITE EMPIRE, C. 3000-C. 500 B.C.E.

OLD PERIOD, C. 3000-C. 1500

Dynasty	*Dates*
Awan Dynasty	c. 2600-c. 2100
Shimashki Dynasty	c. 2100-c. 1900
Elam Dynasty	c.1900-c. 1770
Babylonian Dynasty	c. 1770-c. 1500

MIDDLE PERIOD, C. 1450-C. 1100

Dynasty	*Dates*
Igehalkid Dynasty	c. 1350-c. 1200
Shutrukid Dynasty	c. 1205-c. 1100

LATE OR NEO-ELAMITE PERIOD, C.743-C. 500

Dynasty	*Dates*
Late Elam Dynasty	743-644

ily Sumerian and Akkadian, in the effort to establish general dates for events and stylistic developments in Elamite civilization.

There are three main periods in Elamite history: Old (c. 3000-c. 1500 B.C.E.), Middle (c. 1450-c. 1100 B.C.E.), and Late or Neo-Elamite (c.743-c. 500 B.C.E.). During the Old Elamite period, several ruling dynasties emerged: the kings of Awan (c. 2600-c. 2100 B.C.E.), the kings of Shimashki (c. 2100-c. 1900 B.C.E.), and the so-called grand regents (*sukkalmah* in Sumerian) who were Shimashki as well (c. 1900-c. 1500 B.C.E.). The earliest known king of the Awan Dynasty was Peli.

The Elamite Empire consisted of a loosely organized federation of states united around the powerful royal house. The Elamite system of royal inheritance was one of its chief strengths in maintaining an orderly transfer of power. The king's second-in-command was his brother, and his son was only third in the chain of power. The kingship thus cycled through all the brothers of a generation in a form of matrilineal succession before being passed down and government was a balance of regionalism and federalism. The population was prosperous, politically adept, and militarily confident. The capital city of Susa was a famous cultural center, renowned for its wealth, which resulted from its position as a crossroad of the trade caravan routes. The rulers were considered to be protected by the gods; numerous monuments in different media depict their military victories, enhanced with complex religious and ritualistic activities, created to glorify their deeds and to please their divine protectors. Elamite religion displayed many elements in common with the established belief-systems of other ancient cultures of Mesopotamia, which were predominately focused on earthly preparation for life after death. A professionally trained class of priests and priestesses was in charge of performing ceremonies for the departed that were intended to keep the soul from eternal unrest.

In the Old Elamite period, the empire's chief adversary was the kingdom of Ur. Indeed, King Shulgi of Ur (c. 2094-c. 2097 B.C.E.) conquered Elam for a period, until the Elamites rebelled—an event chiefly known through the laments and dirges written by the overthrown conquerors. Again Elam was conquered by the Babylonian king Hammurabi (c. 1810-c. 1750 B.C.E.), but regained its independence when Hammurabi's empire fell apart after his death. In the Middle Elamite period, the empire faced more aggressive and skilled enemies such as the Assyrians and Persians. During this era, the old system of inheritance broke down and was increasingly replaced by straightforward primogeniture, in which the eldest son inherited the throne.

During the Neo-Elamite period, terrible destruction was inflicted by the Assyrians. King Ashurbanipal was especially cruel: His sack of Susa in 641 B.C.E., in which the usual riot of looting and building destruction was capped by sowing the land with salt to make the fields sterile, mortally wounded the empire. The final days of Elam were recorded during the reign of Darius the Great (522-486 B.C.E.), the famous Achaemenid king who, after his military victory over Elam, tried to rebuild and proclaimed the ancient capital as one of the principal royal residences of the mighty Persian empire. However, Susa never recaptured its original glory, and the city was completely destroyed by Mongol invaders in the thirteenth century C.E.

The earliest Elamite masters were known as the skilled seal-makers. Numerous cylinder seals, often made of black bitumen and faience, were incised with religious scenes of offering and worship. In addition, the artwork expresses preferences for fantastic hybrids, bizarre monsters, and a wide range of horned animals. These objects were commonly used to seal, sign, and identify important documents, storage jars, and other public and private possessions.

An excellent example of Elamite architecture is the sanctuary of Dur Untash (present-day Tchoga Zanbil), near Susa, dating from the thirteenth century B.C.E. Originally the structure had an outer wall that measured

3,937 feet (1,200 meters) by 2,625 feet (800 meters), while an inner wall enclosed the ziggurat, with courts measuring 1,313 feet (400 meters) on each side. The wall was pierced by seven gates, all leading to the central court. The large principal gate, called the Royal Gate, was decorated with glazed bricks and "nails" with pommels holding flat tiles in place. These pommels bore the name of the builder of the entire complex, King Untashagal (c. 1275-c. 1240 B.C.E.). The ziggurat reached a height of 171 feet (52 meters) and had a temple on the top dedicated to the god Inshushinak, "king of gods." The basic structure was built of sun-dried brick with decorative details of glazed tiles and enameled bricks. The presence of nine other temples in the vicinity of this monument, all dedicated to different local gods, emphasize the complexity of the Elamite pantheon.

In addition to applied arts and architecture, Elamite masters were very skilled in metalwork. One of the most celebrated works is the bronze statue from Susa of Queen Napirasu, wife of Untashagal, created c. 1300 B.C.E. It now resides in the Louvre Museum in Paris. The figure is only 51 inches (1.3 meters) tall and weighs 376 pounds (829 kilograms). It is not known how it was made, except that the sculptor cast the statue with a solid bronze core, rather than the hollow core that was the typical technique of the time. The head is missing, but its overall sense of dignity, elegance, and grace reveals the noble character of the depicted individual. The king's wife is presented with her hands crossed in prayer, and according to the inscription preserved on the skirt, it was intended to be a permanent votive offering in the temple, commissioned by the queen herself.

SIGNIFICANCE

The Elamite Empire was chiefly sustained by a flexible governmental system, military prowess, and wealth from trade. Despite periodic conquest by powerful neighbors, the empire lasted for approximately twenty-five hundred years and reached high levels of artistic achievement. Although other empires and dynasties in the ancient Near East came and went, Elam maintained an extraordinary degree of cultural continuity.

—Rozmeri Basic

FURTHER READING

Bottéro, Jean, Clarisse Herrenschmidt, and Jean-Pierre Vernant. *Ancestor of the West: Writing, Reasoning, and Religion in Mesopotamia, Elam, and Greece.* Translated by Teresa Lavender Fagan. Chicago: University of Chicago Press, 2000. Three essays on the ancient world, two of which discuss the position of writing and religion in Elam.

Carter, Elizabeth, and Matthew W. Stopler. *Elam: Surveys of Political History and Archaeology.* Berkeley: University of California Press, 1985. A survey of visual monuments of Elam with numerous archaeological site maps and line drawings.

Edwards, I. E. S., C. J. Gadd, and N. G. L. Hammond, eds. *Early History of the Middle East.* Vol. 1, part 2 of *The Cambridge Ancient History.* 3d ed. New York: Cambridge University Press, 1971. An authoritative history of the ancient world. This volume covers ancient Elam and its relationship with neighboring powers.

Ghirshman, Roman. *Iran from Earliest Times to the Islamic Conquest.* New York: Penguin, 1978. A comprehensive, chronological survey of Iranian history and art.

Potts, D. T. *The Archaeology of Elam: Formation and Transformation of an Ancient Iranian State.* New York: Cambridge University Press, 1999. An up-to-date synthesis of archaeology and history. Includes copious illustrations, plates, and tables.

SEE ALSO: c. 2900-c. 2340 B.C.E., Early Dynastic Period Flourishes in Southern Mesopotamia; c. 1770 B.C.E., Promulgation of Hammurabi's Code; c. 883-c. 824 B.C.E., Second Assyrian Empire Displays Military Prowess; c. 705-330 B.C.E., Founding and Flourishing of the Achaemenian Dynasty.

2953-2838 B.C.E. traditionally
REIGN OF CHINA'S LEGENDARY FIRST RULER, FU XI

Fu Xi, China's mythical first ruler, is said to have developed animal husbandry, musical instruments, the calendar, and the eight trigrams of the Yijing divination text as well as to have made marriage an institution.

LOCALE: China
CATEGORIES: Prehistory and ancient cultures; agriculture; cultural and intellectual history; religion; science and technology

KEY FIGURE

Fu Xi (Fu Hsi; c. 3000-mid-twenty-ninth century B.C.E.), China's legendary and mythical first ruler

SUMMARY OF EVENT

According to Chinese mythology, the creator of the universe, Pangu (P'an-ku), lived during the Creation and Prehistory period, and during the Legendary period (c. 3000-2700 B.C.E.), the three first emperors of China (the San Huang) ruled. Fu Xi was the first of these emperors and the founder of China. The others were Shen Nong (Shen Nung, known as the divine farmer) and Sui Ren (Sui Jen, the fire starter), or alternatively Huangdi (Huang-ti, the Yellow Emperor), and the three of them developed early Chinese civilization.

The only sources of information from this prehistorical period are fragments and various versions of myths or stories preserved through oral traditions. These generally credit Fu Xi with numerous accomplishments. The archaeological evidence suggests Fu Xi might have been a great tribal leader of the Yangshao, a neolithic culture that flourished in the Yellow River region in north China. The discoveries at Banpo (Panp'o), near the present city of Xi'an (Hsien), Shaanxi, show a people who used fishhooks and arrowheads, made pottery, wove cloth, grew crops, and raised animals.

In the historical records, Fu Xi was originally a god. Classical sources from the Zhou Dynasty (1066-256 B.C.E.) mention him as the earliest primeval god and the first of the three cosmogonical gods. However, by the late Han Dynasty (206 B.C.E.-220 C.E.), Fu Xi the god had been reinvented as a historical, part-human king. Wang Yi (89-158 C.E.), in *Chu ci zhang ju* (2d century C.E.; *Ch'u tz'u: The Songs of the South*, 1959), described Fu Xi as an ancient king and composer who created the zither. Wang Jia (fourth century C.E.), in *Shi yi ji* (4th century C.E.; researches into lost records), described him as a god on an earthly throne.

According to legend, Fu Xi had a miraculous conception. In a mythical earthly paradise called Huaxu, a maiden stepped in the giant footprint of the thunder god who lived in Thunder Marsh, then saw a shooting star. She became pregnant and later gave birth to Fu Xi.

Fu Xi became a great tribal ruler and inventor. He discovered how to domesticate wild animals, herd livestock, breed silkworms, hunt wild game, fish for food, cook food over fire, and smelt iron. He invented fishing nets after observing spiders and a knotted cord for measuring distance and computing time. The emperor also established China's first social and political systems. He set up imperial government, different ranks within a state, and a social order using clan names for taxation. He is said to have created the one hundred Chinese family names. Furthermore, Fu Xi established marriage laws, such as the decree that two people must have different family names in order to get married.

During the Han Dynasty, Fu Xi was paired with the popular, mythical creation goddess, Nu Wa (also Nü-kua, Nu Kwa, and Nuwa). Before the Han Dynasty, Nu Wa was a major, independent deity. She was named Jiu Tian Xuannu, the Dark Lady of the Ninth Heaven, before she descended to earth. According to Daoist canon, she created humanity from yellow earth and mud, and she later saved humankind after a disaster.

Han Dynasty pictorial representations of Fu Xi and Nu Wa show the divine couple with human heads and upper torsos and dragon or serpentine lower bodies. They are linked together by intertwined dragon tails. He holds a carpenter's square, representing earth, and she carries compasses, symbolizing sky, so that together they represent order and proper conduct. Early murals from the Eastern Han show a child between them.

According to *Du yi zhi* (ninth century C.E.; records of strange events) by Li Rong of the Tang Dynasty (618-907 C.E.), Fu Xi and Nu Wa were brother and sister, living on Mount Kunlun. Because a devastating flood had destroyed humanity, there were no other people in the world. They wanted to become husband and wife but were ashamed. Therefore, they prayed and asked for a sign from heaven: If all the misty vapor or clouds gathered, they would become husband and wife. The vapor gathered, so they united in a yin-yang (male-female) relationship and created a new race of people. A variation on this is a myth from the southern Yao and Miao peoples. In this story, Fu Xi and Nu Wa are peasant siblings who stayed inside a giant calabash fruit and thus survived a great flood that had drowned everyone else on earth.

Fu Xi is said to have developed the eight trigrams (*bagua*), which were the origin of Chinese writing or calligraphy. His trigrams became the basis of the early *Yijing* (eighth to third century B.C.E.; English translation, 1876; also known as *Book of Changes*, 1986), possibly the most significant ancient Chinese classic that has survived. Fu Xi's discovery of the eight trigrams is documented in the "Great Treatise," which was originally oral instructions developed during the Warring States Period (475-221 B.C.E.) on how to use the *Yijing* and later appended to the work itself. According to the treatise, Fu Xi was standing on the banks of the Yellow River when a dragon-horse (a creature with a dragon's head and a horse's body) suddenly emerged from the water. In another version, the river creature is a tortoise, which was a sacred creature known for its longevity. This dragon steed or tortoise had a series of symbols or markings on its back that formed a meaningful pattern. Fu Xi drew the markings in the sand and interpreted these symbols as a key to understanding the universal laws of existence. Then he wrote these markings, the eight trigrams, in what later became known as the Yellow River map.

The eight trigrams were eight groups, each a different combination of three lines, broken and solid, arranged in ranks. These line groupings represented and classified all naturally occurring phenomena: heaven or sky, earth, water, fire (lightning and the sun), mountains, wind and wood, lake, and thunder. Later the trigrams were developed into sixty-four hexagrams (sixty-four six-line symbols). The trigrams became the first part of the *Yijing* and a system of fortune telling and formed the basis of the Chinese writing system. In Daoist temples, Fu Xi is usually depicted carrying a panel with inscriptions of the eight trigrams. In a Song Dynasty portrait by Ma Lin, he has the long nails typical of scholars, and the eight trigrams are shown on the floor. Looking up at Fu Xi is a tortoise, the animal whose shells were used as oracle bones.

Another essential element in traditional cosmology, *feng shui*, is said to have developed from Fu Xi's discoveries. *Feng* means wind, and *shui* means water, basic elements of the environment. According to traditional Chinese beliefs, these elements, and indeed all aspects of nature, are held in a complex, subtle, but absolutely symmetrical balance, on which life itself depends. By aligning oneself and one's environment through careful positioning with regard to these opposing forces, one can promote the flow of energy and therefore maintain health and prosperity. From comprehensive observations of nature, Fu Xi reportedly became aware of the powerful but invisible forces of life. His idea of *qi* (*chi*), or flowing energy, and the cosmic yin-yang duality (female-male, dark-light, and so on) are at the core of many traditional Chinese sciences (including medicine), aesthetics, and ritual practices. Because the concepts are ancient enough to have been attributed to Fu Xi, it can be seen that progenitors of the earliest Chinese dynasties were quite sophisticated and had already established a consistent philosophical system that would form the intellectual cornerstone of an entire civilization.

THE SAN HUANG AND THE WUDI

THE SAN HUANG (THREE KINGS/AUGUSTS)
Fu Xi
Shen Nong
Sui Ren

THE WUDI (FIVE LEGENDARY EMPERORS)
Huangdi
Zhuanxu
Diku
Yao
Shun

Note: The San Huang are also identified as Fu Xi, Shen Nong, and Huangdi, and the Wudi as Shaohao, Gaoyang, Gaoxin, Yao, and Shun.

SIGNIFICANCE

Fu Xi is one of the most significant mythological and legendary gods or heroes in China. According to the many legends, he was a deity, the first legendary emperor of China, and the brother and husband of Nu Wa. Their union created a new race of humanity. His inventions had an impact in all areas of life. Finally, as a scholar, Fu Xi was the first to observe heavenly and earthly phenomena and conclude that there were universal laws of existence and that everything was composed of *qi*, or energy. His conclusion that everything was subject to change, to the balance and imbalances of yin and yang forces and to symmetries and reactions, became the basis of major Chinese philosophical and intellectual systems.

—*Alice Myers*

FURTHER READING

Birrell, Anne. *Chinese Mythology: An Introduction*. Baltimore: The Johns Hopkins University Press, 1993.

Includes a well-researched discussion of the early sources of information on Fu Xi. Contains a bibliography, illustrations, and glossary.

Christie, Anthony. *Chinese Mythology.* New York: Peter Bedrick Books, 1985. Contains many color plates and illustrations, including the famous Song Dynasty portrait of Fu Xi by Ma Lin. Includes information on the Yangshao culture and the association of Fu Xi and Nu Wa.

Collins, Roy. *The Fu Hsi I Ching*. Lanham, Md.: University Press of America, 1993. Illustrated, with an analysis of Fu Xi's original trigrams and the later changes.

Katz, Brian. *Deities and Demons of the Far East*. New York: Metro Books, 1995. Discusses Fu Xi in the context of the *Yijing*, Nu Wa, and the ten legendary rulers. Illustrated, with a bibliography.

Ke, Yuan. *Dragons and Dynasties*. Selected and translated by Kim Echlin and Nie Zhixiong. New York: Penguin, 1993. Illustrated. Describes Fu Xi in a story about creation.

MacKenzie, Donald A. *China and Japan: Myths and Legends*. London: Studio Editions, 1994. Discusses Fu Xi's accomplishments and the Daoists' view of Fu Xi.

Stevens, Keith G. *Chinese Mythological Gods*. Oxford, England: Oxford University Press, 2001. Discusses Fu Xi and other mythical founders and legendary gods and heroes. Includes color photos, chronology, and bibliography.

SEE ALSO: c. 7500 B.C.E., East Asian Grain Cultivation Begins; c. 6000-c. 1500 B.C.E., Yangshao and Longshan Cultures Flourish in China; c. 2682 B.C.E., Legendary Founding of China by Huangdi; c. 2600 B.C.E., Leizu Discovers Silk Making; c. 500 B.C.E., Acupuncture Develops in China.

c. 2900-c. 2340 B.C.E.

EARLY DYNASTIC PERIOD FLOURISHES IN SOUTHERN MESOPOTAMIA

During the Early Dynastic period, Mesopotamia emerged into history as it pursued urbanization, writing, and the arts and gradually moved away from politically independent city-states.

LOCALE: Mesopotamia (now Iraq and parts of Syria, Iran, and Turkey)

CATEGORY: Prehistory and ancient cultures

KEY FIGURES

Gilgamesh (fl. c. twenty-eighth to twenty-seventh century B.C.E.), semilegendary king of Uruk, r. c. 2700 B.C.E.

Mebaragesi (fl. c. twenty-eighth to twenty-seventh century B.C.E.), earliest historical ruler of Kish, r. c. 2700 B.C.E.

Eannatum (d. c. 2425 B.C.E.), ruler of Lagash, r. c. 2450 B.C.E.

Lugalzagesi (fl. twenty-fourth century B.C.E.), king, r. c. 2375-c. 2350 B.C.E.

SUMMARY OF EVENT

The Early Dynastic period falls between the so-called Jemdet Nasr period (c. 3200-2900 B.C.E.) and the Old Akkadian period (c. 2340-2159) when the northern Semite Sargon of Akkad established the first Mesopotamian empire from his capital Akkad (central Iraq, exact location unknown) by defeating one Sumerian ruler after another. It therefore is sometimes referred to as the Pre-Sargonic period. Archaeological excavations east of Baghdad, Iraq, in the Lower Diyala region and elsewhere have revealed three subdivisions: Early Dynastic I (2900-2700), II (2700-2600), and III (2600-2340).

Although the sources for Early Dynastic I and II are primarily archaeological, documentation exists for Early Dynastic III in the form of administrative, economic, military, religious, and literary texts. Early Dynastic II is also referred to as the Heroic Age because later epics are often set in that time, with such protagonists as Gilgamesh, the semilegendary king of Uruk (modern Warka, site northwest of modern-day Muqaiyir, Iraq).

Mesopotamian tradition holds that a Great Flood destroyed nearly all of humankind in the interval between the Jemdet Nasr and Early Dynastic periods. From a modern perspective, the beginning of the Early Dynastic period does not represent a sharp break from the preceding Jemdet Nasr period, which derives its name from an archaeological site 62 miles (100 kilometers) south of Baghdad. The tendency of modern scholarship is to regard Jemdet Nasr as a local variation of the homogeneous Uruk culture that spread from southern Mesopotamia as far as Egypt.

Therefore, the Early Dynastic period can be viewed as a cultural continuation of the Uruk culture (4000-2900 B.C.E.). Also, the notion that the Sumerians were newcomers who entered southern Mesopotamia shortly before 3000 and that Semites appeared later is no longer generally accepted. The population of southern Iraq is now viewed as widely diverse from the beginning, perhaps as early as 5500.

Continuity aside, two fundamental changes did occur in the Early Dynastic period. First, for reasons still obscure, people actively abandoned small village sites and moved to larger villages, which then developed into great cities. By Early Dynastic III, according to one calculation, 80 percent of the population lived in imposing cities of more than 100 acres (41 hectares). This process, perhaps originally a mode of self-defense against hostile nomadic incursions, may be traced back to the middle of the Uruk period. Though cities less dense and complex did exist earlier, this period was characterized by a relentless urbanization. Second, the wedge-shaped writing that had been invented about 3200 B.C.E. matured and was able to represent complex thoughts rather than mere lists as in the Jemdet Nasr texts. As documentation appeared, individuals and their exploits emerged into the light of history. Literacy was exchanged for protoliteracy.

However, it remains impossible to write a straightforward narrative history of this period because the sources remain problematic. For example, the Sumerian King List, long viewed as fundamental, is a curious mixture of fact and fantasy. In its present form, an inscription on a block of stone dating to the later Isin Dynasty (c. 1800 B.C.E.), it describes kingship as having descended from heaven before the Great Flood. Five antediluvian dynasties in succession hold this kingship, an ill-defined hegemony, for well over 250,000 years. Though from archaeological evidence, Uruk is known to have been an important city in this period, its name does not occur in the antediluvian list. After the flood, kingship is again described as descending from heaven, first to the city of Kish, 9 miles (15 kilometers) east of Babylon, and then passing sequentially by force to thirteen other dynasties in eight different cities.

The twenty-second king of the dynasty of Kish, Mebaragesi, has the distinction of being the earliest historical ruler because two of his royal inscriptions survive. He fought against Elam in southwestern modern-day Iran, an implacable enemy that would later wage war against the Akkadian kings and subjugate the Third Dynasty of Ur (2112-2004). He also dedicated a temple to the god Enlil at Nippur (modern Niffar), which, like Mecca, was the sacred city of the land. The Sumerian King List, however, ascribes to him an incredible reign of nine hundred years. Furthermore, just five other names in the lengthy list are attested elsewhere in inscriptions. Only after Early Dynastic III do the lengths of reigns and royal names become fairly reliable. Finally, the Sumerian King List often presents dynasties as sequential when they may actually have overlapped chronologically. This scheme may reflect the ideology of the Isin Dynasty that rulership from time immemorial passed by divine rotation to one and only one house and was now legitimately in their hands. Probably reliable, however, is the early importance attached to the city-state of Kish located on one of the major bronze routes. In later times, the title "king of Kish" became an honorific implying high hegemonic control.

Despite such troublesome sources, an approximate sketch may be drawn of the period from archaeology and textual materials. In a narrow strip of land about 10,000 square miles (25,900 square kilometers) in extent, there existed a least thirteen and perhaps as many as thirty individual city-states, each of which was dedicated to and in a sense owned by a patron god or goddess. Ur (now Tell al-Muqaiyar), for example, was at the disposal of the moon-god Nanna. Though independent, these population centers may have shared, in the absence of nationalism, some vague sense of belonging to greater Mesopotamia, with its symbolic focal point at Nippur.

A city-state consisted of the city proper and its suburbs, satellite towns and villages, and agricultural and grazing areas. In Early Dynastic III, Lagash (now Al-Hibeh) in the far south included three major centers, twenty-two towns, and about forty villages in an area of about 618 square miles (1,600 square kilometers). Within the city proper, the characteristically oval-shaped temple enclosure figured prominently as a center of economic life. Here were craft workshops, bakeries, and storage facilities for agricultural implements and harvests. By older interpretation, all citizens, including the ruler, as servants of the god or goddess, were constrained to pool labor and resources in the fields and irrigation dikes for their divine masters. Private ownership was virtually nonexistent.

Perhaps partly valid for some city-states, this model of theocratic socialism has now been challenged as an over-generalization from limited source materials. Specialists on Sumer now argue that family groups did own land independently of the temple and that in some instances so-called temple estates were actually the property of the ruler and his family. Certain duties such as shepherding, weaving, and labor details were also a part of citizenship, and secular and sacred spheres of interest were probably not sharply distinguished. Agriculture, including herding, was the principal economic activity, although some luxury trade did exist. Slavery appears to have been an unimportant source of labor. Women were engaged not only as weavers but also as priestesses and high officials in some temple complexes.

In the Early Dynastic period, cities proper were generally encircled by walls. No longer only a bulwark against hostile external pressures, they also reflected the internal warfare between city-states characteristic of this period. Perhaps changing environmental conditions brought about these conflicts that often arose from boundary disputes. The conflicts may even reflect a desire to regain a larger unity as conceived in the time of the Kish hegemony. During this period, at the same time the politically independent city-states were directing their efforts outward (centrifugal particularism), there emerged a tendency toward unification (centripetalism) and wider domineering.

After the idealized hegemony of Kish, power shifted, according to the later epics, to Gilgamesh's Uruk, but more likely, by historical records, to Ur. A hundred years later, Elam and two foreign dynasties, Awan and Hamazi, dominated part of Sumer. The sources then focus on Lagash and its ruler Eannatum, who not only drove out the Elamites but also attacked Ur and Kish. Eannatum's copiously documented war with Umma to the northwest is commemorated in the famous Stela of the Vultures (c. 2450 B.C.E., a clay tablet portraying Eannatum leading a phalanx as they trample over their enemies, whose bodies are being attacked by vultures). His dominion came to end after assaults from Kish and Adab (now Bismaya). A hundred years later, during a period of anarchy, Mari (now Tell Hariri) came to the fore and assisted Umma in an unsuccessful war against Lagash. After corrupt priests had taken over Lagash for twenty years, they were removed by Uruk-Agina (c. 2350), the earliest social reformer. After centuries of defeat (c. 2340), Uruk's ruler Lugalzagesi from Umma destroyed Lagash and established the prototype of an empire.

SIGNIFICANCE

In an area nearly devoid of natural resources, the Mesopotamians set the patterns for later city life. Challenged by a semiarid climate with rainfall inadequate for agriculture, they established a sophisticated irrigation system. Refining cuneiform writing, they left behind some of the world's earliest historical documentation and literature. The institution of the first schools, the extraordinary level of craftsmanship at the burial pits at Ur with their retainer sacrifices, and the building skills found there and elsewhere merely suggest the advances of this period.

—*David J. Ladouceur*

FURTHER READING

Kuhrt, Amelie. *The Ancient Near East, c. 3000-330 B.C.* Vol. 1. New York: Routledge, 1995. An authoritative account that examines Mesopotamia and the surrounding area. Excellent bibliography.

Postgate, J. N. *Early Mesopotamia: Society and Economy at the Dawn of History.* New York: Routledge, 1992. A detailed account of institutions and their roles. Bibliography.

Roux, Georges. *Ancient Iraq*. Baltimore: Pelican Books, 1966. An accessible account of Mesopotamia during ancient times.

Snell, Daniel C. *Life in the Ancient Near East, 3100-332 B.C.* New Haven, Conn.: Yale University Press, 1997. A description of daily life in ancient times in the Near East, including Mesopotamia.

SEE ALSO: c. 6200-c. 3800 B.C.E., Ubaid Culture Thrives in Mesopotamia; c. 5500-c. 4500 B.C.E., Halafian Culture Flourishes in Northern Mesopotamia; c. 4000 B.C.E., Sumerian Civilization Begins in Mesopotamia; c. 3800 B.C.E., Cities and Civic Institutions Are Invented in Mesopotamia; c. 3100 B.C.E., Sumerians Invent Writing; c. 2340 B.C.E., Sumerian Uruk-Agina Makes Social and Political Reforms; c. 2334-c. 2279 B.C.E., Sargon of Akkad Establishes the Akkadian Dynasty; c. 2000 B.C.E., Composition of the Gilgamesh Epic.

RELATED ARTICLE in *Great Lives from History: The Ancient World*: Enheduanna.

c. 2700-c. 1400 B.C.E.
GASH CIVILIZATION THRIVES IN AFRICA

The location of the Gash civilization, at a delta and the crossroads of several cultural zones, made the area an important center of trade.

LOCALE: Gash Delta (near the borders of present-day Sudan and Ethiopia)
CATEGORIES: Prehistory and ancient cultures; trade and commerce

SUMMARY OF EVENT

The Gash civilization was established east of the confluence of the Atbara and Nile Rivers. It emerged from a coalescence of populations using the land in the greater Butana Delta. The people of Gash were a combination of hunting-gathering populations and peoples from at least one of the Nubian chiefdoms that emerged adjacent to the important land routes to the Red Sea. Located at the crossroads of several cultural zones, the Gash society was able to exploit trade opportunities between the river delta lands and the plains west of the Red Sea.

Although the Gash civilization coincided with the Egyptian empires and Kerma's political occupation and control of Upper Nubia in the one thousand years between 2500 and 1500 B.C.E., the Gash political empire can be divided into four distinct periods, each lasting several hundred years. The first period was the early Gash civilization, 2700-2300 B.C.E. The middle Gash civilization, from 2300 to 1900 B.C.E., roughly corresponds to the First Intermediate Period (c. 2160-c. 2055) in Egyptian historiography. The third period, the late Gash civilization, lasted from about 1700 to 1400 B.C.E. After 1400, Gash continued to exist as a distinct culture but was increasingly politically dependent on the emerging kingdom of D'mt, as it was referred to in ancient south Arabian script. The first three periods of Gash development are defined based partially on the types of cultural influences and developments that took place internally and partially on the economic interdependence that developed between this small kingdom and larger states such as Egypt and Nubia, Kerma, Napata, and Meroë. Gash owes its prosperity to its geographic location, which was a benefit because of the fluctuations in Red Sea trade routes. In certain eras, Gash traded primarily with the northern trade circuit, and in other eras, it depended more on the southeastern networks.

The early Gash civilization arose from the settlement of Butuan (Butana) descendants in the Gash Delta lowlands perhaps as early as the fourth and definitely by the third millennium B.C.E. The Butuans had been hunters and gatherers but began to domesticate cattle and grains south of Egypt. There is some archaeological evidence that camels may have been domesticated in this region as early as the fourth millennium B.C.E. Evidence that camels were kept more regularly as domesticated pack animals in this region can be traced back as early as the second millennium B.C.E. The transformation of economic practices and proximity to emerging kingdoms produced a hierarchy in the proto-Gash settlements.

Archaeological evidence of the hierarchical bureaucracies that began to emerge includes lidded pots, maces, staffs, and other such regalia and material culture common to chiefdoms or kingdoms. There is an increased presence of stones marking burial sites and of large residential settlements in the archaeological record beginning with the era designated the early Gash civilization. This archaeological evidence supports the idea that there was a shift in types of material wealth and settlement patterns that accompanied the more sedentary lifestyle of the Gash civilization, which emerged with less food collection and more food production.

SIGNIFICANCE

Gash Delta trade was tied early on to activity in the kingdoms of Egypt and later Kerma in Upper Nubia. Lucrative interregional trade in ancient times was important to political power. Despite its apparent dependence on Egypt and Kerma, trade in the Gash Delta survived the political and economic collapse of those larger and more powerful states. After 2300 B.C.E., traders of the delta region were able to tap into the trade networks in the southeast on the Ethiopian plateau. By shifting from the northern Red Sea networks to the networks on the western edge of the northern Ethiopian plateau (modern-day Eritrea and Tigray), the Gash Delta continued to participate in and benefit from Red Sea trade. Red Sea trade in the fourth and third millennia B.C.E. linked Africa and Arabia in trade exchanges that were accompanied by cultural influences in both directions.

Two separate and distinctive northeastern African pottery styles were traded to the western shores of Arabia via the Gash Delta. The two potteries are known to scholars as Kerma pottery and Tigray pottery. The earliest Tigray pottery created and unearthed in this coastal region has decorative motifs that appear to be variants of one widespread complex. The Kerma style displays signs of Egyptian influence that were most likely brought in through Gash imitation and innovation of the Egyptian fashion. The coastal pottery complex has been dated to between the late fourth and mid-second millennium B.C.E.

The Gash Delta was the intermediary territory that linked the Horn of Africa, the Sudan, Arabia, and Egypt in a complex multiethnic cultural and economic exchange. The Gash civilization was geographically well positioned to act as the liaison among these various cultures of the greater Red Sea region, and it was sufficiently diverse and pioneering to act as mediator in the transmission of cultural knowledge and ideas.

The western part of the Tigray region was associated with Gash Delta culture, and the eastern part belonged to a cultural complex that had links with Nubia and lands across the Red Sea. The eastern and western regions of Tigray were united under the monarchy of D'mt centered in the northern Ethiopian plateau (this area is now known as Eritrea and Tigray). The time referred to as the age of the pharaohs in Egypt was preceded by a period of smaller chiefdoms and kingdoms that benefited from Red Sea and interregional trade. Throughout the time of the pharaohs, there were in fact a number of smaller states, that were able to thrive and perhaps challenged or acted as a counterbalance to Egyptian power outside of the center of the pharaoh's state. At the same time, settlement in the Nile-Red Sea corridor on the borderlands of what became the Nubian and Egyptian kingdoms contributed to the significant outcome of stratified and hierarchical social systems among the Gash.

—*Catherine Cymone Fourshey*

FURTHER READING

Abdel-Magid, Anwar. *Plant Domestication in the Middle Nile Basin: An Archaeoethnobotanical Case Study.* Oxford, England: Oxford University Press, 1989. Focuses on archaeo-ethnobotany of the Nile region, giving a historical sense of ancient plant cultivation in Sudan.

Connah, Graham. *African Civilizations: Precolonial Cities and States in Tropical Africa: An Archaeological Perspective.* Reprint. New York: Cambridge University Press, 1994. A historical account of ancient African towns that draws from archaeological data. Includes a section on ancient Egypt and surrounding urban towns.

Fattovich, Rodolfo, Andrea Manzo, and Donatella Usai. "Gash Delta Archaeological Project: 1991, 1992-1993, 1993-1994 Field Seasons." *Nyame Akuma* 42 (December, 1994): 14-18. This article is somewhat technical and gives an archaeological perspective on the Gash Delta. Fattovich has produced numerous other works on the history of populations and state formation in the Sudan-Ethiopia borderlands.

Iliffe, John. *Africans: The History of a Continent.* New York: Cambridge University Press, 1995. A general textbook on African history from ancient times to the twentieth century.

SEE ALSO: c. 6000-c. 1000 B.C.E., Omotics Advance Farming Practices in Horn of Africa; c. 2687 B.C.E., Old Kingdom Period Begins in Egypt; c. 2200-1500 B.C.E., Kerma Kingdom Develops and Dominates Lower Nubia; c. 1900-1527? B.C.E., Kerma Kingdom Rules Nubia.

c. 2687 B.C.E.

Old Kingdom Period Begins in Egypt

In the Old Kingdom, the Egyptians built on the advances of the Predynastic Period and First and Second Dynasties to achieve an unparalleled level of accomplishments.

Locale: Egypt
Category: Prehistory and ancient cultures

Key Figures

Zoser (c. 2700-c. 2650 B.C.E.), Third Dynasty king, r. 2687-2650 B.C.E.
Imhotep (fl. twenty-seventh century B.C.E.), Zoser's architect
Khufu (Cheops; fl. twenty-sixth century B.C.E.), Fourth Dynasty king, r. 2589-2566 B.C.E.
Khafre (Chephren; fl. twenty-sixth century B.C.E.), Fourth Dynasty king, r. 2558-2532 B.C.E.
Pepi II (fl. twenty-third century B.C.E.), Sixth Dynasty king, r. 2278-2184 B.C.E.

Summary of Event

The Old Kingdom (c. 2687-c. 2125 B.C.E.), the pinnacle of Egyptian civilization, includes the Third through Eighth Dynasties and was characterized by two opposing tendencies. In the early part of this period, there was an evolving concentration of all power in the central figure of the king. The architectural symbol of this centralization, the pyramid, gives this period its second name, the Pyramid Age. Later, a gradual tendency toward decentralization began, which led to the ephemeral reigns of the kings of the Seventh and Eighth Dynasties (c. 2180-c. 2160). They, in turn, ushered in the First Intermediate Period (c. 2160-c. 2055 B.C.E.), once described, in overdrawn terms, as an interval of anarchy.

The term Old Kingdom is an invention of the nineteenth century. From an Egyptian perspective, there may have been no sharp break because the dynasty's founder may have been either related by marriage to or a son of the Second Dynasty (c. 2775-c. 2687 B.C.E.) ruler Khasekemwy. Of the kings of the Third Dynasty (c. 2687-c. 2613), the most illustrious was Netjerikhet, better known as Zoser, but also known as Djoser. He was either the first king of the Third Dynasty (r. c. 2687-c. 2650) or the second king (r. 2667-2650) if an obscure predecessor, Nebka, is inserted.

Twenty-five hundred years after Zoser's death, the priests of the god Khnum at Elephantine, an island near modern Aswān, forged an inscription in his name to assert their rights to land against claims of the priests of Isis, an action testifying to the ruler's enduring prestige. He organized the construction of the first monumental set of stone buildings in the world, the Step Pyramid complex at Saqqara, south of Cairo.

His architect was Imhotep, the Leonardo da Vinci of the Pyramid Age. High priest of Heliopolis (now in a Cairo suburb), royal treasurer, administrator of the Great Palace, builder, and sculptor were just some of the recorded titles and labels of this versatile genius. Imhotep later became the patron saint of scribes and a virtual god of healing, whom the conquering Greeks equated to the healer Aesclepius. Zoser's pyramid, a symbol of the primordial mound on which the god Atum arose to initiate creation, ascended in six unequal steps to 204 feet (62 meters). An encircling wall, thirteen of whose fourteen gates were false, encompassed a mortuary complex in which the spirit of the king could dwell and endlessly celebrate the *heb-sed*, the festival of renewal. Within an enclosed offering structure known as a *serdab* ("cellar" in Arabic) was discovered the earliest-known life-size royal sculpture, a limestone statue of Zoser in which his *ka* (spiritual double) could reside and receive offerings of food or incense.

Zoser's three successors apparently were not as distinguished. Sekhemkhet (r. c. 2648-c. 2640) began but did not complete a similar complex at Saqqara. Khaba (r. c. 2640-c. 2637) also left behind an unfinished smaller step pyramid at Zawiyet el-Aryan, just south of modern Cairo. The unsuccessful attempt to build a geometrically true pyramid at Meidum near the Faiyum region, many scholars now believe, should be ascribed to the Fourth Dynasty king, Snefru (r. c. 2613-2589) and not Huni (r. c. 2637-c. 2613), the final ruler of the Third Dynasty.

The names of three kings of the Fourth Dynasty (c. 2613-2494 B.C.E.)—Khufu, Khafre, and Menkaure (Mycerinus; r. 2532-c. 2503)—stand out, not so much for their recorded exploits but more for their pyramids of extraordinary magnitude on the Giza plateau. The founder of the dynasty was Snefru, perhaps a son of Huni; he apparently legitimized his rule by marrying Hetep-heres, the daughter of Huni and mother-to-be of Khufu.

Unlike his successors, Snefru is remembered in later tradition as a genial sovereign who became the object of cults in certain areas such as the turquoise mines of Sinai. The Meidum pyramid's new east-west orientation perhaps reflects a shift in emphasis from stellar to solar cults. Its smooth-faced sides may also reflect new Heliopolitan doctrines. The strange Bent Pyramid and Red Pyramid are also ascribed to him.

His successor Khufu constructed the Great Pyramid at Giza, one of the Seven Wonders of the Ancient World. Ironically, few sources survive for this king who later developed a tyrannical reputation, perhaps simply inferred from his immense project. One image of him that survives is a 3-inch (8-centimeter) ivory figurine that sharply contrasts with his pyramid, which rose 481 feet (147 meters). A later successor, Khafre, built another pyramid at Giza, 448 feet (136 meters) high, as well as the Sphinx, perhaps a guardian for his complex. Menkaure's pyramid, the smallest at 228 feet (70 meters), completes the tripartite symbol of this period. The shabby tomb of his son and successor, Shepsekhaf (r. c. 2503-c. 2498), suggests declining resources and unrest.

The Westcar papyrus contains a folklore account of the origins of the Fifth Dynasty (c. 2494-c. 2345 B.C.E.). The Sun god Ra (Re) allegedly had relations with the wife of a high priest of Heliopolis. From their union came triplets, all supposedly destined to become kings of Egypt. At least two related historical figures partially confirm this story, Sahure (r. c. 2487-2475) and Neferirkare (r. c. 2475-c. 2455). Dedicated to the god Ra, this line of Sun kings built sun-temples, the first, in the desert at Abu-Gurob between Giza and Saqqara, in the reign of Userkaf (r. c. 2494-c. 2487). Within these temples, large masonry obelisks were built on a podium. At Abusir, they constructed pyramids that were small relative to those at Giza. Despite these changes among the elite, the power of local gods apparently continued unabated.

The reigns of many of these kings are poorly documented. In the pyramid of Unas (r. c. 2375-c. 2345) were the *Pyramid Texts* (c. 2350-2100 B.C.E.; English translation, 1924), the world's earliest religious literature. The purpose of these magical and ritualistic spells was to allow the king to pass into the celestial realms. The death of Unas led to some instability because he left behind no heir.

The Sixth Dynasty (c. 2345-c. 2181 B.C.E.) was marked by possible regicide, conspiracy, decentralization, and the fiscally unsound granting of royal exemptions from taxes and other obligations. Teti (r. c. 2345-2323), the founder of this dynasty, apparently legitimized his rule by marrying Iput, the daughter of Unas. A mere twelve years later, he was dead, the victim of his own bodyguard, according to a later source.

Excluding the scarcely attested Userkare, he was succeeded by a young son Pepi I (r. c. 2321-2287 B.C.E.). In a tomb inscription, the noble Weni refers allusively to involvement in an investigation of an alleged harem conspiracy initiated by Queen Weret-Imtes, a consort of Pepi. The pharaoh's later marriage to two daughters of a powerful southern official is seen by some scholars as an indication of dependency. From the sisters were born the two succeeding kings, Merenre (r. c. 2283-c. 2278) and Pepi II. Pepi I conducted military campaigns against the Syro-Palestinian Aamu, the success of which is difficult to gauge because the sources are one-sided. Nubia in the south also became the more intensive object of commercial and military forays in this period.

Although Merenre ruled for only five uneventful years, his brother Pepi II came to the throne at age six and supposedly held it for ninety-four years, the longest reign in Egyptian history. The inscription of Harkhuf, governer of Elephantine, records the young pharaoh's boyishly enthusiastic

A diorite statue of Khafre, Egyptian king, in the Boulac Museum, Egypt. (Hulton|Archive)

MAJOR RULERS OF THE OLD KINGDOM PERIOD, C. 2687-C. 2125 B.C.E.

THIRD DYNASTY, C. 2687-C. 2613

Ruler	*Reign*
Zoser	c. 2687-c. 2650
Sekhemkhet	c. 2648-c. 2640
Khaba	c. 2640-c. 2637
Huni	c. 2637-c. 2613

FOURTH DYNASTY, C. 2613-C. 2494

Ruler	*Reign*
Snefru	c. 2613-2589
Khufu	c. 2589-2566
Khafre	2558-2532
Menkaure	2532-c. 2503
Shepsekhaf	c. 2503-c. 2498

FIFTH DYNASTY, C. 2494-C. 2345

Ruler	*Reign*
Userkaf	c. 2494-c. 2487
Sahure	c. 2487-2475
Neferirkare	c. 2475-c. 2455
Djedkare	c. 2414-2375
Unas	c. 2375-c. 2345

SIXTH DYNASTY, C. 2345-C. 2181

Ruler	*Reign*
Teti	c. 2345-2323
Pepi I	c. 2321-2287
Merenre	c. 2283-c. 2278
Pepi II	2278-2184
Nitocris	2184-2181

SEVENTH AND EIGHTH DYNASTIES, C. 2180-C. 2160

Note: Dynastic research is ongoing; data are approximate.

reaction to the news that Harkhuf was bringing a pygmy back from Nubia. A Middle Kingdom tale suggests that Pepi II had an irregular, perhaps homosexual, relationship with his general Sasenet. His long rule, probably senescent near the end, is viewed by many scholars as paving the way to the collapse of the Old Kingdom. Particularly singled out are his too frequent grants of immunity from taxation and other burdens to cultic endowments, apparently to shore up his own central position. The effect of these grants was to weaken the economy and thus accelerate decentralization. Climate changes and overexpenditure on building projects are other theoretical explanations of this later collapse.

The fifth century B.C.E. Greek historian Herodotus reported that a queen, Nitocris (r. 2184-2181), ended the dynasty after avenging the death of her predecessor and brother Merenre, but this late story is widely doubted by historians. The female name may be a male name corrupted in transmission. This ruler was followed by more than seventeen queens and kings during the last two dynasties of the Old Kingdom, the Seventh and Eighth.

SIGNIFICANCE

In the Old Kingdom, the achievements of the Predynastic Period and the First and Second Dynasties came to fruition and set a standard for later generations. Among the technological marvels is the first monumental stone complex, the Step Pyramid at Saqqara, which played a part in the evolution of the true pyramid forms of the Fourth Dynasty. The pyramid of Khufu became one of the Seven Wonders of the Ancient World. Relief sculpture was refined, and life-size sculpture first appeared. The centrality and divinity of the kingship, with its emphasis on solar cults, was never again equaled. The pyramid of Unas contained the world's earliest religious texts.

—*David J. Ladouceur*

FURTHER READING

Clayton, Peter A. *Chronicle of the Pharaohs*. London: Thames and Hudson, 1994. A lucid presentation in a well-designed format.

Hornung, Erik. *History of Ancient Egypt: An Introduction*. Translated by David Lortun. Ithaca, N.Y.: Cornell University Press, 1999. A brief but masterly presentation by a major authority.

Shaw, Ian. *The Oxford History of Ancient Egypt*. Oxford, England: Oxford University Press, 2000. A standard but, in parts, a rather lifeless account. Excellent bibliography.

Wilkinson, Toby A. H. *Early Dynastic Egypt*. New York: Routledge, 1999. A current account of the First through Third Dynasties. Excellent bibliography.

SEE ALSO: c. 3050 B.C.E., Unification of Lower and Upper Egypt; c. 2160 B.C.E., First Intermediate Period Begins in Egypt; c. 2055 B.C.E., Middle Kingdom Period Begins in Egypt; c. 1650 B.C.E., Hyksos Create Second Intermediate Period; c. 1570 B.C.E., New Kingdom Period Begins in Egypt.

RELATED ARTICLES in *Great Lives from History: The Ancient World*: Imhotep; Zoser.

c. 2682 B.C.E.
LEGENDARY FOUNDING OF CHINA BY HUANGDI

According to legend, Huangdi, the Yellow Emperor, founded the country that became China and served as an ancestor to the Chinese people.

LOCALE: Yellow River Valley, China
CATEGORIES: Prehistory and ancient cultures; cultural and intellectual history

KEY FIGURE

Huangdi (Huang-ti; c. 2704-c. 2600 B.C.E.), legendary founder of Chinese culture, considered the ancestor of all Chinese people

SUMMARY OF EVENT

Although Huangdi, the Yellow Emperor, is a legendary rather than a historical figure, the beliefs and innovations attributed to him have had a very real and formative effect on Chinese culture and tradition. There is a vast network of tales about Huangdi that includes various contradictory accounts, and those legends continue to inform and vitalize Chinese life.

In *East Asia: The Great Tradition* (1960), Edwin O. Reischauer and John K. Fairbank place Huangdi in context in the legendary account of early China as follows:

> In the beginning there was the creator, P'an-ku [Pangu]. Then followed three series of brothers—twelve Celestial Sovereigns, eleven Terrestrial Sovereigns, and nine Human Sovereigns—representing collectively the triad of Chinese thought: heaven, earth, and man. These three groups were either themselves known as the Three Huang or, in other accounts, they were followed by three individual sovereigns so designated. These in turn were followed by the Five Ti, who included the Yellow Emperor (Huang Ti) and the model rulers, Yao and Shun.

Huangdi, Yao, and Shun played important parts in the religious and moral lives of the Chinese, who have created a way of life that draws from three traditions: Daoism (Taoism), Confucianism, and Buddhism. Huangdi, who appears in a significant number of stories in the works of Zhuangzi (Chuang Tzu), is forever linked with Daoism, and Yao and Shun serve as the models against which all rulers are measured in Confucianism. Huangdi's importance in Daoism can be seen in the fact that when the yin-yang school, which was originally a separate school rather than a part of Daoism, merged the teachings of Huangdi and the teachings of Laozi (Lao Tzu) in the second century B.C.E., the resulting school became known as Huang-Lao. Confucianism and Daoism grew out of Chinese culture, while Buddhism, which originated in India, entered the country at a later date. Buddhism grew rapidly in China and ultimately became hugely influential.

Many versions of the story of Huangdi's origins exist. In one, Huangdi is said to have been born from the combined energies that created the world. However, most stories hold that Huangdi was the leader of a prehistoric tribe that lived in the Yellow (Huang) River Valley. The dates of his life and death (c. 2704-c. 2600 B.C.E.) are traditionally given as 2697-2597 or 2674-2575. Various tribes lived in the Yellow River Valley at that time, and they periodically engaged in wars to extend their territories. Huangdi came to believe that he must put an end to the chaotic and violent situation.

In one legend, Huangdi originally shared power in his tribe with his half brother, Yandi (or Yangdi), who ruled unjustly. Huangdi defeated Yandi and consolidated his power in the tribe. He also formulated a moral code for his people to follow and engaged in raising and thoroughly training an army. In a long series of battles, largely as a result of his careful preparation, he defeated his enemies and became the leader of a group of unified tribes.

The Yellow Emperor's tribe engaged in farming and exalted the fruits of the earth above all things. The word *huang*, which means "yellow," is associated with the tribe because yellow is the color of the earth. The Yellow Emperor is the ruler of farming and of the earth, and legend has it that before his birth, the populations of worms and mole crickets increased dramatically, a portent of the favorable effects that his rule would have on Earth.

According to legend, Huangdi set out during his rule to examine and reform almost every area of Chinese life. It was his idea to create family surnames, and he determined that the surname should precede the personal name. That order still prevails in China. He also divided his territory into provinces. In addition, he created writing, therefore propelling China out of the era of prehistory and into the historical era. Among his other inventions were the potter's wheel and the south-pointing chariot. The south-pointing chariot was a vehicle that carried a wooden figure that always pointed south. Huangdi had created a compass. Huangdi is also thought to have been the first to coin bronze money, and he invented the cart as well as the boat. In innumerable ways, Huangdi's ways of doing things became the Chinese ways of doing things.

Inventions were not limited to Huangdi. His wife, Leizu (Si Ling-Chi), is said to have performed an extremely important act when she introduced sericulture, the making of silk from silkworms, to China. Since that time, China has been known for its high-quality silk. Many of Huangdi's subjects were reportedly inspired to create by observing the creativity displayed by the emperor and empress. Among the inspired were Cang Jie (Ts'ang Chieh), who is credited with the creating of pictographs; Ling Lun, who established the twelve-tone scale in music; and Li Shou, the creator of an array of measuring instruments.

Although generally the legendary figure Pangu, the parts of whose body became the parts of Earth on his death, is considered the first man in Chinese culture, Huangdi is sometimes said to have created the human race. According to tradition, he created earthenware figures and placed them in the four directions, leaving them there for three hundred years so they could be animated by the breath of the world's beginning. When the statues had been sufficiently affected, they became able to move and speak. In this way, the human race was born.

One of the most important contributions Huangdi is said to have made to Chinese culture is the founding of traditional Chinese medicine. The medical work attributed to him, although compiled after his death, *Huangdi nei jing su wen* (compiled c. 300 B.C.E.; *The Yellow Emperor's Classic of Internal Medicine*, 1949), contains concepts of medical theory and practice that served as the foundation for the entire structure of Chinese medicine. The work is still studied by practitioners of traditional Chinese medicine throughout the world.

Daoists associate Huangdi with the tradition of the Daoist Immortals. According to tradition, when Huangdi traveled to the sacred mountains, he encountered the Daoist master Kuan Cheng (K'uan Ch'eng), who instructed him in realizing the Dao. According to the *Zhuangzi* (traditionally c. 300 B.C.E., probably compiled c. 285-160 B.C.E.; *The Divine Classic of Nan-hua*, 1881; also known as *The Complete Works of Chuang Tzu*, 1968; commonly known as *Zhuangzi*, 1991), Kuan Cheng instructed Huangdi as follows:

> See nothing; hear nothing; let your soul be wrapped in quiet, and your body will begin to take proper form. Let there be absolute repose and absolute purity; do not weary your body nor disturb your vitality—and you will live forever. For if the eye sees nothing and the ear hears nothing, and the mind thinks nothing the soul will preserve the body and the body will live forever.

At age 100, Huangdi reportedly developed magical powers and produced the golden elixir of immortality. He attained immortality on Qing Mountain. One story has it that when Huangdi was 110, the king of heaven sent a yellow dragon to bring Huangdi to heaven. As Huangdi was about to ride off on the dragon, his distraught subjects, not wishing him to leave, clutched at his clothes and tried to drag him back to earth. They failed in stopping him but were left with part of his clothing and his hat. They buried all that they had left of Huangdi at Mount Qiaoshan in Shaanxi, and they built a mausoleum there in his honor.

SIGNIFICANCE

The vast network of legends surrounding the legendary Huangdi, the Yellow Emperor, has served as the basis for the growth and development of Chinese culture. In virtually every area of life, the beliefs, practices, and innovations attributed to Huangdi have determined the direction and shape of Chinese culture.

In his role as a major figure in Daoism, the Yellow Emperor served to shape the Chinese worldview. With the exception of Laozi, no figure in Daoism is more significant than Huangdi, who is the subject of various stories in the works of Zhuangzi.

—Shawn Woodyard

FURTHER READING

Chan, Wing-Tsit, comp. and trans. *A Source Book in Chinese Philosophy*. Princeton, N.J.: Princeton University Press, 1963. This volume is perhaps the finest single-volume study of its subject.

De Bary, Theodore, Wing-Tsit Chan, and Burton Watson, comps. *Sources of Chinese Tradition*. Vol. 1. New York: Columbia University Press, 1960. A collection of writings explicating a wide range of Chinese thought.

Fischer-Schreiber, Ingrid. *The Shambhala Dictionary of Taoism*. Translated by Werner Wünsche. Boston: Shambhala, 1996. An essential reference work for anyone interested in any aspect of Daoism.

Huangdi. *The Yellow Emperor's Classic of Internal Medicine*. Translated by Ilza Veith. Rev. ed. Berkeley: University of California Press, 2002. A translation of the classic volume attributed to Huangdi that serves as the foundation of traditional Chinese medicine (TCM) as it is still practiced.

Reischauer, Edwin O., and John K. Fairbank. *East Asia: The Great Tradition*. Boston: Houghton Mifflin, 1960. A succinct and insightful examination of the histories and traditions of China, Korea, and Japan.

Zhuangzi. *The Complete Works of Chuang Tzu*. Translated by Burton Watson. New York: Columbia University Press, 1968. A fine translation of the second most important work in Daoism. An excellent source of legends about Huangdi.

SEE ALSO: 2953-2838 B.C.E. traditionally, Reign of China's Legendary First Ruler, Fu Xi; c. 2600 B.C.E., Leizu Discovers Silk Making; c. 500 B.C.E., Acupuncture Develops in China; 3d century B.C.E. (traditionally 6th century B.C.E.), Laozi Composes the *Dao De Jing*.

RELATED ARTICLES in *Great Lives from History: The Ancient World*: Wang Bi; Zhuangzi.

c. 2600 B.C.E.
LEIZU DISCOVERS SILK MAKING

An ancient and perhaps legendary Chinese empress discovered the technique for unwinding silkworm cocoons and weaving them into fabric.

LOCALE: China
CATEGORIES: Science and technology; agriculture

KEY FIGURE

Leizu (Si Ling-Chi; fl. c. twenty-seventh century B.C.E.), Chinese empress who discovered silk making

SUMMARY OF EVENT

China has long been associated with the production of silk, to the point that ancient Egyptian writers referred to it as Serica, literally "the land of silk." The Chinese so closely guarded the secrets of silk that the Roman historian Pliny the Elder (23-79 C.E.) wrote that it was produced by washing downy fibers from leaves. So old is sericulture (the techniques surrounding the raising of the silkworm moth, *Bombyx mori*, and the unwinding of its cocoons for silk fiber to be woven into fabric) that its origins have become surrounded by myth and legend.

However, one person is generally singled out as having first discovered that a silkworm cocoon could be unwound to make fiber. This is Leizu, who was either a wife or a concubine of the celebrated Yellow Emperor Huangdi (Huang-ti, c. 2704-c. 2600 B.C.E.) in 2640 B.C.E. According to the most common versions of the story, she went to retrieve a cocoon that had fallen into a cup of hot water (some versions say it was tea that she had been making while in the gardens of the Imperial palace). When she withdrew the cocoon, she and all her court were astonished to discover that it came out hanging from a delicate silken thread. The heat of the water had dissolved the gummy substance known as sericen that the silkworm moth uses to bind the silken thread into a solid cocoon and thus enabled the silk fiber to be reeled up for weaving. Although the discovery is generally said to have been an accident, other versions of the tradition suggest that Leizu's husband had assigned her to study the possibility of weaving a useful fiber from silkworm cocoons.

Leizu is said to have developed the techniques by which silkworms could be raised in controlled conditions and invented looms and other equipment with which to transform raw silk fiber into the beautiful, sensuous cloth for which China would become famous throughout the world. So extensive was her contribution to the production of silk that she was deified and joined the sizeable Chinese pantheon as Shantzen (Sien-tsan), the goddess of silkworms. This apotheosis further contributed to the blurring of historical fact with legend, making it difficult if not impossible to determine the boundaries of each.

Archaeological finds have hinted at the substance behind these legends. In 1927, half a silkworm cocoon was unearthed from soil near the Yellow River in Shanxi Province of northern China. It was radiocarbon dated to be from between 2600 and 2300 B.C.E. More recent discoveries have suggested that the beginnings of sericulture and silk weaving may date even earlier, perhaps by as much as one thousand years, although these finds are hotly debated in the archaeological community.

Over the centuries that followed Liezu's discovery, the silkworm became a truly domesticated insect, and selective breeding made it exceedingly docile and incapable of surviving in the wild. The adults became incapable of flight and uninterested in flying away from their cocoons, while the caterpillars became gregarious with no tendency to wander from their feeding beds, as do related species. These transformations made it easier to handle the valuable insects because it was no longer necessary to fully enclose the chambers in which they were raised, as would be the case with a more mobile species.

In the early years of silkworm culture, only members of China's imperial family were permitted to wear silken garments or use items made of silk. However, as time passed, restrictions were relaxed and other aristocrats and officials were permitted the privilege of using this high-status fabric. Ultimately even ordinary people wore silk, and the fabric was used as money during some eras of Chinese history. Eventually, Chinese emperors discovered that a substantial fortune could be made from selling silken cloth abroad, and by the second century B.C.E., the famous Silk Road had come into existence. This trade route or set of trade routes, stretching across Asia, brought not only silk but other exotic Asian goods such as tea and spices to Western Europe and northern Africa. Although China sought to maintain a complete monopoly on the production and sale of silk, within a few centuries, brave spies risked their lives to smuggle live eggs and cocoons abroad. After that point, the primary limit on the growth of sericulture would be the availability of fresh mulberry leaves and willing workers for this labor-intensive industry.

SIGNIFICANCE

Until the development of modern synthetic fibers in the nineteenth and twentieth centuries, silk remained the strongest and finest fiber available for making cloth. These characteristics, as well as the labor-intense methods of raising silkworms, gave silk a reputation for richness and a symbolic association with wealth and power. At the same time, silk was also used in certain precision instruments, such as the cross-hairs of the finest scopes.

—Leigh Husband Kimmel

FURTHER READING

Anquitel, Jacques. *Silk.* Paris: Flammarion, 1996. A closely researched study of the history of sericulture and the impact of silk on society that is accessible to the average reader.

Feltwell, John. *The Story of Silk.* New York: St. Martin's, 1990. An overview of the history of silk, from its discovery in China through the development of the European and American silk industries.

Liu, Xinru. *Silk and Religion: An Exploration of Material Life and the Thought of People, A.D. 600-1200.* 2d ed. New York: Oxford University Press, 1998. Discusses the interaction between China's trade in silk and its religious ideas and institutions.

Major, John S. *The Silk Route: Seven Thousand Miles of History.* New York: Harper Trophy, 1996. Although aimed primarily at younger readers, this book includes copious notes at the end dealing with every aspect of the history of the Silk Road.

Scott, Philippa. *The Book of Silk.* Reprint. New York: Thames and Hudson, 2001. An extensive history of silk and its role in society, includes bibliographic references and index.

SEE ALSO: c. 2682 B.C.E., Legendary Founding of China by Huangdi; 2d century B.C.E., Silk Road Opens.

c. 2575-c. 2566 B.C.E.
BUILDING OF THE GREAT PYRAMID

The building of the Great Pyramid at Giza was a major architectural feat, producing a lasting and impressive monument.

LOCALE: Giza, Egypt
CATEGORY: Architecture

KEY FIGURE

Khufu (Cheops; fl. twenty-sixth century B.C.E.), Fourth Dynasty king, r. c. 2589-2566 B.C.E., builder of the Great Pyramid

SUMMARY OF EVENT

The three great pyramids at Giza in Egypt are undoubtedly the most celebrated group of monuments in the world. Although more than eighty of these great tombs erected over the long span of Egyptian antiquity are known to archaeologists, the specific period known as the Pyramid Age, or the Old Kingdom (c. 2687-c. 2125 B.C.E.), covers the Third through Eighth Dynasties, and the greatest of all these works is that of the pharaoh Khufu. His monument and those of two later kings of the same dynasty, Khafre (Chephren) and Menkaure (Mycerinus), compose the great triad of monuments on the plateau at Giza, at the edge of the Western Desert south of the modern city of Cairo.

The pyramid of Khufu, one of the largest stone structures in the world, is preeminent both for size and quality of workmanship. The Greek historian Herodotus, after visiting the site in 449 B.C.E., stated that the construction required the efforts of a hundred thousand men for a period of twenty years, and these are the figures most often repeated in the later literature. However, modern scholars believe that only between two thousand and four thousand construction workers were actually employed on the working face at any one time, with perhaps four times that number engaged in transport work and in the quarries at the site, in the Mukattam Hills on the east side of the Nile, and at Aswān, some five hundred miles (eight hundred kilometers) upstream. No exact estimate of the amount of hewn stone used is possible because the core of the Great Pyramid consists of a nucleus of living rock, but a likely conjecture is that the completed structure contained some 2.3 million separate blocks of stone weighing an average of 2.5 tons (2.3 metric tons) each and reaching an individual maximum of 15 tons (14 metric tons). The base of each of the four sides measures approximately 755 feet (236 meters) and exhibits an almost true north-south or east-west orientation, so that the four corners are almost perfect right angles. Rising at an incline of 51°52′, the sides originally reached a height of 482 feet (147 meters), but the top 31 feet (9 meters) are now lost. The total area covered by the base measures 13 acres (5 hectare).

Seen from a distance, the Great Pyramid appears to be well preserved, but closer observation shows that it has suffered severe damage over the centuries. Apart from the loss of some twelve courses and the capstone at the top, the entire outer facing of Tura limestone, once about 17 feet (5 meters) in thickness, has been lost. In its original condition, this gleaming white stone, fitted to the closest possible tolerances, presented a smooth and shining surface on all sides that must have dazzled the onlooker. Today, a surviving portion of this facing atop the neighboring Pyramid of Khafre gives the spectator some inkling of the grandeur of these monuments at the time of their completion.

The interior passageways of the Great Pyramid, the plans of which were changed three times during the course of construction, are open at the upper levels to the visitor. As in all pyramids, the entrance is on the north side, in this case 49 feet (15 meters) above ground level. At first the corridor slopes downward for 62 feet (19 meters), then ascends after a point at which the passage was blocked with granite to guard against tomb robbers. The passage rises for a distance of about 60 feet (18 meters) to reach the great chamber, which measures 153 feet (47 meters) in length, 30 feet (9 meters) in height, but only about 7 feet (2 meters) in width. At its upper end, the visitor passes through an antechamber into the royal funerary room, 137 feet (42 meters) above ground level, in which the granite sarcophagus of Khufu stands at the western end. This huge coffin is slightly wider than the passageway and therefore had to be in place when construction reached this level, not after completion of the entire monument.

The Great Pyramid was built mainly of limestone from the quarries nearby and across the Nile, but granite for the columns, architraves, doorjambs, lintels, and other parts of the sepulchral complex that forms the valley temple, covered causeway, funerary temple, and the pyramid itself came from Aswān, far up the Nile. As early as the First Dynasty, the Egyptians had copper saws and chisels capable of cutting any kind of limestone, but special dolorite hammers were required to chip rough slots into the quarry walls of the very hard granite. After wooden wedges were pounded into the slots, they were soaked in water, and the resulting expansion split off chunks of the stone. The finished blocks in all the quarries were moved by work gangs of about eighteen to twenty men using hawsers, levers, log rollers, and sledges. Heavy barges carried the blocks during the journey down the river.

Preparation of the site and construction methods remain to be considered. A rocky knoll at the desert's edge was selected as the substructure to support the great weight of more than 5.5 million tons (5 million metric tons) of the monument. Terraces to serve as the foundations had to be cut into the irregular sides of the hill at an absolute level if the structure was to be true, and to accomplish this, the architects designed a system of water-filled trenches about the base. Then, with the water level as a standard, areas between two trenches were leveled by measurements made from a string stretched between sticks of equal length, each of which was held at the surface of the water. This horizontal string-line provided a perfect level for the work of flattening the terraces.

The basic construction technique for moving the huge blocks up to the ever higher courses, on the other hand, remains a matter of dispute. One theory holds that four mud-brick ramps were built, one starting at each corner, against the outer surface of the casing stones. As each course added to the height, these ramps were extended, with the stones being dragged up three of them by sledge and with the fourth reserved for the descending work gangs. Elegant though it appears at first sight, this theory has serious flaws; I. E. S. Edwards in *The Pyramids of Egypt* (1961) describes an alternate and perhaps more probable method. Edwards rejects the view that one ramp began at each corner of the pyramid and continued in an upward, corkscrew manner around the four faces. Archaeology and engineering both tend to disprove this ingenious but overly complex theory. Such ramps would depend for their support beyond the first stage on the casing-blocks, which it is held were laid in a fairly well-cut, steplike progression. However, no evidence of such ramps has been found at any pyramid site. Undressed casing blocks that lie at the base of the Pyramid of Menkaure are not steplike and would not have supported

The three great pyramids of Giza in Egypt. (Digital Stock)

such a ramp, and it is questionable whether the widest possible step would have provided sufficient room for blocks of the size used at Giza to be unloaded and fixed in place. It is far more likely that a single supply ramp was built to cover the whole of one side of the pyramid. As the building progressed upward, the ramp would not only increase in height but also in length in order to maintain an unchanging gradient for the work gangs dragging the great blocks up the ramp.

The attraction of the ancient Egyptians to the world of the dead is dramatized by their greatest architectural achievement, the Great Pyramid, which exacted an unimaginable cost in human and material resources as a tomb for the pharaoh Khufu. Although the Great Pyramid has lasted for thousands of years, the private and public buildings in which the people lived and worked, as well as the great capital cities of Memphis and Thebes, have all disappeared almost without a trace. The physical explanation for this strange imbalance of surviving objects is an obvious one: Egyptian tombs after the earliest period were all built of stone or hewn out of rock, while the houses and palaces in which the populace resided consisted of mud-brick, wood, and gesso. To the Egyptians, the houses in which they lived were finite and replaceable, but the tomb in which they would rest unendingly had to last forever. This attitude derived from the belief that bliss after death could be achieved only on the fulfillment of two essential conditions: A person's body must be preserved and the physical needs of his or her *ka*, or spirit, must be supplied. Though the form of the final resting place varied many times during the long course of history, the essential purpose of this eternal and enduring last domicile remained unchanged.

Though the conventional photographs of the Giza pyramids invariably show them standing against the stark desert background and a clear sky, the implication that these monuments stand alone and isolated is a false one. Each pyramid complex consisted of four structures: the gate or valley temple, the covered causeway running westward toward the pyramid, the funerary temple in front of the great tomb, and the pyramid itself as the climax of this succession of monuments. The best preserved of these groups belongs to the Pyramid of Khafre not that of Khufu, the auxiliary structures of which have to a large degree been destroyed. To the north of the beginning of the causeway of the valley temple to Khafre's pyramid lies the Sphinx in the form of a colossal, couchant lion with human head. This famous figure measures 65 feet (20 meters) in height and 238 feet (73 meters) in length, and was carved out of the remains of a limestone quarry from which the blocks for the pyramid of Khufu were cut. In Egyptian mythology, the lion is often the guardian of holy places. Incorporated into the majestic figure of the Sphinx at Giza, where it is combined with human facial features depicting the Sun god Ra, the lion represents Khafre acting as divine guardian of the great necropolis.

In the vicinity of each of the three pyramids stand smaller ones for members of the royal family and scores of mastaba tombs for members of the royal household and court. The valley temple or gateway for each of the three pyramids at Giza lay on a branch of the Nile. In the surviving valley temple of Khafre, the simplicity, proportions, and materials make it a structure of great beauty. Sphinxes flanked each of its two entrances on the eastern side. The main halls consist of an inverted T-plan with monolithic granite pillars 13 feet (4 meters) high. Against the walls, there once stood twenty-three statues of Khafre, the best surviving of which was moved to the Cairo Museum. From an oblique side corridor, the 500-yard (457-meter) covered causeway led to the funerary temple standing before the east side of the pyramid itself. This structure was built of local limestone faced with granite and consists of three successive entry halls, the last of which leads into the great court, where sacrifices on behalf of the dead king were offered. Adjoining this court on the west were five chapels, with a statue of the pharaoh in each for worship under one of his five names.

When the king died, his body was borne across the Nile to the great necropolis on the west side. In the valley temple, the corpse was prepared for burial by the process of mummification. On the day of interment, the mummy was hauled up the great causeway in a ritual barge to the funerary temple, where the last rites were performed. Then it was taken up into the great chamber of his pyramid, in which his loyal subjects confidently believed his body would remain for all time.

Significance

Because of their sepulchral purpose and their survival over a span of many millennia, the pyramids at Giza, especially the Great Pyramid of Khufu, remain an impressive sight. They represent both the dominant religious concept and the enduring architectural achievements of the ancient Egyptians.

—*Kevin Herbert*

Further Reading

David, A. Rosalie. *The Pyramid Builders of Ancient Egypt: A Modern Investigation of Pharaoh's Work-*

force. New York: Routledge, 1996. Although this study examines the pyramid of Sesostris II rather than that of Khufu, it centers on the workers who built the pyramids. Bibliography and index.

Dunn, Christopher. *The Giza Power Plant: Technologies of Ancient Egypt*. Santa Fe, N.Mex.: Bear, 1998. Dunn, an engineer, argues that the pyramid was constructed not as a tomb for Khufu but as a power generator. Bibliography and index.

Edwards, I. F. S. *The Pyramids of Egypt*. Rev ed. New York: Penguin, 1993. An excellent survey of the pyramids. Contains a chronological account of the types of pyramids created and a study of construction methods and the purpose of pyramids.

Herz-Fischler, Roger. *The Shape of the Great Pyramid*. Waterloo, Ont.: Wilfrid Laurier University Press, 2000. A study that examines the Great Pyramid by focusing on its dimensions. Bibliography.

Hooghe, Alain d', and Marie-Cecile Brusier. *The Great Pyramids of Giza*. Paris: Vilo, 2000. A pictorial study of the pyramids of Egypt. Index.

Tompkins, Peter. *Secrets of the Great Pyramid*. New York: Galahad Books, 1997. Explores various theories surrounding the Great Pyramid, including the idea that the pyramid was used as a geometric tool for measuring the outside world. Bibliography and index.

See also: c. 3050 B.C.E., Unification of Lower and Upper Egypt; c. 2687 B.C.E., Old Kingdom Period Begins in Egypt; c. 2160 B.C.E., First Intermediate Period Begins in Egypt; c. 2055 B.C.E., Middle Kingdom Period Begins in Egypt; c. 1650 B.C.E., Hyksos Create Second Intermediate Period; c. 1570 B.C.E., New Kingdom Period Begins in Egypt.

Related articles in *Great Lives from History: The Ancient World*: Imhotep; Menkaure.

c. 2500 B.C.E.
Construction of Monumental Architecture at Caral in Peru

Archaeological work on the monumental structures at Caral in Supe Valley, Peru, has pushed back the date for the development of an urban center in the prehistoric Americas more than a thousand years.

Locale: Central coast region of Peru
Categories: Prehistory and ancient cultures; architecture

Summary of Event

Located 120 miles (193 kilometers) north of Lima and 14 miles (22 kilometers) from the Pacific coast, the Caral site in Peru is one of the more notable and significant archaeological discoveries of the late twentieth century. Although the site's existence was known since the early twentieth century and later aerial photography had indicated the existence of some monumental ruins, no evidence was found at the time that would suggest Caral's great antiquity in comparison to better-known sites. Therefore, for more than half a century, this Supe Valley archaeological locale remained neglected.

In 1994, Ruth Shady Solís, director of the Museum of Archaeology and Anthropology at the Greater National University of San Marcos in Lima, first visited Caral and evinced an interest in excavation. Work began with a small crew in 1996. When no pottery fragments turned up in the debris after two months of labor, Shady's excitement arose. If Caral were a preceramic site, then it was associated with an era that preceded Peru's earliest known great populated centers with monumental architecture by more than a millennium. However, more definitive evidence was needed to convince scholars and colleagues who reacted with natural skepticism.

Among numerous artifacts uncovered were bags made from reeds that ancient workers had used to carry stones for construction. These reeds, recovered from various sectors of the site, were taken in 1999 to research institutions in Illinois, where American collaborators Jonathan Haas and Winifred Creamer conducted radiocarbon tests to date Caral's antiquity. The dramatic results, made available in December, 2000, showed the test samples associated with Caral to be forty-six hundred years old. Knowledge of this startling find was first widely disseminated when the magazine *Science* published an article by Shady, Haas, and Creamer in its April 27, 2001, issue.

The evidence uncovered to date suggests that Caral may have been inhabited as far back as 2900 B.C.E., reached its period of splendor in terms of construction three centuries later, and endured for another thousand years until it was abandoned about 1600 B.C.E. The fact that this place was never again inhabited may have contributed to preserving the evidence of its culture in the form of artifacts and ruins that have emerged largely intact. Moreover, the absence of pottery has served to discourage extensive looting of the site through the centuries.

Caral is a 150-acre (60-hectare) complex that contained some three thousand inhabitants. This large monumental center eventually gave rise to seventeen smaller complexes strewn across the 35-square-mile (89-square-kilometer) valley. The ruins, which required mobilization of a large labor force to build, are testimony to the first strong government or state and the first urban civilization of the Americas. Excavation in Caral proper has restored or identified thirty-two major structures including seven large pyramids, residences, altars with fireplaces for burnt sacrificial offerings, tombs, and an impressive circular sunken amphitheater with graduated seating for three hundred spectators. The amphitheater most likely served as the city's center for both ceremonial and civic events during Caral's long history. The city's largest pyramid sprawls over an area equal to four football fields and rises to a height of 60 feet (18 meters). Priests or worshipers gained access to the summit by means of a 30-foot-wide (9-meter-wide) staircase that rose from a sunken plaza and traversed three terraced levels. In addition, the city was divided into numerous residential districts, each possessing its local shire and facility for burnt sacrificial offerings. Caral's principal structures were made of stone and clay. Painted buildings gave the city an exotic, colorful appearance. Walls and floors of structures, including houses, were covered with single colors such as red, yellow, blue, black, and white.

There are strong indications that Caral influenced later well-known Peruvian cultures. A partially excavated monument named Pyramid of the Gallery contains internal passageways very similar to building tunnels at Peru's Chavín de Huantar site, which appeared one thousand years later about 100 miles (160 kilometers) north. Also, the appearance near the city of art styles and symbols like those later associated with Chavín suggests that Caral influenced later sites.

The ancient city was not built over the years in a haphazard manner. Caral's layout conforms to a detailed plan, as would be true of later great centers of pre-Columbian America that designed urban complexes or ceremonial centers in accord with their religious views of the universal order and an understanding of astronomy. Astronomical observations were used primarily for measuring time, developing an agricultural calendar, and interpreting the divine order of the cosmos. In this dawn of prehistoric American civilization, the builders clearly had a substantial grasp of architecture, geometry, and astronomy and knew how to combine forms and lines to harmonize with their own theological and astronomical concepts. In addition, over the centuries Caral's temples and major structures underwent periodic remodeling and enlargement, probably to conform with new astronomical knowledge.

Some of the artifacts unearthed reveal that music was a major part of ritual and daily life. From the environs of the great amphitheater, the sounds of exotic ancient melodies once reverberated. There excavators found a cache of thirty-two flutes made from condor and pelican bones. Carved on each were the same decorative designs and symbols. Later, an even larger number of cornets fashioned from llama and deer bones were found.

Social stratification and class distinctions are among the typical features displayed by early urban civilizations. Surpluses from trade and an abundant food supply led to the appearance of an elite group composed of priests, political leaders, and specialists who planned and built the city. A social hierarchy is evident in an outer sector of the city containing residences grouped in various neighborhood complexes. The elite lived in spacious, fine rooms atop pyramids. Specialists had decent ground-level neighborhoods, while laborers, fishermen, and farmers resided in much poorer quarters located farther out.

One function the ancient city served was that of a spiritual center and sacred place. The influence and pervasiveness of religion in Caral were obvious to Shady and her companions as their work progressed. Everything they uncovered and brought to light was linked in some way to spirituality. Fireplaces for offerings were numerous. The inhabitants conducted religious rituals not only in the major public places and temples but also in individual dwellings. The discovery of human bones in connection with some areas of worship or building construction revealed that some rites involved human sacrifice.

Caral was also an important center for trade. Peru's earliest village cultures in the dry Pacific coast region were located close to or on the seashore, where marine food products were abundant. Caral, however, was located nearly 15 miles (24 kilometers) inland in a desert setting inhospitable to cultivation. Shady theorizes that a diversified economy arose there, which brought about an integrated and interdependent relationship between the interior and the seacoast.

Caral's inhabitants appear to have developed an irrigation system by diverting rivers into canals. Farmers grew cotton, and textiles were manufactured. An important exchange occurred between these farmers and coastal fishermen, who needed cotton for making nets and supplied the city with fish, anchovies, and other marine food products. The discovery of plant fragments from the Amazon rainforest, coca plant seeds, snail necklaces, and other items from regions beyond has reinforced Shady's belief that Caral functioned as a great commercial center linking many settled areas.

SIGNIFICANCE

Caral's major claim to archaeological fame is that its discovery caused a radical revision in the dating scheme for American prehistory, as this Archaic period center is about 1,000-1,500 years older than later Formative period sites in Peru and Mexico's Gulf coast area. While the world's oldest urban civilization, the Sumerians in Mesopotamia, were reaching a peak and as the Egyptians were just initiating their pyramid building near Giza, the inhabitants of Caral were busy constructing pyramids and other monuments in Peru. As a result, Peru is now considered, along with Egypt, Mesopotamia, China, India, and Mesoamerica, as one of the six world centers in which civilization and urban life first emerged.

More of Caral's secrets lie waiting to be revealed. The site presents an opportunity through further work to learn more about the conditions and factors that gave rise to this level of human development. It is noteworthy that Shady sees Caral as the first link in the chain of civilization leading to the Inca state and calls it the "mother city of the Inca civilization."

—*David A. Crain*

FURTHER READING

Pringle, Heather. "The First Urban Center in the Americas." *Science* 292, no. 5517 (April 27, 2001): 621-623. A very readable and interesting short article on the startling revelations about the New World's most ancient city by a prominent writer on science and archaeology subjects. Illustrated.

Ross, John F. "First City in the New World?" *Smithsonian* 33, no. 5 (August, 2002): 56-64. Summarizes the story behind the important discovery of Caral's surprising antiquity and the significance of this site, its ruins, and artifacts. Contains several color photos.

Shady Solís, Ruth, Jonathan Haas, and Winifred Creamer. "A Preceramic Site in the Supe Valley on the Central Coast of Peru." *Science* 292, no. 5517 (April 27, 2001): 723-726. Article in which Caral's chief excavator and her two North American collaborators, who verified the radiocarbon dating of Caral's ruins, went public with the news of this major discovery. Illustrations, map, bibliography, and footnotes.

SEE ALSO: c. 13,000 B.C.E., Humans Enter the South American Continent; c. 8000 B.C.E., Permanent Settlement of the Andean Altiplano Begins; c. 5800-c. 3700 B.C.E., Chinchorro Inhabit the Peruvian and Chilean Coasts; c. 1800-c. 1500 B.C.E., Construction of El Paraíso in Peru; c. 900-c. 200 B.C.E., Chavín de Huántar Is Peru's Urban Center.

2500-1900 B.C.E.
WAWAT CHIEFDOM FLOURISHES IN LOWER NUBIA

The region of Wawat became the Nilotic base of both the C-Group and Pan-Grave peoples, and the groups that settled there provided soldiers for the armies of First Intermediate Period and early Middle Kingdom Egypt.

LOCALE: Lower (northern) Nubian Nile Valley and surrounding desert areas (now in southern Egypt)

CATEGORIES: Expansion and land acquisition; government and politics; prehistory and ancient cultures

SUMMARY OF EVENT

Wawat is the ancient Egyptian name for the region of Lower Nubia and for any state or administrative division within that area. During the Egyptian Old Kingdom (c. 2687-c. 2125 B.C.E.), the Wawat appears to have encompassed all of Lower Nubia, although some scholars believe Wawat, Irtjet, and Setju were all situated within Lower Nubia. The land immediately to the south of Wawat was Irtjet, an area probably including the site of Kerma, the center of a strong Nubian kingdom during the late Middle Kingdom (c. 2055-c. 1650) and the Second Intermediate Period (c. 1650-c. 1570). American Egyptologist George Reisner classified phases of ancient Nubian culture into three groups, of which the A-Group (c. 3100-c. 2700) and C-Group (c. 2300-c. 1550) are currently recognized. The region of Lower Nubia, a center of A-Group Nubian culture, early came under the control of Egyptian pharaohs. Egypt conquered Wawat near the end of the Predynastic Period (c. 3050-c. 2925) and established a major outpost at Buhen during the Old Kingdom. Repeated Egyptian raids into the area appear to have obliterated most traces of Lower Nubian native culture by the end of the First Dynasty (c. 2925-c. 2775), although some archaeological remains fit the space of Reisner's now-discarded B-Group. Lower Nubia appears to have been all but abandoned until the late Fifth Dynasty (c. 2494-c. 2345).

During the latter part of the Old Kingdom and the First Intermediate Period (c. 2160-c. 2055 B.C.E.), the C-Group culture occupied the area. The archaeological vestiges of the C-Group occur in their greatest concentration between Wadi Kubbaniya in the north and the Second Cataract in the south. This culture group had affinities to the west and south and, apparently, spoke a Berber language. They were not a political unity and probably were the population bases of the toponyms Wawat, Irtjet, and Setju.

C-Group settlements are not well known, perhaps because of the accidents of preservation and excavation; most C-Group settlements of the Nile Valley are now lost beneath the Aswān High Dam's reservoir. If, as David O'Connor has suggested, the cemetery locations may provide some evidence of patterns and intensity of settlements, the C-Group may have concentrated in three major areas of Lower Nubia: between Gerf Hussein and Qurta, at Wadi es-Sebua, and around Aniba, with Aniba itself apparently the center of the C-Group. The excavated settlements are primarily of dry stone construction. Areika had rectilinear structures and incorporated some brick architecture as well; Wadi es-Sebua had rectilinear and round structures. Both settlements were walled. Archaeologists have also recognized a so-called Oasis C-Group culture. Although often temporally disparate materials have found a place under this heading, the origins of the C-Group do appear to lie in southwestern Nubia.

The inscriptions of the Sixth Dynasty adventurer Harkhuf (fl. c. 2300-2200 B.C.E.) show that during the late Old Kingdom Wawat, Irtjet, and Setju were able to hinder Egyptian trade and could form an alliance. Yam was apparently a superior power and could provide escort for Harkhuf through Lower Nubia. The Sixth Dynasty ruler Pepi II (r. c. 2278-2184 B.C.E.) mounted a campaign against Wawat and Irtjet, and Old Kingdom Egypt recruited large numbers of Wawat Nubians into the Egyptian service. Inscriptions in the Khor el-Aquiba demonstrate that during the high Old Kingdom, district governors from as far away as the Nile Delta could lead apparent impressment gangs into the area and recruit thousands of soldiers/servants.

During the First Intermediate Period and the Middle Kingdom, the Pan-Grave culture also appears in the region of Wawat. The Pan-Grave people ranged through Lower Nubia, the Eastern Desert, and even much of Upper Egypt. Often associated with strategically important areas, the Pan-Grave people appear to be identical with the Medjay, important auxiliary troops of the Egyptians. The Pan-Grave people appear to have acculturated into Egyptian society during the Middle Kingdom; recruits from the Kerma culture begin to replace them in Egyptian military service during the late Middle Kingdom and the Second Intermediate Periods.

When Montuhotep II (fl. 2055-2004 B.C.E.) reasserted Upper Egyptian control over Lower Nubia following his reunification of Egypt (c. 2055 B.C.E.), Wawat was of particular importance. A fragmentary royal document, probably attributable to the reign of Montuhotep II, records the annexation of Wawat and the oasis road to Wawat. The rock inscriptions of the Nubian soldier Tjehemau reveal that the reason for this interest was a desire to ensure direct Theban access to the military recruiting grounds of Wawat. Tjehemau, an inhabitant of Wawat who joined the Egyptian forces late in the reign of Montuhotep II, served on the loyalist side during a series of conflicts during the internal problems that threatened to destroy the Middle Kingdom during the reign of Amenemhet I (r. c. 1985-1956 B.C.E.) early in the Twelfth Dynasty.

The mercenaries over whom Montuhotep II sought direct Theban control were but the final wave of foreign soldiers, both Nubian and Asiatic, who swelled the ranks of the pharaonic and local armies during the late Old Kingdom and the First Intermediate Period. By the Twelfth Dynasty, the highly militarized society within Egypt, under pressure from now unengaged soldiers, suffered from the depredations of roving bands of brigands originating in the Egyptian, Asiatic, and Nubian elements of the pharaonic realm. Inhabitants of Wawat formed elements of these groups. Perhaps uncertain as to how to solve the problem of the mercenaries within his newly reunified realm, Montuhotep II inadvertently exacerbated the problem.

During the early Middle Kingdom, Lower Nubia remained a problematic area. Several rock inscriptions in the area recorded the establishment of what appear to have been temporary fortifications and the occasional practice of a scorched-earth policy in raiding the riverine Nubians. The early Middle Kingdom established a series of fortresses north of the Second Cataract; during the late Twelfth Dynasty, new hilltop fortresses rose within the

Second Cataract itself. These provided bases for the patrols guarding the routes through Wawat and protection for the caravans and "ships of Wawat," carrying among other things the gold of Wawat coming out of the Eastern Desert. During the Second Intermediate Period, the kingdom of Kush, culturally Classic Kerma, dominated all of Upper and Lower Nubia. Eventually, during the New Kingdom, the Egyptians termed all of Nubia (south of Aswān) Kush. Wawat remained, however, the specific designation for Lower Nubia.

SIGNIFICANCE

Wawat was the northernmost region of Nubia proper and was one of the first areas into which the fledgling pharaonic state began to expand. Essentially depopulated after the late Old Kingdom Egyptian subjugation and perhaps absorption of the A-Group Nubian culture, Wawat became the Nilotic base of both the C-Group and Pan-Grave peoples. The region of Wawat had become a major military recruiting ground by the end of the Old Kingdom, and the new groups that settled there provided desert fighters for the armies of First Intermediate Period and early Middle Kingdom Egypt.

—*John Coleman Darnell*

FURTHER READING

Bourriau, J. "Relations Between Egypt and Kerma in the Middle and New Kingdoms." In *Egypt and Africa: Nubia from Pre-History to Islam*, edited by W. V. Davies. London: British Museum Press, 1991. Pages 129-144 provide an archaeological study of the interrelationships between Kerma and Egypt, particularly focusing on the Second Intermediate Period.

Darnell, J. C. "The Route of Eleventh Dynasty Expansion into Nubia: An Interpretation Based on the Rock Inscriptions of Tjehemau at Abisko." *Zeitschrift für ägyptische Sprache und Altertumskunde* 130 (2003). A discussion of archaeological and epigraphic material demonstrating the importance of Lower Nubia as a military recruiting ground for Eleventh Dynasty Thebes. Also contains a discussion of the mercenary-exacerbated unrest during the reign of Amenemhet I (early Twelfth Dynasty).

O'Connor, David. *Ancient Nubia: Egypt's Rival in Africa*. Philadelphia: University Museum, 1993. A well-illustrated overview of Nubian history, although it does not recognize the Western Desert/Libyan origin of the C-Group. See in particular pages 1-69.

_______. "The Locations of Yam and Kush and Their Historical Implications." *JARCE* 23 (1986): 27-50. Contains a discussion of the toponyms of Nubia, especially helpful in clarifying the extents of the regions—including Wawat—during the Old and Middle Kingdoms.

_______. "Urbanism in Bronze Age Egypt and Northeast Africa." In *The Archaeology of Africa: Food, Metals and Towns*, edited by T. Shaw, P. Sinclair, B. Andah, and A. Okpoko. New York: Routledge, 1993. Pages 570-586 give an overview of the development of settled society in Egypt and Nubia.

Sadr, K. *The Development of Nomadism in Ancient Northeast Africa*. Philadelphia: University of Pennsylvania Press, 1991. A study of the interactions of sedentary and nomadic groups in the area. See in particular pages 95-108.

Säve-Söderbergh, T. "Middle Nubian Sites." *The Scandinavian Joint Expedition to Sudanese Nubia* 4, no. 1 (1989): 6-24. Provides an overview of history and culture in the area. The entire volume is an excellent presentation of archaeological sites from the area.

Trigger, B. *History and Settlement in Lower Nubia*. New Haven, Conn.: Yale University Press, 1965. A slightly dated but still useful study.

Wegner, J. "Regional Control in Middle Kingdom Lower Nubia: The Function and History of the Site of Areika." *Journal of the American Research Center in Egypt* 32 (1995): 127-160. A study of a smaller Nubian fortress, apparently the base of Egyptianized Nubians.

Williams, B. B. "Serra East and the Mission of Middle Kingdom Fortresses in Nubia." In *Gold of Praise*, edited by E. Teeter and J. A. Larson. Studies in Ancient Oriental Civilizations 58. Chicago: Oriental Institute Press, 1999. Pages 435-449 give an overview of the purpose and functioning of the great series of Middle Kingdom fortresses near the Second Cataract.

SEE ALSO: c. 2200-1500 B.C.E., Kerma Kingdom Develops and Dominates Lower Nubia; c. 2160 B.C.E., First Intermediate Period Begins in Egypt; c. 2055 B.C.E., Middle Kingdom Period Begins in Egypt; c. 1900-1527? B.C.E., Kerma Kingdom Rules Nubia; c. 1650 B.C.E., Hyksos Create Second Intermediate Period.

RELATED ARTICLE in *Great Lives from History: The Ancient World*: Montuhotep II.

c. 2500-c. 1500 B.C.E.
SOUTHEAST ASIANS MIGRATE INTO THE SOUTH PACIFIC

Skilled navigators from Southeast Asia, who felt motivated to cross great expanses of water in search of new homes, settled the islands of the South Pacific.

LOCALE: South Pacific (Oceania)
CATEGORY: Expansion and land acquisition

SUMMARY OF EVENT

The South Pacific is believed to be the last place on Earth to be inhabited by humans. The islands of the Pacific are divided into three regions: Polynesia, Melanesia, and Micronesia. Together they form an area four times the size of Europe.

There are several theories as to the origins of the South Pacific people. The most agreed on is that the first inhabitants of the Pacific were hunters and gatherers from what is now Indonesia. Short of stature, dark-skinned with frizzy hair, these immigrants were the direct ancestors of the Aborigines of Australia, the Highland people of Papua New Guinea (Melanesia), and the Negritos still living in the interiors of the Philippines and Malaysia. The path of their migration went from Indonesia to Melanesia, over the Pacific into Micronesia. Travelers continued to migrate to the Pacific in waves, moving from island to island.

Melanesian peoples had lived in the southwest Pacific for more than thirty-five hundred years, but the remote islands of Oceania remained uninhabited. By 2500 B.C.E., a wave of immigrants sailed into the islands in steps from Southeast Asia, reaching the Bismarck Archipelago north of Papua New Guinea by 1600 B.C.E. These new arrivals mixed with the black-skinned Papuan-speaking aborigines, creating the Melanesian culture that eventually moved on to Fiji. Later travelers also sailed north to Micronesia. The first settlers of Melanesia are believed to have deliberately and frequently taken to the seas. These successful settlers were adept at finding and utilizing valuable resources.

At the same time (2500 B.C.E.), Austronesian-speaking people from the Philippines and Indonesia reached Palau, Yap, and the Marianas Islands in western Micronesia. Vegetation on the Micronesian coral islands was very different from the lush vegetation to which they were accustomed. They had to change their methods of farming. They became expert boat builders and navigators. Migration from one island group to another was slow, usually spread over several generations. Many traveled eastward; others stayed and intermarried with Melanesians and other Asian travelers.

Evidence shows that most Micronesian cultures are related to the Polynesian culture in that they can both be traced back to Southeast Asia through the Lapita culture. The peoples of Nukura and Kapingamarangi, two Micronesian atolls, have characteristics similar to Polynesians. This indicates these atolls may have been settled by voyagers from Samoa and Tonga, which are believed to be the first of the Polynesian islands to be settled.

Archaeologists have determined that the true homeland of Polynesia is on the western edge of Polynesia itself. The migration of Polynesians can be traced through pottery. Lapita pottery—named for the location in New Caledonia (Melanesia) where it was found—provides evidence of the general route the ancestors of the Polynesians traveled when migrating into the Pacific in 1500 B.C.E. It proves that ancient Polynesians sailed through Melanesia, not Micronesia, as was originally thought. A particular mix of materials and distinctive designs characterizes this pottery. Though changed over time, these materials and designs remained consistent throughout the regions in which this pottery was found.

Research also indicates that it probably took the Lapita people no more than a few hundred years to move from island to island through Melanesia to Fiji, Tonga, and Samoa. Samples of this pottery have been found on islands from the northeast coast of New Guinea to archipelagos at the western edge of Polynesia. It is believed that the basic ceramic knowledge came from Southeast Asia.

The Lapita who settled in Melanesia became absorbed into the Melanesian population. Those who continued into Polynesia found uninhabited islands and founded their own society. Present-day peoples of Polynesia are direct descendants of the Lapita, evolving with little outside input. They intermarried with the people they encountered on the move into the Pacific. This expansion was the first major movement of Austronesian-speaking people into the Pacific.

The Lapita developed knowledge of seacraft by developing outriggers and double-hulled canoes. They traveled in small numbers, two hundred to four hundred people, without navigational instruments. They traveled upwind, searching in the direction from which they could most easily return in case they did not find land. By 1000 B.C.E., Polynesians moved farther east toward the Hawaiian Islands and farther south and west to New Zealand.

They brought with them root crops such as taro and yams, dogs, chickens, and other poultry. It was at this time that the Lapita culture began to disappear.

SIGNIFICANCE

Discovery of the remote, widely spread Pacific Islands was one of the most remarkable achievements of humanity. Despite the ongoing differences in the scientific community as to the origins of the South Pacific people, it can be agreed on that their travels are unparalleled in ancient times. Voyaging across the great expanse of the Pacific Ocean was not easy. The voyagers traveled in canoes built using tools made of stone, bone, and coral. There was the danger of capsizing in heavy seas, and hulls could be smashed against coral reefs or hidden rocks. The voyagers were often exposed to the elements, with only grass or leaf shelters for protection.

In spite of these hardships, the early travelers continued their move eastward. They navigated without instruments and depended on observations of the stars, currents, and the movement of ocean swells and by traditional knowledge of the patterns of nature for clues to the direction and location of islands. They also studied the seasons of the westerly winds and knew when to avoid hazardous weather.

Quarrels regarding leadership could have been one of the reasons small groups split off and continued moving east. Their migration took place step by step, with only part of those who participated in the first move taking part in the second one. A wave of exploration preceded a wave of colonization. Canoes with explorers were sent out to look for land before the group followed with the women and children.

Modern science has contributed to the studies of the South Pacific expansion with computer-aided simulations, carbon-14 dating and DNA (deoxyribonucleic acid) testing. Computer simulations of exploratory voyages show that explorers traveled upwind in search of islands. Although traveling upwind may have been difficult, if they did not find land, a tailwind would ease their return. This upwind travel may indicate that the voyagers to the South Pacific were strongly motivated to search the ocean and settle it.

The majority of studies have been done on the Polyne-

AUSTRALIA AND THE SOUTH PACIFIC

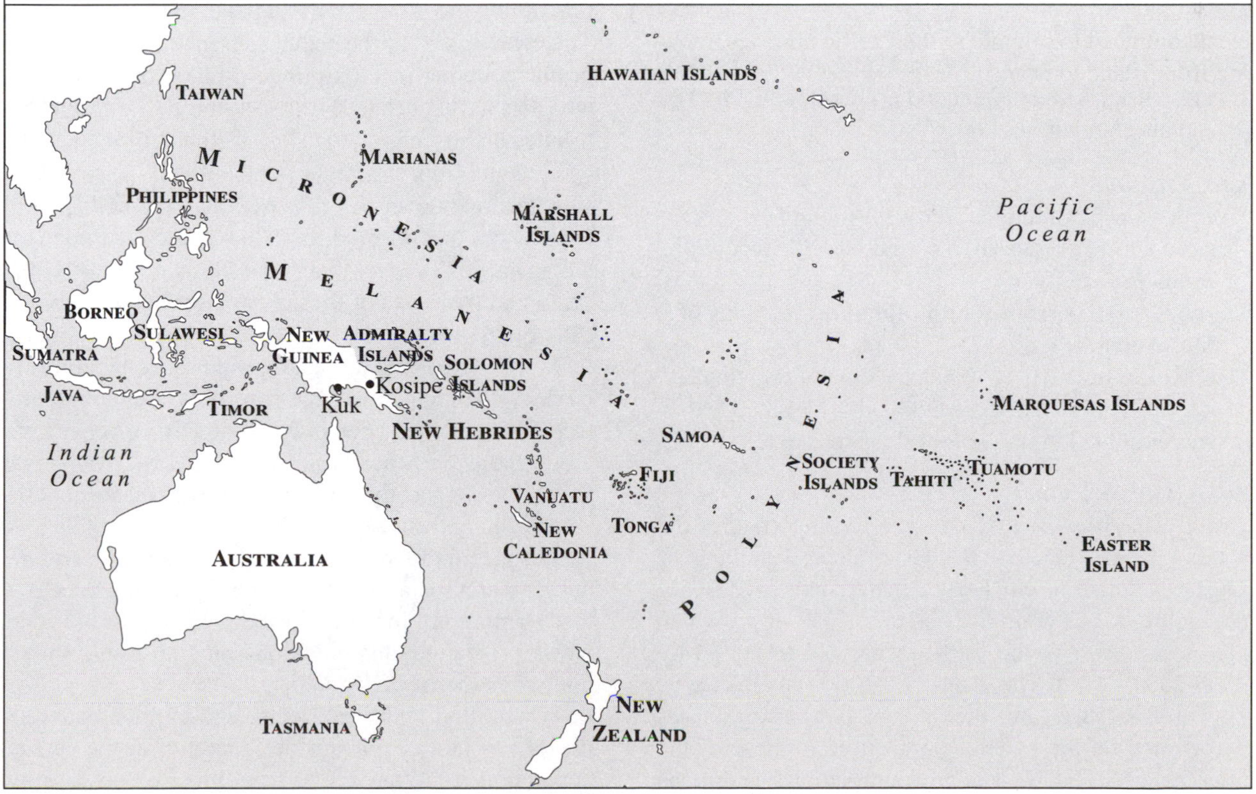

sian movement east; there is very little information on the Micronesians. The contribution of the Polynesians was the development of seafaring and navigation skills and canoe technology that enabled them to travel back and forth across the Pacific. They often returned to central Polynesia and not only related their adventures but also gave directions to the island they had visited, inspiring additional travel.

—*Maryanne Barsotti*

FURTHER READING

Allen, Jim. "In Search of the Lapita Homeland: Reconstructing the Prehistory of the Bismarck Archipelago." *Journal of Pacific History* 19, no. 4 (1984): 186-187. An article on the Lapita pottery culture from its origin in the Bismarck Archipelago to its disappearance c. 1000 B.C.E.

Bellwood, Peter S. *Man's Conquest of the Pacific: The Prehistory of Southeast Asia and Oceania*. New York: Oxford University Press, 1979. A study of the migration of people and cultures into Southeast Asia and the South Pacific Ocean.

_______. *The Polynesians: Prehistory of an Island People*. London: Thames and Hudson, 1978. A detailed study of the history and culture of the Polynesian people of the South Pacific

Heyerdahl, Thor. *American Indians in the Pacific*. London, England: George Allen & Unwin, 1952. A study of the theory that the South Pacific islands were settled by South Americans.

SEE ALSO: c. 1500 B.C.E.-c. 500 C.E., Lapita Culture Colonizes the South Pacific.

c. 2340 B.C.E.
SUMERIAN URUK-AGINA MAKES SOCIAL AND POLITICAL REFORMS

Uruk-Agina was the first ruler to address social ills by proclaiming reforms to alleviate the oppression of the population of the Sumerian city Lagash by its priestly class.

LOCALE: Southern Mesopotamia (modern-day Iraq)
CATEGORIES: Government and politics; prehistory and ancient cultures

KEY FIGURES

Uruk-Agina (Uruinimgina; fl. twenty-fourth century B.C.E.), king of Lagash, r. c. mid-twenty-fourth century B.C.E.

Lugalzagesi (fl. twenty-fourth century B.C.E.), king of Mesopotamia, r. c. 2375-2350 B.C.E.

Hammurabi (c. 1810-1750 B.C.E.), king of Babylonia, r. c. 1792-1750 B.C.E., promulgated a legal code that was exhibited in public for all citizens to see

SUMMARY OF EVENT

Uruk-Agina was the first known social reformer of the ancient world. He was the last independent king of Lagash, a Sumerian city located in the southern Mesopotamian basin. His reign is dated to c. 2340 B.C.E., which places his reign in the Early Dynastic IIIb period (c. 2500-2334 B.C.E.). The series of reforms he effected as king in Lagash were intended to correct economic abuses perpetrated on the general population by those of the priestly class. His reforms are known from inscriptions left on three clay cones and an oval-shaped plaque found at the site of ancient Lagash in 1878.

Uruk-Agina does not appear to have risen to the position of ruler over Lagash through hereditary succession. This is suggested by the notable absence of any reference in his surviving inscriptions to a father or grandfather who may have preceded him on the throne. Further, he attributed his succession to the god Ningirsu, who led him by the hand from the larger population of the city to assume his reign over the city. Although the political circumstances that allowed for his ascent to the throne are unknown, it is known that he used his new position to champion the cause of those who were being economically oppressed.

In the statements he made to introduce his reforms, Uruk-Agina proclaimed that it was his intention to protect those who had been preyed upon by rapacious religious and civic officials. In so doing, Uruk-Agina was the first to suggest that the king, acting as an agent of the patron god of the city, was responsible for providing social justice for the weaker citizens of the state. Therefore, his view of a socially just reign prefigured the lofty goal that Hammurabi included in the preamble to his code, which proclaimed his intention that "the strong should not wrong the weak."

What followed in Uruk-Agina's inscriptions was a series of proclaimed reforms designed to free the general population from various burdens imposed on them by members of the priestly class. First among the complaints of the people was the appropriation of the best fields by priests: As translated by J. N. Postgate in *Early Mesopotamia* (1992), "The oxen of the gods ploughed the garlic plots of the ensi, and the best fields of the gods became the garlic and cucumber plots of the ensi." Uruk-Agina effected a fair redistribution of the use of agricultural lands, considered to be the property of the gods, among the population of the city.

He also identified the abuses of various state inspectors who used their examinations of crops, herds, fisheries, and boat travel on the canals to extract exorbitant taxes from all segments of society. As part of his reforms, Uruk-Agina reduced the number of state inspectors, many of whom had adopted the practice of billeting themselves among the people.

In addition, the population of Lagash had suffered extortion by priests who charged exorbitant fees for officiating at individual burial ceremonies, which from early times involved the interment of the dead in the wall of a house or in a shaft grave underneath a house. Again as part of his reforms, Uruk-Agina prescribed limits for the fees that priests charged for their services at these rites.

One of the more unusual aspects of the reforms that Uruk-Agina effected was his reform of the practice of polyandry—the practice of wives taking more than one husband. This is the only reference found indicating that such social arrangements were contracted. The practice is at odds with the common practices known throughout the cities of the southern Mesopotamian basin. If this was, indeed, a marital practice in Lagash, Uruk-Agina took steps to end or restrict it.

In addition to the inscriptions that relate to Uruk-Agina's reform, there also survives from this period an inscription recording that a large offering of different kinds of fish was sent to Nippur by Uruk-Agina's wife. The reference provides some insight into the complex nature of the inter-state relationships that existed among the several Sumerian cities of the southern Mesopotamian basin.

The reign of Uruk-Agina came to an end when Lagash was attacked by Lugalzagesi, the king of Mesopotamia (Umma) who subjugated all the cities of Mesopotamia from the Persian Gulf to the Taurus Mountains—that is, the entire Mesopotamian river valley. In a lament that survives from that time, Lugalzagesi is identified as the one who committed sacrilege against Lagash's patron god, Ningirsu, by sacking his city's temples and laying waste its fields. In a final statement from this lament, Uruk-Agina's memory is mentioned favorably as the mourner appeals to his gods: "It is not a sin of Uruk-Agina, king of Girsu! May Nisaba, the goddess of Lugalzagesi, ruler of Umma, make him bear the sin!" (Postgate, 1992).

SIGNIFICANCE

Historians of ancient Mesopotamia have long known that Hammurabi, king of Babylon, was not the first to establish laws to provide basic protections for the general population of his realm. Aspects of his law code had precedents in any number of laws proclaimed by earlier Sumerian and Akkadian rulers of the southern Mesopotamian basin. Uruk-Agina was first among Hammurabi's known predecessors.

—*Carlis C. White*

FURTHER READING

Charvat, Petr. *Mesopotamia Before History.* Rev. ed. New York: Routledge, 2002. An archaeological overview of Mesopotamian society. Includes figures, maps, plates, and bibliography.

Cooper, J. S., trans. *Sumerian and Akkadian Royal Inscriptions, I: Presargonic Inscriptions.* New Haven, Conn.: American Oriental Society, 1986. A collection of inscriptions from the ancient cities of the southern Mesopotamian basin dating to the second millennium B.C.E.

Kramer, S. N. *History Begins at Sumer.* 3d ed. Philadelphia: University of Pennsylvania Press, 1989. A general work on the history of the Sumerians.

Postgate, J. N. *Early Mesopotamia: Society and Economy at the Dawn of History.* London: Routledge, 1996. A treatment of the general culture of the ancient societies in Mesopotamia.

Snell, Daniel C. *Life in the Ancient Near East.* New Haven, Conn.: Yale University Press, 1997. A treatment of the full sweep of history in ancient Mesopotamia, which places the reforms of Uruk-Agina in their fuller historical context.

SEE ALSO: c. 2334-c. 2279 B.C.E., Sargon of Akkad Establishes the Akkadian Dynasty; c. 2112 B.C.E., Ur-Nammu Establishes a Code of Law; c. 1770 B.C.E., Promulgation of Hammurabi's Code.

c. 2334-c. 2279 B.C.E.
SARGON OF AKKAD ESTABLISHES THE AKKADIAN DYNASTY

Sargon of Akkad united the city-states along the Tigris and Euphrates Rivers, forming the first empire in world history. This unity permitted a range of developments in art, writing, and technology.

LOCALE: Mesopotamia (present-day Iraq)
CATEGORIES: Expansion and land acquisition; prehistory and ancient cultures

KEY FIGURE

Sargon of Akkad (fl. twenty-fourth to twenty-third century B.C.E.), Mesopotamian ruler, r. c. 2334-2279 B.C.E.

SUMMARY OF EVENT

According to legend, Sargon of Akkad (Šarru-kēn) was born of humble origins. A text written in the 600's B.C.E. tells of how his mother set him adrift on a river and that he was rescued by Akki, a man who was drawing water from the river. Sargon became a royal cup-bearer to Ur-Zababa, the king of Kish.

> My changeling mother conceived me, in secret she bore me. She set me in a basket of rushes, with bitumen she sealed my lid. She cast me into the river which rose not over me. The river bore me up and carried me to Akki, the drawer of water. . . . While I was a gardener, Ishtar granted me her love.

This child eventually would take over the land of his master and go on to found a new kingdom, the kingdom of Akkad. The people of the area would be known as Akkadians.

Originally, the term Mesopotamia (*meso*, "middle," plus *potamia*, "rivers") referred to a region of the Middle East that lies between the Tigris and Euphrates Rivers in what is now Iraq. Because of its rich alluvial soil, people established successful farming communities here from about 3500 B.C.E. During the years of the third millennium, two types of people lived in the area: pastoralists or sheepherders and farmers who raised stock for their subsistence. The farmers were able to settle down near the rivers, but the pastoralists were nomads and are thought to have wandered between the settlements or to have come from the desert to the west or south, which could only be farmed with irrigation. The nomadic pastoralists spoke a Semitic language, whereas most (but not all) farmers spoke Sumerian, a language very different from the Semitic. It seems that before Sargon, Sumerian was the predominant language. However, archaeologists have been able to document a steady rise of the Semitic language and population from about 2300 B.C.E. It seems that the nomads might generally have lived outside the gates of the city with their sheep, whereas the more settled people lived inside. Over a period of about one thousand years, the nomads and the farmers began a process of infiltration and concourse with each other. The nomadic tribes may have even ransacked the towns and settled there themselves.

During the Early Dynastic period, sometimes referred to as pre-Sargonic (c. 2900-c. 2340 B.C.E.), people had begun to live in city-states, each of which had its own ruler and god or goddess, and included suburbs and satellite towns and villages, as well as gardens, palm groves, and fields of barley and wheat. The chief building in each city state was a ziggurat, a huge, many-tiered temple. From these temples, the priests would collect taxes in the form of crops.

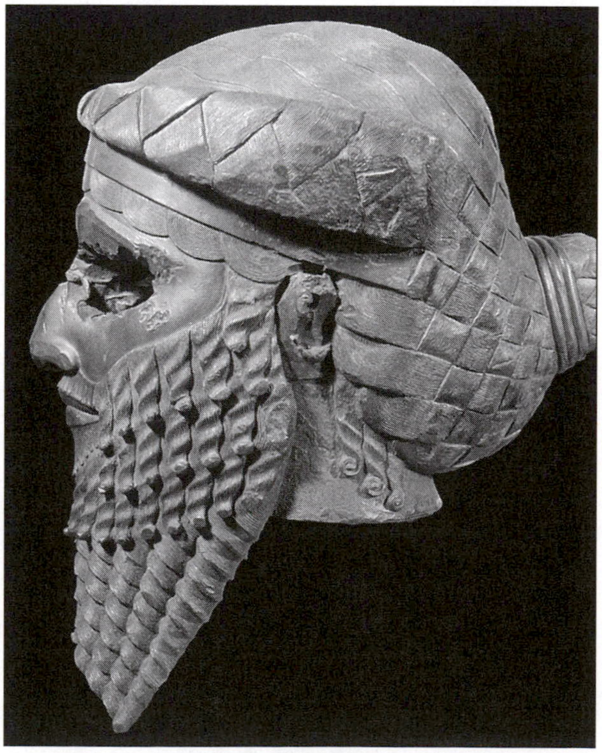

A bronze sculpture of Sargon of Akkad, or possibly his grandson Naram-Sin. (Gianni Dagli Orti/Corbis)

Gradually, political power began to shift between the major cities. When the king of Kish, Ur-Zababa, was conquered in battle by Lugalzagesi of Uruk, Sargon moved to the city of Akkad, the exact location of which has never been determined. He defeated Lugalzagesi, and brought him in chains to Nippur. Sargon then began to extend his control to all of the city-states in the Mesopotamian area, which necessitated uniting the two ethnolinguistic groups. He was an indomitable soldier and powerful administrator, so much so that later monarchs modeled themselves after him. He seems to have destroyed a number of North Syrian cities. He controlled the waterways down to the head of the Persian Gulf. He may even have penetrated central Anatolia. On one stone fragment, Sargon is presented as a terrifying conqueror endowed with an awesome aura. On several fragments, he is compared to a lion.

His empire lasted for just about two hundred years. When Sargon died in 2279, general revolt broke out in Sumer and in Iran. His son and successor, Rimush, repressed it with extreme vigor, but his authority was challenged by his own servants, who killed him in 2270, after a reign of only nine years. Rimush was replaced by Manishtusu, who reigned from 2269 to 2255. Sargon's grandson Naram-Sin, who reigned from 2254 to 2218, became the next hero of the Akkadian Empire. Naram-Sin's reign was filled with military operations. He is commemorated by a rock sculpture and by a masterpiece of Mesopotamian sculpture, the famous stela found at Susa, which is now in the Louvre Museum. He is shown armed with a bow and with the horned tiara of the gods on his head, climbing a steep mountain and treading on the corpses of his enemies.

LIST OF MAJOR AKKADIAN KINGS, 2375-2154 B.C.E.

PRE-AKKADIAN PERIOD

Ruler	*Reign*
Lugalzagesi, king of Uruk	2375-2350
Ur-Zababa, king of Kish	

THE AKKADIAN DYNASTY

Ruler	*Reign*
Sargon I	c. 2334-2279
Rimush, Sargon's son	2278-2270
Manishtusu, Sargon's second son	2269-2255
Naram-Sin, Sargon's grandson	2254-2218
Shar-kali-sharri, son of Naram-Sin	2218-2193
Igigi, king of Babylon	2192
Nanum, king of Babylon	2191
Elulu, king of Baylon	2190
Dudu, king of Babylon	2189-2169
Shudurul, king of Babylon	2168-2154

SIGNIFICANCE

Sargon's reign represents a turning point in the history of Mesopotamia. For the first time, one ruler took over an area that consisted of many small city-states. Civilization—that is, the formation of complex societies—is thought to have begun around 3500 B.C.E. Before Sargon, various peoples had banded together for self-protection or management. During this time there were wars between the city-states and at various times one or another of these would be dominant. Between 2400 and 2334, Sargon conquered these cities. He took over the civilizations of the river valleys and set up a unified empire, integrating all of them into one whole, and inaugurating an Akkadian supremacy. He called himself King of the Lands and King of the Four Quarters. He appointed Semites to high administrative offices and appointed his daughter Enheduanna as chief priestess of Nanna of Ur.

While this empire lasted, many developments took place in technology, art, and literature. Its most outstanding achievement was the invention of a type of writing which the Romans later called cuneiform, from the Latin word for "wedge." Akkadian became the name of a language known for its literary prestige. Indeed, Sargon's daughter Enheduanna is the first writer in the world whose name was preserved for posterity.

—*Winifred O. Whelan*

FURTHER READING

Crawford, Harriet. *Sumer and the Sumerians*. New York: Cambridge University Press, 1991. This book attempts to document the changes that took place on the Mesopotamian plain in the fourth and third millennia B.C.E. It begins with specific aspects of the societies such as the physical environment and the historical background, and combines that with a more traditional, chronological account.

Goodnik, Joan. *Legends of the Kings of Akkade: The Texts*. Winona Lake, Ind.: Eisenhaus, 1997. Illustrates and translates original texts and fragments regarding Sargon and Naram-Sin, his grandson.

Hawkes, Jacquetta. *The Atlas of Early Man: 35000 B.C.-A.D. 500*. New York: St. Martin's Press, 1976. Contains pictures, diagrams, and archaeological findings of ancient civilizations.

Iftikhar, Ahmad, Herbert Brodsky, Marylee Susan Crofts, and Elizabeth Gaynor Ellis. *World Cultures: A Global Mosaic*. New Jersey: Prentice Hall, 1996. The authors here are concerned with the civilizations of the pre-Sargonic and Sargonic periods. They describe the emergence and operation of city-states, and also how archaeologists know what happened in these years through means other than writing.

Roberts, J. H. *Prehistory and the First Civilizations*. Volume 1 in *The Illustrated History of the World*. New York: Oxford University Press, 1999. Describes armies and weapons, irrigation, flood control, and the building of temples in early southern Mesopotamia.

Roux, Georges. *Ancient Iraq*. 3d ed. New York: Penguin Books. 1992. A good introduction for the general reader, covering both political and military history and the history of everyday life.

SEE ALSO: c. 3100 B.C.E., Sumerians Invent Writing; c. 3050 B.C.E., Unification of Lower and Upper Egypt; c. 2900-c. 2340 B.C.E., Early Dynastic Period Flourishes in Southern Mesopotamia; c. 2340 B.C.E., Sumerian Uruk-Agina Makes Social and Political Reforms; c. 2300 B.C.E., Enheduanna Becomes First Named Author.

RELATED ARTICLE in *Great Lives from History: The Ancient World*: Enheduanna.

c. 2333 B.C.E.
OLD CHOSŎN STATE FOUNDED IN KOREA

Legend states that Tangun Wanggom founded Korea by establishing a kingdom now known as Old Chosŏn; these legends remain an important part of the Korean national consciousness.

LOCALE: Northwestern Korea and southern Manchuria
CATEGORIES: Prehistory and ancient cultures; wars, uprisings, and civil unrest

KEY FIGURES

Tangun Wanggom (fl. c. twenty-fourth century B.C.E.), legendary founder of Korea, king of Tangun Chosŏn, r. from 2333 B.C.E.
Kija (fl. twelfth century B.C.E.), king of Kija Chosŏn, r. from c. 1122 B.C.E.
Wiman (fl. c. second century B.C.E.), king of Wiman Chosŏn, r. from 194 B.C.E.

SUMMARY OF EVENT

There is archaeological evidence that the Korean peninsula was inhabited as early as 500,000 years ago. However, most historians place Korea's Paleolithic Age between 40,000 and 50,000 years ago. Artifacts that belong to this period include stone axes, choppers, points, and scrapers. The Paleolithic Age was followed by the Neolithic Age (5000-4000 B.C.E.), Bronze Age (4000-1000 B.C.E.), and Iron Age (1000-400 B.C.E.).

According to legend, Korea was founded by the king Tangun Wanggom in 2333 B.C.E. The earliest known source addressing this origin is *Samguk Yusa* (1281; *Samguk Yusa: Legends and History of the Three Kingdoms of Ancient Korea*, 1972), written by the Korean Buddhist monk Iryŏn (1206-1289) during the Koryŏ Dynasty (918-1392).

Iryŏn based the story of Tangun's founding of Korea on Wei Shou's Chinese history *Wei Shu* (c. late sixth century C.E.; *Treatise on Buddhism and Taoism*, 1956). According to Iryŏn, the *Wei Shu* states that Tangun Wanggom founded the Korean kingdom at Asadal and named it Chosŏn in the fiftieth year of rule by Chinese emperor Yu during the Xia Dynasty (Hsia; c. 2100-1600 B.C.E.); traditionally this date is given as 2333 B.C.E.

Citing another work called *Kogi* (literally "old record," perhaps a name given to all histories written before the mid-Koryŏ Dynasty), Iryŏn wrote in *Samguk Yusa* that Hwanung, son of the creator Hwanin, wished to descend to Earth and rule humankind. After receiving permission from his father, Hwanung, along with three thousand spirits, descended on T'aebaek.

On the mountain, Hwanung encountered a bear and tiger, who beseeched him to make them human. He promised to transform them if they would follow his bidding. Although the bear persevered and was transformed into a woman, the tiger failed to become human. Because the woman wanted to bear a child, Hwanung changed himself into a man and married her. They had a son, Tangun Wanggom, who was made king by the people.

In ancient Korea, the dominant religions were animism, totemism, shamanism, and ancestor worship. In totemism, a natural object or animal is chosen as a patron saint. Given the religious practices of the time, historians have formulated a theory regarding the Tangun Chosŏn origin story. Hwanin and his son Hwanung most likely came from a heaven-worshiping tribe, and the woman who married Hwanung probably came from a bear-totem tribe. These tribes were probably of high status, and their union by marriage would have strengthened their authority. The failure of the tiger to become human suggests that the tiger-totem tribe was of a lower status.

The Old Chosŏn (Ko Chosŏn) period is often divided into three eras: Tangun Chosŏn (2333-1122 B.C.E.), Kija Chosŏn (1122-194), and Wiman Chosŏn (194-108). According to traditional sources, the debauchery of Zhouwang (Chouwang), the last emperor of the Shang Dynasty (1600-1066) in China, brought about his downfall and resulted in the founder of the Zhou Dynasty (Chou; 1066-256) taking over the country. At the end of the Shang Dynasty, a Chinese statesman called Kija (Jizi, or Chi-tzu in Chinese) obtained permission from the new emperor of China to emigrate to Chosŏn with five thousand followers. After arriving in Tangun Chosŏn, he took it over in c. 1122 B.C.E. However, some scholars contend that Kija was just a refugee fleeing wartorn China, and others claim he never came to Korea.

Although the existence of the Kija Chosŏn era is somewhat debatable, the next period, Wiman Chosŏn, is well documented. During the third century B.C.E., China was once again undergoing turmoil and a rapid succession of states. After the Warring States Period (475-221 B.C.E.), China was unified for the first time under the Qin Dynasty (Ch'in; 221-206 B.C.E.), which was soon replaced by the Han Dynasty (206 B.C.E.-220 C.E.).

The turbulence on the continent sent many fugitives across the Yalu River. Among them was Wiman, who came from one of the former Warring States, Yan (Yen). He put his fate in the hands of King Jun of Old Chosŏn. Wiman was well received, given land by the unsuspecting king, and a post guarding the northwestern border. When Wiman collected enough followers, however, he marched on P'yŏngyang (also called Wanggŏm) and usurped the kingdom. King Jun had just enough time to slip away and sail south before Wiman entered the palace, beginning the Wiman Chosŏn era in 194 B.C.E. Some scholars maintain that Wiman was actually a Korean general who served in the Chinese Yan state, which would mean continuous Korean rule instead of the existence of a Chinese state within Korea. The fact that the region occupied by the Yan state had been a part of Old Chosŏn at some point gives the theory some credibility.

Wiman was a capable ruler, and when his kingdom was at its height, it extended from the Han River in the south to southern Manchuria in the north. In 109 B.C.E., the Han emperor, Wudi (Wu-ti), fearful of his empire's security, sent an invading army to stop the expansion of Wiman Chosŏn. King Ugŏ, the grandson of Wiman, mounted a stubborn resistance. The siege lasted until 108 B.C.E., when a traitor assassinated King Ugŏ and fled to the enemy camp, and another opened the gates to the enemy. Wiman Chosŏn fell that year, marking the end of Old Chosŏn.

During the Old Chosŏn period, other political entities existed on the Korean peninsula and southern Manchuria. In the Sungari River basin in Manchuria, there was Puyo, which dates at least as far back as the fourth century B.C.E. Puyo developed into a powerful state, but was taken by Koguryŏ of the Three Kingdoms Period in 370 C.E. South of Puyo, along the Yalu River and Tungchia River basin, were Ye and Maek. Imdun existed in the northeast shore of the peninsula in the South Hamgyŏng Province, and Chinbon was located in the region of Hwanghae Province below the Taedong River.

After Han China defeated Wiman Chosŏn in 108 B.C.E., it established four administrative districts based on the former territories of Imdun, Chinbon, Ye, and Old Chosŏn. Imdun and Chinbon territories became Lintun (Lin-t'un) and Chenfan (Ch'en-fan) Commanderies, respectively. Ye territory became Xuantu (Hsüan-t'u, or Hyundo in Korean) Commandery. Old Chosŏn territory became Lelang (Nangnang in Korean) Commandery, which occupied the region along the Taedong River. Lolang became the political and economic center of the Chinese government. Because of the natives' constant infringement, soon there was much territorial restructuring and readjustment. Only Lolang lasted for more than four centuries and was eventually seized by Koguryŏ in 313 C.E.

South of the Han River, the state of Chin existed around the third century B.C.E. Continuous migration from the north brought more advanced bronze and iron technology. Chin grew in power and was eventually restructured into three Hans (Samhan): Mahan, Chinhan, and Pyonhan. In the first century B.C.E., two powerful kingdoms emerged from these Hans, Silla (57 B.C.E.) and Paekje (Paekche; 17 B.C.E.), which, together with Koguryŏ in the north, formed the Three Kingdoms from which the period takes its name.

SIGNIFICANCE

The founding of Korea is a controversial issue, and some scholars question the existence of Tangun Wanggom as well as the story of his founding of Old Chosŏn. Some scholars prefer to consider Kija the founder of Korea, but his Chinese origins are problematic to some nationalistic Koreans. Further research is needed to settle the numerous controversies. Regardless of the veracity of the Tangun stories, for centuries the Korean people have identified themselves with this early king. In times of crisis, the Korean people have rallied under the banner of Tangun, and Tangun worship has strengthened over time, deepening the Koreans' national consciousness. True or not, the story of Tangun's founding of Korea is deeply ingrained in the people's psyche, where it is likely to remain.

—*Hwa-Soon Choi Meyer*

FURTHER READING

Hulbert, Homer B. *Hulbert's History of Korea*. 2 vols. London: Routledge and Kegan Paul, 1962. Contains a detailed account of the perhaps legendary Kija and a critical treatment of Wiman.

Joe, Wanne J. *Traditional Korea: A Cultural History*. Vol. 1 in *A History of Korean Civilization*. Seoul: Chung'ang University Press, 1972. This history of Korea does not acknowledge the Kija Chosŏn period.

Lee, Ki-baik. *A New History of Korea*. Translated by Edward W. Wagner. Cambridge, Mass.: Harvard University Press, 1984. This history of Korea does not recognize the Tangun Chosŏn period.

Macdonald, Donald Stone. *The Koreans*. San Francisco: Westview Press, 1990. Traces the historical roots of the Korean people and follows the development of their culture. Emphasizes the importance of Korea strategically, economically, and culturally.

Nahm, Andrew C. *Introduction to Korean History and Culture*. Elizabeth, N.J.: Hollym, 1993. Presents the mythical and legendary founding of Old Chosŏn plus a clear overview of various other states during the Old Chosŏn period.

SEE ALSO: c. 2100 B.C.E., Xia Dynasty Marks Start of Historical China; c. 1600 B.C.E., Shang Dynasty Develops Writing and Bronzework; c. 1066 B.C.E., Western Zhou Dynasty Begins in China; 140-87 B.C.E., Wudi Rules Han Dynasty China; c. 300-600 C.E., Three Kingdoms Period Forms Korean Culture.

RELATED ARTICLE in *Great Lives from History: The Ancient World*: Wudi.

c. 2300 B.C.E.
ENHEDUANNA BECOMES FIRST NAMED AUTHOR

Enheduanna, a princess, priestess, and poet, wrote hymns to the goddess Inanna in which she mentions her own name, thus becoming the earliest author in the world whose name is known.

LOCALE: Ur of Sumer (now Iraq)
CATEGORY: Literature

KEY FIGURES

Enheduanna (c. 2320-c. 2250 B.C.E.), first named author

Sargon of Akkad (fl. twenty-fourth to twenty-third century B.C.E.), Enheduanna's father, king of Sumer and Akkad

SUMMARY OF EVENT

Sargon of Akkad united all of Sumer and Akkad into the first real empire on Mesopotamian soil. He also invested his daughter, Enheduanna, with the double office of high priestess of the moon god Nanna (also known as Sin) at Ur and of the sky god An at Uruk. With this appointment, Sargon hoped to exercise more control over the restless and rebellious populations of southern Sumerian cities. He had established a stronghold in the north, not far from Kish, which he named Agade (Akkad).

Enheduanna wrote two large cycles of hymns. One cycle honors the Sumerian goddess Inanna (known in Akkadian as Ishtar), the daughter of the moon couple Nanna and Ningal and goddess of love, her father's patron deity, commemorating her supreme rank in the pantheon as "Queen of Heaven" and consort of the deified heaven, An, king of the gods. This cycle celebrated Enheduanna's father's triumphs in war, though describing them as victories of Inanna. The other cycle, known as the Temple Hymns (1969) honors the temples of Sumer and Akkad. This cycle intended to publicize her father's solicitude for the cults of both halves of his newly established empire, the vanquished Sumerian-speaking south as well as the victorious Akkadian-speaking north.

As a priestess, Enheduanna managed agricultural land around the temple and directed rituals pleasing to Nanna and Ningal. To manage these duties she had a large personal staff, including a steward and a scribe. She took the title *en*, a title denoting highest authority in all matters pertaining to the local cult of a deity. A second title, *dam* (spouse), depicts her as wife to the god Nanna with all the rights and duties that entailed. This title may be metaphoric of the closeness of the religious experience between an immanent deity and a human being.

In 1927, a fragmentary alabaster disc 10 inches (26 centimeters) in diameter was found at her sacred dwelling, the *giparu*, in Ur. The disc is inscribed with Enheduanna's name and shows the high priestess flanked by three of her retainers. She wears a fleeced wool garment; her hair is worn loose with curls flowing down her back. Her right arm is raised in a gesture of salutation. The disc commemorates the dedication of a dais in the temple of Inanna in the city of Ur. The disc is on display in the University Museum of the University of Pennsylvania.

Enheduanna's devotion to Inanna is evident in her poetic trilogy "In-nin me-hus-a" ("The Myth of Inanna and Ebih," 2000), "Nin-me-sar-ra" ("The Exaltation of Inanna," 1968), and "In-nin sa-gur-ra" ("A Hymn to Inanna," 1976). The poems are preserved on clay cuneiform tablets, and many of the poems have survived in twenty to fifty different texts, all written several centuries after Enheduanna's life. This is a testament to the hymns' ongoing popularity and importance in Mesopotamian religion.

In the 153rd line of "The Exaltation of Inanna," as translated on the *Electronic Text Corpus of Sumerian Literature* edited by J. A. Black, et al., a man named Lugalanne or Lugalanna has forced Enheduanna out of the temple into exile. This action is apparent evidence of a revolt against the authority of the Sargonic ruling house. Enheduanna, the theologian, understands this as part of the permissive will of the all-powerful Inanna: "Most precious lady, beloved by An, your holy heart is great; may it be assuaged on my behalf." Enheduanna pleads with Inanna to turn back her displeasure. She has done no wrong:

> But my own trial is not yet concluded, although a hostile verdict encloses me as if it were my own verdict. I did not reach out my hands to the flowered bed. I did not reveal the pronouncements of Ningal to anybody. My lady beloved of An, may your heart be calmed towards me, the brilliant en priestess of Nanna.

Inanna is moved and restores Enheduanna to her rightful place. In turn, Enheduanna exalts Inanna: "Praise be to the destroyer of foreign lands, endowed with divine powers by An, to my lady enveloped in beauty, to Inanna!" This reconstruction and translation is based on ninety-seven different manuscripts, dating five to six hundred years beyond the early Sargonic period.

"A Hymn to Innana" describes Inanna's triumphs over the rebellion that erupted in Sargon's old age. In this text, Sargon's military success is credited to the goddess he worshiped. This hymn is the most effusive in its praise of Inanna. Sjoberg's reconstruction of this poem is based on twenty-nine texts and fragments. "The Myth of Inanna and Ebih" is the story of how the goddess destroys the life of a mountain, Ebih, that refuses to honor her. The independence of the goddess is stressed here, as she first asks the help of An, the chief god of the pantheon, and the council of gods in her vendetta, and when they refuse, acts on her own to redress her wrongs.

SIGNIFICANCE

Enheduanna's combined roles of princess and priestess may have set a precedent in Sumerian history for the next five centuries. The impact of her poetry is evident in the fact that her literary work survives in copies made in the Old Babylonian period, some five hundred years after her death. Enheduanna was the first named author in world history. As such, she has attracted the attention of many scholars of a feminist bent, who emphasize the fact that the world's earliest author was a woman who worshiped a decidedly independent and self-sufficient goddess.

—Mark J. Mangano

FURTHER READING

Black, J. A., G. Cunningham, E. Fluckiger-Hawker, E. Robson, and G. Zolyomi. *The Electronic Text Corpus of Sumerian Literature*. Oxford: University of Oxford, 1998-. http://www-etcsl.orient.ox.ac.uk/. Accessed June 17, 2003. This massive project provides composite texts and translations of nearly all extant Sumerian texts, available on the World Wide Web. An extremely valuable resource.

Hallo, William W. *Origins: The Ancient Near Eastern Background of Some Modern Western Institutions*. Leiden: E. J. Brill, 1996. Hallo discusses Enheduanna's role as a woman of antiquity.

Hallo, William W. and J. J. A. Van Dijk, trans. *The Exaltation of Inanna*. New Haven, Conn.: Yale University Press, 1968. A translation and analysis of Enheduanna's poem "The Exaltation of Inanna."

Meador, Betty De Shong. *Inanna, Lady of Largest Heart: Poems of the Sumerian High Priestess Enheduanna*. Austin: University of Texas Press, 2000. This volume is the most complete treatment of the life and poetry of Enheduanna.

Sjoberg, Ake W. "In-nin-sa-gur-ra: A Hymn to the Goddess Inanna by the en-Priestess Enheduanna." *Zeitschrift für Assyriologie* 65 (1975): 161-253. This article contains a translation and analysis of Enheduanna's poem "A Hymn to Inanna."

Sjoberg, Ake W., and E. Bergmann. *The Collection of the Sumerian Temple Hymns*. Locust Valley, N.Y.: J. J. Augustin, 1969. This work is a compilation of Enheduanna's temple hymns.

Westenholz, Joan Goodnick. "Enheduanna, En-Priestess, Hen of Nanna, Spouse of Nanna." In *DUMU-E-DUB-BA-A: Studies in Honor of Ake W. Sjoberg*, edited by Hermann Behrens, Darlene Loding, and Martha T. Roth. Philadelphia: Occasional Publications of the Samuel Noah Kramer Fund, 1989. This study focuses on Enheduanna in her public persona, her role and functions in the cult and rituals of the god Nanna/Sin.

SEE ALSO: c. 2334-c. 2279 B.C.E., Sargon of Akkad Establishes the Akkadian Dynasty; 1770 c. 580 B.C.E., Greek Poet Sappho Dies; c. 1st century B.C.E., Indian Buddhist Nuns Compile the *Therigatha*; c. 99-105 C.E., Ban Zhao Writes Behavior Guide for Young Women.

RELATED ARTICLES in *Great Lives from History: The Ancient World:* Clodia; Deborah; Enheduanna; Sappho.

c. 2300-c. 2000 B.C.E.

FIRST GREAT EXPANSION OF BERBER PEOPLES ACROSS NORTH AFRICA

The Berber tribes, inhabitants of the increasingly arid Sahara to the west of the Nile Valley whom the Egyptians grouped under the ethnonym Tjemehou, began to expand into the Nubian Nile Valley during the late Old Kingdom period.

LOCALE: Libyan Desert, Egyptian and Nubian Nile Valley

CATEGORIES: Expansion and land acquisition; government and politics; prehistory and ancient cultures

SUMMARY OF EVENT

Between 6000 and 2000 B.C.E., pastoralism developed in the eastern Sahara. At sites such as Nabta Playa and at other more permanently watered regions of the eastern Sahara, cultures in close contact with the Nile Valley developed, but there is at this time no certain evidence of Berber linguistic or ethnic associations for these groups. Nevertheless, groups inhabiting the Western Desert—some of them perhaps Berbers—were of considerable importance for the development of ancient Egyptian culture.

Certain of the early Nilotic cultures, from Khartoum in the south to Badari and Deir Tasa in the north, have many features in common and show affinities with later Nubian cultures. Archaeological evidence suggests that one of these earliest predynastic cultures, the Tasian (c. 4000 B.C.E.; first identified at Deir Tasa), may link the early Nilotic cultures and connect them with groups in the Western Desert. Groups such as the Tasians, operating in the southwestern desert with connections to the Nubian and Egyptian Nile Valley, were perhaps the most prominent agents linking the southern and western Neolithic with the Nile Valley.

The development of pharaonic administration around 3250 B.C.E. contributed to a growing rift between the Nilotic Egyptians and the people of the Western Desert. An early ceremonial cosmetic palette depicts the destruction of strongholds in Tjehenu-Libya. The Sixth Dynasty pharaoh Pepi I (r. c. 2321-2287 B.C.E.) fought a campaign in the region of the Libyans. Slightly later, the Sixth Dynasty Egyptian explorer Harkhuf (fl. c. 2300-c. 2200 B.C.E.) encountered a Nubian army on its way to chastise a group of people the Egyptians called the Tjemehou, usually translated as "Libyans." The Tjemehou threat to Lower Nubia coincided with increasing aridity in North Africa and the Near East, and Tjemehou pressure on the Upper Nile Valley continued during Egypt's First Intermediate Period (c. 2160-c. 2055 B.C.E.). This was a time of disunity and rampant militarism in Egypt proper. The arrival of the Tjemehou in Nubia during the late Old Kingdom corresponds to the appearance of the C-Group (the designation for a Nubian cultural phase, c. 2300-c. 1550 B.C.E.) culture in the archaeological record of that area.

Archaeologically, the C-Group culture that appears in

Nubia during the late Old Kingdom and the First Intermediate Period shows affinities with cultures of the Western Desert. Surviving Berber loan words in Nilotic Nubian languages more recently spoken in the major centers of C-Group occupation—between the Second and Third Cataracts—suggest that the C-Group spoke a Berber language. The Egyptian term Tjemehou may in fact represent the Egyptian designation for Berber-language speakers, corresponding to the term "aamou" for speakers of Semitic languages.

Late in the reign of Amenemhet I (r. c. 1985-1956 B.C.E.) during the early Middle Kingdom, his son Sesostris I (r. c. 1971-1926 B.C.E.) fought against northern Tjemehou, apparently to the northwest of the apex of the Nile Delta. Probably as part of a defensive system planned in the face of potential Tjemehou aggression, Amenemhet I had already constructed at least one fortress in the southern Wadi an-Nazrnn, west of the southern Nile Delta (apparently a western counterpart to Amenemhet's defensive network called Wall of the Ruler, established in the eastern margin of the Delta).

These Berber women spinning fibers in Morocco, photographed in 1950, are probably descendants of the early Berbers in North Africa. (Hulton|Archive)

The C-Group in Nubia appear to have contributed soldiers to the Egyptian armies fighting in the internal conflicts of the First Intermediate Period, and later may have formed the core of Upper Egyptian armies. The great Middle Kingdom (c. 2055-c. 1650 B.C.E.) fortresses of the Second Cataract region in Nubia were built initially to control the Nilotic homeland of the settled C-Group, perhaps the southern Tjemehou, in Nubia.

The earliest C-Group sites appear all to be on the west bank of the Nile. C-Group burials were for the most part round tumuli with dry stone exterior walls, occasionally incorporating small external chapels. The C-Group lost any political power in Nubia with the Middle Kingdom conquest and the late Middle Kingdom expansion of direct Egyptian control over Lower Nubia up to the fortresses at the southern edge of the Second Cataract. The C-Group culture was increasingly influenced and overlaid by Kerma culture, and with the Egyptian return to Lower Nubia in the early part of the New Kingdom (c. 1570-c. 1069 B.C.E.), the discernable C-Group culture disappears.

SIGNIFICANCE

The C-Group people, apparently a Berber-language-speaking population, entered the Nubian Nile Valley in significant numbers during the late Old Kingdom and contributed to the highly militarized society of Egypt in the First Intermediate Period. Early Middle Kingdom Egypt constructed complex fortresses in Lower Nubia in order to dominate the major settlement areas of the C-Group and to ensure a perpetual supply of Nubian troops for the Egyptian army. The C-Group appear to have contributed Berber loan words to later Nilotic languages of Lower Nubia.

—John Coleman Darnell

FURTHER READING

Barker, G. "Prehistoric Settlement." In *Synthesis*, vol. 1 of *Farming the Desert: The UNESCO Libyan Valleys Archaeological Survey*, edited by G. Barker, et al. London: UNESCO, 1996. Pages 83-109 provide a brief overview of the north-central Sahara and the archaeological remains of probable Berber speakers.

Bates, Oric. *The Eastern Libyans: An Essay*. London: MacMillan, 1914. An important work that remains the best overview of Libyan culture using Egyptian and classical textual sources and archaeological remains.

Behrens, P. "Language and Migrations of the Early Saharan Cattle Herders: The Formation of the Berber Branch." In *Libya Antiqua, The General History of Africa: Studies and Documents 11*. Paris: UNESCO, 1986. Pages 29-50 give an English summary of longer German-language studies by Behrens, in which he summarizes the linguistic evidence for the identity of the Tjemehou with Berber-speaking groups.

Bietak, M. "The C-Group and the Pan-Grave Culture in Nubia." In *Nubian Culture: Past and Present*, edited by T. Hägg. Stockholm: Sixth International Congress for Nubian Studies, 1987. Pages 1-17 include a useful overview of these two Nubian cultures.

Spalinger, A. "Some Notes on the Libyans of the Old Kingdom and Later Historical Reflexes." *Journal of the Society for the Study of Egyptian Antiquities* 9 (1979): 144-157. A useful overview of Libyan and Egyptian interrelationships, based primarily on Egyptian textual sources.

Williams, B. B. "Serra East and the Mission of Middle Kingdom Fortresses in Nubia." In *Gold of Praise*, edited by E. Teeter and J. A. Larson. Studies in Ancient Oriental Civilizations 58. Chicago: Oriental Institute Press, 1999. Pages 435-449 provide an overview of the purpose and functioning of the great series of Middle Kingdom fortresses near the Second Cataract.

Zarattini, A. "The Hypothesis of the Saharian-Sudanese Unity." *Origini* 12 (1983): 252-271. A study, primarily on the basis of ceramic remains, of the archaeological interrelationships of Nilotic and Western Desert "Nubian" groups.

SEE ALSO: 2500-1900 B.C.E., Wawat Chiefdom Flourishes in Lower Nubia; c. 2200-1500 B.C.E., Kerma Kingdom Develops and Dominates Lower Nubia; c. 2160 B.C.E., First Intermediate Period Begins in Egypt; c. 2055 B.C.E., Middle Kingdom Period Begins in Egypt; c. 1900-1527? B.C.E., Kerma Kingdom Rules Nubia; c. 1200-c. 1000 B.C.E., Berbers Expand Across North Africa.

c. 2300-c. 1800 B.C.E.
BEAKER PEOPLE LIVE IN WESTERN EUROPE

The Beaker culture introduced metallurgical technology that replaced Neolithic methods and, through the derivative Urnfield culture, endured until the Hallstatt period.

LOCALE: Western Europe and parts of central and Southern Europe

CATEGORIES: Prehistory and ancient cultures; science and technology

SUMMARY OF EVENT

The Beaker (or Bell-Beaker) people derive their name from the distinctive bell-shaped drinking vessels placed in their burial sites. Debate exists regarding the origin of their culture, with some archaeological evidence suggesting the western coast of the Iberian Peninsula. Some scholars have narrowed their probable place of origin to the Tagus River Estuary region. From this point, the culture spread eastward into central Europe, encountering, at some uncertain date and location, the Battle-Ax culture, which had migrated into Europe from the east.

The Battle-Ax people were so named because their (single) graves usually include a flat stone ax head with a central post hole into which a handle could be wedged. Because the graves also usually contained pottery with a pattern around the neck created by imprints of cords wrapped diametrically around the vessels, the Battle-Ax people are sometimes also termed the Corded-Ware culture. The Battle-Ax People are theorized to have been an offshoot of the Kurgan folk of the Russian steppe and to be predominately herdsmen and warriors, having domesticated the horse.

The Battle-Ax and Beaker groups then presumably combined culturally and perhaps physically, migrating westward into eastern Great Britain from the Low Countries and northern France. A parallel theory states that one group of Beaker people journeyed by sea from the Tagus Estuary to Brittany, then eventually proceeded to Cornwall in western Britain (attracted there perhaps by the Cornish tin mines). There also seems to have been a less significant migration of Beaker people from southern France, called the Reflux Movement, into Sardinia and Sicily. Another school of thought (in the minority) places the Beaker origin in the east, where merger with the Battle-Ax culture occurred before migration took the merged group to all of the western archaeological sites.

Unlike the Neolithic peoples among whom they settled or whom they supplanted and who entered their dead in communal long barrows, the Beaker people used single burials in smaller, round barrows. In Beaker graves, the deceased were placed in kneeling or fetal positions with drinking vessels placed on their knees, clutched in their hands. The bell shape of the beakers is unique, and the vessels were decorated horizontally with corded marks or etchings from the sharp edges of seashells. Some horizontal lines run straight across the vessel's diameter; others are in a zigzag or wave pattern. Some have diagonal lines in the spaces between them. The significance of these particular patterns, if any, is unknown. It is uncertain whether the vessels actually contained a beverage, and if so what this would have been; milk, beer, and honey mead have been suggested. It has been postulated that the beaker was provided for the departed soul's refreshment in the afterlife, but scholars are unsure of this. Beakers averaged 8 inches (20 centimeters) in diameter. Because of some regional variation in beaker shapes and surface patterns (for example, the bottoms of beakers at British sites tend to be larger and flatter, and those from sites in the present-day Czech Republic have a smaller, more curved shape at the bottom), the existence of four separate Beaker tribal groupings has been suggested: Maritime, including settlements in southern England, Brittany, and the Tagus; Eastern, for sites in Germany, Austria, Hungary, and Poland; a combination of groupings in the Rhineland, the Netherlands, Austria, and North Italy; and Reflux Movements in central Spain, southern France, Sardinia, and Sicily.

Beaker graves have also been found to contain flint arrowheads; archers' wrist guards, which were often crafted from bone; silver and gold ear rings; bone pendants; copper, silver, and gold pins; fragments of woolen and linen weaves; buttons manufactured from jet, amber, or shale; copper axes and awls; and copper-tanged or riveted knives and daggers.

Physically, the skeletons in Beaker burial sites tend to have skulls that are somewhat rounder than the more longish skulls found in Neolithic communal burial sites. They have been identified as being of stockier build than the earlier Neolithic peoples. The theory that the Beaker people (or a Beaker/Battle-Ax amalgamation) formed a sort of horse-riding military aristocracy over the original Neolithic population cannot be conclusively proven through available evidence.

The Beaker people in southern England, who are thought to have displaced the Windmill Hill folk, added to the already existing megalithic site at Stonehenge. Their contribution is generally referred to as Stonehenge II and mainly includes the outer circle of bluestones. The nearby sites of Avebury, a stone-encircled ditch, and Silbury Hill, Britain's longest manmade mound, can be accurately attributed to the Beaker culture.

The Beaker people are most noted for being the first population of metallurgists in the area. It has been suggested that the Beaker people migrated into various parts of Europe in order to follow metallic deposits of copper, silver, and gold. It is not known from whom the Beaker smiths might have learned their skills. Earlier Beaker graves, especially, reveal that the copper daggers and implements were first hardened by treating them with arsenic. Some bodies reveal a high degree of contamination from arsenic and eventually tin, particularly Cornish tin, which was mixed with copper to form a bronze alloy. The Beaker people who migrated into Ireland were probably the earliest workers in the Irish gold of the Wicklow Mountains.

Like much else concerning the Beaker people, the end of their culture is unknown. The speculative ideas that they were speakers of the earliest Indo-European languages and that the remnants of their language may be found in the surviving Celtic tongues of Europe have no basis in verifiable fact. The Beaker people may have simply assimilated into the existing population, a theory that is suggested by the presence of Beaker burials in certain megalithic tombs in Ireland, France, and Britain and in earlier Sicilian and Sardinian rock tombs. Their style of pottery and their metalworking innovations were adopted and later altered by a succeeding culture, the Urnfield people. Evidence exists that the Beaker people engaged in herding of cattle and sheep and, in some areas, hog and chicken farming. Barley seems to have been their staple grain.

Significance

Few details, apart from the content and layout of their burial sites, are known about the Beaker people; however, it is clear that they initiated the Bronze Age in Europe. Because of their interactions with the Neolithic people and presumably with the Battle-Ax people, the Beaker people were a key element in the diffusion of metallurgic technology throughout western, central, and insular Europe.

—*Raymond Pierre Hylton*

Further Reading

Brodie, Neil. *The Neolithic-Bronze Age Transition in Britain: A Critical Review of Some Archaeological and Craniological Concepts*. Oxford, England: Tempus Reparatum, 1994. A look at the Beaker and Neolithic peoples, with reference to their cranial shapes.

Cavendish, Richard. *Prehistoric Britain*. New York: British Heritage Press, 1983. A conventional rendering, but nonetheless a clear concise account of what set the Beaker people apart from Neolithic Europeans.

Gibson, Alex M. *Beaker Domestic Sites: A Study of the Domestic Pottery of the Late Third and Early Second Millennia B.C. in the British Isles*. 2 vols. Oxford, England: B.A.R., 1982. Looks at the Beaker culture in Great Britain and Ireland through its pottery. Illustrations and bibliography.

Harrison, Richard J. *The Beaker Folk: Copper Age Archaeology in Western Europe*. New York: Thames and Hudson, 1980. An examination of the Beaker culture from an archaeological perspective. Bibliography and index.

_______. *The Bell Beaker Cultures of Spain and Portugal*. Cambridge, Mass.: Peabody Museum of Archaeology and Ethnology, Harvard University Press, 1977. Focuses on the Beaker people in Spain and Portugal.

Piggott, Stuart. *Ancient Europe: From the Beginnings of Agriculture to Classical Antiquity*. Chicago: Aldine, 1970. Uses substantial illustrative material; text attempts to place the Beaker people within the general framework of prehistoric European migrations and technological development.

Vlahos, Olivia. *Battle-Ax People: Beginnings of Western Culture*. New York: Viking Press, 1968. Broader based than its title would suggest; tends to downplay the Beaker culture in favor of the Battle-Ax element.

Waldren, William H. *The Beaker Culture of the Balearic Islands: An Inventory of Evidence from Caves, Rock Shelters, Settlements, and Ritual Sites*. Oxford, England: Archaeopress, 1998. Discusses the Beaker culture and Copper Age on the Balearic Islands in Spain.

SEE ALSO: c. 3100-c. 1550 B.C.E., Building of Stonehenge; 14th-9th centuries B.C.E., Urnfield Culture Flourishes in Northwestern Europe; c. 1100-c. 500 B.C.E., Hallstatt Culture Dominates Northern Europe.

c. 2200-1500 B.C.E.
KERMA KINGDOM DEVELOPS AND DOMINATES LOWER NUBIA

Following the collapse of the Middle Kingdom in Egypt, Kerma controlled all of Upper and Lower Nubia. The Classic Kerma culture ended roughly when the Hyksos were defeated, and Kerma culture vanished during the political reorganization of Nubia under Thutmose I in the Eighteenth Dynasty.

LOCALE: Upper and Lower Nubia, centered at Kerma just south of the Third Cataract of the Nile in modern Sudan

CATEGORIES: Expansion and land acquisition; government and politics; prehistory and ancient cultures

SUMMARY OF EVENT

The site of Kerma—near the Third Cataract of the Nile in the Dongola Reach area of the modern Sudan—is an area of atypically broad cultivation for the Nubian Nile Valley. Although some believe the ancient Nubian kingdoms of Wawat, Irtjet, and Setju were located in Lower Nubia, the ancient evidence appears to argue more persuasively for Wawat corresponding to all of Lower Nubia, with Kerma itself within the domain of the combined Upper Nubian kingdoms of Irtjet and Setju. Although often repeated, an identification of Kerma with the Egyptian toponym Yam is not certain.

The Kerma culture is divided into Early, Middle, and Classic Kerma phases. Early Kerma and the beginnings of Middle Kerma correspond to the time of the kingdoms of Irtjet and Setju in the south, the kingdom of Wawat in Lower Nubia, and the latter part of the Old Kingdom (c. 2687-c. 2125 B.C.E.), the First Intermediate (c. 2160-c. 2055), and early Middle Kingdom (c. 2055-c. 1650) periods in Egypt. The combined kingdoms of Irtjet and Setju, occupying Upper Nubia, formed a coalition against pharaonic Egyptian influence during the Sixth Dynasty (c. 2345-c. 2181). At least for a time, they were able to compel Wawat to join them as well. By the early First Intermediate Period, the Early Kerma culture was well underway, apparently more closely associated with the so-called Khartoum Variant of the far southern Late Neolithic than with the C-Group cultural phase of Lower Nubia.

Toward the middle of the Twelfth Dynasty (c. 1985-c. 1782 B.C.E.) in Egypt, Early Kerma transitions into the Middle Kerma phase, and nascent forms of most elements of Classic Kerma begin to appear. In Upper Nubia, the Middle Kerma culture appears archaeologically to represent the kingdoms of Kush and Shaat. During the Middle Kingdom, Egypt dominated Wawat (Lower Nubia) and established a series of fortifications there. Following the probable construction of smaller fortifications early in the Middle Kingdom and during the early Twelfth Dynasty, the Egyptians built a number of "plains style" fortresses on the low desert, north of the Second Cataract region. They were well-fortified rectilinear structures with outworks. These early fortresses provide little evidence of contact between the Egyptians and the local Nubian populations.

Later in the Middle Kingdom, roughly coinciding with the appearance of the Middle Kerma culture, Egypt constructed a series of irregularly shaped fortresses atop granite outcroppings in the Second Cataract proper, incorporating spur walls. These architectural features suggest a growing threat from a people whose potential siege ability the Egyptians had grown to fear. The new threat from the south was almost certainly the Middle Kerma kingdom.

With the collapse of the Egyptian Middle Kingdom around the middle of the Thirteenth Dynasty, Lower Nubia was lost to Egypt, and all the lands south of Aswān appear to be within the sphere of Classic Kerma. Evidence of destruction at the fortress of Buhen, once attributed to Kerma, now appears to be the result of the Egyptian counterattack at the end of the Second Intermediate Period (c. 1650-c. 1570 B.C.E.). The city of Kerma during the Classic Kerma period was quite large, extending for more than thirty hectares. The *deffufa*, a thick-walled mud-brick temple, towered over the city, and a large, round structure testified to the truly African flavor of much of Kerma architecture. A large fortification wall surrounded the city as well. During the Classic Kerma phase, the elite burials eventually incorporated internal skeleton walls. The bed burials that began in the Middle Kerma period continued, but the funerary beds were now decorated with ivory inlays in the shapes of apotropaic animals. Human sacrifice, also occurring in Middle Kerma, increased along with the tomb sizes during the Classic Kerma Phase.

During the Second Intermediate Period in Egypt, a maritime empire—the Hyksos—dominated the Nile Delta. They directly controlled the eastern Delta, centered at Avaris (now Tell el-Babᶜa), and extended their influence far to the south. The presence of Tell el-Yehudiya ware juglets in Nubia and at Kerma demonstrates that Hyksos trade passed as far south as Kerma. The Theban-centered Seventeenth Dynasty (1580-1570) appears, however, to have controlled the trade routes passing north and south between Kerma and the Mediterranean. During the late Seventeenth Dynasty, the Thebans began open hostilities against the Hyksos, and at the time of the height of Classic Kerma, Egyptian imports at Kerma declined markedly, apparently as a result of the trade war that almost certainly marked the beginning of Theban hostilities.

When the Theban ruler Kamose launched an offensive against the Hyksos capitol at Avaris, the Hyksos ruler Apophis wrote to "the son of the [recently deceased] ruler of Kush [Kerma]." The Thebans intercepted the letter on the oasis road, probably a route passing through Kharga. Rather than indicating close ties, as is sometimes suggested, the letter demonstrates that Kerma had little direct contact with the Hyksos: The Hyksos ruler was only vaguely aware of a change of ruler in Kerma and appears not to know the name of the new ruler. The Hyksos Apophis suggested that the Theban successes against the Hyksos and the current Theban offensive in the north at that time offered an excellent opportunity for a combined Hyksos-Kerma operation against Thebes. If the Kerma ruler answered the summons, he was unsuccessful. Kamose, after destroying the Hyksos merchant fleet beneath the walls of Avaris, if not even earlier, reoccupied the old fortress of Buhen, and the end of Kerma drew near.

The Classic Kerma phase ended around the time of Kamose's campaign against Nubia (apparently before the end of his third regnal year), and the rarely attested and disputed Post-Classic Kerma phase began. The true Kerma culture disappears around the time of Thutmose I (r. c. 1493-1481 B.C.E.), third ruler of the Eighteenth Dynasty, with whom much of what is considered classic New Kingdom Egypt began. On the basis of an inscription from the reign of his successor, Thutmose I appears to have divided Nubia into five districts, each governed by a local chief, all under the administration of the Egyptian viceroy of Kush.

SIGNIFICANCE

The rise of Kerma in the south influenced Egyptian approaches to frontier control and fortification in the area of the Second Cataract. The power of Kerma, based on trade, posed a serious threat to Egyptian long-distance trade with the south and ultimately threatened the existence of the Seventeenth Dynasty. Although Kerma did extend its influence through Lower Egypt to Aswān, the magnitude of any offensive operations it may have mounted against the Seventeenth Dynasty at Thebes is still uncertain. Not all of the Kerma population was uniformly inimical to the Upper Egyptians, and people of Kerma cultural affiliation appear to have replaced the Pan-Grave Medjay—who supplied the most skilled desert fighters of the Upper Egyptian armies since the First Intermediate Period—as Nubian military recruits. The demise of Kerma led to a return of Egyptian control over the gold mining regions of the southeastern desert, contributing greatly to the increased strength of the New Kingdom in Egypt.

—*John Coleman Darnell*

FURTHER READING

Bonnet, C. *Kerma, territoire et métropole*. Cairo: Institut Français d'Archéologie Orientale, 1986. A useful overview of the city by the modern excavator most recently involved in uncovering the ancient metropolis. In French.

Bourriau, J. "Nubians in Egypt During the Second Intermediate Period: An Interpretation Based on the Egyptian Ceramic Evidence." In *Studien zur altägyptischen Keramik*, edited by D. Arnold. Mainz: Philip von Zabern, 1981. A useful archaeological study focusing on the interrelationship of the C-Group, Pan-Grave, and Kerma cultures.

_______. "Relations Between Egypt and Kerma in the Middle and New Kingdoms." In *Egypt and Africa: Nubia from Pre-History to Islam*, edited by W. V. Davies. London: British Museum Press, 1991. Pages 129-144 provide an archaeological study of the interrelationships between Kerma and Egypt, particularly focusing on the Second Intermediate Period.

Kemp, B. J. *Ancient Egypt, Anatomy of a Civilization*. New York: Routledge, 1995. Pages 166-178 contain a stimulating discussion of the Second Cataract fortresses and their wider Egyptian social context.

Lacovara, P. "Egypt and Nubia During the Second Intermediate Period." In *The Hyksos: New Historical and Archaeological Perspectives*, edited by E. D. Oren. Philadelphia: University Museum, 1997. Pages 69-83 provide an accessible and clear summary.

_______. "The Internal Chronology of Kerma." *Beiträge zur Sudanforschung* 2 (1987): 51-74. A useful summary.

O'Connor, David. *Ancient Nubia, Egypt's Rival in Africa*. Philadelphia: University Museum, 1993. A well-illustrated overview of Nubian history, although it does not recognize the Western Desert/Libyan origin of the C-Group.

Ryholt, K. S. B. *The Political Situation in Egypt During the Second Intermediate Period, c. 1800-1550 B.C.*, Carsten Nibuhr Institute Publications 20. Copenhagen: Museum Tusculanum Press, 1997. Pages. 326-327 contain a refutation of the idea that the Hyksos thought of Kerma as a vassal state.

Smith, S. T. *Askut in Nubia*. London: Kegan Paul, 1995. An examination of the Second Cataract Fortresses, focusing primarily on their economic functions.

SEE ALSO: c. 2687 B.C.E., Old Kingdom Period Begins in Egypt; 2500-1900 B.C.E., Wawat Chiefdom Flourishes in Lower Nubia; c. 2200-1500 B.C.E., Kerma Kingdom Develops and Dominates Lower Nubia; c. 2160 B.C.E., First Intermediate Period Begins in Egypt; c. 2055 B.C.E., Middle Kingdom Period Begins in Egypt; c. 1900-1527? B.C.E., Kerma Kingdom Rules Nubia; c. 1650 B.C.E., Hyksos Create Second Intermediate Period; c. 1570 B.C.E., New Kingdom Period Begins in Egypt.

c. 2160 B.C.E.
FIRST INTERMEDIATE PERIOD BEGINS IN EGYPT

During the First Intermediate Period, the Heracleopolitans controlled Egypt, but power shifted to Thebes in the south during the Eleventh Dynasty.

LOCALE: Nile River Valley, Lower Nubia, the oases of the Western Desert

CATEGORIES: Government and politics; prehistory and ancient cultures; wars, uprisings, and civil unrest

SUMMARY OF EVENT

Administrative reforms during the late Old Kingdom (c. 2687-c. 2125 B.C.E.) saw the expansion of agriculture in Middle Egypt and the southern Nile Delta, with control of the area and its wealth centered in the region of Meir in northern Middle Egypt. Following the end of the Sixth Dynasty, the Old Kingdom declined rapidly in prestige and power, until the rulers of the Eighth Dynasty were followed by a successor administration based at Heracleopolis, between the earlier centers of Meir and Memphis. The First Intermediate Period (c. 2160-c. 2055) was at its peak during the Ninth and Tenth Dynasties. The eight southernmost districts of Egypt, the "Head of the South," though nominally loyal to the Heracleopolitan state, quarreled among themselves. The First Intermediate Period ended with the coming of the south to political center stage—the reunification during the Eleventh Dynasty was a product of the Thebaïd (southern Upper Egypt, around Thebes).

During the Egyptian Fifth Dynasty (c. 2494-c. 2345 B.C.E.), local administrators, previously centered around the king and the central administration at the royal residence, began to accumulate power. Under the Fifth Dynasty ruler Djedkare (r. c. 2414-2375 B.C.E.), evidence from a number of necropoles indicate that nome (district) administrators were beginning to be entombed in the "middle provinces" of Upper Egypt. These districts—emphasized in nomarchic titularies of the Fifth Dynasty—were perhaps the most agriculturally wealthy Upper Egyptian nomes (those in the far south have been estimated at low capability); the eight southernmost Upper Egyptian nomes were the Head of the South. The rulers of the Fourth, Fifth, and Sixth Dynasties established a number of funerary domains, "new cities," associated with the royal mortuary cults. Most of these are centered in Middle Egypt (Fourth Dynasty) and in the Delta (increasingly during the Fifth and Sixth Dynasties), with almost none in the eight uppermost (southern) districts.

During the Sixth Dynasty (c. 2345-c. 2181 B.C.E.), perhaps as part of an effort to secure more personal pharaonic control in the far south, Pepi I (r. c. 2321-2287 B.C.E.) established close relations with an important family in Abydos. Plantation-rich Middle Egypt came under the control of the governor of the main tax-receiving center of Meir; Thebes appears to have become the tax collection center for the seven southernmost nomes. In this way, the late Old Kingdom saw the establishment of an agriculturally rich Middle Egypt and southern Delta, administratively centered at Meir and Memphis respectively. The uppermost districts, the Head of the South, were trade oriented, with a loyalist north and a more independent far south.

After the end of the Sixth Dynasty, the ephemeral Seventh and Eighth Dynasties (c. 2180-c. 2160 B.C.E.) increasingly courted Upper Egyptian support through a se-

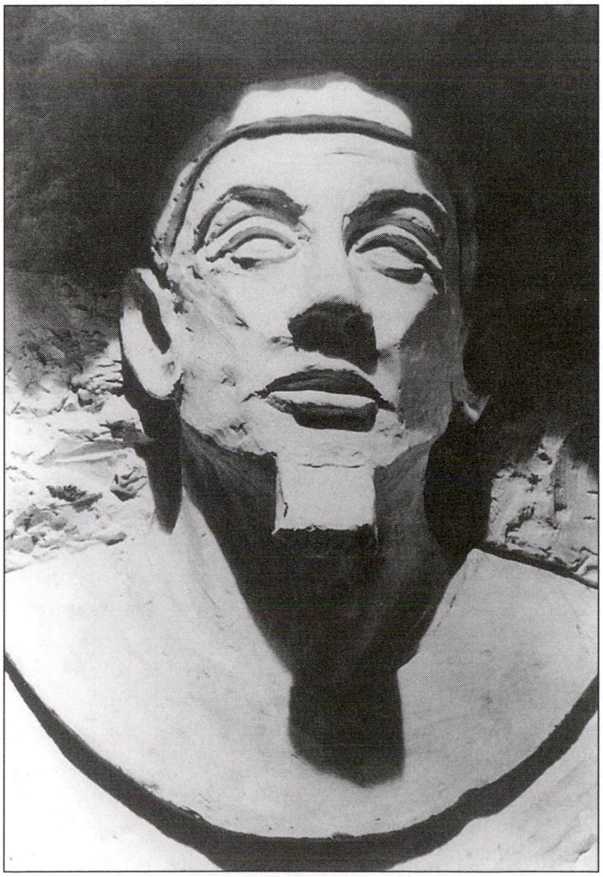

Stone carving of Imhotep. (Library of Congress)

3000 - 2001 B.C.E.

FIRST INTERMEDIATE PERIOD, C. 2160-C. 2055 B.C.E.

NINTH AND TENTH DYNASTIES, C. 2160-C. 2025

ELEVENTH DYNASTY (THEBES ONLY), C. 2025-C. 2055

Ruler	*Reign*
Montuhotep I	c. 2025-c. 2125
Intef I (Sehertawy)	c. 2125-2112
Intef II (Wahankh)	c. 2112-2063
Intef III (Nakhtnebtepnefer)	2063-2055

Note: Dynastic research is ongoing; data are approximate.

ries of exemption decrees for the temple of Coptos in Upper Egypt. The Sixth Dynasty issued a number of decrees concerning the Temple of Min at Coptos; it was primarily concerned with the temple and cult and, secondarily, with the personnel involved. Under the Eighth Dynasty, this changed, and in particular the family of the vizier Shemai—apparently a native Coptite who married the daughter of an Eighth Dynasty ruler—was personally addressed and given much honor and authority. The importance of Coptos to the waning Old Kingdom corresponds to the significance of Qus (near Coptos) during the Middle Ages—accessible from the Red Sea via the Wadi Hamamat Road. A Delta-based power could potentially have controlled Coptos and the gold imports of the Wadi Hamamat Road even if much of the rest of the south had been lost.

Heracleopolis put an end to the Old Kingdom and began the rule of the feudal Ninth and Tenth Dynasties (c. 2160-c. 2025 B.C.E.), based near the mouth of the Fayum oasis in northern Middle Egypt. The new capital was located between the agricultural (Meir) and administrative (Memphis) centers of northern Middle Egypt and controlled Egypt directly up to the southern border of the Fifth District of Upper Egypt. The four southernmost districts of Upper Egypt, although avowing loyalty to Heracleopolis, began to quarrel among themselves.

During the First Intermediate Period, a governor of an Upper Egyptian nome (the third), Ankhtifi, absorbed the two southernmost districts of the south and warred with the Theban (fourth) and Coptite (fifth) nomes to his north. Texts of the period in the south refer to famines, and Ankhtifi evoked the image of people "dying of hunger on the sand bank of Apophis [the chaos serpent]." Although there is evidence for climatic change at the time, the Upper Egyptian famines appear to result less from the total absence of food and more from the breakdown of a central administration capable of redistributing grain. Ankhtifi even stated that he allowed grain ships to pass through the area of his control, except for those going to Thebes. The warring nome rulers initially averred their loyalty to Heracleopolitan rule.

The Heracleopolitans, in imitation of the Eighth Dynasty rulers at Memphis, appear to have attempted to achieve direct control of the Coptite nome. The final pro-Heracleopolitan rulers of the Coptite nome, User and Tjauti, appear to have been members of the Heracleopolitan royal family. These two rulers moved their centers of administration to the area of modern Khozam, at the southern border of the Fifth District, apparently in anticipation of potential trouble from Thebes, the fourth district of Upper Egypt.

After the defeat of Ankhtifi, Thebes under Intef I (r. c. 2125-2112 B.C.E.) attacked toward the north in open hostility to Heracleopolitan rule. The Thebans captured the Coptite nome by annexing the portion of the Western Desert filling the Qena Bend of the Nile, taking control of the routes passing through that desert, and using one of those routes to outflank the Heracleopolitan forces stationed at the southern border of the Coptite nome. They avoided three Upper Egyptian nomes and gained control over the first eight nomes of Upper Egypt. After desultory fighting around Thinis (in the eighth district of the south) under Intef II (r. c. 2112-2063 B.C.E.), including a Heracleopolitan counterattack in which the cemetery of Thinis was destroyed, Intef II advanced into the tenth Upper Egyptian nome and returned to eliminate remaining resistance to the south. Eventually, Montuhotep II of Thebes was able to put an end to the loosely organized Heracleopolitan kingdom (c. 2055 B.C.E.) and ushered in the initial Theban-centered phase of the Middle Kingdom.

As the end drew near, the Heracleopolitans came to rely closely on the governors of another Upper Egyptian nome in Middle Egypt, based at Asyut, for military support. People of Western Asiatic origin appear also to have infilitrated the Nile Delta at this time, and some may have entered Heracleopolitan service. Of particular importance to the Upper Egyptian armies of the First Intermediate Period were the Medjay people of Lower Nubia (Wawat) and the surrounding deserts. A highly militarized society, they appear to be identical to the Pan-Grave culture. A large contingent of Medjay were established at Gebelein, in the southern Thebaïd, during the First Intermediate Period.

Significance

The First Intermediate Period was a time of change and innovation. Pottery shapes change considerably, especially in the south (baglike shapes predominating over high-shouldered, ovoid forms). Cartonnage masks were made for mummies, and small models of workmen and structures were used even in relatively modest burials. The models for much of these new burial goods were the burial equipment of the Old Kingdom elite, so there is a certain "democratization" of the ordered afterlife during the First Intermediate Period. The religious text corpus known as the Coffin Texts (c. 2160-c. 2055 B.C.E.; partial translation as *The Ancient Egyptian Coffin Texts*, 1973-1978)—many derived from the Old Kingdom *Pyramid Texts* (c. 2350-2100 B.C.E.; English translation, 1924)—appear to originate in the First Intermediate Period. Society itself changed, and the often bombastic and egocentric autobiographies of the period demonstrate a new self-confidence and self-consciousness on the part of even lower level officials.

Much of the intense internal turmoil once attributed to the First Intermediate Period is more accurately ascribed to the early Middle Kingdom. The large numbers of Nubians and Western Asiatics who entered Egyptian military service during the First Intermediate Period became lawless bands of unemployed mercenaries after the collapse of the Theban Eleventh Dynasty.

—*John Coleman Darnell*

Further Reading

Butzer, K. *Early Hydraulic Civilization in Egypt*. Chicago: University of Chicago Press, 1976. An important study of irrigation in ancient Egypt; Butzer's work shows the agricultural wealth of the middle districts of Egypt, home of the Heracleopolitan kingdom, and the relative lack of major agricultural production in southern Upper Egypt (the Thebaïd).

Darnell, J. C. "The Message of King Wahankh Antef II to Khety, Ruler of Heracleopolis." *Zeitschrift für ägyptische Sprache und Altertumskunde* 124 (1997): 101-108. A discussion of some events at the end of the First Intermediate Period.

_______. *The Theban Desert Road Survey in the Egyptian Western Desert I: Gebel Tjauti Rock Inscriptions 1-45, and Wadi el-Hôl Rock Inscriptions 1-45*. Oriental Institute Publications 119. Chicago: Oriental Institute Press, 2002. Publication of new inscriptions of the First Intermediate Period from the Theban Western Desert, including an inscription concerning the beginning of the Theban northern expansion during the reigns of Intef I and Intef II. See in particular pages 30-46.

Fischer, H. G. "The Nubian Mercenaries of Gebelein During the First Intermediate Period." *Kush* 9 (1961): 44-80. Contains a useful discussion of the Nubian soldiers well attested in the southern Thebaïd during the First Intermediate Period.

Kanawati, N. *Governmental Reforms in Old Kingdom Egypt*. Warminster, England: Aris and Philips, 1980. A brief but useful attempt to interpret the changes in late Old Kingdom administration, important for understanding the origins of the divisions so prominent during the First Intermediate Period.

Seidlmayer, S. "The First Intermediate Period (c. 2160-2055 B.C.)." In *The Oxford History of Ancient Egypt*, edited by I. Shaw. Oxford, England: Oxford University Press, 2000. Pages 118-147 provide a good, short, and reasonably up-to-date overview of the period (although unfortunately omitting important information from the Western Desert).

See also: c. 2687 B.C.E., Old Kingdom Period Begins in Egypt; c. 2575-c. 2566 B.C.E., Building of the Great Pyramid; 2500-1900 B.C.E., Wawat Chiefdom Flourishes in Lower Nubia; c. 2200-1500 B.C.E., Kerma Kingdom Develops and Dominates Lower Nubia; c. 2055 B.C.E., Middle Kingdom Period Begins in Egypt.

Related articles in *Great Lives from History: The Ancient World*: Montuhotep II; Sesostris III.

c. 2112 B.C.E.
UR-NAMMU ESTABLISHES A CODE OF LAW

Ur-Nammu, first king of the Third Dynasty of the Mesopotamian city of Ur, collected and edited the traditional laws of his culture into a formal legal system.

LOCALE: Ur on the Euphrates River in Mesopotamia (now Tell el-Muquaiyar, near Nasariyah, Iraq)
CATEGORY: Laws, acts, and legal history

KEY FIGURE

Ur-Nammu (late twenty-second century-2095 B.C.E.), king of Ur, r. c. 2112-2095 B.C.E.

SUMMARY OF EVENT

The history of Western jurisprudence begins in Mesopotamia, in the Sumerian city of Ur. The oldest law code for which a surviving written text has been found is that of Ur-Nammu. This text is written on clay tablets in cuneiform, a system of writing using wedge-shaped marks formed with a reed stylus pressed into the moist clay. Because of the fragility of the medium, only fragments of the text of the Ur-Nammu law code survive, and archaeologists have deciphered a mere five of the items in the damaged tablets. However, this has been enough to determine that Ur-Nammu's law code is part of a continuing tradition of Mesopotamian legal thought. Other texts contain references to even older law codes, particularly that of Uruk-Agina compiled three centuries earlier, but no surviving copies of these law codes have been found.

Ur-Nammu was the first king of the Third Dynasty of Ur. He began his career as a governor appointed by Utukhegal of Uruk after the defeat of the nomadic Guti tribes. He subsequently rebelled and established himself as an independent king, creating a sizeable empire among the Sumerian city-states. During his era, Ur was a large and sophisticated city with a high population density and the social pressures that accompany urban development.

Along with an extensive building program intended to secure his position in history, Ur-Nammu set his scribes to collecting and systematically editing the traditional laws of Sumerian society, as well as creating new ones to bridge the gaps revealed by this process. Many scholars believe that the law code may have actually been written by Ur-Nammu's son Shulgi and subsequently credited to the father as a way of honoring his memory. In any case, this law code formed a part of an active judicial tradition, since archaeologists have also discovered court records from the period, dealing with a range of cases from murders to commercial fraud.

The law code of Ur-Nammu reveals a sophisticated grasp of legal concepts. For instance, it established graduated schedules of fines and punishments as a way of making punishments fit the crimes. It established fines as penalties for injuries dealt to others, as opposed to the *lex talionis*, a system by which the culprit was given the same injury as the injured party—"an eye for an eye and a tooth for a tooth," as it was put in the later code of Hammurabi. Ur-Nammu's law code also punished wealthy and clever criminals more harshly than the poor or simple malefactor, perhaps on the rationale that educated and rich people had less excuse for such actions than those who may have been desperate or did not know better.

The compiled code proclaimed Ur-Nammu as the protector of the poor and included a provision for cancelling debts that poor families could not possibly pay. There were also provisions for the dismissal of corrupt officials who oppressed the common people.

However, other aspects of Sumerian law would seem harsh, even barbaric to modern minds. The Sumerians made no distinction between accidents and premeditated crime. Only the act and its consequences mattered, and it was punished accordingly. This may have been an outgrowth of the Sumerian religious idea that human beings were but playthings of the gods and human choice meant little in the face of fate.

SIGNIFICANCE

The development of a written code of laws was a critical turning point in Western history, and its effects have permutated through the centuries to modern times. The idea that laws could be formalized in written form was critical in developing the concept of the rule of law, as was the

THIRD DYNASTY OF UR, C. 2112-2004 B.C.E.

Ruler	*Reign*
Ur-Nammu	c. 2112-2095
Shulgi	c. 2094-c. 2047
Amar-Su'ena	2047-2038
Shu-Sin	2038-2029
Ibbi-Sin	2029-2004

idea that laws could be subject to deliberate review and reform.

The Sumerian law codes also had important effects upon the development of Western religion. The traditional date for the patriarch Abraham's departure from Ur is several decades after the era of Ur-Nammu, so it is possible that some of these legal principles underlie the Hebrew legal and moral tradition. However, most scholars have dated Mesopotamian influence upon the developing Jewish religious law to the later Babylonian captivity. Whatever the precise route of transmission, important Mesopotamian legal principles such as the protection of the poor and the use of punishments commensurate with the offense have become important moral foundations of Judaism, Christianity, and Islam, all of which look to Abraham as an important founding figure.

—*Leigh Husband Kimmel*

FURTHER READING

Bottero, Jean. *Everyday Life in Ancient Mesopotamia.* Baltimore, Md.: The Johns Hopkins University Press, 2001. An overview of the culture of the various Mesopotamian civilizations, the Sumerians and their successors.

Kramer, Samuel Noah. *History Begins at Sumer: Thirty-Nine "Firsts" in Recorded History.* 3d ed. Philadelphia: University of Pennsylvania Press, 1989. Quotations from original Sumerian cunieform texts demonstrate the first instances of many important elements of civilization, including law codes and legal precedents.

Oppenheim, A. Leo. *Ancient Mesopotamia: Portrait of a Dead Civilization.* Chicago: University of Chicago Press, 1977. A comprehensive set of essays on various aspects of ancient Mesopotamian culture, including laws and justice.

Rothman, Michell S. *Uruk Mesopotamia and Its Neighbors: Cross-Cultural Interactions in the Age of State Formation.* Santa Fe, N.Mex.: School of American Research Press, 2001. In-depth study of the development of the apparatus of state in ancient Mesopotamia, including the codification of the legal system.

Roux, Georges. *Ancient Iraq.* New York: Penguin, 1993. An overview of the civilizations of Mesopotamia, from Sumerian beginnings to the modern era, tracing continuity in cultural changes.

SEE ALSO: c. 2340 B.C.E., Sumerian Uruk-Agina Makes Social and Political Reforms; c. 2334-c. 2279 B.C.E., Sargon of Akkad Establishes the Akkadian Dynasty; c. 1770 B.C.E., Promulgation of Hammurabi's Code.

c. 2100 B.C.E.
XIA DYNASTY MARKS START OF HISTORICAL CHINA

The Xia Dynasty moved toward solidifying an empire, establishing dynastic rule, and instituting a range of social and cultural advances.

LOCALE: Central and north central China in the Yellow River region

CATEGORIES: Prehistory and ancient cultures; expansion and land acquisition

KEY FIGURES

Shun (fl. c. twenty-third century B.C.E.), last king before the Xia Dynasty

Xia Yu (Hsia Yü; d. c. 2197 B.C.E.), mythical founder of the Xia Dynasty, who quelled the floods of the Yellow River, r. c. 2205-2197 B.C.E.

Xia Qi (Hsia Ch'i; d. c. 2188 B.C.E.), Xia Yu's son and first recognized emperor of the Xia Dynasty, r. c. 2197-2188 B.C.E.

Xia Jie (Hsia Chieh; d. c. 1783 B.C.E.), last emperor of the Xia Dynasty, r. c. 1818-1783 B.C.E.

SUMMARY OF EVENT

Knowledge of the first Chinese dynasty, the Xia (Hsia), comes from both archaeological digs and ancient texts such as Sima Qian's *Shiji* (first century B.C.E.; *Records of the Grand Historian of China*, 1960, rev. ed. 1993). Although it has long been thought to be a mythical dynasty, its existence has been supported by the findings of modern archaeologists. Remains of the Xia civilization, which corresponds to the late Longshan or Erlitou cultures in archaeological terms, have been found near the Yinghe and Ruhe Rivers, bolstering the foundation myths that place the origin of the dynasty within the context of the Xia people's vulnerability to flooding from the rivers near which they built.

The Xia and its successor Shang and Zhou (Chou)

Dynasties were the first to move toward creating combined empires that would encompass various warring states, clans, and outsiders. Before the Xia Dynasty, much of the Chinese population lived in small villages and had little contact with their government or the outside world. Their worldview was formed by myths that presented their leaders as godlike beings, descended from heaven to rule.

By about 2100 B.C.E., Chinese civilization was centered on the Yellow River in the modern province of Henan. In ancient times, the Yellow River frequently overflowed its banks, flooding the communities nearby and destroying the lives of the peasants who depended on it for water. According to the legend, a man named Gun was executed by King Shun for his failure to control the flooding; his wife, Sewege (Suege), is said to have swallowed a spirit's pearl while pregnant, which resulted in the apparently supernatural powers exhibited by her son, Yu. Following in his father's footsteps, Yu (Yü) solved the problem of flooding by dredging the accumulated sediment from the river. He was so dedicated to the task of taming the river that he refused to enter his house until the task was done, saying that he did not have a family until the waters came under control.

Impressed by Yu's success, King Shun gave him control over a large section of the empire, in equal standing with Shun's son, Di. Shun and Di soon died, leaving Yu in control of both halves of the empire. This combination of the territories of central China represented the end of the prehistoric era in Chinese history. It also began the tradition of inherited control of the Chinese government.

The beginning of the Xia Dynasty has been explained by others in less dramatic terms. Some historians have suggested that Yu was a victorious military leader who defeated the political powers in the Yellow River region. Whichever explanation is accepted, most estimates place the start of the Xia Dynasty c. 2100 B.C.E., ending five centuries later c. 1600 B.C.E.

The Xia Dynasty saw the consolidation of the many tribes of central China into a community. Much of this occurred after Yu's death. Yu had named an adviser and friend, Yi, as his successor, but Yi proved unable to live up to Yu's legendary status. Yi was soon replaced by Yu's son Qi, who garnered the support of the nobility within Xia territory. Upon seizing power, Qi sought out the approval of the major tribal leaders, many of who traveled to his capital and pledged their support to his rule. The Youhu, however, refused to recognize Qi as the ruler of China. Qi responded by sending a large armed force to the Youhu territory and destroying its ruling family. This show of force convinced any rivals that Qi was not to be challenged. However, after gaining control, Qi proved to be an ineffective emperor who drank himself to death. His empire was only held together by his ruthlessness. He was succeeded by his son, Tai Kang, under whose rule the dynasty's decline accelerated. Kang was eventually exiled by a general from a neighboring empire, and Kang's younger brother took over the throne.

Although ancient historians list seventeen emperors of the Xia Dynasty, little is known about most them after Emperor Qi. The considerable political and military conflict that prevailed during the Xia period is seen in the violent deaths of some of the emperors. The emperor Xia Xiang (2146-2079 B.C.E.) was assassinated by a general, who himself was killed by the next emperor, Xia Kang (2079-2057 B.C.E.). The final Xia emperor, Xia Jie (c. 1818-1783 B.C.E.), was sadistic in the treatment of his people. In one bizarre episode, Jie is said to have ordered three thousand of his people to jump into a lake of wine and then enjoyed the spectacle of their struggles as they drowned.

According to legend, Jie pursued a woman, Mei Xi. He built a palace for her and kept her interest by purchasing large quantities of silk, which she enjoyed tearing for the sound it made. This luxurious lifestyle, as well as his declaration that as long as the sun shone he would remain emperor, made Jie vulnerable to outside attack. Cheng Tang, leader of the neighboring Shang clan, defeated Xia Jie in Mingtaio, near the capital of Anyi. Jie's permanent exile and eventual death initiated the fall of the Xia Dynasty and its replacement by the Shang Dynasty (1600-1066 B.C.E.).

SIGNIFICANCE

The Xia Dynasty marked the transformation of the Chinese political system from a disjointed, prehistoric society to one with a developed government and a method for passing on power. The dynasty also marked the beginning of centuries of military and political struggles among dynasty members and with outsiders who sought to overthrow the ruling family and establish their own. The Xia Dynasty also saw the use of governmental power to protect the people from the natural disasters caused by the flooding of the Yellow River.

The reign of the Xia Dynasty saw the creation of a central government that used its power to expand beyond its borders while aiding the commercial advances of the population. It also was the first Chinese civilization to leave some definitive, though limited, record of its achievement and its culture and society.

—*Douglas Clouatre*

FURTHER READING

Chang, Kwang-Chih. *Archaeology of Ancient China*. 4th ed. New Haven, Conn.: Yale University Press, 1987. Covers the archaeological evidence of Xia culture.

Fairbank, John King, and Merle Goldman. *China: A New History*. Enlarged ed. Cambridge, Mass.: Harvard University Press, 1998. Discusses the archaeological evidence for the Xia Dynasty.

Gernet, J. *A History of Chinese Civilization*. Translated by J. R. Foster. 2d ed. New York: Cambridge University Press, 1996. Covers the Xia Dynasty in the context of archaic monarchy in China.

Loewe, Michael, and Edward Shaugnessy, eds. *Cambridge History of Ancient China*. New York: Cambridge University Press, 2001. Chapter 1 reviews the mythology of Xia origins and its relationship to history and archaeology.

Stevens, Keith G. *Chinese Mythological Gods*. New York: Oxford University Press, 2001. Relates the myths surrounding Yu and his taming of the Yellow River.

SEE ALSO: c. 2682 B.C.E., Legendary Founding of China by Huangdi; c. 1600 B.C.E., Shang Dynasty Develops Writing and Bronzework; c. 1066, Western Zhou Dynasty Begins in China; 770 B.C.E., Eastern Zhou Dynasty Begins in China.

c. 2100-c. 600 B.C.E.

MOGOLLON CULTURE RISES IN AMERICAN SOUTHWEST

Mogollon culture formed part of the early Pueblo cultures of the American Southwest, influenced other regional cultures, and later merged with the Anasazi.

LOCALE: East-central Arizona, west-central New Mexico, west Texas, parts of Mexican states of Chihuahua and Sonora

CATEGORY: Prehistory and ancient cultures

SUMMARY OF EVENT

Mogollon culture evolved from the earlier Cochise culture, an adaptation of the widespread Desert culture of the Great Basin, which dated to 6000 or 5000 B.C.E. The Mogollon culture, which has been identified largely by the use of pit houses and brown and dark red pottery, was located in an area bordered by the Verde River on the west, the Little Colorado River on the north, the Pecos River on the east, and the Chihuahua Desert on the south. This area can be subdivided into two areas, a northern or mountainous region and a southern or valley region, which represent both topographical and cultural differences. The southern Mogollon encompasses the Mimbres branch, which is renowned for its fine pottery.

Until the 1930's, the Mogollon were not generally recognized as a separate culture from the neighboring Anasazi to the north and Hohokam to the south and west. The name Mogollon was first used by Emil Haury in 1936, after he had successfully argued for recognizing them as a separate people. The name derived from the Mogollon mountains of central Arizona and New Mexico, which had been named for an eighteenth century governor of New Mexico.

The Mogollon culture inhabited the Gila Cliff Dwellings near modern-day Silver City, New Mexico. (Mark Nohl/courtesy *New Mexico Magazine*)

ANCIENT CIVILIZATIONS OF THE AMERICAN SOUTHWEST

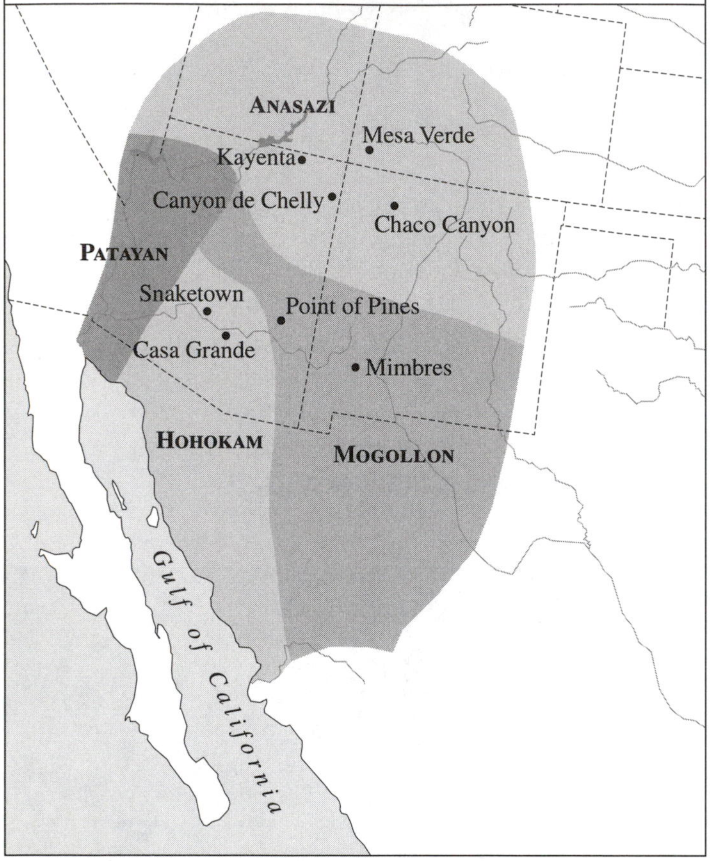

Archaeologists now recognize four distinctive prehistoric civilizations in the southwest: Anasazi, Hohokam, Mogollon, and Patayan, all of which have been referred to as Pueblo, which is the Spanish word for "village." The earliest Mogollon villages were generally composed of roundish or irregularly shaped pit houses ranging in number from four or five to fifty or more. These dwellings consisted of an excavated pit with a depth of 2 to 5 feet (0.6 to 1.5 meters) and a diameter of 10 to 16 feet (3 to 5 meters) covered by a roof made of poles, brush, and mud. The roofs were most often of the umbrella type: one central post with smaller poles coming from it. However, roofs were sometimes constructed using four posts set in a square. Hearths and storage pits were located in or near the house. The entrance, which usually faced the east or southeast, varied in length. The overall effect resembled an igloo.

Most villages contained one or more ceremonial structures, known as kivas, which were larger than the dwellings. The overall construction of villages does not appear to have followed any plan but was rather haphazard. The earliest villages were usually located on high mesas, bluffs, or ridges, which made them easier to defend against raids by hunting-gathering peoples who coveted their food supplies. Later villages were built in valleys or plains near rivers or streams. While less defensible, these locations provided more favorable conditions for farming. There is speculation that the earliest villages were not permanently occupied but were used only seasonally, possibly in the colder months. During the warmer months, after crops were planted, groups may have disbursed to hunt and gather provisions for the winter. As farming began to provide a larger portion of their diet, this situation changed and hunting-and-gathering activities decreased accordingly. This change affected not only the location of villages but also the duration of their occupancy and the size of the dwellings.

It is generally agreed that farming and pottery were the result of diffusion from Mesoamerica. By around 2000-1500 B.C.E. maize, squash, and beans had been introduced into the Southwest from Mexico. These became important in supplementing the diet of the Mogollon, who were still basically a hunting-gathering people. The diet consisted of roots, nuts, seeds, berries, yucca, cactus, sunflowers, insects, small game, deer, and bison. The archaeological sites of Tularosa and Bat Cave in New Mexico have provided information on Mogollon diet.

The relative importance of the different components of the diet is reflected in the frequency with which metates, or grinding stones, and manos, or hand stones, were fashioned. Additional artifacts include polishing stones, grooved mauls, hammer stones, axes, scrappers, choppers, knives, projectile points and tubular pipers. Bone tools include awls, needles, skewers, flakers, fleshers, tubes, and whistles. In general, the tools were more crudely made than those of other contemporary cultures.

The earliest Mogollon pottery was plain, polished brown or dark red. This style of pottery continued throughout Mogollon history, although later other styles were added. Pottery appeared around 500 B.C.E. in the San Simon drainage in Arizona and is believed to have a Mexican influence. Most pots were coiled but some were molded by hand.

SIGNIFICANCE

At the height of its prehistoric development, Southwest civilization was characterized by villages composed of pit houses, horticulture using dry or irrigation techniques, cultivation of maize, squash, beans, and tobacco, hunting and gathering of wild foods, domestication of dogs and turkeys, pottery, and fashioning of stone, bone, and shell artifacts. Overall, the Mogollon culture changed very slowly compared with many other indigenous cultures, and it is not known whether the same language was spoken throughout the region or if they considered themselves to be one people.

—Philip E. Lampe

FURTHER READING

Cordell, Linda. *Ancient Pueblo Peoples*. Washington, D.C.: Smithsonian Books, 1994. A brief cultural history and description of the various civilizations referred to as Pueblo.

Plog, Stephen. *Ancient Peoples of the American Southwest*. New York: Thames and Hudson, 1997. A discussion of the various cultures which inhabited the Southwest from prehistoric to modern times. Contains numerous maps, drawings, and photographs.

Reid, Jefferson, and Stephanie Whittlesey. *Grasshopper Pueblo: A Story of Archaeology and Ancient Life*. Tucson: University of Arizona Press, 1999. Uses a single Mogollon site as the starting point for a general overview of the culture. A good introductory work for the nonspecialist.

Riggs, Charles R. *The Architecture of Grasshopper Pueblo*. Salt Lake City: University of Utah Press, 2001. Focuses on the building techniques and architectural environment of the Mogollon.

SEE ALSO: c. 18,000-c. 11,000 B.C.E., Bering Strait Migrations; c. 9000-c. 8000 B.C.E., Cochise Culture Thrives in American Southwest; c. 8000-c. 1000 B.C.E., Archaic Indians Adapt to Warmer Climates; c. 300 B.C.E., Hohokam Culture Arises in American Southwest; 200-1250 C.E., Anasazi Civilization Flourishes in American Southwest.

c. 2055 B.C.E.
MIDDLE KINGDOM PERIOD BEGINS IN EGYPT

The reunification of Egypt under Montuhotep I of the Eleventh Dynasty ushered in a relatively stable period of increasingly centralized political power during which Egypt flourished in the arts and literature.

LOCALE: Thebes and Lisht, Egypt

CATEGORIES: Cultural and intellectual history; government and politics; Expansion and land acquisition

KEY FIGURES

Montuhotep I (2061-2011 B.C.E.), Egyptian king, r. c. 2025-c. 2125 B.C.E.

Amenemhet I (fl. twentieth century B.C.E.), Egyptian king, r. c. 1985-1956 B.C.E.

Sesostris I (Senwosret I; fl. twentieth century B.C.E.), Egyptian king, r. 1971-1926 B.C.E.

Sesostris III (Senwosret III; d. 1843 B.C.E.), Egyptian king, r. 1878-1843 B.C.E.

Sebeknefru (fl. late nineteenth to mid-eighteenth century B.C.E.), Egyptian queen, r. 1785-1782 B.C.E.

SUMMARY OF EVENT

The conquest of all of Egypt by Montuhotep I in the first half of his reign brought the First Intermediate Period to an end and ushered in the Middle Kingdom (c. 2055-c. 1650 B.C.E.). Montuhotep led armies that defeated independence-minded provincial governors in Upper Egypt and then marched north, uniting the country between 2030 and 2020 B.C.E. One of the most intriguing nonroyal burials at Thebes dates to the militaristic period of his reign, a mass grave of sixty soldiers killed in battle in Nubia and returned to Egypt for burial in an extremely honored location near the funerary temple of their king.

Through his reign and those of his Eleventh Dynasty (c. 2055-c. 1985 B.C.E.) successors, Thebes remained the capital of Egypt, but in the time of Amenemhet I, first king of the Twelfth Dynasty (c. 1985-c. 1782), the capital was moved to a new site south of Memphis. The city was called Amenemhet-itj-tawy (Amenemhet Seizes the Two Lands), usually shortened to Itj-tawy (now Lisht). The king was probably the same Amenemhet who was vizier of the last Montuhotep, and it is unclear whether the transition from one dynasty to the next was completely peaceful. There are no records of an uprising, but the last king of the Eleventh Dynasty is left off later king lists, an omission that may indicate the revision of events in the history as written by a victorious usurper.

MIDDLE KINGDOM PERIOD, C. 2055-C. 1650 B.C.E.

ELEVENTH DYNASTY (ALL EGYPT), C. 2055-C. 1985

Ruler	*Reign*
Montuhotep II (Nebhepetra)	2055-2004
Montuhotep III (Sankhkara)	2004-1992
Montuhotep IV (Nebtawyra)	1992-1985

TWELFTH DYNASTY, C. 1985-C. 1782

Ruler	*Reign*
Amenemhet I	c. 1985-1956
Sesostris I	c. 1971-1926
Amenemhet II	1926-1897
Sesostris II	1897-1878
Sesostris III	1878-1843
Amenemhet III	1843-1798
Amenemhet IV	1802-1785
Sebeknefru	1785-1782

THIRTEENTH DYNASTY, C. 1782-AFTER 1650

Note: Dynastic research is ongoing; data are approximate.

Several literary texts seem to suggest there was at least one attempt on the life of Amenemhet I, but he reigned for a lengthy thirty years, the last ten of which as coruler alongside his son and successor Sesostris I. In the *Instruction of Amenemhet I for His Son Sesostris I* (no original title; c. 1962 B.C.E.; English translation, 1973), Amenemhet tells of an attack against him by his personal guard, an incident that apparently inspired a bitter recommendation to his son that he trust no one, whether a brother or a subordinate or a friend. It has been suggested that this text should be read as an Egyptian ghost story with Amenemhet narrating through a dream or appearing as a full-fledged ghost. A second literary text, *The Story of Sinuhe* (no original title; c. 1928 B.C.E.; English translation, 1973), describes the fearful reaction of an assistant to Sesostris I when he hears of the death of the old king. This is usually taken as an indication that Sinuhe either knew of, or even participated in, a conspiracy against Amenemhet, one that was ultimately successful.

Sesostris I followed his father in taking his son as his coruler during the last part of his reign, a practice that continued throughout the Twelfth Dynasty. This means of assuring the succession probably contributed to the Twelfth being one of the longest-ruling dynasties in one of the most stable periods of Egyptian history. The dynasty controlled Egypt for more than two hundred years, with the throne passing smoothly from father to son (all named Amenemhet or Sesostris) until the last ruler of the period.

During the reign of Sesostris III, a series of governmental reforms decreased the power of provincial governors. Just as he consolidated his control at home, Sesostris III followed a more aggressive foreign policy than any other Twelfth Dynasty king. He conducted military campaigns in Nubia and consolidated his conquests by expanding existing fortifications and constructing a new series of forts along the Nile between the First and Second Cataracts.

The last ruler of the dynasty was a woman, Sebeknefru, possibly a wife of Amenemhet IV, who preceded her on the throne. After Sebeknefru, the dynasty changed in what seems to have been a relatively peaceful transition. Kings grouped by ancient historians as members of the Thirteenth Dynasty include several unrelated and short-ruling kings. They had at least some control over all Egypt, and the period seems relatively prosperous. These kings left few monuments, perhaps an indication of the weakness of their centralized rule. Some were buried in poorly built pyramids at Saqqara, but the best-known burial is that of Awibre Hor, who ruled for less than a year around 1760 B.C.E. His poor but intact burial was found within the funerary precinct of Amenemhet III at Dahshur. The most impressive object from this tomb was a beautiful, life-size statue of the king within a wooden shrine, now in the collection of the Egyptian Museum. The Thirteenth Dynasty faded as a political power through the seventeenth century and was replaced in northern Egypt by the Hyksos and in the south by a new Theban Dynasty during the subsequent era, the Second Intermediate Period.

SIGNIFICANCE

Montuhotep I's successful reunification of Egypt dramatically elevated the importance of his family and their capital of Thebes. Although there was a well-established local style used by the artists who decorated the tombs of the wives of the king, for his own monument Mentuhotep ordered decoration in a style that deliberately copied the style used in monuments of the Fifth and Sixth Dynasty kings at Memphis. It is likely that he transported artists from the north to work at his southern capital. At the same time, however, he did not adopt the Old Kingdom pyramid for his tomb but rather built a temple whose columned porticoes developed from Upper Egyptian First Intermediate Period styles.

The actual site of the Twelfth Dynasty capital city has never been excavated, but the burials of the dynasty's first two kings at Lisht and others elsewhere in the general area have been identified and explored by archaeologists. The pyramid complexes of Amenemhet I and Sesostris I copy the plans and, in the case of Amenemhet I's pyramid, actually use inscribed stones taken from monuments of the Fourth through Sixth Dynasties. This use of Old Kingdom prototypes and materials serves much the same purpose as the transport of artists to the south in the reign of Montuhotep; they serve to symbolically connect the kings of the Middle Kingdom with the golden age before the disorder of the First Intermediate Period.

The stability of the Twelfth Dynasty allowed architecture and art to flourish, with royal portraiture from the reign of Sesostris III particularly distinctive. The face of the king does not display the bland, idealized features found earlier in the dynasty, but rather a newly conceived, distinctive appearance. His eyes are deeply set under heavy brows, there are pouches under his eyes, and deep furrows run from the outside edges of the nose to the sides of the down-turned mouth. The portrait changes through the course of his reign, providing an unusual record of the aging king. In addition to the visual arts, literature also flourished during the Middle Kingdom, with some of the most famous ancient Egyptian texts composed during this period.

A statue of Amenemhet III, from his funeral temple. (Hultonl Archive)

The name Amenemhet contains the name of the god Amen, indicating his place as the family's patron deity. Probably Montu, the hawk-headed war god whose name is part of the name of kings of the Eleventh Dynasty, was the original chief god of the Thebes, but with the ascent of the Twelfth Dynasty, he was eclipsed by Amen. Amen (usually identified with the Sun god Ra and known as Amen-Ra) became the protector of the ruling king, and his cult benefitted from its close association with this family. Although little of the Middle Kingdom temple at Karnak still exists because it was overbuilt in the New Kingdom and later, statues and the finely carved White Shrine of Sesostris I show the importance attached to this Theban god, even after the capital moved to the north. The importance of Amen-Ra continued through the rest of Egyptian history, and he was the patron deity of the next family to rule a united Egypt in the New Kingdom.

—*Sara E. Orel*

FURTHER READING

Bourriau, Janine. *Pharaohs and Mortals: Egyptian Art in the Middle Kingdom*. New York: Cambridge University Press, 1988. A catalogue of a museum exhibition, this has examples of a wide variety of objects, largely from tombs, including coffins, statues, and objects of daily life such as pottery, amulets, and other interesting items.

Clayton, Peter A. *Chronicle of the Pharaohs*. New York: Thames and Hudson, 1994. Reign by reign summary and chronological account of Egyptian history, including even minor rulers.

Lichtheim, Miriam. *The Old and Middle Kingdoms*. Vol. 1 in *Ancient Egyptian Literature*. Berkeley: University of California Press, 1975. Includes *The Story of Sinuhe* and the *Instruction of Amenemhet I*, along with many other classics of Middle Kingdom literature.

Robins, Gay. *The Art of Ancient Egypt*. Cambridge, Mass.: Harvard University Press, 1997. Portions of chapters 5 through 7 present the art of the Middle Kingdom. Bibliography.

Thériault, Carolyn A. "*The Instruction of Amenemhet* as Propaganda." *Journal of the American Research Cen-*

ter in Egypt 30 (1993): 151-60. An intriguing discussion of this important but problematic ancient text. Thériault suggests the *Instruction* was composed by Amenemhet I himself to stress his legitimacy as a ruler after an attempted assassination. This also includes a review of previous interpretations of the composition.

Winlock, Herbert E. *The Slain Soldiers of Neb-hep-et-re' Mentu-hotpe*. New York: Metropolitan Museum of Art, 1945. A short but fascinating excavation report discussing this very early war cemetery. Illustrations.

SEE ALSO: c. 2687 B.C.E., Old Kingdom Period Begins in Egypt; c. 2575-c. 2566 B.C.E., Building of the Great Pyramid; c. 2160 B.C.E., First Intermediate Period Begins in Egypt; c. 1650 B.C.E., Hyksos Create Second Intermediate Period; c. 1570 B.C.E., New Kingdom Period Begins in Egypt; From c. 1500 B.C.E., Dissemination of the Book of the Dead; c. 1338 B.C.E., Failure of Akhenaton's Cultural Revival; 1069 B.C.E., Third Intermediate Period Begins in Egypt.

RELATED ARTICLES in *Great Lives from History: The Ancient World*: Montuhotep II; Sesostris III.

c. 2000 B.C.E.
COMPOSITION OF THE GILGAMESH EPIC

The composition of the oldest surviving epic poem captured Sumerian myth and legend and provided significant comparisons with the later Old Testament.

LOCALE: Sumer, Mesopotamia (now southern Iraq)
CATEGORIES: Literature; religion

KEY FIGURE

Ashurbanipal (c. 685-627 B.C.E.), preserver of the epic of Gilgamesh and king of Assyria, r. 669-627 B.C.E.

SUMMARY OF EVENT

The Gilgamesh epic (translated into English as *Gilgamesh Epic*, 1917) is the oldest extant epic poem and Gilgamesh, legendary king of Uruk, the first literary hero in history. Apart from the similarity of the flood episode to the account given in Genesis 7 of the Bible, Gilgamesh is worthy of study because he reveals the typical pessimism and insecurity felt by man more than twelve hundred years before the time of the Greek poet Homer.

It has been proved by quotations discovered on early Sumerian tablets of the third millennium that parts of the epic existed then, but the main portion was probably composed around 2000 B.C.E. Episodes are written on a large number of cuneiform clay tablets of varying dates unearthed at various places in the Near East, but an almost complete version, consisting of twelve tablets of about three hundred lines each, comes from the library of Ashurbanipal, king of Assyria from 669 to c. 627 B.C.E. The simplicity and clarity of the tale indicates that it was probably designed for recitation rather than reading, and the Semitic parallelism of phrases is characteristic of the ancient epic style.

In the shadowy political history of early Sumer, it is possible that the Gilgamesh of the epic had a human prototype in Gudea of Lagash. Whoever the prototype may have been, in the epic Gilgamesh is part god and part man, which is the source of his tragic dilemma. His mother is an obscure goddess, from whom he inherits his dynamic qualities of beauty, strength, and restlessness, while his father bequeaths to him mortality. Herein rests the tragedy of the conflict between the desires of the god and the destiny of the man. This theme, and the character of Gilgamesh who portrays it, are what give the work its spiritual unity over so many centuries during which it both grew and underwent revision. In a particularly poignant passage after Gilgamesh has told the wine goddess Siduri about his fear of death and his restless search for immortality, she warns him:

> Gilgamesh, where are you hurrying to? You will never find that life for which you are looking. When the gods created man they alloted to him death, but life they retained in their own keeping. As for you, Gilgamesh, fill your belly with good things; day and night, night and day, dance and be merry, feast and rejoice.

Gilgamesh replies: "How can I be silent, how can I rest, when Enkidu whom I love is dust, and I too shall die and be laid in the earth for ever?" This fatalistic philosophy is the distinctive note of the Mesopotamian epic and along with it goes a vivid conception of hell in striking contrast to the Egyptians' optimistic preoccupation with an afterlife akin to heaven. The malaise of Mesopotamian psychology lies in insecurity and the lack of a covenant such as the Hebrews had with Yahweh.

The main plot describes how the people of Uruk beg the gods to relieve them of oppression by their autocratic ruler Gilgamesh. Their prayer is answered when Enkidu,

Ashurbanipal. (Library of Congress)

the counter-hero, enters the city and wrestles with Gilgamesh. Though Gilgamesh proves his physical superiority over Enkidu, the two become firm friends and inseparable companions. They set out to overcome the giant Humbaba, who has been appointed by the god Enlil to guard the cedar forest. Together Gilgamesh and Enkidu succeed in destroying Humbaba.

On their return to Uruk, the goddess lshtar tries to win Gilgamesh as her lover, but he spurns her. In revenge, she prevails upon Anu, father of the gods, to send on Gilgamesh the Bull of Heaven, which represents seven years of drought. Gilgamesh is thus responsible for bringing destruction on many of his own people. Eventually, Gilgamesh kills the bull, but that same night, he learns in a dream that the gods have decreed that one of the two heroes, Gilgamesh or Enkidu, must lose his life for having slain Humbaba and the bull. The penalty falls on Enkidu, and Gilgamesh loses his inseparable companion. Grieving, he sets out to find Utnapishtim, the only human being who survived the Great Flood. Gilgamesh begs Utnapishtim to share with him the secret of immortality, and Utnapishtim gives him a branch from the plant of life. However, on his way home, a snake steals the precious branch while Gilgamesh stops for a swim. Gilgamesh faces the fact that death is his fate. This episode ends the epic, except for an epilogue in which Enkidu in the underworld tries to retrieve two lost objects of Gilgamesh.

This simple adventure tale both conceals and reveals a number of profound human problems and philosophical questions. It raises the question of the purpose of life, and comes to a conclusion characteristic of Mesopotamian culture in its pessimism. Although the Gilgamesh epic does not see death as annihilation of the person, it views existence after death as essentially gloomy. After death, man dwells in a lower world described as a house of dust, where he is a mere shadow of his former self. Thorkild Jacobsen remarks in *The Intellectual Adventure of Ancient Man* (1977) that the Gilgamesh epic does not have a harmonious conclusion; its surging emotions are not alleviated; "nor is there, as in tragedy, any sense of catharsis, any fundamental acceptance of the inevitable." Its ending is unpleasant and disturbing. "An inner turmoil is left to rage on, a vital question finds no answer."

Another theme is the struggle of civilization against barbarism. Enkidu is tamed or "civilized" by succumbing to a woman sent to him for the specific purpose of overcoming him by her charms. The Humbaba episode can also be interpreted as representing the clash between civilization and barbarism, inasmuch as it shows the two heroes struggling against a creature who controls the forest essential to the economy of Uruk.

SIGNIFICANCE

The Gilgamesh epic was forgotten with the decline and disappearance of Sumerian society and its cuneiform writing. It was not brought into view again until the nineteenth century when the ruins of Nineveh were excavated. It is a curious and thought-provoking fact that among the Babylonians themselves the work held no particular position of eminence in literary tradition, as few fragments have been found in Mesopotamia proper and there are few quotations from the epic in other works. After Ashurbanipal's capital, Nineveh, fell to the Medes and Persians in 612 B.C.E., the epic was all but forgotten except for the flood episode. Yet remnants remained in the memory of surrounding civilizations, for there is unmistakable evidence of Gilgamesh elements throughout the Near East and parts of the area around the Aegean Sea.

The relationship of the Gilgamesh epic to the biblical account of the flood in Genesis 7 has been carefully studied by scholars since the parallel was first revealed by George Smith, an English scholar, in 1872. There are striking similarities in the two accounts. Both tell of widespread destruction and the saving of a single man and his family: Utnapishtim in the Gilgamesh account, and Noah in the Bible. The differences, however, are more significant than the similarities in what they tell us about the two cultures. In the biblical account, the flood is a punishment for sin; in Gilgamesh, humankind is not guilty but rather the victim of the caprice of the gods. In Genesis, humankind is given an opportunity to repent in order to avert disaster; no such chance is offered in the Gilgamesh account. In the Mesopotamian version, the salvation of Utnapishtim is a purely personal boon, while in the case of Noah, the conclusion of the drama is a covenant between God and Noah as head of his descendants. The consensus opinion is that the Hebrew and Babylonian versions may have had a common source, but the account in Genesis does not seem to have depended directly on the Gilgamesh epic.

—*Mary Evelyn Jegen*

FURTHER READING

Foster, Benjamin R., Douglas Frayne, and Gary M. Beckman, eds. *The Epic of Gilgamesh*. New York: W. W. Norton, 2001. Includes a new translation of the epic directly from primary sources, a section on analogues to the myth in other world mythologies, a collection of classic critical essays, a glossary of proper names, and a select bibliography. Illustrated.

Frankfort, Henri, et al. *The Intellectual Adventure of Ancient Man: An Essay on Speculative Thought in the Ancient Near East*. Chicago: University of Chicago Press, 1977. Includes an essay on Mesopotamia by Thorkild Jacobsen.

George, Andrew, trans. *The Epic of Gilgamesh: The Babylonian Epic Poem and Other Texts in Akkadian and Sumerian*. Reissue ed. New York: Penguin, 2003. An accessible translation with an introduction that places the epic within its historical and cultural contexts.

Heidel, Alexander. *The Gilgamesh Epic and Old Testament Parallels*. 2d ed. Chicago: University of Chicago Press, 1963. The classic work presenting the parallels between Babylonian and biblical myth.

Jacobsen, Thorkild. *Treasures of Darkness*. New Haven, Conn.: Yale University Press, 1986. One of the best guides to Sumerian culture and literature, with a substantial chapter devoted to Gilgamesh.

Leick, Gwendolyn. *Mesopotamia*. New York: Penguin, 2003. A survey of Mesopotamian culture and mythology relying on archaeological evidence.

SEE ALSO: c. 4000 B.C.E., Sumerian Civilization Begins in Mesopotamia; c. 3100 B.C.E., Sumerians Invent Writing; c. 2300 B.C.E., Enheduanna Becomes First Named Author; 1400-1300 B.C.E., Aqhat Epic Is Composed in Ugarit.

RELATED ARTICLE in *Great Lives from History: The Ancient World*: Ashurbanipal.

c. 2000 B.C.E.
MON-KHMER MIGRATE INTO SOUTHEAST ASIA

People speaking Mon-Khmer languages settled in Southeast Asia, becoming one of the major language groups in the region.

LOCALE: Modern-day southern China, Malaysia, Myanmar, Laos, Thailand, Cambodia, and Vietnam
CATEGORIES: Expansion and land acquisition; prehistory and ancient cultures

SUMMARY OF EVENT

The term "Mon-Khmer" is a linguistic label rather than an ethnic one. It refers to people speaking a number of related languages found primarily in mainland Southeast Asia. Two of the main groups of Mon-Khmer speakers are the Mon (also sometimes spelled Mun), who throughout historical times have lived in eastern Myanmar (formerly Burma) and west central Thailand, and the Khmer (also called Cambodians), who are chiefly concentrated in Cambodia, eastern Thailand, and southern Vietnam. In the past, Vietnamese was not recognized as a Mon-Khmer language, and there are still some scholars who question this linguistic classification, but today it is usually recognized as part of the Mon-Khmer family. Other Mon-Khmer languages include Muong, Khasi, and Wa. Speakers of Mon-Khmer languages make up a large part of the population of Southeast Asia. Languages in this family are spread from western India (mainly the state of Assam) to Vietnam and from southern China to Malaysia. The major language groups of the region that are not Mon-Khmer are Tai (which includes Thai and Lao), Tibeto-Burman (which includes Burmese), and

Austronesian (which includes Malay and a number of languages in the mountains of central Vietnam).

The fact that so many people in this region speak related languages does not necessarily imply that the people themselves have the same ancestry. Languages can spread across unrelated groups through trade and intermarriage. However, languages that are related to each other can be traced back to specific groups of speakers. The Mon-Khmer languages are believed to have been brought to the region from northwest China or from the Khasi Hills in northwest India by about 2000 B.C.E. The Mon, one of the primary subgroups of the Mon-Khmer, followed the Salween River in what is now the nation of Myanmar. Among Mon-Khmer groups, the Mon are generally believed to have retained the greatest cultural continuity with the ancient Mon-Khmer. The subgroup that became known as the Khmer migrated further east into what is now Cambodia (also known as Kampuchea). During the gradual move into Southeast Asia, the Mon-Khmer groups came into contact with speakers of Austronesian languages, which make up one of the world's largest language groups and are believed to have spread from Taiwan throughout Southeast Asia and the islands of Oceania. Speakers of Mon-Khmer languages were already well established in Southeast Asia when the Tai groups began to move southward from the general area of southern China into what are now Thailand and Laos some time before 1000 C.E. Over the centuries, the Mon-Khmer groups, the Austronesian groups, and the Tai groups influenced each other linguistically and culturally.

One of the most notable contributions of prehistoric Mon-Khmer migrants to Southeast Asia may have been the introduction of rice farming. Recent archaeological research suggests that the cultivation of rice developed in the Yangtze Valley of China about 6500 B.C.E., spreading outward through Asia. Sites showing rice cultivation and the domestication of animals along the Mekong River have been dated to about 2200 B.C.E., and it is believed that the farmers at these sites spoke languages that later became Mon, Khmer, and Vietnamese. Rice became the major food crop of the region, and it provided the economic basis for all of the powerful kingdoms of the historical period.

Before the arrival of the Tai groups, most of the politically dominant civilizations of mainland Southeast Asia were founded by Mon-Khmer speakers. In the western part of the region, the Mon came into contact with the civilization of India and became an important avenue for the transmission of Indian culture to Southeast Asia. The Mon became the first people in Southeast Asia to take up the Buddhist religion, adopting the Theravāda Buddhism that predominated in South India and in Ceylon. They also adopted the Indian writing system, which later became the basis of the written languages of the Thai, Lao, Khmer, and Burmese. Two of the most important Mon kingdoms were the Dvaravati, which flourished from the sixth to the thirteenth centuries C.E., and the Haripunjaya, in what is now northwestern Thailand, which was originally founded as a Dvaravati colony in the seventh century and lasted until about the eleventh century. Although the Mon kingdoms were conquered and absorbed by the Burmese, Thai, and Khmer, the Mon greatly influenced the societies of their conquerors.

People thought to have been speakers of the Khmer branch of Mon-Khmer founded the early kingdoms of Funan and Chenla in what is now Cambodia in the first centuries C.E. Funan, located in the Mekong Delta, was described by Chinese records, and the kings of Funan sent missions to China from 226 to 649. Chenla is thought to have risen about 550. Its greatest king may have been Jayavarman I, who reigned from 635 to 680 and greatly centralized control through the development of a sophisticated administrative bureaucracy. Like the Mon, the Khmer were heavily influenced by India, although early Khmer society drew more heavily on Hinduism than on Buddhism. About the third century C.E., the Khmer developed a version of Mon-Khmer writing that became the basis of the Cambodia, Thai, and Lao writing systems. About 790, a prince of a small Khmer kingdom who claimed descent from the kings of Funan took the name Jayavarman II and extended his power over a large part of Cambodia. This was the basis of the influential Angkor civilization, named after the huge temple complex built by the successors of Jayavarman II.

The Angkor civilization survived until the fifteenth century and represents the high point of Khmer society. The statues and buildings of Angkor fell into disrepair and were overtaken by the surrounding jungle until French researchers began to restore and study them in the nineteenth century. During the twentieth century, the remnants of the Angkor civilization became the foremost national symbol of Cambodia.

SIGNIFICANCE

People speaking Mon-Khmer languages came to make up much of the population of mainland Southeast Asia and had enormous influence on the economy, politics, and culture of the region. They may have brought rice farming to the region in prehistoric times. During the times of the great kingdoms, especially those of the Angkor civilization, they developed elaborate systems of agriculture for the rice crop.

The Mon-Khmer speaking kingdoms, especially those of the Angkor civilization, played a large part in shaping ideas about kingship throughout the region. The modern kings of Thailand have inherited many traditions passed down from the old Khmer rulers, even though the Thai kings have been constitutional monarchs since the 1930's. Cambodia, as a nation and a people, originated in the Angkor civilization.

Theravāda Buddhism, first adopted in the region by the Mon, became the predominant religion in Burma, Thailand, Laos, and Cambodia. Through the Mon and the Khmer, Indian influences on literature, music, and dance penetrated the elite cultures of all the Theravāda Buddhist nations. The scripts of these nations, also, are products of the Mon-Khmer transmission of Indian civilization.

—*Carl L. Bankston III*

FURTHER READING

Brown, Robert L. *The Dvaravati Wheels of the Law and the Indianization of Southeast Asia*. New York: E. J. Brill, 1996. Interprets a group of stone sculptures representing the Buddha's Wheel of the Law dating from the Dvaravati period, by connecting the sculptures to the cultures of both India and the Khmer in an effort to trace how Indian influences moved into Southeast Asia.

Coedès, George. *The Indianized States of Southeast Asia*. Honolulu: East-West Center Press, 1968. This is the classic work on the kingdoms of Southeast Asia and on the influence of India on them.

Dumarçay, Jacques, and Michael Smithies. *Cultural Sites of Burma, Thailand, and Cambodia*. New York: Oxford University Press, 1995. A well-illustrated volume that considers the most important ancient cultural centers of Burma, Thailand, and Cambodia. It describes the primary features of each site and explains the importance of each for the region.

Higham, Charles. *The Civilization of Angkor.* Berkeley: University of California Press, 2001. An excellent history of the Khmer civilization of Angkor. Chapter 2, on the prehistoric period, contains conclusions of new research about a little-known time in the history of the region.

Ortner, Jon, Ian W. Mabbett, Eleanor Mannikka, James Goodman, and John Sanday. *Angkor: Celestial Temples of the Khmer.* New York: Abbeville Press, 2002. Illustrated by color photographs and accompanied by a glossary, chronology of construction, and a chart of the kings, this is a unique history and exposition of the cities of Angkor. The text is written by a team of experts on Angkor civilization.

SEE ALSO: c. 7500 B.C.E., East Asian Grain Cultivation Begins; 6th or 5th century B.C.E., Birth of Buddhism; c. 400 B.C.E.-c. 300 C.E., Dong Son Culture Appears in Vietnam; c. 200 B.C.E., Birth of Hinduism; Early 1st century C.E., Pyu Kingdom Develops Urban Culture; 1st century C.E., Tai Peoples Migrate into Southeast Asia; 1st century-c. 627 C.E., Kingdom of Funan Flourishes.

c. 2000 B.C.E.

MONGOLS INHABIT STEPPES NORTH OF CHINA

The Mongols, a nomadic people whose lifestyle involved raiding, grew in power and number, becoming a force that would eventually threaten China and other areas.

LOCALE: The steppe region of Asia (now Russia and northern China)

CATEGORIES: Prehistory and ancient cultures; expansion and land acquisition

SUMMARY OF EVENT

The region known as the Western Steppes is a vast, almost treeless area in Central Asia. The steppes are approximately 1,200 miles (1,935 kilometers) wide and bordered on the west by the Altai Mountains and Tian Shan and in the east by the Khingan Mountains. At 3,000 to 5,000 feet (914 to 1524 meters) above sea level, the area is characterized by extreme temperature variations from dry, hot summers to cold, windy winters. There are few trees in the region except along waterways, but there is a long, grassy blanket of rolling hills. Rainfall amounts remain so small that farming is difficult without irrigation, but the grasslands provide perfect pastures for grazing animal herds.

The Mongols were the most numerous of the groups of nomadic people who occupied the steppes north of China during the Archaic period. The Mongols emerged in the area around Lake Baikal, to the north of present-day Mongolia. They consisted of a number of different tribes with similar heritages and language. Tribal membership was based solely on bloodline or kinship. Mongols frequently fought other nomadic people and sometimes assimilated groups they defeated. Tribal population rose and fell according to food availability, climatic conditions, and warfare, but the functional unit of Mongol life was a group of fifty to one hundred people.

Each tribe was divided into clans. Though the Mongols were a patrilineal society, with children taking the name of their father, clan membership was not based solely on heredity. Captives in war were sometimes adopted into a clan. The tribes were exogamous: People did not marry within their own clan but did marry into other tribes. Leadership of the tribe was not based solely on royal heredity; leaders were chosen from among the most prominent families because of their individual military or hunting skill. A man's accomplishments during battle or his ability to provide food were far more important than birth status in determining his fitness to lead.

The environment shaped Mongol life. Tribes moved frequently, taking all of their possessions with them. Their movements depended on a number of factors, including weather, war, and the constant pursuit of fertile pasturelands. Like most nomadic peoples, the Mongols moved to take advantage of seasonal grazing opportunities for their herds. Tribes camped in the northern regions of the steppe during the summer and moved every few weeks to take advantage of new grasslands as the old ones were grazed down, and in the winter they moved south to a warmer climate.

The Mongols domesticated sheep, goats, horses, and cattle, on which they were dependent for survival. Sheep and cattle provided mutton and beef. Goat's milk was made into cheese and a fermented drink called *koumiss*. Sheepskins and goatskins were tanned, and women pressed and oiled the fur into a feltlike material used to make the coverings for their tents. The same material was used to make clothing and blankets. Tools and weapons were made from animal horn and bone.

Mongols supplemented their food supplies by hunting with bow and arrow and fishing in areas with streams. Mongol men hunted large game including deer, rabbit, gazelle, antelope, and wolves. Women gathered local vegetation. In times of starvation, Mongols were forced to eat from their oxen and horse herds.

Mongol dwellings were well suited to their environment and lifestyle. The primary dwelling type was a tent called a yurt, *maikhan*, or *ger*. These tents, still used by present-day Mongolians, are semicircular dwellings constructed with rounded wooden stakes covered with heavy felt. The interiors were floored with carpets and rugs. Furniture was minimal. To welcome guests, the tent entrance always faced south, frequently adorned with colorful geometric shapes or animal patterns. The tents could be quickly dismantled and easily moved. A hole in the center of the roof allowed smoke from the fire to escape. Wooden fuel was used for cooking and warmth, when available; otherwise, dried dung worked well and was readily available.

The Mongols were among the world's greatest horsemen. They first captured and tamed wild horses that ran in herds across the steppes. The horses pulled wagons and carts, essential to a nomadic lifestyle. Mongol horses were only fourteen to fifteen hands high, with broad chests and foreheads, but they were successfully bred for speed, stamina, and maneuverability. The steeds allowed their riders to speed close to their prey and make their kill at close range. Nomadic steppe tribes fought with one another over prime grasslands, animal herds, and later, manufactured goods. The Mongol horses were essential to Mongol military prowess.

SIGNIFICANCE

Mongol life was built around raiding. While the earliest Mongol peoples only raided their nearby neighbors, by the medieval period their raids took them farther and farther afield, until they were raiding into Europe. Although they developed a concept of empire, with subject nations and peoples submitting to a central Mongol rulership, even at their most widespread, the Mongols retained an essentially nomadic and raiding mentality. Loyalty to the family, clan, and tribe overruled questions of political expediency.

The early Mongols developed into several groups or confederacies that had an enormous impact on world history. The Xiongnu created a vast Central Asian empire beginning in the fifth or fourth century B.C.E., and constituted the dominant enemy of the emerging Chinese empire under the Qin and Han Dynasties, until dissolving in 48 C.E. The descendants of the Xiongnu became the Huns that ravaged Europe in late antiquity. The Mongol Khitans became the Liao Dynasty, which ruled China from 907 to 1125 C.E. Other Mongol descendants included the Tatars and Buryats.

In the early 1200's C.E., the Mongol tribes consolidated under Temüjin, more commonly known as Genghis Khan. Under his leadership, they invaded areas throughout Asia and Eastern Europe, having a profound impact on the future populations of Eurasia. Towns and cities were captured and plundered and thousands of people killed. Genghis Khan eventually controlled the regions that would become Russia, Iraq, Iran, Persia, China, Poland, Hungary, and Turkey. Mongolian domination of these regions altered Asian history for centuries to come.

—Leslie A. Stricker

FURTHER READING

Bold, Bat-Ocher. *Mongolian Nomadic Society: A Reconstruction of the "Medieval" History of Mongolia*. New York: Palgrave Macmillan, 2001. Although the focus of this book is on a later period of Mongol history, it discusses the transition from the earlier, purely nomadic Mongol society to the culture of the Middle Ages in terms of social structure, economics, and religion.

Christian, David. *Inner Eurasia from Prehistory to the Mongol Empire*. Vol. 1 in *A History of Russia, Central Asia, and Mongolia*. Malden, Mass.: Blackwell, 1998. Traces the history of Russia, Central Asia, and Mongolia from the Old Stone Age to the thirteenth century.

Davis-Kimball, Jeannine, Vladimir A. Bashilov, and Leonid T. Yablonsky. *Nomads of the Eurasian Steppes in the Early Iron Age*. Berkeley, Calif.: Zinat Press, 1995. Part 5 covers early nomads in Mongolia and the Late Neolithic, Afanasievo, Slab Grave, and Karasuk cultures.

Morgan, David. *The Mongols*. Malden, Mass.: Blackwell Publishers, 1986. A fundamental history designed for the general reader. Includes maps, diagrams, a chronological list of Mongol events, dynastic tables, and a lengthy bibliography.

Sinor, Denis. *The Cambridge History of Early Inner Asia: From the Earliest Times to the Rise of the Mongols*. New York: Cambridge University Press, 1990. A history of Inner Asia from the Paleolithic to the rise of the Mongol Empire in the thirteenth century.

SEE ALSO: c. 4000 B.C.E., Horse Is Domesticated; 209-174 B.C.E., Maodun Creates a Large Confederation in Central Asia; c. 3d-4th century C.E., Huns Begin Migration West from Central Asia.

c. 1900-1527? B.C.E.

KERMA KINGDOM RULES NUBIA

Independent Nubian polities combined into a single state, with a capital developing at Kerma, while Egypt's central government weakened during the Second Intermediate Period.

LOCALE: Lower Nubian region of the Nile (now in the Republic of Sudan), northeast Africa

CATEGORIES: Expansion and land acquisition; prehistory and ancient cultures

SUMMARY OF EVENT

The portion of the Nile Valley known as Lower Nubia stretches southward from Egypt, roughly between the rocky outcroppings called the First and Second Cataracts. From that point south to the Sixth Cataract is known as Upper Nubia, where the modern village of Kerma is situated, about 430 miles (700 kilometers) from the Egyptian border. Lying on the east bank of the Nile, Kerma stood at the crossing of both river and overland trade routes moving between the African interior and the corridor leading to Egypt. It is believed to be the location of the distant kingdom called Kush that Egyptian inscriptions refer to as a formidable southern neighbor.

What is known about the cultures of early Nubia has been interpreted from material found during excavations and from Egyptian writings. Egyptologist George Reisner referred to the early Nubian culture groups that populated the region around Kerma as the A-Group, which dates from 3100 to 2700 B.C.E., and the C-Group, which extends to around 1550 B.C.E. The observable differences between the groups are in the quality and complexity of their burial objects, which create a picture of the success and development of each society. In 1923, Reisner discovered a cemetery of the C-Group near Kerma that contained several large tumulus graves surrounded by smaller versions. The sizes of these mounded graves seemed to reflect the social status of the person buried there.

The larger of these tumuli, some nearly 295 feet (90 meters) across, incorporated rows of mud-brick corridors that contained skeletons of fifty to four hundred people who appeared to have been buried alive. There were also numerous animal sacrifices, sculptures, and clay vessels found in the many rooms. The central figures in these tombs were placed in a special chamber on a decorative bed. Examples of such beds made of gold-covered wood, blue-glazed quartzite, and slate have been found. The scale of these large tumuli and the number of sacrificed retainers suggests a strong, centralized monarchy.

Similarities among the various Kerma culture burial sites suggest a strong religious tradition lasting generations. Bodies were arranged with legs bent, feet facing west, and heads facing north. They were placed between cowhides or covered and placed on beds that were finely carved and sometimes inlaid with ivory figures. The clothing remains that have been found reveal that men wore goatskin loincloths with beaded belts that held copper daggers. Leather or fabric caps with intricate mica symbols sewn on were common headwear. Headbands with feathers were another popular Kerma style. Pendants in the form of a fly are sometimes found; these were probably awarded for actions in battle. Bows and arrow quivers were also placed close to warriors. Women were buried with jewelry and hair ornaments and wore leather skirts often decorated with hole-punched patterns or beads. Pottery vessels and food offerings were usually included. A distinctive black-topped, red, polished pottery form is an important identifying object in determining the range of Kerma culture.

Another significant site near Kerma that was excavated by Reisner is the Western Deffufa (*deffufa* is Nubian for "large brick ruins"). What remains of this once-massive structure is primarily solid brick and measures 170 by 85 feet (52 by 26 meters) at its base, while reaching 62 feet (19 meters) in height. The structure stood in the middle of a large village and is now believed to have been a religious center. At ground level are brick foundations of a complex of rooms, where pottery, beads, and raw materials used in the manufacture of ornaments and trade objects were found. Fragments of clay seals that had been attached to Egyptian containers and a quantity of ivory attest to the trading activity at the site. Situated among these rooms were workshops, a foundry, and a marketplace.

The role of Kerma as a trading center is well documented in Egyptian writings. The products of inner Africa were highly prized by the Egyptians as well as the Semitic Hyksos people. The Hyksos, in turn, traded with countries of the eastern Mediterranean, which explains the occurrence of examples of Near Eastern pottery in Kerma graves. Ebony wood, ivory, gold, leopards and their hides, baboons, ostrich eggshells and feathers, incense, and gums were all luxury goods prized by people to the north. Kerma acted as an intermediary in this lucrative trading system. Trade goods from Egypt are often found in the graves and among the ruins of the Kerma culture. The history of this north-south relationship extended back to the Old Kingdom period, when another active Nubian center of commerce flourished further north at Buhen. As trade with Egypt grew, so did the wealth and power of the leaders of Kerma. Excavations by Swiss archaeologist Charles Bonnet in the 1970's have uncovered a palace complex just southwest of the Western Deffufa. The king's residence was built in close proximity to warehouses, which suggests the royal control and supervision of commerce.

The recorded history of ancient Egypt between 2900 and 1500 B.C.E. shows that relations with Nubia alternate between cooperation and hostility. Nubian warriors are known to have been employed by the Egyptian pharaohs as mercenaries. Egypt had occupied Lower Nubia and exploited its natural resources, including granite for use in pyramid complexes, semiprecious stones, copper, and gold. Fortified towns were established as Egyptian administrative centers and garrisons. There were occasional raids into Upper Nubia as well. Gradually, however, large numbers of seminomadic herdsmen from the western desert began to settle in the region, forcing the Egyptians to pull back north of the Nile's First Cataract.

Bronze Age Nubia was composed of a loose confederacy of small chiefdoms. Egyptian textual records sometimes mention these population centers by name. During Egypt's Sixth Dynasty it was recorded that Pharaoh Merenre directed the governor of Upper Egypt to lead expeditions to Aswān, the First Cataract, and purchase acacia wood for boats from the chiefs of Wawat, Irtjet, and Setju. At that time Wawat was the northern part of Lower Nubia, Irtjet was in the vicinity of Tomas, while southward to the Second Cataract was the area known as Setju. Another group mentioned was the Medjay, a nomadic people of the eastern desert. Further south lay the chiefdoms of Kaau and Yam. At Elephantine, an inscription on the tomb of an Egyptian official named Harkhuf describes his recruiting and trading expeditions to the land of Yam, in Upper Nubia. On one he reported the chief of Yam to be at war with the chief of Themeh. Inscriptions document his return from another of these journeys along the oasis routes with three hundred donkeys loaded with exotic products from the interior of Africa.

The power of the regional chiefs began to increase during the Sixth Dynasty. Harkhuf recorded that on his second journey there were separate rulers for Setju and Irtjet. By the time of his third journey, both of these regions, and Wawat, were ruled by one man.

The remains of an extensive Kerma culture town and large cemetery have also been found on the island of Sai. Ancient texts mention an Upper Nubian center called Sha'a(t) with its own king. It is believed that the ancient and modern names are for the same location. In comparison with the Kerma cemetery, the smaller scale of even the largest grave sites and an absence of sacrificial remains suggest that the ruler of Sai was a subordinate to the king of Kush. Sai appears to have served as the northern border of the kingdom and the gateway for a caravan route into the Kerma basin.

The growing power of the kings of Kush is illustrated by the appearance of their names on a number of Egyptian artifacts. Two inscriptions (with alternate spellings believed to refer to the same person), "The King of Kush, Awa'wa . . ." on a pot now in the Berlin Museum and "The King of Kush, Utratrerses, born of Teti, his mother, and Awa'a, his father" on a figurine in Cairo, indicate a hereditary ruling dynasty. Two stone stelae found at the fort at Buhen have inscriptions by Egyptian commandants claiming allegiance to the king of Kush. These declarations show that the kings of Kush had taken control of the Egyptian fort at this strategic location near the Second Cataract.

SIGNIFICANCE

During the Thirteenth Dynasty, Egypt weakened, forcing it to abandon its forts in Nubia and withdraw its southern border back to Aswān. The Hyksos invaded and seized control of Lower Egypt while Upper Egypt was ruled by the Theban Seventeenth Dynasty. The Nubians took advantage of this development and by about 1650 B.C.E., all Lower Nubia came under the rule of the kingdom of Kush. With its center at Kerma, the domain now extended from the First to the Fourth Cataract. This period when Upper and Lower Nubia were united as a state is known as the Classic Kerma period.

—*Craig Lloyd*

FURTHER READING

Adams, William. *Nubia: Corridor to Africa*. London: Penguin Books, 1977. A comprehensive examination of the Nubian people, their customs and environment with a history of archaeological work in Nubia. Index and bibliography.

Africa in Antiquity: The Arts of Ancient Nubia and the Sudan. Brooklyn, N.Y.: The Brooklyn Institute of Arts and Sciences, 1978. A two-part volume examining the Nubian culture that traces the history and arts of the region. Index, catalogue and bibliography.

Kendall, Timothy. *Kerma and the Kingdom of Kush: 2500-1500 B.C.* Washington: National Museum of African Art, Smithsonian Institution, 1997. In this exhibition publication, Kendall discusses the history and customs of the people of the Nubian territory known to the Egyptians as Kush. Catalogue and bibliography.

O'Conner, David. *Ancient Nubia: Egypt's Rival in Africa.* Philadelphia: The University Museum, University of Pennsylvania, 1993. O'Conner provides a close look at the archaeology and history of ancient Nubia and details its cultural practices and objects. Index and bibliography.

Török, László. *The Kingdom of Kush: Handbook of the Napatan-Meroitic Civilization.* Leiden, The Netherlands: Konninklijke Brill, 1997. An extensive study of the history and civilizations of Nubia, the environment of the region and archaeological expeditions. Index and bibliography.

Trigger, Bruce. *Nubia: Under the Pharaohs.* New York: Thames and Hudson, 1976. An overview of the archaeology and anthropology of the region, its prehistory, environment, and culture. Index and bibliography.

SEE ALSO: c. 3050 B.C.E., Unification of Lower and Upper Egypt; c. 2687 B.C.E., Old Kingdom Period Begins in Egypt; c. 2160 B.C.E., First Intermediate Period Begins in Egypt; c. 2055 B.C.E., Middle Kingdom Period Begins in Egypt; c. 1650 B.C.E., Hyksos Create Second Intermediate Period; 1069 B.C.E., Third Intermediate Period Begins in Egypt; 8th century B.C.E., Kushite King Piye Conquers Upper Egypt.

c. 1900-c. 1400 B.C.E.
EARLY VILLAGES FORM IN OAXACA

The establishment of villages in the Valley of Oaxaca led to the development of agriculture and early political organization.

LOCALE: Valley of Oaxaca, Mexico
CATEGORIES: Prehistory and ancient cultures; agriculture

SUMMARY OF EVENT

Settlement of the Valley of Oaxaca began as early as 8900 B.C.E. and continued until about 2000 B.C.E. During that time, limited development took place, including the domestication of some plants. Agriculture, which came later, provided the basis for establishing permanent villages and led to advances that resulted in highly developed civilizations and the creation of states that dominated the area.

The Valley of Oaxaca is located in the modern-day state of Oaxaca in southwestern Mexico. The valley has the greatest expanse of flatland in southern Mexico and is shaped like a wishbone. The northern part of the valley is the Etla. Two arms extend southward, the Tlacolula arm to the southeast and the main arm of the valley to the southwest. Both the Etla and Tlacolula arms have narrower flood plains and are higher and less suitable for cultivation than the main valley.

The valley has an average elevation of 5,085 feet (1,550 meters) and is surrounded by mountains on the east, west, and north. The Rio Atoyac and its tributaries drain it. The region is divided into three areas: alluvium near the rivers, piedmont at the base of the mountains, and mountains. Each area has different types of agriculture and resources. The alluvium has the flattest terrain, thickest and richest soil, and easiest water availability. Above the alluvium lies the piedmont or foothills, where there are greater slopes and thinner soil. Cultivation was riskier in the piedmont because the water table is deeper and crops that are not irrigated are dependent on rainfall. Few opportunities for farming existed in the oak- and pine-covered mountains, but there were other resources such as timber and deer.

The valley is semiarid. Even with a rainy season lasting from May through September, annual rainfall averages only 22 inches (56 centimeters). The trade winds from the Gulf of Mexico loose their moisture as they flow over the high eastern mountains. Cultivation is to a large extent dependent on the irrigation water provided by the tributaries of the main rivers flowing down from the mountains. The temperature seldom falls below freezing, except in the higher eastern arm, where frost limits the crops that can be grown.

Near the rivers, the land was heavily forested with willow and alder trees; farther away the forests consisted of evergreen trees. Herbaceous plants and ferns were the only plants that could grow beneath the thick canopy that prevented sunlight from reaching the forest floor. Orchids, vines, and ferns grew in the branches of the trees. In the piedmont, where the water table was farther underground, mesquite grew on the lower hills and thorn scrub on the higher elevation. In the mountains, where rainfall was greater, oak and pine grew.

Small bands of Indians entered the Valley of Oaxaca between 8900 and 2000 B.C.E. The earliest Indians in the valley lived in camps in the open or in caves for varying lengths of time, depending on the resources available. These Indians developed the spear, atlatl (a type of spear-thrower), and roasting pit, as well as baskets, carrying nets, grinding stones, snares, tongs, ropes, and other tools needed to live off wild plants and animals. Tools were made of chert and flint. Obsidian, which is more easily worked and sharper, was not found in the valley. Crude pottery appeared before 2000 B.C.E., and by 1400 B.C.E., more elaborate forms, decorations, and colors were being used. Men hunted deer and peccary with atlatl darts and projectiles with flint points and trapped rabbits, quail, and doves with snares. Women gathered fruits and vegetables, nuts, and acorns in baskets and carrying nets. They kindled fires with fire drills and cooked in rock-lined earthen ovens. The population was so small that there was limited competition for resources.

Between 8000 and 5000 B.C.E., the Oaxaca people began cultivating vegetables, using stone axes, hoes, and wooden digging sticks. One of the first cultivated plants was a variety of squash in the pumpkin family. Before the end of the period maize was cultivated. Because they had neither draft animals nor the wheel, they did not use the plow. When crops were grown, the group would stay for a growing season.

During these early years, the Indians developed knowledge of seasons, plant growth, and the habits and habitats of the animals they hunted. They devised an elaborate system explaining the origins of life. Living and nonliving things were classified based on "vital force," explained as wind, breath, or spirit. The vital force made things warm and filled them with sacred wind that made them move.

Cultivation of domestic plants did not immediately change the life of the Indians of the valley, but it established the basis for significant changes. Agriculturally based villages became the foundation for a new stage of development. As long as the people remained hunter-gatherers, the mountains did not stop the exchange of ideas and food. When people settled down in villages near their fields, the mountains became a barrier. A sense of place and property developed. Other improvements such as permanent houses, storage pits, and irrigation canals were built, and both physical and human defense systems emerged.

The first villages in the Oaxaca Valley were located near the rivers, where fertile soil and water were available. Initially political and social organization was simple. People lived in small groups in an egalitarian society. With the increase in agricultural development came an increase in population. Villages began to be constructed farther up the mountain. Irrigation and terracing provided additional fields. A complex system of large and small villages evolved. The stratification of society began and organized religion developed. Political leaders and priests came to constitute an elite group that controlled village life.

The basic skills of village life such as weaving, pottery making, adobe manufacturing, and stone masonry flourished. A great number of small ceramic feline heads have been found in the area. The number of these heads and their presence in all households probably indicates that they were used in a frequently repeated ritual. Such rituals created a more solid social grouping.

Religion was no longer primarily simple nature worship. A professional priesthood conducted complex and elaborate ceremonies consisting of ancestor worship, bloodletting, and human sacrifice, among other things.

After 1400 B.C.E., strategically located villages were able to dominate the surrounding region either by influence or conquest, and in time states developed out of these villages. The earliest one was Monte Albán, located in the center of the Valley of Oaxaca.

SIGNIFICANCE

The establishment of early villages in the Valley of Oaxaca led to advances in agriculture, art, religion, and social and political organization. Political and religious elites emerged to dominate the village and later the surrounding areas. These advances served as the basis for the great Zapotec civilization that developed in Oaxaca and spread its influence to other areas of Mexico.

—Robert D. Talbott

FURTHER READING

Blanton, Richard E., et al. *Ancient Oaxaca: The Monte Albán State*. New York: Cambridge University Press, 1999. Includes an introduction to pre-Hispanic Mesoamerican civilizations as well as the setting and development of Oaxacan civilizations.

Flannery, Kent V., ed. *The Early Mesoamerican Village*. New York: Academic Press, 1976. Describes and analyzes the rise and development of villages in Oaxaca.

Flannery, Kent, and Joyce Marcus. *The Cloud People: Divergent Evolution of the Zapotec and Mixtec Civilizations*. New York: Academic Press, 1983. Contains a collection of articles by prominent archaeologists on the origins and development of Zapotec and Mixtec civilizations.

Paddock, John, ed. *Ancient Oaxaca: Discoveries in Mexican Archeology and History*. Stanford, Calif.: Stanford University Press, 1966. Gives a discussion of the origins and development of Oaxacan societies. Includes findings of the most knowledgeable archaeologists.

SEE ALSO: c. 3300-c. 1500 B.C.E., Valdivia Culture Forms Villages in Coastal Ecuador; c. 1530 B.C.E., Mixtec Civilization Develops in Western Oaxaca; c. 1500-c. 300 B.C.E., Olmec Civilization Rises in Southern Mexico; c. 500 B.C.E.-c. 700 C.E., Zapotecs Build Monte Albán; c. 300 B.C.E., Izapan Civilization Dominates Mesoamerica; 90 C.E., Founding of the Classic Period Maya Royal Dynasty at Tikal; c. 100-200 C.E., Construction of the Pyramids of the Sun and Moon at Teotihuacán; 200-900 C.E., Maya Civilization Flourishes.

c. 1800-c. 1500 B.C.E.
CONSTRUCTION OF EL PARAÍSO IN PERU

The construction of El Paraíso reflected the continued development of early complex society on the Pacific coast of Peru.

LOCALE: The central Peruvian coast near the mouth of the Rio Chillón, north of the modern city of Lima
CATEGORIES: Prehistory and ancient cultures; architecture

SUMMARY OF EVENT

Early theories of cultural evolution assumed that complex societies and civilization could not have emerged until agriculture became the primary means by which people obtained their subsistence. These theories reasoned that only agriculture could have created sufficient surplus to finance the construction of monumental architecture, long-distance trade, and more complex forms of political organization. These theories were challenged in the 1970's by a number of archaeologists working on the north central Pacific coast of Peru. Prominent among these was Michael Moseley, who developed an alternative theory of emergence of civilization that posited that at least on the north coast of Peru, large architectural complexes and politically advanced societies appeared without substantial investment in agriculture and instead were founded upon the exploitation of highly productive marine resources. Domesticated plants, including gourd and cotton, were not consumed, but used instead to construct fishing gear such as nets and their floats. These technologies enabled the inhabitants of this region to accumulate surplus production of fish and fish meal, which supported extensive building programs. Cultivation of plant subsistence staples were assumed to follow well after the initial occupation and expansion of these sites. At the time, Moseley's theory was highly controversial and, consequently, it stimulated new fieldwork in the region as researchers searched for data to either support or disprove his theory.

The period during which these societies emerged is called the Late Preceramic, dating from c. 2500-1500 B.C.E. More than twenty sites with monumental architecture and hierarchical political organization flourished on the north central Peruvian coast at this time, and the largest and one of the most impressive of them was El Paraíso. Found along the south side of the Chillón River, the site is said to cover at least 125 acres (51 hectares), and probably much more. One author estimates that more than 100,000 tons (more than 90 million kilograms) of locally available rock were quarried to construct the buildings at the site. Because the site is vast, relatively little of it has been either excavated or mapped extensively. At the minimum, structures at the site range from eight or nine stone buildings that contain as few as three rooms to large complexes measuring almost 1,000 feet (300 meters) by more than 300 feet (100 meters). Some of the complexes were massive, with walls greater than 3 feet (1 meter) in thickness. Most of the stone used in construction was cut and trimmed. One of the largest complexes, labeled Unit 1, appears to have been built in several stages and grew by accretion. Earlier rooms were filled in with rubble and leveled, and new, larger rooms were built atop them. This gives Unit 1 and similar complexes a multistory appearance. Unit 1 was at least 20 feet (6 meters) in height in its final stage of construction. Staircases can be found both within the structure and exterior to it, with the latter used as a primary entrance. A number of the rooms of Unit 1 were covered with a red and yellow plaster, and at least one of the rooms contained a hearth that showed no signs of domestic activity, and has been described as a ceremonial feature. Because few artifacts were found in these rooms, it has been difficult to define a function for them.

However, El Paraíso is not typical of Late Preceramic centers with monumental architecture. Unlike many of the contemporary monumental complexes elsewhere on the coast such as Aspero or Huaca la Florida, El Paraíso does not have large, open plazas, circular sunken courts, and U-shaped mound constructions that were clearly planned. The absence of these features has led to considerable speculation about the function of the architecture at El Paraíso and whether it was used for ceremonial or secular activities. Most researchers now agree that the U-shaped complexes and large mound constructions were ceremonial in nature and served a religious function. These constructions were not used as residences; instead they functioned as the sites of rituals, ceremonies, and displays of power and wealth of the local elites who directed their construction.

The obvious differences between El Paraíso and other Late Preceramic sites led to additional excavations during the 1980's designed to determine the range of activities at the site, the use of the monumental architecture, and the basis of social and political power of its inhabitants. American archaeologist Jeffrey Quilter and his colleagues excavated a number of areas of the site, including rooms in building complexes, areas between large complexes, and locations devoid of constructions. They discovered extensive middens, or trash dumps, just below the modern ground surface. Analysis of the remains encountered in these middens confirmed that, consistent with Moseley's theory, fish and mollusks were the primary protein source of the site's inhabitants. The single most important species of fish was the anchovy (*Engraulis ringens*). Although large quantities of mollusks were found at the site, their contribution to diet at El Paraíso was smaller than that at contemporary Late Preceramic sites. Terrestrial sources of protein, such as deer and camelids, were almost nonexistent.

However, the range and types of plant remains recovered were surprising. Domesticated plants included cotton and gourd, both of which had technological roles. Other cultivated plants had roles in the diet, including squash, chili peppers, tubers, and common and lima beans. Fruits were also present, such as guava and lucuma. Although some have suggested these fruits were cultivated, they could also have been gathered in some abundance from the river valley.

These data suggest that diet at El Paraíso was a complex mix of gathered resources, such as fish, shellfish, and some plants, and cultivated plants, such as tubers and beans. However, it is also clear that cultivated plants were not grown in great abundance and did not form the basis of surplus production. Fish and shellfish remained the source of this surplus.

The dominant plant recovered at the site was cotton, and although its was expected to be of economic importance, the quantity of cotton present was far greater than expected. Quilter and his team have suggested that the cotton was the true economic engine that drove the growth and expansion of El Paraíso. They argue that although cotton had a fundamental technological role to play at the site, the vast quantities present may also have been generated by demands for textile production. In the Andes, cloth and fabrics have had a long tradition of being used as prestige goods. High quality fabrics with elaborate designs have been found at other coastal Late Preceramic sites, and it seems likely that El Paraíso was engaged in large-scale cotton farming and textile production. Indeed, the Chillón River Valley is one of the largest in the region, and it is highly suitable for extensive cotton farming.

If this scenario is correct, cotton formed the primary basis of wealth for the site's inhabitants and was extended by surplus production of fish and shellfish. Together, these were used to obtain the labor to construct the large room complexes, which are most likely residences rather than ceremonial spaces, although it is possible that the two functions overlapped in practice. The degree to which this wealth was translated into a more complex political organization remains unclear, however, because burials with costly goods have yet to be found at the site.

SIGNIFICANCE

The importance of El Paraíso lies in its differences when compared to other Late Preceramic sites on the central Peruvian coast. Unlike most other sites, El Paraíso never had a significant ceremonial component and was instead a massive, and wealthy, residential site. Unlike the others, which show clear evidence of hierarchical forms of political order, no such hierarchy is present at El Paraíso. Although the diet of the site's inhabitants was dominated by gathered resources, some cultivated plants were also present. Cotton, while known to be important, was far more central to El Paraíso's economy than suspected. Together, these lines of evidence suggest that while the outlines of Moseley's theory of the maritime foundations of civilization on the Andean coast are correct, there were multiple pathways to complexity and power, and that El Paraíso represents one alternative toward social and political complexity.

—*Mark Aldenderfer*

FURTHER READING

Donnan, Christopher, ed. *Early Ceremonial Architecture in the Andes*. Washington, D.C.: Dumbarton Oaks, 1985. Provides a useful discussion of important sites contemporary with El Paraíso.

Moore, Jerry. *Architecture and Power in the Ancient Andes: The Archaeology of Public Buildings*. New York: Cambridge University Press, 1996. A comprehensive examination of how public buildings were used by different Andean civilizations, including those of the Late Preceramic.

Moseley, Michael. *The Incas and Their Ancestors*. New York: Thames and Hudson, 1992. A useful synthesis of Andean prehistory and archaeology.

_______. *The Maritime Foundations of Andean Civilization*. Menlo Park, Calif.: Cummings Press, 1975. Outlines the foundations of the theory that early Andean civilization was based primarily on marine resources and that plant cultivation came much later in time.

Quilter, Jeffrey, Bernardino Ojeda, Deborah Pearsall, Daniel Sandweiss, John Jones, and Elizabeth Wing. "Subsistence Economy of El Paraíso, an Early Peruvian Site." *Science* 251 (1991): 277-283. A detailed discussion of the subsistence remains recovered from the site.

SEE ALSO: c. 8000 B.C.E., Permanent Settlement of the Andean Altiplano Begins; c. 5800-c. 3700 B.C.E., Chinchorro Inhabit the Peruvian and Chilean Coasts; c. 2500 B.C.E., Construction of Monumental Architecture at Caral in Peru; 700 B.C.E.-100 C.E., Paracas Culture Develops a Sophisticated Textile Tradition; 200 B.C.E.-200 C.E., Nasca Lines Drawn in Desert Near Coast of Peru.

c. 1800-c. 700 B.C.E.
POVERTY POINT CULTURE BUILDS EARTHWORKS

The prehistoric, hunter-gatherer Poverty Point culture created the largest and some of the oldest earthworks found in North America, with trade routes extending from the Great Lakes to the Gulf of Mexico.

LOCALE: Lower Mississippi Delta of the southeastern United States, from the confluence of the Mississippi and Arkansas rivers south to the Gulf of Mexico

CATEGORIES: Prehistory and ancient cultures; trade and commerce

SUMMARY OF EVENT

Archaeologists' findings since the 1950's indicate that the Poverty Point culture was an evolutionary milestone in the American hemisphere. This Native American culture was once thought to be an agricultural society that began about 1730 B.C.E. and became extinct in 1350 B.C.E. Carbon dating of artifacts and other archaeological findings have revealed that Poverty Point was a highly organized hunter-gatherer society that existed from 1800 B.C.E. until 700 B.C.E., and that the society's trade routes extended throughout the eastern half of North America. Historians now believe that the Choctaw, Creek, Shawnee, and Natchez Native Americans have ancestral roots in the Poverty Point civilization.

The first report of artifacts on the Poverty Point site, located west of the Mississippi River on Bayou Macon near the present-day town of Epps in northeastern Louisiana, was that of explorer Jacob Walters about 1840. More than a hundred years later, the discovery of an aerial photograph showing the unusual size and geometric pattern of the massive earthworks on Macon Ridge sparked intense interest in investigating the ancient culture. In the 1950's, archaeologists James Ford and Stuart Neitzel of the American Museum of Natural History began excavating the site. They were followed by others, who have attempted to reconstruct the culture's economic and social organization by comparing it with the earthworks and artifacts of other settlements in the Lower Mississippi Valley.

Archaeologist Jon L. Gibson and contemporary scientists now believe that Poverty Point was a huge commercial center for hunter-gatherers who found plentiful food for the sustenance of a large population in the environment of Bayou Macon. Some believe that several thousand people lived at the central site and that other

Poverty Point people occupied dozens of small villages and hunting camps along the streams and old river channels that radiated out 25 miles (15.5 kilometers) from the central earthworks. Other archaeologists point to the lack of burial mounds and theorize that Poverty Point was a huge common campground used for ceremonial purposes and trade fairs. However, agricultural use and plowing over the past two hundred years have erased much of the evidence usually relied on by archaeologists to determine house types and burial practices. The huge earthworks and the multitude of artifacts found at the site indicate a long-term permanent occupation.

The earthworks dominating the central site were constructed in the shape of six concentric half-hexagons or C-shaped earthen embankments, 4 to 6 feet (1.2 to 2 meters) high and 140 to 200 feet (43 to 61 meters) apart. Ditches made by earth removal separate the embankments or ridges lengthwise. If laid end to end, the earthworks would extend for 7.5 miles (12 kilometers). The embankments consist of six unequal sections separated by five straight aisles ranging from 35 to 160 feet (10 to 49 meters) wide. The aisles may have been boundaries between social and functional areas, astronomical sighting lines, or simply functional aids for the builders to achieve the half-oval design. Parallel to the southwest aisle is an extra ridge—the Causeway—that bisects the outer concentric ridges and extends 300 feet (91 meters) beyond the enclosure, ending near an outer mound called Ballcourt Mound.

At the center of the concentric ridges is a flat, open area covering about 37 acres (15 hectares). Archaeologists suppose this open plaza was used for ceremonies, dances, games, and other public activities. The large number of religious fetishes and charms found at the site indicate that ritual and religion were major forces in the culture. Deep holes on the western side of the plaza suggest the use of huge wooden posts that may have served as calendar markers, casting shadows that enabled people to predict equinoxes or solstices, analogous to the theorized purpose of the British megalithic monument of Stonehenge, which had just reached its final form around this time.

West of the outer ridge, additional earthworks are positioned along a precise north-south line. Mound A,

These clay objects were found at Poverty Point. (AP/Wide World Photos)

shaped like a huge flying bird, measures 640 feet (195 meters) along the wingspread, 710 feet (216 meters) from head to tail, and 70 feet (21 meters) high. The tail section lies in a depression 12 feet (3.7 meters) deep. Mound B, situated about 0.4 miles (0.6 kilometers) north of Mound A, is 180 feet (33 meters) in diameter and 20 feet (6 meters) high. About 1.5 miles (2.4 kilometers) north is Motley Mound, a second bird-shaped mound considered unfinished because it has only a slight bulge to indicate the bird's tail.

Situated about 600 feet (183 meters) south of Mound A is the flat-topped Ballcourt Mound, measuring 100 feet (30 meters) square. Initially, archaeologists thought this mound was a natural knoll that had been shaped to a square, but recent findings indicate that it is entirely artificial, as are all the other mounds. There is no evidence that it was ever used as a ball court. About 1.6 miles (2.6 kilometers) south of Ballcourt Mound, on the same north-south line, lies a second domed mound called the Lower Jackson Mound. Though the Jackson Mound predates the other mounds by at least a thousand years, archaeologists assume a linkage to Poverty Point because there is evidence of a similar C-shaped earthen embankment on the Jackson Place, incorporating mounds inside and outside the enclosure.

Archaeological evidence is convincing that Poverty Point was a major trading center. Occupants of the central site traveled by canoe on the waterways of the Mississippi River system to establish a trading network with other cultures in the Appalachians, the Great Lakes, and in the Ohio, Tennessee, and lower Mississippi River Valleys. Poverty Point's major trade imports were rocks and minerals, including hematite, magnetite, quartz, sandstone, soapstone, various cherts, and copper. From these materials, the Poverty Point people made a variety of polished tools, pipes, ornaments, fetishes and effigies, buttons, and beads—objects they could use in trade with other groups in the Mississippi Valley.

Tools found on the Poverty Point site show that the hunters used stone-tipped spears thrown with atlatls (spear-throwers) to add distance and power. Poverty Point hunters made atlatl weights in varying sizes and shapes, often engraving them with decorations. Stone plummets shaped like plumb bobs and teardrops apparently were used as weights for fishing nets. Game, fish, edible plants, and nuts abounded in the woodlands and streams around the high bluff at the central site. The main source of meat was fish, but other meat sources were wild turkey, ducks, and geese, along with deer, rabbits, squirrels, racoons, opossums, and even reptiles. Wild persimmons, grapes, hackberries, and various nuts and seeds supplemented the diet of the inhabitants. Because rocks and stones had to be imported, the Poverty Point people used clay cooking balls—heated objects placed directly in the pot to cook its contents—using the size and shape of the balls to control the cooking time.

Significance

Discovery and excavation of the prehistoric earthworks at Poverty Point have caused archaeologists and historians to rethink their ideas of ancient civilizations. The Poverty Point culture in northeastern Louisiana flourished at the same time as the Minoan civilization, the rise in Babylon of the law-giving King Hammurabi, and the rule of Akhenaton and Queen Nefertiti in Egypt. The leaders in the Poverty Point culture who wielded political and religious power must have had advanced knowledge and capabilities to plan, construct, inhabit, and maintain such grand earthworks over hundreds of years. The Poverty Point people have left a legacy of magnificent accomplishments in both earthworks construction and commercial networking that modern scientists are still seeking to understand and preserve. Poverty Point is one of three World Heritage Archaeological Sites north of Mexico. The character, size, and age of the 400 acre (162 hectare) site is unique on the North American continent, and its influence can be seen in mound-building Native American cultures encountered by the Europeans who entered the Lower Mississippi Valley in the 1500's to 1700's C.E.

—Marguerite R. Plummer

Further Reading

Byrd, Kathleen, ed. *The Poverty Point Culture, Local Manifestations, Subsistence Practices, and Trade Networks*. Geoscience and Man, Vol. 29. Baton Rouge: Louisiana State University Press, 1991. Contains new interpretations of Poverty Point cultural practices based on discoveries of artifacts and excavations of earthworks. Bibliography.

_______. *Recent Research at the Poverty Point Site*. Louisiana Archaeology Studies, No. 13. Lafayette: Louisiana Archaeological Society, 1986. Presents new information on Poverty Point culture from excavations in the 1980's. Bibliography.

Gibson, Jon L. *Poverty Point: A Terminal Archaic Culture of the Lower Mississippi Valley*. 2d ed. Baton Rouge: Louisiana Division of Archaeology, 1999. State archaeologist's updated overview of earthworks, artifacts, foodways, and cultural practices of Poverty Point people. Bibliography.

_______. "The Poverty Point Earthworks Reconsidered." *Mississippi Archaeology* 22, no. 2 (1987): 14-31. Places Poverty Point in context with other mound builders such as the Mississippi and Hopewell cultures. Bibliography.

_______, ed. *Exchange in the Lower Mississippi Valley and Contiguous Areas at 1100 B.C.* Lafayette: Louisiana Archaeological Society, 1994. Traces trading routes and interaction between Poverty Point and other Indian tribes. Bibliography.

Jackson, H. Edwin. "The Trade Fair in Hunter-Gatherer Interaction: The Role of Intersocietal Trade in the Evolution of Poverty Point Culture." In *Between Bands and Stones*, edited by Susan A. Gregg. Occasional Paper No. 9, Center for Archaeological Investigations. Carbondale: Southern Illinois University, 1991. Focuses on development and range of influence of Poverty Point as a trading center. Bibliography and index.

Webb, Clarence H. "The Extent and Content of Poverty Point Culture." *American Antiquity* 33 (1968): 297-321. Report of amateur archaeologist who assisted with excavations and analysis of artifacts recovered from site. Bibliography.

SEE ALSO: c. 8000-c. 1000 B.C.E., Archaic Indians Adapt to Warmer Climates; c. 2100-c. 600 B.C.E., Mogollon Culture Rises in American Southwest; c. 1000 B.C.E.-c. 100 C.E., Adena Mound Builders Live in North America; c. 700 B.C.E.-c. 500 C.E., Mound Builders Rise in Ohio Valley.

c. 1770 B.C.E.
PROMULGATION OF HAMMURABI'S CODE

The Babylonian king Hammurabi promoted public order by amending and codifying existing laws and carving them on stone pillars in public places so that they were accessible to the entire populace.

LOCALE: Babylonia (now southern Iraq)
CATEGORIES: Laws, acts, and legal history; government and politics

KEY FIGURE

Hammurabi (c. 1810-1750 B.C.E.), ruler of Mesopotamia, r. c. 1792-1750 B.C.E.

SUMMARY OF EVENT

Hammurabi's laws are neither the oldest extant laws nor even a law code as the term is popularly understood, but this does not alter the fact that their promulgation and preservation constitute a landmark in history. Early Sumerian political and religious thought, which became normative for subsequent peoples who invaded or conquered the area between the Tigris and Euphrates Rivers, did not make a clear distinction between divine and human societies. Among the gods, as among their human counterparts, the Sumerians pictured a divine assembly as the ultimate source of authority. This notion of a divine assembly added to the significance of the assembly on Earth. In Sumerian mythology, the cosmic body alone was competent to name the head of the pantheon, regulate the lengths of reigns, and to grant immortality to humans.

Hammurabi was the sixth Amorite king of a Semitic dynasty that had, some two hundred years earlier, imposed its rule on the native Sumerian population of the territory within about a 50-mile (80-kilometer) radius of Babylon. Late in the course of his forty-three-year reign, Hammurabi extended his rule in the direction of Assyria and northern Syria. He published what has come to be known as his code of laws at least in part as a means of unifying this heterogeneous society.

An almost complete copy of the laws, engraved on a diorite column or stela about 8 feet (2.4 meters) tall, was discovered in Susa in 1901. This stela is now in the Louvre Museum in Paris. The laws apparently were engraved on diorite, the most durable substance known to the Babylonians, so that a copy of the laws would stand as a public reference. Many fragments of other copies have been discovered and transcribed, and it is by comparing these that gaps in the Susa stela have been filled, providing a reasonably complete and accurate version of Hammurabi's laws.

The laws are introduced by a prologue in which Hammurabi, in the first person singular, describes his efforts to make law prevail in his lands. He states that the gods Anim and Enlil had appointed him, as a god-fearing prince, to advance the welfare of the people by promoting justice. He was to destroy the wicked and curtail the oppression of the strong over the weak. This divine commission would cause him "to rise like the sun over the black-headed people, and to light up the land."

Following the prologue, 282 articles or laws treat personal property, real estate, business, trade, agriculture, marriage, inheritances, adoption, contracts, and leases. The law also details penalties for injuries both to person and property. Finally, an epilogue recounts in detail Hammurabi's achievements and concludes with a list of blessings for those who keep the laws, and for those who violate them a much longer and more elaborate set of curses.

On the stele that bears his law code, Hammurabi stands in front of the Sun god. (North Wind Picture Archives)

The collection of laws is not a code, but a set of amendments of existing laws. In the prologue, Hammurabi never calls himself a codifier or legislator. Instead, his aim seems to be to promote public order by making easily available current interpretations and applications of the existing law. This becomes clear when his laws are compared with earlier laws in use in Mesopotamia. Sizable fragments of at least three antecedents of Hammurabi's work remain. The threefold division into prologue, the laws themselves, and an epilogue glorifying the lawgiver, was a conventional form in Hammurabi's time.

There are significant differences between Hammuabi's code and law as it is understood in modern Western society. The laws were not enforced by the Babylonian courts; they were more like rules or norms in which the spirit is more important than the letter. This conclusion is based on the fact that there is no evidence of any kind of verbal interpretation of Hammurabi's laws, nor any references to the exact wording of the laws in other Babylonian writings. It follows that the "laws" were not imperative; that is, parties to a dispute were free to make any agreements outside the law in an attempt to settle their differences. The Babylonian documents dealing with property matters should not be seen as contracts but as memoranda of transactions. The statements in the contractlike documents were liable to modification by oral evidence.

Hammurabi's laws provide material for reconstructing the evidence of a remarkable civilization. What emerges is the picture of a society with a defined class system, well-developed agriculture, a viable economy based on foreign as well as internal trade, and a government with a strong judiciary.

At least three social classes are discernible in Babylonian society as reflected in the code: the highest class, including the king, civil and military officials, priests, landed proprietors, rich merchants, and manufacturers; a lower class consisting of laborers and farmers, including many tenant farmers; and finally, a slave class made up of those captured in war, together with men who had lost their freedom through debt. Here it should be noted that in Babylon, as in Israel, a slave was not a mere chattel, as he became later in Roman law and practice. In the ancient Near East, there was little difference between the hired workman and the slave. Indeed, the Hebrew noun for "slave" means simply a "worker."

The role of women was significant in that the law accorded women marriage and property rights in advance of other societies of a considerably later time. Women could divorce, transact business, and inherit or bequeath property. The law recognized a clear distinction between the legitimate wife and the concubine. "If a man take a wife and do not draw up a contract with her, that woman is not his wife." However, even the harlot was protected from wanton exploitation, as were slaves and children. If a man handed over his wife, his son, or his daughter to the service of another, they must work only three years in the house of their purchaser or master; in the fourth year, they secured their freedom.

In many respects, the laws of Hammurabi appear excessively harsh. Criminal law follows the *lex talionis*, the vengeful principle of an eye for an eye. "If a man destroy the eye of another man, they shall destroy his eye. If he break a man's bone, they shall break his bone."

Undergirding the individual laws was an exalted ideal of justice and concern for the vulnerable members of society who were referred to in ancient literature collectively as "the widow and the orphan." In the prologue of his laws, Hammurabi declared that he was the agent of the gods, appointed to protect the weak by enforcing just laws. Again in the epilogue, he stated that his purpose was to hinder the strong from oppressing the weak, to protect widows and orphans from injustice, and to affirm every person's right to equitable treatment.

The legal system of Babylonian society as reflected in Hammurabi's laws had a double function: It reflected the concept of government here described; it also implemented it. Unfortunately, there is little or no extant data about the legal theory that underlay the law. A good case can be made that this is not due to a loss of materials but rather to the fact that the Babylonians of the eighteenth century B.C.E. had not devised a body of legal theory. However, there is much data about legal practice, so that it is possible to reconstruct something of the court system both as to structure and procedure. A partial understanding of Babylonian legal theory can be reconstructed on the basis of two key concepts: *kittum*, which can roughly be translated "truth," and *mesarum*, or "justice."

Mesarum is a process of applying the law equitably, and this is one of the ruler's principal duties. To fulfill his role adequately, the ruler must not only supervise the application of the laws, but must also adapt them to contingencies. The meaning of the lengthy account of his exploits that Hammurabi gives in the epilogue to his set of laws thus becomes clear: It is less a eulogy than an account of the conditions that provide a rationale for his selection and amendments of older and well-known laws.

An analysis of the concept *kittum*, or truth, shows that the king was not the source of the law but only its agent. Here the Babylonian notion is close to the medieval idea that law is something discovered rather than something contrived or constructed. In the Babylonian value system, the cosmos is seen as founded on certain truths. The function of the law is to safeguard these truths, truths that bind the king as well as the lowliest slave. The ruler, therefore, is clearly under the law, not above it. Hammurabi himself succinctly expresses the meaning of *kittum* and *mesarum* when he speaks of himself as "the just king [*sar* mesarum], to whom Shamash [the sun-god] committed the truths." The collected statutes of Hammurabi's code kept alive both the established traditions or customs and also made possible the topical amendments to fit new circumstances.

SIGNIFICANCE

The laws of Babylonia are significant because of the light they throw on the ways of life of an ancient civilization. However, in the case of Hammurabi's redaction, the importance transcends the geographic and historical boundaries of the ancient Near East. Hammurabi's laws coincide with the period that saw a considerable expansion of Babylonian civilization, though recent research shows that the influence was more by commerce than by conquest. Not only Egypt and the Eastern Mediterranean but also the Aegean lands knew the influence of the Babylonian culture. A chief means of transmission of this culture was the law.

It was especially in the case of the Hebrews that this influence was felt, and it was primarily through the Hebrews that some of the political and legal concepts of Hammurabi's laws have become a fundamental part of the heritage of Western civilization and ultimately of the world. In some respects the Babylonian laws reveal a civilization in advance of that of the Hebrews; certainly this is true on the material and economic side. On the other hand, the Hebrew law implies a recognition of a fundamental human equality premised on a recognition of creation by one God, and from this developed a system of ethics far in advance of anything in the Babylonian law. Nevertheless, the historical connections between the two are direct and intimate, and Hammurabi's laws continue to be seen rightly as an early crystallization of some of humankind's deepest aspirations for social justice and public order and ultimately for the good life, conceived in much more than economic or even legal terms.

—*Mary Evelyn Jegen*

FURTHER READING

Bottéro, Jean. *Everyday Life in Ancient Mesopotamia*. Translated by Antonia Nevill. Baltimore, Md.: The Johns Hopkins University Press, 2001. This guide to early Mesopotamian life includes a chapter on law, showing how Hammurabi's code affected daily life.

Harper, Robert Francis. *The Code of Hammurabi, King of Babylon*. Reprint. Stockton, Calif.: University of the Pacific, 2002. This translation of Hammurabi's code was made three years after its discovery. The translation faces a transliteration of the original ideograms, as well as facsimiles of original cuneiform tablets, a glossary, index, lists of proper names, and tables of Babylonian weights and currencies.

Oppenheim, A. Leo. *Ancient Mesopotamia: Portrait of a Dead Civilization*. Rev. ed. Chicago: University of Chicago Press, 1977. A classic survey. Discusses Hammurabi's code in its historical and cultural context.

Skaggs, H. W. *Babylonians*. Berkeley: University of California Press, 2000. An excellent overview of Babylonian civilization, including a chronology, maps, further reading, and indexes of both subjects and biblical names.

SEE ALSO: c. 2112 B.C.E., Ur-Nammu Establishes a Code of Law; 451-449 B.C.E., Twelve Tables of Roman Law Are Formulated; 90 B.C.E., Julian Law Expands Roman Citizenship.

1750-800 B.C.E.
ANDRONOVO CULTURE RISES IN CENTRAL ASIA

The Andronovo culture bridged the Neolithic and Bronze Age cultures in Central Asia.

LOCALE: Kazakhstan, Turkmenistan, the Altai Mountains, and the Ural Mountains
CATEGORY: Prehistory and ancient cultures

SUMMARY OF EVENT

The Andronovo culture was named after a village in the Yenisey Valley near Achinsk, where burials were discovered in 1914 by S. A. Teploukov. This nomadic culture may have resulted from the merging of different Indo-European-speaking tribes to achieve a broad territorial base in the second millennium B.C.E. It extended north to the taiga, south to the Kopet Dag and Pamir Mountains, east to Minusinsk and the Altai Mountains, and west to the Ural steppes. Some people even migrated farther south to form the Indo-Iranian-speaking populations of northern India and Iran. The Andronovo society of the upper Yenisey steppes was marked by a newer, more sedentary way of life. To the south was a semiurban region dominated by the Oxus River (Amu Dar'ya) and nearby oases, encompassing northern Bactria and the Zerafshan valley of present-day Turkmenistan and Tajikistan.

Irrigation discoveries indicate that many of these nomads practiced agriculture, as well as raising sheep, cattle, and horses. On the Andronovo steppes there are early examples of irrigation for farming and stock breeding. Generally, farming developed much earlier in the steppes west of the Ural River, in European lands. The extant pottery from Andronovo also reveals a pastoral society. From the middle of the Amu Dar'ya River to the Fergana valley, pastoralism and farming coexisted. Wild horses were hunted for food, including their milk, but domesticated animals were likewise consumed. In the late Bronze Age (first millennium B.C.E.), the greater dependence on horse culture strengthened the nomadic element in Andronovo culture, and they relied more on herding than farming.

Horse breeding took place in the steppes, and carvings found in the Pamir and Altai Mountains show chariots. These seem to be associated with the Andronovo culture, but to the south, in Bactria, such phenomena are absent. The Indo-Europeans were noted for the prominence of horses in their religious cult. Horse sacrifices were common and combined with a cult of fire. Yet the Andronovo people were not horse riders. They moved on foot, on wagons, and in chariots, but not yet atop their horses.

They lived in earthen huts, supplemented by stone and wood. Brick was sometimes used in the southerly regions. They made pottery decorated with triangles and other geometric patterns on flat-bottomed bowls and flower pots.

Burial sites reveal two principal variations among the eastern Andronovo population. The Fedorovo type maintained earthen burials with bodies in a flexed position. The Alakul type practiced cremation. Both types show evidence of devotion to the Sun god and the god of fire. Burials were in round, narrow embankments, and the graves, in pits, were faced with stone or wooden slabs. Bodies were interred in a supine position with heads turned to the southwest and legs contracted. Some of the graves reveal wooden structures, and variation in the quality of grave goods indicate class differentiation. Graves also contained flint arrowheads, copper beads and earrings, and bronze tools and weapons. Andronovo material culture shows similarities to the cultures of southern Russia, and both reveal relationships with the Indo-Iranian world.

Population movements were marked by competition for pasture lands by the nomadic peoples of the steppes and for farmland and irrigation networks by the more settled societies to the south. Warring East European tribes in this era may have depended on the metallurgical products of the Karasuk, across the Ural River. Andronovo gravesites also reveal the use of knives and spears, flint arrowheads, and bronze weapons. However, such evidence may indicate a hunting rather than a military culture.

SIGNIFICANCE

The Andronovo significantly affected the cultures to the east and south. Like the Karasuk and earlier Afanasiev, they represent the movement of Indo-Europeans eastward across Siberia to Xinjiang and Mongolia. All these westerners brought their iron tools and weapons to the East. The custom of burying chariots in the graves of rulers was common to Mesopotamia and the Andronovo steppes, as well as China. This is evidence to some that the Andronovo culture transmitted this practice from the West to the East. An urban society also existed in the Oxus region to the south, although the population was only semiliterate. David Christian suggests that together these two societies represented a kind of symbiosis between the pastoral north and the urban south. A kind of world economic system may have been created whereby linkages were made between the Inner Asian world (the northern steppes and Mongolia) featuring pastoral lands and woodlands, and the Outer Asian civilizations (China, India, and Mesopotamia) with more extensive urban and agricultural communities.

—*John D. Windhausen*

FURTHER READING

Askarov, A., V. Volkhov, and N. Ser-Odjav. "Pastoral and Nomadic Tribes at the Beginning of the First Millenium." In *The Dawn of Civilization: Earliest Times to 700 B.C.* Vol. 1 in *History of Civilizations of Central Asia*, edited by A. H. Dani and V. M. Masson. Paris: UNESCO, 1992. Demonstrates links between the Andronovo and the Karasuk. Bibliography and index.

Christian, David. *Inner Asia from Prehistory to the Mongol Empire*. Vol. 1 in *A History of Russia, Central Asia, and Mongolia*. Malden, Mass.: Blackwell, 1998. An excellent review of current scholarship for this region by an Australian specialist. Bibliography and index.

Davis-Kimball, Jeannine, Vladimir A. Bashilov, and Leonid T. Yablonsky, eds. *Nomads of The Eurasian Steppes in the Early Iron Age*. Berkeley, Calif.: Zinat Press, 1995. Offers experts' analyses of Soviet studies since 1960. Bibliography and index.

Edwards, I. E. S., et al., eds. *The Cambridge Ancient History*. Vol 1. 3d ed. New York: Cambridge University Press, 1970. An older but indispensable starting point for essential information. Bibliography, maps, and index.

Frye, Richard N. *The Heritage of Central Asia: From Antiquity to the Turkish Expansion*. Princeton, N.J.: Marcus Weiner, 1996. Argues for the Iranian origins of the Andronovo.

Masson, V. M. "The Decline of the Bronze Age Civilization and Movements of the Tribes." In *The Dawn of Civilization: Earliest Times to 700 B.C.* Vol. 1 in *History of Civilizations of Central Asia*, edited by A. H. Dani and V. M. Masson. Paris: UNESCO, 1992. Shows the proto-European elements of the Andronovo. Bibliography and index.

SEE ALSO: c. 7000-c. 4900 B.C.E., Çatalhüyük Flourishes as Center of Anatolian Culture; c. 6800-c. 4900 B.C.E., Kitoi People Live Near Lake Baikal in Siberia; c. 5500-c. 4500 B.C.E., Halafian Culture Flourishes in Northern Mesopotamia; c. 5000-c. 3000 B.C.E., Kelteminar Culture Flourishes in Central Asia; c. 3500 B.C.E., Indus Valley Civilization Begins in South Asia; c. 2000 B.C.E., Mongols Inhabit Steppes North of China; c. 1500-c. 1000 B.C.E., Aryans Appear in India; c. 1250-c. 700 B.C.E., Karasuk Culture Flourishes on Eurasian Steppes; c. 1000-c. 690 B.C.E., Cimmerian Culture Rises in Russia; 8th century B.C.E., Scythians Drive the Cimmerians from Central Asia.

c. 1650 B.C.E.
Hyksos Create Second Intermediate Period

The intrusion of the Middle Eastern Hyksos peoples into Egypt caused the end of the Middle Kingdom and placed Egypt under the rule of conquerors.

Locale: Nile Valley from Lower Egypt's Nile Delta to Nubia (now Egypt and Sudan)
Categories: Expansion and land acquisition; government and politics

Key Figures

Kamose (fl. sixteenth century B.C.E.), last king of Seventeenth Dynasty, r. 1575-1570 B.C.E.
Ahmose I (fl. sixteenth century B.C.E.), brother of Kamose and first king of Eighteenth Dynasty, r. 1570-1546 B.C.E.

Summary of Event

The Second Intermediate Period (c. 1650-c. 1570 B.C.E.) in Egypt succeeded the period of national unification under Theban rulers known as the Middle Kingdom (c. 2055-c. 1650 B.C.E.). In contrast to the preceding and following periods, the Second Intermediate Period was an era of considerable turmoil marked by disorder and conflict. The conflict was both internal and external in nature, probably with its origin in the later part of the Middle Kingdom. Some of the provinces were challenging centralized power, which enabled external forces to make inroads militarily and politically. By 1729, the Hyksos began to challenge the Thirteenth Dynasty's power through invasions of Lower Egypt. They successfully conquered the eastern Delta by 1700 B.C.E. and set up a capital at Avaris (now Tell el-Babᶜa), just northeast of Memphis.

The Egyptians referred to the Hyksos by the indefinite term *Heka-Khaswt* (from which the Greek appellation Hyksos is derived), meaning "rulers of the foreign lands." The exact cultural heritage of the Hyksos remains undetermined, but from all available evidence, they most likely originated from populations in western Asia, the modern Middle East. The Hyksos occupation of the eastern Delta was most likely preceded by a long period of close contact between the Nile Delta and the region to the east from which Hyksos political power came, or where at least there was Egyptian interaction with significant numbers of Hyksos settlers.

In the Second Intermediate Period, the Egyptian state was politically weak and militarily compromised, as provincial leaders took advantage of central weakness to assert their own autonomy. This general state allowed political division and geographic partition to prevail.

During the Second Intermediate Period, foreign heads of state ruled Egypt for a prolonged period. The Hyksos occupation of Lower Egypt, which at times spread as far south as Hermopolis, had a profound effect on the Egyptian nation because it disrupted the long epoch of political unity. Thus, the Second Intermediate Period demonstrates a relatively disunited era in contrast to the Middle and New Kingdoms, but it is not in complete economic, cultural, or political discontinuity with the preceding or subsequent eras.

In fact, although the Hyksos disrupted Egyptian political life, material culture indicates that they adopted Egyptian language, codes of behavior, laws, regalia, and institutions of monarchical rule, becoming at least somewhat Egyptianized. For example, the Hyksos kept in place the long-established Egyptian institutions of divine kingship and declared themselves pharaohs. Although the Hyksos had their own religion they did incorporate the Egyptian god Set into their religious practices, reinterpreting him as their own god of storms. As often occurs in colonial situations, the conquerors took on customs of the conquered. The Hyksos also contributed to Egyptian society, for instance, by introducing the horse, chariot, bronze weaponry, and body armor into Egyptian notions of military strategy and equipment. The Egyptians eventually turned these newly introduced tools of war against their originators to liberate Egypt from Hyksos rule.

The Second Intermediate Period is depicted by some scholars as having lasted about 285 years, from 1785-1500 B.C.E., and having had as many as 230 different rulers, based on the royal scarab-shaped seals found in excavations. The long king lists have led certain scholars to argue that Egypt in this period in fact was not under the domination of a single monarch, but consisted of several independent states under a variety of native Egyptian dynasties and foreign rulers, including the Hyksos in the north and the Nubians in the south.

Many of the names of pharaohs of the Second Intermediate Period have been lost or remain unclear; most of the names of rulers are controversial, including those from the Fifteenth Dynasty lineages, generally considered to be authentically Hyksos. For example, Sheshi was a king of either the Fourteenth or Fifteenth Dynasty. Some scholars believe that a renowned East Delta ruler,

SECOND INTERMEDIATE PERIOD, C. 1650-C. 1570 B.C.E.

FIFTEENTH DYNASTY, HYKSOS OF AVARIS, C. 1650-1540

Ruler	*Reign*
Shamuqenu (Saitês)	
'Aper-'Anati (Bnôn)	
Sakir-Har (Pachnan)	
Khayan (Staan)	
Apepi I (Archlês)	
Apophis (Khamudi/Apepi II)	1605-1565

SIXTEENTH DYNASTY OF THEBES, 1648-1645

Ruler
Djehuty
Sobekhotep VIII
Nebiryraw I
Bebiankh

SEVENTEENTH DYNASTY OF THEBES, 1580-1570

Ruler	*Reign*
Rahotep	
Sobekemsaf I	
Intef VII	
Sobekemsaf II	
Sekenenre (Taa)	c. 1600-1571
Kamose	1575-1570

Note: Dynastic research is ongoing; data are approximate.

Pharaoh Nehsy of Hyksos ancestry, may have been the son and immediate successor of Sheshi. However, due to the nature of the sources available, the names and chronologies of rulers from the Second Intermediate Period are unclear and often contested by scholars.

It is thought that occupying Hyksos colonists established the Fifteenth Dynasty in the Delta concurrently with the collapse of the Thirteenth and Fourteenth Dynasties. Despite the discrepancies over the number of Second Intermediate Period rulers, scholars generally agree that there were at least six Fifteenth Dynasty Hyksos kings of Avaris over a period more than one hundred years (c. 1650-1540). The Turin King List represents the popularly cited theory of Second Intermediate Period political chronology; however, the Turin list is by no means universally accepted. Although the Hyksos rulers are known to have existed, they left no tombs, which makes the issue of documenting names and dates of reign difficult. Scholars maintain that the Seventeenth Dynasty kings, who were based in Thebes and controlled southern Egypt, were independent of the Hyksos in the north. The Fifteenth (Hyksos) Dynasty was most likely contemporary with the Seventeenth (Theban) Dynasty and perhaps even another native Egyptian dynasty centered at Abydos, just north of Thebes on the Nile. The Abydos rulers may be, in fact, the Sixteenth Dynasty.

In the mid-sixteenth century B.C.E., during the Seventeenth Dynasty under the Theban rulers of Upper Egypt, native Egyptians fought their Hyksos kings, effectively utilizing the very military technologies introduced by the Hyksos. Pharaoh Ahmose I, son of Sekenenre and brother of Kamose, finally drove the invaders out of the Delta and recaptured Avaris. Ahmose founded the New Kingdom and the Eighteenth Dynasty in the early sixteenth century B.C.E. The transition from an era of foreign rule and conflict to an era of domestic rule was, in this instance, fertile ground for a renaissance and an era of empire building. The rulers of the Eighteenth Dynasty (c. 1570-1295) are among the best known in modern times: Amenhotep I, Thutmose I, Thutmose II, and Queen Hatshepsut. The New Kingdom was an era of reunification and Egyptian expansion south into Nubia and further north into Palestine and Syria. Although the pharaohs of Egypt were relieved of the antagonism of competing power on domestic lands, for Egyptians outside the imperial class and the state bureaucracy, the reassertion of power by indigenous kings most likely signaled little actual change.

SIGNIFICANCE

The intermediate periods of Egyptian history are distinctive because the events and rulers of these eras are not well documented. The intermediate periods are also characterized by the disunity of political rule; however, these eras are not in complete discontinuity with previous or following eras. They are not as prominently marked by innovation and expansion, yet these are not eras without their own cultural, political, and economic developments. In fact, it may be these eras filled with political fracture and challenge as well as economic recession that allow for the eras of prosperous revitalization and political rebuilding that are so distinctive in the New Kingdom.

—*Catherine Cymone Fourshey*

FURTHER READING

Baker, Rosalie F., and Charles F. Baker. *Ancient Egyptians: People of the Pyramids*. New York: Oxford University Press, 2001. An examination of tradition and grandeur of ancient Egyptians. This book covers the various eras including disruption, rebirth, conquest, and decline. Also includes a section on the life and leadership of Ahmose.

Connah, Graham. *African Civilizations: Precolonial Cities and States in Tropical Africa, an Archaeological Perspective*. New York: Cambridge University Press, 1994. A historical account of ancient African towns which draws from archaeological data. Includes a section on ancient Egypt.

Habachi, Labib. *The Second Stela of Kamose and His Struggle Against the Hyksos Ruler and His Capital*. Blückstadt, Germany: J. J. Augustin, 1972. An archaeological description of the stela and the inscriptions honoring Kamose.

Miosi, F. T. *A Reading Book of Second Intermediate Period Texts*. Toronto: Benben Publications for The Society for the Study of Egyptian Antiquities, 1981. A collection of translated Egyptian language and hieroglyphic texts.

Oren, Eliezer, ed. *The Hyksos: New Historical and Archaeological Perspectives*. Philadelphia: University Museum, University of Pennsylvania, 1997. Contains articles on textual and archaeological sources for the Second Intermediate/Hyksos Period in Egypt and Nubia.

Ryholt, K. S. B. *The Political Situation in Egypt During the Second Intermediate Period, c. 1800-1550 B.C.* Copenhagen: Museum Tusculanum Press, 1997. A controversial reexamination and reinterpretation of Egyptian government and political chronology during the Second Intermediate Period.

Van Seters, John. *The Hyksos: A New Investigation*. New Haven, Conn.: Yale University Press, 1966. This work covers the history of the Hyksos in the ancient Middle East, including the occupation of Egypt.

SEE ALSO: c. 3050 B.C.E., Unification of Lower and Upper Egypt; c. 2687 B.C.E., Old Kingdom Period Begins in Egypt; c. 2160 B.C.E., First Intermediate Period Begins in Egypt; c. 2055 B.C.E., Middle Kingdom Period Begins in Egypt; c. 1570 B.C.E., New Kingdom Period Begins in Egypt; 1069 B.C.E., Third Intermediate Period Begins in Egypt.

1650-1620 B.C.E.
HATTUSILIS I ESTABLISHES THE OLD HITTITE KINGDOM

Hattusilis I established the Old Hittite Kingdom in Central Anatolia (now Turkey) and laid the foundations for the development of the Hittite Empire of the Late Bronze Age.

LOCALE: Anatolia (now Turkey)
CATEGORIES: Expansion and land acquisition; government and politics

KEY FIGURE

Hattusilis I (fl. seventeenth century B.C.E.), second king of the land of Hatti, r. c. 1650-c. 1620 B.C.E.

SUMMARY OF EVENT

During the Late Bronze Age (second millennium-c. 1200 B.C.E.), the Anatolian plateau (now in Turkey) was dominated by confederate tribes known as Hattians, ruling what they called the land of Hatti. Late nineteenth century European scholars who encountered their archaeological remains erroneously designated them "Hittites," from references to Hittites in the Old Testament. Scholars of Hattian history, art, and culture are known as Hittitologists.

It is assumed that the Hattians/Hittites entered Anatolia from the Eurasian steppe zone, overcoming and assimilating the indigenous population. For most of their history, their capital was located at Hattusas (modern Boghazköy). The Hittite language was one of a group of early Indo-European languages found in Anatolia that included Luvian, Lycian, Lydian, and more distantly, Hurrian and Urartian. It was written in what are known as Hittite hieroglyphics, as well as in Akkadian cuneiform. Approximately twenty-five thousand tablets or fragments have been excavated from Hattusas, as well as other sites.

Hittitologists divide Hittite history into three periods: the Old Kingdom, from Labarnas I to Telipinus (c. 1700-c. 1500 B.C.E.); the Middle Kingdom, from Alluwamnas to Muwatallis (c. 1500-c. 1400 B.C.E.); and the Empire, from Tudhaliyas I to Suppiluliumas II (c. 1400-c. 1200 B.C.E.), with a postimperial Neo-Hittite period (c. 1200-c. 700 B.C.E.), associated with Carchemish and other

Hittite successor-states between the Taurus Mountains and the Euphrates River.

Before the establishment of the Old Kingdom by Hattusilis I, earlier attempts at state-formation in the Hittite lands remain obscure, but there are hints of conflicts among small regional kingdoms such as Kanesh/Nesha (modern Kültepe), Hattusas, Zalpa (on the Black Sea coast near modern Bafra), and Mama (perhaps modern Elbistan). Eventually, a father-son team of state-builders emerged who, some time after 1800 B.C.E., united much of central Anatolia. Their original home was Kushshar, an unidentified city located southeast of the Kizil River basin at Shar. From here, the father, Pitkhana, acquired a block of territory, including Kanesh, which he made his capital. His son Anittas, who took the title of Great King, continued his expansionist policies by annexing land north of the Kizil River (later regarded as the Hittite heartland), and what came to be known as the Low Land, the country between the Kizil River and the Salt Lake. When Hattusas rebelled, he captured it and razed it to the ground, laying a curse on whomsoever should rebuild it.

The end of Anittas's career is uncertain, but he had brought under his rule the Kizil River basin, the Pontic coastal region of Zalpa, and the Lower Land south of the Salt Lake. In so doing, he defined the core territories of future Hittite kingdoms. No later Hittite kings claimed descent from Anittas, and it is not clear whether, when Hattusilis I undertook the task of creating an extensive kingdom located in the same general area, the memory of Anittas's conquest lived on, but it may have. Certainly, Hattusilis I, like Anittas, came from Kushshar and it is not impossible that there was a kinship tie, perhaps a very remote one, between them.

Hattusilis's grandfather, Labarnas I, is described in a bilingual inscription found in Hattusas in 1957, as also coming from Kushshar. According to this inscription, Labarnas I set out to subdue his neighbors, thereafter sending his sons to govern his conquests, and in later times, Labarnas I and his wife, Tawanannas, enjoyed such prestige that their names, like Caesar's, were used as royal titles. Thus, when he mounted the throne in 1650 B.C.E., Hattusilis I had before him the precedent of his grandfather's consolidation of the Hittite territory and perhaps a memory of Anittas's more distant conquests. During his thirty-year reign, Hattusilis established a kingdom stretching from the Black Sea to the Mediterranean.

Having consolidated his grandfather's legacy, Hattusilis led an army southeast into Syria, entering Cilicia, where Tarsus and Mersin may have been occupied, and crossed the Amanus range. He reached Alalakh (now Tell-Atçana). Excavators of that site believe that the destruction that marks the end of Level VII at this site confirms the Hittite conquest. On his return northward, he sacked Urshu and two other unidentified cities upstream from Carchemish, but he avoided the powerful city-state of Halab (modern Aleppo).

Major Kings of the Old Hittite Kingdom, c. 1650-c. 1500 B.C.E.

Ruler	*Reign*
Labarnas I	c.1650
Hattusilis I	c. 1650-c. 1620
Mursilis I	c. 1620-c. 1590
Hantilis I	c. 1590-c. 1560
Zidantas I	c. 1560-c. 1550
Ammunas	c. 1550-c. 1530
Huzziyas I	c. 1530-c. 1525
Telipinus	c. 1525-c. 1500

In the following year, he marched west into the region known as Arzawa (the Lydia, Lycia, and Pamphylia of Roman times), perhaps aiming for the Aegean Sea, with its vigorous commercial life. During his absence, disturbances occurred on his eastern frontier associated with the Hurrians of Hanigalbat east of the Euphrates. Forced to call off his western campaigning, he spent the next years restoring his prestige in both the heartland and the southeast. Subsequently, he attacked the Hurrian power of Hashshu, which probably lay east of the Euphrates and which may have been involved in raiding Hittite territories several years previously. Hashshu then allied itself with Halab, but it seems that Hattusilis failed to conquer this latter kingdom, the capture of which was to be the achievement of his grandson, Mursilis I. Hattusilis himself may have been mortally wounded in the struggle against Halab.

Earlier, Hattusilis had rebuilt Hattusas, disregarding Anittas's ancient curse; indeed, his name means "the man from Hattusas." In his *Testament*, one of the most personal documents to emanate from the Bronze Age, he relates how he had intended to nominate as his heir an unnamed sister's son, but after observing this nephew's behavior, he concluded that he had been badly brought up by his sister. The flaws of character in the nephew caused the old king, to the fury of his sister, to put him aside, nominating instead his grandson Mursilis I (r. 1620-1590 B.C.E.), who proved a worthy successor. Mursilis destroyed the city of Halab, led his victorious forces into Mesopotamia, and in c. 1595 B.C.E. sacked Babylon itself, hitherto the capital of Hammurabi's First Babylonian Dynasty (1894-1595 B.C.E.). However, on his return to Hattusas, Mursilis was assassinated by a would-be usurper, and the Hittite Old Kingdom experienced half a century of decline before its fortunes revived under Telipinus (r. 1525-1500 B.C.E.).

There is no reason to suppose that the military forces with which Hattusilis laid the foundation of the Old Kingdom differed from those of the Empire period (c. 1400-c. 1200 B.C.E.), as shown in both Hittite and Egyptian bas-reliefs. Spear-carrying infantry, who made up the bulk of the king's forces, were recruited from the adult male population, stiffened by levies from the vassal kingdoms. The elite shock-troops consisted of chariots with a driver and one (sometimes two) fighting men recruited from the ranks of young aristocratic warriors.

Knowledge of Hattusilis I's reign is based primarily on three texts. The first, the *Annals of Hattusilis* (c. 1650-1620 B.C.E.), records a number of campaigns, although probably not all of them, and the chronology remains extremely vague. The annals are written in the first person, with simple syntax and vocabulary in what would become an established annalistic tradition. The second is the *Testament* of Hattusilis, which describes his arrangements for the succession. Finally, the *Edict of Telepinus* (c. 1500 B.C.E.), the last effective ruler of the Old Kingdom, acclaims the former glory of Hatti, includes a king list from the time of Labarnas I, and acknowledges the central role of Hattusilis I. All three texts survive in both Hittite and Akkadian.

SIGNIFICANCE

Between 1600 B.C.E. and 1200 B.C.E., the Hattians created a powerful kingdom in Anatolia and played a conspicuous role in Late Bronze Age history. Hattusilis I was the founder of that kingdom and defined its institutions and strategic frontiers, laying the ground for future imperial greatness. The texts surviving from his reign, moreover, offer unprecedented insight into the life and politics of Bronze Age Anatolia.

—*Gavin R. G. Hambly*

FURTHER READING

Bryce, Trevor. *The Kingdom of the Hittites*. Oxford, England: Clarendon Press, 1998. An exhaustive account of Hittite history.

_______. *Life and Society in the Hittite Period*. Oxford, England: Oxford University Press, 2002. A sequel to the preceding entry, primarily concerned with social and cultural history.

_______. *The Major Historical Texts of Early Hittite History*. St. Lucia, Brisbane: The University of Queensland Press, 1982. Source material for the period of Hattusilis I.

Gurney, O. R. "Anatolia, c. 1750-1600 B.C." In *The Middle East and the Aegean Region, c. 1380-1000 B.C.* Volume 2, part 1 of *The Cambridge Ancient History*, edited by I. E. S. Richards, C. J. Gadd, N. G. L. Hammond, and E. Sollberger. 3d ed. New York: Cambridge University Press, 1973. The definitive account in English of the Hittite Old Kingdom, down to the assassination of Mursilis I.

_______. *The Hittites*. Rev. ed. New York: Penguin, 1990. An authoritative overview, emphasizing the archaeological evidence.

Macqueen, J. G. *The Hittites and Their Contemporaries in Asia Minor*. Rev. ed. New York: Thames and Hudson, 1986. A very useful introduction to Hittite history and culture.

SEE ALSO: c. 2334-c. 2279 B.C.E., Sargon of Akkad Establishes the Akkadian Dynasty; c. 1650 B.C.E., Hyksos Create Second Intermediate Period; c. 1600-c. 1300 B.C.E., Mitanni Kingdom Flourishes in Upper Mesopotamia; c. 1570 B.C.E., New Kingdom Period Begins in Egypt; c. 1450 B.C.E., International Age of Major Kingdoms Begins in the Near East; c. 1200-c. 1050 B.C.E., Sea Peoples Contribute to Mediterranean Upheaval; c. 883-c. 824 B.C.E., Second Assyrian Empire Displays Military Prowess; 8th-6th centuries B.C.E., Phrygian Kingdom Rises; c. 705-330 B.C.E., Founding and Flourishing of the Achaemenian Dynasty.

c. 1600 B.C.E.
Shang Dynasty Develops Writing and Bronzework

The Shang begin writing in the form of oracle-bone inscriptions and engravings on bronze objects, such as ritual vessels and weapons, becoming the first Chinese dynasty that can be archaeologically authenticated.

Locale: Northern China
Categories: Prehistory and ancient cultures; cultural and intellectual history; science and technology

Summary of Event

In the Neolithic era, several cultures began to develop in China. Chinese histories refer to the oldest dynasties as the Xia (Hsia; c. 2100-1600 B.C.E.) and the Shang (c. 1600-1066 B.C.E.), both of which were considered mythical until the nineteenth century. The finding of characters or *buci* written on oracle bones in the winter of 1899 in Henan Province on the site of Yinxu (Yin-Hsü), the presumed last capital of the Shang Dynasty, provided early evidence that it had indeed existed. Subsequent findings of more oracle bones along with bronze vessels gave substantial information about that civilization.

The *buci* are the only inscriptions to have survived from the Shang era (court records were transcribed onto bamboo rolls, which have long gone to dust). They consist of inscriptions added after the bones or turtle shells had been fired, and were apparently intended to serve as the proper interpretation of the crack patterns the heat had created. The inscription of the *buci* appears to have followed an established practice, and included the date of the divination, the name of the oracle who had performed the ceremony, and two statements with opposite meaning, such as "the king's hunt will be successful" and "the king's hunt will yield nothing." The information stops here. Although the names of at least one hundred oracles have been collated, how they interacted within their caste and how they read the gods' answer to the two propositions is unclear. While there are drawings or patterns older than the *buci*, thus far no equivalent form of writing preceding the Shang Dynasty has been discovered.

When Chinese peasants first discovered the oracle bones in the nineteenth century, they thought these were the remains of a mythical dragon, and ground them into powder for sale as elixir ingredients. Nonetheless, some three thousand pieces were sent to Shanghai, where expert Liu E collected them in a book published in 1903. Archaeologists Lo Chenyu, Wang Guowei, and Dong Zobin pioneered their decipherment. Similar characters found on bronze urns were dated back to the thirteenth century B.C.E. The oldest system, though, utilized turtle shells, and included some three thousand to four thousand characters, about half of which have been deciphered to date.

Like the hieroglyphs of ancient Egypt, the Chinese writing system originated in pictograms. However, the Chinese language structure, which emphasizes monosyllables, allowed the Chinese system to follow and maintain the principle that each syllable had its own character. The writings dating back to the Shang era differ from modern characters, although the principles of writing are the same and their modern script equivalents do exist. There are several groups of characters. Initially, the Shang writings were very close to pictograms. The sun, for example, was a circle with a horizontal bar crossing through it. In addition, there are also some identifiable ideographs—that is, characters that express an idea or a concept rather than an actual thing, such as "one," "two," or "three" (one, two, or three horizontal bars atop one another). Some ideographs could use pictographs to represent an idea. For example, the combination of drawings of a woman and a roof meant "safety." Some pictograms refer to sounds, which is why some Chinese words are homonyms, for they use the same character, are pronounced the same, yet have different meanings. Finally, some characters are used to hint at the phonetic pronunciation of the word, while others form a radical, which allows readers to place the word in a certain category.

The discovery of the *buci* raised new questions about the appearance of writing in China. One theory alludes to the idea of a set of visual characters inspired from Mesopotamian cuneiform that first appeared around 4000 B.C.E. Although the pictograms themselves did not travel, experts who hold this theory consider that, over the centuries, the notion of such a system could have made its way to the Chinese mainland. This does not, however, explain why it was the Shang, rather than the previous dynasty, who implemented a writing system. A combination of factors, including an increase in territory, a stronger centralized power, and economic stability, may have set the stage for seeking to devise a way to transmit and control information that would ensure survival of the dynasty.

Shang culture is also associated with the beginning of the Bronze Age in China, as evidenced by the discovery of weapons and elaborate ceremonial vessels. The discovery of the metal probably dates back to 2000 B.C.E., but it first began to be worked into artifacts under the Shang. The vessels discovered at Yinxu are often of great size, with relief lines, drawings, and pictograms. Although most surviving Shang writing is found on oracle bones, early bronze vessels also display them, alongside representations of animal faces. The latter pattern departs from other Bronze Age civilizations in that, rather than the animal's profile, a frontal, angular representation was chosen, making it into a masklike figure.

Some bronzes had a clear influence in Shang pottery. When considering this information in the context of bronze findings in graves, one can compare and contrast Shang influence in specific regions.

Throughout the twentieth century, a series of bronze finds in areas beyond Yinxu allowed scholars to piece together some of the boundaries of the Shang and to show that it came into contact and conflict with predynastic Chou (Ch'ou) cultures along its western borders, as evidenced by the change in style and patterns of later pottery and bronzes. For example, some Shang style bronzes found in 1976 at the Lingzhi (Ling-Shih) site show different clan emblems not associated with the Shang, suggesting that they had become part of the spoils of war of enemies of the Shang.

Shang craftspeople also worked bronze into weapons such as battle axes and knives, though it appears that they had no bronze daggers initially. These weapons were found mostly on both sides of the Yellow River. Ladles and dippers, important in certain Shang rituals, had snake and frog motifs on the handle. The style they used in shaping their tools and weapons, however, had allowed experts to speculate about the influence and counterinfluence of both succeeding and contemporary cultures on the Shang. Such relationships are not always clear, however, as in the case between the Karasuk and the Yinxu Shang: Although both cultures had similar elements in their bronze designs, they displayed little commonality otherwise.

Other kinds of bronze objects include musical instruments. In particular the *nao* bell, also known, depending on the region of its find, as the *cheng* or the *chung*, remained in use throughout the succeeding Western (1066-771 B.C.E.) and Eastern Zhou (Chou; 770-256 B.C.E.) Dynasties. *Nao* have been found in southern China and include designs with animal masks. These are fairly large, at least 1 to 2 feet (31 to 62 centimeters) in diameter, and weigh anywhere from 30 to 300 pounds (14 to 136 kilograms). Their ceremonial function included military assembly (striking them to call up the troops), sacrifices, and feasts.

Significance

The complicated nature of the Chinese script meant that it took an extremely long time to learn (one needs at least two thousand of the sixty thousand or so characters in existence to be able to read texts). Consequently, only very few members of society were able to master it. On the other hand, the complex nature of the script gave it a special aesthetic value, one that evolved from the oracle-bone writings into the recognized art of calligraphy. In addition, its use by later dynasties as a means of administration made possible the centralization of Chinese bureaucratic practices and overcame the dialects in use throughout China.

The written evidence offered in the oracle bones is further complemented through the multiple bronze artifacts to show the deep religiosity of the Shang people. Multiple worship of the winds, the stars, and their immediate surroundings, as well as the cult of the ancestors explain why the Shang required numbers of ceremonial vessels (and sacrificial victims), to construct the social and religious boundaries of their world. Some of their practices, including the working of bronze, the writing, and the cult of the ancestors, would pass onto subsequent dynasties.

—*Guillaume de Syon*

Further Reading

Allan, Sarah. *The Shape of the Turtle: Myth, Art, and Cosmos in Early China*. Albany: State University of New York Press, 1991. An illustrated book that surveys the myths of Shang China and clarifies some of the foundations of the notion of yin and yang.

Chang, K. C., ed. *Studies in Shang Archeology*. New Haven, Conn.: Yale University Press, 1986. A collection of essays by specialists in the field of Shang China, based on a conference.

Keightley, David N. *The Ancestral Landscape: Time, Space, and Community in Late Shang China c. 1200-1045 B.C.* Berkeley, Calif.: Institute of East Asian Studies, 2000. Deepens the investigation of the author's 1978 work by further discussing the religious social and cultural contexts of the oracle-bone inscriptions.

_______. *Sources of Shang History: The Oracle-Bone Inscriptions of Bronze Age China*. Berkeley: University of California Press, 1978. A foundational book on the interpretation and use of divination in Shang China.

Loewe, Michael, and Edward L. Shaughnessy. *The Cambridge History of Ancient China: From the Origins of Civilization to 221 B.C.* New York: Cambridge University Press, 1999. The standard work for any introduction to the study of ancient China.

Rawson, Jessica, ed. *Mysteries of Ancient China: New Discoveries from the Early Dynasties*. New York: G. Braziller, 1996. A helpful illustrated guide to artifacts used in the study of early Chinese civilizations.

SEE ALSO: c. 6000-c. 1500 B.C.E., Yangshao and Longshan Cultures Flourish in China; c. 3100 B.C.E., Sumerians Invent Writing; c. 2682 B.C.E., Legendary Founding of China by Huangdi; c. 2100 B.C.E., Xia Dynasty Marks Start of Historical China; c. 1066, Western Zhou Dynasty Begins in China.

c. 1600-c. 1500 B.C.E.
FLOWERING OF MINOAN CIVILIZATION

The flowering of the Minoan civilization established the foundations of Mediterranean mythologies, religious practices, and social organization that influenced classical Greek societies.

LOCALE: Crete
CATEGORIES: Prehistory and ancient cultures; religion

SUMMARY OF EVENT

The ancient Greeks of the fourth and fifth centuries B.C.E. inherited legendary accounts of a wealthy, powerful civilization located on the Mediterranean island of Crete. Minos was supposedly the ruler of a thalassocracy (sea-empire) that controlled much of Aegean and mainland Greece in prehistoric times. According to Greek mythology, Minos was semidivine: He was the son of Zeus, ruler of the gods, and Europa, a Phoenician princess. Minos was remarkable for his justice as well as his power.

The Minos legend suggested deep historical roots to classical Greek civilization; but the Minoan civilization named after him remained legendary until 1900. Inspired by the discoveries of Heinrich Schliemann at Troy in the late 1800's and Mycenae, Sir Arthur Evans began to excavate at Knossos. His findings were astonishing and revolutionary. They initiated an ongoing process of revision and reevaluation of classical, Western, and finally world history.

Evans was deeply impressed by the Minos legend. An important part of that legend said that there was a vast labyrinth at Knossos, built by Minos to imprison the mythological Minotaur (a creature which was half-man, half-bull). As Evans excavated, the legend seemed to be confirmed. He unearthed the remains of a multistory building that, on the ground floor, covered roughly 5 acres (2 hectares). The plan of the building was labyrin-

MINOAN PALACES ON CRETE, C. 1600-C. 1500 B.C.E.

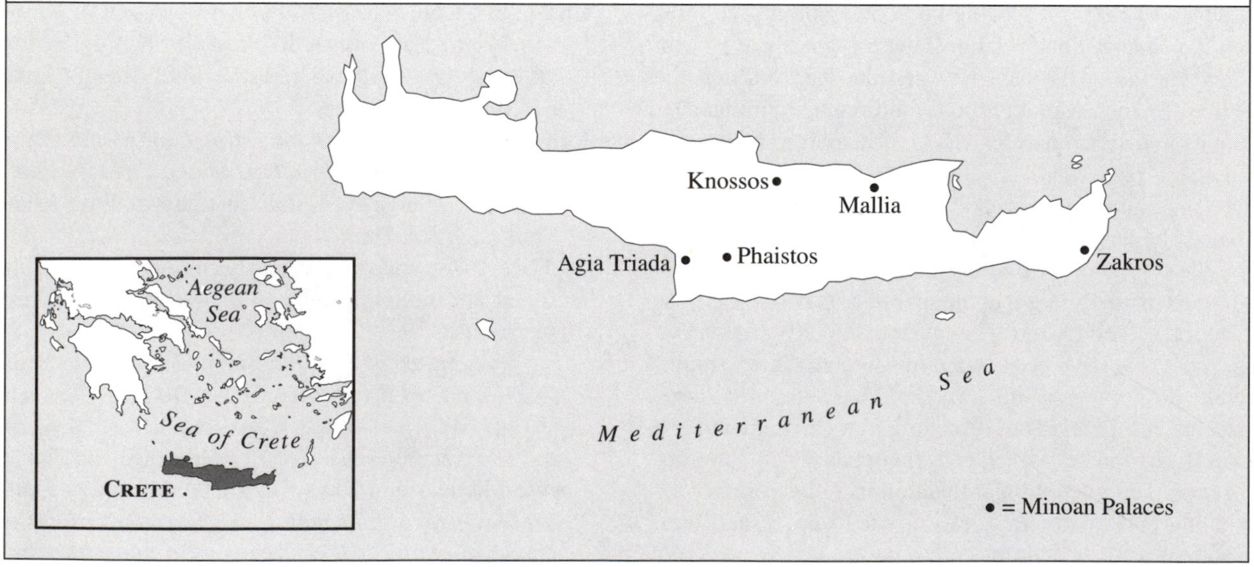

This early 1900's photograph shows the ruins of the palace of Minos at Knossos, excavated by Sir Arthur Evans. (Hulton|Archive)

thine, with intricate corridors and hundreds of rooms arranged around a central court which seemed perfect for containing the Minotaur. Stone building blocks and various artifacts were found marked with the *labrys*, the double-ax, thus making the labyrinth the "house of the double-ax." A vivid fresco depicting male and female acrobats leaping over a powerful, noble bull seemed to refer to Athenian youths and maidens sacrificed as tribute to Minos the Overlord.

As Evans uncovered the ruins and their contents, he believed that he had found the Palace of Minos—that is, the political and administrative headquarters of a powerful monarch who ruled over all or most of Crete, many of the neighboring islands, and portions of the Greek mainland. He interpreted and named sections and rooms accordingly: the Royal Road, the North-West Treasure House, the Royal Magazines, the Corridor of the Procession, the Throne Room, the Central Court, the Hall of the Double-Axes, and the Queen's Toilet (the Minoans invented indoor plumbing, although the technology was lost with the collapse of their civilization). Because virtually all major findings were in ruins or incomplete, Evans and his assistants reconstructed them as they imagined parts of the great palace might have looked.

As the work continued, two facts became evident. The first was the great length of prehistoric human habitation at Knossos. Evans uncovered about 40 feet (12 meters) of human debris, roughly one-half of it from the Minoan period (c. 3000-1150 B.C.E.), one-half from the Neolithic period (6100-3000 B.C.E.). The Palace of Minos was built on the ruins of a prior, probably somewhat smaller, palace, itself built on the ruins of many layers of earlier Minoan and Neolithic buildings. To the extent to which the roots of classical Greek (and thus Western) civilization are Minoan, they are deep in the Cretan soil.

The second fact implied a similar conclusion about deep roots—now religious—in the earth. Classical Greek religion, like classical Greek society, was masculine, competitive, and oriented toward war. Characteristically, Zeus is depicted wielding his mighty thunderbolt:

The Olympian gods are perpetually fighting, either among themselves or in human affairs. Minos as sea emperor fit easily into this scheme of male conquest and domination. Yet the hundreds and then thousands of artifacts—wall and vase paintings, cups, signet rings, cylinder seals and seal stones, jewelry items, rhytons (ritual vessels), and votive offerings—found by Evans and later investigators did not fit this male-warrior picture. They suggested a Minoan religion and civilization of nearly opposite character.

A fundamental insight on religion is offered by the palace itself (and other, smaller palaces subsequently excavated at Phaistos, Mallia, Agia Triada and Zakros on Crete). Unlike mainland palaces, those on Crete had no defensive walls. The obvious implication is a peaceful society; the less obvious one is a society open to nature. Detailed archaeological evidence supports this latter view. The Minoans appear to have loved all aspects of nature—birds, animals, dolphins, fish, bees, flowers, trees and, interestingly, snakes. Aside from the labyrinth itself, the single most famous symbol of Minoan civilization is the figurine of a bare-breasted goddess holding snakes in each hand.

Evans himself was fully aware of the sacred character of many of his findings. However, his view that the palace was the residence of priest-kings has been substantially amended. Archaeological evidence, combined with some documentary evidence from the Linear B tablets (inscribed with an early form of Greek), indicate that the Minoans worshiped and sacrificed to a goddess. The goddess may have taken a number of forms and been attended by one or more younger gods. Nonetheless, at the center of Minoan religion was Potnia (or the Lady). She was the prehistoric Cretan version of the Great Earth/Mother Goddess of Old Europe (7000-3500 B.C.E.). This powerful female deity was understood to be the source of all life and the force behind the annual regeneration of nature.

The place of women in Cretan society paralleled the importance of the goddess. They appear, from graphic representations, to have been at least equal to men. They figured prominently in palace life at Knossos, probably not directly as rulers but as priestesses. It has been suggested that a high priestess impersonated the goddess, who was thus physically present as the lady of the labyrinth.

These considerations suggest that the Palace of Minos was more likely the abode of Potnia. Scholars of Minoan civilization have suggested a number of redesignations for the palace—perhaps it was a temple-palace, or a cult-center, or a temple. Even these names, however, may be misleading, since they imply a specialization of activities into religious, political, administrative, and so forth. Western civilization has inherited this orientation from the classical Greeks. What seems unique about Minoan civilization is that it was leisured, sophisticated, and (relatively) equalitarian, yet viewed life from the perspective of the wholeness of nature. Like the labyrinth, it remained close to the earth.

It is no small irony, then, that the civilization of the earth-worshiping Minoans was very probably ended by the earth. Crete lies in a geologically unstable area and is subject to frequent and severe earthquakes. The Old Palace at Knossos was probably destroyed by an earthquake around 1700 B.C.E. It was rebuilt as the New Palace—excavated by Evans—along the same lines but on a somewhat grander scale. It was in and around this structure, be it termed palace or temple, that Minoan civilization reached its fullest development.

Very much remains uncertain about this "flowering." It is traditionally dated 1700-1450 B.C.E., with the "bloom" of the flowering being 1600-1500. The period 1500-1450 had been thought to correspond to the Thera disaster, when an island 75 miles (121 kilometers) north of Knossos was blown literally to pieces by volcanic eruption. The resulting shock waves, tsunamis, and volcanic fallout, probably combined with local earthquakes, severely damaged Knossos. It has been suggested that this ecological catastrophe forms the historic kernel of the Greek philosopher Plato's myth of Atlantis. Yet considerable scientific evidence indicates a date of 1628 B.C.E. for the Thera eruption, thus raising the "flowering" by roughly a century.

SIGNIFICANCE

It is clear that, at its height, Minoan civilization was a fruitful blending of cultures. Mainland peoples—certainly Mycenaeans, perhaps Luwians from Anatolia and Hyksos from Egypt—mingled with the Cretans, who themselves traveled throughout the eastern Mediterranean. The character of this intercourse is less clear. Did the Minoans colonize and dominate? Were they invaded and conquered? Did both patterns occur, giving rise to ambiguous legends of a "Minos" both powerful and just? Or, was the blending not only peaceful but divine, presided over by a great goddess of nature who nurtured the infant Zeus? Did belief in that Earth Goddess dissipate as the earth repeatedly quaked and destroyed? There are no final answers; Minoan civilization continues to intrigue.

—*John F. Wilson*

FURTHER READING

Castleden, Rodney. *Atlantis Destroyed.* Reprint. New York: Routledge, 2001. Presents the evidence for the theory that Minoan civilization provided the paradigm for Atlantis. Includes a bibliography and an appendix summarizing the controversies over the dating of the eruption of Thera.

_______. *The Knossos Labyrinth.* London: Routledge, 1990. An engaging and often persuasive reinterpretation of the labyrinth as "temple." Castleden stresses the extent of Evans's physical and conceptual reconstruction.

Chadwick, John. *The Decipherment of Linear B.* 2d ed. New York: Cambridge University Press, 1991. Chadwick, the codecipherer of Linear B along with Michael Ventris, provides a narrative of the process by which the script was cracked and an overview of the Minoan and Mycenean worlds it revealed.

Chadwick, John, et al. *Corpus of Mycenean Inscriptions from Knossos.* 4 vols. New York: Cambridge University Press, 1998-1999. Presents thirty years work of translating the entire body of inscriptions in Linear B. Although highly academic, this is the unmediated voice of the Minoans.

Higgins, Reynold. *Minoan and Mycenean Art.* 2d rev. ed. New York: Thames and Hudson, 1997. An abundantly illustrated volume that presents every significant piece of Minoan art known to date. Includes maps and bibliography.

Macgillivray, Joseph Alexander. *Minotaur: Sir Arthur Evans and the Archaeology of the Minoan Myth.* New York: Hill and Wang, 2000. A reassessment of the subjective factors in Evans's reconstruction of Minoan Crete; in the process, provides an overview of contemporary theories about Minoan culture.

Marinatos, Nanno. *Minoan Religion: Ritual, Image, and Symbol.* Columbia: University of South Carolina Press, 1993. The author reconstructs Minoan religious ritual from archaeological evidence, concluding that Knossos was a "cult center."

Willetts, R. F. *The Civilization of Ancient Crete.* Reprint. Las Palmas, Spain: Adolf M. Hakkert, 1992. Perhaps the best single introduction to Minoan civilization, Willetts's work is especially sensitive to problems of interpretation and the resultant controversies.

SEE ALSO: c. 3100 B.C.E., Sumerians Invent Writing; c. 1600-c. 1000 B.C.E., City of Mycenae Flourishes; c. 1250 B.C.E., Transmission of the European Alphabet; c. 1200-c. 1050 B.C.E., Sea Peoples Contribute to Mediterranean Upheaval; c. 1000 B.C.E., Greek Alphabet Is Developed; 775 B.C.E., Delphic Oracle Provides Guidance for City-States.

c. 1600-c. 1300 B.C.E.
MITANNI KINGDOM FLOURISHES IN UPPER MESOPOTAMIA

In the Late Bronze Age, the Hurrians established Mitanni, an empire of confederated states in upper Mesopotamia, and enjoyed diplomatic ties with Egypt, providing a glimpse into the complex interchange among states of the period.

LOCALE: Upper Mesopotamia (now northern Iraq and Syria)

CATEGORIES: Prehistory and ancient cultures; expansion and land acquisition

KEY FIGURES

Paratarna (fl. fifteenth century B.C.E.), Mitannian king, r. c. 1500 B.C.E.

Saustatar I (fl. late fifteenth century B.C.E.), Mitannian king, r. c. 1425 B.C.E.

Tushratta (fl. fourteenth century B.C.E.), Mitannian king, r. c. 1330 B.C.E.

Suppiluliumas I (fourteenth century-c. 1322 B.C.E.), Hittite king, r. c. 1380-1346 B.C.E.

SUMMARY OF EVENT

Mitanni was a kingdom in upper Mesopotamia and Syria carved from territories controlled at various times by the Hittites to its north, the Babylonians to its southeast, and Egyptians to its southwest during the sixteenth through fourteenth centuries B.C.E. The kingdom was known to its neighbors by several names including: Hurri, Hanigalbat and, to the Egyptians, Naharina.

It was sometime during the third millenium B.C.E. that an Indo-European speaking group of people called Hurrians first migrated into northern Mesopotamia and Syria. Their presence in the region became significant by the early centuries of the second millenium B.C.E., as the increasing number of Hurrian names in the archives of

MAJOR MITANNI KINGS, C. 1500-C. 1330 B.C.E.

Ruler	*Reign*
Paratarna	c. 1500
Kirta Shuttarna I	c. 1560?
Saustatar I	c. 1425
Paratarna II?	
Artatama I	c. 1425?
Shuttarna II	c. 1400
Tushratta	c. 1330

Mari, Ebla, Ugarit, and Carchemish attest. Eventually, the Hurrians established their own capital called Washukkanni in a location that has yet to be identified somewhere between the northern reaches of the Tigris and Euphrates Rivers. From c. 1620 to 1590 B.C.E., Hurrian Mitanni succeeded in maintaining a tenuous independence while the Hittite kings Hattusilis I and his adopted son, Mursilis I, engaged in the conquest of Syria and northern Mesopotamia. However, the Hittite conquest of the region ended suddenly in 1590 B.C.E. when Mursilis was assassinated by a rival while attending to affairs in the Hittite capital, Hattusas. This sudden reversal of fortune allowed Mitanni to step into the political void created by the assassination and to establish its own domination of northern Mesopotamia and Syria.

The Mitannians' subjugation of states in Syria brought them into direct competition with Egypt for control of the territory. The Eighteenth Dynasty pharaoh Thutmose I had previously conducted a campaign in the area and erected a victory stela on the upper reaches of the Euphrates River c. 1500 B.C.E.

However, during the subsequent reign of Queen Hatshepsut (r. c. 1503-1482 B.C.E.), Egyptian interests in Syria waned, allowing Mitanni to expand its domination in Syria by incorporating other states once aligned with the Hittites into its own system of confederated vassal states. The kingdom of Mitanni extended its domination over its Syrian neighbors by establishing treaties with them, subjecting them to vassal status and using their indigenous kings as agents of the king of Mitanni. This was the arrangement contracted, for example, by the Mitannian king Paratarna, who settled a disputed succession in Aleppo by installing Idrimi as its king (an event known from two inscriptions: one on a statue of Idrimi found at Alalah and the other a tablet found at the ancient site of Nuzi near Kirkuk).

Through similar arrangements, the kings of Mitanni expanded their rule over such principal Mesopotamian and Syrian cities as Carchemish and Kadesh. Further, all indications point to a Mitannian overlordship of Assyria between the years of 1500 and 1360 B.C.E. Indeed, there remains a record of an invasion of Assyria by Saustatar I, king in Mitanni, that was launched to put down an Assyrian revolt. Assyria had attempted to support its revolt against its Mitannian overlords by seeking an alliance with Egypt. In response, Saustatar I invaded Assyria and looted Ashur, carrying a door made of silver and gold back to Washukkanni as a prize.

When Thutmose III (r. c. 1504-1450 B.C.E.) resumed Egypt's campaigns into the Levant, ultimately extending Egyptian domination throughout Palestine, Lebanon, and into Syria, Mitanni engaged in a struggle to retain control over its confederation. Mitannian opposition against Egypt continued until c. 1420 B.C.E. when a diplomatic accord was reached between Artatarma I of Mitanni and Thutmose IV of Egypt (c. r. 1419-1386 B.C.E.), which Artatarma subsequently sealed by sending his daughter, Kilu-Hepa, to be married to the Egyptian pharaoh. As part of that alliance, the two powers established a border that allowed Egypt to retain Kadesh and Ugarit while conceding territories in the north to Mitanni.

Close diplomatic relations with Egypt were maintained until the reign of Tushratta, who contracted yet another marriage between his daughter, Tadu-Hepa, and the wealthy pharaoh, Amenhotep III (r. 1386-1349 B.C.E.). Nevertheless, this latest marriage alliance was not able to secure the kingdom of Mitanni from destructive forces from both within and without. First, Mitanni was weakened by internal disputes over the issue of Tushratta's succession. Tushratta's brother, another Artatarma, proclaimed himself "king of Hurri" and attempted to advance his claim to the Mitannian throne by seeking support from the Assyrian king, Ashur-uballit I. Second, the kingdom became prey to a resurgent Hittite empire led by the energetic Hittite king Suppiluliumas I. Despite Mitanni's excellent ties with the Egyptian pharaohs of the Eighteenth Dynasty, attested by numerous correspondences with Amenhotep III, Queen Tiy, and the enigmatic Akhenaton found among his archives at Amarna, the new Hittite king was equally careful to forge good relations with Egypt in advance of his conquest of Mitanni. Using the occasion of Tushratta's attack on Nuhasse, a country in Syria aligned with the Hittites, Suppiluliumas swept south of the Taurus Mountains to capture Washukkanni and deprived the Mitannians of all of their holdings except the city of Carchemish. He did so while taking great care to avoid molesting states aligned with Egypt (with the singular exception of Kadesh, which had marched out against Suppiluliumas while he campaigned in Syria). Suppiluliumas commemorated the victory against Mitanni with this statement: "Because of the hostility of Tushratta, the king, I plundered these lands all in a single year, and conveyed them to the Land of Hatti."

Carchemish also fell to the Hittites under Suppiluliumas in a second campaign conducted c. 1350 B.C.E. Although Tushratta escaped from this defeat as well, he was assassinated in a conspiracy that included his own son, Sattiwaza. Having finally subjugated Mitanni, Suppiluliumas installed his sons as viceroys in the several states that had once been part of Mitanni in order to maintain Hittite control of the region.

SIGNIFICANCE

The kingdom of Mitanni was only one of several kingdoms that held portions of Mesopotamia and Syria under its domination during the second millennium B.C.E. Nevertheless, its presence during the sixteenth through fourteenth centuries B.C.E. provides a glimpse into the complex nature of the relationships that were contracted among the (at times) greater powers of Egypt and the Hittites. Indeed, the military and diplomatic interchanges in which Mitanni engaged, attested in numerous inscriptions, reveals how volatile and precarious the fortunes of all the kingdoms in the region were. Further, the discovery of the archives at Amarna, site of the ancient capital of the heretic pharaoh Akhenaton, has yielded numerous letters written between the Mitannian kings and the Egyptian pharaohs of the Eighteenth Dynasty, which provide an intimate glimpse of the ancient Near East in politically turbulent times.

—*Carlis C. White*

FURTHER READING

Bryce, Trevor. *The Kingdom of the Hittites*. New York: Oxford University Press, 1998. An authoritative treatment of the history of the Hittites, which includes discussions of the many military contests waged between the Hittites and Mitannians.

Moran, William. *The Amarna Letters*. Baltimore, Md.: The Johns Hopkins University Press, 1992. An excellent collection of the correspondence (in translation) found in the archives of the heretic pharaoh, Akhenaton, at Amarna. Included among the correspondence are letters written between Tushratta and Akhenaton.

Roux, Georges. *Ancient Iraq*. 3d ed. New York: Penguin Books, 1992. A treatment of the full sweep of history in ancient Mesopotamia, which places the rise and fall of Mitanni in its fuller historical context.

SEE ALSO: c. 1570 B.C.E., New Kingdom Period Begins in Egypt; c. 1338 B.C.E., Failure of Akhenaton's Cultural Revival.

RELATED ARTICLES in *Great Lives from History: The Ancient World*: Akhenaton; Amenhotep III; Thutmose III.

c. 1600-c. 1000 B.C.E.
CITY OF MYCENAE FLOURISHES

Mycenae was one of the most important cultural and political centers during the Heroic Age in Greece. Mycenaean civilization is the term used for the era of Greek civilization immortalized in the myths and legends of the Trojan War; to classical Greeks, it was the formative era of their history and cultural identity.

LOCALE: Mycenae, Greece
CATEGORY: Prehistory and ancient cultures

KEY FIGURES

Perseus (fl. twenty-first century B.C.E.), legendary founder of the city of Mycenae and mythological founder of Mycenae

Aeschylus (525/524-456/455 B.C.E.), Greek dramatist who dramatized the legends of the House of Atreus of Mycenae in the trilogy of plays called the *Oresteia*

Agamemnon (fl. thirteenth-twelfth century B.C.E.), powerful legendary Mycenaean king believed to have led the Greeks against the Trojans in the Trojan War, r. c. thirteenth-twelfth centuries B.C.E.

SUMMARY OF EVENT

In his epics the *Iliad* (c. 750 B.C.E.; English translation, 1611) and *Odyssey* (c. 725 B.C.E.; English translation, 1614), Homer recounted that Mycenae was a city rich in gold. As a general rule, the claims of myth are found to be exaggerated compared with real life, but when excavations of the city began in 1876, it became clear that this city did contain more gold than any other Greek site. The excavations further corroborated Homer's assertions that Mycenae was a powerful city as well as a focal point of the dominant civilization in Greece from 1600 to 1100 B.C.E.

The city itself was located in the northeastern corner of the plain of Argos between two mountains, Mount Prophet Elias to the north and Zara to the south. According to legend, it was founded by the hero Perseus in the twenty-first century B.C.E. Perseus was said to be the son of Zeus and Danaë and was the legendary slayer of the Gorgon, Medusa. When his great-grandson Atreus, son of Pelops, was elected to rule, his brother Thyestes was consumed by jealousy and entered into a love affair with Atreus's wife. In revenge, Atreus killed Thyestes' children and served them as a banquet for their father. After Thyestes had eaten the meal and then learned of its contents, he cursed Atreus, his children, and his children's children. Indeed, according to the *Oresteia* (458 B.C.E.; English translation, 1777) by the playwright Aeschylus, the curse was borne out. When Agamemnon, the son of Atreus, returned from the Trojan War, his wife, Clytemnestra, murdered him in revenge for his sacrifice of their daughter Iphigenia in order to sail for Troy. Eight years later, their son Orestes avenged his father's murder by killing Clytemnestra and her lover Aegisthus. According to Aeschylus, Orestes was then pursued by the Furies, avenging his matricide. Finally, at a trial in Athens, Athena declared that Orestes was not blameworthy for his deeds because the father was the true parent of the child, while the mother's womb was merely the container of the growing fetus. Orestes returned to Mycenae, which was already in decline.

The site of Mycenae was first occupied in the Neolithic period, but the civilization known as Mycenaean belongs to the Late Bronze Age. The first palace complex on the site was probably built c. 1600-c. 1550 B.C.E., at the beginning of the Late Helladic period, with the peak of building occurring during the Late Helladic IIIA period. Mycenaean civilization per se came to an end at the

The Lion Gate at the citadel of Mycenae. (Hulton|Archive)

end of the Late Helladic IIIB period, although the site remained inhabited through Late Helladic IIIC.

Among the oldest of the monuments on the site are the Cyclopean walls that surround the citadel of Mycenae. It was long alleged that Perseus built these walls with the help of the Cyclops, one-eyed giants mentioned in Homer, because the raising of such monumental walls—22 feet (6.7 meters) thick—seemed beyond the power of any human being to build. In actuality, these walls were probably constructed around 1340 C.E. by humans who used ramps to push and pull the blocks of stone into place.

The entrance to the citadel, the Lion Gate, is one of the oldest pieces of monumental sculpture in the Western world. It is noteworthy for its corbel vaulting with sculpted lions. The corbel vaulting consists of blocks of stone carefully placed so that each projects a little beyond the one below it. This creates an empty triangular space over the lintel, which relieves the lintel of the weight of the heavy walls above it. Sculpted figures of two lions (now headless) were placed inside the triangular space with their front paws on an altar, guarding the citadel. Interpretations vary as to the meaning of the Lion Gate. Some say that the lions were a secular emblem of Mycenae, the royal coat of arms; others believe that the lions were a religious symbol. The gate was built around 1250 B.C.E. and attributed to the reign of Atreus.

Inside the Lion Gate, Grave Circle A, a royal cemetery, lies to the right. This cemetery was excavated by Heinrich Schliemann in 1876. Schliemann discovered five shaft graves; another was discovered later. The six graves contained nineteen skeletons—eight men, nine women, and two children—presumably all of royal lineage. In addition to the skeletons, bronze swords and daggers, gold and silver cups, five masks of gold, discs of gold leaf, rhytons of gold and silver, and rings and necklaces were found. Among these artifacts was the so-called mask of Agamemnon. In fact, however, these graves were pre-Mycenean—the sixteenth century B.C.E.

On the east side of Grave Circle A is a great ramp leading up to the palace on the summit. The most important room in the palace was the *megaron*, a long, narrow roofed structure. One entered the *domos*, or main room of the *megaron*, through a vestibule or *prodomos*. The *prodomos* and the *domos* contained fragments of frescoes that were later preserved in the National Archaeological Museum of Athens. The *domos* contained the throne of the king. It was in this room that banquets were held. Additional features of the palace were the grand stairway, domestic and guest quarters, the artist quarters, and the House of Columns, storage rooms for the possessions of the royal family.

In the lower parts of the citadel, houses for the lesser royalty, state dignitaries, and warriors defending the citadel were discovered. Just outside the citadel lived the citizens of Mycenae, their dwellings surrounded by the graves of their ancestors, structures known as chamber tombs. These consisted of a passage known as the *dromos*, open to the sky, and a chamber hollowed out inside a hill.

Graves of royalty were more elaborate than the chamber tombs and were known as *tholos*, or beehive tombs. These were underground and reached by a *dromos*. Nine *tholos* tombs have been discovered at Mycenae to date. Among the best preserved of these tombs is the so-called Treasury of Atreus. It is believed that this tomb was built at the same time as the Lion Gate. The proportions of the tomb are monumental: The width of the *dromos* leading up to the entrance is 19.5 feet (6 meters), and its length is 118 feet (36 meters). Above the lintel in the doorway is the characteristic corbel roof. The ease with which the large stones were fitted into the round structure of the underground tomb make it one of the most impressive architectural achievements of the Mycenaean Age. Grave robbers had emptied all of the known tombs of their contents by the time they were excavated.

Most of modern knowledge of the Mycenaean world comes from artifacts such as frescoes, pottery fragments, metalwork, and jewelry. In 1939, the excavation of another Mycenaean site, Pylos, produced tablets which contained a form of writing known as Linear B. Only seventy of these tablets were discovered at Mycenae; Linear B tablets were also found on Crete associated with the last stages of Minoan civilization. In the early 1950's, linguist Michael Ventris was able to decipher the script. He discovered that the writing dated from just after 1400 B.C.E. and was an archaic form of Greek. The tablets consisted mostly of inventories of stores, livestock, and agricultural products, and catalogs of the citizenry and their occupations. However limited in scope, the tablets have broadened modern understanding of Mycenaean civilization.

Pottery shards remain the chief index of the civilization's extent. At its peak, the Mycenaean trading relations extended west to Italy and Great Britain and north to central Europe. In the east, by the end of the fifteenth century, the Mycenaeans dominated Crete. The culture appears to have been much more aggressive than the previous Minoan culture, with the king, or *wanax*, functioning more as a warlord than a legislator. The epic of the

Trojan War is a heroic representation of the type of raiding and conquest characteristic of Mycenaean culture. Their extensive trade relations created an influx of wealth into the cities—hence the great quantity of gold found at Mycenae—but this remained concentrated in the hands of the ruling class, while the lower classes lived in relative poverty. The later Greeks attributed the collapse of Mycenaean civilization to the invasion of the Dorians, but it may also be that the inequity of Mycenaean class relations led to a fatal imbalance in its social structure.

SIGNIFICANCE

The stories associated with Mycenaean civilization are the basis of a large portion of classical Greek religion and mythology, which is itself central to the art, literature, and drama of Western civilization. The Mycenaean age also saw the beginnings of Greek writing and monumental architecture. It was an era of extensive trade with other Mediterranean civilizations, and it was also a time of increased warfare, indicated by the extensive fortifications of Mycenaean sites. Although the historicity of Mycenaean figures such as Agamemnon, Atreus, Pelops, and Perseus is unknown, Heinrich Schliemann made archaeological history by excavating following the descriptions given by Homer in the *Iliad* and *Odyssey* and unearthed the remains of both Troy and Myceneae. Allowing for poetic license and the passage of time, Homer's descriptions of Mycenaean Age culture and lifestyles appear to have been relatively accurate.

Following the Mycenaean Age, Greece fell into a Dark Age, which is evident in the relative dearth of remains at Mycenae in the Late Helladic IIIC period. When Greece emerged from this Dark Age, it was to bring forth the achievements of the Classical era, but Greeks still looked back to the glories of the Mycenaeans as the foundation of their cultural heritage.

—Jennifer Eastman

FURTHER READING

Aeschylus. *Oresteia*. Translated by Christopher Collard. New York: Oxford University Press, 2002. The legend of the sons of Atreus as reformulated in three plays by a classical Greek dramatist. This edition contains an extensive introduction.

Feuer, Bryan, and John M. Weeks, eds. *Mycenaean Civilization: A Research Guide*. New York: Garland, 1996. An annotated bibliography of over 1100 works dealing with Mycenaean civilization, organized by topic: cultural history and society, material culture, intellectual life, current trends in research, and regional and site reports.

Fitton, J. Lesley. *The Discovery of the Greek Bronze Age*. Cambridge, Mass.: Harvard University Press, 1996. An excellent, up-to-date, and well-illustrated overview of Mycenaean Greece, not only presenting what can be gleaned from archaeological remains, but also relating the story of its discovery and excavation.

Robinson, Andrew. *The Man Who Deciphered Linear B: The Story of Michael Ventris*. New York: Thames and Hudson, 2002. A biography of the linguist whose decipherment of the Mycenaean script led to an expanded understanding of the Greek Bronze Age.

Schliemann, Heinrich. *Mycenae: A Narrative of Researches and Discoveries at Mycenae and Tiryns*. Reprint. Salem, N.H.: Ayer, 1989. First published in 1880, this work provides a firsthand account of Schliemann's excavations and his attempt to fit his findings within the Homeric tradition.

Taylour, Lord William. *The Mycenaeans*. Rev. ed. New York: Thames and Hudson, 1990. A detailed, scholarly account of Mycenaean civilization, written by an archaeologist who himself excavated at Mycenae.

Wood, Michael. *In Search of the Trojan War*. Berkeley: University of California Press, 1998. A companion volume to the Public Broadcasting Service series, this book by a popular classicist presents the archaeological background to Homer's epics, showing the interrelationship of myth and history. Illustrated.

SEE ALSO: c. 1600-c. 1500 B.C.E., Flowering of Minoan Civilization; c. 1000 B.C.E., Greek Alphabet Is Developed; c. 750 B.C.E., Homer Composes the *Iliad*; c. 456/455 B.C.E., Greek Tragedian Aeschylus Dies.

RELATED ARTICLES in *Great Lives from History: The Ancient World*: Aeschylus; Homer.

c. 1570 B.C.E.
NEW KINGDOM PERIOD BEGINS IN EGYPT

Ahmose's military victory reunified Egypt and established the foundation for Egyptian domestic, religious, and cultural achievement throughout the New Kingdom and Near East.

LOCALE: Avaris (now Tell el-Babʿa in the northeastern Nile Delta)

CATEGORIES: Expansion and land acquisition; wars, uprisings, and civil unrest

KEY FIGURES

Apophis (Aa-woserre; fl. seventeenth century B.C.E.), king of the Fifteenth Dynasty, r. 1605-1565 B.C.E.

Kamose (fl. sixteenth century B.C.E.), brother of Ahmose I and last king of the Seventeenth Dynasty, r. 1575-1570 B.C.E.

Ahhotep (c. 1590-c. 1530 B.C.E.), queen, mother of Ahmose I

Ahmose I (fl. sixteenth century B.C.E.), first king of the New Kingdom Eighteenth Dynasty, r. 1570-1546 B.C.E.

Thutmose III (late sixteenth century-1450 B.C.E.), fifth king of the Eighteenth Dynasty, r. 1504-1450 B.C.E.

Ramses II (c. 1300-1213 B.C.E.), third king of the Nineteenth Dynasty, r. 1279-1213 B.C.E.

Ahmose, son of Ebana (fl. sixteenth century B.C.E.), military officer

Ahmose-Pennekheb (fl. sixteenth century B.C.E.), soldier, c. 1550-c. 1525 B.C.E.

SUMMARY OF EVENT

The ancient Egyptian Turin King List identifies an end to Hyksos rule in Egypt by the Seventeenth Dynasty (1580-1570 B.C.E.). Under the leadership of Ahmose I, the expulsion of the Hyksos kings reestablished Thebes as the capital of Egypt and Egyptian dynastic rule throughout a reunified Egypt. Ahmose's reign formed the basis for Theban dynastic dominance and the foundation for the New Kingdom dynasties (Eighteenth through Twentieth, c. 1570-c. 1069 B.C.E.). The Egyptian need, under Ahmose I, to secure and to defend the borders of Egypt led to expansion into the Near East and linked Egypt to the economic prosperity of the New Kingdom empire.

Hyksos is the ancient Greek equivalent for an Egyptian word that translates as "rulers of the foreign countries." Egyptians identify the Hyksos as a group of foreign rulers in Egypt on the Turin King List who occupied Egypt during the Fifteenth Dynasty (c. 1650-1540 B.C.E.).

During the first century C.E., the Roman historian Flavius Josephus erroneously identified the Hyksos with the Shepherd Kings of the Thirteenth and Fourteenth Dynasties (c. 1782-after 1650 B.C.E.). Today, scholars use the term "Hyksos" to identify the kings listed in the Fifteenth and Sixteenth Dynasties of the Turin King List.

There is no clear division between the dynastic rule of the Fifteenth and the Sixteenth Dynasties. Recent scholarship has shown that many of the Sixteenth Dynasty kings ruled simultaneously and based their claim to rule on lineage established during the Fifteenth Dynasty. Interpretations vary, but in general the Sixteenth Dynasty is perceived as a loosely allied group of minor kings whose rule was limited geographically and politically. The Seventeenth Dynasty rulers came from Thebes and were of Egyptian descent. Although evidence provides for earlier battles and thrusts into Hyksos strongholds by the Egyptians, none succeeded to eliminate the Hyksos rule in Egypt until Ahmose's victory at Avaris (Tell el-Babʿa).

After nearly 108 years of control under the Hyksos occupation, Ahmose I reestablished control over both Upper and Lower Egypt through a series of military campaigns that pushed the Hyksos back into southern and coastal Palestine. Ahmose's victory sparked a rebirth of Egyptian domination in Egypt and laid the foundations for future Egyptian military expansion and final annexation of the Near East by Thutmose III. It was not until the treaty of Ramses II with the Hittites that Egyptian control ended in the Near East.

Egypt's attempts to expel the Hyksos can be divided into three distinct efforts. The first clash with the Hyksos was made by Sekenenre (r. c. 1600-1571 B.C.E.), founder of the Seventeenth Dynasty and father of Ahmose. According to the Ramesside Papyrus Sallier I, Egypt is described as a divided land with Sekenenre ruling from Thebes in the south and the Hyksos king, Apophis, from his capital at Avaris in the north. The papyrus does not preserve the results of the battle between Apophis and Sekenenre, but the mummy of Sekenenre is preserved and shows numerous head wounds. Sekenenre's wounds were made by a Syrian-Palestinian type of battle ax and the body was buried only after being left and exposed on the battlefield.

After Sekenenre's death, the offensive against the Hyksos was undertaken by Kamose. His military campaigns against the Hyksos are recorded on the Carnarvon Tablet I and on two Karnak stelae that relate that the begin-

NEW KINGDOM PERIOD, C. 1570-C. 1069 B.C.E.

EIGHTEENTH DYNASTY, C. 1570-1295

Ruler	*Reign*
Ahmose I	1570-1546
Amenhotep I	1546-1524
Thutmose I	1524-1518
Thutmose II	1518-1504
Thutmose III	1504-1450
Hatshepsut	c. 1503-1482
Amenhotep II	1450-1419
Thutmose IV	1419-1386
Amenhotep III	1386-1349
Akhenaton	1360-1334
Smenkhare	1336-1334
Tutankhamen	1334-1325
Ay	1325-1321
Horemheb	1321-1295

NINETEENTH DYNASTY, 1295-1186

Ruler	*Reign*
Ramses I	1295-1294
Seti I	1294-1279
Ramses II	1279-1213
Merenptah	c. 1213-1203
Amenmessu	1203-1200?
Seti II	1200-1194
Saptah	1194-1188
Queen Tausret	1188-1186

TWENTIETH DYNASTY, 1186-1069

Ruler	*Reign*
Sethnakht	1186-1184
Ramses III	1184-1153
Ramses IV	1153-1147
Ramses V	1147-1143
Ramses VI	1143-1136
Ramses VII	1136-1129
Ramses VIII	1129-1126
Ramses IX	1126-1108
Ramses X	1108-1099
Ramses XI	1099-1069

Note: Dynastic research is ongoing; data are approximate.

ning of Kamose's rule was peaceful until the third year of his reign, when he entered into battle. In his first battle, Kamose defeated the vassal Teti, son of Pepi, at Nefrusi (near Beni Hasan). In Kamose's second battle, he tried to secure the Egyptian south and fought against the kingdom of Kush, which held Nubia as far south as the First Cataract, and then he advanced to Buhen. The third encounter by Kamose was in response to Apophis's attempt to reclaim Kush. Kamose returned to fight in the north when Apophis attempted to reestablish strategic control in the south. Apophis attempted to draw Kamose back to the south, but his message never reached Kamose. Instead of returning south, Kamose remained in the north to secure the Faiyum district. Written accounts about Kamose in the north suggest that Kamose attacked the Hyksos fleet in the northern Delta, but there is no evidence that Kamose reached Avaris.

The third phase of the Hyksos wars was taken up by Ahmose I, son of Sekenenre, who succeeded to the Egyptian throne on the death of Kamose, his uncle. Ahmose's mother, Queen Ahhotep, became regent for the young king and is thought by scholars to have had strong ancestral connections in the north, which may have laid the foundations for future military assistance for her son.

Accounts of Ahmose's campaigns against the Hyksos are recorded in autobiographical inscriptions in the tombs of two soldiers who served Ahmose: Ahmose, son of Ebana, and Ahmose-Pennekheb. Both served with Ahmose I in northern Egypt and both followed him into Palestine. Only Ahmose, son of Ebana, served in the south against the Nubians.

Written entries on the reverse of the Rhind Papyrus record Ahmose's victories in Memphis and at the fortress of Sile (Tjel). The battle sequence suggests that Ahmose was a shrewd military strategist. By passing Avaris along the river and taking Memphis and Sile, he effectively cut the Hyksos off from Palestine. The inscription of Ahmose, son of Ebana, indicates that a series of battles, possibly to stabilize the region, took place before Ahmose assaulted Avaris. Manetho, the third century B.C.E. Greco-Roman historian, relates that a long siege of Avaris occurred and that defeat of the Hyksos at Avaris was the result of a treaty, not military force, permitting the inhabitants of Avaris to abandon the city. Both possibilities may be true. The location of the destruction is within the main Hyksos citadel, not throughout the city. The citizens of Avaris could have left peacefully although the Hyksos citadel was destroyed.

Despite the capture of Avaris, Egypt remained vulnerable to incursions and attacks from the northeast Delta. The region of southern Palestine was a valuable economic base for the Hyksos. Ahmose's attack on Sharuhen in southern Palestine recounted by Ahmose, son of Ebana, was a logical military strategy. It stabilized the region for Egypt and made attacks against other Palestinian towns easier. In this way, Ahmose eliminated the Hyksos trading routes along the Pelusaic Branch of the Nile, strategic areas at Tell el-Yahudiyya, and pasture sites at the Wadi Tumilat. The economic benefits of control for Egypt were tremendous.

SIGNIFICANCE

The inland Palestinian cities and northern Syrian sites taken by Thutmose III during the Eighteenth Dynasty reveal the economic importance of Ahmose's earlier inroads. They paved the way for Thutmose III to place the politically powerful kingdom of the Mitanni under the military rule of Egypt.

The economic impact of the Hyksos in Egypt was immense. During Hyksos occupation, Egypt fared badly economically, as it became more and more isolated from the Near East, commercial goods, and natural resources. Once the Hyksos were driven from Egypt under Ahmose I, Egypt was the beneficiary of the Hyksos trade routes, Egypt was again politically united as a nation, and it became a force in the Near East.

The reconquest of Lower Egypt by Ahmose I and the subsequent reunification of Egypt inaugurated an era of unprecedented development for Egypt in the arts, architecture, and trade; expansion through military dominance in the Near East; and the supremacy of the god Amen in Egyptian religion. The Hyksos provided the Egyptians with the means to achieve military power through their introduction of the composite bow, the chariot, and the horse to Egypt.

—*Elizabeth L. Meyers*

FURTHER READING

Baker, Rosalie F., and Charles F, Baker. *Ancient Egyptians: People of the Pyramids*. New York: Oxford University Press, 2001. An overview of Egyptian history and culture, with a section on Ahmose.

Bietak, M. "Egypt and Canaan during the Middle Bronze Age." *Bulletin of the American Schools of Oriental Research* 282 (1991): 28-72. Significant investigation and information for the Middle Bronze Age.

Goedicke, Hans. *Studies About Kamose and Ahmose*. Baltimore, Md.: Halgo, 1995. A collection of essays by a prominent Egyptologist.

Oren, E. D., ed. *The Hyksos: New Historical and Archeological Perspectives*. Philadelphia: University of Pennsylvania Museum, 1997. Excellent summaries of archaeological data, analyses, and theory.

Redford, D. *Egypt, Canaan, and Israel*. Princeton, N.J.: Princeton University Press, 1992. Good overview of the period.

SEE ALSO: c. 1650 B.C.E., Hyksos Create Second Intermediate Period; c. 1600-c. 1300 B.C.E., Mitanni Kingdom Flourishes in Upper Mesopotamia; From c. 1500 B.C.E., Dissemination of the Book of the Dead; c. 1338 B.C.E., Failure of Akhenaton's Cultural Revival.

c. 1530 B.C.E.
MIXTEC CIVILIZATION DEVELOPS IN WESTERN OAXACA

The Mixtecs achieved high artistic development and spread their influence throughout southwestern Mexico. By 700 c.e., they had become the dominant power in Oaxaca.

LOCALE: Mixteca Alta, Oaxaca, Mexico
CATEGORY: Prehistory and ancient cultures

SUMMARY OF EVENT

The earliest settlers of Oaxaca were nomadic hunters and gatherers who entered from the north around 9000 B.C.E. Between c. 9000 and c. 2000 B.C.E., agriculture developed. Before c. 1300 B.C.E., the cultivation of the land led to the development of permanent villages. In time the interaction of these villages resulted in a state with an elite who exercised political and religious power. The political and social stability of this society resulted in advances in writing, numbering, architecture, and artistic excellence. By the end of the seventh century C.E., the Mixtecs replaced the Zapotecs as the dominant power in Oaxaca and extended their influence to other areas of Mexico.

Oaxaca has unusual geographic features. Mountains rising to 9,850 feet (3,000 meters) dominate the area, but most of the land along the Pacific coast is at sea level. Temperatures vary from hot to cold and the land from arid to wet. Mixtec civilization developed in the western part of Oaxaca, an area referred to as Mixteca, where water can be a problem. Rains vary considerably from year to year. Subsurface water is scarce, and streams are dependent on short seasonal rains. There are no open plains or open valleys.

Mixteca is divided into three regions, known as Mixteca Alta in the central area, Mixteca Baja in the northwest, and Costa along the coast. The central area, Mixteca Alta, is a cool region of moist highland hills and valleys. Available mineral resources would have been salt, basalt, chert, gold, mica, and limestone. Animals used for meat, such as deer, turkey, quail, rabbit, and doves, were plentiful. There were a few other wild animals such as foxes, squirrels, and coyotes. Corn, beans, and squash were probably brought to Mixteca as cultivated plants between the middle and end of the Preceramic period. Chilis and gourds were also eventually domesticated. Maguey, avocados, *guajes* (native legumes), and hallucinogenic mushrooms grew wild.

The first inhabitants of Mixteca were the ancestors of the Mixtecs and Zapotecs, the Cloud People, but little is known of the Preceramic and Protoagricultural Village period (c. 6000-c. 1500 B.C.E.) These ancient peoples probably introduced agriculture, which had a profound effect on the cultural development of Mixteca.

The Early Formative period (c. 1500-c. 750 B.C.E.) saw the origin and development of village settlements. Village farmers occupied the Mixteca as early as 1500 B.C.E. Early life in the villages, which were located along streams near fertile bottomland, was simple and uncomplicated. There were no social distinctions.

Even as population increased in the Late Formative period (c.750-c. 200 B.C.E), there seemed to be no pressure on farmland. Villages remained small and separated from each other. Tanware and buffware, produced since the Ceramic period, continued to be made, but the form and style of decoration changed. Many pieces had distinctive decorated rims similar to pottery being made throughout Mesoamerica. Highly expressive figurines were modeled in the stylistic traditions of the Mesoamerican Formative period. Whiteware, blackware, and grayware appeared.

Changes taking place in Mixteca ceramics and figurines during the Formative period indicate that the pattern of village life was an internal development. Settlements were uniform in size, layout, and architectural features. Houses continued to be constructed of adobe blocks and boulders, but differentiations in size began to appear. Large or unusual structures and extensive, elaborate, or diversified complexes did not exist with one exception. At the confluence of the Yucuita and Yanhuitlan Rivers, an earthen platform 656 feet (200 meters) on each side and 33 feet (10 meters) high was constructed. The purpose of the platform is not known. There is no evidence of a sociopolitical hierarchy in the Formative period, but considerable organization was required to build such a structure.

Mixtec civilization ruins in Mitia, Oaxaca. (Corbis)

A precise date for the beginning of a complex pattern of settlement cannot be fixed. Even though small, medium, and large villages were still located on higher ground near fertile bottomlands that were close to hunting and collecting areas, by 200 B.C.E. a hierarchical settlement system had evolved, indicating a significant transformation in Mixtec culture. Settlement systems indicate the existence of a stratified society with a political authority capable of elaborate organization. An urban center served as the regional center or core city for the surrounding area was the system. The first and most elaborate of the urban centers in Mixeca was Yucuita, located in the Nochixtlan Valley. The core city of Yucuita contained a diversified residential area and a civil and ceremonial area. At Yucuita great attention was paid to elaborate and highly organized ceremonies and to major structures. There is abundant evidence of rituals including human sacrifice, cannibalism, and funerary or memorial cults practicing ritual treatment and internment of burned human skulls.

The city possessed great political importance and was the economic center of the region. It also served as the center for trade with other regions of Mixteca. Locally produced ceramic pieces are found in great numbers in the city and at smaller sites in the valley, and there is ample evidence of an extensive interregional trade. Trade goods found in abundance include gray incised ceramics from the Valley of Oaxaca, fish bone from the Pacific Ocean and shells from the Gulf of Mexico, spindle whorls from the lowland cotton-producing area, and obsidian from the Basin of Mexico. As the city developed, its social structure became more stratified and its political authority over the small settlements more centralized.

Other sites in Mixteca Alta underwent similar growth. Smaller and more isolated settlements were not as favorably located as Yucuita, but their settlement patterns, ceramic development, and general complexity and function were similar.

In the Late Classic period (300 to 1000 C.E.), Mixtec civilization experienced great population growth and development. Population growth put pressure on the agricultural resources of the area, and settlements had to be more carefully chosen. Land and mineral deposits of flint, limestone, potting clay, and chert were an important consideration. Hillsides were terraced to provide additional fields. Most settlements were located just below mountaintops or on high hills that could be easily defended. Strategic sites that controlled passes or important trade routes became locations for advanced settlements. The larger, more important centers were located on higher ground and had elaborate ceremonial structures, temples, platforms, plazas, and tombs. Residential areas included large elite structures as well as small houses.

Between 100 and 1520 C.E., the Mixtecs achieved the forms associated with Mixtec culture: pictographic manuscripts, brilliant polychrome pots, and excellent lapidary and metalwork. Military conquests and a network of kinship and marriages linked the small kingdoms surrounding the major cities to form an extensive and workable political system. This was the period of greatest population concentration and most numerous settlements. Religion remained an important part of Mixtec life. Ritual activity continued, but the ceremonial structures built in this period were less impressive and fewer in number. Ritual centers, situated on mountaintops, in caves, or along streams, replaced ritual centers in urban areas.

The influence of other regions is evident. Architecture, murals, and ceramics of the period clearly show an association with Monte Albán, the largest of the Zapotec centers. Although across the mountains from Mixteca, it is possible that Monte Albán, the largest and most powerful site in Oaxaca, may have extended its political control to Mixteca. By 700 C.E., however, the Mixtecs had conquered Monte Albán. Toward the end of the Late Classic period, the influence of Teotihuacán, northeast of present-day Mexico City, became more evident in the Mixteca. Orangeware, slab-footed cylindrical vessels, and figurines with movable arms characteristic of Teotihuacán are numerous in this period. In the Postclassic period, after 1000 C.E., Mixtec culture was influential in the Valley of Oaxaca, Puebla, and the Valley of Mexico. This is the best-known period of Mixtec culture.

SIGNIFICANCE

Mixtec culture became one of the dominant pre-Aztec cultures of Mesoamerica, achieving a high degree of mastery in the arts. Although originally influenced by the neighboring Zapotecs, the Mixtecs eventually dominated their former rivals. In addition, the Mixtecs developed a hieroglyphic writing system that may have influenced the later Aztec system. Much historical, genealogical, religious, and ritual information was preserved in the Mixtec codices dating from the early second millennium C.E.

—*Robert D. Talbott*

FURTHER READING

Blanton, Richard D., et al. *Ancient Oaxaca: The Monte Albán State*. New York: Cambridge University Press, 1999. Includes an introduction to the area and to the beginnings of settlement in Oaxaca.

Flannery, Kent V., and Joyce Marcus, eds. *The Cloud People: Divergent Evolution of the Zapotec and Mixtec Civilizations*. New York: Academic Press, 1983. A collection of articles by eminent archaeologists on the beginnings and development of settlements in Oaxaca.

Paddock, John, ed. *Ancient Oaxaca: Discoveries in Mexican Archeology and History*. Stanford, Calif.: Stanford University Press, 1966. Devotes major attention to dating and development of various aspects of cultural development.

Spores, Ronald. *The Mixtecs in Ancient and Colonial*

Times. Norman: University of Oklahoma Press, 1984. Describes the rise and development of Mixtec civilization through the Colonial period.

SEE ALSO: c. 1500-c. 300 B.C.E., Olmec Civilization Rises in Southern Mexico; c. 500 B.C.E.-c. 700 C.E., Zapotecs Build Monte Albán; c. 300 B.C.E., Izapan Civilization Dominates Mesoamerica; c. 100 B.C.E.-c. 200 C.E., Zapotec State Dominates Oaxaca; c. 1 C.E., Development Begins at Teotihuacán; 90 C.E., Founding of the Classic Period Maya Royal Dynasty at Tikal; c. 100-200 C.E., Construction of the Pyramids of the Sun and Moon at Teotihuacán; 200-900 C.E., Maya Civilization Flourishes.

From c. 1500 B.C.E.
DISSEMINATION OF THE BOOK OF THE DEAD

The Egyptian Book of the Dead offered guidance for the soul in its postmortem judgment and journey to the afterlife.

LOCALE: Egypt
CATEGORY: Religion

SUMMARY OF EVENT

The Egyptian Book of the Dead consists of lists of formulas and rubrics to be used by the soul in order to achieve a satisfactory state after separation from the body. The practice of reciting spells during funeral ceremonies to safeguard the existence and welfare of the deceased dates from an early period in Egyptian history, though most of the texts known to Egyptologists were produced after 1550 B.C.E.

Many spells known from early pyramid texts were adopted for use by the common people over the years, and similar ones were added. These texts were not only recited during funerals but were also considered useful if placed close to the deceased where they could be reached if there was a need. The texts were at one time inscribed on the walls of coffins; only later were they written on papyrus and buried with the dead. At this stage of usage, such texts received the name Book of the Dead, or the Book of Coming Forth by Day. Such books or chapters are not systematic treatises about Egyptian beliefs regarding life after death, but a random collection of magical practices. These spells claim to give to the dead protection against hunger and thirst, the ability to assume various animal forms, and especially the power to come forth by day, that is, to emerge at daylight from the tomb to partake of the funerary offerings.

Survival after death was a conviction firmly anchored in the minds of the Egyptians. They conceived of death as separation of the spiritual and corporal elements of human beings, yet believed that the spirit continued to live close to the corpse and was in some way dependent on it. The Egyptians' inability to abstract the survival of the immortal parts from the continued existence of the body shows how they were bound to ideas of concrete, material reality. Though they admitted both death and survival, they could not imagine existence without a physical basis. The body was seen as the concrete substratum of individuality; the cell or tomb of the body, therefore, was looked on as the eternal dwelling place of the soul. Life of the soul after death tended to be conceived of as gloomy, so that throughout Egyptian history there were efforts to provide a more pleasing substitute for this dismal existence.

At the beginning of the Fifth Dynasty (c. 2494-c.2345 B.C.E.), believers in solar doctrine began to work out a place for the dead in their theology. The most well-developed of these paradises was that of Osiris, or "the West." "The West" was reserved for Osiris's believers, who after death became his subjects for all eternity. At first, the paradise of Osiris was reserved for the pharaoh, but gradually it became accessible to more and more of the population. Entrance into paradise was a favor granted only on certain conditions. Among these was the ordeal of judgment.

One of the most popular religious texts of ancient Egypt was a section of the Book of the Dead known to scholars as Chapter 17. This text, which seems to have been written during the Nineteenth Dynasty, about 1200 B.C.E., opens with a monologue by the high god and expresses a concept quite distinct from the rest of the composition. It indicates a belief, or at least the tendency toward a belief, in one supreme god who first existed as "word" and who manifested or created himself by pronouncing the names of his own limbs.

Chapter 30 of the Book of the Dead provides an example of the attempt to use magical incantations to fulfill the ethical requirements of sinlessness in the judgment. This chapter is addressed to the heart, which Egyptians held to be the most important agent whose favor had to be sought. Although magic had no official place in Egyptian worship of the gods as conducted in the temples, it was the basis of all funeral rites and worship of the dead. It was considered a science whereby, through recited formulas and amulets, protection was obtained against all evil spirits and from all kinds of danger. These formulas and amulets were widely used in all classes of society.

Chapter 125 in the Book of the Dead is probably the best known and is sometimes taken as representative of the whole. In its detailed description of the process of judgment, it exemplifies both the highest ethical component and the most magical features of ancient Egyptian religion. The oldest copy of Chapter 125 dates from about 1550 B.C.E. An accompanying illustration shows the god Osiris seated at one end of a hall and at the other end a dead man who has been brought in by Anubis, the soul leader. In the center of the hall is a set of scales with the heart of the dead man on one side and the symbol of Maat, the goddess of justice, on the other. Anubis supervises the weighing and records the results. The text of the judgment consists of a greeting to the god and then successive declarations of innocence made by the dead man. The declarations are known as the "negative confessions." In these, the man declares he has not committed a whole series of faults that the Egyptian value system saw as immoral.

The negative confessions themselves reflect high moral concepts: The dead man declares that he has not oppressed the members of his family and that he has not been domineering with his servants or filched the property of the lowly man. He further states that he has not inflicted pain, that he has not permitted any man to suffer hunger, that he has neither murdered nor given an order to cause murder, and that he has been just in commercial transactions.

In this scene from Chapter 185 of the Book of the Dead, Ani and his wife (left) stand next to offerings, while the four riders of heaven and the four triads of gods appear on the left. (Hulton|Archive)

Apparently, during most of the millennium or more the "negative confession" formula was in use, its very recital magically won paradise. One did not state the truth; rather one created it. This magic-superstitious approach was offset in Egyptian culture by a more rational ethic, as exemplified in the wisdom literature, which was also popular and flourished throughout Egyptian civilization.

SIGNIFICANCE

Although the Book of the Dead is about the afterlife, it reveals much about the Egyptian view of life, morals, and behavior. The Egyptians viewed the universe as essentially static. This notion of the changeless world provides a useful key to enter the mind of the Egyptians who compiled and used the Book of the Dead. The Egyptians believed that human beings could find immortality and peace by becoming part of one of the cycles of nature. This is the unifying thread connecting so many different religious ideas, customs, and symbols. However, there is a paradox here: The Egyptians conceived of the world as static, yet they thought of immortality as participation in perpetual movement. However, even this movement was in some sense static because it was part of the changeless order of the world. The Egyptians saw the world as an equilibrium of opposites. Death appears to the modern Western mind as a singular event; to the Egyptian it was at most an interruption in life. This attitude is reflected in Egyptian art and writing regarding death, an attitude confident in the ability of the living to continue interpersonal relations with the dead.

However, although the Egyptians could not conceive of a life after death that did not depend on material goods, this led the Egyptians not to view life materialistically but rather to view food spiritually: The same word, *Ka*, denotes both humankind's impalpable, vital force, and its sustenance. This notion provides an understanding of such Egyptian practices as feast day celebrations, including a meal, at the tombs of the dead; and it clarifies much of the subject matter of the Book of the Dead. On one hand, the dead person was considered as having an animated existence. This is the meaning of the term *Ba*, which should not be translated as soul. *Ba* is not part of a living person, but the whole person as he or she appears after death. The Egyptian also regarded a dead person as *Akh* or transfigured spirit. As *Akh*, a dead person had an exalted form of existence, and was seen at night as a star in the sky. Thus, the dead were thought to be incorporated in the cosmic order and, therefore, eternal. For the Egyptian, the righteous person is in harmony with the divine order; therefore, all manifestations of concern with judgment are simply expressions of fear of the unknown.

—*Mary Evelyn Jegen*

FURTHER READING

Assmann, Jan. *The Mind of Egypt*. Translated by Andrew Jenkins. New York: Metropolitan Books, 2002. A rather dense discussion that nonetheless explains the ramifications of the Egyptian view of the cosmos—and thus history—as essentially static.

Faulkner, Raymond, trans. *The Egyptian Book of the Dead*. New York: Chronicle Books, 2000. A straightforward translation of the Book of the Dead by a well-known Egyptologist. There is little commentary, but the translation is placed beneath full-color facsimiles of the papyrus that represent the material in the scroll in its proper order and in its entirety.

Hornung, Erik. *The Ancient Egyptian Books of the Afterlife*. Translated by David Lorton. Ithaca, N.Y.: Cornell University Press, 1999. Discusses the Book of the Dead along with nineteen other texts concerning the afterlife. Places the book in a much broader cultural context than is generally offered. Includes a glossary, bibliography, and index.

Redford, Donald B., ed. *The Ancient Gods Speak: A Guide to Egyptian Religion*. New York: Oxford University Press, 2002. This volume extracts all the articles on Egyptian religion from the authoritative *Oxford Encyclopedia of Ancient Egypt* (2000). Includes nearly one hundred signed articles on all aspects of the subject, providing a handy reference to the subtleties and technicalities of the Egyptian belief in the afterlife.

SEE ALSO: c. 2575-c. 2566 B.C.E., Building of the Great Pyramid; c. 2000 B.C.E., Composition of the Gilgamesh Epic; c. 1338 B.C.E., Failure of Akhenaton's Cultural Revival.

1500-1100 B.C.E.
COMPILATION OF THE VEDAS

As the most revered scriptures of Hinduism and the oldest documentary monument of the Indo-Aryan people, the Vedas occupy an unrivaled place in India's religious and cultural history.

LOCALE: Indus Valley region in Northwestern India (now mostly in the eastern region of Pakistan)
CATEGORIES: Cultural and intellectual history; religion

SUMMARY OF EVENT

The Vedas are the oldest extant texts of the Indo-European language family and the most sacred scriptures of Hinduism. Etymologically, the word *veda* is derived from the Sanskrit root *vid*, meaning "to know" or "to understand," and it is related to other Indo-European words such as the German *wissen*, "to know"; Latine *videre*, " to see"; and English "vision." Compiled over several centuries by many families of authors, these books vary widely in content, length, and literary style. They consist of hymns to forces of nature personified as gods, incantations and magical formulas sung by priests during performances of sacrifices and other religious rituals, and philosophical reflections about the origin and nature of the world, the essence and attributes of the ultimate reality, the deities' relationship to human beings, and the fundamental ethical values that should guide human life on earth.

There are four Vedas: the *Rigveda* (also known as *Ṛgveda*, c. 1500-c. 1000 B.C.E.; English translation, 1896-1897), the *Yajurveda* (c. 1500-c. 1100 B.C.E.; *The Texts of the White Yajurveda*, 1899), the *Sāmaveda* (c. 1500-c. 1100 B.C.E.; *Sama Veda of the Jaiminiyas*, 1938), and the *Atharvaveda* (c. 1500-c. 1100 B.C.E.; *The Hymns of the Arthava-veda*, 1895-1896). Together they comprise the totality of the *sruti* (what is heard) literature, in contrast to the *smriti* (what is remembered) that constitutes some of the later writings of Hinduism. The Hindu scholars divide each Veda into four distinct sections: the Saṃhitās (hymns); the Brāhmanas (explanation and rules of rituals); the Āraṇyakas (forest treatises); and Upaniṣads (philosophical reflections on the meaning of the Vedas). Of these four parts, the Saṃhitās, or collections of hymns, forms the core and the most ancient texts of the Vedas.

By all accounts, the *Rigveda Saṃhitā* is the oldest of the four Vedas and the oldest extant religious book in continuous use by any people on earth. It is a book roughly equivalent in length to the Homeric epic of the *Iliad* (c. 750 B.C.E.; English translation, 1611) and *Odyssey* (c. 725 B.C.E.; English translation, 1614) and consists of 1,028 hymns that total about 10,600 stanzas. Its literary and poetic qualities are remarkably, though not consistently, high. The language of the Vedas is preclassical Sanskrit. The hymns are metrical in form, and each contains, on an average, ten stanzas. The hymns are mostly invocations to gods who inhabit the heavens (*dyaus*), space (*antariksa*), and the earth (*pritvi*). The chief celestial gods are Varuna, Mitra, Surya, Savitr, Pusan, the Asvins, Usas, and Ratri. Gods who make their abode in space are Indra, Rudra, Marut, Vayu, and Parjanya. Earthly gods include Prthivi, Agni, and Soma. Although the hymns are dedicated to these and a multitude of other gods, the *Rigveda* also has some concept of a dominant god called Prajapati, who created everything. Besides gods, the Vedas mention godly creatures such as *apsaras* and demons called *pisacas*. A few hymns deal with purely secular matters such as weddings and gambling.

The *Yajurveda*, which consists of two distinct parts called Krishna (black) and Shukla (white), is a collection of hymns and verses used by priests during religious ceremonies. The *Sāmaveda* repeats much of the *Rigveda* material by setting it to music, facilitating its singing during the performance of religious rituals, and the *Atharvaveda* contain magical formulas and medical treatises. The origin of Indian classical music has its foundation in the seven musical scales employed in the *Sāmaveda*.

The society that is reflected in the Vedas is that of a people occupied in agriculture and cattle raising and who were engaged in making war on the natives. Their family structure was fluid and allowed room both for monogamy and polygamy. Women were generally accorded a higher place than in other early societies and had the ability to choose their husbands. The Vedic people enjoyed chariot racing, gambling, and music for recreation. They believed that truth and righteousness would always triumph in the end, extolled these virtues as the highest ethical values, and searched for knowledge and immortality as the ultimate goals of human life.

Determining the date of the Vedas has always been difficult because of a lack of references in the texts to known historical events and clearly datable items as well as a dearth of archaeological data that can be used as corroborating evidence. Most Indologists are comfortable in assigning 1500 B.C.E. to the earliest parts of the Vedas. One methodology employed by scholars to fix the date of the Vedas is based on their thought patterns and an analysis of the works' linguistic forms. Using this methodology, Max Müller (1823-1900), one of the early European Indologists, estimated that the Vedas are more "ancient and primitive" in thought and expression than any other known texts, including the Babylonian and Akkadian cuneiform tablets. In his judgment, the Vedic concepts and writings are so ancient that they represent the "early growth" of human thinking, leading him to conclude that the Vedas were written no later than 1200 B.C.E. Müller's estimate has since become a point of reference for most Western Vedic scholars.

Some Indian scholars assign the *Rigveda*, the first of the four Vedas, a much older date. For instance, Bala Gangadhar Tilak dates the Vedic hymns to 6000 B.C.E. These Indian scholars claim such extreme antiquity for the Vedas on the basis of astronomical calculations, a claim that is difficult to prove unless one assumes the exactness of those calculations. In any case, because Buddhism began to spread in the fifth century B.C.E., in part as a reaction to the excessive Vedic ritualism and abstract philosophical speculations contained in the Brāhmanas and Upaniṣads, it is safe to assume that the core of the Vedic canon was fixed several centuries before the birth of Buddhism.

Hindu theologians dismiss the question of the origin of the Vedas as inappropriate because of their belief that as eternal (*sanatana*) and impersonal (*apaurusheya*) wisdom revealed to the *rshis*, the Vedas are outside the ken of human history. The difficulties in estimating the date of these books and determining their authorship are themselves theologically interpreted as proof for their ahistorical character. These theologians do not, of course, deny that the written texts originated at some point in history; what they mean to assert is that their content and message are not of human origin.

SIGNIFICANCE

Despite the successive invasions that India suffered at the hands of foreign powers such as the Persians, the Greeks, the Scythians, the Huns, the Arabs, the Persians, the Portuguese, the Dutch, the French and, finally, the British, India succeeded preserving its distinctive cultural identity largely because of its deep roots in the Vedic culture and practices. To the Indians, the Vedas are far more than a literary monument; they are the living foundations of the religious and cultural life of its predominantly Hindu population. The hymns of the *Rigveda* are still being sung, in their original Sanskrit, during religious ceremonies, weddings, funerals, dedications of temples, and other occasions. The Hindus accord no other piece of writing such an exalted position as the Vedas.

The Vedas, and Hindu scriptures in general, have assumed a new political and social significance in recent decades. Led by Hindu nationalists and aided by contemporary Indian political leaders, a potent Hindu revivalism (*Hindutva*) has swept the entire nation, bolstering India's identity and place in the world at a time of increasing globalization. The unparalleled antiquity of the Vedas and the wisdom they contain are touted as pointers to the country's cultural superiority over those who sought to dominate it in the past.

As the oldest written monument of the Indo-European languages, the Vedas also serve as valuable vehicles to understand the relationships among a large family of languages as they shed on the minds of the people who conquered and populated various parts of Asia, Persia, and Western Europe starting in the fifth millennium B.C.E.

—*Mathew J. Kanjirathinkal*

FURTHER READING

Bryant, Edwin. *The Quest for the Origins of Vedic Culture*. New York: Oxford University Press, 2001. Edwin presents an excellent historiographical study of the origin of the Indo-Aryans and carefully examines evidentiary data concerning the date of the Vedas.

Elizarenkova, Tatyana, and Wendy Doninger. *Language and Style of the Vedic Rsis*. Albany: State University of New York Press, 1995. The authors apply the method of semiotics to Vedic philology, providing interesting insights into the linguistic structure of the Vedas.

Lal, B. B., and S. P. Gupta, eds. *Frontiers of the Indus Civilization*. New Delhi: Books and Books, 1984. This edited volume critically reacts to the Western theories about the origins of India's Vedic civilization.

Müller, Max F. *A History of Ancient Sanskrit Literature*. 1859. Reprint. Varanasi, India: Chowkhamba Sanskrit Series Office, 1968. Though dated, Müller's work is still respected as that of a pioneer Indologist.

Patton, Laurie L. *Authority, Anxiety, and Canon: Essays in Vedic Interpretation*. Albany: State University of New York Press, 1994. Going beyond the opposing camps of European philologists and Indian ritualists, the author focuses on the substantive relevance of the Vedas for modern discourse.

Ragozin, Zenaide A. *The Story of Vedic India as Embodied Principally in the Rig Veda*. New York: G. P. Putnam's Sons, 1895. Ragozin's book is a good example of the nineteenth century Western view of ancient India, an interesting reading from a historiographical perspective.

SEE ALSO: c. 3500 B.C.E., Indus Valley Civilization Begins in South Asia; c. 1500-c. 1000 B.C.E., Aryans Appear in India; c. 1000-c. 200 B.C.E., Compilation of the Upaniṣads; c. 200 B.C.E., Birth of Hinduism; c. 200 B.C.E.-200 C.E., *Bhagavad Gita* Is Created; 5th or 6th century C.E., First Major Text on Hinduism's Great Goddess Is Compiled.

c. 1500-c. 1000 B.C.E.
ARYANS APPEAR IN INDIA

The Aryans initiated Vedic culture and introduced an Indo-European language into the Indian subcontinent.

LOCALE: Northern India along the Indus River valley and Ganges plains
CATEGORIES: Prehistory and ancient cultures; expansion and land acquisition

SUMMARY OF EVENT

The theory concerning the appearance of Aryans in Indian history begins with the assumption that there existed a warlike nomadic tribe outside India, probably on the steppes of Central Asia north of the Caspian Sea, who invaded parts of India, the Greek peninsula, Europe, and Iran between 1500 and 1000 B.C.E. Their tribal name is unknown, but in their original scriptures, the Vedas, they called themselves Aryans (the noble ones) as opposed to Dasas (the subservient ones). *Arya* is a Sanskrit word whose root *ar-* refers to such martial virtues as valor, strength, and bravery, or to the plowing and cultivation of the land. Philologists have observed that the Aryans' nature as fierce and warlike is reflected in the Vedic hymns devoted to warrior gods, verses that extol the glories of their weapons and the victories they won against their enemies.

Some scholars believe that the Aryans are not only the founders of India's Vedic culture but also the ancestors of the Celtic and Germanic peoples in northern Europe, the Greeks and Latins of southern Europe, the Persians (Iranians) in the Middle East, and the Hittites and the Kassites in eastern Mediterranean. In India, they established a culture whose most sacred texts are the Vedas; the religion that resulted from this culture is Hinduism, with its rigid caste system that organizes people into the four hierarchical groups of Brahmans (priests and scholars), Kṣatriyas (warriors and rulers), Vaiśyas (farmers and merchants), and Śūdras (peasants and laborers).

The Aryan invasion theory holds that the incursions of the Indo-Aryans into northwestern India occurred in successive waves, eventually conquering and subjugating the native populations of the region. The region in which the Aryans initially settled was the fertile region along the Indus (originally Sindhu) River, which originates in the Hindu Kush mountains in the north and flows into the Arabian Sea near present-day Karachi, Pakistan, after being fed by the five major rivers of the Punjab. The Aryans eventually spread to the east and south.

Three strands of arguments are advanced to support the claim of an Aryan invasion of India. The first hinges on the fact that before the origin of the Vedic civilization, the Harappān civilization of the cities of Mohenjo-Daro and Harappā existed in northern India. This advanced urban civilization may have had its origin as early as 3000 B.C.E. Beginning in the middle of the twentieth century, archaeologists found that the Harappāns had built several well-planned, walled cities with spacious streets and multistory structures that contained indoor plumbing and drainage systems for sanitation. Recent excavations have discovered more such cities along the Indus River and its tributaries. Probably because of floods caused by changes in the course of these rivers, the Harrapāan civilization was already in decline at the time of the settlement of the Aryans in approximately 1500 B.C.E. As reflected in the language of the Vedas, the Aryans fought the natives with superior weapons, including bows and arrows and horse-driven, wheeled chariots. A passage from the *Rigveda* (also known as *Ṛgveda*, c. 1500-1000 B.C.E.; English translation, 1896-1897) indicates that the bow was a weapon that the Aryans loved to use:

> With Bow let us win cattle; with Bow in battle let us win victories in our hot encounters.
>
> The Bow brings grief and sorrow to our foes: armed with Bow let us conquer all regions.

The second strand of argument rests on the physical differences between the Aryans and the Harappāns. It has been observed that the Aryans and their descendants were generally tall, long-nosed, and light-skinned in contrast to the Harappāns and their progeny, who were and are shorter, flat-nosed, and darker. Anthropologists note that today the descendants of Aryans dominate northern India, whereas the descendants of the Harappāns, who were supposedly expelled by the Aryans from their original northern homeland, live in southern India. Added to this, the race theory of the caste system holds that the Aryans invented the system to preserve their racial identity separate from those they had conquered.

The third and perhaps the strongest support for the Aryan invasion theory rests on philological grounds. The language of the Aryans is Sanskrit, which is believed to have developed from a proto-Indo-Aryan root common to all Indo-European languages such as Greek, Latin, German, and English. This shared linguistic root is presented as evidence for a common racial origin of the Indo-European population in the distant past. Philologists note that most North Indian languages of today are derivatives of Sanskrit, in contrast to the South Indian languages, which belong to the Dravidian family.

For livelihood, the Aryans raised cattle and carried out small-scale farming, slashing and burning the forests as they spread east and south. They organized themselves into tribal units called *jana* ruled over by a raja, or chief. Eventually, these tribal units spread far and wide; the *janas* claimed their separate territories, organizing themselves into tribal kingdoms called *janapada*.

SIGNIFICANCE

The Aryan invasion theory is a hotly contested subject among contemporary Indologists, who point out that those European scholars who understood language, race, and culture within the framework of a colonial ideology are the ones who created the Aryan/non-Aryan dichotomy. They reject the validity of arguments that racially distinguish Aryans from Harrappāns and reject as unfounded the theory of the destruction of the Harappān culture by an invading group of nomads. In their view, the Harappāns and the Aryans coexisted at the same time at different locales. They point to evidence uncovered through recent excavations at the Harappān sites, indicating the use of horses and spoked wheels by Harappāns. These archaeological findings, in their view, prove the fact that the Aryans did not import these superior weapons from a foreign land. Apparently, the use of horses in warfare was part of the entire range of known Indian history. They question the description of Aryans as nomads, referring to Vedic passages in which the Aryans are said to have built and lived in cities of their own.

Opponents of the Aryan invasion theory visualize the pre-Aryans and Aryans as forming a continuum of native peoples, who adapted to changing natural conditions by developing new types of settlement and cultural norms. Thus, in their view, the Aryan culture was from the very beginning indigenous and, perhaps, contemporaneous with other ancient cultures such as the Mesopotamian. This would also mean that the Vedas are much older than supposed by scholars such as Max Müller (1823-1900), who assigned to them a date not earlier than 1200 B.C.E.

Referring to the observed physical differences among the Aryans and Dravidians, they explain that there were numerous tribal groups in ancient India, which diverged over the course of centuries in language and culture. However, in their view, these differences do not amount to racial differences but rather are differences that can be easily explained in terms of the influence of environmental factors.

According to indigenous scholars, the practice of linking language and race is the context within which the Aryan invasion theory was developed in the eighteenth century, and this historical context must be understood as part of the British political strategy to make Indians feel inferior by emphasizing the decline of India from the wonder it once was. (The link between language and race is also being contested in other areas of Indo-European studies, especially Celtic studies, where the political agenda of English scholarship is also distrusted.) Interestingly, it was only after the conquest of Bengal and the consolidation of colonial power over India that the British became at all intellectually curious about the Indian culture. When the British philologist Sir William Jones (1746-1794) suggested in 1786 that because of Sanskrit's apparent commonality with other Indo-European languages, the original Indian culture was a high culture created by the Aryans who were also the ancestors of Europeans, he was actually legitimizing the prevalent view that the current Indian culture was in such a decline that the country needed the help of the British (European) rule to bring it back to its original glory. Indigenists also contend that the Aryan invasion hypothesis served to bind the British and the Hindu ruling elite closer together to serve colonial aims. The controversy over the Aryan invasion theory is very interesting from the viewpoint of historiography, and the controversy will not be resolved until more archaeological data are available.

—*Mathew J. Kanjirathinkal*

FURTHER READING

Bryant, Edward. *The Quest for the Origins of Vedic Culture.* New York: Oxford University Press, 2001. Bryant ably summarizes the controversy surrounding the Aryan invasion theory and relates this controversy to the modern nationalist discourse.

Erdosy, George, ed. *The Indo-Aryans of Ancient South Asia: Language, Material Culture, and Ethnicity.* New York: Walter De Gruyter, 1995. The contributors to this edited volume make a remarkable attempt to clarify many of the traditional misconceptions about the Indo-Aryans.

Herman, A. L. *An Introduction to Indian Thought.* Englewood Cliffs, N.J.: Prentice Hall, 1976. A good source for information on the linguistic relationship between Sanskrit and other Indo-European languages, as well as the underlying similarities in many Indo-European philosophies.

Mallory, J. P. *In Search of the Indo-Europeans: Language, Archaeology, and Myth.* New York: Thames and Hudson, 1989. Among the most accessible introductions to Indo-European linguistics and the theorized relationship between Indo-European language and culture.

Manian, Padma. "Harappāns and Aryans: Old and New Perspectives of Ancient Indian History." *The History Teacher* 32 (November, 1998): 17-32. By examining the content of selected world history texts, Manian demonstrates that history courses generally promote a Eurocentric bias when dealing with the history of Indo-Aryans.

Trautmann, Thomas R. *Aryans and British India.* Berkeley: University of California Press, 1997. The book discusses the complex and conflicting attitudes of the British toward the Indo-Aryans and their Vedic culture.

SEE ALSO: c. 3500 B.C.E., Indus Valley Civilization Begins in South Asia; 1500-1100 B.C.E., Compilation of the Vedas; c. 1000-c. 200 B.C.E., Compilation of the Upaniṣads.

c. 1500-c. 300 B.C.E.
OLMEC CIVILIZATION RISES IN SOUTHERN MEXICO

The Olmec were one of the earliest advanced civilizations on the North American continent, developing sophisticated architectural and artistic forms.

LOCALE: Southern Mexico
CATEGORY: Prehistory and ancient cultures

SUMMARY OF EVENT

Olmec civilization is considered to be one of the oldest civilizations of native North America. Recognition and identification of Olmec culture are based exclusively on archaeological evidence because no direct descendants of Olmec civilization have ever been identified. The Olmec heartland included the present Mexican states of Veracruz, Tabasco, and Chiapas, along the southern and western edge of the Gulf of Mexico, but Olmec influence extended across most of southern Mexico and northern Central America. The term "Olmec" is drawn from the Aztec language Nahuatl and loosely translates as "the rubber people," in reference to the production of rubber in the Olmec heartland.

Evidence of Olmec culture first appears about 1500 B.C.E. in the state of Tabasco. The area consists of flat, swampy coastal floodplains crossed by rivers draining from highland mountains to the south into the Gulf of Mexico to the north. Seasonal flooding and the lush tropical environment permitted the development of agriculture and the exploitation of domesticated plants, particularly corn, which led to the development of sedentary societies and advanced forms of social and political organization.

At sites such as San Lorenzo Tenochtitlán, the Olmec constructed large earthen platforms more than 3,000 feet (910 meters) long, 1,000 feet (300 meters) wide, and 150 feet (45 meters) high, on which were erected ritual and ceremonial structures of stone and more perishable materials such as wood or plaster. These platform complexes served several purposes, including providing residences for elite Olmec families and rulers, gathering places for public ceremonies, and burial sites for Olmec royalty. At the site of La Venta, the Olmec constructed conical pyramids in the center of their platform complexes, perhaps meant to imitate mountains or volcanoes not found in the immediate Olmec area. The earthen platforms consisted of layers of worked colored stone laid out in large plazas and covered with as many as a dozen sequential layers of sand and earth piled one on top of the other. The complexity suggests that the process of construction was as important as the final structure.

The Olmecs carved basalt boulders into a variety of shapes, including human heads. (PhotoDisc)

Platforms were engineered and constructed to control water flow throughout the structure. Elaborate drainage systems, composed of sections of carved stone, channeled water throughout the platforms, diverting it for waste runoff and public hygiene and creating decorative and sacred ponds and streams of fresh water within the platform complexes. The scale and complexity of the earthen platforms, along with the evidence of extensive farming and agriculture, suggest that several thousand people may have used or occupied the sites at one time. At least ten large-scale Olmec sites have been identified in the Olmec heartland. Advanced systems of political organization must have been in place to enable the assembly and management of the workforce necessary to construct such elaborate complexes. It is also significant that the Olmec created their buildings and monuments without the wheel, domesticated animals, or metal tools, none of which was used by any Mesoamerican peoples.

Most information regarding Olmec culture that does not come from their architecture is drawn from their remaining artworks. Although the Olmec probably created a wide variety of art forms, such as paintings and textiles, most of these forms have not survived in the archaeological record. What has survived in great abundance is Olmec stone sculpture, and the remaining carved stone images convey a great deal of information about Olmec beliefs. The Olmec were extremely adept at working very hard types of stone, particularly volcanic basalt and jade, neither of which occurs naturally near the Olmec heartland sites. Large basalt boulders, some more than 10 feet (3 meters) tall and weighing several tons, were transported as much as 60 miles (100 kilometers) from volcanic mountain ranges such as the Tuxtla mountains; sacred green jade was imported from areas of western Mexico or eastern Guatemala and Belize.

The basalt boulders were carved into a variety of shapes, usually human but occasionally representing animals or mythological deities, probably originally intended to be displayed in the open plazas of the earthen platforms. Many of the large carved boulders were intentionally defaced or broken and buried within the platforms during Olmec times, suggesting that either the Olmec or a foreign people symbolically killed the sculptures before abandoning the sites.

One of the most common types of boulder sculptures is a series of human heads carved in a lifelike, naturalistic style. Although the specific identity of the subjects is not clear, evidence suggests that the heads portray either former Olmec rulers or defeated enemies. Facial features vary noticeably from one head to the next, suggesting individualized depictions, and each wears a distinctively different type of skullcap or helmet. The caps may represent royal headdress or a type of headgear worn by participants in a ball game similar to modern-day soccer. The losers of this game, which was played on stone, I-shaped courts throughout ancient Mesoamerica, were ritually sacrificed, usually by decapitation. Portions of the ball game may have developed in the Olmec heartland, as that is the source of the rubber used for the ball itself. Regardless of the specific identity of the stone heads, the size and degree of naturalism attest to the Olmec sculptors' ability to manipulate large, hard stones for artistic purposes. Smaller stone objects, such as jewelry, ritual implements, and burial offerings were carved from other hard stones, including jade. The color green was probably considered sacred, and jade was much valued by all pre-Columbian societies. Humans and animals were common subjects, and implements such as ax heads were frequently formed in the shape of humans, suggesting a spiritual tie between the function of the object and its symbolic imagery.

Olmec art reveals much about Olmec political and religious beliefs. Olmec sites were probably governed by elite royal families and kings. Warriors and human prisoners are frequently depicted in Olmec sculpture, suggesting that the Olmec practiced formalized warfare and related forms of human sacrifice. They worshiped a pantheon of natural spirits, chief among which were powerful animals such as the cayman or alligator, the eagle, the shark, and, perhaps most important, the jaguar. The Olmec were similar to most Native American cultures in that the most important religious figures in Olmec society were the shamans, or curers, who were believed to be able to change into animal forms at will and communicate directly with the supernatural world. Olmec sculpture frequently depicts shamans in the act of such transformations.

Between 1000 and 300 B.C.E., Olmec influence stretched far beyond the Olmec heartland. Carved jade and ceramics in Olmec style have been found in central and far west Mexico, and Olmec-style rock carvings, paintings, and earthen platforms occur in areas south of Mexico City. Large Olmec-style carved boulders and upright stones occur along the southern Pacific coast of Guatemala and El Salvador during this period, and Olmec ceramics are found as far east as eastern Guatemala and Belize. The evidence suggests that the Olmec were interacting with a large number of non-Olmec cultures throughout the area at this time. After 500 B.C.E., early examples of hieroglyphic writing, similar to the later hieroglyphic writing of the Maya, appear in a few isolated examples of Olmec art, but these cases are rare, and Olmec civilization appears to have declined before the writing system was fully exploited.

After 300 B.C.E., Olmec culture disappears from the archaeological record. Several later Mesoamerican cultures, particularly the Maya of Guatemala and the Yucatán Peninsula, inherited and continued many aspects of Olmec style and culture, and the Maya, in fact, seem to have considered the Olmec as their divine ancestors.

Significance

The lack of literary material and of cultural descendants makes the Olmec an enigmatic people. However, their influence on the later Maya shows their seminal position in the evolution of Mesoamerican society. Their architecture and their art reveal much about their religious beliefs, which also appear to have influenced those of later cultures.

—*James D. Farmer*

Further Reading

Coe, Michael D. *America's First Civilization*. New York: American Heritage, 1968. One of the earliest comprehensive treatments of Olmec art and culture. Coe was the first scholar to interpret Olmec culture as the precursor to later, more widely known Mesoamerican cultures such as the Maya.

Coe, Michael D., and Richard A. Diehl. *In the Land of the Olmec*. Austin: University of Texas Press, 1980. Extensive report of archaeological investigations at the Olmec site of San Lorenzo Tenochtitlán between 1966 and 1968. Includes numerous detailed maps and line drawings and illustrations of stone monuments from the site.

Coe, Michael D., and Rex Koontz. *Mexico: From the Olmecs to the Aztecs*. 5th ed. New York: Thames and Hudson, 2002. Perceptively presents and interprets the complexities of ancient Mexican history, including the Olmec. Well illustrated.

Miller, Mary Ellen. *The Art of Mesoamerica: From Olmec to Aztec*. 3d ed. New York: Thames and Hudson, 2001. An abundantly illustrated introduction by a well-respected Mesoamerican scholar. One chapter is devoted to Olmec art.

Pina Chan, Roman. *The Olmec: Mother Culture of Mesoamerica*. Translated by Warren McManus. New York: Rizzoli International Publications, 1989. Well-illustrated volume of Olmec art. A thorough summary of Olmec art, archaeology, and culture by a noted Mexican and pre-Columbian scholar.

Sharer, Robert J., and David C. Grove, eds. *Regional Perspectives on the Olmec*. New York: Cambridge University Press, 1989. Discusses Olmec culture in the broader context of greater Mesoamerica. Scholarly treatment of Olmec cultural interaction with other pre-Columbian cultures.

Stuart, George S. "New Light on the Olmec." *National Geographic* 184, no. 5 (November, 1993): 88-115. Discusses revised and up-to-date interpretations of Olmec culture and art, including previously undocumented monuments and controversial translations of Olmec hieroglyphic writing. Includes artists' reproductions of Olmec lifeways.

See also: c. 9500-c. 9000 B.C.E., Clovis Culture Rises in New Mexico; c. 1900-c. 1400 B.C.E., Early Villages Form in Oaxaca; c. 500 B.C.E.-c. 700 C.E., Zapotecs Build Monte Albán; c. 100 B.C.E.-c. 200 C.E., Zapotec State Dominates Oaxaca; 90 C.E., Founding of the Classic Period Maya Royal Dynasty at Tikal; 200-900 C.E., Maya Civilization Flourishes.

c. 1500 B.C.E.-c. 500 C.E.

LAPITA CULTURE COLONIZES THE SOUTH PACIFIC

Inhabitants of Southeast Asia migrated by boat to the islands of the Bismark Archipelago, establishing a sophisticated agricultural society amid the hunter-gatherer peoples already established there.

LOCALE: Melanesia, Polynesia (Bismarck Archipelago)

CATEGORIES: Prehistory and ancient cultures, expansion and land acquisition

SUMMARY OF EVENT

During the time of the establishment of the Shang Dynasty in China (c. 1500 B.C.E.), the first wave of seafaring colonists left the island of Formosa (now Taiwan) to settle the islands of Southeast Asia. Although they probably bypassed the Philippines initially, they settled large islands such as Papua New Guinea and smaller islands to the southwest such as the Solomons and the Bismarck Achipelago. In many cases, the settlers, a light-skinned people of Mongoloid descent, inhabited the coastal regions of islands already inhabited by dark-skinned Negroid peoples, ancestors of modern Melanesian peoples. These original inhabitants had populated these islands for as long as 30,000 years—most likely arriving on foot during ice-age periods that left land-bridge routes from Southeast Asia into what is modern Indonesia and Australia. However, they developed neither seafaring navigation nor the advanced material culture of the light-skinned newcomers.

The so-called Lapita people are named for the archaeological site in the island of New Caledonia in the Bismarck Archipelago, where their distinctive pottery was first identified. The pottery, the earliest of which dates to 1500 B.C.E., is unlike anything previously produced in prehistoric Melanesia or Australia. A comblike device was used to incise elaborate wavelike designs on the wet clay—possible forerunners of the tattoo designs used by Polynesians. Some pots featured anthropomorphic and zoomorphic imagery that may indicate a ritual function. In addition to the pottery, the Lapita exhibited a sophisticated cultural complex that included animal husbandry (raising pigs, dogs, and chickens), intensive agriculture and fishing, stone tools, use of shells and obsidian for purposes of exchange, and a double-hulled outrigger canoe capable of open sea voyage. Their relatively large settlements were situated for defense (possibly against the original inhabitants) and suggest a level of specialization and social hierarchy that may have developed into the theocratic nobilities of Polynesia. By way of contrast, the original inhabitants of Melanesia and Australia lived largely as landbound hunter-gatherers in small, unstratified bands speaking a bewildering number of archaic languages. (It must be noted, however, that recent archaeological finds, such as the possibility of an indigenous pottery in prehistoric New Guinea, may point to greater cultural sophistication among these original inhabitants than previously expected.)

Anthropological debate has arisen regarding the degree of interaction between the Austronesian-speaking Lapita and their neighbors in forming the advanced cultural complex that they spread to Fiji, Tonga, and Samoa, and eventually throughout Polynesia. In a sense, the question dates back to the eighteenth century, when European explorers in the Pacific first noticed the distinction between dark-skinned and light-skinned peoples in the Pacific.

Two main theories have been advanced to explain the rise of the Lapita cultural complex and its importance in the migration to and initial colonization of the Pacific islands. The "express train" model views the Lapita as Austronesian-speaking Asians originally from Formosa who quickly spread their advanced culture throughout Polynesia with little or no input from "less sophisticated" Melanesian neighbors. However, the lack of archaeological evidence of any prototype for the elaborately incised Lapita pottery in Asia has led to the "triple I" (intrusion, innovation, and integration) model of cultural change. According to this theory, Lapita pottery and the advanced skills necessary to populate the widely scattered islands of the Pacific were the result of a gradual process of cultural integration between the Austronesian newcomers and the original inhabitants of Melanesia. It also discredits the implicit, possibly racist, notion that cultural innovation was necessarily the result of light-skinned newcomers rather than dark-skinned original inhabitants. Indeed, the new theory seeks to expose as a Eurocentric construction the tidy and simple division of Pacific cultures into Polynesian, Melanesian, and Micronesian, arguing for more complex patterns of cultural exchange and development in the Pacific islands. Rather than the simple east-to-west migration proposed by the express train theory, the triple-I theory proposes multiple waves of migration, both eastward and westward, "forward" and "reverse," throughout prehistoric Oceania.

SIGNIFICANCE

The debate over the ultimate origins of the Polynesians is both ideological and, increasingly, political. Some twenty-five hundred years before Viking explorers inched along the coast of Greenland to the North American continent, the Lapita people had developed their navigation skills to the degree that they could make open-sea voyages into the wide expanses of the Pacific, taking food and animals with them on their journeys. In simple geographic terms, it qualifies as one of the largest diasporas in world history. Yet this achievement also bears on contemporary politics in Oceania as Melanesian and Polynesians debate land ownership in places such as Bougainville and New Caledonia and seek to reestablish traditional cultural identities as the period of European and American colonization comes to an end.

—*Luke A. Powers*

FURTHER READING

Allen, J., and J. P. White. "The Lapita Homeland: Some New Data and An Interpretation." *Journal of the Polynesian Society* 98 (1989): 129-146. Disputes the theory of Austronesian migration and considers the Lapita cultural complex an indigenous phenomenon.

Bellwood, Peter. *Man's Conquest of the Pacific*. New York: Oxford University Press, 1979. One of the first texts to explore the connections between material cultures and dispersion patterns of Austronesian languages in order to identify the Lapita people.

Bellwood, Peter, ed. *Indo-Pacific Prehistory 1990*. Jakarta, Indonesia: Asosiasi Prehistorisi Indonesia, 1991. A collection of conference papers that presents a broad range of opinion regarding migration theories and the rise of the Lapita cultural complex.

Kirch, P. V. *The Lapita Peoples*. New York: Oxford University Press, 1997. A good overview of the current theories of Lapita origins and migrations, incorporating new archaeological and genetic data.

Sergeantson, S. W., and A. V. S. Hill. *The Colonization of the Pacific: A Genetic Trail*. New York: Oxford University Press, 1989. Argues that certain markers identified in contemporary Polynesians indicate a significant level of non-Austronesian genetic strains.

Spriggs, M. "What Is Southeast Asian about Lapita?" In *Prehistoric Mongoloid Dispersals*, edited by T. Akazawa and E. Szathmáry. New York: Oxford University Press, 1995. Discusses aspects of the proposed migration of Asians from Formosa throughout the Pacific, as opposed to the theory of an indigenous development within the area.

SEE ALSO: c. 2500-c. 1500 B.C.E., Southeast Asians Migrate into the South Pacific.

c. 1450 B.C.E.
INTERNATIONAL AGE OF MAJOR KINGDOMS BEGINS IN THE NEAR EAST

The International Age of Major Kingdoms in the Near East was characterized by diplomacy and long-distance trade; out of this political and economic interaction came significant cultural exchange.

LOCALE: The Near East

CATEGORIES: Prehistory and ancient cultures; government and politics; trade and commerce; cultural and intellectual history

KEY FIGURES

Thutmose III (late sixteenth century-1450 B.C.E.), fifth king of Egypt, Eighteenth Dynasty, r. 1504-1450 B.C.E.

Amenhotep III (c. 1403-c. 1349), Egyptian pharaoh of Egypt, Eighteenth Dynasty, r. 1386-1349 B.C.E.

Akhenaton (Amenhotep IV; c. 1364-c. 1334 B.C.E.), Egyptian pharaoh, tenth king, Eighteenth Dynasty, r. 1350-1334 B.C.E.

SUMMARY OF EVENT

The International Age of Major Kingdoms (c. 1450-1350 B.C.E.) encompasses the second quarter of the Late Bronze Age (c. 1550-1150) in the Near East. Paradoxically, it followed a century and a half of chaos and strife. In central Mesopotamia, a mysterious new people, the Kassites, filled the vacuum created by the fall of the First Dynasty of Babylon (c. 1595). In Syria, Indo-Aryan immigrants mixed with the local Hurrian population, forged the kingdom of Mitanni, and dismembered the kingdom of Assyria (c. 1600-1450). In Anatolia, the Hittite royal family lost control of its eastern territories and degenerated into sultanism (c. 1595-1420). Finally, Egyptian princes dislodged the Hyksos intruders from the Nile Delta and pursued them across the Sinai Peninsula into Canaan (c. 1550-1540).

The International Age of Major Kingdoms arose directly out of Egypto-Mitannian competition in Canaan and Syria. Under Thutmose III, the Egyptian army campaigned seventeen times in the region, reaching as far as the Euphrates River. Egyptian records state, with typical exaggeration, that other rulers became frightened and begged Thutmose III's son, Amenhotep II, for the "breath of life." Reading between the lines, scholars surmise that the Kassites, Mitannians, Hittites, and Egyptians concluded an agreement on boundaries, spheres of influence, and diplomacy. Tensions were eased and peace prevailed.

The Amarna letters, diplomatic documents written in Akkadian cuneiform that were found in Egypt in 1887, reveal the precise mechanisms that sustained the peace. Kings regarded (or pretended to regard) their counterparts as "brothers" and exchanged gifts: metals, precious stones, luxury goods, animals, and slaves. Especially prized were gold (for its decorative uses) and tin (because it was alloyed with copper to make bronze). In theory, kings were supposed to give freely and generously to their brethren, but in reality, they tried to amass presents while avoiding their own obligations. In one letter, the Kassite Burna-Buriyash (early fourteenth century B.C.E.) boasted that he had all he needed but went on to request "much fine gold," noting that an earlier shipment of bullion had been both insufficient and debased. In a whole series of epistles, the Mitannian Tushratta (mid-fourteenth century) complained furiously about receiving a pair of gold-plated statues instead of solid gold ones.

Besides exchanging gifts, royal houses also intermarried. This was a complicated process. The request for a princess-bride usually met with contemptuous surprise, and subsequent petitions were often necessary. Even if these were forthcoming, arrogance, a quality especially common in Egyptian kings, sometimes prevented unions. The pharaoh Amenhotep III, for example, emphatically refused to send his daughter into the harem of the Kassite Kadashman-Enlil I. Humbled, the latter then requested an Egyptian commoner who had been dressed up like a princess. No one in Babylon, he said, would know the difference. Incredibly, Amenhotep III again refused. "From time immemorial," he noted, "no daughter of the king of Egy[pt] is given to anyone."

The fact that princess-brides did not have promising futures may have rendered marriage-alliances even more objectionable. Simply put, such women never became queens. Normally, they were interred among suspicious concubines and scheming eunuchs and disappeared from history. Occasionally, an ambitious princess managed to acquire some power. At the court of the pharaoh Akhenaton, the royal favorite Kiya, who may have been a Mitannian, wielded considerable influence. Still, her life was an exception, not the rule.

As for the mayors and chieftains of Canaan and Syria, they acquired the status of vassals. The more remote their territories were, the more unruly they became. They competed with one another for land, bargained with marauders called Apiru (alternately Hapiru or Habiru), and even conspired against their lords. One of the most notorious strongmen was Abdi-Ashirta, the chief of Amurru in the Bekáa Valley (in modern-day Lebanon), whose constant scheming compelled Amenhotep III to arrest him and convey him to Egypt for questioning. Abdi-Ashirta's son and successor, Aziru, was himself an accomplished rascal, menacing the port of Byblos and pledging loyalty to different masters.

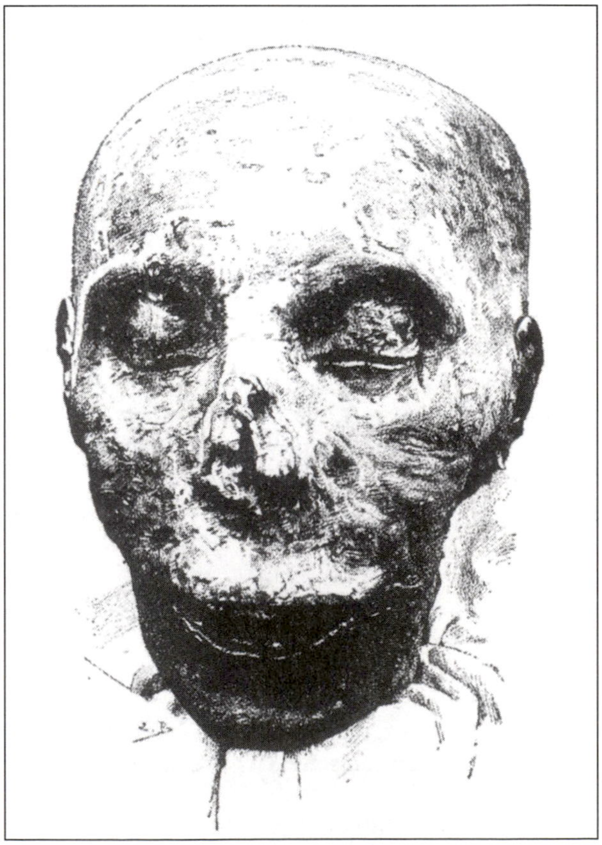

Head of the mummy of Thutmose III. (Library of Congress)

SIGNIFICANCE

Thanks to diplomacy, gift-giving, and intermarriage, the Near East flourished during the International Age of Major Kingdoms. Royal envoys shuttled back and forth through Canaan, caravans crossed Mesopotamia, and trading vessels plied the Aegean Sea. With messengers and merchants went ideas, and an eclectic culture evolved in the region. The cylinder seal of King Shaushtatar of Mitanni (fifteenth century B.C.E.), for example, features an Egyptian winged sun disk, a Hurrian demon, and a generic lion in combat. Similarly, a wall painting from Nuzi, a town near Kirkuk in northern Iraq, depicts the Egyptian goddess Hathor as well as Syrian plants and twists.

Developments in Egypt are particularly interesting. Emissaries, merchants, and princesses, along with captives and hostages, brought new gods into the country. These included the war god Resheph, the sea (and possibly fertility) goddess Astarte, and the sea god Baal Zaphon. In addition, foreign words entered the Egyptian language. In fact, the Egyptian expression "to haggle" became literally "to do business in the Syrian tongue." Finally, new materials such as glass and black bronze inlaid with gold and silver, together with new motifs such as the flying gallop, running spiral, and palmette, inspired vigor, naturalism, and sensuality in art. Perhaps the most striking exemplar of the style is a banqueting scene from the tomb of Nebamun in Thebes (early fourteenth century B.C.E.). In this scene, the artist tried to capture the undulations of two nude dancers, swaying and clapping their hands. He also violated artistic convention and depicted two musicians face-front.

Cultural experimentation in Egypt reached its peak during the reign of Akhenaton. This king founded a new religion with a single god, the Aton (Aten, or solar disk) who nurtured all lands. In addition, he appreciated contemporary trends in art and patronized elegant, gracile sculptures. A painted relief of unknown provenance (possibly from Memphis), shows his daughter, Meritaton, and his coregent, Smenkhare in a garden. The princess offers a bouquet of flowers to her companion, who leans back naturally, almost languidly, on his staff.

The International Age of Major Kingdoms ended with the intrigues and wars of the Hittite king Suppiluliumas I in the mid-fourteenth century B.C.E. Nonetheless, diplomatic mechanisms continued to function until the attack of the Sea Peoples at the end of the thirteenth century. The Hittites encroached on Egypt's sphere of influence and defeated Mitanni, actions that led ultimately to the Battle of Kadesh (c. 1275) between Muwatallis and Ramses II, but they were not savages. Indeed, the famous Ulu Burun shipwreck, which was discovered off the south coast of Anatolia and which carried royal gifts of copper, tin, glass, and other commodities, dates to c. 1325.

Along surviving diplomatic/commercial conduits, elements of Akhenaton's religious hymns appear to have reached Canaan. There, the Hebrews (their name may be derived from Apiru) dovetailed them into the Old Testament, specifically into Psalm 104, which likens the Lord God to the sun in the sky, nourishing all creation with his rays.

—Steven M. Stannish

FURTHER READING

Bass, George F. "Oldest Known Shipwreck Reveals Splendors of the Bronze Age." *National Geographic Magazine* 176, no. 6 (December, 1987): 269-296. A look at the Ulu Burun shipwreck and its cargo. Several photographs.

Cohen, Raymond, and Raymond Westbrook, eds. *Amarna Diplomacy: The Beginnings of International Relations*. Baltimore: The Johns Hopkins University Press, 2000. Essays by various scholars. Bibliography and indices.

Liverani, Mario. *Three Amarna Essays*. Translated by Matthew L. Jaffe. Malibu, Calif.: Undena Publications, 1979. Studies of the Amarna Letters by a brilliant analyst.

Moran, William L., ed. *The Amarna Letters*. Baltimore: The Johns Hopkins University Press, 1992. The standard English translation of the Amarna Letters. Indexes.

O'Connor, David, and Eric H. Cline, eds. *Amenhotep III: Perspectives on His Reign*. Ann Arbor: University of Michigan Press, 2001. Studies of the world of Amenhotep III. Bibliography and indexes.

Snell, Daniel C. *Life in the Ancient Near East*. New Haven, Conn.: Yale University Press, 1997. A study of society and economics in the ancient Near East. Chapter 4, "Retrenchment and Empire, 1600-1100 B.C.E.," is germane. Bibliography and index.

SEE ALSO: 1650-1620 B.C.E., Hattusilis I Establishes the Old Hittite Kingdom; c. 1600-c. 1300 B.C.E., Mitanni Kingdom Flourishes in Upper Mesopotamia; c. 1570 B.C.E., New Kingdom Period Begins in Egypt; c. 1338 B.C.E., Failure of Akhenaton's Cultural Revival; c. 1275 B.C.E., Battle of Kadesh; c. 1200-c. 1050 B.C.E., Sea Peoples Contribute to Mediterranean Upheaval.

14th-9th centuries B.C.E.

URNFIELD CULTURE FLOURISHES IN NORTHWESTERN EUROPE

Urnfield culture, distinguished by its use of cremation and field cemeteries, appeared in central and upper western Europe. It represented the earliest manifestation of what evolved as Celtic civilization, the forerunner to the later civilizations of the region.

LOCALE: Europe
CATEGORY: Prehistory and ancient cultures

SUMMARY OF EVENT

From earliest times in Europe, burial meant interment of an intact corpse. Toward the middle of the second millennium B.C.E., however, a new burial custom appeared. Corpses were cremated, the ashes placed in pots or urns, and the repositories buried with no markers in field cemeteries.

Such burial locations, sometimes with more than one thousand graves, were discovered in modern times at numerous central and northwestern European sites. They indicated that during the late Bronze Age a radical change in a fundamental cultural pattern, human burial, emerged and spread throughout Europe. Modern researchers came to designate this new phenomenon as "Urnfield culture."

Changed burial techniques represented more than altered attitudes toward death. They were a consequence of much larger changes views regarding life. These, moreover, were a consequence of deep changes in economic and social organization that resulted as bronze tools and weapons became the dominant resources of the time.

In previous millennia, humankind had moved from the use of stone to metal as a more effective material for making tools for farming, hunting, and warfare. During the second millennium, the use of bronze, combining copper and tin, produced the hardest metal then known. Copper and tin were scarce materials, so that obtaining them required widespread trade and control of sources.

Those who possessed bronze tools and weapons were a small minority who organized themselves to control and protect their riches and acquire more, forming a warrior elite. The Bronze Age, therefore, saw a greater production of riches through enhanced metallurgy. At the same, however, it also saw the development of class differentiations as a result of the scarcity of the riches and an increase in conflict in order to acquire or defend these riches. The Bronze Age witnessed the first appearance of swords and spears, body armor, horses, and chariots in warfare.

In such an atmosphere, the fragility of life and the vulnerability of the body became more marked. The importance of burying a body intact came to seem less effective as a means for preserving and conducting it to some afterlife. Cremating a body and interring the remains in an urn in a field emerged as an appropriate burial alternative.

The earliest evidence of urn burials in fields appears in the mid-Danube Valley of the Hungarian plain in the fifteenth century B.C.E. However, the Urnfield burial technique came to dominate and emerged strongest in the region of Carpathia during the mid-fourteenth century. This region lies in an area of mountains and river valleys northwest of the Danube River, where it empties into the Black Sea. An area of gold deposits crossed by migrating populations, the region witnessed much conflict. From the fourteenth to the ninth centuries, Urnfield culture advanced from southeastern Europe throughout central and western Europe. Initially it did not spread contiguously but "jumped" from the Carpathian region to the river valley trade centers of modern northwestern Russia, Poland, central Germany, and Italy. It then spread to the areas between the regions and beyond into river valleys of France and Spain and then on to the British Isles. Not only changed burial practices but also greater use of heavy swords and the widespread appearance of fortified villages accompanied the advance of this culture.

The five centuries during which Urnfield culture spread also marked the end of the Bronze Age and the beginning of the Iron Age. This period further spread the use of metal tools and weapons, based now, however, on iron: a metal more plentifully found than copper and tin. The Urnfield period also marked the cultural birth of the Celts, speakers of an Indo-European language, a linguistic family that would come to dominate Europe. The Celts either entered Europe from the east (the area of the presumed birth of the Indo-European language group north of the Black Sea) or differentiated themselves from the rest of the indigenous population of central Europe, coming to occupy much the same areas as Urnfield culture. In the Iron Age, the Hallstatt culture arose in the Austrian and Bavarian Alps, becoming the first truly Celtic culture.

SIGNIFICANCE

Urnfield culture immediately precedes and then accompanies the advance of Celtic civilization in Europe, an Iron Age civilization of the first millennium B.C.E. that marked the advance of the Indo-European languages that came to dominate the continent. Urnfield culture refers to a changed method of burial appearing in the mid-second millennium B.C.E. during the Bronze Age. The culture fostered burial of cremated body remains in urns that were buried in fields. Beyond this changed burial behavior, however, Urnfield culture demonstrated the profound psychosocial transformations of the period. The increase in conflict resulting from greater riches and weapons provoked an awareness of the vulnerability and fragility of the body. A sense spread of the futility of preserving the body through intact interment. It was the combination of warfare, trade, and a noble warrior elite that developed in the Urnfield culture that came to fruition in the subsequent Hallstatt culture. Significantly, however, the Celtic cultures began to return to interment of the full body in its burial customs, although cremation also persisted in some areas.

—*Edward A. Riedinger*

FURTHER READING

Cunliffe, Barry. *The Ancient Celts*. New York: Oxford University Press, 1997. A detailed exploration of the intricacies of the concept of "Celtic culture." The beginning chapters describe the relationship between the Urnfield and Hallstatt cultures.

Haywood, John. *Atlas of the Celtic World*. New York: Thames and Hudson, 2001. Work by a noted scholar of atlases for world and ancient history.

Pare, C. F. E. *Metals Make the World Go Round: The Supply and Circulation of Metals in Bronze Age Europe*. Oxford, England: Oxbow, 2000. Proceedings of a conference in 1997 detailing the spread of bronze and its accompanying cultural transformations in Europe.

Theuws, Frans, and Nico Roymans, eds. *Land and Ancestors: Cultural Dynamics in the Urnfield Period and the Middle Age in the Southern Netherlands*. Amsterdam: University Press, 1999. Several chapters in this work deal with Urnfield culture in the late Bronze and early Iron Ages at its further extensions in northwestern Europe.

Twist, Clint. *Atlas of the Celts*. Buffalo, N.Y.: Firefly Books, 2001. Through detailed maps and illustration, the first two chapters present a clear development of Urnfield culture and relevant aspects of parallel Hallstatt A and B cultures.

SEE ALSO: c. 2300-c. 1800 B.C.E., Beaker People Live in Western Europe; From c. 1500 B.C.E., Dissemination of the Book of the Dead; c. 1500-c. 1000 B.C.E., Aryans Appear in India; c. 1100-c. 500 B.C.E., Hallstatt Culture Dominates Northern Europe; c. 100 B.C.E.-c. 100 C.E., Celtic Hill Forts Are Replaced by *Oppida*; c. 60 B.C.E., Druidism Flourishes in Gaul and Britain.

1400-1300 B.C.E.
AQHAT EPIC IS COMPOSED IN UGARIT

The Aqhat epic recounts the tragic death of Aqhat, Daniel's only son. This epic, together with the whole corpus of Ugaritic literature, reveals a culture that illumines the biblical world.

LOCALE: Ugarit (in modern Syria)
CATEGORIES: Religion; literature

SUMMARY OF EVENT

In 1929, the ancient city of Ugarit (Ras Shamra in modern-day Syria) was discovered. The written texts from this ancient port provide insight into the fabric of the biblical world. The Ugaritic tablets from Ras Shamra are written in an alphabetic cuneiform script known to have been in use by the mid-fourteenth century B.C.E. The literary texts are almost entirely in the form of poetry. One of these principal literary texts is *The Legend of Aqhat*, preserved on three clay tablets found in 1930.

Not a single character from the Aqhat epic is a known historical personage. Neither Aqhat nor his father, Daniel, is known to have ruled as king in Ugarit. The mythic element of the plot compounds the difficulty of identifying the context in which the epic was used. Perhaps the story had no real function but was preserved because it was, in the end, a good story.

The story begins with Daniel, a patriarchal chieftain akin to Abraham who has no son but desires one. In response to prayer, El decrees that Daniel and Danatay, his wife, shall have a son. Daniel is delighted on hearing the divine promise. He will now have a son who will care for him during his lifetime and perform the correct funerary rites. In the words of the epic as translated by Dennis Pardee in William Hallo's *The Context of Scipture*:

> Someone to raise up the stela of his father's god,
> in the sanctuary the votive emblem of his clan;
> To send up from the earth his incense,
> from the dust the song of his place;
> To shut up the jaws of his detractors,
> to drive out anyone who would do him in;
> To take his hand when (he is) drunk,
> to bear him up [when] (he is) full of wine;

1500 - 1001 B.C.E.

> To eat his grain (-offering) in the temple of Ba'lu,
> his portion in the temple of 'Ilu;
> To resurface his roof when rain softens it up,
> to wash his outfit on a muddy day.

Aqhat is born and grows to be a dutiful son. One day, Kothar wa-Hasis (skillful and clever), the craftsman god, visits Daniel, giving to him a special bow and arrows that, in turn, Daniel presents to Aqhat. The goddess Anat sees the bow and wants it for herself. She offers silver and gold for the bow. When Aqhat refuses, she offers life, even eternal life. Aqhat again refuses, perceiving that the goddess is offering what she cannot deliver. Old age and death are the common lot of all humankind.

Enraged, Anat seeks permission from El to destroy Aqhat and calls on the services of her henchman Yatpan to murder him. Disguised as a hawk, Yatpan attacks Aqhat during a meal and kills him. Pughat, the hero's sister, after noticing hovering hawks in the sky, concludes that a murder has been committed. She communicates her suspicions to her father, who then travels around his territory to determine the source of the trouble. He learns of the death of his son and vows vengeance upon the murderer, whose identity is still unknown to him. Daniel begs Baal to bring down the hawks that he may cut them open to see if he can find the remains of his son. No remains are found, so Baal is asked to restore the birds and they fly away. Daniel then spies Hirgabu, the father of the hawks, who is also brought down, but no remains are found. When Samlu, the mother of the hawks, is brought down, Daniel finds the remains of his son, which he then buries.

After seven years of mourning for Aqhat, Pughat discovers that Yatpan was responsible for her brother's death. With a sword hidden in her flowing robes, Pughat disguises herself as Anat and pays a visit to Yatpan. The villain invites the disguised Pughat into his house for a drink. As he drinks, his tongue is loosened, and he boasts of his murderous treachery. Just as Yatpan's confession falls from his lips, and Pughat's revenge is exacted, the clay tablet is broken and the end of the story is lost.

Even though the incompleteness of the text makes the precise meaning and interpretation of the narrative uncertain, many of its themes are familiar from other ancient literature: the concern for a son and successor, mortality, and vengeance for an act of murder. Although the context in which the epic was recited at Ugarit is unknown, it has been speculated that the virtuous king (Daniel), the ideal son (Aqhat), the dutiful daughter (Pughat), and the rash young prince (Aqhat) are sketched as models or as a warning. These models have parallels in the wisdom or sapiential literature of the ancient world such as the biblical Book of Proverbs.

SIGNIFICANCE

The extant literature from Ugarit not only reveals an ancient culture in its own right (Syria in the Late Bronze Age) but also sheds light on the language, literature, and religion of biblical Israel. These ancient cultures valued virtue in the palace (Daniel and Aqhat) and in the home (Aqhat and Pughat). The epic also provides an alternative view of Middle Eastern cultures and religions—such as the worship of Baal—to those presented by the Old Testament. The acts of the goddess Anat furthermore bear a strong resemblance to those of Ishtar in the Gilgamesh epic (c. 2000 B.C.E.; translated into English as *Gilgamesh Epic*, 1917), illustrating the continuity and close relationship among the mythologies of the various cultures of the ancient Middle East.

—*Mark J. Mangano*

FURTHER READING

Coogan, Michael David. *Stories from Ancient Canaan.* Philadelphia: Westminster Press, 1978. Coogan offers a lively translation of the myths of the Canaanites, introducing the reader to the world of the Canaanites and to the world of ancient Israel.

Del Olmo Lete, G. *Mitos y leyendas de Canaan segun la tradicion de Ugarit.* Madrid: Ediciones Cristiandad, 1981. This work is an important Spanish translation of the literary texts from Ugarit.

Pardee, Dennis. "The Aqhatu Legend." In *The Context of Scripture: Canonical Compositions from the Biblical World.* Vol. 1, edited by William W. Hallo. New York: E. Brill, 1997. An English translation by a preeminent scholar in the field.

Smith, Mark S. *Untold Stories: The Bible and Ugaritic Studies in the Twentieth Century.* Peabody, Mass.: Hendrickson, 2001. This work is a delightful survey of the history of Ugaritic scholarship over the course of the twentieth century, focusing attention on its contributions to the study of ancient Israel and the Hebrew Bible (Old Testament).

SEE ALSO: c. 3100 B.C.E., Sumerians Invent Writing; c. 2300 B.C.E., Enheduanna Becomes First Named Author; c. 2000 B.C.E., Composition of the Gilgamesh Epic.

c. 1338 B.C.E.
FAILURE OF AKHENATON'S CULTURAL REVIVAL

Akhenaton attempted to establish a new religion based on the worship of Aton, building a new city where the god could be honored, but the new faith never caught on among the Egyptian people.

LOCALE: Egypt
CATEGORIES: Religion; government and politics

KEY FIGURES

Akhenaton (Amenhotep IV; c. 1364-c. 1334 B.C.E.), pharaoh, tenth king, r. 1350-1334 B.C.E.

Amenhotep III (c. 1403-c. 1349), Egyptian pharaoh of Egypt, Eighteenth Dynasty, r. 1386-1349 B.C.E., Akhenaton's father

Nefertiti (c. 1364-c. 1334 B.C.E.), Akhenaton's queen who supported the Aton cult

SUMMARY OF EVENT

In about 1350 B.C.E., Akhenaton, whose father was Amenhotep III, became pharaoh of the Eighteenth Dynasty of the New Kingdom (c. 1570-c. 1069) of Egypt. Akhenaton began his reign as Amenhotep IV with his capital at Thebes. There is an apparently insoluble dispute about his age at the time he succeeded to the throne, a question of some importance in the light of the claims he made for his achievements.

The reign of Akhenaton's predecessor, Amenhotep III, had been a long and peaceful one of nearly forty years marked by military expeditions in the first decade and followed by three decades of affluent ease. During the latter period, there was a remarkable outpouring of artistic talent resulting in splendid architectural achievements. Amenhotep III was influenced by his queen, Tiy, the daughter of a commoner who became the mother of Akhenaton. In the last decade of his reign, Amenhotep was a sick man, unable to attend to affairs of government. Meanwhile, Syria was restive, and Egypt was suffering from sporadic attacks by invaders. When the outlying districts sent pleas to the capital for military help, their requests were ignored. Conditions called for a vigorous new ruler. Instead, Egypt received a man who was, if not a religious extremist, certainly eccentric.

It is essential to have some grasp of traditional Egyptian religion to penetrate the meaning of the religious movement inaugurated by Akhenaton. Although Egyptian religion was polytheistic and allowed for the worship of distinctive local gods in various regions, Amen, the god of Thebes, had for all intents and purposes become the supreme god of the Egyptian pantheon. Amen, "the hidden one," was exemplified or manifest in the wind and also in breath, the life source of all living creatures.

Another god universally acknowledged among all Egyptians was Ra, the sun god. When Amen and Ra became conceptualized as a single god, Amen-Ra, combining the mysterious life-producing forces of air and the sun, Egypt had come close to the worship of a supreme and universal god. It was a worship built on a theology that saw the gods as essentially immanent in nature because knowledge was not yet sophisticated enough to permit the conception of the sun and wind as purely physical phenomena.

Therefore, at the time of Akhenaton's accession, Egyptian worship was experiencing a growing unification, and along with this tendency, the priesthood was becoming centralized. The priestly class had actually grown so

Akhenaton. (Library of Congress)

FAMILY LINE OF AKHENATON

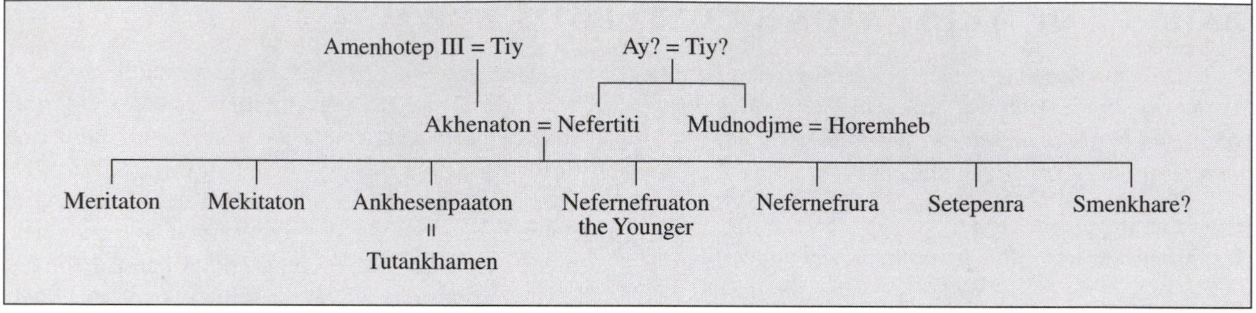

much in wealth and concomitant political power that a struggle between the ecclesiastical and the secular power blocs had begun to arise.

What Akhenaton attempted was a radical reform of the prevailing cult of Amen-Ra. The evidence, relatively abundant for so remote a period, is both archaeological and literary. Among the important documents are letters containing both sides of a diplomatic correspondence.

Akhenaton built an entire city for his god Aton at Akhetaton (now Tell el-ʿAmârna, Egypt), midway between Thebes and Memphis. Here, monuments bear witness to a god represented as a disk or sun, with rays terminating in hands that sometimes hold to the noses of the king and members of the royal family the hieroglyphic sign for "life." Along with the missionary effort to propagate the new faith went a vigorous iconoclastic movement. Images of Amen, who was now seen as a rival to Aton, were ruthlessly destroyed, and the names of those who had promoted his cult, particularly that of Amenhotep III, were effaced from inscriptions. The change of the king's own title from Amenhotep IV to Akhenaton was a part of this movement.

How far the religious reform was accompanied by an effort to break the power of the priests of Amen is a matter of conjecture, with varying interpretations. The dogmatic ideas of the new religion are best expressed in the famous hymn to Aton, ascribed to Akhenaton himself. This psalmlike composition reflects a belief in a supreme provident god who resembles the God of the later Judeo-Christian tradition. These similarities led some historians of the late nineteenth and early twentieth centuries to see in Akhenaton's religion a monotheism that prefigured, if it did not actually influence, the Hebrew idea of one supreme, universal, and transcendent God. Apart from this problem, the hymn stands as a classic of ancient religious literature.

Actually, Akhenaton's religious movement was a failure in almost every respect. On the strictly religious side, it did not take hold of the people, who went on worshiping their old gods in familiar ways. Indeed, the cult of Aton seems to have been restricted almost completely to Akhenaton, his family, and the immediate entourage at Akhetaton, the new capital. The rigidly monotheistic religion of Akhenaton had little appeal to the ordinary Egyptian who saw manifestations, or even emanations, of the divine in all phenomena. The Aton cult ran counter to the popular polytheistic worldview that seemed more tolerant of the complexities of observed realities.

Politically and militarily, Akhenaton's reign was devoid of any outstanding accomplishment, a fact that is generally attributed to his absorption in his attempted religious reform and his lethargy concerning matters of government. In the field of art, however, the era marked a decided turn to a more naturalistic style. Instead of the stylized figures that had become typical of Egyptian art for more than a thousand years, the sculptures depicting Akhenaton are characterized by a photographic realism. The king himself is depicted as a rather grotesque, ill-shapen man, his defects set off by the beauty of his wife, Nefertiti. There are extant a number of groups showing Akhenaton, Nefertiti, and several of their daughters in domestic scenes that until that time were not considered fit subjects for public art.

SIGNIFICANCE

Although the importance of the religious, political, and cultural aspects of Akhenaton's reform are considerable, it was in no sense typical of Egyptian civilization, and there is no evidence of the movement's lasting influence. A few years after his death, a deliberate and successful effort was made to obliterate traces of the cult of Aton. As Akhenaton had caused the very name of Amen-Ra to be erased from monuments—although it could not be eradicated from people's minds—so Akhenaton himself was subjected to the same treatment. Labeled the "heretic king," Akhenaton had his name removed from the list of kings by his successor.

—*Mary Evelyn Jegen*

FURTHER READING

Aldred, Cyril. *Akhenaten, King of Egypt*. New York: Thames and Hudson, 1988. A biography of Akhenaton from an Egyptologist. Bibliography and index.

Freed, Rita E., Yvonne J. Markowitz, and Sue H. D'Auria, eds. *Pharaohs of the Sun: Akhenaten, Nefertiti, Tutankhamen*. Boston: Museum of Fine Arts in association with Bulfinch Press and Little, Brown, 1999. This catalog from an exhibition at the Museum of Fine Arts in Boston in 1999-2000 shows art related to Akhenaton and his wife Nefertiti.

Hari, Robert. *New Kingdom Amarna Period: The Great Hymn to Aten*. Leiden: E. J. Brill, 1985. A look at the hymn to Aton composed by Akhenaton and its religious significance.

Hornung, Erik. *Akhenaton and the Religion of Light*. Translated by David Lorton. Ithaca, N.Y.: Cornell University Press, 1999. An examination of Akhenaton that focuses on his religion, a form of monotheism. Examines the religion's origins.

Montserrat, Dominic. *Akhenaten: History, Fantasy, and Ancient Egypt*. New York: Routledge, 2000. A biography of the king of Egypt that examines his place in history and tries to separate fantasy from fact.

Murnane, William J., and Charles C. Van Siclen III. *The Boundary Stelae of Akhenaten*. New York: Kegan Paul International, 1993. This study of the stelae of Akhenston reproduces their text in English and Egyptian. Bibliography and index.

Reeves, C. N. *Akhenaten: Egypt's False Prophet*. London: Thames and Hudson, 2001. A biography that looks at Akhenaton's efforts to establish a new religion. Bibliography, index, maps.

SEE ALSO: c. 1650 B.C.E., Hyksos Create Second Intermediate Period; c. 1570 B.C.E., New Kingdom Period Begins in Egypt; c. 1450 B.C.E., International Age of Major Kingdoms Begins in the Near East; 1069 B.C.E., Third Intermediate Period Begins in Egypt.

RELATED ARTICLES in *Great Lives from History: The Ancient World*: Akhenaton; Nefertiti; Tiy; Tutankhamen.

c. 1280 B.C.E.
ISRAELITE EXODUS FROM EGYPT

The Exodus marked the birth of Israel as a nation, and the covenant with Yahweh defined many of the stipulations of Israel's relationship with God.

LOCALE: Sinai Peninsula
CATEGORIES: Expansion and land acquisition; religion

KEY FIGURES

Seti I (c. late fourteenth century-c. 1279 B.C.E.), son of Ramses I and pharaoh of Egypt, r. 1294-1279 B.C.E.
Ramses II (c. 1300-1213 B.C.E.), son of Seti I and the most successful pharaoh of the Nineteenth Dynasty, r. 1279-1213 B.C.E.
Moses (c. 1300-c. 1200 B.C.E.), leader of tribal Israel
Aaron (c. 1395-c. 1272 B.C.E.), founder of Jewish priesthood, elder brother of Moses

SUMMARY OF EVENT

The traditional fifteenth century date for the Israelites' Exodus (or escape) from Egypt is calculated by adding the 480 years mentioned in 1 Kings 6:1 as the time that elapsed between the Israelite Exodus and Solomon's building of the temple of Jerusalem c. 966 B.C.E. Israelite participation as slaves in the building of the Egyptian cities before the Exodus (see Exodus 1:11) suggests instead a date after 1302, when Seti I moved the Egyptian capital from Thebes to a site in the eastern Nile Delta near the Mediterranean Sea, eventually known as Pi-Ramesse (domain of Ramses). Many scholars of the Bible see Seti I as the pharaoh who began the Israelites' oppression and whose death is mentioned in Exodus 2:23, and they consider his son Ramses II to be the pharaoh during whose reign the Exodus itself occurred. One archaeological discovery that seems to confirm that view is a stone monument erected c. 1220 by Ramses' successor Merneptah. The monument lists the Israelites as a people he defeated while engaged in a military expedition to Canaan; Israel, then, existed as a nation to be defeated by this time.

Egyptian records available today do not record the successful escape of Israelites from slavery, though the Amarna letters (a group of letters from Canaanite cities to the capital of the Eighteenth Dynasty at Amarna) do mention rebels called "Habiru," as do texts from as early as 2000 B.C.E. in Mesopotamia. Although the name Habiru is similar to "Hebrew" and may be etymologically related to it, there is no reason to suppose the rebels mentioned in the Amarna letters refer to Hebrews/Israelites. The Hebrew Bible, therefore, is the only source of information about the Exodus.

The book of Exodus introduces the flight of the Hebrews with the narrative of the first Passover meal and the death of all first-born Egyptian sons and male animals. Prompted by this tragedy, the pharaoh granted permission for Moses and his brother Aaron to lead the Hebrews to the area of Mount Sinai in the Sinai Peninsula (formed by the two arms of the Red Sea known as the Gulf of Suez and the Gulf of Aqaba). Quickly changing his mind, however, the pharaoh dispatched charioteers to capture the Israelites. Their route is largely unknown, despite the tradition that Israel crossed the "Red Sea." The modern Red Sea cannot be the body of water in question because it lies south of the Sinai Peninsula. Even the Gulf of Suez lies to the south of Pithom and Ramses and of the "land of Goshen" where Israel lived. The biblical text, therefore, seems to envision a more northerly location, yet one south of the main coastal highway to Canaan along the coast of the Mediterranean Sea (see Exodus 13:17). Actually, the Hebrew phrase translated "Red Sea" is more accurately translated "marshy sea" or even "Reed Sea." It may have been one of the small marshy lakes connected in modern times to form the Suez Canal.

The Egyptian army overtook the Israelites at the edge of this "sea." The Bible narrates an event (see Exodus 14:21-29) in which a strong east wind drove the water away from the shore where the Israelites had stopped, thus allowing them to flee from the advancing chariots. The account offers two versions of what happened to the Egyptians. The first (Exodus 14:24-25) says that God caused the wheels of the Egyptian chariots to be stuck in the mud, forcing the Egyptians to abandon their vehicles. The second (Exodus 14:26-28) says that God, acting through Moses, caused the wind to cease blowing, with the result that the water returned, drowning the horses and soldiers (see also Exodus 15:1-5, 21).

A depiction of the Egyptians chasing the Israelites into the sea. (F. R. Niglutsch)

The naming of God as the real actor in the Exodus and the two different (though not necessarily contradictory) explanations of what happened to the Egyptians show that the biblical account is theological narrative and not historiography in the modern sense. The point of the biblical narrative was that God, or Yahweh (Exodus 6:1-3), delivered the Israelites from slavery in Egypt. Elements of the narrative elaborate God's role and make it difficult, if not impossible, to re-create an objective account. For ancient Israelites, however, the event marked their passage from bondage to the beginning of their life as a "nation," as the Hebrew Bible used the term; that is, as a group of related people following their own God to claim their own land.

The route from the "Sea" to Mount Sinai (also called Mount Horeb) also is unknown, partly because the location of the mountain itself is debated. The traditional site, named Jebel Musa, is a rugged mountain near the southern tip of the Sinai Peninsula. A reference to the habitation there of Amalekites (see Exodus 17:8-16), a Canaanite people, suggests a site farther north. In addition, Deuteronomy 1:2 gives the distance of Mount Sinai from Kadesh-barnea, a city near the southern end of Canaan, also suggesting a northern site. Hence, some scholars identify Mount Halal, west of Kadesh-barnea, as Mount Sinai. Regardless, it was the place where Moses had encountered Yahweh for the first time while tending the sheep of his father-in-law and the place to which he was to lead the Israelites to offer sacrifices (see Exodus 3:1, 12).

There, Israel made a covenant with Yahweh. The term "covenant" designates a formal agreement between or among two or more parties, often including stipulations for one or more of the participants. The covenant between Israel and Yahweh at Sinai as reported in the Hebrew Bible extends from Exodus 20 (which records the Ten Commandments) to Numbers 10:10, and includes several smaller codes, a census list, and some narration.

The most famous part of the covenant is the Ten Commandments, possibly originally short commands and prohibitions. The first four deal with how humans should relate to God, the last six with how humans should relate to each other. The commandments set high religious and ethical standards for Israel, standards that became increasingly appealing to other ancients by Greco-Roman times. Other collections of laws set times for the three major harvest festivals of Israel (Exodus 23:14-17), made demands for spiritual and physical purity (Leviticus 17-26), regulated the treatment of other human beings and of personal property (Exodus 21-23), and even gave criteria for diagnosing leprosy (Leviticus 13-14). Laws that aided Israelites in retaining their collective identity in foreign countries (for example during the period of captivity in Babylon in the sixth century) were those requiring circumcision of Hebrew males on the eighth day after birth (Leviticus 12:3) and those setting forth dietary regulations (Exodus 34:26b) that eventually led to kosher rules.

Significance

The Exodus was the most important event in the Hebrew Bible. The Bible's own understanding of the event was twofold. First, it was caused by God's love for God's people. Second, it was the beginning of God's fulfillment of the divine promise to give a land to Abraham and his descendants (see Genesis 12:1-3). Israel's continued possession of the land was conditional on its faithfulness to God in keeping the covenant (see Deuteronomy 8:19-20).

That covenant was the definitive covenant of the Hebrew Bible. One main point was the requirement for Israel to worship Yahweh exclusively. The worship of one god exclusively was the starting point of monotheism, for which the Hebrew Bible is justly famous. Monotheism may be defined as belief in and worship of one god, combined with the denial of the existence of all other gods. Monotheism as such emerges later than the Ten Commandments (see, for example, Isaiah 42:5-9; 44:6-8), but the commandments made the decisive step toward monotheism by limiting Israel's worship to Yahweh alone.

Without doubt the Ten Commandments have influenced the idea of individual rights of humans, endowed by their creator. The commandments also contribute two other innovations. First, the prohibition against making images of God (Exodus 20:4) eventually meant that Jews, Christians, and Muslims would refrain from trying to depict God in two- and three-dimensional art forms and concentrate instead on verbal description and human obedience. Second, the command to observe the Sabbath contributed to the development in all three religions of the idea that humans should take time periodically for rest, worship, and the further nurturance of spirituality.

—*Paul L. Redditt*

Further Reading

Assmann, Jan. *Moses the Egyptian: The Memory of Egypt in Western Monotheism*. Cambridge, Mass.: Harvard University Press, 1997. A prominent Egyptologist discusses the interrelationship between the monotheisms of Moses and Akhenaton.

Childs, Brevard S. *The Book of Exodus*. The Old Testament Library. Philadelphia: Westminster, 1974. A full-length commentary devoted exclusively to the book of Exodus, with lengthy discussions of the Exodus and the laws.

Harrelson, Walter. *The Ten Commandments and Human Rights*. Overtures to Biblical Theology. Rev. ed. Macon, Ga.: Mercer University Press, 1997. A study of the meaning of the commandments in ancient Israel and modern America.

Sarna, Nahum M. *Exploring Exodus: The Origins of Biblical Israel*. New York: Schocken Books, 1996. Compares the narrative of the Exodus with other ancient Middle Eastern religious texts, showing what is unique and what is archetypal about the biblical story. Also discusses current theories about the historicity of the narrative.

SEE ALSO: c. 1000 B.C.E., Establishment of the United Kingdom of Israel; c. 966 B.C.E., Building of the Temple of Jerusalem; c. 950 B.C.E., Composition of the Book of Genesis; c. 922 B.C.E., Establishment of the Kingdom of Israel; 587-423 B.C.E., Birth of Judaism; c. 538-c. 450 B.C.E., Jews Return from the Babylonian Captivity; c. 200 B.C.E.-c. 100 C.E., Composition of the Intertestamental Jewish Apocrypha.

RELATED ARTICLES in *Great Lives from History: The Ancient World*: Moses; Ramses II.

c. 1275 B.C.E.
BATTLE OF KADESH

The Battle of Kadesh decided the areas of influence and the balance of power between the Hittites and Egyptians as they expanded into the regions of Syria and the Levant.

LOCALE: Kadesh (Qadesh), on the Orontes River in western Syria, north of Damascus
CATEGORY: Wars, uprisings, and civil unrest

KEY FIGURES

Muwatallis (fl. fourteenth century-c. 1294 B.C.E.), Hittite king, r. c. 1320-c. 1294 B.C.E.
Ramses II (c. 1300-1213 B.C.E.), Egyptian pharaoh, r. 1279-1213 B.C.E.

SUMMARY OF EVENT

Carved on the walls and pylons of massive temples along the River Nile are pictorial and hieroglyphic reports of a military engagement between the Egyptians and the Hittites in 1275 B.C.E. Egypt had been intermittently at war with the Hittites in Syria for two hundred years, since Thutmose III in the early fifteenth century had extended his sway northward beyond the site of modern Lebanon. Later, however, Hittite kings had invaded Syria as far south as Kadesh, where the best routes inland from the Mediterranean Sea entered the valley of the Orontes River, chief passageway to the north and east. Thutmose III had once devoted an eight-year siege to conquering Kadesh, which became the southern bastion of a widespread Hittite Empire.

When Ramses II came to the throne in 1279, he desired to reassert Egyptian dominance in Syria. In the fourth year of his reign, he sent troops north along the coast beyond modern Beirut to secure harbors, and in his fifth year, he personally led a large force through Palestine. His army was divided into four divisions named after the gods, Ra, Ptah, Amen, and Set, each division numbering about five thousand men. At the heart of this pharaonic army were professional charioteers, experts at using bows and spears.

Aware of the approach of Ramses, the Hittite king Muwatallis mustered a host of approximately equal size, between sixteen thousand and twenty thousand men, collected from vassal units of the Hittite Empire, with at least half of his troops charioteers. Most Hittite chariots depicted in relief sculpture carried a driver along with two fighting men. With remarkable cunning Muwatallis concealed this large force from Egyptian scouts, and he sent several Bedouins to be captured by the Egyptians and to deceive Ramses about the location of the Hittites. Persuaded that the enemy was far to the north, Ramses allowed his army to straggle in its march with wide gaps between the divisions.

Only when the advance division, Amen, led by the pharaoh himself, had crossed the Orontes River west of Kadesh did its members discover, through the interrogation of new Hittite prisoners, that Muwatallis's main force was ominously near, just east of Kadesh. Alarmed, the pharaoh hastily sent back a messenger and a staff officer to hurry forward the Ra division, the next unit in line. At this juncture, however, Muwatallis, using the hill of

In this fanciful depiction of the Battle of Kadesh, Ramses II is shown battling the Hittites with lions.(F. R. Niglutsch)

Kadesh to screen his movement, launched his chariots in a surprise flank attack against the approaching Ra division. The Ra column was scattered in all directions.

Pursuing some Ra fugitives northwestward, Hittite chariots came upon the hill where Ramses with the Amen division was setting up camp; many of these Amen soldiers also broke and fled, leaving the pharaoh with only a small bodyguard of chariots, encircled by the enemy. It was a perilous moment for the young Ramses. Nearly half his army had been slain or scattered, and the remaining units were far to his rear.

When the situation seemed desperate, according to eulogistic records carved later in Egypt, Ramses in his two-horse chariot charged into the midst of more than two thousand Hittite chariots and drove back the enemy. Emphasizing his personal heroism as divine, the sculptural accounts are vague about some troops that arrived in time to rescue Ramses. Modern historians generally credit these fresh troops, perhaps of the Ptah division, with rallying the scattered Egyptian forces at a moment when Hittite charioteers were engaged in pillaging the Egyptian camp and chasing fugitives in several directions. The Hittites were driven back.

Muwatallis then brought into action another Hittite force of a thousand chariots and attempted six successive charges. However, these were driven off as additional Egyptian forces arrived on the scene, and the Hittites suffered heavy losses. The next day Muwatallis may have agreed to a truce once the entire Egyptian army had been assembled; the fresh division of Set had taken no part in the first day's battle. It is also possible that Muwatallis had not used eight thousand foot soldiers stationed east of the river, perhaps because the swiftly changing strategy made less mobile infantry useless.

SIGNIFICANCE

Even though Egyptian inscriptions claimed a triumph for Ramses, portraying the Kadesh plain as strewn with Hittite corpses, the pharaoh's immediate retreat southward nevertheless evacuated the area as far as Damascus and left it in possession of the Hittites. More terse Hittite cuneiform inscriptions reveal that in their home cities the battle was reported as a crushing defeat for Egypt.

In following years, there were minor Egyptian campaigns into Palestine, but archaeologists have discovered both Egyptian and Hittite copies of a peace treaty drawn up fifteen years after the Battle of Kadesh between these two powers. The peace was sealed by a marriage of Ramses II to a Hittite princess, and experts believe that there were no subsequent battles between Egyptians and Hittites comparable to the conflict at Kadesh. The Battle of Kadesh fixed the balance of power between Egypt and the Hittites. Kadesh actually represented a truce between the two powers; it appears to have had a debilitating effect on the Hittites while it checked the rising glory of imperial Egypt. Both powers delineated their spheres of influence and became susceptible to the invading Sea Peoples shortly thereafter.

The pharaoh's retreat from the area and his marriage with the Hittite house do not really suggest the overwhelming victory recorded on the Egyptian inscriptions.

—*Roger B. McShane*

FURTHER READING

Breasted, James Henry. *The Battle of Kadesh: A Study in the Earliest Known Military Strategy*. Chicago: University of Chicago Press, 1903. The first detailed study in English of the numerous Egyptian inscriptions describing the Battle of Kadesh, Breasted's work remains a valuable resource.

Gardiner, Alan H. *The Kadesh Inscriptions of Ramesses II*. Oxford, England: The University Press, for the Griffith Institute, 1960. A distinguished Egyptologist offers a full translation of the various hieroglyphic records concerning Kadesh and a reassessment of their interdependence, considerably differing from Breasted's views. Remains a major work on the topic

Goedicke, Hans, ed. *Perspective on the Battle of Kadesh*. Baltimore: Halgo, 1985. A collection of essays examining the Battle of Kadesh from a variety of perspectives. Bibliography.

Healy, Mark. *Qadesh 1300 B.C.: Clash of the Warrior Kings*. Osprey Military Campaign Series 22. London: Osprey, 1993. An examination of the battle from a military perspective. Illustrations and maps.

SEE ALSO: 1650-1620 B.C.E., Hattusilis I Establishes the Old Hittite Kingdom; c. 1570 B.C.E., New Kingdom Period Begins in Egypt; c. 1450 B.C.E., International Age of Major Kingdoms Begins in the Near East; c. 1338 B.C.E., Failure of Akhenaton's Cultural Revival.

RELATED ARTICLE in *Great Lives from History: The Ancient World*: Ramses II.

c. 1250 B.C.E.
FALL OF TROY MARKS END OF TROJAN WAR

The Mycenaean-Greek invaders defeated and almost completely destroyed Troy; their victory became a symbol of Greek dominance over Asia.

LOCALE: Fortified city of Troy (also called Illium) in the northwestern corner of Asia Minor (now Turkey)

CATEGORY: Wars, uprisings, and civil unrest

KEY FIGURES

Menelaus (fl. thirteenth century B.C.E.), king of Sparta, brother of Agamemnon, and husband of Helen

Helen (fl. thirteenth century B.C.E.), mythological goddess and wife of Menelaus, abducted by Paris

Paris (fl. thirteenth century B.C.E.), prince of Troy, who abducted Helen

Agamemnon (fl. thirteenth-twelfth century B.C.E.), leader of a loose confederation of Greek city-states, leader of Greeks against Trojans in Trojan War, and king of Mycenae, r. c. thirteenth-twelfth century B.C.E.

Achilles (fl. thirteenth century B.C.E.), champion of the Greek invaders

Odysseus (fl. thirteenth century B.C.E.), warrior and king of Ithaca

Priam (fl. thirteenth century B.C.E.), king of Troy

SUMMARY OF EVENT

Knowledge about the legendary Trojan War is based primarily on the Greek Homer's poetic works, with supplementary information obtained from later writers. It is thought that Homer lived in the eighth century B.C.E., which means that he was writing about a war that occurred about five hundred years before his time. Homer relied entirely on legends that had been transmitted orally through the generations. Legends about the war had most likely become mixed with those of other military conflicts. As he was a poet rather than a historian, Homer's primary objective in the *Iliad* (c. 750 B.C.E.; English translation, 1611) and the *Odyssey* (c. 725 B.C.E.;

According to legend, Achilles dragged the body of Hector behind his chariot during the Siege of Troy. (F. R. Niglutsch)

English translation, 1614) was not to relate history "as it actually happened." Clearly, he embellished the heroic aspects of the personalities to tell a good story and appeal to militaristic, aristocratic values. His religious interpretations attributing causation to the gods further diminished his concern about historical accuracy. Still, the majority of modern historians believe that Homeric legends had some foundation in a large-scale war that really occurred.

No factual statements about particular incidents of the Trojan War are established beyond reasonable doubt. According to tradition, the war lasted ten years. Although the dates can only be approximations, it is generally accepted that the war took place during the later years of the Mycenaean-Greek civilization (named after the city of Mycenae), just before the onset of Greece's Dark Ages. Because the term "Greek" was not commonly used during this early period, Homer uses the term "Achaeans" for the invaders from the Greek mainland.

Until the nineteenth century, most scholars believed that Troy and the Trojan War were imaginary. Then in the 1870's, archaeologist Heinrich Schliemann appeared to confirm that Greek tradition had been correct about the location of the legendary city. Later archaeologists discovered layers of nine or more cities located at the site of Schliemann's excavation. Finding that the seventh of the cities was catastrophically destroyed around the traditional date of 1250 B.C.E., Carl Blegen and other scholars argued that these are most likely the remains of the legendary Troy. Others emphasize that it is impossible to determine if the catastrophe was caused by warfare, fire, or an earthquake.

According to legend, the Trojan War resulted from King Menelaus's determination to get back his beautiful wife, the mythological goddess Helen, who had fled to Troy with Prince Paris. Most historians, however, find it unlikely that such a personal matter would have motivated a coalition of city-states to wage a large-scale war in a distant land for ten years. There is evidence that the strategically located Troy was often a prosperous center of trade. Given the history of imperialism, it is entirely possible that the Mycenaean-Greek invaders, under Agamemnon, wanted to obtain colonial hegemony over the region. Ancient writers, however, do not give any support for such a motivation. Some modern historians have concluded that the invaders had the more limited objective of destroying a military and commercial rival, while others have thought it likely that they were simply seeking the benefits of plundering a wealthy city. Possibly the invaders had more than one objective in mind.

After the siege of Troy had lasted about nine years, according to Homer's account, Achilles, the champion fighter of the Greeks, killed Hector, the son of the Trojan king. Achilles then dragged his body around the walls in the dust of his chariot. This infuriated Paris, who shot Achilles in his vulnerable heel with a poisoned arrow. The wound became infected and Achilles died. As the stalemate continued, the Greek invaders were increasingly discouraged, and many of them insisted that they should return to their homes and families.

Before giving up, Odysseus (also known as Ulysses) devised a complex strategy that used a hollow wooden horse large enough to hold from twenty to fifty soldiers. The wooden horse carried an inscription of dedication to the goddess Athena, indicating that it was a religious offering to the goddess meant to ensure a safe return trip to Greece. Knowing that the Trojans venerated horses and had their own temple to Athena within their city, Odysseus expected them to take the structure inside the city gates. The Greeks then pretended to sail for home, but instead they hid their ships behind the nearby island of Tenedos. When the Trojans discovered the wooden horse, according to post-Homeric accounts, a priest of Apollo's temple named Laocoon warned in vain that it was a trick of war. However, two fearful serpents killed Laocoon, and King Priam, fearing Athena's wrath, ordered the Trojans to pull the horse into the city. Cassandra, Priam's daughter who had a gift of prophecy, warned about the danger, but she was ridiculed.

That night, the Trojans celebrated the departure of the Greeks with gaiety and much wine. After most Trojans were asleep or in a drunken stupor, the concealed Greek soldiers descended from the horse with rope ladders, and thus they were able to open the gates for the returning Greek army. Sweeping through the city, the invaders slaughtered much of the population, burned the buildings, looted objects of value, and raped the women. Some versions claim that Odysseus ordered that the sons of Hector and other Trojan heroes be killed in order to prevent them from seeking revenge in the future. Achilles's son Phrrhus killed King Priam, and the Greek soldiers sacrificed his daughter Polyxena at the tomb of Achilles. However, King Menelaus allowed Helen to live as his wife. After leaving Troy in ruins, the victorious Greeks celebrated their victory and boarded their ships. They offered prayers to Zeus for a safe return home.

The dramatic legend of the Trojan Horse is perhaps the most famous story of the Western world. The story does not appear in the *Iliad*, which deals only with a seven-week period during the last year of the war. In the *Odyssey*, the blind bard Demodocus (who perhaps represents Homer) mentions the role of a wooden horse in the Greeks' victory, and Odysseus adds more details later in the poem. Homer's reference to the horse inspired the imaginations of countless writers. Arctinus of Miletus, who lived in the seventh century B.C.E., invented the mythical story of Laocoon in *The Sack of Ilium* (now lost). A few centuries later, the Roman poet Vergil made the story even more dramatic in the *Aeneid* (c. 29-19 B.C.E.; English translation, 1553), claiming that the Trojan prince Aeneas had escaped and traveled to Italy.

In the second century C.E., Latin historian Pausanias the Traveler, in *Periegesis Hellados* (between 143 and 161 C.E.; *Description of Greece*, 1794), refused to take the story of the wooden horse at face value. He suggested that it must have referred to some kind of battering ram or other war machine. There is, however, no evidence that the Greeks ever used such an instrument during either Mycenaean or Homeric times. Some modern historians suggest that the story of the wooden horse might have been based on a tactical ruse that Greek soldiers used at Troy or in another battle. Regardless of its historical validity, the story continues to be a powerful metaphor of deception and foolish gullibility.

SIGNIFICANCE

It appears that the immediate consequences of the Trojan War were limited to the unfortunate residents of Troy. There is no evidence that the Mycenaean Greeks tried to establish military or commercial bases in the region. If the king of Mycenae had led a confederation of city-states, which many historians deny, there is no evidence that the alliance was long-lasting. The Greeks' victory over Troy might possibly have promoted the economic dominance of the Greek mainland, but it is also possible that the costs of the campaign contributed to the decline of the Mycenaean-Greek civilization.

The war later became symbolic of the Greeks' belief that they were destined to dominate southwestern Asia. The stories of Achilles and other heroes, moreover, encouraged values of patriotism and militarism. Alexander the Great was an enthusiastic reader of Homer during his youth. When invading Asia Minor in 335 B.C.E., Alexander apparently imagined himself to be following in the footsteps of Achilles.

—*Thomas Tandy Lewis*

Further Reading

Allen, Susan Henck. *Finding the Walls of Troy: Frank Calvat and Heinrich Schliemann at Hisarlik*. Berkeley: University of California Press, 1999. An examination of the archaeological evidence regarding Troy.

Anderson, Michael J. *The Fall of Troy in Early Greek Poetry and Art*. Oxford, England: Clarendon Press, 1997. A study of how the Trojan War was portrayed in art works and literature.

Erskine, Andrew. *Troy Between Greece and Rome: Local Tradition and Imperial Power.* New York: Oxford University Press, 2001. An analysis of the relationship among Troy, Greece, and Rome.

Luce, John Victor. *Celebrating Homer's Landscapes: Troy and Ithaca Revisited*. New Haven, Conn.: Yale University Press, 1998. Includes excellent discussions of the excavations of Troy and the historical validity of Homeric legends.

Nilsson, Martin. *Homer and Mycenae*. 1933. Reprint. Philadelphia: University of Pennsylvania Press, 1972. Although somewhat dated, it provides a useful analysis of Homer's relationship to Mycenaean history.

Page, Denys. *History and the Homeric "Iliad."* Berkeley: University of California Press, 1966. Examines the archaeological evidence and argues that the *Iliad* was based on a core of historical reality.

Shear, Ione Mylonas. *Tales of Heroes: The Origins of the Homeric Texts*. New York: A.D. Caratzas, 2000. The origin of the *Iliad* and *Odyssey* are analyzed. Discussion of weapons and archaeology included.

Tuchman, Barbara. *The March of Folly: From Troy to Vietnam.* New York: Alfred A. Knopf, 1984. Includes an interesting analysis of the Trojan War, emphasizing the legend of the wooden horse.

Wood, Michael. *In Search of the Trojan War.* 1985. Reprint. Berkeley: University of California Press, 1998. Scholarly and rather technical discussions of the archaeological aspects of the topic, with many beautiful illustrations.

See also: c. 1600-c. 1000 B.C.E., City of Mycenae Flourishes; c. 1200-c. 1050 B.C.E., Sea Peoples Contribute to Mediterranean Upheaval; c. 1000-900 B.C.E., Ionian Confederacy Forms; c. 750 B.C.E., Homer Composes the *Iliad*.

c. 1250 B.C.E.
Transmission of the European Alphabet

The development of an alphabet that could be used regardless of the language it represented constituted a major advance over hieroglyphs and pictograms, greatly affecting the preservation of knowledge throughout the world.

Locale: Mediterranean world
Category: Cultural and intellectual history

Summary of Event

The earliest form of writing was the pictogram. Probably around the beginning of the second millennium B.C.E., the earliest form of what became the Roman alphabet was developed by Semitic peoples of unknown identity.

A cuneiform alphabet of about thirty characters used in writing on clay tablets was discovered at Ras Shamra in 1928. Merchants of this city, located in northern Syria across the sea from Cyprus, traded widely but had close mercantile ties with nearby Phoenicia (present-day Lebanon). According to the view accepted by most scholars, these early Semitic inventors were inspired to develop an alphabet through contact with Egyptian hieroglyphics. Although some of their symbols were Egyptian, the system of writing was distinctly their own, consisting of twenty-two characters representing consonants. In early Semitic writing, the reader had to supply the vowels from knowledge of the language without the aid of written directions.

Symbols were selected on the acrophonic principle: Key Semitic words were selected that each began with a different consonantal sound. Then, stylized pictures portraying the key words, which were generally nouns, were assigned the phonetic value of the initial sound of each word, demonstrating the gradual change from ideograms representing ideas to an alphabet representing sounds. In this manner, the first character of the Semitic alphabet, *aleph*, originally meant and was the symbol for the head of an ox. The second, *beth*, meant "house," and various renderings of the symbol in early Phoenician writing reveal a shelter with a roof, which came to represent the consonantal sound "b." The third, *gimel*, was used for the initial sound of the word for "camel," and all early signs reveal a clear hump. In the same way, *daleth* represented a stylized door, *he* the verb "to behold," *vau* a hook or nail, *zayin* a sickle or weapon, *cheth* a fence, and so on.

The Greeks adopted the Semitic alphabet rather than Egyptian hieroglyphics because it was easier for trading purposes. One Semitic group, the Phoenicians, brought the alphabet to Greece at a very early date, perhaps as early as the thirteenth century B.C.E. That the Greeks obtained their alphabet from Semitic sources is indicated not only by the similarity in the forms of characters in the two systems but also by the fact that the Greek names of the letters, which mean nothing in Greek, are obviously taken from the Semitic names, which are meaningful in that language. *Alpha*, *beta*, *gamma*, and *delta* are clearly modifications of Semitic *aleph*, *beth*, *gimel*, and *daleth*, just as the Greek forms of these letters are clearly based on the corresponding Semitic characters. The Greeks, however, experienced difficulty in expressing the words of their language in written form without using characters for the vowels. Because the Greeks found that they did not need some of the Semitic symbols to express consonants, they used them to take on the value of vowels, and this modification constitutes the greatest contribution of the Greeks to the development of the alphabet. The Semitic *aleph* became the Greek vowel *alpha*, *he* became *epsilon* (short "e"), *cheth* became *eta* (long "e"), *yod* became *iota*, and *ayin* became *omicron* (short "o").

In Greece, the alphabet eventually developed two separate types: the East Greek and the West Greek, which differed in details. For example, the character that modern English uses for X had the sound "kh" in East Greek and "ks" in West Greek. Although the West Greek alphabet eventually died out in Greece, it was used extensively in the Greek colonies in southern Italy and Sicily. From one of these, possibly Cumae, it was borrowed by the Etruscans in about the eighth century B.C.E. Later the Romans also took over the West Greek alphabet, probably directly from the Etruscans, though some argue that the Romans adopted the alphabet independently from some Greek colony.

The Romans made slight changes in the Greek alphabet in adapting it to their own purposes. Certain Greek characters not needed by the Romans as letters were used as numerals. *Theta*, for instance, gives rise to the *C* used for "hundred," *psi* to the *L* used for "fifty," and *phi* both to the *M* used for "thousand" and the *D* (half of *phi*) used for "five hundred." The Latin alphabet, as the West Greek version came to be called, was spread by the Romans throughout the civilized world, so that apart from a few European countries that use the Greek or later-developed Cyrillic alphabet, the entire Western hemisphere has adopted and adapted it.

In its completed form, the Latin alphabet had twenty-three characters. An additional three characters were added in the Middle Ages, when "i" was split into the vocalic "i" and the consonantal "j," "v" was split into the vocalic "u" and the consonantal "v," and "u" was doubled to produce the new character "w." Mixing of the separate traditions has led to variations in spelling, because the Latins invariably corrupted the sound signified by "w" to be pronounced "gu." This accounts for the Anglo-Saxon word *werre*, "war," becoming French *guerre*, or the Old High German *Willihelm* turning up in French as *Guillaume* and in Spanish as *Guillermo*.

Whereas the German and Spanish languages have developed use of the alphabet phonetically, English has not; variations in spelling the same sound in different ways can be accounted for by trying to describe nearly one hundred sounds by twenty-six symbols, as well as by the preservation in modern spelling of archaic pronunciations that have converged over time. Various attempts have been made to introduce so-called universal phonetic alphabets (for instance, the efforts of the Frenchman Paul Passy and the International Phonetic Association in the late nineteenth century), but none has been successful. The difficulty is enhanced in the modern world by different developments in the Middle East. The Semitic alphabet gave rise to the Syriac, from which grew the Arabic alphabet used throughout the Islamic world.

The East Greek was also the parent of several alphabets, including the Coptic, which developed in Egypt in the fourth century C.E. and which incorporated some Egyptian characters. More important, however, in the ninth century, Cyril, the Greek missionary who Christianized the Slavs, invented the Russian or Cyrillic alphabet, based on the East Greek, adding some twelve new characters for Slavonic sounds unknown to the Greeks. In the New World, the Maya developed a glyphic alphabet that confounded linguists for centuries; other African, Asian, and American cultures also developed alphabetical writing systems that died along with the cultures that created them. However, in the twenty-first century, the Cyrillic alphabet is used in Russia, the Arabic is used in Islamic countries, and much of the rest of the world uses the Roman alphabet.

Significance

Alphabets are more efficient and flexible writing systems than glyphs, pictograms, or ideographs, in which each separate object or idea is represented by a different character, as in Chinese or Japanese. By streamlining the process by which information could be written down and preserved, the alphabet promoted the ever-increasing intellectual and technological advance of cultures that used it. The ability to read the texts of a long-vanished civilization also has allowed modern people to gain a greater understanding of their ancestors; cultures such as the Etruscan, whose alphabet has resisted translation, remain enigmatic and their lives can only be guessed at through the relatively subjective medium of interpretation of art and architecture.

—*Chauncey E. Finch*

Further Reading

Diringer, David. *The Alphabet*. Revised by Reinhold Regensburger. 3d ed. 2 vols. New York: Funk and Wagnalls, 1968. The first volume of this monumental work discusses the origins and development of a great number of different systems of writing, concluding with the story of the Greek and Latin alphabets. The second volume consists entirely of high-quality diagrams and photographs illustrating every kind of writing known to humankind, including both inscriptions and manuscripts.

Drucker, Johanna. *The Alphabetic Labyrinth: The Letters in History and Imagination*. New York: Thames and Hudson, 1995. Focuses on the mystical and spiritual power that people have attributed to the letters of the alphabet, regarding them as the key to decoding the meaning of the universe, from the Jewish Cabalists to medieval alchemists.

Man, John. *Alpha Beta: How Twenty-six Letters Shaped the Western World*. New York: John Wiley and Sons, 2001. A clear and succinct history of the Roman alphabet and its importance in the shaping of modern Western civilization.

Robinson, Andrew. *Lost Languages: The Enigma of the World's Undeciphered Scripts*. New York: McGraw-Hill, 2002. Describes the breakthough decipherment of alphabets such as the Minoan Linear B, Egyptian hieroglyphics, and Maya glyphs, as well as the enduring difficulty of breaking the codes of more enigmatic alphabets such as the Etruscan and Easter Island writing systems. Written for a general audience, this book explains complicated issues in clear prose. Includes both a bibliography of works cited and suggestions for further reading.

_______. *The Story of Writing*. New York: Thames and Hudson, 1995. An extremely well-illustrated history of writing systems. Includes step-by-step analyses of the ways in which each alphabet is used. Includes suggestions for further reading.

Sacks, David. *Language Visible: Unraveling the Mystery of the Alphabet from A to Z*. New York: Broadway Books, 2003. Twenty-six fact-filled "biographies" of the letters A through Z, each identifying the letter's particular significance for modern readers, tracing its development from ancient forms, and discussing its noteworthy role in literature and other media. Begins with the earliest known alphabetic inscriptions from about 1800 B.C.E. in Egypt and traces the history of the Roman alphabet from its beginnings in Phoenicia, Greece, and Rome through medieval Europe to the twenty-first century.

See also: c. 3100 B.C.E., Sumerians Invent Writing; c. 1600 B.C.E., Shang Dynasty Develops Writing and Bronzework; c. 1000 B.C.E., Greek Alphabet Is Developed; c. 105 C.E., Cai Lun Invents Paper.

Related articles in *Great Lives from History: The Ancient World*: Dido; Ulfias.

c. 1250-c. 700 B.C.E.
KARASUK CULTURE FLOURISHES ON EURASIAN STEPPES

The Karasuk, primarily a pastoralist culture of aggressive horsemen, were noted for their skill in bronze work and their early ironwork; several thousand of their burial sites have been preserved.

LOCALE: Middle Yenisey River Valley in southern Siberia

CATEGORY: Prehistory and ancient cultures

SUMMARY OF EVENT

The Karasuk culture of the Middle Yenisey River Valley was only a small part of a much broader cultural area affected by the Scythians (whose influence extended from the Danube River in the west, to the Black Sea and Aral Seas in the south, and to the Yenisey River region in the east). Karasuk and related cultures such as the Tagar who replaced them formed a bridge between the Bronze Age and the Iron Age in this region, although they are best known for their bronze work. Among others, they were famous for their horsemanship, many kurgans (burial sites), and jewelry and daggers that they left behind. Pottery, found at many of the burial sites, shows a close association with other cultural groups in central Asia (especially Kazakhstan).

Karasuk culture most likely developed as a blending of indigenous Yenisey cultures with the Andronovo culture (fifteenth-fourteenth centuries B.C.E.) that preceded it. The Andronovo culture is a broad term that covers a series of related cultural traits that were most likely connected to Indo-Iranian peoples and to the Scythians. Styles of bronze work, a preference for animal motifs in their art, and a linguistic connection to proto-Iranian language (as evidenced in place-names across central Siberia) link all these groups together. Thus, the Karasuk were not an isolated or unique group of people but instead were part and parcel of an extensive region of Eurasia connected by trade, burial styles, bronze work, a fascination with and love of horses, and, to some extent, petroglyphs (rock art). Their culture developed during a period of warming in Siberia that made it more habitable than it is today. Therefore, they settled for short periods of time during the several coldest months in homes that were partially subterranean. During the rest of the year, they moved with their horses, cattle, and sheep to find pasture in the hollows and valleys formed by the tributaries of the Middle Yenisey River. A rich collection of knives, daggers, horse bridles, bracelets, and rings found at their burial sites points to their skill in metallurgy. Another interesting aspect of Karasuk culture was their aggressive style of horsemanship. They may have been part of the early formation of "berserk warriors" across Eurasia, whose fierceness and lack of fear as they rode their horses while partially naked during battle made them feared far and wide.

The Karasuk culture probably drew to a close because of the combined effects of a changing climate and competition with other groups of people being displaced by the expansion of the Chinese and Persian civilizations. Maximum average temperatures and humidity occurred around 800 B.C.E. but rapidly cooled over the next several decades and caused a drying period throughout Siberia in general. At the same time, nomadic peoples who lived south and west of the Karasuk were pushed northward and eastward by the expansion of the Chinese and Persian civilizations. The result was the breaking up of some groups and a new blending of peoples and their cultures in the region through competition and new cooperation in order to survive. Thus, what followed was an unsettling period as the old pastoralism contracted and new ways of producing food had to be found. In this transition period, a Scythian people known as the Tagar moved in and supplanted the former cultures of the Yenisey River region.

SIGNIFICANCE

The significance of the Karasuk lies as much in what they left behind for modern archaeologists to study as in their impact on this region for many centuries to come. It is certain that they were one among many groups in the region making the transition from the Bronze Age to the Iron Age, with the changes in technology that this would entail. It is possible that, with other related groups, they made contact with late-Shang Dynasty Chinese and introduced some aspects of bronze work and other forms of metallurgy to them. Moreover, they were most likely part of a larger diffusion of militant horsemanship into the region, which would eventually influence the rise of Mongolian horse cultures that would in turn push into China and westward into Europe centuries later. However, what is most important are the artifacts they left in more than two thousand extant burial sites and their petroglyphs because they provide an invaluable source of information about life and culture at that time and place. These remains also reveal the linkages between different but related groups of people over broad areas (from Europe to the Middle East to India to Siberia) and over a long period of time (from the Neolithic Age through to the Iron Age).

—*Carolyn V. Prorok*

Further Reading

Christian, David. *Inner Eurasia from Prehistory to the Mongol Empire*. Vol. 1 in *History of Russia, Central Asia and Mongolia*. Oxford, England: Blackwell Publishers, 1998. An examination of Eurasia that covers the Karasuk and many other cultures.

Davis, Kimball J., V. Bashilov, and L. T. Yablonsky, eds. *Nomads of the Eurasian Steppes in the Early Iron Age*. Berkeley, Calif.: Zinat Press, 1995. A close look at the nomadic tribes that inhabited the steppes of Eurasia.

Dergachev, V. A. "Climatic Changes During the Holocene in the Eurasian Steppe of Southern Siberia (Miniusinsk and Uyuk Hollows) and the Development of Archaeological Cultures." *Geophysical Research Abstracts* 5 (2003). An examination of the climatic changes as they affected the cultures that lived in the area.

"Karasuk Culture." In *Encyclopedia of Indo-European Culture*, edited by J. P. Mallory and D. Q. Adams. London: Fitzroy Dearborn, 1997. A short overview of the Karasuk culture.

"Pastoral and Nomadic Tribes at the Beginning of the First Millennium B.C." In *The Dawn of Civilization*. Vol. 1 in *History of the Civilizations of Central Asia*, edited by A. H. Dani and V. M. Masson. Paris: UNESCO, 1992. Focuses on early pastoral and nomadic groups during part of the period that the Karasuk flourished.

See also: c. 6800-c. 4900 B.C.E., Kitoi People Live Near Lake Baikal in Siberia; c. 5000-c. 3000 B.C.E., Kelteminar Culture Flourishes in Central Asia; c. 4000 B.C.E., Horse Is Domesticated; 1750-800 B.C.E., Andronovo Culture Rises in Central Asia; 8th century B.C.E., Scythians Drive the Cimmerians from Central Asia; 209-174 B.C.E., Maodun Creates a Large Confederation in Central Asia.

c. 1200-c. 1050 B.C.E.
Sea Peoples Contribute to Mediterranean Upheaval

The Sea Peoples appeared in the eastern Mediterranean amid massive changes in trade and political structures.

Locale: Eastern Mediterranean, from mainland Greece to Egypt
Category: Prehistory and ancient cultures

Summary of Event

Among the most significant events in human history is the emergence of the Sea Peoples in the twelfth century B.C.E. During this era, palace culture collapsed, causing comparative economic hardship throughout the Mycenaean world; the Hittite kingdom disappeared overnight; and a number of city-states in Syro-Palestine were destroyed or depopulated. The empire of the Egyptian New Kingdom also waned at this juncture. The political vacuum created by the collapse of the empires enabled small states, such as Israel and Damascus, to emerge and to play significant roles in the trade and politics of the region. Precisely what role these divergent groups played in these events has become a question of debate.

The Sea Peoples were not a monolithic group but a collection of raiders from various locales. In surviving texts, these groups are mentioned as appearing on occasion as raiders or mercenaries. In some Egyptian texts, for example, the following geographic or ethnic names were assigned to them by scholars (not all of these associations are agreed on by all modern scholars): the Tjekker, Sherdani (Shardana; Sardinia), Lukka (Lycia in Anatolia), Shklsh (also Shekelesh), Trsh (also Teresh; the Tyrsenoi, whom Herodotus asserted migrated from Lydia in Anatolia to Eturia in Italy), 'qwsh (also Ekwesh; Achaeans), Sikila (Sicily), Danuna (either Cilicia in Anatolia or the Greek mainland), Wshsh, and Peleshet (also Peleset; the Philistines, whom the Hebrew Bible asserts came from Crete; some scholars argue for an Anatolian origin). The notion of restless marauders wreaking havoc in the wake of the Trojan War is no longer in vogue among scholars.

The collapse of palace states and economies in Greece and the Aegean at this time is associated with the Sea Peoples, as some sites show signs of destruction and others were abandoned. The variety of material goods attested in the cities was reduced (especially in terms of import goods), which may in turn reflect that social stratification was lessened. Whether the Sea Peoples were the catalyst for these events across the region or were the product of the effect of this collapse is debated; some material culture antecedents preceded their arrival. Cyprus serves as an example, as its economic collapse was the result of warfare. The changing material culture of the island is most likely attributable to these invaders as well. As in the rest of the Aegean, trade resumed on a lesser scale.

The collapse of the Hittite Empire may have been the result of Anatolian Sea Peoples ousting overlords. The Sea Peoples allied themselves with local ethnic groups in the course of their obliteration of the Hittites. Economic collapse in the region closely followed political collapse.

An Ugaritic text refers to the Sikila, who lived in ships, as being the aggressor against the city of Ugarit (near coast of modern-day Syria), ultimately destroying it in perpetuity. Other cities on the Syrian coast were destroyed and others abandoned. Trade was disrupted there as it had been in the Aegean world. Contrary to what occurred in the Aegean world, however, the Syrian sites were not repopulated by the Sea Peoples.

The presence of the Sea Peoples in Palestine (the Roman name for Philistia) at this time is attested in both the Hebrew Bible and Egyptian sources. The Egyptian pharaoh Ramses III proclaimed his victory over the Sea Peoples in a papyrus. The text also describes his subsequent settling of their numerous warriors in the coastal regions of Palestine, with support of the royal treasury. These groups were settled as mercenaries to support the Egyptian administration. The Hebrew Bible indicates that early Israelite society was under either a political or an economic overlordship of these peoples, precipitating the crisis that produced the emergence of the Israelite state. Philistine dominance waned by the second half of the eleventh century B.C.E. Archaeological evidence reveals Philistine cities that were well planned with regard to both defense and economic production. The Philistines engaged in farming as well as metalworking and raiding.

Two battle scenes between the Egyptians and coalitions of Sea Peoples are illustrated on wall reliefs in a temple of Ramses III. These show warriors, in ships or captured, wearing decidedly Aegean dress. One relief depicts a scene with ox carts and civilians near the battle. Traditionally, it has been interpreted to show that there was an intent to settle Egypt after ousting the pharaonic forces, as the Egyptians fought a life-and-death struggle to repel the invaders. However, the context of the text accompanying the relief suggests instead a procession of refugees from Sea People cities in Palestine destroyed by the Egyptians. The Egyptian presence in Palestine ends in the coastal plain with the advent of the Philistines, as its empire recedes. Whether one holds that the Philistines were the product or the cause of all this economic and political chaos, clearly their presence greatly exacerbated the process.

SIGNIFICANCE

The most obvious lasting impact of these events is that the power vacuum created by the actions of the Sea Peoples provided the opportunity for Israel to become a significant state during Iron Age I. The threat of the Philistine presence forced the Israelites to develop a full-fledged state, abandoning their tribal structure. The impact of Israel on Western civilization and world history cannot be overstated.

—Mark Anthony Phelps

FURTHER READING

Dothan, Trude. *The Philistines and Their Material Culture*. New Haven, Conn.: Yale University Press, 1982. This is still the definitive work on the Philistines.

Dothan, Trude, and Moshe Dothan. *People of the Sea*. New York: Macmillan, 1992. The Dothans produce an extremely readable account of their uncovering of Philistine and other Sea People material culture.

Drews, Robert. "Medinet Habu: Oxcarts, Ships, and Migration Theories." *Journal of Near Eastern Studies* 59 (2000): 161-190. An excellent critical essay questioning a number of assumptions by the traditional scholarly consensus concerning the significance of the artwork and texts from Medinet Habu.

Sanders, N. K. *The Sea Peoples: Warriors of the Mediterranean*. London: Thames and Hudson, 1985. Presents the traditional understanding of the impact of the advent of the Sea Peoples in the eastern Mediterranean.

Ward, William, and Martha Sharp Joukowsky, eds. *The Crisis Years: The Twelfth Century B.C. from Beyond the Danube to the Tigris*. Dubuque, Iowa: Kendall/Hunt, 1992. A collection of twenty-three essays by leading scholars that explore the phenomenon of the Sea Peoples from a number of areas, including Europe, Anatolia, Syria-Palestine, Israel, and Mesopotamia.

SEE ALSO: 1650-1620 B.C.E., Hattusilis I Establishes the Old Hittite Kingdom; c. 1600-c. 1000 B.C.E., City of Mycenae Flourishes; c. 1570 B.C.E., New Kingdom Period Begins in Egypt; c. 1450 B.C.E., International Age of Major Kingdoms Begins in the Near East; c. 1000 B.C.E., Establishment of the United Kingdom of Israel.

RELATED ARTICLE in *Great Lives From History: The Ancient World*: Dido.

c. 1200-c. 1000 B.C.E.
BERBERS EXPAND ACROSS NORTH AFRICA

Berber tribes inhabiting the Sahara Desert mounted large-scale invasions of the Nile Valley; although successful Egyptian campaigns drove them back, large numbers of Berber captives became Egyptianized.

LOCALE: Libyan Desert and northern Nile Valley
CATEGORIES: Expansion and land acquisition; government and politics; wars

KEY FIGURES

Merenptah (early to mid-thirteenth century-c. 1203 B.C.E.), Egyptian pharaoh, r. c. 1213-1203 B.C.E.
Merey (fl. thirteenth century B.C.E.), chief of the Libyans during the reign of Merenptah
Ramses III (fl. twelfth century B.C.E.), Egyptian pharaoh, r. 1184-1153 B.C.E.
Meshesher (fl. twelfth century B.C.E.), chief of the Libyans during the reign of Ramses III

SUMMARY OF EVENT

Although Libyan tribes west of Egypt are known from predynastic times, the first concrete evidence of their Berber identity is the appearance of the Berber word for "hound" on the stela of Intef II (r. c. 2112-2063 B.C.E.). The first detailed evidence for the Berber tribes comes from the Nineteenth and Twentieth Dynasties (1295-c. 1069 B.C.E.) in Egypt, when the Libyans became a larger military threat than ever before.

Depictions and brief textual annotations from the reigns of Seti I (r. c. 1294-1279 B.C.E.) and Ramses II (r. 1279-1213 B.C.E.) record Egyptian battles with the Libyan groups but are unclear as to whether these battles were the result of Libyan incursions into the Nile Valley or Egyptian raids into Libyan territory. A chain of fortresses built by Ramses II near the Mediterranean coast west of Egypt also provides archaeological evidence for the growing Libyan threat.

The relationship between Egypt and its western neighbors changed dramatically during the reign of Merenptah (r. c. 1213-1203). Several historical inscriptions dating to the fifth year of his reign (c. 1208 B.C.E.) attest to a massive invasion of Egypt by Berber tribes and their Sea People mercenary allies. According to the Great Karnak Inscription of Merenptah, the longest and most detailed account of the battle, Merey, the chief of the Libyans and son of Dedy, led the invasion of Egypt because of a famine in Libya. Merey was accompanied by native Libyan troops and numerous Sea People groups, including the Ekwesh, Lukka, Teresh, Sherden, and Shekelesh. Although dispute remains about their precise origins, the Sea Peoples appear to have been raiders and pirates from the regions around the northern Mediterranean who fought as armored infantry. Around 1100 B.C.E., the Sea Peoples sacked and pillaged most of the major cities of the Eastern Mediterranean basin and were a major contributing factor to the end of the Bronze Age.

The fortresses constructed by Ramses II forced Merey to avoid the Mediterranean coast and lead his combined Libyan and Sea People army along the roads connecting the large oases in the Western Desert of Egypt. After capturing an unspecified oasis (most likely Siwa Oasis), Merey's troops proceeded to Farafra Oasis, the centrally located and westernmost of the five major oases in the desert west of Egypt. Control of Farafra and access to all the desert routes leading from it enabled Merey to keep the Egyptians uncertain of his final approach into the Nile Valley. The Libyan chief also used the desert routes to form an alliance with Nubian tribes, who created an almost simultaneous diversionary attack in the south.

As the Nubians went into battle against Egypt's southern armies, Merey committed to an attack on the Nile Delta. As evidence from the Great Karnak Inscription indicates, Merey's forces probably traveled from Farafra to Baharīya and then to Fayum, crossing the Nile south of Memphis. Although the vanguard of the Libyan army camped in the eastern Delta, Merey seems to have concentrated his forces around the area around Memphis. In response to this enormous threat, Merenptah marshaled his troops at a place called Perire in the eastern Delta (its exact location is unknown) in about 1208 B.C.E. A six-hour battle ensued and ended in an overwhelming defeat of the Sea Peoples and Libyans. Merey escaped and fled back to Libya, but Egyptian documents suggest that he was later killed by his own tribesmen. Although the tactics of the battle are not explicitly described in any ancient source, Merenptah's texts stress the role of the archers in the Egyptian victory. Merenptah apparently deployed his archers on the wings of his main infantry, preventing the Libyans and their heavily armored mercenaries from engaging in close combat with the lightly armed Egyptians.

Despite Merenptah's defeat of the Libyan armies and their allies, Egyptian documents report that during the civil war at the end of the Nineteenth Dynasty in Egypt, the Berber tribes were successful in penetrating into the western Delta. A coalition of Libyan tribes led by their chief Meshesher also mounted a major invasion in the fifth year of Ramses III (r. 1184-1153) in 1179 B.C.E., only twenty-nine years after the Battle of Perire; in Ramses III's eleventh regnal year, the Meshwesh Libyan tribe led yet another attack on the Nile Valley. Because the mortuary temple of Ramses III on the west bank of Thebes at Medinet Habu is extremely well preserved, the two Libyan invasions (Year 5 and Year 11) are known from large-scale relief depictions in addition to extensive historical texts. As during Merenptah's reign, the desire for land in the fertile Nile Delta drove the Libyan invasions under Ramses III. Although Ramses III's texts do not describe the specific battles of his Libyan wars, the Year 5 text relates Ramses's attempt to establish an Egyptianized Libyan boy as the leader of the Libyan tribes. This practice of educating foreign princes in Egypt to gain influence over other kingdoms is well attested earlier during Eighteenth Dynasty (c. 1570-1295 B.C.E.) relations with Syria-Palestine but seems never to have been applied to Libya. Unfortunately, it is not clear whether the attempt to establish an Egyptianized Libyan ruler caused the Year 5 invasion or whether the action was an attempt to prevent a seemingly inevitable invasion.

The impetus for the Year 11 invasion under Ramses III is similarly obscure, but the texts at Medinet Habu seem to imply that the Meshwesh were now at the head of a Libyan coalition and that they were intent on seizing Egyptian territory. The superiority of the Meshwesh among the Libyan groups was perhaps because of their possession of long swords, much like the swords of the Sea Peoples (from whom they probably acquired the technology). The reliefs at Medinet Habu vividly depict the sword-bearing Meshwesh infantry, but the Libyans are not shown with body armor, so again Egyptian archers probably played a crucial role in the battles.

In addition to providing information about the armaments of the Libyans during the invasions under Ramses III, the reliefs at Medinet Habu contain some of the only preclassical evidence for Libyan dress and culture. The Libyans are predominantly shown with long, open leather cloaks, often painted with colored designs. Underneath the cloaks, Libyan warriors wore either a short kilt or elaborate penis-sheath. In well-preserved painted depictions, the Libyans are shown with tattoos. The plunder lists of Merenptah and Ramses indicate that some of the Libyan tribes possessed horses and chariots. Painted rock depictions from the region of Tassili n'Ajjer in the southwestern corner of Libya also reveal details of Libyan dress and chariot culture roughly contemporaneous with late New Kingdom Egypt. Finally, the nomadic nature of Libyan society at this time can be deduced from the huge numbers of cattle, sheep, and goats captured from the Libyans after their unsuccessful invasions.

SIGNIFICANCE

The Berber invasions of Egypt from 1200-1000 B.C.E. had a significant impact on later periods of Egyptian history. Ramses III settled the Libyan captives from the Year 5 and 11 invasions in Egyptian territory to be used as mercenaries. The thousands of Libyans settled by Ramses III, in addition to the other successful infiltrations, led directly into the Third Intermediate Period (1069-664 B.C.E.), when Libyan kinglets in the Delta fought for control of all of Egypt and even became Egyptian pharaohs with all the traditional iconography.

—*Colleen Manassa*

FURTHER READING

Bates, Oric. *The Eastern Libyans: An Essay.* London: Macmillan, 1914. The only comprehensive treatment of all aspects of ancient Berber society using Egyptian and classical sources, Bates's work remains important.

Brett, M., and E. Fentress. *The Berbers*. Oxford, England: Blackwell, 1996. A general overview of Berber culture, with illustrations of Saharan rock art.

Drews, Robert. *The End of the Bronze Age: Changes in Warfare and the Catastrophe ca. 1200 B.C.* Princeton, N.J.: Princeton University Press, 1993. Covers Sea Peoples, their origins, and military technology.

Leahy, Anthony, ed. *Libya and Egypt, c. 1300-750 B.C.* London: Center of Near and Middle Eastern Studies, 1990. Relevant articles by Donald Redford and Kenneth Kitchen on Libyan society and the history of the invasions.

Manassa, Colleen. *The Great Karnak Inscription of Merneptah: Grand Strategy in the Thirteenth Century B.C.* New Haven, Conn.: Yale Egyptological Seminar, 2003. Translation and commentary on the Great Karnak Inscription, with military analysis.

Peden, A. J. *Egyptian Historical Inscriptions of the Twentieth Dynasty.* Stockholm: Paul Aströms Förlag, 1994. Translations of inscriptions from Medinet Habu.

SEE ALSO: c. 2300-c. 2000 B.C.E., First Great Expansion of Berber Peoples Across North Africa; c. 1570 B.C.E., New Kingdom Period Begins in Egypt; c. 1450 B.C.E., International Age of Major Kingdoms Begins in the Near East; c. 1200-c. 1050 B.C.E., Sea Peoples Contribute to Mediterranean Upheaval; 1069 B.C.E., Third Intermediate Period Begins in Egypt.

RELATED ARTICLE in *Great Lives from History: The Ancient World*: Masinissa.

c. 1100 B.C.E.
ARAMEANS EMERGE IN SYRIA AND MESOPOTAMIA

Aramean groups settled regions throughout Syria-Palestine and Mesopotamia in the wake of the political vacuum of the twelfth century B.C.E.

LOCALE: Syria, Mesopotamia (now Iraq), and Palestine
CATEGORY: Prehistory and ancient cultures

SUMMARY OF EVENT

The great political vacuum created by the chaotic close of the Late Bronze Age (c. 1200 B.C.E.) in Syria-Palestine allowed smaller states to emerge into the fore of ancient Near Eastern political and economic life. The Arameans were one such group widely attested during this period.

The origin of the Arameans is a topic of debate among scholars. Some scholars view these groups as pastoralists from the fringes of the Syrian Desert who infiltrated the region, initially in Upper Mesopotamia (northern present-day Syria and Iraq), and later swept southwest into Syria and southeast into southern Mesopotamia. One model holds that pastoralists were especially equipped to survive the economic upheavals of the end of the Late Bronze Age. This view holds that the exchanges made by pastoralists were not dependent on the palace economy of the region but on small-scale production that did not wane. This model holds that when the urban centers were depopulated, these pastoralists were the economic successors to the urban elite.

Other scholars prefer to view these groups as descendants from long-attested West Semitic groups based primarily in Syria, the same groups that produced the Amorite kingdoms, including Hammurabi's Babylonian kingdom, in the second millennium B.C.E. These groups reemerged after the collapse of Hurrians and the Hittites at the end of the Late Bronze Age.

It is not clear what relationship these groups had with one another. The Arameans were not a single ethnic entity. Aside from their language, there is little cultural continuity among these groups. What material culture has been found is clearly influenced strongly by Phoenician or neo-Hittite forms. Scholars are hard-pressed to identify Aramean remains, apart from association with inscriptions.

The first attestation to Arameans is found in the late twelfth century B.C.E. in the annals of the Assyrian king Tiglath-pileser I (r. c. 1115-1077 B.C.E.) as he faced an Aramean enemy west of the Euphrates. Arameans lived on the fringes of the Assyrian state and were the constant object of military attention. After a century-long dark age, the Arameans had penetrated and settled in Assyria and Babylonia, and they were constantly engaged militarily with the Assyrian armies. Eventually (by the end of the eighth century B.C.E.), most of the Aramaic-speaking world, from Syria to Babylonia, was under the control of the Assyrian Empire.

The eleventh century B.C.E. kings of united Israel encountered Aramean peoples, generally appearing in the Hebrew Bible in the context of armed conflict. Aramaic inscriptions became common in the ninth century B.C.E. and thus shed little light on the Arameans' period of entry into the land. There may be two Egyptian references to Arameans before 1100 B.C.E. and perhaps an Ugaritic reference before 1200 B.C.E., but all three are at best suspect identifications. The presence of Aramean states occurred in the political vacuum of the events following the advent of the Sea Peoples and the collapse of the major political powers in Syria-Palestine at the beginning of the Iron Age.

The Aramean states that emerged were separate tribal entities, often known by their patronyms. The political structures of the states evolved into monarchies. The bulk of the population was pastoral or agricultural, as indicated by Assyrian booty lists, which normally consist of agricultural products. Political unity never occurred, as there was never anything resembling a single state or empire of the Aramean world. Shifting alliances instead governed political relations, reflected in a number of ninth and eighth century B.C.E. accounts (usually involving Damascus) in the Hebrew Bible.

Little is known about the religion of the Arameans. Religion, like every other aspect of Aramean culture, has been the victim of a comparative lack of interest among former generations of archaeologists. Aside from oaths in treaties and occasional mentions in cuneiform sources or in the Hebrew Bible, little written evidence regarding religion is preserved from this (or for that matter, any other) period.

SIGNIFICANCE

The most significant contribution of the Arameans was doubtless their language, which became the *lingua franca* of successive empires for more than one thousand years. The Assyrians, Babylonians, and Persians all used the language for official correspondence. The spoken language was dominant in the region from the seventh century B.C.E. until after the advent of the Islamic caliphate, which began in the seventh century C.E. The legacy of the literature of these peoples is not limited to what these individual city-states produced. Rather, through the media of Jewish and Christian religious writings, an enormous corpus of writing exists in a number of dialects of Aramaic.

The presence of the Arameans in the region influenced the theology of the Hebrew Bible. The ancient Israelites perceived a kinship with all Semitic peoples, especially the Arameans (see Genesis 10:22). Abraham is called "a wandering Aramean" (Deuteronomy 26:5), a reference, perhaps anachronistically, to kin-group ties in the region of Padam-Aram (Genesis 25:20 and 31:20; compare 22:21). The veracity of this claim is the subject of debate. A distant common cultural milieu is theoretically possible, though one distant enough to precede the emergence of Hebrew and Aramaic begs the question of the cultural influence of these peoples on later Israelite society.

—*Mark Anthony Phelps*

FURTHER READING

Dion, Paul. "Aramean Tribes and Nations of the First-Millennium Western Asia." In *Civilizations of the Ancient Near East*, edited by Jack Sasson. New York: Scribner, 1995. Excellent brief summary of the topic.

Greenfield, Jonas. "Aspects of Aramean Religion." In *Ancient Israelite Religion: Essays in Honor of Frank Moore Cross*, edited by Paul Hanson, S. Dean McBride, and Patrick Miller. Philadelphia: Fortress, 1987. A magisterial work on a neglected topic.

Hawkins, J. D. "The Neo-Hittite States in Syria and Anatolia." In *The Cambridge Ancient History.* Vol. 31. New York: Cambridge University Press, 1982. A meticulous essay on the material culture and history of Iron Age Syria.

Pitard, Wayne. *Ancient Damascus: A Historical Study of the Syrian City-State from Earliest Times Until Its Fall to the Assyrians in 732 B.C.E.* Winona Lake, Ind.: Eisenbrauns, 1987. Focuses on the best-documented city-state of the Arameans, with a methodology that is fitting to apply to all other sites.

_______. "The Arameans." In *Peoples of the Old Testament World*, edited by Alfred J. Hoerth, Gerald Mattingly, and Edwin Yamauchi. Grand Rapids, Mich.: Baker Books, 1994. A good general introduction to Aramean history and culture.

SEE ALSO: c. 1450 B.C.E., International Age of Major Kingdoms Begins in the Near East; c. 1200-c. 1050 B.C.E., Sea Peoples Contribute to Mediterranean Upheaval; c. 1000 B.C.E., Establishment of the United Kingdom of Israel; c. 922 B.C.E., Establishment of the Kingdom of Israel; c. 883-c. 824 B.C.E., Second Assyrian Empire Displays Military Prowess.

RELATED ARTICLE in *Great Lives from History: The Ancient World*: Abraham.

c. 1100-c. 500 B.C.E.

HALLSTATT CULTURE DOMINATES NORTHERN EUROPE

The Hallstatt culture ushered in the European Iron Age, setting the pattern of urban civilization in northern Europe for the next two thousand years.

LOCALE: Northern Europe, particularly the Bavarian and Austrian Alps

CATEGORIES: Prehistory and ancient cultures; science and technology

SUMMARY OF EVENT

In the early 1800's, Europeans were experiencing a revolution in thinking about the past. The world was then believed to be only a few thousand years old; however, discoveries of the bones of extinct animals along with stone tools led people to consider a world that was vastly older. In 1836, Danish archaeologist Christian Jürgensen Thomsen wrote a guidebook to the Danish National Museum in Copenhagen that divided the past into a succession of ages: Stone Age, Bronze Age, and Iron Age. This three-age system has continued to serve as a fundamental framework for prehistoric studies.

In 1824, Austrian K. P. Pollhammer uncovered an ancient tomb outside the small Austrian town of Hallstatt. Located by a lake in a picturesque Alpine valley some 30 miles (50 kilometers) southeast of the city of Salzburg, the community had been important for centuries as a source of salt. The tomb itself came from above the valley on the slope of a mountain named Salzberg, literally "salt mountain."

George Ramsauer, the manager of the local salt mines in 1846, followed up on Pollhammer's discovery. On the same slope, Ramsauer located a vast cemetery that covered nearly 100,000 square feet (more than 9,000 square meters). He conducted excavations there until 1863, uncovering nearly one thousand graves. Ramsauer's meticulous drawings recorded nearly twenty thousand items, including pottery, bronze vessels of Greek and local origins, jewelry of gold and Baltic amber, and many weapons of an unexpected material, iron.

More than one thousand additional graves have been discovered near Hallstatt since 1863. These graves have been shown to fall into two major periods: Hallstatt A and B, covering the time of the Late Bronze Age Urnfield culture (1300-800 B.C.E.), and Hallstatt C and D, covering the early Iron Age (800-500 B.C.E.). It is to this latter phase that Hallstatt gives its name—the First Iron Age of northern Europe.

The Urnfield peoples helped to spread bronze working throughout Europe. They were named for their custom of cremating bodies and placing the ashes in urns for burial. Ramsauer excavated many such burials at Hallstatt, and it seems clear that the Hallstatt culture evolved from Urnfield roots.

There were changes, however, which produced a culture now believed to be that of the early Celts. The advent of ironworking was accompanied by the custom of inhumation (burial of the entire body) instead of cremation. Groups of people began building and using large hill forts, and chiefs were buried with costly grave goods, including four-wheeled carts, indicating that strong social differentiation was emerging, based on an energetic trade.

Mountain ranges, such as the Cévennes of France and the Maritime Alps between southern France and Italy, created a formidable barrier between temperate Europe and the Mediterranean world. The classic Hallstatt heartland developed where passes and rivers made access to trade routes possible. From the area of the Black Forest, headwaters of the Rhine River flow all the way to the North Sea, those of the Danube reach the Black Sea, and the Rhône joins the Saône on its way to the Mediterranean. Alpine passes, such as the Brenner Pass, connect Austria with Italy. Mediterranean wine, oil, bronzes, jewelry, and ironworking skills moved north, paid for with tin, copper, hides, textiles, amber, salt, and salt-cured fish and pork.

From Spain to Hungary, hill forts and settlements arose along these trade routes, evolving into industrial and commercial centers. Indeed, it has been suggested that so-called Celtic culture evolved not in conjunction with an anthropologically definable tribe united by blood but as a linguistically defined group united by a language spread by trade. Desirable objects were more easy to obtain when the buyer and seller spoke the same language, and the trade in these objects—particularly metalwork—inspired an expanding number of peoples to adopt the material culture that was fostered by the shared trading language.

In eastern France, the Hallstatt D hill fort on Mount Lassois dominated the headwaters of the Seine River. In an associated barrow located in the nearby village of Vix in 1953, archaeologist René Joffroy discovered the spectacular tomb of a Celtic princess. Beneath the mound, in a wooden chamber, she had been buried on a dismantled wagon, its wheels lined along one wall. She bore a golden crown, its ends terminating in winged horses. Her grave goods included jewelry of bronze and amber, a Greek

Black Figure pot, and silver and bronze vessels. Dominating the chamber was a huge bronze jar, or krater, with a broad body, a wide neck, and two handles. A magnificent specimen of Greek manufacture, the jar stood 5 feet (1.5 meters) tall, measured 13 feet (4 meters) in circumference, and weighed 460 pounds (210 kilograms). The jar's decorated rim features a frieze showing a Greek charioteer, four horses, and hoplite infantrymen.

Iron continued to be relatively rare during the Hallstatt period, but its impact was evident in materials excavated from the Hohmichele barrow, located near the Heuneburg hill fortress overlooking the Danube River in southern Germany. Forty feet (12 meters) in height, the barrow contained thirteen burials. Two were wagon burials, one containing a man and a woman, the other containing a solitary woman. Although the chambers had been looted by grave robbers, intriguing traces of their richness remained, including the earliest known appearance of silk cloth in Europe. Iron arrowheads were found along with an archer's bow measuring 6 feet (nearly 2 meters) in length. Scholars were particularly interested in the planks used to construct the main chamber. Twenty

HALLSTATT AND LA TÈNE SITES

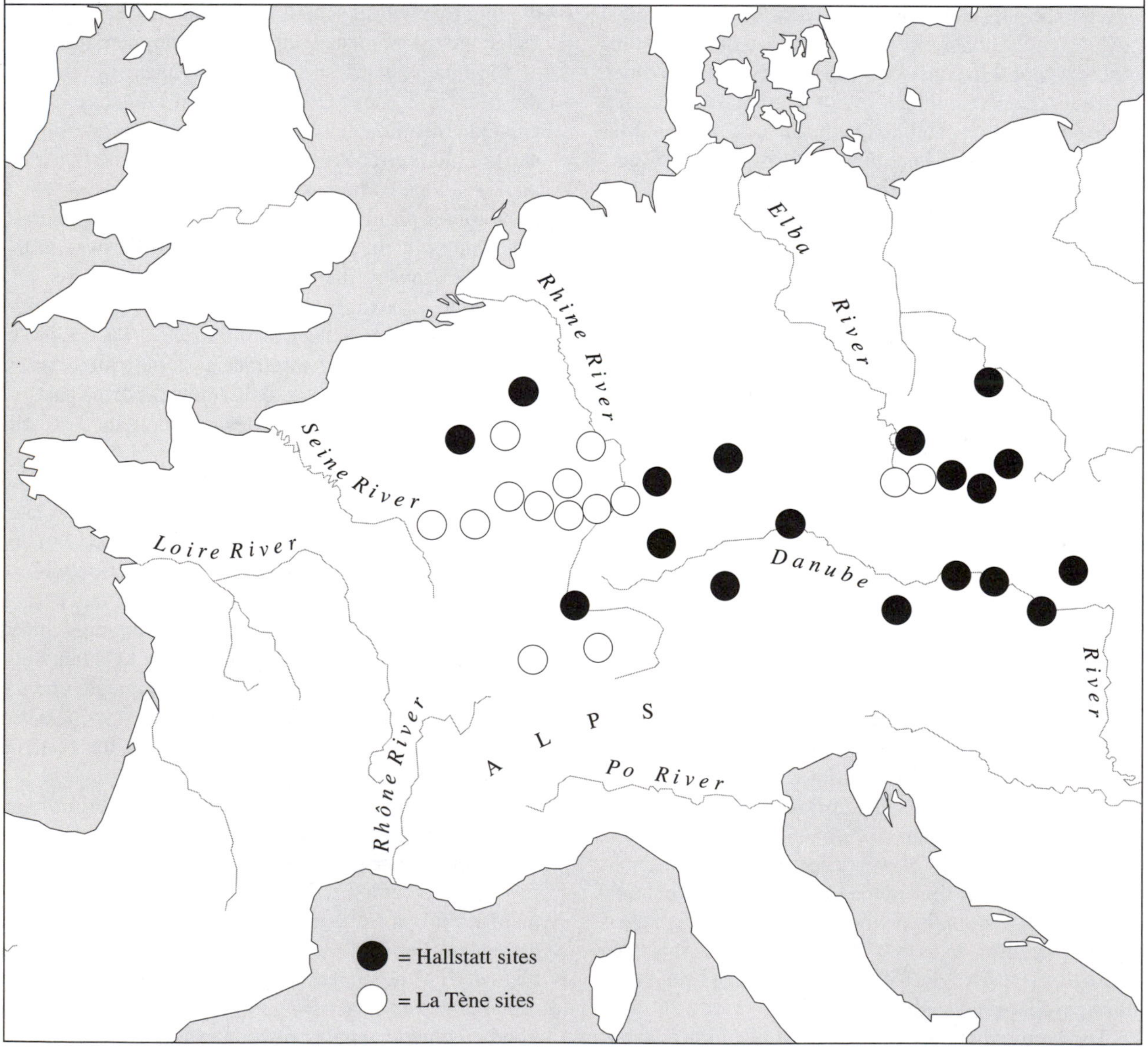

feet (6 meters) long, these planks apparently were sawn from logs with a two-man iron saw. Saws, adzes, and other tools of iron were transforming woodworking and other industrial activities.

Excavation of another wagon burial in 1978 at Hochdorf, Germany, uncovered other uses of the metal. The wagon itself was plated with sheets of iron. The grave's burial offerings included an iron drinking horn measuring more than 3 feet (90 centimeters) in length.

Early Celtic art of the Hallstatt period shows a concern with nature. Human beings are also portrayed, but they are rather rigid or patterned almost abstractly, using triangles and circles. Fine pottery shows bold geometric incising of lozenges and circles. Animals, especially birds, are shown more realistically. One common design is the "Hallstatt duck" motif, usually associated with concentric circles.

SIGNIFICANCE

The First and Second Iron Ages of Europe—the Hallstatt culture and the La Tène culture that began in about 500 B.C.E. and lasted through Roman times—laid the social and economic foundation of northern European civilization. The La Tène culture, named for a site on Lake Neuchâtel in Switzerland, clearly evolved out of the Hallstatt culture. Conical helmets and oval shields found at sites from both periods were identical. "Hallstatt duck" and "solar" symbols continued. Wagon burials of chieftains also continued, although in two-wheeled chariots at La Tène sites. High status for women continued to be reflected in the richness of many of their burials.

In addition to continuing many of the Hallstatt traditions, the La Tène culture introduced some new practices. At places such as Manching in southern Germany, the hill forts evolved into true urban centers, known as *oppida*, where there were industries in copper, iron, glass, amber, pottery, and textiles, as well as important ritual centers. Even coins were minted there. Objects began to exhibit art styles that represented a true Celtic art and culture. The difference in standards of living between the elite and the common folk became even more pronounced, and although the Hallstatt culture introduced significant advances in the technology of weapon making, it was the La Tène culture that created the stereotype of the Celtic warrior who fought naked in a battle frenzy. It was this aggressive La Tène Celtic culture which, probably for reasons of population pressure, began to raid throughout the Mediterranean world in the fourth century B.C.E., striking fear into the Romans to such an extent that they developed their highly efficient and regimented military to prevent the city of Rome ever again being sacked, as the Celts had done in 390 B.C.E.

Although the various Celtic peoples did not constitute a single united empire, they are jointly credited with an industrial revolution that produced horseshoes, iron-rimmed wheels, standardized tools, soap, the rotary flour mill, a harvester on wheels, and an iron plow that could open the heavier and more fertile soils for cultivation. They established courts, created a common market, and accorded rights to women. These developments, built on the Hallstatt culture, are reflected in many later northern and central European civilizations.

—Gary A. Olson

FURTHER READING

Audoze, Françoise, and Olivier Buchsenschutz. *Towns, Villages, and Countryside of Celtic Europe: From the Beginning of the Second Millennium to the End of the First Century B.C.* Translated by Henry Cleere. Bloomington: Indiana University Press, 1992. A comprehensive survey of the archaeological remains of Celtic Europe. Rather academic, but contains a depth of information that is rarely found elsewhere.

Cunliffe, Barry. *The Ancient Celts*. New York: Oxford University Press, 1997. A responsible, middle-of-the-road presentation of a topic that has become increasingly acrimonious since 1990. Cunliffe surveys the whole spectrum of Celtic civilization throughout Europe, from the Urnfield culture through modern Ireland, Wales, and Scotland. Well illustrated, with many very helpful maps.

________. "Iron Age Societies in Western Europe and Beyond, 800-140 B.C.E." In *The Oxford Illustrated Prehistory of Europe*. New York: Oxford University Press, 1994. A comprehensive overview focusing on the relationship between Iron Age society and the environment.

Hodson, Frank Roy. *Hallstatt: Dry Bones and Flesh*. New York: Oxford University Press, 1986. An examination of excavations and findings from the Hallstatt site in Austria. Bibliography.

James, Simon. *The World of the Celts*. New York: Thames and Hudson, 1993. An overview written by an archaeologist, intended to update and supplement T. G. E. Powell's classic 1958 work of the same title.

Moscati, Sabatino, et al., eds. *The Celts*. New York: Rizzoli, 2000. Originally the catalog of the massive *I Celti* exhibit held in Venice in 1991, this volume, at over 700 pages, offers the best representation of Celtic material culture anywhere. Essays written by top scholars cover all aspects of Celtic life and culture, touching on areas (especially in Eastern Europe) and objects often overlooked.

Rankin, David. *The Celts and the Classical World*. Reprint. New York: Routledge, 1996. A succinct overview of the relationship between the northern European Celts and the Mediterranean Roman and Greek cultures, offering useful insight into the biases of the Classical writers that shaped their descriptions of Celtic life and culture. Much more in-depth than most coverage of this material in general "Celtic world" surveys.

SEE ALSO: 14th-9th centuries B.C.E., Urnfield Culture Flourishes in Northwestern Europe; c. 100 B.C.E.-c. 100 C.E., Celtic Hill Forts Are Replaced by *Oppida*; c. 60 B.C.E., Druidism Flourishes in Gaul and Britain; 58-51 B.C.E., Caesar Conquers Gaul; 43-130 C.E., Roman Conquest of Britain; c. 450 C.E., Conversion of Ireland to Christianity.

1069 B.C.E.
THIRD INTERMEDIATE PERIOD BEGINS IN EGYPT

Political disunity after the New Kingdom left Egypt open to invasion, and the country was successively ruled from Nubia, Assyria, and Persia, until finally conquered by Alexander the Great.

LOCALE: Egypt and Nubia
CATEGORIES: Government and politics; wars, uprisings, and civil unrest

KEY FIGURES

Psusennes I (fl. eleventh-tenth centuries B.C.E.), Egyptian king, r. 1045-c. 991 B.C.E.
Piye (Piankhi, c. 769-716 B.C.E.), Kushite king, r. 742-716 B.C.E.
Psamtik I (c. 684-610 B.C.E.), Egyptian king, r. 664-610 B.C.E.
Darius the Great (550-486 B.C.E.), third king of Persia, r. 522-486 B.C.E., expanded the Persian empire
Nectanebo II (fl. fourth century B.C.E.), Egyptian king, r. 360-343 B.C.E.

SUMMARY OF EVENT

The Third Intermediate Period (1069-c. 332 B.C.E., which is sometimes broken into the Third Intermediate Period, 1069-644, and the Late Period, 644-c. 332) covers the time between the end of the powerful and centralized New Kingdom government and the conquest of Egypt by Alexander the Great in 332 B.C.E. Already by the end of the Twentieth Dynasty (1186-1069), Upper Egypt was effectively ruled by a family of High Priests of Amen, a family whose power continued unabated into the Twenty-first Dynasty (1069-945), whose nominal kings ruled from the Nile Delta. There was extensive intermarriage between the two families, and the Twenty-first Dynasty king Psusennes I was the grandson of Ramses XI and the son of Pinedjem, one of the High Priests of Amen.

The kings of the Twenty-first Dynasty were buried at their Delta capital of Tanis. The tomb of Psusennes I, within the precinct of a temple to Amen, is the only intact pharaonic grave ever found (the tomb of Tutankhamen had been looted at least twice). The king was buried in three nested coffins, the outer one pink granite and the middle of black granite, both originally used in the Nineteenth Dynasty, and the inner one of solid silver made for this king. Within the silver coffin lay Psusennes himself. A solid gold mask covered his head, and elaborate jewelry was placed on his body. The other partially robbed burials of kings and high officials at Tanis also yielded rich grave goods, but their excavation at the beginning of World War II limited the publicity surrounding their discovery, and they remain less well known than the burials of New Kingdom kings.

The succession of overlapping dynasties in the northern part of the country ended with the Nubian king Piye's conquest of Egypt in the eighth century B.C.E. His kingdom of Napata had grown into the vacuum left after the Egyptians pulled back from direct control over their southern neighbors in the Twentieth Dynasty. The kings styled themselves as Egyptian kings, using titles and royal regalia based on Egyptian prototypes, and the chief deity of the kingdom was a local version of Amen. Although Piye conquered Egypt, he retained his capital at Napata in Nubia, and it was his successor Shabaka (r. 716-c. 702/698) who killed the rebellious Delta king in battle and moved his capital to the traditional Egyptian site of Memphis. Therefore, Shabaka is often credited with the foundation of the Twenty-fifth (Kushite) Dynasty, sometimes referred to as the Kushite kings. The rulers of the Twenty-fifth Dynasty were confronted with the surging Neo-Assyrian Empire, which invaded Egypt first in 671 B.C.E. and again sometime between 663 and 657 B.C.E. This latter invasion, during which the Assyrian king Ashurbanipal led his armies in the sack of Thebes, ended the Napatan domination of Egypt.

The Assyrians established an alliance with the kings of Saïs, who ruled Egypt after the Assyrians pulled back to attend to disunity closer to home. The Saite (Twenty-sixth) Dynasty (664-525 B.C.E.) began with Psamtik I, who ruled Egypt for more than fifty years and oversaw a renaissance in Egyptian art and religion. The emphasis on traditional artistic styles means that it is sometimes difficult to determine whether a sculpture from a Saite context is a Twenty-sixth Dynasty work or one from the Middle Kingdom transported to the site. There are Old Kingdom works on which a grid of the Saite period has been drawn, allowing an exact copy of the earlier work to be manufactured. A distinctive Saite style developed in parallel with the archaizing trend, and the sculptural production of the period provides the most beautiful examples of Egyptian art during the first millennium B.C.E.

The Twenty-sixth Dynasty was brought to an end in 525 B.C.E. by the armies of Persia under Cambyses II. However, the Persians were never popular with their Egyptian vassals, and as the Persians under Darius the Great fought a series of losing battles against the Greeks (beginning with the Battle of Marathon in 490 B.C.E.), the Egyptians organized to throw off the foreign yoke. The success of Amyrtaeus of Saïs (r. 404-399), who was at least partially successful in leading the rebellion and united the Delta with the Nile Valley as far south as Aswān, was short-lived. He was unable to pass on his empire to any of his children and is the single king of the Twenty-eighth Dynasty. The last native Egyptian rulers were those of the Thirtieth Dynasty. Nectanebo II, the last king of that dynasty, lost control of Egypt to the Persians in 343 B.C.E. and fled to Nubia. He was the last ethnically native Egyptian to rule the country until the twentieth century of the common era.

Significance

During the Third Intermediate Period, Egypt became politically less isolated from the rest of the Mediterranean. This was manifested in the succes-

Third Intermediate Period, 1069-c. 332 B.C.E.

Twenty-first Dynasty, 1069-945

Ruler	*Reign*
Smendes	1069-1043
Amenemnisu	1043-1039
Psusennes I	1045-c. 991
Amenemope	993-984
Osorkon the Elder	984-978
Siamun	978-959
Psusennes II	959-945

Twenty-second (Libyan) Dynasty, 945-715

Twenty-third Dynasty, 818-715

Twenty-fourth Dynasty, 730-715

Ruler	*Reign*
Tefnakht	730-720
Bakenranef (Bocchoris)	720-715

Twenty-fifth (Kushite) Dynasty, c. 742-c. 656

Ruler	*Reign*
Piye	742-716
Shabaka	716-702/698
Shebitku	698-690
Taharqa	690-664
Tanutamuni	664-656

Twenty-sixth (Saite) Dynasty, 664-525

Ruler	*Reign*
Psamtik I	664-610
Necho II	610-595
Psamtik II	595-589
Apries	589-570
Ahmose II	570-526
Psamtik III	526-525

Twenty-seventh (First Persian) Dynasty, 525-404

Twenty-eighth Dynasty, 404-399

Ruler	*Reign*
Amyrtaeus	404-399

Twenty-ninth Dynasty, 399-380

Thirtieth Dynasty, 380-343

Ruler	*Reign*
Nectanebo II	360-343

Thirty-first (Second Persian) Dynasty, 343-332

Note: Dynastic research is ongoing; data are approximate.

sive conquests of Egypt by rulers from both its north and its south. In addition, foreigners (including large numbers of Greeks) were recruited into the Egyptian armed forces as mercenaries and rewarded for their service with grants of land in the Delta and Fayum. The close relationship between Egypt and Greece set the stage for the conquest of Egypt by Alexander the Great.

—*Sara E. Orel*

FURTHER READING

Clayton, Peter A. *Chronicle of the Pharaohs*. London: Thames and Hudson, 1994. Reign-by-reign chronological account of Egyptian history, including even minor rulers.

Hope, Colin A. *Gold of the Pharaohs*. Sydney: International Cultural Corporation of Australia, 1988. Catalogue of an exhibition of material from the royal tombs of Tanis, dating to the Twenty-first and Twenty-second Dynasties. Extensive illustrations.

Robins, Gay. *The Art of Ancient Egypt*. Cambridge, Mass.: Harvard University Press, 1997. Chapters 11 and 12 present the art of the period under discussion. Bibliography.

Welsby, Derek A. *The Kingdom of Kush*. London: British Museum Press, 1996. Discussion of the Napatan Dynasty (which includes the kings of the Egyptian Twenty-fifth Dynasty) and its Nubian successors, including history and archaeological material. Appendix with list of rulers, bibliography, index.

SEE ALSO: c. 1570 B.C.E., New Kingdom Period Begins in Egypt; c. 1450 B.C.E., International Age of Major Kingdoms Begins in the Near East; c. 1338 B.C.E., Failure of Akhenaton's Cultural Revival; 8th century B.C.E., Kushite King Piye Conquers Upper Egypt; c. 783-c. 591 B.C.E., Napata Kingdom Flourishes in Kush; c. 712-698 B.C.E., Shabaka Reunites the Nile Valley; 664 B.C.E., Saite Dynasty Begins in Egypt.

RELATED ARTICLES in *Great Lives from History: The Ancient World*: Alexander the Great; Darius the Great; Piye; Psamtik I.

c. 1066 B.C.E.
WESTERN ZHOU DYNASTY BEGINS IN CHINA

The Western Zhou Dynasty introduced a mechanism of using kinship as a political institution and the idea of using the mandate of heaven to legitimize the ruling power of the royal line.

LOCALE: Haojing (near present-day Xian, Shaanxi Province) and the areas from the Wei Valley to Shangdong and from southern Manchuria to the middle and lower Changjiang (Yangtze) Valley

CATEGORIES: Government and politics; expansion and land acquisition

KEY FIGURES

Wenwang (Wen-wang; fl. c. eleventh century B.C.E.), Zhou ruler, r. c. eleventh century B.C.E.

Wuwang (Wu-wang; fl. c. eleventh century B.C.E.), first ruler of Western Zhou Dynasty, r. c. eleventh century B.C.E., Wenwang's son

Duke of Zhou (Chou-kung; fl. eleventh century B.C.E.), Wuwang's brother

SUMMARY OF EVENT

The Zhou people began as a semiagricultural and seminomadic clan that lived to the west of the Shang Dynasty (c. 1600-1066 B.C.E.). Although the Zhou themselves were an agricultural people, they interacted with the sheepherding nomads of the northwest and gradually adopted a nomadic way of life. This nomadic lifestyle enabled them to deal with people of different cultures. They later settled in the Wei Valley, west of the great bend of the Yellow River, and became vassals of the Shang, protecting the western regions of the realm.

By the early eleventh century B.C.E., the Zhou had become powerful and had begun their expansion. They attacked their neighboring states and finally came into sharp conflict with the Shang. At one point, King Zhou of the Shang imprisoned Wenwang. To obtain Wenwang's release, the Zhou presented tributes of treasures and beautiful women to King Zhou. After his release, Wenwang began preparing to attack the Shang, whose moral corruption had already incited much internal dissension. After the death of Wenwang, his successor Wuwang, assisted by his brother Zhou, allied with the neighboring states and deployed a large army to march east. The Shang army collapsed in the face of the Zhou attack. King Zhou of Shang fled and committed suicide. This marked the beginning of the Western Zhou Dynasty.

Traditionally, the start of the Western Zhou Dynasty has been placed at c. 1122, however, other scholars suggest dates such as c. 1066 and c. 1050.

The Western Zhou controlled the area formerly dominated by the Shang and other smaller states. The Western Zhou territory stretched from the Wei Valley in the west to Shangdong in the east, and from southern Manchuria to the middle and lower Yangtze (Changjiang) Valley. The ruler of Zhou had to solve the problem of how to govern the vast expanse of land. He eventually resolved to adopt a policy of *feng zhu hou, jian jiang tu* (enfeoffing relatives and establishing principalities), which has been interpreted by Western scholars as a form of feudalism. However, it is worth noting that the feudalism of Western Zhou and the successive dynasties in China differs from that practiced in Europe and Japan two millennia later. In Europe, feudalism was a political and economic system based on the relation of lord to vassals held on legal or contractual bonds; however, in China, the system depended on familial ties—bonds between the lord and the vassals based on blood or pseudo-blood relations. The Zhou rulers delegated authority to a large number of vassals. The vassals were for the most part the descendants or relatives of the Zhou royal family but also included unrelated subordinates and local aristocrats who had acknowledged Zhou suzerainty.

After Wuwang's unexpected death, his son succeeded to the throne and became King Cheng (Chengwang). As Cheng was too young to rule, his uncle, the duke of Zhou, acted as a regent, who loyally and successfully assisted Cheng. In addition to the primary capital Haojing (west of Changan County, near present-day Xian, Shaanxi Province), the Zhou established a secondary capital at Luoyi (near present Louyang, Henan Province), in the heartland of the old Shang. Soon both the cities of Haojing and Luoyi became political, military, and cultural centers of the Western Zhou. Cheng and Zhou also moved the unruly Shang aristocrats to Luoyi to keep a close eye on them and to prevent any potential revolts by them.

The Western Zhou achieved further social economic development. It was a sharply divided class society, in which the hereditary lord, supported by his aristocratic vassals and warriors, ruled over the peasant masses and the slaves, who were primarily used as domestic servants or exploited in producing the products of the handicraft industry. The bronze-casting industry became more prominent. In addition to the royal bronze workshop, there were feoff-owned workshops. During this time, the quality and quantity of bronzes were increased, and bronze became more popular among people. The development of the bronze industry prompted the start of other industries. Chinese script became more widely used. Inscriptions appeared not only on oracle bones but also on bronze utensils. Noticeable progress was also made in agriculture, animal husbandry, textiles, metallurgy, architecture, astrology, and geography.

In the Western Zhou, reportedly, eight farming families, each with their own field, collectively cultivated a central field for the support of the lord. As the system resembles the Chinese character for "well," which depicts the pattern of nine fields as a unit, it has been called the well-field system. Although the well-field system may be a later idealization rather than a historical reality, it certainly reflects a time when farmland and agricultural produce were shared within a community.

The royal succession during the Western Zhou was from father to son. The Zhou worshiped *tian* (heaven) as their chief deity, and each Zhou king called himself the Son of Heaven and further justified his conquest and rule on the grounds that he had received the mandate of heaven.

During the reign of King Li (Liwang), the tenth king of Zhou, conflicts between the royal family and the people began to surface. The despotic rule of King Li, which included exorbitant taxation, ruthless oppression of people, and prohibition of public discussion of state affairs, eventually provoked a revolt in 841 B.C.E. In that year, cit-

MAJOR KINGS OF THE WESTERN ZHOU DYNASTY

King	*Reign*
Wuwang	c. 1050-c. 1047
Chengwang	c. 1047-c. 1017
Kangwang	c. 1017-c. 992
Zhaowang	c. 992-c. 973
Muwang	c. 973-c. 918
Gongwang	c. 918-c. 903
Yiwang	c. 903-c. 900
Xiaowang	c. 900-c. 893
Yiwang	c. 893-c. 861
Liwang	c. 861-c. 827
Zuanwang	c. 827-c. 781
Youwang	c. 781-c. 771

Note: Reign dates for kings (*wang*) of the Western Zhou Dynasty (c. 1066-c. 771 B.C.E.) vary widely; these dates are based on an assumption that the dynasty began in c. 1050 B.C.E., not 1066.

izens drove King Li out of the capital. The event was hailed by the Marxist Chinese historians as the first popular uprising in Chinese history. During the reign of King You (Yu; Youwang), the thirteenth king of Zhou, rebels, allied with the barbarians from outside Zhou, destroyed the capital in 771, thus ending the Western Zhou Dynasty. Although the royal line was restored at the secondary capital of Louyi, the Zhou kings never again exercised any significant political or military power.

SIGNIFICANCE

The Western Zhou introduced kinship as a main element of political institutions. The Chinese form of feudalism therefore endured over the centuries and was often used by rulers of later dynasties alternately with centralization (the concentration of power in the ruler or the central government). The Western Zhou also created a new basis of legitimacy for their rule by instilling the theory of the mandate of heaven. The Zhou kings claimed that their right to rule came from a supernatural and powerful source, heaven, whose mandate could be bestowed to any family that was morally deserving of the responsibility and power. This doctrine asserts the divine right of rulers, theoretically legitimizing the ruling power of the royal house. The theory of the mandate of heaven also asserts a ruler's accountability to a supreme moral force that is above humankind.

The Western Zhou expansion necessitated that they acculturate, at least to some degree, those cultures who submitted to them and that they commingle with the mainstream culture of the central plains (the middle and lower reaches of the Yellow River) and the peripheral cultures of the non-Chinese, including seminomadic groups of the north, northeast, and northwest, and tribal peoples of South China. Although the central plains had reached the zenith of the Bronze Age, the neighboring regions still lagged behind. The cultural mingling continued throughout the following periods, becoming a significant element of Chinese history.

—*Huping Ling*

FURTHER READING

Adler, Joseph A. *Chinese Religious Traditions*. Upper Saddle River, N.J.: Prentice Hall, 2002. A study of Chinese religions starting with the Zhou Dynasty.

Cullen, Christopher. *Astronomy and Mathematics in Ancient China: The Zhou bi suan jing*. New York: Cambridge University Press, 1996. An intellectual history on the scientific development of the Zhou.

Embree, Ainslie T., and Carol Gluck, eds. *Asia in Western and World History: A Guide for Teaching*. Armonk, N.Y.: M.E. Sharpe, 1997. A useful guide for teaching Asian history.

Fairbank, John King. *China: A New History*. Cambridge, Mass.: Belknap Press of Harvard University Press, 1992. A comprehensive Chinese history from antiquity to the present.

Gernet, Jacques. *Ancient China from the Beginning to Empire*. Translated by Raymond Rudorff. Berkeley: University of California Press, 1968. A comprehensive ancient Chinese history.

Hsu, Cho-yun, and Katheryn M. Linduff. *Western Chou Civilization*. New Haven, Conn.: Yale University Press, 1988. A history of the Zhou Dynasty.

Li, Jun. *Chinese Civilization in the Making, 1766-221 B.C.* New York: St. Martin's Press, 1996. Ancient Chinese history from the Shang Dynasty to the beginning of the Qin Dynasty.

Loewe, Michael, and Edward L. Shaughnessy, eds. *The Cambridge History of Ancient China: From the Origins of Civilization to 221 B.C.* New York: Cambridge University Press, 1999. Ancient Chinese history from antiquity to the end of the Zhou Dynasty.

Meyer, Milton W. *China: A Concise History*. 2d ed. Lanham, Md.: Rowman and Littlefield, 1994. A comprehensive Chinese history, covering from antiquity to the present.

Wang, Aihe. *Cosmology and Political Culture in Early China*. New York: Cambridge University Press, 2000. An intellectual history of ancient China.

SEE ALSO: 2953-2838 B.C.E. traditionally, Reign of China's Legendary First Ruler, Fu Xi; c. 2682 B.C.E., Legendary Founding of China by Huangdi; c. 2100 B.C.E., Xia Dynasty Marks Start of Historical China; c. 1600 B.C.E., Shang Dynasty Develops Writing and Bronzework; 770 B.C.E., Eastern Zhou Dynasty Begins in China; 221 B.C.E., Qin Dynasty Founded in China.

c. 10th century B.C.E.
QUEEN OF SHEBA LEGENDS ARISE

In the biblical account, the queen of Sheba visited King Solomon and witnessed his wisdom and power, inspiring more legends in Jewish, Christian, and Muslim traditions. Sheba's origin continues to be a matter of historical conjecture.

LOCALE: Israel and Sheba (Saba, now in Yemen)
CATEGORIES: Religion; cultural and intellectual history

KEY FIGURES

Queen of Sheba (fl. c. tenth century B.C.E.), Arabian queen, r. c. tenth century B.C.E.
Solomon (c. 991-930 B.C.E.), king of Israel, r. c. 961-930 B.C.E.

SUMMARY OF EVENT

In the brief biblical story of I Kings 10:1-13, the queen of Sheba came to test King Solomon and was overcome by his wealth and wisdom, which surpassed her own mystifying riddles and riches.

The earliest recorded account of the nameless queen takes place in the court of Solomon in the tenth century B.C.E. but probably was composed in the post-exilic period (sixth century B.C.E.) from earlier traditional materials. Even if the queen cannot be named, can her kingdom be located? If she is a historical figure, it is most likely that she came from a wealthy culture of the Arabian peninsula. No clear geographical or archaeological proofs substantiate the origin and existence of the queen, though there is some evidence of one or more queens in regions of the Arabian peninsula.

Saba (Sheba) was the most prominent of several kingdoms in southern Arabia (present-day Yemen); however, the spice-trading culture flourished sometime after the time of Solomon, in the eighth or seventh century B.C.E. Although this Sabaean culture is anachronistically linked to the story in I Kings, the rich land certainly would have been known to the tellers of that story in post-exilic Israel. The Sabaeans had a caravan economy situated between the Near East and Africa and India, carrying spices, metals, and other trade goods. They were particularly envied for their frankincense and myrrh, resins harvested from trees exclusive to the region. Linguistic and archaeological evidence suggests that the Sabaeans influenced the surrounding cultures of the entire south Arabian region. Thus, it is likely that the opulence of the trade goods coming from Saba contributed to typical ideological tales, such as those found in the biblical accounts. Speculation continues about the queen's historicity, for which there is no direct evidence. Her land has been associated with Arabia, Africa, and Egypt.

This indirect evidence can be misleading or fruitless unless contextualized by another historical approach, which is to inquire of the histories of the traditional tales themselves that accrued in each of the western monotheisms (Judaism, Christianity, and Islam) and not to take them merely literally. That is, the event of the queen of Sheba is not tied securely to facts but more significantly to a web of religion and culture.

The historical consequence of the queen of Sheba is paradoxically to be located in her various fictional representations. Rather than attempt to search out the queen's elusive historical presence, scholars can uncover the pur-

A nineteenth century depiction of the queen of Sheba. (Hulton| Archive)

poses of the storytellers. In pursuing the varied and abundant avenues of her legends, scholars find that the queen plays many roles. In the brief story in I Kings (repeated in II Chronicles), the queen of Sheba visits Solomon bearing lavish gifts; she tests the king with riddles and is overcome by his wealth and wisdom, offering up a testimony to Solomon and his god. It is a typical ethnic legend that boasts of Solomon by overshadowing the legendary power of Sheba. Given the politics of theocracy, it is possible that in early versions of the tale, the queen of Sheba represented Astarte, a goddess of rival religious sensibilities, humbled and narratively demoted to human status before the presence of Yahweh, God of Israel.

Jewish, Christian, and Muslim narratives have continued to elaborate the story into the present time. In the New Testament, the woman of the legend is called the Queen of the South and is used as an apocalyptic figure of judgment (Matt. 12:42). In Jewish folklore, the enigmatic queen is linked with Lilith, a demonic figure and the first wife of Adam. In the medieval Christian tradition, the queen is associated with the legend of the True Cross, being an allegory of the church. She has been linked with the woman of the "Song of Songs"; although implausible historically, the connection indicates part of the rich literary and religious tradition of the queen, a fluid figure who becomes part of many narratives.

In the Qur'ān (Surah 27:15-45), the queen serves as a miniature emblem of the entire message of the Muslim tradition; Solomon subdues her (named Bilqis in the Qur'ān), so that she submits to Allah (God). Solomon's magical abilities with the language of birds and his transportation of the queen's throne disadvantage her, and the queen is tricked into revealing her unacceptably hairy leg. Ethiopia plants its origin story in the erotic encounter between Solomon and Sheba, who gives birth to their founding emperor, Menelik. The Jewish tradition focuses on the "hard questions," the riddles, with which she tests him. In later literary and artistic versions of her story, she is an emblem of transgressive womanhood: overreaching and sexual. The legend is the source for orientalist romance (as in the works of French novelist Gustave Flaubert or English writer Rudyard Kipling): The story is often an allegory of gender politics.

SIGNIFICANCE

Thus, it is the tracing of and considering the legends of the queen, rather than the searching for the elusive and literal queen, that is of historical significance. The queen who visited Solomon has many permutations, political, artistic, and religious, that extend through Jewish, Christian, and Muslim traditions in numerous locales. The legend continues to diverge and to flourish in religion and the arts.

—Lynda Sexson

FURTHER READING

Clapp, Nicholas. *Sheba: Through the Desert in Search of the Legendary Queen*. New York: Houghton Mifflin, 2002. Fast-paced travelogue, history, and speculation.

Cogan, Mordechai. *I Kings*. Anchor Bible Series. New York: Doubleday, 2000. This source clarifies historical and textual issues in the biblical narrative.

De Voragine, Jacobus. *The Golden Legend*. Vols. 1-2 in *Readings on the Saints*. Translated by William Granger Ryan. Princeton, N.J.: Princeton University Press, 1995. This medieval collection, *Aurea Legenda*, compiled around 1260, records the Queen of Sheba's role in the Legend of the True Cross, a popular theme in devotional painting.

Lassner, Jacob. *Demonizing the Queen of Shea: Boundaries of Gender and Culture in Postbiblical Judaism and Medieval Islam*. Chicago: University of Chicago Press, 1993. The book traces transmutations of the Sheba story from testimonies of political and religious dominance to anxieties of gender and culture.

Pritchard, James B., ed. *Solomon and Sheba*. London: Phaidon, 1974. Survey essays trace the diffusion of the legend through Jewish, Muslim, Ethiopian, and medieval Christian legends, with lucid overview by Pritchard.

Simpson, St. John, ed. *Queen of Sheba: Treasures from Ancient Yemen*. London: British Museum Press, 2002. Twelve scholars contribute essays on the legend of Sheba, including artistic and religious traditions up through the present and archaeological finds in Yemen and surrounding areas.

SEE ALSO: c. 1280 B.C.E., Israelite Exodus from Egypt; c. 1000 B.C.E., Establishment of the United Kingdom of Israel; c. 922 B.C.E., Establishment of the Kingdom of Israel; c. 750-c. 500 B.C.E., Marib Dam Is Built in Yemen.

RELATED ARTICLE in *Great Lives from History: The Ancient World*: Solomon.

c. 1000 B.C.E.
ESTABLISHMENT OF THE UNITED KINGDOM OF ISRAEL

David established a politically united Israel, an empire that enjoyed a vibrant economy and culture as well as international renown for less than a century.

LOCALE: Palestine
CATEGORIES: Government and politics; wars, uprisings, and civil unrest

KEY FIGURES

Saul (fl. eleventh century B.C.E.), Benjamite peasant, first king of Israel, r. c. 1020-1000 B.C.E.
Samuel (c. 1090-c. 1020 B.C.E.), Hebrew visionary of Ramah appearing c. 1070 B.C.E., sponsor of Saul
David (c. 1030-c. 962 B.C.E.), Judaean peasant, king of Judah, r. c. 1000, and later of Israel, r. c. 1000-c. 962 B.C.E.
Ishbaal (fl. eleventh century-early tenth century B.C.E.), fourth son and successor of Saul as king of Israel, r. c. 1000-993 B.C.E.
Abner (fl. eleventh century B.C.E.), military commander of Saul's troops

SUMMARY OF EVENT

The settlement of the Philistines along the southern coast of Palestine at the beginning of the eleventh century B.C.E. presented the Hebrew tribes occupying the central and southern hills with a challenge that could not be met through the military institutions of Israel's loose tribal confederacy. Coming from Crete, where they had been displaced along with many other Aegean peoples in the turbulent era following the Dorian invasion, the Philistines brought with them the first iron tools and weapons known in Palestine. They organized themselves into five strong city-states and soon began to thrust inland into Hebrew territory. For two centuries, the Hebrew tribes had successfully put together armies of peasantry led by temporary charismatic leaders, or "judges," to meet crises of invasion or threat from Canaanite city-states, but in a battle fought about 1050 B.C.E., the Hebrews were decisively defeated and the Ark of the Covenant itself was captured, after which the Philistines established garrisons in the central hill country.

With Israel pressed by the Philistines on the west, the Ammonites east of the Jordan seized the opportunity to regain territories previously lost to the Hebrew tribe of Gilead to their north and laid siege to the Gileadite city of Jabesh. At this point, Saul emerged as a charismatic military leader of combined tribal forces that routed the Ammonites and relieved the Siege of Jabesh. On their return across the Jordan, the Israelite militia elected Saul king, and for the next several years, he maintained a standing army and engaged Philistine troops in battle with varying degrees of success.

The Hebrew tradition regarding the emergence of the monarchy in this crisis is contained in the first book of Samuel in the Bible; it is a composite narrative woven together from two sources, each of which has its own distinct and antithetical account of events and their evaluation. One source gives the account presented above, that Saul emerged as a political leader with a standing army following his successful leadership of the campaign against the Ammonites. The other source presents Saul as a figure subordinate to Samuel, who is portrayed as the last judge and the first prophet. Samuel, according to this account, commissioned Saul as a prince and anointed him as king over Israel after strongly protesting Israel's demand for a king in order to be "like the nations" and after warning of the dangers to be expected by Israel from the institution of dynastic monarchy. On Saul's failure to fulfill to the letter Samuel's instructions to conduct a holy war against the Amalekites in the south, Samuel proclaimed Saul's rejection by Yahweh and anointed David to be king in his stead. Saul did, however, continue in actuality to exercise rule over Israel in spite of the specific action of Samuel in "deposing" him in favor of David.

The traditions regarding the emergence of Saul's successor, David, are partly legendary. As a young man, David was a member of Saul's court and a close friend of Saul's son Jonathan and was given Saul's daughter Michal as his wife. His popularity aroused Saul's jealousy, and eventually, he fled to the south, where he organized a guerrilla band and ingratiated himself with Hebrew tribesmen of Judah by warring on Amalekites and other groups that had long harassed them. At the same time, he took service with the Philistine Achish, king of Gath, as a mercenary leader of his warrior band. The fortunes of Saul continued to fall as a consequence of his alienation of the priesthood of Yahweh and his own mentally disturbed condition. He was finally decisively defeated and met his death in battle with the Philistines at Mount Gilboa. Saul's surving son, Ishbaal, was taken by Abner, his commander, to Mahanaim, east of the Jordan, and nominally made king. David, in the meantime, was elected king of Judah by tribal elders at Hebron. In the ensuing period of intrigue, Abner and Ishbaal were both assassinated, and in a second assembly at Hebron, elders of the northern tribes made David king over Israel. All the Hebrew tribes were thus bound to David in a united monarchy over Israel and Judah.

David consolidated his hold on the kingdom by decisive victories over the Philistines, Ammonites, Arameans, Moabites, and Edomites; by bringing the Canaanite city-states of Palestine under his own power; and by conquering the centrally situated Jebusite city of Jerusalem, which he made the capital of his kingdom. There he established a centralized political administration and gave his state a solid legitimacy by bringing the Ark of the Covenant to Jerusalem and establishing the cult of Yahweh as an official institution.

This illustration depicts Saul committing suicide during a battle with the Philistines, as described in the Book of Samuel. (Hulton|Archive)

SIGNIFICANCE

David created a regime that was an amalgam of Hebraic and Canaanite types of monarchy bound together in the person of the king. In the dynastic succession of David's son Solomon to the throne, the old concept of Yahweh's designation of commander by charisma was replaced by the new concept of Yahweh's covenant with the house of David, but this conception was accepted only by Judah, and at Solomon's death the whole imperial structure of Palestine, based as it was on the personal union of distinct political entities, fell apart and reverted to earlier conditions: the coexistence of several ethnic polities in Palestine. However, for the brief period of less than a century of rule by David and Solomon, Israel enjoyed political unity, a considerable empire with international prestige, a flourishing economy, and a culture expressing the high spirits of successful nationalism.

—*Carl W. Conrad*

FURTHER READING

Ahlström, Gösta. *Ancient Palestine: A Historical Introduction*. Rev. ed. Minneapolis, Minn.: Fortress Press, 2002. This revised version of her earlier work examines the historicity of biblical events and includes archaeological discoveries.

Fox, E. *Give Us a King: Samuel, Saul, and David*. New York: Schocken Books, 1999. Examines the early kings of Israel and the formation of the United Kingdom of Israel.

Marcus, Amy Dockser. *The View from Nebo: How Archaeology Is Rewriting the Bible and Reshaping the Middle East*. Boston: Little, Brown, 2000. Marcus looks at how the findings of modern archaeology have altered some biblical views and interpretations of Scripture. Bibliography and index.

Matthews, Victor Harold. *A Brief History of Ancient Israel*. Louisville, Ky.: Westminster John Knox Press, 2002. A history of Israel, with emphasis on social customs and daily life. Index.

Shanks, Hershel, ed. *Ancient Israel: From Abraham to*

the Roman Destruction of the Temple. Rev. ed. Washington, D.C.: Biblical Archaeology Society, 1999. Examines the history of Israel from biblical and archaeological viewpoints. Bibliography.

Soggin, J. Alberto. *An Introduction to the History of Israel and Judah*. 3d ed. London: SCM, 1999. A general history of ancient Israel, covering the period of the United Kingdom of Israel.

SEE ALSO: c. 1280 B.C.E., Israelite Exodus from Egypt; c. 966 B.C.E., Building of the Temple of Jerusalem; c. 950 B.C.E., Composition of the Book of Genesis; c. 922 B.C.E., Establishment of the Kingdom of Israel; 587-423 B.C.E., Birth of Judaism; c. 538-c. 450 B.C.E., Jews Return from the Babylonian Captivity.

RELATED ARTICLES in *Great Lives from History: The Ancient World*: David; Samuel; Solomon.

c. 1000 B.C.E.
GREEK ALPHABET IS DEVELOPED

The Greek alphabet became the ancestor of all modern European alphabets, including the English.

LOCALE: Greece
CATEGORY: Cultural and intellectual history

SUMMARY OF EVENT

An alphabet is a system of writing consisting of generally less than thirty symbols that represent all the spoken sounds of a language. The Greeks were the first to assign a single sound to a single letter; hence, they were the first to develop a completely phonetic alphabet.

Every system of writing in existence ultimately derived from pictures used to represent words. Such pictographic writing emerged independently in many places around the world. In Mesopotamia around 3000 B.C.E., Sumerians had a form of picture writing, followed by cuneiform in 2500 C.E. This was also the time of the earliest Egyptian hieroglyphs. China in 1500 C.E. developed a system in which each symbol designated a word. The Canaanites along the western shore of the Mediterranean had a pictographic writing system also, but they developed a syllabic alphabet around 1700 C.E. Syllables consisting of vowels and consonants were depicted as symbols, and peoples of the area, including a North Semitic group the Greeks came to call the Phoenicians, gradually devised alphabets consisting solely of consonants. All the several hundred alphabets that came into existence can be traced back to this area of the Middle East.

The Mycenaean peoples inhabiting the area on and around the Greek mainland also had a writing system c. 1500-1100 C.E. Designated by twentieth century translators as Linear B, it derived from Crete, an island south of Greece, where Minoans devised a system designated Linear A to record items of commerce and official records. Linear B had at least eighty-eight signs with a few vowels, but it was a clumsy syllabic method of writing used only by the elite. During the twelfth century B.C.E., Doric-speaking invaders from the northwest or possibly Doric-speaking Greeks who were already part of the Mycenaean culture overthrew the nobility. Greece was then illiterate for the four centuries around the time of Homer.

The twelfth century C.E. also saw the Phoenicians of the Canaanite region venture out to establish trade and colonies in the Mediterranean. They settled such places as Kition, Cyprus, Malta, Sicily, Sardinia, Spain, and possibly Carthage and Utica. Their alphabet was a series of consonants that is the distant ancestor of the modern Hebrew alphabet. The Phoenicians might have provided the alphabet to the Greeks as they traveled around the Mediterranean trading with various peoples, yet it is not unlikely that Greeks and Phoenicians lived together in a bilingual settlement in which the Greeks could learn the script at their leisure. Around 1000 B.C.E., the Greeks adapted the alphabet to fit the needs of their own speech.

The twenty-two-character Phoenician alphabet from *aleph* (Greek *alpha*) to *taw* (Greek *tau*) was accepted by the Greeks with few deletions. The Greeks were forced to add letters, however, for sounds that were present in their language but not used by the Phoenicians. The Greeks added *psi* for "ps," *chi* for "kh," and *phi* for "ph" around 800 C.E. Yet the most radical change that the Greeks accomplished was to create vowels as letters that stood alone for the first time in history. Phoenician sounds at the beginning of some of the letter names were hard for the Greeks to pronounce, so they emphasized a vowel sound of their own speech, which became the new sound of the letter. *Alpha* ("a"), *epsilon* (short "e"), *eta* (long "e"), *iota* ("i"), *omicron* (short "o"), *upsilon* ("u"), and *omega* (long "o") formed the seven vowels in the twenty-four-character eastern Greek dialect of Ionian. The alphabet varied from region to region in the city-states of

Greece. Some dialects, for example, adopted the Semitic *qoph* (an ancestor of the modern "q") and *digamma* (an ancestor of the modern "f"). The Ionian dialect, however, was declared the official alphabet of Greece in a decree of Athens in 403 B.C.E., and it became the classical Greek alphabet.

Another important development attributed to the Greeks is the direction the letters eventually took. Every European language that is derived from the Greek alphabet writes from left to right. Phoenician, like modern Hebrew and Arabic, ran right to left, but early Greek inscriptions were not consistent. Some have been found running right to left, left to right, vertically either top to bottom or bottom to top, and even in a hairpin fashion that flipped some letters in reverse. Also common was the Greek practice of *boustrophedon*, or "as the ox plows." The letters in *boustrophedon* ran left to right, then right to left, so that they appear backward, then back to left to right, taking curves as they went. It must not have bothered readers of the time to read letters backward or upside-down. The practice is not as odd as it seems, for the readers would not have to automatically jerk their eyes back to the left margin in an unnatural fashion (yet one that is acceptable to readers of European alphabets). The Greeks standardized the left to right method around 600-500 B.C.E.

The orientation of symbols in the Phoenician language was important, because they were supposed to represent objects, albeit in an abstract way. The Greeks, however, were not constrained, for example, to leave *aleph*, the Phoenician word for "ox," as an upside-down "A," which representated an ox face, because the word *alpha* to them only meant the name of the first letter of their alphabet. With all the different directions the Greeks gave their scripts originally, letters flipped back and forth (for example, a backward "B" flipped over to become a forward "B") before settling down to become the familiar ones of most modern European languages. Another possible reason the Greeks had to adjust the letters was to make them all taller than they were wide for uniform inscriptions into stone.

SIGNIFICANCE

The versatility of a totally phonetic alphabet led to a widespread acceptance of the Greek alphabet. The alphabet was simpler to memorize than systems of writing based on thousands of picture symbols, so more people were able to master reading and writing. The concept of an alphabet worked its way to Egypt, where the Coptic alphabet replaced hieroglyphs. The phonetic system has even been applied in the transliteration of Asian symbols so that they can be read by speakers of European languages. The Greek alphabet was sent east around the ninth century C.E. at the hands of the Greek missionary Saint Cyril, making it the direct ancestor of the Cyrillic alphabet used in Slavic countries.

The most significant Greek influence came from the speakers of the Chalcidian dialect of eastern Greece. Unlike the Ionian dialect, it was not established as Greece's official alphabet. Nevertheless, the Chalcidian dialect traveled west from Kyme, Boeotia, and Euboia on the eastern shores of Greece to colonies on the island of Pithecusa (present-day Ischia) around 775 B.C.E., as well as near the city of Cumae on Italy itself. The peoples of the area were called the Etruscans, and they accepted this Greek alphabet that had an "f" and a "q" for use in writing their language. Etruscan symbols are the direct ancestor of the Roman alphabet, and, from there, all European alphabets.

—*Rose Secrest*

FURTHER READING

Drucker, Johanna. *The Alphabetic Labyrinth: The Letters in History and Imagination*. New York: Thames and Hudson, 1995. For advanced students, the chapters "The Alphabet in Context," "Origins and Historians," and "The Alphabet in Classical History, Philosophy, and Divination" are a detailed but succinct summary of speculations concerning the origin of the Greek alphabet.

Jeffery, L. H. *The Local Scripts of Archaic Greece: A Study of the Origin of the Greek Alphabet and Its Development from the Eighth to the Fifth Centuries B.C.* London: Oxford University Press, 1961. Despite its age and scholarly tone, this is still the definitive study of the Greek writing system. The first two chapters, "The Origin and Transmission of the Greek Alphabet" and "Writing in Ancient Greece," yield a clear analysis of scripts.

McCarter, P. Kyle, Jr. *The Antiquity of the Greek Alphabet and the Early Phoenician Scripts*. Missoula, Mont.: Scholars Press, 1975. Technical and full of detail, yet a fascinating look at where, how, and when the Greek alphabet originated.

Moleas, Wendy. *The Development of the Greek Language*. New Rochelle, N.Y.: Aristide D. Caratzas, 1989. Useful appendices show early Mycenaean and Greek signs, while the first chapter, "Prehistoric and Ancient Greek," is an easily accessible introduction to the Greek alphabet.

Robinson, Andrew. *The Story of Writing: Alphabets, Hieroglyphs, and Pictographs*. New York: Thames and Hudson, 1995. A colorful book with plenty of illustrations, it traverses the history of writing from cuneiform and hieroglyphics to the 1990's.

SEE ALSO: c. 3100 B.C.E., Sumerians Invent Writing; c. 1600-c. 1500 B.C.E., Flowering of Minoan Civilization; c. 1600-c. 1000 B.C.E., City of Mycenae Flourishes; c. 1250 B.C.E., Transmission of the European Alphabet.

c. 1000 B.C.E.
SUB-SAHARAN IRONWORKING BEGINS

The discovery of abundant iron ore in the Central African region greatly affected African life through the creation of ironworking tools and iron goods that changed the structures of some societal hierarchies.

LOCALE: Central Africa around Lake Chad and the Rwanda Great Lakes
CATEGORIES: Prehistory and ancient cultures; science and technology

SUMMARY OF EVENT

According to archaeological evidence, the art of iron metallurgy in Africa originated in the Central African territories between Lake Chad and modern-day Rwanda's Great Lakes region before 1000 B.C.E. By 500 B.C.E., ironworking was well established in these two separate anchor regions of Central Africa. A third area of iron smelting has been located in the Nigeria-Cameroon corridor, where smelting seems to have taken hold by the last half of the last millennium B.C.E. Although the technology of iron metallurgy was established in a few localized settings by the commencement of the last millennium, the technology did not become more widespread in sub-Saharan Africa until the sixth century B.C.E. The gradual and uneven nature by which iron became an integral part of sub-Saharan life can be seen at Daima, southwest of Lake Chad. One archaeological level of a continuous settlement shows that herders in that area acquired iron only in the first century B.C.E.

The landscape between the Lake Chad Basin in the north, the Great Lakes region to the east, the Nigeria-Cameroon corridor in the west, and the Congo Basin in the south has been composed of dense forests, woodlands, and savannas for at least the last twenty centuries (since c. 2000 B.C.E.). The peoples inhabiting the inter-Chad-Rwandan lands would have relied on local resources found in their regions, not long-distance trade for goods. Among the important resources of Central Africa around Lake Chad and in the region of modern-day Rwanda were the clay soil used for pottery and the iron ore used for iron metallurgy.

Cultivating raw iron into a workable product typically involved a corporate group such as a clan or other communal group. Though only men were permitted and sanctioned to perform the smelting and smithing processes, women and children were involved in the management of the resources and site preparation for the smelt. Scholars have contended that women and children were most likely included in looking for and mining iron, constructing pots for transporting the ore, and providing provision of food and drinks to distant smelting camps.

The process began with the mining of suitable ore. Lumps of ore were chipped away with hammers and anvils and stockpiled. Then, in order to make the iron ore malleable, a smelting process had to take place. Made of a clay composite, the furnaces for smelting were of varying shapes and sizes. It is suspected that the great variation in furnace types throughout Central Africa reflects the diversity and quality of ores found throughout the Central Africa region. Despite the structural differences, all furnaces were loaded with a mixture of crushed charcoal and iron ore. Air was hand-pumped into the furnace through bellowed air pipes, which acted as vents. An ironworker had to calculate the ratio of air to ore precisely, so as to ensure a suitable product. After the process was complete, the mixture was removed from the furnace and set to cool. The African furnaces were highly complex to operate and have been difficult for modern-day scholars to re-create. In ancient Africa, only skilled specialists who had completed years of apprenticeship could have succeeded in conducting the smelting process.

In the last millennium B.C.E., central Africans mined and smelted iron ore into useful items such as rings, bangles, hammers, chisels, and hoes. Iron served several purposes throughout society, being formed into products that ranged from weapons to tools to jewelry and currencies. Reflecting the importance of iron ore to the communities of Bantu descent is the inclusion of iron-related terms in various branches of the Bantu-descended languages. Words for "ore," "iron," "anvil," "charcoal," and related concepts are prevalent in Bantu-speaking areas. Scholars have been able to examine such language through historical linguistics, archaeological findings, and ethnographic surveys to understand the early history of iron in Africa. In many instances, the root words for terms related to iron technology are common across the Bantu landscape. Although many of these terms may at one point have referred to stone tools, their meanings shifted as iron became more important and abundant. Distribution of shared iron terms follows a pattern that appears to be directly related to a center of diffusion originating in central Africa, on the borderlands, where Mashariki Bantu and other Bantu peoples of the western and central savannas meet. The language patterns imply that the Great Lakes area might have served as this center of diffusion, though further research in Congo, Gabon, and Cameroon is necessary before any clear conclusions can be drawn about the centers from which iron technologies were dispersed.

SIGNIFICANCE

The significance of the Iron Age in sub-Saharan Africa is twofold. First, because the evidence indicates that iron-smelting technology in sub-Saharan Africa developed separately from iron technologies in other parts of the world and seems not to have been introduced from outside the continent, scholars believe that iron smelting was most likely invented by Sudanian and Sahelian speakers of the Great Lakes zone, was adopted by Bantu speakers, and then spread out with Bantu population movements.

Second, iron shifted the basic economies of sub-Saharan peoples. The advent of iron metallurgy in sub-Saharan Africa opened the door to the development of specialized technologies, trade, and social stratification, which in turn placed ironworkers at the center of several socioeconomic circles. Though economic activities such as hunting, cattle raising, and farming were integral to these societies, no profession required as much skill as that of the ironworker.

The smiths' production of tools for farming, hunting, and warfare helped to make smelters and smiths an indispensable and respected group in society. When iron became the center of economic, political, and even ritual life, ironworkers became men of great wealth. In later eras (between the sixteenth and nineteenth centuries C.E.) in the Rwandan and Burundian kingdoms, kingship and smithing were hereditary, and oral traditions frequently make mention of the interconnection through the figure of the "smith-king." These traditions also refer to ironworking as that which "mediates the passage from sterility to fecundity." As in other places in Central Africa, the kings of Rwanda were known to keep an iron hammer at hand even when they slept, as it was the symbol of royal power. In the Great Lakes region of East Africa, rulers claimed that their chiefs had invented metallurgy and were responsible for bringing it to the region. For example, according to oral tradition, the founder of the Rwandan kingdom, Gihanga, was a blacksmith. The link, which is often seen as purely symbolic, demonstrates the alliance of kingship and ironworking.

Perhaps the greatest testament to the importance of early ironworking can be seen in the role it plays in origin myths. A common theme in several Bantu origin myths portrays ironworkers as divine heroes from whom civilization was created. According to oral tradition, ironworkers produced the ax for the creation of the village and the razor to cut the umbilical cord—clear references to creation, fertility, and birth.

Marriage was at times closely connected to wealth in iron. Iron eventually became the material used for currency, repositories of value, and social payments (including the bride price). Iron helped to make patrilineality important in certain regions, in that the possession of iron meant heightened access to the woman of one's choosing. Iron also made marriage a difficult achievement for men who could not acquire the desired wealth in iron. Because of their wealth and social status, smiths often came to be viewed as possessing magical or supernatural powers. Sometimes they were feared for their potential power both to curse individuals and communities and to withhold iron production.

The shift from a stone-tool-based society to one centered on iron brought about the possibility of centralized control of tool production by those who guarded the knowledge of this technology, which in turn influenced foodways, warfare, and political organization. Previously, salt and stone tools were the commodities at the center of any short-distance trade, but the rarity of suitable ores and specialized knowledge shifted the importance and value to iron, which elevated the economic and political influence of those regions where pockets of good ore were located. As the metal in refined form and the techniques for refining the ores spread across the continent, sub-Saharan access to iron ore proved to be invaluable.

—*Candace R. Ellington*

FURTHER READING

Digombe, Lazare, et al. "Gabon: the Earliest Iron Age of West Central Africa." *Nyame Akuma* 28 (1987): 9-11. This article discusses the western side of Central Africa and its history of iron production.

Ehret, Christopher. *The Civilizations of Africa: A History to 1800*. Charlottesville: University Press of Virginia, 2002. A textbook that examines early African civilizations.

Phillipson, David W. *African Archaeology*. Cambridge, England: Cambridge University Press, 1993. Particularly useful is the chapter titled "Iron Using Peoples Before A.D. 1000."

Schmidt, Peter R., ed. *The Culture and Technology of African Iron Production*. Gainesville: University Press of Florida, 1996. Contains chapters authored by various scholars discussing iron production in Africa. Of particular interest is a chapter by Pierre de Maret and G. Thiry, "How Old Is the Iron Age in Central Africa?"

SEE ALSO: c. 6500-c. 5000 B.C.E., Nilo-Saharan Farmers Spread Cultivation and Herding; c. 6000-c. 1000 B.C.E., Omotics Advance Farming Practices in Horn of Africa; c. 5500-c. 4500 B.C.E., Niger-Congo Peoples Spread Agriculture in Africa; c. 1000-c. 700 B.C.E., Mashariki Bantu Establish Chifumbaze Ironworking Culture; c. 1000 B.C.E.-c. 300 C.E., Urban Commerce Develops in the Sudan Belt; c. 800-c. 600 B.C.E., Ironworking Spreads into Sub-Saharan Africa; 290-300 C.E., West African Gold First Reaches North Africa; 300-400 C.E., Bantu People Invent Copper Metallurgy.

c. 1000-900 B.C.E.
IONIAN CONFEDERACY FORMS

The Ionian confederacy brought together large settlements of Ionian Greeks who were responsible for the birth of Greek epic poetry, history writing, and natural philosophy.

LOCALE: The western coast of Anatolia (modern Turkey)

CATEGORIES: Expansion and land acquisition; cultural and intellectual history

KEY FIGURES

Neleus (fl. c. eleventh-tenth century B.C.E.), son of King Codrus and founder of Miletus

Androclus (fl. c. eleventh-tenth century B.C.E.), son of King Codrus of Athens and founder of Ephesus

SUMMARY OF EVENT

The central portion of the west coast of Anatolia has had a long and varied history. In the first half of the second millennium B.C.E., Minoan merchants from Crete established trading posts throughout the Aegean and eastern Mediterranean. Archaeologists have found Minoan-type pottery on the west central coast of Anatolia in an area that would later be called Ionia. Moreover, Minoan settlements have also been found at Miletus.

The preclassical mainland Greeks, known as Mycenaeans, also colonized the west coast of Anatolia, as evidenced by the beehive-shaped *tholos* tombs (dated from the fourteenth to the twelfth centuries B.C.E.) found at Colophon along the central coast. Hittite cuneiform records found in central Anatolia and dating to about 1300 B.C.E. mention a city named Milawata, probably the later Ionian city of Miletus. The records imply that Milawata was under the control of a polity known as Ahhiyawa, possibly the Hittite name for the Achaeans of mainland Greece during the Mycenaean period. It is not clear, however, who composed the indigenous population of the area during the second millennium B.C.E., although later tradition claims that they were a local Anatolian people called the Carians. By the twelfth century B.C.E., the Mycenaean and Hittite kingdoms were either destroyed or had become decentralized. Archaeological research has shown that the Mycenaean levels of Miletus were destroyed at this time, and Greek tradition claims that this period coincided with the sack of Troy.

At about this time, the Greek mainland was overrun by the Dorians, a group that had originated north of Greece. Greek historical tradition holds that migrations of Greeks from the mainland to Ionia began in response to the destruction of their cities at the end of the Bronze Age around 1200 B.C.E. Aeolian Greeks sailed to some of the Aegean islands, including Lesbos, and to the northwest Anatolian coast. Some Dorians evidently settled in the southern regions, and Greeks known as Ionians settled on the central coast. Their presence is evidenced by archaeological finds at Miletus, where the Mycenaean civilization settlement was succeeded by a group using pottery akin to that found in Attica on the mainland of Greece. This pottery type, called Protogeometric, has been found throughout Ionia.

The material remains concerning the Ionian migration can be complemented by a series of fragmented literary accounts in Greek. The memory of Ionians living in the mainland of Greece is recounted in Greek poet Homer's *Iliad* (c. 750 B.C.E.; English translation, 1611), which mentions them once in association with the Boeotians. A fragment written by Athenian lawgiver Solon (c. 630-c. 560 B.C.E.) implies that the Ionians had come from Attica. The Greek historian Herodotus noted in his *Historiai Herodotou* (c. 424 B.C.E.; *The History*, 1709) that there had been Ionians in Boeotia, Attica, and the Peloponnesus. The earliest extant account of the Ionian migration was written by the Athenian historian Pherecydes (c. 500 B.C.E.) and was paraphrased by the Roman geographer Strabo as well as by Pausanias the Traveler (with slight variations). These accounts tell that the sons of Codrus, the Ionian king of Athens, and others migrated from there sometime around 1100 B.C.E. Miletus was founded by Neleus, a son of Codrus. The Ionians led by him killed the local male inhabitants and married the local women. Androclus, another son of Codrus, was the founder of the city of Ephesus. According to these accounts, Androclus drove out the Lydians but, unlike Neleus, was friendly with the local inhabitants. Tradition holds that others founded the remaining Ionian cities on the islands of Chios, Samos, and Mycale, as well as the mainland sites of Colophon, Priene, Lebedos, Phocaea, and Teos, among others.

The Ionian city-states forged a defensive confederacy that fostered a sense of community among them. The Greek writers state, however, that the Ionians fought among themselves and against the Carians, the local Anatolian inhabitants. In the eighth century B.C.E., the Ionians were successful in sending out colonies in the Aegean, the western Mediterranean (notably Sicily and southern Italy), inland Anatolia, and even the Egyptian Delta region. By the early seventh century B.C.E., the Ionians were attacked by the Lydian king Gyges, who threatened their existence. Even more dangerous was the threat posed by the Cimmerians and the Scythians later in the century who, according to Herodotus, plundered Ionia but did not destroy the cities. The Ionian confederacy was later forced to pay tribute to Lydia and soon thereafter was conquered by Persia late in the sixth century B.C.E. In the beginning of the fifth century B.C.E., with the support of Athens and other mainland Greek cities, Ionia staged an unsuccessful revolt against Persian rule. According to Herodotus, this revolt sparked the beginning of the great Persian Wars of the period.

SIGNIFICANCE

Notwithstanding their importance to eastern Mediterranean political history, the Ionians were at the forefront of Greek civilization in the first half of the first millennium B.C.E. The great epic poetry of Greece, exemplified by Homer's *Iliad* and *Odyssey* (c. 725 B.C.E.; English translation, 1614), originated on the Asiatic Greek coast during the eighth century B.C.E. Moreover, the Ionians appear to have been the first to promote a rational view of the world, thus founding the study of natural philosophy. Many of the greatest thinkers of the ancient world came from Ionia, including Thales of Miletus, Anaximander, Heraclitus of Ephesus, Anaximenes of Miletus, and Pythagoras, who was from Samos. Furthermore, critical history writing originated from the Ionian coast with Hecataeus of Miletus, a forerunner of Herodotus. Finally, the Ionians made great innovations in art and architecture, creating a distinct style of sculpture known as Ionia. Thus, the Ionian impact on European poetry, philosophy, historiography, and sculpture is incalculable.

—*Mark W. Chavalas*

FURTHER READING

Bouzek, J. *The Aegean, Anatolia and Europe: Cultural Interaction in the Second Millennium B.C.* Göteburg, Sweden: Paul Astroms, 1985. This work surveys the cultural and artistic interconnections in the Aegean world during the Late Bronze and Early Iron ages, the periods of the Ionian migration to Anatolia.

Drews, R. *The Coming of the Greeks: Indo-European Conquests in the Aegean and the Near East.* Princeton, N.J.: Princeton University Press, 1988. A look at the entry of Greeks into Anatolia and other regions.

_______. *The End of the Bronze Age: Changes in Warfare and the Catastrophe ca. 1200 B.C.* Princeton, N.J.: Princeton University Press, 1993. Drews provides the background for understanding the major cultural and political changes that occurred in the eastern Mediterranean from the Bronze to Iron Ages, leading to the Ionian settlement of the Anatolian coast.

Emlyn-Jones, C. J. *The Ionians and Hellenism: A Study of the Cultural Achievement of the Early Greek Inhabitants of Asia Minor.* London: Routledge & Kegan Paul, 1980. Surveys the cultural attributes of Ionia in the first half of the first millennium B.C.E. and the interaction of the Ionians with the local Anatolian populations.

Huxley, G. L. *The Early Ionians*. New York: Barnes & Noble, 1972. A general survey of Ionia from the beginning of the first millennium B.C.E. to the revolt against Persia five centuries later. Huxley studies both the literary traditions concerning early Ionia and the existing material remains.

Souyoudzoglou-Haywood, Christina. *The Ionian Islands in the Bronze Age and Early Iron Age, 3000-800 B.C.* Liverpool, England: Liverpool University Press, 1999. An examination of the Ionian Islands before and during the confederacy.

SEE ALSO: c. 1200-c. 1050 B.C.E., Sea Peoples Contribute to Mediterranean Upheaval; 8th century B.C.E., Scythians Drive the Cimmerians from Central Asia; 8th-6th centuries B.C.E., Phrygian Kingdom Rises; c. 734-c. 580 B.C.E., Greeks Colonize the Mediterranean and Black Sea Regions; 499-494 B.C.E., Ionian Revolt.

RELATED ARTICLE in *Great Lives from History: The Ancient World*: Homer.

c. 1000-c. 700 B.C.E.
MASHARIKI BANTU ESTABLISH CHIFUMBAZE IRONWORKING CULTURE

The Chifumbaze segment of Bantu culture produced pottery and iron tools that have been uncovered by archaeologists in eastern, central, and southern Africa.

LOCALE: Eastern and southern Africa, especially present-day Rwanda and Burundi

CATEGORIES: Prehistory and ancient cultures; science and technology

SUMMARY OF EVENT

Chifumbaze material culture encompasses pottery, iron tools, and perhaps even architectural styles. Chifumbaze refers more generally to the early Iron Age industrial complex and material culture uncovered in Rwanda and Burundi, which resembles other eastern and southern African regional variants of the same broad era. Some scholars have even applied the term Chifumbaze as nomenclature for the various and diverse populations who produced the material culture identified as Chifumbaze wares.

The Chifumbaze pottery complex had developed in the region west of Lake Victoria in Eastern Africa by the beginning of the last millennium B.C.E. (by 1000 B.C.E.). Archaeology across several regions of Africa reveals that Chifumbaze pottery arose out of Urewe ware, also with origins in the Great Lakes region of eastern Africa. Chifumbaze ware began in the west Rift region, spread into Rwanda and Burundi, and then extended out further from the Great Lakes center. Chifumbaze culture extended north of Lake Victoria by the middle of the last millennium B.C.E., and by the third century C.E., Chifumbaze ware had spread east and south from the Great Lakes region into Natal in the eastern enclave of southern Africa. This pottery, which covers eastern and southern Africa and seems to be closely linked to Bantu populations and cultures, appears to have spread over approximately 1,850 miles (3,000 kilometers) north to south in two centuries' time.

The Chifumbaze pottery and iron tool tradition has a basic common form and yet is manifested in a variety of stylistic expressions across southern and eastern Africa. Chifumbaze pottery is fired stoneware and is characterized by the beveled, fluted rims, narrow slits, and stamped bands decorating the exterior. The various facies of Chifumbaze have been identified outside the Great Lakes proper, for example in northern Angola near Luanda, in Botswana at Toutswe sites, and in coastal East Africa as Kwale ware; in central Tanzania as Lelesu ware; south of the Zambezi as Matola ware; in Shaba Province of Zaire; and in Malawi and Zambia in several manifestations.

In conjunction with the fluted, fired pottery produced from the Chifumbaze complex, Great Lakes smiths of the Early Iron Age smelted iron from local ores to produce tools and items for adornment. The pottery and iron production are closely interconnected technologies in the Chifumbaze archaeological sites, indicating that the two skills spread together and perhaps were produced in tandem as complementary items for consumption. The introduction of the Chifumbaze tool kit provided farmers with iron technology for field preparation and other economic endeavors such as hunting and fishing. Tools of this complex, which have been excavated at sites, include iron

CHIFUMBAZE TRADITIONS, 1ST TO 11TH CENTURIES C.E.

Facie	*Location*	*Dates*
	North Angola at Benifica	First centuries
Kalambo	Tanzania/Zambia/Malawi	
Mwabulambo	Zambia/Congo	
Muteteshi	Central Zambia	First century
Matola	Southern Africa	Second century
Nampula	Malawi/Mozambique	Second century
Kwale	Northeast coastal Tanzania/Southeast coastal Kenya	Second century
	Situmpa/Salumano	Third century
Monapo	North Mozambique/South Tanzania	Fourth century
Nkope/Gokomere	Malawi/East Zambia/Zimbabwe	
Toutswe	East Botswana Limpopo Valley	Seventh century
Lyndenburg	Southern Africa	First millennium

Source: Data compiled from *African Archaeology* (1993) by David W. Phillipson.

axes, hoes, knives, and arrows, more indicative of farming life than of a strictly gathering and hunting system.

Extant evidence indicates that the innovators and subsequent makers of Chifumbaze wares were agriculturalists who produced domesticated millets, sorghums, beans, and gourds that scholars have long associated with Bantu-speaking farmers. Green vegetables, root crops, and grains evidenced in excavations demonstrate the varied diet of the Bantu, who descended from those who had come into contact with cattle-raising and grain-cultivating Central and Eastern Sudanians and adapted some of those techniques, an idea that has long been established among scholars in the field of African history. Foodways and nutritional evidence are important sources of historical information and lend additional support to a history of Bantu production and spreading of Chifumbaze potteries.

Because the tools and potteries of the Chifumbaze genre did not include insignia in written language, scholars have not been able to establish definitively if this is a Bantu innovation. However, the motifs and decorations on the excavated items recovered thus far, together with the economic lifestyle uncovered in the paleobotanical record and other archaeological evidence, strongly suggest that the Chifumbaze wares were spread by speakers of Bantu languages practicing agriculture in settled communities. Archaeological evidence includes Chifumbaze potteries, iron tools, grindstones, and pollens of both grain and vegetal plants, all of which indicate what kinds of foods were consumed, how they were prepared, and some of the other cultural practices that may have been associated with the communities leaving behind such evidence. With some variation, Chifumbaze-producing communities tended to erect residential structures with burnt-thatch roofs and clay walls and floors. At least up to the tenth century C.E., Chifumbaze material culture was one unifying feature of a larger and extremely diverse Bantu continuum of cultures.

Based on archaeological and linguistic data, scholars believe that a core group of Bantu speakers gained knowledge of iron technology from grain-cultivating and cattle-raising communities speaking Central and Eastern Sudanian languages by the last millennium B.C.E. The technologies were adopted and innovated by Bantu speakers and then diffused out from the western side of Lake Victoria eastward across eastern Africa, southward into southern Africa, and even westward into the Congo Basin as a supplement to western production between c. 500 B.C.E. and 200 C.E. These iron- and pottery-producing Bantu lived in relatively small, dispersed village settlements and probably frequently incorporated a variety of non-Bantu speaking cultures and individuals into the life of the settlements.

SIGNIFICANCE

The pottery of Chifumbaze style found in Rwanda dates as early as the eighth and seventh centuries B.C.E., making it one of Africa's ancient potteries. Chifumbaze belongs to one of the most contentious eras in terms of the scholarly debate on Bantu Africa. Chifumbaze potteries are linked to a spread of culture which may have marked a set or series of population movements, but Africanist scholars have yet to agree how, when, and why they occurred.

The eastward expansion of Bantu culture and language into the Great Lakes Basin may be the result of multiple movements out of the western half of the continent over centuries; it may be a result of population booms; it may be a consequence of non-Bantu adopting some key aspects of Bantu culture; or, more likely, it is the result of multiple factors that resulted in the presence of a community of Mashariki Bantu located in the east, in contrast to the Bantu of equatorial and woodland western Africa. Each migration in all probability involved movement of numerous subgroups over an extended period of centuries. Some scholars have referred to the particular era of Chifumbaze expansion out of the Great Lakes core area as the middle Mashariki era, when two distinctive branches of Mashariki Bantu began to form: the Kusi and Kaskazi. It is entirely possible that the multiple migrations resulted not only in divergences but also in convergences as well as reconvergences, which makes historical analysis of Bantu peoples an exciting challenge for scholars.

Chifumbaze culture notably marks an archaeological break with the types of material culture present prior to the arrival of Chifumbaze wares and tools in most parts of eastern, central, and southern Africa. Chifumbaze makers interacted with and in some cases displaced hunter-gatherer populations who produced little or no pottery and, it seems, smelted no iron or other metal. It appears from available evidence that Chifumbaze economic activities of agriculture, cattle raising, pottery making, and iron smelting spread with Bantu and even non-Bantu speakers who took up the Chifumbaze way of life. Pottery style and iron smelting traditions characteristic of the Eastern and Southern African Iron Age were most likely linked with the spread of Bantu speakers from the Great Lakes region into eastern and southern parts of the African subcontinent.

—*Catherine Cymone Fourshey*

FURTHER READING

Bisson, Michael S., et al. *Ancient African Metallurgy: The Sociocultural Context*. Edited by Joseph O. Vogel. Walnut Creek, Calif.: AltaMira Press, 2000. Four scholars examine the evidence and elucidate the debates surrounding when and where iron and copper technology arose in Africa and the role metallurgy played politically, economically, socially, and ideologically. Bibliographical references, index.

Ehret, Christopher. *The Civilizations of Africa: A History to 1800*. Charlottesville: University Press of Virginia, 2002. This textbook examines early African civilizations and the cultures they introduced.

Hall, M. *Archaeology Africa*. London: James Currey, 1996. Discussion of significant archaeological finds in Africa with some attention to the material's cultural and historical significance.

Musonda, F. B. "The Significance of Pottery in the Later Stone Age Sites." *African Archaeological Review* 5 (1987): 147-158. Explains why pottery is significant in human culture and particularly how this technology emerged in southern central Africa.

Phillipson, David W. *African Archaeology*. New York: Cambridge University Press, 1993. Discussion of archaeological finds in Africa and explanation of what those finds mean, with some special attention to iron production.

Van Grunderbeeck, M. C., et al. *Le Premier Âge du fer au Rwanda et au Burundi: Archéologie et environment*. Butare, Rwanda: Institut National de Recherche Scientifique, 1983. Presents primary research data on ancient iron production in Rwanda and Burundi. In French.

SEE ALSO: c. 6500-c. 5000 B.C.E., Nilo-Saharan Farmers Spread Cultivation and Herding; c. 6000-c. 1000 B.C.E., Omotics Advance Farming Practices in Horn of Africa; c. 5500-c. 4500 B.C.E., Niger-Congo Peoples Spread Agriculture in Africa; c. 1000 B.C.E., Sub-Saharan Ironworking Begins; c. 1000 B.C.E.-c. 300 C.E., Urban Commerce Develops in the Sudan Belt; c. 800-c. 600 B.C.E., Ironworking Spreads into Sub-Saharan Africa; 290-300 C.E., West African Gold First Reaches North Africa; 300-400 C.E., Bantu People Invent Copper Metallurgy.

c. 1000-c. 690 B.C.E.
CIMMERIAN CULTURE RISES IN RUSSIA

The nomadic Cimmerians, the first people to domesticate the horse and use it in warfare, arose in what would later become European Russia and the Ukraine.

LOCALE: Areas north of the Black Sea (now in Ukraine and European Russia)
CATEGORY: Prehistory and ancient cultures

SUMMARY OF EVENT

The Cimmerians were an early people whose existence is shrouded in myth and legend. In the eighth century B.C.E., the Greek Homer referred to them in his epics as living in the far north, in perpetual darkness. This may have been the ancient Greeks' way of attempting to describe the peculiar patterns of night and day near the Arctic Circle, where the sun barely sets in summer and scarcely rises in winter. Several Assyrian texts mention them as Ga-mir or Ga-mir-a-a, which roughly means "people traveling back and forth," that is, nomads. In the Jewish Torah (which also constitutes the first five books of the Christian Old Testament), Moses referred to the Cimmerians as the Gomer horde. In the twentieth century, fantasy author Robert E. Howard made his sword-and-sorcery hero Conan the Barbarian a member of the Cimmerian tribe, and his works became so popular that many casual readers associate the name "Cimmerian" primarily with those fictional adventures. As a result, it might be easy for a modern reader to conclude that the Cimmerians were an entirely mythical people.

However, archaeological research in the areas of modern Ukraine and European Russia has found that the Cimmerians were indeed a real ethnic group that lived north of the Black Sea. In fact, the name Crimea for the peninsula on the Black Sea shores of Ukraine comes from their occupation of that territory. Archaeological research has linked the Cimmerians with the Novocherkassk culture, which was located on the grassy plains of the Prut and the lower Don Rivers. Because the Cimmerians had no written language, it is impossible to say for certain what language they spoke, but it is probable that they were an Iranian people, speaking a language similar to the Farsi spoken in modern Iran. Some scholars have suggested a possible connection with the Sumerians who founded the first Mesopotamian civilization on the Tigris and Euphrates Rivers (modern Iraq), but this theory depends on similarities of names and artifacts that may be attributable to chance rather than historic descent.

The Cimmerians were a Bronze Age people who produced numerous metal artifacts, including some very sophisticated sculptural representations of various animals familiar to them. They also produced striking bas-relief sculptures of men riding horses. Cimmerian men were buried with bow, sword, and spear among their grave goods, and there is ample evidence that they fought as mounted archers. It was said that their women fought as fiercely as their men and were not permitted to marry until they had killed an enemy. These warrior women may have been the basis for the Greek myth of the Amazons.

The horse was a major factor in the culture of the Cimmerians. In fact, it appears that they were the first people to domesticate and ride the horse and that they invented the mounted nomad lifestyle. Domestication of the horse gave them considerable military advantages over their neighbors and enabled them to increase their territory greatly. By the eighth century, they were encroaching on the plains to the north of the Caucasus (the area between modern Rostov-na-Donu and Astrakhan), which alarmed the kingdom of Urartu (predecessor of modern Armenia). In 720 B.C.E., the Urartuan king, Rusa, made a preemptive attack on Cimmerian forces, only to be defeated. As a result, the Cimmerians invaded and looted the entire area.

This brought the Cimmerians into contact with Phrygia, a kingdom in what would become Turkey. The Phrygian king, called Mit-ta in Assyrian sources and Midas in the Greek (who may have served as the basis for the legendary King Midas of the golden touch and the donkey's ears), called on the assistance of King Sargon II of Assyria but was defeated in battle and committed suicide rather than be captured. Subsequently, a new kingdom, Lydia, rose from the ruins of Phrygia and fought numerous battles with the Cimmerians over the next century. By 610 B.C.E., the Lydians were able to inflict several major defeats on the Cimmerians, who subsequently disappeared from history. Apparently they were subsumed by the Scythians, also horse-riding nomads.

SIGNIFICANCE

The Cimmerians' domestication of the horse has had profound effects on human history that have extended into modern industrial times. Horses completely revolutionized the lifestyles of every nomadic tribe that acquired them, from the Cimmerians themselves to the Huns and Mongols and even the native peoples of the North American Great Plains. Only with the development of gunpowder weapons, which must be produced by a settled civilization, was the perpetual threat of the mounted nomadic horde broken for good. From then on, civilizations remained vulnerable only to one another or internal decay. The importance of the horse in other areas of life, including agriculture and transportation, remained paramount until the development of steam and internal-combustion engines by industrial societies.

—*Leigh Husband Kimmel*

FURTHER READING

Davis-Kimball, Jeaninne, Vladimir A. Bashilov, and Leonid T. Yablonsky, eds. *Nomads of the Eurasian Steppes in the Early Iron Age*. Berkeley, Calif.: Zinat, 1995. A collection of articles dealing with early nomadic tribes in the area of modern Russia and Ukraine.

Rolle, Renate. *The World of the Scythians*. Translated by F. G. Walls. Berkeley: University of California Press, 1989. An overview of the world of early horse-nomad tribes. Includes index and bibliography.

Trippett, Frank. *The First Horsemen*. New York: Time-Life Books, 1974. Discusses archaeological evidence of the earliest mounted nomad tribes. Includes index.

Wells, Peter S. *Beyond Celts, Germans, and Scythians: Archaeology and Identity in Bronze-Age Europe*. London: Duckworth, 2001. Deals with the problem of relying upon Greek and Roman texts, with their built-in biases, in understanding preliterate ancient peoples, particularly nomads.

SEE ALSO: 8th century B.C.E., Scythians Drive the Cimmerians from Central Asia; c. 420 B.C.E.-c. 100 C.E., Yuezhi Culture Links Persia and China; 15 B.C.E.-15 C.E., Rhine-Danube Frontier Is Established; c. 3d-4th century C.E., Huns Begin Migration West from Central Asia.

c. 1000-c. 500 B.C.E.
NOK ARTISTS DEVELOP TERRA-COTTA SCULPTURE

The Iron Age African culture that flourished near the tin-mining village of Nok in Nigeria produced finely crafted figurative sculpture out of clay, using sophisticated firing techniques.

LOCALE: Jos Plateau between the Niger and Benue Rivers in north-central Nigeria, Africa

CATEGORIES: Prehistory and ancient cultures; cultural and intellectual history; science and technology

SUMMARY OF EVENT

Some of the earliest ironworking communities in Africa were those of the Nok culture in northern Nigeria. Their knowledge of furnaces and iron smelting apparently carried over into the firing of pottery and clay sculpture, as relics of this little-known group of people have shown. The most striking of the pieces unearthed from this area are figurative terra-cotta sculptures representing distinct individuals and crafted with a high degree of sophistication. They are unique in African art history for both their technical mastery and their artistic expression.

While the period during which the Nok sculptures were created is generally accepted to be between 800 B.C.E. and 500 C.E., recent improvements in technology are extending this time range. The radiocarbon dating system used to analyze the pieces has recently been recalibrated to more current standards. This process has expanded the chronology of the Nok culture to a period of around 900 B.C.E. to 875 C.E. Another dating technique known as thermoluminescence has been added to cross-date the objects for a more accurate history of the Nok culture. Using this cross-dating system, some scholars place the earliest emergence of the Nok at 1000 B.C.E.

The name Nok refers to a village in a region known as the Jos Plateau, which lies between the Niger and Benue Rivers. It was there, in 1928, that the first small terra-cotta head was uncovered by a worker at a tin mine. In 1942 a larger and more elaborately sculpted head was found some 40 miles (65 kilometers) away, near Jemaa. The find was reported to local administrative officer Bernard Fagg, who had experience in archaeology. Fagg sent out an appeal to all who worked in the minefields of the region to preserve any more examples found. Further excavations brought to light more fragments that revealed the heads were once part of complete figures. They displayed a wide range of facial characteristics and gestures; some pieces were in the form of animals. Despite the variety of characters and poses the Nok terra-cottas portray, there is strong stylistic continuity that makes them immediately recognizable as a group.

Close examination of Nok sculptures has revealed their method of construction. They were made from local clay, employing the same coiling method used in bowls and cooking vessels found nearby. The clay was mixed with gravel containing rock and quartz fragments, perhaps to add strength. In some of the larger sculptures, the head and other appendages were crafted separately and then joined to a hollow body. Finger marks of the artist are visible on the interior of the clay forms. The eyes and sometimes the ears are pierced. Details such as elaborate hairstyles, facial hair, necklaces, amulets, beads, armbands, and bracelets were carefully modeled and attached next. Liquid clay (slip) was applied as a final step to achieve a smooth surface. In order to support the soft clay for the larger pieces, they were built around a simple wooden frame with branches for the arms. This support would burn away during the firing process.

The precise function of the Nok terra-cottas is still being researched. The majority of sculptures found have been in soils deposited over time by flooding, which makes an accurate archaeological context difficult to establish. Excavations have not shown that the sculptures were buried with human remains. They seem to be representations of royalty and important members of society, such as priests and diviners. It is most likely that they were placed in altars, similar to the way native cultures of more recent times displayed their ancestor figures.

Many technical and stylistic factors in Nok sculpture point to a connection with later generations of African art, though a direct link has yet to be established. Terra-cotta figures of a style different from Nok have been discovered in the northern Nigerian state of Sokoto. They date from between 200 B.C.E. and 200 C.E. Still another style from the same time period may originate from the region of Katsina, also in the north. Both share certain technical features with those of Nok. There are also similarities in technique with the highly realistic terra-cotta sculpture of Ife, created between the eleventh and fourteenth century C.E. in southern Nigeria. Specific details such as hairstyles and headbands are found in both groups. The Ife tradition, which also included bronze portrait heads, is known to have had a direct influence on the bronze sculpture produced in Benin starting around the fourteenth century C.E. Masks still being made up to the present day by the Yoruba people of Nigeria use a method of facial stylization that has much in common with Nok examples. Eyes are enlarged and slightly bulging, with holes for the pupils, a detail that has no practical function because the masks are worn on the top of the head.

SIGNIFICANCE

One constant within the design of Nok sculptures is a proportional standard. The head is used as a unit of measure, and the total piece is three or four times this length. African art historian William Fagg termed this "the African Proportion." It is used in many sculptures throughout Africa, regardless of the materials chosen. It is possible that elements of this Nok style spread gradually throughout what is now Nigeria and Cameroon. Linguists working in this region have traced a two-thousand-year movement of Bantu languages from a cradle area that includes the Jos Plateau. As those early people migrated, they brought with them cultural traditions including pottery techniques and modes of artistic expression. Gestures and proportions that are repeated in the Nok terra-cottas are also found in sculptures from the tribes of this Bantu language group, which range as far as the Congo and beyond. The absence of any similar art in Africa before the Nok culture's advances in terra-cotta sculpture places it as a seminal event in the artistic development of the continent.

—*Craig Lloyd*

FURTHER READING

De Grunne, Bernard. *The Birth of Art in Black Africa: Nok Statuary in Nigeria*. Paris: Adam Biro, 1998. A comprehensive study of the Nok culture, including archaeological history, theories on functions of the objects, influence on other cultures, and recent dating methodology. Bibliography.

Fagg, Bernard. *Nok Terracottas*. London: Ethnographica, 1990. A detailed account of the author's discovery, excavation, documentation, and interpretation of the Nok terra-cottas. Index and bibliography.

Jemkur, J. F. *Aspects of Nok Culture*. Zaria, Nigeria: Ahmadu Bello University Press, 1992. Covers what is known about Nok culture, particularly their sculpture.

Willet, Frank. *African Art*. New York: Thames and Hudson, 1993. A survey of African art history with a discussion of Nok art that covers its archaeological origins, dating, meaning, and influence on later cultures. Index and bibliography.

SEE ALSO: c. 9000-c. 7000 B.C.E., Nilo-Saharan Peoples Produce Food and Pottery; c. 1000 B.C.E.-c. 300 C.E., Urban Commerce Develops in the Sudan Belt; c. 5th century C.E., Lydenburg Bantus Sculpt Life-Size Terra-cotta Heads.

c. 1000-c. 200 B.C.E.

Compilation of the Upaniṣads

As a major source of Indian philosophy and culture, the Upaniṣads are second only to the Vedas in importance, and they purport to explain the hidden meaning of the Vedas.

Locale: Indus Valley region in the Northwestern India (now mostly in the eastern region of Pakistan)

Categories: Religion; cultural and intellectual history

Summary of Event

The Upaniṣads (or Upanishads) are a group of classical Sanskrit texts in prose and verse that interpret and elaborate in philosophical language the "central aim and the meaning of the teaching of the Veda," according to philosopher Sarvepalli Radhakrishnan. Because they are appended to the Vedas (writings concerning aspects of religious thought and customs compiled 1500-1100 B.C.E.), the Upaniṣads are also called the Vedānta, meaning the end of the Vedas. Etymologically, the compound word *upaniṣad* is derived from Sanskrit roots that imply "to sit down near," which apparently refers to the practice of trusted disciples sitting down at the feet of spiritual masters to gain a deeper understanding of the Vedas. Their compilation spanned several centuries from 1000 to 200 B.C.E.

To understand the broader sociohistorical context leading to the compilation of the Upaniṣads, it is important to note that the majority of these texts were committed to writing during the period that the German thinker Karl Jaspers (1883-1969) described as the Axial Age. Jaspers thought that the period between 800 and 400 B.C.E. was axial because the cultural axis of the world today was established during this time through the emergence of what were to become the major philosophical systems and world religions in both Asia and the West: China (Daoism and Confucianism), India (Hinduism and Buddhism), Greece (Western philosophy), Persia (Zoroastrianism), and Palestine (Judaism). They offer collective, though differing, responses to the perennial questions about the meaning and purpose of life and how human beings are to live. The beginnings of the Indian axial age are characterized by the compilation of the Upaniṣads, followed by the founding of Buddhism.

The concerns of this period sharply contrast with those of the Vedic age. The thrust of the Vedic age was to understand and manipulate the forces of nature, personified as powerful and capricious divine beings, to serve human purposes. Attributing human emotions to the behavior of these gods, the Vedic authors believed that they could be controlled by prayers and sacrifices offered at proper times in proper ways. Elaborate rituals and expensive sacrifices were devised and performed by Brahman priests to invoke the favor of these gods and to ask their forgiveness for human offenses. Vedic religion eventually became little more than a shell of ceremonialism, and it failed to answer the fundamental questions about the meaning and purpose of life and human beings' ethical obligations to one another. Brahmanism, the ritualized socioreligious system created by the Brahman priests, legitimized its dominance and social control by an elaborate belief system that included such notions as karma (the belief that one's station in life is the consequence of one's actions in a previous life), dharma (the moral obligation to follow the established rules of the social and cosmic order), and *varṇa* (the caste system), which gradually became the hallmarks of Hinduism. Known as *varṇaśrama dharma*, Brahmanism forced people into a pre-established social categories that determined their occupational choices and social interactions. Understandably, the majority of the people were disillusioned by the oppressive effects of Brahmanism and was eager to find alternatives means of achieving liberation from life's sufferings.

A major reaction to Brahmanism emerged in movements that rejected its ritualism and sought refuge in ascetic and meditative practices promoted by thinkers and religious figures who had chosen to withdraw from the world. Leaders of these movements also turned to philosophical reflection that reinterpreted the Vedic religion in new ways. These reflections crystallized in oral teachings that were eventually committed to writing to help propagate these teachings. Though they differ in emphasis, reflecting independent but related schools of thought, the Upaniṣads provide a distinctive pattern of answers that supports the view that redemption from suffering can be achieved through one's own effort without resorting to sacrifices and rituals. They teach that freedom from desire would assure freedom from suffering, and consequently, the cycle of birth and rebirth will be broken because desire lies at the root of all suffering, a theme that Buddha was to pursue much later. The means recommended by the Upaniṣads to extinguish desire is *tapas*, or asceticism, and meditation leading to self-knowledge and achieving oneness with the supreme being.

The actual authors of the Upaniṣads are unknown. However, some of the names to which the authorship of the major Upaniṣads has been traditionally attributed include Yajñavalkya, Svetāśvatara, Pratradana, Bhṛgu, Trisanku, Maitrī, Uddālaka, Śvetaketu, Aitareya, Kauśītaki, Kaikeya, Ajātaśatru, Pippalada, Sandilya, Sanatakumara, and Aruni. They were mystics, poets, critics, metaphysicians, moralists, and cosmologists. The Upaniṣads in their extant form probably are the result of additions and alterations made to original texts by the leaders of the various schools of thought that flourished between 1000 and 200 B.C.E. There is little consensus on the exact number of the Upaniṣads. Estimates range from several dozen to approximately two hundred. Many texts are believed to have been lost, but most scholars agree that of those extant, about 108 are authentic. According to most commentators, the principal Upaniṣads are *Bṛhad-āraṇyaka*, *Chāndogya*, *Aitareya*, *Taittirīya*, *Īśa*, *Kena*, *Kaṭha*, *Praśna*, *Muṇḍaka*, *Māṇḍūkya*, *Svetāśvatara*, *Kauṣītakī*, *Maitrī*, *Subāla*, *Jābāla*, *Paiṅgala*, *Kaivalya*, and *Vajrasūcikā*.

The longest and the oldest Upaniṣad is *Bṛhad-āraṇyaka*, which expounds the doctrine of the identity of the individual self and the universal self. Its main thrust is reflected in the following prayer: "From the unreal lead me to the real, from darkness lead me to light, from death lead me to immortality" (as translated by Radhakrishnan). Critical of the excesses of the Brahmanic ritualism, the *Chāndogya* Upaniṣad explains the symbolic meaning of sacrifices. It also lays the foundation for a philosophy of sound and music as it analyzes the famous meditative syllable *aum*, which is said to contain all possible sounds.

Picking up on the theme of sacrifice as a symbolic action, the *Aitareya* Upaniṣad urges readers to focus on the inner meaning of sacrifices rather than on their outer forms. It also suggests that inner freedom is achievable by all regardless of the differences in their lifestyles. The nature of Brahman, the ultimate reality, is the focus of the *Taittirīya* Upaniṣad, and the *Īśa* Upaniṣad explains the role of knowledge in attaining eternal life. The *Kena* Upaniṣad distinguishes between the popular conception of God (*Iśvara*) and the absolute reality (Brahman), assigning superiority to the latter. The *Kaṭha* Upaniṣad unequivocally asserts the fundamental identity of everything and warns the readers that failure to grasp this truth will lead to rebirth, and *Muṇḍaka* explains that desire is the root of ignorance itself. Unrivaled in its analysis of consciousness, the *Muṇḍaka* Upaniṣad inquires into the progressive levels or states of consciousness represented by simple wakefulness, dream, dreamless sleep, and transcendental consciousness to argue that only transcendental consciousness is capable of grasping the essential oneness of all reality.

It would be incorrect to state that all Upaniṣadic texts are equally lofty in their philosophical intent. Also scattered throughout these texts are reflections on many mundane concerns. However, they are overwhelmingly devoted to philosophical and mystical thinking.

SIGNIFICANCE

The effect the Upaniṣads have had on Indian history and civilization is immeasurable. Although Brahmanism eventually co-opted the Upaniṣads by appending them to the Vedas, it was profoundly transformed by the communities that generated these texts. Arguably, the dominant themes of the Upaniṣads also underscore the general character of the Indian civilization, which is to be inward looking, reflective, and tolerant. The ascetic and spiritual practices the Upaniṣads promote have profoundly influenced the cultural ethos of India, in particular the veneration of ascetics, the teaching of the value of nonviolence, and the practicing of vegetarianism.

The emergence of Buddhism, which ultimately rejected Brahmanism, would also not have been possible without a Buddha being culturally predisposed, at the moment of his enlightenment, to accept the Upaniṣads' fundamental teaching that desire is the cause of all suffering. Many sophisticated techniques of mediation and the practice of yoga were also spawned by the Upaniṣads' focus on self-knowledge and asceticism as means of liberation.

—*Mathew J. Kanjirathinkal*

FURTHER READING

Gotshalk, Richard, *The Beginnings of Philosophy in India*. Lanham, Md.: University Press of America, 1988. Gotshalk discusses the emergence of the Upaniṣads against the social and historical background of early India.

Pershad, Guru. *An Introduction to the Vedas and the Upaniṣads: A Compilation from the Writings of Sri Aurobindo*. Hyderabad, India: Sri Aurobindo Society, 1991. This is a compilation of essays written by one of India's foremost scholars on Indian thought.

Radhakrishnan, S. *The Principal Upaniṣads*. 1935. Reprint. London: George Allen and Unwin, 1968. Radhakrishnan, a highly respected Indian philosopher, presents the texts and his own translation of eighteen principal Upaniṣads with a comprehensive introduction to their main themes.

Ranade, R. D. *A Constructive Survey of Upaniṣadic Philosophy.* Bombay: Bharatiya Vidya Bhavan, 1968. Ranade provides an excellent discussion of the background of the Upaniṣads as well as a masterly exposition of their contents.

SEE ALSO: 1500-1100 B.C.E., Compilation of the Vedas; 6th or 5th century B.C.E., Birth of Buddhism; c. 200 B.C.E., Birth of Hinduism.

RELATED ARTICLE in *Great Lives from History: The Ancient World*: Vardhamāna.

c. 1000 B.C.E.-c. 100 C.E.
ADENA MOUND BUILDERS LIVE IN NORTH AMERICA

The Adena were a prehistoric farming society in North America who left evidence of their lives in the mounds they constructed.

LOCALE: Ohio River Valley (in Ohio, Indiana, Illinois, West Virginia, Kentucky, New York, and Pennsylvania)

CATEGORY: Prehistory and ancient cultures

SUMMARY OF EVENT

The Eastern Woodland period, which began around 1000 B.C.E., was characterized by several developments, the most notable of which was the introduction of an early form of agriculture. The Adena were an Early Woodland people who lived around the Ohio River Valley from about 1000 B.C.E. to 100 C.E. Evidence of Adena settlements has been found in Ohio, Indiana, Illinois, West Virginia, Kentucky, New York, and Pennsylvania. The Adena lived in an environment of dense forests, rich with game and foraging foods, drained by numerous rivers and streams. The weather changed significantly during the year from cold, harsh winters to hot summers. However, the length of the growing season, the rich soil, and ample rainfall proved well suited for farming.

The Adena are most noted for the hundreds of earthen effigy mounds they left behind. These large hills varied in size from a few feet to hundreds of yards across and hundreds of feet tall. Most Adena mounds are circular, but some were constructed in geometric and animal shapes, and others were surrounded by moats, walls, or embankments. The most famous of these and one of the longest, the Serpent Mound near Cincinnati, Ohio, is a series of mounds, 20 feet (7 meters) wide and 5 feet (nearly 2 meters) tall, that stretch almost a quarter of a mile (nearly half a kilometer). From the sky, the mound appears to be an open-mouthed snake.

Thousands of mounds once dotted the Ohio River Valley. Over the years, many were destroyed, cleared away by early nonnative farmers or raided by the curious. Hundreds remained, however, and both professional and amateur archaeologists have excavated many of them. Through the examination and study of the artifacts found inside, archaeologists and anthropologists have learned much about the foods the Adena ate, the clothing and jewelry they wore, the tools they used, and even how they may have worn their hair.

A great deal of labor and organized community effort was used to construct the mounds. The Adena moved thousands of tons of earth to the sites using only woven baskets to carry the soil. The mounds were constructed for various purposes. Some were dumping places for tribal garbage. Some mounds are believed to have had religious or ritual significance, and celebration headdresses and masks were unearthed from small interior dwellings that were possibly ceremonial rooms or buildings. The mounds might have begun with a round dwelling house that was converted into a mortuary.

Most Adena mounds were used as burial sites for the dead and contain human and animal remains along with various grave goods, including copper beads and bracelets, carvings on stone tablets, river pearls, mica, weapons, tools, cooking utensils, and pipes. Some pipes, weapons, and bowls were decorated with carvings of animals and humans. The human remains have provided scientists with clues as to the age, sex, and size of the Adena; when they died; and the causes of their deaths. Bodies of some of the dead were cremated before their ashes were placed in the mounds. Others were cached in hollow tree trunks or logs. Several graves contained small vaults constructed of wood or bark. A few of the bodies were decorated with headdresses, helmets, bracelets, pendants, and rings. Bodies dating to the end of the Adena era, c. 100 C.E., have been found sprinkled with powdered ocher derived from a red clay in the area that was also used to decorate pottery.

Some mounds were not completed after the first group of remains was interred. They contained multiple layers and dozens of bodies buried over many generations. The bodies were interred, sealed, and covered with another layer of earth. By excavating the mounds in horizontal slices, anthropologists have been able to track the progression of Adena culture over the years, revealing that as the centuries passed, the Adena developed more advanced tools and weapons, produced more refined jewelry, and made advancements in agricultural methods.

The Adena were some of the earliest Native American farmers. Cultivation may have begun when tribal people stuck seeds or nuts from foods they already gathered into the ground. If they bore fruit, the people planted more in areas closer to their villages. Agriculture supplemented the diets of the Early Woodland people rather than acting as their main source of nutrition. The Adena diet included hazelnuts, walnuts, and hickory nuts. They also appear to have eaten grown sunflower and goosefoot seeds, raspberries, strawberries, knotwood, and grapes. Toward the end of the period, there is evidence that the Adena were planting the corn and squash that would later become staples for many Eastern American tribes.

The Adena continued to hunt and gather to supplement their diet. Many different animal bones were found in the mounds. Evidence suggests the Adena hunted deer, bear, elk, wolf, and small game such as raccoon, squirrel, and beaver. Fish and wild birds such as turkey, duck, and grouse were also a part of their diet. The Adena broiled or grilled their food over an open fire or boiled it in leather or wooden containers. Meals were eaten from wooden or stone bowls. Gourds were dried and used as bowls and spoons as well as eaten.

Hunting tools included spears with pointed flint blades and stone knives for cutting and scraping. Spearheads were sharpened to a point by chipping away at flint with knife blades or other stones. Hides from hunted animals were used for clothing and blankets. Evidence indicates the Adena wove and twined local grasses for mats and sandal-like footwear.

The Adena lived in small, semipermanent villages. They used lumber from the forests around them to construct circular wooden homes. The outside walls were erected with sunken wooden tree posts that were pointed outward to support the roof. The outside walls were covered with bark or long, thin sticks interwoven into wattle for support and insulation. The conical-shaped roof was also constructed of wooden poles and covered with slabs

The Great Serpent Mound in Adams County, Ohio, represents a giant snake holding an egg in its mouth.(Hulton|Archive)

of bark. Each home was approximately 18 to 40 feet (6 to 12 meters) in diameter.

Pottery was found in a number of mound sites. Some anthropologists believe the Adena were one of the first tribes in the eastern United States to make pottery. Pottery was made from carved stone or clay that was abundant in the area. Clay was gathered from nearby creek beds, formed into bowls and pots, and dried in the sun. Many vessels were decorated with geometric and animal shapes. Serpent decorations were found carved into bowls and pipes and painted on pottery. Pottery was used for cooking and storing food and as eating utensils.

Evidence suggests that the Adena traded extensively with other tribes, including tribes hundreds of miles away. Grizzly bear teeth and obsidian from the Rocky Mountain region were found in the burial mounds along with copper from north of the Great Lakes and seashells from the coastlines of both the Atlantic Ocean and the Gulf of Mexico.

Significance

It is not known why the Adena civilization disappeared. Somewhere around 100 C.E., the Adena may have dispersed or been driven away to other regions. They may have merged with the Hopewell tribe, another mound-building Eastern Woodland group that later occupied the same areas of the Ohio River Valley. The Hopewell constructed more refined metal tools and ornamentation and produced mounds that were even more elaborate than those of the Adena. However, the artifacts the Adena left behind in the mounds they constructed provided future generations with vital clues about their culture and way of life.

—*Leslie A. Stricker*

Further Reading

Ceram, C. W. *The First American: A Story of Native American Archaeology*. New York: Harcourt, Brace, Jovanovich, 1971. Describes mounds and the artifacts that have been found in them.

Jennings, Jesse D. *Ancient Native Americans*. San Francisco: W. H. Freeman, 1978. Provides information on the Adena way of life. Bibliography and index.

Kennedy, Roger G. *Hidden Cities: The Discovery and Loss of Ancient North American Civilizations*. New York: Free Press, 1994. Describes Native American architecture, its excavation, and prominent theories.

Silverberg, Robert. *Mound Builders of Ancient America: The Archaeology of a Myth*. Athens: Ohio University Press, 1968. Maps and details the excavation of mounds.

Webb, William S., and C. E. Snow. *The Adena People*. Reprint. Knoxville: University of Tennessee Press, 1988. A classic study of the Adena originally appearing in 1945.

Woodward, Susan L. *Indian Mounds of the Middle Ohio Valley: A Guide to Adena and Hopewell Sites*. Newark, Ohio: McDonald & Woodward, 1986. A brief but valuable guide, including a bibliography.

See also: c. 5000 B.C.E.-c. 1 C.E., Red Paint Culture Flourishes in Eastern North America; c. 4000-c. 1000 B.C.E., Old Copper Complex Flourishes in North America; c. 1800-c. 700 B.C.E., Poverty Point Culture Builds Earthworks; c. 1000 B.C.E.-c. 900 C.E., Woodland Culture Flourishes in Northern America; c. 700 B.C.E.-c. 500 C.E., Mound Builders Rise in Ohio Valley; c. 200 B.C.E.-c. 500 C.E., Hopewell People Construct Earthworks.

c. 1000 B.C.E.-c. 300 C.E.
URBAN COMMERCE DEVELOPS IN THE SUDAN BELT

Inhabitants of Africa's Sudan Belt cities and towns had extensive contacts with the Mediterranean regions through trade in a wide variety of goods, of which the most important were salt and gold.

LOCALE: Djenné, the Sudanic belt, the Sahel, and the Sahara.

CATEGORIES: Prehistory and ancient cultures; trade and commerce

SUMMARY OF EVENT

Geographers and historians define the Sudan belt of the ancient world as the area that extends from the Sahara in the north to the Bay of Niger (present-day southern Nigeria) in the south and from the Atlantic in the east to the Indian Ocean in the west. In the western part of this broad environmental region, in a subregion called the Sahel, Africans established towns and cities that served as inland ports between Africa's interior and coastal areas and the people beyond those areas.

Western Africa is characterized by several environmental zones. The Sahel, an Arabic word meaning "shore" or "coast," is located between the Sahara in the north and the rain forest in the south. It is a mixed zone of grass-covered plains (steppe), brush, thicket, and sparse forests (savanna). The ancients knew it as the southern boundary of the Sahara, a desert so huge it seemed to them to be a kind of "sea." Cities developed in the Sahel and prospered as a result of trade they carried on across the Sahara. Trade items from the Berbers of northern Africa—salt, textiles, spices, sword blades, and metal tools and utensils—were carried south across the Saharan "sea" on the backs of camels, animals ideally suited to endure long treks of thirty to forty days. Of these trade goods, salt was the most valuable. Produced in salt mines in the Sahara, such as the one at Taghaza, salt was so valued—as a taste enhancer and preservative for food—that it was used as currency. At various outposts along the way, the salt, spices, and sword blades were broken down into smaller or larger packages and repacked for the next stage of the journey. Rests were taken at desert oases. The termini for the trade goods were the towns of the Sahel: Koumbi Saleh, Timbuktu, Gao, Kano, and Ngazaragamu. The goods were then traded for gold, ivory, animal hides, and slaves for the trip north. Farther south, traders transferred their loads into dugout canoes or used other modes of transport. In this way, they ventured to cities of the rain forest where they were traded for bronze and iron items. Foodstuffs, in the form of rice, beans, sorghum, and millet, were also exchanged. Trade in iron weapons and tools was also important. The people of the Nok culture were smelting iron in western Africa by the first century C.E.

Several cities arose in the Sahel of western Africa that became famous as a result of trade and commerce carried on there: Dhar Tichitt, Djenné, Timbuktu, Gao, Mali, Ghana, and Walata. They comprised the leading commercial centers of the kingdom of Mali. The inhabitants of these centers were both local people and migrants from the north escaping the gradual spread of the Sahara desert. The promise of productive farmland in the south lured them into the Sahel, and the growth of trade and trade routes hastened the migrations. As people moved from north to south and around subregions within this larger region, they settled villages and towns, ostensibly with the aim of farming. Over time, however, the strategic locations of these towns and villages along Sahara, Sahel, and savanna trade routes led the inhabitants to turn from agriculture to trade. Gradually, they developed networks of interregional trade.

One of the earliest trading centers was Djenné (in present-day Mali). Located in the Niger River Delta, it was first settled c. 250 B.C.E. and grew steadily over the centuries. By 450 C.E., Djenné spread over at least 60 acres (24 hectares). At first, the people of Djenné lived from herding, fishing, farming, and exchanging their produce with others within their immediate locale. Over time, circles of trade expanded. At the center of the regional trade was Djenné, where people would gather to exchange goods. Archaeologists have discovered Roman and Hellenistic beans in the remains of ancient Djenné, suggesting that these trade items were reaching West Africa.

SIGNIFICANCE

The trading cities of the Sudanic belt entered their peak during the Islamic era. These included Koumbi Saleh, a trading center for salt and gold in what was to become the kingdom of Ghana. Mined in the Sahara, salt was carried to Koumbi or Awdaghast. Koumbi became the liveliest trading center in West Africa. Salt and gold were the most important trading items but other things were traded as well: cattle from the south, wheat from the north, cloth, leather goods, seashells (used for decoration and as currency), copper, and ivory. Craftspeople in Koumbi worked the gold and copper into jewelry or other items.

Gao, the city that became the capital of the Songhai Empire, rose up around 500 C.E. Its important trading items were salt and gold. Luxury items that flowed into Gao from trade included glass, copperware, and cloth.

The trade and commerce of the Sudanic Belt towns and cities of Africa extended over a wide area and touched diverse peoples. Berbers were among the main traders across the Sahara to the West African Sahel. Different groups within the Sahel rose up as vital traders of goods such as gold and iron and also produced some of the leading trade items, such as gold and ivory jewelry. Of all the trade items in the trans-Saharan trade, salt was the most important. Gold was also highly desired.

—*Adriane Ruggiero*

FURTHER READING

Davidson, Basil. *The Lost Cities of Africa*. Rev. ed. Boston: Little, Brown, 1959. A classic study of ancient sub-Saharan African civilizations

Newman, James L. *The Peopling of Africa: A Geographic Interpretation*. New Haven, Conn.: Yale University Press, 1995. A geography of Africa that focuses on the development of cultures within the continent's different regions from prehistoric times to colonization.

Time-Life Editors. *Africa's Glorious Legacy*. Alexandria, Va.: Time-Life Books, 1994. A pictorial overview of African civilizations.

SEE ALSO: c. 10,000 B.C.E.-c. 1 C.E., Saharan Peoples Create Rock Art; c. 9000-c. 7000 B.C.E., Nilo-Saharan Peoples Produce Food and Pottery; c. 6500-c. 5000 B.C.E., Nilo-Saharan Farmers Spread Cultivation and Herding; c. 1000 B.C.E., Sub-Saharan Ironworking Begins; 3d century B.C.E., Commercial City of Djenné Is Founded on Niger River; c. 100 B.C.E.-c. 300 C.E., East African Trading Port of Rhapta Flourishes; 290-300 C.E., West African Gold First Reaches North Africa.

RELATED ARTICLES in *Great Lives from History: The Ancient World*: Amenhotep III; Ramses II.

c. 1000 B.C.E.-c. 900 C.E.
WOODLAND CULTURE FLOURISHES IN NORTHERN AMERICA

The Indians of the Woodland period established the hunting-and-gathering style that was still in place when Europeans arrived in North America in the sixteenth century.

LOCALE: Northeastern North America (present-day Canada and the United States)
CATEGORY: Prehistory and ancient cultures

SUMMARY OF EVENT

The Indians of the Woodland period lived in an enormously wide range of territory in the eastern portion of North America. The region extended from the vast forest regions of Canada to the southern extreme of Florida. The main habitat of the people was east of the Mississippi River and along the waterways of large rivers and lakes, as well as the tributaries that flowed into those bodies of waters. The tribespeople that belonged to the region spoke in one of the three main language groups: Siouan, Iroquois-Caddoan, and Algonquian.

The tribes of the southern woodland region were hunters and fishermen, but mainly farmers of squash, corn, beans, and tobacco. The tribes of the northeastern woodland region were primarily hunters and gatherers, and the spoken language was either Iroquois or Algonquian. Those tribes of the northwestern woodland region were also primarily hunters and gatherers, and they spoke Iroquois, Algonquian, or Siouan.

The success of the native people's lifestyle was based on the region in which they lived. The climate allowed for successful crop growing and provided an abundance of wildlife and plenty of natural materials for shelter and warmth. The people adapted well, and they prospered. The Woodland period saw an enormous change in lifestyle based on technology.

The Old Copper period immediately preceded the Woodland period; from an archaeological perspective, this was an Archaic culture. During the Old Copper period, the use of copper products, such as knives and other tools, made life for the Indians much easier. Two major inventions of the Woodland period produced even more significant changes. The bow and arrow were developed, displacing spears as the weapon of choice. The bow and arrow allowed the archer to be some distance away from the prey or the enemy and yet be successful. No longer did the hunter have to be so close to the target, where danger might be lurking. The second major change in the period was the invention of the clay pot. Water and food supplies could be successfully carried or stored. Both of these inventions made life much easier, and because of this, the clans and families flourished.

The native cultures became somewhat more complex as tribes established more permanent living places, forsaking the nomadic lifestyle. The Woodland people developed settlements and lived in small villages of twenty to two hundred people. Most of these villages maintained the same lifestyle and political framework. Although it was an informal existence, it was a distinctive way of life that, in some areas, is known as the Adena or Hopewell culture. Not all the Woodland people were part of this lifestyle, but it did impact their lives.

The Woodland period saw the development of a social structure that was divided into clans grouped by family and controlled by the female line of ancestry. The eldest female in the family was the leader, and the leadership of the clan traced directly down the female line. Marriage could take place only within the clan and was prohibited from taking place outside that social structure.

During the latter part of the Woodland period, an increase in warfare led to the fortification of the more permanent villages. It was more or less expected that war was a constant and sustained occurrence in Woodland society. The warfare was based on revenge, not bloodletting. The activity used only small groups of warriors, which would go out and ambush neighboring enemy tribes. The capture of slaves was a key to the survival of the society, although after a captured person lived with the group for a time, he or she often became accepted as a tribal member and then had all the same rights and privileges.

SIGNIFICANCE

Two significant Native American cultures are associated with the Woodland period: the Adena and the Hopewell. The Adena first appeared in what is now the state of Ohio and then spread to the west and south. They are known as mound builders; their earthworks were built to represent specific designs and shapes, most of them snakes, birds, and various symbols of the sky universe. The Hopewell people were also builders of earthen mounds. Both people lived along major rivers and controlled the flow of trade goods in and out of the region. The Adena and Hopewell people served as a link to the other tribes in North America, from the Rocky Mountains in the west to the swamps in the south. Archaeologists suggest that the Woodland cultures were very similar to the Archaic culture in that they were primarily hunters and gatherers, and that they tended to migrate from season to season. The major difference was that the Woodland culture developed pottery production, farmed a little, and buried their dead in earthen mounds. They also made the transition to more permanent, although not completely permanent, settlements.

Archaeologists suggest that the Adena people lived a rather simple life; the culture spread from the Great Lakes region to the Gulf Coast and stayed mainly to the west of the Appalachian Mountains. The Hopewell people culture tended to be more complex, with larger populations that were organized and covered a larger geographical area. It also appears that the Hopewells cremated their deceased and placed influential families in special, dominant mounds. In comparison to the Adena, theirs was a more highly structured society that relied on close management skills.

—*Earl R. Andresen*

FURTHER READING

Anderson, David G., and Robert C. Mainfort, Jr., eds. *The Woodland Southeast.* Tuscaloosa: University of Alabama Press, 2002. Covers the culture and archaeology of the Woodland period.

Mainfort, Robert C., Jr., and Lynne P. Sullivan, eds. *Ancient Earthen Enclosures of the Eastern Woodlands.* Gainesville: University Press of Florida, 1998. A collection of strictly archaeological papers on the interpretation of Woodland sites. Illustrations, maps.

Sattler, Helen R. *The Earliest Americans.* New York: Clarion Books, 1993. A close look at the Native Americans in the northeast portion of North America.

Shaffer, Lynda Norene. *Native Americans Before 1492: The Moundbuilding Centers of the Eastern Woodlands.* Armonk, N.Y.: M. E. Sharpe, 1992. Although this book's focus is on a somewhat later stage of Woodland culture, it offers a concise introduction to the mound building of the Adena and Hopewell cultures.

Trigger, Bruce G. *Northeast.* Vol. 15 in *Handbook of North American Indians.* Washington, D.C.: Smithsonian Institution Press, 1988. A review of all the tribes in the northeast portion of North America.

SEE ALSO: c. 13,000-c. 7000 B.C.E., Paleo-Indian Culture Flourishes in North America; c. 8000-c. 1000 B.C.E., Archaic Indians Adapt to Warmer Climates; c. 4000-c. 1000 B.C.E., Old Copper Complex Flourishes in North America; c. 1800-c. 700 B.C.E., Poverty Point Culture Builds Earthworks; c. 1000 b.c.e.-c. 100 C.E., Adena Mound Builders Live in North America; c. 700-c. 500 B.C.E., Dorset Culture Extends into Labrador, Newfoundland, and Greenland; c. 700 B.C.E.-c. 500 C.E., Mound Builders Rise in Ohio Valley; c. 200 B.C.E.-c. 500 C.E., Hopewell People Construct Earthworks.

c. 966 B.C.E.
BUILDING OF THE TEMPLE OF JERUSALEM

The temple built at Jerusalem and dedicated exclusively to Yahweh became the religious and national center for Judaism for nearly one thousand years.

LOCALE: Jerusalem (now in Israel)
CATEGORIES: Architecture; religion

KEY FIGURES

David (c. 1030-c. 962 B.C.E.), king of Israel, r. c. 1000-c. 962 B.C.E.
Nathan (fl. tenth century B.C.E.), prophet at the royal court
Solomon (c. 991-930 B.C.E.), king of Israel, r. c. 961-930 B.C.E.

SUMMARY OF EVENT

Scripture states that David consulted the prophet Nathan about building a temple to Yahweh, presumably as an offering in gratitude for his successes and as an adornment for his new capital at Jerusalem. Whatever the initial inspiration, Nathan encouraged David's project, but a later vision revealed to the prophet that although David enjoyed God's favor, the building of the temple would be reserved for a descendant of his house.

The temple was built under Solomon, who, through a commercial alliance, employed architects from Tyre (now in south Lebanon) and imported the famous cedars of Lebanon in its construction. According to Scripture, the dedication ceremonies featured special sacrifices and an address by Solomon. The temple played a dominant role in the religious and national life of Judaism, and the religion's followers saw it as an assurance of God's abiding presence among his Chosen People.

The site of the temple, on Mount Zion in eastern Jerusalem, was chosen by Solomon because it was a holy place, connected by tradition with the threshing floor of Araunah. The temple itself was modest in size, smaller than the palace Solomon built for himself; many consider it basically a royal chapel attached to the palace. Wrought exquisitely in traditional Phoenician architectural style, the new shrine was rectangular in shape, composed of three chambers, and faced over its entire width with a porch or vestibule. Temples of similar design have been unearthed in Syria and at Hazor in Galilee (in northern Israel). As with all ancient places of worship, the sanctuary provided no seats because there were no specified requirements for indoor worship. Although the courtyard was used for the celebration of great national festivals, the main function of the edifice was to provide a venerable place for the offering of sacrifices.

THE KINGS OF ISRAEL, C. 1020-930 B.C.E.

Ruler	*Reign*
Saul	c. 1020-1000
David	c. 1000-c. 962
Solomon	c. 961-930

The erection of the temple may be interpreted as part of Solomon's campaign to centralize his government and reinforce his larger program of administrative changes. He intended to establish new governmental districts cutting across old tribal boundaries, a plan designed to encourage centralization of power in the city of Jerusalem by breaking down tribal loyalties and other competing outlying vested centers of power. Solomon's building of a central sanctuary in Jerusalem could have facilitated such a program of organization, but the temple probably was not significant in this respect before the reign of Josiah in the seventh century B.C.E. The temple's influence became so decisive, however, that foreign conquerors always regarded the Jewish polity as a temple-state.

SIGNIFICANCE

The Deuteronomic authors who later centered about the temple glorified Solomon for his role in constructing the shrine, although at the time of its building, it seems to have introduced no significant revolution in religious belief or practice. Syncretism was still much in evidence, and many local high places of cult worship and sacrifice, such as those at Hebron (now in Jordan) and Bethel (in Israel-occupied Jordan), continued to function during Solomon's reign. With the reforms of Josiah, the temple at Jerusalem finally became the sole center of worship. As the edifice gradually grew in importance under the Deuteronomists, Solomon grew correspondingly famous as its designer and builder, despite the idolatrous practices that he allowed to remain in vogue during his rule.

A depiction of the building of the Temple of Jerusalem. (Hulton|Archive)

The major cultist innovation of the Deuteronomists was the centralization of worship at Jerusalem. They believed that the unity of God must be mirrored in unity of worship, that a multiplicity of sanctuaries corrupted the worship of God by associating it with a polytheistic paganism that worshiped in many temples nestled in high places. This centralizing reform around the temple was, in turn, a direct stepping-stone to the pure ethical monotheism of the eighth century B.C.E. prophet Isaiah, who enunciated clearly that there was only one god: Yahweh. Within the framework of his single temple, his central sanctuary, Yahweh became the single god for Israel. His temple became a concrete expression of his uniqueness. It was destroyed and rebuilt several times until it was demolished along with much of Jerusalem in 70 C.E.

—*Joseph R. Rosenbloom*

FURTHER READING

Backhouse, Robert. *The Kregel Pictorial Guide to the Temple*. Grand Rapids, Mich.: Kregel Publications, 1996. A pictorial presentation of the temple and its architecture.

Berman, Joshua. *The Temple: Its Symbolism and Meaning Then and Now.* Northvale, N.J.: J. Aronson, 1995. Berman looks at the history of the temple, emphasizing its significance over the years. Bibliography and index.

Hayward, C. T. R., ed. *The Jewish Temple: A Nonbiblical Sourcebook*. New York: Routledge, 1996. A history of the temple at Jerusalem that concentrates on nonbiblical sources, particularly the Greek historians. Bibliography and indexes.

McCormick, Clifford Mark. *Palace and Temple: A Study of Architectural and Verbal Icons*. New York: Walter de Gruyter, 2002. A study that compares and contrasts the temple of Jerusalem and the palace of Sennacherib in Nineveh. Bibliography and index.

Schwartz, Max. *The Biblical Engineer: How the Temple in Jerusalem Was Built*. Hoboken, N.J.: KTAV, 2002. Schwartz describes the construction of the temple, adding to his discussion with his own illustrations. Bibliography and index.

SEE ALSO: c. 922 B.C.E., Establishment of the Kingdom of Israel; c. 607-562 B.C.E., Nebuchadnezzar Creates the First Neo-Babylonian State; 587-423 B.C.E., Birth of Judaism; c. 538-c. 450 B.C.E., Jews Return from the Babylonian Captivity; September 8, 70 C.E., Roman Destruction of the Temple of Jerusalem.

RELATED ARTICLES in *Great Lives from History: The Ancient World*: David; Solomon.

c. 950 B.C.E.
COMPOSITION OF THE BOOK OF GENESIS

The Yahwist compiled a number of traditions regarding Israel's history, its religious beliefs, and a story of humankind's origins to form the book of Genesis, a significant book for not only Judaism but also Christianity and Islam.

LOCALE: Jerusalem (now in Israel)
CATEGORIES: Literature; religion

KEY FIGURES

Yahwist (c. 950 B.C.E.), principal compiler of Israel's sacral and folk tradition in the essential framework of the Pentateuch

Elohist (c. 900-700 B.C.E.), principal compiler of the settlement and patriarchal traditions of the northern tribes of Israel

SUMMARY OF EVENT

The reign of Solomon (c. 961-930 B.C.E.), king of Israel, was the culmination of two generations of an immense political and social transformation in Palestine. A weak and loosely organized confederation of Israelite tribes had been welded by the military and political astuteness of David into a powerful monarchy with a centralized national administration and religious center at Jerusalem. The Philistine harassment had been conclusively ended, the hitherto unconquered Canaanite cities had been absorbed into the new state, and the burgeoning Israelite empire had come to encompass the neighboring peoples of Aram, Ammon, Moab, and Edom. Under Solomon, trade flourished and wealth flowed into the new capital. Israel had become conscious of its national identity and now began to mold its ancient traditions, which had long been transmitted orally, into an epic of its national destiny.

Modern biblical criticism has determined that the essential pattern into which these ancient traditions were consolidated was developed by an anonymous tenth century writer whom scholars designate the Yahwist in recognition of the divine name Yahweh in those portions of the Pentateuch (first five books of the Bible) assigned by literary criticism to him. The fundamental framework of the epic was provided by the settlement traditions: The ancestors of the Israelites had been slaves in Egypt when their god Yahweh called them forth into freedom and gave them the land of Canaan in which to dwell. A second tradition, incorporated by the Yahwist into the framework of the settlement narrative, told of the solemn covenant made at the sacred mountain Sinai by Yahweh with Israel and of Yahweh's covenant legislation by which Israel was bound. A third body of traditions concerning Israel's patriarchal ancestors, Abraham, Isaac, and Jacob, to whom that land had been promised by Yahweh as a habitation for their descendants and who had sojourned in it before the Egyptian enslavement, was prefixed to the settlement narrative. The whole scheme, finally, was introduced by a fourth block of traditional materials dealing with the primeval history of humankind. Thus four groups of traditional material were incorporated into a single narrative tracing the divine providence of Yahweh by which the Israelite tribes had taken possession of Canaan in fulfillment of their national destiny.

The Yahwist not only molded the traditions together but also infused the work as a whole with a theological perspective that makes the Hebrew epic more than a glorification of national success or a religious justification of Israel's claim to a conquered land. By means of the primeval history, which traces the progressive alienation of humankind from God from the time of creation to the dispersal of peoples from Mesopotamia, the Yahwist set Hebrew national history in the context of Yahweh's redemptive purposes for all humankind: The departure of Abraham toward the Promised Land is heralded with the promise that the nation to be formed by his descendants will be implicated in the blessing of all communities of human beings. By means of the patriarchal history, the Yahwist formulated the theological perspective on history that was to characterize the prophets of Israel: secular history, wherein people freely and responsibly interact to shape their own destinies, is the sphere in which Yahweh's historical purposes for Israel and all nations are worked out. Finally, through the incorporation of the Sinai tradition into the settlement account, the Yahwist enunciated another theological concept that was to be fundamental in the prophetic tradition: Israel's tenure of the Promised Land and its very national identity is intimately bound up with its obedience to Yahweh, its sole legitimate sovereign, and to his covenant demand for justice and brotherhood in national corporate life.

Several additional blocks of material were incorporated into the Yahwist narrative before the Pentateuch assumed its authoritative form toward the end of the sixth century B.C.E. A second epic incorporating the settlement and patriarchal traditions of the northern tribes was composed in the ninth century B.C.E. by a second anonymous writer termed the Elohist by scholars, to distinguish him from the Yahwist, because of his characteristic use of the divine name Elohim in his narrative. In the course of the seventh century B.C.E., materials from the premonarchic covenant-renewal ceremony of the tribes were edited into the core of the book of Deuteronomy (fifth book of the Bible). Finally, during and after the exile of the Jews in Babylon, the traditional ritual law and theology of history of the Jerusalem priesthood was formally written down as a framework binding together the whole complex of historical and cultic traditions of Israel into a literary whole. The resultant literary corpus is a complex document representing several distinct eras and theological perspectives and reflecting the richness and diversity of Israel's national religious experience.

SIGNIFICANCE

Although the Priestly Writers of the Pentateuch in its final form seem to have intended the document to serve as a constitutional foundation for the theocratic life of the second temple, the theological concepts of the Yahwist, most clearly evident in Genesis, where his contributions bulk largest, mark the book as one of religious significance extending beyond Judaism to the Christian and Islamic traditions and as a major constitutive element of Western European culture.

—*Carl W. Conrad*

FURTHER READING

Davies, Philip R., and David J. A. Clines, eds. *The World of Genesis: Persons, Places, Perspectives*. Sheffield, England: Sheffield Academic Press, 1998. Criticism and interpretation of the book of Genesis. Supplement to the *Journal for the Study of the Old Testament*. Bibliography and indexes.

Garrtt, Duane A. *Rethinking Genesis: The Sources and Authorship of the First Book of the Bible*. 1991. Reprint. Fearn, England: Mentor, 2000. Garrett examines the sources and authorship of the various traditions that make up Genesis, arguing that the seven days of Genesis are actually revelations made to Moses. Bibliography.

Lemche, Niels Peter. *Prelude to Israel's Past: Background and Beginnings of Israelite History and Identity.* Peabody, Mass.: Hendrickson, 1998. An examination of the history of Israel that deals with the book of Genesis.

Van Seters, John. *Prologue to History: The Yahwist as Historian in Genesis*. Louisville, Ky.: Westminister/ J. Knox Press, 1992. Looks at the role of the Yahwist in writing Genesis as well as the history of Israel. Bibliography and index.

Wénin, A., ed. *Studies in the Book of Genesis: Literature, Redation, and History*. Sterling, Va.: Uitgeverij Peeters, 2001. A collection of papers presented at the Forty-eighth Colloquium Biblicum Lovaniense, in July, 1999, on the book of Genesis. Bibliography and indexes.

SEE ALSO: c. 966 B.C.E., Building of the Temple of Jerusalem; c. 922 B.C.E., Establishment of the Kingdom of Israel; 587-423 B.C.E., Birth of Judaism; c. 538-c. 450 B.C.E., Jews Return from the Babylonian Captivity; 250-130 B.C.E., Commissioning of the Septuagint; c. 250 B.C.E.-70 C.E., Dead Sea Scrolls Are Composed; c. 200 B.C.E.-c. 100 C.E., Composition of the Intertestamental Jewish Apocrypha; c. 90 C.E., Synod of Jamnia.

c. 922 B.C.E.
Establishment of the Kingdom of Israel

The Kingdom of Israel marked the high point of Israelite political unity, and its memory has been a focal point of Jewish identity even into the present. The existence of this ancient kingdom is the justification for the establishment of the modern state of Israel in 1948.

Locale: Palestine
Categories: Government and politics; religion; wars, uprisings, and civil unrest

Key Figures
Sheba (fl. tenth century B.C.E.), a Benjamite
Solomon (c. 991-930 B.C.E.), king of the united nation, r. c. 961-930 B.C.E.
Rehoboam (fl. tenth century B.C.E.), son of Solomon and king of Judah, r. c. 930-915 B.C.E.
Jeroboam I (c. tenth century-c. 910 B.C.E.), first king of Israel, r. c. 925-901 B.C.E.
Ahijah (fl. tenth century B.C.E.), a prophet

Summary of Event
Around the turn of the first millennium B.C.E., the pressing problem of the Hebrews was to forge a group of independent tribes into a strong functioning nation in order to conquer Canaan and subdue the Philistines and their allies. Although there had been some feeling of unity among the Hebrew tribes that settled in Canaan, it took approximately two hundred years for a unified state to evolve. Even when organized, the kingdom apparently never overcame the vested interests of groups and individuals, for it survived for less than a century.

At first the tribes acted together, occasionally under the temporary leadership of a hero called a "judge" in the Bible. By 1000 B.C.E., it became evident that a more stable unity under a permanent king was desirable, and Saul was called on to rule the double kingdom of Israel and Judah. Saul's death at the hands of the Philistines on Mount Gilboa allowed David, who had to some extent already usurped power under Saul, to be declared next leader of the united tribes. He appears to have won confirmation as king through a covenant with the tribes that left them some autonomy as well as the right to confirm his successors in office. Symptomatic of the lack of full acquiescence, especially on the part of the northern tribes, were the rebellions by David's son, Absalom, and by Sheba, a Benjamite. According to 2 Sam. 20:2, only "the men of Judah followed their king steadfastly."

Resentment against the monarchy increased, especially in the north, during the reign of Solomon. The heavy exactions in money and men necessitated by his ambitious building programs became increasingly distasteful, as did his commercial alliance with Tyre involving repayment for supplies and services employed in the construction of the Temple of Jerusalem. The tribal covenant entered into by David was virtually ignored; Judah, the kingdom and tribe of the ruling family, was preferentially exempted from many of the onerous provisions demanded

An artist's depiction of King David, holding Goliath's severed head. (Library of Congress)

of the other tribes. More disturbing was Solomon's program of centralization, which weakened the power of individual tribes by destroying their traditional boundaries through the creation of new administrative districts.

After Solomon's death, his son Rehoboam was immediately accepted as king by Judah. When Israel demurred, Rehoboam went to Shechem, the historic covenant center where Jacob had gone after his return from Harran and where the national assembly had been held in the time of Joshua. The assembled Israelites demanded that the oppressive rule imposed by Solomon be lightened, and they reminded Rehoboam that a king could not take the principle of hereditary monarchy for granted; nor did they intend to tolerate a second Solomon with a resplendent court resulting in extravagant demands for taxes and labor drafts.

When Rehoboam unfortunately heeded the advice of his luxury-minded young courtiers to ignore the demands of the northern Israelites, Jeroboam, a seditious leader of one of Solomon's labor battalions who had been forced to flee to Egypt for asylum, returned to take advantage of the new discontent. He was supported by the prophet Ahijah, who announced symbolically, by tearing a garment in ten pieces, that ten tribes would follow Jeroboam. Consequently, Jeroboam was proclaimed king at the Shechem assembly. He established his capital first at Shechem and then at Tirzah, placing sanctuaries at Dan and Bethel, thus ending the united kingdom.

Although the immediate cause of the breakup was the heavy-handed reign of the despotic Solomon, which curtailed tribal freedoms and favored the south, the schism had deeper underlying causes. The hilly terrain encouraged sectional insularity. Each section had a different geography and therefore a different economic orientation. The north, facing toward the plains, was agricultural and commercial; Judah, oriented toward the desert, was pastoral and nomadic. Moreover, the original separation of the northern or Jacob Hebrews and the southern or Abraham Hebrews was too deeply rooted to be wiped out in one or two generations. Although Jeroboam and others had a personal interest in the breakup of the kingdom, the vital factor was the constant reassertion of tribal sympathies with all their religious implications. Whenever the northern Israelites established new religious centers, they implied the tacit rebellion of localism against the centralized regime in Jerusalem.

The northern branch of the Hebrew nation proved much stronger in population, economic resources, and cultural initiative. It possessed more fertile lands, and its plain of Esdraelon controlled international highways. However, when great new empires arose in the vicinity, the more isolated and poorer Judah survived longer. Israel was destroyed by Assyria in 721 B.C.E. and became another "lost nation"; the survival of Judaism was left to the weaker Judah.

Significance

The period of the united Hebrew kingdom was the high point of ancient Jewish history, even though it soon decayed. During a single century, the United Kingdom of Israel solved many serious problems and precociously passed through all the successive stages of development: youth, manhood, and declining old age. Saul awakened the nation to a consciousness of its strength. Under David it reached its zenith of power and entered on a course of vigorous development. During the reign of Solomon the first signs of decadence appeared; advances in expansion of trade, increase in wealth and luxury, and other refinements of civilization were dimming the great goals of the nation.

The unity imposed on the Jews was purchased dearly at the price of absolute, disciplined tyranny. Pompous religious ceremonial betraying a secularizing spirit obscured Israel's distinctive, yet simple, spiritual mission and character. Jeroboam adroitly marshaled the attitude of general disaffection with the monarchy. As an overseer of the work on the fortifications for Jerusalem, he had a good opportunity to learn the temper of Solomon's subjects and apparently sympathized with their complaints, encouraging a spirit of sedition. His action forced him into exile in Egypt. After Solomon's death Jeroboam returned to lead the rebellion.

The division of the kingdom was fatal to the nation's prosperity and disastrous in other respects. The elements of inner discord, which had been conciliated or suppressed while the kingdom was united, now revived and prevented further growth. The nation wore itself out in fifty years, never again to rise to its former glory. Religious life also suffered irreparably. Rather than advancing along the line David chartered for it, the state reverted to the conditions of previous anarchic periods.

—*Joseph R. Rosenbloom*

Further Reading

Coogan, David Michael. *The Oxford History of the Biblical World*. New York: Oxford University Press, 2001. Chapters 4 through 6 cover the periods of the judges, the early monarchy, and the ages of David and Solomon. Includes maps, chronology, and a general bibliography.

Finkelstein, Israel, and Neil Silberman. *The Bible Unearthed: Archaeology's New Vision of Ancient Israel and the Origin of Its Sacred Texts*. New York: Free Press, 2001. Two well-known scholars present the archaeological case against a historical reading of the Bible's narrative of Israelite history. They hold that the historical books of the Old Testament were codified in the seventh century B.C.E. in order to create and promote Jewish identity.

Isserlin, B. S. J. *The Israelites*. Minneapolis, Minn.: Fortress, 2001. A good overview of what is known and what is conjectured about the history of ancient Israel.

Shanks, Herschel, ed. *Ancient Israel: From Abraham to the Roman Destruction of the Temple*. 2d ed. New York: Prentice Hall, 1999. Chapters 4 and 5 of this volume edited by the editor of *Biblical Archaeology Review* cover the period of the united and divided monarchies. Includes color plates, maps, charts, and index.

Thompson, Thomas L. *The Mythic Past: Biblical Archaeology and the Myth of Israel*. New York: Basic Books, 1999. A dense but well-argued case against the historicity of the ages of David and Solomon.

See also: c. 1450 B.C.E., International Age of Major Kingdoms Begins in the Near East; c. 1280 B.C.E., Israelite Exodus from Egypt; c. 10th century B.C.E., Queen of Sheba Legends Arise; c. 1000 B.C.E., Establishment of the United Kingdom of Israel; c. 966 B.C.E., Building of the Temple of Jerusalem; 587-423 B.C.E., Birth of Judaism; c. 538-c. 450 B.C.E., Jews Return from the Babylonian Captivity; September 8, 70 C.E., Roman Destruction of the Temple of Jerusalem.

Related articles in *Great Lives from History: The Ancient World*: Abraham; Bathsheba; David; Deborah; Ezra; Ezekiel; Isaiah; Jeremiah; Johanan ben Zakkai; Solomon.

c. 900-c. 200 B.C.E.
CHAVÍN DE HUÁNTAR IS PERU'S URBAN CENTER

Chavín de Huántar was an important religious and urban center of ancient Peru, noted for its temple complex, stylized stone carvings, and association with a widely diffused art style.

LOCALE: Northeastern Highlands of Peru
CATEGORIES: Prehistory and ancient cultures; religion; architecture

SUMMARY OF EVENT

The ruins of the Chavín de Huántar site lie in a small Andean mountain valley about 10,000 feet (3000 meters) above sea level at the junction of two small tributaries to the Marañon River. Chavín is strategically placed almost midway between the tropical rain-forest region to the east and the arid coastal plains to the west. Moreover, being positioned at an intersection of major north-south routes facilitated connections and interaction with cultures ranging from the current Ecuadorian border to the north to Ica on the southern coast of Peru.

The time line for this site falls within the later part of the archaeological era known as the Formative period (c. 1700-c. 200 B.C.E.), which arose shortly after the rapid dissemination of agriculture. Although there is evidence of some human activity as early as 1300 B.C.E., the major ruins date from about 900 to 200 B.C.E. The period of Chavín's flourishing and external influence occurred during the last two centuries. The complex of buildings and residences found here served as an important religious or ceremonial center with a relatively small population until after 400 B.C.E., when it grew to an urban settlement of around 2,000 to 3,000 inhabitants and consisted of 104 acres (42 hectares).

Important features of this center include intriguing stone carvings of anthropomorphic deities and also of animals from the tropical Amazon lowlands such as the cayman, anaconda, jaguar, and harpy eagle. Carvings and sculpture are rendered in a distinctive art style also known as Chavín, associated with a Peruvian religious cult and culture that began to appear as early as 1400 B.C.E. In Chavín art, animal fangs and claws also appeared on nonanimal and human representations as indicators of divinity. Furthermore, physical features such as hair were represented by snakes, faces were shown with snarling feline or cayman fangs, and limbs ended in feet with claws. Many experts believe that these features serve as visual metaphors that the indigenous viewers would understand or recognize through comparison or substitution, a process known as kenning.

The building complexes at Chavín are characterized by sunken courts and pyramidal platforms in U-shaped configurations. Most notable are two monumental tem-

SELECTED SITES IN THE CHAVÍN CULTURE AND THE CENTRAL ANDES

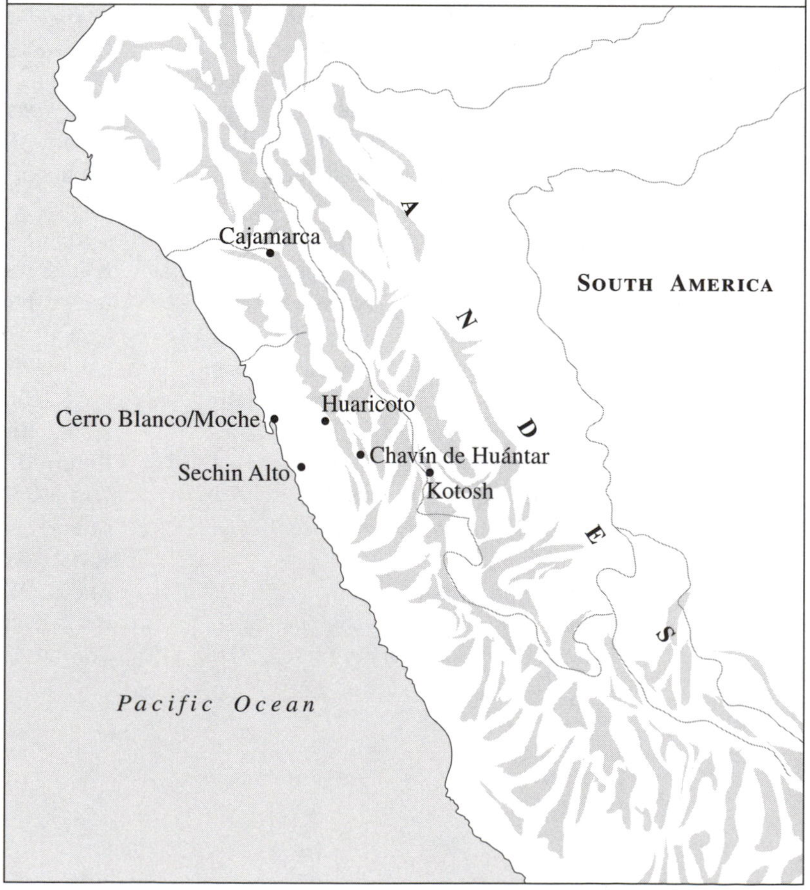

ples characterized by sunken plazas accessed by stone stairways and containing interior subterranean passages or galleries. The exteriors display cut and polished masonry decorated with stone carvings of animals in the Chavín style. The outer courtyards most likely served as centers for open-air public ceremonies.

The Old Temple, built during the late Initial period (c. 900 B.C.E.), became a great sanctuary of supernatural power and authority. At its center, reached by an interior passageway, is found the Lanzón Gallery. The Lanzón, named for its lancelike form, represents the supreme deity of this site, an anthropomorphic figure 14.5 feet (4.4 meters) tall displaying a feline head with grinning fanged facial features, and a human torso. In the era preceding the Chavín culture and art style, the jaguar image represented the main deity. In this later period, the purely feline symbol had evolved into an anthropomorphic figure. The Old Temple also contains a system of canals channeled from a glacially fed river to run through the temple, an impressive engineering achievement. Water, probably used for ritual purposes, passed through the large temple platform and beneath the sunken circular courtyard. As a result, the galleries reverberated with the roaring sound of rushing water.

The New Temple in most aspects is very similar to the older structure with a few minor variations such as the rendering of its Lanzón. This newer structure, however, did not displace the Old Temple and its plaza, which continued to be used for both spiritual and storage purposes. Numerous artifacts testifying to the inhabitants' creative and artistic abilities are found at Chavín de Huántar. These items include limestone sculptures; conch-shell trumpets, implements, and utensils; and fine tapestries and textiles usually decorated in the distinctive Chavín art style.

Late in the site's history, by around 300 B.C.E., evidence of social stratification appears. Excavated burial sites reveal that an elite class received elaborate and impressive interments. These tombs contained many valuable objects such as colorful textiles and jewelry. On the other hand, the great majority of graves representing the humbler or less elevated classes were shallow pits containing remains wrapped in simple cotton-cloth garments and accompanied by only mundane burial objects such as tools.

It should be noted that findings in recent years have revised older interpretations of the site's role in Peruvian prehistory. Many scholars once regarded Chavín de Huántar as Peru's "mother culture" and one of the earliest centers of a complex civilization that originated and disseminated the art style that bears its name and the religious cult associated with it. Archaeologists now realize that the site's monumental architecture, with features such as sunken courtyards and its stylized art forms, originated with earlier cultures from both the coast and highlands. Chavín's decline and collapse came during the third century B.C.E., a time of turbulence and instability. New construction was suddenly left unfinished, and structures eventually began to fall into ruin, while the land began to be used for agriculture or pasture.

Significance

In its heyday, Chavín was a very important center of interregional trade and a site of religious pilgrimage. In spite of recent discoveries about the important role of earlier urban and cultural centers in Peruvian prehistory, Chavín de Huántar is still regarded as a very important and influential archaeological site. One recently excavated sensational find, the urban center of Caral in the Supe Valley near the coast, precedes Chavín by well over a thousand years and parallels similar developments in the Old World. Yet the latter must still regarded as a focus of one of ancient Peru's early and most advanced complex societies to develop in the Central Andean region.

In addition, the synthesis of older cultural patterns and styles at Chavín de Huántar produced a distinctive blend now regarded as one of the major artistic achievements of South American prehistory. This style clearly influenced later high cultures such as the Moche, Nazca, Huari, and Inca. Dissemination of the Chavín style during the site's later phase in the form of stone carvings, metallurgy, textiles, and ceramics indicates that Chavín de Huántar was this region's most prestigious religious and urban center.

—*David A. Crain*

Further Reading

Benson, Elizabeth P., ed. *Dumbarton Oaks Conference on Chavín.* Washington, D.C.: Dumbarton Oaks Research Library and Collection, 1971. Collection of articles by specialists in the field from a conference held in October, 1968. Illustrations and maps.

Burger, Richard L. *Chavín and the Origins of Andean Civilization.* New York: Thames and Hudson, 1992. Good overview by a noted specialist on prehistoric Peru of the Chavín culture, its origins, development, fall, and influence on the later Nazca, Moche, Huari, and Inca civilizations. Bibliography, index, illustrations.

_______. *The Prehistoric Occupation of Chavín de*

Huántar, Peru. Berkeley: University of California Press, 1984. Presents archaeological evidence on the background and early settlement at Chavín prior to that site's period of flourishing. Bibliography and index.

_______. "Unity and Heterogeneity Within the Chavín Horizon." In *Peruvian Prehistory*, edited by Richard W. Keatinge. New York: Cambridge University Press, 1988. An excellent synthesis of the archaeological research on Chavín. Maps and illustrations.

Kano, Chiaki. *The Origins of the Chavín Culture*. Washington, D.C.: Dumbarton Oaks Trustees for Harvard University, 1979. Traces the relationship between early pre-Chavín cultures and Chavín, focusing on changes in the artistic style using the feline motif as a base. Illustrations and bibliography.

Lumbreras, Luis G. *The Peoples and Cultures of Ancient Peru*. Translated by Betty J. Meggers. Washington, D.C.: Smithsonian Institution Press, 1974. The section on Peru's Formative period (c. 1800 B.C.E.-c. 100 C.E.) contains an informative discussion of the Chavín culture, the famous ceremonial site, and its influence on other ancient Peruvian centers. Bibliography, index, and illustrations.

Rowe, John H. *Chavín Art: An Inquiry into Its Form and Meaning*. New York: The Museum of Primitive Art, 1963. One of the best-known interpretative studies on the Chavín art style. Illustrations, map.

Von Hagen, Adriana, and Craig Morris. *The Cities of the Ancient Andes*. New York: Thames and Hudson, 1998. Uses archaeological evidence to trace the development of the great Andean cities, including Chavín de Huántar. Illustrations, site plans, and photos.

SEE ALSO: c. 5800-c. 3700 B.C.E., Chinchorro Inhabit the Peruvian and Chilean Coasts; c. 2500 B.C.E., Construction of Monumental Architecture at Caral in Peru; c. 1800-c. 1500 B.C.E., Construction of El Paraíso in Peru; 700 B.C.E.-100 C.E., Paracas Culture Develops a Sophisticated Textile Tradition; c. 500 B.C.E.-c. 700 C.E., Zapotecs Build Monte Albán; 200 B.C.E.-200 C.E., Nasca Lines Drawn in Desert Near Coast of Peru; 200-800 C.E., Lima Culture Flourishes on the Central Andean Coast.

c. 883-c. 824 B.C.E.
SECOND ASSYRIAN EMPIRE DISPLAYS MILITARY PROWESS

The reestablishment of Assyria's strategic power capabilities by Ashurnasirpal II and Shalmaneser III formalized the empire's efficient yet brutal strategic military dominance of the Near East, the Middle East, and the surrounding ancient world.

LOCALE: Assyria (centered in Mesopotamia, reaching Central Asia and the Mediterranean)

CATEGORIES: Expansion and land acquisition; wars, uprisings, and civil unrest; government and politics

KEY FIGURES

Ashurnasirpal II (c. 915-859 B.C.E.), strategic leader of Assyrian Empire, r. c. 883-859 B.C.E.

Shalmaneser III (fl. ninth century B.C.E.), son of Ashurnasirpal II, r. c. 858-824 B.C.E.

SUMMARY OF EVENT

The first Assyrian Empire began with Shamshi-Adad I (r. c. 1814-1782 B.C.E.), who established limited Assyrian rule in the ancient Middle Eastern region with the purpose of controlling strategic trade routes in and near the Tigris and Euphrates river valleys. However, the great king of the Babylonian Empire, Hammurabi, defeated the Assyrian's son, Ishme-Dagan I (1782-c. 1741 B.C.E.), and the first Assyrian Empire collapsed. With the fall of Babylon in the sixteenth century B.C.E. as a result of a very powerful Kassite invasion force, Assyria also succumbed to the Kassites and endured repeated invasions by various marauding nomadic tribes. In the fifteenth century B.C.E., the powerful Mitanni kingdom invaded and enslaved the Assyrian heartland, as well as other states within the northern Mesopotamia region, for more than two centuries. In the thirteenth century B.C.E., the once mighty Mitanni kingdom collapsed because of a massive and successful Hittite invasion. The Assyrian king Ashur-uballit I (r. c. 1363-1330 B.C.E.), taking full advantage of the regional turmoil with the fall of the Mitanni kingdom, temporarily restored Assyria's independence and freedom of action by strengthening the field army and using it to recapture Assyrian territories.

Between the thirteenth and ninth centuries B.C.E., the talented Assyrian kings who followed Ashur-uballit also

Ashurnasirpal II. (Library of Congress)

sought to consolidate Assyria's territorial sovereignty and political independence in a number of important ways. First, they extended Assyrian territory against the wild and dangerous mountain tribes in the east, the enemy states located in the Lake Van region in the north, the powerful Babylonian Empire in the south, and the states in the Mediterranean region in the west. Second, they built an extremely powerful army and security forces that were capable of extended military field operations against enemy states and marauding nomadic tribes in the Near East and Middle Eastern regions. Third, they greatly strengthened the Assyrian economy (which was based primarily on animal husbandry, agriculture, and trade) as well as strengthening its commercial links with neighboring friendly states to pay for and sustain foreign military operations. Finally, they erected geographical and military defensive barriers to prevent foreign invasions from belligerent neighbors such as Lullubi, Urartu, and Babylon into the heartland of Assyria.

However, the reestablishment of Assyrian military hegemony in the Near East, the Middle East, and the surrounding ancient world occurred with Assyria's House of Ashur-rabi, which successfully produced, among other outstanding rulers, two excellent strategic leaders, Ashurnasirpal II and his famous son, Shalmaneser III.

Ashurnasirpal II, the son of Tukulti-Ninurta II (r. c. 890-884 B.C.E.), came to the throne of Assyria around 883 B.C.E. with the singular purpose of subjugating kings on both sides of Assyria. Ashurnasirpal II was an extremely complex, very ambitious, and gifted individual who was determined to put Assyria on the path of world conquest and military glory. His strategic political policy toward all enemies and friends of the Assyrian state was to threaten to use or actually to use massive military power brutally and ruthlessly, both to advance Assyria's national interests and to extend the geostrategic reach of the emerging Assyrian Empire. Surrounded by extremely aggressive enemy states on all sides in the Near East and Middle Eastern regions, Ashurnasirpal II was determined to improve the organizational efficiency, military effectiveness, and the military shock power of the Assyrian army.

In this context, Ashurnasirpal II (and the Assyrian rulers who followed him) introduced revolutionary reforms to strengthen fighting capabilities of the Assyrian field army. They included the following force structure reforms: the development of all-weather and all-terrain capabilities for field combat operations; the development of extremely sophisticated logistics capabilities to support all types of field combat operations in all weather and all terrain; the development of a highly efficient transport system with camels and mules as the main transportation and logistical units; the development of a very powerful, well-trained, and combat-ready Assyrian cavalry force (supplementing and inevitably replacing war chariots); the development of heavy mobile siege towers, mobile battering rams, and massive wall breakers to break down and collapse the walls of enemy capitals and cities; the development of a national system for horse procurement to maintain the overall combat readiness of Assyrian cavalry divisions; military technological improvement of the three most important organizational components of the Assyrian infantry division (slingmen, spearmen, and archers); the maximization of the combat organization of Assyrian field army divisions, compa-

MAJOR ASSYRIAN RULERS, C. 1814-824 B.C.E.

Ruler	*Reign*
Shamshi-Adad I	c. 1814-1782
Ishme-Dagan I	1782-c. 1741
Ashur-uballit I	c. 1363-1330
Tukulti-Ninurta II	c. 890-884
Ashurnasirpal II	c. 883-859
Shalmaneser III	c. 858-824

nies, and units to maximize maneuverability, fighting ability, overall discipline, and killing power; and finally, the development and application of advanced psychological and propaganda strategy and tactics.

By producing one of the most battle-ready and highly disciplined armies in the history of the ancient Near East and Middle East, Ashurnasirpal II increased the efficiency and functionality of Assyria's military and domestic intelligence organization and improved the overall administrative and economic organization of Assyria in preparation for sustained military operations against its many enemies. As the historical record indicates, Ashurnasirpal II conducted a series of merciless "total war" campaigns against Lebanon, Armenia, Babylon, Syria, Kurdistan, Urartu, the land of the Hittites, the cities of Phoenicia, and other enemy states in the Near East and the Middle East. His campaigns had the political consequence of securing Assyria's long borders, expanding its external territorial control, expertly terrorizing its enemies and friends, and satisfying its national interests. The political legacy of Ashurnasirpal II is that his extremely successful military campaigns and raids in the Near East, the Middle East, and the surrounding ancient world led to the unequaled primacy of Assyrian strategic military power, which was increased even further by his son, Shalmaneser III.

Shalmaneser III came to power c. 858 B.C.E., continuing the expansionary foreign military policy of his father, Ashurnasirpal II. His general military campaigns against Syria, Turkey, Urartu, Palestine, Israel, Babylon, Iran, and other enemy states in the Near East and the Middle East demonstrated the combat effectiveness and brutal shock power of the Assyrian field army. In particular, his campaigns against Urartu in 858 B.C.E., 849 B.C.E., and 831 B.C.E. to secure Assyria's northern passes were instances of Assyria pursuing its national interests through military means. However, he was less successful than his father in politically exploiting his numerous tactical military victories, especially with regard to the birthplace of Assyrian civilization, a still powerful Babylon, the emerging empire of Urartu in eastern Turkey, and the various major and minor kings in Iran, Syria, and Palestine. Moreover, Shalmaneser III's foreign military strategy faced very serious domestic problems, including a damaging conflict between his two sons on who would succeed him, which broke out into civil war, and independent provincial governors who had built their power bases and were at odds with Shalmaneser III's authority. These problems cast a shadow over the political legacy of Shalmaneser III, and they would play a major role in the ultimate collapse of the Assyrian Empire.

SIGNIFICANCE

The strategic significance of the rule of Ashurnasirpal II and Shalmaneser III is that both sought to strengthen the Assyrian state and transform it into an empire by pursuing a foreign military policy that was aggressive, expansionary, and consistent with overall national security interests. The evidence shows that Ashurnasirpal II was the more successful in pursuing these objectives and that his son Shalmaneser III was less so for foreign policy and domestic political reasons.

—*Michael J. Siler*

FURTHER READING

Gabriel, Richard A., and Karen S. Metz. *From Sumer to Rome: The Military Capabilities of Ancient Armies*. Westport, Conn.: Greenwood Press, 1991. Discusses the advanced military capabilities of ancient armies from Sumer to the Roman Empire.

Luckenbill, Daniel David. *Ancient Records of Assyria and Babylon*. London: Histories and Mysteries of Man, 1989. A comprehensive review of the ancient records on the Assyrian and Babylonian civilizations.

Roux, Georges. *Ancient Iraq*. 3d ed. New York: Penguin, 1992. An excellent examination of the history, culture, and governmental and military capabilities of ancient Iraq.

Saggs, H. W. F. *The Might That Was Assyria*. London: Sidgwick and Jackson, 1984. The author examines the military capabilities and strategic accomplishments of ancient Assyria.

Wiseman, D. J. "The Assyrians." In *Warfare in the Ancient World*, edited by Sir John Hackett. London: Sidgwick and Jackson, 1989. Focuses on the military capabilities and successful campaigns of the Assyrian Empire and its leaders.

SEE ALSO: c. 1450 B.C.E., International Age of Major Kingdoms Begins in the Near East; c. 1100 B.C.E., Arameans Emerge in Syria and Mesopotamia; 745 B.C.E., Tiglath-pileser III Rules Assyria; 701 B.C.E., Sennacherib Invades Syro-Palestine; c. 607-562 B.C.E., Nebuchadnezzar Creates the First Neo-Babylonian State.

RELATED ARTICLES in *Great Lives from History: The Ancient World:* Ashurnasirpal II; Hammurabi; Sammu-ramat.

8th century B.C.E.
KUSHITE KING PIYE CONQUERS UPPER EGYPT

Piye conquered Egypt and restored its splendor, renewing its cultural traditions as well as increasing its political power.

LOCALE: Kush (present-day northern Sudan) and Egypt

CATEGORIES: Government and politics; expansion and land acquisition; cultural and intellectual history

KEY FIGURES

Kashta (d. c. 747/746 B.C.E.), Kushite ruler and father of Piye, r. c. 783-747/746 B.C.E.

Piye (Piankhi; c. 769-716 B.C.E.), Kushite conqueror of Egypt and founder of the Twenty-fifth Dynasty, r. 742-716 B.C.E.

Tefnakht (early eighth century-c. 720 B.C.E.), Twenty-fourth Dynasty ruler of Saïs in the Nile Delta, r. 730-720 B.C.E.

Harwa (mid-eighth century-c. 680 B.C.E.), Egyptian priest installed by Piye as governor of Thebes

Taharqa (fl. seventh century-656 B.C.E.), Kushite ruler of Egypt, r. 690-664 B.C.E.

SUMMARY OF EVENT

The vast expanse of Sudan, Africa's largest nation in modern times, contains much evidence of advanced ancient civilizations. In northern Sudan, several early cultures exerted influences that spread to Egypt, which eventually dominated the lower half of the Nile River basin. Lured by the region's gold, the Egyptians conquered the Sudanese kingdom of Kush, the region known later in the ancient period as Nubia. So valued was this colony that one of the highest offices meted out by the pharaohs was that of viceroy (governor) of Kush. As Egypt's power waxed, Kush's contributions to its powerful northern neighbor's civilization were often obscured.

The New Kingdom period (c. 1570-c. 1069 B.C.E.), the zenith of Egypt's power, ended when Kush freed itself from Egyptian rule. Around 1087, Viceroy Panehsy of Kush led a rebellion against Egypt and occupied the Upper Egyptian capital, Thebes. Around 1080, Theban high priest Herihor successfully led the priests of the sun god Amen-Ra in a revolt against the Kushites, and Upper Egypt became a theocracy. The Kushites then created an independent kingdom in the south, while the kings of the Twenty-first Dynasty (1069-945) ruled the Nile Delta from Tanis.

By the eighth century B.C.E., Egypt's glorious achievements had become distant memories. The land of the pharaohs, embroiled in civil strife, had been divided into competing states. By 945 B.C.E., Lower Egypt was overwhelmed by the gradual encroachment of Libyans, many of whom had been mercenaries in the pharaoh's army. For the next three millennia, Egypt would be ruled by foreigners. The Twenty-second, or Libyan, Dynasty ruled Egypt from 945 to 715. The second half of this dynasty was marked by chaos. To the south in Kush, Alara rose as the ambitious ruler of Napata, a city near the Fourth Cataract. Alara's brother and heir, Kashta, invaded Upper Egypt, captured Aswān, and took control of Egypt's gold fields.

In 747 B.C.E., Kashta's son Piye rapidly completed his father's conquest of Upper Egypt with help from the Theban priesthood of Amen-Ra. Piye is an elusive figure. His many wives include a daughter and a niece of Alara. No surviving statue or painting shows Piye clearly, and historians are faced with numerous difficulties in dating events in his life. He adopted different throne names during various parts of his reign, including the names of previous rulers, such as Usermaetre (Ramses II). Numerous inscriptions show that he was particularly fond of using the name and titles of the Eighteenth Dynasty pharaoh Menkheperre' Thutmose (Thutmose III). Many scholars have been confused by the mistaken assumption that every inscription that bears the name Menkheperre' Thutmose was authored by the fifteenth century Thutmose III.

Piye's campaign in Upper Egypt may have stemmed from a tour to renew oaths of allegiance pledged to his fa-

RULERS OF THE TWENTY-FIFTH (KUSHITE) DYNASTY, 742-656 B.C.E.

Ruler	*Reign*
Piye	742-716
Shabaka	716-702/698
Shebitku	698-690
Taharqa	690-664
Tanutamuni	664-656

Note: Dynastic research is ongoing; data are approximate.

ther by his northern vassals. He may also have intervened to protect the cult of Amen-Ra from conquest by Tefnakht of the Delta state of Saïs, which rebelled against the Libyans around 740 B.C.E. Piye's flotillas and cavalry soon became dominant. To many Egyptians, the Kushites were morally upright liberators who had come to save Egypt from the degenerate petty nobles who had dominated the land of the pharaohs. Others saw Piye as an unsophisticated moralist meddling in Egyptian affairs.

The end of Piye's conquest of Upper Egypt is the subject of the dark-granite victory stela of Piye, found at the temple of Amen at Gebel Barkal in 1862. This find was the inspiration for Giuseppe Verdi's 1874 opera *Aïda*. This inscribed stone shows the defeat of Nimlot of Khemenu (Hermopolis, modern-day Al-Ashmünein) and Peftjauawybast of Nen-nesut (Heracleopolis, modern Ihnasya), whose lands formed the northern third of Upper Egypt. Piye was described as an attacking bull; however, when the fortress of Per-Sekhemkheperre surrendered, the often merciful Piye ordered his men not to kill the surviving occupants.

Piye put an end to Egypt's chaotic decline. He maintained direct control over the theocratic state of Thebes by promoting his sister Amenirdis as divine adoratrice (high priestess and governor). His coronation as pharaoh in 742 B.C.E. marked the beginning of the Twenty-fifth, or Kushite, Dynasty (742-c. 656). He then returned in triumph to his beloved Napata, with the spoils of his campaigns and tributes from his new vassals.

When Piye conquered Upper Egypt, a priest named Harwa embraced the Kushite cause, and his subsequent loyalty to the Twenty-fifth Dynasty led to his appointment as grand steward of the divine adoratrice, a position he held for some forty years. Portrayed in statues as a fat, bald man with a large face, almond-shaped eyes, and thin lips, he was from an elite family of Theban priests. The number of statues made in his image and the vastness of his funerary monument and inscriptions found by Italian archaeologists in Luxor in 1997 suggest that Harwa, called the Great of the Greats, was the de facto governor of at least Thebes and possibly all of Upper Egypt during the reign of Piye and his three successors, Shabaka, Shebitku (Shabataka), and Taharqa. Only the pharaohs ranked above him. His elaborate tomb later become the center of the Assassif necropolis, which suggests that his powers were more than just priestly.

Tefnakht of Saïs ruled the northern half of Egypt very briefly before it was fragmented into numerous feuding states. Lower Egypt languished under the control of five different kings, each reigning over a limited area but each claiming to be the sole pharaoh. Around 725 B.C.E., they formed an unsuccessful coalition against Piye, who captured Memphis and Heliopolis three years later. Tefnakht and his son Bakenranef, whose reigns are listed as part of the Twenty-fourth Dynasty (730-715), were the last to be conquered. With the defeat of the Lower Egyptian kings, Piye united the Nile Valley from Meroë to the Mediterranean Sea. He generously appointed four of the former kings to rule on his behalf as governors of their territories.

Noted for his devotion to Amen-Ra, Piye showed great reverence for traditional New Year's celebrations and Thebes' Opet Festival. A just ruler, he sought to restore Egypt to its past splendors, and Egypt and Kush experienced a cultural revival.

Having ruled over a united empire on the Nile for almost a decade, Piye died in 716 B.C.E. His great love of horses, a common Kushite trait, was demonstrated by his having eight horses buried near his tomb. The Kushite throne tended to pass from brother to brother, and Piye was succeeded by his brother, Shabaka, who moved his capital from Napata to Thebes. On his death c. 702-698, Shabaka was succeeded by Shebitku, who in turn was succeeded by his nephew Taharqa (the biblical Tirhakah) in 690. A prolific builder and capable administrator, Taharqa ruled for twenty-six years. However, the final decade of Taharqa's rule was dominated by a series of invasions by three successive Assyrian emperors, who had already conquered Mesopotamia, Phoenicia, and Palestine. Taharqa's successor, Tanutamuni, failed to hold Egypt, and his reign marked the end of the Twenty-fifth Dynasty.

After its rise to world power under Piye and his successors, Kush was isolated from the Mediterranean and Middle Eastern civilizations to the north. The iron-working center of Meroë, Nubia's medieval Christian kingdoms of Nobatia, Makouria, and Alodia and the Muslim Funj Sultanate of Sennar were the geographical heirs to Kush but hardly displayed the brilliance of Piye's glory.

SIGNIFICANCE

Piye's conquest of Egypt and his establishment of the Twenty-Fifth, or Kushite, Dynasty ushered in a renascence of the ancient Egyptian civilization. It brought about a hopeful revival of eons-old political and religious norms. However, conquest by the more advanced and more ruthless Assyrians heralded Egypt's subjugation and Kush's isolation for many centuries to come.

—*Randall Fegley*

FURTHER READING

Adams, William Y. *Nubia: Corridor to Africa*. Princeton, N.J.: Princeton University Press, 1977. Although later findings have changed much of the body of scholarship on Nubia, this work remains the most thorough reference on the archaeology and history of Kush.

Kendall, Timothy. *Kerma and the Kingdom of Kush, 2500-1500 B.C.: The Archaeological Discovery of an Ancient Nubian Empire*. Washington, D.C.: National Museum of Africa Art, Smithsonian Institution, 1997. Kendall surveys the archaeological work that has been conducted on the earliest periods of Kushite history.

Morkot, Robert G. *The Black Pharaohs: Egypt's Nubian Rulers*. London: The Rubicon Press, 2000. A good work on the Twenty-fifth Dynasty. Focuses on the roles of the Kushites (Nubians) during Egypt's conflicts with Libya and Assyria.

Török, Lásló. *The Kingdom of Kush: Handbook of the Napatan-Meroitic Civilization*. New York: Brill, 1998. Török provides a good reference on ancient Kush, from its emergence to the Meroitic period. Contains a genealogy of the kings of Kush.

Wildung, Dietrich. *Sudan: Ancient Kingdoms of the Nile*. New York: Flammarion, 1997. This large, illustrated work concentrates on artifacts from ancient Sudan but also provides a good chronological survey.

SEE ALSO: c. 1900-1527? B.C.E., Kerma Kingdom Rules Nubia; c. 1570 B.C.E., New Kingdom Period Begins in Egypt; c. 1450 B.C.E., International Age of Major Kingdoms Begins in the Near East; c. 1200-c. 1000 B.C.E., Berbers Expand Across North Africa; c. 783-c. 591 B.C.E., Napata Kingdom Flourishes in Kush; 745 B.C.E., Tiglath-pileser III Rules Assyria; c. 712-698 B.C.E., Shabaka Reunites the Nile Valley; 664 B.C.E., Saite Dynasty Begins in Egypt; c. 6th century B.C.E.-c. 350 C.E., Meroitic Empire Rules from Southern Egypt to the Blue Nile.

RELATED ARTICLE in *Great Lives from History: The Ancient World*: Piye.

8th century B.C.E.
SCYTHIANS DRIVE THE CIMMERIANS FROM CENTRAL ASIA

The Scythians hunted the Cimmerians, driving them out of the Volga River Valley, Armenia, the borders of Assyria, and Asia Minor.

LOCALE: Armenia, Iran, Iraq, Russia, Turkey, Ukraine
CATEGORIES: Expansion and land acquisition; prehistory and ancient cultures

SUMMARY OF EVENT

The Cimmerians, a nomadic people referred to in the Bible as the Gomer, were a militarily aggressive Indo-European people of Iranian lineage. The Cimmerians settled along the northern coast of what is today known as the Black Sea (known in ancient Greek literature as the Southern Sea), specifically in modern Ukraine east of the Dnieper River. Modern scholars believe that Cimmerian culture arose on what is now known as the Crimean Peninsula in the late eleventh century B.C.E. The first known reference to the Cimmerians appears in the poetry of Homer and dates from c. 714 B.C.E., when the Cimmerians defeated a number of peoples and occupied the lands of several civilizations in Asia Minor and the Near East, particularly the kingdom of Media in present-day Iran and the Assyrian Empire in modern-day Iraq.

The Cimmerians' antagonists, the Scythians (also known as the Scyths), shared with them an Indo-European origin. The Scythians spoke a language that belonged to the Iranian linguistic group and most likely originated in the steppe of southwestern Russia. Of all the extant ancient historians, Herodotus is the only one to

05

discuss the nomadic Scythians and their interaction with the Cimmerians in any detail. Herodotus's knowledge of the Scythians' exploits came from the fact that groups of Greek settlers, with whom Herodotus had lived, encountered the Scythians during their colonization of territory of what is today southern Russia.

In his detailed historical narrative *Historiai Herodotou* (c. 424 B.C.E.; *The History*, 1709), Herodotus mentions that the Scythians, who he noted were formidable warriors, invaded Cimmerian territory. This event, which is also mentioned in Chinese records of the time, probably occurred in the eighth century B.C.E. (ancient accounts disagree regarding the exact time of this episode). According to Herodotus, the Scythians crossed the Araxes River (located in present-day Armenia), which had been controlled by the Cimmerians. On learning of the Scythians' impending arrival, the Cimmerians convened a meeting of their legislative council to determine a course of action. Herodotus notes that the session was unable to reach a consensus on how to deal with the Scythian threat, and consequently two factions emerged. One group resolved to leave the area immediately and avoid a confrontation with the Scythians, who were well known throughout western Asia and the Mediterranean region as accomplished soldiers. The other coalition, whom Herodotus refers to as the Royal Tribe, decided to remain and fight the Scythian invaders. These individuals were killed in their failed bid to turn back the marauding Scythians. Herodotus indicates that the graves of the Cimmerian defenders were still visible near the Tyras (modern-day Dniester) River. The Scythian onslaught compelled those Cimmerians who had chosen not to fight to abandon their territories along the Volga River Valley in southern Russia as well as their lands in the southern Caucasus Mountains. After relinquishing these holdings to the Scythians, the remaining Cimmerians fled across the Caucasus west into Asia Minor (modern-day Turkey).

SIGNIFICANCE

Despite their expulsion from the Volga region and Armenia at the hands of the Scythians, the Cimmerians and their civilization were not completely extinguished. The writings of Herodotus reveal that Cimmerian culture survived the Scythian invasion. He notes that Cimmerian castles were still present during his day (the fifth century B.C.E.) and that some locations retained their Cimmerian names. Furthermore, Herodotus remarks that after fleeing the Scythians, the Cimmerians built settlements that would later serve as the foundations for the Greek colonies that arose in the Black Sea region during Herodotus's day, particularly the Greek city of Sinope (modern-day Sinop, Turkey).

The Cimmerians' experience with the Scythians led them to take up arms and seek new lands to the west. The Cimmerians' luck improved after they crossed the Caucasus—they successfully plundered the Lydian city of Sardis in present-day western Turkey and destroyed another important Lydian city, Magnesia. Eventually, however, the Lydians were able to turn the tide against the newcomers, and the Cimmerians were defeated by the seventh century B.C.E. Apparently, Cimmerian civilization did not survive beyond this period, as no records of the Cimmerians exist after their encounter with the Lydians.

As for the Scythians, their encounter with the Cimmerians did not signal the end of their territorial expansion. Before its decline in the late third century B.C.E., the Scythian Empire extended over 2,000 miles (3,200 kilometers), from Ukraine in the west to present-day Kazakhstan in the east. The Scythians' significance in the ancient world is clear given Herodotus's lengthy discussion of their activities as well as the biblical reference to the Scythians (Colossians 3:11).

—*Christopher J. Ward*

FURTHER READING

Boren, Henry C. *The Ancient World: An Historical Perspective*. 2d ed. Englewood Cliffs, N.J.: Prentice-Hall, 1986. A classic text that covers the ancient cultures that occupied western Russia, the Caucasus, and the Near East.

Herodotus. *The Histories*. Translated by Robin A. Waterfield, edited by Carolyn Dewald. New York: Oxford University Press, 1999. This is the definitive ancient source on the Cimmerians and Scythians—particularly books 1, 4, and 7—from arguably the greatest of ancient historians.

Rice, Tamara Talbot. *The Scythians*. 3d ed. New York: Thames and Hudson, 1961. A classic work on the Scythians that covers their interactions with the Cimmerians. Well illustrated.

Von Soden, Wolfram. *The Ancient Orient: An Introduction to the Study of the Ancient Near East*. Grand Rapids, Mich.: William B. Eerdmans, 1994. An approachable introduction to the Cimmerians and their relationship with the Scythians.

Wells, Peter S. *Beyond Celts, Germans, and Scythians: Archaeology and Identity in Iron Age Europe*. London: Duckworth, 2001. Discusses the process of identifying and discussing a nomadic or migratory "people" solely from archaeological evidence and commentary by outside writers. Discusses the movements of and conflicts among the Scythians and Cimmerians.

SEE ALSO: c. 6800-c. 4900 B.C.E., Kitoi People Live Near Lake Baikal in Siberia; c. 4000 B.C.E., Horse Is Domesticated; c. 2000 B.C.E., Mongols Inhabit Steppes North of China; c. 1500-c. 1000 B.C.E., Aryans Appear in India; c. 1000-c. 690 B.C.E., Cimmerian Culture Rises in Russia; c. 420 B.C.E.-c. 100 C.E., Yuezhi Culture Links Persia and China; 95-69 B.C.E., Armenian Empire Reaches Its Peak Under Tigranes the Great.

RELATED ARTICLES in *Great Lives from History: The Ancient World*: Herodotus; Miltiades the Younger; Sennacherib.

8th-6th centuries B.C.E.
PHRYGIAN KINGDOM RISES

The Phrygians, an Iron Age people, founded a kingdom in western Anatolia with its capital at Gordium, an important cultural and religious center during the reign of the legendary king Midas, son of Gordios.

LOCALE: Phyrgia, western Anatolia (now in Turkey)
CATEGORY: Prehistory and ancient cultures

KEY FIGURES

Midas (738-c. 696/695 B.C.E.), king of Phrygia, r. c. 730-709 B.C.E., son of Gordios
Alexander the Great (356-323 B.C.E.), king of Macedonia, r. 336-323 B.C.E.

SUMMARY OF EVENT

The Phrygians were originally a Thracian tribe who arrived in Anatolia around 1200 B.C.E. and participated in the destruction of Troy VII (near modern-day Hissarlik, Turkey) and the former Hittite capital of Hattusa (Bogazköy, Turkey). Their king Midas (Mit-ta) is mentioned in the annals of the Assyrian king Sargon II (second half of eighth century-705 B.C.E.) and records of Eusebius of Caesarea (c. 260-339 C.E.) as Mita or Mushki. This is the same legendary mythological figure whose ears were transformed into those of an ass and who had power to turn everything he touched to gold. However, the well-known geographer Strabo (64/63 B.C.E.-after 23 C.E.) refers to Midas as a king who committed suicide by drinking the blood of the bull during the invasions of the Cimmerian tribes that attacked and burned the ancient capital at Gordium (Yassi Höyük, Turkey) around 700 B.C.E.

The result was a transfer of hegemony of western Anatolia to the indigenous Lydians, the representatives of the old pre-Hittite civilization in Anatolia. During the Lidyans' rule between 675 and 585 B.C.E., the kingdom lost its political and cultural power. After 585 B.C.E., the Phrygians were allowed to be ruled by their own princes, and although subjects of Lydia, they experienced a second golden age. It was a brief period, yet numerous well-preserved monuments erected in the districts of present-day Eskişehir and Afyon document the final prosperous years of this great culture. In 546 B.C.E., under the Persian occupation, the ancient kingdom became weak and inefficient. Alexander the Great entered Asia Minor in 334 B.C.E. and, within a short time, gained control over the region. Later, under the successive rulers of Anatolia, the Phrygians were considered slow and stupid and were valued only as slaves.

The Phrygian society consisted of high priests, landowners, merchants, and craftspeople who were highly cultured and educated. They had their own Indo-European language, related to Thracian dialects, with script based on the early Greek alphabet in use from about 730 B.C.E.

Gordium, the capital of the Phrygian kingdom, was at its best between 725 and 675 B.C.E. Originally, the city was surrounded by a massive fortification of walls with three gates, and the centrally located palace had inner rooms arranged like a megaron (large room). The name of the city comes from that of Gordius, the first legendary king of Phrygia, who tied the original knot on the walls of the city, prophesying that whoever loosened the knot would become the leader of all Asia. In winter of 333 B.C.E., Alexander the Great cut through the knot with his sword. From his act arose the phrase "cutting the Gordian knot," which denotes a bold solution to a complex problem. Although the story of Gordius, of a peasant who became king and who dedicated his chariot to Zeus, has been handed down from ancient times, no records support a historical status for Gordius, and archaeologists have not found the remains of the temple in which the chariot was reportedly kept.

In addition to this fortress, the so-called Midas Monument at Midas City (Yazilkaya, Turkey) is in a good state of preservation. Proposed dates for it have ranged between the eighth and sixth centuries B.C.E. The imposing carved rock surface bears two inscriptions, of which the upper one contains the name Midas (MIDAI). The monument imitates the facade of a building that served as an architectural frame for the niche in which the figure of great Phrygian mother goddess Cybele was displayed at public festivals.

Elaborate funeral ceremonies and burial customs resulted in the creation of tumuli of various sizes, erected between the eighth and sixth centuries B.C.E. There are about eighty mounds in the area around Gordium, of which the Midas Mound is the largest and most luxurious. This tomb is famous for both its dimensions—170 feet (53 meters) in height with a diameter of close to 1,000 feet (300 meters)—and the finds made there. The timber chamber, constructed of pine, measured 17 by 20 feet (5 by 6 meters) and included the skeleton of a man who had lived to be at least sixty years old and had no traces of any physical deformity. Originally, the body was placed in an open cedar coffin surrounded with exceptionally fine furniture and two hundred bronze and pottery vessels, several of which contained solid food and liquids. The reconstructed interior of the chamber is on permanent display in the Museum of Anatolian Civilizations in Ankara, Turkey. Although some researchers believe the tomb's occupant to be King Midas, the latest research dates the tomb to 718 B.C.E., which calls this identification into question.

Significance

The Phrygians were an Iron Age people whose king Midas founded a short-lived kingdom in western Anatolia. They were known to be creative, and their art and culture occupy an outstanding position in recorded history of ancient civilizations.

Phrygian architecture, particularly its carved facades and tumuli, may have influenced the Etruscan rock-cut tombs of Norchia and burial mounds of Tarquinia (both in Italy), which they resemble. Furthermore, there is strong evidence that Phrygian religion influenced beliefs in Greece and Rome, including the early cult of the goddess Cybele and her association with Demeter and Rhea. The influence of Phrygian design and technique, especially in woodwork, textiles, and tapestry, can be recognized in Ionian artistic production of the seventh century B.C.E.

—Rozmeri Basic

Further Reading

Akurgal, Ekrem. *Ancient Civilizations and Ruins of Turkey.* New York: Kegan Paul International, 2002. An archaeological survey of visual monuments of Turkey with maps and illustrations.

Boardman, John, et al., eds. "The Phrygian Kingdom." In *The Cambridge Ancient History.* Vol. 3. New York: Cambridge University Press, 1991. A comprehensive depiction of historical events relevant to the Phrygian kingdom from the eighth to the sixth centuries B.C.E.

De Vries, Keith. "Gordion and Phrygia in the Sixth Century B.C." *Source: Notes in the History of Art* 7, nos. 3/4 (Spring/Summer, 1988): 51-60. This special issue is dedicated to Phrygian art and archaeology.

Ramsay, William Mitchell. *The Cities and Bishoprics of Phrygia.* New York: Arno Press, 1975. A comprehensive history of Phrygia from the earliest times to the Turkish conquest.

Sams, Kenneth G. "The Early Phrygian Period at Gordion: Toward a Cultural Identity." *Source: Notes in the History of Art* 7, nos. 3/4 (Spring/Summer, 1988): 9-16. A brief analysis of Phrygian early pottery from Gordium.

Simpson, Elizabeth. "Celebrating Midas." *Archaeology* 54, no. 4 (July/August, 2001): 27-33. A report on the latest excavations at Gordium.

_______. "Phrygian Artistic Intellect." *Source: Notes in the History of Art* 7, nos. 3/4 (Spring/Summer, 1988): 24-43. An excellent analysis of artifacts from three early tumuli at Gordium.

See also: c. 7000-c. 4900 B.C.E., Çatalhüyük Flourishes as Center of Anatolian Culture; c. 1250 B.C.E., Fall of Troy Marks End of Trojan War; c. 1000-c. 690 B.C.E., Cimmerian Culture Rises in Russia; 8th century B.C.E., Scythians Drive the Cimmerians from Central Asia; 336 B.C.E., Alexander the Great Begins Expansion of Macedonia.

Related article in *Great Lives from History: The Ancient World*: Alexander the Great.

c. 800 B.C.E.
Phoenicians from Tyre Found Carthage

The emergence of Carthage shifted political and economic power from the Middle East to the Western Mediterranean.

Locale: Carthage (modern Tunisia)
Categories: Expansion and land acquisition; trade and commerce

Key Figure

Dido (mid-ninth century-late ninth or early eighth century B.C.E.), legendary queen who founded Carthage

Summary of Event

The founding of Carthage represented a major shift in economic and political power in the Mediterranean world. Carthage represented the first major center of Western influence outside the Middle East, the traditional cradle of political influence represented by the Sumerians, Egyptians, Assyrians, and Hittites. As such, Carthage embodied the future of Western civilization, foreshadowing the rise of the Greeks, Etruscans, and Romans. By locating in the western Mediterranean, Carthage retained the best elements of the traditional empires of the east, while enjoying new discoveries and assets present only in the location that Carthage enjoyed. As a result, Carthage quickly emerged as a new political force that first surpassed its originating culture, then dominated the western Mediterranean until the rise of the Roman Republic.

Like many ancient cities, Carthage had both mythological and empirical origins. According to Greek legend, the princess Dido founded the city as a haven after her brother, Pygmalion, murdered her husband and uncle Cicerbas. There she ruled as queen. Roman legend added to Carthage's legend by casting Dido as the scorned lover of Aeneas, as described in Vergil's *Aeneid* (29-19 B.C.E.; English translation, 1553). The Roman story provided a mythological explanation for the Punic Wars between Carthage (the descendants of Dido) and Rome (the descendants of Aeneas).

On a more practical level, Carthage emerged because of shifting power in the eastern Mediterranean. By the eighth century B.C.E., the decline of the Hittite Empire permitted the rise of the Phoenician culture, a cluster of city-states on the eastern shore of the Mediterranean in the region now occupied by Israel and Lebanon. A commercial culture, Phoenicia established a wide-ranging trade network that soon expanded to modern-day Greece, Cyprus, Sicily, and Spain. Around 814 B.C.E. (the traditional date of the founding of Carthage), traders from the Phoenician city of Tyre, seeking additional trading opportunities and raw materials, planted a trading colony on the African coast opposite Sicily in modern-day Tunisia. The city was named Kart Hadasht (new city), later Romanized into Carthage.

The tiny city survived because of mutually beneficial trade agreements arranged between the Phoenicians and the indigenous peoples, the Berbers (from the Greek work *barbaros* meaning strange or savage, from which derives the word "barbarian"). Surrounded by the more numerous Berbers, the Carthaginians embraced local food and culture while exchanging the goods of the eastern Mediterranean for local products, chiefly gold and tin. As a result, the Berbers became a key element of Carthage's success, comprising a large percentage of the city's population and military force.

Carthage remained a remote Phoenician trading post for two hundred years, until events transformed it into a major commercial center. Just as the decline of the Hittites permitted the emergence of the Phoenicians, the expansion of the Babylonian Empire destroyed Phoenician influence in the eastern Mediterranean, and Carthage's influence increased in proportion. At the same time, new economic powers changed the situation in the western Mediterranean. Greek trading colonies at Selinus and Syracuse challenged Carthaginian dominance in Sicily, forcing Carthage to fight a series of wars to halt Greek expansion. The wars between Greece and Carthage ended in 480 B.C.E. when the Greeks defeated a Carthaginian fleet at the Battle of Himera, temporarily giving the Greeks naval dominance in the western Mediterranean. The Greeks, however, faced a greater threat from the Persian Empire in the east and could not capitalize on their advantage.

Although Carthage could never consolidate its control over Sicily, it emerged from the Greek wars as an empire in its own right, with commercial contacts expanded to modern-day Sardinia, France, and even the west coast of Africa beyond the Strait of Gibraltar. Carthage jealously protected these commercial contacts, going so far as to mandate the execution of any foreign trader found in their ports, a practice that ensured the Carthaginians success and wealth. According to the Greek historian Strabo, Carthage boasted a population of 700,000 and controlled an empire of seven hundred cities. Carthage also benefited from trade contacts with the Romans, a new culture consolidating its power across the Mediterranean in modern-day Italy. Although Carthage would later fight a series of wars with the Romans, trade benefited both cultures, and the Romans signed treaties of peace and commerce with Carthage in 508 and 450 B.C.E.

The success of Carthage rested on its population, stability, location, and ingenuity. Because of its close cooperation with the local Berbers, Carthage possessed wider opportunities to expand its commercial interests than other rising cultures, who faced opposition from local cultures who did not welcome outside influence. This advantage was particularly useful to the Carthaginians after their defeat in Sicily led them to emphasize expansion on the African continent instead of into the eastern Mediterranean. Also unlike other cultures, Carthage enjoyed relative political stability over the course of its history. Although a popularly elected assembly existed to manage city affairs, it had little influence, and political power rested instead with the wealthy commercial families. These families controlled the politics of the empire through a small but powerful senate, overseen by two magistrates (*suffetes*) named by the senate in manner reminiscent of the later Roman Empire. Although hardly a democratic government, the Carthaginian senate did at least rule consistently, balancing political power between the two major political interests: one that comprised the external commercial business of the empire and the other made up of the internal agricultural interests. Families engaged in external commerce tended to dominate in the senate, although they had to address the demands of the internal agricultural faction, which included the large numbers of Berbers essential for Carthaginian economic success.

The next great advantage that led to Carthage's suc-

CARTHAGE, C. 800-146 B.C.E.

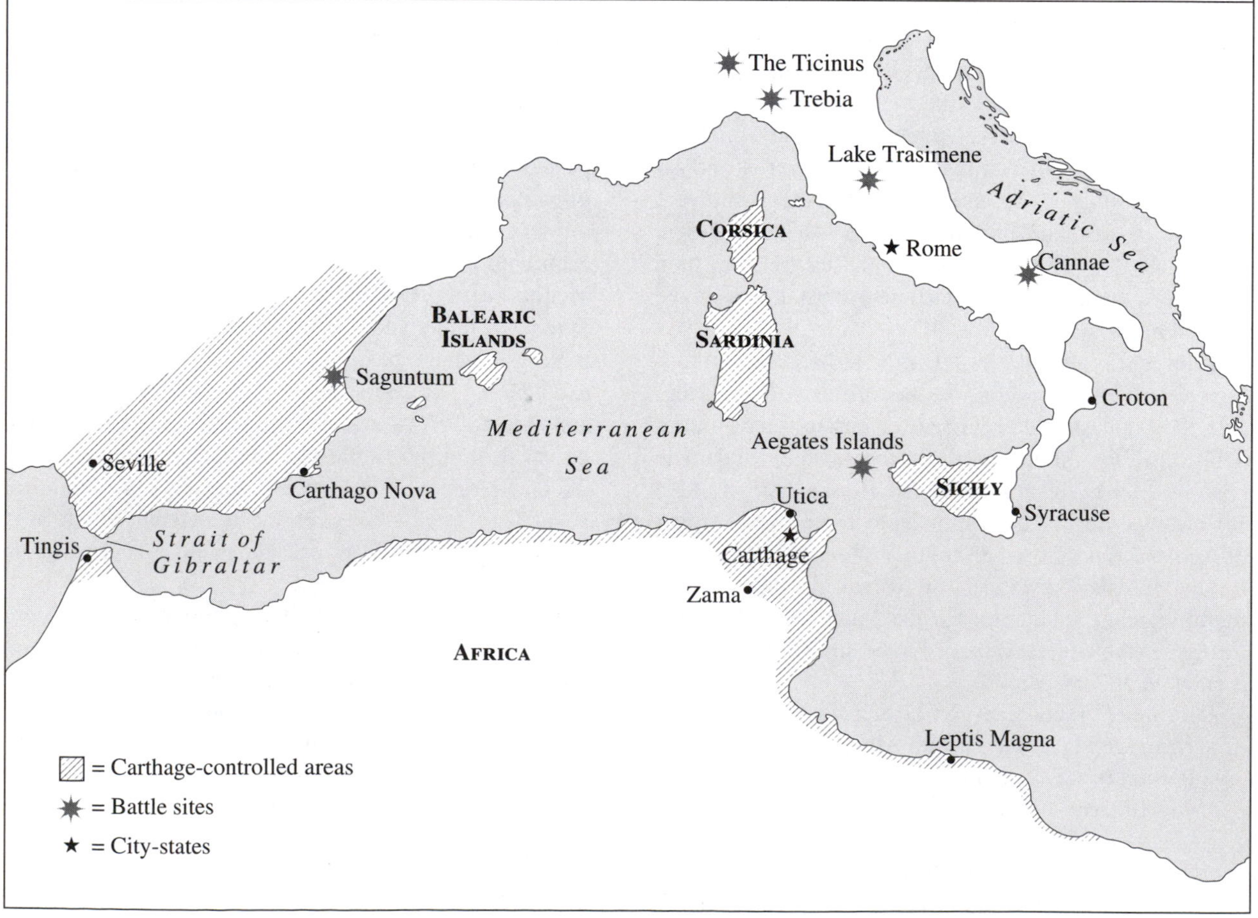

The city of Carthage, which, according to legend, was founded by Dido. (F. R. Niglutsch)

cess was a location well suited for both commercial expansion and long-term survival. From a commercial standpoint, Carthage is ideally located at the narrowest point of the Mediterranean Sea. Modern-day Tunisia is located at the northernmost point of Africa immediately opposite the point where Italy juts into the Mediterranean. In between, like a cork in a bottleneck, is Sicily. The only sea passage between Sicily and Italy is through the narrow and treacherous Straits of Messina, location of Scylla and Charybdis in Greek legend. The southern sea passage, much wider and less treacherous, passed right by Carthage, which was thus in a prime position to regulate not only the east-west sea traffic but also the north-south land traffic across the Mediterranean. This central location also meant that Carthaginian ships did not have to range the entire length of the Mediterranean, but instead sat in the middle.

From a military viewpoint, Carthage's location was equally advantageous. Carthage sat on a peninsula jutting out from the mainland that limited landward access from the west. To the east was the open Mediterranean. Flanking the city to north and south were two enclosed bodies of water, the southern Bay of Tunis and the northern Stagnum Marinum (dead ocean), the shallow, salty mouth of the Medjerda River. All of these geographical features made Carthage a daunting place to attack. An immense wall, 18 miles (29 kilometers) long, surrounded the city, with the thickest defenses—40 feet (12 meters) high and 30 feet (9 meters) thick—across the base of the peninsula, which was 3 miles (5 kilometers) long. This sealed off any landward attack from the west. The northern and southern bodies of water also aided Carthage's defense. With two access points to the sea, a sea-borne enemy had to possess a huge naval force to entirely blockade the Carthaginian navy or halt its sea trade. The Medjerda River was another factor that ensured Carthage's survival. It provided a secure source of fresh water, its fertile banks kept the city fed, and it served as a natural highway into the African interior and to Carthage's Berber allies.

Carthaginian ingenuity took these existing advantages and made them better. Chief among Carthage's innovations were two titanic manmade harbors, each with an entrance to the sea and internally connected by a canal. Located in the southeast corner of the city off the Bay of Tunis, the harbors consisted of a large rectangular commercial harbor and a round harbor with an island in the center for military vessels. Each harbor was manmade, with the commercial harbor requiring the excavation of approximately 157,000 cubic yards (120,000 cubic meters) of earth and the military harbor 150,000 cubic yards (115,000 cubic meters); the latter was capable of accommodating 220 warships.

Given these advantages, the long history of Carthage is no surprise. Utilizing the advantages of position, allies, and opportunities, Carthage soon emerged as a major Mediterranean power.

SIGNIFICANCE

The creation of Carthage began a major transition of cultural, military, political, and economic power in the ancient world. As the first great civilization beyond the traditional cradle of civilizations in the Middle East, Carthage laid the groundwork for the elements of culture that marked a separate Western civilization. Although created by an eastern culture, Carthage soon developed its own identity and independence. Carthage pioneered the sense of nationalism, the diversified economy of agriculture and commerce, the military balanced between land and sea power, and the urge to explore and expand that led to the success of other empires, notably Rome.

—Steven J. Ramold

FURTHER READING

Aubet, Maria E. *The Phoenicians and the West: Politics, Colonies, and Trade*. New York: Cambridge University Press, 1993. A study of Phoenician expansion into the Western Mediterranean.

Charles-Picard, Gilbert. *The Life and Death of Carthage*. London: Sidgwick, 1968. A very comprehensive history of Carthage.

Lancel, Serge. *Carthage: A History*. Translated by Antonia Nevill. New York: Blackwell, 1997. A good history of Carthage, incorporating up-to-date archaeological research.

Pisano, Giovanna. *Phoenicians and Carthaginians in the Western Mediterranean*. Rome: University of Rome, 1999. Emphasizes the Phoenician origins of Carthage and its connection to the Eastern Mediterranean.

SEE ALSO: c. 1200-c. 1000 B.C.E., Berbers Expand Across North Africa; 439 C.E., Vandals Seize Carthage.

RELATED ARTICLES in *Great Lives from History: The Ancient World*: Dido; Hamilcar Barca; Hannibal; Hanno.

c. 800-c. 600 B.C.E.
IRONWORKING SPREADS INTO SUB-SAHARAN AFRICA

Iron production gradually extended out of North Africa and into East and West Africa, eventually covering the entire continent by the first century C.E.

LOCALE: Africa

CATEGORIES: Science and technology; prehistory and ancient cultures

SUMMARY OF EVENT

Ironworking, a significant technological advancement in any society, slowly made its way into sub-Saharan Africa after 800 B.C.E. Scholars, however, do not know the exact routes of transmission. Most suggest that a slow diffusion occurred along one or more links from Meroë, Africa's first industrial city.

In Meroë, ironworking dates to 800-600 B.C.E. Artisans in Meroë benefited from ample supplies of coal, which was used to heat furnaces to more than 1,300 degrees Fahrenheit (700 degrees Celsius). They also had rich deposits of iron ore. Because of their special skills in iron smelting, craftspeople in Meroë most likely occupied a higher rung in society. Thus, iron production was perfected by smiths in Meroë in the first millennia B.C.E.

How Meroë acquired the iron-smelting process has engendered some debate. Some scholars suggest that the Phoenicians brought the technology to North Africa. They claim that the trans-Saharan trade probably carried the process across the desert and eventually into West Africa. Other historians believe that the Assyrians, with their iron weapons, introduced iron smelting to North Africa when they attacked the Egyptians. Evidence supports both groups of scholars.

Remnants of iron production have been discovered along the Jos Plateau in Nigeria, at an elevation of more than 1,000 feet (300 meters). Fragments of iron and furnaces have been recovered throughout Africa in sites from Egypt to Tutankhamen's tomb and in West Africa as well as in the Horn of Africa. Iron recovered from the tomb of Tutankhamen indicates that it was present there around 1340 B.C.E. and perhaps even earlier. Iron daggers and blades were used in Egypt during the same time period, pointing to an earlier introduction. From Egypt, the technology spread out along the Nile River and reached the kingdom of Kush sometime around 500 B.C.E., perhaps even a century before.

The diffusion of iron-smelting technology presents another problem to scholars, who do not agree on one single route of transmission. One possible path took the technology out of Meroë and into Rwanda-Uganda and even into northwestern Tanzania. It may have reached West Africa across the western portion of the Sahara Desert, carried by trans-Saharan traders. Still another avenue could have taken the process to the Mediterranean coast from the central Sahara Desert, from Meroë to Morocco.

By the first century C.E., iron smelting in Africa had progressed to cover most of the continent, from north to south. Trade probably facilitated its spread, and the cutting of trees to support hot fires in various types of furnaces most likely contributed to some deforestation.

The significance of iron production and its diffusion is that the African continent skipped over a lengthy period of bronze and copper production and went directly into iron smelting. Although it is possible that copper was also worked during this period, most of Africa advanced as a result of an Iron Age that occurred well before the technology of ironworking was commonly used in many other areas of the world.

Significance

Iron smelting in sub-Saharan Africa represents a major step forward in human history. Rather than going through the bronze and copper stages, Africa for the most part leaped into an Iron Age. With Meroë as a center for industrial Africa, the process of smelting spread throughout sub-Saharan Africa between 800 and 600 B.C.E., finally covering the entire continent by the first century C.E.

—*Jackie R. Booker*

Further Reading

July, Robert W. *A History of the African People*. Prospect Heights, Ill: Waveland, 1998. This book provides important background to iron technology in Africa. Maps, bibliography, and index.

Miller, Duncan E., and Nikolaas J. Van Der Merwe. "Early Metal Working in Sub-Sahara Africa: A Review of Recent Research." *Journal of African History* 35 (1994): 1-36. Provides good background to the scholarly argument concerning the spread of iron smelting in Africa. Maps and dictionary of key terms.

Munson, Patrick J. "Africa's Prehistoric Past." In *Africa*, edited by Phyllis M. Martin and Patrick O. O'Meara. Bloomington: Indiana University Press, 1977. Gives background on iron smelting. Maps.

Oliver, Roland, and Brian M. Fagan. *Africa in the Iron Age*. New York: Cambridge University Press, 1975. This book furnishes background on iron smelting and technology in Africa to 500 C.E. Maps, bibliography, and index.

See also: c. 1000 B.C.E., Sub-Saharan Ironworking Begins; c. 1000-c. 700 B.C.E., Mashariki Bantu Establish Chifumbaze Ironworking Culture; c. 1000 B.C.E.-c. 300 C.E., Urban Commerce Develops in the Sudan Belt; c. 783-c. 591 B.C.E., Napata Kingdom Flourishes in Kush.

c. 783-c. 591 B.C.E.
NAPATA KINGDOM FLOURISHES IN KUSH

The Kushites, centered in Napata, gained power over much of Egypt and created a great civilization that produced many monuments and temples before losing Egypt to the Assyrians.

LOCALE: Kush (present-day northern Sudan) and Egypt

CATEGORIES: Government and politics; expansion and land acquisition

KEY FIGURES

Piye (Piankhi; c. 769-716 B.C.E.), Kushite conqueror of Egypt and founder of the Twenty-fifth Dynasty, r. 742-716 B.C.E.

Taharqa (fl. seventh century-656 B.C.E.), last Kushite ruler of Egypt, r. 690-664 B.C.E.

SUMMARY OF EVENT

Dominating the Nile's cataracts south of Egypt, Kush was one of Africa's great civilizations. Much modern scholarship suggests that the ancient northern Sudan, later known as Nubia, contributed greatly to the Nile's cradle of civilization. However, Kushite political, religious, and cultural contributions were overshadowed by Egypt's hegemony, and archaeological finds in the region have often been attributed to Egypt.

Immediately south of Upper Egypt lay Wawat, known later as Egyptian Nubia. The limited agricultural potential of the Nile's stony, high banks in this region separated the rich lands of Egypt from the Dongola Reach, Kush's fertile heartland between the Third and Fourth Cataracts. Egypt's New Kingdom pharaohs enviously cast their eyes south of Wawat. Thutmose III (r. c. 1504-1450 B.C.E.) penetrated south of the Third Cataract, conquered Kerma, and established forts at Sai and Tombos. Later Thutmose III conquered the Dongola Reach. By 1400 B.C.E., the pharaohs' empire reached from the Fourth Cataract in Kush to Syria in the north. After several unsuccessful rebellions, the Kushites acquiesced to Egyptian occupation. Forts dotted the region. Egyptian-influenced script, iconography, and religion followed. Amenhotep III erected a temple at Soleb. Farther south at Sesibi, others were built by Akhenaton (Amenhotep IV). Major settlements south of the Third Cataract included Kerma, Kawa, and Tabu on Argo Island.

By the time of the Nineteenth Dynasty (1295-1186 B.C.E.), Kush was an integral part of the Egyptian empire, ruled by a viceroy who collected tribute and delivered it to the pharaoh personally. This viceroy's titles included King's Son in Kush and Overseer of the Gold Lands of the Lord of the Two Lands. Renowned as skilled horsemen, the thoroughly Egyptianized Kushites exported gold, ebony, gum, ivory, ostrich feathers and eggs, perfumes, cattle, and exotic animals to their powerful northern neighbors. Often keeping Egyptian traditions more faithfully than the Egyptians themselves, they worshiped the same gods, particularly the sun god Amen-Ra (Re, or Amen). Kush's rapid adoption of Egyptian culture is unique in ancient times and suggests that much that underlay Egyptian civilization must have been already present in Kush.

Kush slipped out of Egyptian control in 1087 B.C.E., when Viceroy Panehsy rebelled and marched on Thebes. This incident effectively marked the end of the zenith of Egypt's power. Around 1080, Theban high priest Herihor led a coup that defeated the Kushites, who created an independent kingdom in the south. Upper Egypt was a theocracy ruled by the priests of Amen-Ra, and the kings of the Twenty-first Dynasty (1069-945) ruled the Nile Delta from Tanis. Meanwhile, the Kushite capital, Napata, became a center of power.

Situated west of the modern Sudanese town of Karima on the Nile's right bank, about 25 miles (40 kilometers) downstream from the Fourth Cataract, Napata was a major river crossing for overland routes linking the Sixth Cataract with the Third. However, its strategic value was overshadowed by its religious importance, which derived from Gebel Barkal, the later Arabic name of a nearby sandstone butte. Although at least one military outpost lay farther up the Nile, near the Fifth Cataract, this isolated mountain marked the southern limit of Egypt's New Kingdom and was the pharaoh's most remote religious sanctuary.

The Kushites and later the Egyptians attached sacred significance to Gebel Barkal, possibly because of its odd flat shape. Calling the mountain Dju-wa'ab (pure mountain), the Egyptians believed it was the original home of their state god Amen-Ra, who dwelt behind the mountain's sheer southern cliff, hidden from mortal view. Two great temples were built there, dedicated to Amen's northern and southern aspects, a situation similar to Thebes, some 715 miles (1,150 kilometers) downstream, where the Luxor temple is dedicated to Amen's southern aspect and Karnak to his northern. The Karnak and Napata temples were both called Ipet-sut (sanctuary of the thrones). Known as the Thrones of the Two Lands, the mountain was possibly the source of Karnak's name. Gebel Barkal was the primary center of Kushite royal coronations and religious ritual. Early Kushite monarchs were buried at el-Kurru, 10 miles (16 kilometers) downstream from Napata, and at Nuri, upstream on the opposite bank from the capital, a pyramid field marks the tombs of later rulers.

By the eighth century B.C.E., Egypt's glorious achievements had become distant memories. Embroiled in frequent strife, the land of the pharaohs was divided into competing states. By 945, Lower Egypt was overwhelmed by the gradual encroachment of Libyans, many of whom had been mercenaries for the pharaohs. Three millennia of foreign occupation followed, and no Egyptian would rule all of Egypt again until Gamal Abdel Nasser's rise in 1952 C.E. The Twenty-second, or Libyan, Dynasty (945-715 B.C.E.) maintained order for about a century, when two chaotic dynasties ensued.

In the south, Kushite ruler Kashta (r. c. 783-747 B.C.E.), invaded Upper Egypt, captured Aswān, and took control of the gold fields. His son Piye completed his father's conquest of Upper Egypt and annexed Lower Egypt to a vast empire stretching from the Mediterranean to the Fifth Cataract. Piye sought to restore Egypt to its past splendor. He was succeeded by his brother, Shabaka (r. 716-c. 702/698 B.C.E.), who moved the capital from Napata to Thebes. Shabaka was succeeded by Shebitku (Shabataka; r. 698-690 B.C.E.), who encouraged the Hebrew king Hezekiah of Judah to resist the rising Assyrian Empire.

Following Shebitku's death, his nephew Taharqa became pharaoh. A prolific builder and capable administrator, he ruled for twenty-six years, the first sixteen of which were filled with great achievements at a time when heavy Nile floods brought record harvests. Taharqa built Kawa's gilded sandstone temple and a huge colonnade at the temple at Karnak. He restored the columns of Gebel Barkal's temples. His pyramid in the royal field at Nuri was the largest of his dynasty. The greatest of the Twenty-fifth Dynasty pharaohs, he is the only Kushite ruler mentioned by name (Tirhakah) in the Bible.

Around 674 B.C.E., Taharqa unwisely provoked war with Assyrian ruler Esarhaddon (r. 680-669 B.C.E.) and faced a series of invasions by the Assyrians, who had already swept through western Asia. Armed with superior iron weapons, the all-conquering Assyrians under Esarhaddon captured, lost, and recaptured Lower Egypt. Taharqa fled to Napata, after Esarhaddon's successor Ashurbanipal (r. 669-627 B.C.E.) took Upper Egypt in 669. However, Ashurbanipal's hand-picked vassal Psamtik I was not recognized in Upper Egypt, which remained loyal to Kush. Priests continued to record events as if Taharqa's rule continued, and in Taharqa's name, Prince Mentuemhat of Thebes restored temples damaged by the Assyrians. However, Taharqa's successor, Tanutamuni, failed to recapture Egypt, and his death in 656 B.C.E. marked the end of the Twenty-fifth Dynasty.

In 591 B.C.E., Psamtik II sent a punitive expedition south. Following their king Aspelta, the Kushites withdrew to Meroë, a city between the Fifth and Sixth Cataracts, beyond the reach of invaders. The seat of a branch of the Kushite royal family, Meroë became the new capital. Adopting the technologies of the Assyrian invaders, it became a major ironworking center and transmitted knowledge of ironworking throughout Africa. Furnaces and slag heaps stood beside Egyptian-style palaces and temples. Although a huge temple, known as the Table of the Sun, was dedicated to Amen-Ra, the most important Meroitic deity was the lion-headed Apedemak. Eventually, a distinct Meroitic civilization arose with its own still undeciphered script.

In 24 B.C.E., Napata was destroyed in a Roman raid. The Meroitic royal couple Natakamani and Amanitare oversaw the last major restoration of its temples in the first century C.E. After the establishment of the Christian kingdom of Makouria, Napata faded from history. Western travelers first saw Gebel Barkal in 1820, and Piye's famous victory stela was found in 1862. Much of Napata was excavated by archaeologists in the twentieth century.

SIGNIFICANCE

Enriching each other throughout ancient times, Kush and Egypt were intertwined, sometimes in conflict, but usually in peace. As Egypt spiraled into its slow decline, Napata's rulers rose to give the empire on the Nile one last era of glory. Although Kush's successors, the ironworking Meroitic civilization and medieval Christian Nubia, would rise as flourishing cultures, northern Sudan would never again be the focus of power it was during the Twenty-fifth Dynasty.

—*Randall Fegley*

FURTHER READING

Adams, William Y. *Nubia: Corridor to Africa*. Princeton, N.J.: Princeton University Press, 1977. Despite many later findings, this work remains the most thorough reference on the archaeology and history of Kush/Nubia.

Kendall, Timothy. *Kerma and the Kingdom of Kush, 2500-1500 B.C.: The Archaeological Discovery of an*

Ancient Nubian Empire. Washington, D.C.: National Museum of African Art, Smithsonian Institution, 1997. Kendall surveys the archaeological work conducted on the earliest periods of Kushite history.

Morkot, Robert G. *The Black Pharaohs: Egypt's Nubian Rulers*. London: The Rubicon Press, 2000. Focuses on the roles of the Kushites (Nubians) during Egypt's conflicts with Libya and Assyria.

Török, L. *The Kingdom of Kush: Handbook of the Napatan-Meroitic Civilization*. Leiden: E. J. Brill, 1997. Török provides a good reference on ancient Kush, from its emergence to the Meroitic period. Contains a genealogy of the kings of Kush.

Wildung, Dietrich. *Sudan: Ancient Kingdoms of the Nile*. New York: Flammarion, 1997. This large, illustrated work concentrates on artifacts from ancient Sudan but also provides a good chronological survey.

SEE ALSO: c. 1900-1527? B.C.E., Kerma Kingdom Rules Nubia; c. 1570 B.C.E., New Kingdom Period Begins in Egypt; c. 1450 B.C.E., International Age of Major Kingdoms Begins in the Near East; 1069 B.C.E., Third Intermediate Period Begins in Egypt; 8th century B.C.E., Kushite King Piye Conquers Upper Egypt; c. 712-698 B.C.E., Shabaka Reunites the Nile Valley; c. 6th century B.C.E.-c. 350 C.E., Meroitic Empire Rules from Southern Egypt to the Blue Nile.

RELATED ARTICLES in *Great Lives from History: The Ancient World*: Akhenaton; Ashurbanipal; Piye; Psamtik I; Thutmose III.

776 B.C.E.
OLYMPIC GAMES ARE FIRST RECORDED

The Olympic Games were established as one of four Panhellenic (all-Greek) games and helped provide unity in a region otherwise isolated into competing city-states.

LOCALE: Olympia, Greece
CATEGORIES: Cultural and intellectual history; government and politics

KEY FIGURES

Pindar (c. 518-c. 438 B.C.E.), lyric poet whose works celebrated the perfection of the human body and the mythical importance of the Games

Phidias (c. 490-c. 430 B.C.E.), sculptor who created a massive statue of Zeus at Olympia

Theodosius the Great (346/347-395 C.E.), Eastern Roman emperor, r. 379-395 C.E.

Theodosius II (401-450 C.E.), Eastern Roman emperor, r. 408-450 C.E., and grandson of Theodosius the Great

SUMMARY OF EVENT

It is unknown whether the date 776 C.E. represents the first Olympic Games or the first *recorded* celebration of the Olympic Festival. If the former, the Olympic Games arose at the end of the Greek Dark Ages, a period of roughly four hundred years extending from the fall of Mycenae (c. 1100 B.C.E.) until the dawn of the Archaic period. If the latter is true, however, the year 776 C.E. represents the point when writing returned to the Greek mainland, allowing people to begin preserving records of a celebration that began centuries earlier. Whichever of these is true (and evidence seems to support the second alternative), winners of each Olympic Festival were recorded from 776 B.C.E. until 217 C.E. in a list appearing in the writings of the chronographer Eusebius of Caesarea (c. 260-339 C.E.). Winners of the earliest recorded events were thus roughly contemporary with the founding of Rome (April 21, 753 B.C.E.) and the earliest settlements on the Palatine Hill (c. 750 B.C.E.).

Olympia is located in the region of Elis, roughly 10 miles (16 kilometers) inland from the Ionian Sea in the west-central Peloponnese. The festival celebrated there was, along with a common language and shared religion, one of the few aspects of Greek life promoting unity among the highly disparate city-states. Divided by local traditions, variant dialects, and diverse forms of government, the Greek poleis (singular: polis), or city-states, were often rivals. At the Olympic Games, however, a truce was declared for the duration of the festival, and political disputes were not allowed to interfere with the celebration. The Greeks believed, probably without foundation, that the Olympic Festival had been proposed by the Delphic Oracle as a means of promoting peace.

The Olympic Games were one of four Panhellenic Festivals or all-Greek athletic competitions held periodically in Greece. At the Pythian Games honoring Apollo at Delphi, the prize awarded to victors was a wreath of bay leaves gathered in the Vale of Tempe. The Nemean

Men participate in a foot race at the Olympic Games. (F. R. Niglutsch)

Games were held in honor of Zeus at Nemea, with winners receiving a wreath of wild parsley. At the Isthmian Games dedicated to Poseidon at Corinth, victors received a wreath of wild celery. Of these four festivals, the Olympic Games were by far the most prestigious, held once every four years in honor of Zeus at Olympia. The prize awarded to victors was a wreath made of wild olive leaves. The four-year period between Olympic Festivals was known as an Olympiad and could be used as a means of calculating dates. The games began at Olympia at the first full moon after the summer solstice.

Like the other Panhellenic festivals, the Olympic Games had a religious as well as an athletic and political importance. The perfection of the human body was seen as an act of worship by which human beings tried to imitate the perfection of the eternal gods. In the odes of the Greek poet Pindar, this physical achievement is often placed in a religious or mythological context. To aristocrats such as Pindar, the competition and the prize that the victor received were important not because they were useful but because they were useless. Time spent in activities having no practical utility must be the result of sheer love of the activity itself, not the pursuit of material gain. Honors and prizes conferred on the victors by their native cities were, however, usually so large that they became rich for the rest of their lives.

Certain restrictions applied to those who were eligible for competition. Free men (and, after 632 B.C.E., boys) whose native language was Greek were allowed to participate in the Games. Those whose native language was not Greek were permitted to watch the Games but could not compete in them. (In the Roman period, this restriction was waived for the Romans.) Slaves and all women, except for the local priestess of Demeter, were forbidden from entering the sacred area while the Games were in progress. Those violating this prohibition were hurled to their deaths from the Typaeon Rock.

The stadium that was built for the Olympic Festival was the earliest ever built by the Greeks, and it influenced the design of all that succeeded it. In Greece, a stadium was always used for footraces; it was never used, like Roman circuses, as an arena for chariot races. (A longer track, called a hippodrome, was built for horse racing.) The term "stadium" is derived from the Greek word *stade* or *stadion*, a unit of measurement corresponding to 600 Greek feet, each foot measuring slightly more than 13 inches (33 centimeters). A *stade* was thus 606.75 English feet (198 meters) in length. This became a standard unit of measurement in Greek racetracks of all periods. Because of the fierce independence of Greek city-states, however, some regional differences did occur.

The earliest events at Olympia appear to have been footraces, wrestling, and throwing events. As early as the seventh century B.C.E., races for chariots and individual horses occurred. In races, it was always the owner of the horse, not its rider, who was awarded the victory. From 472 B.C.E. onward, events at the Olympic Games were expanded to include horse races, the discus throw, the javelin throw, boxing, the pentathlon (jumping, wrestling, the javelin, the discus, and running), and the *pancration* (a type of no-holds-barred wrestling). Contestants in the Games had to be in training for a minimum of ten months before their competition. For the last thirty days before the festival, athletes trained in a special gymnasium at Olympia itself, where they ran and threw the javelin or discus. This final month of training was supervised by the Hellenodicae, a board of ten men who also served as referees during the Games themselves.

As an important religious center, Olympia was also the location of the ancient world's most famous statue of Zeus, considered one of the Seven Wonders of the Ancient World. The statue was a 40-foot-high (12-meter-high) representation of the god in gold and ivory by the artist Phidias that stood within the Temple of Zeus. Though about the same size as Phidias's statue of Athena in the Athenian Parthenon, this statue of Zeus was said to seem taller because it was a seated statue. The geographer Strabo (64/63 B.C.E.-after 23 C.E.) noted that if Zeus had risen from his chair, he would easily have lifted off the roof from the temple. The rhetorician Quintilian claimed that this statue "could be said to have added something to traditional religion." The Roman statesman Cicero noted that the statue was not based on any living model but rather on an idealized view of beauty, somewhat like that to which the athletes themselves aspired. Zeus was depicted as a bearded man, crowned with an olive wreath, and holding a life-size Winged Victory in his right hand.

SIGNIFICANCE

In 393 C.E., the Roman emperor Theodosius the Great, a Christian, ended all pagan athletic games in Greece. In 426, his successor Theodosius II ordered the destruction of the temples at Olympia. Then, in 1880-1881, the starting blocks and lines used for footraces in the ancient stadium were rediscovered. The modern Olympic Games began in the spring of 1896, largely through the efforts of the French educator Baron Pierre de Coubertin. In 1924, the Winter Olympics were added to this existing competition (now often called the Summer Olympics). For seventy years, both festivals were held in the same year. Beginning in 1994, however, winter and summer festivals began to alternate in even-numbered years. Like the ancient Olympic Festival, the modern Games are viewed as a means of promoting peace among peoples of different cultures.

—*Jeffrey L. Buller*

FURTHER READING

Golden, Mark. *Sport and Society in Ancient Greece*. New York: Cambridge University Press, 1998. Golden examines the social aspects of the Olympic Games in ancient Greece. Bibliography and index.

Ross, Stewart. *The Original Olympics*. Lincolnwood, Ill.: P. Bedrick Books, 1999. Covers the history of the Games as well as the traditions and athletic events themselves. Bibliography and index.

Sinn, Ulrich. *Olympia: Cult, Sport, and Ancient Festival*. Princeton, N.J.: Markus Wiener, 2000. A study of the Olympic Games in ancient Greece and the associated archaeological discoveries.

Swaddling, Judith. *The Ancient Olympic Games*. 2d ed. Austin: University of Texas Press, 1999. A general discussion of the ancient Games, with illustrations and maps. Bibliography and index.

Woff, Richard. *The Ancient Greek Olympics*. New York: Oxford University Press, 1999. A scholarly treatment of the traditions, history, and events of the ancient Olympic Games. Bibliography and index.

SEE ALSO: 775 B.C.E., Delphic Oracle Provides Guidance for City-States; c. 438 B.C.E., Greek Lyric Poet Pindar Dies; 380-392 C.E., Theodosius's Edicts Promote Christian Orthodoxy.

RELATED ARTICLES in *Great Lives from History: The Ancient World*: Erātosthenes of Cyrene; Pausanius the Traveler; Phidias; Pindar; Theodosius the Great.

775 B.C.E.
DELPHIC ORACLE PROVIDES GUIDANCE FOR CITY-STATES

The Oracle at Delphi provided a common meeting ground for early Greek city-states and a religious ratification for individual cities' decisions.

LOCALE: Central Greece
CATEGORIES: Government and politics; religion

KEY FIGURE

Phemonoe (fl. eighth century B.C.E.), traditional first priestess of Apollo's temple at Delphi, daughter of Apollo

SUMMARY OF EVENT

The ancient Greek cities, as they entered recorded history about 800 B.C.E., were disunited. Except for temporary, often strained alliances against foreign enemies, they developed no common political institutions. They were permanently in competition with one another and often at war. Decisions had to be made, mostly about internal matters, but also about war, colonization, and occasional joint enterprises. These decisions were fundamentally matters of individual sovereignty. Yet there was enough sense of being Hellenes—Greeks—to permit the Oracle of Apollo at Delphi to emerge as somewhat of a common center. To understand this development, it is necessary to glance at prior religious and political arrangements.

From roughly 2000 until 1250 B.C.E., the brilliant, powerful "palace societies" of Crete and Mycenae dominated the area. The political-administrative form of these societies appears to have been bureaucratic aristocracy. Palace societies were originally worshipers of the Great (Earth) Goddess, but with increasing male military influence, Poseidon, the earth-shaking lord of the sea, and then Zeus, the weather/sky god, emerged as major deities.

The period from 1200 through 800 C.E. is termed the Greek Dark Age. The rich archaeological and even documentary evidence of a half millennium earlier does not exist. From what is known, Dark Age Greece was rudimentary and disorganized. The classical philosopher Aristotle (384-322 B.C.E.), in his *Politica* (335-323 B.C.E.; *Politics*, 1598), held that the early Greeks lived "scattered about." Each clan was a little kingdom, ruled absolutely by an elder male who was father, master, and king. Aristotle may be overstating the extent of patriarchy, which he sees as analogous to Zeus's ascendancy as father and king of the Olympian gods. It was, however, precisely during this period that Zeus became dominant. His cult was established at Olympia in the early tenth century B.C.E.

Zeus was a deity appropriate to a period dominated by small-scale, quasi-feudal monarchy. Slowly, however, and no doubt in part because of the relative order provided by authoritarian patriarchy-monarchy, the small Greek communities began to recover and grow. The classical Greek form of political organization, the polis, or city-state, emerged. These early political communities were not yet the powerful, populous, often democratic cities of several centuries later, but neither were they scattered rural citadels of warrior chieftains. They represented the partial reemergence in Greece of civilized urban life, and as such required a revised religious orientation.

The god most related to this development was Apollo. The terms "Apollo" and "Apollonian" convey an image of beauty and harmony. Apollo is *the* god of Greek classicism, especially as Phoibos Apollo, the Radiant Apollo. He is the god of healing, purification, and music. Yet the Greeks could never forget the connotations of his name. With his characteristic bow and arrow, Apollo the "far-darter" seemed to be "The Destroyer." Even the adjective *phoibos* was frighteningly close to the noun *phobos*, "fear" or "terror."

This moral ambiguity is present in the tales of Apollo's arrival at Delphi. Apollo was the son of Zeus, begotten on the nymph Leto. Enraged, Zeus's sister-wife Hera sent the dragon-serpent Python to pursue Leto. Apollo was born on the Aegean island of Delos, met Python on Mount Parnassus and wounded him, and pursued Python to Delphi, where he killed him. Thus Apollo was established at Delphi.

At issue in the establishment is the question of precedence. Scholars debate whether the cult of Apollo took over an earlier oracle of the Earth goddess Ge, or Gaia. Complicating things is the question of whether Ge, Gaia, and Hera are all later personifications of the original Great (Earth) Goddess. Mythic traditions, combined with some archaeological and linguistic evidence, tend to affirm both prior occupation and theological identity. The moral implication is that both Zeus and Apollo acted unjustly and that redress was required. Zeus appears to have suffered only through the growing influence of Apollo's cult. Yet Apollo is purified (on Crete, the Great Goddess's center); he shares the shrine with the Pythia, his priestess and Oracle; and he further honors the memory of the slain Python with the Pythian Games, begun in 586 B.C.E.

There seems, then, to be an inner logic to the concomitant emergence of the Oracle of Apollo at Delphi and the polis. Apollo is the new, young god. He represents a fresh beginning, a break with the obvious patriarchal order but also with the dimly remembered maternal religion lying behind it. Nevertheless, there is an evident compromise and implicit alliance of son and mother against father. Apollo is the personification of beauty and harmony but with an undercurrent of violence and injustice in his nature.

Given these characteristics, Apollo is the appropriate god for the classical Greek cities. They too represent a new principle, that of politics. Politics is the free intercourse of equal citizens, who conduct their affairs by speaking. Its authority stems not from the ancestral but from individual, often youthful excellence. Politics is also a spirited, often violent, sometimes terrible competition. It is a kind of order deeply in need of a neutral ground, and of moderation.

The Delphic Oracle issues a decree. (F. R. Niglutsch)

Delphi provided that ground and attempted to provide the moderation. Supposedly carved over the entrance of one of the several successive temples of Apollo were the sayings "Nothing in Excess" and "Know Thyself." These famous pieces of advice capture much of the permanent spirit of the Oracle—a spirit communicated to cities and individuals with decreasing effectiveness as time passed. Yet they are not themselves utterances of Apollo's Pythian priestess, Phemonoe. To imagine the priestess "prophesying," that is, foretelling the future or uttering pithy, cryptic sayings, is to misunderstand, according to modern scholarship, normal Delphic procedure. (In this sense, Phemonoe, "prophetic mind," seems misnamed.) The Oracle functioned approximately as a divine court of appeals. The "judges" were Apollo and, behind Apollo, at the omphalos stone marking the navel of the world, Earth herself.

Representatives of cities or, less frequently, private individuals initiated an inquiry. They did not, however, do so at their own convenience. The Pythia gave responses nine times each year, on the seventh of each nonwinter month. She did so seated on a tripod in the innermost sanctuary of Apollo's temple. There is scholarly agreement that the most usual form of the response was "yes" or "no" to a policy question previously deliberated by a city and, moreover, that the reply was almost always to affirm the policy. This simple, nearly automatic sort of "oracle" renders irrelevant the interesting question of the Pythia's state of mind when pronouncing. The traditional view, that she spoke under the influence of vapors emitted from a chasm in the earth, has been discarded. Those who admit as genuine some of the longer, more substantive responses reported speculate that the Pythia inhaled narcotic fumes or induced self-hypnosis.

Given that the Oracle's usual response was an affirmation of policy proposals, it is understandable that Delphi's greatest influence occurred in the first few centuries of its existence. The characteristic early political problems were the devising of law codes and the establishment of colonies. These proposals were both relatively easy to affirm and conducive to good reputation because they provided both internal stability and widening Greek influence. The most famous examples of legislation, Lycurgus's at Sparta and Solon's at Athens, were noted for their balance and moderation, and closely associated with Delphi.

SIGNIFICANCE

Delphi's broad political program appears to have been twofold—acquiescence in particular polis decisions while encouraging development of moderate institutions. This program implicitly acknowledged Delphi's own limitations. At best, it might provide an opportunity for policy reconsideration in a setting suggestive of both a common Greekness and a superhuman perspective. Delphic moderation tended toward passivity, and was successful insofar as its member cities tended in the same direction. Early, most did; later, some, especially Athens, did not, and Delphi declined accordingly.

—*John F. Wilson*

FURTHER READING

Burkert, Walter. *Greek Religion*. Translated by John Raffan. Cambridge, Mass.: Harvard University Press, 1985. Widely recognized as the standard source, this book includes clear and balanced accounts of the Minoan-Mycenaean Great Goddess, sanctuaries and oracles, and Apollo.

Clay, Jenny Strauss. *The Politics of Olympus: Form and Meaning in the Major Homeric Hymns*. Princeton, N.J.: Princeton University Press, 1989. This interesting work emphasizes the gender aspects of divine politics, including the Gaia-Python-Apollo relationship.

Dempsey, Reverend T. *The Delphic Oracle: Its Early History Influence and Fall*. New York: Benjamin Blom, 1972. Superseded in scholarly terms, this short book is a useful, widely available introduction to the subject.

Fontenrose, Joseph. *The Delphic Oracle: Its Responses and Operations*. Berkeley: University of California Press, 1978. An important scholarly effort, this work consists largely of an exhaustive, sometimes controversial evaluation of the historicity of the oracle's responses.

Morgan, Catherine. *Athletics and Oracles: The Transformation of Olympia and Delphi in the Eighth Century B.C.* New York: Cambridge University Press, 1990. This work effectively links the rise of the Delphic Oracle to early Greek city-state development.

Parke, H. W., and D. E. W. Wormell. *The History*. Vol. 1 in *The Delphic Oracle*. Oxford: Basil Blackwell, 1956. The classic source, this well-balanced account takes a middle position on the historicity of responses.

SEE ALSO: 8th-6th centuries B.C.E., Phrygian Kingdom Rises; c. 736-716 B.C.E., Spartan Conquest of Messenia; c. 734-c. 580 B.C.E., Greeks Colonize the Mediterranean and Black Sea Regions; c. 640 B.C.E., Greek City-States Use Coins as Means of Exchange; Before 600 B.C.E., Celebration of the Eleusinian Mysteries; c. 594-580 B.C.E., Legislation of Solon.

RELATED ARTICLE in *Great Lives from History: The Ancient World*: Solon.

770 B.C.E.
EASTERN ZHOU DYNASTY BEGINS IN CHINA

During the Eastern Zhou Dynasty, the Chinese experienced political division but witnessed economic growth, political and social innovation, and major intellectual achievements.

LOCALE: Luoyi, Eastern Zhou (near present-day Luoyang, Henan Province, China) and the surrounding area

CATEGORIES: Government and politics; cultural and intellectual history

KEY FIGURES

Pingwang (P'ingwang; fl. c. eighth century B.C.E.), first king of the Eastern Zhou, r. c. 770-720 B.C.E.

Qin Xiaogong (Ch'in Hsiaokung; fl. fourth century B.C.E.), ruler of Qin, r. c. 361-338 B.C.E.

Shang Yang (d. c. 337 B.C.E.), chief minister under Qin Xiaogong

Confucius (551-479 B.C.E.), founder of Confucianism

Mencius (c. 372-c. 289 B.C.E.), disciple of Confucius

Xunzi (Hsün-tzu; c. 307-c. 235 B.C.E.), disciple of Confucius

SUMMARY OF EVENT

The Eastern Zhou Dynasty (Chou; 770-256 B.C.E.) began in 770 B.C.E., after the rebels and northern barbarians drove the royal family of the Western Zhou out of the capital, Haojing (west of Changan County, near present Xian, Shaanxi Province), and killed King You (Yu), the last king of the Western Zhou. Pingwang, King You's son, was forced east to the secondary capital at Luoyi

MAJOR KINGS OF THE EASTERN ZHOU DYNASTY, 770-256 B.C.E.

Ruler	*Reign*
Pingwang	c. 770-720
Huanwang	c. 719-696
Zhuangwang	696-681
Xiwang	681-676
Huiwang	676-651
Xiangwang	651-618
Qingwang	618-612
Kuangwang	612-606
Dingwang	606-585
Jianwang	585-571
Lingwang	571-544
Jingwang	544-520
Daowang	520
Jingwang	519-475
Yuanwang	475-468
Zhen Dingwang	468-441
Aiwang (co-rulers)	441
Siwang	441
Kaowang	440-425
Wei Liewang	425-401
Anwang	401-375
Liewang	375-368
Xianwang	368-320
Shen Jingwang	320-314
Nanwang	314-256

Note: Wang means "king."

(near present Louyang, Henan Province) and became the first king of the Eastern Zhou, which covered the area from the Wei Valley to Shangdong, and from southern Manchuria to the middle and lower Changjiang (Yangtze) Valley.

During the Western Zhou Dynasty, the royal house was sufficiently powerful to control its vassal states and prevented them from attacking and annexing each other. During the Eastern Zhou, although the royal line was restored and the king retained his position as a nominal overlord, he was no longer able to control the activities of his vassals. Economic imbalance of the states led to some of the stronger states declaring war on the weaker ones and annexing them regardless of the prohibition by the Zhou king. Thus, unlike the Western Zhou, which maintained its suzerainty, the Eastern Zhou was politically divided and weakened by the contending vassal states.

The Eastern Zhou is further divided into two time periods, the Spring and Autumn Period and the Warring States Period. The Spring and Autumn Period (770-476 B.C.E.) is named after *Chunqiu* (fifth century B.C.E.; *The Ch'un Ts'ew with the Tso Chuen*, 1872; commonly known as *Spring and Autumn Annals*), a history of Lu, one of the vassal states of the Eastern Zhou, which was adapted by Confucius. The Warring States Period (475-221 B.C.E.) took its name from the power struggles between the large states that were trying to gain control over all of China.

During the Spring and Autumn Period, there were more than 150 kingdoms. One of these kingdoms, the Eastern Zhou, declined in power. The stronger kingdoms included Qi (Ch'i), Lu, Jin (Chin), Yan (Yen), Qin (Ch'in), Chu (Ch'u), Wu, and Yue (Yüeh). These powerful states, relying on their economic and military advantages, launched wars to expand their territories and forced small states to follow them in order to establish their dominance as overlords. At one time, five dukes—Huangong of the Qi state, Xianggong of the Song, Wengong of the Jin, Mugong of the Qin, and Zhuangwang of the Chu, known as the Five Overlords of the Spring and Autumn Period—fought for the overlordship (*ba*, or hegemon). The system of hegemony gave China only brief and sporadic stability, lasting no longer than the lifetime of each strong man who was able to establish himself as hegemon.

During the sixth century B.C.E., some stability was achieved through a formalized balance of power between Jin in the north and Chu in the south. In 579 and 546 B.C.E., two treaties were made between the states of Jin and Chu, resulting in a short peace in the central plains. Continuous wars created many problems for the people. According to historical records, during this period, a total of thirty-six kings were killed, and fifty-two vassal states were destroyed. After this period of drastic upheavals, reshufflings, and regroupings, seven states—Qi, Chu, Yan, Han, Zhao (Chao), Wei, and Qin—eventually emerged, and China entered the Warring States Period.

To expand their forces and territories, the seven states, known as the Seven Overlords of the Warring States, carried out internal reforms designed to increase their strength. Meanwhile, they constantly waged war against each other and schemed to annex other states. Among the seven states, Qin gradually emerged as the most powerful.

Situated in the remote west, Qin was once to be a vassal state enfeoffed by Pingwang to reward Qin Mugong's contribution of escorting the Zhou king on his move east. During the Spring and Autumn Period, Qin Mugong annexed twelve states, largely expanding his territory and making himself an overlord. During the Warring States Period, Qin was more backward than the states in the central plains because of its remote locale. When Qin Xiaogong gained power, he made Shang Yang, an aristocratic descendant of the Wei state, his chief minister. Shang Yang carried out a series of reforms in 359 and 350 B.C.E. to strengthen the power of Qin. Shang Yang's reforms included abolishing the outdated well-field system, legalizing the private ownership of land, canceling the hereditary system of rank, and establishing a county system.

Qin also improved its agriculture by encouraging new farming technologies and building dams. Around 250 B.C.E., Libing, governor of Shu Prefecture (present-day Sichuan Province), along with his son, directed the construction of Dujiangyan Irrigation Project. The completed project not only controlled flooding but also irrigated the entire Chengdu Plain.

Because of its reforms and economic improvements, Qin soon became a powerful state, laying a solid foundation for the future unification of China. In 256 B.C.E., Qin dispatched an army and destroyed the Eastern Zhou Dynasty. Ten years later, Yingzheng, the young king of Qin, succeeded to the throne. He continued the effort of expansion and annexation, and finally in 221 B.C.E. united China, establishing a unified, autocratic, and politically centralized state and ending the Warring States Period.

Although sociopolitically turbulent and tumultuous, the Eastern Zhou Dynasty witnessed technological and economic growth and cultural brilliance. By the end of eighth century B.C.E., China was the most populous land on Earth and about twenty million Chinese resided in the seven largest states. Iron became common in China by the fifth century B.C.E. and was used to make weapons and farming tools. Grain yields also were increased as a result of large-scale irrigation and water-control projects. The rapid development in trade helped formulate a society consisting of four classes (in descending order): the warrior-administrators, the peasants or primary producers, the artisans or secondary producers, and the merchants.

The Eastern Zhou was also a period of great intellectual development, in which a wide array of philosophical and religious approaches, known as the Hundred Schools, were contending for the attention and patronage of lords of the various states. Among the Hundred Schools, Confucianism, Legalism, and Daoism (Taoism) captured the fascination of the ruling houses and intellectuals.

Confucianism traced its origin to Confucius, a member of a lower aristocratic family and a minor official in the state of Lu. Confucius repeatedly tried to convince rulers that a ruler should cultivate moral perfection in order to set a good example for his subjects and that only a benevolent ruler could earn the respect of the people. The two prominent disciples of Confucius, Mencius and Xunzi, each developed opposite views of human nature. While Mencius asserted that human nature was fundamentally good as everyone was born with the capacity to recognize what was right and act on it, Xunzi believed that people were born selfish and that it was only through education and ritual that they learned to give up evil and return to good.

The Legalist school sought to strengthen the state and increase its agricultural capabilities and military power. The Legalists defined the duties of people in society by creating detailed laws and determining rewards and penalties for the following or flouting of these laws. Unlike the other two schools, the Daoists preferred to understand the Dao (Tao) as the way of nature as a whole, advocating a lifestyle of spontaneity and harmony.

SIGNIFICANCE

Although the royal house of the Zhou restored its line in the east, it never really exercised political and economic power over its vassal states. Politically divided and socially turbulent, the Eastern Zhou nevertheless saw great economic and technological growth, social changes, political development, and intellectual advances. Above all, the Hundred Schools have proved to be the most influential philosophical contributions of China.

—*Huping Ling*

FURTHER READING

Adler, Joseph A. *Chinese Religious Traditions*. Upper Saddle River, N.J.: Prentice Hall, 2002. A study on Chinese religions, beginning with the Zhou Dynasty.

Cullen, Christopher. *Astronomy and Mathematics in Ancient China: The Zhou bi suan jing*. New York: Cambridge University Press, 1996. An intellectual history of the scientific development of the Zhou.

Embree, Ainslie T., and Carol Gluck, eds. *Asia in Western and World History: A Guide for Teaching*. Armonk, N.Y.: M. E. Sharpe, 1997. A useful guide for teaching Asian history.

Fairbank, John King. *China: A New History*. Cambridge, Mass.: Belknap Press of Harvard University Press, 1992. A comprehensive Chinese history from antiquity to the present.

Gernet, Jacques. *Ancient China from the Beginning to*

Empire. Berkeley: University of California Press, 1968. A comprehensive history of ancient China.

Hsu, Cho-yun, and Katheryn M. Linduff. *Western Chou Civilization*. New Haven, Conn.: Yale University Press, 1988. A history of the Zhou Dynasty.

Li, Jun. *Chinese Civilization in the Making, 1766-221 B.C.* New York: St. Martin's Press, 1996. Ancient Chinese history from the Shang Dynasty to the beginning of the Qin Dynasty.

Li, Xueqin. *Eastern Zhou and Qin Civilizations*. New Haven, Conn.: Yale University Press, 1985. A history of the Eastern Zhou and Qin Dynasties.

Loewe, Michael, and Edward L. Shaughnessy, eds. *The Cambridge History of Ancient China: From the Origins of Civilization to 221 B.C.* New York: Cambridge University Press, 1999. Ancient Chinese history from antiquity to the end of the Zhou Dynasty.

Meyer, Milton W. *China: A Concise History*. 2d ed. Lanham, Md.: Rowman and Littlefield, 1994. A comprehensive Chinese history from antiquity to the present.

Wang, Aihe. *Cosmology and Political Culture in Early China*. New York: Cambridge University Press, 2000. An intellectual history of ancient China.

SEE ALSO: c. 1066, Western Zhou Dynasty Begins in China; 5th century B.C.E., Composition of the *Spring and Autumn Annals*; 5th-1st century B.C.E., Composition of *The Great Learning*; 500-400 B.C.E., Creation of the *Wujing*; 479 B.C.E., Confucius's Death Leads to the Creation of *The Analects*; 475-221 B.C.E., China Enters Chaotic Warring States Period; Early 4th century B.C.E., Founding of Mohism; 3d century B.C.E. (traditionally 6th century B.C.E.), Laozi Composes the *Dao De Jing*; c. 285-c. 255 B.C.E, Xunzi Develops Teachings That Lead to Legalism; 285-160 B.C.E. (traditionally, c. 300 B.C.E.), Composition of the *Zhuangzi*; 221 B.C.E., Qin Dynasty Founded in China; 221-206 B.C.E., Legalist Movement in China.

RELATED ARTICLES in *Great Lives from History: The Ancient World*: Confucius; Hanfeizi; Laozi; Mencius; Mozi; Shi Huangdi; Xunzi; Zhuangzi.

c. 750 B.C.E.
HOMER COMPOSES THE *ILIAD*

Homer's composition of the Iliad *established the epic poem as a genre in Western literature and influenced the culture and literature of Europe for centuries.*

LOCALE: Ionia, on the coast of Asia Minor (now in Turkey)
CATEGORIES: Cultural and intellectual history; literature

KEY FIGURE

Homer (fl. c. eighth century B.C.E.), Greek poet and author of the *Iliad* and the *Odyssey*

SUMMARY OF EVENT

The *Iliad* (English translation, 1616) is a Greek epic poem of 15,693 lines that tells the story of the fall of the city of Troy to the Greeks. Written in dactylic hexameter, the poem was divided sometime in the third century B.C.E. into twenty-four books, each having from 424 to 909 lines.

The composition of the *Iliad* can be seen as both the beginning of Western literature and the culmination of a long tradition of oral epic poetry that probably dates from the height of Mycenaean civilization in the thirteenth and twelfth centuries B.C.E. Controversy has raged for years over the authorship of the *Iliad*. Some scholars see the epic as the work of one person, whereas others see it as the work of several individuals. Although the epic does contain inconsistencies—some probably caused by the inclusion of pieces of earlier epics, others doubtless the result of additions made by post-Homeric scribes and editors—the modern consensus seems to be that one controlling artistic imagination must have shaped the whole, regardless of the origin of its components. The consistent characterizations, the epic similes with their sympathetic glimpses into the life of the common people of Homer's day, and above all, the unifying theme of the tragedy of Achilles can hardly have resulted from the work of a number of poets working separately.

Although few facts can be verified about the identity of Homer and the time and place of the composition of his epic poem, the *Iliad* itself provides evidence that can support some educated guesses as to its authorship and provenance. References to Homer's material in later Greek writings suggest that the epic must have been widely circulated by 700 B.C.E., and descriptions of sculpture and certain types of shields that can be closely dated by archaeologists indicate that the final version of the *Iliad* is unlikely to have been composed much before 750 B.C.E.

Elements of the Aeolic and Ionic dialects used in the poem have encouraged scholars to believe that its author lived in one of the Greek colonies on the coast of Asia Minor, where Hellenes, who had been powerful in Mycenaean days, had taken refuge from Dorian invaders during the eleventh century B.C.E. Somehow, in the nearly five hundred years between the legendary fall of Troy and the writing of the *Iliad*, the Ionian courts preserved the names of the Mycenaean heroes and cities powerful in the Aegean culture of the Bronze Age, as well as stories of events related to some conflict between Greeks and Trojans.

The preservation of these elements of a dead civilization has been attributed to the existence of a strong oral tradition. In books 7 and 22, the *Odyssey* (c. 725 B.C.E.; English translation, 1616) describes court poets who entertained visitors with recitations of the deeds of heroes, and the characters of Demodocus and Phemius probably reflect Homer's own role in Ionian society. Scholars have postulated the existence of poetic guilds that preserved and passed on, with their own embellishments, bodies of historical and legendary materials.

These Ionian bards, like later ones who preserved and transmitted the Germanic sagas, developed sophisticated techniques to assist them in their composition. At some point in the growth of the oral epic, dactylic hexameter became the accepted metrical form. It is a complex meter, hardly more natural to the Greek language than it is to the English language. The bards therefore developed formulas, or stock phrases that fit the meter. Frequent use of the same epithets, such as "fleet-footed Achilles" or "Agamemnon, king of men," illustrates the technique; Hera is called "white-armed" or "Hera of the golden throne" according to whether she is mentioned at the beginning or end of a line, not because of the context in which she is mentioned.

In this depiction of the events of the Trojan War, the priest Laocoon stands behind the Trojan horse. (F. R. Niglutsch)

800 - 701 B.C.E.

Learning hundreds of these formulas must have been part of the training of Ionian court poets, for the same phrases seem to have been handed down for generations. Once a satisfactory pattern had been established, it appears to have been preserved, even though its words might have vanished from ordinary speech. The use of formulas probably explains why, for example, there are contradictory descriptions of weapons in the *Iliad*.

In addition, entire passages, such as the catalog of ships in book 2 of the *Iliad*, seem to have been handed down almost intact. Many of the cities mentioned were centers of commerce during Mycenaean times but were obliterated long before Homer lived. It is interesting to note that Homer considered the list of heroes important enough to preserve in his poem, even though many of the leaders mentioned play little or no part in the epic itself.

Little is actually known about Homer's audience. Nevertheless, the nature of the *Iliad* makes it clear that the events surrounding the Trojan War were familiar to the poet's audience, for he begins in the middle of the action. There is no need to discuss the causes of the war or its conclusion, and the characters evidently need no introduction. The greatness of the poet was not his originality as a creator of plot but rather his ability to bring a unified whole out of the masses of material at his disposal.

Perhaps even less is known about Homer as an individual. When the Greeks became interested in biography, nothing had been recorded about the man to whom they ascribed their greatest literary treasures. It is simply a romantic story that claims that Homer was a blind minstrel.

Homer used traditional materials and forms to create a work that embodied a radical and consistent interpretation of the world and of the position of humankind. As far as possible, he cleared away everything that could distract attention from his main theme: the terrible contrast of life and death. The hero of Homer's epics represents the summit of human greatness, and his struggle to face death is fascinating enough to attract the gaze of the immortal gods, thus exalting human life to a level at which it achieves significance and becomes a fit subject for the song that celebrates its fragility and its greatness.

The *Iliad* says that the natural human state in this world can be comprehended in human terms and that human life can be more than an insignificant or ignoble struggle in the dark. The human soul can rise to the height of the challenges and the suffering that are the lot of all humankind. That spirit, chastened but not despairing, which sees the world without illusion and confronts it without self-pity or evasion, was the gift of Greece to the world, and it is the deepest element in the thought of Homer.

SIGNIFICANCE

It is nearly impossible to assess the enormous impact of the composition of the *Iliad* on Western civilization. The story of the fall of Troy has been part of the education of many Westerners for nearly three thousand years, testifying to the significance of the Homeric understanding of the nature of human beings and their place in the world. The values expressed in the work persisted not only into Roman times but also into the Renaissance. In addition, Homer's use of the epic poem established it as a genre in Western literature. Many epic poems have been created based on Homer's model, and the story of the *Iliad* has inspired many great works of European literature in other genres.

—Elizabeth Johnston Lipscomb and Susan M. Taylor

FURTHER READING

Frazer, Richard M. *A Reading of the "Iliad."* Lanham, Md.: University Press of America, 1993. Frazer discusses the history and literary criticism surrounding epic poetry, using the *Iliad* as an example. Bibliography and index.

Hammer, Dean. *The "Iliad" as Politics: The Performance of Political Thought.* Norman: University of Oklahoma Press, 2002. An analysis of the political and social views of Homer as well as the relationship between literature and politics in ancient Greece. Bibliography and indexes.

Kim, Jinyo. *The Pity of Achilles: Oral Style and the Unity of the "Iliad."* Lanham, Md.: Rowman and Littlefield, 2000. Kim examines the oral tradition and its effect on the *Iliad*. Bibliography and indexes.

Luce, John Victor. *Celebrating Homer's Landscapes: Troy and Ithaca Revisited.* New Haven, Conn.: Yale University Press, 1998. Luce examines what is known of Troy and Ithaca, where Homer's epics took place. Includes archaeological information on Troy. Bibliography and indexes.

Morrison, James V. *Homeric Misdirection: False Predictions of the "Iliad."* Ann Arbor: University of Michigan Press, 1992. Morrison provides a detailed discussion of Homeric technique and explores truths and falsehoods in literature. Bibliography and indexes.

Van Duzer, Chet A. *Duality and Structure in the "Iliad" and the "Odyssey."* New York: Peter Lang, 1996. Homer's technique is discussed at length, as well as the use of logic and polarity in literature. Bibliography and indexes.

Wilson, John. *Sense and Nonsense in Homer: A Consideration of the Inconsistencies and Incoherencies in the Texts of the "Iliad" and the "Odyssey."* Oxford, England: Archaeopress, 2000. An examination of the discrepancies in the text of the *Iliad* as well as of the *Odyssey*. Bibliography.

SEE ALSO: c. 1250 B.C.E., Fall of Troy Marks End of Trojan War; c. 580 B.C.E., Greek Poet Sappho Dies; c. 500-470 B.C.E., Hecataeus of Miletus Writes the First Geography Book; c. 456/455 B.C.E., Greek Tragedian Aeschylus Dies; c. 438 B.C.E., Greek Lyric Poet Pindar Dies; 406 B.C.E., Greek Dramatist Euripides Dies; c. 385 B.C.E., Greek Playwright Aristophanes Dies; c. 335-323 B.C.E., Aristotle Writes the *Politics*.

RELATED ARTICLE in *Great Lives from History: The Ancient World:* Homer.

c. 750-c. 500 B.C.E.

MARIB DAM IS BUILT IN YEMEN

The construction of the Marib Dam in Yemen provided water for irrigation for nearly one thousand years and created a rich farming region on the edge of the desert in south-central Arabia.

LOCALE: Kingdom of Sheba, Arabian Peninsula (now Marib Governate, Yemen)

CATEGORIES: Science and technology; agriculture

SUMMARY OF EVENT

The area around the ancient city of Marib has been important commercially and agriculturally for several thousand years. Once known as Sheba (or Sabah, or Sabaa), the region lay on trade routes stretching by sea to the Persian Gulf and India and by land to Mesopotamia and the eastern shores of the Mediterranean. Equally important, Sheba was a rich agricultural region. The Old Testament of the Bible records a queen of Sheba, believed to have lived about 950 B.C.E., as visiting Solomon, king of Israel. Today the region lies in the nation of Yemen in southern Arabia.

Heavy rains fall in Yemen only two or three times a year, briefly flooding the hills only to disappear into the sand or evaporate. In order to channel this water for farming, Sheba's inhabitants developed an extensive and sophisticated irrigation system, some of whose diversion dams and canals have been dated to the middle of the third millennium B.C.E.

The greatest component of Sheba's irrigation system was the Marib Dam, built about 5 miles (8 kilometers) west of Marib across the Wadi (watercourse) Adana. The Adana flows in a northeasterly direction from the eastern highlands of Yemen and gathers the runoff of many other wadis. The original earth dam, which was begun about 750 B.C.E., was about 13 feet (4 meters) high and 1,900 feet (580 meters) long. It fed water into a single, naturally occurring spillway lying nearly 10 feet (3 meters) below the top of the dam and located between the northern end of the dam and a high cliff. The water then flowed into a basin 75 feet (23 meters) wide and 213 feet (65 meters) long in which silt could settle. A canal 92 feet (28 meters) wide and 3,068 feet (935 meters) long led from the basin to twelve separate ditches. As a result, Sheba's inhabitants were able to bring the land north of the wadi under cultivation.

Some two and a half centuries later, beginning about 500 B.C.E., the dam was heightened to 23 feet (7 meters). The slope of its sides now lay at about 45 degrees, and its upstream surface was faced with stone set in mortar to prevent seepage and erosion. A sluice was cut and an adjoining canal built at the dam's southern end, allowing for irrigation of the southern banks of the Wadi Adana. Later construction raised the height of the dam to 46 feet (14 meters) and improved the irrigation system's efficiency.

SIGNIFICANCE

Thanks to the dam and its extensive series of canals, settling ponds, and ditches, much of the rainwater falling in the highlands of Sheba was caught and channeled to the lands around Marib. Although the region lay at the edge of the forbidding desert known as the Rub al Khali, or Empty Quarter, it grew into a rich farming community. Some 24,000 acres (9,600 hectares) were brought under cultivation, an area large enough to feed as many as fifty thousand people. The region's farmers produced barley, maze, millet, dates, grapes, and other crops. The immense structure that made this possible came to be known simply as the Great Dam, and the fertile lands north and south of the Wadi Adana were known as the Garden of the Two Paradises.

The accumulation of silt and other debris was cleared from behind the dam every one hundred years. Unusually heavy floods overtopped the dam more frequently, approximately every fifty years, necessitating periodic repairs. However, the damage caused by a major flood in 575 C.E. was never repaired, and subsequently the dam washed away. The loss was devastating, an event so catastrophic that it is memorialized in the Qur'ān, the Muslim holy book. Most inhabitants fled the region.

Beginning in 1984, a new earth dam was built across the Wadi Adana upstream from the location of the ancient structure.

—*Grove Koger*

FURTHER READING

Clapp, Nicholas. *Sheba: Through the Desert in Search of the Legendary Queen*. Boston: Houghton Mifflin, 2001. Popular account of a journey through the lands associated with the queen of Sheba, with a chapter devoted to Marib and its dam. Photographs, plans, and extensive bibliography.

Dayton, J. E. "A Discussion of the Hydrology of Marib." *Proceedings of the Seminar for Arabian Studies* 9 (1979): 124-129. Examines possible causes for the destruction of the dam. Includes two plans of the south sluice and a photograph.

_______. "Marib Revisited." *Proceedings of the Seminar for Arabian Studies* 11 (1981): 7-26. Summary of a brief visit to the site in 1979. Plans and numerous photographs.

Ganchikov, V. G., and Z. I. Munavvarov. "The Marib Dam (History and the Present Time)." *Hydrotechnical Construction* 25 (1991): 242-248. Discusses the ancient dam and its modern counterpart. Includes plans, excellent drawings, a cross section of the ancient dam, a schematic cross section of the modern dam, and a table summarizing its measurements.

Hehmeyer, Ingrid. "Irrigation Farming in the Ancient Oasis of Marib." *Proceedings of the Seminar for Arabian Studies* 19 (1989): 33-44. Analyzes the irrigation systems in use in ancient Marib, methods of preparation of the soil, and the variety of crops grown.

Schnitter, Nicholas J. *Dams: The Useful Pyramids*. Rotterdam, The Netherlands: A. A. Balkema, 1994. Discusses the Marib Dam as one of several ancient dams. Includes a photograph, detailed plan of the dam in its final configuration, table of other dams in the area, and bibliography.

Smith, Norman. *A History of Dams*. Secaucus, N.J.: Citadel Press, 1972. Smith devotes several pages to the Marib Dam in his survey of the dams of antiquity, discussing its construction, maintenance, and eventual abandonment.

SEE ALSO: c. 10th century B.C.E., Queen of Sheba Legends Arise; c. 420 B.C.E.-c. 100 C.E., Yuezhi Culture Links Persia and China.

745 B.C.E.
TIGLATH-PILESER III RULES ASSYRIA

Tiglath-pileser III reorganized Assyria, its foreign policy, and its army, thus creating an empire that would dominate the Fertile Crescent for the next century.

LOCALE: Assyria, Mesopotamia (now northern Iraq)
CATEGORIES: Expansion and land acquisition; government and politics

KEY FIGURE

Tiglath-pileser III (Tukulti-Apil-Esharra; early eighth century-727 B.C.E.), king of Assyria, r. 745-727 B.C.E.

SUMMARY OF EVENT

The accession of Tiglath-pileser III to the throne in 745 B.C.E. brought Assyria out of a century-long period of relative weakness. Internal revolt and stagnation had followed Assyria's spectacular military successes of the mid-ninth century B.C.E. In addition, the emergence of Urartu as a large and powerful kingdom in modern-day Armenia had stymied Assyria throughout the first half of the eighth century B.C.E. Tiglath-pileser (whose name means "my trust is in the son of Esharra [Ashur]") was a vigorous and intelligent ruler who changed his nation's fortunes. Some inscriptions imply he was of royal blood, but Tiglath-pileser seized the throne after a rebellion killed his weak predecessor, Ashur-nirâri V. As king, he brought about an administrative reform, modified Assyrian policy toward subjugated areas, and reorganized the army. The successes of these actions coupled with his successful military campaigns made Tiglath-pileser the true founder of the Assyrian Empire.

Before Tiglath-pileser III, administrative districts had operated semi-independently under old noble families that treated their governorships as hereditary in nature. Tiglath-pileser reduced these districts in size and multiplied their number, placing them under governors responsible directly to the king. This system and an efficient communications network increased royal authority and control within Assyria proper. Other changes affected the oversight of conquered territory.

The glorified campaigns of the Assyrian kings Ashurnasirpal II and Shalmaneser III in the ninth century B.C.E. had resulted in tribute but only minimal territorial gains. Tiglath-pileser organized his conquests into an efficient empire. Conquered nations beyond Assyria itself were made vassals under native rule but placed under the watchful eye of an "overseer." As long as the imposed tribute was paid and the "overseer" was accepted, the local ruling families were left independent with regard to internal matters and protected against external attack or rebellion. For example, an Aramean king of Sam'al described in his own inscription how Tiglath-pileser III had reinstalled his father after quelling a rebellion. For more troublesome territories in which local rule did not produce the desired result, however, Tiglath-pileser instituted a policy of incorporating them as Assyrian provinces. War was waged against more distant states that had not yet submitted to the Assyrian yoke. As was the case with his predecessors, scenes of the Assyrian army in action—besieging and conquering cities and dispatching leaders of resistance—remained the primary subject of Assyrian royal bas-reliefs.

Tiglath-pileser III also initiated the practice of mass deportation from conquered territories. Entire towns and even districts of subjugated lands were emptied, the former inhabitants were resettled in distant parts of the empire, and other populations were moved in to take their place. This practice served to limit continued nationalism and dedication to old ruling families on the part of the deportees. Occasional scenes in the royal bas-reliefs show long lines of deportees carrying small bundles of belongings, holding the hands of pitiful children, with women sometimes riding in carts alongside. Despite the fact that this practice was in part to punish recalcitrant states, the deportees themselves were cared for on their journey and were not considered slaves. At their destination, they were regular citizens of Assyria, with the same status as the original Assyrian population. Tens of thousands of persons were deported by Tiglath-pileser on single campaigns. Subsequent rulers of both Assyria and Babylon continued this practice, and one estimate puts the number of displaced over a three-century span in the Near East at about 4.5 million.

Before Tiglath-pileser III, the Assyrian army had been composed primarily of peasants and slaves conscripted by noble landowners of Assyria and men doing military service in exchange for royal grants of land and provisions—an institution called *ilkum*, introduced by Hammurabi of Babylon centuries earlier. Tiglath-pileser added to this a permanent professional army recruited mainly in the peripheral provinces. He developed cavalry in addition to the traditional chariotry, perhaps because of the necessity of fighting the Urartu and other mountain peoples on their ground.

The particular details and chronology of Tiglath-pileser's campaigns are far from certain, as the annals and bas-reliefs from his capital Calah (modern Nimrud) are very badly preserved. Their condition results from their removal from his palace walls for reuse in a successor's building project and the recovery methods used by nineteenth century excavators. Work by scholar Hayim Tadmor in collating the available material permits the following general overview.

In his first campaign, Tiglath-pileser marched to southern Mesopotamia, removing Aramean threats and reminding Babylon of Assyrian superiority. Then Tiglath-pileser led his army in a protracted six-year campaign to the west (probably 743-738 B.C.E.). He first faced Neo-Hittite and Aramean princes loyal to Sarduri II, king of Urartu. Sarduri attempted to intervene but was defeated and fled. Arpad, capital of the Aramean leader Mati'il, was besieged for three years. After its fall, about 741 B.C.E., Arpad became the chief town of an Assyrian province. Before Arpad's fall, Tiglath-pileser had annexed the territory of enemies on the Syrian coast and probably Phoenicia as well. By the end of the campaign

This wall carving depicts the siege of a city during the reign of Tiglath-pileser III. (Hulton|Archive)

KINGS OF THE NEO-ASSYRIAN EMPIRE, 745-609 B.C.E.

King	*Reign*
Tiglath-pileser III	745-727
Shalmaneser V	726-722
Sargon II	721-705
Sennacherib	704-681
Esarhaddon	680-669
Ashurbanipal	669-627
Ashur-etil-ilāni, Sin-shum-lishir, and Sīn-shar-ishkun	627-612
Ashur-uballit II	612-609

(about 738 B.C.E.), several kings of neighboring states took fright and brought "presents" and tribute to Tiglath-pileser at Arpad. According to the annals, tributaries included Zabibê, queen of the Arabs; Rezin, king of Aram-Damascus; and Menachem, king of Israel. The tribute of the latter is recorded in 2 Kings 15:19-20, in which Tiglath-pileser is called Pul, derived from his nickname, Pulu.

For the next few years, Tiglath-pileser III concentrated his efforts in the east in moves against the interests of Urartu. The temporary withdrawal of the main Assyrian army from Syria perhaps encouraged anti-Assyrian coalitions there. The best known of these is the alliance reported in the Bible between Rezin of Aram-Damascus and the usurper Pekah of Israel. Ahaz, king of Judah, apparently refused to join the effort, causing the coalition to turn against him in an attempt to effect a regime change (2 Kings 16:5-9; Isaiah 7). Ahaz called on Tiglath-pileser for assistance, sending a "present" to the Assyrian. In 734 B.C.E., Tiglath-pileser campaigned to Philistia, capturing Gaza and receiving tribute from neighboring states. The following year, he reduced Israel to the area surrounding Samaria and confirmed Hosea as a vassal king in place of the deposed Pekah. In 732, Damascus was destroyed, and Assyrian provinces were created from its territory and that taken from Israel. This episode illustrates various levels of Tiglath-pileser's policy toward conquered areas. Judah willingly entered into a vassal relationship and was protected, but with the yoke of Assyrian domination (cf. 2 Kings 16:10-18). Israel, where a coup had replaced a dynasty loyal to Assyria with a rebellious king, was reduced, returned to local rule, and saddled with tribute. It was the last straw, however, for Damascus, where the former vassal king himself rebelled.

In the meantime, a Chaldean tribal leader had seized the throne in Babylon. Assyrian intervention there was met with mixed feelings. One preserved letter gives an account of negotiations at the gates of Babylon between Assyrian officials and the people of the city. Just as in the later negotiation at Jerusalem reported in the Bible (2 Kings 18:17-36; Isaiah 36), the Assyrian officers attempted to appeal to the people directly, bypassing the rebel leaders. It took Tiglath-pileser three years to settle the situation in Babylon through a combination of diplomacy and force. In the end, the Chaldean usurper fled and Tiglath-pileser "took the hand of Marduk" in the Akitu (New Year) Festival of Babylon. Tiglath-pileser thus assumed the throne of Babylon for himself, the first Assyrian king to do so for more than four centuries.

SIGNIFICANCE

In 727 B.C.E., Tiglath-pileser died, leaving Assyria with an empire stretching from the Persian Gulf in the east to the border of Egypt in the west and extending north into Cilicia and Anatolia. The western expansion brought Assyria into conflict with Egyptian interests; this conflict lies behind Egypt's role in fomenting rebellion against Assyria in Palestine and Syria in the following years. Because of the Bible, the best-known consequence of this interference is the Assyrian investment of Samaria and subsequent fall of the remnant of Israel (722-720 B.C.E.; cf. 2 Kings 17:3-5). These Egyptian efforts notwithstanding, Tiglath-pileser had reestablished Assyria as the dominant power of the Near East, a position it retained for the next century. His policies of keeping vassal states under native rule where possible, incorporating recalcitrant regions, and mass deportation were followed by subsequent rulers in the region, setting the tone for the great empires of the later Iron Age.

—*Daniel C. Browning, Jr.*

FURTHER READING

Barnett, R. D., and M. Falkner. *The Sculptures of Tiglath-pileser III, 745-727 B.C.* London: British Museum, 1962. Relevant objects in the British Museum.

Grayson, A. K. "Assyria: Tiglath-pileser III to Sargon II (744-705 B.C.)." In Vol. 3 of *The Cambridge Ancient History*, edited by J. Boardman, I. E. S. Edwards, N. G. L. Hammond, and S. Sollberger. New York: Cambridge University Press, 1991. A standard history.

Hallo, William W. "From Qarqar to Carchemish: Assyria and Israel in the Light of New Discoveries." *Biblical*

Archaeologist 23, no. 2 (May, 1960): 33-61. A review of Assyrian influence in Palestine with a special reference to biblical data.

Saggs, H. W. F. *The Might That Was Assyria*. London: Sidgwick & Jackson, 1984. An excellent general treatment of Assyria with a helpful section on Tiglath-pileser.

Tadmor, Hayim. *The Inscriptions of Tiglath-pileser III of Assyria*. Jerusalem: The Israel Academy of Sciences and Humanities, 1994. A modern critical edition of known inscriptions of Tiglath-pileser with introductory essays, translation, and commentary.

SEE ALSO: c. 1100 B.C.E., Arameans Emerge in Syria and Mesopotamia; c. 883-c. 824 B.C.E., Second Assyrian Empire Displays Military Prowess; 701 B.C.E., Sennacherib Invades Syro-Palestine.

RELATED ARTICLES in *Great Lives from History: The Ancient World*: Ashurnasirpal II; Tiglath-pileser III.

c. 736-716 B.C.E.
SPARTAN CONQUEST OF MESSENIA

The Spartan conquest of Messenia reduced the Messenian population to servitude and helped Sparta become the dominant military state in Greece.

LOCALE: Sparta and Messenia (now in the southern Peloponnese, Greece)

CATEGORIES: Wars, uprisings, and civil unrest; expansion and land acquisition

KEY FIGURES

Theopompus I (fl. mid-eighth to early seventh century B.C.E.), Spartan king, r. late eighth century B.C.E., and commander in the First Messenian War

Tyrtaeus (fl. mid-seventh century B.C.E.), Spartan poet at the time of the Second Messenian War

SUMMARY OF EVENT

In the fifth and fourth centuries B.C.E., the Peloponnesian city-state of Sparta in Laconia developed some unique institutions. Although these institutions were not precisely imitated by other states, they were admired by many, including the Athenian philosopher Plato. In a Greek environment increasingly dominated by economic commerce, Sparta remained almost exclusively agrarian. In a world in which other states had developed social diversity and rich cultural expression, Sparta retained a strict and simple social structure and a spiritual character rich in strength but seemingly wanting in creative artistic expression. Scholarly studies have shown the existence of some Spartan artistic creativity. Because archaeological and literary evidence indicates that Sparta was in the mainstream of Greek cultural development until the beginning of the seventh century B.C.E., the reason for Sparta's later uniqueness must have its origins in developments later in that century. The most likely explanation is to be found in the deliberate crystallization of permanent military institutions made necessary by Sparta's conquest of Messenia as a response to the problem of overpopulation in the eighth century B.C.E.

The Dorian invaders of Laconia, who settled in the valley of the Eurotas River during the twelfth century B.C.E., remained ethnically distinct from the residual non-Dorian inhabitants whom they had conquered and over whom they exercised administrative jurisdiction. The distinction seems to have been preserved especially by maintenance of a social code from the period of conquest that featured strict separation of the sexes, early military training for boys in kinship groups, and common daily gatherings of adult males within kinship groups.

During the eighth century B.C.E., most communities in the Greek world faced the problem of overpopulation and responded to the challenge by establishing overseas colonies throughout the Mediterranean world. Sparta stood aloof from the general movement of colonization, founding only a few colonies and solving its problem of overpopulation by conquering the neighboring province of Messenia. Located to the southwest, Messenia was one of the richest agricultural districts in a region known for its generally rocky, mountainous, and infertile terrain. The war between Sparta and Messenia extended over a twenty-year period from approximately 736 to 716 C.E. According to tradition, the Spartan army was led by Theopompus I, one of its hereditary kings. There are abundant legends about the war, but little more can be firmly established beyond the bare facts recounted above and the Spartan organization of the land and its people following the conquest. Because the war had been fought in response to the challenge of overpopulation, Messenian land was divided into estates that were distributed

Ancient Sparta. (F. R. Niglutsch)

among the victorious Spartan soldiers. The Messenians themselves continued to work the land as serfs and were obliged to pay one-half of their produce to the new Spartan landowners. The conquered Messenians were called helots, a term that probably had the original meaning of "prisoners of war."

Encouraged by Sparta's involvement in local wars against Argos, Arcadia, and Elis in the mid-seventh century B.C.E., the Messenians attempted to throw off Spartan domination after several generations of servitude. The ensuing struggle was bitterly fought and apparently engendered a constitutional crisis from which Sparta emerged as a permanently militarist society with a rigid social and political structure. Primary sources describing events of this period include the poems of Tyrtaeus, exhortations of Spartan soldiers to resolution in the war with Messenia, a paraphrase of an Oracle of Delphi sanctioning the constitution (apparently adopted or amended at this time), and the text of a document called the Great Rhetra (quoted by Plutarch in his "Life of Lycurgus" in *Bioi paralleloi*, c. 105-115; *Parallel Lives*, 1579) containing information about the provisions of this constitution.

A major factor in this political crisis involved a shift in military tactics from fighting based on spear carriers and aristocratic cavalry to reliance on the close-knit phalanx of heavily armed foot soldiers known as hoplites. In Sparta and throughout the Greek world, the shifting of the burden of community defense to the shoulders of the hoplite infantry was accompanied by a demand by these soldiers for greater political authority. The imperative economic necessity of the reconquest of Messenia forced aristocratic leaders to grant concessions that were formalized by the Great Rhetra. In addition, the Spartan assembly (*apella*) of nine thousand warriors adopted the framework of a military organization based on local considerations rather than one based solely on claims of kinship. According to the Great Rhetra, this assembly was to be sovereign in the state and would hold final authority over the *gerousia*, an aristocratic council of thirty elders. Some adjustment of land distribution was evidently involved as well, for the nine thousand were henceforth called "equals" and were so content with their new lot that they did not resist the formulation of an amendment to the Great Rhetra granting veto power to the *gerousia* over decisions made by the *apella*.

SIGNIFICANCE

Although they successfully conquered the Messenians and suppressed the revolt, the Spartans were fully conscious that their economic security depended on the continued subjection of a large population of serfs under the control of a relatively small Spartan army. The Spartan commitment to a life of relentless military preparedness was maintained at the cost of cultural stagnation—a price that the Spartans were willing to pay.

—*Carl W. Conrad, updated by Mark W. Chavalas*

FURTHER READING

Atkinson, Kathleen Mary Tyrer Chrims. *Ancient Sparta: A Re-examination of the Evidence*. Manchester, England: Manchester University Press, 1999. Atkinson examines the traditional and archaeological sources on Sparta, separating myth and fact. Bibliography and index.

Cartledge, Paul. *Sparta and Lakonia: A Regional History, 1300-362 B.C.* 2d ed. New York: Routledge, 2002. A history of Sparta and Laconia that draws from both traditional sources and archaeological findings. Bibliography and index.

_______. *The Spartans: An Epic History*. London: Four Books, 2002. In this volume, which has a television tie-in, noted scholar Cartledge covers the history of the city-state.

Jones, A. H. M. *Sparta*. 1967. New York: Barnes & Noble, 1993. A history of the ancient city and its environs. Maps, genealogy tables, bibliography, and index.

Powell, Anton, and Stephen Hodkinson, eds. *Sparta: Beyond the Mirage*. London: Classical Press of Wales and Duckworth, 2002. A collection of essays presenting various views of Sparta, originally presented at a conference at the National University of Ireland in September, 2000. Bibliography and index.

SEE ALSO: c. 734-c. 580 B.C.E., Greeks Colonize the Mediterranean and Black Sea Regions; 508-507 B.C.E., Reforms of Cleisthenes; 499-494 B.C.E., Ionian Revolt; September 17, 490 B.C.E., Battle of Marathon; 480-479 B.C.E., Persian Invasion of Greece; May, 431-September, 404 B.C.E., Peloponnesian War; June, 415-September, 413 B.C.E., Athenian Invasion of Sicily.

RELATED ARTICLES in *Great Lives from History: The Ancient World*: Agesilaus II of Sparta; Epaminondas; Pericles.

c. 734-c. 580 B.C.E.
GREEKS COLONIZE THE MEDITERRANEAN AND BLACK SEA REGIONS

Excess population forced the Greek city-states to establish colonies throughout the Mediterranean world.

LOCALE: Mediterranean region
CATEGORY: Expansion and land acquisition

SUMMARY OF EVENT

By 1100 B.C.E. the Greek civilizations of the second millennium B.C.E. (Mycenaean and Minoan) had been overrun by other Greek speakers from the north. For three hundred years, the Greek world entered into the Dark Age. When the Greek culture emerged with a new alphabet borrowed from the Phoenicians, it made a dramatic reappearance—as witnessed by the epic poetry of Homer that capsulized its mythological history and religion.

The Greeks imported the alphabet in an attempt to support their excess population. The numerous valleys of Greece, which is on a mountainous peninsula, created a political system of hundreds of independent city-states (the poleis) and a terrain unsuitable for meeting the food needs of the population. The Greeks, forced to become merchants as well as farmers because of the need to import grain and other necessities, needed a commercial alphabet like that of the Phoenicians. They also solved their overcrowding problem by sending Greeks to other regions.

The age of Greek colonization lasted from 734 to 580 B.C.E. The Greek city-states established new settlements on both shores of the Mediterranean and around the littoral of the Black Sea. These colonies shared religious and communal affinities with their mother cities but were entirely independent in their politics. Early colonies were settled by people from a number of cities, leading to divided loyalties. In many cases, this, plus the fact that some settlers were driven from the mother cities by force and coercion, led to tension between the colony and the founding city. One of the causes of the Peloponnesian

War (431-404 B.C.E.) was a conflict between Corinth and Corcyra (now Corfu), one of the former's own colonies.

Some Greeks were already familiar with the Mediterranean and knew the best locations for settlements. Others relied on the advice of seafarers or oracles, particularly the Oracle of Delphi, who was also consulted for decision on the rules of government. The Greek colony was called *apoikia*; the mother city, metropolis.

The two major Greek city-states, Athens and Sparta, did not participate in the creation of colonies with the exception of Tarentum, founded by the latter in the early seventh century. Both controlled large areas during the period and did not suffer the land hunger of the smaller city-states. Furthermore, Sparta's enslavement of the native Laconians as helots provided an economy that precluded colonization and the exportation of citizens.

The major colonizing city-states were the commercial cities of Corinth and Megara. Sometimes two or more cities established a colony, but settlers from only one took over the leadership. Historian Herodotus relates that the citizens of Thera chose by lot and forcibly expelled about two hundred people, who founded Cyrene (now Shaḩḩāt, Libya) in North Africa, because of a prolonged famine. Trade was another possible reason for colonization, but the evidence that most colonies were founded in plains suitable for agriculture supports land hunger as the chief motive. Some city-states, however, did establish merchant colonies. One example Herodotus mentions is Naucratis in Egypt, where Greek settlers lived in special sections of the city for mercantile reasons. Another commercial colony was Mina in Syria.

Modern scholars generally date the founding of Greek colonies by studying the pottery found at the locations, but ancient authors such as the Greek historian Thucydides give the dates of the founding of the *apoikias*. The Mediterranean offered a suitable climate, arable unoccupied land, and minerals—tin, iron, silver, and copper. They were able to establish colonies along the Black Sea coast as the native inhabitants preferred the interior. These new Greek cities were important for trade with the interior populations.

Sicily was an early and favorite area for Greek colonizations. The Greeks occupied most of the eastern half of the island and its western coast, and many city-states sent their citizens there. The first recorded settlers came from Chalkis (now Khalkís) on the island of Euboea to Naxos in 734 B.C.E. In 733 B.C.E., Corinth founded Syracuse and, the same year, Corcyra in the Adriatic. These first settlers were followed by colonists from all over Greece, including Megara, Rhodes, Crete, and other cities on Euboea, over the next two centuries. Southern Italy, called Greater Greece, also was a mecca for the city-states, but Greeks were slower to settle the rest of the Adriatic coast. The Euboens, followed by Corinth and city-states of the Peloponnese, established settlements there, and the western cities then moved to what is now France and Spain.

According to tradition, Cumae (in Campania, Italy), the northernmost Greek colony that was settled by Euboeans, was the oldest colony west of the mainland. Settlers from Achaea founded the major cities of Sybaris (near present-day Terranova di Sibari) and Croton (now Crotone) in southern Italy. Phocaea in Balkan Ionia founded Massilia (now Marseilles, France) around 600 B.C.E., and settlers from there set up trading colonies along the coast into northeast Spain. In the seventh century B.C.E., settlers from Andros and Chalkis founded many colonies on the Chalkidace (named after the latter) Peninsula. Around 685 B.C.E., Corinth founded the major colony of Poteidaea on the Pallene isthmus, also on the Chalkidice Peninsula. Control of Poteidaea was an issue in the Peloponnesian War. Megaran settlers founded Calchedon (now Kadiköy) on the Bosporus, and seventeen years later, nearby Byzantium (now Istanbul), less fertile but fated to become more prosperous and famous. Asia Minor Greek cities led by Miletus founded many colonies along the Black Sea in the eighth and seventh centuries B.C.E.

In the Eastern Mediterranean, the colonists' way was blocked by the presence of older, established civilizations, but Libya was open. The Phoenicians, however, colonized Carthage in northern Africa while the Greeks were moving into Sicily and southern Italy.

SIGNIFICANCE

Greek colonization in the eighth and seventh centuries B.C.E. spread Hellenic culture throughout the Mediterranean world and established the basis for what would become the classical legacy of European civilization. The variety and independence of the Greek city-states in both the metropoleis and the *apoikias* led to the success of the Greek world as a leading culture of the ancient world but at the same time led to the multitude of conflicts that resulted in the political downfall of Greece at the hands of the Macedonians and Romans.

—*Frederick B. Chary*

FURTHER READING

Graham, A. J. *Collected Papers on Greek Colonization*. Leiden: Brill, 2001. A collection of articles by leading scholars on the subject.

Herodotus. *The Histories*. Edited by Aubrey De Sélincourt and John Marincola. London: Penguin, 2003. The ancient historian records the reasons and details of several colonies.

Malkin, Irad. *Religion and Colonization in Ancient Greece*. Leiden, Netherlands: E. J. Brill, 1987. An important work by a leading scholar on Greek colonization.

Thucydides. *The Peloponnesian War*. Indianapolis: Hackett, 1998. Describes the colonization of Sicily.

SEE ALSO: c. 1000 B.C.E., Greek Alphabet Is Developed; 775 B.C.E., Delphic Oracle Provides Guidance for City-States; c. 736-716 B.C.E., Spartan Conquest of Messenia; c. 733 B.C.E., Founding of Syracuse; c. 640 B.C.E., Greek City-States Use Coins as Means of Exchange; 625-509 B.C.E., Rise of Etruscan Civilization in Rome.

RELATED ARTICLES in *Great Lives from History: The Ancient World*: Agesilaus II of Sparta; Epaminondas; Herodotus; Homer; Thucydides.

c. 733 B.C.E.
FOUNDING OF SYRACUSE

The founding of Syracuse by the Greek city-state of Corinth on the island of Sicily established one of the major political and cultural centers of the Greek world in the western Mediterranean.

LOCALE: The southeastern coast of Sicily (now in Italy)
CATEGORIES: Expansion and land acquisition; government and politics

KEY FIGURE

Archias (fl. eighth century B.C.E.), Corinthian nobleman and founder of Syracuse

SUMMARY OF EVENT

Greece has sparse natural resources. Its deposits of minerals are not extensive, and the soil is thin and stony. Much of the terrain is covered by mountains, limiting its arable land to only one-quarter of its surface. At the dawn of Greek history, the poet Homer wrote that Hellas (Greece) was married to poverty. As time passed and the population of Greece grew, many city-states found themselves unable to support their citizens. The acute need for more land could be satisfied only by emigration overseas. As a result, Greek city-states began a program of colonization around 750 B.C.E. that continued for nearly five centuries.

One of the first states to establish overseas colonies was Corinth, even though it possessed notable wealth by Greek standards. Corinth's position on the isthmus placed it at an important crossroads, where the land route between the Peloponnesus and central Greece intersected the short overland connection between the Gulf of Corinth and the Saronic Gulf. The city-state charged tolls on both routes, but the revenue received was insufficient to pay for much-needed imported food. As a result, Corinth decided to dispatch two expeditions overseas sometime around 733 B.C.E. Archias, a member of the noble family of the Bacchiadae, was selected to be the founder of the colony that settled on the east coast of the fertile island of Sicily. It is possible that the Corinthians consulted the god Apollo at Delphi to receive his sanction for the venture and to seek useful advice.

Virtually nothing is known of the story of the voyage to Sicily or of the early years of the new colony. Scholars believe that the risks faced by the Corinthians were similar to those encountered by European settlers who colonized North and South America in the seventeenth century C.E. Although the Atlantic Ocean was more dangerous than the Mediterranean Sea, such dangers were mitigated by the larger and stronger ships used by seventeenth century colonists, as well as the compasses they used and their superior knowledge of celestial navigation. These later colonists also had firearms and armor to defend themselves in encounters with the original inhabitants of the lands they claimed, whereas the Greeks had essentially the same weapons as the people they dispossessed. Archias and his Corinthian force succeeded in establishing their colony, and within a generation or two, Syracuse became a large and flourishing state.

As a colony, Syracuse was not governed by Corinth, but was fully autonomous. Corinth and Syracuse enjoyed the typically friendly relationship that developed between most Greek city-states and their offshoots; war between a colony and its mother city was considered to be a particularly shameful occurrence. There were exceptions, however, as in the case of Corcyra (now Corfu), another colony founded by Corinth around 733 B.C.E. Historians are aware of two wars fought between Corcyra and Corinth before the end of the fifth century B.C.E., and there are indications that there were other conflicts as well.

Syracuse became so powerful and populous that it was forced to establish its own colonies in other parts of Sicily; these daughter states also came to play an important role in the life and history of Sicily. Under the rule of the tyrant Dionysius at the beginning of the fourth century B.C.E., Syracuse temporarily imposed its hegemony on all of Sicily and much of southern Italy. The city became a brilliant center of Greek learning and culture and served as a conduit for transmitting elements of Hellenic culture from the Greek mainland and from Hellenized Alexandria to later Roman civilization.

After 650 B.C.E., a second motive for colonization supplemented the drive for agricultural expansion: Many colonies were founded for commercial gain. For example, the colony of Naucratis was established in Egypt shortly before 600 B.C.E. by Miletus, Aegina, Samos, and some smaller city-states as a depot for exporting much-needed grain from Egypt to Greece. In the west, Massilia (modern Marseilles, France) founded the city of Emporium, whose name may be translated from the Greek as "trading station," thus indicating the intention of its founders. Massilia also propagated Greek civilization up the valley of the Rhone River into southern Gaul.

SIGNIFICANCE

Corinth was not the only city to colonize extensively. Other important colonizers included Eretria, located on the island of Euboea, which settled many colonies on the northern coast of the Aegean Sea, and Miletus (now in Turkey), an Ionian city with numerous colonies along the coast of the Black Sea. This colonizing activity was of great significance not only because it furnished the city-states with the necessary food supplies and goods for prosperity and continued growth but also because the Black Sea, virtually all of Sicily, and the coastal regions of southern Italy were Hellenized by descendants of the original settlers of the western Mediterranean.

—*Samuel K. Eddy, updated by Mark W. Chavalas*

FURTHER READING

Berger, Shlomo. *Revolution and Society in Greek Sicily and Southern Italy.* Stuttgart, Germany: Steiner, 1992. A survey of the social and political institutions of Magna Grecia, or western Greece (Sicily and southern Italy), before and after the Roman conquest. Berger places special emphasis on the study of Syracuse and the impact of Greek tyranny.

Bernabo Brea, Luigi. *Sicily Before the Greeks.* Translated by C. M. Preston and L. Guido. Rev. ed. New York: F. A. Praeger, 1966. An important summary of Sicilian material culture that existed before Greek colonization.

Boardman, John. *The Greeks Overseas: Their Early Colonies and Trade.* 4th ed. New York: Thames & Hudson, 1999. One of the more concise works on Greek colonization, with pertinent information concerning Sicily and southern Italy as well as areas in other parts of the Mediterranean and near the Black Sea.

Dunbabin, Thomas James. *The Western Greeks.* 2d ed. Chicago: Ares, 1979. The fundamental study of Magna Grecia, surveying political history, natural philosophy, art, architecture, and other important subjects.

Finley, M. I. *Ancient Sicily.* Rev. ed. Totowa, N.J.: Rowman and Littlefield, 1979. A comprehensive historical survey of Sicily until Byzantine times. Index.

Fischer-Hansen, Tobias, ed. *Ancient Sicily.* Copenhagen: Museum Tusculanum Press, 1995. A collection of papers from a seminar held in May, 1993, on the history of Sicily and its antiquities. Bibliography.

Malkin, Irad. *Religion and Colonization in Ancient Greece.* Leiden, the Netherlands: E. J. Brill, 1987. This volume surveys the religious aspects of Greek colonization in the Mediterranean and near the Black Sea. It also focuses on syncretism between Greek religious customs and those of the local inhabitants.

SEE ALSO: c. 736-716 B.C.E., Spartan Conquest of Messenia; c. 734-c. 580 B.C.E., Greeks Colonize the Mediterranean and Black Sea Regions; c. 640 B.C.E., Greek City-States Use Coins as Means of Exchange; June, 415-September, 413 B.C.E., Athenian Invasion of Sicily.

c. 712-698 B.C.E.
SHABAKA REUNITES THE NILE VALLEY

Shabaka, successor to the Kushite ruler Piye, moved his capital to Thebes and assumed the title of pharaoh over all of Egypt and Kush.

LOCALE: Egypt and Nubia (now Republic of Sudan), northeast Africa

CATEGORIES: Government and politics; expansion and land acquisition

KEY FIGURES

Shabaka (d. c. 702/698 B.C.E.), king of Kush and Egypt, 716-c. 702/698 B.C.E., ruler of the Egyptian Twenty-fifth Dynasty

Piye (c. 769-716 B.C.E.), Shabaka's older brother and king of Kush, r. 742-716 B.C.E.

Sennacherib (c. 735-681 B.C.E.), king of Assyria, r. 704-681 B.C.E., who attempted to invade Egypt during Shabaka's reign

SUMMARY OF EVENT

In the early years of the New Kingdom (c. 1570-c. 1069 B.C.E.), Egypt conquered and annexed all of the Nubian territory to its south down to the Fourth Cataract (rapids) of the Nile River, the land called Kush. Between the eleventh and eighth century B.C.E., rival Egyptian dynasties split up the country while power weakened, resulting in a gradual withdrawal of administration from Nubia. In the region of Napata, near the Fourth Cataract, an influential family of local origin began to emerge. A strong chieftain known as Alara rose as the first in a long succession of Kushite rulers. His reign lasted twenty years, starting around 780 B.C.E. His brother Kashta followed, assuming the title "son of Ra" and embarking on a campaign of territorial expansion. He eventually was able to gain control of Lower Nubia as far north as Aswān.

Khasta's son Piye was faced with competition from Tefnakht, the ruler of Saïs, who, after overpowering Lower Egypt, began to threaten regions to the south. Piye continued the Nubian conquest of Egypt, defeating Tefnakht and capturing Memphis before returning to Napata, calling himself Lord of Two Lands. The campaigns of Piye are recorded on a stela he had installed at Gebel Barkal. Piye nonetheless chose to remain in Napata until the end of his reign, as Kushite control of Egypt slipped. When he died, his younger brother Shabaka ascended to the throne, according to the Kushite custom that allowed brothers, under certain conditions, priority over sons in the royal succession. He was married to a woman who was not a member of the female line of princesses.

Shabaka, having witnessed the rapid growth of the kingdom of Kush, sought to renew the quest to conquer Egypt. Tefnakht's son Bakenranef attempted to regain the territory captured by his father but was defeated and killed by Shabaka. Expanding on the accomplishments of Piye, Shabaka went on to subdue other rival princes and build a sizable empire that extended some 2,100 miles (3,379 kilometers) along the Nile. After establishing control over all of Egypt, he moved the capital of Kush from Napata to Thebes and assumed the title of pharaoh.

The Egyptian priest and author Manetho (third century B.C.E.) wrote an orderly account of the history of the Egyptian pharaohs that established the numbering of the dynasties. He credits Shabaka as founder of the Twenty-fifth Dynasty, although sometimes Piye is regarded as the founder of this dynasty.

The Kushite kings sought harmony between their kingdom and the people of Egypt. They brought an Egyptian style of government to their homeland. They promoted the worship of Egyptian deities, particularly the god Amen, which developed into a state cult. A temple dedicated to Amen was erected at Gebel Barkal and became the center for a powerful priesthood. Because the mountain there was already sacred in local tradition, it made an ideal location for a religious center. The Kushite kings also erected new temples at Meroë and Sanam.

At Kawa, in the northern part of Kush, Shabaka built a small temple near one from earlier times that is attributed to Tutankhamen. In the area around Thebes, he continued a plan of temple restoration and enlargement. The fourth pylon at Karnak bears an inscription describing Shabaka's restoration of the gate. At the same complex, he began work on the second pylon in front of the temple of Tuthmose III.

Shabaka strengthened his connection to Egyptian tradition and culture through the placement of his family in key leadership roles. His sister, Amenirdis, held an important religious and political position. She was given the title God's Wife of Amen at Thebes, a virgin princess and chief of the female priesthood. Her installation into this office was an important moment in the Kushite takeover of Egypt. A funerary temple was constructed for her at Medinet Habu near the temple of Ramses III. Shabaka's son, Haremakhet, became the high priest of Amen of Thebes, a post that had not been active for fifty years.

The desire to restore Egypt's ancient customs and encourage religious renewal was part of the motive for the creation of an important monument dating from Shabaka's reign: the Memphite Theology. Sometimes referred to as the Shabaka stone, it is a black basalt tablet measuring 54 by 37 inches (138 by 93 centimeters) that is now located in the British Museum in London. Though portions are damaged, the inscriptions still visible on it present an account describing Memphis as origin both of the creation of the world and of pharaonic kingship. It refers to Ptah, the deity of Memphis, as the creator god. In the first part, Shabaka is quoted as having inspected the temple of Ptah, where he found the most sacred scrolls worm-eaten. He then states how he set out to preserve those sacred words in stone. When completed, the tablet was installed in the temple of Ptah in Memphis, where it gave new prestige to the city's patron deity. The project may have been designed to create an accord with this important city, which had only recently been conquered by the Kushites.

The Kushite kings adopted many Egyptian cultural attributes, including its written language, titles, and clothing styles. At the same time, they chose to retain certain ties to their origins. They continued to use their Kushite names and were returned to their homeland for burial. They also combined the royal trappings of Egypt with their own insignia, such as the distinctive skullcap the kings of Kush had always worn. King Piye's stela at Gebel Barkal shows the god Amen presenting him with both the red crown of Lower Egypt and the skullcap of Kush.

Both the Egyptian crowns and Kushite caps were usually fitted with a diadem (royal headband) and a representation of the sacred asp called a uraeus. The Kushite headdress often had a pair of streamers hung from the back and two uraei above the forehead. The double uraeus became the symbol of the kings' sovereignty over a united Kush and Egypt.

Unlike their Egyptian counterparts, the Kushite kings wore wide armbands, anklets, bracelets, and a distinctive ram's-head pendant. Several of these pendants, depicting a ram with a sun disk between its horns, might be worn around their necks. The symbol probably dated from their ancestral Kerma culture, with its pastoralist history. Because the ram's head was also the symbol of the state god of Egypt, it served the kings well in both contexts.

Several sculptures and reliefs of Shabaka have survived. They depict him in the Kushite style with southern features. Perhaps the best example is a bronze statuette in the collection of the Athens National Museum. The king is kneeling in an offering pose. He is dressed in a short kilt and patterned belt with a buckle bearing his name. On his head is the traditional Kushite skullcap with the double uraeus in front and streamers trailing from the back. A cord around his neck has three ram's heads attached. He is shown with the characteristically straight Nubian neck and muscular torso. The face is full, with high cheekbones, prominent lips, and slightly enlarged eyes. Lines running horizontally from the sides of the nose are consistent with a detail found in many Nubian images that is known as the Kushite fold. The bronze figure, with its meticulous detail and modeling, is considered to be the best likeness of Shabaka.

In 701 B.C.E., Shabaka faced an invasion from the powerful empire of Assyria. He assigned the command of the army to his nephew Taharqa, who marched to Palestine in a defensive maneuver. However, an outbreak of the plague stopped the advance of the Assyrian forces under Emperor Sennacherib. Fragments of a clay tablet with Shabaka's royal seal and that of an Assyrian king indicate that a truce was eventually arranged.

Shabaka, along with other kings of the Twenty-fifth Dynasty—Piye, Shabataka, and Tanutamuni—is buried in the cemetery at El-Kurru near the Nile, about 10 miles (16 kilometers) downstream from Gebel Barkal. Their Egyptian-style tombs are constructed beneath narrow pyramids measuring between 26 and 36 feet (8 and 11 meters) square. There are also fourteen queens' pyramids located nearby. The importance that the kings placed on their royal chariot horses was made evident by the discovery of four rows of horse burials, the second row belonging to Shabaka. American archaeologist George Reisner and a team from Harvard University and the Boston Museum excavated the site in 1918-1919.

Significance

Following the remarkable triumphs of Piye, Shabaka advanced the dynasty of Kushite pharaohs that endured for more than eighty years. For the first and only time in history, an African power had gained control over all of Egypt. Shabaka and his successors worked to restore the glory of Egypt through traditional government, architecture, and religious orthodoxy. Most important, they brought a period of unity, economic recovery, and peace to a divided Egypt.

—Craig Lloyd

Further Reading

Adams, William. *Nubia: Corridor to Africa*. Princeton, N.J.: Princeton University Press, 1977. A detailed examination of Nubian history with a discussion of

Shabaka's reign and a chronology of the Kushite rulers. Index and bibliography.

Africa in Antiquity: The Arts of Ancient Nubia and the Sudan. 2 vols. Brooklyn, N.Y.: Brooklyn Museum, 1978. A study of Nubian arts and history that describes the rise of Shabaka and provides a number of illustrations of Shabaka as he is portrayed in sculpture. Index and bibliography.

Gaballa, Gaballa Ai. ed. *The History and Culture of Nubia*. Aswān, Egypt: Nubia Museum, 1997. A concise history of Nubia divided into significant time periods that describes Shabaka's place in the succession of Kushite kings.

O'Conner, David. *Ancient Nubia: Egypt's Rival in Africa*. Philadelphia: The University Museum, University of Pennsylvania, 1993. O'Conner provides a close look at the archaeology and history of ancient Nubia including a description of Shabaka's pyramid at El-Kurru. Index and bibliography.

Török, László. *The Kingdom of Kush: Handbook of the Napatan-Meroitic Civilization*. New York: Brill, 1997. An extensive study of the history and civilizations of Nubia, with detailed information on the Kushite kings, Shabaka's accomplishments, and his family. Tables, index, and bibliography.

Welsby, Derek. *The Kingdom of Kush: The Napatan and Meroitic Empires*. Princeton, N.J.: Markus Weiner, 1998. Welsby explores the archaeology, history, economy, arts, and architecture of the ancient kingdoms of Nubia with Shabaka's contributions. Index and bibliography.

See also: 2500-1900 B.C.E., Wawat Chiefdom Flourishes in Lower Nubia; c. 2112 B.C.E., Ur-Nammu Establishes a Code of Law; c. 1900-1527? B.C.E., Kerma Kingdom Rules Nubia; c. 1570 B.C.E., New Kingdom Period Begins in Egypt; 1069 B.C.E., Third Intermediate Period Begins in Egypt; 8th century B.C.E., Kushite King Piye Conquers Upper Egypt; c. 783-c. 591 B.C.E., Napata Kingdom Flourishes in Kush; c. 6th century B.C.E.-c. 350 C.E., Meroitic Empire Rules from Southern Egypt to the Blue Nile.

Related articles in *Great Lives from History: The Ancient World*: Piye; Sennacherib.

c. 705-330 B.C.E.
Founding and Flourishing of the Achaemenian Dynasty

Reaching its peak under the leadership of Cyrus the Great, the Achaemenid Dynasty dominated the region between India and Asia Minor.

Locale: Middle East between Turkey and India (mostly present-day Iran)

Categories: Government and politics; expansion and land acquisition

Key Figures

Achaemenes (c. 700-675 B.C.E.), founder of the Achaemenian Dynasty and its first monarch, r. c. seventh century B.C.E.

Cyrus the Great (c. 601/590-c. 530 B.C.E.), ruler who consolidated the Persian Empire, r. c. 559-c. 530 B.C.E.

Darius the Great (550-486 B.C.E.), king of the Persian Empire during the peak of its expansion, r. 522-486 B.C.E.

Summary of Event

During the fifteen hundred years between the origins of the Persian Empire c. 705 and its conversion to an Islam state in the seventh century C.E., four major dynasties ruled present-day Iran: the Achaemenids, Seleucids, Parthians, and Sāsānians. The empire reached its peak with the reigns of Cyrus the Great and Darius the Great, the most dominant of the Achaemenid rulers; during this period, the empire stretched over much of the Middle East between present-day Turkey and India.

The origins of the Achaemenid Dynasty are shrouded in mystery and myth. Even the existence of a historical Achaemenes is based on indirect evidence. The Greek historian Herodotus, writing in the fifth century B.C.E., makes reference to a Persian ruler named Teispes, "son of Achaemenes (Hakhamanish)," the eponymous ancestor of the dynasty. Later, Darius the Great named one of his sons Achaemenes, appointing him satrap in Egypt. On the Behistun inscription, carved by Darius into the side of a cliff, Darius also provides an Achaemenian genealogy that begins with Achaemenes.

At the time of the founding of the Achaemenid Dynasty, the region between the Tigris and Euphrates Rivers (Mesopotamia) was a scene of war and chaos. The area was dominated by the Assyrians, who maintained an em-

THE ACHAEMENID DYNASTY, C. 7TH CENTURY-330 B.C.E. (REIGN YEARS)

Achaemenes (c. 7th century B.C.E.)

Teispes (c. 675-c. 640)

Cyrus I (fl. 7th century B.C.E.) — Cambyses I (c. 600-559) — Cyrus the Great (c. 559-c. 530) — Cambyses II (529-522) → Darius the Great (522-486)

Ariaramnes (c. 640-c. 615) — Arsames (590-550) — Hystaspes (Vishtaspa, fl. 6th century B.C.E.) — Darius the Great (522-486)

Darius the Great (522-486)
Xerxes I (486-465)
Artaxerxes (465-423)
Darius II (424-405)
Artaxerxes II (405-359)
Artaxerxes III (359-338)
Arses (Xerxes III, 338-336)
Darius III (336-330)

pire that stretched from Egypt to much of present-day Iraq. The Parsua (Persians) existed as a series of ten to twelve Aryan (Indo-European) tribes, of which one, the Pasargadae, included a clan known as the Hakhamanish; the Greek translation gave rise to the name Achaemenes.

The only source directly describing the origins of the Persian dynasty is a work by Herodotus. According to the Greek historian, the Parsua emerged from the mountain during the eighth century B.C.E., founding a new kingdom in the region previously dominated by the Elamite Empire. Herodotus's only reference to Achaemenes is indirect, in relation to his son Teispes. Nevertheless, several sources note that Teispes was head of the royal house at the time of a revolt against Assyria by the weakened kingdom of Elam and several small kingdoms or vassal states. It is likely Teispes, the Great King in Anshan (Fars), was instrumental in establishing the dynasty within the region, following formation of an alliance with Elam.

Regardless of who actually represented the beginning of the dynasty, during the late eighth century B.C.E., the region referred to as the Land of the Medes (Madai) and Persians was one of turmoil. Not only were there periodic revolts against the Assyrian rulers, but also problems developed because of inherent differences among the people themselves. Both the Persians and the Medes, their close relations, had migrated from the steppes of Russia over a period of centuries, settling in the mountains of what was to become western Iran. It remains unclear as to which represented the dominant tribe; fighting between these peoples would continue until the region was united under Cyrus the Great.

Following the death of Teispes (c. 640 B.C.E.), it has been suggested that the kingdom was divided between his sons, with Cyrus I becoming king of Anshan and the younger Ariaramnes inheriting Parsua/Parsumash. However, the sites of Anshan and Parsua probably represent the same region north of the Persian Gulf, suggesting the younger brother was actually the ruler of a small kingdom somewhere in the region to the east. Elamite inscriptions from a later period, as well as contemporary Assyrian inscriptions, refer to Cyrus as king of the land of Parsumash, adding further confirmation to how the kingdom was divided after the death of Teispes. Little is known of the reign of Cyrus I. His son, Cambyses I, married Mandana, daughter of Astyages, the ruler of Media, in what was probably a marriage of convenience. Nevertheless, according to Herodotus, the Persians remained a vassal to the Medes.

The union of Mandana and Cambyses resulted in a son, Cyrus the Great. Cyrus was arguably the most important of the Achaemenid kings, in part because of his founding of the Persian Empire. Much of what is known of Persian history from the period is derived from inscriptions on the Cyrus Cylinder, a clay cylinder probably deposited by Cyrus in the city of Babylon after its fall. In addition to extensive political propaganda, Cyrus inscribed a description of his conquests as well as his toleration of the religious rites of the conquered peoples. There are a number of references to Cyrus in the Old Testament, in which he is explicitly called the *moshiach* (Messiah) in granting permission to the Jews to return to their lands. An additional contemporary source was the Babylonian/Nabonidus Chronicle, which recorded events over a several-hundred-year period beginning about 745 B.C.E.

Cyrus began his rule in 559 B.C.E., shortly afterward leading a revolt against his grandfather, Astyages. He defeated the Medes in two decisive battles, the last in the plain of Pasargadae (550), where he later established his capital. Herodotus notes that Cyrus captured Astyages, allowing him to survive under "house arrest" for the remainder of his life. Cyrus spent much of his reign in extending his empire and establishing the roots of Persian culture throughout the region. In 547 B.C.E., he defeated the Lydians in the plain of Sardis. Then he turned east to face the empire of Babylonia.

In 540/539 B.C.E., Cyrus began the siege of the capital, Babylon. Cyrus diverted the Euphrates River that ran outside the city, allowing his troops passage into the capital. Reference to the event is found in Daniel 5 of the Old Testament. Nabonidus, the king of Babylon, was spared and sent into exile. The fair treatment of the conquered was characteristic of Cyrus's rule. Cyrus, as well as his son Cambyses II, repaired the Babylonian temples, restoring sacred objects. He also gave permission for the Jews to return to Judaea, even providing funds for the rebuilding of the temple that had been destroyed by the Babylonians.

In 530 B.C.E., Cyrus began a campaign in the northeastern portion of his empire against Tomyris, queen of the nomadic Massagetae. By this time nearly seventy years old, Cyrus was killed in July of that year.

Cyrus was succeeded by his son, Cambyses II, often described as a tyrant. Under Cambyses, the empire reached its peak with the incorporation of Egypt. In 522 B.C.E., Cambyses died as a result of infection incurred from a fall from his horse. Leaving no male offspring, he was succeeded by Darius the Great, great-grandson of Ariaramnes, the younger son of Teispes.

Darius spent much of his reign putting down revolts in various parts of the kingdom. Among his achievements was construction of the Royal Road, a 1,700-mile (2,740-kilometer) road connecting the parts of his kingdom. It was Darius who was defeated by the Greeks at Marathon in 490. The remaining years of the dynasty were characterized by progressive decline in both culture and territory, as the Persian influence was gradually replaced by that of the Greeks. The last of the Achaemenid kings, Darius III, was defeated by Alexander the Great in campaigns during 331/330.

Significance

Cultural and social conditions established during the period of the Achaemenid rulers set the tone for much of the twenty-five hundred years of history of Persia/Iran. To a significant degree, it was during the reign of Cyrus the Great that cultural influences that continue until today were begun. By establishing an empire that consisted of much of what is now termed the Middle East, Cyrus was able to spread Persian art, writings, and even monotheism (via the Zoroastrian religion) over much of the region. Architecture that has withstood the passage of time still represents some of the most significant period art forms in existence in the region.

—Richard Adler

Further Reading

Adler, Richard. "The Achaemenid Dynasty." *Scott Stamp Monthly* 9, no. 12 (October, 1991). A history of the dynasty as depicted on stamps, including the tomb of Cyrus the Great.

Boyle, J. A., ed. *Persia: History and Heritage*. New York: Routledge, 1978. An extensive description of early Persian development and history.

Gershevitch, Ilya, ed. *Cambridge History of Iran*. Vol. 2. New York: Cambridge University Press, 1985. The definitive history of the subject.

Herodotus. *The Histories*. Translated by David Grene. Chicago: University of Chicago Press, 1988. A history of Persian and Greek civilizations.

Huart, Clement. *Ancient Persia and Iranian Civilization*. New York: Barnes & Noble, 1972. Reprint of an earlier text. Extensively illustrated.

Mackey, Sandra. *The Iranians: Persia, Islam, and the Soul of a Nation*. New York: Penguin, 1996. A history of both the Persian and Iranian periods.

Olmstead, A. T. *History of the Persian Empire*. Chicago: University of Chicago Press, 1948. Emphasizes a cultural description of the empire and its effects in the region.

Yamauchi, Edwin. *Persia and the Bible*. Grand Rapids, Mich.: Baker Books, 1990. An extensive view of ancient Persia as depicted in writings and archaeology.

SEE ALSO: 745 B.C.E., Tiglath-pileser III Rules Assyria; 701 B.C.E., Sennacherib Invades Syro-Palestine; c. 645-546 B.C.E., Lydia Rises to Power Under the Mermnad Family; c. 607-562 B.C.E., Nebuchadnezzar Creates the First Neo-Babylonian State; 547 B.C.E., Cyrus the Great Founds the Persian Empire; October, 539 B.C.E., Fall of Babylon; 520-518 B.C.E., Darius the Great Conquers the Indus Valley; 520-518 B.C.E., Scylax of Caryanda Voyages the Indian Ocean; September 17, 490 B.C.E., Battle of Marathon.

RELATED ARTICLES in *Great Lives from History: The Ancient World*: Alexander the Great; Cyrus the Great; Darius the Great; Nebuchadnezzar II; Sennacherib; Tiglath-pileser III.

701 B.C.E.
SENNACHERIB INVADES SYRO-PALESTINE

The Assyrian king Sennacherib invaded Syro-Palestine to end a rebellion against Assyrian hegemony. Though his campaign was successful, his army did not take Jerusalem but instead ended the siege of the city and withdrew.

LOCALE: The Levant, Jerusalem (now in Israel)
CATEGORY: Wars, uprisings, and civil unrest

KEY FIGURES

Sennacherib (c. 735-681 B.C.E.), king of Assyria, r. 704-681 B.C.E.
Hezekiah (c. 740-c. 687 B.C.E.), king of Judah, r. 715-c. 687 B.C.E.

SUMMARY OF EVENT

Sennacherib came to the throne of Assyria (later Mesopotamia) after his father Sargon II died in a war against the Cimmerians in 705 B.C.E. The national states subject to Assyria used the interregnum as an opportunity to rebel against Assyrian domination. Merodachbaladan (Marduk-apal-iddina) declared Babylon's independence in 704 B.C.E. The states in the west, led by Luli of Tyre (now in south Lebanon) and Hezekiah of Judah (now in Israel), followed suit. Sennacherib first dealt with Babylon (near modern Al Ḩillah, Iraq), bringing it back into the Assyrian orbit and deposing Merodachbaladan by 702 B.C.E. Sennacherib then turned his attention to the west.

Because the rebels in Syro-Palestine made no attempt to concentrate their forces against Sennacherib, he was able to face and defeat them individually. The first to fall was Tyre, in 701 B.C.E. Luli fled in the face of the Assyrian invasion, and Tyre and the cities dependent on it offered almost no resistance. In the Bible (Isaiah 23), the Hebrew prophet Isaiah derided Tyre's impotence and Luli's flight to Cyrus. After the fall of Tyre, the anti-Assyrian coalition in Syro-Palestine began to disintegrate. The Phoenician cities, the Transjordanian kingdoms, and most of the Philistine city-states submitted to Assyria. Only Ashqelon (now in Israel) and Judah refused to concede defeat, hoping Egypt's support would enable them to resist successfully.

After ending the rebellion in Tyre, Sennacherib moved down the Mediterranean coast to deal with Ashqelon. Again, the Assyrian army had little difficulty in subduing that city and its dependencies. Sennacherib deposed Sidqa, Ashqelon's king, replacing him with Sharru-lu-dari, an Assyrian sympathizer. Before Sennacherib could deal with Judah, he had to face an Egyptian army that came to aid the rebels. He repulsed the Egyptians at Eltekeh (Tell esh-Shallaf, near Yavneh, Israel), although the Egyptians were to threaten the Assyrian army again during the campaign in Judah. After the Egyptian retreat, Sennacherib led his army to Ekron (now in Israel), which submitted without a siege. Before Sennacherib began his campaign in Syro-Palestine, Padi, Ekron's king, was deposed by an anti-Assyrian faction of Ekron and sent to Jerusalem, where Hezekiah had him imprisoned. Sennacherib reinstated Padi to Ekron's throne, although it is not clear when this happened.

With Ekron neutralized, Sennacherib invaded Hezekiah's kingdom. The first town that the Assyrians took was Azekah (Tell Zakariyeh). Forty-five other towns and numerous villages in Judah were devastated in the course of the campaign because Hezekiah did not surrender. Sennacherib met significant resistance at three cities: Libnah, Lachish (Tell ed-Duweir), and Jerusalem. The Bible does not mention the fall of Lachish, but the city's fate is depicted on reliefs from Sennacherib's palace in Nineveh, as noted by scholar James B. Pritchard. While the Assyrian army was dealing with Lachish, Sennacherib sent a delegation led by his chief cupbearer (*rabshakeh*) to Jerusalem to demand the city's surrender (2 Kings 18:17-18). Sennacherib most likely wanted to end his campaign without a lengthy siege of Jerusalem that would only delay the inevitable and take Assyrian lives in the process. Certainly he knew of the steps Hezekiah undertook in preparation for an Assyrian siege. The Judaean king reorganized and refitted his army, strengthened Jerusalem's walls, made access to the city's water supply possible during a siege, and stockpiled food (2 Kings 20:20; 2 Chronicles 32:3, 5, 29, and 35:5-6).

The *rabshakeh* pointed out the futility of resistance, noting that the cities of Judah had all fallen to Assyrian might, that Egypt was in no position to offer Judah any relief, and that Jerusalem's own patron deity had abandoned it to Assyria (2 Kings 18:19-37). Because Hezekiah refused to surrender, Sennacherib probably tightened his siege on Jerusalem, boasting that he had Hezekiah imprisoned in his capital "like a bird in a cage," according to Pritchard. The siege of Jerusalem, however, did not end with the city's surrender and the deposition of its king. The Assyrians lifted their siege and withdrew.

There are two probable reasons for Sennacherib's willingness to accept something other than total victory. First, the Egyptian army repulsed by Sennacherib at Eltekeh had reorganized and had begun marching north from Gaza. Second, the Assyrian army besieging Jerusalem was seriously degraded by the effects of a contagious disease that swept through its camp. Sennacherib probably concluded that his forces were not sufficient to carry on the siege of Jerusalem and to face the Egyptians, so he decided to end his campaign. Before Sennacherib left for Nineveh, however, he exacted a heavy indemnity from Hezekiah (2 Kings 18:13-16).

The Bible and Sennacherib's annals (written on a clay prism known as the Taylor Prism) do not agree on the timing of the tribute. The Bible asserts that the tribute was given before the siege, whereas Sennacherib asserts that it was delivered to Nineveh after the siege was lifted. The Assyrian and biblical sources fail to concur on several other details of Sennacherib's campaign in Judah. This lack of consistency has led to the hypothesis that the

This drawing of a wall carving shows Sennacherib riding in his war chariot, with warriors following. (F. R. Niglutsch)

biblical and Assyrian narratives recount two different campaigns. Although both took place during the reign of Hezekiah, the "first" Assyrian advance on Jerusalem ended after the payment of tribute by Judah to Assyria. It was during a "second" Assyrian campaign in Judah that Lachish and later Jerusalem came under siege. The former fell, but the latter was relieved when the Assyrian army retreated after some disaster in its camp. The two-campaign hypothesis is best exemplified by scholar John Bright, who suggests that the second and unrecorded campaign took place c. 688 B.C.E. Supposedly Sennacherib preserved no record of the second campaign because it ended in a humiliating disaster.

The Assyrian and biblical sources will understandably differ in describing Sennacherib's siege of Jerusalem. Neither is a historical account in the modern sense of the term. Still, both can contribute to the reconstruction of the events that took place during the Assyrian campaign of 701 B.C.E. The differences in detail do not reflect two different events but rather two different perspectives on the same event. Both the Assyrian and biblical accounts claim success, and both are right to some extent. Assyrian objectives were met because Hezekiah ended his rebellion and paid tribute as a token of his submission to Sennacherib. Assyria remained dominant in all of Syro-Palestine. Still, Jerusalem did not fall, and Hezekiah was not deposed. The Judahite state and the Davidic dynasty continued to exist.

SIGNIFICANCE

Though the Assyrian siege of Jerusalem was lifted and the city spared, the rebellion cost Judah much. Besides the substantial tribute Hezekiah had to pay to Assyria, he lost effective control over a substantial part of his territory. It is likely that Judah became a city-state consisting of Jerusalem, its immediate environs, and the Judaean wilderness. Lachish was ruled by an Assyrian governor. Edomites probably infiltrated and controlled the southern portion of the Negev, and Sennacherib handed over some Judaean territory in the southwest to the Philistines.

Hezekiah remained a compliant Assyrian vassal until his death in c. 687 B.C.E. He was succeeded by his son Manasseh (r. c. 687-642 B.C.E.), whom the annals of Esarhaddon, Sennacherib's youngest son, describe as "the king of the city of Judah," reflecting the reduction of Judaean territory following Sennacherib's campaign. Manasseh's reign in Jerusalem coincided with the acme of Assyrian hegemony over Syro-Palestine. Manasseh was a loyal Assyrian vassal because political and military realities left him no other choice. He quelled dissent against his pro-Assyrian stance (2 Kings 21:16), continued to send tribute to Nineveh, and introduced Assyrian liturgical practices in the Temple of Jerusalem (2 Kings 21:2-9) to demonstrate his loyalty to his Assyrian masters.

The people of Jerusalem—especially the supporters of the Davidic dynasty—remembered the withdrawal of Assyrian forces before the gates of Jerusalem in 701 B.C.E. as a miraculous sign of the city's inviolability. When faced with a similar crisis in 587 B.C.E., Jerusalem refused to accept the seriousness of the threat that the Babylonians presented, believing that a miracle would save it from Nebuchadnezzar II, as it had saved it from Sennacherib (2 Kings 19:35). The Book of Jeremiah reflects the frustration of the prophet who tried, in vain, to lead Jerusalem to recognize the peril that the Babylonians represented.

—*Leslie J. Hoppe*

FURTHER READING

Bright, John. *A History of Israel*. 4th ed. Introduction and appendix by William P. Brown. Louisville, Ky.: Westminster J. Knox Press, 2000. The classic scholarly account of more than five hundred pages, reissued many times since its original publication in 1956. This edition offers color illustrations, maps, bibliographical references, and indexes.

Childs, Brevard S. *Isaiah and the Assyrian Crisis*. Studies in Biblical Theology 2/3. London: SCM, 1967. A study of the prophet's interaction with the royal establishment of Judah during the period of Assyrian domination of Judah.

Clements, Ronald E. *Isaiah and the Deliverance of Jerusalem: A Study of the Interpretation of Prophecy in the Old Testament*. Sheffield: JSOT Press, 1980. An analysis of Isaiah's understanding of the threat that Assyria posed to Jerusalem.

Cogan, Morton. *Imperialism and Religion: Assyria, Judah, and Israel in the Eighth and Seventh Centuries B.C.E.* Missoula, Mont.: Scholars Press, 1974. A description of the role of religion in neo-Assyrian militarism and expansionism.

Gallagher, William R. *Sennacherib's Campaign to Judah: New Studies*. Leiden: E. J. Brill, 1999. Argues that Sennacherib made one campaign to Judah and that the Assyrian and biblical sources are reliable, producing a coherent picture of the war.

Pritchard, James B. *The Ancient Near East: An Anthology of Text and Pictures*. 2 vols. Princeton, N.J.:

Princeton University Press, 1980. This set combines Pritchard's *The Ancient Near East in Pictures Relating to the Old Testament* and *Ancient Near Eastern Texts Relating to the Old Testament*, both standard resources on the subject. Includes meticulous illustrations, maps, plans.

SEE ALSO: c. 966 B.C.E., Building of the Temple of Jerusalem; c. 922 B.C.E., Establishment of the Kingdom of Israel; c. 883-c. 824 B.C.E., Second Assyrian Empire Displays Military Prowess; 8th century B.C.E., Kushite King Piye Conquers Upper Egypt; 8th century B.C.E., Scythians Drive the Cimmerians from Central Asia; 745 B.C.E., Tiglath-pileser III Rules Assyria; 664 B.C.E., Saite Dynasty Begins in Egypt; c. 607-562 B.C.E., Nebuchadnezzar Creates the First Neo-Babylonian State.

RELATED ARTICLES in *Great Lives from History: The Ancient World:* Nebuchadnezzar II; Piye; Sennacherib; Tiglath-pileser III.

c. 700 B.C.E.
HESIOD COMPOSES *THEOGONY* AND *WORKS AND DAYS*

Hesiod's composition of Theogony *and* Works and Days *signaled a departure from oral epic poetry toward set compositions by a single author.*

LOCALE: Ascra and Mount Helicon in Boeotia, central Greece

CATEGORIES: Literature; religion

KEY FIGURE

Hesiod (fl. c. 700 B.C.E.), Greek poet and author of *Theogony* and *Works and Days*

SUMMARY OF EVENT

Two of Hesiod's epic poems have survived: *Theogony* (English translation, 1728), which narrates the creation of the earth, sky, and ocean and the origin of the gods, and the later *Erga kai Emerai* (*Works and Days*, 1618), a collection of technical advice, moral instruction, and maxims about the virtues of hard work. Homer and Hesiod are often considered together as the progenitors of two divergent forms of epic poetry. Yet unlike Homer, who is believed to have lived two generations earlier and reveals nothing about himself in his poems, Hesiod does tell the reader some details about his life. His father was an unsuccessful shipping merchant from Cyme in Aeolia, on the coast of Asia Minor. Settling in Ascra, Boeotia, he fathered two sons, Hesiod and Perses. Hesiod characterizes his brother as a wastrel and a spendthrift, and accuses him of stealing the greater share of their patrimony and bribing the judges who found in his favor.

Hesiod himself was a shepherd, pasturing his sheep on nearby Mount Helicon. There, he says, he had a vision of the Muses, who appeared before him and gave him the knowledge and inspiration to compose *Theogony*. On another occasion he won first prize for a song in a singing contest in nearby Chalcis. He dedicated the prize, a tripod, to the Muses on Mount Helicon. Other stories told about Hesiod in the centuries after his death, such as winning a poetic contest against Homer, or that he seduced a young woman and was murdered by her brothers, are fiction.

Theogony, a 1022-line epic, differs from the Homeric epics in several important ways. Whereas the compositions of Homer reflect the culmination of several generations of a strong underlying oral tradition, Hesiod's work is clearly that of a single poet composing at a specific point in time. Even their subject matter differed, since Homer relates the legendary action of mortal heroes in which the gods play an important but peripheral role, whereas Hesiod deals with the creation of the gods and their relationships.

Hesiod was not the only Greek to compose a theogony (the word literally refers to the birth of the gods), but his is the only one to have survived intact. Enough fragments and citations from other theogonies remain to show that they at times differed radically, but it was Hesiod's version that became standard.

Earlier civilizations had their own theogonic stories. Some of these show definite similarities to *Theogony*, in particular the Hittite *Song of Kumarbi* and the Babylonian *Enuma Elish*. Though they precede the composition of *Theogony* by several centuries, the eighth and seventh centuries B.C.E. were a time of close contact between Greece and its neighbors in Mesopotamia and Western Asia. Even though the evidence suggests that Hesiod did not travel widely from his rural village, he did have access to stories from other lands told by visiting traders or immigrants.

Despite the parallels with other theogonic poetry, Hesiod's poem is a unified whole. It begins with the creation of Earth, Sky, and Ocean, all gods or goddesses from whom all other gods derive. They are represented as members of a family, marrying and bearing children over a series of generations. Family trees and genealogies are recounted showing their relationships with one another. Divinity extends to positive and negative forces of nature, such as Love, Victory, Strife, Sleep, and Death. More extended narration of certain myths, such as the succession myth of the gods, the creation of Pandora, or the story of Prometheus, are also featured. Hesiod's aim is to describe how his world, and humankind's lot in it, came into being.

Some years later Hesiod composed *Works and Days*, a poem of 828 lines. It, too, deals with humankind's lot in the world, but in the form of practical advice on the value of hard, honest work. Ostensibly addressing himself to his profligate brother, Hesiod exhorts Perses to change his ways and follow his advice. The poet uses myth, proverbs, and examples of divine retribution to make his point. Though scholars in the past argued that Perses was not a real person but a poetic fiction, the consensus today is that Perses was the brother of Hesiod.

Works and Days is written from the point of view of the peasant farmer, and just over one-quarter of the poem outlines the agricultural year. Hesiod advises when specific plants should be sown, and when harvested, and what jobs and repairs are best performed at different times of the year. Even in winter there is repair work to be done around the farm, which is preferable to spending the day socializing with one's friends.

Reminding Perses of their father, Hesiod suggests avoiding the seafaring life because it is financially risky and physically dangerous. Despite his distrust of the sea, he gives the seafarer sound advice, such as the best times of the year to sail, and suggests that the trader put only some of his goods on board any one ship. Hesiod continues the poem with various, disjointed recommendations about civic, social, domestic, and religious matters and concludes with a discussion of the favorable and unfavorable days of the month.

Works and Days is a valuable source for the social history of Archaic Greece. In addition, unlike most literature from ancient Greece, which reflects the views of the elite, *Works and Days* illustrates the feelings and opinions of an articulate man somewhat lower on the social scale. The realities of village life are mirrored in Hesiod's comments on the value of good neighbors and the importance of treating them fairly. Advice on the age of marriage of men and women, the necessity of choosing one's wife wisely, the ideal number of sons to raise, all illuminate the social and economic world of Archaic Greek village life.

Hesiod's personal outlook on life comes through in both poems, but particularly in *Works and Days*. He appears to have been a dour man, aware of the gods' control over human fate, disappointed by his father's lack of accomplishment, and disgusted by Perses' behavior. Nor was he proud of his polis, as an Athenian or Spartan would be proud of his. He refers to Ascra as a wretched, pitiable village, miserable in winter, hard in summer, and never good during any season. Life itself held few rewards, and it took constant, hard work to make it bearable.

In his attitude toward women Hesiod, like most Greek men, was a misogynist. Both *Theogony* and *Works and Days* relate the myth of Pandora, the first woman and the bearer of evil to humankind. Yet marriage is preferable to lonely old age and, after death, an estate divided among kinsmen. Care should be taken in choosing a wife: She should be a virgin and live nearby so that her reputation, or lack of one, will be well known. A good wife is the best thing a man can have, but a bad wife the worst.

SIGNIFICANCE

The impact of *Theogony* on Greek literature was enormous, as poets and philosophers for centuries after would express their view of the development of the world in theogonic terms. Hesiod's version of the myths of the gods became the starting point from which poets, dramatists, and mythographers would narrate their versions. *Works and Days* similarly started a trend in Greek and Latin literature, and there is a direct line of influence between the agricultural section of the poem and the Roman poet Vergil's *Georgics* (c. 37-29 B.C.E.; English translation, 1589). It was a literary form emulated by seventeenth and eighteenth century gentlemen farmers.

—*Robert Rousselle*

FURTHER READING

Hamilton, Richard. *The Architecture of Hesiod's Poetry.* Baltimore, Md.: The Johns Hopkins University Press, 1989. Hamilton shows how the digressions in Hesiod's poetry illuminate the entire poem.

Hesiod. *"Theogony" and "Works and Days."* Edited and translated by Martin L. West. New York: Oxford University Press, 1999. West provides an introduction, Greek text, and a full and thorough commentary on the poems.

Lefkowitz, Mary. "Hesiod." In *The Lives of the Greek*

Poets. Baltimore, Md.: The Johns Hopkins University Press, 1981. Classicist Lefkowitz analyzes the biographical evidence for the life of Hesiod.

Nelson, S. *God and Land: The Metaphysics of Farming in Hesiod and Virgil*. New York: Oxford University Press, 1998. Nelson argues that *Works and Days* is a unified, coherent composition rather than a collection of aphorisms and sayings.

Penglase, Charles. *Greek Myths and Mesopotamia: Parallels and Influence in the Homeric Hymns and Hesiod*. New York: Routledge, 1994. Penglase examines the influence of Sumerian and Akkadian myth on Hesiod.

West, Martin L. *The East Face of Helicon: West Asiatic Elements in Greek Poetry and Myth*. Oxford, England: Oxford University Press, 1997. Classicist West documents the parallels between Mesopotamian, Anatolian, and Jewish literature and early Greek, and identifies the avenues of transmission.

SEE ALSO: c. 750 B.C.E., Homer Composes the *Iliad*; 600-500 B.C.E., Greek Philosophers Formulate Theories of the Cosmos; c. 456/455 B.C.E., Greek Tragedian Aeschylus Dies.

RELATED ARTICLES in *Great Lives from History: The Ancient World*: Aeschylus; Hesiod; Homer.

c. 700-c. 500 B.C.E.
DORSET CULTURE EXTENDS INTO LABRADOR, NEWFOUNDLAND, AND GREENLAND

The Dorset culture appeared in the Canadian high Arctic and northwestern Greenland around 800 B.C.E., spread to Labrador by 700 B.C.E., and eventually crossed the Strait of Belle Isle into Newfoundland, where until 500 C.E. Dorset people may have been the only inhabitants.

LOCALE: Arctic, Canada, and Greenland
CATEGORY: Prehistory and ancient cultures

SUMMARY OF EVENT

The Paleo-Eskimos, or Old Eskimos, originated in the central and high Arctic regions sometime between 1000 and 500 B.C.E. and gave way to today's Neo-Eskimos, or Inuits, between 500 and 1000 C.E. In 1924 at Cape Dorset on southwestern Baffin Island, Canadian ethnologist Diamond Jenness discovered a large collection of artifacts from a previously unknown early way of life that he named the Dorset culture. No evidence exists to link the Dorset culture to modern Eskimos, and therefore, knowledge of Dorset life has to be inferred solely from archaeological evidence. All the Paleo-Eskimos may have been related to the ancestors of modern Chukchi living in northeastern Siberia, and scholar Robert McGhee conjectures a migration from Siberia across the north slope of Alaska to the eastern Arctic, Greenland, and Labrador.

McGhee points out that the earliest Paleo-Eskimo settlements between Baffin Island and the Arctic mainland date to 2,500 B.C.E. and, as a consequence of geological uplift, are now at elevations 165 feet (50 meters) above sea level. The progression of pre-Dorset camps occupies beaches 165 to 80 feet (50 to 24 meters) above today's coastline, and the regular succession of campsites from ridge to ridge parallels steady changes in artifact styles. The evidence suggests that the period of 1000 to 500 B.C.E. was a time of great changes among the Paleo-Eskimos, leading to the emergence of the Early Dorset culture around 500 B.C.E.

New artifacts (flat needles, burins for chiseling bone, chipped-stone blades with side notches) have been found in far southern Dorset camps established around 500 B.C.E. along the coast of Labrador and in Newfoundland, where the so-called Groswater Dorset culture (named for Labrador's Groswater Bay) occupied the shores around the Gulf of St. Lawrence to take harp seals on the spring ice. New knives and other implements appeared, the bow and arrow gave way to the handheld lance, and temperatures became colder. The fact that the Dorset people built winter houses of earth, boulders, skins, and driftwood implies that they were proficient at hunting sea mammals, from which they extracted oil for fuel and light. The many well-preserved Dorset villages reveal talented workers in jade, flint, and quartz with a keen aesthetic sense. Their tools were remarkably small, necessitating a variety of handles to hold them. The Dorset people—probably the Tunits described later by the Inuits—trapped fish in weirs, and they constructed lines of boulders to form lanes that guided caribou to rivers for easy slaughter.

Some of the changes found in the Dorset culture are hard to explain. Why did the Dorset people not use the bow and arrow? Why did they use gouging tools instead of drills? Why is there no evidence of dogsleds? Why did they not use kayaks? Why are the only human remains found in western Newfoundland in limestone caves? These questions are typical of the mysteries surrounding the Dorset people's everyday lives.

SIGNIFICANCE

Given the relative paucity of historical evidence, it is difficult to judge the impact of the Dorset culture during its own time and that of its successors. McGhee surmises that climatic changes may have influenced both the appearance and the disappearance of the Dorset people. Their migration southward coincided with the onset of colder temperatures, which, instead of deterring them, created the sea ice that facilitated their killing of sea mammals from the ice edge. This change in living conditions probably led, in turn, to innovations in implements for hunting and other uses. Conversely, around 600 C.E., when a warming trend that would last several centuries began, their ice-edge hunting economy would have suffered, a transition perhaps accounting for the complete disappearance of the Late Dorset culture from the Labrador and Newfoundland coasts soon after 500 C.E. At this same time, Dorset settlements expanded in the High Arctic and in northern and southwestern Greenland. On the basis of his investigation of a Late Dorset site at Brooman Point on eastern Bathurst Island, McGhee imaginatively recreated what might have happened when the Inuits, moving east, encountered the Dorset settlement and defeated its dwellers, but he could only speculate. Just when they seemed to be flourishing, building impressive longhouses and creating what McGhee called an "artistic florescence," they vanished for unascertainable reasons, and their territories were occupied by the Inuit.

—*Frank Day*

FURTHER READING

Harp, Elmer, Jr. "An Archaeological Reconnaissance in the Strait of Belle Isle Area." *American Antiquarian* 16 (1951): 203-220. Detailed and scholarly account of the Dorset culture.

_______. *Cultural Affinities of the Newfoundland Dorset Eskimo*. Bulletin 200. Hull, Quebec: National Museum of Canada, 1964. Includes history of research and discoveries.

Ingstad, Helge. *Westward to Vinland: The Discovery of Pre-Columbian Norse House-Sites in North America*. Translated by Erik J. Friis. New York: Harper & Row, 1969. Puts Dorset culture in context of Norse explorations. Richly illustrated.

Jenness, Diamond. "A New Eskimo Culture in Hudson Bay." *The Geographical Review* 15 (1925): 428-437. The article that announced Jenness's discovery of the Dorset culture.

McGhee, Robert. *Ancient Peoples of the Arctic*. Vancouver: University of British Columbia Press, 1996. Surveys the Paleo-Eskimos' history through the end of the Dorset culture. Many illustrations, sixteen pages in color. Thorough and indispensable.

_______. *Canadian Arctic Prehistory*. Hull, Quebec: Canadian Museum of Civilization, 1990. Concise, with maps and excellent illustrations.

Nagy, Murielle. "A Critical Review of the Pre-Dorset/Dorset Transition." In *Threads of Arctic Prehistory: Papers in Honour of William E. Taylor, Jr.*, edited by David Morrison and Jean-Luc Pilon. Hull, Quebec: Canadian Museum of Civilization, 1994. A concise treatment of the Dorset culture. Good bibliography.

Such, Peter. *Vanished Peoples: The Archaic Dorset and Beothuk People of Newfoundland*. Toronto: NC Press, 1978. Map of Dorset settlement sites and photographs of Dorset artifacts.

Tuck, James A. *Newfoundland and Labrador Prehistory*. Ottawa: National Museum of Man, 1976. Informative chapter on Dorset Eskimos with excellent illustrations and a map showing Dorset settlement sites.

SEE ALSO: c. 13,000-c. 7000 B.C.E., Paleo-Indian Culture Flourishes in North America; c. 8000-c. 1000 B.C.E., Archaic Indians Adapt to Warmer Climates; c. 5000 B.C.E., Aleutian Coastal Hunters Flourish; c. 5000 B.C.E.-c. 1 C.E., Red Paint Culture Flourishes in Eastern North America.

c. 700-330 B.C.E.
PHALANX IS DEVELOPED AS A MILITARY UNIT

The phalanx created the first truly cohesive unit in Western warfare and made heavy infantry supreme on the battlefield.

LOCALE: Greece and Macedonia
CATEGORIES: Science and technology; wars, uprisings, and civil unrest

KEY FIGURES

Miltiades the Younger (c. 554-489 B.C.E.), Athenian general who defeated the Persians at Marathon

Epaminondas (c. 410-362 B.C.E.), Theban general who brought new flexibility to the phalanx

Alexander the Great (356-323 B.C.E.), king of Macedonia, r. 336-323 B.C.E., who combined the phalanx with light infantry and cavalry to conquer the Persian Empire

SUMMARY OF EVENT

Although many factors help determine the characteristic military tactics of a time and place, culture and geography are certainly key among them. These were undoubtedly the two most important elements leading to the rise of the phalanx as the essential military unit among the ancient Greeks.

Quite early in their development, the inhabitants of Greece coalesced around a surprisingly large number of city-states, each of which controlled a limited portion of the Hellenic countryside. Arable lands on the slopes and hillsides were used to raise vines and olive trees for wine and oil; the relatively small amounts of flat lands were reserved for growing the cereal crops that formed the basis of the Greek diet. During the frequent wars between the city-states, it was the practice of the invader to attempt to seize the level farmland and destroy the crops, thus bringing about their opponent's eventual starvation and surrender. The natural defensive strategy was therefore to meet the invader as quickly and as close to the border as possible, defeating him in one climactic battle. Thus was born the need for quick decision in ancient Greek warfare.

Because Greece is a highly uneven land, often mountainous and with few expanses of level land—and those often narrow and hemmed in by hills and other rough terrain—even moderately sized forces could be deployed in relatively few areas. This meant that the focus on quick, decisive battle limited the type of warfare and the range of tactics that were available. Essentially it came down to the clash of two forces confined to a limited space; out of this necessity the phalanx was developed as a military unit.

The word "phalanx" itself comes from a Greek term which means, essentially, "a roller," and that is precisely what the unit was intended to do: roll over the enemy's battle line through sheer weight of mass and momentum. Throughout most of its career, the essence of phalanx warfare was to push forward until the opposing line broke; once that happened, defeat for the enemy was almost always inevitable.

The phalanx developed, apparently simultaneously throughout Greece, sometime during the eighth century B.C.E. It seems to have grown out of informal, small infantry units of citizen-soldiers armed with spears and shields. To increase their cohesiveness and impact, these units generally ranked shoulder to shoulder in a compact mass. The Greeks seemed to have found that eight ranks was the optimum depth for the spear. This length allowed at least three lines of spearpoints to project beyond the front rank, confronting the enemy with an imposing threat.

By the end of the eighth century, these troops were uniformly equipped. As citizens and landowners, however, each man was expected to purchase his own arms and armor. The primary weapon was the spear, typically 6 to 8 feet (1.8 to 2.4 meters) long and approximately 1 inch (2.5 centimeters) in diameter. It was usually made of ash or cornel wood with an iron spearhead and a bronze butt spike, and generally seems to have weighed only 2 to 4 pounds (0.9 to 1.8 kilograms). The spear was invariably held in the right hand, while the shield was grasped in the left.

Armor consisted of a helmet, breastplate, greaves (shin guards), and a round, bowl-shaped shield, which seems to have been about 3 feet (nearly 1 meter) in diameter and which may have weighed around 16 pounds (7 kilograms). It was clearly unwieldy and difficult to hold, for there are numerous references to those facts by ancient writers. Still, it seems to have offered considerable physical protection, and even greater psychological comfort, during the initial clash of lines in a phalanx battle. This shield was known in Greek as the *hoplon*, thus giving birth to the term for such a Greek soldier, a hoplite; the phalanx is hoplite warfare par excellence.

From ancient sources such as Thucydides (c. 459-c. 402 B.C.E.) and more recent archaeological evidence, hoplite warfare seems to have been highly ritualistic. Battles were often agreed to beforehand by the combatants and followed a prescribed course. This agreement was, for all practical purposes, necessary, because the phalanx was maneuverable only on fairly level ground; an army that had no wish to fight could simply withdraw into more rugged terrain. Such a shameful act, however, would have been unthinkable to the ancient Greeks. Before battle, each army offered sacrifices, followed by a ceremonial communal breakfast. Once ranged into position, the hoplites heard rousing speeches by their commanders. Then, shouting their battle cry, or *paean*, they charged.

Throughout most of phalanx warfare, this straightforward charge was the essence of the battle. As the two front lines collided, those in the front sought to find some opening through which to push their spearpoints; failing that, they resorted to a simple push of their *hoplon* against their opponent's, seeking to knock him off balance or at least force him backward.

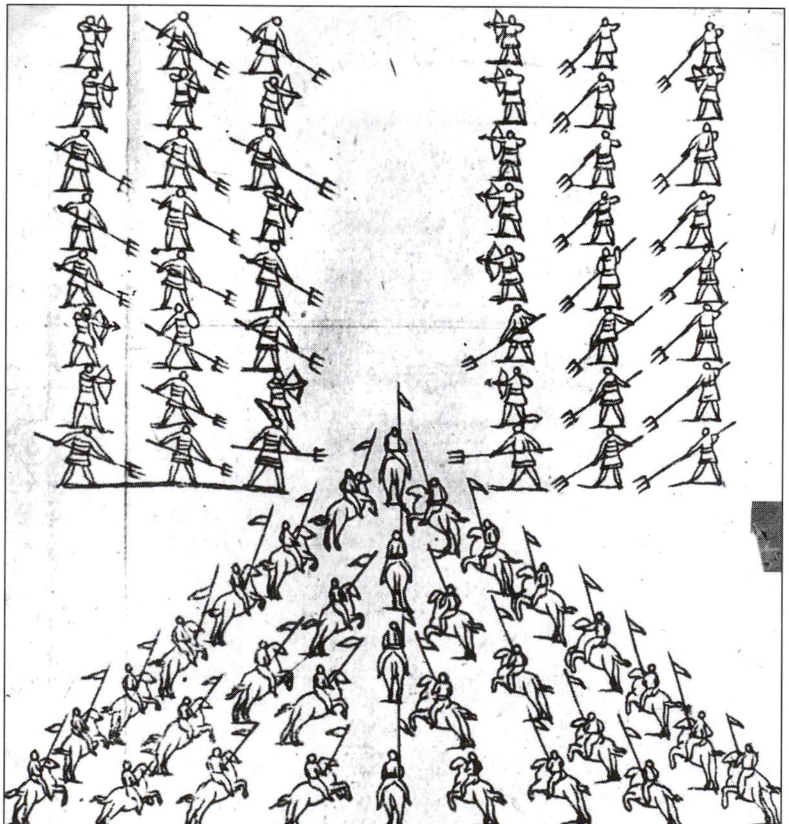
This diagram illustrates the infantry battle order followed by ancient Greeks. (Hulton|Archive)

As this struggle went on at the front, the men behind them pushed forward, adding their weight and impetus to the struggle. Eventually, one front line was pushed back until it began to break up in disorder, allowing its opponents to exploit the gap by striking into the heart of the phalanx. That was generally the point when the defeated phalanx collapsed and its men fled, many of them to be slaughtered from behind as they sought to escape. If there were any light troops or cavalry with the victorious army, this would be the time when they might be most useful in pursuing a beaten enemy. Even so, such pursuit seems to have been relatively limited, for generally speaking, the purpose of a phalanx battle was to repulse the enemy, not annihilate him.

After the battle, the ritualistic aspects of Greek warfare would continue, for there would be a truce that allowed for the exchange of the bodies of the dead, followed by their ceremonial burial on the field, often with memorials to honor them. As Homer's *Iliad* (c. 750 B.C.E.; English translation, 1611) and Sophocles' *Antigonē* (441 B.C.E.; *Antigone*, 1729) clearly show, refusal to permit proper burial was a shocking and indeed sacrilegious action.

The power of the traditional phalanx was convincingly demonstrated at the battle of Marathon (490 B.C.E.) in which Miltiades the Younger, the Athenian commander, completely defeated a Persian force overwhelmingly superior in numbers. Ancient writers remark on how shocked the Persians were by the ferocity and power of the attack of the Greek phalanx.

The brilliant Theban general Epaminondas made further refinements to the phalanx by increasing its flexibility. The ancient historian Thucydides, among others, had noticed that in battle a phalanx tended to shift to the right, as each soldier unconsciously moved toward the protection of his neighbor's shield. Others had sought to make use of this fact, but Epaminondas and the Thebans achieved the greatest flexibility and, therefore, the greatest results. At the battles of Leuctra (371 B.C.E.) and Mantinea (362 B.C.E.), Epaminondas defeated the Spartans by skillfully swinging a select force against their exposed and drifting flank.

The ultimate development of phalanx warfare came under the Macedonians, especially in the conquering army of Alexander the Great. The Macedonians, northern neighbors of the Greeks, doubled the length of the spear; this *sarissa* was held in both hands. The first five rows of *sarissas* projected beyond the front rank; the other rows held their *sarissas* at increasing angles of elevation, giving the formation a "hedgehog" effect. The Macedonians also further improved the flexibility of the phalanx and trained it to act as a unit.

Even under Alexander the Great, however, the phalanx remained essentially the same: a compact body of heavily armed spearmen, willing to form up and charge equally courageous and well-armed opponents, until the issue was decided.

SIGNIFICANCE

The phalanx was an efficient military unit in the environmental and cultural context of ancient Greece. From a military standpoint, it made the best use of its men in the typically constricted areas in which Greek battles were fought. However, the phalanx's efficiency also depended on the bravery of the soldiers within it, a characteristic encouraged by Greek culture, which admired and rewarded courage and despised and punished cowardice. In larger battlefields with more pragmatic soldiers, the unit would be less optimal.

The phalanx was also developed for a specific type of weaponry: the spear and shield. In situations in which the sword was the dominant weapon, the phalanx was too tightly packed to allow for a free sword arm, and against warriors on horseback, it was less maneuverable. In essence, phalanx warfare operated like a large, armed rugby scrum, in which the mass and momentum of the soldiers/players are the key to victory. This is in contrast to the type of heroic, single combat model of warfare depicted in the *liad* or practiced by the marauding Celtic tribes. However, whatever military unit was favored, warfare in the ancient world was often as much concerned with ritual and honor as it was with the acquisition of land and goods.

—*Michael Witkoski*

FURTHER READING

Devine, Albert. "Alexander the Great." In *Warfare in the Ancient World*, edited by General Sir John Hackett. New York: Facts On File, 1989. A brief but informative explanation of the weaponry and organization of the Macedonian phalanx.

Hanson, Victor Davis. *The Western Way of War: Infantry Battle in Classical Greece*. 2d ed. Berkeley: University of California Press, 2000. An outstanding work that presents the full range of phalanx warfare, including its psychological and sociological aspects.

Jones, Archer. *The Art of War in the Western World*. 1987. Reprint. Urbana: University of Illinois Press, 2001. An eminent scholar clearly and concisely presents the tactical nature of battle between opposing phalanxes, and explains how victories such as Leuctra came about.

Keegan, John. *A History of Warfare*. New York: Alfred A. Knopf, 1993. Within this general survey of human conflict this work presents an outstanding section on phalanx and hoplite warfare, written in Keegan's unmistakable and entirely admirable style.

Pritchett, W. K. *The Greek State at War*. 4 vols. 1965-1985. Reprint. Berkeley: University of California Press, 1997. A classic, multivolume set which provides extensive detail about all aspects of ancient Greek warfare.

Sekunda, Nicholas Victor. *The Greek Hoplite, 480-323 B.C.* Oxford, England: Osprey Publishing, 2000. A short overview of the typical armor and equipment of a Greek hoplite. Plates, illustrations.

SEE ALSO: c. 550 B.C.E., Construction of Trireme Changes Naval Warfare; 483 B.C.E., Naval Law of Themistocles Is Instituted; 480-479 B.C.E., Persian Invasion of Greece; May, 431-September, 404 B.C.E., Peloponnesian War; 336 B.C.E., Alexander the Great Begins Expansion of Macedonia.

RELATED ARTICLES in *Great Lives from History: The Ancient World*: Alexander the Great; Epaminondas; Miltiades the Younger; Thucydides.

700 B.C.E.-100 C.E.

PARACAS CULTURE DEVELOPS A SOPHISTICATED TEXTILE TRADITION

The Paracas culture, known for the production of spectacular textiles and complex mortuary rites, was an eight-hundred-year tradition in which social institutions adapted to a coastal maritime environment.

LOCALE: Paracas Peninsula and the south coast of Peru

CATEGORY: Prehistory and ancient cultures

SUMMARY OF EVENT

The term "Paracas" refers to a specific archaeological site, an art style, and an archaeological culture. The culture is found along the south coast of Peru, through six major river valleys, and in the coastal desert region of the Paracas Peninsula.

Collections of Paracas cultural material began to be amassed in the 1870's and progressed through the early twentieth century. Wilhelm Gretzer, a collector, and Max Uhle, an early archaeologist, recognized the distinctive and sophisticated nature of Paracas textiles and ceramics. A number of dilettantes, grave robbers, and professional archaeologists, including Alfred Kroeber, were involved with Paracas material culture during the early decades of the twentieth century.

It was not, however, until 1925 that the Peruvian archaeologist Julio Tello named the culture and designated a specific chronological framework emanating from his peninsular excavations. With assistant Toribio Mejia Xesspe, he began excavation in a cemetery known as the Paracas Cavernas. In 1927, yet another Paracas cemetery, the Necropolis, was excavated by Mejia, revealing more than four hundred burials, which had been interred in subterranean chambers. During the 1950's, significant advancement was made in understanding the chronology, spatial distribution, and cultural variability of Paracas by the American archaeologists John Howland Rowe, William Duncan Strong, Donald Lathrap, Edward Lanning, and Dwight Wallace. Much remains to be learned as well as resolved about the Paracas cultural experience.

The settlement pattern is imperfectly understood, as are the dynamics of political organization and social structure. The harsh, arid peninsular environment suggests that Paracas farmers faced severe problems of adaptation. Dietary remains recovered from sites suggest a wide range of marine foodstuffs, rich in protein, as well as vegetal remains, among them maize, peanuts, beans, and chili peppers. Modern archaeologists have neither resolved nor agreed upon the dynamics of the Paracas productive economy.

The two most enduring Paracas legacies are textiles and ceramics. Textile recovery has been the result of twentieth century grave robbing and scientific archaeology. Two types of burials have been recognized from the Paracas Peninsula. In the Cavernas-type burials, the dead were placed in bottle-shaped chambers constructed by digging through the sand and cutting into the underlying rock formations. Necropolis burials consist of masses of bundles, sometimes up to forty, placed in subterranean vaults. Modern archaeologists have assumed these groupings of bundles in single mortuary vaults suggest kinship affiliation. Both sexes and a wide range of ages are represented in both forms. In the burial ceremony, the unattired corpse was positioned in a flexed, or sitting, position with the knees placed against the chest and tightly wrapped with cords. The body was then wrapped in numerous layers of textiles and placed within a large basket. Grave offerings were deposited in the basket: slings, pottery, jewelry, food remains, tools, and other cultural artifacts. The entire funerary bundle was then wrapped in layers of cotton cloth. The bodies were not prepared prior to interment: The arid environment alone was responsible for their extraordinary preservation.

Certain individuals, presumably because of their elevated social status, were buried with larger quantities of grave goods than others, and also were swathed in increased layers of textiles. The textiles that were wrapped around the corpses are among the most sophisticated and complex manufactured in the prehistoric world.

Textiles were manufactured from a wide variety of fibers, including cotton, llama, and alpaca. Presumably certain yarns, such as alpaca, were imported into the arid region. The spectacular textiles were composed of a number of primary colors and many hues. Green, blue, black, red, brown, and orange were among the basic colors. Studies on dyes have been inconclusive. Chemicals and substances found in Paracas yarns include phosphorus, sulfur, sodium, indigo, and calcium. The dyeing technology remains unknown. Weaving was accomplished through twining procedures, as well as the backstrap and heddle loom.

A wide range of textile types was created by Paracas textile workers: loincloths, mantles, headbands, turbans, ponchos, and hangings and cloths of various sizes. The embroidered motifs on the fabrics represent both animals and plants found in the Peruvian coastal environment. These included marine life such as killer whales and sharks, fish, sea lions and seals; various birds, of which the condor and falcon were the most representative; mammals such as foxes, monkeys, and rodents, as well as feline images. Other images included spiders and reptiles such as the boa constrictor. Many images are fantastic and exotic: curved-fin fish, creatures with fishlike appendages, and some with birdlike features. Embroidered figures occasionally are depicted carrying human trophy heads. Plants and vegetal products are occasionally depicted on textiles: beans or complex plant/animal figures. Another prominent image is known as the Oculate Being, a figure found in various forms but always with large eyes. Cultural influence from the highland center of Chavín de Huantár is apparent in the representations of the Staff God found on cotton textiles. The Staff God is depicted as a humanlike figure with claws and a three-point mouth. Other motifs include supernatural figures and geometric designs. Scholars have suggested that the Paracas textiles provide a window into understanding the early Peruvian calendrical system. Solar and lunar cycles, and the movements of stars and constellations have been interpreted on an embroidered mantle.

The Paracas ceramic tradition includes both polychrome and monochrome examples. Polychrome wares, particularly libation vessels, were short with single and double spouts. Bowls were constructed into varied shapes without the benefit of a potter's wheel. Designs on monochrome ware were incised; after firing they were painted with brightly pigmented colors. Ceramic motifs included felines, birds, geometric design, dots, and vertical stripes.

Paracas architecture, both domestic and civic or religious, remains imperfectly understood. Mound structures of adobe mud brick, with courts and walls, have been recognized in the Chincha Valley. Artifacts retrieved from Paracas sites include items of daily use such as shells, stone tools, food remains, bone needles, wood and bone panpipes, and fragments of pottery.

SIGNIFICANCE

The Necropolis burials reflect social stratification within Paracas society. These were high-status individuals who were entombed with spectacular textiles. The leadership pattern that evolved on the Peruvian south coast remains unknown. It may have been a highly developed regional chiefdom or the early stages of a formative state. It has been suggested that Paracas burials were transported to the coast for interment from an inland locale. These were a sophisticated people who practiced skull deformation, presumably to provide visible recognition of elevated status. Skull trepanation to alleviate internal pressure or pain was also practiced and testifies to the culture's level of medical knowledge. The textiles, however, are an enduring memorial to a highly complex and somewhat mysterious archaeological culture.

A major dilemma since the 1930's has been tomb looting for textiles, which are then sold to collectors in Peru and elsewhere. This is enormously detrimental to modern archaeology. The irreversible destruction of the archaeological record in an effort to retrieve only the high-quality textiles retards the progress of cultural reconstruction.

—Rene M. Descartes

FURTHER READING

Atwood, Roger. "Guardians of the Dead." *Archaeology* 56, no. 1 (2003): 42-49. Discusses the ways in which modern Peruvians are protecting their archaeological heritage.

Burger, Richard L. *Chavín and the Origins of Andean Civilization*. New York: Thames and Hudson, 1995. An important study of archaeological culture which influenced Paracas development. Appendix and bibliography.

Gundrum, Darrell S. "Fabric of Time." *Archaeology* 53, no. 2 (2000): 46-51. A compelling discussion which offers evidence on the evolution of Peruvian calendrics.

Moseley, Michael E. *The Incas and Their Ancestors: The Archaeology of Peru*. Rev. ed. New York: Thames and Hudson, 2001. A modern reconstruction of Peruvian prehistory, which places the Paracas within an overall cultural and chronological context. Bibliography.

Paul, Anne. *Paracas Ritual Attire: Symbols of Authority in Ancient Peru*. Norman: University of Oklahoma Press, 1990. An in-depth analysis which suggests that the Paracas textiles convey information on the social, religious and political institutions, in addition to Paracas cosmology.

________. "The Use of Color in Paracas Necropolis Fabrics: What Does It Reveal About the Organization of Dyeing and Designing?" *National Geographic Research* 6, no. 2 (1990): 7-21. Discusses various aspects of the technology which produced the Paracas textiles.

_______, ed. *Paracas Art and Architecture: Object and Context in South Coastal Peru*. Iowa City: University of Iowa Press, 1991. A collection of nine articles on what is known and controversial on Paracas culture. Bibliography.

Paul, Anne, and Solveig Turpin. "The Ecstatic Shaman Theme of Paracas Textiles." *Archaeology* 39, no. 5 (1986): 20-27. Discusses the embroidered image of the shaman on textiles.

Wallace, Dwight T. "The Process of Weaving Development on the Peruvian South Coast." In *The Junius B. Bird Pre-Columbian Textile Conference, 1979*, edited by Ann Pollard Rowe, E. P. Benson, and A. L. Schaffer. Washington, D.C.: Textile Museum and Dumbarton Oaks. A discussion of the evolution of Paracas weaving techniques.

SEE ALSO: c. 5800-c. 3700 B.C.E., Chinchorro Inhabit the Peruvian and Chilean Coasts; c. 2500 B.C.E., Construction of Monumental Architecture at Caral in Peru; c. 900-c. 200 B.C.E., Chavín de Huántar Is Peru's Urban Center; c. 500 B.C.E.-c. 700 C.E., Zapotecs Build Monte Albán; 200 B.C.E.-200 C.E., Nasca Lines Drawn in Desert Near Coast of Peru; 200-800 C.E., Lima Culture Flourishes on the Central Andean Coast.

c. 700 B.C.E.-c. 500 C.E.
MOUND BUILDERS RISE IN OHIO VALLEY

The earliest architects in North America built elaborate burial mounds in the Ohio Valley.

LOCALE: Valleys and tributaries of the Ohio River
CATEGORIES: Architecture; prehistory and ancient cultures

SUMMARY OF EVENT

When a large number of burial mounds were found in the Ohio River drainage and other parts of eastern North America in the nineteenth century, the ancestors of native North Americans seemed an unlikely source for their grandeur to the European mind. Various non-Indian mound builders were hypothesized: the lost tribes of Israel, the Vikings, and other Old World groups. The oversight of Native Americans is surprising, given the high culture developed by the Native Americans in Mexico and Peru. In fact, other hypotheses suggested that the Mound Builders were an offshoot of, or ancestral to, these Middle American cultures, but few explanations allowed for a relationship to North American Indians. Late in the nineteenth century, however, careful studies by the Smithsonian Institution's Bureau of Ethnology demonstrated that the mounds were built by ancestors of the historic North American tribes.

Although it is not yet possible to determine how the builders of such elaborate structures, presumably sedentary agriculturalists of high culture, developed, or how they gave rise to the more mobile, and seemingly less highly cultured, natives encountered by European pioneers, there is much known about the Mound Builders, and reasonable hypotheses for their origin and relationship to the historic Indian tribes have been developed. Most evidence suggests that the original natives of North and South America were members of Siberian tribes that crossed the Bering Strait from Siberia to Alaska some time after 13,000 B.C.E. This was during the early stages of the last glacial retreat, when the Bering Strait was dry land. These tribes were big-game hunters who moved south into North, Central, and South America as the ice sheets melted. These people, called Paleo-Indians, moved into the eastern part of North America and came to live in sparse, wide-ranging populations in the forests that developed there after the glacier melted.

Archaeologists recognize a second Native American culture, the Archaic, beginning about 6000 B.C.E. Directly descended from Paleo-Indians, the Archaic Indians are thought to have given rise to the Mound Builders around 700 B.C.E. Some Late Archaic woodland groups buried their dead in small, natural hills, and a few built small burial mounds, the presumed progenitors of the more elaborate burial mounds built by the Woodland Indians. The larger burial mounds are widespread throughout eastern North America but are centered in the Ohio River drainage.

The earliest of the Ohio River Mound Builders were the Adena and are thought to have lived between 700 B.C.E. and 200 C.E. Their culture is characterized by the development of fiber-tempered pottery, domestication of several kinds of native plants, and the development of elaborate rituals and practices for burying their dead, including the mounds in which they were buried. They also worked stone to make pipes and various ornaments. In addition to cultivating plants, they gathered wild plant products and hunted available animals. They used a spear-throwing device called an atlatl (developed by Archaic or late Paleo-Indians) to produce greater flight speed in their spears. They added burials to individual mounds through time and were more sedentary than their Archaic predecessors. There is evidence that trading networks developed between the Adena people and contemporaneous American Indian cultures.

The Adena gave rise to the Hopewell culture, which was also centered in the valleys of the Ohio River and its tributaries. The Ohio Hopewell culture is recognized from around 100 B.C.E. until about 400 or 500 C.E. The Hopewell tradition is characterized by advanced pottery production and stoneworking, more intensive cultivation of native plants, some cultivation of corn (*Zea mays*, ultimately obtained from Mexico), and more elaborate funeral procedures and burial mounds.

Although corn was grown by the Hopewell people, it was not the staple it became in Middle American and Mississippian cultures. Instead, corn seemed to be grown more for symbolic and religious ceremonies. There is some anthropological evidence that the Hopewell people's more diversified diet, based on the cultivation of several native plant species and supplemented by hunting and gathering, produced a healthier population than did the corn-intensive diet of the Mississippians.

The Hopewell Indians also developed vast, nearly continent-wide trading networks. This trade may have been associated with another cultural development that differentiates the Hopewell from the Adena. Researchers have hypothesized that some Hopewell men obtained privileged positions in society because of their trading skill and trade contacts. These men were buried with more elaborate material goods and in larger and more complex mounds than were other members of the population. As a result, Hopewell burials suggest a class structure not seen in the more egalitarian Adena burials.

Adena and Hopewell mounds were built by people carrying baskets full of dirt from a source region, called a borrow pit, and depositing the dirt on the growing mound. Large mounds with many burials were built in stages, with one set of burials superposed on an earlier group. Many artifacts, presumably prized possessions and tools needed for the next life, were buried with the dead. More of these are found in Hopewell burials than in Adena burials. The Hopewell differentiation of class, and contrasting Adena egalitarianism, are hypothesized on the basis of such artifacts and specific conditions of the burials.

Hopewell characteristics are all elaborations of Adena characteristics. It is impossible to determine the point in time at which the Adena culture ended and the Hopewell began; instead, there is a lengthy transition period. Clearly, the Hopewell tradition is a continuation of the Adena culture.

The Hopewell culture peaked in the Ohio River Valley around 200 C.E., and their mound-building activities, at least, disappeared between 400 and 500 C.E. Numerous hypotheses have been proposed for the decline of Hopewellian peoples, at least as Mound Builders. The theories range from an environmental catastrophe, brought on by larger population concentrations and intensive agriculture, to changes in trade balances that brought an end to the Hopewell people's strategic central position between the northern and southern and between the eastern and western sources of raw materials and finished goods.

The last North American mound-building culture, the Mississippian, was centered along the Mississippi River at Cahokia, where East St. Louis, Illinois, now stands. It developed around 700 C.E. and flourished until after 1500. Adena and Hopewell mounds were primarily burial mounds, but many Mississippian mounds were platforms on which temples, houses, and other structures were built. Many scholars believe that these Mississippian Mound Builders were descendants of the Hopewell through intermediates who, for unknown reasons, abandoned mound-building activities. Many also believe that the Mississippians were directly ancestral to the Cherokee, Sioux, and other historic American Indian tribes. Some researchers posit that Hopewellians were ancestral to the Iroquois.

SIGNIFICANCE

The Ohio Valley Mound Builders maintained a developing culture for more than a millennium and played a central role in North American prehistory for much of that time. Their descendants gave rise to the prehistoric Mississippian culture and to historic Indian tribes. In addition, North American archaeology traces its professional roots to the exploration of their mounds.

—*Carl W. Hoagstrom*

FURTHER READING

Fagan, Brian M. *Ancient North America: The Archeology of a Continent.* 2d ed. New York: Thames and Hudson, 1995. Describes the Mound Builders and their place in prehistory. Chapter 2 gives a brief history of the European Mound Builder hypothesis. Illustrations, maps, index, and bibliography.

Shaffer, Lynda Norene. *Native Americans Before 1492: The Moundbuilding Centers of the Eastern Wood-*

lands. Armonk, N.Y.: M. E. Sharpe, 1992. Explores Mound Builder cultures and the interactions and interrelationships between those cultures and other Native American cultures. Illustrations, maps, index, and bibliography.

Silverberg, Robert. *The Mound Builders*. Athens: Ohio University Press, 1970. Discusses the hypothesis that the Mound Builders were European, and its demise. Also describes the American Indian Mound Builder cultures. Illustrations, maps, index, and bibliography.

Snow, Dean R. *The Archaeology of North America*. New York: Chelsea House, 1989. Outlines the prehistory of the Mound Builders. Chapter 1 covers the Mound Builder mystery and its importance in American archaeology. Illustrations, maps, index, glossary, and bibliography.

Thomas, Cyrus. *Report on the Mound Explorations of the Bureau of Ethnology*. 1894. Reprint. Washington, D.C.: Smithsonian Institution Press, 1985. Describes the Bureau of Ethnology's mound work. The introduction to the 1985 edition adds historical perspective. Illustrations, maps, and index.

Webb, William S., and Charles E. Snow. *The Adena People*. Knoxville: University of Tennessee Press, 1974. Descriptions of the mounds, pottery, pipes, and other artifacts of the Adena and Hopewell people. Illustrations, maps, index, and bibliography.

Woodward, Susan L., and Jerry N. McDonald. *Indian Mounds of the Middle Ohio Valley: A Guide to Adena and Hopewell Sites*. Blacksburg, Va.: McDonald and Woodward, 1986. A guide to Adena and Hopewell sites that can be visited by the public. Illustrations, maps, index, and lists of pertinent topographic maps and publications.

SEE ALSO: c. 18,000-c. 11,000 B.C.E., Bering Strait Migrations; c. 1800-c. 700 B.C.E., Poverty Point Culture Builds Earthworks; c. 1000 B.C.E.-c. 100 C.E., Adena Mound Builders Live in North America; c. 200 B.C.E.-c. 500 C.E., Hopewell People Construct Earthworks.

664 B.C.E.
SAITE DYNASTY BEGINS IN EGYPT

After defeating the Kushites and Assyrians, Psamtik I unified Egypt and founded the Twenty-sixth Dynasty in Egypt, a time of relative peace and cultural renaissance.

LOCALE: Saïs, Egypt
CATEGORIES: Government and politics; wars, uprisings, and civil unrest

KEY FIGURES

Necho I (fl. seventh century B.C.E.), Egyptian vassal of Assyria, r. c. 672-664 B.C.E.
Tanutamuni (fl. seventh century B.C.E.), Kushite pharaoh, final ruler of the Twenty-fifth Dynasty, r. 664-656 B.C.E.
Psamtik I (c. 684-610 B.C.E.), pharaoh of Egypt, founder of the Twenty-sixth (Saite) Dynasty, r. 664-610 B.C.E., son of Necho I
Mentuemhat (fl. seventh century B.C.E.), mayor of Thebes
Nitocris (fl. seventh century B.C.E.), daughter of Psamtik I

SUMMARY OF EVENT

The Saite Dynasty (664-525 B.C.E.), the Twenty-sixth Dynasty of Egypt, originated in the conflicts between the Kushite pharaohs of the Twenty-fifth Dynasty and the Assyrian Empire, according to the historian Manetho. Toward the end of the Twenty-fifth Dynasty, the Kushite rulers reversed their earlier conciliatory stance toward the rising might of Assyria and assisted the kingdoms of Syro-Palestine in their efforts to cast off the Assyrian yoke. This Egyptian interference provided the pretext for the Assyrian king Esarhaddon (r. 680-669 B.C.E.) to attempt an invasion of Egypt in 674 B.C.E., but he was successfully repelled by the Kushite ruler Taharqa (r. 690-664). However, in 671 B.C.E., Esarhaddon managed to capture Memphis and drive Taharqa into the south.

Esarhaddon's successor, Ashurbanipal (r. 669-627 B.C.E.), expanded Assyrian control of Egypt during his invasion in 667/666 B.C.E., which penetrated all the way to Thebes and drove Taharqa back to his capital Napata, far in the south. Vassal rulers were then established in the Nile Delta, including Necho I, ruler of Saïs, a descendant of Tefnakht and Bakenranef, rulers of Saïs who had fought against the Twenty-fifth Dynasty pharaoh Piye (r. 742-716 B.C.E.). Despite Necho's family history, he entered into an alliance with Taharqa against the Assyrians and was taken with his son Psamtik I (who is called

Nabushezibanni in the Assyrian documents) to Nineveh by Ashurbanipal. For unknown reasons, Necho I was the only Delta ruler spared execution, and he was returned to Egypt and given control over Saïs and Memphis, while Psamtik I ruled over Athribis.

Meanwhile, in the south, Tanutamuni succeeded Taharqa. As the well-known Dream stela reports, Tanutamuni received a prophetic dream that he was destined to rule all of Egypt, and soon after his accession, he captured Thebes, Middle Egypt, and Memphis. During the battles between the Delta rulers and Tanutamuni, Necho I was killed (664 B.C.E.). This new threat from Kush brought Ashurbanipal back to Egypt, and he reconquered Memphis and sacked Thebes in 663 B.C.E. with the aid of Psamtik I and northern Egyptian troops. Psamtik I returned to Saïs again as an Assyrian vassal, but he quickly asserted dominance within the Delta and was probably in control of most of northern Egypt by 660 B.C.E.

By 658 B.C.E., Psamtik I had expelled the Assyrians and created an independent Egyptian state under the Twenty-sixth Dynasty. Several factors allowed Psamtik to take control. First, he allied himself with Gyges of Lydia, giving him access to Ionian and Carian mercenaries, the "bronze men of the sea" as reported by the Greek historian Herodotus. Additionally, Assyria at this time faced internal instability and pressure from its eastern and northeastern neighbors and therefore was unable to commit military forces to far-off Egypt. Finally, the Assyrians may have known that Egypt would become their ally once independent, which did indeed happen by the end of the reign of Psamtik I, when the Egyptian pharaoh sent troops to help the Assyrians in their struggles with the Neo-Babylonians.

After the battles with the Kushites and the Assyrians, the fifty-four-year reign of Psamtik I, by far the longest of the Saite Dynasty, ushered in a long period of stability. Except for brief skirmishes with the Scythians and Libyans, the remaining reign of Psamtik I was relatively peaceful. During this time, Egypt developed strong ties with other powers in the eastern Mediterranean basin and became especially reliant on Greek mercenaries. To guard the eastern edge of the Delta, Psamtik I constructed fortresses at Daphnae (now Tall al-Dafana) and other sites in the eastern Delta and western Sinai. Archaeological evidence from these sites indicates that they may have had garrisons of foreign mercenaries. The trading city of Naucratis in the central Delta—a site that became a center for Greek settlers in Egypt—was probably founded late in the reign of Psamtik I.

From 656 B.C.E., Psamtik I also gained control of Upper Egypt (at this time still dating documents to the Kushite pharaoh Tanutamuni), not through conquest, but by means of skillful diplomacy. To secure their own rule over Thebes and Upper Egypt, the Kushite pharaohs had resurrected the office of the god's wife of Amen, a high priestess. As the well-known Adoption stela reports, Psamtik I had his daughter Nitocris adopted by the god's wife Shepenwepet II and her already adopted successor Amenirdis II (both daughters of Kushite pharaohs) so that she could be the next god's wife of Amen. Psamtik I's success in Upper Egypt was also caused by the cooperation of Mentuemhat, the mayor of Thebes who was the de facto ruler of Upper Egypt during the transition between the Twenty-fifth and Twenty-sixth Dynasties and the Assyrian invasions.

TWENTY-SIXTH (SAITE) DYNASTY, 664-525 B.C.E.

Ruler	*Reign*
Psamtik I	664-610
Necho II	610-595
Psamtik II	595-589
Apries	589-570
Ahmose II	570-526
Psamtik III	526-525

Note: Dynastic research is ongoing; data are approximate.

In addition to his political role, Mentuemhat occupies an important position in the art history of the Saite Dynasty because his large tomb on the west bank of Thebes is one of the best-preserved tombs of the period, and his statues are excellent examples of Saite sculpture. Although the Egyptians did not use the term renaissance for the beginning of the Twenty-sixth Dynasty, the artistic production that marked its start has caused scholars to call the period the Saite Renaissance. Saite art is characterized by archaistic tendencies and the production of exact replicas of earlier art, especially Old Kingdom reliefs. Sculpture of the period also draws on Old, Middle, and New Kingdom models but often mixes elements from different periods to create entirely new styles. The sculpture of the Twenty-sixth Dynasty is distinctive in its use of hard stones such as granite and quartzite and the highly polished surfaces of the statues.

The Saite Dynasty was also a time of prolific temple construction, especially during the prosperous and peaceful reign of Psamtik I. Almost all the major monuments of the Twenty-sixth Dynasty were built in the

Delta, where very few archaeological sites have remained intact (in contrast to those in Upper Egypt). Thus, it is difficult to reconstruct the architectural style of the Saite Dynasty, but the limited evidence available suggests that many of the innovative features of later Ptolemaic temples can be traced back to the seventh century B.C.E., most notably composite columns. The recent redating of the earliest composite columns to the Twenty-sixth Dynasty indicates that early Greek Corinthian columns were influenced by Egyptian columns, and not vice versa as was previously assumed.

SIGNIFICANCE

The Saite Dynasty, as one of the last independent Egyptian dynasties, influenced later attempts to reestablish Egyptian independence after the First and Second Persian periods. From the Saite Dynasty onward, Egyptian independence was closely linked to foreign mercenaries; these mercenaries enabled Psamtik I's successors to briefly control Syro-Palestine, and foreign naval forces in addition to infantry were recruited by Twenty-sixth Dynasty pharaohs. However, the resulting conflicts with local Egyptian *machimoi* (warrior class) would become a major problem for the Saites, causing civil war during the reign of Apries (r. 589-570) and the subsequent usurpation by Ahmose II (r. 570-526). The establishment of Naucratis paved the way for increased trade interactions between Greece and Egypt. The Delta origin of the Saite rulers also led to the adoption of the northern Demotic (as opposed to the southern abnormal hieratic) as the official administrative script. This Demotic script survived until the fifth century, when Coptic was adopted as the writing system of Christian Egypt.

—*Colleen Manassa*

FURTHER READING

Arnold, Dieter. *The Temples of the Last Pharaohs*. New York: Oxford University Press, 1999. An analysis of Egyptian architecture during the Late period, including its influence on Greece.

Boardman, John. *The Greeks Overseas*. London: Thames and Hudson, 1980. Discusses the development of Naucratis and other Greek settlements in Egypt, along with Egyptian influences on Greek art and architecture.

Bothmer, Bernard. *Egyptian Sculpture of the Late Period, 700 B.C. to A.D. 100*. Brooklyn, N.Y.: The Brooklyn Museum, 1960. Catalogue of an exhibit with a discussion of Saite Dynasty art.

Der Manuelian, Peter. *Living in the Past: Studies in the Archaism of the Egyptian Twenty-sixth Dynasty*. London: Kegan Paul International, 1994. Includes translations of Saite historical texts.

Lloyd, Alan. In *Ancient Egypt: A Social History*. New York: Cambridge University Press, 1983. The chapter "The Late Period" addresses the Saite Dynasty.

Myœliwiec, Karol. *The Twilight of Ancient Egypt*. Ithaca, N.Y.: Cornell University Press, 2000. Historical overview with discussion of primary sources.

SEE ALSO: 8th century B.C.E., Kushite King Piye Conquers Upper Egypt; c. 783-c. 591 B.C.E., Napata Kingdom Flourishes in Kush; 745 B.C.E., Tiglath-pileser III Rules Assyria; 701 B.C.E., Sennacherib Invades Syro-Palestine; c. 645-546 B.C.E., Lydia Rises to Power Under the Mermnad Family; 547 B.C.E., Cyrus the Great Founds the Persian Empire.

RELATED ARTICLES in *Great Lives from History: The Ancient World*: Ashurbanipal; Cyrus the Great; Piye; Sennacherib; Psamtik I; Tiglath-pileser III.

c. 645-546 B.C.E.
LYDIA RISES TO POWER UNDER THE MERMNAD FAMILY

The Mermnad family brought Lydia to a state of power and prosperity before being conquered by Cyrus the Great.

LOCALE: Sardis, capital of Lydia in Asia Minor (now near Izmir, Turkey)
CATEGORIES: Expansion and land acquisition; government and politics

KEY FIGURES

Gyges (c. 705-c. 645 B.C.E.), the founder of the Mermnad Dynasty, r. c. 680-c. 645 B.C.E.
Ardys (d. 600 B.C.E.), son of Gyges, r. c. 645-600 B.C.E.
Sadyattes (d. 588 B.C.E.), son of Ardys, r. c. 600-588 B.C.E.
Alyattes (d. c. 560 B.C.E.), son of Sadyattes, r. c. 588-c. 560 B.C.E.
Croesus (c. 595-546 B.C.E.), son of Alyattes, king of Lydia, and last king of Mermnad Dynasty, r. c. 560-546 B.C.E.
Cyrus the Great (601/590-c. 530 B.C.E.), king of Persia, r. c. 559-c. 530 B.C.E., conqueror of Lydia who ended the rule of the Mermnad Dynasty

SUMMARY OF EVENT

The best written source on this period is the Greek historian Herodotus, who gives an account of each Lydian king of the Mermnad Dynasty, telling famous anecdotes about each king, especially Gyges and Croesus, the first and last dynasts. Although his narration provides lengths of rule that cannot be acceptable for each king, especially for Ardys and Alyattes, to whom he gives lengths of reigns of 49 and 57 years respectively, Herodotus provides a better understanding of events that can also be reconstructed in the archaeological excavations, such as the siege of Sardis by Cyrus the Great in 546 B.C.E.

Gyges, who founded the Mermnad Dynasty around 645 B.C.E., is known from Herodotus's tale, which reveals how he chose to take the throne after the former king Candaules compelled him secretly to view his beautiful queen naked in her tent. When the queen discovered Gyges, she forced him to choose between losing his life to her guards and killing her husband and taking his place as king. Gyges wisely chose the latter option of survival and later expanded the Lydian kingdom into the territories of Miletus and Smyrna. He is also famous for his gifts of gold and silver to Delphi, becoming the first barbarian to make such gifts after Midas, son of Gordius of Phrygia. His gifts were most likely to derive from the Delphic Oracle's confirmation of him as king (although the Oracle "predicted" his dynasty would last for five generations), and these gifts to Delphi were known henceforth as Gygian.

Ardys was the son of Gyges and ruled Lydia for some decades after his father. Herodotus maintains that Ardys expanded military campaigns against Priene and the Milesians, but his kingdom was attacked by the Cimmerians, who sacked nearly all of Sardis. His rule was followed by that of his son, Sadyattes, who drove the Cimmerians out of Asia with the help of Cyaxares and the Medes and continued the long-term war against the Milesians. According to Herodotus, Sadyattes often left the Milesian buildings intact but destroyed the crops and trees. His aim reportedly was not to drive the Milesians away but to let them continue living in the area and produce more crops and goods so that he would have more to plunder in the next campaign.

Alyattes, the son of Sadyattes, continued the Milesian wars. He burned down a temple of Assesian Athena in Milesia but became sick and sent a request to Delphi for wisdom. Herodotus said the Delphic Oracle then replied that no answer would come until the temple was rebuilt. Alyattes tried to negotiate a truce with Thrasybulus, king of the Milesians, that would be favorable to Lydia, but the king tricked him into believing that the Milesians had great supplies of wheat and food. Thinking the Milesians would be able to withstand a long siege, Alyattes made peace quickly and then built two temples instead of one. Herodotus claimed Alyattes recovered from his sickness and was the second Lydian to give gifts to Delphi, vessels made of silver and inlaid steel in gratitude. The tomb of Alyattes at the royal necropolis of Bin Tepe is famous for the still extant great marker over the tumulus.

Croesus is the most famous of the Mermnad kings. He attacked Ephesus and subdued all the Ionian and Aeolian states of Asia Minor, which he ruled. His legendary wealth—which reportedly made him the richest king in his area—was such that not only was he the first to mint coins, which portrayed the Lydian lion struck in electrum, an alloy of gold and silver, but also he was proud of and confident in his wealth and thought it made him the happiest man on earth. Solon, the self-exiled Athenian lawgiver, was traveling through Asia Minor when Croesus wanted to impress him with his happiness derived from material wealth. Solon was unimpressed and said that a

KINGS OF THE MERMNAD DYNASTY, C. 680-546 B.C.E.

Ruler	*Reign*
Gyges	c. 680-c. 645
Ardys	c. 645-600
Sadyattes	c. 600-588
Alyattes	c. 588-c. 560
Croesus	c. 560-546

man's happiness could only be measured at death and that a poor man could live a long life happily in good health until the end with children of whom he could be proud.

Fearing the Persian rise under Cyrus the Great, Croesus sent messengers to inquire at Delphi and also dedicated sacrifices on a pyre with three thousand animals and an immense treasure of gold and silver couches, golden goblets, purple mantles, and vests. From this pyre, Croesus melted down the equivalent of several tons of gold and silver into ingots, which he sent to Delphi in the shape of a lion statue (the symbol of Lydia) along with immense gold and silver bowls, silver chests, a gold statue of a female around 4.5 feet (1.4 meters) tall, his wife's gold and silver filigree necklaces, and belts inlaid with gems. As Herodotus related, the Delphic Oracle replied in typical ambiguity that if Croesus attacked the Persians "he would destroy an empire"; he did not realize that it would be his own. Croesus battled evenly against Cyrus and the Persians in Cappadocia and in Sinope on the Black Sea, then disbanded his mercenary army, thinking himself safe. However, Cyrus continued to advance with alacrity and took Lydia, even with its Spartan allies, using camels in the battles against Croesus's vaunted cavalry because horses feared camels.

Perhaps Croesus's late-acquired wisdom showed when, in 546 B.C.E., Cyrus conquered Sardis after a fourteen-day siege. After a storm put out the flames rising from Croesus's self-made pyre, Cyrus removed Croesus from the smoldering pile. Croesus, remembering the words of Solon, asked Cyrus what his men were doing. Cyrus pointed out to Croesus that sackers were burning Croesus's capital city. Croesus looked at burning Sardis and replied, "No, it's your city," which made Cyrus stop the complete sacking of Sardis after conquering Lydia.

SIGNIFICANCE

One of the most significant measures of Lydian wealth is that this kingdom under Croesus is generally accepted as the first to mint coins of precious metal, especially the electrum (gold and silver), a small elliptical ingot stamped with the Lydian lion seal. The Lydians were also instrumental in extending greater Greek influence to Asia Minor, such as through the counsel of Solon. Several of their wealthy kings, including Gyges and Croesus, gave magnificent gold gifts to Delphi. Another compelling influence of Lydian history is seen in the narration of Herodotus, which brings to life customs of ancient Lydia for his Greek readers. These famous stories of Gyges and Croesus influenced subsequent Western literature and history and are still memorable today.

—*Patrick Norman Hunt*

FURTHER READING

Greenewalt, Crawford H., and Marcus L. Rautman. "The Sardis Campaigns of 1994 and 1995." *American Journal of Archaeology* 102, no. 3 (1998): 469-505. Extensive report of excavating the Lydian capital of Sardis, especially the archaic walls of the Mermnad Dynasty and the Bin Tepe funeral mounds of the Lydian royal necropolis. Includes studies on the tumulus of Alyattes.

Guralnick, Eleanor, ed. *Sardis: Twenty-seven Years of Discovery.* Chicago: Chicago Society of the Archaeological Institute of America, 1987. A collection of papers presented at a symposium in 1987 held in conjunction with a traveling exhibition on the archaeological finds at Sardis. Covers metal working and the arts.

Komroff, Manuel, ed. *The History of Herodotus*. Translated by George Rawlinson. 1928. Reprint. New York: Tudor, 1947. Herodotus (especially in book 1) discusses the succession of the Mermnad Dynasty, including the anecdotal history and famous stories associated with each ruler, especially Gyges and Croesus.

Mellink, Machteld. "Archaeology in Anatolia: Lydia." *American Journal of Archaeology* 95, no. 1 (1991): 147. Describes recent excavations in chamber tombs at Bin Tepe, the royal Lydian necropolis and skeletal remains of a soldier killed in the siege of Sardis by Cyrus.

SEE ALSO: 775 B.C.E., Delphic Oracle Provides Guidance for City-States; c. 640 B.C.E., Greek City-States Use Coins as Means of Exchange; c. 594-580 B.C.E., Legislation of Solon; 547 B.C.E., Cyrus the Great Founds the Persian Empire.

RELATED ARTICLES in *Great Lives from History: The Ancient World*: Croesus; Cyrus the Great; Solon.

c. 640 B.C.E.
GREEK CITY-STATES USE COINS AS MEANS OF EXCHANGE

The Greek city-states used coins as a means of exchange as they expanded their area of settlement and became economically sophisticated in their trade relations.

LOCALE: Greece
CATEGORY: Trade and commerce

SUMMARY OF EVENT

The earliest Greek trade occurred during the Neolithic era and was opportunistic in nature. In response to a particular need or an unusual situation, Greeks ventured on the sea and engaged in rudimentary barter to secure what they needed or to gain an economic advantage. The leaders of the earliest Greek communities were eager to import luxury goods such as jewelry, decorative pottery, and ornamented weapons that they ultimately used as grave goods. The Greeks usually obtained their luxury goods from Levantine or Minoan traders who called on the Greeks of the mainland at infrequent intervals.

When the Greeks needed additional food supplies or raw materials such as wood or metals, they sought to trade their locally grown produce or locally manufactured goods for that which they needed from various traders who happened into the area. In terms of competition, however, the earliest Greek traders were at a decided disadvantage because Greece offered little in the way of natural resources to use as beginning trading capital. To compensate for this deficiency, the Greeks participated in a combination of commerce and piracy, trading with or attacking passing ships as the occasion allowed.

Greek merchant adventurers traded with the people who inhabited the Aegean islands and the various peoples who lived along the coasts of the Black, Ionian, and Mediterranean Seas. With increased experience at sea and a growing familiarity with overseas territories and peoples, the Greeks began the process of overseas colonization. Over an extended period of time, from the Late Bronze Age through the Iron Age, mainland Greeks colonized the islands of the Aegean and the coastal areas of Asia Minor. The greatest period of colonization, however, occurred from about 734 to 580 B.C.E., when the Greeks succeeded in founding more than three hundred Greek communities along the Mediterranean coasts of present-day Africa, Spain, France, southern Italy, and the northern shore of the Black Sea. With the notable exception of the Greek communities of the Black Sea region, all these Greek colonies developed into independent city-states.

For the most part, the newer areas of colonization had climates similar to that of mainland Greece. This factor not only enabled the Greeks overseas to practice their usual forms of agriculture without change but also helped them to adapt to their new surroundings quickly. In addition, the colonial areas commonly offered the Greeks more economic opportunities than they ever had before. The Greeks in colonial areas wanted to have the foods and products they were used to having in their former homelands. There developed a significant and steady trade between the mother cities of mainland Greece and the daughter cities overseas in foodstuffs (olives, olive oil, wine, grain, and fish), raw materials (timber, marble, and metal ores), and manufactured goods (such as pottery).

Through their trade and colonization efforts, the Greeks came into contact with a number of people (particularly in Asia Minor and the Levant) who were more economically advanced than they were and who had developed more sophisticated political organizations than they had. Some of these people had writing and numerical systems through which they could record tax collections and maintain inventory lists of produce and weapons. The traders from these more advanced economies were able to conduct more complex economic transactions than just barter. To participate in these more complicated and many times more lucrative economic transactions, the Greeks had to adjust to these new realities. In addition to adapting the Phoenician alphabet to the Greek language, the Greeks adopted and improved on a new economic development—coinage.

Both archaeology and Greek tradition attribute the beginnings of coinage to the Lydians of the interior of Asia Minor. The Greeks, having colonized the coastal areas of Asia Minor, would have come into economic contact with the Lydians at a very early date and would have been one of the first people introduced to the concept of coinage. Coinage is simply a method of designating value on a specific amount of precious metal. When a state struck or marked a coin with its mint mark, it certified the purity and weight of the precious metal in the coin and guaranteed its value. Coinage enabled an individual or state to store value or wealth in the form of a coin of precious metal that could be used again at some time in the future. The earliest coins, however, represented relatively high values and were probably issued to facilitate large payments between and among the various independent states of Asia Minor.

The Lydians appear to have struck their first coins sometime around 640 B.C.E., and the Greeks soon followed suit. The earliest Lydian coins were of electrum, an alloy of gold and silver, and the Greeks usually struck their coins in silver. Although both the Lydians and the Greeks had access to gold, they rarely coined it because it represented such a high value in relationship to silver. It was the Greeks who developed, refined, and expanded the use of coinage. The island of Aegina off the Greek mainland was the first Greek city-state to issue a large number of silver coins and struck them with the image of a sea turtle. Soon, the Greeks recognized the Aeginetan "turtles" as a practical coin standard and used them as a medium of exchange throughout their trading area. Aegina came to dominate the seaborne trade within Greece and the Greek trade with Egypt and the other countries of the eastern Mediterranean. With the expansion of trade, other Greek city-states struck coins and used mint marks unique to their cities as their guarantee of value.

Although there was no international regulation of coinage, the Greeks realized early that there would be economic chaos if every Greek city-state issued coins according to its own arbitrary standard of weights and measures. Although Aegina was the earliest Greek city-state of the mainland to strike coins, its standard did not end up the sole standard for Greece. Greek city-states roughly adhered to, with local variations, one of two standards of coin weights and measures—the Aeginetan standard and the Euboic standard. Of the two weight systems, the Aeginetan system possessed the heavier weights, since it contained more silver in its coins. During the history of ancient Greece, the Euboic system gradually replaced the Aeginetan standard as the most common coin standard.

SIGNIFICANCE

Whether coins were used as tribute payment or for payment for goods and services, the advent of coinage marked a great advance for the Greek city-states. When a state had to pay an obligation, the obligation did not have to be paid in bullion that would have to be weighed and assayed each time it was used in a transaction. This made trading simpler and allowed for far more complicated deals than could be accomplished by barter. Gradually by the fifth century B.C.E., Greek city-states began to mint smaller denomination coinage to facilitate the economic transactions of the average person. This brought the convenience and standardization provided by the use of coins in trade to the level of the ordinary person, thereby increasing the level of economic transaction that an individual could make.

—Peter L. Viscusi

FURTHER READING

Carradice, Ian. *Greek Coins*. Austin: University of Texas Press, 1995. An up-to-date and thorough publication written by one of the leading authorities on Greek and Roman coinage.

Hasebroek, Johannes. *Trade and Politics in Ancient Greece*. Translated by L. M. Fraser and D. C. Macgregor. Chicago: Ares, 1978. Originally published in German in 1928, this book has been recognized by the world's leading authorities as a classic work for a topical overview of the subject.

Lowry, S. Todd. *The Archaeology of Economic Ideas: The Classical Greek Tradition*. Durham, N.C.: Duke University Press, 1987. An unusual economic history that examines archaeological finds in the light of their economic significance and their relationship to the overall evolution of classical Greece.

Malkin, Irad. *Religion and Colonization in Ancient Greece*. Leiden: Brill, 1987. An important work by a leading scholar on Greek colonization.

Meadows, Andrew, and Kirsty Shipton, eds. *Money and Its Uses in the Ancient Greek World*. New York: Oxford University, 2001. A collection of papers presented at two conferences in 1995 and 1997 on money in ancient Greece. Bibliography and index.

SEE ALSO: c. 1000 B.C.E., Greek Alphabet Is Developed; c. 734-c. 580 B.C.E., Greeks Colonize the Mediterranean and Black Sea Regions; c. 733 B.C.E., Founding of Syracuse; c. 645-546 B.C.E., Lydia Rises to Power Under the Mermnad Family.

625-509 B.C.E.
RISE OF ETRUSCAN CIVILIZATION IN ROME

The rise of the Etruscan civilization in Rome transformed scattered agricultural villages into an advanced city-state with the capacity to grow into a major world empire.

LOCALE: Etruria (now in Tuscany) and Rome
CATEGORIES: Prehistory and ancient cultures; cultural and intellectual history

KEY FIGURES

Lucius Tarquinius Priscus (seventh century-579 B.C.E.), first Etruscan king, r. 616-579 B.C.E.
Servius Tullius (fl. sixth century B.C.E.), second Etruscan king, r. 579-535 B.C.E.
Lucius Tarquinius Superbus (sixth century-after 510 B.C.E.), third and last Etruscan king of Rome, r. 534-510 B.C.E.
Lucretia (sixth century-c. 509 B.C.E.), legendary figure whose rape and subsequent suicide set the overthrow of the Roman monarchy in motion
Lucius Junius Brutus (sixth century-c. 508 B.C.E.), leader of the revolution to expel the Etruscans in 509 B.C.E.

SUMMARY OF EVENT

Modern scholars continue to disagree about the origins of the Etruscans. The non-Indo-European language of these remarkable civilizers of what became Italy has not yet been satisfactorily translated. Between 800 and 600 B.C.E., the Etruscans expanded into west-central Italy, establishing Etruria (now in Tuscany) as a home base. The Etruscans became neighbors of the Latins, who had established villages in Rome as early as 1000 B.C.E.

The Etruscans grew wealthy on the copper, tin, zinc, lead, and iron deposits in Etruria. Fertile soil and favorable climate led to abundant crops of wheat, olives, and grapes. The Etruscans traded widely with the ancient world. They were trading partners and periodic hostile adversaries of two other maritime powers, the Greek city-states and the Phoenicians.

The Etruscans built a loose confederation of twelve independent city-states including Veii (now Velo), Caere (now Cerveteri), Tarquinii, and Vulci, and a number of large towns. Judging from paintings depicting scenes from everyday life, the realistic figures of the dead placed on top of sarcophagi or funerary urns, and artifacts uncovered from tombs, the Etruscans were a luxury- and pleasure-loving people with much leisure time and were voracious consumers. Splendor was enjoyed even in death, for the Etruscans built large cities of the dead (necropoleis), laid out in grid fashion. Etruscan women enjoyed the luxury of fine jewelry, elegant clothing, and diverse cosmetics and appear to have been granted a high degree of equality in Etruscan life.

Militarily, the Etruscans developed an excellent navy and a formidable army that was based on heavy body armor and the use of bronze chariots. Cities were built on defensible hilltops, protected by heavy walls and gates as well as ravines. Their military power was projected south into the Bay of Naples and toward the Latin villages of Rome, which the Etruscans easily dominated as an aristocratic military ruling elite from 616 to 509 B.C.E. The seven hills of Rome, situated in the middle of a coastal plain, and the potential of the area as the hub of major trade routes, was not lost on the Etruscans.

In the course of a century, Etruscan Rome rapidly developed from a collection of villages into a major city. For Rome, the Etruscan cultural and technological legacy was immense. In building the city, the Etruscans first used the arch and vault, which could support considerable weight. Later, the arch would be used with great proficiency by the Romans. The practice of placing temples on a high platform (podium) at the far end of a sacred enclosure so as to elevate both the structure and the gods, making the individual feel relatively insignificant, would later become a standard Roman practice. The Romans also adopted the science of boundaries (*limitatio*), which divided land into rectangular grids. Also the marking of formal city boundaries in a circle (*pomerium*) to define a holy and protected space became a basic Roman preoccupation. To expand land for cultivation and to eliminate unhealthy marshlands, the Etruscans employed the tunnel method of draining river bottoms (*cuniculus*), a method that the Romans would continue. The general use of drainage and irrigation systems, the construction of excellent hydraulics works, and the building of roads, bridges, and sewers were all aspects of Etruscan technology that the Romans would borrow and continue.

In relation to religious beliefs, the Etruscans also had a major impact. Their preoccupation with foretelling the future (divination) also became a Roman preoccupation, though one that was usually relegated only to times of emergency. Examination of animal entrails, most commonly the liver, became a pseudo-science designed to uncover the will of the gods. Similarly, the interpretation of lightning and thunder was used by the Etruscans to decipher the will of the gods, a practice the Romans would continue. In fact the Romans would insist on discovering signs (*auspices*) before making any major decision.

Like the Greeks, the Etruscans pictured their gods as having human form. The three major Etruscan gods—Tinia, Uni, and Menrva—were adapted by the Romans. Having much leisure time, the Etruscans celebrated many official holidays in honor of their gods. The Romans would also mark the year with many religious festivals.

For recreation during religious festivals, the Etruscans staged gladiator duels. Although these Etruscan duels may have been basic martial contests when compared with the later Roman gladiatorial extravaganzas, still the Romans appear to have first developed their love of gladiator shows from the Etruscan experience. Tomb paintings also indicate that chariot racing was a favorite Etruscan recreation. This entertainment also became popular in Rome, with the Circus Maximus later outdoing anything the Etruscans could have imagined. Undoubtedly, the major event in Etruscan Rome was the

IMPORTANT ETRUSCAN CITIES, 530-520 B.C.E.

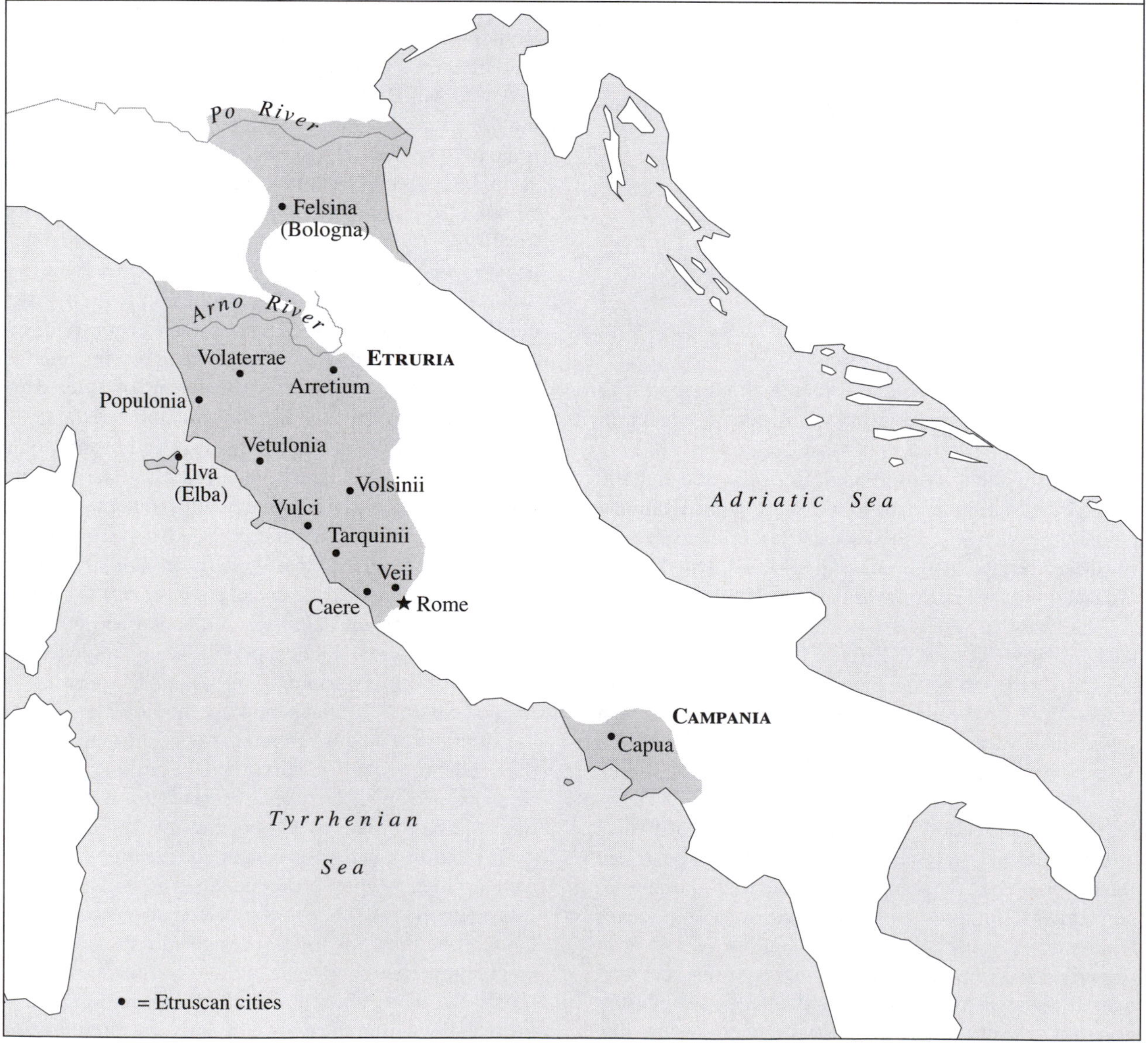

elaborate, semireligious procession following victorious campaigns, containing victors, captive prisoners, displays of seized treasures, musicians, and dancers. This ritual of the triumphant victory processional would continue throughout the Roman Republican and Imperial eras. The Etruscan propinquity toward rampant consumerism, fine foods, and elaborate banquets provided a hedonistic model that the Romans would first reject during the early centuries of the Republic and eventually follow to an extent that would have made the Etruscans envious.

Roman hero Horatius defends the Tiber Bridge against the Etruscan forces; his victory was the turning point in the Etruscan War. (Hulton|Archive)

Politically, the Romans were ruled by Etruscan kings. The king's power, or imperium, was conferred by a popular assembly. Imperium was symbolized by an eagle-headed scepter and an ax bound in a bundle of rods (*fasces*). After the Etruscans, both these symbols continued as Roman symbols, as did the concept of imperium.

The first Etruscan king, Lucius Tarquinius Priscus according to tradition, consolidated Roman villages and began the building of the city. His successor, Servius Tullius, extended the city boundaries and continued building projects, including fortified city walls. He also implemented social reform, dividing the population into six classes, according to wealth. He introduced the system of centuries into the Roman citizen army, grouped in phalanx formation into legions. According to Roman historian Livy, he also cemented bonds with the Latin nobles (patricians) who formed an advisory council to the king. The patricians were grouped into clans and were known by both personal name and clan name. The common people (plebeians) were divided into thirty wards, which constituted a committee, and could only discuss matters set by the king on the agenda. In embryonic form, Rome's second king set up the senate and assembly of tribes.

The third and last Etruscan king, Lucius Tarquinius Superbus, reversed the Servian Reforms, established absolute rule, and succeeded in antagonizing both plebeians and patricians. Arrogant, tyrannical, and a lavish spender, Tarquinius built a temple to Jupiter larger than the Parthenon. He is also credited with building Rome's great sewer, the Cloaca Maxima. According to legend, Tarquinius's son raped Lucretia, the wife of a friend. To regain her honor, Lucretia stabbed herself, inspiring a friend, Lucius Junius Brutus, to lead a revolt against Tarquinius's tyranny. In 509 B.C.E., the revolt was successful. In reaction to monarchical tyranny, the Romans turned legislative power over to the senate. Preventing overbearing executive power, Rome established a system of two consuls, elected only for a single one-year term, each with the power to veto the other. Junius Brutus was the first consul of the newly established Republic of Rome.

Following its defeat in Rome, Etruscan power received a serious setback. In 474 B.C.E., the Etruscan navy was defeated by the Greeks off of Cumae. Rome and its Latin allies gradually expanded toward the Etruscan cities. In 396 B.C.E., Veii fell after a long siege. By 250 B.C.E., what was left of Etruscan autonomy was integrated into the Roman system.

SIGNIFICANCE

The Etruscan concept of civilization and the technological know-how that enabled them to live in this advanced manner were integrated into the Roman civilization that followed. Much of what characterized the Roman Empire can be traced back to the Romans' predecessors, the Etruscans.

—*Irwin Halfond*

FURTHER READING

Barker, Graeme, and Tom Rasmussen. *The Etruscans*. Malden, Mass.: Blackwell Publishers, 1998. An overview of the Etruscan civilization. Bibliography and index.

Haynes, Sybille. *Etruscan Civilization: A Cultural History*. Los Angeles: J. Paul Getty Museum, 2000. Concentrates on the culture of the Etruscan civilization and how it influenced Italy. Bibliography and index.

Heurgon, Jacques. *Daily Life of the Etruscans*. London: Phoenix, 2002. A study of the everyday life of the Etruscans. Bibliography and index.

Pallottino, Massimo. *A History of Earliest Italy*. Translated by M. Ryle and K. Soper. Ann Arbor: University of Michigan Press, 1991. A scholarly and well-illustrated treatment of the development of early Italy and the Etruscan role in that development.

Ridgway, David. *The World of the Early Etruscans*. Jonsered: Paul Aströms Förlag, 2002. Part of the Studies in Mediterranean Archaeology series, this book examines the ancient Etruscans and their society. Bibliography.

Spivey, Nigel J., and S. Stoddart. *Etruscan Italy*. London: Batsford, 1990. An excellent portrayal of Etruscan settlement, their technology, social and political organization, economic activity, methods of warfare, and religious beliefs.

SEE ALSO: 509 B.C.E., Rape of Lucretia; c. 509 B.C.E., Roman Republic Replaces Monarchy; 312 B.C.E., First Roman Aqueduct Is Built; 312-264 B.C.E., Building of the Appian Way; 245-140 B.C.E., Rise of Parthia.

RELATED ARTICLES in *Great Lives from History: The Ancient World*: Lucretia; Tarquins.

621 or 620 B.C.E.
DRACO'S CODE IS INSTITUTED

Draco's code represented the beginning of Athenian legal and constitutional history and, for the first time in Europe, formulated a distinction between intentional and unintentional homicide.

LOCALE: Athens
CATEGORIES: Laws, acts, and legal history; government and politics

KEY FIGURE

Draco (fl. c. seventh century B.C.E.), semimythical lawgiver

SUMMARY OF EVENT

According to ancient traditions, Draco was a Greek statesman who drew up the first code of law for the Athenians during the archonship of Aristaechmus in 621/620 B.C.E. Although Draco and his laws are mentioned more than fifty times in various sources, the evidence is so conflicting that it is difficult to determine the nature and extent of his legislation. It has even been denied by some noted scholars that there ever was a human lawgiver with this name, the Greek *drakon* referring instead to a "serpent god" that the Athenians credited with drawing up their first legal code. However, Draco was also a common personal name. The Greek Sophist Prodicus was aware of the difficulty surrounding the word *drakon*, and his famous pun reported in Aristotle's *Technē rhetorikēs* (335-323 B.C.E.; *Rhetoric*, 1686) scarcely makes sense if the Athenians believed that their lawgiver was a snake: "They are not the laws of a man but of a 'snake,' so severe are they."

Other scholars have maintained that much of the evidence regarding Draco's legislation is the product of fourth century B.C.E. research and merely proves, if anything, that Draco drew up some laws regarding homicide. Such narrow interpretation of his activities, however, does not agree with all the evidence. Aristotle obviously attributed laws other than those on homicide to Draco. He states in his *Athenaiōn politeia* (335-323 B.C.E.; *The Athenian Constitution*, 1812), for instance, that after the Athenian statesman Solon had drawn up a constitution and enacted new laws, "the ordinances of Draco ceased to be used, with the exception of those pertaining to murder." Writers as early as Xenophon (c. 431-c. 354 B.C.E.) and Lysias (c. 445-c. 380 B.C.E.) refer to Draconian laws that were no longer in force. In 403 B.C.E., Greek statesman Tisamenus enacted a decree providing for the enforcement of the laws of Solon and of Draco as in earlier times. Various sources indicate that the legislation of Draco appeared to cover, in addition to homicide, such crimes as theft, vagrancy, adultery, the corruption of youth, neglect of the gods, and violation of the oath taken by jurors.

Like other early lawgivers, Draco probably did not so much initiate new legislation as reduce customary law to an orderly and usable form in writing. He may also have drawn on the decisions of earlier magistrates as recorded by the *thesmothetes*, or judges. According to Aristotle's *Politica* (335-323 B.C.E.; *Politics*, 1598), there was nothing unusual enough to mention about Draco's laws "except the greatness and severity of their penalties." Indeed, the severity of these laws had become legendary; Greek biographer Plutarch in his life of Solon reports that Draco's laws, except those relating to homicide, were repealed by Solon because they prescribed punishments regarded as too severe. Idleness or stealing a cabbage or an apple were capital offenses as serious as sacrilege or murder, and it was held that his laws were written not in ink but in blood. When Draco was asked why he assigned the death penalty for most offenses, he is reputed to have replied: "Small ones deserve that, and I have no higher for the greater crimes."

Such severity should not cause surprise. Most early codes of law were harsh in assigning severe penalties for petty crimes, as attested by early Hebrew law, Zaleucus's code, and the Twelve Tables of Rome. Not until the time of the Enlightenment was there much concern to make the punishment fit the crime, and in England some severe and unreasonable penalties prescribed in Elizabethan times remained in force throughout the nineteenth century. Consequently, Draco's harshness, considering the times, can be exaggerated. Death was not the only penalty inflicted on violators; lesser infringements drew fines, disfranchisement, or exile. In the case of homicide, his legislation appears enlightened in that it drew careful distinction between willful murder and accidental or justifiable manslaughter. Evidence for such a view comes not only from the legal procedures that were established in his day but also from a copy of his homicide law that was erected in front of the Royal Portico in 409/408 B.C.E. by a decree of the Council and People initiated by Xenophanes.

SIGNIFICANCE

Draco's laws marked definite advances. By designating crimes, fixing penalties, and establishing rules of procedure, he made it easier for the poor and the weak to obtain justice. His laws on homicide so effectively put an end to the blood feuds that had plagued Athens that other primitive communities adopted Athenian laws generally.

The ancient city developed out of a gradual federation of groups, and it never was an "assembly of individuals." Draco's code represents the time when the coalescing city was forced to curtail the sovereignty of the tribe and family and to interfere first of all, for the sake of peace, in its prerogative of the blood feud. In the case of intentional homicide, old tribal rights were still honored; in the case of self-defense, however, the new city saw a reasonable place to begin its encroachments on tribal rights. In the case of involuntary homicide, probably often occurring between persons of different groups and unknown to each other, the city again saw wisdom in restricting old tribal blood feuds. Consequently, Draco's code is interesting not only as a history of Athenian jurisprudence but also as an index of the growing jurisdiction of the city of Athens itself. That the "state" did not concern itself with murder in the Greek poet Homer's day is quite likely inasmuch as the "city" in that era had not developed out of tribal associations but still represented the concerns of a noble family.

—*M. Joseph Costelloe, updated by Jeffrey L. Buller*

FURTHER READING

Arnaoutoglou, Ilias. *Ancient Greek Laws: A Sourcebook.* New York: Routledge, 1998. A source book on the laws of ancient Greece. Includes maps, bibliography, and index.

Carawan, Edwin. *Rhetoric and the Law of Draco.* New York: Oxford University Press, 1998. Looks at homicide and Draco's law in ancient Greece. Bibliography and indexes.

Gagarin, Michael. *Drakon and Early Athenian Homicide Law.* New Haven, Conn.: Yale University Press, 1981. The most complete academic analysis of Draco's law code, with attention to its historicity and impact, by a distinguished scholar of early Greek law.

Stroud, Ronald S. *Drakon's Law on Homicide.* Berkeley: University of California Press, 1968. Contains the complete text of Draco's law code, with an English translation and commentary, using the text appearing on a marble inscription of 409/408 B.C.E. now in the Epigraphical Museum in Athens.

Todd, S. C. *The Shape of Athenian Law.* Oxford, England: Clarendon, 1993. An overview of law in Athens and how it affected social life. Bibliography and indexes.

Tulin, Alexander. *Dike Phonou: The Right of Prosecution and Attic Homicide Procedure.* Stuttgart, Germany: B. G. Teubner, 1996. An examination of early Greek law as it pertained to homicide and the right of prosecution. Indexes.

SEE ALSO: c. 594-580 B.C.E., Legislation of Solon; 508-507 B.C.E., Reforms of Cleisthenes; 483 B.C.E., Naval Law of Themistocles Is Instituted; 451-449 B.C.E.,

Twelve Tables of Roman Law Are Formulated; 445 B.C.E., Establishment of the Canuleian Law; 287 B.C.E., *Lex Hortensia* Reforms the Roman Constitution; 180 B.C.E., Establishment of the *Cursus honorum*; 90 B.C.E., Julian Law Expands Roman Citizenship; c. 165 C.E., Gaius Creates Edition of the *Institutes* of Roman Law; c. 220 C.E., Ulpian Issues Dictum in Rome.

RELATED ARTICLES in *Great Lives from History: The Ancient World*: Draco; Hammurabi; Solon.

c. 607-562 B.C.E.
NEBUCHADNEZZAR CREATES THE FIRST NEO-BABYLONIAN STATE

The Neo-Babylonian state was the second of five great ancient empires—the Assyrian, the Medo-Persian, the Greek, and the Roman—that facilitated the spread of civilization in the Middle East and the Mediterranean.

LOCALE: Neo-Babylonian Empire (now Iraq, Kuwait, Syria, Lebanon, Israel/Palestine, Jordan, and Egypt)
CATEGORIES: Expansion and land acquisition; government and politics

KEY FIGURES

Nabopolassar (fl. seventh century B.C.E.), father of Nebuchadnezzar II and founder of the Neo-Babylonian Empire, r. c. 626-605 B.C.E.
Nebuchadnezzar II (c. 630-562 B.C.E.), greatest ruler of the Neo-Babylonian Empire, r. c. 605-562 B.C.E.

SUMMARY OF EVENT

The Neo-Babylonian Empire (626-539 B.C.E.) arose in Mesopotamia (present-day Iraq), which had been a center of culture for more than thirty-five hundred years before the birth of Nebuchadnezzar II. Great societies had come and gone—the Sumerian, the Akkadian, and the Babylonian. All these cultures had been included in the first world empire of the Middle East, that of the Assyrians (722-612 B.C.E.), which united the entire Fertile Crescent from modern-day Iraq to Egypt. With its impressive capital at Nineveh and its seemingly invincible army, Assyria seemed unstoppable.

In 626 B.C.E., Nabopolassar, an Assyrian official, led a successful revolt and was crowned king in Babylon. Within ten years, Nabopolassar had expelled the Assyrians from Babylon, and in 612, Nineveh, its walls weakened by a flood on the Tigris River, fell. This freed Nabopolassar to found the Neo-Babylonian, or Chaldean, Empire.

From an early age, Nabopolassar's son Nebuchadnezzar II assisted his father. Nebuchadnezzar was given the Akkadian name Nabu-Kudurri-User, which means "O Nabu, watch over my heir." The crown prince claimed Naram-Sin, an Akkadian ruler of the third millennium, as an ancestor. Such pretentiousness was soon to be validated in war. In 607/606 B.C.E., crown prince Nebuchadnezzar led an army north of Assyria, and by 606/605, he was the commander in chief of his father's forces, defeating the Egyptians at Carchemish and Hamath (now Hamāh) and gaining control of the Levantine coast.

After the death of his father in 605 B.C.E., Nebuchadnezzar returned home and ascended the throne. He suppressed opposition and, with a refurbished army, began the conquest of the west. Having pacified northwest Arabia, Nebuchadnezzar subdued the state of Judah. In 597, he deported the Jewish king Jehoiachin to Babylon, and in 587/586, he destroyed the city of Jerusalem, exiling its leading citizens to Mesopotamia and starting what became known among Jews as the Babylonian captivity. Nebuchadnezzar is featured prominently in the Jewish Bible in such books as Daniel, Ezekiel, and Jeremiah. Concurrently, Nebuchadnezzar lay siege to the coastal city of Tyre (Jewish historian Flavius Josephus contends that conquest required thirteen years).

During his reign, Nebuchadnezzar was able to unite the entire Fertile Crescent, from the Persian Gulf to the Nile Delta. By war and by diplomacy, he confirmed his conquests as a universal ruler, claiming that he had "no opponent from the horizon to the sky."

A builder as well as a warrior, Nebuchadnezzar was

MAJOR RULERS OF THE NEO-BABYLONIAN EMPIRE, C. 626-539 B.C.E.

Ruler	*Reign*
Nabopolassar	c. 626-605
Nebuchadnezzar II	c. 605-562
Awil-Marduk	562-556
Nabonidus	556-539

Nebuchadnezzar II expels the Jews from Jerusalem. (F. R. Niglutsch)

noted for the moat and fortifications that he had built around the city of Babylon. The Processional Way was paved with limestone, canals were dug, and the principal temples were refurbished. It was said that Nebuchadnezzar was "the one who set in the mouth of the people reverence for the great gods."

According to tradition, one of his wives was a Median princess who was homesick for the hills of her native country. To make her feel more at home, Nebuchadnezzar is said to have constructed a step pyramid, or ziggurat, known as the Hanging Gardens of Babylon, one of the Seven Wonders of the Ancient World. In the literature of the Jewish Bible, Nebuchadnezzar is—despite his anti-Jewish acts—regarded favorably as a protector of the prophets Jeremiah and Daniel, as a divine defender against evildoers (in Ezekiel, Daniel, 1 Esdras), and as one miraculously cured after seven years of insanity (Daniel). Classical historians as varied as Strabo, Diodorus Siculus, and Berossus were also fascinated by him. On his death, he was succeeded by his son Awil-Marduk (the evil Merodach of 2 Kings).

The last ruler of the Neo-Babylonian Empire was Nabonidus. While Nabonidus was absent from the capital, his regent Belshazzar allowed the Persians to seize Babylon in 539, ending the Neo-Babylonian Empire.

SIGNIFICANCE

The impact of the reign of Nebuchadnezzar for world history was sixfold:

Militarily, he demonstrated the possibility of creating a vast regional empire that stretched more than 1,000 miles (620 kilometers) from its eastern to its western frontiers. This example encouraged others to follow in his footsteps, including Cyrus the Great (r. c. 559-c. 530 B.C.E.) and Darius the Great (r. 522-486), who created the vast Persian Empire, a state of twenty-two provinces reaching from India to Macedonia. In turn, that commonwealth was surpassed by the vast empire created by Alexander the Great (r. 336-323); Alexander's achievements were eclipsed by those of the Romans. It is not by chance that the Babylonians were called "the Romans of the ancient East" and that Rome was nicknamed "Babylon" by early Christian writers. Nebuchadnezzar is the first of a long line of world conquerors.

Administratively, Nebuchadnezzar showed that it was possible to rule a vast empire composed of people of many cultures, customs, creeds, languages, and traditions. This idea of a cosmopolitan world state would inspire many later attempts—Persian, Greek, and Roman—to create what the stoic philosophers later named "the single house of all humanity."

Socially, Nebuchadnezzar set a pattern of the ruler as the benefactor of the people through the construction of vast public works. It is not surprising that the Greeks and Romans, who expected their leaders to enhance their cities, credited him with building one of the Seven Wonders of the Ancient World.

Religiously, Nebuchadnezzar was important for the Judaeo-Christian tradition in many ways—the deportation of the Jews from Jerusalem in 587/586 B.C.E. began the vast Jewish diaspora, the exile of the Hebrew people, which caused Judaism to interact creatively with other cultures and to provide, in the diaspora, the nursery of early Christianity. Because of Nebuchadnezzar's role in the Jewish Bible, he has become a figure of legendary proportions in Western literature. Perhaps this reflects the historical reality that the Babylonian conquest forced the Hebrew prophets to develop not just a national but also a global view of their God.

Economically, Nebuchadnezzar's unification of the Middle East created a gigantic "common market" that was later expanded and enhanced by the Persians and the Greeks. This led to times of great prosperity and leisure, which facilitated the growth of the arts, sciences, and letters.

Intellectually, Nebuchadnezzar's reign was the apex of thirty-five hundred years of cultural evolution in Mesopotamia. The results of that civilization—literacy, science, architecture, and astronomy—were disseminated widely in the region. It is not an exaggeration to state that the Neo-Babylonian Empire was a bridge over which ideas and inventions passed from the east to the west. It is hard to imagine the later splendor of Hellenistic times without the preliminary labors of the Babylonians.

Few figures of antiquity have captured the modern imagination more than Nebuchadnezzar. Danish philosopher Søren Kierkegaard puzzled over his meaning, and the king's alleged madness inspired English artist William Blake's picture "Nebuchadnezzar." The Italian musician Giuseppi Verdi featured him in his 1842 opera *Nabucco*, and many historians have named him the "Napoleon of Ancient Iraq." Behind the rich and contradictory images stands the reality of one of the greatest conquerors of antiquity, a warrior comparable to Alexander the Great and Julius Caesar.

—*C. George Fry*

FURTHER READING

Henze, Matthias. *The Madness of King Nebuchadnezzar: The Ancient Near Eastern Origins and Early History of Interpretation of Daniel 4*. Boston: Brill, 1999. Examines the portrayal of Nebuchadnezzar, particularly in regard to animalization, in Daniel 4.

Roux, Georges. *Ancient Iraq*. 3d ed. New York: Penguin Books, 1992. Especially valuable for the military campaigns of Nebuchadnezzar. Bibliography and index.

Sack, Ronald Herbert. *Images of Nebuchadnezzar: The Emergence of a Legend*. Cranbury, N.J.: Associated University Presses, 1991. Provides a look at the life of Nebuchadnezzar, using secondary classical and Hebrew sources.

Skaggs, H. W. F. *Babylonians*. Berkeley: University of California Press, 2000. A study of the Babylonians by a specialist. Bibliography and indexes.

Wiseman, D. J. *Nebuchadnezzar and Babylon*. New York: Oxford University Press, 1985. A collection of lectures about the Babylonian ruler and the land in which he lived. Bibliography and indexes.

SEE ALSO: c. 922 B.C.E., Establishment of the Kingdom of Israel; 745 B.C.E., Tiglath-pileser III Rules Assyria; 701 B.C.E., Sennacherib Invades Syro-Palestine; 547 B.C.E., Cyrus the Great Founds the Persian Empire; October, 539 B.C.E., Fall of Babylon; c. 538-c. 450 B.C.E., Jews Return from the Babylonian Captivity; 520-518 B.C.E., Darius the Great Conquers the Indus Valley.

RELATED ARTICLES in *Great Lives from History: The Ancient World*: Cyrus the Great; Darius the Great; Nebuchadnezzar II; Sennacherib; Tiglath-pileser III.

Before 600 B.C.E.
CELEBRATION OF THE ELEUSINIAN MYSTERIES

The Eleusinian Mysteries were the longest-lasting and most important mystery cult of the ancient world. Initiates were forbidden to reveal the final revelations of the ritual and none ever did; however, it is known that the result of the initiation was to remove all fear of death.

LOCALE: Eleusis, a small town northwest of Athens
CATEGORY: Religion

KEY FIGURE
Pisistratus (c. 612-527 B.C.E.), tyrant of Athens

SUMMARY OF EVENT
In classical antiquity there were many secret cults or "mysteries," each of which characteristically required initiatory rites before full knowledge of its beliefs and liturgy would be revealed. Demeter and Dionysos were the deities with whom the most famous ancient Greek mysteries were associated, and the Eleusinian Mysteries, celebrated in honor of Demeter and her daughter Persephone, were perhaps the most renowned of all. The name is derived from Eleusis, a town some fourteen miles northwest of Athens, its acropolis facing the Bay of Salamis and dominating the rich Thriasian plain. It is with this city that one of the principal myths of antiquity became associated some time in the latter half of the second millennium B.C.E.; as a result, Eleusis became famous and wealthy as the site of a major sanctuary.

According to the early Greek poets, the goddess Demeter was a daughter of the Titans Kronos and Rhea. Like many of the Hellenic female deities she was a fertility goddess, her province being the care of agriculture in general, specifically of grain. By Zeus, she had a daughter Persephone, known in the earliest myths as Kore, the Greek word for "maiden." One day as the beautiful Persephone was picking flowers—according to one version, in the lush fields of Sicily—Hades, god of the underworld, violently carried her off to make her queen of his realm. Her mother searched for the maiden all over the world, even, in one version of the story, lighting torches by the fires of the volcano Etna to continue her quest by night. In her wanderings, she eventually came to Eleusis, where in her weariness she was received hospitably and was entrusted with the care of the prince's newborn son, who is called Demophon in the Homeric hymn but is alternately known as Triptolemus. Demeter decided to reward the hospitality of her hosts by holding the infant in the hearth fire to make him immortal. However, she was interrupted in the process and forced to admit her divinity in explanation of this strange act. The people of Eleusis were ordered to erect a temple in her honor.

Because the crops and fruits withered and the earth became barren because of Demeter's sorrow and neglect, Zeus ordered Hades to release his captive queen. Hades agreed, but before Persephone left, he gave her some pomegranate seeds to eat. Unaware that they would make impossible her permanent return from the underworld, she ate them. Consequently while Persephone might spend eight months of each year with her mother, she had to pass the remaining four in the company of Hades. The restriction could not tarnish Demeter's joy at seeing her daughter once more; in celebration she rewarded the Eleusians by teaching them the rites by which she was to be worshiped thereafter. According to one version of the tale, she subsequently dispatched Triptolemus to go about the world teaching the arts of agriculture to humankind.

Upon Persephone's return to earth, the barren fields had blossomed anew, and therefore the myth of Demeter and Persephone may be said to symbolize the annual turn of the seasons from spring growth to summer harvest, and thence to the sterile time of late fall and winter. More specifically it can refer to the fact that in Greece the seed grain was stored in the ground from the harvest in June until the sowing in October, when it was brought forth for the festival of planting.

Originally the Eleusinian Mysteries were an agrarian cult celebrated in the fall at the time of sowing. After the union of Eleusis with Athens some time before 600 B.C.E., the festival of the Greater Mysteries included a procession from Athens to the sanctuary in Eleusis. The Athenian tyrant Pisistratus not only encouraged the mysteries but subsidized them so that they could be celebrated with great formal and official pomp. Occasionally the state even paid the initiation fees for poor candidates.

The Greater Mysteries were held every year for eight days in the month of Boedromion, which corresponds to September and early October in the modern Western calendar. The sacred activities began in Athens on the first day of the festival when the cult herald proclaimed to the people an invitation to take part in the ceremonies and be initiated. The only ones banned were those who had committed homicide, those otherwise unclean, and foreigners who could not speak Greek. On the next day all the acceptable initiates went down to the sea, each with a sacrificial pig, in order to purify themselves and the animals in the sea waters. On the return to the city, the pigs presumably were sacrificed. Nothing specific is known about the third day, but it probably centered on a formal ceremony for the two goddesses in their temple, the Eleusinion, situated below the Acropolis on the north side. The fourth day honored Asclepius, the god of healing, and finally on the fifth day a great procession of priests and priestesses, officials, initiates, and their escorts set out for Eleusis, fourteen miles away. Because of the distance, the latter part of the journey had to be completed by torchlight. On the sixth day, after resting and feasting, the initiation rites began in the evening with the drinking of the *kykeon*, a mixture of meal, water, and mint.

The rites began in the evening in the Telesterion or Great Hall of the Mysteries, but because the cult practices themselves were carefully guarded secrets throughout antiquity, almost nothing is known about them. The chief priest displayed certain holy objects, as indicated by his Greek title *hierophant*, meaning one who shows something sacred; a chorus recited and chanted various hymns; and ritual acts were performed. For the participants in the liturgy there appear to have been three stages: initiation, preliminary confirmation, and final revelation. While some early Church Fathers, notably Clement of Alexandria (c. 150-c. 215 C.E.), report that sexual objects were uncovered in the final stage, it is more likely that the ultimate manifestation of the mysteries was an ear of wheat, which could well embody the wonder of the changing seasons as well as food and famine, or life and death. However, the actual content of the final revelation remains unknown. Completion of all ritual activity came on the evening of the seventh day, and on the eighth there were libations and rites for the dead. The return of the pilgrims to Athens occupied the ninth day, and on the tenth the Athenian Council of the Five Hundred convened in the Eleusinion to receive a formal report on the celebration.

The main building of the sanctuary of Demeter at Eleusis was the Telesterion, a large structure some 170

Pisistratus, the Athenian tyrant, is carried through the streets by Athenians celebrating his return. (F. R. Niglutsch)

feet (52 meters) square at its base. Its roof was supported by forty-two columns, with banks of steps on all sides of the interior which perhaps served as seats. Here the *mystai* or initiates observed the sacred rites on the floor in front of them. The building was a final evolution of a first structure that had been small and rectangular and a second that had been square but only one fourth the size of the last building, which was designed and built by the architect Ictinus (fl. fifth century B.C.E.) in the Periclean age. Other structures in the area were the Temple of Artemis Propylaea, the Greater and Lesser Propylaea, all of Roman times, and numerous altars and stelae with inscriptions and dedications within the sanctuary proper.

Excavations at Eleusis were begun in 1882 by the Greek Archaeological Society, and have continued at varying times until the present.

Significance

The Eleusinian Mysteries offered the hope of a happy afterlife to its initiates for over one thousand years. In some ways, it bore similarities to other Greek festivals such as the Thesmophoria (which also included the sacrifice of piglets), and in some it foreshadowed the promises of Christianity. This was probably one source of the hostility exhibited toward the mysteries by early Christians. The festival also transcended the strictly local nature of most ancient cults, eventually drawing initiates from throughout the Mediterranean world. The myth and worship of Demeter and Persephone was one of the most important in Greek religion and in many ways provide the paradigm for goddess worship in the Western mind.

—*Kevin Herbert*

Further Reading

Cosmopoulos, Michael B., ed. *Greek Mysteries: The Archaeology of Ancient Greek Secret Religions*. New York: Routledge, 2003. A collection of essays that take an archaeological approach to understanding Greek religions. The first three essays discuss the Eleusinian Mysteries.

Downing, Christine, ed. *The Long Journey Home: Re-Visioning the Myth of Demeter and Persephone for Our Time*. Boston: Shambhala, 1995. A collection of essays that offers a variety of approaches to the contemporary meaning of the myth that underlies the Mysteries.

Hard, Robin, and H. J. Rose. *The Routledge Handbook of Greek Mythology: Based on H. J. Rose's "A Handbook of Greek Mythology."* New York: Routledge, 2003. A standard work containing basic information on Demeter, Persephone, and other deities.

Kerenyi, Karl. *Eleusis*. Translated by Ralph Manheim. Reprint. Princeton, N.J.: Princeton University Press, 1991. A psychological analysis of the Mysteries and Greek religion. Draws on archaeology, art history, religious history, and comparative religion.

Mylonas, George F. *Eleusis and the Eleusinian Mysteries*. Princeton, N.J.: Princeton University Press, 1961. This book sums up the archaeological research up to the middle of the twentieth century on the site of Eleusis, and also examines what is known about the mysteries celebrated there in antiquity. The book concludes with a glossary of ancient Greek terms, a selected bibliography, an index, and eighty-eight illustrations, including a map, plans, and photographs of the site.

Nilsson, Martin P. *Greek Folk Religion*. Reprint. Philadelphia: University of Pennsylvania Press, 1998. A substantial chapter in this classic study is devoted to Eleusis.

SEE ALSO: 775 B.C.E., Delphic Oracle Provides Guidance for City-States.

6th or 5th century B.C.E.
BIRTH OF BUDDHISM

The teachings of Siddhārtha Gautama, known as the Buddha, gave rise to one of the world's major religions.

LOCALE: Northern India
CATEGORY: Religion

KEY FIGURE

Buddha (Siddhārtha Gautama; c. 566-c. 486 B.C.E.), founder of Buddhism

SUMMARY OF EVENT

Buddhism is one of the world's major religions. The teachings known as the Four Noble Truths are generally recognized as the core of Buddhism. The first truth is that life is suffering. Suffering continues through an endless chain of rebirths. The second truth is that suffering is caused by desire. The third is that desire can be ended, and the fourth is that right living according to Buddhist precepts (known as the Eightfold Path) is the way to end desire. With the ceasing of desire, beings enter nirvana, a state of release from existence. The striving toward nirvana also involves dedication to the Three Jewels. The first jewel is Buddha himself. The second is the dharma, or "universal law," the truth taught by Buddha. The Saṅgha, or community of monks, is the third.

The founder of Buddhism, Siddhārtha Gautama, also known as Gautama Śākyamuni, was born in the kingdom of the Śākyas in northeastern India. The most commonly accepted dates for his life are c. 566 to c. 486 B.C.E. During this period, India was in a state of rapid political, social, and economic change. By about 600 B.C.E., a number of republics and kingdoms had arisen in northern India, and settled towns became a prominent part of life. Trade with western Asia and other parts of the world contributed to the growth of merchant and artisan classes.

The development of new urban centers and new social classes led to a tendency to pose fundamental philosophical questions, and the time was rich in philosophical and religious teachers. One of those was Vardhamāna, the founder of India's Jain religion, who lived and taught at roughly the same time as Buddha. According to Vardhamāna, the universe works according to an eternal law and everything in the universe has a soul. The purpose of living, in Jainism, is the purification of the soul in order to release the soul from the body. Although there are important differences between Jainism and Buddhism, there are also similarities, such as the idea of universal law, adherence to the principle of nonviolence, and the view of life as a movement toward release. These similarities suggest some of the ideas that were current at the time of the birth of Buddhism.

The details of the life of Siddhārtha Gautama are based on tradition because the first written accounts of his life and actions date from about two hundred years after his death. Siddhārtha is said to have been a prince. At his birth, the Brahmans, or priests, at his father's court foretold that the prince would either become a world-conquering monarch or a Buddha, which means "awakened one" or "enlightened one" in the classical Indian language of Sanskrit. Wishing to keep his son from taking up the life of a holy man, King Śuddhodana attempted to surround the child with luxury and comfort. Nevertheless, as a young man, Gautama saw old age, sickness, and death, which convinced him of the misery of the world. He also saw a wandering holy man and was inspired to leave home to seek wisdom.

For a time, Gautama starved himself and followed a regimen of extreme asceticism and self-mortification. He decided that his self-imposed suffering would not lead him to enlightenment, and he began to live in a more moderate manner. One morning, he sat down under an banyan tree, and according to Buddhist teaching, he vowed not to rise until he had achieved enlightenment. After struggles with the evil spirit Mara, the lord of passion, Gautama realized the truth about existence.

Buddha, as he had become, meditated on his realization for several weeks and then began to teach others. He preached his first sermon at the Deer Park in Sārnāth, about five miles from modern Banāras. As a result of this sermon, Buddha attracted his first five disciples, and these were followed by others. The full-time disciples of Buddha became monks and were known as the Saṅgha, which means "community" or "order."

At the age of eighty, Buddha became sick and died. About a year later, the First Buddhist Council took place and, in the absence of the founder of the religion, Buddhism split into four factions. At this time, a book of Buddha's teachings and a book on monastic discipline were written down. Monks traveled about spreading the religion, and monasteries were established in various places. These monasteries contributed to the spread of literacy and the growth of education because they became centers for teaching.

Part of the appeal of Buddhism lay in its rejection of

the caste system of ancient India. The established Indian religion, which much later became known as Hinduism, taught that relations among people should be based on a social hierarchy of birth, and that social position was a result of deeds in past lives. Buddhists accepted men and women from all social ranks as monks and nuns. While Buddha was alive, he taught in the popular language of Magadhi, rather than in classical Sanskrit, so that he could be understood by the common people. This relative egalitarianism, another trait that Buddhism shared with Jainism, attracted people from the lower castes and people from the merchant class, who lacked social prestige to match their economic power.

Early Buddhism also denied other aspects of the faith of India's Brahman priest caste. The Buddhists rejected the authority of the Vedas, the sacred writing of the Brahmans, and they attached no value to Brahman sacred rituals. Animal sacrifices, a central practice of the established religion of ancient India, were contrary to the teachings of both Buddhism and Jainism. Despite this turning away from the ruling religion, though, early Buddhism tended to be open to influences from popular beliefs. Reverence for funeral mounds and tree worship were among the originally non-Buddhist cults that were accepted by Buddhists and were incorporated as Buddhist religious practices. Although Buddhism did not require belief in a god or gods, it also did not reject the existence of deities or other supernatural beings. Spirits, heaven and hell, and divine beings therefore became part of popular Buddhism in many locations, and the religion's ability to absorb different traditions contributed to its spread.

A second Buddhist council was held about a century after Buddha's death. At this meeting, known as the Council of Veśālī, the different approaches to Buddhism began to develop into the split that would gradually lead to the develop of the two major sects or schools of Buddhism, Theravāda (also called Hīnayāna) and Mahāyāna. The primary difference between these was that Theravāda Buddhism emphasized the importance of an individual's own efforts in striving toward nirvana, while Mahāyāna Buddhism gave more emphasis to the ability of beings who had already achieved enlightenment to make salvation possible for others.

In the fourth century B.C.E., the rulers of the Mauryan Dynasty united much of northern India in a single empire. The Mauryan emperor Aśoka, who ruled from c. 273/265 to 238 B.C.E., supported the Buddhist teachings and became the ideal of the Buddhist king. Some historical accounts report that during Aśoka's reign, a Third Buddhist Council was convened at Pataliputra in 250. Soon afterward, Buddhist missionaries traveled to countries outside of India, possibly as a result of policies set at Pataliputra.

SIGNIFICANCE

Although Buddhism largely disappeared in India by about 700 C.E., elements of Buddhism were absorbed into Hinduism. However, different versions of the faith preached by Siddhārtha Gautama spread throughout other parts of Asia. In 251 B.C.E., Aśoka's son Mahinda went to Ceylon (Sri Lanka) as a Buddhist missionary. Theravāda Buddhism would later spread from Ceylon to the Southeast Asian lands of Burma (Myanmar), Siam (Thailand), Laos, and Cambodia. Buddhism entered China about 61 C.E., and Mahāyāna Buddhism became one of the dominant religions in China, Japan, Korea, and Vietnam. During the fifth to the seventh centuries C.E., another major school, known as Vajrayāna Buddhism, developed in eastern India and became the faith of Nepal and Tibet.

Buddhist statues and painting became central to the arts in these lands. Monasteries became fundamental social institutions throughout Asia. Political ideas, such as views on the nature of kingship, were often based on concepts of the Buddhist ruler.

—*Carl L. Bankston III*

FURTHER READING

Armstrong, Karen. *Buddha*. New York: Viking, 2001. A short, well-written biography of Buddha and introduction to his teachings. Glossary.

Keay, John. *India: A History*. New York: Atlantic Monthly Press, 2000. A general history of India that places the birth of Buddhism in its social and historical context.

Lopez, Donald S. *The Story of Buddhism: A Concise Guide to Its History and Teachings*. Harper San Francisco, 2001. A short history of the origins and transformations of Buddhism. Pronunciation guide, bibliography, glossary, and index.

Nelson, Walter H. *Buddha: His Life and Teaching*. Los Angeles: J. P. Tarcher, 2000. An introduction to the basic teachings of Buddha. Glossary, bibliography, index.

SEE ALSO: c. 5th-4th century B.C.E., Creation of the *Jātakas*; 300 B.C.E.-600 C.E., Construction of the Māhabodhi Temple; c. 273/265-c. 238 B.C.E., Aśoka Reigns over India; c. 250 B.C.E., Third Buddhist Council Convenes; c. 250 B.C.E., *Tipiṭaka* Is Compiled;

c. 247-207 B.C.E., Buddhism Established in Sri Lanka; c. 1st century B.C.E., Indian Buddhist Nuns Compile the *Therigatha*; 1st century B.C.E.-1st century C.E., Compilation of the *Lotus Sutra*; 1st-2d century C.E., Fourth Buddhist Council Convenes; c. 60-68 C.E., Buddhism Enters China; Late 4th-5th century C.E., Asanga Helps Spread Mahāyāna Buddhism; 399 C.E., Chinese Monk Faxian Travels to India; c. 470 C.E., Bodhidharma Brings Chan Buddhism to China.

RELATED ARTICLES in *Great Lives from History: The Ancient World*: Aśoka; Bodhidharma; Buddha; Faxian.

c. 6th century B.C.E.-c. 350 C.E.
MEROITIC EMPIRE RULES FROM SOUTHERN EGYPT TO THE BLUE NILE

After the capital of Kush was moved from Napata southward to Meroë, the Meroitic Empire became one of the most powerful states of the ancient world and a corridor for commerce and cultural exchange.

LOCALE: Kush, Nubia (now northern and central Sudan)

CATEGORIES: Government and politics; trade and commerce

KEY FIGURE

Aspelta (fl. sixth century B.C.E.), king of the Meroitic Empire

SUMMARY OF EVENT

The ancient kingdom of Meroë, known to its inhabitants as Kush or Kash, developed in the Upper Nile River Valley. It extended from Egypt's southern border to a point south of Khartoum, capital of the modern Republic of Sudan. Classical writers called the kingdom Meroë in reference to the city that replaced Napata as its center of government. It became one of the most important empires of the ancient world.

Kush's power rivaled that of Egypt. After years of Egyptian invasion and dominion, Kushite kings became strong and expansion minded. During the eighth and seventh centuries B.C.E., they took control of their northern neighbor and formed Egypt's Twenty-fifth (Kushite) Dynasty (c. 742-c. 656 B.C.E.). They ruled for nearly a century before they were driven out in 656. In 594, the Egyptian pharoah Psamtik II carried out a campaign against Kush, then under the rule of Aspelta, and may have sacked the original Kushite capital of Napata.

Fear of Egyptian incursion was probably one reason for moving Kush's capital from Napata to Meroë, a site about 180 miles (290 kilometers) southeast. The relocation of the capital occurred over a period of time, probably during the sixth century B.C.E. The city of Meroë became the administrative capital, but the Napata area remained the religious center and the site of royal burials for two more centuries. During the transition, rulers may have kept royal residences in both cities.

Little is known of specific events from the time of Aspelta to the Meroitic decline in the fourth century C.E. As no related languages or sufficient bilingual translations have yet been found, the Meroitic language has not been deciphered. Other literary sources from Egyptians, Greeks, Romans, or Aksumites are limited. Although a list of Kushite kings has been developed from identifiable burial places marked with small pyramids and commemorative inscriptions, many of these sites have suffered damage from time and vandalism. Archaeological evidence is rich but incomplete, and much of the history and chronology remains speculative.

Kush's power was concentrated along the Nile, although some settlements developed in the grasslands around the city of Meroë. Most towns were located along a 1,250-mile (2,000-kilometer) stretch that started near Maharraqa in the north. The border shared with Egypt fluctuated. A fort built at the Second Cataract of the Nile may once have served as an Egyptian outpost, but in the fourth century B.C.E., the Meroitic Empire asserted control beyond the First Cataract near Aswān. After the establishment of Ptolemaic rule in Egypt, archaeological evidence indicates alternating Egyptian and Meroitic occupation of the disputed region. With the Roman conquest of Egypt, the border dispute intensified. A Meroitic attack on Aswān resulted in a Roman retaliation (described by historians Strabo and the elder Pliny), which went as far upstream as Napata. A tentative peace was established with the boundary fixed at Aswān in 24 B.C.E. Deserts to the east and west of the Nile provided natural frontiers, and specific borders were probably ill defined. As there were no major forces to challenge Meroitic expansion into central Africa, the southern borders of

Meroë reached as far as the modern town of Sennar, Sudan, located on the Blue Nile 160 miles (250 kilometers) upstream from Khartoum, Sudan.

The city of Meroë, located between the Sixth Cataract and the Nile-Atbara confluence, had been inhabited for perhaps four centuries before it became the seat of government. It has been suggested that the original town was built on an island that fused with the east bank of the Nile in the third or fourth century B.C.E. Because the city and grasslands to the east were surrounded by rivers, the general region came to be designated the Island of Meroë. The city itself had a population as large as 20,000. Excavations of the area indicate a great royal walled compound, a temple complex (including a large building dedicated to the Egyptian god Amen), an extensive residential area of timber huts and later mud-brick buildings, an ironworking area, and pyramid cemeteries.

The southward shift in political power from Napata to the city of Meroë had advantages in addition to military security. Whereas the Napata area was undergoing desiccation, the southern region had sufficient rainfall to facilitate the growth of crops and the use of land as pasture. By the fifth century B.C.E., the city of Meroë was an established ironworking center with sources of iron ore and timber necessary for smelting. In addition, the new capital was well placed for trade; it was located on the Sudanese Nile near regions that provided products valued in the Mediterranean world, and it was situated near caravan routes that crossed to ports on the Red Sea. It has been suggested that the city of Meroë rose to importance because it was home territory to powerful families who eventually came to control the empire. Whether its origins were due to economic factors or dynastic considerations, the southern capital became a major center.

With the move of the capital to the southern part of the kingdom, Meroites were exposed to long-established African traditions at the same time that Egyptian influences were decreasing. There is no doubt that Egyptian occupation left an imprint on early Kushites, but as the kingdom emerged, it developed its own distinct civilization. Although the Kushites worshipped Egyptian gods (especially Amen), they also developed their own deities and religious idioms. The lion-headed war god Apedemak, for example, was distinctively Kushite. They used pyramids for royal burials but did not adopt Egyptian building and burial customs. Inhabitants of the Meroitic Empire

The Meroitic Empire. (Library of Congress)

retained their own language. They first wrote with Egyptian hieroglyphs, but during the three centuries before the Common Era, they developed their own written script, now known as Meroitic cursive. Although they adopted features of pharaonic rule, they also had uncommonly powerful queens called *kandake*, a term from which the name Candace derives. They recruited Egyptian craftspeople and utilized many of their artistic techniques, but Egyptian elements were blended with other influences to develop a distinctively Meroitic style.

With its prosperity and influence peaking in the centuries between c. 300 B.C.E. and c. 100 C.E., the kingdom of Meroë played a central role in an international trading system that extended to southeast Asia, the Mediterranean world, and parts of the African interior. Meroë's rise was aided by Ptolemaic development of additional Red Sea trade routes that provided outlets for exports such as iron, tortoise shell, ostrich feathers, slaves, animal skins, gold, and ivory. The rarity of Meroitic manufactures beyond its own frontiers suggests to some that goods from the African interior were acquired through expropriation rather than trade. Nevertheless, it was a time of unprecedented wealth, expansion, and construction in the Upper Nile River Valley.

By the third century C.E., the Meroitic Empire was encountering a host of problems. As Rome declined, sources of wealth diminished and shifts occurred in the trade markets. Commercial routes from the Nile to the Red Sea came under control of the Aksumites. Desert groups, especially the Noba, staged incursions. The empire fell into slow decline. Aksum rose to power, and fourth century inscriptions indicate Aksumite suzerainty over Meroë. It is generally believed that c. 350 C.E., Ezana, king of Aksum, led a campaign into territories previously held by the Meroitic Empire. His inscriptions describe the defeated enemy as the Noba, who were already occupying areas in the heartland of the former kingdom. It is evident that central control had already fragmented, but Ezana's victory is used to mark the official end of the Meroitic Empire as an independent political entity.

SIGNIFICANCE

The importance of the Meroitic Empire has not always been recognized in accounts of the ancient world, perhaps because of its geographic distance from the Mediterranean basin and to the misconception that it was a copy of Egypt. Meroë was a corridor of cultural exchange, but despite many examples of syncretism, a distinctive civilization emerged. The empire was a key component of international trade; it may have been one of the main channels through which ironworking technology was transmitted into sub-Saharan Africa. The vacuum created by Aksum's eclipse of Meroë enabled consolidation among the Noba peoples and the founding of the new Christian successor states of Alwa (Alodia), Makouria, and Nobatia.

—*Cassandra Lee Tellier*

FURTHER READING

Adams, William Y. *Nubia: Corridor to Africa*. Princeton, N.J.: Princeton University Press, 1977. Although slightly outdated, a detailed history of this area. Bibliography and index.

Burnstein, Stanley, ed. *Ancient African Civilizations: Kush and Axum*. Princeton, N.J.: Marcus Wiener, 1998. A compilation of primary sources including geographic and ethnographic texts, secular and church histories, inscriptions, and commercial documents. Notes, bibliography, and index.

O'Connor, David. *Ancient Nubia: Egypt's Rival in Africa*. Philadelphia: University of Pennsylvania, 1993. Discusses the rise and fall of Nubian kingdoms and documents many artifacts included in the title exhibition. Index and photographs.

Shinnie, P. L. *Meroë: A Civilization of the Sudan*. New York: Frederick A. Praeger, 1967. Although slightly out of date, a detailed survey of the history and culture of Meroë. Notes, bibliography, and index.

Welsby, Derek A. *The Kingdom of Kush: The Napatan and Meroitic Empires*. Princeton, N.J.: Markus Wiener, 1998. A modern analysis of Kushite civilization. Discusses the problems involved in developing a balanced account of the kingdom's thousand-year history. Notes, bibliography, and index.

SEE ALSO: c. 2700-c. 1400 B.C.E., Gash Civilization Thrives in Africa; 2500-1900 B.C.E., Wawat Chiefdom Flourishes in Lower Nubia; c. 2200-1500 B.C.E., Kerma Kingdom Develops and Dominates Lower Nubia; c. 1900-1527? B.C.E., Kerma Kingdom Rules Nubia; 8th century B.C.E., Kushite King Piye Conquers Upper Egypt; c. 783-c. 591 B.C.E., Napata Kingdom Flourishes in Kush; c. 712-698 B.C.E., Shabaka Reunites the Nile Valley; 664 B.C.E., Saite Dynasty Begins in Egypt.

RELATED ARTICLE in *Great Lives from History: The Ancient World*: Ezana.

6th-4th century B.C.E. (traditionally, 1st millennium B.C.E.)
Suśruta, Indian Physician, Writes Medical Compendium

Suśruta, a physician and sage, wrote Suśruta Samhitā, *a medical compendium of verses about health, disease, and longevity; it is a cornerstone of Āyurvedic medicine and is particularly renowned for the chapter on surgery.*

Locale: Benares (now Varanasi), India
Category: Health and medicine

Key Figure

Suśruta of Benares (c. 450-380 B.C.E.), Indian physician and sage

Summary of Event

Suśruta of Benares (now Varanasi, a Hindu holy city on the Ganges River in India) was a sage and physician. In India, he is known as the Father of Surgery and the Pioneer Anatomist. His name is sometimes spelled Sushruta or Suśrata. He wrote *Suśruta Samhitā* (*An English Translation of the Sushrata Samhita*, 1907-1916), a medical treatise that is renowned for its descriptions of sophisticated surgical techniques and its lengthy plant-based pharmacopoeia. The treatise is one of the key texts of Āyurveda (literally, knowledge of life), a classical system of ancient medicine, and is written in Sanskrit verse.

Orthodox Hindus believe that Āyurveda is derived from the *Atharvaveda* (c. 1500-1100 B.C.E.; *The Hymns of the Atharva-veda*, 1895-1896), one of the holy Vedas said to have been revealed before 5000 B.C.E. It was a gift from Brahmā, the creator of the universe, who gave the knowledge of life to a succession of teachers. Eventually, Dhanvantari, the god-king of Kāúi (Varanasi), revealed Āyurvedic medicine to Suśruta. The codification of Āyurveda, however, probably took place during the sixth century B.C.E. Much of the Vedas are hymns of praise and worship, as well as prayers for health, longevity, and sons. The families of priests or *brāhmana* memorized thousands of Vedic verses and orally transmitted them throughout the ages. Hence, an Āyurvedic physician would prescribe a regimen of care or would opt for a particular surgical procedure depending on the verses he recalled from his memory.

Contemporary scholars, such as Roy Porter, the British historian of science, and Dominik Wujastyk, a Sanskrit specialist, dispute the ancient Vedic origin of Āyurveda and attribute this claim to religious fundamentalism or nationalism. They posit that Āyurveda may have come from heterodox ascetic communities, especially Buddhist monastic groups, no earlier than the fourth century B.C.E. Nevertheless, faithful Hindus believed (and still believe) that the ancient holy Vedas were revealed by the gods to the sages and that the Āyurveda has divine origins.

Āyurveda is the foundation for much of the *Suśruta Samhitā*. Āyurveda and Suśruta's treatise are more rational and empirical than *The Hymns of the Atharva-veda*. Suśruta described herbal and mineral therapeutics and wrote commentaries on health and disease, longevity, and living well. His tone is more pragmatic than magico-religious.

The Vedics believed that all matter is made of five elements: earth, air, fire, water, and ether. The elements are vivified by the *prānas* (vital breaths), which act on the three humors: *vāta* (wind, breath, or air), *pitta* (bile or fire), and *kapha* (phlegm, mucus, or water). Humoral balance depends, in part, on climate and diet. Humoral imbalance is symptomatic of disease or human suffering, and the root cause of disease is sin, either in this life or in a previous life. To cure sickness, promote health, and enhance longevity, the humors are brought into equilibrium by means of diet, botanical and mineral therapeutics, surgery, and prayer.

Suśruta believed that the good physician should treat a patient like a son because the patient has faith in the doctor; in an emergency, the physician must respond as if his house were on fire. Moreover, a good surgeon is bold and swift, with a steady hand and instruments of steel sharp enough to split a hair. Among the blunt instruments, such as his own feet, magnets, linen, stones, and hammers, the surgeon's hands are the most important.

Suśruta described operations resembling modern reconstructive plastic surgery, as well as methods for extracting arrows and splinters. He detailed how to make an incision to extract urinary stones, couching for cataracts (a procedure that displaces the cloudy lens), suturing, and the anatomical study of corpses. He wrote of etiology and symptoms of disease and appropriate therapeutics. As part of the materia medica, he classified about seven hundred plants by structure, exudates, and extracts, such as oil and ash, and listed animal by-products such as ghee (an oil from clarified butter), honey, and milk. Common methods for redressing humoral imbalance included enemas and purgatives for intestinal evacuation, emetics to induce vomiting, bloodletting, cupping, and the application of leeches.

Suśruta also gave advice regarding a healthful diet and exercise regimen. For example, one should eat good food in moderate amounts with due consideration of the humors and season. To reduce fat and gain strength, one should exercise every day regardless of the season, exercising just up to the point of rapid breathing.

Although many of the surgical techniques are surprisingly modern, the context of care is more spiritual than is typical of Western medicine. The operations commence with prayer and offerings. For an auspicious outcome, the patient is placed facing east and the physician facing west. After the operation, Vedic hymns are sung to ward off evil spirits.

With regard to severed or displaced body parts, Suśruta suggested that ears should be stitched in place, stumps of legs should be cauterized, and eyes out of sockets should be gently replaced by exerting pressure over lotus leaves. If the belly is opened and the guts have come out, they should be cleaned with ghee and milk; if there is a rupture, black ants may be applied to the edges of the perforation until they bite; then their bodies should be cut off and the belly sutured.

The surgical methods of Suśruta appear to have been neglected for hundreds of years. Scholars hypothesize that as the caste system became more rigid, taboos prohibiting physical contact grew stricter. Physicians were less inclined to invade the body. Diagnostic techniques, such as reading the pulse, smelling and tasting urine, and examining the tongue took precedence over surgery, along with a range of less invasive therapies, such as purging, sweating, and massage. Furthermore, no ancient or medieval surgical instruments have survived that could corroborate the idea that the methods of Suśruta were practiced by educated physicians in later periods. On the other hand, his methods probably were passed down as caste skills outside the Āyurveda mainstream.

There is a famous anecdote supporting caste transmission of Suśruta's surgical methods. In the late eighteenth century, a man named Cowasjee, who had served in the English army, was captured by the forces of Tipu Sultan. They cut off one hand and his nose, traditionally a punishment for adultery. A year later, Cowasjee found a man from the brickmakers' caste near Poona who rebuilt his nose with consummate skill. The eyewitness reports of two British surgeons, Thomas Cruso and James Trindlay, were published in London in 1794. The superior skin-grafting and reconstruction of the nose were astounding; Europeans adopted the new procedure for rhinoplasty and referred to it as the Hindu method.

In his treatise, Suśruta wrote that rhinoplasty is similar to repairing a cleft palate, except that two reeds for lifting the skin flap are unnecessary in the latter procedure. Also, to qualify as royal physician, a man must be capable of successfully performing both of these operations.

SIGNIFICANCE

In the Western world, Āyurveda is viewed as an alternative to mainstream medicine. According to physician K. D. Sharma of New Delhi, India, 20 percent of the world's population makes use of Āyurveda today. The ancient system for healing the sick and injured and for promoting health and longevity is especially popular in the rural villages of India. Even in cosmopolitan areas, traditional medicine is practiced alongside biomedicine, commonly typified as Western. Contemporary caregivers familiar with the canonical texts, including *Suśruta Samhitā*, are able to design and deliver programs that meet the needs of women and men of all castes who turn to Āyurveda.

—*Tanja Bekhuis*

FURTHER READING

Leslie, Charles, and Allan Young, eds. *Paths to Asian Medical Knowledge*. Berkeley: University of California Press, 1992. In the chapter "Death and Nurturance in Indian Systems of Healing," Margaret Trawick, an anthropologist, discusses four indigenous systems, including Āyurvedic medicine, and Suśruta's role. Transcription of a modern Āyurvedic healer's interview of a patient with commentary is included.

Ninivaggi, Frank John. *An Elementary Textbook of Āyurveda: Medicine with a Six-Thousand-Year-Old Tradition*. Madison, Wis.: Psychosocial Press, 2001. First chapter is a historical overview of Āyurvedic medicine up to the modern period. Includes a discussion of Suśruta's contribution. Appendices include time line of Āyurveda, a glossary of Sanskrit terms, a classification of diseases, and clinical cases.

Porter, Roy. *The Greatest Benefit to Mankind: A Medical History of Humanity*. New York: W. W. Norton, 1997. Chapter 6, "Indian Medicine," is a very good introduction with some mention of research controversies. Includes comments on *Suśruta Samhitā*. Suggested sources for further reading by chapter. Index.

Singhal, G. D., and T. J. S. Patterson. *Synopsis of Āyurveda: Based on a Translation of the "Suśruta Samhitā" (The Treatise of Suśruta)*. Delhi: Oxford University Press, 1993. A summary in English of Suśruta's medical compendium with citations given for the relevant canto(s), chapter(s), and verse(s). English and Sanskrit keywords in margins serve as pointers to topics. Index of Sanskrit terms for drugs, minerals, and recipes. General index.

Suśruta. *An English Translation of the "Sushruta Samhita."* 3d ed. Varanasi: Chowkhamba Sanskrit Series Office, 1981. A revised edition of the translation originally published in 1907-1916.

SEE ALSO: 1500-1100 B.C.E., Compilation of the Vedas; c. 500-400 B.C.E., Greek Physicians Begin Scientific Practice of Medicine; c. 200 B.C.E., Birth of Hinduism; c. 157-201 C.E., Galen Synthesizes Ancient Medical Knowledge.

c. 600 B.C.E.
APPEARANCE OF ZOROASTRIAN DITHEISM

Zoroaster founded a new faith, which featured a dual godhead, an idea that has affected both Judaism and Christianity.

LOCALE: Persia (now Iran)
CATEGORY: Religion

KEY FIGURES

Zoroaster (c. 628-c. 551 B.C.E.), founder and prophet of the new faith

Vishtaspa (b. c. 630 B.C.E.), a prince in Media, r. from c. 610 B.C.E.

SUMMARY OF EVENT

Ditheism, or belief in two gods as in Zoroastrianism, attempts to provide a satisfactory answer to one of the serious problems of religion: the explanation of evil. To some extent the concept of a dual godhead has penetrated both Judaism and Christianity. The god of darkness or evil found its way into the former in attenuated fashion in the form of Satan. The Dead Sea Scrolls, for instance, speak of the war between the sons of light and the sons of darkness. In Christianity, the force of evil becomes the Devil.

Zoroastrian ditheism was a theological position reached only with difficulty. The religion was developed by Indo-Europeans who wandered into the Iranian plateau about 2000 B.C.E. and reflects to a great extent the environment of the old religion before the invasion.

Zoroaster may have been the son of a landed proprietor. His name seems derived from a Greek corruption of the old Iranian word Zarathustra, possibly meaning "one who plows with camels" or "one whose camels are old." According to tradition, at the age of twenty, Zoroaster left home to ponder religious questions and, after ten years, was rewarded with a series of revelatory visions in which an angel called him to ascend a mountain as a disembodied soul to meet with the old Iranian god Ahura Mazda and his heavenly host. In eight days, he was fully instructed as the god's new prophet in the doctrines and duties of true religion. For ten more years, his preaching bore no tangible results beyond the conversion of his cousin, even though he inveighed against religious inadequacies and the social injustices visited on peasants and herdsman.

His first important conversion, of a prince named Vishtaspa, came at a crucial time when he needed support in his struggle with the Magi, the entrenched priests of the traditional cults. When Vishtaspa contributed his influence to the new religion, the whole court was converted. For the next twenty years, Zoroaster propagated the new faith, but its greatest success came only after his death at seventy-seven, victim of an assassin in a religious uprising. Darius the Great might have been the first Achaemenid converted. In general, however, the Persian kings were never militant supporters of the religion.

Zoroaster's message was reasonably simple: He was Ahura Mazda's prophet sent to teach religion and the end of the world. Worship was to be directed toward this one god who brought everything into existence and who in a final apocalyptic event would crush evil forever and establish right and truth. Ahura Mazda was said to express his will through the Holy Spirit, *Spenta Mainyu*, and various "modes" of divine action, such as good thought, power, prosperity, piety, and immortality. Just how Zoroaster envisaged these modes is difficult to say. As forces in their own right, as good *genii*, or angels, or as personalized abstractions, they represented a compromise with the local polytheism, a concession that makes it debatable whether Zoroaster was altogether a monotheist. Although Ahura Mazda was supreme, he was not unopposed. A polarity implicit in creation characterized all existence. Over against right, *Asha*, stood the lie, *Druj*; truth was confronted with falsehood, life with death, the good spirit by the bad.

Zoroaster's cardinal principle of ethics taught that each person's soul was the seat of war between good and evil. At creation, Ahura Mazda gave each person the

Ancient walls in the city of Balkh, Afghanistan. Balkh was once in Bactria and is the legendary birthplace of Zoroaster, who probably was born in Rhages, Media (now Rey, Iran). (AP/Wide World Photos)

freedom to determine his or her own actions and the power to choose between right and wrong. Good people would naturally accept the true religion, while the evil, especially those who continued to practice old rites, would reject it. The old local sacrifices were eliminated, and rituals were purged of what Zoroaster termed magic and idolatry. The sacred fire was kept, but only as a symbol of Ahura Mazda and not as an object of worship in itself. Zoroaster believed in individual judgment after death, with the state of the soul remaining fixed until a general resurrection at the end of the world when evil would be destroyed forever. Those whose record of evil was greater than their good report would dwell in the House of the Lie, Zoroaster's hell, while the righteous would go to the House of Song, or paradise.

With the popularization of Zoroastrianism, more compromises entered into its original "monotheistic" theology. Moreover, the old Magi succeeded in molding a syncretistic system out of Zoroaster's teaching and the old Iranian polytheism. Old Aryan gods were raised to a prominence far greater than the old modes. Thus Mithra was elevated along with a female figure, Anhita, the Spotless One, a counterpart of Ishtar, the goddess of fertility, to form a trinity: Ahura Mazda, Mithra, and Anhita. Zoroaster was raised from human status to that of a godlike personage. His coming was said to have been foretold for three thousand years. His birth became miraculous through Ahura Mazda's intervention, and he became celebrated as an outstanding miracle worker.

Spells and formulas again became popular to ward off evil, and ceremonial purity took more and more precedence over inward regeneration. Eventually Zoroastrianism became a religion of a book, the *Avesta* (1000-600 B.C.E.), a collection of hymns broken into five parts—Yasna, Yasht, Wispered, Vendidad, and Khorde—that were once part of a far larger literature that has since disappeared. Zoroaster's hymns, the *Gathas*, are in the Yasna; they are less legalized and simpler than the later writings.

Eventually in the Sāsānian period, the ditheism developed fully. The many contending gods were again demoted, and a god of evil rose in importance to contend

Ahura Mazda's monopoly. Although Zoroaster had spoken bitterly, but not very tangibly, of the evil spirit Shanitin or Satin, his successors rendered this figure more concrete in the form of an almost equal opponent of Ahura Mazda, the archfiend Ahariman, the cause of darkness and evil straining to nullify every good Ahura Mazda arranged, whether by killing frost in winter, excessive heat in summer, snakes, locusts, or by disbelief and death.

SIGNIFICANCE

The impact of Zoroastrianism on the West is difficult to assess. The old Iranian god Mithra, greatly "Zoroastrianized," became popular in the early Roman Empire; Gnosticism and Manichaeanism appear to owe some debt to the Zoroastrianism of the Sāsānian period.

—*Joseph R. Rosenbloom*

FURTHER READING

Bausani, Alessandro. *Religion in Iran: From Zoroaster to Baha'ullah*. New York: Bibliotheca Persica Press, 2000. An overview of the religions of Iran, which touches on Zoroastrianism.

Boyce, Mary. *Zoroastrians: Their Religious Beliefs and Practices*. 1979. Reprint. New York: Routledge, 2001. A study of the followers of Zoroastrianism that includes a history of the belief.

Clark, Peter. *Zoroastrianism: An Introduction to an Ancient Faith*. Sussex, England: Sussex Academic Press, 1999. Examines all aspects of Zoroastrianism, from its history to present.

Hartz, Paula R. *Zoroastrianism*. New York: Facts on File, 1999. An overview of the religion.

Kellens, Jean, ed. *Essays on Zarathustra and Zoroastrianism*. Costa Mesa, Calif: Mazda, 2000. A collection of essays on Zoroastrianism that cover topics such as the *Avesta* and specific beliefs.

Kriwaczek, Paul. *In Search of Zarathustra: The First Prophet and the Ideas That Changed the World*. London: Weidenfeld and Nicolson, 2002. Focuses on Zoroaster and how his beliefs influenced those who came after him.

Neusner, Jacob. *Judaism and Zoroastrianism at the Dusk of Late Antiquity: How Two Ancient Faiths Wrote Down Their Great Traditions*. Atlanta: Scholars Press, 1993. A comparison and contrast of Zoroastrianism and Judaism in antiquity.

Nigosian, Solomon A. *The Zoroastrian Faith: Tradition and Modern Research*. Toronto: McGill-Queens University Press, 1993. This study looks at the Zoroastrian religion, examining the traditions and legends as well as scholarly research.

SEE ALSO: 520-518 B.C.E., Darius the Great Conquers the Indus Valley; c. 500 B.C.E.-c. 600 C.E., Mithraism Emerges as Significant Religion.

RELATED ARTICLES in *Great Lives from History: The Ancient World*: Darius the Great; Zoroaster.

600-500 B.C.E.
GREEK PHILOSOPHERS FORMULATE THEORIES OF THE COSMOS

In Greece, the presocratic philosophers formulated theories of the cosmos, setting aside previous mythopoeic explanations and launching an empirical and scientific intellectual revolution.

LOCALE: Greece
CATEGORIES: Philosophy; science and technology

KEY FIGURES

Hesiod (fl. c. 700 B.C.E.), Greek epic poet
Thales of Miletus (c. 624-c. 548 B.C.E.), Greek philosopher and scientist
Anaximander (c. 610-c. 547 B.C.E.), Greek philosopher often called the founder of astronomy
Anaximenes of Miletus (early sixth century-latter sixth century B.C.E.), Greek philosopher and scientist
Xenophanes (c. 570-c. 478 B.C.E.), Greek philosopher and poet
Pythagoras (c. 580-c. 500 B.C.E.), Greek philosopher, astronomer, and mathematician
Heraclitus of Ephesus (c. 540-c. 480 B.C.E.), Greek philosopher known for his book *On Nature*
Parmenides (c. 515-after 436 B.C.E.), Greek philosopher of metaphysics
Democritus (c. 460-c. 370 B.C.E.), Greek philosopher associated with atomism

SUMMARY OF EVENT

Before the sixth century B.C.E., human beings everywhere explained the world in mythological terms. These myths depicted humankind dependent on the wills of inscrutable gods who created the world and acted on their all-too-human personal whims. Nonliving and powerful natural forces were "animated," given living souls by the prelogical mentality of early people, otherwise quite sophisticated in building pyramids or irrigation canals. No other explanation was available to them, no scientific foundation on which to build a real understanding of the world and nature.

Similarly, most Greeks honored the epic poets Homer (early ninth century-late ninth century B.C.E.) and Hesiod as their teachers. Hesiod's *Theogony* (c. 700 B.C.E.; English translation, 1728) is the earliest Greek version of the origins of the cosmos. The Greek term *kosmos* means the organized world order. In Hesiod's account, the origin of all things was *chaos*, formless space or yawning watery deep, the opposite of *kosmos*. In time there emerged, either independently or by sexual union, Gaia (Earth), Tartaros (Hades), Eros (Love), Night, Day, and Aither (upper air), Sea, and Ouranos (Sky), and boundless Okeanos (Ocean). A generation of powerful Titans was engendered, and finally the Olympian gods descended from Ouranos and Gaia.

About 600 B.C.E., in Ionia (western Turkey), a new way of perceiving the world was beginning. Confronted by the confusing mythologies of ancient Near Eastern peoples, their own no better, a handful of Greeks over three generations attempted to explain the origins and components of the seen world without mythology. Their great discovery was that to one seeking knowledge—the philosopher—the world manifests internal order and discernible regularity. Nature can be understood. The world is a *kosmos*.

From allusions in Homer and Hesiod came hints. The sky was thought to be a metallic hemispheric bowl covering the disk of earth. The lower space immediately above the disk was *aër*, breathable air; the upper part of the bowl-space was *ouranos* or *aither*. Below its surface, the earth's deep roots reached down to *Tartaros*, the deepest part of Hades (the underworld realm of the dead), as far below earth as sky is above it. *Okeanos*, infinitely wide, encircled the disk of earth and was the source of all fresh and salt waters. Such a mixture of the empirical and the imaginative was common to most mythopoeic cosmologies.

Thales of Miletus was the first to rationalize the myths. He conceived the earth-disk as floating on the ocean and held the single substance of the world to be water. His reasoning, according to Aristotle, was that water can be gaseous, liquid, and solid; life requires water; Homer had surrounded the earth by *Okeanos*. As a unified source of all things, Thales' choice of water was a good guess, but it begged for alternatives. More important, in reducing multiple things to water, Thales had taken a first step in establishing inductive reasoning (from particular examples to general principles) as a scientific methodology.

Anaximander, companion of Thales, was a polymath: astronomer, geographer, evolutionist, philosopher-cosmologist. It is nearly impossible to do justice to his intellectual achievement. He was the first Greek to write in prose. He said that animal life began in the sea and that humans evolved from other animals. He made the first world map, a circle showing Europe and Asia plus Africa equal in size, all surrounded by ocean. Anaximander's cosmos was a sphere with a drum-shaped earth floating in space at its center. The sun, stars, and moon revolved around the earth, seen through openings in the metallic dome of the sky.

In place of Thales' water, Anaximander offered *apeiron*, an eternal, undefined, and inexhaustible basic stuff from which everything came to be and to which everything returns. It is a sophisticated *chaos*. Convinced by his own logic, Anaximander imputed an ethical necessity to this process. Things coming to be and claiming their share of *apeiron* thus deprive others of existence. So, in his words, "they must render atonement each to the other according to the ordinances of Time." This eternal process operates throughout the cosmos. Using terms such as *kosmos* (order), *diké* (justice), and *tisis* (retribution), Anaximander enunciated the exalted idea that nature itself is subject to universal moral laws.

The contributions of Anaximenes of Miletus pale before those of Anaximander. What best defines Anaximenes is his empirical approach. He posited air as the primal stuff that gives rise to all things. Observing air condensing into water, he conceived a maximum condensation of air into stone. Similarly, by rarefaction, air becomes fire or soul. The earth and other heavenly bodies, being flat, ride on air in its constant motion.

Xenophanes, an Ionian who had moved to Italy, represents a new generation of thinkers. He interpreted the new natural explanations of the universe that had challenged the older Hesiodic mythopoeic construct as the abandonment of the old, often immoral, anthropomorphic gods, who dressed in clothes and spoke Greek. He posited a single spiritual creator god who controls the universe without effort, by pure thought. In this monotheism, he was alone among the Greeks.

Insightfully, Xenophanes said human knowledge about the universe is limited and the whole truth may never be known. He taught that natural events have natural, not divine, causes. The rainbow is only a colored cloud. The sea is the source of all waters, winds, and clouds. From sea fossils found in rocks, his cosmogony deduced a time when land was under water. Civilization was the work of men, not gods. Xenophanes was a skeptic who trusted only his own observations about the world.

Pythagoras, an Ionian mathematician in southern Italy, had noticed that the sounds of lyre strings varied according to their length and that harmonies were mathematically related. He saw that proportion can be visually perceived in geometrical figures. From these notions he and his followers described a cosmos structured on a mathematical model. Instead of adopting Anaximander's "justice" or Heraclitus of Ephesus's *logos* as the dominant organizing principle, the Pythagoreans preferred numerical harmony. Pythagoras thus added a dimension to the ancient concepts of due proportion and the golden mean that pervaded Greek thought. These concepts are seen in Greek sculpture and architecture and as moral principles in lyric and dramatic poetry and historical interpretations, where *hybris* (excess) and *sophrosyné* (moderation) were fundamental principles of human behavior.

Inevitably, Greek physical philosophy began to investigate the process of knowing. Number is unchanging; ten is always ten. In a world of apparently infinite diversity and flux, numbers can be known more perfectly than other objects of experience. Though the Pythagoreans went too far in trying to explain everything by numbers, they taught that a nature based on mathematical harmony and proportion was knowable.

Heraclitus argued that change, though sometimes imperceptible, is the common element in all things. All change, he said, takes place along continuums of opposite qualities, such as the hot-cold line or dry-moist line. His contribution, however, was his idea of *logos* as the hidden organizing principle of the cosmos. *Logos* maintains a protective balance (the golden mean again) among all the oppositional tensions in the world.

Although Parmenides and Democritus fall outside the chronological scope of the sixth century B.C.E., their contributions of logic to the Greek discovery of the cosmos merit some attention. In the mid-fifth century, Democritus reasoned to a world built of the smallest thinkable indivisible particles, atoms. Parmenides—struck by the constant flux of the physical world and seeking, as Pythagoras, an unchanging object of knowledge that mind can grasp—saw existence, or Being, as the common element of things in the cosmos. He proposed the logic that while things change, Being itself cannot change, for nothing and no place exists outside of the sphere of Being, so nothing could enter or leave. He is thus the most metaphysical of the philosophers, initiating ideas that would only be completed by Plato and Aristotle, the greatest of the philosophers.

SIGNIFICANCE

The significance of the Ionian philosophers is that, within little more than a century after breaking with mythopoeic interpretations of the world, they had asserted its atomic makeup, conceived human evolution, discovered induction and logic, and practiced a curiosity about all natural phenomena. This was one of history's great intellectual revolutions, the origins of scientific speculation.

—*Daniel C. Scavone*

FURTHER READING

Kirk, G. S., and J. E. Raven. *The Presocratic Philosophers*. 2d ed. New York: Cambridge University Press, 1984. A collection of Greek texts and English translations, with commentary based upon the words of individual philosophers.

Long, A. A. *The Cambridge Companion to Early Greek Philosophy*. New York: Cambridge University Press, 1999. Includes essays on both individual philosophers and overarching themes.

Morgan, Kathryn A. *Myth and Philosophy from the Presocratics to Plato*. New York: Cambridge University Press, 2000. Explores the interactions between mythological and scientific thinking in classical Greece culture.

Popper, Karl R. *The World of Parmenides: Essays on the Presocratic Enlightenment*. Edited by Arne F. Petersen and Jørgen Mejer. New York: Routledge, 1998. One of the most influential philosophers of the twentieth century assesses the work and worldview of the Presocratics, focusing on Parmenides. The essays attempt to illuminate the ways in which Presocratic philosophy still guides modern conceptions of the scientific process.

Ring, Merrill. *Beginning with the Presocratics*. 2d ed. New York: McGraw-Hill, 1999. A short and accessible introduction to the Presocratic philosophers, intended as an introductory college text.

Wakefield, Robin, ed. *The First Philosophers: The Presocratics and the Sophists*. New York: Oxford University Press, 2000. A collection of translations of the important Presocratic philosophers, including Thales, Anaximander, Anaximenes of Miletus, Heraclitus of Ephesus, Xenophanes, and Parmenides. Textual and explanatory notes, chronology, bibliography, concordance, and index.

SEE ALSO: c. 750 B.C.E., Homer Composes the *Iliad*; c. 700 B.C.E., Hesiod Composes *Theogony* and *Works and Days*; c. 530 B.C.E., Founding of the Pythagorean Brotherhood; c. 500-400 B.C.E., Greek Physicians Begin Scientific Practice of Medicine; c. 450-c. 425 B.C.E., History Develops as a Scholarly Discipline; c. 440 B.C.E., Sophists Train the Greeks in Rhetoric and Politics; 399 B.C.E., Death of Socrates; c. 380 B.C.E., Plato Develops His Theory of Ideas; c. 335-323 B.C.E., Aristotle Writes the *Politics*.

RELATED ARTICLES in *Great Lives from History: The Ancient World*: Anaximander; Anaximenes of Miletus; Aristotle; Democritus; Heraclitus of Ephesus; Hesiod; Parmenides; Plato; Pythagoras; Socrates; Thales of Miletus; Xenophanes.

c. 594-580 B.C.E.
LEGISLATION OF SOLON

The legislation of Solon allowed Athens temporarily to avoid revolution in the sixth century B.C.E. and gave greater rights and authority to the nonnoble citizens of Athens.

LOCALE: Athens
CATEGORY: Laws, acts, and legal history

KEY FIGURE

Solon (c. 630-c. 560 B.C.E.), Athenian aristocrat who revised Athenian laws that established the political and social foundations for the development of classical democracy

SUMMARY OF EVENT

At the beginning of the sixth century B.C.E., Athens was threatened with disaster. The aristocratic families fought among themselves for supremacy, and their struggles sometimes verged on civil war. The nobles also used their power against farmers of middle and low income in order to expand their own estates. Some poor farmers became serfs or were enslaved through debt. The resultant tendency was to diminish the class of men on which the military strength and safety of Athens depended.

Other states solved similar problems by resorting to tyranny, a kind of one-man benevolent despotism which tended to favor the nonaristocrats, including the poor. The great magnates of Athens, fearful lest such a tyrant might arise and dispossess them, agreed to have limits set upon their power. Solon, himself a member of the aristocracy, was chosen archon, or ruler, about 594 B.C.E. In that year, and probably later as well, as special "conciliator" he brought about social and political relief by revising the laws of Athens.

Solon's social reforms were important; he himself referred to them as the "lifting of burdens." He abolished serfdom and slavery for debt, ridding Athens of those curses once and for all. New laws on debt were enacted, though details have been lost, and in this way the number of men eligible for military service was maintained.

Solon also appears to have considered building up the commerce of Athens, possibly to provide employment for skilled foreigners such as potters and shipbuilders who were allowed to settle in Athens with the protected status of *metic*, or resident alien. How far Solon went along these lines is disputed. The tyrant Pisistratus (c. 612-527 B.C.E.) undoubtedly did more later, so that by the end of the sixth century, Athens was successfully competing with important trading states such as Aegina and Corinth.

To protect his social gains, Solon sought to strengthen political institutions through which the middle income group could voice its desires. The citizens were divided into four census classes based on wealth: The richest men were the *pentacosiomedimni* with an income of five hundred measures of olive oil, wine, or grain, a measure being 11.5 gallons (43.5 liters) wet or 1.85 bushels (0.65 hectoliter) dry; next came the *hippeis* or cavalry, whose farms produced three hundred measures and enabled them to keep a warhorse; then there were the *zeugitae*, who plowed their land with a yoke of oxen, had an income of two hundred measures, could afford armor, and served as infantrymen; and last were the remaining citizens, who belonged to the lowest class of the *thetes*, the laborers or hired men.

The top three classes had certain duties and privileges in the public affairs of the city and served in the first-line field army. Only members of the two richest classes, however, could hold the office of archon. Three archons were selected annually, each having jurisdiction over a specific sphere of public business. The *archon eponymus* had charge of internal affairs and presided over the assembly. The *archon basileus* was responsible for the conduct of the state religion. The *archon polemarchos* commanded the army. These three officials and the other six archons called *thesmothetes* were also magistrates of the courts. Solon probably believed that only the nobility, by reason of birth and training, had sufficient knowledge and experience to carry out these important duties. The archons were, however, selected by lot by the people sitting as the *Ecclesia* or assembly. It is disputed whether the *thetes* were members of this body. The same people differently organized were the *heliaea*, or court. All citizens now had the right of appeal to this court from a judgment handed down by one of the archons, an advantage for the poor. This right, and the right of the assembly to examine the acceptability of candidates for archonship and to scrutinize the conduct of the magistrates in office, were safeguards of the few rights enjoyed by nonnoble Athenians. There is no reason to believe that the assembly did more than elect the archons once a year and assent to declarations of war. There is no sure evidence that it passed laws, although it may have done so from time to time. How the laws of Solon were enacted is not known.

Solon is also said to have created an annual Council of Four Hundred whose function was to act as a steering committee for the whole assembly. Considerable doubt has been cast on the existence of this body. There was certainly another council at this time, the *areopagus*, made up of former archons serving for life, and it was also important. Although scholars are unsure of its exact duties, it had some sort of power to safeguard the laws. It was also claimed in antiquity that Solon handed down a mass of detailed legislation amounting to a whole written code. It is extremely unlikely that he did, in fact, do so.

SIGNIFICANCE

Solon's work was of great significance for Athens. He found the state dominated by a hereditary aristocracy, and he left it an aristocratic republic. The nobles had accepted limitation of their power, which gave the downtrodden peasantry a chance to develop. This paved the way for the reforms of Cleisthenes of Athens in 508 B.C.E. and eventually for the democratic system of government that is one of ancient Greece's major contributions to the world.

—*Samuel K. Eddy, updated by Jeffrey L. Buller*

FURTHER READING

Anhalt, Emily Katz. *Solon the Singer.* Lanham, Md.: Rowman & Littlefield, 1993. A broad analysis of Solon and his influence, exploring not only his political contributions but also his poetry.

Brock, Roger, and Stephen Hodkinson, eds. *Alternatives to Athens: Varieties of Political Organization and Community in Ancient Greece.* New York: Oxford University Press, 2001. A collection of essays that illuminates the alternatives to democracy that existed in ancient Greece, contextualizing why Athens was different from its surrounding city-states.

Mitchell, Lynette G. "New Wine in Old Wineskins: Solon, *Arete*, and the *Agathos*." In *The Development of the Polis in Archaic Greece*, edited by Lynette G. Mitchell and P. J. Rhodes. New York: Routledge, 1997. Solon's legislation is placed in the context of the civic institutions of Greece as a whole. Discusses the significance of written legislation in the development of the polis.

O'Neil, James. *The Origins and Development of Ancient Greek Democracy.* Lanham, Md.: Rowman & Littlefield, 2002. Solon's position in Greece's political history is analyzed.

Sealey, Raphael. *A History of the Greek City States, 700-338 B.C.* Berkeley: University of California Press, 1976. A clear analysis of the distinction between the historical and mythical elements in the tradition of Solon.

Stroud, Ronald S. *The Axones and Kyrbeis of Drakon and Solon.* Berkeley: University of California Press, 1979. A brief but scholarly examination of the legal codes of Draco and Solon. (*Axones* and *kyrbeis* are technical terms for legal codes and are derived from the tablets on which laws were inscribed.)

SEE ALSO: 508-507 B.C.E., Reforms of Cleisthenes; 478-448 B.C.E., Athenian Empire Is Created; c. 335-323 B.C.E., Aristotle Writes the *Politics*; c. 300 B.C.E., Stoics Conceptualize Natural Law.

RELATED ARTICLES in *Great Lives from History: The Ancient World*: Alcibiades of Athens; Cleisthenes of Athens; Draco; Pausanias of Sparta; Pericles; Pisistratus; Solon.

587-423 B.C.E.
BIRTH OF JUDAISM

Judaism developed from the religion of ancient Israel following the Babylonian exile, with the impetus provided by the Persian policy of restoring local cults and codifying local laws.

LOCALE: Jerusalem
CATEGORY: Religion

KEY FIGURES

Cyrus the Great (c. 601/590-c. 530 B.C.E.), king of Persia, r. c. 559-c. 530 B.C.E.
Darius the Great (550-486 B.C.E.), king of Persia, r. 522-486 B.C.E.
Artaxerxes I (d. c. 423 B.C.E.), king of Persia, r. 465-c. 423 B.C.E.
Ezra (fl. late sixth-early fifth century B.C.E.), Jewish scribe

SUMMARY OF EVENT

The English word "Judaism" is derived from a Greek word, *ioudaïsmos*, which appears for the first time in the Bible, in 2 Maccabees (see 2:21, 8:1, 14:38). There is no ancient Hebrew or Aramaic equivalent of this Greek word. Despite the origin of the term "Judaism" in the Hellenistic period, the phenomenon of Judaism is a product of events that began with the fall of Jerusalem to the Babylonians in 587/586 B.C.E.

Since the eighth century B.C.E., the kingdom of Judah had enjoyed only nominal independence. It was a vassal state subject first to Assyria, then to Egypt, and finally to Babylon. After an unsuccessful revolt against Babylon in 587 B.C.E., the kingdom of Judah ceased to exist and its territory was incorporated into the Babylonian provincial system. According to the Bible, Zedekiah, the last king of Judah, was led off to exile after witnessing the execution of his sons (2 Kings 25:7). The Temple of Jerusalem was destroyed and its priesthood scattered. The city was sacked and its leading citizens were exiled from the land and taken to Babylon (2 Kings 25:8-12). The institutions that gave the people of Judah their identity were no more.

Although the Judaean exiles were not slaves, they were no longer part of society's elite as they had been in Judah. Most were sent to work in agriculturally marginal regions in Babylon, and a few were recruited to work as civil servants in the Babylonian bureaucracy. The exile lasted a little more than two generations. In 539 B.C.E., the Persians under Cyrus the Great conquered the Babylonian Empire, and Cyrus encouraged the exiles from Judah to return to their ancestral homeland and rebuild the Temple of Jerusalem (2 Chron. 36:22-23; Ezra 1:1-4).

The anonymous prophet whose words have been preserved in Isaiah 40-55 asserted that God used Cyrus as an instrument to effect the restoration of a righteous remnant, who would return to Jerusalem (Isaiah 45:1). The words of prophets such as Jeremiah and Ezekiel helped the returnees interpret the fall of Jerusalem and the exile in ways that made it possible for them to look to the future with some measure of hope. According to these prophets, the disasters that befell Judah were the just punishment for its infidelity, but judgment was not to be God's last word to Judah.

The territory of the former kingdom of Judah was reduced to the city of Jerusalem and its immediate environs. This region was a Persian colony known as Yehud. Its residents were the *yehudim* (Hebrew) or the *yehudin* (Aramaic). It is from these words that the English term "Jews" derives. *Yehudim* had more than one meaning, however. From a political perspective, it meant the residents of the Persian colony of Yehud. It also had an ethnic connotation, referring to the descendants of those who had lived in Yehud. For example, the mercenaries who formed the Persian garrison at Elephantine Island in Egypt called themselves *yehudin* because their ancestors came from Judah. *Yehudim* also came to have a religious meaning, describing people whose religious beliefs and practices derived from the Mosaic Torah. These beliefs and practices have become known as Judaism.

Judaism was rooted in the beliefs, practices, and institutions of the religion of ancient Israel—that is, the religion practiced in the two nation-states of Israel and Judah. Still, Judaism was not simply synonymous or continuous with Israelite religion. The religion of ancient Israel was concerned with communal salvation, with the welfare and survival of the state and its ruling dynasty. This was achieved through the temple service, which brought the blessing of fertility to the land and protection from external enemies. The political realities faced by Yehud made it clear, however, that neither the Judahite national state nor the Davidic dynasty was going to be restored. Judaism's focus shifted from the welfare of the state to the salvation of the individual, which would be achieved through the observance of the Torah. Although this transformation began with the events of 587 B.C.E., it would not be complete until the emergence of the rabbinic movement as the dominant force in Judaism following the destruction of the second Temple of Jerusalem in 70 C.E.

There were two pivotal developments in the formative period of Judaism following the return from exile: the building of the second Temple of Jerusalem and the promulgation of the Torah. Ironically, both came at the initiative of the Persian authorities. The inhabitants of Yehud were not consumed with a desire to rebuild the temple destroyed in 587 B.C.E. There is no evidence that the Babylonians forbade the temple's reconstruction, but the inhabitants of Jerusalem who were not taken into exile made no effort to restore the building. They offered sacrifices on the ruins of the temple, which appeared to be sufficient for them. Cyrus encouraged the returnees to undertake the rebuilding of the temple in 539 B.C.E., but nothing was done for seventeen years. Work began on the second temple only after Darius the Great commanded that the rebuilding project begin, funded it from his treasury, and sent emissaries to check on its progress (Ezra 4:24-6:18).

The Hebrew prophet and scribe Ezra delivers a sermon. (Hultonl Archives)

Darius the Great was also responsible for the promulgation of the Torah of Moses as the code to govern the lives of the *yehudim*. The Persians did not attempt to create a single law code for their empire. The imperial authorities used local traditions as the basis of what came to be known as the King's Law (see Ezra 7:26). Darius the Great then provided an administrative structure that allowed Yehud to codify its traditional legal practices, and once codified, these laws had the force of imperial law. About fifty years later, Artaxerxes I sent Ezra, a Jew serving in the Persian bureaucracy, to Yehud to enforce the "the Law of God," which was the King's Law for the *yehudim* (Ezra 7:1-26).

The rebuilding of the temple appeared to make Judaism as temple-centered a religion as was that of ancient Israel. There was one important difference, however: The first Temple of Jerusalem provided theological support for the Judahite nation-state and the Davidic dynasty, but the second temple was a project initiated and supported by the Persians. Although there was some local support for this project (see Haggai and Zechariah 1-8), initially the second temple was seen as a symbol of the Persian domination of Yehud. The temple was the center for the worship of the ancestral deity of the *yehudim*, so it did serve another symbolic function. Still, Judaism was only loosely focused on the temple because of the other force set in motion by Darius: the codification of ancient Israel's legal traditions.

The codification of ancient Israel's legal traditions under the impetus provided by the Persian imperial authorities led to a shift in the central focus of early Judaism from the temple to the Torah. This process led to the collection and transmission of not only legal but also prophetic and wisdom texts that soon began to be recognized as normative in varying degrees. Judaism was in the process of becoming a "religion of the book." While this shift in focus took place over hundreds of years, it began in the Persian period.

SIGNIFICANCE

With the rebuilding of the Temple of Jerusalem and the codification of ancient Israel's legal traditions, Judaism began to emerge out of the disaster of the exile. While centuries of development were yet to take place, the foundation of Judaism's fundamental character as a religion based on a written, authoritative text was laid in the Persian period.

Judaism's shift from a religion focused on temple worship to a religion that is centered primarily on a sacred text made it possible for Judaism to survive the loss of the second temple following an unsuccessful revolt against Rome in 70 C.E. and to persist throughout the diaspora. Ultimately, this focus on a written, authoritative text influenced Christianity, which continued to regard the Jewish Scriptures as authoritative while producing its own distinctive texts as well. Still later, Islam too was based on an authoritative text that is clearly indebted to the Scriptures of both Judaism and Christianity. Increasing focus on a text, which can be transported along with the worshiper, rather than a temple, which exists in a single location, laid the foundation for the propagation of global rather than local religions.

—*Leslie J. Hoppe*

FURTHER READING

Berquist, Jon L. *Judaism in Persia's Shadow: A Social and Historical Approach*. Minneapolis, Minn.: Fortress Press, 1995. A study of the political and intellectual history of Judaism in the Persian period.

Boccaccini, Gabriele. *Roots of Rabbinic Judaism: An Intellectual History from Ezekiel to Daniel*. Grand Rapids, Mich.: William B. Eerdmans, 2002. Describes three types of Judaism from the Persian period: sapiential, Zadokite, and Enochic.

Jaffee, Martin S. *Early Judaism*. Upper Saddle River, N.J.: Prentice Hall, 1997. Emphasizes the role of ethnic identification as the means of continuity of Judaism with ancient Israelite religion.

Nodet, Étienne. *A Search for the Origins of Judaism*. Sheffield, England: Sheffield Academic Press, 1997. Argues that the two major sources of Judaism are Joshua's laws established at the Shechem assembly and the Mishnah.

VanderKam, James. *Introduction to Early Judaism*. Grand Rapids, Mich.: William B. Eerdmans, 2001. Sketches the history, literature, and religious institutions of early Judaism.

SEE ALSO: c. 1280 B.C.E., Israelite Exodus from Egypt; c. 966 B.C.E., Building of the Temple of Jerusalem; c. 950 B.C.E., Composition of the Book of Genesis; c. 922 B.C.E., Establishment of the Kingdom of Israel; 547 B.C.E., Cyrus the Great Founds the Persian Empire; c. 538-c. 450 B.C.E., Jews Return from the Babylonian Captivity; 520-518 B.C.E., Darius the Great Conquers the Indus Valley.

RELATED ARTICLES in *Great Lives from History: The Ancient World:* Aaron; Abraham; Cyrus the Great; Darius the Great; David; Ezekiel; Ezra; Isaiah; Jeremiah; Jesus; Johanan ben Zakkai; Josephus, Flavius; Moses; Solomon.

c. 580 B.C.E.
GREEK POET SAPPHO DIES

Sappho was one of the first female authors whose name is known and one of the most revered poets of Greece. She expressed her personal, female experience through lyric love poetry and allegedly took her own life over a failed love affair.

LOCALE: Lesbos, Greece (now Lesvos, Greece)
CATEGORY: Literature

KEY FIGURES

Sappho (c. 630-c. 580 B.C.E.), Greek lyric poet
Alcaeus of Lesbos (c. 625-c. 575 B.C.E.), Greek lyric poet

SUMMARY OF EVENT

When Sappho died c. 580 B.C.E., Greece was in its Archaic period (roughly 750-500 B.C.E.). Having emerged from a Dark Age of four centuries' length around 800 B.C.E., Greece rapidly developed its literary and artistic traditions. During the Archaic period, Greece was not a unified nation but a collection of city-states with differing forms of government. Greeks worshiped many gods, who were imagined to have both human form and emotions as well as immortality and supernatural powers. Humanism was a hallmark of ancient Greece, reflected in its anthropomorphic gods, focus on the human figure in art, and recognition of human achievement.

Sappho and Alcaeus of Lesbos were the two great leaders of the Aeolian school of lyric poetry. To the Greeks, "lyric" poetry was poetry accompanied by a lyre, although the term now describes poetry of a personal nature, expressing the poet's emotional response to the world.

Facts are rare and contradictory regarding Sappho's life. The Roman poet Horace (65-8 B.C.E.) made the earli-

The Greek poet Sappho stands, surrounded by her students. (F. R. Niglutsch)

est reference to Sappho in literature, some six hundred years after her death. Other references to Sappho occur in the New Comedies of the third century B.C.E. These references were compiled and presented as biographical information in the tenth century C.E. in an encyclopedic Byzantine compilation of literature, biography, and history called the *Suda*. Here it is stated that Sappho, a native of the island of Lesbos from the town of Eresus, was a lyric poet, active in the forty-second Olympiad (612-608 B.C.E.), and a contemporary of the poets Alcaeus of Lesbos, Stesichorus (632/29-556/53 B.C.E.), and Pitticus. The *Suda* relates that Sappho married a wealthy trader from Andros named Cercylas, and they had a daughter, Kleis. Sappho had three friends named Atthis, Telesippa, and Megara, and because of her "shameful" friendship with them—presumably a reference to her alleged lesbianism—earned a bad reputation.

Sappho taught Anagora from Miletus, Gongyla from Colophon, and Euneica from Salamis; wrote nine books of lyric poetry; and invented the plectum (a pick for stringed instruments). She also wrote epigrams, elegiacs, iambics, and solo songs. This information was all compiled in the *Suda* more than fifteen hundred years after Sappho's death, so its accuracy is questionable. For example, Cercylas, the husband cited in the *Suda*, is mentioned in none of her poetry, and his name only turns up in a later comedy. The name "Cercylas" is an obscene pun meaning "Prick from the Isle of Males."

None of Sappho's original manuscripts survive. It is not known whether Sappho wrote down her poems, but they were not published in her lifetime. Her poems would have been sung to music, perhaps accompanied by dance, and were most likely recorded at a later date, perhaps soon after her death. By the fifth century B.C.E. production of manuscripts on papyrus rolls was established. By the third century B.C.E. the library at Alexandria, Egypt, was established, and Sappho's works were collected. At that time, Aristophanes of Byzantium (c. 257-180 B.C.E.) and Aristarchus of Samothrace (c. 217-c. 145 B.C.E.), both librarians of the Alexandria library, edited Sappho's poems into nine books according to meter. One book was devoted to Sappho's *epithalamia*, wedding songs. One of her poems was reportedly1,320 lines in length. The earliest surviving written poems of Sappho are from the second or third centuries C.E. and were found on papyrus fragments that had been used as mummy wrappings and were discovered in the late nineteenth century.

Other speculative information about Sappho is drawn from people or places mentioned in her poems or from later writings. Fragments of her poetry reveal that Sappho was probably born in the town of Eresos to an aristocratic, socially prominent family, and lived most of her life in Mytilene, the most important city on Lesbos. She was orphaned at the age of six. Two of her brothers are mentioned in her poems: Charaxos, a wine merchant in Egypt, and Larichos, the wine pourer at the Mytilenean town hall. The latter position was one generally reserved for men of aristocratic birth.

It is generally believed that Sappho conducted a school for girls devoted to instruction in poetry, music, and dance: the three elements associated with lyric poetry. It may have been a type of "finishing school" to prepare aristocratic girls for marriage and was dedicated to the goddess of love, Aphrodite. Sappho was allegedly exiled to Sicily in her thirties, perhaps as a result of her father's political activities, but returned to Lesbos—this according to Ovid in his *Heroides* (before 8 B.C.E.; English translation, 1567). Even Ovid's account is cast in doubt, though, because Sappho is presented as a comic character in the *Heroides*.

Ovid, in poem 15, line 1 of his *Epistulae ex Ponto* (after 8 B.C.E.; *Letters from the Black Sea*, 1639) and Strabo in his description of Leucas in book 10, chapter 2, line 9 of *Geōgraphica* (c. 7 B.C.E.; *Geography*, 1917-1933) relate the legend that Sappho jumped from a cliff to her death because of her unrequited love for a man named Phaon. The idea that Sappho committed suicide because of Phaon spurning her love may be the result of the conflation of an Adonis-like myth of Phaon and a myth that Sappho threw herself off a cliff at Leucas after being spurned. The comedy *The Woman of Leucas*, by the playwright Menander (c. 342-c. 291 B.C.E.), whose survival is very fragmentary, may refer to the latter. This is the first surviving account of Sappho's "suicide."

SIGNIFICANCE

The fact that a woman could be as accomplished in Archaic Greece as Sappho appears to have been is remarkable. Sappho's aristocratic birth may have afforded her the education that most Greek girls of the time lacked, or the island of Lesbos afforded more rights to women than the rest of Greece, where boys were favored, women did not count as citizens, and female infanticide was commonly practiced.

One of the most revered poets of Greece, Sappho is known as the first female Greek author and the only extant female Greek poet from the Archaic period. Sappho used love as the subject of all her poetry, some directed to men, some to women. The term "lesbian" (from Lesbos, the name of the island on which Sappho lived) originated because of Sappho's poetry, which often expresses love between women. Ironically, the cause of her leap is alleged to be the unrequited love of a man.

No poetry from Lesbos before that of Sappho survives. Sappho's poems quickly became famous in the Greek world, revered by teachers, influencing later lyric and choral poets and dramatists, both Greek and Roman. Later poets, especially the Romans Catullus (c. 84-c. 54 B.C.E.) and Horace, imitated Sappho's four-line stanza, which is known as the Sapphic, consisting of three identical lines, and a fourth, shorter line.

Sappho explored human values through her own, female experience. She tells of the prayers and rites of women, as well as their longings. As such, Sappho was the first poet to make love and its accompanying human emotions her theme. In terms of entering into a personal relationship with the reader, she is matched by only Archilochus (seventh century B.C.E.) and Alcaeus. In addition to her monodic lyric poetry, she wrote poetic elegies, hymns, odes and epithalamia in the Aeolic dialect. The Greeks called her the Tenth Muse, and ranked her equal to the epic poet Homer (early ninth century-late ninth century B.C.E.).

Although Sappho was prolific and highly popular in ancient times, today just over two hundred fragments survive, most of which are only a few lines in length. Dramatic stories explain the destruction of Sappho's poems: The Fourth Crusade's sack of Constantinople in 1204 destroyed most of the corpus of Sappho's poetry; Pope Gregory VII burned Sappho's poems publicly in 1073 and banned them. In actuality, Sappho's poems do not survive because they became unpopular. Before printing presses, manuscripts had to be laboriously hand-copied. As the Aeolic dialect and lyric poetry became less popular, fewer copies of Sappho's poems were made, and she slipped into obscurity. Until the late 1890's, only one complete poem by Sappho survived: "Artfully Adorned Aphrodite," which was quoted by Dionysius of Halicarnassus in his book *De compositione verborum* (c. 30 B.C.E.; *On Literary Composition*, 1910). Since the late nineteenth century, more than one hundred fragments have been discovered, but only about five hundred verses survive.

—*Sally A. Struthers*

FURTHER READING

Carson, Ann, trans. *If Not, Winter: Fragments of Sappho*. New York: Alfred A. Knopf, 2002. This bilingual translation indicates, with brackets, where text is missing. The book includes a brief introduction to Sappho, the text, and on marks and lacks. Extensive notes on the text.

Powell, Jim, trans. *Sappho: A Garland*. New York: Farrar, Straus, Giroux, 1993. Powell's translation reorders Sappho's fragments into a meaningful thread through a faithful, literal translation. Includes valuable "Afterwards" on Sappho, Sappho's fragments, measures and translation, and bibliography.

Raynor, Diane, trans. *Sappho's Lyre: Archaic Lyric and Women Poets of Ancient Greece*. Berkeley: University of California Press, 1991. Annotated translations of Archilochos, Alcman, Stesichoros, Sappho, Alcaios, Ibykos, Anacreon and Simonides.

Reynolds, Margaret. *The Sappho Companion*. New York: Palgrave, 2001. Nicely illustrated work that documents the influence of Sappho and her poetry throughout history. Includes poetry, literary references and artwork about Sappho, as well as different translations of Sappho's poems over the centuries. Includes bibliography.

Williamson, Margaret. *Sappho's Immortal Daughters*. Cambridge, Mass.: Harvard University Press, 1995. Williamson's book is a search for Sappho through her poetry, her culture, and the myths surrounding her.

Wilson, Lyn Hatherly. *Sappho's Sweetbitter Songs: Configurations of Female and Male in Ancient Greek Lyric*. New York: Routledge, 1996. Through gender study, the author compares Sappho's works to those of Greek male poets and attempts to recreate the world of Sappho. Bibliography.

SEE ALSO: c. 2300 B.C.E., Enheduanna Becomes First Named Author; c. 750 B.C.E., Homer Composes the *Iliad*; c. 700 B.C.E., Hesiod Composes *Theogony* and *Works and Days*; c. 456/455 B.C.E., Greek Tragedian Aeschylus Dies; c. 438 B.C.E., Greek Lyric Poet Pindar Dies; 406 B.C.E., Greek Dramatist Euripides Dies, c. 385 B.C.E., Greek Playwright Aristophanes Dies.

RELATED ARTICLES in *Great Lives from History: The Ancient World:* Clodia; Enheduanna; Homer; Horace; Menander (dramatist); Ovid; Sappho; Simonides.

c. 550 B.C.E.

CONSTRUCTION OF TRIREME CHANGES NAVAL WARFARE

The construction of the trireme changed naval warfare, making possible the sophisticated ramming tactics that dominated Mediterranean naval warfare during the fifth and fourth centuries B.C.E.

LOCALE: Greece
CATEGORIES: Science and technology; wars, uprisings, and civil unrest

KEY FIGURES

Ameinocles (fl. seventh century B.C.E.), early Corinthian shipwright who built the first trireme
Phormion (d. c. 428 B.C.E.), expert Athenian naval commander during the Peloponnesian War
Themistocles (c. 524-c. 460 B.C.E.), Athenian general at the time of the Persian Wars who advocated the building of triremes for a strong navy

SUMMARY OF EVENT

Although warships with rams appeared early in the Mediterranean region, sophisticated ramming tactics had to await the evolution of specialized warships designed specifically for optimum use of the ram. As early as the eighth century B.C.E., Greek vase paintings depict warships with rams and a single file of rowers on each side. Like most ancient warships, these vessels could cruise under sail but relied on oar power in battle. Later literary sources refer to larger and smaller versions of this type of ship: a *triakontor* (thirty-oared ship) with fifteen rowers per file, and a *pentekontor* (fifty-oared ship) with twenty-five rowers per file. With only two files of rowers at one level, these ships had roomy holds and considerable capacity for passengers and cargo in addition to their rowing crews. This roominess suited a style of warfare that involved the transport of sizable numbers of soldiers for coastal raids and boarding attacks on other ships. In naval battles between fleets, the *pentekontors* primarily functioned as fighting platforms from which armored soldiers, javelin throwers, and archers fought for control of immobilized adjacent vessels. Rams were no doubt used when the opportunity to hole an enemy ship presented itself, but the *pentekontor*'s limited rowing power restricted its effectiveness as a ram.

Because the *pentekontor*'s length approached the ancient design limit of twenty-five to thirty rowers, in order to substantially augment rowing power, it was necessary to increase the number of files. The bireme accomplished this by putting two additional files of oar men in the hold area, so that there were now two banks of rowers on each side of the ship. The trireme, with three banks of rowers per side, simply took this concept one step further to produce a vessel with more than three times the oar power of a *pentekontor.*

For centuries, historians have argued over the exact design and rowing configuration of the trireme, but the recent construction of a functioning full-scale replica appears to settle most questions. In particular, it demonstrates that with outriggers, rowers at three different levels can operate efficiently using oars of the same length. With 170 rowers in three banks packed within its narrow, lightly built hull, the trireme sacrificed strength, stability, and cargo capacity for speed and maneuverability. An improved bronze ram at the bow's waterline completed the transformation of the *pentekontor.* The result was a virtual guided missile perfectly matched to the hit-and-run ramming tactics that would rule naval warfare in the two centuries following the trireme's widespread adoption.

Although the overall evolution from *pentekontor* to bireme to trireme seems clear enough, the question of the date and place of trireme's invention is still debated. The earliest explicit report of triremes used in war refers to ships built in Egypt by the pharaoh Necho I (r. c. 672-664 B.C.E.). Because of Egypt's proximity to Phoenicia and the later fame of Phoenician triremes, some historians attribute the innovation to the Phoenicians. Other scholars note Necho's close relations with the Greeks and prefer to credit them with the breakthrough. According to the Greek historian Thucydides (c. 459-c. 402 B.C.E.), the earliest naval battle took place when the Corcyraeans fought the Corinthians, who were the first among the Greeks to build triremes. Thucydides also names a noted Corinthian shipwright, Ameinocles, who built four triremes for the island city-state of Samos. If these events are correctly dated to the middle and late seventh century, then Necho may well have learned about triremes from Corinth. Regardless of who is given credit for the invention, in later times both the Phoenicians and the Greeks were acknowledged as masters of trireme construction and use.

Despite its early invention and its superiority as a ramming weapon, the expense of building and operating the

Triremes on the water. (Library of Congress)

trireme slowed its adoption. The construction of first-class triremes required not only skilled shipwrights but also costly materials such as pitch and wax for waterproofing, and fir, which gave lightweight strength to hull and oars. In addition, because each ship required a skilled crew of two hundred, the operational cost of a fleet of triremes exceeded the means of all but the wealthiest states. Thus, in addition to Necho in Egypt, early trireme users included commercially prominent city-states such as Corinth in Greece and Sidon in Phoenicia, and the powerful Greek tyrant Polycrates of Samos, who replaced his fleet of one hundred *pentekontors* with one of triremes.

In the late sixth century, the adoption of the trireme by the superpower of the day, Persia, guaranteed its predominance and made it the warship of choice for those Greek states that wished to resist the expansion of the Persian Empire into the Aegean region. Drawing on his Phoenician, Egyptian, and eastern Greek subjects, Xerxes put together a gigantic fleet of twelve hundred triremes for his invasion of Greece in 480 B.C.E., an assault that may well have succeeded except for the Greeks' historic naval victory at Salamis. Greek triremes were the key to this victory, above all the two hundred ships that Themistocles had convinced the Athenians to build using the proceeds of a fortunate silver strike. Following the defeat of Xerxes, triremes and the tactics associated with them dominated Greek naval warfare for more than a century.

Although it was used sometimes in what Thucydides called the "old-fashioned manner," with marines in boarding attacks, the trireme excelled when the ship itself was used as a ramming weapon. Rival fleets of triremes typically faced each other in line abreast, and the defender attempted to avoid presenting vulnerable sides and sterns to the rams of the enemy. A drastically inferior force might form a defensive circle with bows facing outward. The attacking force sought to achieve *diekplous*, a breakthrough by a squadron of ships in line, or *periplous*, a flanking maneuver, either of which permitted ramming the enemy broadside. Once a ship had been holed, the attacker quickly disengaged to avoid a counterattack and resumed the offensive. Given these tactics, the advantage normally went to the swifter and more agile ships, a status determined partly by their design but also by how long the ships had been in the water and the expertness of their crews. In the victory at Salamis, for example, the normally slower Greek triremes probably had the advantage of speed, because their ships were drier and their crews more rested than those of the Persian force. The Athenians were renowned for the speed of their triremes, and their mastery of hit-and-run ramming tactics regularly let them defeat larger, less-skilled forces. In a famous encounter early in the Peloponnesian War, for example, a twenty-ship Athenian squadron commanded by the expert Phormion twice defeated larger Peloponnesian fleets.

Significance

As long as ramming tactics prevailed and skilled oarsmen were available, the trireme dominated ancient naval warfare. Beginning in the fourth century, however, a shortage of skilled crewmen encouraged the development of new rowing configurations that made use of less-skilled personnel. By manning each oar with a pair of rowers, only one of whom needed real expertise, it was possible to produce a two-banked "four," which required one third fewer expert rowers but maintained the sleekness and speed of the trireme. The first "four" is attributed to the Phoenicians at Carthage. By 323 B.C.E., the Athenians planned a new fleet based primarily on "fours" rather than triremes. The use of rowers in teams of three or more produced ships of broader beam, which were slower and less agile than the trireme, but by the end of the fourth century new tactics were beginning to favor larger, more stable ships. By using various combinations of rowers in gangs of three, four, or more per oar, Hellenistic navies introduced much larger warships, from "fives" up to huge "sixteens," that provided stable firing platforms for catapults and excellent protection to their large crews of rowers and marines. Aptly suited to naval combat in the "old-fashioned manner," these vessels marked a return to tactics completely alien to the trireme and relegated it to an ancillary role in Hellenistic warfare.

—*James T. Chambers*

Further Reading

Casson, Lionel. *Ships and Seamanship in the Ancient World*. 1971. Reprint. Baltimore, Md.: The Johns Hopkins University Press, 1995. This study offers a general overview of ancient seafaring and includes a chapter on the trireme.

Gabrielsen, Vincent. *Financing the Athenian Fleet: Public Taxation and Social Relations*. Baltimore, Md.: The Johns Hopkins University Press, 1994. Provides background on the financial aspects of maintaining a fleet in ancient Greece.

Morrison, John S., J. F. Coates, and N. B. Rankov. *The Athenian Trireme: The History and Reconstruction of an Ancient Greek Warship*. 2d ed. New York: Cambridge University Press, 2000. The most important volume on this subject, this study analyzes all aspects of the trireme's history and incorporates knowledge gained from the modern replica.

Shaw, Timothy, ed. *The Trireme Project: Operational Experience 1987-90, Lessons Learnt.* Oxford, England: Oxbow Books, 1993. This anthology contains essays, some quite technical, on many aspects of the construction and operation of the full-scale replica.

SEE ALSO: c. 700-330 B.C.E., Phalanx Is Developed as a Military Unit; 483 B.C.E., Naval Law of Themistocles Is Instituted; 480-479 B.C.E., Persian Invasion of Greece; 478-448 B.C.E., Athenian Empire Is Created; May, 431-September, 404 B.C.E., Peloponnesian War.

RELATED ARTICLES in *Great Lives from History: The Ancient World*: Themistocles; Thucydides; Xerxes I.

c. 550 B.C.E.
VĀLMĪKI COMPOSES THE *RĀMĀYAṆA*

The Rāmāyaṇa, *a Sanskrit poem attributed to Vālmīki, became the national epic of India and has continued to influence poetry, art, drama, and religion in South and Southeast Asia.*

LOCALE: Kosala in east-central India (now in Uttar Pradesh)

CATEGORY: Cultural and intellectual history

KEY FIGURE

Vālmīki (fl. c. 500 B.C.E.), a legendary bard

SUMMARY OF EVENT

The *Rāmāyaṇa* (c. 550 B.C.E.; English translation, 1870-1889) or *Vālmīki-Rāmāyaṇa*, is an epic poem of ancient India. The title is taken to mean "the adventures of Rāma." The epic's central narrative is a romance, recounting the birth of Rāmacandra, heir to the throne of the city-state Ayodhyā (a town by that name still exists); his banishment through a palace intrigue; and his subsequent wanderings throughout central and southern India, accompanied by both his wife, Sītā, and brother Lakṣmaṇa. Sītā is abducted but is rescued, and Rāma is eventually restored to his rightful place as king in Ayodhyā.

The poem's long sixth book is a detailed description of a battle pitting Rām and his allies, the monkey army (*vānaras*), against Rāvaṇa, the demon-king of Lanka who has abducted Sītā. A prominent character is the monkey Hanumān, Rāma's friend and helper. In some parts of the epic, Hanumān is said to be the son of the wind god, a status that grants him supernormal abilities.

The *vānaras* have produced much commentary, especially in India. Some readers have interpreted them as human beings of tribal origin. Such a theory, however, does not adequately account for their tails and other monkeylike attributes. They represent a fairy-tale or fable motif in the epic: talking monkeys with admirable traits who aid the hero. Sītā, Rāma's wife, also has significant connections with early Vedic myth and may be divine in origin. This is suggested by her wondrous birth in a furrow (the meaning of her name), as recounted in book 1.

The poem, in its shortest version, consists of more than eighteen thousand stanzas, divided into seven books (called *kāṇḍas*), and about six hundred cantos (called *sargas*). It was composed in a style of Sanskrit comparable in most ways to the style of India's other ancient epic poem, the *Mahābhārata* (400 B.C.E.-400 C.E., present form by c. 400 C.E.; *The Mahabharata of Krishna-Dwaipayana Vyasa*, 1887-1896). However, the Sanskrit text also has earned the name *ādi-kāvya*, "the first art poem," making it the first in a tradition of elaborate court poems, such as those by Kālidāsa in the fourth century C.E. The date of composition of the *Rāmāyaṇa* can only be estimated to between 750 and 500 B.C.E., although an important scholarly study by Alf Hiltebeitel has redated the epic to 150 B.C.E. or a century later. Most of the action of the epic takes place in the far southern region of the Indian subcontinent. Sītā is abducted to Lanka, a legendary isle often identified with modern Sri Lanka (formerly Ceylon). This distinguishes the *Rāmāyaṇa* from the *Mahābhārata*, which takes place in the northern Gangetic plain. The precise place of composition can only be surmised: Because it is the royal family of Kosala that is celebrated, that region may be where the epic originally arose.

Certain features—most prominently the use of formulaic repetitions with slight variations—suggest an origin in ancient oral tradition. Extant, however, are two main manuscript traditions, associated with north and south India. It is controversial among textual scholars which of the two manuscript traditions preserve the more original text. The Baroda Oriental Institute, which edited the standard edition, the seven-volume *The Vālmīki-Rāmayana* (1960-1975), decided in favor of the southern recension.

Of the epic's seven books, books 2-6 are generally agreed to represent the older core of the poem, and this section can be ascribed to the poet Vālmīki. The first book (*Bāla-kāṇḍa*, or the book of the boy-prince) was seemingly added at a later time to explain the birth and youth of the hero of the epic, Rāma or Rāmacandra. This first section also relates the story of the sage Vālmīki, including how he came to compose the epic and, in the process, to invent the most common epic poetic meter, the *anuṣṭubh* or *śloka*. The latter is a thirty-two-syllable stanza constructed in four quarters of eight syllables each. It is easily memorized and flexible enough to allow an oral poet to compose new stanzas extemporaneously in front of an audience.

The *Rāmāyaṇa* contains an apparently old core (books 2-6) and two later sections, books 1 and 7, although parts of book 1 might also be early (see Robert Goldman's translation, *The Rāmāyaṇa of Vālmīki*). In these later sections, Rāma is clearly an incarnation of Vishnu, the important central deity in later Hinduism. The earlier books, by contrast, do not portray Rāma's godhood as explicitly, which has led some scholars to theorize that Rāma, as a human hero, came to be valued as a god only subsequently, as the text grew and developed through retelling. Thus, between the period the older books represent and the creation of the later books, storytellers elevated Rāma from prince to an incarnation of Vishnu—a theory known as euhemerism in the history of religions. Sheldon Pollock dealt with this topic and cast doubt on such theories in an article, "The Divine King in the Indian Epic," that appeared in *Journal of the American Oriental Society* in 1984. Pollock focuses on a key feature of the Rāma narrative: Rāvana, the chief villain of the epic, received the boon that no god or other celestial power could harm him, yet he neglected to obtain protection from humans or animals, for they were beneath his notice. As Pollock points out, men were powerless to harm the demon king, but Rāma was special—a god-man. This suggests, perhaps, that some idea of Rāma's divinity was present from the earliest composition of the poem. Moreover, the tradition of divine kingship in ancient India is known from other sources.

The final, seventh book, was added to tell the story of what happened to Rāma after the conclusion of his central adventure. Throughout the poem, however, are found lines, passages, or entire groups of cantos that textual critics label as later interpolations.

Significance

Who was the intended audience for this poem? Book 1 suggests the answer: In the prologue to the epic (book 1, chapters 1-4), a pair of bards, who in this case happen also to be Rāma's own sons, after learning the entire epic by heart from its author Vālmīki, "sing" the epic before an audience consisting of sages, learned Brahmans, and ascetics. Later they repeat the recitation to King Rāmacandra and his royal assembly. From this one can assume a twofold audience for the epic: the Brahmans, or priestly class, and the ruling class, for whom the poem is a court epic, or *mahākāvya*. Thus elements appealing to both groups are incorporated into the epic. There is no mention here of a recitation before the less exalted classes of either city people or villagers. Later the text became broadly popular and was understood to be a religious scripture.

The Sanskrit *Rāmāyaṇa* has given rise to later versions in various languages, most prominently the *Raghuvaṁśa* (traditionally c. 50 B.C.E., probably c. 390 C.E.; *The Dynasty of Raghu*, 1872-1895), composed in polished Sanskrit by Kālidāsa, and the *Rāmcaritmānas* in Avadhi from North India by Tulsidās (late sixteenth to early seventeenth century C.E.), the latter often thought of as the bible of northern India. Folk drama, sophisticated stage plays, and puppet shows have been based on the Rāma story. Television and film adaptations, as well as comic-book versions, remain very popular. Its popularity spread to the Indianized states of Southeast Asia, particularly to Indonesia. Hanumān is hugely popular in India, where he is understood as the paragon of religious devotion. As a result, the *Rāmāyaṇa*, in its various versions, is probably the single most influential literary work India has produced.

—*Burt Thorp*

Further Reading

Brockington, John. *The Sanskrit Epics*. Leiden, the Netherlands: Brill, 1998. A basic reference work on famous Sanskrit epic works, including the *Rāmāyaṇa*.

Goldman, Robert P., ed. *The Rāmāyaṇa of Vālmīki*. 5 vols. Princeton, N.J.: Princeton University Press, 1984-1996. The latest scholarly translation of the epic, as yet incomplete; includes valuable introductions and detailed annotations.

Hiltebeitel, Alf. *Rethinking the Mahābhārata: A Reader's Guide to the Dharma King*. Chicago: University of Chicago Press, 2001. An important study that argues for redating the Rāmāyana.

Pollock, Sheldon. "The Divine King in the Indian Epic."

Journal of the American Oriental Society 104 (1984): 505-528. Examines the divine and human nature of Rāma.

Richman, Paula, ed. *Many Rāmāyaṇas: The Diversity of Narrative Tradition in South Asia*. Berkeley: University of California Press, 1991. Focuses on the retellings of the *Rāmāyaṇa*.

Thorp, Burt. "When Bhīmasena Met Hanumān." In *The Persistence of Religions*, edited by Sara J. Denning-Bolle and Edwin Gerow. Malibu, Calif.: Undena Publications, 1996. An article discussing the relationship of the *Rāmāyaṇa* and the *Mahābhārata* and the character of Hanumān.

SEE ALSO: 1500-1100 B.C.E., Compilation of the Vedas; c. 1000-c. 200 B.C.E., Compilation of the Upaniṣads; c. 500 B.C.E., Pāṇini Composes Sanskrit Work of Grammar; c. 400 B.C.E.-400 C.E., Composition of the *Mahābhārata*; c. 200 B.C.E.-200 C.E., *Bhagavad Gita* Is Created.

RELATED ARTICLES in *Great Lives from History: The Ancient World:* Kālidāsa; Vālmīki.

547 B.C.E.
CYRUS THE GREAT FOUNDS THE PERSIAN EMPIRE

Cyrus's march against Croesus, whose rich kingdom of Lydia controlled most of western Antolia, led to the capture of the Lydian capital of Sardis and the founding of the Persian Empire, led by the Achaemenian kings until it was conquered by Alexander the Great in 330 B.C.E.

LOCALE: Lydia, western Anatolia (now Turkey); Babylonia (now Iraq, Syria, Lebanon, Israel); and Iran

CATEGORIES: Expansion and land acquisition; government and politics; wars, uprisings, and civil unrest

KEY FIGURES

Cyrus the Great (c. 601/590-c. 530 B.C.E.), an Achaemenian king who founded and ruled the Persian Empire, r. c. 559-c. 530 B.C.E.

Astyages (fl. sixth century B.C.E.), king of the Median Empire, r. c. 585-550 B.C.E.

Croesus (c. 595-546 B.C.E.), king of Lydia, r. c. 560-546 B.C.E.

Nebuchadnezzar II (c. 630-562 B.C.E.), greatest ruler of the Neo-Babylonian Empire, r. c. 605-562 B.C.E.

SUMMARY OF EVENT

Cyrus the Great, the first Achaemenian emperor, founded Persia by uniting the two original Iranian tribes, the Medes and Persians, in 549 B.C.E. Cyrus's name in Old Persian was Kurush, which probably meant "old dog" or possibly just "son" in a local dialect. According to the Greek historian Herodotus (c. 484-c. 424 B.C.E.), Cyrus's father was the Iranian nobleman Cambyses I (c. 530 B.C.E.) and his mother, the Median princess Mandane, was the daughter of Astyages, the last king of the Medes, who ruled the area of Persia at the time of Cyrus's birth. However, other notable historians, such as Ctesias (fl. c. 400 B.C.E.), claimed that many accounts of Cyrus's life were merely legends. Although intertribal marriages to solidify power were common, it may also be that the account of Cambyses' Median marriage was fabricated to encourage Median acceptance of Cyrus's rule.

Cyrus inherited the throne of the district of Anshan in 559 B.C.E. and quickly gathered under his leadership local tribes in Iran, especially in Pars, now the province of Fars. (The form "Pars" is the root of the word "Persian," while the later form "Fars" underlies the name of the Persian language Farsi.) Cyrus revolted five years later against his Median overlord Astyages and made the Median capital of Ecbatana (modern Hamadan, Iran) the center of what became the Persian Empire. Cyrus became disturbed at the cruelty of previous Median rule after observing Astyages slay his own general's son in punishment for a minor misdeed by the father; his own rule emphasized reconciliation and respect instead of brutality and humiliation. Cyrus took over the loosely organized Median government, including its subject states of Armenia, Cappadocia, Parthia, Drangiana, and Aria, which were ruled by semiautonomous vassal kings called satraps. However, he left in place most of the existing governments of regions he conquered, allowing most midlevel officials to retain power and thus to maintain nearly all their indigenous traditions and cultures for the good of the empire.

In 547 B.C.E., Cyrus marched against Croesus, whose rich kingdom of Lydia controlled most of western Anatolia, and besieged the capital of Sardis (near modern Izmir). Croesus, Nabonidus of the Neo-Babylonia Empire, and Ahmose II of the Saite Dynasty in Egypt, joined briefly by the Greek city-state Sparta, attempted an unsuccessful alliance against Cyrus's advance. The Ionian Greek cities along the coast of the Aegean Sea in Asia Minor revolted against his expansion one year later but were crushed before Cyrus turned toward Babylonia. Cyrus is said to have invaded Egypt, a claim most historians doubt; nonetheless, his victories gave him the largest empire in the world at that time and paved the way for future Persian victories.

Cyrus's innovative government utilized both Median and Persian nobles as civilian officials. Unlike previous emperors, Cyrus was remarkably humane and did not force conquered nations into a single mold; rather, he left the major institutions of each subject kingdom relatively unchanged. Cyrus showed forbearance and respect toward the religious beliefs and cultural traditions of his newly conquered subjects. Cyrus even honored the gods of his captured subjects, notably the Babylonian god Marduk. The Assyrians and Babylonians, by contrast, had brutally massacred and exiled whole peoples in the hope of preventing later rebellions against their rule. Even the Greeks, who at this time considered the Persians to be their chief threat to independence, considered Cyrus a highly capable and just ruler. Addressing his newly conquered subjects in their own languages, Cyrus took the title king of Babylon, king of the land. His policies enabled peace to prevail in the region until the conquest of Persia two centuries later by Macedonian king Alexander the Great (356-323 B.C.E.); the region was then divided among four Greek generals on Alexander's death.

Cyrus the Great, shown restoring the sacred vessels to the Jews, built a vast empire. (F. R. Niglutsch)

In 539 B.C.E., Cyrus's conquest of Babylon—the ancient world's center of scholarship and science, which encompassed modern Iraq, Syria, Lebanon, and Israel—was well received by the Jewish community, which had been held captive there for the previous seventy years. Cyrus allowed more than forty thousand of his Jewish subjects to return to Palestine to reestablish the kingdom of Judah and commanded them to build the second temple of King Solomon in Jerusalem. Cyrus may have had as a secondary motive the fact that a Jewish government in Palestine would create a buffer state between the western border of Persia and Egypt in anticipation of Egyptian aggression.

The Jews took their deliverance as a fulfillment of prophecy: Nearly 160 years before Cyrus was born, the prophet Isaiah had proclaimed that Yahweh would raise up a king who would allow the Jewish nation to reclaim their homeland, even though Jerusalem was prospering at the time and another century would pass before it was destroyed by the Babylonian king Nebuchadnezzar II. Cyrus besieged Babylon and, according to Herodotus, diverted the Euphrates River, which passed under the city walls, by building a canal, thus enabling his army to assault the city when the river became low enough. According to the Bible, the Babylonians were recklessly unaware of Cyrus's advance; as he entered the city, Nabonidus's son, Belshazzar, was holding a festival of dancing and revelry (Daniel 5). With the conquest of Babylon, Cyrus gained control over much of the Middle East from the Mediterranean Sea to the borders of India.

With the conquest of Asia Minor complete, Cyrus marched east to Central Asia, where he was killed in battle with a nomadic, horse-riding tribe called the Massagetae at the river Araxes. The precise limits of Cyrus's eastern conquests remain debatable; many historical accounts suggest that his empire might have progressed to the Peshawar region of what is now Pakistan. Cyrus's primary capitals were Susa, Ecbatana, and Babylon, and he was buried at his magnificent palace at Pasargadae. He left his name on a city in central Asia called Kureskhata (later called Kurkath) near Khojert in modern Leninabad, Russia. Cyrus was succeeded by his eldest son, who took the royal name Cambyses II in 529 B.C.E., despite opposition by another son, Smerdis.

SIGNIFICANCE

Although Cyrus the Great was a great military conqueror who consolidated the Persian Empire into the world's most powerful state, he is best remembered for his unprecedented religious tolerance, cultural understanding, and benevolent attitude toward his defeated subjects. The fusion of disparate cultures into the first world state was his most important legacy. The Hellenes referred to him as "lawgiver" and the Jews as the "anointed of the Lord." The doctrines of Cyrus were continued by future emperors of the Achaemenian Dynasty, most notably Darius the Great (r. 522-486 B.C.E.), who brought together skilled craftspeople from all parts of the empire to build the city of Persepolis.

Cyrus can also be credited with creating gold and silver coinage and developing the first postal service: He built a series of stations, at distances based on how far a horse could travel in one day, to facilitate efficient communication between his satraps. Cyrus ordered all governors to treat their subjects as if they were their own children, disallowed slavery, and refused to allow anyone to be executed for a first-offense crime. The Athenian author Xenophon (c. 431-c. 354 B.C.E.) wrote a famous biography known as the "Cyrus saga," which depicted him as a model ruler with impeccable moral and ethical values. Cyrus later came to be considered the father of the Iranian monarchy: In 1971, Iran celebrated the twenty-five hundredth anniversary of its foundation, tracing that date to the end of Cyrus's reign.

On his conquest of Babylon, Cyrus issued a famous decree inscribed on a clay cylinder discovered in Babylon in the late nineteenth century, now housed in London's British Museum, which is considered by many to be the first declaration of human rights. Cyrus's policy regarding captives, inscribed on the cylinder, was to "gather all their [former] inhabitants and return [to them] their habitations." A replica of this cylinder is on display at the headquarters of the United Nations in New York City.

—*Daniel G. Graetzer*

FURTHER READING

Finegan, Jack. *Light from the Ancient Past*. Princeton, N.J.: Princeton University Press, 1946. Noted scholar relates the importance of the Cyrus Cylinder in the declaration of human rights.

Pritchard, James B. *The Ancient Near East*. Princeton, N.J.: Princeton University Press, 1958. A text which relates the science of archaeology to numerous sacred scriptures. The name Cyrus is mentioned twenty-two times in the Bible, giving evidence to his prominence during this critical period in the history of Judaism.

Whiston, William. *Josephus: The Complete Works*. Nashville, Tenn.: Thomas Nelson Publishers, 1998. The often-referenced writings of a famous author from Jewish roots who had access to numerous now lost historical records.

Wiesehöfer, Josef. *Ancient Persia*. Translated by Azizeh Azodi. New York: I. B. Tauris, 2001. A history of the origins of Persia written from a Near Eastern perspective. The first half of the book is on the Achaemenian period.

SEE ALSO: c. 607-562 B.C.E., Nebuchadnezzar Creates the First Neo-Babylonian State; c. 538-c. 450 B.C.E., Jews Return from the Babylonian Captivity; 480-479 B.C.E., Persian Invasion of Greece.

RELATED ARTICLES in *Great Lives from History: The Ancient World:* Alexander the Great; Croesus; Cyrus the Great; Darius the Great; Isaiah; Flavius; Nebuchadnezzar II; Xenophon.

October, 539 B.C.E.
FALL OF BABYLON

Nabonidus's unpopular religious reforms in favor of the moon god Sin led his people to favor rule by the Persian Cyrus the Great. Although the fall of Babylon ended one of the largest empires of the ancient Near East, the city itself lived on as an important cultural center.

LOCALE: Babylon (south of modern Baghdad, Iraq)
CATEGORIES: Government and politics; wars, uprisings, and civil unrest

KEY FIGURES

Nebuchadnezzar II (c. 630-562 B.C.E.), last king of the Neo-Babylonian Empire, r. c. 605-562 B.C.E.
Nabonidus (fl. sixth century-c. 539 B.C.E.), last independent king of Babylon, r. 556-539 B.C.E.
Belshazzar (d. 539 B.C.E.), crown prince of Babylonia, ruled during his father Nabonidus's exile, r. 550-c.540 B.C.E.
Cyrus the Great (c. 601/590-c. 530 B.C.E.), Achaemenian king of Persia, r. c. 559-c. 530 B.C.E.

SUMMARY OF EVENT

Babylon, centrally located in the Tigris-Euphrates valley, had been the capital city of Semitic kings who ruled most of the Fertile Crescent from 1900 to 1600 B.C.E. Best known of these rulers was Hammurabi. During the following millennium Babylon remained a vital economic and cultural center, acknowledged as a sacred city by the Assyrians and others. After the fall of Nineveh in 612, Babylon became the capital of a new dynasty of Chaldean rulers, beginning with Nabopolassar, who had shared with the Medes in the overthrow of Assyria.

The next Chaldean king, Nebuchadnezzar II, known in the Hebrew Bible as the conqueror of Jerusalem, controlled the entire Fertile Crescent and Phoenicia, even going so far as to invade Egypt. He enlarged and beautified many cities as his part in a religious revival. Even by modern standards, Babylon became a huge city, covering 500 acres (202 hectares) with paved streets, more than a thousand temples, elaborate gateways, and sumptuous palaces. For a Median princess whom he married, the king created the famous Hanging Gardens of Babylon. He designed formidable defenses, including a triple circle of walls around Babylon itself and earthworks connecting the two rivers in a wider fortification that enclosed many other cities.

After Nebuchadnezzar, a short period of disorder ended in 556 B.C.E. when an official not directly of royal descent was crowned king. Nabonidus was more than sixty years old at the time, a pious man from a priestly family who devoted much energy to religious affairs. In an attempt to make the moon god, Sin, the supreme deity over his kingdom, he had huge temples erected for him as well as for other gods. Fascination with the past led him to dig for ancient foundation stones and to collect histori-

Babylon, after the fall. (F. R. Niglutsch)

cal records. During much of his reign, he was absent from Babylon on expeditions to Arabia and Syria, leaving affairs at home in charge of his son Belshazzar.

When Nabonidus sought to rebuild a temple of Sin in Harran, the strategic center of northern Mesopotamia then held by the Medes, he sought military aid from Cyrus the Great, the ruler of Persia. Cyrus used Babylonian support to overcome the Medes, and then he marched westward to capture large areas of territory formerly subject to Nebuchadnezzar. By 546 B.C.E., his Persian troops dominated western Asia Minor and Greek cities along the eastern Mediterranean coast. Cyrus then marched eastward into India. Only Babylon remained unconquered.

In 540 B.C.E., the elderly Nabonidus returned to Babylon to defend his kingdom. Lacking soldiers to maintain all the fortifications developed by Nebuchadnezzar, he concentrated on a smaller area. Belshazzar was put in charge of troops guarding a defensive rectangle including the cities of Opis, Sippar, Cutha, and Borsippa, which were considered essential to the defense of Babylon. Inscriptions record efforts during a four-month period to bring into Babylon the gods of other, more distant cities, making these unprotected cities dependent.

Through propaganda, Cyrus had gained the admiration or respect of certain residents in Babylonia. His later reputation for religious tolerance and mercy is known through the Greek historian Herodotus (c. 484-c. 424 B.C.E.) and through Hebrew prophets who saw Cyrus as a savior of the oppressed. Some historians believe there was resentment in Babylonian cities against Nabonidus's religious programs or as a result of economic difficulties. Perhaps it was a desire to reconcile native Babylonians that led Nabonidus, at the beginning of 539, to participate in the New Year festival at Babylon, for the first time in eleven years. This was an ancient rite invoking the triumph of Marduk over forces of evil; it also purified and reinstated the king.

Also in 539 B.C.E., Cyrus the Great came. With overwhelming numerical superiority and with the support of a "fifth column" within some Babylonian cities, the Persian army quickly breached the Chaldean defenses. Early in October, Cyrus attacked the city of Opis, aided by a turncoat Babylonian governor. There was rioting within the defensive perimeter, and a battle was fought in which Belshazzar was killed. Within a few more days, remaining key cities were seized or surrendered without siege, and Nabonidus fled from Babylon.

Herodotus enlivens his account of Babylon's capture with a story that Cyrus diverted the Euphrates River into an old floodway, allowing his army to enter the city through a nearly dry riverbed. The older cuneiform record simply states that "the army of Cyrus entered Babylon without a battle" to receive the acclaim of many citizens.

SIGNIFICANCE

Although the fall of the Chaldean Dynasty ended Babylon's political supremacy, it did not cause the decline of the city as an economic and cultural center. Cyrus granted the area considerable autonomy and made Babylon his winter headquarters. A century later Herodotus described it as still "surpassing in splendor any city in the known world." Indeed, one result of Cyrus's victory was the economic unification of Mesopotamia with the Iranian plateau, a move that was important for later Parthian and Muslim cultures.

—*Roger B. McShane*

FURTHER READING

Beaulieu, Paul-Alain. *The Reign of Nabonidus, King of Babylon, 556-539 B.C.* New Haven, Conn.: Yale University Press, 1999. This study of Nabonidus's reign draws chiefly on archaeological evidence.

Dougherty, Raymond P. *Nabonidus and Belshazzar.* 1929. Reprint. Brooklyn, N.Y.: AMS Press, 1978. Translations of the cuneiform sources on the last Chaldean ruler of Babylon, with commentaries.

Herodotus. *The Histories.* Translated by Aubrey de Selincourt. New York: Penguin, 2003. One of the primary sources on the fall of Babylon, although Herodotus's account is biased, or at least sensationalized.

Pritchard, James B. *Ancient Near Eastern Texts Relating to the Old Testament.* 3d ed. Princeton, N.J.: Princeton University Press, 1969. A scholarly work including Babylonian texts.

Roux, Georges. *Ancient Iraq.* 3d ed. New York: Penguin, 1993. A popular survey of Mesopotamian empires, with a brief account of Cyrus's conquests.

Skaggs, Henry W. F. *Babylonians.* Berkeley: University of California Press, 2000. An archaeologically based history. The final chapter focuses on the Neo-Babylonian Empire and its downfall.

SEE ALSO: c. 607-562 B.C.E., Nebuchadnezzar Creates the First Neo-Babylonian State; 547 B.C.E., Cyrus the Great Founds the Persian Empire; c. 538-c. 450 B.C.E., Jews Return from the Babylonian Captivity.

RELATED ARTICLES in *Great Lives from History: The Ancient World*: Darius the Great; Cyrus the Great; Nebuchadnezzar II.

c. 538-c. 450 B.C.E.
JEWS RETURN FROM THE BABYLONIAN CAPTIVITY

Cyrus the Great's program of encouraging local religious cults allowed the Jews to return to Palestine, rebuild the Temple of Jerusalem, and codify their religious practices.

LOCALE: Palestine
CATEGORIES: Government and politics; religion

KEY FIGURES

Cyrus the Great (c. 601/590-c. 530 B.C.E.), king of Persia, r. c. 559-c. 530 B.C.E.
Zerubbabel (fl. sixth century B.C.E.), a descendant of King David, governor of Judah, and rebuilder of the temple, 520-516 B.C.E.
Haggai (fl. sixth century B.C.E.), a Hebrew prophet who encouraged the rebuilding of the temple
Zechariah (fl. late sixth century B.C.E.), a Hebrew prophet who helped persuade the Jews to rebuild the temple
Nehemiah (fl. fifth century B.C.E.), the governor of Palestine, c. mid-fifth century B.C.E., authorized to rebuild Jerusalem
Ezra (fl. late sixth-early fifth century B.C.E.), a Jewish scribe and priest, c. 425 B.C.E.
Sanballat (fl. fifth century B.C.E.), a Samaritan leader who opposed the rebuilding of Jerusalem

SUMMARY OF EVENT

The four centuries of Jewish history from 586 until 166 B.C.E. constituted a period of physical weakness but of religious growth and strength. The very destruction of the Temple of Jerusalem and the nation encouraged the author of Second Isaiah to reach such a lofty concept as the universality of God.

The return from the Babylonian exile was made possible by an edict of Cyrus the Great in 538 B.C.E., which gave evidence of his appreciation for local autonomy and for the cultural and religious integrity of his peoples. The books of Chronicles record that 42,360 Jews with their servants returned under the combined leadership of the prince Zerubbabel and the high priest Joshua. The numbers appear to be exaggerated when compared to those suggested by the prophets Haggai and Zechariah, who imply that the community was weak and struggling. To develop a new central shrine, a second temple was built and completed, probably by 516. Though not as large or grandiose as that of Solomon, it stood as a symbol of triumph and hope to a revived Judaism until Jerusalem was destroyed by the Romans in 70 C.E.

The returned exiles, however, had their problems. First of all, Zerubbabel, a legitimate descendant of David, plotted to reestablish the old dynasty. Taking advantage of the death of Cyrus the Great's son Cambyses II, with its consequent turmoil and open rebellion in the Persian Empire, he established himself as king in Jerusalem, but was either executed or deported.

Once the exuberance of the return had passed, the Jews were faced with the harsh realities of the situation. Palestine was agriculturally poor and isolated from trade routes. On to this mixed scene of joy and despair appeared first Nehemiah and then Ezra, presumably in that order because Nehemiah seems to set the stage for Ezra. Nehemiah, a cupbearer to the Persian king Artaxerxes I, requested permission to go to Jerusalem as governor to help his coreligionists struggling to adjust to Palestine. The temple had been rebuilt, but it had been as quickly defiled, the Sabbath was regularly desecrated with commercial activities, and the city's defenses were in disrepair. Intensive work enabled Nehemiah to rebuild the city's walls and consequently to guarantee the integrity of the Jewish cult by isolating his people from their neighbors, including even the Samaritans, despite the fact that under the leadership of Sanballat they had sought some political and religious rapprochement with the Jews. Disregarding considerable intermarriage between the two groups, Nehemiah preferred to exclude the Samaritans as a mixed people, even going to the length of trying to separate couples who had intermarried. To thwart religious syncretism and to maintain a pure Yahwism, Nehemiah would unify only those Jews who, because of their experiences in the exile, were highly motivated religiously.

Hoping to solidify Nehemiah's program, Ezra, a scribe, established the Law of the Pentateuch as the politico-religious constitution of the Jews. This official promulgation of the law, tantamount to its canonization as the first part of the Hebrew Scriptures, was the first important effort since the Deuteronomic reform of Josiah, king of Judah, to establish the Jewish community on the basis of the written word of God. Ezra's dispensation fixed the basis for Judaism so effectively that normative Judaism continued to develop as a legalistic and exclusive community for the next thousand years.

The only vindication for the parochialism of both Nehemiah and Ezra is its desire to enable biblical faith to prosper in a protected environment. A new type of optimistic prophecy encouraged men such as Haggai, Zechariah, Malachi, Third Isaiah, and Joel, who labored in turn by emphasizing the temple, institutional reform, and the cult to provide a religious structure which could replace the crumbled political order. Concern for social justice and for a universal worship of God took second place.

The Jews maintained their peaceful isolation during virtually the whole Persian period, not even participating in the sole rebellion of the Syro-Palestinian provinces, that of the Phoenician cities in 351 B.C.E. Except for the abortive aspirations of Zerubbabel, the Jews devoted themselves to internal affairs, mainly the purification of Judaism and the maintenance of the law as the undisputed cornerstone of the community. The solidity and depth of this reformed Judaism was soon to be tested by the impact of Hellenism, which came with the Greek conquests of Alexander the Great in the fourth century.

Significance

Although the return from the exile is remembered among Jews as a reinstatement of the kingdom that had been lost, there were significant differences in the way in which Judaism was re-formed during this period. The program itself emphasized a studied hostility on the part of Jews toward alien life in general and justified their reaction against the outside world as a means to restore their own peculiar life and renew the conditions of the past.

This conservative course based on institutionalized religion was decisive in determining the future. Jewish leaders rejected the extreme proposals of Ezekiel, including the restoration of the kingdom with a descendant of Jehoiachim, the eighteenth king of Judah, on the throne, allotting equal portions of land to the twelve tribes (Jews of the dispersion) to unify them, and placing the temple and the priests outside the capital. He would have new laws for priestly temple service as well as new royal obligations to the cult. The new leaders chose instead to reinstate an ancient Levitical (Old Testament) law. Yet because conditions were different, some changes in the cult had to be made. The injunction of appearing in Jerusalem three times each year was quietly dropped because of the widespread Jewish dispersion. An offering sent to the temple would suffice. The temple with an elaborate priesthood and liturgy became a symbol of unity for a people bent solely on enriching their relationship with God.

Although all those developments gave a *raison d'être* to the life of the scattered nation, they still offered little opportunity for personal involvement. This gap between corporate and individual life was bridged by the development of an elaborate scheme of penitential atonement, an arrangement that tied the individual Jew to both God and the temple through sacrifices as means of justification. In this intensified ritual system, sin itself became chiefly ceremonial defilement rather than moral transgression as in the Mosaic and prophetic systems. However, this religion of outward forms and signs succeeded in enabling the Jews to sense quickly in a visible way any invading influences from their heathen surroundings. Sabbath observance and circumcision naturally assumed new importance in distinguishing Jews from the polyglot population of the Palestine to which the exiles returned. Although such stressing of the outward signs of nationality caused the faith to lose some of its prophetic universalism, the times called for a Judaism more interested in preserving itself than in enlightening the world.

—*Joseph R. Rosenbloom*

Further Reading

Anderson, Jeff S. *The Internal Diversification of Second Temple Judaism*. Lanham, Md.: University Press of America, 2002. An overview of the developments in Judaism in the postexilic period.

Davies, W. D., and Louis Finkelstein, eds. *Introduction: The Persian Period* and *The Hellenistic Age*. Vols. 1 and 2 in *The Cambridge History of Judaism*. New York: Cambridge University Press, 1990-1999. A thorough history of the development of Judaism during the exile and postexilic period; looks especially at the interrelationships between Judaism and surrounding cultures and religions.

Grabbe, Lester L. *Judaic Religion in the Second Temple Period: Belief and Practice from the Exile to Yavneh*. New York: Routledge, 2000. This overview gives both a chronological account of the evolution of Judaism and discussion of thematic topics.

Hjelm, Ingrid. *Samaritans and Early Judaism*. Sheffield, England: Sheffield University Press, 2001. Discusses the questions of Jewish relationship to Samaritans, which was a fulcrum in Jewish postexilic self-definition. Includes a bibliography, index of references, and index of authors.

Shanks, Herschel, ed. *Ancient Israel: From Abraham to the Roman Destruction of the Temple*. 2d ed. New York: Prentice Hall, 1999. This history of Israel, edited by the editor of *The Biblical Archaeology Review*, includes separate chapters on the major eras of Judaism, including one on the period of exile and return. Maps, charts, illustrations, color plates, and bibliography.

SEE ALSO: c. 1000 B.C.E., Establishment of the United Kingdom of Israel; c. 966 B.C.E., Building of the Temple of Jerusalem; c. 922 B.C.E., Establishment of the Kingdom of Israel; c. 607-562 B.C.E., Nebuchadnezzar Creates the First Neo-Babylonian State; 587-423 B.C.E., Birth of Judaism; October, 539 B.C.E., Fall of Babylon.

RELATED TITLES in *Great Lives from History: The Ancient World*: Cyrus the Great; David; Ezra; Isaiah; Solomon.

c. 530 B.C.E.

FOUNDING OF THE PYTHAGOREAN BROTHERHOOD

The Pythagorean brotherhood developed ideas about knowledge that influenced classical Greek philosophers and lasted more than one thousand years. Pythagoras's mathematical theorems were intended to show the relation between the abstract, mystical concept of number and the physical universe.

LOCALE: Croton, in southern Italy
CATEGORIES: Mathematics; philosophy

KEY FIGURES

Archytas of Tarentum (fl. 400-350 B.C.E.), Pythagorean philosopher and mathematician
Philolaus of Croton (fl. fifth century B.C.E.), Pythagorean philosopher
Pythagoras (c. 580-c. 500 B.C.E.), Ionian polymath and philosopher

SUMMARY OF EVENT

The doctrines espoused by the Pythagorean brotherhood were repeated by a number of thinkers. For example, the final conversations of Socrates with his friends as described in the *Phaedōn* (c. 388-368 B.C.E.; *Phaedo*, 1675) reveal Plato's immense debt to Pythagoras and his school. In addition, the Pythagoreans stand out in the history of science as precursors to the later understanding of the structure of the universe in terms of mathematics. Even Nicolaus Copernicus and Johannes Kepler incorporated the mystical importance of "number" in their heliocentric theories of the sixteenth and seventeenth centuries C.E. It is unfortunate, then, that the facts about Pythagoras and his brotherhood are shrouded in legends that began in his own lifetime and grew more colorful during the millennium after his death. Adding to the confusion is the fact that the followers of Pythagoras usually signed his name to their own writings, which did not necessarily contain orthodox Pythagorean philosophy.

Although reliable information is scant, it can be stated that Pythagoras was born about 580 B.C.E. and lived until maturity on the Ionian island of Samos during the period when it was economically and culturally prominent. He had already acquired fame as a sage well versed in the learning of his age and also as an exponent of doctrine about the immortality of the soul when he left Samos about 540 B.C.E. According to tradition, he left Samos because he was opposed to the tyranny of Polycrates. He then settled in Croton, one of the Greek cities in southern Italy and Sicily that made up the region known as Magna Graecia. In Croton, he organized a secret society of mixed religious, philosophic, and political interests that had become dominant by 510, and he played a leading role in the war between Croton and Sybaris, which established the hegemony of Croton over the other cities of Magna Graecia. In 509 B.C.E., a democratic rebellion expelled the Pythagorean party from power in Croton, and Pythagoras moved to Metapontum, where he died about 500 B.C.E.

His followers founded a number of Pythagorean societies of an oligarchic nature. These groups played a leading role in several cities of Magna Graecia until about the middle of the fifth century B.C.E., when they were expelled in a violent upheaval. Afterward, several survivors migrated to the Greek mainland and established communities in Thebes and in Phlius. The foremost of these Pythagoreans was Philolaus of Croton. He is referred to in the *Phaedo* even though he wrote only one genuine book. In this work, he argued that "unlimited" and "limiting" substances were bound together through harmony to form the natural world. After the beginning of the fourth century, Pythagorean influence in southern Italy was reestablished with its center at Tarentum under the leadership of Archytas. This philosopher is noted for his collection of a variety of evidence in an attempt to prove that there is a relationship between the pitch of a musical note and its "speed," or measure.

Pythagoras addresses a group of people. (F. R. Niglutsch)

It is a matter of debate which doctrines may reasonably be attributed to Pythagoras and the society that he founded. The most prevalent view is that the society's activities were based on a curious fusion of religious belief and speculative cosmology dominated by mathematics. The religious doctrine shared an affinity with so-called Orphic conceptions of the transmigration of souls. The soul, according to this doctrine, is distinct in origin from the body, in which it is imprisoned during a person's lifespan. Originally akin to the fires of heaven, it has entered at birth into a body from which it is released at death, only to enter anew into another body in a continuing cycle of successive reincarnations. The soul cannot free itself permanently from the cycle of reincarnation until it has successfully purified itself of the corruption to which its bodily imprisonment has subjected it. The distinctive element of the Pythagorean concept of purification is that, although one must engage in ascetic practices of bodily denial, the primary purifying activity is the intellectual endeavor to understand the nature of the heavenly bodies and their harmony.

This endeavor was based on the assumption that understanding the essence of the astral harmony enables the soul to "recollect" its primal astral purity and actualize at last its divine nature. The Pythagoreans believed that the essence of the heavenly bodies and their interrelationships was number: One came to understand the heavens by understanding the geometrical and arithmetical ratios involved in the constitution of the cosmos. They noted that harmonious sounds were in whole number ratios, and they believed that these ratios could be extended to describe all natural objects. The resulting cosmos was a single and nonmaterial system of reality which included a correspondence between inanimate and living objects. The Pythagoreans claimed, however, that only the elite could achieve this mystical process of knowing. Aristotle reported on the Pythagorean view of the ultimate reality in the *Metaphysica* (335-323 B.C.E.; *Metaphysics*, 1801), although he on occasion purposely misunderstood them in his works in order to minimize their philosophical influence.

SIGNIFICANCE

Plato had visited the Pythagoreans and incorporated the concept of number as the essence of reality into his theory of matter. His sharp distinction between the sense-experience mediated by organs of the body and the intellectual awareness of pure concepts is essentially Pythagorean, as is the notion that mathematical relationships are eternal objects of knowledge. Once Plato had taken the step of identifying the eternally valid moral concepts that Socrates sought to define as of the same nature with the Pythagorean eternal mathematical objects of knowledge, the ground was laid for the doctrine of Ideas.

It was probably also through the mediation of the Pythagorean tradition that Plato came to appropriate the notions of the soul's eternal nature, of its transmigration, and of learning as a process of "recollection" of truths once known by the soul when free from the corrupting influences of the bodily prison.

All these notions find expression in the *Phaedo* of Plato, a dialogue deliberately fashioned so as to present Socrates as a Pythagorean sage and a paradigm of the disciplined philosophic life of progressive actualization of one's innate potential divinity through the acquisition of wisdom. Through Plato the influence of the Pythagorean brotherhood continued throughout the history of Western philosophy.

—*Carl W. Conrad,*
updated by Amy Ackerberg-Hastings

FURTHER READING

Barnes, Jonathan. *The Presocratic Philosophers*. 2 vols. London: Routledge & Kegan Paul, 1979. Single-volume revised reprint, 1982. Pythagorean scholars of the 1980's and 1990's, among others, have drawn upon this book for background information and issues to be discussed.

Furley, David. *The Formation of the Atomic Theory and Its Earliest Critics*. Vol. 1 in *The Greek Cosmologists*. New York: Cambridge University Press, 1987. Furley keeps a general audience in mind while discussing the Pythagoreans in terms of the early Greek theories of the universe.

Guthrie, Kenneth Sylvan, trans. *The Pythagorean Sourcebook and Library*. Introduction by David Fideler. Grand Rapids, Mich.: Phanes Press, 1991. A voluminous anthology of ancient writings related to Pythagoras and Pythagorean philosophy and practice. Fideler's introduction places the material in cultural and historical context. Includes a glossary of Pythagorean terms, bibliography, and indexes of proper names and topics.

Huffman, Carl A. *Philolaus of Croton: Pythagorean and Presocratic*. New York: Cambridge University Press, 1993. Huffman's book includes scholarly commentary on the fragments attributed to Philolaus as well as essays on his life and philosophy.

Kingsley, Peter. *Ancient Philosophy, Mystery, and Magic: Empedocles and Pythagorean Tradition*. New York: Oxford University Press, 1997. A study of Pythagorean influence on Plato's philosophy as well as on medieval alchemy and Islamic science.

Kirk, G. S., J. E. Raven, and M. Schofield. *The Presocratic Philosophers*. 2d ed. New York: Cambridge University Press, 1983. The landmark work that has been stimulating discussion since the 1960's and 1970's.

Lloyd, G. E. R. *Early Greek Science: Thales to Aristotle*. New York: W. W. Norton, 1970. The classic textbook for the beginning scholar, providing assistance with placing the Pythagoreans in context in the history of science and with explaining their mathematics.

Navia, Luis E. *Pythagoras: An Annotated Bibliography*. New York: Garland, 1990. A reference which contains detailed information on more than eleven hundred journal articles, books, and dissertations on a variety of topics related to Pythagoras.

SEE ALSO: 600-500 B.C.E., Greek Philosophers Formulate Theories of the Cosmos; c. 440 B.C.E., Sophists Train the Greeks in Rhetoric and Politics; 399 B.C.E., Death of Socrates; c. 380 B.C.E., Plato Develops His Theory of Ideas; c. 335-323 B.C.E., Aristotle Writes the *Politics*; c. 300 B.C.E., Stoics Conceptualize Natural Law.

RELATED ARTICLES in *Great Lives from History: The Ancient World*: Alcmaeon; Aristotle; Plato; Pythagoras; Socrates.

527 B.C.E.
DEATH OF VARDHAMĀNA, FOUNDER OF JAINISM

Vardhamāna broke with certain aspects of contemporary Hinduism and established the movement that resulted in the religion of Jainism.

LOCALE: India
CATEGORY: Religion

KEY FIGURE
Vardhamāna (c. 599-527 B.C.E.), founder of Jainism

SUMMARY OF EVENT

Vardhamāna's original name was Nataputta Vardhamānam, and he was also known as Māhavīra, which means "great man" or "great hero." Vardhamāna is generally recognized as the founder of Jainism, one of several important religions, including Hinduism and Buddhism, which developed in the Indian subcontinent before the common era.

The traditional dates for his birth and death are 599 B.C.E. and 527 B.C.E., but some scholars suggest that a more accurate chronology might place his dates about sixty years later. Siddhārtha Gautama, the Buddha (c. 566-c. 486 B.C.E.), was a near contemporary of Vardhamāna, and their traditional histories show similarities, as do some, but not all, of their religious ideas and practices. As with many other figures from the ancient world, there are no existing written historical sources about the life of Vardhamāna from his own era. The earliest surviving written accounts of his life and accomplishments were composed approximately one thousand years after his death.

Vardhamāna was born in Magadha, present-day north Bihār in northeastern India. His family, the Jnatrikas, belonged to the Kṣatriya caste, the second of India's traditional four-caste system, which included Brahmans, or the priests, Kṣatriya, or the warrior-rulers, Vaiśya, who were the small landholders and artisans, and the Śūdra, or the workers, the lowest of the four castes. Below the four castes were outcastes. Vardhamāna's father was a raja, or local ruler, and his mother was belonged to the Licchavis, an important royal family, and his childhood and youth was a life filled with material comforts. Here, too, is a parallel with the Buddha, whose father was also a local chieftain in northern India, and whose early life was equally privileged. As young adults, both turned their backs on their luxurious pasts and pursued their separate quests for spiritual and theological understanding.

Because Vardhamāna was a younger son, his elder brother would inherit their father's position, thus making it less difficult for Vardhamāna eventually to leave his family. At about the age of thirty, after the death of his parents and with his brother's consent, he seriously began his spiritual search, leaving the palace to join a body of ascetic monks. For the next twelve years, he followed an itinerant existence, wandering in woods and forests and the hills of north India, begging for his food, and living a life of increasing austerity.

Unlike the Buddha's Middle Way between the extremes of material pleasure and excessive asceticism, Vardhamāna practiced a rigorous ascetic discipline in his pursuit to free himself from the desire for material things and to achieve deliverance and release, *mokṣa* or nirvana, from this world. Vowing to neglect his physical body, he pulled out the hair on his head, abandoned his clothes, and wandered naked, a practice that he followed for the rest of his life. He never spent more than a day or two at any single location, and he conversed only rarely, as he wished to form no attachments to anything that would tie him to the material world. In his early forties, while meditating, he achieved nirvana. He had overcome the desires that held him to this world, becoming the *Jina* (the Sanskrit word for conqueror) or *Kevalin* (completed soul). Vardhamāna's followers would be known as Jains. The remainder of his life was devoted to preaching his beliefs and gathering around him a group of a naked ascetics like himself who would continue his practices and preserve his teachings.

As with Buddhism, it is difficult to ascertain entirely which beliefs and practices were those of the founder and which were adopted later. Both Vardhamāna and Buddha rejected certain aspects of the prevailing religion of their era, the religion known as Hinduism. Whether Vardhamāna and Buddha were intentionally founding new religions is a disputed point among scholars. Jains believe that Vardhamāna was the twenty-fourth and last of the savior beings, and that there were twenty-three previous *tīrthaṅkaras* who taught the way to salvation, or nirvana.

Jains believe the world to be divided into lifeless matter (*ajiva*) and living beings, or souls (*jiva*), which exist everywhere, in both animate as well as inanimate objects. Both lifeless matter and souls are eternal. Matter is made up of atoms that come together to form all things, some being heavy and some light, the latter of which is called karma-matter. Desires and unethical conduct thicken the karma-matter, but ethical conduct and the abandonment of desire rids the soul of its karma-matter, eventually freeing the soul from its cycle of rebirth or reincarnation (*samsāra*), and thus nirvana is finally achieved. There are five levels of souls, with gods, men, and animals having five senses, down to plants, earth, water, and fire, having only one sense. Jains strive to limit the pain caused to the numerous souls in order to avoid as much bad karma as possible.

To avoid bad karma resulting from pain inflicted upon the *jiva*, the concept and practice of nonviolence, or *ahiṁsā*, is central to Jainism. This is not just a moral and ethical imperative, but also the knowledge that violence against souls or *jivas* will impede any hope for release from the cycle of death and rebirth, from reincarnation. Vardhamāna carried a soft broom to sweep the path before him so he would not inadvertently step on any insects. He would eat only food prepared for someone else so that he would not be the cause of the injury to any souls, even those of plants, and he would always search the ground before he sat or slept so that he would not injure any living beings.

By avoiding bad karma, ultimately the soul will be freed from matter and the cycle of reincarnation, becoming *Siddha*, or a liberated soul. Siddhas lack matter but they are conscious and eternal. Although there are various celestial "heavens," there is no creator god in Jainism. There are higher beings that might be called gods, or *arhats*, but they provide no aid or help to the soul in freeing itself. Prayers will not help, and thus there is no role for priests, or Brahmans, as in Hinduism. Salvation is achieved by the self, by getting rid of one's bad karma through proper conduct and avoiding causing pain to *jivas*.

Vardhamāna established a community of monks, as did the Buddha. Jain monks were to follow the Five Great Vows, including practicing nonviolence, telling the truth, taking only what is given, abstaining from sexual activity, and renouncing all attachments. The rigorous ascetic demands that Vardhamāna followed and laid down for Jain monks was too rigorous for ordinary people, so a modified series of rules was created for laypersons, which included allowing sexual relations for those who were married.

By the traditional accounts, in the year 527 B.C.E., near the modern city of Patna, at the age of seventy-two, Vardhamāna willingly starved himself to death, in a practice called *sallakhana*. According to Jain belief, he would no longer be subject to the pain of rebirth and reincarnation and would enter that place at the top of the universe, *Siddha-sila*, or the place of the perfect souls.

SIGNIFICANCE

Like most religions, Jainism divided into several sects. Svetambaras monks allow the wearing of white clothes and allowed women into their monastic order, but the Digambaras hold to strict nudity whenever engaged in any religious duty. The latter do not allow women in their order, thus rigorously following Vardhamāna's claim that women are only a temptation. The Digambaras believe that women can only achieve salvation after first being reborn as men.

Both Jainism and Buddhism were greatly influenced by earlier Hindu beliefs and practices, but both rejected certain aspects of Hinduism. Unlike Buddhism, Jainism has few adherents beyond the borders of India, perhaps because of its strict ascetic requirements. Tradition has it that Chandragupta Maurya (r. c. 321-301 B.C.E.), one of India's greatest rulers, became a Jain monk late in his life and starved himself to death. Although the Jain community in India today is only about two million out of a total population of approximately one billion, its beliefs and practices, such as vegetarianism and *ahiṁsā*, as practiced by the Hindu Mahatma Gandhi, have been influential among non-Jains.

—*Eugene Larson*

FURTHER READING

Chapple, Christopher, ed. *Jainism and Ecology*. Cambridge, Mass.: Harvard University Press, 2002. A provocative collective of essays about Jainism, ecology, and the practice of *ahiṁsā*.

Dundas, Paul. *The Jains*. London: Routledge, 2002. A comprehensive summary of Jainism by a western scholar.

Jain, Hiralal, and A. D. Upadhye. *Māhavīra, His Times and Philosophy of Life*. New Delhi: Bharatiya Jnanprith Publishers, 1974. A sympathetic account of Vardhamāna's life and ideas.

Jain, Kailash Chand. *Lord Māhavīra and His Times*. One of a number of works written to commemorate the twenty-five-hundredth anniversary of Vardhamāna's death and his nirvana. Delhi: Motilal Banarsidass, 1974.

Laidlaw, James. *Riches and Renunciation: Religion, Economy, and Society Among the Jains*. New York: Oxford University Press, 1995. A discussion of the Jain community in the modern world.

Schubring, Walther. *The Doctrine of the Jainas*. Translated by Wolfgang Beurlen. Delhi: Motilal Banarsidass, 1962. A classic account of the beliefs and practices of Jainism.

SEE ALSO: 1500-1100 B.C.E., Compilation of the Vedas; c. 1000-c. 200 B.C.E., Compilation of the Upaniṣads; 6th or 5th century B.C.E., Birth of Buddhism; c. 467 B.C.E., Gośāla Maskarīputra, Founder of Ājīvika Sect, Dies; c. 321 B.C.E., Mauryan Empire Rises in India; c. 200 B.C.E., Birth of Hinduism; c. 200 B.C.E.-200 C.E., *Bhagavad Gita* Is Created.

RELATED ARTICLES in *Great Lives from History: The Ancient World*: Buddha; Chandragupta Maurya; Gośāla Maskarīputra; Vardhamāna.

c. 525 B.C.E.
SIBYLLINE BOOKS ARE COMPILED

The Sibylline Books were developed early in Roman history as a means of state divination and as a senatorial mechanism for effecting collective religious responses to critical situations.

LOCALE: Rome (now in Italy)
CATEGORIES: Cultural and intellectual history; religion

KEY FIGURES

Dionysius of Halicarnassus (30-8 B.C.E.), Roman historian and rhetorician who passed on the legend surrounding the origin of the Sibylline Books

Lucius Tarquinius Superbus (sixth century-after 510 B.C.E.), last king of Rome, r. 534-510 B.C.E., who acquired three of nine Sibylline Books and provided for their safekeeping

Marcus Terentius Varro (116-27 B.C.E.), politician and author who compiled the Sibylline Books

SUMMARY OF EVENT

The Sibylline Books were a collection of oracles written in Greek hexameters that were carefully guarded in ancient Rome and were consulted in times of great distress as a result of war, famine, pestilence, or other public calamity.

The Sibyls, from whom the adjective "Sibylline" is derived, were women oracles who gave responses to questions posed to them. The etymology of "Sibyl" is unknown, although numerous attempts have been made in ancient and modern times to explain it. The Sibyls originated in Asia Minor during the seventh century B.C.E. and spread from there to various sites throughout the Mediterranean world. The philosopher Heraclitus of Ephesus (c. 540-c. 480 B.C.E.) was the first writer to refer to women of this type, but he knew of only one Sibyl. Heraclides Ponticus (c. 388-c. 310 B.C.E.), a philosopher and writer, was aware of two Sibyls, and later authors mention three, four, eight, ten, and twelve of them, or leave the number indefinite. The most famous listing of these seers is that given by Marcus Terentius Varro in his *Antiquitates rerum humanarum et divinarum libri XLI* (first century B.C.E., now lost; of matters human and divine), in which he names all sorts of Sibyls: Persian, Libyan, Delphic, Cimmerian, Erythraean, Samian, Cumaean, Hellespontic, Phrygian, and Tiburtine.

The Sibyls could be consulted on a private or public basis, and collections of their responses were compiled and circulated. One of these collections reached Rome toward the end of the sixth century B.C.E. There, it received official approval and came to be known as the *Libri Sibillini*, or Sibylline Books.

The famous story connected with the advent of these books is a legend devised to increase their prestige. The story is related by both Greek and Latin authors with some minor alterations in detail. The fullest account is that found in Dionysius of Halicarnassus, who taught history and rhetoric in Rome. According to him, Rome, through the favor of some divinity, was the recipient of wonderfully good fortune during the reign of Lucius Tarquinius Superbus (also known as Tarquin the Proud). A foreign woman tried to sell the king nine books of Sibylline oracles. When he refused to buy them, she burned three of the nine books and then offered him the remaining six at the original price. Rebuffed again, she burned three more of the books. When she finally offered the remaining three for the same price as the original nine, the baffled king asked the advice of his augurs, or official diviners. These augurs decided by certain signs that he had rejected a divine blessing in not buying all the books and urged him to purchase at least those that remained.

Tarquinius appointed two prominent men to guard the books and gave them two public slaves to assist them in their task. Dionysius states that these books were kept in a stone chest beneath the temple of Jupiter on the Capitoline hill until the time of the Roman Civil War in 91-88 B.C.E., and that they perished in the fire that destroyed the temple in 83 B.C.E. The books were replaced with oracles gathered from other Italian cities, from Erythrae in Asia Minor, and other places. According to Dionysius, these oracles were the most guarded possession of the Romans, whether sacred or profane, so that the senate decreed that they could be consulted only during times of strife and misfortune in war or when some baffling prodigy or apparition appeared.

Some attempts have been made to derive the Sibylline Books from Etruria because of their resemblance to the *Libri fatales*, or Books of Fate, which are assumed to be of Etruscan origin. This title, however, is a generic term used for both Etruscan and Greek rituals. It seems more probable that the oracles were brought to Rome from Cumae, whence they had originally come from Erythrae. Unlike the Greeks, who freely allowed private persons as well as public officials to consult their oracles and even permitted private copies of the responses to be made, the Romans surrounded the books with great secrecy and restricted their use to state officials. Not even the priests in charge could consult them without a special order of the senate.

Significance

Scholars have traditionally credited the Sibylline Books with the progressive introduction of Greek and Eastern deities and modes of worship into Rome. Among the gods introduced in this manner were Demeter, Dionysus, and Kore under the Latin names Ceres, Liber, and Libera; the most famous of all was Cybele. Among the rites introduced were the *lectisternium*, or public offering of food to the gods as they were displayed on pillows or couches; the *supplicatio*, a general thanksgiving in honor of the gods; and the *ver sacrum* (sacred spring), a sacrifice of all fruits and animals produced in a particular spring. In a paper presented to the American Philosophical Association's annual meeting in 1994, Eric Orlin showed that the introduction of some of the so-called Greek cults and practices represented the senate's attempt to strengthen ties with south Italy and Sicily and that the Sibylline Books were thus used to sanction senatorial diplomatic policy rather than to serve as a mechanism for importing foreign religious customs.

The original priesthood in charge of the books, the *Duoviri sacris faciundis*, was increased from two to ten individuals, known as the *Decemviri*, and then to fifteen, the *Quindecimviri*. This priesthood formed one of the four major priestly colleges. As part of his religious reform, Augustus (r. 27 B.C.E.-14 C.E.) ordered a revision to be made of the oracles and had them transferred to the temple of Apollo on the Palatine hill, but by then their days of influence had largely passed. Although interest in them revived under the emperors Aurelian and Julian the Apostate, the Sibylline Books were reportedly burned during the reign of Honorius (r. 393-423 C.E.) by order of his general Stilicho.

—*M. Joseph Costelloe,*
updated by Richard D. Weigel

Further Reading

Beard, Mary, and John North. *Pagan Priests*. Ithaca, N.Y.: Cornell University Press, 1990. A collection of essays that focus not only on Roman divination and priesthoods but also on the activities of other pagan societies.

Boyce, Aline. "The Development of the *Decemviri Sacris Faciundis*." *Transactions of the American Philological Association* 69 (1938): 161-187. Provides an overview of the rituals prescribed by the priesthood charged with consulting the Sibylline Books.

Coulter, Cornelia. "The Transfiguration of the Sibyl." *Classical Journal* 46 (1950-1951): 65-71, 78, 121-126. The author surveys the changing role of the books over time.

Momigliano, Arnaldo. "Sibylline Oracles." In *The Encyclopedia of Religion*. Vol. 13. New York: Macmillan, 1987. An account of Sibylline oracles in different religious traditions.

North, John. "Religion in Republican Rome." In *The Rise of Rome to 220 B.C.* Vol. 7, part 2 in *The Cambridge Ancient History*, edited by F. W. Walbank et al. New York: Cambridge University Press, 1989. North provides an overview of the development of Roman cults, games, and traditions during the course of the Republic.

Parke, H. W. *Sibyls and Sibylline Prophecy in Classical Antiquity*. London: Oxford University Press, 1988. A study of Sibyls and their prophecies in religion, poetry, and politics of the ancient world.

Turcan, Robert. *The Gods of Ancient Rome: Religion in Everyday Life from Archaic to Imperial Times*. Translated by Antonia Nevill. New York: Routledge, 2001. This overview of Roman religion is divided into sections on family religion, state religion, and imperial religion, providing a context for understanding the use of oracles in Roman life.

See also: 775 B.C.E., Delphic Oracle Provides Guidance for City-States; 625-509 B.C.E., Rise of Etruscan Civilization in Rome; 494/493 B.C.E., Institution of the Plebeian Tribunate; 451-449 B.C.E., Twelve Tables of Roman Law Are Formulated; 445 B.C.E., Establishment of the Canuleian Law; 287 B.C.E., *Lex Hortensia* Reforms the Roman Constitution.

RELATED ARTICLES in *Great Lives from History: The Ancient World*: Heraclitus of Ephesus; Flavius Stilicho; Marcus Terentius Varro.

520-518 B.C.E.
DARIUS THE GREAT CONQUERS THE INDUS VALLEY

Darius the Great of Persia explored and added the Indus Valley to his empire, allowing commerce and ideas to flow easily between east and west.

LOCALE: Province of Hindush (now in Pakistan)
CATEGORIES: Expansion and land acquisition; wars, uprisings, and civil unrest

KEY FIGURES

Cyrus the Great (c. 601/590-c. 530 B.C.E.), king of Persia, r. c. 559-c. 530 B.C.E., extended empire east to the Indus River

Darius the Great (550-486 B.C.E.), third king of Persia, r. 522-486 B.C.E.

SUMMARY OF EVENT

The Persian Empire under its Achaemenid rulers (705-330 B.C.E.) was the largest political entity in the Near East until Alexander the Great (356-323 B.C.E.) briefly united all the countries from Greece to India. No historical narratives composed by the Persians have survived, and it is likely that none were ever written. However, Persian monarchs often commissioned monumental inscriptions to be placed in public places at decisive moments during their reigns. These impressive inscriptions functioned as political propaganda, lauding the ruler and his most recent public works and conquests. They often concluded with a list of the provinces subject to Persian rule at the time. The growth of the empire is related in these lists.

Greek writers constitute the only other major source of information about the Achaemenid Empire. Chief among these is the historian Herodotus (c. 484-c. 425 B.C.E.), whose *Historiai Herodotou* (c. 424 B.C.E.; *The History*, 1709) is devoted to the rise of Persia and its relations with Greece. A few other Greek writers provide occasional nuggets of information, as do some books in the Hebrew Bible.

The Persian Empire included a part of the Indus River Valley on its eastern frontier almost from the beginning. The first great Achaemenid king, Cyrus the Great, created an empire in the area now occupied by Iran and Iraq before expanding both east and west. By 545 B.C.E. he had extended his holdings in the east to, or nearly to, the banks of the Indus River, east of modern Kabul and Peshawar. Cyrus named this new eastern province Paruparaesanna, "the land beyond the mountains." Later, it was called by its native name, Gandhara.

After Cyrus the Great's death in 530 B.C.E., his son Cambyses II (r. 529-522 B.C.E.) became king. Cambyses reigned for only eight years before dying under mysterious circumstances. In the ensuing chaos, Darius the Great, a distant relative of Cyrus without a direct claim to the throne, used intrigue and assassination to obtain the kingship, which he held from 522 to 486 B.C.E.

The new king's first order of business was to quell the uprisings that had begun after Cambyses died. Once his base of power was secure, Darius turned his thoughts to expansion. He seems to have been both eager for fame as a great conqueror and practical in his desire to extend the commercial horizons of his empire. In the west, his failure to seize the Greek mainland is well known and forms the focal point of Herodotus's work. The Persian defeat in 490 B.C.E. on the plain of Marathon became the rallying cry for the Greek city-states ten years later when they expelled Darius's successor Xerxes I (r. 486-465 B.C.E.) and forever ended the threat of Persian domination in Greece.

In the east, Darius's conquests seem to have had an additional motivation: the need to protect his holdings from invaders from the north. Herodotus recounted fabulous stories of gold, apes, peacocks, ivory, and other exotic goods that may also have influenced Darius to press farther south along the Indus River in search of trade routes. Because there is no Indian equivalent of Herodotus, evidence regarding Darius's eastern campaigns remains sketchy. The details of his movements have generated much scholarly disagreement.

Herodotus states clearly that the Persian king commissioned an expedition to sail down the Indus River from some northern point in order to find out where it debouched into the Indian Ocean. Trustworthy sailors, including a Greek-speaking Persian subject named Scylax, then returned home, probably traveling along the Iranian coast, around the Arabian peninsula, and back to a port in Egypt. As a result of the information gained by this expedition Darius took over a new province somewhere east or south of Gandhara and proceeded to make use of the Indian Ocean, presumably for trade.

One of the few aspects of the Indian campaign that can be stated with certainty is its date. In 520 B.C.E., after he had reunited dissident factions in Persia, Darius commissioned a massive trilingual inscription to commemorate his triumph. It still stands today on a cliff at Bisitun, high above the road from Babylon to Ecbatana (now Hamadan, Iran), one of the ancient capitals of Persia. The list of subject provinces at the end includes Gandhara as the easternmost province. The inscription carved to commemorate Darius's building of a wall around Persepolis in 518 B.C.E. contains Gandhara and a new eastern province, Hindush. This province, whose name reproduces the Persian pronunciation of "Indus" (from which derives the word "Hindu"), must have been acquired sometime between 520 and 518 B.C.E.

The location of the newly conquered territory is in dispute, but it clearly lay somewhere along the Indus River. Persian dominion in the region seems to have been limited to the area along the Indus River and its tributaries. It did not extend to the Ganges River Valley, at that time a thriving region in northern India. Most scholars feel that the new Persian possession was the area around the mouth of the Indus River, known today as the province of Sind in Pakistan. A few believe that Darius proceeded northeast of the existing province of Gandhara and conquered territory there. This latter view makes the expeditionary voyage irrelevant to the military action.

Herodotus states clearly that Darius sent the expedition before beginning his takeover of the new province, and most agree. Some scholars feel that a naval expedition unprotected by the Persian military force would not have survived hostile natives, but it is not known how the inhabitants of the Indus Valley at that time would have responded to the Persians. It seems most likely that before mounting an invasion the cautious Darius would have sent out scouts to explore the area, both for its purported wealth and for information that would help his forces succeed.

Little is known about the administration of the province of Hindush while under Achaemenid dominion. The Persians did build forts along the rivers in their eastern holdings, and there is evidence for a fort on the Indus that may have housed the provincial governor. Hindush contributed a massive amount of gold as tribute to the Persian treasury: Herodotus says it made the largest contribution of all the provinces, 360 talents of gold dust per year, nearly half the crown's revenues. Later, Indian soldiers from this province, both on foot and in chariots, were conscripted to fight for Persia in Greece.

How long Persian hegemony lasted in the Indus Valley is unclear. Hindush appears in the province lists of Darius's successor Xerxes and may still have belonged to the Persians in the fourth century B.C.E. if the identification in the biblical book of Esther of the Persian king Ahasuerus with Artaxerxes II (405-359 B.C.E.) is correct. Persian control must have slipped soon after that, for, when Alexander crossed the Indus River in 326 B.C.E., he found local kings, not Persian governors, awaiting him.

Significance

The Persian incursion into the Indus Valley established much broader communications between east and west. Such contact had existed for millennia in the form of

Darius the Great. (Library of Congress)

commercial relations. Now a well-organized, efficient administration linked the Persian capital and its territories. The results were felt in both India and the West.

In the East, stamped coins came into use in the Ganges Valley shortly after the arrival of the Persians in the lower Indus Valley. Scholars believe the Aramaic language and letters, used by the Persians as a sort of *lingua franca*, were probably introduced into India around the same time. Later Sanskrit texts suggest that Babylonian astrological writings were translated into Indian languages around 500 B.C.E. The first inscriptions found in India, of a monumental type similar to the records of the Achaemenid kings, date from the reign of the emperor Aśoka (r. c. 273/265-238 B.C.E.). The script used in these monuments is consistent with a development from Aramaic letters over the course of several hundred years.

Eastern ideas had an equally great influence on the West. Concepts of transmigration of souls, strikingly similar to Indian ideas about reincarnation, appear about this time in the teachings of the early Greek philosophers, especially Pythagoras (c. 580-c. 500 B.C.E.). They influenced many later Greek and Near Eastern religious ideas.

The desire to facilitate access to the gold of India, and presumably also to India's trading partners to the east, may have persuaded Darius to reopen an Egyptian canal that is the ancestor of the modern Suez canal. Originally created by the Egyptian pharaoh Seti I (c. late fourteenth century-c. 1279 B.C.E.), it was cleaned of silt by Pharaoh Necho II (610-595 B.C.E.) but fell into disuse again. Ancient sources are divided in their opinion as to whether Darius actually used the canal. However, most believe he did, and Darius's own inscriptions state proudly, "This canal was dug."

A book titled *Periplus* (voyage around by sea) written by Scylax, a member of Darius's exploratory expedition down the Indus River, became the foundation for two new genres of Greek writing, geography and ethnography. The book influenced all later Greek historians, including Herodotus, and through them later historical writing. It remained the source for all Greek knowledge about India until the time of Alexander the Great.

—*Julie A. Williams*

FURTHER READING

Cook. J. M. *The Persian Empire*. New York: Schocken Books, 1983. Covers the growth of the Achaemenid Empire through the conquest of Alexander. Many photographs and maps.

Herodotus. *The Histories*. Translated by Robin Waterfield. New York: Oxford University Press, 1998. Useful and extensive notes. The description of Darius's conquest of the Indus appears in book 4, chapter 44.

Kuhrt, Amelie. *The Ancient Near East, c. 3000-330 B.C.* 2 vols. New York: Routledge, 1995. Volume 2, chapter 13, covers the Achaemenid Empire. Detailed bibliography.

Olmstead, A. T. *History of the Persian Empire*. Chicago: University of Chicago Press, 1948. Somewhat outdated but still the starting point for all histories of the Achaemenid Empire. Photographs and maps.

Pingree, David. *From Astral Omens to Astrology, from Babylon to Bikaner.* Rome, Italy: Serie Orientale, 1997. Presents the transmission of celestial omens, astronomy and astrology in the area from Greece to India as a model for the way many other kinds of knowledge were shared in antiquity.

SEE ALSO: 547 B.C.E., Cyrus the Great Founds the Persian Empire; 520-518 B.C.E., Scylax of Caryanda Voyages the Indian Ocean; 480-479 B.C.E., Persian Invasion of Greece; 327-325 B.C.E., Alexander the Great Invades the Indian Subcontinent.

RELATED ARTICLES in *Great Lives from History: The Ancient World*: Alexander the Great; Cyrus the Great; Darius the Great; Herodotus; Xerxes I.

520-518 B.C.E.
SCYLAX OF CARYANDA VOYAGES THE INDIAN OCEAN

Scylax of Caryanda's voyage expanded communication among India, the Near East, and Greece. His account marked the beginning of the genres of geography and ethnography and was one of the first Greek works written in prose rather than poetry.

LOCALE: Indus River Valley (now in Pakistan)
CATEGORY: Cultural and intellectual history

KEY FIGURES

Scylax of Caryanda (fl. sixth century B.C.E.), geographer and explorer who documented the voyage
Herodotus (c. 484-c. 425 B.C.E.), Greek historian who is the source for the story of the expedition
Darius the Great (550-486 B.C.E.), third king of Persia, r. 522-486 B.C.E., who commissioned Scylax's voyage

SUMMARY OF EVENT

The *Historiai Herodotou* (c. 424 B.C.E.; *The History*, 1709) of the Greek historian Herodotus is the main source for the story of a fabulous expedition down the Indus River undertaken by Scylax of Caryanda. According to Herodotus, the Persian king Darius the Great was anxious to expand his empire, both for personal glory and to open lucrative trade channels. He wanted to know where the Indus River met the sea, and thus sent a group of trustworthy men, including a Greek-speaking Persian subject named Scylax, to sail east down the river to the ocean, and thence back to a port in Egypt. The trip lasted thirty months. The information Darius received from Scylax and the others led him to conquer a part of India and to begin sailing the Indian Ocean, presumably for commercial ventures.

The few lines in Herodotus concerning Scylax and his voyage have produced an ocean of discussion about the details. Scholars disagree on nearly every aspect of the voyage, but most believe it did take place.

Herodotus is almost the only source for information on Scylax, a native of the coastal town of Caryanda, close to the hometown of Herodotus, in a region of Ionia (now Turkey) heavily settled by Greeks. His name, Scylax, suggests that he was not Greek but Carian. The Carians inhabited the inner, mountainous regions of southern Ionia and spoke a language which has not yet been deciphered. At the time of the expedition, Caria was subject to Persian rule. Herodotus implies but does not state directly that Scylax was the leader of the Indus River expedition.

Herodotus does not give a date for the expedition, but he presents it as a necessary prelude to Darius's acquisition of the province of Hindush. More precise dating can be obtained from two monumental inscriptions commissioned by Darius to commemorate important events in his reign because these inscriptions contain a current list of subject provinces. Hindush is absent from the list of provinces of an inscription in Bisitun (near modern-dayHamadan, Iran), dating to 520 B.C.E., but appears on an inscription just two years later.

A particularly vexed question concerns the point of departure of the expedition. Herodotus says that it left from the town Caspatyrus in the region of Pactyice. Numerous attempts to identify locations for these names have proved fruitless. Some believe the most logical place from which Scylax and his expedition would have set sail is the point at which the Kabul and Indus Rivers join, near modern Peshawar, Afghanistan.

The statement by Herodotus that the expedition sailed east down the river to the sea further complicates an understanding of the voyage. The Indus in fact flows southwest to the Indian Ocean, not east. To meet this objection, some scholars suggest that the expedition may have begun farther north of the confluence of the Indus and Kabul Rivers, along the Kabul River itself, which flows east before joining the Indus. It is possible that Herodotus has simply misunderstood his source here. Classical scholar J. L. Myers suggested in 1896 that the expedition actually sailed along the Ganges, which does flow east to the Bay of Bengal, and thence around the Indian subcontinent. This theory has the virtue of explaining why the return voyage took thirty months but does not account for the fact that the Persians never explored or conquered the Ganges Valley.

Scholars are unable to establish with certainty the locations and boundaries of the eastern provinces of the Persian Empire, and thus the location of Hindush is in dispute. It clearly lies somewhere along the Indus River, but possibilities have ranged from the north end of the Indus River to the river's mouth, where it meets the Arabian Sea. A majority of scholars support the latter area.

It is not known whether Scylax presented a written account of the voyage to Darius the Great or simply reported his information in person. At some point, Scylax wrote a book titled *Periplus* (voyage around by sea). The work was lost, probably fairly early, judging from the inaccurate and confused quotations from it even by early

Greek historians. A fourth century B.C.E. work attributed to Scylax was actually composed more than a century after the voyage and does not appear to have any information from the real Scylax.

Only five fragments from the original book have survived in the works of other Greek writers. They are sufficient to show that the *Periplus* was not merely a series of notes but rather a connected narrative covering the course of the entire voyage from India to Africa. Scylax recorded the sea route and commented on the topography, flora and fauna, and people he saw and their customs. According to the Greek philosopher Aristotle (384-322 B.C.E.), Scylax noticed a great difference between Indian kings and their subjects; unfortunately the nature of this difference was either not related or has been lost.

SIGNIFICANCE

The voyage of Scylax paved the way for the Persian conquest of all of northwest India (now Pakistan) and made possible the sharing of intellectual, scientific, and religious ideas between east and west on a scale much greater than before.

The genres of geographical writing and ethnography begin with Scylax. His little book made such a large impact because Scylax wrote in the east Greek dialect of his region, called Ionic. At the time Scylax lived, the Ionian coast was home to an intellectual explosion in science and philosophy. Many of these early scientific and philosophical works were composed in poetic meters, but prose was starting to take its place as the medium for the straightforward exposition of facts. Scylax, as one of the first writers in Greek to use prose, helped foster its development as a scientific medium. His writings constituted the main source of information about India for the early Greek historians, the philosophers Plato (c. 427-347 B.C.E.) and Aristotle, and through them most of the Western world.

—*Julie A. Williams*

FURTHER READING

Herodotus. *The Histories*. Translated by Robin Waterfield. New York: Oxford University Press, 1998. Darius's conquest of the Indus appears in book 4, chapter 44. Detailed notes.

Karttunen, Klaus. *India in Early Greek Literature*. Helsinki: Studia Orientalia, 1989. Chapters 2 and 3 discuss the Persian conquest and the accuracy of Greek historical writers. Detailed bibliography.

Lesky, Albin. *A History of Greek Literature*. New York: Thomas Crowell, 1966. The section entitled "The Beginnings of Science and Historiography" outlines the beginnings of prose writing on geography.

Obregon, Mauricio. *Beyond the Edge of the Sea: Sailing with Jason and the Argonauts, Ulysses, the Vikings, and Other Explorers of the Ancient World*. New York: Modern Library, 2002. Scylax's voyage is mentioned and contextualized in relation to ancient travel and exploration.

SEE ALSO: c. 734-c. 580 B.C.E., Greeks Colonize the Mediterranean and Black Sea Regions; 520-518 B.C.E., Darius the Great Conquers the Indus Valley

RELATED ARTICLES in *Great Lives from History: The Ancient World*: Darius the Great; Herodotus.

509 B.C.E.
RAPE OF LUCRETIA

Lucretia, a Roman noblewoman, was raped by Tarquinius Sextus, the king's son. Her appeal to her husband and father for vengeance brought about the end of the Roman monarchy and the beginning of the Roman Republic.

LOCALE: Rome (now in Italy)
CATEGORIES: Cultural and intellectual history; wars, uprisings, and civil unrest

KEY FIGURES

Lucretia (sixth century-c. 509 B.C.E.), legendary figure whose rape by Tarquinius Sextus, plea for vengeance, and then suicide set in motion the end of the Roman monarchy
Lucius Tarquinius Superbus (sixth century-after 510 B.C.E.), last king of Rome, r. 534-510 B.C.E.
Tarquinius Sextus (sixth century-c. 500 B.C.E.), son of Superbus, who raped Lucretia
Lucius Tarquinius Collatinus (fl. sixth century B.C.E.), husband of Lucretia and briefly consul of Rome, 509 B.C.E.
Lucretius (sixth century-c. 508 B.C.E.), Lucretia's father and briefly consul of Rome, after Collatinus
Publius Valerius (sixth century-c. 507 B.C.E.), avenger of Lucretia and consul of Rome, following Lucretius
Lucius Junius Brutus (sixth century-c. 508 B.C.E.), avenger of Lucretia and first consul of Rome, late sixth century B.C.E.

SUMMARY OF EVENT

The traditional date for the end of the Roman monarchy and the beginning of the Roman Republic is 509 B.C.E. The canonical version of the story was written by Titus Livius, better known as Livy (59 B.C.E.-17 C.E.), in his *Ab urbe condita libre* (c. 26 B.C.E.-15 C.E.; *The History of Rome*, 1600). According to Livy, the seventh and last king of Rome, Lucius Tarquinius Superbus, was a tyrant who treated the Roman people like slaves and executed those who might oppose him or whose wealth he coveted. During the siege of the wealthy town of Ardea, the leading young men—including Superbus's son, Tarquinius Sextus—spent their evenings drinking and talking. One night, the discussion turned to wives. Each man argued that his own wife was the most beautiful and virtuous. Then Lucius Tarquinius Collatinus, nephew of the king and a cousin of Sextus, declared that they should all ride to Rome and to Collatia, where they would see that his wife, Lucretia, was by far the best.

The intoxicated young men agreed and rode first to Rome, where they found their wives spending time eating and talking with friends. When they arrived at Collatinus's house, they found Lucretia with her maidservants working wool by lamplight. She received them graciously, and as a result, Collatinus was declared the winner. While the men enjoyed Lucretia's hospitality, Sextus took special note of Lucretia's beauty and modesty, and an immoral lust began to grow in him.

A few days later, Sextus secretly returned to Collatinus's home. Because Sextus was her husband's cousin, Lucretia invited him in and offered him hospitality. After she and the rest of the household retired for the night, Sextus, sword in hand, crept into Lucretia's bedroom and woke her by placing his hand over her mouth. He warned her that he would kill her if she cried out. Then he confessed his love and begged Lucretia to acquiesce to his desire. When she refused, he threatened her with death. She still refused. He then threatened to kill a male slave, put him naked in Lucretia's bed with her body and tell all that he found them together. Faced with the prospect of both death and dishonor without the chance of clearing her name, Lucretia submitted to Sextus's lust, and Sextus returned to the camp.

Lucretia sent messages to her father and husband to come immediately with trusted friends. Lucretius (Lucretia's father) with Publius Valerius and Collatinus with Lucius Junius Brutus arrived at the house without delay. When Collatinus asked his wife if she was well, Lucretia responded that no woman could be well who had lost her honor. Through her tears, she informed the men that Tarquinius Sextus had raped her and demanded that they avenge her. She said, however, that she could not forget that her body had been defiled and vowed to commit suicide. The men tried to dissuade her, but Lucretia ignored their pleas, responding that no immoral woman should be allowed to live. She then drew a knife from under her garment and ended her life.

While her father and husband raised a lament, Brutus (who had for some time pretended to be a half-wit to prevent Superbus from considering him a threat) seized Lucretia's knife and vowed that by her most sacred blood the Tarquins would be expelled. Then the men carried Lucretia's body out of the house and into the forum of

Collatia, where all could see and hear what had happened. From there they rode to Rome, where Brutus summoned the people to the Roman Forum and delivered a fiery speech detailing the wrongs Superbus had committed against the Roman people and rallying them to expel the family. Superbus's sons and his wife fled, and Superbus found the gates of Rome locked against him when he returned to the city to quell the rebellion. The Romans then elected two consuls (magistrates) to serve yearly terms. The first to hold the new office were Brutus and Collatinus, but because Collatinus was related to the former king, he was asked to step down and to leave Rome; he was replaced by Lucretius, and after Lucretius's death, by Valerius.

SIGNIFICANCE

The truth of this tradition has sometimes been questioned by scholars, but what is most important in this story is not whether it happened exactly as Livy told it, but what this story shows of the Romans' view of themselves as a people.

The first glimpse of the Roman character comes in the Roman response to the rule of the city by the Tarquins, an Etruscan family. The archaeological record does show that Etruscans ruled the city during the sixth century B.C.E. and brought their symbols and customs to Rome. That Etruscan rule did not disappear immediately is represented through the figure of Lucius Junius Brutus, who was himself related to the Tarquins (his mother was the daughter of Superbus) and was the first to hold a consulship. Yet, the "Roman" aspect of Brutus did not emerge until the Tarquin family had done something so horrible it could not be overlooked. Even though Superbus had killed Brutus's own father and uncles and had forced Brutus to pretend to be stupid (*brutus* is Latin for "dull" or "stupid"), it was not until the Tarquins had turned their illicit use of power against a woman that he and the other Romans were willing to revolt against the king. These elements of the tradition represent the Romans as a people who willingly accepted influence from other cultures. Moreover, the Romans respected power and did not easily resort to rebellion. Abuse of men was not sufficient reason for rebellion, but abuse of women could not be tolerated.

A second statement about Rome and the Romans comes through Lucretia. She is presented as a young Ro-

A meeting between Lucretia and Tarquinius Sextus (third from left). (F. R. Niglutsch)

THE TARQUINS

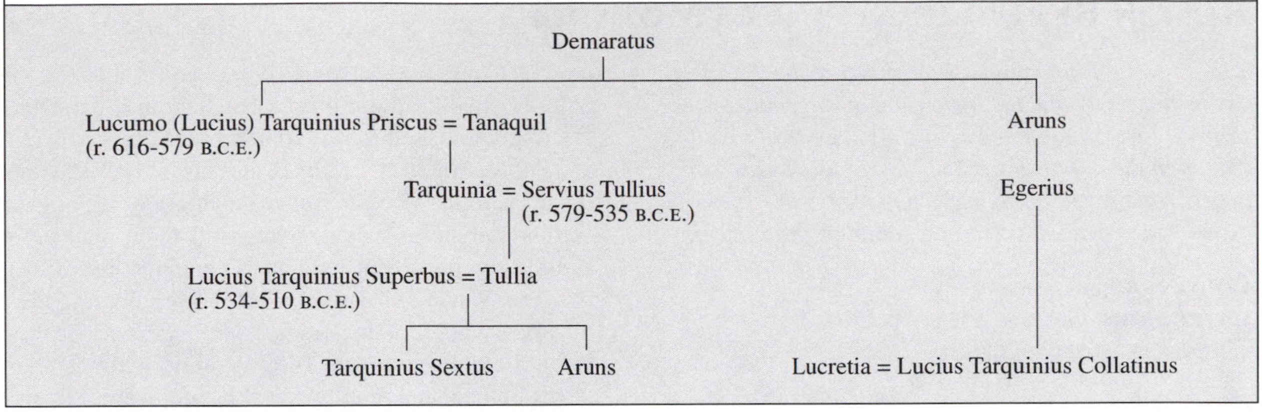

man woman married to a member of the Tarquin family. When the men, mostly members of the Tarquin family, began to argue about who had the best wife, no one hesitated to show off his wife to the others. Scholars have argued that in Etruscan society, women were very visible and lived lives closer to those of men than either their Greek or even Roman counterparts. Livy's story conveys this idea through the actions of the wives the men find in the palace—they, like the men, are spending time with friends. Only Lucretia was found participating in work that was specific to women: She was working wool.

More important, through Lucretia, Livy demonstrates Roman bravery, Roman morality, and the ability of women to change the course of history. First Lucretia acted with kindness and respect, greeting her husband and his friends when they arrived unexpectedly and greeting her husband's cousin when he returned a few days later. Lucretia was willing to face death rather than give in to Sextus's lust, but death with dishonor—the knowledge that her reputation would be destroyed—she could not accept. By choosing to submit, Lucretia determined that it was more important for her to have the opportunity to speak out, to name her attacker, and to ensure that he would pay. As a married woman inside her own home, she had the authority to give orders to the men in her family and they were expected to listen and to determine the proper course of action outside the home. Lucretia's further refusal to live as a compromised woman, one whose story others could manipulate for their own purposes, sealed her reputation as the brave and virtuous woman who brought an end to the hated monarchy of Lucius Tarquinius Superbus and thereby initiated the Roman Republic.

—T. Davina McClain

FURTHER READING

Bonfante, Larissa. "Etruscan Women." *Archaeology* 26 (1973): 242-249. Bonfante argues for an elevated role of women in Etruscan culture.

Cornell, T. J. *The Beginnings of Rome: Italy and Rome from the Bronze Age to the Punic Wars, c. 1000-264 B.C.E.* New York: Routledge, 1995. A detailed study of the archaeological evidence as well as the historical tradition surrounding Rome's founding and development.

Dixon, Suzanne. *The Roman Mother.* Norman: University of Oklahoma Press, 1988. Dixon surveys the nature of a woman's authority within the home and within Roman society.

Livy. *The Early History of Rome, Books I-V.* Translated by Aubrey de Selincourt, introduction by R. M. Ogilvie. Reprint. New York: Penguin, 2002. The story of Lucretia and the founding of the Republic occurs in book 1.

McDougall, I. "Livy and Etruscan Woman." *Ancient Historical Bulletin* 4 (1990): 24-30. McDougall questions Bonfante's view that Etruscan women had political power to match their social freedom.

Vandiver, E. "The Founding Mothers of Livy's Rome." In *The Eye Expanded: Life and the Arts in Greco-Roman Antiquity,* edited by F. B. Titchener and R. F. Moorton. Berkeley: University of California Press, 1999. Vandiver demonstrates the central role of women in founding Rome, first as a monarchy and then as a republic.

SEE ALSO: 625-509 B.C.E., Rise of Etruscan Civilization in Rome; c. 509 B.C.E., Roman Republic Replaces Monarchy.

RELATED ARTICLES in *Great Lives from History: The Ancient World*: Livy; Lucretia; Tarquins.

c. 509 B.C.E.
ROMAN REPUBLIC REPLACES MONARCHY

The rape of a Roman noblewoman led to the downfall of the monarchy and the institution of a republican form of government to counter the excesses of royalty. Although the overthrow of the monarchy was an aristocratic rebellion, it led to a move toward democratic representation in a complex government.

LOCALE: Rome (now in Italy)
CATEGORIES: Government and politics; wars, uprisings, and civil unrest

KEY FIGURES

Lucius Tarquinius Superbus (sixth century-after 510 B.C.E.), last king of Rome, r. 534-510 B.C.E.
Tarquinius Sextus (sixth century-c. 500 B.C.E.), son of Superbus, who raped Lucretia
Lucretia (sixth century-c. 509 B.C.E.), legendary figure whose rape initiated the fall of the Roman monarchy
Lucius Junius Brutus (sixth century-c. 508 B.C.E.), avenger of Lucretia and first consul of Rome, late sixth century B.C.E.
Lucius Tarquinius Collatinus (fl. sixth century B.C.E.), husband of Lucretia and briefly consul of Rome, 509 B.C.E.

SUMMARY OF EVENT

In 509 B.C.E., King Lucius Tarquinius Superbus and his family were driven out of Rome, and a new Republican government was instituted.

By traditional accounts, Rome was founded in 753 B.C.E. by Romulus, a descendant of the hero Aeneas who fled Troy after the Greeks sacked the city. An elective monarchy was adopted, and from 753 to 509 B.C.E. Rome was ruled by a series of seven kings. The nature of the kingship evolved while the Roman state developed. As the state grew and prospered, the monarchy became populist in character. The kings courted the favor of the people at the expense of the aristocrats. The kings of Rome are credited with developing political assemblies, instituting public services (such as the first sewers in the city), and undertaking large-scale building projects. The fall of the monarchy in 509 B.C.E. was the work of aristocrats, not the common people.

Roman writers, including Livy (59 B.C.E.-17 C.E.), record that the fall of the monarchy was a private family affair and not a political movement. Tarquinius Sextus, the second son of Lucius Tarquinius Superbus, raped the noblewoman Lucretia, the virtuous wife of Lucius Tarquinius Collatinus. Lucretia committed suicide, but not before revealing the crime to her husband, her father Lucretius, and their trusted friends Lucius Junius Brutus and Publius Valerius. Led by Brutus, the friends and family of Lucretia vowed to avenge her injury by driving out Sextus Tarquinius and his tyrannical father and never again allowing anyone to reign as king in Rome. Superbus, who was waging war against the neighboring town of Ardea, was prohibited from reentering Rome. He went into exile in Etruria (now Tuscany, Italy) with members of his immediate family. A republican government was established and Lucius Junius Brutus and Lucius Tarquinius Collatinus were elected to the newly created office of consul. To protect the young republic from a return to monarchy, a law was soon passed banishing from Rome all members of the Tarquin clan. Collatinus, though a leading member of the uprising against the king, resigned his post as consul and went into exile. Lucretius was appointed in his place, followed by Publius Valerius.

Some scholars reject this traditional account with its focus on the personal tale of Lucretia and prefer a political explanation for the fall of the monarchy in Rome. This interpretation is supported by a comparative study of political developments occurring at this time throughout the Greco-Roman world. In the sixth century B.C.E. leading aristocrats were rising up against monarchs and tyrants throughout the Mediterranean, establishing new aristocratic (oligarchic) governments. The events in Rome fit into this larger framework of regional political changes.

The two views, however, are best reconciled. The leading role of Brutus and Collatinus, both of whom came from prominent families, suggests that frustration over the antiaristocratic policies of the king and the lack of opportunity for political advancement may have contributed to the fall of the monarchy. The rape of Lucretia served as the catalyst for action. Under the new Republican system, citizens in the centuriate assembly would elect two aristocrats to hold annual consulships and serve as military and executive officers. Though open to all Roman citizens, the centuriate assembly was organized on the basis of property classes and gave significantly more political power to the wealthiest citizens. The new Roman Republic was thus at its core aristocratic and antimonarchic, not democratic. The aristocratic friends of Lucretia who led the revolt against the monarchy directly benefited from the change of regime.

As the chief officers of the state, the consuls adopted many of the powers and symbols of the kings; however, their authority was not absolute. Power was limited by the collegial and annual nature of the office. These important restrictions on individual power would become the hallmark of Roman magistracies, almost all of which were limited to one year and required the sharing of powers among colleagues. The senate, first organized by Romulus, became the chief deliberative body of the republican system. The popular assemblies took on the new responsibilities of electing magistrates and voting on legislation. The second century B.C.E. Greek historian and political observer Polybius noted the multiple components of Roman government and recognized it as a major factor contributing to Rome's success. The consuls, senate, and people each held a share of the power, but significant checks were in place to maintain a balance between the three governmental bodies. The result was a political system of exceptional stability, lasting for almost five centuries without significant interruption and forming the foundation for the system later instituted by the emperors.

The date for the fall of the monarchy in Rome is commonly held to be 509 B.C.E. This is confirmed by the consular Fasti, the official lists of annual consuls in Rome. Public records of the chief annual magistrates were kept in Rome throughout the republican and imperial periods. These records provided a chronology for Roman historical writers, and fragments of the Fasti survive to the present day. This evidence, together with the literary sources, clearly indicates the institution of a new political system in the years shortly before 500 B.C.E.

The fall of the monarchy and the establishment of the new republican government in Rome correspond with the decline of Etruscan civilization in Italy. The Etruscans had spread their influence through the northern and central portions of the Italian peninsula during the seventh and sixth centuries B.C.E. The last three kings of Rome (Tarquinius Priscus, Servius Tullius, and Tarquinius Superbus) were Etruscan, and Rome seems to have served as an important base for extending Etruscan influence into the regions of Latium and Campania (present-day Lazio and Campagnia, Italy). Some modern scholars have viewed the fall of the monarchy in Rome as a revolt against Etruscan political control. Indeed, the expulsion of the Tarquins meant the removal of a leading Etruscan family from Rome. Etruscan influence in Italy continued to decline throughout the fifth century. Not long after the establishment of the republic in Rome, the Etruscans were defeated by western Greek forces at the Battle of Cumae (474 B.C.E.) and their holdings in northern Italy were reduced by Celtic invasions (c. 400 B.C.E.). The decline of Etruscan civilization left the way open for the new Roman Republic to rise to power in central Italy and later the Mediterranean world.

Significance

The fall of the monarchy in Rome led to new developments in Roman government. The pair of annually elected consuls allowed for a sharing and rotation of power among the leading men in the state. The senate and people also enjoyed a measure of authority. It was as a republic that the Roman state enjoyed centuries of unprecedented success that led to the conquest of the Mediterranean world. With its mixture of executive, deliberative, and popular elements, the Roman Republic has served for centuries as a model for modern Western states.

—*Darryl A. Phillips*

Traditional Dates of the Early Kings of Rome and Their Wives, 753-510 B.C.E.

King and Wife	*Reign*
Romulus (Alba Longa) + Hersilia (Sabine)	753-715
Numa Pompilius (Sabine) + unnamed poet	715-673
Tullus Hostilius (Latin)	673-642
Ancus Marcus (Latin) + unnamed mother of two sons	642-617
Lucius Tarquinius Priscus (Etruscan) + Tanaquil	616-579
Servius Tullius (Etruscan) + daughter of Tanaquil	579-535
Lucius Tarquinius Superbus (Etruscan) + Tullia	534-510

Note: Ethnicity appears in parentheses.

Further Reading

Cornell, T. J. *The Beginnings of Rome: Italy and Rome from the Bronze Age to the Punic Wars, c. 1000-264 B.C.E.* New York: Routledge, 1995. A comprehensive historical analysis of early Rome with detailed discussions of current controversies. Bibliography, indexes, and maps.

Heurgon, Jacques. *The Rise of Rome to 264 B.C.* Translated by James Willis. Berkeley: University of California Press, 1973. Historical account of Rome's development. Maps.

Lintott, Andrew. *The Constitution of the Roman Republic*. New York: Oxford University Press, 1999. Lintott provides a detailed examination of the fully developed Roman Republican government institutions.

Livy. *The Early History of Rome*. Translated by Aubrey de Selincourt. Reprint. New York: Penguin, 2002. An ancient Roman historian's account of the founding and development of the Roman state.

Walbank, F. W., A. E. Astin, M. W. Frederiksen, R. M. Ogilvie, and A. Drummond, eds. *The Rise of Rome to 220 B.C.* Vol. 7, part 2 of *The Cambridge Ancient History*. 2d ed. New York: Cambridge University Press, 1990. A comprehensive study of the sources and controversies related to early Roman history.

SEE ALSO: 625-509 B.C.E., Rise of Etruscan Civilization in Rome; 509 B.C.E., Rape of Lucretia; c. 50 C.E., Creation of the Roman Imperial Bureaucracy; September 4, 476 C.E., Fall of Rome.

RELATED ARTICLES in *Great Lives from History: The Ancient World*: Livy; Lucretia; Polybius; Tarquins.

508-507 B.C.E.
REFORMS OF CLEISTHENES

The reforms of Cleisthenes decreased the authority of the noble factions in Athens and established the foundations of Athenian direct democracy.

LOCALE: Athens
CATEGORY: Government and politics

KEY FIGURES

Cleisthenes of Athens (c. 570-after 507 B.C.E.), aristocrat of the Alcmaeonid family, architect of Athenian direct democracy

Cleomenes I (d. c. 490 B.C.E.), king of Sparta, r. c. 519-c. 490 B.C.E., urged by Cleisthenes to overthrow Athenian tyrannical rule

Isagoras (fl. sixth century B.C.E.), Athenian aristocrat who opposed Cleisthenes, elected archon 508/507 B.C.E.

SUMMARY OF EVENT

After the passage of Solon's legislation early in the sixth century B.C.E., Athens continued to experience political turmoil. Pisistratus established a tyranny which, after his death in 527, passed to his two sons, one of whom was assassinated in 514 and the other expelled with the assistance of King Cleomenes I of Sparta in 510. The tyranny was followed by government by the nobility, apparently a narrow oligarchy whose leader was the aristocrat Isagoras. Cleisthenes of Athens, of the noble family of the Alcmaeonidae, incited the common people against the oligarchs. In 508-507 B.C.E., he besieged the conservatives and their Spartan supporters on the Acropolis. The Spartans acknowledged defeat and were permitted to withdraw, whereupon the aristocratic faction surrendered. Cleisthenes, with the support of most Athenians, then drew up a fresh series of laws which superseded the constitution established by Solon. The reform was essentially political in nature, although it inevitably had repercussions on Attic society as a whole.

Social change was made mainly through abolishing the four traditional tribes of citizens and creating new ones which were not territorial, although they were made up of members of the old *demes*, the villages of Attica. There were then about 170 *demes* of varying sizes. Groups of ten *demes* called *trittyes* were formed by assigning *demes* by lot from the three geographical regions of Attica: the city itself and the countryside immediately around it; the coastal district; and the interior. The *demes* were not necessarily contiguous, especially as Cleisthenes intended to break up regional interest groups of the nobility that had hitherto caused civil unrest, but they were approximately equal in population. New cults were created for the tribes with the approval of the Delphic Apollo in order to bind new loyalties.

The organization of Solon's assembly was also changed, and there is reason to suppose that Cleisthenes assigned to it a more active and important role. It continued to supervise the annual election of magistrates and to be consulted on the issue of war or peace, but it now passed new laws from time to time. With thirty thousand male citizens including the *thetes* (lower-class citizens) eligible to attend, though not to vote, the assembly was unwieldy. An important constitutional innovation of Cleisthenes was creation of the *Boule* or council, an executive committee of the assembly made up of five hundred councilors, fifty from each tribe. Each *deme* elected councilors in proportion to its population. It is a matter of controversy whether the *Boule* was a new institution or merely replaced the Council of Four Hundred said to have been constituted by Solon.

Though the precise functions of the *Boule* in the time of Cleisthenes are not clear, it began somewhat later to draw up formal bills for consideration by the assembly, receive foreign embassies, discharge certain judicial functions, and look after the construction of warships, fortifications, and other public works.

Each tribal group of fifty men, a *prytany*, lived continuously at public expense in the city of Athens for a tenth of the year, an arrangement that was the closest Cleisthenes came to giving payment for holding public office. These groups were ready in emergency to call either the full *Boule* or the assembly into session. One man of the *prytany* was chosen each day to be the *prytanis* or "president" of Athens for twenty-four hours. He was responsible for the safekeeping of keys to the temples and treasuries, and he presided over any sessions of the council or assembly that might take place on his day in office. The *Boule* familiarized the people of Athens with the organization, finances, and resources of the state. It also prepared the generation that followed Cleisthenes for the more democratic 460's and 450's under Pericles.

The nine archons (rulers) continued to function as heretofore, but Cleisthenes has also been credited by some authorities with creating the new office of "general" or *strategos*, which was a more democratic office than archon because generals were elected without regard to census rating. As the office actually dates from 501/500 B.C.E., it was probably the creation of some other man, because Cleisthenes drops out of Athenian history abruptly after 507 B.C.E. Some ancient writers also ascribed to him the honorable form of legalized exile known as "ostracism," but since it was not used until 487 B.C.E., it, too, was in all probability the creation of someone else.

SIGNIFICANCE

Cleisthenes' governmental reforms marked a significant advance in the concept of democracy. His version of elected representation, as embodied in the *prytany* and the *Boule*, provided a workable compromise between oligarchy or monarchy and the unwieldy assembly created by Solon. His creation of *trittyes* also served to break up regionalism and opened citizens' eyes to wider interests, as did the practice of sharing oversight of the government through the office of *prytanis*. The *Boule* also inaugurated the creation of laws by a representative assembly. In many ways, Cleisthenes' reforms sowed the seeds of modern democratic government.

—*Samuel K. Eddy, updated by Jeffrey L. Buller*

FURTHER READING

Fornara, Charles W., and Loren J. Samons. *Athens from Cleisthenes to Pericles*. Berkeley: University of California Press, 1991. A legal and constitutional history of Athens that treats Cleisthenes as a pivotal figure in the development of the Athenian constitution.

Jones, A. H. M. *Athenian Democracy*. Reprint. Baltimore, Md.: The Johns Hopkins University Press, 1986. Describes the day-to-day functioning of the Athenian government, providing an excellent picture of the political bodies developed or reformed by Cleisthenes.

Sealey, Raphael. *A History of the Greek City States, 700-338 B.C.* Berkeley: University of California Press, 1976. Provides a concise yet reliable summary of the reforms by Cleisthenes and details his political conflicts with Isagoras.

Stockton, David. *The Classical Athenian Democracy*. New York: Oxford University Press, 1990. Traces the evolution of Athenian democracy from the reforms of Solon in the early sixth century to those of Ephialtes in the late 460's B.C.E. Gives definitions of Greek terms and suggestions for further reading. Intended as an introduction to the subject for high school and college students.

Thorley, John. *Athenian Democracy*. New York: Routledge, 1996. A short overview of the development of democracy in Athens, contrasting theory and practice.

SEE ALSO: 621 or 620 B.C.E., Draco's Code Is Instituted; c. 594-580 B.C.E., Legislation of Solon; 483 B.C.E., Naval Law of Themistocles Is Instituted; 478-448 B.C.E., Athenian Empire Is Created; May, 431-September, 404 B.C.E., Peloponnesian War.

RELATED ARTICLES in *Great Lives from History: The Ancient World*: Cleisthenes of Athens; Cleomenes; Pericles; Pisistratus; Solon.

5th century B.C.E.

COMPOSITION OF THE *SPRING AND AUTUMN ANNALS*

The Spring and Autumn Annals *established a Chinese historiographic tradition based on the rational observation of events and delineation of historic patterns.*

LOCALE: China
CATEGORY: Historiography

KEY FIGURE

Confucius (551-479 B.C.E.), Chinese philosopher, historian, and probable author of the *Spring and Autumn Annals*

SUMMARY OF EVENT

The *Chunqiu* (*Ch'un-ch'iu*; *The Ch'un Ts'ew with the Tso Chuen*, 1872; commonly known as *Spring and Autumn Annals*) is the earliest complete chronicle extant in China. Attributed to Confucius, it records events in his home state of Lu during the Zhou Dynasty (Chou; 1066-256 B.C.E.). The work's title (literally, spring, autumn) is derived from its format, which contains references to a season for most entries. The entries themselves tend to be brief, at times gnomic; they record everything from affairs of state, wars, and matters of dynastic succession to astronomical signs and even sightings of a *lin* (purported to be a Chinese unicorn). The work covers a span of some twelve rulers, from 722 to 476 B.C.E., an epoch in Chinese history often referred to as the Spring and Autumn Period in honor of the work. Although it deals primarily with events in the tiny state of Lu and its more powerful neighbors, the work suggests the general atmosphere of change and uncertainty during the middle Zhou period and prefigures the dynasty's disintegration during the subsequent Warring States Period (475-221 B.C.E.). The work's title has become symbolic as it records the "rise-and-fall" of Zhou culture as illustrated by the vicissitudes of Lu.

The *Spring and Autumn Annals* is the only book of the Five Classics claimed to be actually written, rather than merely edited, by Confucius. According to the later philosopher Mencius (Mengzi, Meng-tzu; c. 372-c. 289 B.C.E.), Confucius was so devoted to the work that he once told his disciples that his literary reputation would rise or fall by it alone. Another tradition indicates that the original text of the work was copied from the walls of Confucius's family mansion. To most modern scholars, Confucius's authorship of the *Spring and Autumn Annals*, as with his editorship of the other classics, remains open to debate. Although its ultimate origin is uncertain, the text does seem to derive from authentic records dating to the Spring and Autumn Period. Unlike many other histories, it survived the burning of the books in 213 B.C.E. by the Qin Dynasty (Ch'in; 221-206 B.C.E.) and was elevated to classic status during the subsequent Confucian revival of the Han Dynasty (206 B.C.E.-220 C.E.).

Perhaps the least accessible of the Five Classics, the work attracted the attention of ardent Confucianists seeking to discern hidden meanings in the brief, obscure entries. This tradition of close reading looked back to the very source of history writing in China (and, indeed, of writing itself) in the collection and interpretation of oracle inscriptions on bones and tortoise shells. This oracular impulse is evident in the text's inclusion of astronomical events as portents of change and indications of the "will of Heaven." The *Spring and Autumn Annals* mentions thirty-seven solar eclipses and includes the first recorded sighting of Halley's Comet. With its emphasis on pure observation and causation, the text acts as a meeting place between older divination processes and an emergent scientific tradition.

According to tradition, the text is deliberately opaque as Confucius's strict notions of propriety prevented him from directly criticizing the social elite. For instance, an apparently innocent entry in the *Spring and Autumn Annals* (as translated in *Classical Chinese Literature*, edited by John Minford and Joseph S. M. Lau) reads: "In the third month, the late duke's wife returned to Qi"; however, later commentaries explain the woman's departure as a result of her involvement in incest and murder. Another entry reports: "In winter, the duke and an officer of Qi hunted in Zhuo"; yet later commentaries see the incident as an indication of the duke of Lu's declining status in that he would hunt in a neighboring state with a mere "officer." Of course, such interpretations may simply represent excessive zeal on the part of commentators, quick to look for Confucian signs of "praise or blame" in the original text written centuries before. However, they may document authentic oral traditions dating back to the time of Confucius, who may have used the original text as a guide for more frank oral discussions of history with his students.

Ironically, the *Spring and Autumn Annals*' ultimate importance seems to lie not so much in its own text but in the commentary traditions to which it gave rise. Indeed, three of these commentaries join the *Spring and Autumn Annals* in the Thirteen Classics of Confucianism. According to Sima Qian (Ssu-ma Ch'ien; 145-86 B.C.E.), the earliest written commentary of the text, the *Zuo Zhuan* (between fifth and third centuries B.C.E.; c. fourth century B.C.E.; *Zuo Commentary*, in Vol. 5 of *The Chinese Classics*, 1872) was compiled to sift through various oral traditions surrounding the incidents recorded in the work. Although the *Zuo Zhuan* may have originally been an independent work, it shares the annalistic structure of the *Spring and Autumn Annals*; however, it expands the earlier text's spare entries into dramatic episodes with motivated characters similar to those in the classical Greek histories of Herodotus or Thucydides. The other major commentaries, the *Gongyang Zhuang* (*Kung-yang Chuan*; c. third century B.C.E.) and the *Guliang Zhuan* (*Ku-liang Chuan*; c. third century B.C.E.), are more formalistic in their approach, seeking to systematize the *Spring and Autumn Annals* into a consistent program of Confucian ideology.

Confucius plays the lute in this twelfth century drawing. (Library of Congress)

Although the interpretations of particular events in the *Spring and Autumn Annals* may vary, the commentaries seem to agree in the basic assumption that the original text contains a consistent, if submerged, ideology. If read correctly, each event is potentially a microcosm of the whole of Confucian thought. Taken as a whole, the work's structure implies an essential conservatism, if not pessimism: The same mistakes get repeated from generation to generation and the subjects of the chronicle inevitably ignore the disastrous consequences of their actions to pursue a short-term or selfish gain. As such, not only the text reflects the tumultuous Spring and Autumn Period but also becomes a model of Chinese history as a whole—a dynasty's rise followed by its inevitable fall.

In the elevation of the work to canonical status, as perhaps the ur-text of Chinese history, one is tempted to read an unflinching fatalism into the subsequent Chinese historiographic impulse. At the same time, the text illustrates the preference in Confucian ideology, and perhaps in Chinese thought itself, for inductive rather than deductive thought. Like both the *Shijing* (*Shih Ching*, compiled fifth century B.C.E.; *The Book of Songs*, 1937) and the *Liji* (*Li Chi*, compiled fifth century B.C.E.; *The Liki*, 1885; commonly known as *Classic of Rituals*), the *Spring and Autumn Annals* calls on its reader to come to terms with often opaque particulars before establishing patterns and making generalizations. As with the other classics, close reading and attention to detail are required for the reader to wrest a meaning from the text. To some degree, this confrontation with the text becomes its ultimate meaning.

SIGNIFICANCE

The *Spring and Autumn Annals* established the role of historian in Chinese culture as an objective rationalistic observer of events, a person able to distill complex historic detail into its moral and ideological essence. Despite the self-imposed censorship based on notions of propriety, the work's continued influence and subsequent commentary traditions illustrate how Chinese historians became political figures in their own right who not only passed final judgment on the elite but also, more important, discerned the broad social and historic patterns that led to cultural triumph or tragedy.

—*Luke A. Powers*

Further Reading

Durrant, Stephen. "The Literary Features of Historical Writing." In *The Columbia History of Chinese Literature*, edited by Victor Mair. New York: Columbia University Press, 2001. This accessible overview of early Chinese historical writing places the *Spring and Summer Annals* within the tradition of the *shih* or scribe.

Legge, James. *The Chinese Classics*. 5 vols. Taipei: Literature House Reprints, 1966. A facsimile edition that includes Legge's translation of the *Chunqiu* (supported by his translation of the *Zuo Zhuan*) as volume 5. Though originally published in 1872, this text remains the standard edition in English.

Minford, John, and Joseph S. M. Lau, eds. *Classical Chinese Literature*. New York: Columbia University Press, 1996. This excellent anthology of Chinese literature includes representative selections from the *Spring and Summer Annals* annotated with selections from with later commentaries.

Pines, Yuri. *Foundations of Confucian Thought: Intellectual Life in the Chunqiu Period, 722-453 B.C.E.* Honolulu: University of Hawaii Press, 2002. This work examines the intellectual ferment in China during the Spring and Autumn Period that gave rise to the Confucian school and the *Spring and Summer Annals*.

Schaberg, David. *A Patterned Past: Form and Thought in Early Chinese Historiography*. Cambridge, Mass.: Harvard University Asia Center, 2001. An examination of the emergence of Chinese historical writing during the Spring and Autumn Period, with close study of the relationship between the *Spring and Summer Annals* and the *Zuo Zhuan*.

Watson, Burton. *Early Chinese Literature*. New York: Columbia University Press, 1962. A good general introduction to Chinese historiography (and its beginning with the *Spring and Summer Annals*) in the broader context of Chinese literature.

Yutang, Lin, ed. *The Wisdom of Confucius*. New York: Modern Library, 1994. This work couples a good sampling of major Confucian literature in translation with an able introduction that places the *Spring and Summer Annals* within the context of the larger Confucian canon.

See also: c. 1066, Western Zhou Dynasty Begins in China; 770 B.C.E., Eastern Zhou Dynasty Begins in China; 5th-1st century B.C.E., Composition of *The Great Learning*; 479 B.C.E., Confucius's Death Leads to the Creation of *The Analects*; 475-221 B.C.E., China Enters Chaotic Warring States Period; c. 450-c. 425 B.C.E., History Develops as a Scholarly Discipline; 221 B.C.E., Qin Dynasty Founded in China; 1st century B.C.E., Sima Qian Writes Chinese History; c. 99-105 C.E., Ban Zhao Writes Behavior Guide for Young Women.

Related articles in *Great Lives from History: The Ancient World*: Ban Gu; Ban Zhao; Confucius; Mencius; Sima Qian; Xunzi.

c. 5th-4th century B.C.E.
Creation of the *Jātakas*

The Jātakas*, the stories of the earlier lives of Buddha, have been a popular means of disseminating Buddhist ideas and have inspired artworks in Buddhist countries.*

Locale: India

Categories: Religion; cultural and intellectual history; literature

Key Figure

Buddha (Siddhārtha Gautama; c. 566-c. 486 B.C.E.), founder of Buddhism

Summary of Event

The *Jātakas* (*Buddhist Birth-Stories*, 1925) are the stories of the previous lives of Śākyamuni, the historical Buddha, before he attained final enlightenment. The most well-known collection of these stories is in the Pāli canon. In the canon, the *Jātakas* are the tenth book of the *Khuddaka Nikāya* of the *Sutta Piṭaka*. Each of the 547 stories consists of verse and prose. The stories range from very short animal fables to long *jātakas* that run on for pages. Strictly speaking only the verses, with a few exceptions, are considered canonical. The *Jātakas* are divided up into *nipātas*, according to the number of verses they contain. For example, the first *nipāta* has stories that have a single verse; however, among the higher numbered *nipātas*, the number does not always match the number of verses. The last *nipāta*, known as the *Mahāni-pāta*, consists of ten long *jātakas*.

In the Pāli *Jātakas*, the texts usually begin by describing a particular incident in the present, which prompts Buddha to tell about his previous incarnation. The verses are usually embedded in the telling of the story. The text ends with Buddha identifying the characters in the story with the members of Buddha's present circle.

A commentary, called the *Nidānakathā*, has been attached to the Pāli *Jātakas*, introducing the background of these stories. It begins by relating the story of Sumedha, who resolves to become enlightened, and proceeds down to the events leading up to and following the enlightenment of Buddha, ending with the establishment of the Jetavana Retreat.

According to the tradition in Sri Lanka, the *Jātakas* originally consisted of verses to which a commentary was added with the stories. This text was in Singhalese, the language of Sri Lanka. In the fifth century C.E., Buddhaghosa is said to have translated these verses and commentary into Pāli. After the work of twentieth century scholar T. W. Rhys Davids, this tradition has not found acceptance, primarily because the *Jātakas* commentary is unlike other translations made by Buddhaghosa.

The question remains as to when the *Jātakas* first appeared. The earliest concrete evidence for the *Jātakas* is found in the relief sculptures of the Bhārhut stupa from the third or second century B.C.E. Of twenty-four scenes identified as illustrating the *Jātakas*, eighteen can be traced to the present collection. These reliefs seem to indicate that stories of the previous lives of Buddha were circulating before the third century B.C.E. This dating seems to be confirmed by scholar K. R. Norman's arguments. He has noted that Sanskrit versions of the *Jātaka* stories are at times almost identical with their Pāli counterparts. This implies that the two versions are based on earlier material. Because Sanskrit was not in common use in translating Buddhist works until the third century B.C.E., it is likely that the source of the Pāli and Sanskrit versions goes back at least to the fourth century B.C.E.

There has been a long argument as to whether the verse or the prose of the stories is older. Norman has pointed out differences between the verses and the prose stories surrounding them; he believes these indicate that the writer of the prose parts misunderstood the verses. This would seem to show that the prose was a later addition. However, Norman also readily acknowledges that it is difficult, if not impossible at times, to understand the verses without the surrounding stories.

It is also clear that most of the stories were not Buddhist in origin but were adapted into a Buddhist context through references to Buddhist doctrines and by identifying the main character as a bodhisattva (a future Buddha). There are exceptions, most notably the "Kaliṅgabodhi Jātaka" (number 479), in which King Kaliṅga honors the Bodhi tree, under which Buddha attained enlightenment.

That the stories were not Buddhist in origin is demonstrated by their appearance elsewhere in India, outside their Buddhist guise. Similar stories are found in the Indian fable collections *Pañcatantra* (c. 200 B.C.E.; *The Fables of Pilpay*, 1699) and *Hitopadeśa* (after 200 B.C.E.; English translation, 1880). The "Dasaratha Jātaka" (number 461) is a miniature retelling of the *Rāmāyaṇa* (c. 500 B.C.E., some material added later; English translation, 1870-1889), one of the major Hindu epics. Stories similar to the *Jātakas* appear not only in India but also all over the world.

Since the nineteenth century, it has often been argued that the fable tradition began in India and migrated to Europe. Although this idea has not won universal approval, interesting parallels can be seen between the stories found in the *Jātakas* and those found elsewhere. Rhys Davids, for example, noted that the story of the ass in the lion skin (number 189 in the *Jātaka*) turns up in Aesop and other Western fable collections. In number 67 of the *Jātaka*s, a woman attempts to free her husband, brother, and son, who have been mistakenly imprisoned for a crime. The king asks that she decide which of the three she would have released. She chooses her brother because she is able to find another husband and have another son. A similar line of reasoning is found in Herodotus's *Historiai Herodotou* (c. 424 B.C.E.; *The History*, 1709) 3.118-120 and Sophocles' *Antigonē* (441 B.C.E.; *Antigone*, 1729) 902-12.

SIGNIFICANCE

The *Jātaka* stories have been translated into the languages of all Buddhist lands and have proved to be a popular means of teaching Buddhist values. It is interesting to note that a noncanonical Pāli collection of fifty *jātakas*, the *Paññāsa Jātaka*, is found in Thailand, Cambodia, and Burma. Although some of the stories are based on Indian material, others appear to be of local origin.

The *Jātakas* not only have appeared in literature but also have played a major role in the artwork of Buddhist countries. As mentioned before, the earliest evidence for the *Jātakas* in India is found in the relief sculptures in Bharhut. The *Jātakas* are also portrayed in artworks in *Sāñcī* (second century B.C.E.), *Bodh Gayā* (first century B.C.E.), *Amāravatī* (second century C.E.), *Nāgārjunakoṇḍa* (third century C.E.), and *Ajaṇṭā* (sixth century C.E.). From India, the *Jātaka* stories have migrated and found their place in the artistic traditions of other Buddhist countries.

—*Albert T. Watanabe*

FURTHER READING

Ahir, D. C. *The Influence of the Jātakas on Art and Literature*. Delhi: B.R. Publishing, 2000. A collection of essays on the influence of the *Jātakas* on art and literature, both inside and outside India. Indexes.

Cowell, E. B. *The Jātaka: Or, The Stories of the Buddha's Former Births*. 7 vols. 1895-1913. Reprint. Boston: Routledge and Kegan Paul, 1981. The standard translation of all the *Jātakas* in the Pāli canon. The preface gives a description of the development of the *Jātakas*. Indexes.

Norman, K. R. *Pali Literature*. Wiesbaden, Germany: Otto Harrossowitz, 1983. This standard account of Pāli literature gives a concise description of the *Jātakas*. Bibliography and indexes.

Rhys Davids, T. W. *Buddhist Birth Stories: The Oldest Collection of Folk-Lore Extant*. Translated by T. W. Rhys Davids. 1880. Reprint. London: Routledge, 2000. Translation of the *Nidānakathā* and selected *Jātakas*. The lengthy introduction gives a detailed discussion of the development of the *Jātakas*. Also it cites various parallels from the literature of other countries. Index of *Jātakas*.

Wray, Elizabeth, Clare Rosenfield, and Dorothy Bailey. *Ten Lives of the Buddha: Siamese Painting and Jātaka Tales*. Rev. ed. New York: Weatherhill, 1996. This book offers versions of the last ten *Jātakas*, with illustrations from Thai temples. The appendices consist of the history of the development of the *Jātakas* and an essay on Siamese temple painting. Thirty-two plates. Bibliography.

SEE ALSO: 6th or 5th century B.C.E., Birth of Buddhism; c. 273/265-c. 238 B.C.E., Aśoka Reigns over India; c. 250 B.C.E., Third Buddhist Council Convenes; c. 250 B.C.E., *Tipiṭaka* Is Compiled; c. 1st century B.C.E., Indian Buddhist Nuns Compile the *Therigatha*; 1st century B.C.E.-1st century C.E., Compilation of the *Lotus Sutra*; 1st-2d century C.E., Fourth Buddhist Council Convenes; c. 60-68 C.E., Buddhism Enters China; Late 4th-5th century C.E., Asanga Helps Spread Mahāyāna Buddhism; 399 C.E., Chinese Monk Faxian Travels to India; c. 470 C.E., Bodhidharma Brings Chan Buddhism to China.

RELATED ARTICLES in *Great Lives from History: The Ancient World*: Bodhidharma; Buddha; Faxian; Menander (Greco-Bactrian ruler).

c. 5th-3d century B.C.E.
COMPOSITION OF *THE ART OF WAR*

Sunzi's writing of The Art of War *established the foundation of Chinese and East Asian military thought.*

LOCALE: State of Qi (now Shandong, China)
CATEGORY: Cultural and intellectual history

KEY FIGURE

Sunzi (Sun Tzu; fl. c. 500 B.C.E.), Chinese general and putative author of *The Art of War*

SUMMARY OF EVENT

Sunzi Bingfa (*The Art of War*, 1910) is a Chinese treatise, divided into thirteen *pian*, that provides detailed advice on the conduct of war. Written in terse classical Chinese, its thirteen basic divisions were sometimes grouped into three *zhuan* and accompanied by numerous and widely varied commentaries written over the succeeding two millennia.

The writing of *The Art of War* is the beginning of the intellectual tradition of Chinese considerations of war. Considerable controversy surrounds the authorship of the text, whether the work is a departure from past practice or the inheritor of a long tradition of writing about war, and when it was actually written. Very little consensus exists on any of these questions, and archaeological finds have resolved very few of the problems. The core of the disputes is whether *The Art of War* can be used as a description of warfare in early Chinese history and, if so, in which period. Given the broader controversies over early Chinese history and society and the often ambiguous archaeological record, much is at stake for scholars of early China.

Sunzi (Master Sun), or Sun Wu, was active from the late sixth to the early fifth century B.C.E. according to Sima Qian's biography of him in the *Shiji* (first century B.C.E.; *Records of the Grand Historian of China*, 1960, rev. ed. 1993). *The Art of War* has traditionally been attributed entirely to Sunzi, with any discrepancies of language or style brushed aside as transmission errors. As

Sunzi was a near contemporary of Confucius, and a successful general, the text's pedigree as a classic would therefore be quite impeccable. Later scholars called this attribution into question, arguing that no such person existed, that the writing style was not compatible with Sunzi's time, that the ideas expressed were not available until several centuries later, or that the description of warfare was consistent with a later period.

Moreover, the text appears to be a compilation of the works of different writers rather than the work of a single author. The most obvious reason to deny Sunzi's direct authorship is the repeated use of the preamble "Master Sun said." This leaves open the possibility that *The Art of War* could be attributed to Sunzi in the same way that the *Lunyu* (later sixth-early fifth centuries B.C.E.; *The Analects*, 1861) is attributed to Confucius. None of these issues has been conclusively proven or disproved, but it does seem likely that the text was compiled over time, possibly as the received wisdom of a school of thought associated with, if not originating from, Sunzi, and that its core contents were stable by the second century B.C.E.

There are three ranges of dates for *The Art of War*, but general agreement has proven impossible because each of these ranges has its own problems. The first possibility is that the text was actually composed by Sunzi shortly before his death in the early fifth century B.C.E. This position assumes that the attribution of the text to Sunzi is correct, and therefore, the work must have been written during his lifetime. The two other proposed ranges, both based on internal evidence (such as writing styles and content), are the last half of the fifth century B.C.E. and the fourth to third centuries B.C.E. These latter two datings obviously deny Sunzi's authorship and attempt to situate the text within a particular literary and intellectual milieu. Without an unambiguous archaeological find to clarify these issues, however, they will remain unresolved.

The sophistication of the understanding of war represented in the text, the simplicity of its language, and the comprehensiveness of its consideration has convinced many modern scholars that *The Art of War* must be the inheritor of a long and well-developed tradition of discussions of war rather than the originator of a tradition. It is probably true that the writer or writers of the text had a profound understanding of war, extending from its relationship to the ruler and state all the way down to tactical issues. This does not preclude, however, the possibility that the author or authors were the first to write these understandings down and to shift an oral tradition to a written one. Regardless, either because of the loss of any earlier texts or because *The Art of War* was actually the beginning of the tradition of Chinese military thought, the work effectively became the starting point of all subsequent Chinese writing on war.

SIGNIFICANCE

Sunzi's *The Art of War* has been the most important treatise on military strategy in East Asia for more than two thousand years. The 1972 archaeological discovery of an early version of *The Art of War* at Yinqueshan (Linch'üeh-shan) has confirmed the mostly faithful transmission of the work from its early form in the second century B.C.E. to the eleventh century edition, which is the basis of the current version. It is the second most frequently translated Chinese work, after Laozi's *Dao De Jing* (possibly sixth century B.C.E., probably compiled late third century B.C.E.; *The Speculations on Metaphysics, Polity, and Morality of "the Old Philosopher, Lau-Tsze,"* 1868; better known as the *Dao De Jing*), and is now widely recognized within Western culture, demonstrating a remarkable staying power and attraction for a text squarely focused on military strategy.

The concepts in *The Art of War* developed during a time of intense, prolonged interstate warfare and assume the presence of professional generals, large infantry armies, and organized logistical support systems. These were newer military developments that conflicted with an earlier feudal aristocratic practice based on chariot warfare and precampaign divination. Both traditions are represented in the text, with Sunzi consistently arguing for professionalism and rational calculation over aristocratic honor and superstitious practice. War was too important a matter to be left to the untrained or ignorant because the existence of the state itself was at stake. Sunzi is concerned only with the continued existence of the state and assumes that it can be maintained or expanded only through skill at war.

As is characteristic of a composite text assembled over time with much of the material derived from oral tradition, the organization is haphazard and unsystematic. Perhaps as a result of its oral origins or because of its target audience, much of the information and advice is given in the form of lists. These lists provide convenient memory devices for systematically responding to the different concerns of a field commander, such as what to do in various kinds of terrain. In general, much of what *The Art of War* says seems to be common sense, but that is precisely why the book has been so valuable over the centuries.

The Art of War's relationship with actual strategic, operational, or tactical events is uncertain. Most generals were illiterate, and there are extremely few documented instances in which *The Art of War* was specifically cited in policy or strategy discussions in support of a particular proposal. However, the continued reproduction of the book and its frequent prohibitions from private ownership indicate that its utility in military affairs was well accepted.

The Art of War's most direct influence was probably as the intellectual counterbalance to the more utopian strains of Chinese political thought. Unlike Confucianism, Daoism, or Buddhism, *The Art of War* takes a purely pragmatic approach to war, accepting it as intrinsic to the continued existence of the state and arguing that it must be waged ruthlessly. No higher ideals inform the text, though its warnings about the dangers of war and its ideal of defeating the enemy's plans without engaging in battle have led many to erroneously conclude that it is antiwar. Rather, the book opens by pointing out how crucial war is and that it cannot be ignored. Given that war is going to take place, *The Art of War* points out that the goal is not to win battles but to win the war, that is, to achieve the state's objectives. It is to one's own advantage to achieve those objectives with a minimum of violence, because battles are uncertain and destruction benefits no one. This ideal cannot always, or even ever, be achieved, so the text suggests the other possibilities in descending order of desirability, from attacking alliances to attempting to capture a city by escalade.

Sunzi's *The Art of War* is more widely read now than it ever was in the past and, with the rise in the general education level of armies, is more widely read in many militaries and therefore more influential than before. Moreover, the many translations of the work have spread its influence across the world. Its earlier, erroneous reading as the diametric opposite of the Western way in warfare, the indirect versus the direct method of fighting, is beginning to fade, and a more accurate, nuanced understanding of the text is beginning to emerge. The work is now read not as an exotic or quaint piece of ancient Chinese wisdom but as a valuable contribution to the general understanding of war whose precepts were precociously written down two millennia ago and have thus stood the test of time. More than two thousand years after it was written, *The Art of War* is not only still read and used by commanders and statesmen but appears to be growing in influence.

—*Peter A. Lorge*

FURTHER READING

Graff, David. *Medieval Chinese Warfare, 300-900*. New York: Routledge, 2002. An outstanding military history of China's medieval period that places battlefield results in the larger context of strategic thought, social change, and political struggle.

Graff, David, and Robin Higham, eds. *A Military History of China*. Boulder, Colo.: Westview, 2002. A wide-ranging collection of articles written for the lay reader covering aspects of both ancient and modern Chinese military history.

Kierman, Frank, and John K. Fairbank, eds. *Chinese Ways in Warfare*. Cambridge, Mass.: Harvard University Press, 1974. Somewhat dated but still solid scholarship on a variety of Chinese military topics.

Johnston, Alastair Iain. *Cultural Realism: Strategic Culture and Grand Strategy in Chinese History*. Princeton, N.J.: Princeton University Press, 1995. A worthwhile attempt to describe Chinese strategic culture, which is occasionally overwhelmed by a perplexing theoretical framework.

Sawyer, Ralph, trans. *The Seven Military Classics of Ancient China*. Boulder, Colo.: Westview, 1993. A complete English translation of China's seven military classics; includes useful introductions to the works and current scholarship on them.

SEE ALSO: 479 B.C.E., Confucius's Death Leads to the Creation of *The Analects*; 475-221 B.C.E., China Enters Chaotic Warring States Period; 221 B.C.E., Qin Dynasty Founded in China; 206 B.C.E., Liu Bang Captures Qin Capital, Founds Han Dynasty.

RELATED ARTICLES in *Great Lives from History: The Ancient World*: Cao Cao; Confucius; Laozi.

5th-1st century B.C.E.
COMPOSITION OF *THE GREAT LEARNING*

The Great Learning *provided a capsule statement of the connections among philosophical inquiry, good character, and government/social order and was established as the first of the Confucian Four Books.*

LOCALE: Lu and adjacent states (now northeast China)
CATEGORIES: Philosophy; cultural and intellectual history

KEY FIGURES

Confucius (551-479 B.C.E.), Chinese ethicist and political philosopher
Zengzi (Tseng-Tzu; c. 500-436 B.C.E.), Confucius's pupil, Chinese scholar and philosopher
Zhu Xi (Chu Hsi; 1130-1200 C.E.), Chinese scholar and philosopher

SUMMARY OF EVENT

Political turmoil forms the backdrop to the composition of *Da Xue* (*The Great Learning*, 1861). In the late sixth and early fifth centuries B.C.E., the kingdoms that would become China had been warring with one another for three hundred years. This warfare would only increase in intensity and brutality during the ensuing Warring States Period (475-221 B.C.E.). The Zhou Dynasty (Chou; c. 1066-256 B.C.E.), headed by the Tian Zi (T'ien Tzu, or the son of heaven), performed a ceremonial and symbolic function but was increasingly unable to provide peace and harmony. *The Great Learning*'s great editor and commentator, Zhu Xi, attributes the failure of the Zhou to the absence of good and wise sovereigns.

Confucius and his followers attempted to rectify this troubled situation, largely through affirming traditional political morality against the amoral Legalism of the aggressive kingdom of Qin (Ch'in). Their philosophical statement intended to instruct active rulers—*The Great Learning*—is appropriately brief. The main text may be easily accommodated on a single printed page. This original portion is now divided into seven sections, each only a sentence or two long, but the pivotal central sections, four and five, are each rendered as one very long sentence. *The Great Learning* is framed by a preface and a postscript by Zhu Xi, who also contributed two notes and two comments. The classic portion is followed by a commentary traditionally attributed to Confucius's devoted follower Zengzi. This commentary consists of ten very short chapters, with 9 and 10 being the longest by far—a page or two. In all, *The Great Learning*, with the commentary and Zhu Xi's remarks included, runs about ten standard book pages.

Given its brevity, the authority of this text must be considered; first, however, a small but significant point: Traditionally, *Da Xue* (*Ta-hsueh*) has been translated as *The Great Learning*. Recently, however, the tendency has been to speak of *The Greater Learning*, because in Zhu Xi's preface, the "greater" learning is contrasted with the "lesser." He argues that gradually in the course of the three dynasties—Xia (Hsia; c. 2100-1600 B.C.E.), Shang (1600-1066 B.C.E.), and Zhou—widely attended schools of lesser learning were established. These schools instructed in good manners and in the six arts of ritual, music, archery, charioteering, calligraphy, and mathematics. Following this instruction, the sons of aristocrats and the most gifted young (male) commoners advanced to the school of greater learning, which was a school of philosophy, especially moral and political philosophy. The comprehensive educational pattern is very similar to that proposed in the ancient Greek philosopher Plato's *Politeia* (388-368 B.C.E.; *Republic*, 1701) but with the striking differences that it was realized practically much earlier and on a much larger scale.

According to the Confucian tradition as represented by Zhu Xi, the authority behind *The Great Learning* is a vast expanse of time. The much-disputed issue of authorship must be seen within this temporal framework. Zhu Xi's premise is that fundamental understanding is characteristic of the very best human beings. In the course of two or three millennia, the number of such persons will be very small. It is these connected persons, the Confucian line of "transmission of the Way, *Dao tong* (*Tao-t'ung*)," who are the joint "authors" of *The Great Learning*.

More specifically, the line of transmission begins (according to Zhu Xi) long before Confucius, with "sovereign-instructors" who discovered and practiced the Way. The implication is vitally important: The Way is found through practical action, especially governing, and is transmitted not primarily in words but through correct, effective behavior that manifests sound character. In a word, those who govern, learn; and those who learn, govern. This suggests that writing down the Way is of relatively little value or, in historical context, is an indication of a much-deteriorated educational and political situation.

This is Zhu Xi's interpretation of Confucius's situation. The integration of understanding and governing had all but ended. Through a heroic combination of study, thought, and experience—that is, through "learning" broadly understood—Confucius recovered this Way, but he did not hold practical governing power. He was able only to suggest the philosophical and educational foundations of political order. Zhu Xi intimates that Confucius did not write *The Great Learning* but instead transmitted it to his followers orally and exemplified his words with actions.

The historical point at which *The Great Learning* was written, and by whom, remains in dispute. This is a lesser problem, given the Confucian "transmission" orientation; however, the question deserves attention. Examination of the wording of Zengzi's commentary in relation to the main text suggests that one of Zhu Xi's speculations on textual creation may be correct: that Confucius repeated certain inherited words and phrases in a certain order and that his listeners remembered, recalled, repeated, and recorded this "text" with general accuracy but some variations. This process may have continued, from master to disciple, until a written text stabilized.

Ironically, once this great text was created it was, in a sense, lost. *The Great Learning* was included in the *Liji* (compiled first century B.C.E.; *The Liki*, 1885; commonly known as *Classic of Rituals*), buried as the thirty-ninth "book" of a mixed assortment. The *Classic of Rituals* is traditionally attributed to Dai Sheng (Tai Sheng; fl. 51 B.C.E.). *The Great Learning* was then all but ignored for one thousand years, until Neo-Confucians sought to recover the "true" Way, in opposition to Daoism (Taoism) and Buddhism. Zhu Xi gives principal credit to the Cheng (Ch'eng) brothers, Cheng Hao (Ch'eng Hao; 1032-1088 C.E.) and Cheng Yi (Ch'eng I; 1033-1107 C.E.), for continuing the Way (*Dao tong*). However, it was Sima Guang (Ssu-ma Kuang; 1019-1086 C.E.) who separated *The Great Learning*, together with the *Zhong yong* (*Chung-yung*; written c. 500 B.C.E.; *The Doctrine of the Mean*, 1861), from the *Classic of Rituals*, and thus began the process that resulted in their establishment as the first and the fourth, respectively, of the Confucian Four Books.

SIGNIFICANCE

The influence of *The Great Learning*, as the first book, may best be compared with that of the first four chapters of the biblical book of Genesis or with the first three or four chapters of the ancient Greek philosopher Aristotle's *Ethica Nicomachea* (335-323 B.C.E.; *Nicomachean Ethics*, 1797) and *Politica* (335-323 B.C.E.; *Politics*, 1598). Each of these brief texts establishes the fundamentals of a distinctive way of human existence, respectively the Confucian, the Judeo-Christian, and the Western classical. If anything, the influence of *The Great Learning* is greater, in that it was more authoritative for more people. In 1313, the Yuan Dynasty (1271-1368) established the Four Books—identified by Zhu Xi as *Sishu* (*Ssu-shu*, or the four masters)—as the basis of the empire's civil service examinations. They shaped the minds of those who ruled China until 1912, date of the final overthrow of the Qing Dynasty (Ch'ing; 1644-1912)—just as Confucius and his followers believed that *The Great Learning* expressed the Way of those who created China three to four millennia ago. Small wonder that today, even after *The Great Learning* has lost official status, scholars continue to discuss the authenticity and meaning of every word.

This connection between past and present is a part of the (Confucian) Way. More of the Way lies in the sustained effort to understand fully the line *zhi zhi zai ge wu* (*chih chih tsai ko wu*), which lies at the center of the main text. This stretching of people's understanding by endeavoring to grasp the principle or essence of things remains an interpretive, philosophical, and practical challenge to every reader of *The Great Learning*. More than this, however, the effort to understand connects humanity, people's activities, their social institutions, and their aspirations to permanent reality and thus intimates a Way that transcends time itself.

—*John F. Wilson*

FURTHER READING

Chan, Wing-tsit, ed. *Chu Hsi and Neo-Confucianism*. Honolulu: University of Hawaii Press, 1986. An outstanding collection of papers from the International Conference on Zhu Xi. The papers by A. C. Graham (chapter 10) and Kao Ming (chapter 19) are especially relevant for *The Great Learning*. Chapter notes and glossaries, appendices, and index.

Finer, S. E. *Ancient Monarchies and Empires*. Vol. 1 in *The History of Government*. Oxford, England: Oxford University Press, 1999. The paperback edition of Finer's masterwork discusses the historical and political philosophical context of *The Great Learning* in book 2, chapters 5 and 6. Chronologies, tables, footnotes, and bibliography.

Gardner, Daniel K. *Chu Hsi and the Ta-hsueh: Neo-Confucian Reflection on the Confucian Canon*. Cambridge, Mass.: Harvard University Press, 1986. An important commentary on and edition of the text that Gardner identifies as *The Greater Learning*. He traces the history of the text through its establishment as canonical. Includes Gardner's study, English translation with extensive notes, the Chinese text, bibliography, glossary, and index.

Hall, David L., and Roger T. Ames. *Thinking Through Confucius*. Albany: State University of New York Press, 1987. The first work in the Hall and Ames series interpreting Confucian thought in relation to Western philosophy. Especially relevant to *The Great Learning* is the discussion of learning (*xue*), reflecting (*si*), and realizing (*zhi*). Wade-Giles/Pinyin conversion table, notes, bibliography, and index.

Moore, Charles A., ed. *The Chinese Mind: Essentials of Chinese Philosophy and Culture*. Honolulu: University of Hawaii Press, 1968. A widely used paperback treatment of the Chinese tradition. Regarded as fundamental to Confucian philosophy, *The Great Learning* is discussed throughout. Chapter notes, appendix, and index.

See also: c. 1066, Western Zhou Dynasty Begins in China; 770 B.C.E., Eastern Zhou Dynasty Begins in China; 5th century B.C.E., Composition of the *Spring and Autumn Annals*; 500-400 B.C.E., Creation of the *Wujing*; 479 B.C.E., Confucius's Death Leads to the Creation of *The Analects*; 475-221 B.C.E., China Enters Chaotic Warring States Period; 221-206 B.C.E., Legalist Movement in China.

Related articles in *Great Lives from History: The Ancient World:* Confucius; Mencius; Xunzi.

c. 500 B.C.E.
Acupuncture Develops in China

Acupuncture, deeply rooted in the basic principles undergirding Chinese culture, evolved from obscure predynastic origins into a highly complex system of medicine during the Zhou Dynasty.

Locale: The north central Chinese plain
Category: Health and medicine

Summary of Event

Acupuncture, an ancient technique of traditional Chinese medicine, consists of treating health disorders by inserting thin needles at various points on a patient's body. This therapeutic procedure has a long history in China.

Certain archaeologists have traced it to the Chinese stone age, but other scientists doubt that the crude stone needles that have been unearthed warrant such an interpretation. During the dynastic periods, the Chinese attributed their pivotal inventions to fabulously eminent exemplars of predynastic times, and acupuncture typifies this practice of honorable attribution. According to these myths, which may or may not have a basis in reality, the legendary ruler Shen Nong (Shen Nung, known as the divine farmer) and the Yellow Emperor, Huangdi (Huang-ti, c. 2704-c. 2600 B.C.E.), originated acupuncture. Shen Nong and Huangdi may have lived in the third millennium B.C.E., but many modern scholars consider their existence doubtful and believe they may have been created by later Confucian functionaries to provide China with a noble past.

Some historians of Chinese religion emphasize the connection between Daoism (Taoism) and medicine. Daoist ideas of maintaining the harmony of the body's internal organs (and of the state and cosmos) became an integral part of the philosophical system underpinning acupuncture. Also connected with Daoism was the belief that both the world and the human body were realms of benevolent and malevolent spirits; the Chinese character for "physician" conveys the meaning of a priest who uses strong weapons to conquer the demons of disease. During the Zhou Dynasty (Chou, 1066-256 B.C.E.), medicine passed from the hands of priests to those of physicians, and many scholars believe that acupuncture first developed around 500 B.C.E., when its chief doctrines were systematized.

Much of what is known about early acupuncture comes from the *Huangdi nei jing su wen* (compiled c. 300 B.C.E.; *The Yellow Emperor's Classic of Internal Medicine*, 1949), a manual of medicine often called the most important medical text of Chinese antiquity. Though traditionally attributed to the legendary Huangdi, most scholars believe that the text was compiled between 479 and 300 B.C.E. and put into its final form in the first century B.C.E. *The Yellow Emperor's Classic of Internal Medicine*, which influenced Chinese medicine for the next twenty-five hundred years, was based on the doctrines of yin and yang, the five elements, and the elaborate correlations between macrocosm (the universe) and microcosm (the human body).

The chief idea supporting the practice of acupuncture is *qi* (*chi*), the vital life energy whose balanced flow throughout the body maintains good health. *Qi* circulates through twelve channels in the body, and these twelve meridians are linked to such organs as the heart, lungs, stomach, spleen, and kidneys. Early acupuncturists located more than one thousand points on these meridians. By inserting a needle at a specific meridianal point, the flow of *qi* to an organ could be controlled. In this way, an overactive organ could be moderated and a lethargic one stimulated.

The insertion of needles was the method of treatment by ancient acupuncturists, but why they should be inserted and what they were intended to accomplish was more complex, deriving from the Chinese doctrines of yin and yang, the five elements, and the resonances between internal and external energy. For Chinese of the Zhou era, yin, the negative principle, and its complement yang, the positive principle, constituted all things. The five ancient Chinese elements—water, fire, wood, metal, and earth—were not basic kinds of matter (as in the four ancient Greek elements) but five kinds of fundamental processes, such as fluidity, combustibility, solidity, and nutrivity. Both yin and yang and the five elements were involved in the composition and functioning of the universe as well as with the physiological processes of specific organs. For example, the heart, which was associated with the element fire and its concomitant emotion joy, had further associations with a hot climate, the planet Mars, and even the Zhou Dynasty itself. Thus the Chinese physician had to establish whether the season, day, hour, location, and all else were propitious for the practice of acupuncture.

From a set of several needles, he would then choose one and insert it in the point determined by his understanding of the patient's symptoms and the particularities of time and place. If the needle were inserted at the wrong point, a worsening of the condition, even death, could result. During the Zhou Dynasty, physicians became part of the state system and were assessed on their cure-to-failure ratio. Together with scholars, these physicians made acupuncture into an extremely detailed doctrine and practice that dominated Chinese medicine for the next twenty-five hundred years.

SIGNIFICANCE

Though it differs somewhat from region to region, acupuncture became Chinese medicine's most characteristic therapy. Because this practice was based on a holistic conception of the body and the world, its major impact was in China and in those Eastern cultures that shared its organic view of nature. The practice spread into all the countries bordering on China, and its influence was particularly strong in Japan.

Western countries did not learn about acupuncture until the seventeenth and eighteenth centuries, when Jesuit missionaries communicated knowledge of it to Europe. However, the practice had little influence in the West until the twentieth century. Because of their mechanistic view of the body, Western physicians found it absurd to believe that a needle stuck into a patient's foot could cure a liver disorder. Similarly, the scientific medicine of Europe failed to impress Chinese physicians. The highly structured system associated with acupuncture was not susceptible to empirical falsification.

It was not until the nineteenth and twentieth centuries that Chinese doctors began to modernize their treatment of patients with Western scientific techniques. However, acupuncture continued to be practiced, and modern and traditional medicines evolved cooperatively. During this time, a controversy developed in Western countries between those who accepted acupuncture as an effective system of medicine and those who believed that it had no scientific basis. Western researchers found no anatomical or physiological evidence for the existence of meridians, and they attributed acupuncturists' cures to the placebo effect.

Joseph Needham, who was both a Western scientist and a Sinologist, argued against this critique by scientists. He pointed to his statistical study of the impressive successes of acupuncture therapy. Some Eastern researchers believe that scientific reasons for acupuncture's effectiveness will eventually be discovered and that a place will be found for this ancient practice alongside modern Western medicine.

—*Robert J. Paradowski*

FURTHER READING

Bivens, Roberta E. *Acupuncture, Expertise, and Cross-Cultural Medicine*. New York: Palgrave Macmillan, 2001. This history of the fortunes of acupuncture in Britain, from the seventeenth century to the twenty-first, is a good assessment of the changing Western attitudes toward the practice.

Lu Gwei-Djen and Joseph Needham. *Celestial Lancets: A History and Rationale of Acupuncture and Moxa*. Introduction by Vivian Lo. Reprint. New York: Curzon Press, 2002. A wide-ranging historical account of acupuncture and moxibustion in the theoretical structure of Chinese medicine, combined with a rationale of the two techniques in the light of modern scientific knowledge. Includes a substantial introduction surveying new sources and research methodologies that have developed since first publication in 1980.

Needham, Joseph. *Clerks and Craftsmen in China and the West: Lectures and Addresses on the History of Science and Technology.* New York: Cambridge University Press, 1970. The fourteenth chapter of this book, "Medicine and Chinese Culture," which the author wrote with Lu Gwei-Djen, provides an overview of the healing arts, including acupuncture, from ancient to Marxist China.

_______. *Science and Civilisation in China.* Vol. 6 in *Biology and Biological Technology.* Part 6. *Medicine.* Assisted by Lu Gwei-Djen. Edited by Nathan Sivin. New York: Cambridge University Press, 2000. Needham died in 1995, and Sivin, while praising the pioneering work of Needham and Lu Gwei-Djen, updates their treatment by showing how medical practices, including acupuncture, were socially constructed in different historical and cultural contexts within China.

_______. *Science in Traditional China: A Comparative Perspective.* Cambridge, Mass.: Harvard University Press, 1981. This book's fourth chapter, "The History and Rationale of Acupuncture and Moxibustion," contains a detailed historical analysis informed by the author's knowledge of both Western science and Chinese culture.

SEE ALSO: 600-500 B.C.E., Greek Philosophers Formulate Theories of the Cosmos; 6th-4th century B.C.E. (traditionally, 1st millennium B.C.E.), Suśruta, Indian Physician, Writes Medical Compendium; 479 B.C.E., Confucius's Death Leads to the Creation of *The Analects*; c. 157-201 C.E., Galen Synthesizes Ancient Medical Knowledge.

c. 500 B.C.E.
PĀṆINI COMPOSES SANSKRIT WORK OF GRAMMAR

Pāṇini composed a grammar of the Sanskrit language, which set an enduring standard that continues to interest linguists for its systematic approach to language description.

LOCALE: Śalātura, Gandhara (now Lahūr, Pakistan)
CATEGORY: Cultural and intellectual history

KEY FIGURES

Pāṇini (Dakṣiputra Pāṇini, fl. c. 500 B.C.E.), grammarian

Patañjali (fl. second century B.C.E.), grammarian and chief early commentator on Pāṇini

SUMMARY OF EVENT

Pāṇini (also known as Dakṣiputra Pāṇini) and his forerunners in India, stimulated by a religious sanction to preserve the correct interpretation of ritual texts, pioneered the study of language. He composed the *Aṣṭādhyāyī* (c. 500 B.C.E.; *Astakam Paniniyam: Panini's Eight Books of Grammatical Sutras*, 1887), the earliest extant systematic grammar (*vyakarana*) of any language—in his case Sanskrit, the classical language of ancient Indian literature and philosophy. This work has interested modern grammarians for its almost mathematical approach to describing language and its profound influence on all later grammatical tradition in India. The *Aṣṭādhyāyī* became the most important authority on correct Sanskrit and is perhaps the oldest scientific treatise available.

Little is known about Pāṇini's life except that he was born in a small town in the ancient province of Gandhara (in modern Pakistan). His date of birth can only be approximated to the fifth or sixth century B.C.E. He is remembered primarily for the *Aṣṭādhyāyī*, the title of which is interpreted to mean a "work consisting of eight chapters" or "a collection of eight chapters." Composed in Sanskrit (Old Indic), it consists of nearly four thousand concise rules or formulas that prescribe the correct forms of the spoken language known to Pāṇini. The form of his grammar, called the *sūtra* style, suggests that the text was composed orally. Though writing was known to Pāṇini, each of his rules is loaded with such condensed meaning and function that any student must already have been familiar with them in order to use the grammar. During Pāṇini's time and continuing until the modern period in India, the prestige of oral texts, which had to be preserved in memory and passed down through oral instruction, was high, while written texts were not as highly esteemed.

The eight chapters of Pāṇini's grammar are a string of *sūtras*, each brief and precise but also difficult to interpret without the aid of an explanatory commentary. An example is the final *sūtra* of the work, "a a," whose mean-

WORDS WITH COMMON INDO-EUROPEAN LINGUISTIC ROOTS

Sanskrit	*Greek*	*Latin*	*German*	*English*
pitr	pater	pater	vater	father
matr	meter	mater	mutter	mother
str	aster	stella	stern	star
na	ne	ne	nein	nay (no)
vid	oida	videre	wissen	vision

ing is too complex to explain adequately in a few sentences. The brevity of the rules in *sūtra* style was an aid to memorization. In Pāṇini's time, the master himself would provide the commentary, while the students learned the *sūtras* by heart. Ancient written commentaries have also survived; two of the most famous are the *Mahābhāṣya* by Patañjali (second century B.C.E.; English translation, 1856) and the *Kāśikā-vrtti* by two authors of the seventh century C.E.

Pāṇini's grammar is prefaced by a table, organized to produce all the needed sounds of the language. Then the grammar proper moves on to a discussion of rules of interpretation, definitions, and the technical language of the grammar itself. The section on metalanguage, or the technical vocabulary and rules that govern the rules, is the key to understanding the *sūtras* and their astonishing brevity. In other words, Pāṇini had to invent an artificial language, a metalanguage, to allow a concise and scientific description of his object language, Sanskrit. The rules that produce sentences follow. Added to the grammar is a list of roots. The exact interpretation of many features of Pāṇini's grammar has remained a topic of debate and study by scholars, both traditional scholars in India, who continue to produce commentaries, and linguists in the West.

The language described by Pāṇini was the language spoken by educated people of the region in which he lived, the language he considered a standard for correct speech. Pāṇini also mentions regional variants to this standard language as well as earlier dialects, which have been preserved in older literature. The oldest existing literary monument of India is the *Rigveda* (also known as *Ṛgveda*, c. 1500-1000 B.C.E.; English translation, 1896-1897); between this text and Pāṇini's time, other works were produced, such as commentaries on the prevailing ritual and the philosophical texts known as Upaniṣads. Pāṇini shows his awareness of these materials and some of their unique linguistic features. He does not, however, deal with the popular language spoken by an uneducated class. Theirs was most likely a language closer to the Prakrit (Middle Indian) language preserved in inscriptions dating from the third century B.C.E. Though Pāṇini does mention predecessors, earlier grammarians, their works have not survived. Perhaps the excellence and prestige of Pāṇini's grammar eclipsed earlier authors.

SIGNIFICANCE

Pāṇini's influence in India was immense. Most later grammarians based their work on his system. When Sanskrit ceased to be a living language and became instead a literary and sacred language, his rules, though originally descriptive, came to be understood as prescriptive, normative, and authoritative. They were memorized as a regular part of education; poets and scholars were expected to know many of Pāṇini's most important rules. In traditional schools young boys would sit around a teacher and recite Pāṇini's formulas, learning them by rote. Only much later would a discussion of the meaning of the rules ensue. Pāṇini's grammar was therefore established as the standard for correct usage. Almost all later works of Sanskrit grammar depended on his approach, which filtered down through commentaries and adaptations. Even today, Sanskritists who wish to make use of any of the classical commentaries, such as those on the fourth century C.E. poet Kālidāsa, need to recognize citations from Pāṇini.

The Western discovery of Pāṇini's system influenced the development of nineteenth century comparative philology and, through that, modern linguistics. In the twentieth century he has also interested linguists as a precursor of modern theories which construct ordered rule-based descriptions of language.

—*Burt Thorp*

FURTHER READING

Cardona, George. *Recent Research in Paninian Studies*. Delhi: Motilal, 1999. An overview of scholarly work on Pāṇini.

Katre, Sumitra M., trans. *Astadhyayi of Panini*. Austin: University of Texas Press, 1987. Contains the Sanskrit text along with a close translation.

Mahulkar, D. D., ed. *Essays on Panini*. Simla: Indian Institute of Advanced Study, 1998. Articles on a variety of topics.

Scharfe, Hartmut. *Grammatical Literature*. Wiesbaden, Germany: Harrassowitz, 1977. A history of the entire grammatical tradition in India. Pāṇini is discussed in chapter 2.

_______. *Panini's Metalanguage*. Philadelphia: Ameri-

can Philosophical Society, 1971. A technical account of an important and unique feature of Pāṇini's work.
Staal, J. F., ed. *A Reader on the Sanskrit Grammarians*. Cambridge, Mass.: MIT Press, 1972. Contains substantial material on Pāṇini.

See also: c. 3100 B.C.E., Sumerians Invent Writing; c. 1600 B.C.E., Shang Dynasty Develops Writing and Bronzework; 6th or 5th century B.C.E., Birth of Buddhism; c. 5th-4th century B.C.E., Creation of the *Jātakas*; c. 467 B.C.E., Gośāla Maskarīputra, Founder of Ājīvika Sect, Dies; c. 321 B.C.E., Mauryan Empire Rises in India.

Related articles in *Great Lives from History: The Ancient World:* Ānanda; Asanga; Bodhidharma; Buddha; Kālidāsa; Kanishka; Vālmīki.

c. 500-470 B.C.E.
Hecataeus of Miletus Writes the First Geography Book

Greek geographer and historian Hecataeus of Miletus developed a comprehensive view of the Mediterranean physical world and wrote the first geography book, which included a map.

Locale: Miletus (now in Turkey)
Category: Cultural and intellectual history

Key Figure

Hecataeus of Miletus (fl. c. sixth-fifth century B.C.E.), Greek historian and geographer

Summary of Event

Hecataeus of Miletus wrote the first comprehensive description of the Mediterranean world, the *Ges Periodos* (fifth century B.C.E.; tour around the world). In this work, which included a map, Hecataeus participated in the intellectual revolution of fifth century B.C.E. Greece, using techniques developed by earlier thinkers in Asia Minor and setting the stage for later Greek historians such as Herodotus and Thucydides.

The roots of this intellectual revolution can be found in epic poets such as Homer and Hesiod, who had created elaborate genealogies and mythologies to explain the structure of the world. However, the so-called natural philosophers of sixth century B.C.E. Miletus turned to explanations outside mythology for natural events. In particular, Anaximander of Miletus connected meteorological and geographic phenomena to form a comprehensive system, developing both a cosmological view of the heavens and a map of the Mediterranean world.

Hecataeus applied both mythology and natural philosophy to ethnography, writing works on genealogy and history in addition to his geography. Whether he created three separate works or one is debatable; evidence exists in the modern world only in some three hundred fragments, many of which are merely place-names recorded by the Byzantine commentator Stephanus in the sixth century C.E. Hecataeus's geography book was probably in two parts, dealing with Europe and Asia (including Africa). Modern suggestions that he did not write the second part have not been accepted.

Hecataeus used data collected during extensive travels as well as observations he made throughout the Mediterranean world. A reconstruction of his book suggests that he began at the Pillars of Heracles in Gibraltar and traveled clockwise around the Mediterranean. Although he focused on Mediterranean coastal sites, he had knowledge of the Black Sea through his contact with colonists sent there by his hometown Miletus. He also had access to Persian court records, Egyptian temple carvings, and Babylonian scientific works. Hecataeus was no armchair speculator but an active participant in the affairs of the day.

Although Hecataeus did not pursue Anaximander's concern for cosmology, both men tried to understand the Earth systematically, by reducing it to a simplified scheme. Anaximander had drawn a map in the form of a circular representation on a tablet, viewed from an overhead perspective. This corresponded to the circular shape he accorded to the cosmos. Hecataeus also described the world as round and surrounded by ocean; the title of his book translates literally as "the way around land," and he may have been able to grasp the earth as anchored in water at the center of a wider cosmos.

Hecataeus may have improved on existing maps by measuring the earth using standard distances and geometric figures and by describing places in relation to constellations in the cosmos. According to the historian Herodotus in his *Historiai Herodotou* (c. 424 B.C.E.; *The History*, 1709), the tyrant Aristagoras of Miletus used a map, possibly drawn by Hecataeus, in 499 B.C.E. when he asked Athens and Sparta for assistance in a revolt against Persian rule.

Herodotus wrote critically of Hecataeus's map:

> I smile when I see that many have drawn circuits of the earth, and none of them has explained the matter sensibly; they draw Ocean running around the earth, which is drawn as though with a compass, and make Asia equal to Africa.

The Greeks were concerned with order, symmetry, and balance, and such ideas may have led Hecataeus to balance Europe against Asia/Africa in his geography. This suggests that Hecataeus reasoned from certain fundamental ideas in an attempt to bring order to his wide-ranging observations.

SIGNIFICANCE

Despite the disdain of Herodotus, who used Hecataeus's work in order to improve on it, Hecataeus made groundbreaking advancements in spatial and historical understanding. He participated in a tradition that connected philosophy to a systematic understanding of the physical world. By the fourth century B.C.E., Aristotle (384-322 B.C.E.) and others were able to see Earth and its climatic zones in relation to the wider cosmos. The Greek explorer Pytheas of Massalia (c. 350/325-after 300 B.C.E.) probably used maps similar to that of Hecataeus to explore beyond Gibraltar, possibly as far north as Ireland or even Iceland. Geographer and mathematician Eratosthenes of Cyrene (c. 285-c. 205 B.C.E.) drew on Aristotle and possibly Hecataeus by using heavenly bodies to more accurately measure the size of the earth.

Diogenes Laertius, the third century C.E. biographer, says that Hecataeus saw Earth as a spherical heavenly body. However, the spherical idea is a later discovery, and Hecataeus, like Anaximander, probably envisaged the earth as a cylinder at the center of the cosmos. Nevertheless, attempts by Hecataeus to reduce spatial complexities to a simplified graphic picture not only provided a more precise geographic guide to the earth but also advanced people's ability to conceive of things from a perspective different from that available to their senses. He presaged the maps that would be used by explorer Christopher Columbus and others in the European Age of Exploration two thousand years later. A crater on the Moon has been named after him.

—*John Lewis*

FURTHER READING

Bunbury, E. H. *A History of Ancient Geography.* Loughton, England: Prometheus Books, 1979. Includes a concise overview of Hecataeus's place in the history of geography.

Fornara, Charles William. *The Nature of History in Ancient Greece and Rome.* Berkeley: University of California Press, 1983. A discussion of genres of ancient historical writing; covers Hecataeus.

Heidel, W. *Hecataeus and the Egyptian Priests in Herodotus.* Vol. 2. New York: Garland, 1988. Examines Herodotus's use of Hecataeus when investigating the history of Egypt.

Herodotus. *Histories.* Translated by Aubrey De Selincourt. New York: Penguin, 1996. Book 2 contains firsthand mentions of Hecataeus.

Momigliano, Arnaldo. *The Classical Foundations of Modern Historiography.* Berkeley: University of California Press, 1990. A discussion of the influence of ancient historical writers such as Hecataeus on modern historical writing.

SEE ALSO: 600-500 B.C.E., Greek Philosophers Formulate Theories of the Cosmos; 499-494 B.C.E., Ionian Revolt; c. 450-c. 425 B.C.E., History Develops as a Scholarly Discipline.

RELATED ARTICLES in *Great Lives from History: The Ancient World*: Anaximander; Eratosthenes of Cyrene; Herodotus; Homer.

500-400 B.C.E.
CREATION OF THE *WUJING*

The Wujing*, or Five Classics, which becomes the foundation for classical Chinese scholarship and statecraft, is purportedly compiled by Confucius and passed down to his disciples.*

LOCALE: State of Lu, Eastern China (now part of Shandong Province)
CATEGORY: Cultural and intellectual history

KEY FIGURE

Confucius (551-479 B.C.E.), teacher and traditional founder of Confucian tradition

SUMMARY OF EVENT

The *rujia*, or school of literati, commonly referred to as Confucianism in the West, has been a dominant force in Chinese political and social thought for more than two millennia. Centered on the teachings of Confucius and the *Wujing* (Five Classics), Confucianism serves as far more than a religion or philosophical tradition. In fact, many scholars dispute whether it can actually be referred to as a religion. Although Confucianism contains certain elements that lend themselves to such a characterization, such as sacrifices to Heaven and ancestor veneration, the scope of its impact on Chinese—and East Asian civilization as a whole—goes far beyond its religious practices. Without exaggeration, it is fair to say that the tradition represents and embodies a unique way of life and a traditional system of values. It has affected the religious, philosophical, political, social, ethical, and cultural values of countless millions, and although it is no longer the dominant force it once was, Confucianism continues to demand the attention of philosophers, diplomats, and theoreticians.

As scholar William de Bary wrote in *Sources of Chinese Tradition* (1960),

> If we were to characterize in one word the Chinese way of life for the last two thousand years, the word could be "Confucian." No other individual in Chinese history has so deeply influenced the life and thought of his people, as a transmitter, teacher and creative interpreter of the ancient culture and literature and as a molder of the Chinese mind and character.

The primary literary vehicle for the transmission of the Confucian tradition has been the group of texts known as the *Wujing*, or the Five Classics. In customary order, the Five Classics are: the *Yijing* (eighth to third century B.C.E.; English translation, 1876; also known as *Book of Changes*, 1986), *Shijing* (compiled fifth century B.C.E.; *The Book of Songs*, 1937), *Shujing* (compiled after first century B.C.E.; English translation in *The Chinese Classics*, Vol. 5, Parts 1 and 2, 1872; commonly know as *Classic of History*), *Liji* (compiled fifth century B.C.E.; *The Liki*, 1885; commonly known as *Classic of Rituals*), and *Chunqiu* (fifth century B.C.E.; *The Ch'un Ts'ew with the Tso Chuen*, 1872; commonly known as *Spring and Autumn Annals*). A sixth text, the *Yue Jing* (book of music), is thought to have originally been included in this grouping, but it was lost before or during the Qin Dynasty (221-206 B.C.E.), perhaps as a result of the Qin emperor's decree that all Confucian texts were to be burned (213 B.C.E.). Thus, the earliest mention of these texts as a set comes in the Daoist work, the *Zhuangzi* (traditionally c. 300 B.C.E., probably compiled c. 285-160 B.C.E.; *The Divine Classic of Nan-hua*, 1881; also known as *The Complete Works of Chuang Tzu*, 1968; commonly known as *Zhuangzi*, 1991), which describes five classics: "Confucius told Laozi, 'I have labored on the *Shi, Shu, Li, Yue* and *Chunqiu* for a long time.'" The *Zhuangzi* also characterizes the works in this way: "The *Shi* describes aims; the *Shu* describes events; the *Li* describes conduct; the *Yue* secures harmony; the *Yi* shows the principles of yin and yang; the *Chunqiu* shows distinctions and duties."

Based in part on the work of the Han historian Sima Qian (145-86 B.C.E.), tradition has ascribed the texts to the hand, or editorial efforts, of Confucius himself. After the fall of the Qin and ascendancy of the new Han Dynasty (206 B.C.E.-220 C.E.), the texts became the foundation and source of ideological unity for the governmental bureaucracy. After the Han, and in particular following Emperor Wu (r. 154-87 B.C.E.), the classics served as the official texts for learning and the basis for the evolving civil examination system. With few significant modifications, this system would prevail until the beginning of the twentieth century (1905). Young boys memorized the classics, imitated their literary style, and incorporated their ideas into their worldviews and political policies if fortunate enough to pass the examinations. As "classics" (*jing*), the texts were believed to be true, in the most literal sense of the word. They faithfully and accurately depicted the history, morals, and practices of the sages of old. The classics' effectiveness and value was embedded in their irrefutable truth.

The content and composition of the Five Classics varies widely. Although tradition holds that Confucius shaped the texts, either personally authoring some or all of them or editing already existing manuscripts, there is little evidence for this assertion. Scholars almost unanimously see the classics as the products of hundreds of years of accumulated material, widely divergent in terms of style, literary quality, regional derivation, and content. Although it is impossible to date them with any definitiveness, general consensus holds that the five texts were composed from the tenth to the first century B.C.E. Debate continues as to whether Confucius and his disciples purposely edited and collected the Five Classics or simply preserved and transmitted an already existing body of texts. It is most likely that the classics represent a combination of the two, with Confucius utilizing an already established set of writings in a unique manner consistent with his educational goals for his disciples.

As for content, the *Yijing* reflects ancient divination practices. In an effort to comprehend and interpret the regular patterns of cosmic change, a system of prognostication was developed based on the sixty-four possible combinations of *yin* (broken) and *yang* (intact) lines. The present text is composed of two main parts. The oldest, which may be a systemized redaction of ancient oracle-bone practices, contains the sixty-four hexagrams and brief explanations. The second part, the so-called Ten Wings, consists of commentaries attributed to Confucius, although this claim is widely disputed. By tossing yarrow stalks, or alternatively coins, the practitioner constructs a hexagram in response to their inquiry and then consults the text and commentaries for guidance.

The Book of Songs contains 305 poems, most likely composed during the early Zhou Dynasty (Chou; c. 1066-256 B.C.E.). Again, tradition records that Confucius culled these odes out of more than 3,000 and compiled them into a single text as an educational tool. Among the diverse poems are folk songs, religious liturgy, hymns of praise, and accounts of local customs and festivals. The *Classic of History* is the earliest work on history in China and consists of accounts purporting to record the words and exhortations of the kings and ministers of the Xia (Hsia; c. 2100-1600 B.C.E.), Shang (c. 1600-1066 B.C.E.), and Zhou Dynasties. Inasmuch as Confucius viewed himself as merely a transmitter of ancient wisdom and looked back on the early Zhou as a "golden age" of harmony and well-being, this work played an important role as a textbook for his disciples and subsequent generations.

The fourth classic, the *Classic of Rituals*, is a compendium of rituals, gathered from a multitude of regional and historically diverse sources. In addition to texts on proper etiquette, marriage and funeral services, the nature and structure of government, and daily behavior, it contains two works that eventually stood on their own and became part of the Four Books during the Song Dynasty (Sung; 420-479). Both the *Da Xue* (fifth-first century B.C.E.; *The Great Learning*, 1861) and *Zhong yong* (*Chung-yung*; written c. 500 B.C.E.; *The Doctrine of the Mean*, 1861) emphasize personal moral cultivation as the foundation for societal harmony and are singled out as independent works by the great Neo-Confucian Zhi Xi (Chu Hsi; 1130-1200). Along with the *Lunyu* (later sixth-early fifth centuries B.C.E.; *The Analects*, 1861) and *Mengzi* (first transcribed in the early third century B.C.E.; English translation in *The Confucian Classics*, 1861; commonly known as *Mencius*), these texts become additional compulsory reading for scholars.

The *Spring and Autumn Annals* is a chronological history of Confucius's home state, Lu. Each year of the chronicle is divided into two seasons, spring and autumn, with each entry beginning, "In the Spring [or "Autumn"] of . . . ," thus providing the name. Covering the years 722-481 B.C.E., the annals are purportedly the work of Confucius, who used the history as a means of passing moral judgment on the decadence of his own age. As with the other texts, there is little evidence that such is the case. Regardless of its original authorship, the text has been the subject of a continuous tradition of commentary, which sees the *Spring and Autumn Annals* as the quintessential tool for establishing proper government and ordering society.

Significance

As noted above, the classics gained national prominence as a result of the actions of Wudi. Determined to reverse the policies of the Qin and seeing the tenets of the Confucian tradition as the most suitable for the ordering of a new society, in 136 B.C.E., Wu banned all non-Confucian schools and proclaimed Confucianism the orthodox state religion.

He then established the Imperial Academy for the nation in the capital (124 B.C.E.) and appointed learned scholars to act as "imperial academicians" (*bo shih*). A typical course of study at the academy included two years on two classics, followed by an examination; those who passed and wished to continue proceeded to study the three remaining texts for two years apiece, after which time they would be examined again. The creation of the Imperial Academy, combined with state sponsorship, propelled the classics and the Confucian tradition into a dominant political role. Henceforth, every aspiring official would diligently study the texts in preparation for the civil examinations required for government service.

As the examination system evolved, the classics became the mandatory textbook of the educated elite, thereby permeating every aspect of Chinese society. Not only did the texts shape the literati's view of the world; they also became the primary source of moral examples, erudite sayings, allusions, and metaphors. Despite occasional challenges from Daoism and Buddhism, the Confucian classics remained the bedrock of Chinese political and social thought well into the twentieth century.

—*Jeffrey W. Dippmann*

FURTHER READING

De Bary, William Theodore, Wing-tsit Chan, and Burton Watson, eds. *Sources of Chinese Tradition*. 2 vols. New York: Columbia University Press, 1960. An excellent resource of primary text materials and solid introductions to the traditional culture of China.

Jingpan, Chen. *Confucius as a Teacher: Philosophy of Confucius with Special Reference to Its Educational Implications*. Beijing: Foreign Languages Press, 1990. Contains an extensive and well-written discussion of the Confucian classics.

Legge, James, trans. *The Chinese Classics*. 5 vols. 1867-1875. Reprint. Hong Kong: Hong Kong University Press, 1960. Though somewhat outdated, Legge's translations remain among the best for several of the texts. Included are the *Shujing, Shijing, Lunyu, Mengzi, Chunqui*, the *Da Xue* and the *Zhong Yong*.

_______, trans. *The Sacred Books of China: The Texts of Confucianism*. 4 vols. 1879-1885. Reprint. Delhi: Motilal Banarsidass, 1966. Along with his translations of the *Shujing* and *Shijing*, this collection includes Legge's versions of the *Yijing* and *Li Ji*.

Nylan, Michael. *The Five "Confucian" Classics*. New Haven, Conn.: Yale University Press, 2001. An excellent critical analysis of the origins, formation, and impact of the classics on traditional Chinese society and politics.

SEE ALSO: 770 B.C.E., Eastern Zhou Dynasty Begins in China; 5th century B.C.E., Composition of the *Spring and Autumn Annals*; 5th-1st century B.C.E., Composition of *The Great Learning*; 479 B.C.E., Confucius's Death Leads to the Creation of *The Analects*; 475-221 B.C.E., China Enters Chaotic Warring States Period; 3d century B.C.E. (traditionally 6th century B.C.E.), Laozi Composes the *Dao De Jing*; 221 B.C.E., Qin Dynasty Founded in China.

RELATED ARTICLES in *Great Lives from History: The Ancient World*: Confucius; Mencius; Xunzi.

c. 500-400 B.C.E.
GREEK PHYSICIANS BEGIN SCIENTIFIC PRACTICE OF MEDICINE

Greek physicians developed the scientific practice of medicine, allowing reason to triumph over superstition in their search for knowledge about disease and its treatment.

LOCALE: Greece
CATEGORIES: Health and medicine; science and technology

KEY FIGURE

Hippocrates (c. 460-c. 370 B.C.E.), Greek physician associated with a medical school on Cos and a body of early medical writings

SUMMARY OF EVENT

One of the great accomplishments of the ancient Greek world was the development in the late fifth century B.C.E. of the scientific practice of medicine. Doctoring is as old as civilization itself, but only when the Greeks developed a purely rational way of looking at the world did medicine become a science.

Early Greek thought resembles that of other peoples: Illness, like all other facets of human life, was believed to be in the hands of the gods. Two of the brilliant masterpieces of Greek literature, Homer's *Iliad* (c. 750 B.C.E.; English translation, 1611) and Sophocles' *Oidipous Tyrannos* (c. 429 B.C.E., *Oedipus Tyrannus*, 1715), begin with plagues sent by an angered Apollo. The idea that God is responsible for causing and for curing illness is also found in biblical writings, especially in the New Testament, where among the principal activities of Jesus are the casting out of demons and the healing of the sick. Curative powers were attributed to the pagan gods, and among the most common archaeological finds are votive offerings (many of which are models of the affected parts needing cure) and amulets. As attested by the *Oneirocritica* of Artemidorus (second century C.E.; *The Interpretation of Dreams*, 1644), Greeks also believed in the curative power of dreams. These nonscientific medical views were never abandoned by the ancient world but existed side by side with scientific medicine.

The fifty years following the Persian Wars saw spectacular intellectual development in the Greek world. Philosophy, which started with Thales in the preceding century, came into its own. The natural philosophers of Ionia (now the western part of Turkey) sought an explanation of nature that did not rely on supernatural causation. They sought, instead, to show that all nature operated by the same set of physical laws. They offered different solutions to the questions of what the world was made from and how it functioned, and their theories were developed from arbitrary assumptions. Anaximenes of Miletus asserted air to be the basic element; Anaxagoras, a substance of indeterminate nature; Heraclitus of Ephesus, fire; and Empedocles, the four elements air, earth, fire, and water.

Because of the tremendous success of Greek mathematics, and of geometry in particular with its system of deductive reasoning based on very few axioms, there was a tendency among natural philosophers to seek systems of the physical universe that were deductive. Deductive reasoning produces the highest degree of certainty, and Aristotle is typical of the Greeks in affording the prize for scientific knowledge to sciences such as geometry and logic, sciences whose conclusions are reached through deductive reasoning from axioms and definitions.

The results of the natural philosophers, however, were not satisfying: The material world does not yield to deductive reasoning. Medical writers of the fifth century B.C.E. and later very much wanted to separate themselves from the arbitrary axioms of the natural philosophers, and Celsus (fl. c. 178 C.E.) claims that Hippocrates was the first actually to do so. Hippocrates criticizes those physicians who claim that because humans are a unity, they are composed of only one of the four elements. He says that their proofs amount to nothing and that victory in their debates goes to the one with the glibbest tongue. Yet the same author, though attacking others for their lack of evidence, accepts as axiomatic that humans are made of four humours—blood, yellow bile, black bile, and phlegm, each derived from one of the four elements.

A key feature of Greek medical science is its rejection of gods and magic in the interpretation of disease. In popular Greek language, epilepsy was called the "sacred disease." The Hippocratic author who wrote the treatise *On the Sacred Disease* (translated into English in 1923) claims that this disease is no more sacred than any other:

> I do not believe that the "Sacred Disease" is any more divine or sacred than any other disease, but, on the contrary, has specific characteristics and a definite cause. Nevertheless, because it is completely different from other diseases, it has been regarded as a divine visitation by those who, being only human, view it with ignorance and astonishment.

He continues by attacking as charlatans and quacks those who try to cure the disease by means of charms. He himself explains the disease as resulting from a discharge in the brain, and he supports this theory with the dissection of a goat that had suffered from the same disease. In addition to the physiological explanation, what is remarkable is that the author sees the same laws of nature operative in both humans and goats.

The man most identified with the development of Greek medicine is Hippocrates of Cos, who is said to have established a medical school on his native island. Virtually nothing is known of Hippocrates himself, though he is treated respectfully by writers of his era. Plato refers to him as a typical doctor, and Aristotle calls him the perfect example of a physician. Plato attributes to Hippocrates the revolutionary idea that in order to understand the body, it is necessary to understand it as an organic whole, that is, as a unity whose parts function together. This organic view, however, is not explicitly stated in any of the extant Hippocratic books, which were most likely compiled in the fifth to four century B.C.E. The consensus of scholarly opinion is that there was no single author "Hippocrates." None of the fifty to seventy surviving books of the so-called Hippocratic corpus agree with the views attributed in antiquity to Hippocrates, and moreover, the contents of these books are often at odds with one another. Nevertheless, even if his actual works are not known, he appears to have been a real person and to have had—if Plato may be credited—a scientific outlook.

One of the important features of Greek medicine is the inquiry into the causes of disease. As in the case of natural philosophy, where a variety of views explained the universe, so in medicine there are various theoretical formulations, ranging from a single unitary cause for all disease to specific causes for each. The author of the Hippocratic work *Peri physon* (*On Breaths*; 1923), for example, thinks that because some breathing irregularity accompanies illness, breath is at the root of every disease.

On the other hand, the author of *Peri archaiēs iētrikēs* (*Ancient Medicine*, 1849) criticizes physicians who do not distinguish between symptoms and causes. He also criticizes those who think that if a disease follows a certain action, the action was the cause of disease—a mistake known in philosophy as the *post hoc propter hoc* fallacy. An example would be eating a certain food and, when illness followed shortly after, assuming the food to be the cause of the illness.

Another feature of Hippocratic medicine, as detailed in the work *Prognostics* (translated into English in 1819), was the careful study of the progress of diseases. Once a physician had diagnosed a particular illness, he could tell the patient what to expect in the future as the disease ran its course. The ability to predict was certainly essential in establishing medicine's status as a science.

Diagnosis and prognostication both incorporate the fundamental principle of Hippocratic medicine that disease is a part of nature and acts in accordance with natural laws. As humans share a common nature and as diseases share a nature that is regular and hence predictable, a science of medicine is possible. For a disease to be treatable, what works for one patient must work for another. Thus, medicine must carefully analyze nature, catalog the types of diseases, and define the appropriate treatment for each. The underlying assumption of ancient medicine, as of modern medicine, is that the body functions best when its nature is maintained. Hence the physician's job is twofold: First, he should not interfere with the body's nature but should maintain it by means of preventive medicine, the principal forms of which are diet and exercise; second, when the patient is already ill, the physician, using therapeutic medicine, should restore the body to its nature.

SIGNIFICANCE

From its birth in fifth century B.C.E. Greece, the scientific practice of medicine has been continually alive in the West. The centuries following Hippocrates saw advances in anatomy, as *post mortem* dissections became common. Specialized work in gynecology, orthopedics, and other branches of medicine continued and flourished. Later, in the Roman period, there followed major advances in public health, and the Romans bequeathed to posterity insights about hygiene, sanitation, water supplies, and public health.

—*James A. Arieti*

FURTHER READING

King, Helen. *Greek and Roman Medicine.* London: Bristol Classical, 2001. An examination of the practice and science of medicine during Greek and Roman times. Bibliography and index.

Lloyd, G. E. R., and Nathan Sivin. *The Way and the Word: Science and Medicine in Early China and Greece.* New Haven, Conn.: Yale University Press, 2002. The authors compare and contrast the approaches to medicine and science in ancient Greece and China. Bibliography and index.

Longrigg, James. *Greek Medicine: From the Heroic to the Hellenistic Age.* New York: Routledge, 1998. A source book on ancient Greek medicine. Includes bibliography and index.

_______. *Greek Rational Medicine: Philosophy and Medicine from Alcmaeon to the Alexandrians.* New York: Routledge, 1993. Longrigg examines the part that philosophy and rationality played in ancient Greek medicine. Bibliography and index.

Magner, Lois. *A History of Medicine.* New York: Marcel Dekker, 1992. Magner's work offers a fine introduction to Greek contributions to the study of medicine.

Sargent, Frederick. *Hippocratic Heritage: A History of Ideas About Weather and Human Health.* New York: Pergamon Press, 1982. Sargent focuses on the legacy of Hippocrates and his impact on modern medical science.

SEE ALSO: 6th-4th century B.C.E. (traditionally, 1st millennium B.C.E.), Suśruta, Indian Physician, Writes Medical Compendium; c. 500 B.C.E., Acupuncture Develops in China; 325-323 B.C.E., Aristotle Isolates Science as a Discipline; c. 157-201 C.E., Galen Synthesizes Ancient Medical Knowledge.

RELATED ARTICLES in *Great Lives from History: The Ancient World*: Galen; Hippocrates.

c. 500 B.C.E.-c. 200 C.E.
LIBYAN GARAMANTES FLOURISH AS FARMERS AND TRADERS

The Garamantes harnessed the water beneath the Sahara, through networks of underground canals called foggara, *to supply oases, where they carried on farming.*

LOCALE: Northern Sahara Desert in present-day Libya
CATEGORIES: Agriculture; prehistory and ancient cultures; trade and commerce

SUMMARY OF EVENT

The Garamantes were an ancient people who inhabited the Sahara Desert from around 500 B.C.E. to 200 C.E. They lived in three large cities—the capital of Germa (ancient Garama), Zinchera, and Saniat Gebril—and in about twenty other settlements in the Fazzan, a region in the southwest of Libya. The remains of the Garamantes' settlements have been uncovered by archaeologists who believe the Garamantes were not nomadic people, as described by ancient historians, but were, in fact, an advanced civilization adept at building a 3,000-mile (4,840- kilometer) network of irrigation canals (*foggara* in Arabic) buried under the desert sands. The Garamantian canals tapped into aquifers beneath the surface of the Sahara and carried the precious water via low-grade gravity to nearby oases. In these oases, the Garamantes grew foodstuffs such as cereals, grapes, olives, and dates in quantities significant enough to allow them to survive, enlarge their settlements, and expand their control over the Fezzan.

Historians know very little about the Garamantes and their way of life. Scholars differ about their origins, with some maintaining that they were Berbers (a people of northern Africa linked through language) who made their way into the Sahara in the first thousand years B.C.E. Other scholars believe the Garamantes originated from a Neolithic people who lived in northern Africa when it was covered by lakes and inland oceans. Archaeologists have examined rock paintings of humanlike stick figures hunting animals and existing alongside cattle to support their claim that the Garamantes evolved from a nomadic people who hunted to survive to a settled people who raised and herded cattle. Because livestock need reliable water supplies to survive, scholars believe that the Garamantes had access to such reserves.

At some point in their history, the Garamantes developed a method of constructing many hundreds of underground irrigation channels. In northern Africa, these desert irrigation channels are called *foggara*; in other areas of the Middle East they are called *qanat*. Where the Garamantes learned the technology of desert irrigation channeling is still a mystery, although scientists suggest they may have acquired the technique of oasis farming from the Egyptians and other peoples to the east. More puzzling is why and when the Garamantes abandoned the *foggara* and with them their settlements. Falling water levels in underground aquifers could be one reason.

Ancient historians, beginning with the Greek Herodotus (c. 484-c. 425 B.C.E.), depict the Garamantes in a variety of ways. In book 4 of his *Historiai Herodotou* (c. 424 B.C.E.; *The History*, 1709), Herodotus describes the salt hills of the Libyan interior and the streams which flow from them. The Garamantes, according to Herodotus, are one of several tribes who

> are the last inhabitants of Libya on the side of the desert, living as they do, more inland than the wild-beast district.... The Garamantians, a very powerful people... cover the salt with mould, and then sow their crops.... The Garamantians have four-horse chariots, in which they chase the... Ethiopians.

In his *Naturalis historia* (77 C.E.; *Natural History*, 1938-1963), the Roman writer Pliny the Elder (23-79 C.E.) recounts their hostile behavior during the military conquest by Lucius Cornelius Balbus the Minor in 19 B.C.E. In *Ab excessu divi Augusti* (c. 116 C.E., also known as *Annales*; *Annals*, 1598), the Roman historian Tacitus (c. 56-c. 120 C.E.) recalls how the Garamantes raided cities on Libya's Mediterranean coast.

Knowledge of the Garamantian way of life has grown slowly during the modern era. The Italian archaeologist Giacomo Caputo excavated in the Fezzan during 1930's. His work led to the discovery of sixty thousand tombs. Another archaeologist, Mohammed S. Ayoub, excavated the area around Germa from 1962 to 1966. He uncovered cemeteries and what he believed to be the foundations of a royal palace. From the late 1960's through the 1970's, Charles Daniels excavated around the oasis of Wadi el-Agial, one of three oases in the Fezzan. His work revealed more burial grounds as well as irrigation systems. Daniels's work suggests that humans had been making use of the oasis for at least the past twelve thousand years.

Archaeological work continues at sites such as Germa, the hilltop fortress of Zinchara, the oasis of Saniat Gebril, and the burial ground of Saniat Ben Howedi. Germa was the capital of the Garamantes and has been called a metropolis by ancient Roman writers. It is believed that Germa started out as a settlement of mud-brick buildings in or before the fourth century B.C.E. Stone buildings date from around the first or second century C.E. During this time, trade between the Garamantes and the Mediterranean region was at its height. The Garamantes had turned from making war on their neighbors and the Roman occupiers of Libya into an important trading partner with the Rome. Goods traded by the Garamantes included salt, gold, ivory, and slaves.

Taking off where Daniels's work ended, present-day archaeologists believe that the Garamantes tapped into desert groundwater (deposited when the Sahara experienced plentiful rain) and transported it via canals to their oases. In one oasis, Wadi al-Agial, the inhabitants were able to irrigate approximately 300 square miles (777 square kilometers) of soil.

The Garamantes were at the mercy of their changing environment and adapted accordingly. When groundwater levels fell below the underground canal system, the Garamantes drove hundreds of wells into the Sahara to tap the lowered water level. They must have been successful in harnessing their diminishing water supplies because the Garamantes were able to support a state with a population of fifty thousand at the height of their power in the second and third centuries C.E. As the Sahara became increasingly dry, however, the Garamantes' civilization declined. By the sixth century C.E., it had all but disappeared. Small settlements continued to survive clustered around oases fed by wells.

SIGNIFICANCE

The Garamantes succeeded in harnessing the water beneath the Sahara through a system of underground canals which allowed them to irrigate oases, where they carried on farming. They may have learned the technique of building these *foggara* from other ancient peoples such as the Egyptians. The Garamantes thus made use of the scarce resources of their dry environment to build a thriving civilization. The key factors of their civilization were the *foggara*, oasis settlements, a capital noted for its size and building type, and numerous burial mounds.

—*Adriane Ruggiero*

FURTHER READING

Ayoub, M. S. "The Royal Cemetery at Germa. A Preliminary Report." *Libya Antiqua* 3/4 (1966/1967): 213-219. An account of archaeological findings that led to increased knowledge about the Garamantes' way of life.

Brett, Michael, and Elizabeth Fentress. *The Berbers*. Cambridge, Mass.: Basil Blackwell, 1996. The Garamantes are covered in the first chapter as an early Berber people. Illustrations and maps.

Daniels, C. M. *The Garamantes of Southern Libya*. Stoughton, Wis.: Oleander Press, 1970. An archaeologically based study of Garamantean history.

Lhote, Henri. *Les Chars rupestres saharien: Des Syrtes au Niger, par le pays des Garamantes et des Atlantes*. Toulouse, France: Éditions des Hésperides, 1982. Although written in French, this book contains pictures of Garamantean rock paintings and petroglyphs.

Mattingly, D. J., et al. "The Fezzan Project, 1997: Methodologies and Results of the First Season." *Libyan Studies* 28 (1997): 11-26. Archaeological findings about the Garamantes.

SEE ALSO: c. 2300-c. 2000 B.C.E., First Great Expansion of Berber Peoples Across North; c. 1200-c. 1000 B.C.E., Berbers Expand Across North Africa; c. 800 B.C.E., Phoenicians from Tyre Found Carthage; c. 300-c. 100 B.C.E., Berber Kingdoms of Numidia and Mauretania Flourish.

c. 500 B.C.E.-c. 300 C.E.

SOCIALLY STRATIFIED KINGDOMS ARISE AROUND THE MIDDLE NIGER RIVER

Kingdoms developed around the Middle Niger River in Africa, becoming socially stratified and increasingly complex.

LOCALE: Middle Niger River, Africa
CATEGORY: Prehistory and ancient cultures

SUMMARY OF EVENT

The Niger River has its source in present-day Guinea and meanders through Mali, Niger, Benin, and Nigeria. It is the third largest river in Africa, rising within 150 miles (240 kilometers) of the sea in the Fouta Jallon highlands on the borders of Sierra Leone and Guinea. It extends for 2,600 miles (4,180 kilometers), and its basin covers an area of approximately 580,000 square miles (1.5 million square kilometers), including the lake region between Sansanding and Kabara. The Benue River, a tributary of the Niger, has its source in the Cameroon highlands.

Artificial earth mounds, reflecting either settlement sites or graves (*tumuli*), are found in the three main areas of the Middle Niger region: the Niger-Bani confluence in the Bani valley, north and northeast of Masina and Segu, and the area to the extreme east of the bend of the Niger river, in present-day Burkina Faso. According to African archaeologist Bassey Wai Andah, thick-walled wares served as burial pots in all three areas. In Burkina Faso (Niger Rim), researchers found iron or polished-and-ground stone tools as well as domestic pottery. Bronze and copper implements were found in the Niger bend area. At Masina and Segu, fine dishes and bowls with thin walls, footed cups, jugs, and conical jars were found. The people were generally farmers of the Iron Age, cultivating millet and rice, and others were fisherfolk who used nets with terra-cotta weights as opposed to bone harpoons.

Archaeological evidence found in what was known as the Western Sudan and is now Nigeria and Mali suggests that desiccation and the constant growth of the Sahara precipitated the movement of pastoralists and agricultural producers southward and from the north and northeast between 5000 and 2000 B.C.E. There is some basis to suggest that certain species of rice such as the *Oryza Barthii A. Chev* (hardy rice) and *Oryza breviligulata A. Chev* and *Oryza Roer* may have been originally planted in West Africa in the middle Niger River region and that the delta of the Middle Niger was the point for varietal diversification of the rice species. Certain distinctive characteristics of the rice species such as the deciduous spikelets, the anthocyanin pigmentation of the flowers, the purple seed coats and the "floating" form, indicate a center of primary variation.

Oral traditions in West Africa, particularly in Northern Nigeria, from Wukari on the Benue tributary to Busa on the Niger, describe the Kisra Legend, which speaks about a royal ruler named Kisra from the east who migrated and forged numerous kingdoms. Remnants of this anecdote are also found in Songhai. Kisra has been associated with the Hausa words, *Sarki* or *Seraki*, and the Busa word, *ki-shira*. Traditions of eastern roots of ancient migrants to the Western Sudan are especially strong in Nupe and Borgu.

Archaeological sites such as Taruga, and to some extent, Bonga, Amo, Gurun, and Mongon in the Nok Valley in central Nigeria demonstrate the use of furnaces, indicating that ironworking was prominent and paved the way for the use of iron agricultural implements such as hoes and cutlasses, which revolutionized earlier agricultural practices. Findings of large beads of quartz, pottery, and bangles point to a thriving and increasingly sophisticated lifestyle of people in the Nok Valley. Just as the proximity of the Nile led to the emergence of the earliest civilizations around the Nile River Valley, so too, the communities that lived close to the Niger River in West Africa experienced radical changes in the evolution of their lifestyles and cultures.

Iron use changed the kinds of weapons and tools used by the people around the wooded Niger Valley in the middle of the first millennium B.C.E. Removal of trees for human cultivation in forested areas through fires and bark peeling was probably considered a time-consuming and energy-intensive process. Africans in the Middle Niger River Valley may thus have become more receptive toward developing a more energy-efficient technology to meet increased subsistence needs. Iron use provided an important avenue to relieve physical stress and harness resources of the material environment for better living in a more effective manner. Iron-ended hoes and axes replaced those made of wood or stone.

Another important factor was the sedentary lifestyle of the communities in the middle Niger River Valley. The archaeological evidence suggests that these communities engaged in iron production periodically and not perennially. Further, the task of iron smelting was left to the specialist blacksmiths and master smelters, using the wood and ore available in the forested regions of West Africa. It is also probable that gold and silver mining occurred in parts of West Africa at close proximity to the Middle Niger region from the beginning of the first century C.E., even though excavations at Jenne-Jeno later unearthed a gold earring from 800 C.E. Jenne-Jeno became a fully settled center starting in 300 C.E. What is evident is that technological skills were expanding in West Africa with the inception of the Iron Age.

As populations increased and social organization became more complex, the peoples of the middle Niger River Valley took to forming larger political structures that resembled states or institutions of governance and social maintenance. Trade began to expand, and with trade came enhanced economic prosperity, which beckoned people to organize themselves. Some became kings or community leaders and others the ruled or subjects. In other communities of West Africa, people collectively organized themselves into clans and familial units with no centralized authority, except a council of elders, as is the case in many African societies today. The net result of these evolutionary changes, the beginning of earnest trade and commerce, the emergence of marketing relations, and the formations of towns and villages, was the sparking of greater social differences and the exacerbation of social stratification among different segments of communities in the Middle Niger River Valley.

Graham Konnah, a Euro-Australian archaeologist, notes that the *tumuli* point to a formalizing of power by African leaders, derived from their control of iron and later gold deposits that led to further social stratification. It was this process of accumulation of wealth from mining and agricultural expansion that preceded the emergence of the vast Ghana Kingdom in the eighth century C.E. and the successive urban centers of the first millennium C.E.

SIGNIFICANCE

What is clear in the chronology of events from 500 B.C.E. to 300 C.E. in the Middle Niger River region is that African civilizations were evolving as numerous other civilizations were in Asia, the Americas, and Europe. West Africa skipped the Bronze Age, showing that there is no law of historical evolution that demands a region go through such a stage of cultural and technological development. The view that Africans were undeveloped and West Africa was a land devoid of civilizations before European colonialism is shattered by the preponderant archaeological evidence demonstrating some of the most sophisticated civilizations of the era, equaling or exceeding cultures in other parts of the world. The Middle Niger River region's cultures, from the first millennium B.C.E. through the first millennium C.E., reflect consistent technological innovation and social complexities that paved the way for the towering civilizations in Ghana, Mali, and Songhai that would last through the fifteenth century.

—Julian Kunnie

FURTHER READING

Ajayi, J. F. A., and Michael Crowder, eds. *History of West Africa*. New York: Columbia University Press, 1972. A foundational text for understanding West African history, including ancient civilizations of the Niger River Valley.

Alagoa, E. J., F. N. Anoizie, and Nwanna Nzewunwa in association with the University of Port Harcourt, eds. *The Early History of the Niger Delta*. Hamburg, Germany: Helmut Buske Verlag, 1988. A valuable work by African archaeologists discussing the economic, cultural, and linguistic history of early West Africa.

Diop, Cheikh Anta. *The Origin of African Civilizations: Myth or Reality?* New York: Lawrence Hill, 1975. A good reference text that argues for a continuity of ancient Egyptian civilizations with that of the rest of ancient Africa.

Fage, J. D., and R. A. Oliver, eds. *Papers in African Prehistory*. New York: Cambridge University Press, 1970. An important work of diverse essays discussing among other topics on African civilizations, botanic arguments on the origins of agriculture in tropical Africa.

Kense, François. *African Occasional Papers, No. 1: Traditional African Iron Working*. Calgary, Alta., Canada: Department of Archaeology, University of Calgary, 1983. An informative book discussing the complexities of iron technology in Africa.

Konnah, Graham. *African Civilizations: Precolonial Cities and States in Tropical Africa: An Archaeological Perspective*. New York: Cambridge University Press, 1987. This work provides a good discussion of archaeological evidence found in Africa substantiating the complexity of precolonial African societies, including a section on Middle Niger River findings.

Mokhtar, G., ed. *Ancient Civilizations of Africa*. Vol. 2 in *General History of Africa*. Paris: UNESCO and London: Heinemann Educational Books, 1981. This book provides important archaeological information on ancient African civilizations.

Olaniyan, Richard, ed. *African History and Culture*. Lagos, Nigeria: Longman Nigeria, 1982. This work contains important essays by African scholars on the evolution of African societies from the ancient period to the present

Osae, T. A., S. N. Nwabara, and A. T. O. Odunsi. *A Short History of West Africa: A.D. 1000 to the Present*. New York: Hill and Wang, 1975. Though this book covers a later period of West Africa, the background information provided in the first chapter is informative, particularly in discussing influences on West African civilizations.

Sorgwe, C. M. *A Textbook of Niger Delta History*. Oyo State, Nigeria: Rescue Publications, 1997. A basic history of the area that covers ancient times.

SEE ALSO: c. 6th century B.C.E.-c. 350 C.E., Meroitic Empire Rules from Southern Egypt to the Blue Nile; c. 500 B.C.E.-c. 200 C.E., Libyan Garamantes Flourish as Farmers and Traders; 450-100 B.C.E., City-State of Yeha Flourishes in the Northern Ethiopian Highlands; 4th-11th centuries C.E., Ancient Ghana Emerges.

c. 500 B.C.E.-c. 600 C.E.

MITHRAISM EMERGES AS SIGNIFICANT RELIGION

Mithraism, a dynamic religion developed over the previous millennium, took root in the newly created Persian Empire and played an influential role in religious developments over the next thousand years.

LOCALE: Persia (now Iran), India, and the Roman Empire
CATEGORY: Religion

KEY FIGURE

Zoroaster (c. 628-c. 551 B.C.E.), prophet who revised Mithraism

SUMMARY OF EVENT

By 500 B.C.E., Persia had become the largest empire the world had ever known. Its subject peoples had multiple religions, which were tolerated, and the Persians themselves had a well-developed belief system that had evolved over the previous millennium. This religion, Mithraism (also Mithrism), continued to evolve during the next thousand years and had a revolutionary impact on other Western religions. By the late Roman Empire, Mithraism was the most popular religion among Roman soldiers and a major competitor of Christianity.

Mithra emerged as an important deity in the world's earliest religious texts. In the Indian *Rigveda* (also known as *Ṛgveda*, c. 1500-1000 B.C.E.; English translation, 1896-1897) and the later Persian *Avesta* (1000-600 B.C.E.), Mithra is the god who rewards those who keep their contracts and punishes those who violate their commitments. In an increasingly complex commercial world, Mithra played an important role in interactions between the universe of the gods and the mundane affairs of humans. In Old Iranian, the name Mithra means contract, and his name was invoked to make binding a fourteenth century B.C.E. Hittite-Mitanni treaty that was discovered in the 1907 excavation at Bogazköy, Turkey. The form that worship of Mithra took at this time is not known.

In the earliest religious texts, Mithra is also associated with the light of the sun. By 500 B.C.E., Mithra was considered second only to Ahura Mazda, the supreme god of cosmic light, good, truth, and righteousness who is locked in a cosmic battle with Ahriman, the god of evil and darkness who is considered by many scholars to be the prototype of the devil. To help wage this battle on earth, Mithra took human form before the advent of civilization by being born from a rock (which he himself formed by divine concentration) on December 25. He was attended by shepherds and magi (representative of earlier Persian animistic beliefs) bearing gifts. By the sixth century B.C.E., Mithra's birth was attributed to the immaculate conception of the virgin mother goddess Anahita (who had first emerged in Persian religion as a fertility goddess).

In the earliest texts, Mithra is linked to the slaying of a sacred bull with a dagger. From the blood and body of the dying bull grew all food plants and animals useful to humankind. With the slaying of the bull, the battle between good and evil, one front in a cosmic conflagration, began on earth. As humankind developed, Ahriman sent droughts and a great flood; however, Mithra interceded during each disaster to save humankind. As the threat of humankind's extinction vanished, Mithra ate a sacramental meal of bread, the body of the bull, and wine (*haoma*). He then ascended to heaven in a fiery chariot to continue the cosmic battle against the forces of evil as an intermediary between the forces of light and humankind.

Early Persian worship of Mithra appears to have involved sacrificing a bull; a cleansing involving the bull's blood was an important part of the sacramental ritual. In the seventh century B.C.E., the prophet Zoroaster (also called Zarathustra) attacked this sacrificial practice and transferred many of Mithra's powers to Mazda. Zoroaster created a belief system more lofty and abstract than Mithraism, but one still containing Mithra as a major lieutenant of Mazda and his chief intermediary on earth. Eternally watchful of all affairs on earth, Mithra would be the judger of souls at the last judgment when the good would receive eternal heavenly bliss and the evil would join Ahriman in a fiery hell. Starting with Darius the Great, Persian kings followed Zoroastrianism but tolerated the older Mithraic belief.

Mithra, in a relief from an altar in a third to fourth century C.E. temple near a Roman fort on Hadrian's Wall at Carrawburgh, England. (Hulton|Archive)

SIGNIFICANCE

Mithraism remained a powerful belief in the Persian Empire and may have influenced the Hebrew concepts of heaven and hell and good versus evil after Cyrus the Great freed the Hebrews from the Babylonian captivity (538 B.C.E.). It coexisted with a multitude of eschatological beliefs during the succeeding Hellenistic Age, then spread rapidly after 100 C.E., becoming the major belief of the Roman army. Remains of Mithraic temples, usually in underground caves, can be found throughout the Roman Empire, including fringe areas such as Britain and the Rhine.

The exact impact of Mithraism on Judaism, Christianity, and Islam remains a source of considerable scholarly debate. That its impact was great is difficult to refute. Mithraism's practices and doctrines—including a ritual of baptism, ceremonies involving a sacred meal, the concept of a virgin birth on December 25, sacredness of worship on Sundays, and practice of calling all initiates "brother" and priests "father"—are similar to those of Christianity, and in the fifth century C.E. the faith was a powerful rival to the newly expanding religion of Christianity. However, Mithraism's division into separate religious communities lacking any central administration and its refusal to allow female initiates helped doom the belief to oblivion.

—*Irwin Halfond*

FURTHER READING

Clauss, Manfred. *The Roman Cult of Mithras: The God and His Mysteries*. New York: Routledge, 2000. A most reliable and readable account of the Roman form of the Mithras cult based on recent research and new archaeological discoveries. Bibliography and indexes.

Colpe, Carsten. "Development of Religious Thought." In Vol. 3 of *The Cambridge History of Iran*, edited by Ehsan Yarshater. Vol. 3. New York: Cambridge University Press, 1983. A clear treatment of the historical evolution of Persian Mithraism.

Cumont, Franz V. *The Mysteries of Mithra*. Translated by Thomas J McCormack. New York: Dover Publications, 1956. The landmark study of Mithraism, originally published in English in 1903, by the scholar who started Mithraic studies. Bibliographic footnotes.

Hinnells, John R. *Persian Mythology*. New York: P. Bedrick Books, 1985. A very readable treatment of the re-

ligions and mythology of ancient Persia, most notably Mithraism and Zoroastrianism. Bibliography.
Ulansey, David. *The Origins of the Mithraic Mysteries: Cosmology and Salvation in the Ancient World*. New York: Oxford University Press, 1989. A scholarly study of the development of mythologies related to Mithraism. Bibliography.

SEE ALSO: c. 600 B.C.E., Appearance of Zoroastrian Ditheism; 547 B.C.E., Cyrus the Great Founds the Persian Empire; 520-518 B.C.E., Darius the Great Conquers the Indus Valley; 520-518 B.C.E., Scylax of Caryanda Voyages the Indian Ocean.

RELATED ARTICLES in *Great Lives from History: The Ancient World*: Cyrus the Great; Zoroaster.

c. 500 B.C.E.-c. 700 C.E.
ZAPOTECS BUILD MONTE ALBÁN

Inhabitants of Monte Albán, one of the earliest and biggest cities in the Western Hemisphere, pioneered the construction of astronomically oriented public buildings; the use of adobe, stone masonry, and lime plaster; the development of a 260-day ritual calendar; and the carving and painting of hieroglyphs.

LOCALE: Monte Albán, Oaxaca, Mexico
CATEGORIES: Architecture; prehistory and ancient cultures

SUMMARY OF EVENT

Monte Albán, founded by the Zapotecs, was the first and largest urban center in the Oaxaca Valley of Mexico, reaching an extension of 12 square miles (31 square kilometers). The Y-shaped valley is 60 miles long by 15 miles wide (97 by 19 kilometers) and is surrounded by forested mountains. It has an altitude of 5,000 feet (1,524 meters), with little rainfall and a permanent dry condition. The Salado River and its tributaries provide irrigation for agriculture.

The entire urban complex, at the summit of a hill 1,320 feet (402 meters) high, covers 45 acres (18 hectares). Outcrops of sedimentary rock provided construction material for its many residences, palaces, temples, ball courts, stelae, and other structures. Less than 1 percent of the total area has been excavated. The Zapotec name for the metropolis is still unknown. Its current name derives from the conquistador Diego López de Monte Albán, who received this area as part of his *encomienda* (commissioned) territory in the sixteenth century. The city's central location on a hilltop implies its dominant role within the region.

Over the course of its twelve-hundred-year existence, which included a number of phases, Monte Albán reached a maximum population of about twenty-five thousand inhabitants. The urban phase, called Monte Albán I, lasted from 500 to 200 B.C.E. The Protoclassic period, or Monte Albán II, lasted from 100 B.C.E. to 200 C.E. The Classic period, from 200 to 700 C.E., is divided into Monte Albán IIIa and IIIb. During the city's final phase, archaeological evidence implies political breakdown and depletion of resources.

In 500 B.C.E., at the end of the Rosario phase, there was a radical change in the Oaxaca Valley. San José Mogote, the largest community in the valley for more than eight hundred years, suddenly lost most of its population. This was possibly because of internal conflict. At the same time, some two thousand inhabitants left their villages on the valley floor to relocate on the slopes of Monte Albán. Soon afterward, about a dozen communities in the valley were established on defensible hilltops with walls.

Social stratification developed during Monte Albán I. There is no evidence that a supreme ruler existed but rather a privileged class of priests, warriors, rulers, and artists controlled other Zapotecs and their labor. A market flourished in Monte Albán, where imported goods such as obsidian, pottery, salt, lime, and other items were bartered.

The first permanent structure constructed during this era was Building L, containing the Wall of the Danzantes. The Spanish conquistadors mistakenly believed that these carvings of naked upright figures represented dancers. The wall contains four alternating rows of so-called dancers and swimmers, who appear in smaller rectangular blocks in an outstretched horizontal position. More than three hundred of these varied figures are recorded at Monte Albán. Each stone has a single naked male figure, eyes closed, mouth open, some with elaborate hairstyles, earspools, and bead necklaces. They could signify an awesome display of military strength or a historical narrative.

By 100 B.C.E., Monte Albán had gradually subjugated more than three hundred tribute-paying communities in the Oaxaca Valley to create the Zapotec empire. It cannot be determined how many of these towns were taken by military conquest, or how many weaker ones succumbed to colonization. The metropolis was protected by a long defensive wall 15 feet (4.6 meters) high and 60 feet (18 meters) wide on the easily climbed western slopes of the mountain.

During the second period, Monte Albán II (100 B.C.E.-200 C.E.), there were an estimated seven hundred Oaxaca Valley communities with some fifty thousand inhabitants, while Monte Albán's population had grown to ten thousand. New construction included the 8-acre (3-hectare) Main Plaza and a ball court, shaped like a capital I, with bilateral inclined surfaces of smooth stucco. There is a large increase in public buildings and temples, most of which are oriented toward the cardinal directions. The temple-patio-altar compound emerged as a ritual-ceremonial precinct. The largest of these is the Sunken Patio in the North Platform, measuring 54 yards (about 50 meters) on each side. A cistern was built in the Main Plaza. Drains lined with stone were used to evacuate inundations in the plazas and patios into dams and a large reservoir at the bottom of the hill.

Building J, an arrowhead-shaped structure, was constructed during this era. It has the ruins of a temple on top and its unusual shape is believed to be an astronomical indicator. Its outer walls contain about forty large slabs, weighing several tons each, with a variety of incised glyphs. Each depiction has a place glyph in the center, with an inverted adorned human head below it and a symbol unique to the slab above it. The glyphs are sometimes accompanied by a text with place-names and dates. Alfonso Caso, in charge of archaeological explorations at Monte Albán from 1931 to 1943, described these glyphs as signifying places conquered by Monte Albán. A contrasting theory is that the slabs commemorate important allied communities. A few recycled danzante stones also appear in sections of the Building J walls.

The classic era of Zapotec civilization is known as Monte Albán IIIa (200-500 C.E.) and IIIb (500-700 C.E.). The Oaxaca Valley population grew to 100,000 inhabitants distributed in some thousand communities. Zapotec art, symbols, and writing, which is limited to the elite families, flourished during this epoch, while carved stones are relatively rare. Monte Albán's twenty-five thousand residents occupied more than two thousand family homes of three different styles. They all have a common floor plan of rooms surrounding a central patio, which contained a burial place, and roofs of wood beams and thatch. The simplest dwellings had wattle-and-daub walls with an open or semiclosed format. Their patios contained work areas, storage pits, ovens, and family graves. Intermediate-size homes, with adobe walls on stone foundations, had a central patio with adjacent rooms and a modest tomb. Elite families lived in grand-scale palaces. Rooms with thick walls and stucco floors surrounded an inner courtyard with stairways, an altar, and a decorative tomb. These burial chambers, including Tombs 103, 104, 105, 112, and 125 at Monte Albán, were adorned with colorful murals and contained offerings of elaborate funerary urns, carved bone, and jewelry.

The South Platform, containing carved stelae on its northern corners, was constructed during Period III. The Plain Stela and the Lápida de Bazán depict significant Teotihuacán elements. Strong political and cultural ties with Teotihuacán are reflected in the Monte Albán murals and the new scapulary *tablero* (vertical panel) architecture. Likewise, a Oaxaca residential section appears at

A rock carving at Monte Albán. (Corbis)

Teotihuacán, with Zapotec-style pottery, urns, and a tomb. A Monte Albán mural on Tomb 105 shows the Teotihuacán influence of profiled speech-scroll figures, with one wearing the goggles of the rain god.

The Zapotecs were animistic, believing in a pantheon of gods that included a supreme being and Cocijo, the water god. Cocijo's image is often depicted on urns. During this era there also appeared two other deities, the Wide-Billed Bird and a crocodile-like creature with an up-curled snout.

The demise of Monte Albán began by 600 C.E., the result of a scarcity of basic resources after the tribute system collapsed; possibly there was also a loss of ecological equilibrium. As the overextended Zapotec empire receded back to the Oaxaca Valley, by 700 C.E. Monte Albán was largely abandoned and fell into ruins. There is no archaeological evidence of warfare or wanton destruction. The Zapotecs then retreated into city-states, from where they fought against each other and against outside invaders such as the Mixtecs, who had been migrating into the Oaxaca Valley from the mountains of northwestern Oaxaca state.

SIGNIFICANCE

Monte Albán was the focal point of the Zapotec empire, which expanded outward from the city over the course of seven hundred years. The metropolis was a center of religious and political power. Its inhabitants developed a class society that confronted its neighbors with warfare and diplomacy to maintain a system of trade and tribute. The Mixtecs would later adopt many of their cultural traditions and architecture.

—Antonio Rafael de la Cova

FURTHER READING

Blanton, Richard E., et al. *Ancient Oaxaca: The Monte Albán State*. New York: Cambridge University Press, 1999. Investigates the emergence of social complexity and state formation in a New World region.

Marcus, Joyce, and Kent V. Flannery. *Zapotec Civilization*. New York: Thames and Hudson, 1996. An overview of the origins and the rise of Zapotec civilization up to the abandonment of Monte Albán.

Whitecotton, Joseph W. *The Zapotecs: Princes, Priests, and Peasants*. Norman: University of Oklahoma Press, 1977. An anthropological history of Zapotec civilization.

Winter, Marcus. *Oaxaca: The Archaeological Record*. 1989. Reprint. Mexico City: Minutiae Mexicana, 2001. An examination of excavations and findings in the Oaxaca Valley.

SEE ALSO: c. 1500-c. 300 B.C.E., Olmec Civilization Rises in Southern Mexico; c. 300 B.C.E., Izapan Civilization Dominates Mesoamerica; c. 100 B.C.E.-c. 200 C.E., Zapotec State Dominates Oaxaca; 90 C.E., Founding of the Classic Period Maya Royal Dynasty at Tikal.

499-494 B.C.E.
IONIAN REVOLT

The Greek city-states of Ionia in Asia Minor revolted against their Persian rulers, an event that was the opening chapter of the Greco-Persian War, a war in which the Greeks were ultimately victorious.

LOCALE: Ionia (now in Turkey and Greece)
CATEGORY: Wars, uprisings, and civil unrest

KEY FIGURES

Aristagoras (d. 494 B.C.E.), tyrant of the Ionian city of Miletus, son-in-law of Histiaeus, and legendary instigator of the revolt

Artaphernes (fl. sixth-fifth centuries B.C.E.), brother of Darius and a satrap of Asia Minor, who helped suppress revolt

Cyrus the Great (550-486 B.C.E.), Persian king, r. 522-486 B.C.E.

Histiaeus of Miletus (mid-sixth century-493 B.C.E.), former tyrant of Miletus

Cleomenes I (d. c. 490 B.C.E.), king of Sparta, r. c. 521-c. 490 B.C.E.

SUMMARY OF EVENT

Ionia, in western Asia Minor (now Turkey), was made up of independent Greek-speaking city-states. The city-state, or polis, was the basic form of political, social, and economic organization in the Greek world, which included Ionia, the Aegean islands, and the Greek mainland. However, in the mid-sixth century B.C.E., Cyrus the Great established the Persian Empire, which expanded to include Asia Minor. By the end of the sixth century B.C.E., the city-states of Ionia had been under Persian rule for several decades, and some of the Aegean islands had recently come under Persian control. The cities in mainland Greece were still beyond the borders of Persia's ever-expanding empire.

In 499 B.C.E., a revolt against Persian domination began in Ionia, the beginning of a two-decade conflict between the Persians and the Greeks. The major historical source for the Greco-Persian War, including the Ionian Revolt, is the Greek historian Herodotus. Some of the stories he relates seem problematic, but whatever his limitations as a historian, all subsequent histories of the Greco-Persian War must by necessity rely on Herodotus.

The Persians governed the Ionian cities through tyrants, or dictators. Individual tyrants could be either good or bad, but what all tyrants had in common was that they were above any laws, ruling without the legal consent of the populace. Miletus, located in the southwest coast of Asia Minor, was the largest and richest polis in Ionia. Its ruling tyrant was Aristagoras, the major figure in Herodotus's account of the Ionian Revolt and, according to the historian, the primary cause of the conflict. However, there were other causes. Some Ionians resented the Persian-backed local tyrants; others the military conscription policies of the Persian army. The high taxes that Persia imposed on the Ionian cities was also a factor. More generally, all Greeks shared a broad cultural distrust of and bias against non-Greeks, which included the Persians, and the individual poleis prized their freedom above all else.

According to Herodotus, exiles from the Aegean island of Naxos approached Aristagoras, requesting his support in overthrowing the island's ruling regime and enticing Aristagoras with the role he might play after the exiles were restored. Aristagoras was eager, but believing his Miletian forces insufficient, requested additional military support from Artaphernes, the Persian satrap, or governor, of Asia Minor and brother of Darius the Great, the Persian king. Aristagoras promised to reward Artaphernes personally with Naxos's wealth and claimed that control of Naxos would facilitate further Persian expansion in the Aegean. Darius gave his approval, and authorized two hundred ships to take part in the Naxos expedition. Although Aristagoras had intended to lead the attack, command was given to Darius's nephew, Megabates. Friction developed between the leaders, and Herodotus states that after a confrontation, Megabates secretly warned the Naxos defenders of the impending invasion. After an unsuccessful four-month siege, Aristagoras was forced to call off the assault.

Fearing disgrace and possible punishment for his failure to fulfill his promises to the Persians, Aristagoras turned to rebellion, a decision that was supported secretly by Histiaeus, the former tyrant of Miletus and Aristagoras's uncle and father-in-law, who was then residing in the Persian capital of Susa. Those with whom Aristagoras consulted were supportive of the revolt, with the exception of the historian Hecataeus, who claimed that Persian power was too great. He said that the only chance of Ionian victory was to seize the treasury of a prominent religious temple and use the wealth to build a fleet to resist the Persians. Hecataeus's proposal was rejected, perhaps in fear of religious consequences.

To gain support, Aristagoras resigned his position as tyrant and encouraged other Ionian cities to rid themselves of their tyrants. Cognizant of Ionian military weakness, Aristagoras journeyed to Sparta, located in Greece's Peloponnese, to appeal for assistance to free the Ionians from the Persian yoke. Oligarchic Sparta was famed for its phalanx army of hoplite warriors, the best in the Greek world, but its king, Cleomenes I refused to aid the uprising, arguing that the Persian Empire was too extensive to be defeated. In addition, the Spartans were Dorian Greeks rather than Ionian Greeks; the Ionian-Dorian divide was one of the traditional causes of rivalry in the Greek world. Aristagoras then turned to democratic Athens, the largest and richest polis in Greece, and the Athenians promised to send twenty ships in support of their fellow Ionians. Five ships were also contributed by Eritrea. Aristagoras undoubtedly hoped for more than those twenty-five.

In 498 B.C.E., the rebels, mainly Miletians, Athenians, and Eretrians, sailed from Miletus to Ephesus, Ionia's second-largest city. Joined by the Ephesians, they marched to Sardis, the Persian administrative center of Asia Minor. Most of Sardis was captured and burned, including a temple of the goddess Cybele, which led to later accusations of sacrilege, but Artaphernes, controlling the Sardis acropolis, or citadel, held out. During the Greek retreat from Sardis, the Persians inflicted a severe defeat on the Ionians. In the aftermath, the surviving Athenians and Eretrians abandoned the Ionian cause and sailed back to Greece, taking no further part in the Ionian stage of the Greco-Persian War.

The revolt spread, and several non-Greek cities joined the uprising, some perhaps unwillingly. An Ionian fleet sailed north, seizing the Hellespont, the body of water dividing Europe from Asia Minor, and the polis of Byzantium, thus threatening Persia's link to its European province of Thrace. Onesilus, a ruler on the island of Cyprus, embraced the rebellion, but because of its close proximity to the Near East, the Persians reacted quickly. Although the Ionian fleet was victorious on the sea, on land the Persian army quickly quelled the Cyprus rebellion, in part because of treachery and divisions within the Greek-Cypriot contingent.

The tide turned against the rebels. Persian armies, led by sons-in-law of Darius, were sent to crush the rebels in Ionia. The Hellespont region was successfully retaken, and Ionian resistance began to weaken elsewhere. In 496 B.C.E., Aristagoras fled Miletus and later died in battle in European Thrace, leaving a vacuum of leadership among the Ionians. Hisiataeus, having abandoned the Persians, failed in his attempt to regain power in Miletus.

The final battle took place at Lades, an island near Miletus. A Persian fleet of six hundred ships was assembled, many of them Phoenician, whose people were formidable seafarers. By 494 B.C.E., many of the Greek poleis had abandoned resistance, intimidated by Persian power, bribed by Persian wealth, or succumbed to the perennial inter-Greek rivalries. Herodotus reported that only nine cities provided ships at Lades, with 100 ships from Chios and 80 from Miletus forming the largest contingents, for a total of 353 ships. Ephesus did not join the last Ionian resistance. The Persians wisely moved only slowly to battle. Divisions and rivalries occurred among the Ionians, and they lost faith in their commander, Dionysus of Phocae. The ships from Samos deserted to the Persians, possibly the result of Persian bribery, and the ships from Lesbos fled at the beginning of the battle. Persia was victorious. Miletus, under Aristagoras, began the Ionian Revolt in Ionia, and after the Persian naval victory at Lades, the city was destroyed and its population killed or enslaved and removed to the mouth of the Tigris River, or modern Iraq.

SIGNIFICANCE

The failure of the Ionian Revolt led to such grief in Athens that the dramatist Phrynichus was fined and his play about the capture of Miletus was banned for the sorrow it caused. The road to the Greek mainland was open, and in 492 B.C.E., Darius the Great invaded Greece but suffered defeat at the Battle of Marathon in 490. After his death, his son Xerxes I invaded Greece in 482. A Spartan army of seven hundred was defeated at Thermopylae, Athens was sacked, but the Greeks triumphed at the naval battle of Salamis and the land battle at Plataea. The Ionian Revolt was a disaster, but the Greco-Persian War ended in 479, with a glorious victory for the Greek city-states.

—*Eugene Larson*

FURTHER READING

Burn, A. R. *Persia and the Greeks: The Defense of the West*. 2d ed. Stanford, Calif.: Stanford University Press, 1984. The classic account of the Persian-Greek confrontation.

Davis, Victor Hanson. *The Wars of the Ancient Greeks*. London: Cassell, 1999. One of the foremost military historians of ancient Greece and expert on its military culture writes about the Greek wars, including the Ionian Revolt.

Gillis, Daniel. *Collaboration with the Persians*. Wiesbaden, Germany: Steiner, 1979. One of the few studies that focuses solely upon the Ionian rebellion portion of the Greco-Persian War.

Herodotus. *The Persian Wars*. Translated by George Rawlinson. New York: Random House, 1942. The classic account of the Greek-Persian conflict, by the "father of history."

Lateiner, Donald. *The Historical Method of Herodotus*. Toronto: University of Toronto Press, 1989. A historian's analysis of Herodotus and his history of the Greco-Persian War.

SEE ALSO: 547 B.C.E., Cyrus the Great Founds the Persian Empire; 520-518 B.C.E., Darius the Great Conquers the Indus Valley; September 17, 490 B.C.E., Battle of Marathon; 480-479 B.C.E., Persian Invasion of Greece.

RELATED ARTICLES in *Great Lives from History: The Ancient World*: Cleomenes I; Cyrus the Great; Darius the Great.

494/493 B.C.E.
INSTITUTION OF THE PLEBEIAN TRIBUNATE

The institution of the plebeian tribunate by the Roman senate recognized the rights of the lower orders of Roman society.

LOCALE: Rome (now in Italy)
CATEGORY: Government and politics

KEY FIGURES

Manius Valerius (fl. sixth-fifth century B.C.E.), Roman dictator, r. c. 500/494 B.C.E.
Sicinius (fl. sixth-fifth century B.C.E.), leader of the plebeian revolt

SUMMARY OF EVENT

Because of the lack of contemporary sources and because evidence was at times deliberately suppressed and falsified for purposes of family aggrandizement or moral and artistic edification, much early Roman history lies shrouded in obscurity and myth. Despite conflicting details, however, there seems to be a core of fact relating to the institution of the plebeian tribunate as described by the historians Dionysius of Halicarnassus and Livy. A secession of the plebs, prompted by their abuse at the hands of the patricians, was followed by the election of officers to represent plebeians and defend their rights. Ultimately, an oath was sworn by the plebeians to regard as inviolable the persons of their new tribunes. Conflicting accounts exist about the place of secession, whether on the Aventine hill or the Sacred Mount; about the number of tribunes elected, whether two, four, or five; about the manner of their election; and about the oath taken making them sacrosanct.

According to Livy, trouble broke out during the consulship of Appius Claudius Sabinus Inregillensis and Publius Servilius in 495 B.C.E. The plebeians complained that while they were fighting in the army to preserve Roman independence, they were being enslaved at home by patrician creditors. They were particularly exasperated by the pitiful sight of a former soldier who, having lost his home and his crops to the enemy, had to borrow money in order to pay his taxes. To induce plebeians to take up arms against a Volscian army, Servilius was forced to order that no Roman citizen should be held in chains or in prison to prevent him from enlisting, that no one should seize or sell a soldier's property while he was in service, and that no one should harass his children or grandchildren.

Continued pressure on debtors, however, caused the plebs to become violent. They began to assemble at night on the Aventine and Esquiline, and they refused to fight against the invading Sabines. An edict by the dictator Manius Valerius giving greater protection to plebeians from their creditors made it possible to muster an army. In the absence of permanent adjustments, however, the plebs took the advice of a certain Sicinius and withdrew to the Sacred Mount 3 miles (5 kilometers) from the city across the Anio River. This secession caused panic in the city among the patricians, who were afraid of hostile foreign invaders and those plebeians who remained behind. According to Livy, the senate compromised with a constitutional innovation.

This new agreement, a milestone in the struggle between the orders, created an exclusive plebeian office to protect "the people" from the aristocratic consuls. The "tribunes of the people" at first had only a negative function because they could do no more than "forbid" an overt act inimical to a plebeian at the instant of its perpetration. Moreover, aid had to be initiated by a complaining plebeian, so a tribune could not absent himself from the city for a whole night or shut his doors at any time. The person of the tribune was declared sacrosanct by a *lex sacrata*; anyone who interfered with a tribune doing his duty became an outlaw, liable to be killed by plebeians.

At first, there were two tribunes—or possibly four or five, according to some sources. That number, however, eventually grew to ten. This strange negative office, creating a set of parallel officials working at cross-purposes with the old magistrates of the state, was intended partly to satisfy plebeian unrest and partly to keep plebeians from becoming regular magistrates, thus usurping the prerogative of the nobility. In 471 B.C.E., a law transferred the election of tribunes from the assembly of the *curiae* to the *comitia tributa*, an event and date that Eduard Meyer and some other scholars have associated with the actual creation of the plebeian tribunate itself.

SIGNIFICANCE

Eventually, the veto of a plebeian tribune permitted him to negate the passage of any legislation prejudicial to plebeian concerns. Thus, it was only natural that tribunes began to sit in the senate to make known their objections to laws before they were actually passed, or to suggest legislation and even to call together the senate. The tribunes were also able to veto acts of the consuls and other magistrates, with the exception of dictators. In 287 B.C.E., plebiscites of their *comitia tributa* were given the same force as laws passed by the senate or the *comitia centuriata*.

Because of its invaluable power of veto, the office of plebeian tribune came to be sought avidly. Even patricians had themselves adopted by plebeians to become eligible. It is ironic that this weak, makeshift office became so powerful that the emperor Augustus used the authority of the plebeian tribunate to rule Rome in preference to consular *imperium* because of the unique right of the former to initiate or veto legislation.

—M. Joseph Costelloe, updated by Jeffrey L. Buller

FURTHER READING

Ferenczy, Endre. *From the Patrician State to the Patricio-Plebeian State*. Translated by G. Dedinsky. Amsterdam: A. M. Hakkert, 1976. An excellent survey of the major reforms in the Roman government expanding the legal rights of non-nobles.

Lintott, A. W. *The Roman Republic*. Stroud, Glouestershire: Sutton, 2000. This volume in the Sutton Pocket Histories series provides a concise overview of the history of the Roman Republic, including its politics and government. Bibliography and index.

Mitchell, Richard E. *Patricians and Plebeians: The Origin of the Roman State*. Ithaca, N.Y.: Cornell University Press, 1990. An examination of the relationship between patricians and plebeians in the early Roman Republic. Bibiliography and indexes.

Münzer, Friedrich. *Roman Aristocratic Parties and Families*. Baltimore: Johns Hopkins University Press, 1999. This work on the aristocracy in Rome sheds light on the class structure in Republican Rome. Bibliography and index.

Sandberg, Kaj. *Magistrates and Assemblies: A Study of Legislative Practice in Republican Rome*. Rome: Institutum Romanum Finlandiae, 2001. An examination of the legislative process under the Roman Republic. Bibliography and index.

Stewart, Roberta. *Public Office in Early Rome*. Ann Arbor: University of Michigan Press, 1998. Stewart looks at public officials in Rome, specifically examining the roles of patricians and plebeians in the fourth century B.C.E. Bibliography and index.

SEE ALSO: c. 509 B.C.E., Roman Republic Replaces Monarchy; 483 B.C.E., Naval Law of Themistocles Is Instituted; 451-449 B.C.E., Twelve Tables of Roman Law Are Formulated; 445 B.C.E., Establishment of the Canuleian Law; 340-338 B.C.E., Origin of *Municipia*; 287 B.C.E., *Lex Hortensia* Reforms the Roman Constitution; 180 B.C.E., Establishment of the *Cursus honorum*.

September 17, 490 B.C.E.
BATTLE OF MARATHON

At the Battle of Marathon, soldiers of the democratic city-state of Athens inflicted a spectacular defeat on a much larger Persian force.

LOCALE: A plain named for the village of Marathon in northeast Attica (now in Greece)
CATEGORY: Wars, uprisings, and civil unrest

KEY FIGURES

Datis (fl. early fifth century B.C.E.), joint commander of Persian forces at Marathon
Artaphernes (fl. sixth-fifth century B.C.E.), joint commander of Persian forces at Marathon
Darius the Great (550-486 B.C.E.), king of the Persian Empire, r. 522-486 B.C.E.
Hippias of Athens (c. 570-490 B.C.E.), Athenian tyrant
Miltiades the Younger (c. 554-489 B.C.E.), Athenian general in command at Marathon

SUMMARY OF EVENT

In the late summer of 490 B.C.E., a Persian force of some twenty-five thousand arrived by sea at the plain of Marathon in northeast Attica, about 26 miles (42 kilometers) from the city of Athens. Its leaders were Datis and Artaphernes, agents of Darius the Great, known as the Great King, the King of Kings, and the King by the Grace of Ahura Mazda. They had chosen this particular landing point because it allowed deployment of their cavalry and because they were accompanied by the exiled former tyrant of Athens, Hippias, whose family had holdings and supporters in this region of Attica. Hippias probably anticipated an exchange of intelligence, supplies, and cooperation for the position of satrap (provincial governor) in a conquered Attica and perhaps in a Persian-dominated Greece as a whole.

Whatever his ultimate designs, Darius the Great's immediate intent was punitive because the Athenians had

The Battle of Marathon. (F. R. Niglutsch)

sent twenty ships to assist their fellow Greeks across the Aegean Sea during the Ionian Revolt of 499-494 B.C.E., taking part in the destruction of Sardis, the capital of the Persian satrapy in western Asia Minor (498). Though the revolt had been crushed and the Ionian city of Miletus destroyed in retaliation, the Athenians had not been made to pay the price of their interference. This was an intolerable situation for Darius the Great. The historian Herodotus reports that Darius had a servant whose sole function was to utter the words "remember the Athenians" every time the king took a meal. The army landing at Marathon was charged with settling the score with the Athenians.

The Athenian assembly of citizens met in emergency session and, rather than postpone the inevitable by sitting behind the city walls and allowing the Persians a free hand in Attica, authorized an expedition to Marathon. A force of nine thousand hoplites (heavily armored infantrymen) marched to the plain and set up an encampment. They were joined by an additional one thousand or so hoplites from the neighboring Boeotian town of Plataea. In both cases, these numbers represented every man that could be put in the field. Still, they were outnumbered at least two-to-one. A professional, all-day runner named Philippides (or Pheidippides) was sent to Sparta to request assistance. He set out one day and arrived the next, covering a distance of about 150 miles (240 kilometers). The Spartans, who possessed the finest hoplite warriors in the world, promised to send reinforcements in a few days, as soon as they had completed an important religious festival. They arrived a day late.

The Athenian force was led by its "joint chiefs," the committee of ten *strategoi* (generals). Most of the panel recognized Miltiades the Younger as their best military mind and ceded to him their turns as commander in chief (the position rotated on a daily basis). As it happened, the battle occurred on his designated day of command. Miltiades' tactical arrangements largely determined the outcome of the battle.

The battle probably commenced in the morning because Herodotus says that the fighting lasted "a long time," probably most of the day. Miltiades met the danger of envelopment by the larger enemy force by thinning the center of his phalanx battle formation (typically eight ranks deep) both to stretch his line to equal that of the Persians and to strengthen his wings. As the battle opened, he ordered his advancing formation to move at the double once they came in range of Persian javelins and arrows (their preferred weapons). Having reduced the effect of that barrage, the Greek army closed fast on the opposing foot soldiers, attacking them with thrusting spears and swords. Both enemy wings were beaten back and put to flight. The Persian center pushed back the thinned Greek center but soon found itself enclosed by the redirected phalanxes of the victorious Greek wings. A slaughterous rout resulted. The Greek forces pursued the enemy some 3 to 4 miles (5 to 6 kilometers) across the Marathon plain back to the Persian camp and to the ships beached along the shore. There was fierce fighting here as the Persians desperately scrambled aboard their ships and embarked. Several vessels were actually captured by the Greeks.

A day or two later, the Persian fleet made the 70-mile (113-kilometer) journey around Attica and put into the Athenian harbor at Phaleron. There they sighted the Greek hoplites awaiting them, arrayed in good order. Opting not to confront those formidable infantrymen again, the Persians set sail for home.

SIGNIFICANCE

The "barbarian" menace was repelled with crushing effectiveness at Marathon: Persian dead numbered 6,400 as opposed to 192 on the Greek side. As a special honor, the Athenians buried their dead on the site, where their tomb-mound (the *soros*) may still be seen today.

The victory of the Athenians, particularly because it was won without the assistance of Sparta's vaunted infantry, was a source of intense pride. Veterans of the battle were known as *Marathonomachoi* (Marathon warriors). The Greek playwright Aeschylus, whose tragedies are masterpieces of world literature, chose to record in his epitaph only his service at Marathon, where his brother had been killed in the fighting along the shore. Famous panel paintings depicted scenes from the battle in the Stoa Poecile (Painted Stoa) in Athens' *agora* (city-center). As the Greek Thucydides reports in his history of the Peloponnesian War, the Athenians could still—sixty years later—throw it in the Spartans' faces that at Marathon they (with a few Plataeans) had stood alone to save the Greek world.

The threat of Persian dominance recurred in 480 B.C.E., when Xerxes I, Darius's son and successor, led an enormous expeditionary force into the Greek mainland. Then, a federation of some thirty-one city-states joined forces to repel the invasion and save Greek civilization. However, this did not diminish the achievement or the example of the stalwart infantrymen whom Miltiades led in defense of the soil of democratic Athens against overwhelming odds on a hot and bloody summer's day in 490 B.C.E.

—*James P. Holoka*

FURTHER READING

Hammond, N. G. L. "The Campaign and the Battle of Marathon." In *Studies in Greek History: A Companion Volume to A History of Greece to 322 B.C.* Oxford, England: Oxford University Press, 1973. The author, for many years the leading English-speaking ancient historian, possessed a masterly knowledge of the sources for the battle and made detailed inspections of the Marathon plain; this is still the authoritative modern discussion.

Hanson, Victor D. *The Western Way of War: Infantry Battle in Classical Greece*. 2d ed. Berkeley: University of California Press, 2000. Hanson vividly reconstructs the experience of heavy infantry combat in ancient Greece.

Herodotus. *Herodotus: The Histories*. Translated by Aubrey de Sélincourt. New York: Penguin Books, 1996. A new revised edition, with new introductory material by John Marincola. Book 6 is the earliest and best ancient source for the Battle of Marathon; a stirring account.

Holoka, James P. "Marathon and the Myth of the Same-Day March." *Greek, Roman, and Byzantine Studies* 38 (1997): 329-53. A corrective to misleading claims, both ancient and modern, about the movements of Greek and Persian forces during the battle and its aftermath.

Lazenby, J. F. *The Defence of Greece, 490-479 B.C.* Warminster, England: Aris & Phillips, 1993. A reliable and very readable history of the Greco-Persian wars in general and of the Battle of Marathon in particular.

SEE ALSO: c. 700-330 B.C.E., Phalanx Is Developed as a Military Unit; 547 B.C.E., Cyrus the Great Founds the Persian Empire; 520-518 B.C.E., Darius the Great Conquers the Indus Valley; 499-494 B.C.E., Ionian Revolt; 483 B.C.E., Naval Law of Themistocles Is Instituted; 480-479 B.C.E., Persian Invasion of Greece; 478-448 B.C.E., Athenian Empire Is Created.

RELATED ARTICLES in *Great Lives from History: The Ancient World*: Darius the Great; Miltiades the Younger; Pheidippides; Themistocles; Xerxes I.

483 B.C.E.
NAVAL LAW OF THEMISTOCLES IS INSTITUTED

The naval law of Themistocles was intended as a limited defensive measure but became essential to the defense of Greece against Persia and provided the foundation for the Athenian Empire.

LOCALE: Athens
CATEGORIES: Laws, acts, and legal history; government and politics

KEY FIGURES

Themistocles (c. 524-c. 460 B.C.E.), Athenian archon and general whose naval strategy included building a new type of warship
Darius the Great (550-486 B.C.E.), king of the Persian Empire, r. 522-486 B.C.E.
Xerxes I (c. 519-465 B.C.E.), king of the kings of the Persian Empire, r. 486-465 B.C.E.

SUMMARY OF EVENT

In 483 B.C.E., Themistocles, one of several political leaders in the recently established Athenian democracy, made a proposal to the assembly that had far-reaching implications for Athens and the whole of Greece. For many years, the Athenians had obtained silver from their state-owned mines at Laurium and frequently distributed the modest annual output as a bonus to citizens. In 483 B.C.E., however, spectacularly rich veins of silver were exposed, and a debate ensued as to the disposal of this bonanza. Many argued for the customary (if unusually large) distribution to citizens, but Themistocles proposed that the windfall be used to build two hundred warships of the advanced trireme type. His proposal carried the day, and by 480 B.C.E. Athens had a fleet that made it a major naval power in Greece. To understand how Themistocles achieved acceptance of his proposal and his rationale, one must consider the democratic constitution of Athens, its previous troubled encounters with Persia and Aegina, and changes in naval technology.

Before this buildup, Athens had a small fleet of old-fashioned *pentekontors* (fifty-oared ships), which served well for coastal raids and boarding attacks on other ships but had limited effectiveness in the ramming tactics that were emerging with the spread of a newer style of warship, the trireme. With three banks of rowers per side, providing more than three times the oar power of a *pentekontor*, the trireme had great speed and ramming power. Despite its early invention and its superiority as a ramming weapon, however, the expense of building and operating the trireme slowed its adoption. Because each ship required a skilled crew of two hundred men, the operational cost of a fleet of triremes exceeded the means of all but the wealthiest states, such as Persia, Sidon, and a few of the richest Greek city-states. The silver strike at Laurium gave Athens the opportunity to join this elite group.

In advancing his naval policy, Themistocles operated within the democratic constitution, which had been instituted by Cleisthenes of Athens in 509 B.C.E. This reform placed primary power in the hands of an assembly composed of all adult male citizens and a council of five hundred selected annually by lot, while retaining limited aristocratic features. For example, only wealthier citizens could hold the office of archon and serve on the council of the Areopagus. Pay was not provided for service on the councils or for jury duty. The new arrangement was also prone to factionalism, as rival aristocratic leaders competed for popular support. Fortunately, the system included the peculiar procedure of ostracism, whereby the Athenians might annually vote to exile one individual for ten years. Designed to preempt a revival of tyranny, it emerged in the 480's B.C.E. as a political weapon that allowed a leader such as Themistocles to eliminate rivals and forge a consensus for a policy such as the naval law.

In proposing this costly program, Themistocles had in mind two potential threats: Aegina and Persia. Situated less than 15 miles (24 kilometers) from the Athenian harbor, the island city-state of Aegina had achieved commercial and naval power well ahead of Athens. Rivalry between the two city-states went back many years, and since at least 506 B.C.E., an undeclared state of war had existed between them, with Aegina getting the better of the conflict. A naval expedition to avenge an Aeginetan raid on the Athenian harbor district had failed miserably and demonstrated Athenian naval inferiority. By building the new fleet, Themistocles hoped to put Athens in a position to retaliate for earlier aggressions and make the harbors of Attica safe from future Aeginetan predations. Punishment of Aegina had to wait, however, because the Persians presented a greater and more immediate threat.

In 545 B.C.E., the Persian king Cyrus the Great had conquered Asia Minor and incorporated the Greek city-states of Ionia into the Persian Empire. His successor Darius the Great asserted power across the Bosporus into

European Thrace. When the Ionian city-states rebelled against Persian rule in 499 B.C.E., the Athenians alone of the mainland Greeks sent military support, an act that greatly incensed Darius. After suppressing the revolt by 494 B.C.E., he resolved to punish the Athenians for their interference. In 490 B.C.E., Darius sent an expeditionary force by sea, which landed at Marathon and suffered a humiliating defeat at the hands of the Athenians. Outraged at this outcome, Darius began preparations for a full-scale invasion of Greece, but his death in 486 B.C.E. forestalled this attack. His successor Xerxes I took up Darius's plan for invading Greece, and, by 483 B.C.E. (the year of the silver strike at Laurium), Persian advance forces were already in Thrace and cutting the famous canal across the Athos Peninsula that would facilitate passage of their fleet.

In proposing his naval law, Themistocles surely had this threat in mind as well as the continuing Aeginetan nuisance. Themistocles possessed the strategic insight to see the weakness of the immense Persian army: Its very size made it dependent on seaborne supplies, which were protected by the Persian navy of more than one thousand triremes. Thanks to Themistocles, when the Persian onslaught came, the Greeks had an effective naval strategy and a substantial fleet to implement it. In the decisive naval battle at Salamis in 480 B.C.E., Athenian triremes made up more than half the combined Greek fleet that defeated the larger Persian force and broke the back of Xerxes' invasion. Ironically, the Aeginetans, who had temporarily suspended hostilities with Athens in the face of the Persian threat, were awarded the prize for valor at Salamis.

Once Xerxes' invasion had been repulsed, the Athenians eagerly assumed leadership of a continuing offensive against the Persians. In 478 B.C.E., they organized the Delian League, a voluntary alliance of Aegean city-states in which members contributed either triremes or money to support the league's common navy. In that same year, Themistocles employed a clever diplomatic ruse to secure the rebuilding of the city walls of Athens over the objections of other city-states, and he oversaw the fortification of the Athenian harbor at Piraeus. His

Themistocles and his soldiers enjoy the triumph after the victory at the Battle of Salamis. (F. R. Niglutsch)

antagonistic attitude toward Sparta led to his own ostracism in 473 B.C.E., but by this time the Athenians were committed to maintaining the navy program and pursuing the war against the Persians.

During the next two decades under Athenian command, the forces of the Delian League expelled the Persians from Greek waters and liberated the city-states of Ionia. At the same time, however, the Athenians used the fleet to coerce Greek states to join or remain in the league, which rapidly became the Athenian empire. Aegina, the original target of Themistocles' naval buildup, succumbed in 458 B.C.E. and became a tribute-paying member of the Delian League. That same year also saw construction on the final part of the defensive system begun by Themistocles—the famous Long Walls that linked the city of Athens with its harbor. Secure within these walls and with its commerce and imperial tribute protected by its navy, Athens now entered its greatest period of power and prosperity.

SIGNIFICANCE

The naval empire provided great material benefits to Athenians of all classes in the form of jobs, grants of land confiscated from subject city-states, and magnificent public buildings, most famously the Parthenon. It also greatly enhanced the influence of the poorest class of citizens and engendered constitutional changes that resulted in the "radical democracy" so hated by conservative critics. The security of Athens now depended less on the wealthier citizens who made up the infantry and cavalry forces than on the poorer citizens, called *thetes*, who rowed the triremes. Recognition of the increased importance of the lower classes led statesmen such as Pericles to introduce reforms that further democratized the political system. Thus, the wealth qualification for the office of archon was lowered; the powers of the council of the Areopagus were drastically limited; and pay was now extended to members of the council of five hundred and to jurors. Since the aristocrats and conservative theorists who attacked these constitutional changes clearly associated them with the rise of the navy, it is not surprising that they singled out Themistocles for special condemnation.

—*James T. Chambers*

FURTHER READING

Jordan, Borimir. *The Athenian Navy in the Classical Period*. Berkeley: University of California Press, 1975. A detailed study of the navy created by Themistocles.

Morrison, John S., and J. F. Coates. *The Athenian Trireme: The History and Reconstruction of an Ancient Greek Warship*. 2d ed. New York: Cambridge University Press, 2000. The most important volume on this subject, this study analyzes all aspects of the trireme's history.

Osborne, Robin, ed. *The Athenian Empire*. 4th ed. London: London Association of Classical Teachers, 2000. An analysis of the empire's origins, course, and effects on Athens and the Greek world as a whole.

Plutarch. *The Rise and Fall of Athens*. Translated by Ian Scott-Kilvert. New York: Penguin Books, 1960. This excellent translation of nine of Plutarch's biographies has the lives of nine Athenian statesmen, including Themistocles.

Starr, Chester G. *The Influence of Sea Power on Ancient History*. New York: Oxford University Press, 1989. Chapter 3, "Athens on the Sea," provides an excellent overview of the rise and decline of Athens as a naval power.

SEE ALSO: c. 550 B.C.E., Construction of Trireme Changes Naval Warfare; 508-507 B.C.E., Reforms of Cleisthenes; 499-494 B.C.E., Ionian Revolt; September 17, 490 B.C.E., Battle of Marathon; 480-479 B.C.E., Persian Invasion of Greece; 478-448 B.C.E., Athenian Empire Is Created.

RELATED ARTICLES in *Great Lives from History: The Ancient World*: Cimon; Darius the Great; Leonidas; Themistocles; Xerxes I.

480-479 B.C.E.
PERSIAN INVASION OF GREECE

The Persian invasion of Greece was repulsed by Greek city-states, who joined together to defeat Persia, halting future invasions.

LOCALE: Greece, the Aegean Sea, and western Asia Minor

CATEGORIES: Expansion and land acquisition; wars, uprisings, and civil unrest

KEY FIGURES

Xerxes I (c. 519-465 B.C.E.), king of the kings of the Persian Empire, r. 486-465 B.C.E.

Eurybiades (fl. fifth century B.C.E.), Spartan admiral, commander in chief of the Greek fleet, c. 481-480 B.C.E.

Themistocles (c. 524-c. 460 B.C.E.), Athenian general

Adeimantus (fl. fifth century B.C.E.), Corinthian general, 480 B.C.E.

Leonidas (c. 510-480 B.C.E.), king of Sparta, r. 490-480 B.C.E.

Pausanias of Sparta (late sixth century-c. 470 B.C.E.), nephew of Leonidas and regent of Sparta, r. 480-c. 470 B.C.E.

SUMMARY OF EVENT

Cyrus the Great, founder of the Persian Empire, subjugated the Ionian Greek states of western Asia Minor to Persia. The Ionians resented the loss of their sovereignty, and in 499 B.C.E., they rebelled against Cyrus's successor, Darius the Great. Their action was supported by two states in Old Hellas, Eretria and Athens. At first the Ionian Revolt went well, but Darius soon gathered overwhelming forces and had reimposed Persian authority by 494 B.C.E. He then determined to invade Old Greece, to punish the states that had assisted the Ionian cities, and to end a vexatious frontier problem. Persia had been reasserting its strength along its western boundaries, but a campaign against Greece required different strategies, including a much greater reliance on naval battle than Persia had experienced before.

Darius's first attack in 492 B.C.E. miscarried when much of the Persian fleet was wrecked in a storm, and his second attempt in 490 B.C.E. failed when his army was driven into the sea at Marathon in Attica. He therefore planned a third invasion on a lavish scale. Darius, however, died in 486 B.C.E., and it fell to his son Xerxes I to complete the preparation of his empire's forces.

The great invasion finally began in the spring of 480 B.C.E. An enormous host of more than one hundred thousand soldiers was supported by a fleet of six hundred warships. For fifty years, part of the Persian military strategy had been to let the opponents know that the Persian army was coming. They counted on terror and the effects of psychological warfare rather than the element of military surprise. The Greeks could not fail to learn about

The Battle of Thermopylae. (F. R. Niglutsch)

Major Greek Battles Against Darius and Xerxes, 490-479 B.C.E.

the assembling of such masses, and in the winter of 481-480 B.C.E., representatives of the larger states met at Corinth to discuss resistance. The Delphic Oracle had to be persuaded to modify its initial prophecy of doom to one of doubtful outcome, and it was with some trepidation that a decision was taken to fight under Spartan leadership. Appeals to other Greek states to join the patriotic cities were rejected by some of the more important ones, notably anti-Spartan Argos. Ultimately, only thirty-one states fought on the Greek side. There were actually more Greek states on the side of Xerxes, although these served under compulsion.

The Greeks decided to delay the Persians' advance by holding the narrow pass at Thermopylae with eight thousand men and the adjacent strait between Thermopylae and the island of Euboea with their fleet. It was not until August that the Persians came up against these fortified positions. Three days passed as Xerxes vainly sent his best troops against the well-armored Peloponnesian infantry fighting under King Leonidas of Sparta. Simultaneously, a series of inconclusive but costly naval engagements were fought off Cape Artemisium on Euboea; the Persians had earlier lost about two hundred warships in a storm. Xerxes, however, turned the position at Thermopylae by marching around it through the mountains. Most of the Greeks escaped encirclement in time, but Leonidas with his bodyguard of three hundred Spartans and the seven-hundred-man army of Tespiae were cut off and could only die resisting bravely to the end.

With the position on land lost, the Greek fleet retreated and took station on the island of Salamis off the western coast of Attica. The population of Athens had already been evacuated to the Peloponnesus. There was more wavering among the Greeks at Salamis, some even considering defection, but at last honor prevailed, and led by Eurybiades of Sparta, Themistocles of Athens, and Adeimantus of Corinth, the Greek sailors prepared to fight. The Persians, fearing that the Greek fleet might escape westward, decided on an immediate attack, and late in September the Battle of Salamis was fought in the narrow strait between the island and the mainland. The Persians had about 350 ships, the Greeks probably 310, of which the majority were Athenian. The conflict lasted most of the day, and by sunset the Greeks were victorious. With the campaigning season nearly over, Xerxes withdrew from devastated Attica and left half his army to winter in Boeotia. The rest of the army and the shattered fleet retired with the king to Asia.

The war was resumed the following spring. After a second Persian devastation of Attica, a hard-fought land battle took place at Plataea, a small state between Athens and Boeotia. Under the command of the Spartan regent Pausanias, the Greeks gained the victory, and the Spartan infantry showed once more their undoubted excellence. The Persian army was forced into rapid retreat.

While this campaign was being fought in Greece, the Hellenic fleet had crossed the Aegean to seek out the remnants of Xerxes' navy. Off the island of Mycale, the Greeks completed its destruction. Thus, the great force that Xerxes had led against the Hellenes was either destroyed or forced back into Asia, and, as the poet Simonides wrote, "Hellas put on the crown of freedom."

These victories did not end the war with Persia, but they did end Persian efforts to invade Greece. The liberation of Ionia now became the goal of the Greek states, and by 477 B.C.E. most of it had been freed. As a result of these campaigns Athens became one of the most important military powers of Greece.

SIGNIFICANCE

After these wars, the Persian Empire never again seriously threatened the Greek city-states. Greece became the major power in the Mediterranean Sea, and this allowed the city-states to prosper through trade and to increase their political power. Athens' role in leading the fight against Persia continued in time of peace, as Athens was the most influential of the Greek city-states and the center of Hellenic cooperation. In contrast, the Persian Empire began its slow shrinking that set the stage for Alexander the Great's conquest nearly one hundred fifty years later.

In the centuries after the Greco-Persian wars, Greek culture blossomed, expanding into the greatest variety of its classical period. The cultural vibrancy came to expression in literature such as the drama of Aeschylus of Athens and the poetry of Pindar of Thebes, as well as in the philosophy, mathematics, and athletics that flourished in this period. Greek hegemony over the eastern Mediterranean allowed its wealth to grow and its Hellenistic culture to begin its spread throughout the region, preparing the way for the later military conquests of what became Alexander the Great's empire.

—*Samuel K. Eddy, updated by Jon L. Berquist*

FURTHER READING

Bengston, Hermann, ed. *The Greeks and the Persians from the Sixth to the Fourth Centuries*. New York: Delacorte Press, 1968. A collection of essays dealing with different aspects of Persian-Greek relations surrounding the invasion.

Boardman, John, N. G. L. Hammond, D. M. Lewis, and M. Ostwald, eds. *Persia, Greece and the Western Mediterranean, c. 525 to 479 B.C.* Vol. 4 in *The Cambridge Ancient History*. 2d ed. New York: Cambridge University Press, 1988. The most complete analysis of events from before the invasion through Persia's defeat.

Burn, A. R. *Persia and the Greeks*. 2d ed. Stanford, Calif.: Stanford University Press, 1984. A narrative covering events from the sixth century to Xerxes' defeats in 479 B.C.E.

Dandamaev, M. A. *A Political History of the Achaemenid Empire*. 1989. Reprint. Leiden, the Netherlands: E. J. Brill, 1997. A remarkably thorough treatment of the Persian involvement in the war.

Green, Peter. *The Greco-Persian Wars*. Reprint. Berkeley: University of California Press, 1998. An engaging history of the wars, offering exciting narrative as well as analysis.

Herodotus. *The History*. Translated by David Grene. Chicago: University of Chicago Press, 1987. The standard translation of the famous Greek historian who records (and interprets) the Persian invasion from the Greek perspective.

Olmstead, A. T. *History of the Persian Empire*. Chicago: University of Chicago Press, 1948. A somewhat uncritical account of the wars from the Persian viewpoint.

SEE ALSO: c. 550 B.C.E., Construction of Trireme Changes Naval Warfare; 547 B.C.E., Cyrus the Great Founds the Persian Empire; 520-518 B.C.E., Darius the Great Conquers the Indus Valley; 499-494 B.C.E., Ionian Revolt; September 17, 490 B.C.E., Battle of Marathon; 483 B.C.E., Naval Law of Themistocles Is Instituted; 478-448 B.C.E., Athenian Empire Is Created; May, 431-September, 404 B.C.E., Peloponnesian War; 336 B.C.E., Alexander the Great Begins Expansion of Macedonia.

RELATED ARTICLES in *Great Lives from History: The Ancient World*: Cyrus the Great; Darius the Great; Leonidas; Pausanias of Sparta; Themistocles; Xerxes I.

479 B.C.E.
CONFUCIUS'S DEATH LEADS TO THE CREATION OF *THE ANALECTS*

In recording the scholar-philosopher Confucius's conversations, his followers epitomized his life and teachings, providing the foundation for Confucianism, a philosophical outlook that has shaped Chinese and other East Asian societies.

LOCALE: Lu and adjacent ancient states (now northeast China)
CATEGORIES: Philosophy; cultural and intellectual history

KEY FIGURES

Confucius (551-479 B.C.E.), Chinese ethicist and political philosopher
Zigong (Tsu-kung; 520-c. 460 B.C.E.), Chinese scholar, merchant, and government official
You Zi (Yu Tzu; c. late sixth century-c. mid-fifth century B.C.E.), Chinese scholar and philosopher
Zengzi (Tseng-Tzu; c. 500-436 B.C.E.), Chinese scholar and philosopher

SUMMARY OF EVENT

On the eleventh day of the fourth month, 479 B.C.E., Confucius died. His death was not dramatic; according to tradition, he sensed that his time had come, took to his bed, and seven days later, expired. His life—which has been reconstructed by modern scholars largely from the *Lunyu* (later sixth-early fifth centuries B.C.E.; *The Analects*, 1861)—was neither especially dramatic nor especially successful.

Briefly, according to *The Analects*, Confucius was a person of the highest intelligence and moral character. Both drawing on and augmenting a tradition of legendary sage-emperors, he conceived a project of political reform. Educated gentlemen of good character, or *junzi*, were to advise and assist rulers: Perhaps they would be able to develop wisdom in the ruler, and perhaps one of them would become a sage, or *shengren*, who held or strongly influenced governmental power. Stymied in the principality of Lu by the infighting among powerful clans, Confucius and his followers traveled for many years to adjoining states (c. 497-484 B.C.E.). Evidently, the Confucians were not welcomed with open arms by the nobles who ruled these states. No one turned over the reins of power to them or appointed Confucius to high office. Returning to Lu, he became embroiled in the conflict between its duke and the dominant Qi family, again with no happy result. He is generally supposed to have died disappointed and even embittered by the failure of his reformist project.

Confucius's life does not seem to have been distinguished by the successful exercise of practical wisdom. He is represented in *The Analects* not as a philosophical innovator but instead as a traditionalist who followed established ways, especially those of the Zhou Dynasty (Chou; c. 1066-256 B.C.E.). His reformist project, which constitutes a "traditionalist revolution,"did not succeed.

It is necessary, then, to consider the reasons for Confucius's prominence and especially the great esteem accorded him by his younger associates. According to the *Liji* (compiled first century B.C.E.; *The Liki*, 1885; commonly known as *Classic of Rituals*), Confucius's followers mourned him as they would a father, that is, for three years. One of the most noteworthy, Zigong, extended this to six years, living in a hut that he built on the burial grounds. Zigong was one of two adherents who might have succeeded the master: He was considered by some in Lu to be superior to Confucius, an opinion that Zigong repudiated in apparent good faith, according to *The Analects*.

The other possible successor was You Zi. A story from the *Classic of Rituals* indicates that You Zi resembled Confucius, probably not physically but in thought and speech. Three of the leading Confucians—Zuxia (Tzu-hsia), Zizang (Tzu-chang), and Ziyou (Tsu-yu)—desired that You Zi replace the master whom he resembled. You Zi does not appear to have demurred concerning this proposal. However, Zengzi was deeply offended. In his view, Confucius was incomparable and therefore irreplaceable. He refused to participate in this scheme of succession, thus ending it.

It was in this context that *The Analects* was created. Despite lengthy and continuing, even intensifying, scholarly efforts, there are no definitive answers to the questions of who composed *The Analects*, when, and why. There is, however, general agreement on a number of points concerning the text, those primarily responsible for it, the existence of chronologically differing "layers" or "strata" in it, and the date when *The Analects* was crafted into final form. The question of the purposes of this multi-authored text is, inevitably, controversial and interpretative.

For a text central to the shaping of billions on billions of human lives, *The Analects* is almost shockingly short and, on its face, simple. It consists of twenty "books"; but these books are short chapters of a few pages apiece. Most of the books consist of Confucius's statements or very short dialogues with followers (or both), although famously book 10 characterizes Confucius's habitual behavior and book 19 contains only statements from prominent followers.

Book 19 is crucial in understanding the formation of *The Analects*. Most scholars hold that it was the five "major disciples" of book 19 (with You Zi included, Zigong excluded) who began the process of remembering Confucius. Zigong's evident humility and Zengzi's pronounced filial piety established that neither You Zi nor anyone else would replace Confucius. If the rapidly splintering groups of Confucians were to maintain relative coherence and harmony, a central focus was indispensable. It had been Confucius who brought together the seventy-odd identified "Confucians." It was to be shared memories of Confucius's person, his words, his actions, and not least, his hesitations and misfortunes that would loosely bind together his followers and their followers.

Enormous critical energy has been expended in attempting to determine the order in which the pieces of *The Analects* originated and were recorded, transmitted, revised, and assembled. Very likely, the process of remembering occurred during the century following Confucius's death; but some would extend this period to two and even three centuries. It is appropriate to suggest that a text recording conversations was itself developed slowly and conversationally. Sustained and persuasive analysis has discerned the presence of at least two and probably three (or more) "strata" in *The Analects*, the oldest of them being books 3 through 15, but with 8 joining 1 and 2 in a middle layer, and 10 together with 16 through 20 in the most recent. Three different versions of *The Analects* were extant early in the Han Dynasty (206 B.C.E.-220 C.E.); but these were synthesized into a single generally adopted version by Zhang Yu (Chang Yu) toward the end of the first century B.C.E.

SIGNIFICANCE

Every seminal text speaks differently to different times, cultures, and people. Given the uncertainties of its composition, this is especially true of *The Analects*. This uncertainty is fitting and indicative because one of the important themes of the work is the uncertainties encountered in any attempt to influence those possessing governmental power. If Confucius set out to rule directly or to be the wise and moral power behind some great throne, then his life was a failure, probably an embittering failure.

His followers, however, certainly did not regard him as such. *The Analects* is a memorial and not merely to a remarkable and beloved teacher. Its gradual, deliberate composition permitted reflection on Confucius's experiences and conversations. Viewed comprehensively, *The Analects* is a record of a life devoted to learning. Some of the learning was derived from old, inherited writings, which Confucius—and his younger associates—studied, commented on, and rearranged until they became the Five (once Six) Classics. A very important part of the learning was derived from trying to improve humanity. No doubt, this experience was often painful and frustrating, especially as it involved dealing with powerful, recalcitrant men; but it must have been steadily instructive. Finally, Confucius learned of the irreducible diversity of human beings as every attentive teacher learns, from the characteristic questions, preoccupations, and ambitions of his students.

This devotion to complex learning, manifested in *The Analects*, constitutes the Confucian tradition. The life of learning complexly is a mean, an equipoise, between solitary thinking and unreflective action. Confucius's gift to his followers, in the fifth century B.C.E. and for two millennia thereafter, was the life of learning. People tend to speak of a way of life, but what the Confucian tradition offers is a life of the Way, the Dao, which finds and follows the path of balance and harmony. According to *The Analects*, intrinsic to this harmony of being is a sincere effort to improve public life, although these situations might appear to be hopeless.

—*John F. Wilson*

Further Reading

Ames, Roger T., and Henry Rosemont, Jr. *The Analects of Confucius: A Philosophical Translation.* New York: Ballantine Books, 1998. Ames and Rosemont incorporate the recently discovered Dingzhou (partial) text of *The Analects* and provide both a complete text and studies of *The Analects*, in paperback. They include the Chinese text chapter-by-chapter with translations; a lengthy historical, textual, and philosophical introduction; extensive notes; appendices; and a bibliography.

Confucius. *The Analects* (*Lun yu*). Translated by D. C. Lau. New York: Penguin Books, 1979. The standard paperback translation. Lau's approach is traditional, relating Confucius's life and followers to *The Analects.* Introduction, useful appendices, and glossary of persons and places.

Creel, H. G. *Confucius and the Chinese Way.* New York: Harper Torchbooks, 1960. Originally published in 1949 as *Confucius: The Man and the Myth.* A standard, widely available biography and interpretation, the book treats Confucius and his followers as progressive reformers. An appendix on *The Analects*, notes, references, bibliography, and index.

Fingarette, Herbert. *Confucius: The Secular as Sacred.* 1972. Reprint. Prospect Heights, Ill.: Waveland Press, 1998. A very short but interesting and influential work. Treating core Confucian terms, Fingarette endeavors to demonstrate the gap between traditional Chinese and individualistic Western thinking. Fundamental and provocative, with a few notes and a very short bibliography.

Schwartz, Benjamin I. *The World of Thought in Ancient China.* Cambridge, Mass.: Harvard University Press, 1985. A scholarly but relatively accessible study. Schwartz interprets Confucius as an idealistic traditionalist seeking to restore a comprehensive normative sociopolitical order. Notes, bibliography, glossary, and index.

See also: c. 1066, Western Zhou Dynasty Begins in China; 770 B.C.E., Eastern Zhou Dynasty Begins in China; 5th century B.C.E., Composition of the *Spring and Autumn Annals*; 5th-1st century B.C.E., Composition of *The Great Learning*; 500-400 B.C.E., Creation of the *Wujing*; 475-221 B.C.E., China Enters Chaotic Warring States Period; 206 B.C.E., Liu Bang Captures Qin Capital, Founds Han Dynasty; 104 B.C.E., Dong Zhongshu Systematizes Confucianism.

Related articles in *Great Lives from History: The Ancient World:* Confucius; Mencius; Xunzi.

478-448 B.C.E.
ATHENIAN EMPIRE IS CREATED

The Athenian Empire was created, transforming a defensive alliance against Persia into a political empire that prevented the peaceful unification of Greece and led to the Peloponnesian War.

LOCALE: Athens, Ionia, and other Greek city-states
CATEGORIES: Expansion and land acquisition; government and politics

KEY FIGURES

Aristides of Athens (c. 525-c. 467 B.C.E.), Athenian statesman and leading organizer of Delian League
Cimon (c. 510-c. 451 B.C.E.), Athenian general and conservative political leader
Ephialtes of Athens (c. late sixth century-461 B.C.E.), Athenian democratic political leader and reformer
Pericles (c. 495-429 B.C.E.), Athenian general and democratic political leader

SUMMARY OF EVENT

After the Persian invasion of Greece had been repulsed in the spring of 479 B.C.E., delegates from the liberated Greek cities of Ionia and Athens assembled and agreed to combine forces in a league whose stated aims were to protect the Aegean area from fresh Persian offensives and to ravage Xerxes I's territory. Pausanias of Sparta (c. late sixth century-c. 470 B.C.E.) had been the commander in chief of the allied Greeks. His behavior was so arrogant and brutal, however, that the allies rejected all Spartan leadership. Aristides of Athens became the allied leader, accompanied by his younger colleague Cimon.

The headquarters of this confederacy was located on the sacred island of Delos, and it came to be called the Delian League. In the beginning an assembly of representatives determined policy, with each state, large or small, exercising one vote. Each member contributed either ships or money; the respective assessments of ships and money were the work of Aristides, whose determinations were so fair that he was called "The Just." The money was kept on Delos under the supervision of a board of Athenians called Hellenic Treasurers. Fleet and army were both commanded by Athenians because Athens was the largest and most powerful of the allied states, and Athenians had won great prestige in both war and peace.

At first, all went well. The league fleet maintained the security of the Aegean and even successfully attacked the Persian-held island of Cyprus. Such victories led some members of the confederacy to regard the Persian menace as broken, and about 470 B.C.E., Naxos, tired of onerous naval service, seceded. The Athenians, supported by a majority of the allies, felt that the withdrawal of Naxos might portend the dissolution of the league to Persia's advantage. Naxos was therefore besieged and reduced to obedience. This act set an important precedent. Moreover, the league's assessment of the situation was confirmed the next year, when the reconstituted Persian navy sailed toward the Aegean but was defeated in the Battle of Eurymedon (c. 467 B.C.E.) by the league fleet ably commanded by Athens' Cimon.

Because providing ships year after year was a hardship for some members, Athens, on the suggestion of Cimon, introduced the policy of allowing any state to convert its obligation to one of paying money. The exact date of this change is unknown; it probably occurred in the mid-460's B.C.E., at the height of Cimon's power and prestige. Gradually most confederates made payments until, by 445, only seven states of a regular membership of some 150 still contributed triremes. At the time the change must have seemed statesmanlike, but it actually cloaked a great danger to the league. As time went on, only the Athenians and the few other states with fleets were capable of serious naval action; the ships of the money-paying cities decayed, and their crews lacked practice. The Athenians, meanwhile, not only increased the size of their navy but also introduced improved models of triremes and new naval tactics, so that their navy was a virtually invincible force by the 440's.

In another unintended way, Cimon furthered Athenian imperialism. League member Thasos seceded in 465 B.C.E. It was defeated at sea and then besieged by the Athenians, and it finally appealed to Sparta for help. Athens and Sparta remained formally allied, but Sparta, fearing Athens' growing power, agreed to aid Thasos. Before they could act, a severe earthquake struck Sparta, causing much destruction and many deaths. Seizing this opportunity, Sparta's subject-peoples revolted and eventually were besieged at Ithome. Meanwhile, the Thasians, lacking Spartan aid, surrendered.

Sparta, recognizing Athenian prowess in siege operations, appealed to Athens for help. Cimon, relatively conservative and pro-Spartan, argued in favor; his more democratic, anti-Spartan opponent Ephialtes of Athens, against. Cimon prevailed and was chosen to lead the assisting army. Yet the Spartans, probably fearing both the presence of an Athenian army in their territory and the effects of Athenian liberalism on current and would-be rebels, changed their minds. Delivering a "slap in the face," they asked the Athenians to leave but retained their other allies. As a result, Cimon's pro-Spartan policy was repudiated, and he was ostracized in 461 B.C.E. His conservative institutional ally, the council of the Areopagus, was stripped of most of its powers by Ephialtes. Athens became more democratic, more anti-Spartan, and almost immediately, more imperial.

In 460 B.C.E., the Delian confederates attacked the Persians in Egypt, but the offensive ended with the annihilation of a league fleet in 454 B.C.E. For a time, it seemed that Persian naval forces might again invade the Aegean. To meet the immediate danger posed to the league's treasure on the unfortified island of Delos, it was agreed to move the fund to the heavily guarded Acropolis at Athens. When peace was made with Persia in 448 B.C.E., however, the money was not moved back. The leaders of Athens assumed sole control of this enormous sum of five thousand talents and insisted that the annual sums thereafter be paid to Athens. During the following decades, this money was used to maintain the Athenian navy, to erect the remarkable series of buildings on the Acropolis, and to finance future wars. Meetings of the league's assembly stopped; the league had become the Athenian Empire.

Some members of the league strongly objected to this new regime and rebelled against it, but their naval weakness made them easy to suppress. Rebellious states were

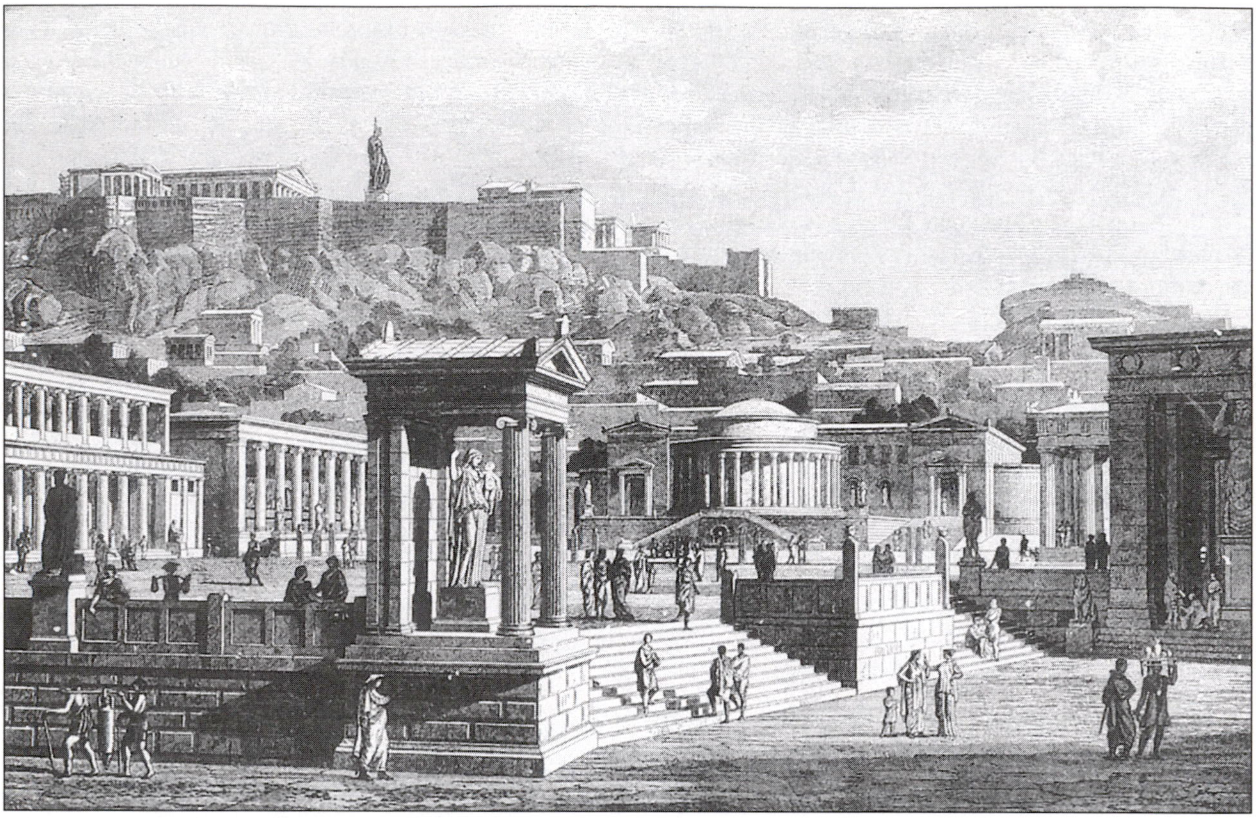

The marketplace at Athens. (F. R. Niglutsch)

compelled to accept democratic, pro-Athenian governments; other states had their legal and commercial relations with Athens subjected to regulation. A few were forced to accept Athenian garrisons or to cede territory for Athenian settlers. Pericles was mainly responsible for this program. He envisioned an idealized Athens, both as a supreme military power and as a model of political organization and advanced culture. "Our state," he said, "is the education of Hellas."

Pericles' more extreme acts of imperialism were condemned by conservatives such as the statesman and historian Thucydides (c. 459-c. 402 B.C.E.), but by the 440's some thousands of Athenians received wages for various services from the annual payments of the allies. As a result the majority backed Pericles, and Thucydides was ostracized. "It may have been wrong to acquire the empire," said Pericles, "but it would certainly be dangerous to let it go." Therefore, while defense had dictated the punishment of Naxos, imperial power compelled the Athenians to keep their grip on their former allies. Athens, in its own eyes "the educator of Hellas," was the tyrant-city to other Greeks. When the Peloponnesian War broke out in 431 B.C.E., most Greeks supported Sparta in the hope of seeing Athenian power destroyed.

SIGNIFICANCE

Athenian imperialism was regrettable because it was, in most respects, the most advanced state in Greece. Athens was democratic. It tolerated free speech to a remarkable degree. Athens provided work for its poor and treated its slaves with relative humanity. Artists, poets, and scholars came to Athens from all parts of the Hellenic world so that the city became the cultural and philosophical center of Greece, a first "world city." Yet the Athenians' passion for empire turned much of the world against them and perhaps prevented the Delian League from becoming a vehicle for the gradual and voluntary unification of the numerous small, quarrelsome Greek states.

The possibility of this transformation highlights the relationship between internal politics and foreign policy. The early Delian League was nonimperial largely because Athens was balanced internally—in leadership, between Ephialtes and Cimon; institutionally, between the council of Areopagus and a popular assembly. The events about 462 B.C.E. permanently upset these balances, opening the way for imperial policies. In time, Pericles became as dominant internally as Athens did externally. Each had ceased to be a first among equals, the condition necessary for a peaceful transformation.

—*Samuel K. Eddy, updated by John F. Wilson*

Further Reading

Fornara, Charles W., and Loren J. Samons II. *Athens from Cleisthenes to Pericles*. Berkeley: University of California Press, 1991. Comprehensive in historical scope and interestingly detailed, this work emphasizes the interplay of Athenian democracy and the acquisition of empire.

Hornblower, Simon. *The Greek World, 479-323 B.C.* 3d ed. New York: Routledge, 2002. Covers the Athenian Empire from its start to finish, including Athenian supremacy, the Peloponnesian War, and the Macedonian expansion.

Kagan, Donald. *Pericles of Athens and the Birth of Democracy*. New York: Free Press, 1991. Part history, part biography, this semipopular work presents Pericles as a commanding Athenian figure and model for contemporary democratic leadership.

Meier, Christian. *Athens: A Portrait of the City in Its Golden Age*. New York: Metropolitan Books/H. Holt, 1998. A study that examines Athens at the peak of its power. Discusses the influence of the Battle of Salamis and the Greco-Persian Wars. Bibliography and index.

Podlecki, Anthony J. *Perikles and His Circle*. New York: Routledge, 1998. A close look at Pericles and other important Athenians. Bibliography and index.

Wartenberg, Ute. *After Marathon: War, Society, and Money in Fifth-Century Greece*. London: British Museum Press, 1995. A museum catalog featuring Greek coins that examines the period in which Athens was supreme. Bibliography and index.

See also: September 17, 490 B.C.E., Battle of Marathon; 483 B.C.E., Naval Law of Themistocles Is Instituted, 480-479 B.C.E., Persian Invasion of Greece; May, 431-September, 404 B.C.E., Peloponnesian War; June, 415-September, 413 B.C.E., Athenian Invasion of Sicily; September, 404-May, 403 B.C.E., Thirty Tyrants Rule Athens for Eight Months; 401-400 B.C.E., March of the Ten Thousand; 336 B.C.E., Alexander the Great Begins Expansion of Macedonia.

Related articles in *Great Lives from History: The Ancient World*: Cimon; Pausanias of Sparta; Pericles; Thucydides.

475-221 B.C.E.
China Enters Chaotic Warring States Period

During the Warring States Period, China broke down into seven major feudal states and entered into two and a half centuries of political and social chaos.

Locale: Central and northeastern part of modern-day China

Category: Wars, uprisings, and civil unrest

Key Figures

Confucius (551-479 B.C.E.), Chinese ethicist, political philosopher, and founder of Confucianism

Xunzi (Hsün-tzu; c. 307-c. 235 B.C.E.), Chinese philosopher and proponent of authoritarian Legalism

Hanfeizi (Han Fei-tzu; 280-233 B.C.E.), Chinese philosopher and popularizer of authoritarian Legalism

Summary of Event

The Warring States Period is one of the most important eras in Chinese history. The social, political, and philosophical systems that emerged during this time would form the foundation of Chinese civilization for almost two millennia. Politically, this era is seen as a crisis of the old regime. The ancient political power structure rested on the relationship between the emperor and the traditional noble families. This noble class formed the foundation of the early Chinese military. The most important strategic weapon at this time was the war chariot. This mode of warfare demanded horses, bronze weapons, and the chariot itself. The nobles were the only segment of Chinese society that could afford to maintain this equipment. This made these aristocrats extremely important to the welfare of the nation.

As the Zhou Dynasty (Chou; 1066-256 B.C.E.) began to decline, the rulers of the seven major provinces attempted to enrich themselves through military conquest. Traditionally, battles among groups of nobles were regulated by codes of conduct that controlled the actions on the battlefield. A new form of warfare emerged that ignored these traditional codes of conduct. The acceptance of a military philosophy in which the end justified the means increased the carnage and casualties and plunged China into an era of disastrous civil war. The Warring States Period also witnessed the rise of a new group of military professionals who accelerated the decline of the traditional aristocracy. This new martial class directed its energies to the development of strategic and tactical doctrines and laws of warfare that displaced the traditional codes of military conduct. Success on the battlefield based on inflicting heavy casualties on one's enemy became an acceptable practice among this new officer class.

Socially as the acquisition and retention of these professional warriors became more important, the leaders of the warring states were willing to give land, honors, and power to the most successful officers in exchange for their military expertise. This new landed gentry would in time replace the traditional noble families in China's new social structure.

The most important military change was the new emphasis on the use of infantry. To be an effective power, a state had to field and maintain a large standing army. Forces in excess of 250,000 men were commonplace. This in turn necessitated that greater emphasis be placed on the quality of training. The publication of training manuals that codified rules of discipline, training, and tactics became routine. This standardization increased the effectiveness of fighting forces, which in turn increased the likelihood of war. This incessant warfare placed a great economic burden on the leaders of the warring states and forced them to increase their agricultural output; therefore, many of their military campaigns targeted rich agricultural areas.

The political and social upheaval that was so characteristic of the end of the Zhou Dynasty, also known as the Spring and Autumn Period (770-476 B.C.E.), and the subsequent chaos of the Warring States Period set the stage for a Chinese intellectual renaissance. This philosophical golden age created systems that explored every aspect of human behavior, the structure of government, and military theory. This intellectual explosion has been designated by historians as the Hundred Schools of Thought. Scholars of the period have reduced these differing philosophical schools into three main schools: Confucianism, Daoism (Taoism), and Legalism.

The most influential of these schools was Confucianism. Confucius lived during the declining period of the Zhou Dynasty. He was a member of one of the traditional noble families that had fallen on hard times during the chaotic social restructuring of the Spring and Autumn Period. Confucius based his social system on the early, successful days of the Zhou Dynasty. He believed that an orderly, prosperous society was based on the natural social stratification found in the traditional Chinese class system. Confucius wrote that if everyone followed the strict code of ethical conduct found within the confines of his particular class, the nation would prosper. The foundation of this ethical conduct was virtue, and everyone—emperor, noble, warrior, and peasant alike—was expected to follow its dictates. The model for this social paradigm was to be found in the patriarchal structure of the Chinese family. Confucius believed that harsh Legalist codes of law were the result of the breakdown of the family structure, and a nation with an extensive legal structure was exhibiting the major characteristic of a society in decline. Confucius spent his life trying to obtain a position at the court of one of the regional rulers. He was unsuccessful in this quest and went to his grave believing that he was a failure.

The antithesis of the Confucian model was Legalism, the authoritarian response to the social and political chaos of the Warring States Period. Its original proponent was a disciple of the Confucian school, Xunzi, but this theory was popularized by Hanfeizi. The basic principle of Legalism was that people are basically evil, and the carnage and chaos of the period seemed to confirm this negative view of humanity.

The structure of Legalism rested on three concepts: law, legitimacy, and the act of governing. Legalists believed that everyone was equal under the law, and to ensure proper behavior, laws had to be codified and published for all to see. Adherence to these laws formed the basis of a well-run society. Because a Legalist state was theoretically a nation of laws, not people, the legitimacy of a ruler was not based on Confucian virtue but strictly on the individual's ability to gain and hold power. The ruler, in fact, could be considered part of a larger legal apparatus whose primary function was the enforcement of a strict legal code. Legalists believed that the Confucian model of a virtuous leader looking out for the welfare of his people would eventually lead to disorder and failure because most people would mistake kindness for weakness and rise up to overthrow the king. Strict, harsh, authoritarian rule was the only way to ensure a safe, stable society.

The Daoist school was a rejection of the attempt by the first two models to create a human structure to govern society. Daoists believed that all such attempts were futile because they challenged the natural order of the cosmos. Disciples practiced a lifestyle that was in tune with the rhythms of nature in an attempt to find inner peace.

The philosophical inquiries concerning the proper role of government and virtuous personal conduct flowed over into discussions concerning military philosophy. Six of the seven major military classics of early China were either popularized or composed during this time. Military philosophers composed works that encompassed every aspect of military theory. These theories can be subdivided into three categories: the interrelationship between warfare and the state, proper conduct on the battlefield, and the human aspect of war.

All six military classics recognized that warfare and the welfare of the state were closely linked and a government that ignores the possibility of war does so at its own risk. At the same time, most military philosophers warned that if a state focused too much on war and conquest, it would most likely perish by the sword. A sound, well-ordered government would ensure a highly efficient, balanced military establishment.

The military classics also described proper conduct on the battlefield. All theorists believed the first guiding principle should be restraint, whether in deciding to go to war or in determining actions taken in battle and, especially, in victory. The enemy should always be soundly defeated, but after hostilities cease, great care should be taken to treat the surviving forces in humane fashion. Such actions not only are virtuous but also eliminate the possibility of creating a new set of hatreds that in the end could create conditions for another conflict. Finally, every military philosopher believed that it was necessary to have a training program for military personnel that emphasized honor, courage, and self-reliance.

SIGNIFICANCE

The social and political chaos of the Warring States Period created a Chinese culture that demanded stability. The Qin Dynasty (Ch'in; 221-206 B.C.E.) developed a strong central government that subdued the seven warring states and created the beginning of modern China. The new emperor used the authoritarian principles of Legalism to maintain his control. Great emphasis was placed on uniformity, especially in the area of philosophical thought. Books were burned, and dissenting intellectuals were executed. This need for conformity and orthodoxy is a major characteristic of Chinese culture to the present day.

—Richard D. Fitzgerald

FURTHER READING

De Barry, William Theodore, et al., eds. *Sources of Chinese Tradition*. New York: Columbia University Press, 1999. An excellent source for early Chinese cultural history. Index.

Loewe, Michael, and Edward L. Shaughnessy. *The Cambridge History of Ancient China: From the Origins of Civilization to 221 B.C.E.* New York: Cambridge University Press, 1999. A comprehensive overview of the time period. Maps, bibliography, and index.

Sawyer, Ralph. D. *The Seven Military Classics of Ancient China: Translations and Commentary.* San Francisco: Westview Press, 1993. The best collection of Chinese military history available. Index.

Sun-tzu. *The Art of War.* Translated by Samuel B. Griffith. New York: Oxford University Press, 1972. The most important Chinese philosophy of war. Index.

SEE ALSO: 770 B.C.E., Eastern Zhou Dynasty Begins in China; 5th century B.C.E., Composition of the *Spring and Autumn Annals*; 5th-1st century B.C.E., Composition of *The Great Learning*; 500-400 B.C.E., Creation of the *Wujing*; 479 B.C.E., Confucius's Death Leads to the Creation of *The Analects*; c. 285-c. 255 B.C.E, Xunzi Develops Teachings That Lead to Legalism; 285-160 B.C.E. (traditionally, c. 300 B.C.E.), Composition of the *Zhuangzi*; 221 B.C.E., Qin Dynasty Founded in China; 221-206 B.C.E., Legalist Movement in China; 140-87 B.C.E., Wudi Rules Han Dynasty China; 104 B.C.E., Dong Zhongshu Systematizes Confucianism; 9-23 C.E., Wang Mang's Rise to Power; 25 C.E., Guang Wudi Restores the Han Dynasty.

RELATED ARTICLES in *Great Lives from History: The Ancient World*: Confucius; Hanfeizi; Xunzi; Zhuangzi.

c. 467 B.C.E.

GOŚĀLA MASKARĪPUTRA, FOUNDER OF ĀJĪVIKA SECT, DIES

Gośāla Maskarīputra founded a religious and philosophical sect of radical determinists, during the same era when the Jain and Buddhist religions were being established.

LOCALE: Savatthi, Magadha (now in India)
CATEGORIES: Philosophy; religion

KEY FIGURES

Vardhamāna (c. 599-527 B.C.E.), ascetic monk who revived Jainism and is considered its historical founder

Gośāla Maskarīputra (sixth century-c. 467 B.C.E.), founder of Ājīvika sect

SUMMARY OF EVENT

The story of the death of Gośāla Maskarīputra (also known as Gośāla Mankhaliputta, Markali, and Goshala Maskariputra) is recorded in the *Bhagavati Sūtra* (c. fourth century C.E.; *Sudharma Svami's Bhagavati Sutra* 1973), a text of the Jain religion written probably about eight hundred years after Gośāla died. Because the tale was recorded so long after the event and because the Jains regarded the Ājīvika sect founded by Gośāla as a heresy, many of its details should therefore be regarded with a great deal of skepticism.

The historical period of Gośāla's life and death was a time of great social and religious change in India. About a century before Gośāla's time, kingdoms and republics began to rise in India, replacing the earlier tribal organization of society. The emergence of stable, organized political institutions was accompanied by increasing trade and commerce. Social change led to philosophical and religious questions about the nature of life and the place of humanity in the universe. The old Vedantic faith of India, which would develop into the religious tradition that eventually became known as Hinduism, was unsatisfying to many people. New religious teachings began to offer fresh answers. One of these teachings, Buddhism, spread from India through much of Asia and became a major world faith. Another, Jainism, continues to exist today as a minority religion in India. The Ājīvika faith was a third teaching that survived for about a thousand years after its founder but eventually disappeared or was dissolved into Hinduism. There are references to the Ājīvikas and to Gośāla Maskarīputra in the texts of both the Buddhists and the Jains, but the Jain writings give the most attention to the sect. This is apparently because of the close connections between the Jains and the Ājīvikas during the early years of the two teachings.

In the Jain version of Gośāla's end, the founder of the Ājīvikas died as a result of a conflict with Vardhamāna, the great teacher of the Jain faith. According to the *Bhagavati Sūtra*, the two religious leaders had been companions earlier in their lives. This Sanskrit language text tells us that Vardhamāna was living in a shed at the village of Nalanda when Gośāla went to the Jain sage and begged to be allowed to become Vardhamāna's disciple. After several rejections, Gośāla was accepted, and the two holy men wandered together for six years. During their wanderings and adventures together, Gośāla was impressed by Vardhamāna's magical powers and wanted to acquire these kinds of powers for himself. After observing Vardhamāna's ascetic practices, Gośāla sat down by a lake facing the sun, with his hands raised above his head. He remained in this position for six months, eating only a handful of beans every three days. At the end of this period, Gośāla is said to have acquired the magical powers he desired. Afterward, the two parted ways, becoming rival teachers.

Gośāla apparently lived for another sixteen years after acquiring his powers, establishing his headquarters in a pottery shop in the town of Savatthi. His teachings attracted a number of disciples among the seekers of his age. The disciples who gathered around him at Savatthi were the first of the Ājīvika communities that were to spread and persist long after his death. The meaning of the term *ājīvika* is unclear, but many scholars believe that it can be translated as "one who follows the ascetic way."

Toward the end of his life, in the account given by the *Bhagavati Sutra*, Gośāla was visited at Savatthi by six holy men known as the *disacaras*. This is apparently a reference to a conference or council held at Savatthi by Gośāla and his major disciples. The Ājīvika doctrines seem to have been discussed and refined at this conference, and it probably began the process of assembling the Ājīvika scriptures from earlier writings. These scriptures have been lost in the centuries since the disappearance of the Ājīvika religion, but selections from them have survived as disapproving quotations in Buddhist and Jain texts.

Gośāla is supposed to have visited Vardhamāna not long after the meeting with the six holy men. The Ājīvika sage was angry because the Jain leader had talked about

Gośāla's lowly birth and about shameful incidents during the time the two were together. Gośāla threatened Vardhamāna with magic, but Vardhamāna simply answered that the magic would only affect Gośāla himself, who would soon be stricken with fever and die.

Gośāla made his way back to his shed and fell into the foretold fever. During his sickness, he is said to have proclaimed some of the last doctrines of his religion. He then gave instructions for an elaborate funeral, during which his followers would proclaim the death of the last *tīrthaṅkara*, or ford-maker. Before dying, though, Gośāla repented and announced that he was a fraud and that Vardhamāna was the true ford-maker. The Ājīvika leader told his followers to tie a rope around his foot and to drag his body through the streets of Savatthi, praising Vardhamāna. The followers, though, only drew a map of Savatthi on the floor of the pottery shop and, after dragging the body over the map, held funeral celebrations according to the original instructions before cremating the body.

The tale of Gośāla's repentance and death-bed conversion should be regarded with skepticism because it is the Jain version. Still, it does indicate that the Jains and the Ājīvikas had once been closely connected, possibly even members of the same sect, and that there was some bitterness when the two went their separate ways.

Both the Ājīvikas and Jains held that humankind had been visited by twenty-three *tīrthaṅkaras* who brought sacred truth. However, the Jains maintained that the twenty-fourth and last *tīrthaṅkara* was their sage, Vardhamāna, while the Ājīvikas believed that Gośāla was the twenty-fourth *tīrthaṅkara*. The Jains believed that the human spirit had to struggle for salvation from the material world and that the spirit could conquer the material world by practicing nonviolence and by renouncing the passions and the bodily senses. By contrast, the Ājīvikas believed that nothing existed except the material world, which was locked into an unbreakable chain of cause and effect. The basic principle of Gośāla's teaching was the concept of *niyata*, which is translated as "order" or "fate." In his view, the universe was a system of interconnected forces in which every event happened by necessity. Gośāla accepted the common Indian idea of the rebirth of souls. However, although other Indian religions hold that rebirth is influenced by good or bad actions, Gośāla maintained that all sin and virtue had no effect. One's past, present, and future births and all other events were simply the working out of a completely determined destiny. It was not simply that one's will could change nothing. Free will itself was an illusion. Every individual was destined to go through a chain of births before ultimately ending in extinction. Faced with this utter powerlessness, the Ājīvikas believed that all one could do was to follow a life of simplicity and renunciation.

Significance

Communities of Ājīvika believers continued to exist in India for about a thousand years after Gośāla's death. Although the Ājīvikas diappeared by about the fourteenth or fifteenth century, many scholars believe that they left influences on some of the Hindu sects of southern India. Gośāla Maskarīputra therefore left a heritage that occupies a notable, although minor, place in the religious history of India.

The life and death of Gośāla Maskarīputra are also significant for any study of the intellectual history of a critical period in ancient India. Gośāla's teachings illustrate the variety of philosophical and religious perspectives that flourished when Buddhism and Jainism appeared. His thorough determinism, his materialism, and his rejection of the idea of free will contrast sharply with the gods and rituals of India's earlier religious beliefs. These teachings of Gośāla also have much in common with many modern scientific world views.

—*Carl L. Bankston III*

Further Reading

Basham, A. L. *History and Doctrines of the Ājīvikas: A Vanished Indian Religon*. 1951. Reprint. New Delhi, India: Motilal Banarsidass, 1981. An essential work on the Ājīvikas that contains an extensive discussion of the Buddhist and Jain versions of the life of Gośāla.

Charoborti, Haripada. *Asceticism in Ancient India: In Brahmanical, Buddhist, Jaina, and Ājīvika Societies (From the Earliest Times to the Period of Sankaracharya)*. Columbia, Mo.: South Asian Books, 1993. A useful work on the religious communities of ancient India and one of the few that devotes substantial attention to the Ājīvikas.

Dundas, Paul. *The Jains*. New York: Routledge, 2002. An excellent book on the history and practice of Jainism.

See also: 6th or 5th century B.C.E., Birth of Buddhism; 527 B.C.E., Death of Vardhamāna, Founder of Jainism; c. 200 B.C.E., Birth of Hinduism.

Related articles in *Great Lives from History: The Ancient World*: Buddha; Gośāla Maskarīputra; Vardhamāna.

c. 456/455 B.C.E.
GREEK TRAGEDIAN AESCHYLUS DIES

Aeschylus, the acknowledged master of Greek tragedy even during his lifetime, established many of the artistic and literary conventions of Western theater.

LOCALE: Gela, Sicily
CATEGORIES: Cultural and intellectual history; literature

KEY FIGURES

Aeschylus (525/524-456/455 B.C.E.), the earliest of the three extant Greek tragedians, known as the father of Greek tragedy, who developed the ideas of protagonist, antagonist, and supporting actor

Hieron I of Syracuse (c. sixth century-466 B.C.E.), tyrant of Syracuse, patron of the arts, and friend of Aeschylus, who died in his kingdom

SUMMARY OF EVENT

It is beyond doubt that Aeschylus died in the town of Gela, Sicily, in about 456 or 455 B.C.E. Even so, as often happens when famous personages die, especially suddenly and in cultures that privilege mythic explanations of historical events, a clearly apocryphal version of that death is the one that survives. Such is the case for Aeschylus. Supposedly an eagle, while attempting to crack the shell of a tortoise for food, dropped it on the playwright's bald head, mistaking it for a stone. As with most such explanations, this fanciful version of the event fastens on Aeschylus's self-imposed exile to Sicily; the playwright's sudden death, ironically after having survived three of the most devastating battles of the Greco-Persian War; and the undeniable fact that in regions with the topography of Sicily, birds of prey actually do obtain their food by cracking the tortoise shells on large rocks.

The indignity that the folkloric version of Aeschylus's death ascribes to the most dignified of all the Greek tragedians also lampoons Aeschylus's sober, conservative appearance and artistic outlook. The bust of Aeschylus in Rome's Capitoline Museum portrays a man with piercing eyes, an aquiline nose, a full beard, and a high noble forehead, an unusual man for whom baldness actually enhances his appearance. Aeschylus was also a soldier of conspicuous bravery who had fought the Persians at the battles of Marathon (490 B.C.E.), Salamis (480 B.C.E.), and Plataea (479 B.C.E.). He came from one of Eleusis's most noble families, and his brother Cynegirus met his death at Marathon.

It is clear that Athenians considered Aeschylus a great artist as well as a patriot. Soon after his death, all the clans (or *phratries*) of the city's most ancient families displayed his bust adorned with the laurel wreath presented to victorious playwrights at the theater contest known as the Dionysia. Aristophanes' comedy *Batrachoi* (405 B.C.E.; *The Frogs*, 1780) has his character of Aeschylus declare, "I am dead, but my poetry lives." Even Sophocles stands aside in Aristophanes' play rather than presume to challenge Aeschylus as the master of Greek tragedy. The herald of the ancient Athenian murder court known as the Areopagus blew the Tyrrhenian trumpet that traditionally opened its sessions in honor of Aeschylus. In doing so, he recalled the playwright who had celebrated both that court and Athens' patron goddess Athena in his play *Eumenides*, part of his trilogy *Oresteia* (458 B.C.E.; English translation, 1777). All of these are measures of Aeschylus's fame.

The question to be answered is why a playwright so obviously celebrated, even during his lifetime, would have died so obscurely so far from the city he loved. Why would Aeschylus have remained for two extended periods of his life at the court of a Syracusan tyrant? It is clear that Aeschylus always had his detractors. Some viewed his plays as overly conservative, or they criticized the formalism of his set speeches and linear plotlines. In doing so, they privileged the dramatic tension of the tragedies of Sophocles (c. 496-406 B.C.E.), the irreverence of the tragicomedies of Euripides (c. 485-406 B.C.E.), or the elegant rhetoric of Thespis (before 535-after 501 B.C.E.) and Phrynichus (c. 510-c. 476 B.C.E.).

The Greek lexicographer Suidas (fl. 970 C.E.) claims that Aeschylus was brought before the very same Areopagus that had honored him, charged with having indirectly caused the deaths that occurred in the collapse of a theater that was staging one of his works. Rather than face a verdict, Aeschylus exercised the option available to every person accused of a criminal charge and chose voluntary exile, at Hieron I of Syracuse's court. However, Aelian, a Greek historian of the second century C.E., declared that Aeschylus, who was a full member of the Demeter cult at his native Eleusis, had blasphemed by revealing the secrets of the Eleusinian Mysteries, and that to avoid a charge of religious impiety elected an extended residence in Sicily following 470 B.C.E.

Far more likely than either of these alternatives is the explanation that Aeschylus simply accepted Hieron's invitation to stay at his court in the role of a distinguished literary personage. It was, indeed, the policy of the Sicilian tyrant to grant subventions to the famous artists of the day. The lyric poets Pindar (c. 518-c. 438 B.C.E.) and Simonides (c. 556-c. 467 B.C.E.) were definitely recipients of Hireon's largess. This would also account for the second visit that Aeschylus made to Hieron's court in the year before his death.

Aeschylus certainly had his detractors, but no indication exists that there is anything suspicious in his death. Alone among the tragedians, his plays, numbering anywhere between seventy-two and ninety depending on the list one consults, received the extraordinary privilege of revival to compete with newly written plays. Neither Sophocles nor Euripides received such an honor. Indeed, it can be argued that the right of revival combined with the overwhelming power of Aeschylus's output was one element paradoxically responsible for discouraging new playwrights after his death. Based on contemporary testimony, Aeschylus's plays continued to win more than half of the theater contests held after their author's death.

What appears to be a consistent pattern of recognition during Aeschylus's lifetime seems only to have increased after his death. The orator Lycurgus of Athens (396-325 B.C.E.) called for a bronze statue of Aeschylus to be erected at Athens. Bronze was reserved for larger-than-life statues of deities. At Gela, the town in which Aeschylus died, an epitaph said to have been written by the playwright himself is noteworthy for several reasons. It may be translated as follows:

> This tomb hides the dust of Aeschylus,
> Son of Euphorion and pride of Gela.
> Marathon may tell how tried was his valor,
> And the long-haired Medes, who knew it well, May do so too.

The epitaph is extraordinary, especially if Aeschylus did write it himself, first because it does not refer at all to Aeschylus as a playwright. Second, while it identifies Aeschylus as son of a noble of Eleusis, it mentions neither that city nor the city of Athens, in which Aeschylus had achieved his fame. Rather, it appears to adopt Gela as the playwright's native city. It gives prominent mention, however, to Aeschylus's heroism in the Greco-Persian War, and it forces this acknowledgment even from his enemies.

As with so much of the folklore surrounding Aeschylus's death, in the case of the epitaph one must also read past the metaphor. Certainly, the death of Aeschylus was unexpected. An eagle, Zeus's bird, was said to have been its agent; in other words, divine destiny took him. The epitaph that records a death far from home at the court of a tyrant who privileged the arts as well as military achievement would naturally focus on Aeschylus's heroism in the Greco-Persian War. While extolling this, it simultaneously adopts the playwright as Gela's honorary citizen, making Aeschylus's tomb both a local shrine and a place of pilgrimage.

Aeschylus. (Library of Congress)

SIGNIFICANCE

Aeschylus moved Greek drama clearly and finally away from a purely choral art to one that featured three primary actors in dialogue with the chorus. Sophocles' plays would feature this device, thereby creating the exceptional dramatic tension which identifies his plays.

The three most famous Greek tragedians, Aeschylus, Sophocles, and Euripides, all flourished within the fifth century. The productions of their plays dovetail and Greek dramatic style moves quickly from Aeschylus's conservative patriotism to Euripides' tragicomedy. The comic playwright Aristophanes poses the aesthetic question implicit in the contemporaneous lives of these three playwrights in his play *Frogs*, produced in 405 B.C.E., one year after the deaths of both Sophocles and Euripides. The central feature of the play is a rhetoric contest held between Aeschylus and Euripides in the Underworld to see who should receive the laurel crown.

Significantly, Sophocles withdraws from the contest in favor of Aeschylus, though Euripides remains—and loses to Aeschylus. This outcome reflects Aeschylus's desire for a more elegant, rhetorically based dramatic form than it does public taste of the late fifth century.

—*Robert J. Forman*

FURTHER READING

Aylen, Leo. *The Greek Theater.* Rutherford, N.J.: Fairleigh Dickinson University Press, 1985. A nontechnical survey written from the perspective of a theater director contemplating the production of a Greek play. Contains a brief examination of theater logistics with separate chapters on production, choral dance, and a good discussion of Aeschylus's *Prometheus Bound*.

Bieber, Margarite. *History of the Greek and Roman Theater.* 1939. Reprint. Princeton, N.J.: Princeton University Press, 1961. A profusely illustrated volume that traces the development of ancient theater with chapters on every phase of ancient theater development.

Bloom, Harold, ed. *Aeschylus: Comprehensive Research and Study Guide*. New York: Chelsea House, 2001. Presents important twentieth century criticism from a variety of perspectives, as well as a critical biography, a chronology of Aeschylus's life, an index, and an introductory essay by Bloom.

Csapo, Eric, William J. Slater, and Judith Barringer. *The Context of Ancient Drama*. Ann Arbor: University of Michigan Press, 1995. An excellent work on the cultural, political, and historical context in which the ancient plays were produced.

Forman, Robert J. *Classical Greek and Roman Drama: An Annotated Bibliography.* Pasadena, Calif.: Salem Press, 1989. A survey of the development of Greek and Roman drama with annotated references to editions, translations, as well as primary and secondary works of criticism.

Green, Richard, and Eric Handley. *Images of the Greek Theater.* Austin: University of Texas Press, 1995. An impressive collection of depictions of performances, productions, actors, and stage settings as represented on ancient Greek pottery.

Mylonas, George E. *Eleusis and the Eleusinian Mysteries*. Princeton, N.J.: Princeton University Press, 1961. Remains an excellent source on information about the rites of Demeter that were held in Aeschylus's place of birth.

Pickard-Cambridge, A. W. *The Dramatic Festivals of Athens*. 2d rev. ed. Edited by S. Gould and D. Lewis. New York: Oxford University Press, 1989. Contains information of the Greater Dionysia at Eleusis, the major Pan-Hellenic theater festival. Has been revised in line with modern archaeological findings.

_______. *The Theater of Dionysus in Athens*. New York: Oxford University Press, 1946. Remains the major source of information for the site of the Lesser Dionysia, the theater festival held at Athens.

SEE ALSO: c. 750 B.C.E., Homer Composes the *Iliad*; c. 700 B.C.E., Hesiod Composes *Theogony* and *Works and Days*; Before 600 B.C.E., Celebration of the Eleusinian Mysteries; c. 580 B.C.E., Greek Poet Sappho Dies; c. 438 B.C.E., Greek Lyric Poet Pindar Dies; 406 B.C.E., Greek Dramatist Euripides Dies; c. 385 B.C.E., Greek Playwright Aristophanes Dies.

RELATED ARTICLES in *Great Lives from History: The Ancient World:* Aeschylus; Aristophanes; Euripides; Menander (dramatist); Pindar; Simonides; Sophocles; Thespis.

451-449 B.C.E.
TWELVE TABLES OF ROMAN LAW ARE FORMULATED

The Twelve Tables of Roman law established a code of laws to check the power of the patricians against the lower orders of Roman society.

LOCALE: Rome (now in Italy)
CATEGORY: Laws, acts, and legal history

KEY FIGURES

Gaius Terentilius Harsa (fl. fifth century B.C.E.), plebeian tribune who led opposition against the excessive, tyrannical authority of the consuls

Appius Claudius Crassus (fl. fifth century B.C.E.), chair of first decemvirate, decemvir 450-451 B.C.E., consul 471 and 451 B.C.E.

SUMMARY OF EVENT

The formulation of the Twelve Tables of Roman Law, as recorded by Livy (59-17 B.C.E.) and Dionysius of Halicarnassus (fl. c. 20 C.E.), was one of the most significant events in the "struggle of the orders" between patricians and plebeians in Rome during the fifth century B.C.E. In 462 B.C.E., according to the traditional date, Gaius Terentilius Harsa, a tribune of the plebs, made a spirited attack on the authority of the consuls, charging that their unregulated and unlimited power brought down all the terrors and penalties of the law on the plebs. Harsa suggested that five men should be appointed to compose a code of laws that would put a check on the patricians, who, as judges, were interpreters of the unwritten customary law and, as priests, determined the validity of the complex legal procedures. His proposal was rejected, as was another in 454 when the tribunes suggested that a commission composed of both patricians and plebeians should draw up the code.

In 452 B.C.E., the tribunes insisted that the work of codification should begin. To expedite the task, it was decided that the ordinary magistracies should be suspended and that, instead, *decemviri legibus scribundis* (ten men for writing the laws) should be chosen to rule the state the following year without being subject to appeal. After some debate, the plebeians agreed to surrender their demand to be represented on the board along with the patricians, but they did so with the understanding that their sacral laws would not be abrogated.

The ten elected decemvirs set about framing the laws and set them up on ten tables in the Forum. After amending them according to suggestions received, they presented their work to the *comitia centuriata* for formal ratification. It soon became apparent that two more tables would have to be added to make the corpus complete, and so the decemvirs were again elected by the *comitia centuriata* after considerable canvassing. Appius Claudius Crassus, who had been chairman of the first decemvirate, was reelected with nine new colleagues.

The second decemvirate is traditionally pictured as drafting the two additional tables amid a reign of terror. For some unknown reason, they began to act like tyrants by oppressing the plebeians, and only a secession of the plebs forced them out of office at the expiration of their commission. Legendary though much of this account of the formulation of the Twelve Tables may be, there is little doubt about the antiquity of the ancient code, which Livy, with some exaggeration, describes as "the source of all public and private law" for Rome.

Although the original text of the Twelve Tables is said to have been lost in the sack of Rome by the Gauls around 390 B.C.E., copies remained so that Cicero (106-43 B.C.E.) reported in his *De legibus* (52 B.C.E.; *On the Laws*, 1841) that boys still had to memorize them in his day. Provisions of the code were never repealed, although many lapsed through neglect and irrelevancy. Some 140 fragments or paraphrases show that the code was genuinely Roman in content and largely a codification of already existing custom. The code had only two constitutional provisions: one forbidding *privilegia*, and the other forbidding trial of a citizen on a capital charge by any assembly except the *comitia centuriata*.

Dealing with private, public, and sacral law, the code concerned itself, among other matters, with the guardianship and status of women and property, the guardianship of lunatics and prodigals, division of inheritances, and rights concerning land. Assembly at night was forbidden. The laws were absolute imperatives and protected property above life; an insolvent debtor, for example, could be fettered for sixty days and then executed or put up for sale. Many believed that the code allowed dismemberment of a debtor's body to satisfy several creditors. A person was permitted to kill a thief only if the thief came at night or actually used a weapon. Deformed children were to be killed. Blood revenge was recognized if satisfaction was denied in other ways. As absolute head of the family, the father could, with certain safeguards, sell his sons into slavery. Although marriage rites were simple, intermarriage between plebeian and patrician was forbidden.

Penalties were harsh, and death was meted out in five different ways, including burning at the stake and casting from the Tarpeian rock. Bribery, libel, sorcery, cutting other people's crops, and even theft were capital offenses. Besides the death penalty, other forms of punishments that were recognized included being fined, fettered, or flogged; retaliation in kind; civil disgrace; banishment, and slavery. Fines for injuring persons were graduated according to the value traditionally ascribed to individuals. Plebeians gained benefits through a law allowing a thirty-day interval to discharge a debt before the infliction of penalty. Interest was fixed, probably at 8.3 percent, and "not according to the free choice of the wealthy."

SIGNIFICANCE

Apart from their legal significance, the Twelve Tables are of great interest to philologists because of the archaic language used and to historians because the ordinances provide the best information available on the economic and social conditions of Rome during the fifth century B.C.E. However, it is their legal legacy that is most important, as the Roman Empire spread, not only the Latin language, but also Roman law throughout most of Europe and the Mediterranean world. In many of Rome's provinces, Roman law formed the basis of later medieval law, albeit syncretized with elements of local custom.

—*M. Joseph Costelloe, updated by Jeffrey L. Buller*

FURTHER READING

Coleman-Norton, P. R. *The Twelve Tables Prefaced, Arranged, Translated, Annotated*. Princeton, N.J.: Princeton University Press, 1952. The best place to begin for readers interested in examining the primary source material on the Twelve Tables.

Cornell, Tim. *The Beginnings of Rome: Italy and Rome from the Bronze Age to the Punic Wars (c. 1000-264 B.C.)*. New York: Routledge, 1995. This general history contains a chapter specifically on the Twelve Tables and their role in the formation of Roman identity.

Diosdi, Gyorgy. *Contract in Roman Law: From the Twelve Tables to the Glossators*. Translated by J. Szabo. Budapest: Akademiai Kiado, 1981. Limited to only one aspect of the legal code, this work traces the development of Roman contract law from its origins in the Twelve Tables.

Gardner, Jane F. *Being a Roman Citizen*. New York: Routledge, 1993. A good introduction for the general reader on the impact of Roman law upon private life. Written in a popular style but well researched.

Lobingier, Charles Sumner. *The Evolution of the Roman Law*. Littleton, Colo.: F. B. Rothman, 1987. Although now somewhat dated (it was originally released in 1923), this work is still an excellent survey of Roman law from the period before the Twelve Tables to the major legal codes of the late Empire.

Stein, Peter. *Roman Law in European History*. New York: Cambridge University Press, 1999. A short but illuminating introduction to the influence and legacy of Roman law, beginning with the Twelve Tables.

Watson, Alan. *The Evolution of Law*. Baltimore: The Johns Hopkins University Press, 1985. A good general introduction on the history and development of Roman law.

SEE ALSO: 445 B.C.E., Establishment of the Canuleian Law; 340-338 B.C.E., Origin of *Municipia*; c. 300 B.C.E., Stoics Conceptualize Natural Law; 287 B.C.E., *Lex Hortensia* Reforms the Roman Constitution; 90 B.C.E., Julian Law Expands Roman Citizenship.

c. 450-c. 425 B.C.E.
HISTORY DEVELOPS AS A SCHOLARLY DISCIPLINE

History developed as scholarly discipline, establishing historiography as a literary and scientific genre.

LOCALE: Samos, Athens, and the Greek colony of Thurii in Italy

CATEGORIES: Historiography; cultural and intellectual history

KEY FIGURES

Hecataeus of Miletus (fl. c. sixth-fifth century B.C.E.), early geographer and genealogist who made geography and history into a science

Herodotus (c. 484-c. 425 B.C.E.), Greek historian who wrote the first work of history

Thucydides (c. 459-c. 402 B.C.E.), Greek historian who was an early founder of history as a discipline

SUMMARY OF EVENT

Herodotus's monumental history of the Greco-Persian Wars, *Historiai Herodotou* (c. 424 B.C.E.; *The History*, 1709), established its author as "the father of history," in the words of the Roman philosopher and statesman Cicero (106-43 B.C.E.). It is an extraordinary work, combining history in the modern sense with geography, anthropology, and comparative religion.

As part of the unprecedented intellectual movement that began in the fifth century B.C.E., Herodotus was in the midst of a philosophical revolution initiated by Socrates (c. 470-399 B.C.E.), perfected by Plato (c. 427-347 B.C.E.), and culminating with Aristotle (384-322 B.C.E.). In an analogous fashion, Herodotus initiated the new style of historiography, Hecataeus of Miletus (fl. sixth-fifth centuries B.C.E.) solidified the notion of scientific historical and geographical evidence, and Thucydides crowned their efforts.

Like most genres, history did not achieve maturity in its first form. Herodotus, while groping for the historical perspective mastered by Thucydides a generation later, retained many characteristics of his diverse predecessors. The Greek poet Homer (early ninth century-late ninth century B.C.E.) influenced him significantly; critics have pointed out that epic poetry, for centuries the repository of records of the Greek past, probably hindered the development of history as a discipline through its emphasis on the biographical rather than the institutional, its theistic-humanistic philosophy, and its appeal to romance and excitement.

Herodotus clearly derived much from the poets: the art of holding interest by intermingling digressions with narrative, the significance put on characterization of leaders, and, most important, a view of history as controlled to a great degree by the gods. Like his contemporaries, the great dramatists Sophocles (c. 496-c. 406 B.C.E.) and Aeschylus (525/524-456/455 B.C.E.), Herodotus followed Homer in viewing human affairs as divinely ordained: Man is a creature of fate, often a suffering victim. Like the heroes of classical tragedy, Herodotus's kings and princes become arrogant in their wealth and power and bring catastrophe on themselves. Once the Persian prince Xerxes I (c. 519-465 B.C.E.) chastises the sea, the reader knows his great host crossing the Hellespont is headed toward destruction.

Although Herodotus worked objectively, sometimes resembling a modern-day anthropologist or ethnographer, he imbued his work with divine plans and predestinations in the Homeric tradition. The use of history to defend the existence of a divine power is common in ancient and modern historiography. The eighteenth century historian Edward Gibbon believed in divine cycles in history, each of which was initiated by a divine figure such as Moses, Jesus, or Muḥammad. Thucydides, in contrast to Herodotus, treated history in a more dispassionate manner. He was interested in the simple formula of "Who, what, where, and when?" His *Historia tou Peloponnesiacou polemou* (431-404 B.C.E.; *History of the Peloponnesian War*, 1550) is a masterpiece of historiography. He advised historians not to be "masked by exaggerated fancies of the poets" or the stories of chroniclers who "seek to please the ear rather than to speak the truth."

Although epic was the most popular record of the past in the Greek world of the seventh and sixth centuries B.C.E., Ionian writers were gradually developing prose accounts of the geography and customs of the areas they visited as they sailed on trading expeditions around the Mediterranean. The exposure to a variety of cultures seems to have developed in them a rational, often skeptical spirit, and they began to cast the eye of reason on the myths that passed for history among their people. Only fragments have survived to indicate the nature of these semihistorical works. The remains of two treatises by Hecataeus of Miletus, who wrote during the latter part of the sixth century B.C.E., are probably representative of the new school of thought. In his *Genealogia* (c. 500 B.C.E.; genealogies), he attempted to give rational expla-

Herodotus. (Library of Congress)

nations for familiar tales of the gods and heroes who were purportedly the ancestors of the Greeks of his own day. More significant for Herodotus was Hecataeus's *Ges Periodos* (c. 500 B.C.E.; tour around the world), his account of his observations on his journeys into Egypt, Persia, mainland Greece, and the countries near the Black Sea.

Thus, Herodotus began his work with a foundation in the epic concept of the relationship of god and humankind, and an Ionian-inspired curiosity about humankind and society, along with a rationalistic and skeptical approach to mythical history. To these perspectives must be added his strong pro-Athenian bias. Born in the Dorian city of Halicarnassus on the coast of Asia Minor, Herodotus lived in Athens for much of the period between 454 and 443, when he helped to colonize Thurii in Italy. He was thus a part of the flowering of Periclean Athens during the years between the end of the Greco-Persian Wars in 479 and the beginning of the Peloponnesian War in 431. It was during these years that he probably derived his strong faith in the free state and its ability to triumph over tyranny, a belief that becomes a significant theme in the histories.

To assess *The History* as history, it is perhaps useful to note that the Greek word *histor* means "observer," or "recorder," rather than "analyst of facts," and Herodotus is a historian in this sense more than in the modern one. Especially in the first six books, he refers repeatedly to what he has seen or what he has been told. He does not uncritically accept everything he hears, but neither does he attempt to sort out every conflicting account.

Like Thucydides, Herodotus was committed to objective reporting. In book 7, he writes, "My duty is to report all that is said, but I am not obliged to believe it all alike." For the most part he was fair and impartial. For example, despite his fervent Greek patriotism, he gave a meticulous and largely accurate account of the enemy's history and cultural practices.

Herodotus's work begins with a discussion of the earliest conflicts between the Near Eastern and western Mediterranean cultures and an account of the growth of the Persian Empire. As he recounts each new conquest, he digresses to describe the customs of the soon-to-be invaded nation: Lydia, Assyria, Egypt, Ethiopia, Scythia, India, and Arabia. He traces the careers of successive Persian monarchs, Cyrus the Great (c. 601/590-530 B.C.E.), Cambyses II (d. 522 B.C.E.), and Darius the Great (550-486 B.C.E.), setting the stage for the massive expedition of Xerxes I against the Greeks. Initially more digression than narrative, Herodotus's work sharpens its focus as it moves toward the climax, the account of the battles that culminated in the Persian defeat at Salamis in 480 B.C.E.

SIGNIFICANCE

Herodotus was criticized by ancient and modern historians on various charges. The Greek biographer Plutarch (c. 46-after 120 C.E.) dubbed him "the flatterer of Athens." He was considered by various historians a mere industrious compiler of gossip, a moralizer, inept in military tactics and statistics. For example, he reported the size of the Persian army as five million—too inflated by any ancient or modern estimation. He was also accused of plagiarism, dishonestly using Ionian chronicles as eyewitness reports and even doing that uncritically. Some downplayed his *History* as inconsistent, lacking unity of purpose or direction.

Some of these accusations have been proven false or exaggerated. Herodotus worked within the limitations of his time. He had little evidence to verify the accounts of his eyewitnesses. He was careful in crediting what he noted, distinguishing between things he saw and things he only heard. He revisited battlefields and alleged army routes. He often used inscriptions on monuments and quoted extensively from temple records at Delphi. As a tourist-historian at Egyptian pyramids, he gave a meticulous, although at times speculative, account of what he saw. Only in the last two centuries have geographers, archaeologists, and anthropologists confirmed many of his observations.

Herodotus was an intelligent and observant historian with good faith and tolerance for diverse cultures. The unity of his work comes from his deep religious convictions and notion of history as divine epic. Many historians consider him the father of history without whose work modern readers would have been deprived of invaluable insights into the ancient world.

—Elizabeth Johnston Lipscomb,
updated by Chogollah Maroufi

Further Reading

Brunt, P. A. *Studies in Greek History and Thought.* New York: Oxford University Press, 1993. Meticulous accounts of early Greek ideas on historiography and historical analysis.

Derow, Peter, Robert Parker, and Robert A. Sedgewick, eds. *Herodotus and His World.* New York: Oxford University Press, 2003. A lively and diverse set of essays on Herodotus in his cultural, historical, and literary context. Discusses topics such as Herodotus's attitudes toward ethnicity, tradition and history, the supernatural, religion, chronology, and epigraphy.

Harrison, Thomas. *Divinity and History: The Religion of Herodotus.* New York: Oxford University Press, 2002. Scholars have tended to view Herodotus's depictions of religion as separate from his conception of history; this work shows how the two are intimately interrelated and discusses how this relationship should affect the reading of his work.

Hornblower, Simon, ed. *Greek Historiography.* Oxford: Clarendon Press, 1994. This is a challenging and rich book. It has a thorough and extensive introduction (seventy-two pages) and an extensive bibliography.

Luraghi, Nino, ed. *The Historian's Craft in the Age of Herodotus.* New York: Oxford University Press, 2002. A collection of essays on a wide variety of topics in fifth century B.C.E. historiography.

Thomas, Rosalind. *Herodotus in Context: Ethnography, Science, and the Art of Persuasion.* New York: Cambridge University Press, 2002. Examines the intellectual context of Herodotus's work, particularly in his descriptions of foreign and exotic lands and peoples.

See also: 480-479 B.C.E., Persian Invasion of Greece; c. 440 B.C.E., Sophists Train the Greeks in Rhetoric and Politics; May, 431-September, 404 B.C.E., Peloponnesian War; c. 380 B.C.E., Plato Develops His Theory of Ideas; May, 431-September, 404 B.C.E., Peloponnesian War; 1st century B.C.E., Sima Qian Writes Chinese History; 54 B.C.E., Roman Poet Catullus Dies; c. 99-105 C.E., Ban Zhao Writes Behavior Guide for Young Women.

Related articles in *Great Lives from History: The Ancient World*: Cyrus the Great; Darius the Great; Herodotus; Homer; Flavius Josephus; Livy; Polybius; Sima Qian; Tacitus; Thucydides; Xerxes I.

450-100 B.C.E.
CITY-STATE OF YEHA FLOURISHES IN THE ETHIOPIAN HIGHLANDS

Yeha, an ancient city and the center of the earliest kingdom in Ethiopia, influenced subsequent cultural and political developments in that region.

LOCALE: Tigray highlands, northern Ethiopia (now in Eritrea)
CATEGORY: Prehistory and ancient cultures

SUMMARY OF EVENT

The northern highlands of Ethiopia, including present-day Eritrea, with its temperate climate, summer rains, and fertile soil, are believed to be one of the earliest centers of agrarian development and large-scale settlements. The noted Russian plant geneticist, Nikolay Vavilov, who investigated Ethiopian crops, concluded that the cultivation of barley and other cereals, such as teff (*Eragrostis abyssinica*) and noug (*Guizotia abyssinica*), developed autonomously in Ethiopia quite early in the Neolithic revolution.

Trade between Egypt and this region of the Horn of Africa (referred to by the Egyptians as the land of Punt) is known to have existed as far back as the Fifth Dynasty in the middle of the third millennium B.C.E. This Egyptian contact continued down to the time of Ramses III around 1200 B.C.E. Rodolfo Fattovich, who has studied the history of ancient urbanization in northeast Africa, suggests that traders from the plateau of eastern Tigray played an important role as intermediaries between the hinterland and the coast. The material culture dating back at least to the early first millennium B.C.E. also indicates that there existed a sustained commercial interaction between the communities of northern Ethiopia bordering the Red Sea and those on the South Arabian side. Evidence indicates that more complex societies that participated in long-distance trade evolved among the mixture of Cushitic and Semitic-speaking peoples that inhabited the plateau of Tigray and the Eritrean highlands by the beginning of the first millennium B.C.E.

Although a number of petty political principalities may have appeared in the region as early as the beginning of the second millennium B.C.E., the first recorded state in Ethiopian history dates to around the fifth century B.C.E. with the rise of Yeha (in western Tigray) as a vigorous city-state. In due time, Yeha absorbed the surrounding chiefdoms and became the center of what is known as the kingdom of Da'amat. The kingdom covered parts of Tigray and what is now Eritrea, extending to Adulis on the Red Sea coast. The rulers of Da'amat called themselves *mukarribs* (a title that was also used by the Sabaean states in South Arabia) and may have combined the function of chief priest and ruler.

Linguistic, monumental, and epigraphic evidence points to a strong South Arabian (particularly Sabaean) influence in Yeha during this time. Contacts between the two sides of the Red Sea were frequent. Available evidence suggests that a steady trickle of South Arabians (possibly for commercial and hunting purposes) penetrated into the interior and fused with the Cushitic (mostly Agaw) peoples of northern Ethiopia.

First highlighted by a German archaeological expedition at the beginning of the twentieth century, the ancient city of Yeha has yielded a trove of artifacts that have proved useful in reconstructing the architectural, linguistic, religious, and cultural features of this ancient kingdom. Although extensive excavation of the site has not yet been undertaken, archaeologists have uncovered large numbers of fragments of Sabaean (one of the Semitic languages) inscriptions that mention names of tribes and a mix of local deities and South Arabian gods. Although not conclusively established, there is a general agreement that the oldest Sabaean inscription discovered in Yeha dates to the fifth century B.C.E.

Also found in Yeha is the oldest known standing monument in Ethiopia. This imposing rectangular temple (which has lost its roof and upper stories) is about 60 feet (18 meters) in length, 48 feet (14.5 meters) wide, and 50 feet (15 meters) in height. It stands on a hill overlooking the surrounding area. The temple may have been dedicated to Almuqah, the South Arabian god of the moon. Palace ruins, royal cemeteries, elite residences, pottery, and tools and relics found in the graves near the temple attest to the flourishing of an urban community that drew its prosperity from trade and the rich agricultural resources of the surrounding areas.

SIGNIFICANCE

The embryonic Ethiopian state that developed with its center at Yeha collapsed by the end of the first millennium B.C.E., but it had considerable influence on its successor state, Aksum (first century C.E.). The meshing of Semitic and Cushitic cultures evidenced in fifth century B.C.E. Yeha became the most prominent feature of Ethiopian society. The evolution of a new Ethiopic script and language called Ge'ez by the first century C.E. is testimony to the continuing fusion of the Semitic and Cushitic elements and its spread over wider areas of northern and central Ethiopia.

—*Shumet Sishagne*

Further Reading

Anfray, F. "Yeha, berceau d'une civilization." *Archeologia* 64 (1973). Prominent arachaeologist Anfray, who has done extensive work on ancient sites in northern Ethiopia, discusses Yeha. In French.

Fattovich, Rodolfo. "Pre-Aksumite Civilization of Ethiopia: A Provisional Review." *Proceedings of the Seminar for Arabian Studies* 7 (1977). An outline of the major political and commercial centers that grew in northern Ethiopia before the rise of Aksum in the first century C.E.

_______. "Remarks on the Pre-Aksumite Period in Northern Ethiopia." *Journal of Ethiopian Studies* 23 (1990). This work incorporates some of the latest findings on the pre-Aksumite period.

Littman, Enno, Daniel Krenker, and Theodore von Lüpke. *Der deutschen Aksum Expedition* I-IV. Berlin: Reimer Verlong, 1913. An account of the first German expedition that carried out extensive excavations in northern Ethiopia, including at Yeha. In German.

Save-Soderbergh, T. *The Navy of the Eighteenth Egyptian Dynasty.* Uppsala, Sweden: A. B. Lundequistska Bokhandeln, 1946. Provides a fairly extensive account of ancient contacts between Egypt and the Horn of Africa.

Sergew Hable Sellassie. *Ancient and Medieval Ethiopian History to 1270.* Addis Ababa, Ethiopia: United Printers, 1972. Covers the most important highlights of Ethiopian history from the earliest times to the medieval period with detailed reproductions of the ancient Sabaean, Greek, and Geez inscriptions and Aksumite coins.

Vavilov, Nikolay. "The Problem of the Origin of the World's Agriculture in the Light of the Latest Investigations." In *Science at the Crossroads.* London: Frank Cass, 1931. An exploration of the major centers of the Neolithic revolution by a noted Russian plant geneticist.

See also: c. 6th century B.C.E.-c. 350 C.E., Meroitic Empire Rules from Southern Egypt to the Blue Nile; c. 500 B.C.E.-c. 200 C.E., Libyan Garamantes Flourish as Farmers and Traders; 3d century B.C.E., Commercial City of Jenne Is Founded on Niger River; c. 300-c. 100 B.C.E., Berber Kingdoms of Numidia and Mauretania Flourish; c. 300 B.C.E.-c. 100 C.E., Khoikhoi and Kwadi Adopt Pastoral Lifestyle; 3d-5th century C.E., Giant Stelae Are Raised at Aksum; 4th century C.E., Ezana Expands Aksum, Later Converts to Christianity.

Related article in *Great Lives from History: The Ancient World:* Ezana.

447-438 B.C.E.
Building of the Parthenon

The Parthenon was built using a revolutionary combination of Doric and Ionic orders to create a high standard of architectural excellence while giving rise to new forms in Greek art.

Locale: Athens

Categories: Architecture; cultural and intellectual history

Key Figures

Pericles (c. 495-429 B.C.E.), political leader of Athens, 460-429 B.C.E., who helped beautify the city through architecture and statuary

Ictinus (fl. fifth century B.C.E.), architect, along with Callicrates, in charge of design and construction of the Parthenon

Callicrates (fl. fifth century B.C.E.), architect, along with Ictinus, in charge of design and construction of the Parthenon

Phidias (c. 490-c. 430 B.C.E.), master sculptor and overseer of artwork for the Parthenon

Summary of Event

The Parthenon, dedicated to Athena the Maiden, is the most famous of Greek temples, the crowning monument of the Athenian Acropolis. It was built on the remains of an older temple begun in 490 B.C.E. to celebrate the Athenian victory over the Persians in the Battle of Marathon. This temple was destroyed when the Persians returned and invaded Athens in 480. With the help of Sparta, Athens was able to defeat the Persians in 479 near Plataea. There, on the battlefield, the Greeks took an oath not to rebuild the ruined temples as a reminder of the devastation caused by the Persian invasion. By 449, Athens had made peace with Persia and this oath was no longer binding.

In 447 B.C.E., Athens began to build a new Parthenon. Of the Doric order but with Ionic architectural features such as the continuous frieze, the new Parthenon was built under Pericles in 447-438 B.C.E. by the architects Ictinus and Callicrates. The sculptor Phidias was responsible for the design and composition of its decorative reliefs and statuary, which continued to be added to the structure through 432 B.C.E.

Constructed entirely of Pentelic marble on a limestone foundation, it is peripteral octastyle in plan, being encompassed by a single row of columns, with eight at each end and, in this instance, seventeen on each side. At the top step of the stylobate, or substructure, the building measures 228 by 101 feet (69 by 31 meters), so that it is exceptionally wide in proportion to its length. Within the peristyle of columns stood the enclosed cella, or main room, and a back chamber, each fronted by a porch with six columns. At both ends, metal grilles between these columns completely enclosed the two chambers. The cella, with its door facing east, had interior columns in two levels at the sides and rear. Within this main gallery, visitors could view the colossal cult statue, the gold and ivory *Athena of Phidias*, set at the far end of the room. The foundation of the pedestal, all that remains of this great work, measures 26 by 13 feet (8 by 4 meters). The back chamber, or opistodomos, with its door opening to the west and with four interior columns, may have served as a treasury for gifts dedicated to the goddess. It was this chamber, officially known as the Parthenon, that gave rise to the name of the building as a whole. The chamber of the virgin, or the Parthenon, was that room set aside in Athenian homes for the use of the virgin daughter before her marriage.

Chief among the sculptural decorations of the Parthenon were the metopes in high relief on the entablature, the continuous frieze in low relief above the wall of the two chambers, and the fully sculptured groups in the pediments at each end of the temple. The themes of this art glorify the goddess and the city of which she was patron; the metopes depicted notable combats—Lapiths against

The Parthenon. (PhotoDisc)

Centaurs, Olympians against giants, and Greeks against Amazons—to symbolize the victory of civilization over barbarism, which was how the Athenians viewed their victory over the Persians. The frieze was remarkable in that it showed the Athenian citizenry involved in the contemporary event of the great Panathenaic procession in honor of the goddess. This procession took place every four years. Until this time, Greeks had been ambivalent about depicting current historical events. Although the procession was in honor of Athena, the goddess, many of the human beings portrayed embody godlike qualities.

The western pediment portrayed the contest between Athena and Poseidon for dominion over the city, and the eastern one depicted the birth of Athena. The gods portrayed on the pediments exhibited humanlike qualities. Of the purely architectural features, the columns stand 34.5 feet (11 meters) high, the equal of about five and a half lower diameters of the columns. From the stylobate to the peak of the gabled roof, the structure stood more than 61 feet (19 meters) in height. Rectangular coffered blocks of marble supported by a sequence of pillars, beams, and walls made up the ceiling, above which was a network of timbers to sustain the low-pitched roof. Even the roof tiles were cut from marble.

The earliest Greek temples were constructed of sun-dried brick and wood, but hard limestone, conglomerate, and marble became the chief materials after the seventh century B.C.E. Athens was well endowed with marble from Mount Pentelicus to the northeast of the city. After being roughly cut in the quarries there, the blocks were brought to the Acropolis in wagons. Hoisting was accomplished by means of pulleys and tongs, the lewis, or iron tenon, fitting into a dove-tailed mortise in the stone. To bond the stones set vertically, such as the individual drums of the columns, iron or bronze dowels set in molten lead connected the top of one drum to the bottom of the one above it. Horizontal bonding of stone beams was achieved by the double-T- or H-type of clamp. The Greeks never used mortar or nails in this kind of construction, and great care was taken to assure perfect contacts along the surface joints of the marble. Even in the twentieth century, many of these joints were so tight that a razor blade could not be inserted between the blocks.

Many elements in the Hellenic temple came from other Mediterranean cultures—the floor plan from Crete, the columnar structure from Egypt, and the capitals from Assyria—but the genius of the evolving Doric form was typically Greek in its simplicity, its balance of proportions, and its complementary use of Ionic sculpture and decoration. As the perfection of this type, the Parthenon also includes a number of unique refinements that make it a dynamic creation and a moving visual experience. Among these are the drooping or horizontal curvature of the stylobate toward all four corners, so that, for example, on the long sides, the rise from the ends to the center of the structure is about 4 inches (10 centimeters). The columns have both diminution or tapering of the shaft from the bottom up and also entasis, or a slight convex swelling, in the shaft. Furthermore, all the outside columns incline slightly toward the cella walls; the four angle columns are thicker than the others and by virtue of their position have a double inclination. Last, the chief vertical surfaces such as the cella wall have a backward slope, but the entablature above the columns has a slightly forward tilt. These and other refinements were probably incorporated to correct optical illusions that would otherwise make the stylobate appear to sag, the entablature to recede, and the angle columns to appear thin against the sky.

Significance

The architectural refinements combined with other features of the Parthenon, such as the Ionic frieze and the tendency of the overall sculpture in the building to deify the humans and to humanize the gods, to make it a nearly perfect building. At the same time it revolutionized conceptions of what was human and divine and brought into question what would be the future basis of architectural forms in Greek society.

The Parthenon survived in fairly whole condition until 1687, when it was badly damaged by an explosion during a war between the Turks and the Venetians. More than a century later, Lord Elgin brought most of the surviving sculptures to London to save them from piecemeal destruction. Consequently, a full appreciation of the Parthenon requires a visit to the British Museum in London, where the Elgin Marbles are on display, and to Athens, to view the partially restored temple.

—Kevin Herbert, updated by Jennifer Eastman

Further Reading

Beard, Mary. *The Parthenon*. London: Profile, 2002. Contains a history of the building of the Parthenon and background on Athens as well as a list of sculptures and numerous illustrations.

Bruno, Vincent J., ed. *The Parthenon*. 1974. Reprint. New York: W. W. Norton, 1996. Collection of essays and illustrations on the history and construction of the Parthenon.

Cook, B. F. *The Elgin Marbles*. 2d ed. London: British Museum Press, 1997. A closer look at the sculptures from the Parthenon, most of which have been collected at the British Museum. Bibliography and index.

Korres, M. *Stones of the Parthenon*. Los Angeles: J. Paul Getty Museum, 2000. A study of the marble used in the Parthenon: where it came from and how it was quarried, transported, and shaped.

Neils, Jenifer. *The Parthenon Frieze*. New York: Cambridge University Press, 2001. An examination of the frieze of the Parthenon. Contains folded leaf of illustrations in a pocket, bibliography, index, and CD-ROM with virtual films of the relief.

Rhodes, Robin Francis. *Architecture and Meaning on the Athenian Acropolis*. New York: Cambridge University Press, 1995. Rhodes stresses the importance of the combination of the Doric and Ionic orders and the tendency to deify the human and humanize the divine in the building of the Parthenon.

SEE ALSO: 480-479 B.C.E., Persian Invasion of Greece; 478-448 B.C.E., Athenian Empire Is Created; 312 B.C.E., First Roman Aqueduct Is Built; 245-140 B.C.E., Rise of Parthia.

RELATED ARTICLES in *Great Lives from History: The Ancient World*: Pericles; Phidias.

445 B.C.E.
ESTABLISHMENT OF THE CANULEIAN LAW

The Canuleian Law continued a process of Roman political reform by making it possible for the plebeian class to attain patrician status.

LOCALE: Roman Empire
CATEGORY: Laws, acts, and legal history

KEY FIGURE

Gaius Canuleius (fl. fifth century B.C.E.), plebeian tribune of Rome in 445 B.C.E.

SUMMARY OF EVENT

During the last decade of the sixth century B.C.E., the political community already established in Rome took its first steps toward the Republican constitution of the first century B.C.E. The traditional system of kingship was overthrown and replaced by two magistrates equipped with broad executive powers who were elected annually. Legislative initiative and political power were vested in the senate, a self-sustaining body of elder counselors. Although both these organs of government appeared to be republican in character, they were unable to forestall civil strife at Rome and reflected the basic discrepancy in Roman society behind that strife. This dichotomy was the so-called struggle of the orders, a class conflict that was contested on almost all levels of communal life.

The two classes engaged in the struggle were known as patricians and plebeians. After 509 B.C.E., the traditional date for the beginning of the Roman Republic, the plebeians held an inferior position within the Roman state. They were excluded from political office and the senate because such honors were reserved for the patricians. Furthermore, the plebeians were barred from the official religious bodies of the state and, by one of the laws in the Twelve Tables, from intermarriage with the patricians. The cause and significance of these prohibitions can be found in the underlying social structure of Rome.

The predominant social unit was the *gens*, or clan, which consisted of a group of families linked by a common name and the veneration of a common male ancestor. The origin of the *gens* structure has been keenly disputed, but there is general agreement among scholars that it was an outgrowth of the economic progress within the early agrarian society of Rome. Increased wealth caused a split into upper and lower classes that hardened into richer and poorer families. Members of the richer and more powerful clans called themselves patricians from their exclusive hold on the senate, whose original members were termed *patres*, or fathers. This nobility of wealth eventually became a nobility of blood that claimed for itself full citizenship and total dominance in all aspects of political life. For the fifth century B.C.E., scholars have found evidence of the existence of fifty such patrician clans, entrenched in power and maintained by privilege.

Opposed to the patricians were the plebeians. Scholars have debated their origin, but plebeians were probably not racially distinct from the patricians. In general, plebeians were the poorer elements of Roman society who had not shared in the economic advances of the early years of Roman history. This original core was augmented by the workers and peasants who had either been attracted to Rome by its commercial growth or engulfed by the spread of Roman conquest. Together, these various strands formed the *plebs*, or multitude. The plebeians were not a servile class; they always possessed a number of political and civil rights. Furthermore, the plebeians also had a *gens* structure within which individual plebeian clans gradually increased in size and wealth. They eventually became discontented with their second-class status; throughout the first half of the fifth century, they repeatedly demanded, and obtained, greater equity within the state. The plebeians acquired their own officials, the tribunes of the *plebs*, to act as their protectors and leaders. In 449 B.C.E., a special commission completed the first written codification of law at Rome, the famous Twelve Tables, which made knowledge of the law accessible to everyone. These gains were not obtained without patrician resistance, however, as evidenced by the inclusion in the Twelve Tables of the ban on intermarriage—a blatant reminder that the plebeians did not enjoy total equality.

It is misleading to say that marriage between the two groups was completely forbidden. Roman law recognized various forms of marriage, the simplest being the mere cohabitation of a man and a woman. If such an arrangement persisted without interruption for one year, the two parties were considered legally married, except in the case of patricians and plebeians. A plebeian woman could share the house of a patrician man for the required period without becoming patrician, and the children of such a union were not considered patrician. The decisive factor in this arrangement was a religious one. The only valid marriage ceremony for patricians was the solemn religious ritual called *confarreatio*. For a valid marriage between the two groups, therefore, the plebeians would have to be permitted entrance into the tenaciously guarded domain of patrician religion.

This impasse was circumvented in 445 B.C.E. by Gaius Canuleius, a tribune of the people, who proposed a law rescinding the ban on intermarriage. The law did not eliminate the exclusion of plebeians from the ceremony of *confarreatio*; instead, it recognized cohabitation and another secular form of marriage as legally binding so that a wife and her children gained patrician status. It seems probable that the patricians at first rejected even this compromise, which left their religion intact. The plebeians countered with their most effective weapon, a mass withdrawal from the communal life of the city. This drastic measure compelled the patricians to accept the law.

SIGNIFICANCE

With the enactment of the Canuleian Law, the plebeians shed another vestige of their inferior status. Civil strife between the two classes persisted, but for the plebeians, the new law came to stand as one of their more gratifying victories.

—George M. Pepe, updated by Jeffrey L. Buller

FURTHER READING

Aubert, Jean-Jacques, and Boudewijn Sirks, eds. *Speulum iuris: Roman Law as a Reflection of Social and Economic Life in Antiquity.* Ann Arbor: University of Michigan Press, 2002. A collection of essays examining the relationship between Roman law and the social and economic life of the Romans. Bibliography and index.

Buckland, W. W. *A Manual of Roman Private Law.* 2d ed. Holmes Beach, Fla.: Wm. W. Gaunt, 1994. A detailed analysis of the major laws affecting Roman citizenship and private life.

Ferenczy, Endre. *From the Patrician State to the Patricio-Plebeian State.* Translated by G. Dedinsky. Amsterdam: A. M. Hakkert, 1976. An excellent survey of the major reforms in the Roman government expanding the legal rights of non-nobles.

Gardner, Jane F. *Being a Roman Citizen.* New York: Routledge, 1993. A good introduction for the general reader on the impact of Roman law upon private life. Written in a popular style but well researched.

Mitchell, Richard E. *Patricians and Plebeians: The Origin of the Roman State.* Ithaca, N.Y.: Cornell University Press, 1990. An examination of the relationship between patricians and plebeians in the early Roman Republic. Bibiliography and indexes.

Münzer, Friedrich. *Roman Aristocratic Parties and Families.* Baltimore: The Johns Hopkins University Press, 1999. This work on the aristocracy in Rome sheds light on the class structure in Republican Rome. Bibliography and index.

Sandberg, Kaj. *Magistrates and Assemblies: A Study of Legislative Practice in Republican Rome.* Rome: Institutum Romanum Finlandiae, 2001. An examination of the legislative process under the Roman Republic. Bibliography and index.

SEE ALSO: 494/493 B.C.E., Institution of the Plebeian Tribunate; 451-449 B.C.E., Twelve Tables of Roman Law Are Formulated; 340-338 B.C.E., Origin of *Municipia*; c. 300 B.C.E., Stoics Conceptualize Natural Law; 287 B.C.E., *Lex Hortensia* Reforms the Roman Constitution; 180 B.C.E., Establishment of the *Cursus honorum.*

c. 440 B.C.E.

SOPHISTS TRAIN THE GREEKS IN RHETORIC AND POLITICS

The teachings of the Sophists marked the emergence of an educational movement that supplemented traditional learning in ancient Greece.

LOCALE: Greek-speaking communities throughout the Mediterranean world
CATEGORY: Cultural and intellectual history

KEY FIGURES

Protagoras (c. 485-c. 410 B.C.E.), Greek Sophist prominent for doctrines of epistemological relativism and agnosticism
Gorgias (c. 480-c. 370 B.C.E.), Greek Sophist important in the development of rhetorical theory
Thrasymachus of Chalcedon (fl. fifth century B.C.E.), Greek Sophist known for his belief that justice is a matter of human convention

SUMMARY OF EVENT

The Sophists, literally "wise ones," arose in the second half of the fifth century B.C.E. in response to a recognized need in the more advanced Greek states for training in the skills needed for active participation in political life. Traditional education consisted of appropriation of aristocratic ideals embodied in the poetic tradition and in military education, but this training was felt to be inadequate to impart the skills of political leadership in states in which success depended on the ability to sway votes in the courts and the popular assembly and on awareness of the principles of community organization.

To meet this need, the Sophists emerged as itinerant educators making the rounds of Greek cities and offering courses of instruction to anyone willing to pay. Although their name suggests they were organized into a school, the Sophists had no direct affiliation with one another. They did, however, all claim to teach *politite arete*, the civic virtues considered necessary for a life of public service. One of the better-known Sophists, Protagoras, claimed that any man who went through his course of instruction would learn "to order his own house in the best manner and be able to speak and act for the best in the affairs of the state."

Although the Sophists offered courses of instruction in a variety of subjects, including history, mathematics, and literature, the ability to sway votes in courtroom or assembly was a fundamental political skill, so the Sophists placed special emphasis on the teaching of rhetoric and were the first to organize it into an art. Credited with being the first to suggest that there were two sides to every controversial question, Protagoras defined the nature and function of the orator as the ability to speak with equal persuasiveness to them both and to fortify a weaker argument so as to make it more convincing. The Sophist Gorgias simply defined rhetoric as "the art of persuasion."

The methods of rhetorical training employed by the Sophists were the debate and the set speech. The debate was an imitation of the courtroom situation, wherein speakers had to present, as convincingly as possible, the arguments for both the prosecution and the defense. The set speech might exemplify the presentation of a policy before the popular assembly or present a persuasive reinterpretation of some conventional myth, offering a convincing reversal of value judgments on characters in the myth. Thus, the *Encomium of Helen*, a set speech by Gorgias, argued the view that Helen, far from being guilty of criminal adultery, was the innocent victim of forces beyond her control. Gorgias's *Encomium of Helen* neatly exemplifies some of the assumptions of Sophistic rhetorical theory: that human psychology may be understood in terms of physiochemical causation, that speech bears no necessary relationship to objective reality but plays on people's hopes and fears to dislodge firmly held convictions and moral principles and to implant new perspectives with the same inevitable efficacy that drugs have when administered to the body.

Unlike their most immediate intellectual predecessors, the Greek natural philosophers, the Sophists were more interested in exploring the relation of human beings to each other than to the cosmos. Sophistic anthropology and political science were consciously founded on humanistic assumptions rather than on traditionally recognized divinely sanctioned principles. Protagoras made the first widely publicized open declaration of agnosticism concerning the nature and activities of the gods, and he also propounded the doctrine of the relativity of human knowledge: "Of all things the measure is [each single] man, of things that are, that they are, and of things that are not, that they are not." With the logical priority of the individual over the group thus assumed, it is only reasonable to argue that the Sophists saw the values of any particular human community as artificial conventions, distinct from the conventions of other communities and imposing arbitrary limitations on an individual human being, whose natural inclination could be empirically recognized as essentially self-interested and aggressive. That *nomos*, the conventional values and laws of a particular community, were artificial limitations imposed on the universally self-assertive nature, or *physics*, of the individual thus became a widely accepted view in the later years of the fifth century B.C.E., a view finding varied expression in literature as well as in formulations of public policy.

As a consequence of this view of the nature of individuals and of human communities, the principle of justice came to be defined by some Sophists, most notably by Thrasymachus of Chalcedon, as the "advantage of the stronger party" in any community. Traditionally, justice had been held to be a divinely sanctioned principle of distribution of rights and privileges in the human community, but it was now held by the Sophists to be a reflection of the power structure of any state. For example, in an oligarchy, a minority, by virtue of its control of the army and the police, enforces a distribution of wealth and privileges that benefits itself; in a democracy, the majority has seized and maintains power to assure an equality of distribution of rights and privileges. In Plato's *Politeia* (388-368 B.C.E.; *Republic*, 1701), Socrates sharply criticizes Thrasymachus's view of justice and argues that not only justice but also all moral virtues are objectively real and good in themselves. In other dialogues, Socrates opposes additional Sophistic teachings, including the idea that virtue is teachable. Socrates is arguably the most famous Athenian opposed to the views and practices of the Sophists; however, their oligarchical associations, their skepticism about traditional beliefs concerning the gods, and their educational emphasis on the credibility of an argument rather than its truth made them the objects of criticism of many Athenian citizens.

SIGNIFICANCE

The impact of Sophistic rhetorical training on Athenian life is clearly evident in the literature of the later years of the fifth century B.C.E., especially in the history of Thucydides and the plays of Euripides and Aristophanes. A critical disposition of mind toward traditional values was fostered; eloquence of speech came to be admired and often to be practiced with a cynical awareness that an argument need not be valid to be persuasive; and there were growing doubts of the efficacy of traditional values to govern human conduct, which was increasingly viewed as governed by nonpredictable compulsions.

The impact of this analysis of human society in terms divorced from traditional moral sanctions was to undermine public confidence in, and voluntary submission to, constituted authority. Encouraged by the new perspective on humankind and society, groups of young noblemen, who were naturally most directly influenced because they were best able to afford Sophistic instruction, carefully studied the means of gaining power without scruples, and the later years of the Peloponnesian War were marked by violent social upheavals in many Greek states, upheavals made the more violent by the undermining of traditional moral scruples.

—*Carl W. Conrad, updated by Diane P. Michelfelder*

FURTHER READING

Gleason, Maud W. *Making Men: Sophists and Self-Presentation in Ancient Rome*. Princeton, N.J.: Princeton University Press, 1995. A discussion of how the Sophist ideas about rhetoric influenced ancient Romans.

Irvin, Terence, ed. *Socrates and His Contemporaries. Vol. 2 in Classical Philosophy*. New York: Garland, 1995. Contains recent and classical essays concerning the moral and political views of the Sophists, as well as their relation to Socrates and Plato.

Jarratt, Susan Carole Funderburgh, ed. *Rereading the Sophists: Classical Rhetoric Refigured*. 1991. Reprint. Carbondale: Southern Illinois University Press, 1998. An examination of the Sophists and their teachings from a feminist perspective. Bibliography and index.

McComiskey, Bruce. *Gorgias and the New Sophistic Rhetoric*. Carbondale: Southern Illinois University Press, 2002. A study of the life and works of Gorgias, a major Sophist. Bibliography and index.

Poulakos, John. *Sophistical Rhetoric in Classical Greece*. Columbia: University of South Carolina Press, 1995. A discussion of rhetoric, including the Sophists' reception by Plato, Isocrates, and Aristotle.

SEE ALSO: 399 B.C.E., Death of Socrates; c. 380 B.C.E., Plato Develops His Theory of Ideas; c. 335-323 B.C.E., Aristotle Writes the *Politics*.

RELATED ARTICLES in *Great Lives from History: The Ancient World*: Isocrates; Plato; Protagoras; Socrates.

c. 438 B.C.E.

GREEK LYRIC POET PINDAR DIES

Pindar, the greatest Greek lyric poet, perfected the genre of choral poetry, performed in celebration of gods and men, especially athletic victors, and bequeathed to Western literature the grand Pindaric ode.

LOCALE: Greece
CATEGORY: Literature

KEY FIGURE

Pindar (c. 518-c. 438 B.C.E.), author of choral odes

SUMMARY OF EVENT

The death of Pindar, a native of Thebes, marked the end of archaic choral lyric poetry, one of the greatest literary achievements of the ancient Greeks. Like J. S. Bach, whose work came at the end of an artistic era (the Baroque) and summed up, while surpassing, the works of his contemporaries, Pindar was universally acknowledged as the greatest Greek lyric poet. His poems express the fullest flowering of the genre of extremely complex choral odes that combined song, dance, and musical accompaniment by lyres and pipes (reed instruments similar to oboes). Also, just as the generation following Bach was turning to new forms of music that made Bach's music seem outdated, so Athenian drama, oratory, history, philosophy, and new forms of poetry were eclipsing Pindar's lyric poetry.

His poems were collected into seventeen books (actually papyrus rolls) and edited by Alexandrian scholars, beginning around 250 B.C.E. They included hymns, songs addressed to various gods (1 book); *paeans*, hymns addressed to Apollo (1 book); *dithyrambs*, hymns addressed to Dionysus (2 books); *prosodia*, hymns for approaching a god's shrine (2 books); *partheneia*, hymns sung by maidens (3 books); *hyporchemata*, dancing hymns (2 books); *enkomia*, songs of praise for men (1 book); *threnoi*, songs of lament for deceased men (1 book); and *epinikia*, victory songs (four books). Only the four books of victory odes (about one-fourth of Pindar's total work) have survived in manuscripts.

Choral lyric poetry first flourished with the poet Alcman in Sparta around 625 B.C.E. At that time, the genre was already marked by brief mythical narratives, gnomic reflections, and allusive, metaphorical language. Studies have shown that the performance of choral poetry served various important functions, such as physical, aesthetic, and moral education; ritual worship of the gods; and the initiation and integration of young women and men into their societies.

Pindar's odes serve these and other purposes. Some, like the *enkomia* (songs of praise), are less formal and contain praise suitable for *symposia* (communal drinking parties). Others, like the *hymns*, *paeans*, and *dithyrambs*, are communal and formed part of ritual celebrations of the gods, while the *threnoi* are solemn songs of lament and consolation for a death.

The other thirteen of Pindar's books have survived only in fragments, through chance discoveries of papyrus in Egypt or as quotations in the works of later Greek authors. However, the four books of *epinikia* are very well preserved in manuscripts through a long chain of copying and recopying from the original papyrus rolls. These four books contain forty-five poems, varying in length from 20 to 299 verses. They celebrate athletes from cities all over Greece (and Greek colonies throughout the Mediterranean) who were victorious in the most prestigious games, Olympian, Pythian, Nemean, and Isthmian. Each of the four books is devoted to victors in each of these games. Those celebrated range from boy victors from small towns (such as Asopichos of Orchomenos) to some of the most powerful rulers at the time (Hieron of Syracuse, Theron of Acragas, and Arcesilas of Cyrene), whose horses and four-horse chariots had won for them prestigious victories. Pindar's reputation as the greatest praise poet of Greece rests on these poems.

The odes consist of extremely complex metrical arrangements. The verses are organized into stanzas called strophes, antistrophes, and epodes. A strophe contains from three to thirteen verses. It is matched by a metrically identical stanza called an antistrophe, and a metrically different stanza called an epode—the three combining to form a triad, which is typically repeated from three to five times in a poem. The longest and most complex ode, *Pythian* 4, contains thirteen triads. Odes often have an ABA structure: praise—mythical narrative—praise. Pindar's language is rich in metaphor, bold images, newly coined words, and very complex syntax and word order, all making his poetry extremely dense and difficult to interpret.

In each ode, Pindar sets the achievements of the victor within the context of his city's traditions, Greek history, mythology, and traditional wisdom. The odes often contain myths, recounting heroic or divine stories that serve as backdrops for the athlete and his city, maxims, prayers and addresses to gods, and sometimes catalogs of past victories of the victor or his family. In Pindar's odes to powerful kings such as Hieron and Arcesilas, the poet adopts the position of a Panhellenic adviser, offering precepts of statesmanship such as "Guide your people with a rudder of justice; on an anvil of truth forge your tongue" (*Pythian* 1.86-87).

SIGNIFICANCE

Pindar's lifetime spanned the end of the Archaic period and the beginning of the Classical, divided by the repulsion of two Persian invasions in 490 and 479 B.C.E. In the ensuing decades, the Greek world split into two opposing camps. Whereas Athenian democracy promoted innovation, aggressive economic imperialism, and radically new philosophical ideas, Spartan conservatism grounded itself in aristocratic institutions, Doric traditions, defensive foreign policy, and traditional ideas. Pindar was a spokesperson for the conservative outlook. He regularly praises aristocratic leaders and governments, Doric laws and institutions, and political stability; he looks back to the traditional legends and wisdom; and he is wary of what is not tried and true. His poetry is full of warnings about humans' dependence on the gods and their limitations: "From the gods come all the means for human achievements" (*Pythian* 1.41); "Do not, my soul, strive for the life of the immortals, but exhaust the practical means at your disposal" (*Pythian* 3.61-62); "Creatures of a day! What is someone? What is no one? A dream of a shadow is man" (*Pythian* 8.95-96).

Yet, Pindar's vision was universal, for he aspired to be "foremost in wisdom among Hellenes everywhere" (*Olympian* 1.116) and consistently gave praise where it was fairly earned. The international reputation Pindar gained in the century following his death is illustrated by the story that when Alexander the Great razed the city of Thebes in 335 B.C.E., Pindar's house was the only building he spared. In this way, the commander who venerated Homer and was uniting all Greece paid homage to the Panhellenic poet who had celebrated the deeds of great men.

With the death of Pindar came the end of the independent genre. Choral lyric poetry survived for a while in a diminished role in the tragic choruses of Sophocles and Euripides and in the comic choruses of Aristophanes. The expense of outfitting and training these choruses (the most expensive part of producing tragedies and comedies) indicates how lavish the performance of Pindaric odes must have been, requiring talented singers, dancers, and musicians dressed in fine costumes. Within a couple more generations, their performance ceased altogether. The last attested victory ode was composed by Euripides

Pindar, with lute in hand, recites his poetry. (Library of Congress)

in 416 B.C.E. Even knowledge of their poetic conventions and details of performance were soon lost. The remarks of the earliest Alexandrian commentators two centuries after Pindar's time show that his poetic language was perplexing and performance no longer understood.

Pindar's odes, however, continued to influence the European tradition. The Roman poet Horace measured his smaller (Horatian) odes against Pindar's grand poems. The Renaissance poet Pierre de Ronsard imitated Pindar and aspired to become the French Pindar. In the seventeenth century, the English poets Ben Jonson, Abraham Cowley, and John Milton composed Pindaric odes, as did Thomas Gray in the eighteenth century. Even the grand odes of Samuel Taylor Coleridge, William Wordsworth, John Keats, and Gerard Manley Hopkins are distant relatives of Pindaric odes.

—*William H. Race*

FURTHER READING

Bundy, Elroy L. *Studia Pindarica*. 1962. Reprint. Berkeley: University of California Press, 1986. A pioneering, dense, scholarly analysis of the poetic and rhetorical aspects of Pindar's praise that revealed the sophistication of his poetry and challenged its usefulness in providing historical or biographical information.

Race, W. H. *Pindar*. Boston: Twayne, 1986. A survey for the general reader of Pindar's work addressing its influence on Western literature.

_______. *Pindar*. 2 vols. Cambridge, Mass.: Harvard University Press, 1997. Facing Greek text and English translation of all the odes and principal fragments.

Rutherford, I. *Pindar's Paeans: A Reading of the Fragments with a Survey of the Genre*. New York: Oxford University Press, 2001. A scholarly edition of the fragmentary paeans, recovered on papyrus from Egypt in the early twentieth century.

Steiner, D. *The Crown of Song: Metaphor in Pindar*. London: Duckworth, 1986. A readable survey of Pindar's extensive use of metaphor.

SEE ALSO: 8th-6th centuries B.C.E., Phrygian Kingdom Rises; c. 750 B.C.E., Homer Composes the *Iliad*; c. 580 B.C.E., Greek Poet Sappho Dies; c. 456/455 B.C.E., Greek Tragedian Aeschylus Dies; 406 B.C.E., Greek Dramatist Euripides Dies; c. 385 B.C.E., Greek Playwright Aristophanes Dies; 336 B.C.E., Alexander the Great Begins Expansion of Macedonia.

RELATED ARTICLES in *Great Lives from History: The Ancient World*: Aeschylus; Aristophanes; Euripides; Homer; Horace; Pindar; Sappho; Sophocles.

May, 431-September, 404 B.C.E.
PELOPONNESIAN WAR

The Peloponnesian War, a military conflict between the two greatest powers of ancient Greece, Athens and Sparta, was also the final stage of a long-standing struggle between conflicting political, economic, and social systems.

LOCALE: Greece

CATEGORIES: Expansion and land acquisition; wars, uprisings, and civil unrest

KEY FIGURES

Pericles (c. 495-429 B.C.E.), Athenian statesman and general of the mid-fifth century B.C.E.

Cleon of Athens (c. 465-422 B.C.E.), Athenian demagogue and political leader

Demosthenes (d. 413 B.C.E.), Athenian general

Nicias of Athens (c. 470-413 B.C.E.), general who led the peace party in Athens

Brasidas of Sparta (c. 460-422 B.C.E.), Spartan general

Alcibiades of Athens (c. 450-404 B.C.E.), Athenian general who betrayed his city to the Spartans

Lysander of Sparta (d. 395 B.C.E.), Spartan statesman and general who finally defeated Athens

SUMMARY OF EVENT

In the late spring of 431 B.C.E., the tensions that had existed between Athens and Sparta since the end of the Greco-Persian War suddenly erupted into open conflict. The resulting war became known as the Peloponnesian War because Sparta's area of greatest influence was the Peloponnese, the peninsula on which it was located. The causes of the war were long-standing. The Great Peloponnesian War (also known as the First Peloponnesian War; 459-445 B.C.E.), largely a conflict between Athens and Corinth, with Sparta also participating, had ended with a truce between Athens and Sparta, but neither side had abided completely by its terms.

In 433 B.C.E., Athens defended the island of Corcyra against Corinth and excluded the city of Megara from commerce with any city in the Athenian empire. Both Corinth and Megara were Spartan allies, and the Athenians' actions were taken as open acts of aggression, provoking a war between the two cities that had long vied for domination in Greece. In May, 431, Athens and Sparta finally erupted into war.

The military leader Pericles developed a strategy intended to win an easy victory for Athens. Pericles avoided direct conflicts with the much larger Spartan land army and took his forces to the sea, where Athens had an advantage. The entire population of Attica, the region in which Athens was located, withdrew behind the Long Walls, a defensive structure that connected the city to its port. Safe behind these defenses, the Athenians allowed the Spartans to invade Attica. The loss of Attic grain caused by this invasion was not a significant problem. The protection of the Long Walls permitted the Athenians to import substantially all the food they needed by sea.

Nevertheless, the crowding that resulted in Athens because of Pericles' strategy had one effect that the general had not foreseen: the spread of disease. After the first year of the war, a plague erupted in Athens, killing as much as one-quarter of the population. Pericles was fined and not selected as general for the following year. In the intervening period, Pericles himself became ill and died of the plague in the autumn of 429 B.C.E. Without the guidance of Pericles, the Athenians began to take increasingly brutal measures against their adversaries.

In 428 B.C.E., Mitylene, a city on the island of Lesbos, attempted to free itself from the Athenian empire. The Athenians resisted this action and starved the city into submission by May of 427 B.C.E. Back in Athens, the assembly decreed that all Mitylenaean men were to be killed, with the women and children sold into slavery. After a ship had already been dispatched to carry out this decree, the assembly reconvened to examine the severity of its sentence. Cleon of Athens, a politician popular with the masses, argued that the punishment of Mitylene had to be carried out as planned. He described the Athenian empire as a tyranny, saying that the state was now compelled to act like a despot and use terror and cruelty to keep its subjects in check. In the end, Cleon's arguments failed. The Athenians voted to "lighten" Mitylene's penalty by executing "only" about one thousand of the rebels, seizing the island's fleet, and destroying its defensive walls. Within six years, however, the harsh penalties proposed by Cleon would be used against rebel cities as a matter of ordinary policy, without any further opposition from the assembly.

By 425 B.C.E., the Athenians appeared to be winning the Peloponnesian War. Demosthenes (not the famous

Lysander of Sparta. (Hulton|Archive)

orator, but an earlier general of the same name) established a stronghold at Pylos on the southwest coast of the Peloponnesian peninsula. When the Athenians could not be dislodged from this base, the Spartans sued for peace. Nicias of Athens—who was often accused of being pro-Spartan—wanted the Athenian assembly to accept this proposal, but he was resisted by Cleon, who argued that Athens should hold out for better terms. As a result of this argument, Cleon was placed in command of the Athenian force on the Peloponnese and arrived in Pylos to discover that the army there was already planning a massive attack against the Spartans. When this attack occurred, the Spartans endured a loss of nearly a third of their troops and then surrendered, providing the Athenians with a group of hostages that included 120 full Spartan citizens. As Cleon had hoped, the Spartans then offered peace without concessions, proposing that Athens be allowed to keep its empire and all of its possessions.

Cleon sought an even greater victory. He suggested an aggressive campaign against the Spartans that would compel them to yield territory. In 424 B.C.E., the Spartan general Brasidas captured an Athenian ally (Amphipolis) in northern Greece through a combination of negotiation and strategy. In 422 B.C.E., in a second battle over

Amphipolis, both Cleon and Brasidas were killed. With the death of the leading Athenian opponent to peace, Sparta and Athens signed a treaty in March of 421 B.C.E. This treaty, known as the Peace of Nicias after its leading negotiator, held until the summer of 416 B.C.E., when the Athenians attacked the island of Melos, forcing it to join the empire. When Melos was captured, all men of military age were executed, and all other citizens were enslaved.

In the following year, the Athenians also began a campaign to extend their empire westward into Sicily. The plan proved to be a disaster. Alcibiades of Athens, the former ward of Pericles and one of the Athenian generals sent to Sicily, was recalled just before the battle began on suspicion of having profaned the religious rites of Demeter. On his way back to Athens, Alcibiades slipped his guard and fled to Sparta. Partly because of Alcibiades' betrayal and partly because of the arrival of the Spartan commander Gylippus, a major portion of the Athenian fleet was destroyed in the campaign. Of a total force of forty thousand, only seven thousand soldiers survived the battle and a subsequent retreat inland. Nicias and Demosthenes were killed. The rest of the troops were imprisoned in a quarry, where the harsh conditions killed many.

Although its economy was nearly ruined, Athens used its limited resources to build additional ships and recruit soldiers. The Spartans also chose a new commander, Lysander, an incorruptible politician who had distinguished himself both as a diplomat and as an admiral. In 405 B.C.E., Lysander captured the Athenian fleet at Aegospotami along the Hellespont. Some 170 ships were seized and four thousand Athenian soldiers were executed after the battle. Lysander then swept the coast of Asia Minor, forcing all Athenians and Athenian supporters to return to Athens. Filled with this excess population and with no means of importing food, Athens was starved out, finally offering unconditional surrender to Sparta in 404 B.C.E.

SIGNIFICANCE

The terms imposed by the Spartans were relatively mild: Athens had to adopt Sparta's foreign policy, allow its exiles to return, reduce its fleet to a defensive force of twelve ships, and breach the Long Walls. The defeat of Athens prevented what might otherwise have been a spread of direct democracy throughout much of Greece (and possibly elsewhere in Europe as well). The Peloponnesian War also came to symbolize for many people the conflict between democracy and military oligarchy, freedom and totalitarianism, and passion and control.

—*Jeffrey L. Buller*

FURTHER READING

Forrest, William George Grieve. *A History of Sparta, 950-192 B.C.* 2d ed. London: Duckworth, 1980. The standard history of Sparta for the general reader; Forrest condenses the Peloponnesian War to a concise account of fewer than twenty pages.

Hornblower, Simon. *The Greek World, 479-323 B.C.* 3d ed. New York: Routledge, 2002. An examination of the rise of Athens and its conflict with Sparta in the Peloponnesian War.

McGregor, Malcolm Francis. *The Athenians and Their Empire*. Vancouver: University of British Columbia Press, 1987. Focuses on the period of Athenian supremacy from the end of the Greco-Persian Wars through the fall of Athens in the closing days of the Peloponnesian War.

Powell, Anton. *Athens and Sparta: Constructing Greek Political and Social History from 478 B.C.* 2d ed. New York: Routledge, 2001. An excellent study of the political and social relationship between Athens and Sparta from 478 B.C.E. onward, with special attention given to the period of the Peloponnesian War.

Roisman, Joseph. *The General Demosthenes and His Use of Military Surprise*. Stuttgart: F. Stiner, 1993. A look at the role of the general Demosthenes in the Peloponnesian War.

Wartenberg, Ute. *After Marathon: War, Society, and Money in Fifth Century Greece*. London: British Museum Press, 1995. This catalog of coins from the collection of the British Museum discusses the Athenians and the Peloponnesian War.

SEE ALSO: c. 736-716 B.C.E., Spartan Conquest of Messenia; c. 550 B.C.E., Construction of Trireme Changes Naval Warfare; 478-448 B.C.E., Athenian Empire Is Created; June, 415-September, 413 B.C.E., Athenian Invasion of Sicily.

RELATED ARTICLES in *Great Lives from History: The Ancient World*: Alcibiades of Athens; Pericles.

c. 420 B.C.E.-c. 100 C.E.
YUEZHI CULTURE LINKS PERSIA AND CHINA

The nomadic Indo-European Yuezhi linked Persian and Chinese civilizations at various periods over five centuries.

LOCALE: Mongolia, northern China, eastern Persia, and northern India

CATEGORIES: Prehistory and ancient cultures; trade and commerce

KEY FIGURES

Zhang Qian (Chang Ch'ien; d. 114 B.C.E.), Han courtier and ambassador sent by Wudi, the Han emperor, to the Yuezhi

Kujūla Kadphises I (d. c. 80 C.E.), unifier of the Oxus Valley Yuezhi, conqueror of the Śakas, and founder and first king of the Kushān Dynasty, r. c. 30-80 C.E.

SUMMARY OF EVENT

Though the earliest known home of the Yuezhi (Yüeh-Chih) people of Central Asia is northern China south of the Gobi Desert (modern Gansu Province), they were apparently, if the images on later Yuezhi coins are accurate, ethnic Caucasians and spoke an Indo-European language called Tokharian by the Greeks. The earliest references to them are in Chinese sources, where they appear as nomads in more or less constant conflict with another nomadic group, the Xiongnu (Hsiung-nu) in the late fifth century B.C.E.

Immediately after the last Ice Age, c. 4000 B.C.E., Central Asia had been lush farmland, irrigated by the retreating ice. It continued to be so when Indo-Europeans, the probable ancestors of the Yuezhi, entered the area around 2500 B.C.E. However, in the ensuing millennia, the glacier runoff dried up, leaving vast grasslands less suitable to farming. The Xiongnu finally expelled the Yuezhi from the fiercely contested land around 300 B.C.E., and they settled farther west, establishing a similar nomadic grazing society between the Altai Mountains in western Mongolia and Lake Balkhash in modern Kazakhstan.

Even there they were not safe from the Xiongnu, who found them again a century later and resumed warfare between 176 and 160 B.C.E. The Yuezhi fled to the Oxus Valley in modern Turkmenistan, just north of the Afghan border. This area had been the eastern frontier of Alexander the Great's Greek expansion of the Persian empire (the Greeks called it Bactria), and here the Yuezhi became the aggressors, conquering the Persian-Greek residents of the Oxus Valley. The Yuezhi maintained their hold on the conquered people by marrying their leaders to the five royal families in the region and adopting Greco-Bactrian culture.

It was this settled Yuezhi pentocracy that the Han Dynasty of China, under Emperor Wu (Wu-ti; 156-87 B.C.E.), contacted in 138 B.C.E. The courtier Zhang Qian was sent out to seek allies to fight against the Xiongnu, who were beginning to raid the Han empire from the north. When he heard the Xiongnu boast of conquering the Yuezhi—they claimed to have a goblet made from the skull of the Yuezhi chief—Zhang Qian felt that revenge might motivate the Yuezhi to join the Chinese against the Xiongnu. He was mistaken. Life was too good in the Oxus Valley, and the Xiongnu were enemies of a past generation.

Nonetheless, almost a century later, the Xiongnu found them again, invading the Oxus Valley in 73 B.C.E. This time, the Yuezhi welcomed an alliance with the Chinese, and with their help repelled the Xiongnu for good in 44 B.C.E.

Sometime around 30 C.E., one of the five Yuezhi kings, Kujūla Kadphises, overpowered his four rivals and created a powerful state that would be the nucleus of a North Indian empire, known to the Chinese as Guishang (Kueh Shen)—the Kushān Dynasty. Not content with ruling the Oxus Valley, Kujūla defeated the Śakas of northern India, expanding into the headwaters of the Ganges and the whole of the Indus valley, and reigning from 30 to 80 C.E. His successor, Vima Takhto, maintained the empire until his death c. 100 C.E., and Vima's son Vima Kadphises I (r. c. 100-c. 127 C.E.) expanded it into Afghanistan.

SIGNIFICANCE

The Yuezhi were a significant influence on the development of a number of different cultures. To the Chinese of the Han Dynasty, they represented the first liaison with any group outside of China's borders. To the Bactrians, they represented a fellow Indo-European culture that began as their conquerors but ended up synthesizing Greco-Bactrian culture with their own. To India, they represented an early empire to the north.

To the later history of the region, the Yuezhi also represent a model for another nomadic group who, a millennium later, would create the largest land empire in history: the Mongols. In fact, horses are a direct historic connection between the Yuezhi contact with China and a major factor in the success of the great khans of the twelfth century. When the Han courtier Zhang Qian visited the Yuezhi in 138 B.C.E., he may have come away without their military aid, but he did not leave empty-handed. He acquired a strategic understanding of the importance of what his report called *tien ma*, "heavenly horses," larger by far than any ever seen in China.

These horses must have been Arabians, half again the size of the Asian ponies then in China. Han horse breeders crossed the Chinese pony with these *tien ma* to produce the hybrid that propelled the armies of the great khans across the steppes of Central Asia, combining the strength and endurance of the Arabian with the agility of the pony. Ironically enough, the battle style of the Mongols—shooting a longbow from a running horse, a skill made possible by the invention of the stirrup—was learned not from the Yuezhi who sold the Han their horses, but from the Xiongnu who used it over the centuries to harass the Yuezhi.

—*John R. Holmes*

FURTHER READING

Christian, David. *A History of Russia, Central Asia, and Mongolia: Inner Eurasia from Prehistory to the Mongol Empire*. Malden, Mass.: Blackwell, 1999. Section 3, "The Scythic and Hunnic Eras, 1000 B.C.E.-500 C.E.," includes coverage of the Xiongnu and their interations with the Yuezhi. Although highly academic, this is one of the best sources on this extremely under-studied area and time. Maps.

Lowe, Michael. *Records of Han Administration*. New York: Cambridge University Press, 1967. Primary source for the first contact between China and the Yuezhi.

So, Jenny F., and Emma C. Bunker. *Traders and Raiders on China's Northern Frontier.* Seattle: University of Washington Press, 1995. Detailed history of China's nomadic neighbors throughout history, including the Yuezhi.

Sun, Alex. *The Saga of Zhang Qian*. Hong Kong: Orchid Pavilion, 2003. Though a historical novel, this fictional work gives more detail of the daily life of the Yuezhi than any purely historical work available.

Worden, Robert L., and Andrea Matles Savada, eds. *Mongolia: A Country Study.* Washington, D.C.: Library of Congress, 1989. U.S. Federal Research Division study on Mongolia; the opening chapter concerns the Yuezhi and their struggle with the Xiongnu.

SEE ALSO: c. 4000 B.C.E., Horse Is Domesticated; c. 2000 B.C.E., Mongols Inhabit Steppes North of China; c. 1500-c. 1000 B.C.E., Aryans Appear in India; c. 1100-c. 500 B.C.E., Hallstatt Culture Dominates Northern Europe; 209-174 B.C.E., Maodun Creates a Large Confederation in Central Asia.

June, 415-September, 413 B.C.E.
ATHENIAN INVASION OF SICILY

The Athenian invasion of Sicily failed when the invasion force sent by Athens to Sicily was totally destroyed, setting Athens on its course to inevitable defeat in the Peloponnesian War.

LOCALE: Syracuse and its environs, island of Sicily
CATEGORIES: Wars, uprisings, and civil unrest; expansion and land acquisition;

KEY FIGURES

Nicias of Athens (c. 470-413 B.C.E.), conservative Athenian politician and general
Alcibiades of Athens (c. 450-404 B.C.E.), radical Athenian politician and general
Gylippus (c. 450-400 B.C.E.), Spartan general
Demosthenes (d. 413 B.C.E.), Athenian general

SUMMARY OF EVENT

Following the successful conclusion of the series of wars with Persia during the sixth century B.C.E., the Greek city-states gradually settled into a system of conflicting alliances headed by Athens on the one hand and Sparta on the other, or they tried to maintain neutrality between these two great powers. In 477 B.C.E., Athens became head of the Delian League, supposedly a purely defensive association of some 150 Greek city-states. Within fifty years, the Delian League had grown to encompass more than 250 city-states and was, for all practical purposes, the Athenian Empire, with all league riches flowing into Athens and with Athens setting league foreign policy.

Sparta, Athens' major Greek rival, watched its northern neighbor grow steadily more powerful, especially at

The Athenians are defeated in the Battle of Syracuse. (F. R. Niglutsch)

sea, where the Spartans were weakest. According to the early historian Thucydides, it was this fear of Athenian expansion that led to the outbreak of the Peloponnesian War in 431 B.C.E. It would last, with several interruptions caused by uneasy truces that pretended to be peace, until the final and apparently utter defeat of Athens in 404 B.C.E. One of the factors that led directly to the downfall of Athens was the disaster that overtook its expedition against the city of Syracuse, on the island of Sicily, in 415-413 B.C.E.

The first phase of the war, known as the Archidamian War for the name of the Spartan king who began it, ended inconclusively in 421 B.C.E. The years from 421 through 415 B.C.E. were known as the Peace of Nicias, for Nicias, the Athenian leader who negotiated a treaty with the Spartans. In Athens, the young and brilliant but unscrupulous Alcibiades, a ward of the great Athenian leader Pericles, urged a renewal of the conflict and an invasion of Sicily. He claimed this invasion would cut off Sparta's vital supply of Sicilian wheat. It is also thought that Alcibiades may have dreamed of further conquests of southern Italy or Carthage.

Although the invasion plan was vigorously resisted by Nicias of Athens and other conservative leaders, it was enormously popular, and, in June, 415 B.C.E., the Athenians launched what was then an enormous fleet of at least 134 warships carrying between 5,000 and 6,500 heavy infantry (hoplites) and light armed troops. In joint command of the expedition were Alcibiades, Nicias, and Lamachus, the last more a professional soldier than a politician.

Just before the armada sailed (some sources say the very night before), a number of religious statues throughout Athens were mutilated. Because these Herms, as they were known, were sacred to Hermes, the god of travel, the act could be seen either as a bad omen or as a deliberate sacrilege; in either event, considerable suspicion fell on Alcibiades, largely because of his scandalous past, which included participation in mocking celebrations of some of the Greeks' most solemn religious mysteries. Alcibiades was recalled after the fleet had sailed. Fearing for his life, he fled to Sparta and urged a strong defense of Syracuse and a prompt attack on Athens.

In the absence of Alcibiades, the Athenian expedition sailed on and landed in Sicily. Lamachus urged an immediate attack on Syracuse, which might well have carried the city, but Nicias preferred caution. When Lamachus was killed in an early skirmish, Nicias procrastinated and the campaigning season of 415 B.C.E. ended with Syracuse scarcely damaged. The Athenians were forced to withdraw into winter quarters, while the Syracusans appealed for and received help from their mother city of Corinth and its ally Sparta. The Spartans sent one contingent under Gylippus and the Corinthians another under Gongylus.

In 414 B.C.E., Athenian reinforcements arrived in Sicily, and Nicias pressed the Siege of Syracuse, a strong, walled city built on a peninsula that separates a large bay, the Grand Harbor, from the sea. The Athenians seized part of the Grand Harbor, fortified it, and blockaded the city by the sea, hoping by building a wall across the landward end of the peninsula to isolate Syracuse completely and force its surrender through lack of food. Lacking a siege train of battering rams, catapults, and similar weapons, the Athenians had no choice but to attempt the long and arduous process of starving out their opponents—or to have the city betrayed by a faction within its walls. Starvation or betrayal were, in fact, the typical fashion in which sieges were conducted during classical times because a walled city such as Syracuse was, for all practical purposes, invulnerable to assault. After months of inaction, and at the moment when the Athenian strategy seemed about to force the city's surrender, Gongylus slipped inside the city to report Gylippus's approach with relief forces. Gylippus's strategy was to extend a counterwall from Syracuse at right angles to Nicias's wall and head off its completion. During the summer, fierce combat ranged around the ends of the two walls. By a narrow margin, Gylippus carried his fortifications past those of Nicias and thus frustrated the Athenian offensive. In the autumn, operations stalled, and Nicias asked for reinforcements.

During the winter of 414-413 B.C.E., although under Spartan attack on the Greek mainland, the Athenians dispatched seventy-three additional triremes and five thousand hoplites under the command of Demosthenes. Their arrival barely restored the balance in favor of the Athenians. Fresh naval forces had reached Syracuse from the Peloponnesus and parts of Sicily. The Syracusans had made a bid for victory, and in June and July, 413 B.C.E., they had won a series of naval actions in the Grand Harbor. It was at this point that Demosthenes had arrived, reestablished Athenian naval supremacy, and dashed Syracusan hopes.

Demosthenes and Nicias next decided to capture Gylippus's counterwall to retrieve gains made in the campaign of the year before. The Athenian army went forward by night and came extremely close to success, but in the darkness, it lost cohesion and was repulsed. Demosthenes promptly advised Nicias to begin immediate withdrawal by sea, but once more Nicias delayed, believing an eclipse of the moon an omen against evacuation. The Syracusans then resumed their naval offensive and, in September, defeated the Athenian fleet in a great battle in the Grand Harbor, compelling Nicias to resort to the forlorn hope of escaping by land. Complete disaster followed. The Syracusan cavalry and light troops harried their enemy and wore them down under a hail of missiles until Nicias surrendered. The Syracusans executed both Nicias and Demosthenes and imprisoned their men in stone quarries for months. Those who did not die under these conditions were sold into slavery.

SIGNIFICANCE

This military defeat of Athens marked the beginning of the end for the city's struggle in the Peloponnesian War, primarily because it struck at Athens' political solidarity. At first enthusiastically united behind Alcibiades' scheme, the city was devastated first by his defection to the Spartans and then by the complete disaster that overtook the bulk of its relatively limited armed forces. Athens experienced a crisis of confidence from which it never fully recovered.

Although the Sicilian disaster encouraged some revolts within the Athenian Empire and lured Persia into an alliance with Sparta, its main effect—and Alcibiades' enduring legacy—was to sow distrust and dissension within Athens. It was this internal disarray, which brought distrust to its citizens and timidity to its military commanders, that led to its eventual collapse and final surrender in 404 B.C.E.

—*Samuel K. Eddy, updated by Michael Witkoski*

FURTHER READING

Ellis, Walter M. *Alcibiades*. New York: Routledge, 1989. A brief but penetrating study of the Athenian who, almost single-handedly, convinced his native city to embark upon its most dangerous and ultimately disastrous adventure during the long war with Sparta.

Hornblower, Simon. *The Greek World, 479-323 B.C.* 3d ed. New York: Routledge, 2002. An examination of the rise of Athens and its conflict with Sparta in the Peloponnesian War.

Kagan, Donald. *The Peace of Nicias and the Sicilian Expedition*. Ithaca, N.Y.: Cornell University Press, 1981. The best, most extensive and most scholarly modern treatment of the subject, exhaustive in its scope but exhilarating in its narrative. Kagan places the events into their wider historical perspective while maintaining the vividness of an almost firsthand account.

Roisman, Joseph. *The General Demosthenes and His Use of Military Surprise*. Stuttgart: F. Stiner, 1993. A look at the role of the general Demosthenes in the Peloponnesian War.

Strauss, Barry S., and Josiah Ober. *The Anatomy of Error: Ancient Military Disasters and Their Lessons for Modern Strategists*. New York: St. Martin's Press, 1990. In addition to providing a brief but clear explanation of what happened, Strauss and Ober explain in more detail why the Athenian expedition met such a disastrous fate—and indeed, why the entire war resulted in an Athenian defeat.

Thucydides. *The Peloponnesian War.* Translated by Richard Crawley. Edited by Robert B. Strassler, with an introduction by Victor Davis Hanson. New York: Simon and Schuster, 1998. The definitive source for the Sicilian expedition are books 6 and 7 of Thucydides' history of the war. Contains maps, appendices, and index.

See also: 480-479 b.c.e., Persian Invasion of Greece; 478-448 b.c.e., Athenian Empire Is Created; May, 431-September, 404 b.c.e., Peloponnesian War.

Related articles in *Great Lives from History: The Ancient World*: Alcibiades of Athens; Thucydides.

406 B.C.E.
Greek Dramatist Euripides Dies

The death of Greek dramatist Euripides marked the end of the Classical Age; his work set the pattern for complex and melodramatic drama for centuries to come.

Locale: Athens, Greece, and Macedonia (now in Greece)

Categories: Literature; cultural and intellectual history

Key Figures

Euripides (c. 485-406 b.c.e.), Greek dramatist and tragic poet

Archelaus (d. 399 b.c.e.), king of Macedonia, r. c. 413-399 b.c.e.

Protagoras (c. 485-c. 410 b.c.e.), Greek philosopher

Thucydides (c. 459-c. 402 b.c.e.), Greek historian

Summary of Event

Euripides, the youngest of ancient Athens' three greatest tragic poets, lived most of his life in Athens. He retired to the court of Archelaus, king of Macedonia, in 408 b.c.e. and died there two years later.

Few certainties exist about the death of Euripides. Of the sources for his life, composed mostly of ancient quotes, gossip, anecdotes, and criticism dating from the second century b.c.e. to the eleventh century c.e. or later, the best authority is the *Atthis* (n.d.; English translation of more than 170 fragments, 1949) of Philochorus. Philochorus, an early third century b.c.e. historian, composed a treatise on Euripides that calls into question the loosely assembled bits of information.

Generally, it is believed that the events depicted in Euripides' plays reflected what was occurring in his private life. One of the oft-repeated traditional views of Euripides is that his mother was a greengrocer who sold herbs. Another common belief centers on the assumption that Euripides' treatment of women in his plays reproduced his personal hatred and hostility toward them (thought to be the result of two disastrous marriages). In addition, contemporary Athenian comic poets made many jokes about Euripides. Though these stories have been shown to have no basis in fact, the frequency with which they are repeated necessarily render narratives of Euripides' later life and death equally unreliable.

However, owing to the large output of plays toward the end of his life, which provide points of reference, and the customary emphasis placed on the latter period of life by Greek annalists of antiquity, certain events about the end of Euripides' life have some degree of certainty.

By the year 415 b.c.e., Euripides had undergone a period of change evident in a series of plays written about this time. The Peloponnesian War, which had begun in 431 b.c.e., had raged for sixteen years and had taken its toll on Euripides. Although his early plays often adopt

Euripides. (Library of Congress)

500 - 401 b.c.e.

the theme of revenge, his later ones are imbued with an emphasis on forgiveness and peace. Also, whereas his early wartime plays had suggested that he believed war to be honorable and necessary to defend the oppressed, his series of plays in 415 B.C.E. depict inhuman brutality. As he was writing the plays, in 416 B.C.E., Athenians besieged and captured the small neutral island of Melos, massacring all the adult men and enslaving all the women and children. Euripides was critical of Athens because he believed it had been false to its ideals.

The war dragged on, and Euripides, akin to characters in his tragedies who long for a means of escape from their terrible circumstances, spent more time away from Athens. Many Athenians detested him for his denouncement of war and his insistence that the doings of the gods were evil. They were confused by the innovation and complexity of his tragedies. He had seemed to vent a deep antipathy toward women; however, he strangely defended adultresses in his plays. Philochorus depicts Euripides at this time in his life with a long beard and moles on his face. A bust of him in his old age shows a worn, fine face, thin hair, and somewhat sunken lips. He lived very much alone, despising visitors and living on the island of Salamis in a cave that looked out on the sea. Reputedly, he spent his days thinking and writing.

By this time, some of Euripides' old friends had been driven out of Athens. The poet's master, Anaxagoras, had died long before; the famed Sophist Protagoras, who had read his famous book, *On the Gods*, in Euripides' own house, had drowned at sea, proving to many Athenians how the gods regarded his ideas. Timotheus, the Ionian musician whose failed first performance brought thoughts of suicide until Euripides encouraged him, had forsaken Athens for Macedonia.

Perhaps some darker event befell Euripides, because in 408 B.C.E., he left Athens in voluntary exile. Early sources insist that he left in grief and almost all Athens rejoiced in his misfortune. More gossipy commentaries maintain that his shame for his wife's immorality occasioned his departure, but his motives remain obscure. He stayed for a while in Magnesia, near Ephesus, but soon continued on to Macedonia, a barbaric or semibarbaric country of rivers, forests, and wild mountain ranges.

As an invited guest of Archelaus, king of Macedonia, Euripides was treated with respect, sharing the company of other wise men including Thucydides, the historian. While at court, he continued to compose plays. One narrative of his time there reports that a Macedonian who insulted Euripides was given to him by Archelaus to be scourged.

The event of his death in 406 B.C.E. was given a dramatic turn by traditional sources. According to one, Euripides was sitting alone, in a wood, when the king's hounds fell on him and tore him to pieces. Another one related that he was torn from limb to limb by a mob of irate women. How Euripides really died is not known, although at the age of seventy-eight, he may well have died of natural causes. He was buried in a magnificent tomb at the confluence of two streams in a valley in Macedonia.

SIGNIFICANCE

With the death of Euripides, the age of Classical Greece was drawing to a close. His death occurred two years before the fall of Athens in 404 B.C.E., and his plays seem to indicate a crisis of conscience that occurred during the waning years of his life.

Euripides was by far the most modern of the ancient dramatists. Thought to have hastened the demise of tragedy through his more realistic depictions of characters, he appears to reflect the cultural strains that existed in fifth century B.C.E. Greece. Embittered by the lengthy Peloponnesian War, Euripides seems to have adopted the new sophistic questioning to suggest a new moral atmosphere in which he despairs over meaningless human suffering. He depicted men and women as the people they actually were, as opposed to their ideal images, and placed them among familiar and household things and had them speak simple dialogues. By the end of his life, he had also written tragicomic plays, pointing to the drama of fourth century B.C.E. and, ultimately, toward the tragedies of the English playwright William Shakespeare.

—*Mary Hurd*

FURTHER READING

Dunn, Frances M. *Tragedy's End: Closure and Innovation in Euripidean Drama*. Oxford, England: Oxford University Press, 1996. Dunn argues that Euripides' techniques in plot and endings opened tragedy to comic impulses.

Highet, Gilbert. *The Classical Tradition: Greek and Roman Influences on Western Literature*. Oxford, England: Oxford University Press, 1992. Well-researched and interesting source for the beginnings of Western literature. Follows Greek and Roman authors who managed to survive through the ages and helps the reader understand what they meant to civilization.

Jones, Nicholas F. *Ancient Greece: State and Society*. New York: Prentice Hall, 1996. An interesting book describing the fifth and fourth centuries B.C.E. in Athens, focusing on the physical arrangement of the city, government, religion, political and economic groups, family structure, and typical occupations.

Lloyd, Michael. *The Agon in Euripides*. Oxford, England: Clarendon Press, 1992. A study of the *agon*, or formal debate, a technique used in Euripides' tragedies in which two characters confront each other, often before an arbitrator or judge, and make long speeches as if they were opponents in a court of law. Lloyd believes the *agon* is often of crucial importance to the central conflict of the play.

Morford, Mark P. O., et al. *Classical Mythology*. Oxford, England: Oxford University Press, 2001. An excellent introduction to the myths and legends of Greece and Rome. Contains useful illustrations.

Murray, Gilbert. *Euripides and His Age*. Westport, Conn.: Greenwood, 1979. Classic study of Euripides. Reconstructs his life and times, the conventions of Greek tragedy, and how Euripides worked within them and liberated them.

Rabinowitz, Nancy Sorkin. *Anxiety Veiled: Euripides and the Traffic in Women*. Ithaca, N.Y.: Cornell University Press, 1993. The author argues that the prominence of female characters in Euripides' plays suggests a structure of male dominance while simultaneously applauding the strength of women.

Thucydides. *History of the Peloponnesian War*. Translated by Rex Warner. Reprint. New York: Viking Press, 1954. Written four hundred years before the birth of Christ, this volume details contemporary accounts of the war between Athens and Sparta, which eventually plunged the entire Greek world into twenty-seven years of struggle.

SEE ALSO: c. 456/455 B.C.E., Greek Tragedian Aeschylus Dies; c. 440 B.C.E., Sophists Train the Greeks in Rhetoric and Politics; c. 438 B.C.E., Greek Lyric Poet Pindar Dies; May, 431-September, 404 B.C.E., Peloponnesian War; June, 415-September, 413 B.C.E., Athenian Invasion of Sicily; September, 404-May, 403 B.C.E., Thirty Tyrants Rule Athens for Eight Months; c. 385 B.C.E., Greek Playwright Aristophanes Dies.

RELATED ARTICLES in *Great Lives from History: The Ancient World*: Aeschylus; Anaxagoras; Aristophanes; Euripides; Menander (dramatist); Pindar; Protagoras; Thucydides.

September, 404-May, 403 B.C.E.
THIRTY TYRANTS RULE ATHENS FOR EIGHT MONTHS

Following its defeat in the Peloponnesian War, Athens was ruled by thirty oligarchic, pro-Spartan tyrants, whose despotic behavior quickly led to civil war and the restoration of the democracy.

LOCALE: Athens
CATEGORIES: Government and politics; wars, uprisings, and civil unrest

KEY FIGURES

Lysander of Sparta (d. 395 B.C.E.), Spartan general
Pausanias of Sparta (d. c. 385 B.C.E.), king of Sparta, r. c. 408-c. 385 B.C.E.
Theramenes (d. 403 B.C.E.), Athenian politician
Critias of Athens (c. 460-403 B.C.E.), Athenian politician
Thrasybulus (d. 388 B.C.E.), Athenian politician

SUMMARY OF EVENT

In 405 B.C.E., a Spartan fleet under the command of Lysander of Sparta won a devastating victory over the Athenians at Aegospotami. Having crippled Athenian naval power, Lysander proceeded to blockade Athens by sea while the Spartan kings, Pausanias and Agis (r. c. 427-400), besieged the city by land. The threat of starvation forced the Athenians to capitulate the following year, finally bringing the Peloponnesian War (431-404) to an end. The Athenian politician Theramenes helped negotiate the surrender terms, which required the Athenians to become subordinate allies of Sparta, recall all exiles, limit their navy to twelve ships, give up most foreign territory, and dismantle both the harbor fortifications at Piraeus and the Long Wall connecting the port to the city of Athens 4 miles (6.5 kilometers) away.

In the summer of 404 B.C.E., the Thirty, a group of Athenian oligarchs, formed a new government at Athens, replacing the democracy. Chief among the Thirty were Critias of Athens and Theramenes. Critias, a relative of Plato and friend of Socrates, was a politician, philosopher, and playwright who had been exiled from Athens in 406. Like many upper-class Greeks, he greatly admired the aristocratic and authoritarian Spartan political system. Theramenes, though he had participated in two short-lived oligarchic governments in 411, favored less extreme policies. It is unclear precisely how the Thirty came to power, but they were probably installed at the instigation of Lysander, who created similar puppet governments in other conquered cities. Apparently the Thirty were not meant to be a permanent ruling body but merely had a mandate to draw up a new constitution for the Athenians along more conservative lines.

The Thirty quickly consolidated power, establishing a council of five hundred, appointing magistrates, abolishing democratic laws and institutions, and providing themselves with a bodyguard. Under the leadership of Critias, they began to try to execute men who had acted as informers under the democracy. Soon the Thirty moved against pro-democratic leaders and potential rivals. They may even have been responsible for the assassination of the notorious politician and general Alcibiades of Athens (c. 450-404 B.C.E.), who had sought refuge with the Persians. Some were executed, and others were exiled. In Plato's *Apologia Sōkratous* (399-390 B.C.E.; *Apology*, 1675), Socrates claims to have defied the Thirty's order to help arrest one individual sentenced to death and thereby risked arrest and execution himself. According to Aristotle, the Thirty killed about fifteen hundred men during their short reign. Such practices soon caused these oligarchs to be known as the Thirty Tyrants.

At some point (the precise chronology is unclear), Theramenes began to question the policies of Critias. Favoring a more moderate and inclusive government, he opposed both the executions and Critias's scheme to limit the franchise to only three thousand Athenians. Backed by the other members of the Thirty, Critias had Theramenes put to death.

Having established a citizen body of three thousand, the Thirty proceeded to disarm all other Athenians and expel them from the city. Resident aliens, or *metics*, were soon threatened as well. Either because of their wealth or opposition to the regime, the Thirty executed a number of wealthy *metics* and confiscated their property. To discourage opposition and enforce their commands, at some point (again the precise chronology is unclear), the Thirty also requested and received a garrison of about seven hundred soldiers from Sparta.

Many Athenians fled the Thirty's reign of terror, seeking refuge in neighboring Greek city-states such as Argos, Megara, and Thebes. The Spartans responded by ordering their allies to surrender any Athenian exiles to the Thirty, but some states, increasingly disenchanted with Spartan hegemony, refused to do so. Thrasybulus, a staunchly pro-democratic Athenian politician and general who had been banished by the Thirty, began to organize the refugees in Thebes.

During the winter of 404/403 B.C.E., Thrasybulus invaded Attica with a small group of men and occupied the fortress at Phyle, 12 miles (19 kilometers) north of Athens. The Thirty sent the Three Thousand to retake Phyle, but they were unable to dislodge the democrats. Buoyed by this initial success and strengthened by reinforcements, Thrasybulus now began to raid the surrounding countryside. The Thirty deployed the Spartan garrison and some Athenian cavalry to contain the pro-democratic forces. Thrasybulus responded by launching a dawn surprise attack on the Spartan camp. He won a major victory, inflicting many casualties and forcing the Spartans to flee.

Thrasybulus and his followers proceeded to march on Piraeus, where they took up a strong defensive position at Munichia, a steep hill on the outskirts of the port city. The Thirty, whose army still greatly outnumbered that of Thrasybulus, foolishly decided to attack. Thanks in part to his use of light-armed *peltasts* (javelin-throwers), Thrasybulus was able to defeat the oligarchs' army, killing more than seventy men. Of the Thirty, both Critias and Hippomachus died in the fighting.

The surviving oligarchs retreated with their army to the city of Athens, where the Three Thousand, increasingly unhappy with the leadership of the Thirty, deposed them and installed a new ruling council of ten. The Thirty and their remaining supporters withdrew to Eleusis, a city in Attica approximately 10 miles (16 kilometers) northwest of Athens. As a precaution, the Thirty had seized this town sometime earlier, expelling and executing its inhabitants.

Thrasybulus's support continued to grow, and the democrats soon threatened to take Athens itself. After both the Thirty at Eleusis and the Ten at Athens requested Spartan assistance, Lysander responded by lending the oligarchs money, sending a fleet to blockade Piraeus, and gathering an army at Eleusis. Pausanias, perhaps fearful of Lysander's growing power and reputation, soon arrived with another army. By the summer of 403 B.C.E., a combined force of Spartan and pro-oligarchic Athenian troops proceeded to attack the democrats at Piraeus. After a few inconclusive engagements, Pausanias managed to broker a new settlement between the various Athenian factions. Thrasybulus and his followers were allowed to return to Athens while the Thirty and their close associates would retain control of Eleusis. Those who had remained at Athens during the reign of the Thirty were allowed to choose whether they wanted to stay there or relocate to Eleusis. In early October of 403, Thrasybulus and his army entered Athens, and democratic government was restored. The Athenians all swore to observe an amnesty and not punish anyone for his actions under the oligarchic regime.

Two years later in 401 B.C.E., the democrats, fearing renewed attacks from the Thirty, marched on Eleusis. At a parley, they surprised and killed the leaders of the oligarchs. The democrats then reached a peaceful settlement with the inhabitants of Eleusis, who once again became part of the Athenian polity.

SIGNIFICANCE

The reign of the Thirty Tyrants was significant for a number of reasons. Most famously, Socrates' close association with Critias and other oligarchs probably led to his trial and execution in 399 B.C.E. despite the amnesty agreement. The harsh policies of the Thirty helped make Thebes, which had called for the complete destruction of Athens in 404, sympathetic to Athenian democrats. The Thebans aided Thrasybulus and soon formed an alliance with Athens. Together they resisted Spartan imperialism during the Corinthian War (395-386). Thrasybulus's victories further tarnished Sparta's military reputation and demonstrated how effective light-armed troops could be against hoplites. Finally, Athens, unlike many other Greek city-states that suffered periods of civil strife, managed to avoid a debilitating cycle of revenge and retribution following the bloody reign of the Thirty. For the most part, the amnesty worked, and Athens was able to begin rebuilding its power.

—*David B. Hollander*

FURTHER READING

Aristotle. T*he Athenian Constitution: The Eudemian Ethics; On Virtues and Vices*. Translated by H. Rackham. Cambridge, Mass.: Harvard University Press, 1981. A history of Athenian political institutions from the archaic period down to the fourth century B.C.E.

Buck, Robert J. *Thrasybulus and the Athenian Democracy: The Life of an Athenian Statesman*. Stuttgart, Germany: Franz Steiner Verlag, 1998. Buck examines Thrasybulus's role in the conflict involving the Thirty Tyrants.

Krenz, Peter. *The Thirty at Athens*. Ithaca, N.Y.: Cornell University Press, 1982. A comprehensive modern study of the Thirty's reign. Bibliography and index.

Wolpert, Andrew. *Remembering Defeat: Civil War and Civic Memory in Ancient Athens*. Baltimore: The Johns Hopkins University Press, 2002. A discussion of the civil war and how Athenians coped with the memory of it. Bibliography and index.

Xenophon. *Hellenica*. New York: Arno Press, 1979. A history of Greece from 411 to 362 B.C.E. written by a contemporary Athenian.

SEE ALSO: 499-494 B.C.E., Ionian Revolt; 478-448 B.C.E., Athenian Empire Is Created; May, 431-September, 404 B.C.E., Peloponnesian War; June, 415-September, 413 B.C.E., Athenian Invasion of Sicily.

RELATED ARTICLES in *Great Lives from History: The Ancient World*: Pausanias of Sparta; Socrates; Xenophon.

401-400 B.C.E.
MARCH OF THE TEN THOUSAND

The March of the Ten Thousand was a failed military expedition against Persia, but it confirmed the superiority of Greek hoplites over Asian infantry and revealed the growing importance of mercenaries in Greek warfare.

LOCALE: Western Persian Empire in Asia Minor (now Turkey, Syria, and Iraq)

CATEGORIES: Wars, uprisings, and civil unrest; expansion and land acquisition

KEY FIGURES

Xenophon (c. 431-c. 354 B.C.E.), Athenian officer, historian, and chronicler of the march

Cyrus the Younger (c. 424-401 B.C.E.), Persian prince and satrap in Asia Minor, brother of Artaxerxes II

Artaxerxes II (d. c. 359 B.C.E.), king of Persia, r. 405-359 B.C.E.

Tissaphernes (d. 395 B.C.E.), Persian satrap in Asia Minor, general at the Battle of Cunaxa

Clearchus (fl. fifth century B.C.E.), Spartan exile, chief commander of the Greek mercenaries

SUMMARY OF EVENT

The March of the Ten Thousand refers to the 1,500-mile (2,400-kilometer) journey of a Greek mercenary army into the heart of the Persian Empire, its valorous but vain combat near Babylon (now in central Iraq), and its arduous trek back to Greek territory more than a year later. The story is vividly recounted in the *Kurou anabasis* (between 394 and 371 B.C.E.; *Anabasis*, also known as

Expedition of Cyrus and *March Up Country*, 1623) by Xenophon, an Athenian officer who participated in the expedition. This adventure made a huge impression on contemporary Greeks, who took it as an indication of the vulnerability of the Persian Empire, and the campaign greatly influenced relations between Persia and Sparta. Nevertheless, the expedition arose out of Persian dynastic strife and is best understood in that context.

The ambitious Persian prince, Cyrus the Younger, organized this expedition in order to depose his older brother, Artaxerxes II, who had recently assumed the Persian throne on the death of their father, Darius II, in 404 B.C.E. Under Darius II, Persia had played a key role in the later phase of the Peloponnesian War (431-404) between Athens and Sparta, when it intervened on the side of the Spartans by subsidizing the fleet that brought about the defeat of Athens. In return for this Persian support, the Spartans agreed to allow the Persians to reassert their control of the Ionian Greek cities, which had been part of the Athenian Empire. Sent out to Asia Minor in 407 B.C.E. to implement this pro-Spartan policy and given an extraordinary command at the age of sixteen, Cyrus quickly displayed his regal ambitions. Among those he offended were the Ionian satrap, Tissaphernes, whose authority and policies Cyrus largely displaced, and two of Cyrus's royal cousins, whom he later had executed for refusing to go along with his kingly ceremonial pretensions. When Artaxerxes assumed the throne in 404 B.C.E., Cyrus immediately plotted to dethrone him but was denounced by Tissaphernes and placed under arrest at the imperial capital. He escaped execution thanks to the intercession of his mother and was allowed to return to Ionia, although with drastically reduced authority. There, he immediately began preparations for a military challenge to Artaxerxes. To augment his sizable force of Asian troops, Cyrus recruited approximately thirteen thousand mercenary soldiers from many areas of Greece. Most were heavily armored infantry, or hoplites, whose superiority to Asian infantry had been demonstrated in earlier conflicts. By sending a company of soldiers under a Spartan general and providing naval support, the Spartans became the only Greeks to participate as a city-state.

Xenophon and the Ten Thousand at the sea's edge. (F. R. Niglutsch)

Cyrus the Younger attempted to disguise his treasonous objective by saying that the army would be used against rebellious tribes in Asia Minor, but he did not fool Tissaphernes, who dashed to alert Artaxerxes as soon as Cyrus's army left Sardis in the spring of 401 B.C.E. As the march progressed, the Greeks became suspicious of their destination and mutinied twice. Only the exhortations of the Spartan general, Clearchus, and promises of huge increases in pay induced the mercenaries to continue the march and cross the Euphrates River into Mesopotamia. By turning south toward Babylon instead of proceeding east against the northern capital city of Ecbatana (now Hamadān, Iran), Cyrus may have surprised Artaxerxes, who had to defend Babylon without his full army. In the Battle of Cunaxa during September, 401 B.C.E., the Greeks acquitted themselves well, routing the more numerous Asian troops opposite them and beating off a counterattack organized by Tissaphernes. Not until the next day did they learn that Cyrus's Asian troops had been defeated and that Cyrus himself had died leading a cavalry charge against the king.

Demoralized by the death of Cyrus the Younger and aware of their precarious position, the Greeks nevertheless refused to surrender their weapons and acknowledged Clearchus as their leader. Clearchus entered into an uneasy truce with Tissaphernes, who promised the Greeks safe conduct on their return home and began to escort them out of Mesopotamia by way of the Tigris Valley. Either out of pure treacherous impulse, as Xenophon would have it, or because he had learned that Clearchus was plotting to kill him, Tissaphernes surprised the Greeks by calling a parley at which he arrested their generals and executed the officers attending them. Clearchus and the other generals were put on display in Babylon before being put to death.

The leaderless army showed its resilience by electing new leaders, including Xenophon, and continued its march up the Tigris River. Leaving Mesopotamia and Persian harassment behind, the mercenaries faced many hardships during the winter of 401-400 B.C.E., as they made their way through the mountains of Kurdistan and Armenia. In the spring of 400 B.C.E., they arrived at Trapezus (now Trabzon, Turkey) on the Black Sea coast, where they rejoiced at the sight of the sea and recuperated before continuing their journey west by land and ship. At one point, Xenophon suggested that they settle and found a new city, but this idea was not well received by his fellow soldiers, who were determined to return to Greece. When they finally reached the Bosporus in the autumn of 400, their number had shrunk to approximately six thousand. After their return, most of the Cyreans, as they were called, did not go back to their home city-states but reentered mercenary service. They first served the Thracian king, Seuthes, and then crossed back to Asia Minor in 399 B.C.E. to fight for the Spartans, who had decided to go to war with the Persians in Ionia.

SIGNIFICANCE

Xenophon's straightforward style in the *Anabasis* makes his account an ideal primer for students of classical Greek, and generations of modern students are familiar with the saga of the Ten Thousand, which reveals much about Greek military practice and the non-Greek peoples encountered by the army.

Contemporary Greeks may have exaggerated the significance of the army's successful retreat out of Asia as a sign of Persian weakness, for Artaxerxes II certainly could have isolated and destroyed them if he had wished to do so. His primary concern, however, was to get them out of the rich province of Mesopotamia with a minimum of damage. Still, the encounter at Cunaxa confirmed the superiority of the Greek infantry phalanx over Asian troops and would inspire future invaders of the Persian Empire. The ease with which Cyrus the Younger recruited these soldiers, the first large mercenary Greek army, demonstrated the wide appeal of mercenary service among impoverished Greeks with no better means of earning a living. In coming years, such mercenaries would play an important role in Greek warfare.

The expedition also brought about a change in Spartan-Persian relations that had enormous importance for the future of Sparta. Spartan support of Cyrus's failed attack on Artaxerxes soured relations between the empire and its former allies and led to Sparta's decision to fight the Persians in Asia. This Asian war weakened Sparta and prompted Artaxerxes to organize a coalition of Greek city-states to fight the bitter Corinthian War (395-386 B.C.E.) against Sparta. To face this conflict at home, Sparta abandoned the contest in Asia and acknowledged Persian overlordship of the Ionian Greeks. Sparta eventually won the war in Greece but emerged with its manpower drained and its prestige among the Greeks badly damaged.

—*James T. Chambers*

FURTHER READING

Anderson, J. K. *Xenophon*. Bristol, England: Bristol Classical, 2001. A biography of the general Xenophon, written by a classicist, that examines the evidence regarding his life in his major works. Bibliography and index.

Hackett, John, ed. *Warfare in the Ancient World*. New York: Facts On File, 1989. This excellently illustrated volume contrasts Greek and Persian styles of warfare in two chapters, "Hoplite Warfare" and "The Persians."

Nussbaum, G. B. *The Ten Thousand: A Study in Social Organization and Action in Xenophon's "Anabasis."* Leiden, the Netherlands: Brill, 1967. This study analyzes the decision-making process of the Greeks during their retreat and argues that the army functioned as a mobile city-state.

Prevas, John. *Xenophon's March: Into the Lair of the Persian Lion*. Cambridge, Mass.: Da Capo Press, 2002. An examination of the expedition of Cyprus. Bibliography and index.

Stronk, Jan P. *The Ten Thousand in Thrace: An Archaeological and Historical Commentary on Xenophon's*

"Anabasis." Amsterdam: J. C. Gieben, 1995. A comparison and contrast of Xenophon's account and the historical and archaeological evidence. Bibliography and index.

Xenophon. *The Persian Expedition*. Translated by Rex Warner. New York: Penguin, 1972. An entertaining firsthand record of the expedition. The extended introduction by George Cawkwell alerts the reader to the shortcomings of Xenophon's account and discusses some of the larger strategic and tactical problems associated with the march.

SEE ALSO: c. 700-330 B.C.E., Phalanx Is Developed as a Military Unit; 480-479 B.C.E., Persian Invasion of Greece; 478-448 B.C.E., Athenian Empire Is Created; c. 450-c. 425 B.C.E., History Develops as a Scholarly Discipline; May, 431-September, 404 B.C.E., Peloponnesian War; September, 404-May, 403 B.C.E., Thirty Tyrants Rule Athens for Eight Months; Between 394 and 371 B.C.E., Xenophon Writes the *Anabasis*.

RELATED ARTICLE in *Great Lives from History: The Ancient World*: Xenophon.

c. 4th century B.C.E.-3d century C.E.
KAUṬILYA COMPILES A TREATISE ON PRACTICAL STATECRAFT

Kauṭilya's Treatise on the Good *is the most famous treatise on statecraft and administration belonging to the Arthaśāstra (science of government) school of thought.*

LOCALE: Pataliputra in Magadha (near present-day Bankipur in Bihar, India)

CATEGORIES: Cultural and intellectual history; government and politics

KEY FIGURE

Kauṭilya (fl. 300 B.C.E.), Brahman scholar from Taxila

SUMMARY OF EVENT

Kauṭilya (the politician), also known as Viṣugupta (the astronomer) and Cāṇakya (the moralist), was a peripatetic pundit from Taxila in the northwestern border of India (now a part of Pakistan). According to Jain tradition, Kauṭilya was born in Chanaka, a village in the Golla district of Taxila, son of a poor Brahman called Chani and his wife, Chaneshwari. After his wife suffered the humiliation of being poor at her wedding, Kauṭilya determined to become wealthy. He studied metallurgy to learn how to mint coins. Then he traveled to Pataliputra, capital city of the prosperous and powerful kingdom of Magadha, to serve King Dhanananda, who was reputed to be wealthy and haughty but generous to Brahmans. At the Nanda court, Kauṭilya prospered for a time, becoming the head of the royal alms office. He lost his job when he fell out of royal favor because of his unattractive looks and insolent manners. He thereupon vowed to put an end to the Nanda rule and began his wanderings as an Ājīvika ascetic in search of ways and means to realize his objective.

During his sojourn, Kauṭilya chanced on a boy named Chandragupta of striking personality and disposition in a Magadhan village, bought him from his foster parents, and took him to Taxila, where he could train in a school. With the wealth Kauṭilya had accumulated through his minting skill, he raised an army, made Chandragupta its commander, and laid siege to Pataliputra. However, the siege failed to subdue the Nanda ruler, and the besiegers decamped. After a short while, however, they tried another strategy and defeated the Magadhan king. Chandragupta Maurya founded the Mauryan Dynasty, named after Chandragupta's clan. The story of the Kauṭilya-Chandragupta connection, originating probably with works such as Kāmandaka's *Nītisāra* (first half of eighth century C.E.; *Kamandakiya Nitisara: Or, The Elements of Polity*, 1896) and Viśākhadatta's play *Mudrārākṣasa* (possibly fourth century C.E. or later; *Mudraraksasam*, 1900), is preserved in present-day Indian juvenile literature.

According to popular accounts, Kauṭilya fell out of favor with his royal disciple toward the end of his career, left Pataliputra, and became a forest-dwelling ascetic (*vanaprastha*). The *Arthaśāstra* (dates vary, c. fourth century B.C.E.-third century C.E.; *Treatise on the Good*, 1961) was probably composed in retirement.

Arthaśāstra means the *śāstra* (science) of *artha* (wealth or territory inhabited by humans). However, the term is best interpreted as "science of politics" or "science of government." According to Kauṭilya, the source of people's livelihood is Earth, which is inhabited by human beings, and the means of the attainment and protection of Earth is the *arthaśāstra*. The *arthaśāstra*, which eventually represented a school of political thought, was developed as an independent discipline beginning in the sixth century B.C.E. It arose as a reaction to the Buddhist teachings that emphasized the transience of the world and the lasting value of liberation (*mokṣa*). Prefering materialism over morality, the *arthaśāstra* writers divided the goals of human life into four categories: *dharma* (morality and justice), *artha* (wealth or material well-being), *kāma* (desires), and *mokṣa* (liberation or salvation). Among them, *artha* occupied the most prominent place. In his *Treatise on the Good*, Kauṭilya claimed that material well-being alone is supreme because spiritual and sensual pleasures depend on it. Accordingly, the *arthaśāstras* included the study of agriculture, commerce, animal husbandry, and other allied occupations, though by far the single most important subject was the art of governance and the ways and means of attaining sovereign authority. In short, the object of the *arthaśāstra* was to counsel the prince in the attainment of material welfare and in the art of good government.

Kauṭilya's *Treatise on the Good* echoes all the earlier *arthaśāstras* and even harks back to a number of authorities mentioned in the Hindu epic *Mahābhārata* (400 B.C.E.-400 C.E., present form by c. 400 C.E.; *The Mahabharata of Krishna-Dwaipayana Vyasa*, 1887-1896), which stated that the king's duty (*rājadharma*) consisted in providing security for his subjects and protecting morality and justice. *Rājadharma* is founded on *daṇḍa* (literally, rod or stick), or legitimate coercive authority, which is the basis of a political society or the state. For example, Vaivasata Manu, the first elected ruler of humankind in Hindu mythology, maintained that if the king did not employ *daṇḍa* when necessary, the strong would torment the weak, just as the larger fish devour the smaller ones in the river. Thus, the law of the fish results in the absence of either *daṇḍa* or the king. However, although Manu exercised coercive authority, he was no more than a dispenser of *daṇḍa*, which he held as sacred as *dharma*. Kauṭilya endorses the principles of *daṇḍa* by declaring that its administration constitutes the science of politics.

The central theme of Kauṭilya's *Treatise on the Good* is the study of the state. The work is divided into fifteen books, 150 chapters, 180 sections, about 5,000 verses, and about 5,370 pithy statements (sutras). The first book deals with the education and upbringing of the prince. The second addresses civil administration, including the formation of village units, construction of forts, and the revenue system. Books 3-5 deal with civil law, legal proceedings, and punishments and duties of courtiers and councillors. The sixth book discusses the seven elements of politics—king, ministers, land, fort, treasury, army, and ally—and analyzes interstate relations. The seventh book deals with the six diplomatic policies. The eighth book enumerates and elucidates the various calamities befalling a kingdom, including their causes and cures. The problems of war occupy books 9-10, and the subsequent three books deal with diplomacy and espionage. The fourteenth book discusses the various magical ways and means of eliminating the enemy. Finally, the last book outlines the thirty-two methodological principles, or the method of science.

According to the *Treatise on the Good*, the state has a moral purpose: to bring about order. The ruler of the state must at all times be guided by *dharma* (righteousness or duty). Even though he wields the rod for the sake of maintaining order, he must, nevertheless, use his coercive authority judiciously. The king who is too severe with the rod, says Kauṭilya, inspires terror in his people, while the king who is too mild with the rod incurs his people's displeasure, but the king who is just with the rod is honored by all. A truly Kauṭilyan ruler is a saintly king who has conquered the six basic drives pernicious to human nature: *kāma* (lust), *kopa* or *krodha* (anger), *lobha* (avarice), *mana* (vanity), *mada* (insolence), and *harṣa* (levity). In addition, he must be well versed in the four sciences: *trayī* (the three Vedas: *Rigveda*, *Samāveda*, and *Yajurveda*), *anviksiki* (the philosophy of Sāṁkhya, Yoga, and Lokāyata), *varta* (the science of economics consisting of agriculture, cattle breeding, and trade), and *dandaniti* (the science of government). In short, a ruler of men must be adept in the arts of virtue and valor.

The ruler is also enjoined to expand his realm by means of what Kauṭilya calls *dharmavijaya* (righteous conquest). He counsels against any victory by wanton destruction (*asuravijaya*) or because of excessive greed (*lobhavijaya*). He encourages aggression only against an enemy who is both active (*śatru*) and passive (*ari*). Hence, he insists on the total destruction of the enemy even by foul means in a strategic battle (*kutayuddha*). The *Treatise on the Good* devotes an entire book to describing the secret means such as magic or medicinal charms to injure an enemy. However, the victor must be guided by a strict code of conduct. After gaining new territory, he should cover the enemy's faults with his own virtues and the enemy's virtues with double virtues. In other words, the conqueror should govern all his conquered people strictly in accordance with the duties prescribed to kings.

SIGNIFICANCE

Kauṭilya inspired subsequent generations of philosophers, poets, and political thinkers of India, including the poet Kālidāsa. In the eighth century C.E., the *Treatise on the Good* was taught formally in the schools of Varanasi, India. The influence of the *Treatise on the Good* declined after the Turkish conquest of northern India in the thirteenth century; however, as late as the eighteenth century, Kauṭilya continued to be ranked with such great political thinkers of ancient India as Vrihaspati and Shukracharya.

—*Narasingha P. Sil*

FURTHER READING

Bandyopadhyaya, Narain C. *Kauṭilya, Or, An Exposition on His Social Ideal and Political Theory.* 1927. Reprint. Varanasi, India: Indological Book House, 1982. Extremely useful biographical information on Kauṭilya.

Kangle, R. P. *The Kautiliya "Arthaśāstra."* Bombay: University of Bombay, 1965-1969. The first part contains a magisterial translation of the *Arthaśāstra* and the third part a superb critical analysis of the work.

Mookerji, Radha K. *Chandragupta Maurya and His Times.* 4th ed. Delhi: Motilal Banarasidass, 1966. Important information on the Kauṭilya-Chandragupta connection and on the *Treatise on the Good* by a distinguished historian.

Ray, Ranjan K. *An Introductory Study of Kauṭilya's "Arthaśāstra."* Calcutta, India: K. Ray, 1966. A basic overview of the theories and concepts of the *Treatise on the Good.*

Raychaudhuri, Hemchandra. *Political History of Ancient India from the Accession of Parikshit to the Extinction of the Gupta Dynasty.* 7th ed. Delhi: Oxford University Press, 1996. A classic work, first published in 1923, on the political history of India.

Sil, Narasingha P. *Kauṭilya's "Arthaśāstra": A Comparative Study.* 2d ed. New York: Peter Lang, 1989. A bibliography on Kauṭilya and a comprehensive comparative analysis of the texts of Plato, Aristotle, and Machiavelli, as well as of the *Arthaśāstra.*

_______. "Political Morality Versus Political Necessity: Kauṭilya and Machiavelli Revisited." *Journal of Asian History* 9, no. 2 (1985). A revisionist study of an older standard comparison between the ideas of both authors.

SEE ALSO: c. 321 B.C.E., Mauryan Empire Rises in India.

RELATED ARTICLE in *Great Lives from History: The Ancient World*: Chandragupta Maurya.

Early 4th century B.C.E.
FOUNDING OF MOHISM

The founding of the Mohist school ushered in ideas and practices involving meritocratic, law-based systems of government that helped shape the development of empire and civil service for twenty-three thousand years.

LOCALE: Central States (now the regions around the Yellow and Yangtze Rivers, in China)

CATEGORIES: Cultural and intellectual history; religion; philosophy

KEY FIGURE

Mozi (Mo-tzu; c. 470-c. 391 B.C.E.), Chinese philosopher

SUMMARY OF EVENT

Mo Di, referred to posthumously and by his own disciples as Mozi, is renowned as an ethicist, political philosopher, and man of irreproachable behavior. He is the purported founder of Mohism, a school of thought that was perpetuated and developed under the aegis of several main disciples and leaders, or *juzi*. The various schools of Mohism flourished throughout the Central States (the core group of states that participated in a wide cultural, political, and economic sphere associated with the Zhou Dynasty), rivaling the Confucians for centuries until their sudden disappearance sometime during the late third or early second centuries B.C.E.

Mozi's thought and the preoccupations of his school are preserved in a text known as *Mozi* (fourth-third centuries B.C.E.; partial translation as *The Ethical and Political Works of Motse*, 1929; known as *Mozi*). *Mozi* was written over a period of about two hundred years and reflects the thinking of at least two main phases of the school, commonly referred to as the Early Mohist phase (fourth century B.C.E.) and the Later Mohist phase (third-second centuries B.C.E.).

Early Mohists concerned themselves primarily with ethics, political philosophy, and religion. They advocated a radical ideology of utilitarianism and universal human adherence to objective, heavenly law. This ideology strongly supports a meritocratic system of government, referred to as a politics of "advancing those who achieve" (*jin xian*) through official appointment commensurate to merit. In addition, early Mohists made an appeal to an original concept known as "universal caring" (*jian ai*). This concept recommends that individuals show similar concern for those people belonging to the impersonal, public realm as they would for their own loved ones, relatives, and friends.

Their religious views uphold many traditional Zhou beliefs in the efficacy of ghosts and spirits as agents of heaven. Heaven is seen as an absolute moral force that responds directly to individual human behavior through reward and punishment. On the basis of this religious vision of heaven lies the early Mohist belief in utilitarianism. According to their beliefs, since heaven rewards and punishes according to objective standards of what is right and since what is right brings benefit to people, one can make calculations of benefit to establish just, impartial laws that reflect heaven's wishes.

Early Mohists assembled in groups according to a rigid, authoritarian hierarchy. All disciples paid their allegiance to the group leader, or *juzi*, who served as the chief commander in military service. As staunch advocates of defensive warfare, the Mohists used their groups to participate frequently in military activity. Groups were called on by lords and kings of states to serve in times of need. Loyalty to the group and *juzi* was of primary importance, as evidenced in stories about Mohists who made great sacrifices in order to uphold Mohist law and the oaths of allegiance. The structured organization of the Mohist unit lends itself better to the category of "school" than any other early Chinese intellectual group—even more so than the Confucians.

The founding of Mohism is associated with a few main teachers and *juzi*, some of whom might have been the immediate disciples of Mozi himself. Very little of their lives, including their dates, is known, but early sources suggest that they were leading intellectuals who perpetuated Mohism by setting up separate branches of the organization throughout the Central States. Each branch vied with the others for authority over what they claimed to be an authentic line of Mohist thought. Among the Mohist leaders who are associated with the founding of competing branches of Mohism are Qin Guli (Ch'in Ku-li), Xiang Li (Hsiang Li, also Xiang Liqin/Hsiang Li-ch'in), Deng Ling (Teng Ling, also Deng Lingzi/Teng Ling-tzu), Xiang Fu (Hsiang Fu), Wu Hou, Ku Huo (K'u Huo), and Ji Zhi (Chi Chih).

Early Mohists also became famous for their stance in opposition to certain Confucian practices of the day. Early Mohist precepts include the denunciation of elaborate burial practices and musical performances, which the Confucians deemed critical to the perpetuation of ritual, a key concept in Confucianism. In addition, the Mohist school disagreed with a proclaimed Confucian belief in fatalism. Although this disagreement appears to stem from a Mohist exaggeration of Confucian belief (the textual doctrines associated with Confucianism do not imply the kind of fatalism for which they are accused), it is plausible that there existed Confucians of the period who espoused a fatalistic belief in the ultimate powers of heaven. Lastly, disagreement with the Confucians arose concerning beliefs about the family. Encouraging an attitude of impartiality and transcendence over one's personal and familial contexts, Mohists directly negated the Confucian belief in the priority of family relations.

Later Mohists lived and wrote from about 300 to 200 B.C.E. Their concerns appear on the surface to diverge radically from those of their predecessors. In reality, they preserved the basic tenets of ethical and political Mohism while adding new interests in specialized matters of defense, "scientific" knowledge, and disputation. Later Mohists organized themselves into three main schools that viewed each other as rivals, or heretical Mohists, rather than in fraternity with each other. The perceived rift was expressed through a claim by each group that it maintained exclusive hold on the correct transmission of Mohist ideals and practices. The many treatises on military science, logic, and language stem most likely from the Later Mohist phase of the school.

Significance

Mohist philosophy had a profound effect on Warring States culture and politics as well as on the political structure of the imperial Chinese state for the next twenty-three hundred years. Several sources hint that Mohists and Confucians dominated the intellectual and political scene of the fourth to third centuries B.C.E. Mohist beliefs in meritocracy and impartial law were absorbed so thoroughly in political discourse that they quickly became associated with non-Mohist intellectual activity involving ideas on statecraft, later referred to as Legalism. Early Mohist influence on Legalistic thought and figures as well as its direct influence on the courts of the day helped shape governments and move them toward the development of the first Chinese empire in 221 B.C.E. Their concern with meritocracy helped fuel policies, and institutions would establish a means by which worthy and able men might be rewarded for their merit through government service. This ideal formed the basis for what later became the Chinese civil service examination system, which dominated the political scene in many states throughout East Asia from the eighth and ninth centuries until the twentieth century.

The disappearance of Mohism coincided with the rise of the Qin (Ch'in; 221-206 B.C.E.) and Han (206 B.C.E.-220 C.E.) Dynasties. Some scholars speculate that the group's sudden demise can be attributed to the wide popularity enjoyed by the Mohists during the roughly two centuries of their existence. This claim states that Mohist ideals became so absorbed into intellectual culture that there no longer was a need for the school itself. However, without more data on the particular contexts and circumstances surrounding their demise, such a claim cannot be confirmed.

Mohist writings were largely neglected for two millennia, until recent Western influence sparked a renewed interest in the scientific and logical foundations of Chinese thought. As a result of this general neglect, the text of *Mozi*, and especially the work of the Later Mohists, did not receive the scribal recopying, editing and textual reworking, and interpreting and exegesis that its counterparts in the Confucian or Daoist traditions received. It is therefore extremely difficult for any contemporary scholar to gain solid comprehension of the complexities of Later Mohist intellectual concerns.

—*Erica Brindley*

FURTHER READING

Forke, Alfred, trans. *Me Ti des Sozialethikers und seiner Schüler philosophische Werke*. Berlin: Kommissionsverlag der Vereinigung Wissenschaftlicher Verleger, 1922. In German. The only complete translation of the entire Mohist corpus in a Western language. While translations of the core chapters of the early Mohist school are acceptable, translations of the specialized, later works are not reliable.

Fung, Yu-lan. *A History of Chinese Philosophy*. Vols. 1-2. Translated by Derk Bodde. Princeton, N.J.: Princeton University Press, 1967. Thorough overview of Chinese philosophy that includes a narrative of the Mohists and their place in the history of early thought.

Graham, A. C. *Disputers of the Tao: Philosophical Argument in Ancient China*. LaSalle, Ill.: Open Court, 1989. Provides one of the best discussions of the role of Mohist thought as a radical reaction to contemporary debates of the time.

________. *Divisions in Early Mohism Reflected in the Core Chapters of Mo-tzu*. Singapore: Institute of East Asian Philosophies, 1985. Argues for the division of Mohist schools of thought on the basis of apparent differences in the Mohist corpus.

________. *Later Mohist Logic, Ethics and Science*. Hong Kong: The Chinese University Press, 1978. The most thorough discussion of the later Mohist "Canon," its "Explanations," and other treatises that attest to the depth of later Mohist involvement in science and language, as well as more standard ethical pursuits.

Hu, Shih. *The Development of the Logical Method in Ancient China*. 2d ed. New York: Paragon Book Reprint Corporation, 1963. A twentieth century Chinese thinker's restatement of the value of China's own past. This view makes a claim for the indigenous roots of logic as reflected in Mohist writings of the classical period.

Mozi. *Mo Tzu: Baisc Writings*. Translated by Burton Watson. New York: Columbia Universtiy Press, 1963. Selected translations of the core chapters of Early Mohist ethical writings. Despite the limited content of this translation, it is still the most used and readable version of the Mohists' early writings.

Schwartz, Benjamin. *The World of Thought in Ancient China*. Cambridge, Mass.: Harvard University Press, 1985. Provides a very good overview of early Chinese thought that includes Mohist concerns and pursuits.

SEE ALSO: 479 B.C.E., Confucius's Death Leads to the Creation of *The Analects*; c. 285-c. 255 B.C.E, Xunzi Develops Teachings That Lead to Legalism; 221 B.C.E., Qin Dynasty Founded in China; 221-206 B.C.E., Legalist Movement in China.

RELATED ARTICLES in *Great Lives from History: The Ancient World*: Confucius; Hanfeizi; Mozi; Xunzi.

c. 400 B.C.E.-c. 300 C.E.
BANTU PEOPLES SPREAD FARMING ACROSS SOUTHERN AFRICA

The movement of the Kusi Bantu across the eastern and southern parts of Africa spread a variety of agricultural practices, as well as the Bantu languages.

LOCALE: Southern and southern central Africa (present-day Angola, Zambia, Mozambique, Zimbabwe, and South Africa)

CATEGORIES: Agriculture; expansion and land acquisition

SUMMARY OF EVENT

Between 400 B.C.E. and 300 C.E., a process of population relocation was under way in southern and south-central Africa, initiated by Bantu communities. This population movement and resettlement was a continuation of the expansion of Bantu communities within eastern Africa beginning around 1000 B.C.E. Several factors contributed to these demographic shifts among the Bantu-speaking communities, in both eastern and southern Africa. The most significant and ecologically visible dynamic spurring migration was a prolonged population growth. Large demographic increases for an extended period of time over several centuries likely threatened the stability of the food supply in the western parts of East Africa, ultimately leading to the expansion of Bantu populations out of eastern Africa and into southern Africa.

Speakers of non-Bantu languages with hunting-and-gathering economies were the primary inhabitants of southern Africa until the latter part of the last millennium B.C.E., when the Bantu agriculturalists began to emerge. The primary inhabitants of southern Africa before the Bantu arrival spoke ancestral Khoikhoi languages, which are related to the few remaining Khoisan languages of modern-day southern Africa. In contrast to the strictly hunting-and-gathering lifestyle of the semi-desert-dwelling populations of southern Africa, the earliest Bantu had combined hunting and gathering with root-crop agriculture in the tropical forests of western and central Africa, and their descendants continued this system of food production with some modifications.

By the last millennium B.C.E., the Bantu agriculturalists of western Africa were, like their later eastern African counterparts, faced with growing populations requiring intensified production. The intensification of cultivation in western and eastern Africa resulted in a need for more land on which to grow crops; however, the same land was also in progressively greater demand for settlement by the increasing populations. The food supply was steadily enhanced in quantity and variety, but intensification of cultivation meant there was greater pressure on the land as a resource. The option chosen by some segments of the Bantu in eastern Africa was to relocate away from the western side of East Africa. Thus, a population expansion and migration into far eastern and southern Africa was well under way by the fifth century B.C.E. Settlement was expanded through many parts of the forest and to the edges of woodland savannas to the south and east.

In the east, the non-Bantu Sahelians, who were already well established, introduced to the Bantu speakers both grain cultivation and the domestication of animals such as sheep and cattle. The spread of Bantu populations into southern Africa was greatly facilitated by the introduction of grain crops. Unlike root crops, which require relatively high rainfall levels or irrigation for each plant, grains such as sorghum and certain millets grow well in dry environments. The southern and eastern parts of Africa, which were too dry for traditional forest crops, were perfectly suitable for grains. Thus the Bantu incorporated new economic practices from eastern Sahelian grain cultivators and turned again to migration as a means of alleviating population pressures and resource competition within the western Great Lakes region of East Africa. In some areas of eastern Africa, the eastern Sahelian speakers and Bantu had extensive social contact; in the case of the central Sudanic and Sog peoples, many began to be assimilated into Bantu-speaking communities.

The most commonly followed routes of migration must have been through the generally tsetse-free corridors of East Africa, which extend south and southeast of modern-day Tanzania from the Rungwe Mountains along the western side of the Lwangwa River Valley to the Batoka Plateau of southern Zambia. The Mashariki Bantu spread farther east and into the south across East Africa into the regions known today as Uganda, Kenya, and Tanzania. Other Bantu peoples, known to scholars as Kusi Bantu, spread directly south from the savanna into areas of southern Zaire and into modern Angola, Zambia, Mozambique, Zimbabwe, and South Africa. In the southern regions, the Kusi Bantu encountered Khoisan-speaking peoples who engaged predominantly in hunting-and-gathering economies.

A complex of crops allowed for settlement in a greater variety of regions, and the increase in both quality and quantity of food production continued the trend of Bantu population growth. The smelting of iron allowed production of tools such as axes, hoes, arrows, spears, and knives, which, scholars conclude, facilitated movement into a diversity of environments in which new communities could be pioneered. The introduction of luxury goods, as well as new apparatuses and technologies of food production, made trade with neighboring communities attractive. New tools made from iron alleviated the difficulties of acquiring the heavily demanded firewood for cooking, pottery making, and ultimately more iron smelting. Iron production allowed for the making of equipment and tools more durable than their stone or wooden counterparts. In the dry regions of eastern and southern Africa, where grain was typically grown, there were not many forested areas to be continuously cut down for wooden tool production. Iron could be smelted in forested areas at local smelting sites, and then the iron that was produced could be carried back to the more distant settlements in savanna and nonforested areas.

SIGNIFICANCE

The spread of Bantu populations over most of southern and eastern Africa spread Bantu languages through eastern and southern Africa, which has had a tremendous impact on the linguistic landscape even into present times. Over centuries, Bantu-speaking communities seem to have absorbed speakers of Khoikhoi languages and reduced the number of descendant Khoisan-speaking communities. In the twenty-first century, more than one-third of the African continent speaks Bantu languages because of the large area over which the Bantu spread, although in most previously Khoikhoi-speaking regions there are some Khoisan root words and linguistic features, such as clicks, which have been preserved through incorporation into the Bantu languages.

The concept of grain cultivation moved with the Bantu into areas that were once habitable only by hunters and gatherers because few known indigenous plants could be domesticated and cultivated as staple crops in these areas of southern Africa. The Bantu can be credited with introducing cultivated grains and cattle raising, two new subsistence practices, to a variety of areas within Africa, particularly in the arid south and east. Because domestic animals reproduce more rapidly and frequently than humans, cattle raising, along with grain production, created a secure supply of foodstuffs. With increased agriculture in southern Africa came the opportunity for villages and town centers to develop, as people were typically drawn to the new agricultural areas. Before the arrival of Bantu agriculturalists, the population density of the indigenous Khoisan across southern Africa was low. The expansion of the Bantu therefore was characteristically rapid, because there was a very modest population to deter Bantu establishment of settlements in many areas.

The use of iron was expanded into new regions as the cultivation of grain was spread with Bantu population movement. This dispersion of technology led to increased modifications of iron smelting and smithing within southern Africa. Social and economic changes emerged as different groups of people spread and lost their connections to other Bantu communities from which they had diverged geographically and culturally. Some of the cultural changes included a shift from a double-descent system (wherein matriclans, matrilineage, and patrilineages were significant) to a system wherein such bilateral lineage connections became irrelevant. In southern Africa, either matrilineages were central or, in a few select locations, patrilineages became the principal unit of social organization. In some areas of southern Africa, the distribution of iron wealth gave rise to communities in which clan became more important than lineage in social precedence.

—*Katherine B. Beem*

FURTHER READING

Collins, Robert O., ed. *Problems in African History: The Precolonial Centuries*. New York: Markus Wiener, 1991. A synthesis of major issues in early African history. One chapter of this book provides an overview of the changes that took place as a result of the Bantu population movements and how they impacted other African peoples.

Ehret, Christopher. *An African Classical Age: Eastern and Southern Africa in World History, 1000 B.C. to A.D. 400*. Charlottesville: University Press of Virginia, 1998. Includes an outline as well as a detailed historical and social account of the population movements among Bantu peoples in eastern and southern Africa between 1000 B.C.E. and 400 C.E., based primarily on linguistic evidence.

SEE ALSO: c. 7000-c. 6000 B.C.E., Khoisan Peoples Disperse Throughout Southern Africa; c. 6500-c. 5000 B.C.E., Nilo-Saharan Farmers Spread Cultivation and Herding; c. 6000-c. 1000 B.C.E., Omotics Advance Farming Practices in Horn of Africa; c. 5500-c. 4500 B.C.E., Niger-Congo Peoples Spread Agriculture in Africa; c. 1000-c. 700 B.C.E., Mashariki Bantu Establish Chifumbaze Ironworking Culture; c. 300 B.C.E.-c. 100 C.E., Khoikhoi and Kwadi Adopt Pastoral Lifestyle.

c. 400 B.C.E.-c. 300 C.E.
DONG SON CULTURE APPEARS IN VIETNAM

The Dong Son, a Bronze Age civilization of skilled artisans, farmers, and seafaring traders, appeared in northern and central Vietnam on the eve of the emergence of historical Vietnam.

LOCALE: Southeast Asia, primarily northern and central Vietnam
CATEGORY: Prehistory and ancient cultures

SUMMARY OF EVENT

The Dong Son culture was a society of highly skilled artisans, farmers, and seagoing traders centered in the northern part of Vietnam. It is named after the village of Dōngson on the Ma River in the Thanh-hóa Province of central Vietnam, where some of the most important Vietnamese archaeological finds have been made. The existence of the ancient drums characteristic of the culture had been recognized even before the discoveries in this village. In 1902, the Austrian ethnographer Franz Heger produced a monograph in which he classified the ancient bronze drums into four categories according to weight, shape, design, composition, and casting technique. However, the history of the Dong Son culture in modern scholarship is usually regarded as having begun in 1924, when a Vietnamese fisherman from this village came across a number of ancient bronze objects. He sold these to a French collector named Émile Pajot, who proceeded to hunt for more of the antiquities. In 1929, a French scholar named Victor Goloubew published a study of Pajot's artifacts that brought them to public attention.

Most early scholars believed that the ancient objects found in Vietnam were results of influences from other, presumably more advanced, civilizations. Goloubew believed that the artistic and metalworking techniques had been introduced by the invading Chinese army of Ma Yüan in 43 C.E. or by other Chinese during the early period of Chinese domination. However, archaeological work since the time of Goloubew has established that the Dong Son products were developed in the region in which they were found, during centuries of technical progress.

The roots of the Dong Son culture may go as far back as 1000 B.C.E., when people in Southeast Asia began to make objects from bronze and sometimes iron. The earliest bronze objects in the region were plowshares, axes, spearheads, fishhooks, and ornaments. By about 500 B.C.E., characteristic Dong Son objects began to appear. These included skillfully wrought bracelets, bronze arrowheads, containers, knives, items made from jade, and pottery. The objects also included the bronze drums that have become recognized as the symbols of Dong Son craft and civilization. These drums were shaped like mushrooms, with flat tops and side handles. Sometimes weighing more than 150 pounds (68 kilograms), they were decorated with scenes and human figures. Apart from the artistic value of the drums, the decorations are important to archaeology because they provide images of life in ancient Vietnam. The drums were apparently used in burial and funeral rites, and they are often found with other artifacts in tombs.

The Dong Son drums follow a fairly standard pattern in their design. At the center of the top face of the drum, known as the tympanum, there is usually a star. The star is surrounded by circular panels of scenes of humans and animals among abstract geometric designs. Some conclusions about religious beliefs may be drawn from the decorations on the sides of drums and from other artifacts. The people of this society held a strong belief in the afterlife, and many of the objects placed in tombs may have been intended to be of use to the dead, who would sail away in boats to some type of paradise in the west. This last idea was probably suggested to them by their seagoing society and by the daily path of the sun.

Life in this world, as well as in the next, is represented on the drums. There are frequent scenes of boat races, thought to indicate the importance of water in this culture, which depended on water both for agriculture and for its seagoing activities. Images of warriors and a wide variety of weapons, including crossbows, hatchets, spears, javelins, daggers, and shields, indicate that warfare was a common part of life. As might be expected from a culture with a drum as a symbol, music seems to have been central to the activities of the Dong Son people. Musicians and dancers appear often in the illustrations. Among the instruments are khens (a wind instrument made of long pipes still found in Southeast Asia), bells, castanets, and rattles, as well as the big drums themselves. On some of the drums, there are images of drummers sitting on the floor while dancers move around in circles.

The Dong Son people lived in houses built on stilts or pilings, similar to houses sometimes still used in Southeast Asia. Their domesticated animals included dogs, pigs, and water buffalo. On land, they were farmers and their staple crop was apparently rice, so that they set the agricultural pattern for later people in the region. They were also a seafaring people who built large boats and traveled about the Asian area. Drums in the Dong Son style have been found from China in the north to Indonesia in the south, possibly as a result of cultural contacts from the traveling and trading of the Dong Son people. They apparently had extensive links with Tibeto-Burman culture, with the Thai culture of Yunnan in southern China and of Laos, and with the Mon-Khmer cultures of Southeast Asia, notably that of the Plain of Jars in contemporary Laos. Bronze Dong Son drums have been found in south and southwest China, Burma, Thailand, Laos, and Indonesia.

Although there were Dong Son colonies, the center of the culture appears to have remained in Vietnam. It reached its highest point of development during the third century B.C.E., but evidence of it can be found as late as the third century C.E., and some scholars believe they have found traces of this culture surviving until as late as the sixteenth century.

The Dong Son overlapped with the origins of the Vietnamese nation. Many Vietnamese believe that Dong Son was closely connected to the foundation of Van Lang, the first kingdom of Vietnam under the Hung kings, which was supposed to have lasted two thousand years, up to the third century B.C.E. Although scholars are often skeptical of these claims, it does appear that Vietnamese nationhood took shape while elements of the more ancient culture still existed. As information about the Dong Son has emerged, the culture has become an important part of the self-image of the Vietnamese nation.

SIGNIFICANCE

Scholars used to believe that the cultures of Southeast Asia were based primarily on influences from other regions, chiefly influences from India and China. However, excavations of Dong Son artifacts indicate that they came from a civilization that was native to the region and that the society that produced these artifacts was the origin of Bronze Age culture throughout Southeast Asia. The Dong Son people are also believed to have been responsible for turning the Red River Delta in Vietnam into the rice-growing area that it continued to be throughout historical times. Moreover, the archaeological discoveries about this culture suggest that Southeast Asia contained an advanced society that not only was skilled in artistic production but also engaged in seagoing trade over a wide geographic expanse. The artistic influence of the culture extended to a large part of the Southeast Asian region, and traces of it can still be found in many places. The Dong Son culture is particularly important to nationalist Vietnamese historians, who regard it as the origin of the Vietnamese nation.

—*Carl L. Bankston III*

FURTHER READING

Girard-Geslan, Maud, ed. *Art of Southeast Asia*. New York: Harry N. Abrams, 1998. A comprehensive work on historical and contemporary art in the region that contains a chapter by the editor on the Dong Son culture and its descendants. Bibliography, illustrations, glossary, index.

Huyen, Van Nguyen. *The Bronze Dong Son Drums*. Singapore: Dong Son Editions, 1989. A compilation of surveys on the Dong Son drums, essential for those who are interested in this culture from the perspective of art history. Illustrations.

Taylor, Keith W. *The Birth of Vietnam*. Berkeley: University of California Press, 1991. An excellent work on the history of Vietnam from prehistory until the tenth century C.E. Taylor touches on the Dong Son culture at a number of points in the book, but readers interested in this topic may want to look in particular at the first half of the first chapter. Bibliography and index.

Wagner, Frits. A. *Indonesia: The Art of an Island Group*. New York: Greystone Press, 1967. This volume is now somewhat dated, but the third chapter gives a good overview of the significance of Dong Son artistic traditions for various parts of the islands of Indonesia. Illustrations and index.

SEE ALSO: c. 2000 B.C.E., Mon-Khmer Migrate into Southeast Asia; c. 1600 B.C.E., Shang Dynasty Develops Writing and Bronzework; 1st century C.E., Tai Peoples Migrate into Southeast Asia; 40-43 C.E., Trung Sisters Lead Vietnamese Rebellion Against Chinese.

c. 400 b.c.e.-400 c.e.
Composition of the *Mahābhārata*

The Mahābhārata, *the great epic of India, is a monumental Sanskrit poem, composed for a popular audience, that records ancient Indian political, ethical, mythological, and philosophical thought.*

Locale: India
Categories: Literature; cultural and intellectual history

Summary of Event

Called the great epic of India, the *Mahābhārata* (*The Mahabharata of Krishna-Dwaipayana Vyasa*, 1887-1896) is composed in Sanskrit, the chief classical language of ancient India, and is seemingly the longest single poem extant in any language. In its shortest version, the poem consists of more than 74,000 stanzas, divided into sections of varying length. The main poetic meter of the *Mahābhārata* is the *anuṣṭubh* stanza, which consists of thirty-two syllables divided into quarters of eight syllables each. Other meters also occur, most prominently the *triṣṭubh*, used for especially lyrical passages, with its four eleven-syllable lines.

Certain features of the poem—most prominently the use of formulaic repetitions with slight variations—suggest an origin in ancient oral tradition. Such orality is described many times in the poem itself: During the intervals between the performances of elaborate rituals, for example, a bard (*sūta*) is asked to tell a story of ancient gods or kings, and he does so at length. Alternatively, such a bard appears at the court of a king, where he is honored as a sage and asked to tell stories, both for entertainment and for edification. According to the poem, the bards recited from memory, and the poem makes little reference to writing, except in one very late passage tacked on to the beginning of the text. The legendary bard of the entire *Mahābhārata* is said to be Vyāsa, a name that means "the arranger," indicating, perhaps, that he was an ancient editor or redactor.

Extant are two main manuscript traditions, associated with north and south India. The standard edition of the Sanskrit text, the multivolume Critical Edition (published at Poona, India, 1927-1966), has based its text on a collation of manuscripts from all over India, north and south. None of these manuscripts, however, dates to anywhere close to the time of the poem's composition. India's climate has led to a loss of fragile handwritten books: The oldest manuscript of Book 1, for instance, is dated 1511 c.e.

The variations among manuscripts and other features of the text—for instance, contradictions in the story line—have led many researchers to conclude that the extant poem is the product of a long period of historical development, with some sections older than others. The poem's complex overlay of diverse features suggests a composite authorship, stretching over centuries and carried out in different locales. Such a theory would account for the many long sections that interrupt the story with religious and philosophical teachings, most notably the *Santi-parvan*, more than 15,000 stanzas in length. These didactic sections are filled with narratives, anecdotes, and parables meant to illustrate the teachings. This is a traditional mode of religious instruction in India—a mixture of storytelling and sermon.

The peculiar dating of the work in a range from 400 b.c.e. to 400 c.e. reflects its gradual composition. It has proved difficult, however, to distinguish these different historical layers because the style of the poem is uniform, with some minor exceptions. One example of such an exception to this stylistic uniformity is the *Pauṣya-parvan*, a chapter occurring in the first major book of the epic. This section is composed in prose rather than verse. However, it is debatable whether that peculiarity should be taken as a sign of greater or lesser antiquity. Sometimes episodes within the poem are told two or more times, a short version immediately followed by a longer version. Is the longer version a later expansion, or is the shorter version a summary of an earlier longer text? Also problematic are the first two chapters of the epic, which describe the contents and extent of the entire *Mahābhārata*, but whose enumerations do not precisely fit any available version of the epic. As research continues, it is possible that computer-aided studies of meter and other stylistic features may provide objective evidence to determine the history of the text. Modern scholarly work, however, has cast some doubt on both the orality of the poem and its dating: The *Mahābhārata*, according to scholar Alf Hiltebeitel, was composed in the range 150 b.c.e.-1 c.e. and was originally a written text.

The title *Mahābhārata* means "the narrative of the great war of the *Bhāratas*," the latter a dynasty of northern India that gives modern India its official name *Bharat*. The epic's central narrative records in great detail a succession dispute between two branches of this dynasty and the resultant war said to involve most of the ruling families of known India. A large part of the poem (books 6-9) describes in copious violent detail an eighteen-day battle that ends with the tragic deaths of most participants. The historicity of this war and the poem's political details have proved difficult to confirm. The war is thus legendary—fictional, though with a historical core.

The *Mahābhārata* displays features known from national epics elsewhere: genealogies and tales of ancestors; descriptions of the youth and adventures of important heroes; embassies, debates, and parleys before the decisive battle; the involvement of deities and related mythological digressions; descriptions of weapons and battle tactics; and taunts and the issuing of challenges. Religious episodes, such as legends of saints and the description of pilgrimage sites, occur frequently.

In some of its sections, such as one narrating a great cattle raid, the *Mahābhārata* foregrounds a culture like that of other archaic Indo-Europeans—nomadic cattle-herders. However, the text also refers to city-dwellers and slash-and-burn agriculturalists.

Kṛṣṇa (or Krishna) figures both as an important deity and as a human character in the epic, the friend of the great hero Arjuna, one of the Pāṇḍava brothers. Kṛṣṇa relates the most famous episode of the *Mahābhārata*, the *Bhagavadgītā* (c. 200 B.C.E.-200 C.E.; *The Bhagavad Gita*, 1785), literally, "the mystic teaching sung by the Lord."It is a matter of debate among scholars whether Kṛṣṇa was originally part of the epic story. He appears sometimes as a human figure, a ruler of a people of western India, and a political ally of the Pāṇḍava brothers. However, at key moments in the story, he reveals himself a divine, a deity dwelling on Earth for a time. In fact, passages in book 1 of the epic describe how most of the central figures are either incarnations of various deities or alternatively the sons of deities by mortal mothers. The villains of the story, the Kauravas, are described as incarnations of demons, the mythical enemies of the gods. No attempt is made to harmonize these various ideas. Historically minded readers thus could conclude that they are seeing different interpretations of the story—some theological, some legendary—layered one on the other by different authors writing sometimes centuries apart.

Among studies of the epic are attempts to interpret the poem in its entirety. One prominent scholar who advanced such a theory about the *Mahābhārata* was Georges Dumézil. For him, the epic had its origin in myths stemming from a prehistoric Indo-European tradition. The heroes are thus not only incarnations or sons of deities but also "transposed" from divine figures that existed in Indo-European myth: Beneath the epic as it exists is a very archaic mythology. So, for example, the epic hero Arjuna mirrors an Indo-European sky-god, who appears under the name Indra in the oldest stratum of Indian mythology and as Zeus in ancient Greece. Myth has become epic; an epic myth was once current in traditions from Iceland and Ireland to Iran and India.

SIGNIFICANCE

The immense influence of the *Mahābhārata* ranges from the arts—poetry, drama, sculpture—to philosophy, religion, and political science. India's most renowned classical dramatist, Kālidāsa (c. 340-c. 400 C.E.), based his admired play *Abhijñānaśākuntala* (c. 45 B.C.E. or c. 395 C.E. (*Śakuntalā: Or, The Lost Ring*, 1789) on a version of a story first recorded in the *Mahābhārata*. The epic's vast treasure trove of narratives has always been a source book for India's storytellers, who have continued to produce versions of the epic and its parts, both written and oral (the latter often in the form of tales told to children). There exist translations in most of India's regional languages as well as novelizations, adaptations, and dramatizations in English and other languages. Today, film, television, and graphic narratives (comic books) also keep the story of the five brothers and their adventures alive in the consciousness of Indian audiences.

J. A. B. van Buitenen's translation of the *Mahābhārata* (3 vols., 1973-1978) is incomplete, covering only the first five books. The Peter Brook-directed stage play (script by Jean-Claude Carriére, 1985) and subsequent film, which aimed to universalize the story by using an international cast, have been widely viewed in the West. As a significant episode in the *Mahābhārata*, *The Bhagavad Gita* (first translated into English by Charles Wilkins) remains the best-known and most widely translated religious text from India.

—*Burt Thorp*

FURTHER READING

Brockington, John. *The Sanskrit Epics*. Leiden, Netherlands: E. J. Brill, 1998. A basic reference work on the epics written in Sanskrit.

Buitenen, J. A. B. van, trans. *The Mahābhārata*. 3 vols. Chicago: University of Chicago Press, 1973-1978. A scholarly and readable modern translation. Contains valuable introductions to each book.

Carrière, Jean-Claude. *The Mahābhārata: A Play Based upon the Indian Classic Epic*. Translated from the French by Peter Brook. New York: Harper & Row, 1987. An admired dramatic rendition.

Dumézil, Georges. *The Destiny of the Warrior*. Translated by Alf Hiltebeitel. Chicago: University of Chi-

cago Press, 1970. Sees the epic's origins residing in prehistoric Indo-European myth.
Hiltebeitel, Alf. *Rethinking the Mahābhārata: A Reader's Guide to the Education of the Dharma King*. Chicago: University of Chicago Press, 2001. Argues for a different interpretation of the epic's provenance and dating.
Sharma, Arvind, ed. *Essays on the Mahābhārata*. Leiden, Netherlands: E. J. Brill, 1991. Scholarly essays on a variety of topics concerning the *Mahābhārata*.
Van Nooten, Barend A. *The Mahābhārata: Attributed to Kṛṣṇa Dvaipayaṇa Vyāsa*. New York: Twayne, 1971. An accessible account of the epic; includes a plot summary.
Williams, David, ed. *Peter Brook and the Mahābhārata: Critical Perspectives*. London: Routledge, 1991. Contains much information on the epic and its modern adaptation.

SEE ALSO: c. 550 B.C.E., Vālmīki Composes the *Rāmāyaṇa*; c. 4th century B.C.E.-3d century C.E., Kauṭilya Compiles a Treatise on Practical Statecraft; c. 200 B.C.E., Birth of Hinduism; c. 200 B.C.E.-200 C.E., *Bhagavad Gita* Is Created; c. 400 C.E., Kālidāsa Composes Sanskrit Poetry and Plays.
RELATED ARTICLE in *Great Lives from History: The Ancient World:* Kālidāsa.

399 B.C.E.
DEATH OF SOCRATES

The death of Socrates was decreed after he was tried, found guilty, and sentenced to die by an Athenian jury for crimes against the state, but his final days offered a lasting model of moral integrity and composure in the face of death.

LOCALE: Athens
CATEGORIES: Philosophy; cultural and intellectual history; government and politics

KEY FIGURES

Socrates (c. 470-399 B.C.E.), Athenian citizen and informal teacher
Meletus and
Anytus (both fl. fifth-fourth century B.C.E.), Athenian citizens who brought the indictment against Socrates
Plato (c. 427-347 B.C.E.), Athenian disciple of Socrates who wrote an account of the trial, imprisonment, and death of Socrates
Xanthippe (c. 445-early to mid-fourth century B.C.E.), wife of Socrates
Crito (fl. fifth-fourth century B.C.E.), wealthy Athenian disciple of Socrates

SUMMARY OF EVENT

The conclusion and aftermath of the Peloponnesian War left Athenian democrats bitter and resentful. By the time this war ended in 404 B.C.E., the empire had crumbled, and the fleet and walls of Athens had been dismantled. Democracy had finally been restored in 403 B.C.E. following two periods of oligarchic rule, one beginning in 411 B.C.E. under a group of aristocrats known as the Four Hundred, the other under the Thirty Tyrants in 404 B.C.E. In the person of Socrates, there seemed to stand the symbol, if not the principal cause, of all the factors of intellectual and moral enervation that had destroyed from within the power of Athenian democracy to prosecute the war successfully and to sustain the integrity of its own governmental institutions.

An indictment was therefore brought against Socrates in 399 B.C.E. by a religious fanatic, Meletus, supported by the politician Anytus and by the orator Lycon, on the charge of impiety. Socrates was officially charged with failing to worship the gods of the state, introducing new gods of his own, and corrupting the youth of Athens. Although his accusers demanded the death penalty, their intention seems to have been to drive Socrates into self-imposed exile, a sentence which they believed he himself would propose if found guilty.

Plato's *Apologia Sōkratous* (399-390 B.C.E.; *Apology*, 1675) makes it clear that Socrates was identified in his accusers' minds with the natural philosophers and Sophists, whose teaching had indeed contributed to the deterioration of the traditional Athenian religious and political values. The natural philosophers had promulgated doctrines of a world sustained by impersonal laws rather than by personal deities, and the Sophists had encouraged their young noble pupils to be skeptical of all forms of institutional authority. Most damaging of all in their teaching was the doctrine of political power based on the assumptions that every individual's natural inclination was toward self-aggrandizement, and that the law of the state was an artificial restriction on the individual's self-realization.

It was the Sophists, rather than Socrates, who were responsible for these demoralizing ideas. Socrates himself scrupulously lived by the laws of Athens and fully participated in the formal religion of the states. He did, however, openly criticize the tendency of the democracy to entrust tasks of professional competence to amateurs chosen by popularity or, worse still, by lot. Moreover, he freely associated with the young aristocrats who were then the most conspicuous pupils of the Sophists. To the Athenians who did not know him intimately, Socrates must have appeared to be a typical Sophist, and it was as such that he was caricatured in *Nephelai* (423 B.C.E.; *The Clouds*, 1708) by Aristophanes, a play that must have left an indelible impression on many Athenian minds. After the double humiliation of defeat and revolution in 404 B.C.E., people remembered Alcibiades of Athens, who had deserted to the enemy during the war and severely damaged the Athenian war effort by helping to bring about a major Athenian naval defeat at the Battle of Syracuse, and Critias of Athens, who was despised by Athenian democrats for his role as leader of the Thirty Tyrants. They also recalled that these two men had been pupils of Socrates in their youth, and so Socrates seemed an ideal scapegoat for the frustrated resentment of many Athenians.

Despite these considerations, the vote to convict Socrates was fairly close. Out of a total of 500 jurors, 280 voted to find him guilty; a switch of only 30 jurors would have acquitted him. As Plato shows in his *Apology*, Socrates spoke forcefully in his own defense, denying all the charges brought against him. The *Apology* of Plato presents a portrait of Socrates as an earnest moralist who, though no Sophist, was indeed a real threat to whatever aspects of the Athenian traditional could not be rationally grounded. Far from the atheist his accusers would have proved him, Socrates believed in objective moral values and a transcendent deity of truth. Athenians who were personally confronted by him were faced with a relentless challenge to their pretense of certain knowledge in matters of religion and morals. Although he himself pro-

After being sentenced to die, Socrates drinks the hemlock. (F. R. Niglutsch)

fessed ignorance in these areas, he claimed a wisdom unique among people by virtue of his awareness of ignorance.

Socrates stood on common ground with the Sophists in refusing to acknowledge any self-evident authority in traditional Greek theological and moral ideals. Yet he differed from them in that his skepticism was methodological rather than radical; he believed that valid moral ideals could ultimately be grounded rationally, although the effort might be long and arduous. To this end, he committed himself to a life of intellectual inquiry through conversation with any who would join him, and he honestly believed that his informal intercourse with the Athenian man-in-the-street was a divine commission of vital concern to Athens. The only life worth living, he insisted, was the life based on values formulated through rigorous, honest, personal self-examination. Through such individual self-examination alone might come about eventual moral regeneration in the state.

Once found guilty on the counts brought against him, Socrates refused the traditional option of voluntary exile and obstinately insisted, goading the jury, that only death would make him cease from his customary activities in Athens, whereupon the jury felt compelled to sentence him, this time by a larger margin, to execution by poison. During the interval between his trial and death, Socrates conversed freely with his disciples, who sought to persuade him to go into exile. Plato's *Kritōn* (399-390 B.C.E.; *Crito*, 1804) gives Socrates' reason for resisting these entreaties: The command of the state, which he had heeded throughout his life, must be heeded now even though the condemnation was unjust.

SIGNIFICANCE

The death of Socrates is dramatically portrayed in the *Phaedōn* (399-390 B.C.E.; *Phaedo*, 1675) of Plato. On the day of his execution, Socrates appeared calm and relaxed. After a final reunion with his wife, Xanthippe, distraught over the idea that her husband would no longer be able to have philosophical conversations with his disciples, Socrates dismissively ordered his disciple Crito to take her home. Before drinking, without any protest, the cup of hemlock that would bring about his death, Socrates had one last philosophical conversation with his disciples, in which he argued for the immortality of the soul and the nature of human existence as a constant struggle between the body and the mind. The lasting value of this conversation, however, goes beyond the substance of Socrates' arguments, as Plato's *Phaedo* exalts the pattern of philosophic life consummated in Socrates' death to a transcendent ideal for all people.

—Carl W. Conrad, updated by Diane P. Michelfelder

FURTHER READING

Brickhouse, Thomas C., and Nicholas D. Smith. *The Philosophy of Socrates*. Boulder, Colo.: Westview Press, 2000. An analysis of the philosophy of Socrates. Bibliography and indexes.

Brickhouse, Thomas C., and Nicholas D. Smith, comp. *The Trial and Execution of Socrates: Sources and Controversies*. New York: Oxford University Press, 2002. A collection of ancient sources, including Plato's work, and modern scholarship on Socrates' trial. Bibliography.

Colaiaco, James A. *Socrates Against Athens: Philosophy on Trial*. New York: Routledge, 2001. A study of Socrates's trial and the ethical questions raised. Bibliography and index.

Green, Rickey K. *Democratic Virtue in the Trial and Death of Socrates: Resistance to Imperialism in Classical Athens*. New York: Peter Lang, 2001. Green examines Socrates' trial from the standpoints of ethics and politics.

Hansen, Mogens Herman. *The Trial of Socrates: From the Athenian Point of View*. Copenhagen: Kongelige Danske Videnskabernes Selskab, 1995. A close look at the trial of Socrates from the Athenian viewpoint.

Stone, I. F. *The Trial of Socrates*. New York: Doubleday, 1989. This best-selling book by a famous independent journalist is a lively investigation of the democratic values of ancient Athens and Socrates' relation to them.

SEE ALSO: 478-448 B.C.E., Athenian Empire Is Created; c. 440 B.C.E., Sophists Train the Greeks in Rhetoric and Politics; May, 431-September, 404 B.C.E., Peloponnesian War; September, 404-May, 403 B.C.E., Thirty Tyrants Rule Athens for Eight Months; c. 380 B.C.E., Plato Develops His Theory of Ideas.

RELATED ARTICLES in *Great Lives from History: The Ancient World*: Aristophanes; Plato; Socrates.

Between 394 and 371 B.C.E.
XENOPHON WRITES THE *ANABASIS*

In his landmark memoirs and travelogue, Xenophon recounted a two-year-long retreat by Greek mercenaries after fighting in the failed attempt of Cyrus the Younger to wrest control of the Persian Empire from his brother, King Artaxerxes II.

LOCALE: Western Persian Empire in Asia Minor (now Turkey, Syria, and Iraq)
CATEGORIES: Cultural and intellectual history; wars, uprisings, and civil unrest

KEY FIGURES

Xenophon (c. 431-c. 354 B.C.E.), Athenian soldier, historian, and philosopher
Cyrus the Younger (c. 424-401 B.C.E.), Persian prince and satrap, brother of Artaxerxes II
Tissaphernes (d. 395 B.C.E.), Persian satrap and general
Artaxerxes II (d. c. 359 B.C.E.), king of the Persian Empire, r. 405-359 B.C.E.

SUMMARY OF EVENT

While in retirement, the Athenian aristocrat Xenophon wrote his memoirs about a military campaign that made him famous in the world of ancient Greece. The book, which later became known as *Kurou anabasis* (*Anabasis*, also known as *Expedition of Cyrus* and *March Up Country*, 1623), describes one of the longest, most grueling tactical retreats in all military history. For modern historians, the book reveals a distinct evolution in Golden Age Greek military tactics and politics.

In 401 B.C.E., Xenophon, a student of Socrates, found himself under suspicion in Athens for his earlier support of the rule of the Thirty Tyrants. His home city no longer congenial, he gladly accepted an offer to become a member of a Greek mercenary force hired by the Achaemenid prince Cyrus the Younger. Cyrus was a powerful satrap (regional governor) in the northwestern Persian Empire. Apparently the victim of false accusations of treason by another leading satrap, Tissaphernes, Cyrus had been arrested by his brother, King Artaxerxes II, and nearly executed. Through his mother's intercession, Cyrus was freed and restored to his satrapy, but according to Xenophon, the incident so angered him that he resolved to overthrow Artaxerxes.

Cyrus had financed Sparta's naval campaign in the Peloponnesian War, and in return, Sparta helped Cyrus form a corps of Greek hoplites (heavy infantry) and peltasts (lighter, more mobile auxiliary troops). He brought together as many as thirteen thousand soldiers drawn from city-states throughout Greece, although the largest groups came from Sparta, Elis, and Arcadia. They were to be the spearhead in Cyrus's larger army of Persian troops.

Under the pretext of quelling rebellious tribes near his satrapy, Cyrus assembled his army at Sardis (now in western Turkey) and marched south to capture the Persian capital at Babylon (now in central Iraq). Artaxerxes led a massive army north to stop him, with Tissaphernes, his most able general, at his side. The two armies met at Cunaxa, just north of Babylon, in the summer of 401. A Greek attack was on the verge of routing the royal forces when Cyrus was killed. Artaxerxes counterattacked, and Cyrus's Persian troops fled.

The Greeks remained a coherent fighting force, and it was not until the day after the battle that they realized their side had lost. The Greek commander, Clearchus of Sparta, concluded an uneasy truce with the Tissaphernes on behalf of the king, but soon afterward, Tissaphernes lured many of the Greek leaders to a conference and killed or imprisoned them. He then demanded that the rest of the Greek soldiers surrender. The Greeks were understandably downhearted. They were nearly surrounded by a much larger army in the center of a hostile nation, hundreds of miles from the nearest Greek city.

However, at a late-night meeting, several prominent captains argued against surrender and convinced nearly all the Greeks to abandon the bulk of their gear and force-march northward in one unit toward the Black Sea, where they would follow the coast west to Byzantium (now Istanbul, Turkey). According to his own account, Xenophon was one of these speakers and, because of it, was elected commander of the rear guard. Those Greeks that participated in the retreat became known as the March of the Ten Thousand.

The Greek departure caught Tissaphernes by surprise, and his unwieldy army could not catch up to the Ten Thousand. Although he managed to attack several times with his swiftest forces, the Greeks countered his advantage in horsemen by hastily creating a small cavalry of their own and fought off his archers with a detachment of slingers. Tissaphernes was thereafter content to press the Ten Thousand northward until they climbed over a mountain pass into a region dominated by fierce, semi-independent tribes in what is now eastern Turkey.

There their hardships began in earnest. They endured cold that killed anyone who rested too long on the ground, fought through ambushes by tribe after tribe, and nearly ran out of supplies several times. In fact, procuring food, by whatever means necessary, was the army's chief concern. In the many pitched battles that the Ten Thousand fought, the force won by quick, aggressive assaults, then confiscated provisions and outran their pursuers with relentless, united movement forward.

The Ten Thousand reached the Black Sea at Trapezus (now Trabzon, Turkey) in February, 400 B.C.E., after a five-month trek. The army rested and held sports events in celebration, then continued on its way to Byzantium. However, dissension began to create factions within the ranks. Groups broke off to enrich themselves by plundering villages and taking captives for sale into slavery. The Greek colonies along the way treated the Ten Thousand with suspicion. A prominent leader abandoned them after being sent on a mission to find ships for passage. One large division split off to march on its own and barely escaped annihilation by an indigenous army. Even Xenophon felt the urge to quit the long march: He proposed founding a new colony with the Ten Thousand, an idea most of them rebuffed angrily.

Partly by sea, partly by land, the Ten Thousand finally reached Byzantium, their numbers reduced to between eight thousand and nine thousand. Their troubles were not over, however. Spartan authorities were uneasy about having a large, battle-hardened army with unclear loyalties nearby and tried to starve them into submission and divide them. Xenophon wrote that it was largely through his efforts that the remnant army stayed together. For a while, the Ten Thousand served the Thracian prince Seuthes, an unsatisfactory arrangement that made Xenophon unpopular with both the Thracians and the Greeks.

Xenophon. (Library of Congress)

At that point, during the spring of 399 B.C.E., Xenophon left the Ten Thousand to return to Greece, and the *Anabasis* ends. Most of the remaining Ten Thousand eventually became part of Sparta's forces. Such professional mercenary armies afterward grew increasingly prominent in struggles between Greek city-states.

Significance

Fragmentary accounts exist by other authors concerning Cyrus's campaign and the Ten Thousand, and they sometimes contradict Xenophon's version of events, especially about the importance of his leadership. This fact led scholars, such as Hans R. Breitenbach, to propose that Xenophon wrote the *Anabasis* to amplify his role and justify his actions. However, this view lost favor, and scholars proposed other motivations for the book. Josef Moor and others think it is basically propaganda that extols Greek political systems and ideals and, in comparison, implies that the Persians were corrupt and weak. William Higgins finds a philosophical theme in the narrative: The story betrays the inevitable self-deception of leaders as they pursue their ambitions. Werner Jaeger believes the book was intended to instruct readers on military tactics and leadership qualities. To Steven W. Hirsch and others, the story reveals the effects of suspicion, deceit, and trust in politics. Scholars generally agree, however, that Xenophon emphasizes one theme throughout the narrative of the retreat: The Ten Thousand—and, by implication, Greece itself—stood the best chance of remaining free through unity.

The *Anabasis* is credited with encouraging innovations in warfare, such as setting a high standard for military leadership and the use of tactical reserves and the emphasis on auxiliary forces. Certainly, such themes strongly influenced subsequent generations of leaders, including the Romans Julius Caesar and Scipio Africanus. Xenophon's forthright, lucid prose style found admirers in the writers Cicero and Quintilian and the historian Arrian. In the standard curriculum of Western Europe well into the twentieth century, the *Anabasis* served as a basic text for beginning students of classical Greek and thereby impressed on young minds the heroic steadfastness of the Ten Thousand.

—*Roger Smith*

FURTHER READING

Anderson, J. K. *Xenophon*. New York: Scribner's, 1974. Written by a classicist, this biography follows Xenophon's life on the basis of the evidence in his major works and explains the cultural and political context of Golden Age Greece as it does.

Georges, Pericles. *Barbarian Asia and the Greek Experience: From the Archaic Period to the Age of Xenophon*. Baltimore: The Johns Hopkins University Press, 1994. Georges devotes a chapter to Xenophon's ambivalent attitudes toward the Persians and his idolization of Cyrus.

Hirsch, Steven W. *The Friendship of Barbarians: Xenophon and the Persian Empire*. Hanover, N.H.: University Press of New England, 1985. Hirsch examines Xenophon's writings, including *Anabasis*, to assess contemporary Greek attitudes to the Persian Empire and how these attitudes affected the clash of the two civilizations.

Hunt, Peter. *Slaves, Warfare, and Ideology in the Greek Historians*. New York: Cambridge University Press, 1998. Hunt argues that slaves and commoners played a greater role in Greek mercenary armies than previously acknowledged, armies that changed warfare and Greek politics. He discusses Xenophon's account of the Ten Thousand in three chapters.

Xenophon. *The Persian Expedition*. Translated by Rex Warner. London: Penguin Books, 1972. A widely available translation of the *Anabasis* with a lengthy introduction by George Cawkwell that summarizes the political setting, Xenophon's life, and Xenophon's reasons for writing it.

SEE ALSO: c. 700-330 B.C.E., Phalanx Is Developed as a Military Unit; 480-479 B.C.E., Persian Invasion of Greece; 478-448 B.C.E., Athenian Empire Is Created; May, 431-September, 404 B.C.E., Peloponnesian War; September, 404-May, 403 B.C.E., Thirty Tyrants Rule Athens for Eight Months; 401-400 B.C.E., March of the Ten Thousand.

RELATED ARTICLE in *Great Lives from History: The Ancient World*: Xenophon.

386 B.C.E.
KING'S PEACE ENDS CORINTHIAN WAR

Although dictated by Persia, the King's Peace, also known as the Peace of Antalcidas, which ended the Corinthian War, had autonomy as its governing principle and served as the beginning of later Hellenic peace movements.

LOCALE: Sardis, Lydia, and Asia Minor (northeast of the modern Izmir, Turkey)

CATEGORIES: Expansion and land acquisition; laws, acts, and legal history; wars, uprisings, and civil unrest

KEY FIGURES

Agesilaus II of Sparta (c. 444-c. 360 B.C.E.), king of Sparta, r. 400-360 B.C.E.

Antalcidas (fl. 4th c. B.C.E.), Spartan general and ambassador

Artaxerxes II (d. c. 359 B.C.E.), king of Persia, r. 405-359 B.C.E.

Epaminondas (c. 410-362 B.C.E.), Theban general

SUMMARY OF EVENT

About a decade after the end of the Peloponnesian War (431-404 B.C.E.), the cities of Thebes and Corinth, former allies of Sparta in that conflict, had become alienated by Sparta's tyrannical interference in Greek affairs. The two cities took advantage of Sparta's involvement in a war with Persia to challenge Spartan supremacy. They declared war on Sparta and were followed in this act by Argos (a perennial enemy of Sparta), Athens, and a few lesser states. At this juncture, the Persians offered the Greeks money and aid to wage war against Sparta in order to remove the Spartan king Agesilaus II and his troops from Asia.

The ensuing war, the Corinthian War (395-386 B.C.E.), pitted Sparta against a Hellenic coalition well funded by Persia. The Spartan admiral Lysander died at the outset of the war, which led to the recall of Agesilaus from Asia. Although the Spartans made small gains, these were offset by the decisive victory by the Athenian admiral Conon and the Persian fleet over Sparta at

Cnidus (394) in southwest Asia Minor. Conon returned to Athens and played a large part in rebuilding the Long Walls destroyed there following the Peloponnesian War, assisted by Persian men and money. Athens also recovered the islands of Lemnos (now Límnos), Scyros (now Skíros), and Imbros (now Gökçeada).

As the war dragged on, casualties mounted on both sides. In the largest hoplite battle the Greeks had ever fought, the Battle of Nemea (394 B.C.E.) in the northeast Peloponnesus, more than four thousand men were killed fighting. The Spartans tried to ally with the Persians and even convinced their satrap Tiribazus that it was them, and not the Athenians, who were the Persians' better allies. However, the peace negotiations initiated in 392 ultimately failed, and fighting resumed.

Recent trends in warfare greatly aided the coalition forces. The years following the Peloponnesian War witnessed a rapid development of lightly armed infantry forces, including archers, slingers, and javelin throwers, particularly peltasts named after the small round wicker shield they carried (the Theban *peltē*). These forces could also play pivotal roles in hoplite confrontations, as they could easily harass the heavily armed hoplites from a distance. Perhaps because of their history of success at hoplite warfare, the Spartans never really learned to make use of light-armed troops. A master of this new type of warfare was the Athenian general Iphicrates. With a force of light infantry, he attacked a division of Spartan hoplites at the Corinthian port of Lechaeum in 390 B.C.E. and annihilated it. This achievement stunned the Greek world and made the reputation of Iphicrates, who became one of Athens' best known generals.

As the tide of war turned against Sparta, its agent in Persia, Antalcidas, urged negotiations for peace. Artaxerxes II had recently become disenchanted with Athens and its involvement in the political affairs of Egypt and Cyprus, both of which were traditionally Persian areas of influence. Antalcidas therefore won the support of Artaxerxes, who determined the provisions of the peace agreement known as the King's Peace or the Peace of Antalcidas. At the summons of Tiribazus, deputies from the Greek states met at the city of Sardis in Asia Minor to hear the terms of the peace. At this conference at Sardis, Tiribazus read the edict of the king. According to the historians Xenophon and Diodorus of Sicily, Artaxerxes claimed possession of all the cities of Asia Minor and the islands of Cyprus and Clazomenae (now Klazümen); recognized Athenian rights over Lemnos, Imbros, and Scyros; declared that all other Greek cities were autonomous; and asserted that he was prepared to enforce these terms by force if necessary.

Agesilaus II of Sparta. (Library of Congress)

The ambassadors thereafter returned to their cities to report the terms of the peace. They met at Sparta to declare their acceptance, but negotiations nearly broke down over the difficult issue of Boeotian representation. The delegates from the chief city in Boeotia, Thebes, wanted to ratify the treaty on behalf of all Boeotia as a confederation. King Agesilaus demanded that they swear to leave all the Boeotian cities autonomous, according to the provisions of the peace. When he met resistance, he began mobilizing forces to invade Boeotia. In the face of a Spartan attack, the Thebans reluctantly agreed to Agesilaus's terms.

The end result of the King's Peace is that Sparta had essentially transformed itself into an instrument of Persia in order to maintain its dominant position in Greece. It was a humiliating situation for the Greeks, and the Greek cities of Asia Minor were subsequently returned to Persian rule.

SIGNIFICANCE

The King's Peace was the first of several fourth century B.C.E. attempts to establish a common peace applicable to all Greek states and whose primary principle was that of autonomy. However, as Persia had drafted the particular provisions of this agreement, it intended the peace to demonstrate the influence that it had in Hellenic affairs.

Sparta rapidly assumed the role of Persia's ally and the guarantor of this peace, although Sparta's disregard for the autonomy of the other Greek states had instigated the Corinthian War in the first place. Under the pretense of enforcing the provisions of the peace, Sparta immediately thereafter started using force or the threat of force to dismantle a variety of existing arrangements in Greece. In 384 B.C.E., Sparta commanded the city of Mantinea to dismantle its walls and dissolve into five villages. It later dissolved the brief experiment in political union between Corinth and Argos.

During the 380's B.C.E., the Thebans were divided between a pro-Spartan faction led by Leontiades and a pro-Athenian group led by Ismenias. In 382, Leontiades persuaded the Spartan commander Phoebidas to occupy the Theban acropolis and install a pro-Spartan government. Ismenias was then accused of conspiring with Persia and accepting Persian money and was executed.

Seven of Ismenias's followers who had sought refuge in Athens secretly returned to their native Thebes. In 379 B.C.E., they overthrew the pro-Spartan government, killed Leontiades, and, with Athenian aid, expelled the Spartan garrison. In the following year, the Spartan officer Sphodrias attempted to seize Athens' port of Piraeus.

Because of Spartan aggression under the guise of enforcing its terms, the King's Peace ultimately failed. The Spartan attempt to take Piraeus caused Athens to seek an alliance with Thebes. Athens also proceeded to create a new naval league, called by historians the Second Athenian Confederation, as a revived form of the fifth century B.C.E. Delian League. Unlike its predecessor, however, this league would not become a vehicle for Athenian imperialism as its government was bicameral, consisting of both the Athenian assembly and an assembly of allies, and all proposals required the approval of both bodies.

Soon thereafter the league won a naval victory over the Spartans at Naxos. Because of this defeat and its concern over Jason of Pherae's attempts to unite Thessaly, Sparta therefore agreed, along with Athens and Thebes, to a new common peace in 375 B.C.E. that acknowledged the existence of the Athenian league. However, fighting soon broke out, and another attempt at a common peace was made in 371. This peace initiative, however, was thwarted by Thebes. Its general Epaminondas had spent much of the 370's trying to reconstitute the Boeotian Confederation, and as in 377, Thebes once again tried to claim to speak for all of Boeotia. When Agesilaus refused, Epaminondas walked out of the peace congress. Sparta subsequently prepared for war.

As the Spartans attempted to invade Boeotia, the Thebans met them at Leuctra (371 B.C.E.). Using innovative military techniques, such as a slanting attack by the left wing, Epaminondas shattered both the Spartan hoplite force and the myth of Spartan invincibility. He subsequently raided deep into Spartan territory, liberating Messenia and freeing the helots. He again defeated the Spartans at Mantinea (362) but died of his wounds soon afterward. Nevertheless, the failure of the third common peace and the subsequent humiliation at Leuctra led to the end of Sparta's status as an international power.

—Andrew G. Traver

FURTHER READING

Cartledge, Paul. *Agesilaos and the Crisis of Sparta*. London: Duckworth, 1987. A detailed study of the life of the Spartan king. Bibliography and indices.

_______. *Spartan Reflections*. Berkeley: University of California Press, 2001. An interesting and scholarly reassessment of Spartan society and politics. Bibliography and index.

Hamilton, Charles D. *Agesilaus and the Failure of Spartan Hegemony*. Ithaca, N.Y.: Cornell University Press, 1991. An in-depth analysis of Sparta's foreign policy in the fourth century B.C.E. Bibliography and index.

_______. *Sparta's Bitter Victories: Politics and Diplomacy in the Corinthian War*. Ithaca, N.Y.: Cornell University Press, 1979. A very useful study of the Corinthian War and the King's Peace. Bibliography and index.

SEE ALSO: c. 736-716 B.C.E., Spartan Conquest of Messenia; May, 431-September, 404 B.C.E., Peloponnesian War; 401-400 B.C.E., March of the Ten Thousand; Between 394 and 371 B.C.E., Xenophon Writes the *Anabasis*; August 2, 338 B.C.E., Battle of Chaeronea; 333 B.C.E., Battle of Issus.

RELATED ARTICLES in *Great Lives from History: The Ancient World*: Agesilaus II of Sparta; Epaminondas.

c. 385 B.C.E.
GREEK PLAYWRIGHT ARISTOPHANES DIES

During his lifetime, Greek playwright Aristophanes was able to perfect the literary form now known as comedy.

LOCALE: Athens
CATEGORY: Literature

KEY FIGURE

Aristophanes (c. 450-c. 385 B.C.E.), Athenian comic dramatist and poet

SUMMARY OF EVENT

The death of Aristophanes signaled the complete demise of what has come to be known as Greek Old Comedy, a form perfected by Aristophanes. Prior to Aristophanes, there were comic works, farces, and various humorous skits performed in ancient Greece, but none of these survives as a written document. Historic commentary and evidence taken from such sources as vase paintings and terra-cotta statuary indicate that types of comic performance are as old as Greek civilization. The term comedy comes from the Greek word *Komos*, which literally means a wild celebration or party. Aristotle in his *De poetica* (c. 335-323 B.C.E.; *Poetics*, 1705) indicates that comedy originated in fertility celebrations in which a chorus, often dressed in animal costume and led by a leader carrying a phallic pole, danced and sang "phallic songs." The members of this chorus would also interact with spectators by making fun of them or hurling obscene insults at them. Tradition has it that comedy was a Doric invention and gradually migrated to Attica. From the first half of the fifth century B.C.E. onward, a comic playwriting contest was formally introduced into the Lenaea festival, which occurred in January and had originally been devoted to marriage ceremonies. In 487 B.C.E., a comic competition was also added to the tragic playwriting contests of the City Dionysia., a springtime festival devoted to Dionysus, god of fertility. Before 487 B.C.E., the City Dionysia, the main dramatic festival of Athens, had been limited to tragedies and satyr plays.

Aristophanes entered the Lenaea comic contest at the age of twenty with *Acharnēs* (425 B.C.E.; *The Acharnians*, 1812), a play that was produced under the pseudonym of Callistratus. Athens was at the time engaged in the Peloponnesian War (431-404 B.C.E.) with Sparta, and the play is fiercely antiwar, a theme that was to be repeated throughout Aristophanes' works. *The Acharnians* won first prize at the festival, and the young comic genius was on his way to an illustrious career. In all, Aristophanes is credited with writing forty-four plays, eleven of which are preserved in their complete form.

Aristophanes' second play and the first to be produced under his own name, *Hippēs* (424 B.C.E.; *The Knights*, 1812), won the first prize at the Lenaea of 424 B.C.E. Like its predecessor, *The Knights* is adamantly antiwar. Seemingly fearless in his criticism of the Athenian war party, Aristophanes introduces the Athenian tyrant Cleon as a character and satirizes him brutally for rejecting a Spartan peace offer. In 423 B.C.E., Aristophanes entered the Dionysian festival and won second prize with *Nephelai* (423 B.C.E.; *The Clouds*, 1708). Although the play did not win the comic competition, *The Clouds* has become one of Aristophanes' most studied works. This is, perhaps, because Socrates is the butt of much of the satire of the play. Indeed, tradition has it that when the character playing Socrates first entered the playing area, the philosopher, who was in the audience, stood up so that his face could be compared with that of the character in the play. Because all Greek actors wore complete head masks, the story is a compliment to the mask designer, but it also indicates how personally Aristophanes aimed his satire. *The Clouds*—centered on a school for young boys—is an attack on the Sophistic philosophers, a group of teachers of argumentation and law whom Aristophanes despised as manipulators of truth. He included Socrates in the Sophistic group, although Socrates was not an avowed Sophist. The play had such an impact on Athenian audiences that it is said to be one of the main causes of the ultimate execution of Socrates for corrupting Athenian youth.

Aristophanes returned to the Lenaea in 423 B.C.E. to win first prize there with *Sphēkes* (422 B.C.E.; *The Wasps*, 1812), another play viciously attacking the Athenian ruler Cleon. *The Wasps* was followed in 421 B.C.E. by *Eirēnē* (421 B.C.E.; *Peace*, 1837), which won second prize at the Dionysian festival. Although Aristophanes had introduced an element of fantasy in *The Wasps*, *Peace* is his first full fantasia, in which he has a war-weary Athenian fly to heaven on the back of a dung beetle to beg the gods for peace. The gods have abandoned the goddess Peace, and the hero has to rescue her from entombment by the god War. Another full-blown fantasy, *Ornithes* (414 B.C.E.; *The Birds*, 1824), won second prize at the City Dionysia of 414 B.C.E.

Perhaps Aristophanes' most widely known work, the one many consider his masterpiece, is *Lysistratē* (411

Aristophanes. (Library of Congress)

B.C.E.; *Lysistrata*, 1837), produced at the Lenaea under his pseudonym, Callistratus. The play's theme of the women of Greece going on a sex strike to end the Peloponnesian War is wildly funny, especially the scene with the young, panting husband begging his wife to return home for the "sake of the children," but on the whole, the play is filled with a sad war-weariness and argues that the only solution is a Panhellenic peace accepted by all sides. It is also a sympathetic presentation of the lonesome suffering that war forces on a nation's women.

Weary of the endless war and its destruction of the precious fabric of Athens' democracy, Aristophanes turned his attention to literary criticism, especially the works of the tragic poets in two comic fantasies: *Batrachoi* (405 B.C.E.; *The Frogs*, 1780) and *Thesmophoriazousai* (411 B.C.E.; *Thesmophoriazusae*, 1837). In the first play, Aristophanes features a chorus of frogs who aid the god Dionysus descending to Hades to bring back Euripides because there are no longer any good tragic poets writing in Athens. Euripides is also the subject of *Thesmophoriazusae* (women celebrating the Thesmophoria), in which a group of women put the tragedian on trial for debasing their sex. In less than a year after the production of this play, Sparta defeated Athens in 404 B.C.E. and destroyed the freedoms of the ancient democracy. One thing that was not allowed was political satire, the very meat of Aristophanic comedy. Old Comedy, the form created by Aristophanes and the form devoted to the criticism and satire of public figures and social practice, was dead.

Old Comedy was replaced by a form known as Middle Comedy, which put its emphasis on comedy of manners, drawing humor from such general human types as misers or lovesick suitors rather than from the foibles of particular living persons. Aristophanes tried his hand at two such comic forms with in *Ekklesiazousai* (392 B.C.E.?; *Ecclesiazusae*, 1837) and *Ploutos* (388 B.C.E.; *Plutus*, 1651), but neither play has the bite and brilliance of his work in Old Comedy. By the time of Aristophanes' death c. 385 B.C.E., the great period of classic Athenian dramatic art in both its tragic and comic forms was clearly finished. Only one Greek playwright, Menander, who brought the comedy of manners to new heights in New Comedy, would be Aristophanes' successor.

SIGNIFICANCE

Aristophanes perfected the form of the literary genre now called comedy. He took the wild singing and dancing of the *komos* celebrants and added poetry and structure to bring comedy in line with the tragedies being performed at the City Dionysia. His plot structure made use of a chorus, sometimes of people, sometimes costumed as birds or frogs. Known as Old Comedy, his comic structure employed a complicated plot brought to a point of ultimate conflict. At this point, the chorus stepped forward in a movement known as the *parabasis* and presented the thematic issues of the play. The plot was then resolved.

Although the change in government in Athens meant that Old Comedy with its social and political themes was no longer possible, the theatrical form realized by Aristophanes was rekindled later by the Greek playwright Menander and traveled from Greece to Rome and thence through the ages to modern Western culture. Finally, as Western culture began to develop an educated middle class much like ancient Athens, comedy as social and political satire has flourished in the Aristophanic tradition wherever there is freedom of speech in a society or wherever brave persons wish to call attention to social and governmental injustices or malpractice. From satires on religious hypocrisy such as Molière's *Tartuffe: Ou, L'Imposteur* (pr. 1664, revised pr. 1667, pb. 1669; *Tartuffe*, 1732) to the delightful wit of W. S. Gilbert and Sir Arthur Sullivan and the sharp political criticism of writers such as Bertolt Brecht with his *Die Dreigroschenoper* (pr. 1928, pb. 1929, libretto; *The Threepenny Opera*, 1949), and the modern attacks on dictators such as Adolf Hitler in Charlie Chaplin's 1940 film *The Great Dictator*, the influence of Aristophanes burns brightly.

—*August W. Staub*

FURTHER READING

Bieber, Margrete. *The History of the Greek and Roman Theater.* Princeton, N.J.: Princeton University Press, 1961. This study remains the basic and most comprehensive presentation of Greek theater history.

Brockett, Oscar. *History of the Theater.* New York: Allyn and Bacon, 2000. The most respected of the general theater histories, with an excellent section on Greek theater and Aristophanes.

Crane, Gregory. *The City as Comedy: Society and Representation in Ancient Greece.* Chapel Hill: University of North Carolina Press, 1997. Gives great insight into Old Comedy themes.

Hadas, Moses. *The Complete Plays of Aristophanes.* New York: Bantam Books, 1962. Excellent and readable translations of all the extant plays.

Norwood, Gilbert. *Greek Comedy.* New York: Hill and Wang, 1963. A study of the whole range of Greek comedy.

Segal, Eric. *The Death of Comedy.* Cambridge, Mass.: Harvard University Press, 2001. A study of the history of theatrical comedy with an excellent chapter on the importance and influence of Aristophanes.

SEE ALSO: c. 440 B.C.E., Sophists Train the Greeks in Rhetoric and Politics; c. 438 B.C.E., Greek Lyric Poet Pindar Dies; May, 431-September, 404 B.C.E., Peloponnesian War; 406 B.C.E., Greek Dramatist Euripides Dies; 399 B.C.E., Death of Socrates; 159 B.C.E., Roman Playwright Terence Dies.

RELATED ARTICLES in *Great Lives from History: The Ancient World*: Aristophanes; Euripides; Menander (dramatist); Pindar; Socrates; Terence.

c. 380 B.C.E.
PLATO DEVELOPS HIS THEORY OF IDEAS

Greek philosopher Plato developed his theory of Ideas, providing a philosophical formulation of the concept of the ultimate reality.

LOCALE: Athens and Sicily (now in Italy)
CATEGORIES: Philosophy; cultural and intellectual history

KEY FIGURES

Plato (c. 427-347 B.C.E.), Athenian philosopher, disciple of Socrates and founder of the Academy
Socrates (c. 470-399 B.C.E.), Athenian citizen and informal teacher

SUMMARY OF EVENT

Plato's concept of *eidos*, meaning "vision" in Greek, has influenced thinkers from Aristotle to medieval scholastics and theologians to modern philosophers such as René Descartes, Baruch Spinoza, Gottfried Wilhelm Leibniz, and even the twentieth century German mathematician Gottlob Frege.

The Forms, or Ideas, are the penultimate reality of things. The Platonic realm of ideas contains the pure Forms of mathematical entities, such as numbers and geometrical shapes, and moral and aesthetic ideas, such as "the just," "the beautiful," and "the good." These Forms are immutable and timeless, unlike phenomena in the actual world, which are shadowy, unreliable reflections of their Forms. Although humans can never fully articulate or define the Forms using limited conceptual terms, they can grasp them intuitively. The purer the mirror of the mind, the clearer the reflection received from the realm of Ideas.

In one sense, the emergence of this theory is the consummate logical expression of the classical Greek way of viewing human experience of the world, but in another, it is possible to trace the emergence of Plato's theory in the context of pre-Socratic and Socratic thought.

For example, from Parmenides and the Sophists, Plato borrowed language for describing the nature of the Forms and their relationship to things in the actual world; from Heraclitus of Ephesus, he derived the idea of self-sufficiency and completeness of the Forms; from the Pythagoreans, he abstracted the idea of transcendence of the Forms and how the human soul has access to that heavenly realm from the lower realm of phenomena.

Plato's master and spiritual father, Socrates, had sought in the later years of the fifth century B.C.E. to discover a science of life, an objective system of knowledge of life's goals, and the means by which such goals might be achieved. While questioning his young aristocratic friends, Socrates found that no person had made this discovery, and that all people held no more than mere opinions about these ends and means of life. Yet Socrates was convinced that the technique of life was a matter of the mind's knowing objective principles and, once they were known, communicating them rationally. At the divine level, he was convinced that they were grasped by a deity essentially good and truthful. The individual mind, or psyche, had intuitive access to these divinely known principles; moreover, Socrates believed that the psyche was obligated to bring them to explicit rational formulation in dialogue with other people. The earlier Socratic dialogues, notably the *Euthyphrōn* (399-390 B.C.E.; *Euthyphro*, 1804), *Charmidēs* (399-390 B.C.E.; *Charmides*, 1804), and *Lachēs* (399-390 B.C.E.; *Laches*, 1804) of Plato, which are generally held to be reasonably accurate descriptions of the characteristic aims and procedures of Socrates, portray him as engaged in the effort to define inductively the precise nature of the traditional Greek moral virtues of piety, temperance, and courage. Thus, implicit in the philosophical activity of Socrates is a dualism of common opinion and transcendental moral truth to which the psyche has intuitive access.

Plato. (Library of Congress)

In Plato's account of the Forms, however, there is no dualism, because the only things that genuinely exist are the Forms. Everything else, such as rocks, plants, and animals, are mere shadows of the Forms. This explains Plato's abhorrence of poetry and the arts. If the actual world is mere shadows of the Forms, then art and poetry are shadows of shadows. Ironically, Plato himself used a poetic and fictional literary style to narrate his philosophy.

Plato, however, preferred the speculative and analytic mode of thought over imaginative ones. He argued that to speculate about the Forms, humans must avoid the realm of opinion (*doxa*) and embrace the science of knowledge (*epitome*) or the pure intellect, which uses logical inferences to abstract the truth of the Forms. Thus, Plato separated the knowing subject from the knowledge of the realm of Ideas.

The Ionian philosophical tradition had already distinguished two types of experience: that of the senses on one hand, revealing a multiplicity of distinct impressions; and that of the mind on the other, comprehending a rational pattern having the character of unity, order, and permanence. It was characteristic of the Greek mind, moreover, to value more highly, and attribute greater reality to, the static pattern of order—visualized by the mind and recognized as a recurrent feature of experience—than the continually shifting flux of concrete phenomena. Greek art and literature, especially the richly exploited store of mythical paradigms, amply exemplify this Greek preoccupation with the eternal and recurrent pattern. It is consistent with this intellectual perspective that the Pythagorean community of southern Italy discovered that meaningful patterns of sense-experience are based on mathematical relations grasped not by the senses but by the psyche alone in inner vision. It was thus the Pythagoreans who distinguished the universal (the triangle, the square, the circle), seen by the mind alone, from the particular mode of the universal seen by the eye and found meaningful only by virtue of the psyche's grasp of the universal.

Plato, who spent some time following the death of Socrates in 399 B.C.E. in southern Italy and Sicily in company with Pythagoreans, appears to have brought together the Pythagorean idea of the universal and the Socratic idea of the objective and eternally valid moral concept. All meaningful patterns of human experience, Plato felt, must be founded on an eternal Form or Idea known by the psyche through intuitive experience and recognized by the senses as immanent in or imitated by concrete particular objects or phenomena. In the *Menōn* (388-368 B.C.E.; *Meno*, 1769), a transitional dialogue between his early and middle period, Plato gave the first clear formulation of this doctrine in terms of Orphic-Pythagorean dualistic mysticism. The doctrine is given ample expression in several dialogues of the middle period of Plato, notably in *Phaedōn* (388-368 B.C.E.; *Phaedo*, 1675) and *Politeia* (388-368 B.C.E.; *Republic*, 1701). The destiny of the individual psyche is a function of its participation in successive life-periods, in two distinct realms of experience: a transcendental realm in which the psyche, free from the bodily limitations of sense-experience, apprehends the eternal forms in their purity, and a physical realm of generation and corruption in which the psyche, through the bodily medium of the senses, apprehends imperfect and perishable concrete exemplifications of eternal forms. The function of philosophers is to purify their vision of the eternal forms in their ideal transcendental order so that in the physical realm they may creatively order their own lives and, if permitted, the lives of their human community, in accordance with this vision.

Plato was keenly aware of the difficulties and paradoxes involved in his notion of Forms. There are allusions to these difficulties throughout his work, especially in *Parmenidēs* (388-368 B.C.E.; *Parmenides*, 1793) and *Meno*, where learning and teaching become paradoxical because humans are supposed to have access to knowledge of the Forms before their experience with the world.

Significance

The impact of this doctrine on the history of philosophy, however, is immeasurable. Some believe that philosophy started with Plato's famous dialogues. With certain modifications, Aristotle made it the basis of the first great systematic understanding of all human experience. The ontological status of Forms, be they mathematical concepts or moral ideals, has been a major subject of controversy between opposing philosophical schools throughout the Western tradition, and empiricists' logical objections to the Doctrine of Ideas have never fully succeeded in dismissing its cogency and appeal as a necessary foundation for a secure epistemology.

—*Carl W. Conrad, updated by Chogollah Maroufi*

Further Reading

Beck, Martha C. *Plato's Self-Corrective Development of the Concepts of Soul, Forms, and Immortality in Three Arguments of the "Phaedo."* Lewiston, N.Y.: E. Mellen Press, 1999. Examines Plato's philosophy, including his views of the Forms.

Fine, Gail. *On Ideas: Aristotle's Criticism of Plato's Theory of Forms*. New York: Clarendon Press, 1993. A rigorous and insightful account of how Aristotle incorporated his teacher's conception of the Forms.

Fine, Gail, ed. *Plato 1: Metaphysics and Epistemology*. New York: Oxford University Press, 1999. Examines Plato's theories of metaphysics, including forms.

Hare, R. M. *Plato*. New York: Oxford University Press, 1989. Written by an eminent philosopher, this book lucidly and briefly describes Plato's major theories. Especially see chapter 6, "Definition, Dialectic, and the Good."

Morgan, Kathryn A. *Myth and Philosophy from the Pre-Socratics to Plato*. New York: Cambridge University Press, 2000. Provides background to Plato's philosophical ideas by describing those that came before him.

Reynold, Noel. *Interpreting Plato's "Euthyphro" and "Meno."* Provo, Utah: Brigham Young University Press, 1988. A comparative look at different notions of the Forms in *Euthyphro*, *Meno*, and other dialogues.

Ross, William David. *Plato's Theory of Ideas*. 1951. Reprint. Westport, Conn.: Greenwood Press, 1976. An account of the development and ramifications of Plato's theory.

See also: 600-500 B.C.E., Greek Philosophers Formulate Theories of the Cosmos; c. 440 B.C.E., Sophists Train the Greeks in Rhetoric and Politics; 399 B.C.E., Death of Socrates; c. 335-323 B.C.E., Aristotle Writes the *Politics*.

Related articles in *Great Lives from History: The Ancient World*: Aristotle; Heraclitus of Ephesus; Plato; Pythagoras; Socrates.

359-336 B.C.E.

PHILIP II EXPANDS AND EMPOWERS MACEDONIA

Philip II built a powerful military, united surrounding territories under Macedonian rule, conquered Greece, and set the stage for a combined Greco-Macedonian invasion of Persia.

LOCALE: Macedonia (now in Greece) and Greece
CATEGORIES: Expansion and land acquisition; government and politics

KEY FIGURES

Philip II of Macedonia (382-336 B.C.E.), king of Macedonia, r. 359-336 B.C.E.
Isocrates (436-338 B.C.E.), Athenian orator
Demosthenes (c. 384-322 B.C.E.), Athenian statesman and orator
Alexander III (Alexander the Great; 356-323 B.C.E.), king of Macedonia, r. 336-323 B.C.E.

SUMMARY OF EVENT

Macedonia was an unstable band of feuding rural clans, loosely united under a hereditary kingship, when Philip II of the Argead Dynasty came to power. Historians debate the actual date of Philip's assumption of Macedonian leadership. Traditionally, historians set the date at 359 B.C.E., but some scholars, such as Eugene Borza, have moved the date back to 360 B.C.E. as they refine knowledge of the Macedonian calendar. Also clouding the issue is the debate, in which historians are about equally divided, regarding whether Philip first served as regent for his infant nephew before assuming kingship in his own right.

According to Plutarch, Philip was born in 382 B.C.E., the third son of King Amyntas III and therefore not the immediate heir to the throne. Philip gleaned a modest education from his mother, Eurydice, who had learned to read in order to educate her children. Philip's schooling was cut short by the death of his father and turmoil in Macedonian affairs. Philip's older brother, Alexander II, had led an unsuccessful attempt to undermine Theban influence in Thessaly, and as a result, young Philip was taken hostage and held in Thebes (369-367). While in Thebes, Philip was able to observe the superior culture and military might of this important Greek city-state. Philip learned at first hand of the infighting among the Greek city-states and perceived that the Greeks were vulnerable to outside forces. He also learned the importance of a powerful military in conquering and ruling other territories. In addition, he was able to experience the beauty and sophistication of Greek culture, for which he developed a lifelong admiration. When Philip returned to his homeland, he took with him these lessons that he would later turn to his advantage as king of Macedonia.

The Macedonia that Philip encountered on his return was in chaos, even within the royal household. During the 360's B.C.E., no less than three kings had ruled, the last of which was Philip's brother Perdiccas III. When Perdiccas III died fending off an Illyrian (now Albanian) invasion in 360/359, Philip moved quickly to consolidate power and to quell outsiders' efforts to weaken Macedonia. The Paeonians and the Thracians, to the north and the east (now Kosovo, Yugoslavia, and Bulgaria), were bought off, and Illyria, to the west, was defeated and incorporated into the Macedonian kingdom.

Philip's success was in large part due to his knowledge of the superior Theban military tactics. Philip organized his troops into uniform phalanxes (tightly packed lines of soldiers with interlocking shields), which overpowered the disorganized local militias. Philip also equipped his soldiers with 17-foot-long (5-meter-long) pikes, significantly longer than those of his opponents, thus putting Philip's troops at a distinct advantage.

In addition to military might, Philip used shrewd diplomacy in dealing with his adversaries. When Athens backed an attempted coup against his rule, Philip foiled the plot and then defused Athenian hostility by offering the Athenians the return of their prisoners. When diplomacy failed, Philip did not hesitate to use bribery, coercion, and marriage alliances to achieve his objectives.

By 358 B.C.E., Philip had incorporated the fiercely independent clans of upper Macedonia into his kingdom. In a show of statesmanship, Philip invited the clan leaders to join the Companions, a prestigious group of aristocrats who served as Philip's advisers and comrades-in-arms. To secure the loyalty of the commoners, Philip created the Foot Companions, thus elevating the status of ordinary soldiers.

Philip did not follow the practice of many of his contemporary generals, who directed battles from a distance, but instead fought alongside his troops—a tactic that gained him the admiration and loyalty of his men but cost him the loss of his right eye during one battle. Much of the land that Philip acquired in his military endeavors was distributed among his followers. The wealth from captured gold and silver mines was used to finance additional military campaigns, to buy favors from foreign diplomats, and to support Philip's lavish lifestyle, which was legendary, even in his own time.

In 357 B.C.E., Philip moved against Athenian interests by conquering, annexing, and allying with Athens' territories and allies in northern Greece. As Philip's power and land holdings grew, so did the fear of the citizens in Athens, and fierce debates arose about Philip and his intentions. Isocrates, a prominent Athenian orator, published the *Philippus* (346 B.C.E.; English translation, 1927), in which he called on Philip to do the one thing that the Greeks could not do for themselves: unite Greece and bring an end to generations of infighting among the Greek city-states. Isocrates even proposed that Philip lead a united Greco-Macedonian campaign against their mutual archrivals, the Persians.

A fellow Athenian, Demosthenes, strongly disagreed, and in a series of speeches known as the *Philippics* (344 B.C.E.; *The Philippics of Demosthenes*, 1875), he denounced Philip as a threat to Greece and warned the Greek city-states against negotiating for peace with Philip. Demosthenes went so far as to appeal to Persia to unite with Greece against Philip, but before that alliance was realized, Philip moved against both Thebes and Athens. The pivotal battle was played out at Chaeronea in 338, with Demosthenes and Philip both engaged in the fighting, and Philip's sixteen-year-old son, Alexander III (later the Great), heading up the elite Macedonian cavalry. The Greek forces were no match for the superior Macedonian troops, and Philip achieved his dream of conquering Greece.

Philip immediately established garrisons across Greece to enforce his dominion and set himself up as *hegemon* (leader) of the Greek city-states. With his typical flair for diplomacy, Philip made it clear that his intention was to allow the Greeks a large measure of domestic self-rule, as long as the Greeks joined the Macedonians in what was, by this time, Philip's ultimate goal—to conquer the great Persian Empire to the east. In 336 B.C.E., Philip sent an expedition force to Asia Minor to begin his conquest of the longtime rival.

Back at home in Aegae (now Vergina), the Macedonian capital, domestic rivalries were undermining Philip's aspirations for a successful campaign against Persia. Philip, a blatant polygamist, had taken a seventh wife, Cleopatra, but this time he ventured so far as to place his new wife in a position of status above that of his first wife and queen, Olympias, the mother of his son, Alexander. When Cleopatra became pregnant, Olympias feared a new son might usurp Alexander's right to the throne. Olympias left the royal palace in anger, and Alexander was forced into ex-

An assassin attacks Philip II of Macedonia. (F. R. Niglutsch)

KINGS OF THE ARGEAD DYNASTY, C. 700-311 B.C.E.

King	*Reign*
Perdiccas I	c. 670-652
Argaios I	652-621
Philip I	621-588
Aeropos I	588-568
Alketas	568-540
Amyntas I	c. 540-498
Alexander I	before 492-c. 540
Perdiccas II	c. 450-c. 413
Archelaus	c. 413-399
Orestes	399-396
Aeropos II	396-393
Pausanias	393
Amyntas II	393
Amyntas III	393/392-370/369
Argaios II	390
Alexander II	370-368
Ptolemy Alorites	368-365
Perdiccas III	365-360/359
Philip II	359-336
Alexander the Great	336-323
Philip III Arrhidaeus	323-317
Alexander IV	323-311

ile. The new child turned out to be a girl, and an uneasy reconciliation was made between Philip and Alexander.

In the autumn of 336 B.C.E., while participating in a procession in celebration of his daughter's marriage, Philip was attacked and killed by a disgruntled bodyguard. Sources differ as to whether this was the act of a lone assassin or part of a larger plot perhaps spearheaded by Olympias. Historians generally exonerate Alexander in his father's assassination, however, citing Philip's favorable treatment and training of the young Alexander, which indicates that Philip was preparing Alexander to take the throne of Macedonia.

Philip left a powerful legacy for the twenty-year-old Alexander: He left the best trained and best equipped military machine of the era, a united Greece and Macedonia, vast wealth from silver and gold mines, and the vision of conquering Persia, the greatest empire the world had yet known. Alexander took this legacy and, within twelve years, fulfilled Philip's dream.

SIGNIFICANCE

Through creative diplomacy and military genius, Philip II transformed Macedonia from a backward group of warring clans into the first large-scale unified state on the continent of Europe. By conquering and uniting with Greece, Philip set the stage for his son, Alexander III (later Alexander the Great), to amass one of the greatest empires in history.

—*Sonia Sorrell*

FURTHER READING

Borza, Eugene N. *Before Alexander: Constructing Early Macedonia*. Publications of the Association of Ancient Historians 6. Claremont, Calif.: Regina Books, 1999. An excellent update on recent scholarship on Philip II and early Macedonia.

_______. *In the Shadow of Olympus: The Emergence of Macedon*. Princeton, N.J.: Princeton University Press, 1990. Macedonian history until Philip II.

Ellis, J. R. *Philip II and Macedonian Imperialism*. London: Thames and Hudson, 1976. The career of Philip II from the Macedonian viewpoint.

Errington, R. M. *A History of Macedonia*. Translated by Caroline Errington. Berkeley: University of California Press, 1990. A detailed history including good analyses of ancient sources.

Green, Peter. *Alexander of Macedon, 356-323 B.C.* Berkeley: University of California Press, 1991. Begins with an excellent chapter on Philip II, which, although based on sound scholarship, reads like a historical novel.

Hammond, N. G. L. *The Macedonian State: Origins, Institutions, and History*. Oxford, England: Oxford University Press, 1989. A useful overview of traditional Macedonian scholarship for the general audience.

Roisman, Joseph, ed. "The Macedonian Background: Macedonia, Philip II, and Alexander." In *Alexander the Great: Ancient and Modern Perspectives*. Lexington, Mass.: D.C. Heath, 1995. Excerpts from the ancient writers Arrian, Diodorus, and Plutarch, as well as contemporary scholars A. B. Bosworth and Stanley M. Burstein.

SEE ALSO: August 2, 338 B.C.E., Battle of Chaeronea; 336 B.C.E., Alexander the Great Begins Expansion of Macedonia; 332 B.C.E., Founding of Alexandria; 327-325 B.C.E., Alexander the Great Invades the Indian Subcontinent; c. 323-275 B.C.E., Diadochi Divide Alexander the Great's Empire.

RELATED ARTICLES in *Great Lives from History: The Ancient World*: Alexander the Great; Demosthenes; Isocrates; Olympias; Philip II of Macedonia.

c. 350 B.C.E.
DIOGENES POPULARIZES CYNICISM

Diogenes' teachings and his unconventional lifestyle led to the establishment of the Cynic philosophical school.

LOCALE: Athens
CATEGORIES: Philosophy; cultural and intellectual history

KEY FIGURE

Diogenes (c. 412/403-c. 324/321 B.C.E.), Greek philosopher

SUMMARY OF EVENT

Diogenes is considered by a number of ancient traditions as the founder of the Cynic school of philosophy. His thought represented a rejection of all existing philosophical systems as well as of conventional morality and social custom. Diogenes' philosophical convictions translated into public behavior that scandalized his contemporaries. Although none of Diogenes' works has survived into modern times, details of his life and aspects of his thought have been preserved by a number of classical historians and authors. Of special note is the work of Diogenes Laertius, who, in his *Peri biōn dogmatōn kai apophthegmatōn tōn en philosophia eudokimīsantōn* (third century C.E.; *The Lives and Opinions of the Philosophers*, 1853), provides information from a diverse body of sources, including Diogenes' own writings.

Diogenes was born in the city of Sinope, a Greek colony on the southern coast of the Black Sea. According to one version, his father, Hicesias, was a banker in charge of the public finances, but when it was discovered that he had debased the currency, he was forced into exile along with Diogenes. According to other versions, including Diogenes' own work *Pordalus* (now lost), it was Diogenes himself who adulterated the currency and was forced to leave his native city in disgrace.

Whatever the exact circumstances of his departure from Sinope, Diogenes was living in the city of Athens by the mid-fourth century B.C.E. On his arrival in Athens, Diogenes reportedly became a student of Antisthenes, who, in turn, had been a student of Socrates. Some ancient writers claim that Antisthenes was the first philosopher with whom the word "cynic" was associated, probably because he met with his followers at the gymnasium of Cynoserges (the white dog). Antisthenes reportedly was the first philosopher to wear a cloak and carry a staff and a knapsack, clothing and accessories that, along with the Phrygian felt cap, later became the trademarks of Cynic philosophers. Although the extent to which Antisthenes influenced Diogenes is not known, Diogenes' thought and behavior clearly represented a radical departure from all previous philosophical propositions.

Obtaining a clear biographical portrait of Diogenes is difficult because there are no contemporary historical accounts of his life. Furthermore, events in the life of the historical Diogenes are intertwined with anecdotes that are part of the literary persona that emerged in his own writings and the works of writers from the Roman period such as Lucian and Dio Chrysostom. As the founder of the Cynic school, Diogenes became a paradigmatic figure to whom many philosophical authors and biographers attributed countless acts and aphorisms. The most detailed surviving biography of Diogenes comes from Diogenes Laertius, a writer who probably lived in the third century C.E. Laertius himself implicitly acknowledged the difficulty in reconstructing an accurate biographical portrait of his subject when he included several versions of important events in Diogenes' life.

Whether historical or fictional, all actions and words attributed to Diogenes conjure the image of an individual whose mission in life became to ridicule all philosophical systems and to challenge all social and moral practices. Every source mentions that Diogenes rejected material possessions. He wore a coarse cloak, went about barefoot, held his few possessions in a knapsack, carried a walking staff, and never groomed his hair or beard. Diogenes rejected the idea of work and relied on the charity of friends and strangers for his basic needs. Because he did not own a house, Diogenes slept at friends' houses, on the steps of public buildings, on the streets, and most famously, in a bathtub.

Every story about Diogenes illustrates his disregard for rank, wealth, and power; his defiance of authority; and his desire to provoke outrage. After Philip II of Macedonia defeated Athens and its allies at the Battle of Chaeronea in 338 B.C.E., Diogenes was brought to the Macedonian king as a captive. The king asked him who he was, to which Diogenes responded, "A spy upon your insatiable greed." A few years later Philip's successor, Alexander the Great, came to meet Diogenes. When he found the cynic taking a sunbath, the young king told Diogenes that he could request anything from him, to which the philosopher replied, "Stand out of my light." Alexander is quoted as having said that if he had not been Alex-

Diogenes. (F. R. Niglutsch)

ander, he would have liked to have been Diogenes.

Diogenes was equally defiant toward those who presumed of intellectual authority. When Diogenes heard Plato lecturing about his theory of Ideas and using such terms as "tablehood" and "cuphood," Diogenes commented that he could see a table and a cup, but he was unable to see "tablehood" and "cuphood." During another lecture, Plato pompously defined humans as bipedal animals with no feathers. Diogenes ran outside, found a chicken, and plucked its feathers; he came back to the lecture hall and presented the bird to the crowd saying, "Here is Plato's man."

No institution was immune to the cynic's attacks. Diogenes was critical of organized religion. When he saw temple officials arresting a man who had stolen a bowl, he said that the great thieves were taking away the little thief. He had no use for revered social institutions. When asked what the appropriate time for marriage was, he responded that "for a young man not yet and for an old man never at all." Diogenes held no national allegiances. When asked where he was from, he responded that he was a citizen of the world. He is believed to have coined the word "cosmopolitan."

According to several sources, while traveling by sea, Diogenes was captured by pirates and subsequently sold as a slave. When asked at the auction block what kind of tasks he could perform, Diogenes replied that he could rule men. On hearing this, a Corinthian by the name of Xeniades bought Diogenes, brought him to Corinth, and entrusted him with the education of his sons. Diogenes spent the rest of his life in Corinth growing old at Xeniades' household. He died at the age of about ninety. Although he had requested that his dead body be left unburied so that the wild beasts could feed off him, Xeniades' sons buried him. One account claims that Diogenes' life ended on the same day that Alexander the Great died in Babylon.

SIGNIFICANCE

The rise of Cynicism marks the end of the classical period in Greek philosophy and the beginning of Hellenistic thought. After the formalism of Plato and Aristotle, embodied in the rival institutions of the Academy and the Lyceum, Diogenes emerged as the philosopher of the antiestablishment.

Plato once described Diogenes as "a Socrates gone mad." The comparison to Socrates is apt because, like the martyred Athenian, Diogenes spent his life exposing the hypocrisy of society, the presumptuousness of intellectuals, and the greed of the powerful. However, unlike Socrates, whose life and thought reflect deep trust in humankind's inherent rationality and a desire to improve society through example, Diogenes, through his behavior, projected a complete lack of confidence in humankind's rational abilities and hopelessness about the future of humanity.

—Gilmar E. Visoni

FURTHER READING

Branham, R. "Diogenes and the Invention of Cynicism." In *The Cynics: The Cynic Movement in Antiquity and Its Legacy*, edited by R. Branhman and M. Goulet-Caze. Berkeley: University of California Press, 1996. Essay provides a good summary of Diogenes's role in the development of Cynicism. Bibliography and index.

Diogenes Laertius. *Lives of Eminent Philosophers*. Translated by R. D. Hicks. Cambridge, Mass.: Harvard University Press, 2000. Primary source containing the most extensive extant account of Diogenes's life. Diogenes Laertius also provides references to other ancient works now lost. Index.

Long, A. "Diogenes, Crates and Hellenistic Ethics." In *The Cynics: The Cynic Movement in Antiquity and Its Legacy*, edited by R. Branhman and M. Goulet-Caze. Berkeley: University of California Press, 1996. Essay dealing with the influences of the first Cynics on the field of ethics. Bibliography and index.

SEE ALSO: c. 440 B.C.E., Sophists Train the Greeks in Rhetoric and Politics; c. 438 B.C.E., Greek Lyric Poet Pindar Dies; c. 380 B.C.E., Plato Develops His Theory of Ideas; 359-336 B.C.E., Philip II Expands and Empowers Macedonia; August 2, 338 B.C.E., Battle of Chaeronea; 336 B.C.E., Alexander the Great Begins Expansion of Macedonia

RELATED ARTICLES in *Great Lives from History: The Ancient World*: Alexander the Great; Diogenes; Philip II of Macedonia; Socrates.

340-338 B.C.E.
ORIGIN OF *MUNICIPIA*

The origin of municipia *represented an advance in the development of diplomatic relations between Rome and its neighbors.*

LOCALE: Rome, Latium, and Campania (now in Italy)
CATEGORIES: Expansion and land acquisition; government and politics

KEY FIGURE

Titus Manlius Imperiosus Torquatus (fl. fourth century B.C.E.), military tribune, dictator, and consul, later general in 340 B.C.E. for Rome

SUMMARY OF EVENT

Vital to the expansion of Roman dominance in Italy was the discovery of a way to cement close relationships with small neighboring states. Although the bonds gradually forged with Italian towns and tribal groups since the mid-500's B.C.E. were diverse in character, Roman diplomacy exhibited unprecedented sophistication in the terms imposed in the settlement in 338 B.C.E.

Some thirty to forty smaller communities in Latium, south of Rome, had long been united for mutual defense and common religious rites before Rome itself entered into agreement with them, possibly as early as 493 B.C.E. Surviving records reflect a Roman bias, according to which Rome dominated Latin League decisions; in the 400's, all members cooperated in rough equality against the Aequi and Volsci in the hills east of Latium. By the 300's, the chief enemies were farther afield: Gauls in northern Italy, who had sacked Rome in 390, and Samnite tribes in the southern Apennine mountains, whom overpopulation and poor soil compelled to attack the Latins of the rich coastal plain. Latin League members exchanged some citizenship privileges such as intermarriage and recognition of commercial contracts; individuals could also abandon their homes and acquire new citizenship by establishing residence in another league town. The league occasionally founded colonies at strategic sites to serve as garrisons against its enemies; the *coloniae* became new members. From the 380's, Rome achieved a supremacy that its partners resented. About 358 B.C.E., several league towns supported an attack on Rome, and in 340 B.C.E. almost the entire league and a number of places in Campania took up arms against Roman hegemony.

Led by Titus Manlius Imperiosus Torquatus, hero of a famous duel against a giant Gaul, the Romans defeated their opponents by 338 B.C.E. The terms imposed at the restoration of peace are a milestone in Italian history, for the Roman senators established the principle of flexible treatment of beaten enemies. Rome retained and adapted the essential features of this settlement for centuries. Two points preface the ensuing discussion. First, as in civil law, Romans distinguished categories of people (free-slave, citizen-foreigner, *in patria potestate-sui juris*, and so forth), so in diplomacy they distinguished types of community; consequently, some technical terms are essential. Second, at the time citizenship was membership in one's home community, not some larger unit. Two hundred fifty years later, the Romans devised a national citizenship: The Julian Law of 90 B.C.E. built on the principles formulated in 338 B.C.E. and applied over the next century, as it extended Roman citizenship to all free inhabitants of Italy.

In 338 B.C.E., Rome disbanded the old Latin League and replaced it with a new system. With the addition of other peoples, it became the Roman alliance system. (This is a modern term of convenience; it was not a federation, which implies an approximate equality among members.) The victor ended the independence of five nearby towns by incorporating their inhabitants as citizens of Rome. These places, at least as old as Rome, became the first *municipia* (*municipium* in the singular) and their residents Roman *municipes* (*municeps* in the singular), so called because they undertook (*ceperunt*) the obligations (*munera*) of citizenship. *Coloniae* were new foundations, whether on a new site or replacing a destroyed town. Fresh treaties with the other Latin cities, chiefly league colonies, defined them as allies (*socii*) of Rome. These peoples retained their old rights, but henceforward only with Rome.

Farther south there were a number of populous communities that controlled the fertile lowland plain called Campania, situated between the Samnites to the east and south and the Romans to the north. Capua, the largest city in Campania, appealed in 343 B.C.E. for Roman aid against Samnite aggression and received help. During the Latin War of 340-338 B.C.E., citizens of Capua and a few other Campanian communities assisted the Latins against Rome, but the upper-class Campanian cavalry remained loyal to Rome. Rome consequently rewarded the nobles of Capua and several smaller towns in Campania with what the historian Livy calls *civitas romana*, that is, Roman citizenship. Also described as *civitas sine suffragio*, or "citizenship without suffrage," this qualified citizenship specifically excluded the right to vote in Roman elections or to hold offices in Rome, but it did include the obligation to serve with the Roman legions when called on to do so. These towns were also designated as *municipia*. *Cives sine suffragio* were similar to Latin *socii*: Already citizens of Rome, they had the rights of marriage and commerce with Romans; neither group could vote or hold office at Rome. This partial Roman citizenship subordinated the *municipia* to the military and diplomatic dominance of Rome, but it also allowed Italian cities to retain almost complete freedom in local self-government. This autonomy was a practical necessity, as Rome lacked the machinery to govern its enlarged territory. Itinerant prefects (*praefecti*) sent out from Rome kept a watch on the *municipia*. Inscriptions reveal a considerable variety in the titles of municipal magistrates for years; for instance, Capua continued to be governed by its own traditional magistrates.

SIGNIFICANCE

The *municipium* with *civitas sine suffragio* was one of two highly effective political weapons in Rome's steady expansion after 338 B.C.E.: Nineteen were established in 303-270 B.C.E., the first few among the Volsci but most in central Italy outside Latium. The other was the Latin colony, of which eighteen were founded in 338-268 B.C.E. The *municipia sine suffragio* and *coloniae Latinae* showed remarkable loyalty during the Second and Third Samnite Wars between 326 and 290 B.C.E.; slowly they confined the Samnites to their mountain homelands and cut them off from potential allies such as the Etruscans. Though Rome probably intended *civitas sine suffragio* to be a permanent condition, it gradually elevated these *municipia* to full citizenship (*civitas optimo iure*). Some Sabine communities moved up in 268 B.C.E., the first block grant of full citizenship to non-Latin people; the rest followed in 241 B.C.E.; and the people of Arpinum (including the families of Marius and Cicero) and Formiae received *civitas optimo iure* in 188 B.C.E., a consequence of loyalty during Hannibal's invasion of Italy. *Civitas sine suffragio* disappeared over the second century. The Latins, however, did not acquire *civitas Romana*, though like the *cives sine suffragio* they shared some of the fruits of Roman military victories and preserved their own self-government. Of less importance was the Roman citizen colony: Few in number (eight by 264 B.C.E.) and small in size (three hundred families), their inhabitants remained full citizens of Rome with little autonomy. Diplomacy was as important as battlefield superiority in the spread of Roman political power. Some fifty-five communities below a line from Cosa on the west to Ariminum on the east combined with the growing mass of Roman citizens to extend Roman culture and Latin language throughout peninsular Italy.

Incorporation of the remaining people of Italy as allies (*socii*) completed the Roman alliance system. These groups lacked the relatively privileged status of the Latins and *cives sine suffragio*, for though allowed a measure of autonomy, they could not intermarry or conduct business with Romans and had no hope of full citizenship. This inferior treatment explains why the revolt of 90 B.C.E. was almost entirely confined to the Italian allies.

As Rome's domination extended in later centuries beyond Italy, terms such as *municipia* changed in meaning. The Julian Law of 90 B.C.E. extended citizenship to all people south of the Po River. Existing towns easily converted into *municipia*, and the less urbanized people formed *municipia* by amalgamating their villages and hamlets (*fora*, *conciliabula*, and so forth). Over the next century, these towns gradually adopted annual *quattuorviri* (two *duoviri iure dicundo*, judicial officials modeled on Rome's consuls, and two *aediles*). From then on, all Italian towns were either *coloniae* or *municipia*.

In the Roman Empire, the institution of the *municipium* spread widely. Grants of municipal status in the form of charters conferring increased rights to manage local affairs with Roman-style government emanated from the capital. Town elites became Roman citizens by holding local office, a practice appearing in the 120's B.C.E., in Italy. The process is best known in Spain, where Vespasian, recognizing their Romanization, elevated all the native (noncolonial) communities to Latin municipalities in 70-79 C.E.

—*Roger B. McShane, updated by Thomas H. Watkins*

FURTHER READING

Bruun, Christer, ed. *The Roman Middle Republic: Politics, Religion, and Historiography.* Rome: Institutum Romanum Finlandiae, 2000. A collection of papers from a 1998 conference on Roman history from c. 400-133 B.C.E. that provides a background for understanding the colonies. Bibliography and index.

Lintott, A. W. *The Roman Republic*. Stroud, Gloucestershire, England: Sutton, 2000. A concise history of the Roman Republic that deals with politics and government.

Salmon, E. T. *The Making of Roman Italy.* Ithaca, N.Y.: Cornell University Press, 1982.

_______. *Roman Colonization Under the Republic.* Ithaca, N.Y.: Cornell University Press, 1970.

_______. *Samnium and the Samnites.* New York: Cambridge University Press, 1967. These three works are probably the best introduction to the role and historical context of *coloniae* and *municipia*; consequences of enfranchisement from 90 B.C.E. forward.

Sherwin-White, A. N. *The Roman Citizenship*. 2d ed. New York: Oxford University Press, 1980. An authoritative and technical source.

SEE ALSO: 494/493 B.C.E., Institution of the Plebeian Tribunate; 451-449 B.C.E., Twelve Tables of Roman Law Are Formulated; 445 B.C.E., Establishment of the Canuleian Law; 287 B.C.E., *Lex Hortensia* Reforms the Roman Constitution; 90 B.C.E., Julian Law Expands Roman Citizenship.

August 2, 338 B.C.E.
BATTLE OF CHAERONEA

The Battle of Chaeronea resulted in a Macedonian victory that heralded the dawn of the Hellenistic age.

LOCALE: Chaeronea, in Boeotia northwest of Thebes (now in Greece)

CATEGORY: Wars, uprisings, and civil unrest

KEY FIGURES

Alexander the Great (356-323 B.C.E.), son of Philip and his successor as king, r. 336-323 B.C.E.

Demosthenes (c. 384-322 B.C.E.), Athenian statesman and orator

Isocrates (436-338 B.C.E.), Athenian publicist, orator, and rhetorician

Philip II of Macedonia (382-336 B.C.E.), king of Macedonia, r. 359-336 B.C.E.

SUMMARY OF EVENT

The Peloponnesian War (431-404 B.C.E.) ended Athens' hegemony in Greece and marked the beginning of Spartan dominance. The result was the outbreak of new destructive wars aimed at the overthrow of Sparta. At the Battle of Leuctra in 371 B.C.E., the Thebans, allies of Athens, inflicted a decisive defeat on the Spartans, and Greece passed to the hegemony of Thebes. This hegemony proved to be exceedingly short-lived. Athens changed sides and, in concert with Sparta and other states, overcame Thebes in the closely fought Battle of Mantinea in 362 B.C.E. Meanwhile, Athens had revived the Delian confederacy, but most of its allies successfully revolted against Athens in the Social War of 357-355, and Athenian power was badly shaken.

Men who participated in these unsuccessful wars for the hegemony of Greece called out for relief from conflict. Understanding the vital necessity for escaping continual competition and bloodshed, the Athenian Isocrates advocated the unification of Greece under the leadership of a strong state with a strong ruler. Demosthenes of Athens dreamed of an Athens revitalized culturally and militarily and preeminent in Greece. The philosopher Plato hoped for government by philosophers.

A more likely savior than one of Plato's scholars appeared in Philip II of Macedonia, who began his reign in 359 B.C.E. He set about to Hellenize and modernize Macedonia with ingenuity and energy. He brought the factious nobility of his country to heel and taught them to serve him with heavy cavalry. He also created a phalanx better drilled and more effective than that of the Greeks. His army was of professional quality, far superior to the citizen militias or hired mercenaries that made up the bulk of the armies of the Hellenic cities. The Macedonian army was, moreover, supported by efficient financial institutions. Philip intended to establish his own hegemony over Greece, although he wished it to be merciful and enlightened. In the 340's, he began to penetrate southward through Thessaly. The principal Greek states of Athens, Sparta, and Thebes, distracted by their own perpetual feuds and weakened by their precarious fiscal circumstances, only halfheartedly resisted Philip.

In 340 B.C.E., the decisive war broke out between Macedonia and the Greeks. In August of 338 B.C.E., the Macedonian army of two thousand cavalry and thirty thousand infantry came face to face with the united Greek armies of weak cavalry and thirty-five thousand infantry near the small town of Chaeronea in northwestern Boeotia. The Greeks deployed with their right flank near a small stream; it was held by twelve thousand Thebans and Boeotians. The center was composed of various allies from central Greece and the Peloponnesus, and the left was made up of ten thousand Athenians. The Greek phalanx was to make its usual straightforward attack, hoping to crush the enemy by the weight of its charge. On the other side, Philip was a master of more subtle tactics, combining the use of cavalry and infantry. His own left, opposite the Thebans, was headed by his cavalry, which was to thrust itself into a gap to be made in the Greek line. The gap would be opened by luring the Athenians into charging Philip's own right as it purposefully drew back in pretended retreat.

The battle was probably fought on August 2, 338 B.C.E., and everything went according to Philip's plan. The Athenians rushed forward, shouting "On to Pella!" (the capital of Macedonia), and when the Greek center and the Theban left moved obliquely to keep in close ranks, a hole opened in the Theban line. Led by the eighteen-year-old crown prince Alexander, the Macedonian heavy cavalry charged into this gap in wedge formation. They were followed by crack formations of infantry, which attacked the flanks on either side of the gap. The Thebans, after heroic resistance, were beaten; the Greek center and left, panic-stricken, broke and ran. The result was a decisive victory for Philip.

During the next few weeks, the Greek states surrendered one after the other. In 337 B.C.E., Philip organized them into a Hellenic League with its seat at Corinth. He served as president of the league, and members were forced to follow his foreign policy. Wars among them were forbidden, as was internal constitutional change except by constitutional methods. Philip's intentions were to secure a tranquil and contented Greece as the necessary first step in his new plan to liberate the Greeks of Asia Minor from the Persian Empire.

SIGNIFICANCE

The Battle of Chaeronea was the great event that destroyed the sovereignty of the Greek states. There was a revolt against Macedonia in 323-321 B.C.E. called the Lamian War, and several more occurred in the third century B.C.E., bringing temporary freedom. Nevertheless, the old, unbridled parochialism and imperialism of Athens, Sparta, and Thebes was extinguished.

—*Samuel K. Eddy, updated by Jeffrey L. Buller*

FURTHER READING

Borza, Eugene N. *Before Alexander: Constructing Early Macedonia*. Publications of the Association of Ancient Historians 6. Claremont, Calif.: Regina Books, 1999. An excellent update on recent scholarship on Philip II and early Macedonia.

Bradford, Alfred S., ed. and trans. *Philip II of Macedon*. Westport, Conn.: Praeger, 1992. A lavishly illustrated biography of Philip with its texts drawn from ancient sources. Also includes a good set of maps.

Cawkwell, George. *Philip of Macedon*. Boston: Faber & Faber, 1978. A good biographical introduction to Philip II and the events leading up to the Battle of Chaeronea; intended for the general reader.

Hammond, Nicholas. *Philip of Macedon*. Baltimore: Johns Hopkins University Press, 1994. Includes extensive information on the Battle of Chaeronea and valuable bibliographic references.

Hatzopoulos, Miltiades B., and Louisa D. Loukopulos, eds. *Philip of Macedon*. Athens, Greece: Ekdotike Athenon, 1980. An overview of the historical, cultural, and military aspects of Philip II's reign. Includes maps that are particularly useful in illustrating the background to the Battle of Chaeronea.

Montgomery, Hugo. *The Way to Chaeronea*. New York: Columbia University Press, 1983. Primarily focusing on Demosthenes' role before the Battle of Chaeronea, this work provides a thorough analysis of Athenian foreign policy in the period before Philip's conquest.

SEE ALSO: 478-448 B.C.E., Athenian Empire Is Created; May, 431-September, 404 B.C.E., Peloponnesian War; September, 404-May, 403 B.C.E., Thirty Tyrants Rule

Athens for Eight Months; 401-400 B.C.E., March of the Ten Thousand; 386 B.C.E., King's Peace Ends Corinthian War; 359-336 B.C.E., Philip II Expands and Empowers Macedonia; 336 B.C.E., Alexander the Great Begins Expansion of Macedonia; 333 B.C.E., Battle of Issus; October 1, 331 B.C.E., Battle of Gaugamela.

RELATED ARTICLES in *Great Lives from History: The Ancient World*: Alexander the Great; Philip II of Macedonia.

336 B.C.E.
ALEXANDER THE GREAT BEGINS EXPANSION OF MACEDONIA

Following the assassination of his father, Alexander the Great was proclaimed king of Macedonia, setting the stage for his military campaigns that would extend from Egypt to India and create the foundation of a vast empire.

LOCALE: Macedonian capital of Aegae (now Verghina, Greece)

CATEGORY: Expansion and land acquisition; wars, uprisings, and civil unrest; government and politics

KEY FIGURES

Alexander the Great (356-323 B.C.E.), king of Macedonia, r. 336-323 B.C.E.

Philip II of Macedonia (382-336 B.C.E.), king of Macedonia, r. 359-336 B.C.E.

Olympias (c. 375-316 B.C.E.), wife of Philip II and mother of Alexander

SUMMARY OF EVENT

Philip II, during his reign of more than twenty years, consolidated the Macedonian kingdom and achieved hegemony over the Greek city-states of Europe, thus making possible the famous exploits of his son, Alexander the Great. Philip's success was due in part to his skillful diplomacy, but even more important was his reorganization of the army into an effective killing machine. Rather than amateurs, Philip's soldiers were well-paid and well-trained professionals. Fighting in phalanx formations of eight to sixteen rows, they were armed with the *sarisa*, a 15-foot-long (4.5-meter-long) wooden spear with a metal tip. Philip supplemented the phalanx with many archers and a large cavalry. When these components worked together as intended, Philip's army was almost invincible.

After defeating Athens and Thebes in the Battle of Chaeronea in 338, Philip was the recognized master of all Greece. The following year, to preserve peace, he established the League of Corinth, which included all the Greek states except Sparta. As president of the league's council of representatives, Philip influenced the decisions of its representatives and had the authority to execute their orders. Not long before Philip's death, the council approved a joint invasion of Asia Minor (now Turkey) to drive out the Persians and further expand Macedonian hegemony.

Philip did much to prepare Alexander for future political and military leadership. Alexander's first teacher was Leonidas, a strict disciplinarian who helped develop his ascetic nature. At the age of thirteen, his personal tutor was the famous philosopher Aristotle. In 340 B.C.E., when Philip led a campaign against Byzantium, he authorized his sixteen-year-old son to rule over Macedonia as regent in his absence. While regent, Alexander led the army to suppress a tribal revolt in northern Macedonia. Two years later, he commanded a decisive cavalry charge at Chaeronea, thus acquiring the reputation of a fearless warrior. These political and military experiences developed the young man's leadership skills, and they also made him extremely popular among the soldiers, who exercised significant influence in governmental affairs.

Alexander was very close to his ambitious mother, Olympias, but he did not get along with Philip, who had seven wives and many concubines. In 337 B.C.E., a wedding between Philip and Cleopatra, the daughter of a Macedonian nobleman, was especially painful for Alexander and his mother. At a drinking party to celebrate the event, Cleopatra's uncle and protector, Attalus, asked those present to pray for a legitimate heir to the throne, referring indirectly to the fact that Philip's other wives, including Olympias, were of foreign birth. Alexander was so angry that he hurled his cup at Attalus. This act enraged Philip. However, when the intoxicated king tried to strike his son, he stumbled and fell on his face. Alexander then publicly ridiculed him. Within a few months, however, Alexander was reconciled with his father and was scheduled to be a commander in the invasion of Asia Minor.

MILESTONES IN ALEXANDER'S CONQUESTS, 334-323 B.C.E.

Date	*Action*
April, 334	Crosses into Asia in order to conquer Persia
May, 334	Meets and defeats Persian army at the River Granicus; liberates Miletus and other Greek coastal cities of Asia Minor
September-November, 334	Takes coastal city of Halicarnassus after a siege
Winter, 334-August, 333	Captures coastal cities of Phrygia, Gordium, and Cappodocia
September, 333	Seizes vital pass at Cilician Gates
November, 333	Decisively defeats Persian army along Pinarus River near Issus, capturing family of Emperor Darius IV
January-August, 332	Besieges then destroys Phoenician seaport of Tyre; takes control of Phoenicia; refuses peace offer from Darius
September-October, 332	Besieges, then storms and sacks Gaza
November, 332-April, 331	Occupies Egypt; founds city of Alexandria
April-September, 331	Marches into northern Mesopotamia through Tyre in pursuit of Darius; refuses second peace offer
October, 331	Defeats Persian army under Darius at Arbela/Gaugamela; occupies Babylon
November-December, 331	Occupies Susa; captures Persian Gates
December, 331-March, 330	Occupies, destroys Persepolis; continues pursuit of Darius
May, 330	Occupies Ecbatana
July, 330	Finds Darius murdered by Persian nobles; becomes ruler of Persian Empire
July-October, 330	Conquers tribes on southern shore of Caspian sea; subdues Parthia and Aria
January-May, 329	Invades Arachosia, then Bactria
August-October, 329	Defeats Scythians near Oxus River
February-August, 328	Puts down revolt in Sogdiana
January-February, 327	Captures fortresses at Sogdian and Chiorenes Rocks
July-September, 327	Invades India by the Khyber Pass and other passes north of the Kabul Valley
March-April, 326	Besieges and storms citadel of Aornas; crosses Indus River
May, 326	Defeats and captures King Porus at Hydaspes
July, 326	Decides to return to Persia after army mutinies
August, 326-July, 325	Travels down Indus River to the sea, subduing Mallians
September-November, 325	Leads grueling march through Gedrosian desert on way to Persepolis
July, 324	Tries to reunite empire by melding Greek and Persian cultures
Spring, 323	Arrives in Babylon
June, 323	Dies of a fever in Babylon

As Philip was preparing for the campaign, he held a large celebration for his daughter's marriage to Olympias's brother. Delegations from most of the Greek states were gathered at Aegae for the occasion. When Philip was leaving the palace to go to the theater, he was fatally stabbed by Pausanius, a disgruntled young Macedonian nobleman (rumored to be Philip's lover) who was furious about a personal injustice that Philip had ignored. Soldiers immediately killed Pausanius, which made it impossible to gain accurate information about a possible conspiracy. Because Alexander and Olympias had the most to gain from Philip's death, some writers have suspected that one or both of them might have been involved, even though it appears unlikely that either would have risked cooperation with a person such as Pausanius.

The assassination of Philip created a condition of turmoil and uncertainty for the next several days. Alexander, only twenty years old, was not the only pretender to the vacant throne, but once the army recognized him as the legitimate successor, he quickly obtained the support of the most powerful noblemen of the country. Ancient historians, unfortunately, did not provide many details about the process and ceremonies for installing a Macedonian king. They did report that within a few weeks, Alexander promised the assembly at Aegae that he would continue the policies of his father.

Alexander's first official act was to punish all those who were suspected of involvement in Philip's murder. About a dozen alleged conspirators were quickly tried and executed before large crowds. The decision to execute these individuals publicly rather than secretly suggested that Alexander probably had no part in his father's death. After these acts of vengeance were completed, the body of Philip was cremated and interred in a large royal tomb (excavated by Manolis Andronikos in 1977).

Alexander further demonstrated his ruthlessness by eliminating all his major rivals as well as the faction that opposed him. Attalus, who was in Asia Minor, desperately tried to reconcile with Alexander, but it was too late. Alexander ordered the assassination of both Attalus and his close relatives. However, Alexander limited the executions to those persons considered a threat to his rule. Philip's only other surviving son, Arrhidaeus, who was mentally disabled, was allowed to live. Olympias, however, was determined to get revenge. She personally engineered the death of Cleopatra and her infant daughter. Although Alexander expressed horror about their deaths, he took no action to protect them or to punish his mother.

After consolidating his power in Macedonia, Alexander then asserted his authority over the League of Corinth. The city-states of Thebes and Athens, not wanting to be ruled by a twenty-year-old youth, decided that the time was ripe to declare their independence. Without delay, Alexander marched to Thebes with thirty thousand troops. When Thebes rejected his ultimatum, his soldiers stormed the city, killed about six thousand Thebans, burned most of the buildings, and sold thousands of the population into slavery. Faced with this cruel example, Athens wisely ceased its revolt. Shortly thereafter, the council of the league appointed Alexander commander (*hegemon*) of Greek forces for the anticipated war against Persia.

SIGNIFICANCE

Alexander the Great was primarily a warrior, and during his thirteen-year reign, he achieved unprecedented military conquests that included much of the known world. Between 335 and 327 B.C.E., he established control over Asia Minor, Syria, Egypt, Mesopotamia (now Iraq), and Persia. During the next two years, he took control over much of Afghanistan and several small kingdoms of India. His commanders, however, forced him to return to Mesopotamia in 325. After Alexander died two years later, his kingdom was divided into several Hellenistic (or Greek-like) empires. For the next three hundred years, three of these empires achieved great accomplishments in science, technology, art, and literature.

Historians disagree about whether Alexander's legacy was primarily good or bad. Those who admire Alexander argue that he was tolerant of different races and cultures and that he spread the blessings of Greek civilization, including government based on the rule of law, the practice of political representation, and Greek ideas of rationality and science. They insist that the Macedonian Empire promoted relative peace, stability, and prosperity. Critics of Alexander, on the other hand, tend to concentrate on the bloodshed and the cruel reprisals associated with his conquests. They maintain that almost none of the conquered peoples joined the Macedonian Empire voluntarily and that the Macedonians exploited the peoples with oppressive taxes. They further argue that the science and technology of the Hellenistic era was the result more of the impact of peaceful trade and cultural contact than of Alexander's military expansionism.

—Thomas Tandy Lewis

FURTHER READING

Bosworth, A. Brian. *Conquest and Empire: The Reign of Alexander the Great*. New York: Cambridge University Press, 1988. A scholarly work with detailed footnotes referring to ancient sources; takes a moralistic and negative view of Alexander's conquests.

Curtius, Quinntus. *History of Alexander.* New York: Penguin, 1984. Classic work of the first century that is filled with controversy, scandals, and intrigues.

Fox, Robin Lane. *Alexander the Great*. New York: Viking Penguin, 1997. A scholarly and extremely readable book, which takes a skeptical approach to the ancient historians.

Green, Peter. *Alexander of Macedon: A Historical Biography.* Berkeley: University of California Press, 1991. A scholarly and very interesting book that frequently accepts sensationalist stories of questionable validity, including the assertion that Alexander was involved in the murder of his father.

Hammond, Nicholas. *Philip of Macedon*. Baltimore: Johns Hopkins University Press, 1994. A scholarly and detailed work arguing that Alexander's conquests were possible only because of his father's achievements.

Plutarch. "Alexander." In *Lives of Noble Grecians and Romans*, edited by Arthur Clough. New York: Modern Library, 1992. Although Plutarch uncritically accepted sensationalist stories and wrote four hundred years after Alexander's time, he had access to sources no longer available.

Renault, Mary. *The Nature of Alexander.* New York: Pantheon Books, 1975. A readable and generally dependable work of medium size, with many beautiful illustrations.

Tarn, William. *Alexander the Great*. New York: Cambridge University Press, 1948. A dated but standard biography that takes a very favorable view of Alexander's achievements.

SEE ALSO: 359-336 B.C.E., Philip II Expands and Empowers Macedonia; August 2, 338 B.C.E., Battle of Chaeronea; 333 B.C.E., Battle of Issus; 332 B.C.E., Founding of Alexandria; 327-325 B.C.E., Alexander the Great Invades the Indian Subcontinent; c. 323-275 B.C.E., Diadochi Divide Alexander the Great's Empire.

RELATED ARTICLES in *Great Lives from History: The Ancient World*: Alexander the Great; Philip II of Macedonia; Olympias.

c. 335-323 B.C.E.
ARISTOTLE WRITES THE *POLITICS*

In writing the Politics, *Aristotle established a classic body of political concepts capable of being applied by later generations of Western political analysts.*

LOCALE: Athens
CATEGORIES: Cultural and intellectual history; government and politics

KEY FIGURE

Aristotle (384-322 B.C.E.), major Greek philosopher who developed what is now known as the scientific method and the founder of the Lyceum

SUMMARY OF EVENT

Aristotle's *Politica* (*Politics*, 1598) is but one of a number of treatises compiled in the Lyceum from school discussions of the philosopher on every conceivable realm of phenomena that was of interest to the Greek mind. In his discussion of politics, Aristotle did not seek, as the philosopher Plato had done, to lay foundations for a moral reconstruction of human community existence; instead, he sought to understand the distinctive form of Greek community life, the polis.

Characteristic of Aristotle's organismic perspective on the whole spectrum of phenomena is his concept of the city-state as a natural entity developing in response to inherent needs and drives in humans. Humans have a natural place in a hierarchy of life in which each genus and species of creature has its own distinctive inherent possibilities of development and modes of formal self-realization. At their own level in this hierarchy, human beings not only enjoy and participate in the plant and animal forms of development and realization but, as creatures uniquely endowed with reason, also build on the foundation of these nonhuman life activities a distinctively human mode of development and formal perfection.

Because they have the power of reason, humans are able not only to experience pain and pleasure like nonhuman animals but also to discriminate between good and evil, justice and injustice, and to share with others of their kind a community of values. For this reason, human beings, more than any other animal, fulfill themselves naturally in forms of shared existence. The forms of community are themselves derived from a natural complementarity of the differing natures of human beings participating in a community. At the most primitive level, the household reaps the advantages of the association of man and woman for procreation and of ruler and ruled for mutual security. In those suited by nature for rule, the power of reason is sufficiently developed to discern what is advantageous for the common welfare, while in those who are by nature servile resides the physical power to effect such policy and sufficient reason to recognize the advantage of obedience to their wiser master.

Beyond the primitive community of the household is the village, a community of households established in order to secure, on a more permanent basis, the advantages of shared existence. Beyond the village-community stands the natural form of fully realized community life—the association of villages, or polis. Although the polis came into existence, according to Aristotle, to sustain human life in a fully self-sufficient form, it continues to exist to achieve the optimal state of human existence.

It should be noted that in designating the polis as the natural form of fully realized human community, Aristotle was thinking not of the large nation-state or of the industrial state or other historical times and places but specifically of the relatively small Greek city-states, whose members could be reasonably familiar with one another. Once these circumstances are understood, the meaning of Aristotle's dictum "Man is by nature a polis-animal" can be appreciated in its uniquely Greek and Aristotelian context.

Polis communities may differ widely from one another, but the factor determining the distinctive form of each is its *politeia*, or constitution, which defines who the citizens of the polis are and in what category of citizens the primary authority for judicial and policy decisions resides. According to Aristotle, the citizen is that individual who participates in dispensing justice and determining policy. Although a constitution may confer supreme authority on one man, a few, or all freeborn members of the polis, Aristotle viewed a legitimate constitution to be one in which the authoritative body in the polis dispenses justice and formulates policy with a view to the well-being of all freeborn citizens and not the well-being of the authoritative body itself alone. In the latter case, the constitution would not be a legitimate form but a perversion. On this basis, Aristotle distinguished between three legitimate forms, which he terms monarchy, aristocracy, and *politeia* (in a distinctive sense that could be translated as "republic" or "constitutional democracy"), and three corresponding perversions, which he called tyranny, oligarchy, and *demokratia* (which might perhaps be translated as "rule of the proletariat").

A survey of the functions necessary to a fully self-sufficient polis that maximizes the potentials of human well-being and of Aristotle's distribution of status among those who perform these functions makes fully clear to the modern mind that Aristotle's political theory was not so much a universally applicable conceptual scheme as it was a distillation of distinctively Greek aristocratic notions of what constituted optimal human well-being in a polis community. These necessary functions included food production, provision of essential goods and services, maintenance of internal order and defense against enemies, accumulation of surplus wealth to sustain private expenditures and security forces, cultic functions of polis religion, and policymaking and dispensation of justice. In Aristotle's view, the farmers and laborers who performed the first two of these functions, while essential to the self-sufficiency and well-being of the polis, could not be citizens. Lacking the higher uses of reason necessary to participate in judicial and policymaking decisions, farmers and laborers were servants sustaining the plant and animal functions of a corporate body, of which only the true citizens could achieve full realization of the well-being possible to humans. The last three of the necessary functions were performed by the true citizens at the ages at which they were best suited by nature to discharge them, and surplus wealth would also be in the possession of the citizens proper.

Several ideas emerge from a reading of Aristotle's *Politics*. First, the state has a natural history, and part of its meaning must be sought in its development. Second, the state has a natural basis in economics, family structure, and ethics. Third, there are basic state forms into which political activity falls, and the art of politics lies in the choice among those forms and their combinations. Fourth, the art of government is the art of finding a proper equilibrium for the forces in the state. Aristotle was interested in the rise and fall of political systems, but he did not make the mistake of tracing that rise and fall to autonomous factors within politics. Like Plato, he believed that much in politics depended on the image that was stamped on the young by birth, education, nature, and habit. Above all, Aristotle was interested in what constituted the strength and weakness of the political community. He saw that the strength of the state depends not so much on the machinery of government as on the moral sense of the community.

Aristotle said "man is by nature a political animal" and "he who by nature and not by mere accident is without a state, is either above humanity or below it." By this, he meant that in their origin and impulses, in terms of the end toward which their development tends, human beings must be part of a whole that is greater than the sum of its parts. Except as a member of a collectivity, a person ceases to be a person and becomes either something greater or something less. The most important element of strength in a community is the sense of greatness that it can generate. The most important political emotion in human beings is the thirst for greatness, which, under pressure, stretches them beyond their everyday selves so that they reach the full outline of their human personality.

SIGNIFICANCE

In creating the *Politics*, Aristotle established a classic body of normative political concepts capable of being applied by later generations of Western political analysts.

—*Carl W. Conrad, updated by Susan M. Taylor*

FURTHER READING

Chuska, Jeff. *Aristotle's Best Regime: A Reading of Aristotle's "Politics."* Lanham, Md.: University Press of America, 2000. A look at *Politics* and Aristotle's views on political science.

Davis, Michael. *The Politics of Philosophy: A Commentary on Aristotle's "Politics."* Lanham, Md.: Rowman & Littlefield, 1996. This work provides a sound discussion of Aristotle's contributions to political science.

Johnson, Curtis N. *Aristotle's Theory of the State*. New York: St. Martin's Press, 1990. Johnson discusses Aristotle's conception of the polis as a natural entity fulfilling a human impulse toward perfection.

Loizou, Andros, and Harry Lesser, eds. *Polis and Politics: Essays in Greek Moral and Political Philosophy*. Brookfield, Vt.: Avebury Press, 1990. A series of papers that concentrate on Greek political thought.

Miller, Fred Dycus. *Nature, Justice, and Rights in Aristotle's "Politics."* Oxford, England: Clarendon Press, 1995. Focusing on Aristotle's concept of natural law and justice, Miller provides a good analysis of Aristotle's contributions not only to law but also to political science.

Nichols, Mary P. *Citizens and Statesmen: A Study of Aristotle's "Politics."* Lanham, Md.: Rowman & Littlefield, 1992. Contains useful insights into Aristotle's view of the polis and how he has contributed to modern ideas of political science.

Simon, Peter. *A Philosophical Commentary on the "Politics" of Aristotle*. Chapel Hill: University of North Carolina Press, 1998. An examination of the philosophical views of Aristotle as expressed in *Politics*.

SEE ALSO: 600-500 B.C.E., Greek Philosophers Formulate Theories of the Cosmos; c. 440 B.C.E., Sophists Train the Greeks in Rhetoric and Politics; c. 380 B.C.E., Plato Develops His Theory of Ideas; 325-323 B.C.E., Aristotle Isolates Science as a Discipline.

RELATED ARTICLES in *Great Lives from History: The Ancient World*: Aristotle; Plato.

333 B.C.E.
BATTLE OF ISSUS

The Battle of Issus was a significant victory for Alexander the Great in his conquest of the Persian Empire.

LOCALE: Issus, Anatolia (now in Turkey)
CATEGORY: Wars, uprisings, and civil unrest

KEY FIGURES

Alexander the Great (356-323 B.C.E.), king of Macedonia, r. 336-323 B.C.E.

Darius III (c. 380-330 B.C.E.), king of Persia, r. 336-330 B.C.E.

SUMMARY OF EVENT

Following his invasion of the Persian Empire in the spring of 334 B.C.E., Alexander the Great won an important battle at the Granicus River, in Asia Minor, against a Persian force of comparable size. This victory permitted Alexander to liberate the Greek city-states of Anatolia and to neutralize the Persian navy through the capture of key ports and bases in the Levant.

The need to entirely deny the Persian fleet portage along the eastern Mediterranean Sea compelled Alexander to move his army from Asia Minor southeastward toward the Syrian coast in the autumn of 333 B.C.E. This action would ultimately bring the Greco-Macedonian army into direct confrontation with a numerically superior Persian force advancing northward from the Euphrates River under the command of the Persian king, Darius III.

As the Greek army continued its southward march into Syria along the coastal road toward the settlement of Myriandros, the Persian army advanced northward through a more difficult eastern mountain pass called the Amanian Gates, which crossed Mount Amanus, near the plain of Issus. By these movements, the two armies unknowingly passed one another.

On learning that Darius was behind his position, Alexander turned his army north so as to intercept the Persian host before it could escape the confines of the coastal hill country. Near the village of Issus on the Gulf of Iskenderun and north of the settlement of Myriandros, the two armies met. The battle developed on a small coastal plain, forcing both armies to deploy according to the geographical constraints of the space available. Movement was further hampered by the Pinarus River, whose course effectively divided the battlefield. Dominating the plain to the east was Mount Amanus.

Alexander's battle line stretched the length of the plain, forcing the Macedonian king to anchor the army's left wing on the shoreline of the Iskenderun and its right

A damaged rendering of the Battle of Issus. (Library of Congress)

near the Amanic foothills. Thessalian, Peloponnesian, and other allied cavalry were then deployed on the left flank, with a second force of cavalry, including the Companions, positioned on the right. Elements of light and heavy infantry were placed in support of these forces or held in reserve, with the Macedonian phalanx securing the center.

On the approach of the Greek army, Darius temporarily dispatched a sizable force of cavalry and light infantry south across the Pinarus River to serve as a protective screen while the remainder of the army arrayed for battle on the north bank of the river. Fully deployed, the Persian front line ranged the full length of the Greek formation and beyond. On the left, units of light infantry extended into the Amanic foothills, where they threatened to turn Alexander's extreme right flank. At the center of Darius's main vanguard was a large concentration of some thirty thousand Greek mercenaries, flanked by divisions of Persian heavy infantry called *Kardakes*. Arrayed behind this front was a sizable reserve of light and heavy infantry. On the extreme right, opposite the Greek allied cavalry, Darius stationed a large contingent of Persian horses. Though the Persian army was formidably arrayed, the narrowness of the plain of Issus neutralized the numerical advantage of the larger force and handicapped any effort by Darius to use his superior numbers of cavalry to best effect against the Macedonian formations.

Alexander sought to check the threat posed by the Persian forces on the high ground to the east by ordering a mixed contingent of archers and cavalry to form a salient on his right. Elements of this reconstituted force then launched an assault that quickly scattered the Persians on the foothills. Following this skirmish, Alexander briefly rested his army before initiating the primary attack against the Persian host.

Alexander opened the main battle with an intense cavalry charge that immediately shattered the Persian left wing. Advancing to the attack, the Macedonian phalanx crossed the shallow Pinarus but was stalled by the steepness of the opposing bank and the stiff resistance of the Greek mercenaries. As the phalanx continued to press its assault, the cohesion of the Macedonian front weakened, exposing gaps in the line, which the Greeks exploited to full advantage. The result was a violent struggle of heavy infantry that, for a time, left the outcome of the engagement in question. Pressure on the phalanx was finally relieved when Alexander, fresh from his victory on the right, outflanked the remnants of the Persian left and delivered a flank attack that crumpled the mercenary formation. As the Persian center began to disintegrate, Alexander wheeled the remainder of his force to the left in order to drive against Darius's position in the center. This charge unnerved the Persian king, who turned his war-chariot and fled the field.

Simultaneous with these events, the Persian cavalry, on the north bank of the Pinarus River near its juncture with the Gulf of Iskenderun, having witnessed Alexander's charge on the left, launched a massive charge that threatened to overwhelm the squadrons of Thessalian horses deployed near the shoreline. The momentum of this assault was checked only when the king was seen to flee the battlefield following the destruction of the Persian left and center. What followed was a complete rout of the entire Persian army, followed by a sustained pursuit by the forces of Alexander.

SIGNIFICANCE

The Battle of Issus was instrumental in breaking Persian power in the eastern Mediterranean. After the engagement, Darius III proposed a treaty of friendship and alliance between the two kingdoms, offering Alexander control of all Persian territories west of the Euphrates River. The Macedonian king's rejection ultimately precipitated the Persian army's stunning defeat at Gaugamela in 331 B.C.E. This latter engagement ensured Alexander control of the Persian crown.

—Donathan Taylor

FURTHER READING

Arrian. *History of Alexander and Indica*. Translated by P. A. Brunt. Cambridge, Mass.: Harvard University Press, 1976-1983. An account by an ancient historian, writing four hundred years later, of the exploits of Alexander the Great.

Bosworth, A. Brian. *Conquest and Empire: The Reign of Alexander the Great*. New York: Cambridge University Press, 1988. Bosworth relates the story of how Alexander the Great built his empire.

Curtius, Quintus. *The History of Alexander.* Translated by John Yardley. New York: Viking Penguin, 1984. A examination of the life of Alexander the Great.

Dodge, Theodore Ayrault. *Alexander.* London: Greenhill Books, 1993. A biography of Alexander the Great, with reference to the Battle of Issus.

SEE ALSO: 359-336 B.C.E., Philip II Expands and Empowers Macedonia; 336 B.C.E., Alexander the Great Begins Expansion of Macedonia; 332 B.C.E., Founding of Alexandria; October 1, 331 B.C.E., Battle of Gaugamela; 327-325 B.C.E., Alexander the Great Invades the Indian Subcontinent.

RELATED ARTICLES in *Great Lives from History: The Ancient World*: Alexander the Great; Philip II of Macedonia.

332 B.C.E.
FOUNDING OF ALEXANDRIA

The founding of Alexandria created a new city that became a center of Hellenistic culture and learning in North Africa and throughout the Mediterranean.

LOCALE: The Nile Delta in Egypt
CATEGORIES: Cultural and intellectual history; expansion and land acquisition

KEY FIGURES

Alexander the Great (356-323 B.C.E.), king of Macedonia, r. 336-323 B.C.E.

Ptolemy Soter (367/366-283/282 B.C.E.), king of Egypt, r. 305-285 B.C.E.

Ptolemy Philadelphus (308-246 B.C.E.), king of Egypt, r. 288-246 B.C.E.

Dinocrates (fl. fourth century B.C.E.), architect who planned Alexandria

Sostratus of Cnidus (fl. fourth-third century B.C.E.), architect of the lighthouse at Alexandria

SUMMARY OF EVENT

When Alexander the Great took Egypt from the Persians in 332 B.C.E., he had no intention of restoring the country as an independent kingdom. He meant to make it a province of his own, and he believed that a new Hellenic city would make a more suitable capital than one of the old Egyptian towns. This capital was to be named Alexandria in honor of himself as its founder. The site chosen was on the coast, on the western edge of the Nile Delta, where the city would have easy communications with the interior by river and with the outside world by sea. Labor was conscripted from adjacent villages of Egyptian peasants and fishermen, and the work began in 331 B.C.E. with impressive religious ceremonies. Greek seers prophesied that the city would become "large and prosperous, a source of nourishment to many lands." Construction of the metropolis took years to complete and was still proceeding in the time of Alexander's succes-

The library at Alexandria. (North Wind Picture Archives)

sors, Ptolemy Soter and Ptolemy Philadelphus.

The original plan of the city was prepared by the architect Dinocrates, who had it laid out on the grid pattern developed in the fifth century B.C.E. It was divided into four large quarters by two broad avenues. Canopus Street, a processional boulevard 100 feet (30 meters) wide, ran east and west along the long axis; a lesser street running north and south bisected it. At this intersection was the civic center containing the Court of Justice; the Gymnasium, a handsome, colonnaded building whose front stretched 600 feet (183 meters); a series of sacred groves; and, most remarkable of all, an artificial hill dedicated to the god Pan. Its summit could easily be reached by a spiral path, and from this point, visitors—of whom there were many—could survey the entire metropolis.

The most striking characteristic of Alexandria was its size. By the third century B.C.E., its population had already reached perhaps half a million. By the beginning of the Christian era, it stood at nearly one million, rivaling even the capital of the Roman Empire. One quarter of the city was inhabited by Egyptians and half-caste Greeks, who had no civic rights and performed the menial labor of the city. Another quarter was the residence of the Jews, who came to Egypt in considerable numbers during the reign of Ptolemy Soter. They enjoyed a certain autonomy under their own ethnarch (governor of an ethnic group) and council and constituted one of the most important Jewish settlements in all the ancient world.

The Greco-Macedonian quarter seems to have been near the sea breezes of the waterfront. It is probable that the Europeans were organized into demes and tribes, with an autonomous council and assembly. From east to west along the waterfront stretched warehouses and harbors that received merchant ships from upriver, from Mediterranean ports, and even, via a canal connecting the Nile River with the Red Sea, from the Far East. By the second century B.C.E., there was contact with India, and Buddhist missionaries visited the port. Here, too, were the efficient dockyards of the Ptolemaic navy.

The Royal Quarter was the most imposing of all. It was ornamented with the palaces of the Ptolemies and the nearby monumental tomb of Alexander. Here also was the great Serapeum, a magnificent temple dedicated to the dynasty's new god, Serapis. The palace complex contained the famous library and museum, where the first two Ptolemies gathered the most distinguished minds of the third century for science and scholarship.

Dominating the skyline and even overshadowing the palace itself was the great stone lighthouse designed by Sostratus of Cnidus. It stood on the island of Pharos, which was connected to the mainland by a manmade mole nearly three-quarters of a mile (a little over a kilometer) long, pierced by two bridged channels for ships. The tower was more than 400 feet (120 meters) high and was provided with a windlass so that firewood could be drawn to the top. Here, fires blazed by night in front of a reflector of polished bronze, warning ships of dangers and guiding them into the harbor.

In the third century, the culture of Alexandria eclipsed even that of Athens. The scholarship of Aristophanes of Byzantium (c. 257-180 B.C.E.), the astronomy of Aristarchus of Samos (c. 310-c. 230 B.C.E.), the poetry of Callimachus (c. 305-c. 240 B.C.E.), and the medical studies of Erasistratus (c. 304-c. 250 B.C.E.) all were the products of Alexandria. The city was also an important bridge between the cultures of the Greeks and the Jews. The Septuagint, the Greek translation of the Old Testament, was begun in Alexandria in the third century, and the Jewish scholar Philo of Alexandria (c. 20 B.C.E.-c. 45 C.E.) later worked there.

SIGNIFICANCE

Alexandria contained both the positive and negative qualities of Hellenistic culture. Although the city was the birthplace of much that was good, it was also infected with urban ills. Mobs of the poor sometimes rioted against the government and staged massacres. The city's pleasure domes housed the most sophisticated debauchery; its slums, the most sordid depravity. There was conflict between ethnic groups, with Egyptians swelling the ranks of the proletariat while most Greek immigrants enjoyed lives of privilege. Because intermarriage between Egyptians and Greeks was prohibited by law, few Egyptians found themselves sharing fully in the benefits of Greek civic culture. It was, in fact, a classic example of colonialism, with the conquering people living well, the indigenous population living poorly, and a hybrid culture arising out of it.

—*Samuel K. Eddy, updated by Jeffrey L. Buller*

FURTHER READING

Canfora, Luciano. *The Vanished Library*. Translated by Martin Ryle. Berkeley: University of California Press, 1990. A wide-ranging discussion of the Library of Alexandria, covering its contents, its role in ancient scholarship, and its eventual destruction. Part 1 provides a narrative history of the library, while part 2 discusses the sources of information on it.

Empereur, Jean-Yves. *Alexandria: Jewel of Egypt*. New York: Harry N. Abrams, 2002. An overview of Alexandria's history and archaeology.

_______. *Alexandria Rediscovered*. London: British Museum Press, 1998. A truly breathtaking book describing the archaeological discoveries in Alexandria in the late twentieth century. Abundantly illustrated.

Green. Peter. *Alexander of Macedon, 356-323 B.C.: A Historical Biography*. Reprint. Berkeley: University of California Press, 1992. One of the best biographies of Alexander, with great attention paid to the cultural context of the fourth century Mediterranean world. Includes maps and battle plans, a table of dates, bibliography, and genealogical table.

Haas, Christopher. *Alexandria in Late Antiquity: Topography and Social Conflict*. Baltimore, Md.: The Johns Hopkins University Press, 1997. Discusses the interrelationships between the pagan, Jewish, and Christian communities in Alexandria. Includes a chronological table of emperors, prefects, and patriarchs in the fourth and fifth centuries C.E.

Hammond, Nicholas Geoffrey Lempriere. *Alexander the Great*. 1980. Reprint. London: Duckworth, 2002. Detailed biography of Alexander by one of the twentieth century's foremost scholars of the Hellenistic Age.

Sly, Dorothy I. *Philo's Alexandria*. New York: Routledge, 1996. Uses the writings of Philo of Alexandria to construct a picture of Alexandrian life in the first century C.E.

Vrettos, Theodore. *Alexandria: City of the Western Mind*. New York: Free Press, 2001. A lively, fact-filled overview of Alexandrian culture, written by a well-known classicist. Most chapters cover thematic topics, while the first and last discuss the city's founding and its fall. Includes bibliography, notes, index, and a list of principal figures.

SEE ALSO: August 2, 338 B.C.E., Battle of Chaeronea; 336 B.C.E., Alexander the Great Begins Expansion of Macedonia; 323 B.C.E., Founding of the Ptolemaic Dynasty and Seleucid Kingdom; c. 300 B.C.E., Euclid Compiles a Treatise on Geometry; c. 275 B.C.E., Greeks Advance Hellenistic Astronomy; c. 250 B.C.E., Discoveries of Archimedes; 415 C.E., Mathematician and Philosopher Hypatia Is Killed in Alexandria.

RELATED ARTICLES in *Great Lives from History: The Ancient World*: Alexander the Great; Archimedes; Athanasius of Alexandria, Saint; Callimachus; Cleopatra VII; Ctesebius of Alexandria; Erastistratus; Eratosthenes of Cyrene; Hero of Alexandria; Herophilus; Hypatia; Origen; Pappus; Philo of Alexandria; Ptolemy Philadelphus; Ptolemy Soter; Sosigenes; Valentinus.

October 1, 331 B.C.E.
BATTLE OF GAUGAMELA

The Battle of Gaugamela pitted Alexander the Great's Macedonian forces against the Persians in a decisive battle for supremacy in Asia Minor.

LOCALE: Gaugamela (Tel Gomel in modern Iraq)
CATEGORIES: Expansion and land acquisition; wars, uprisings, and civil unrest

KEY FIGURES

Alexander the Great (356-323 B.C.E.), king of Macedonia, r. 336-323 B.C.E.
Bessus (d. c. 329 B.C.E.), Persian satrap of Bactria, who ruled as Artaxerxes IV after Darius III's death in 330 B.C.E.
Darius III (c. 380-330 B.C.E.), king of the Persian Empire, r. 336-330 B.C.E.
Parmenio (c. 400-330 B.C.E.), Macedonian general who served as Alexander's second in command in conquest of Persia

SUMMARY OF EVENT

After King Philip II of Macedonia had defeated the Greek states in the Battle of Chaeronea (338 B.C.E.), he made plans to invade the Persian Empire. His assassination in 336, however, forestalled this scheme until his son Alexander made his succession to the throne secure. In 334, Alexander the Great invaded Asia Minor and quickly defeated the Persians on the Granicus River. Alexander advanced eastward and, at the town of Issus in northern Syria, defeated King Darius II himself in 333. Next, Alexander took the wealthy province of Egypt in 332.

By 331 B.C.E., Alexander was ready for a second and decisive battle with Darius for the supremacy of Asia. The Persian king had been collecting a large army, and he came westward as far as the plains near the village of Gaugamela (Tel Gomel in modern Iraq), where he waited to be attacked. Darius's army consisted mainly of cavalry posted in long lines on level ground. The left wing was made up of his good Iranian horsemen, the Persians, some heavily mailed Śaka, and the Bactrians, all commanded by Bessus, the satrap of Bactria. Syrian, Mesopotamian, and Median cavalry took stations on the right. Behind the cavalry was the infantry, mostly troops of little fighting value who had been conscripted recently. Behind the center of the two fighting lines was Darius, with his personal bodyguard and fifteen elephants. The Persian forces numbered more than fifty thousand men.

Alexander arrived in Gaugamela in the autumn and, on October 1, he led his army out of camp. Alexander had forty thousand infantry and seven thousand horsemen,

The Battle of Gaugamela. (Library of Congress)

Alexander's Early Campaign Against the Persian Empire, 334-331 B.C.E.

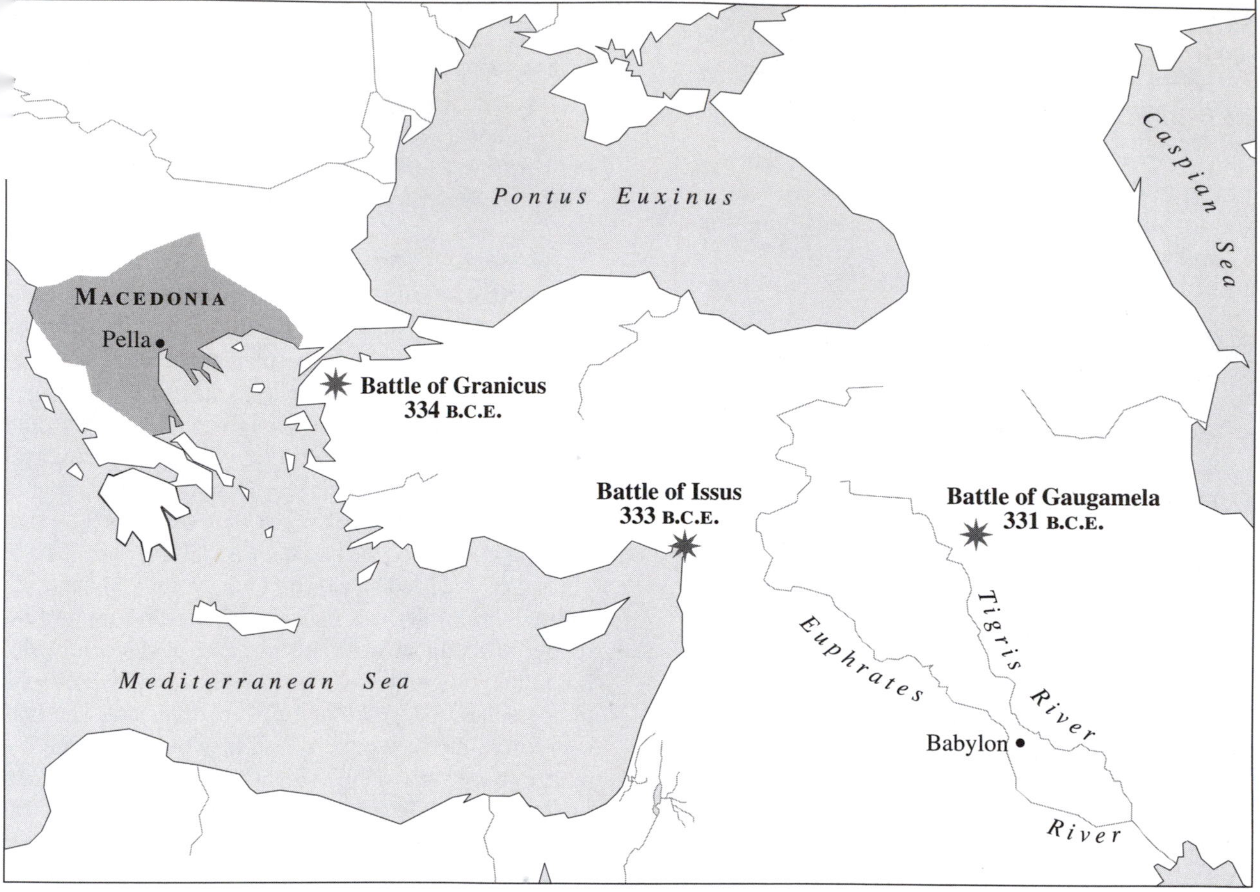

both Greek and Macedonian. His army was also in long lines, with the infantry placed in the center and half the cavalry on either flank. Parmenio commanded the left, while Alexander himself took charge of the right with his best squadrons of Macedonian heavy cavalry. Alexander's chief virtues as a general were his understanding of how to use cavalry and infantry together and his gift for inspiring his men, either in battle or in the relentless, disciplined pursuit of a disorganized and fleeing foe. He now slowly advanced to his right while studying the enemy's array until the Hypaspists, a brigade of crack Macedonian infantry, were facing scythed chariots in front of the Persian center. Alexander turned to confront the enemy. Bessus sent the Śaka charging at the extreme right of Alexander's cavalry. Alexander countered by bringing forward squadrons deployed behind them. There was a sharp fight with losses on both sides until Bessus's cavalry drew off to regroup. Meanwhile, the scythed chariots bounded forward against the Macedonian center, but here Alexander had posted troops armed with arrows and javelins who were able to shoot down most of the chariot horses before they reached the phalanx. The chariots, which did little damage to the Macedonians, were routed.

The cavalry action on Alexander's front had opened a gap between Bessus and the center of the long line of Persian horsemen. As soon as Alexander had his own horsemen under control, he charged into this gap, with the infantry phalanx following him on the run. This blow was irresistible, and the Persian lines began to crumple and stream toward the rear. For the second time, Darius turned to flee. His personal guard of two thousand Greek mercenaries stood their ground and lost five hundred men, sacrificed to win time for Darius to escape. As Alexander was reforming his troops to pursue Darius, he received distress messages from Parmenio that the Persian right was pressing him hard. Alexander rushed across the field with his own cavalry, and his timely arrival sent the

Persian right reeling back. As the battle became a general rout, Alexander drove his horseman rapidly after the remnants of the Persian army, dispersing large numbers of fugitives until he reached the city of Arbela (modern Arbīl, Iraq) after nightfall. Despite these efforts, Alexander did not succeed in catching up with Darius.

SIGNIFICANCE

The Battle of Gaugamela, also known as the Battle of Arbela, was decisive. The Persian forces were so scattered that they could not be reorganized. The Persian nobles believed that Darius was responsible for the debacle, and they accordingly deposed and killed him. Bessus, whose troops were the only ones to withdraw in fairly good order, became king as Artaxerxes IV. He was unable, however, to collect enough men to oppose Alexander's swift and inexorable advance. The Persians quickly lost their wealthiest provinces, and the rich plains of Babylonia surrendered without resistance. Persis, the heartland of the Persian Empire, fell, and the religious capital of Persepolis was also taken, along with some fourteen years' worth of accumulated tribute. Alexander eventually caught Artaxerxes and had him executed, alleging the murder of Darius as an excuse. Alexander also burned the magnificent royal buildings at Persepolis. This act signaled the fall of the Persian Empire, the beginning of Alexander's own empire, and the subjugation of the East to Macedonian imperialism.

—*Samuel K. Eddy, updated by Jeffrey L. Buller*

FURTHER READING

Adcock, F. E. *The Greek and Macedonian Art of War.* Reprint. Berkeley: University of California, 1974. A reprint of Adcock's Sather lectures delivered at the University of California, this slim volume provides insight into Alexander's military strategy. Adcock regards Gaugamela as the Persian army's only serious attempt to win a battle by using chariots; this was a strategy that failed utterly.

Fuller, J. F. C. *The Generalship of Alexander the Great.* 1960. Reprint. Ware, Hertshire, England: Wordsworth, 1998. Still the most thorough analysis of Alexander's military strategy. The Battle of Gaugamela is covered as the Battle of Arbela. Written by a British major general who was himself renowned as a strategist.

Green, Peter. *Alexander of Macedon, 356-323 B.C.: A Historical Biography.* Reprint. Berkeley: University of California Press, 1992. One of the best biographies of Alexander, with great attention paid to the cultural context of the fourth century Mediterranean world. Includes maps and battle plans, a table of dates, bibliography, and genealogical table.

Hammond, Nicholas Geoffrey Lempriere. *Alexander the Great.* 1980. Reprint. London: Duckworth, 2002. Detailed biography of Alexander by one of the twentieth century's foremost scholars of the Hellenistic Age.

Lane Fox, Robin. *The Search for Alexander.* Boston: Little, Brown, 1980. Intended for the general reader, this work provides an excellent mix of current research, photographs, and readable narration. Contains an extensive discussion of the Battle of Gaugamela.

Marsden, Eric William. *The Campaign of Gaugamela.* Liverpool, England: Liverpool University Press, 1964. A brief but comprehensive account of nearly every aspect of the battle. Also contains a useful map and a list of helpful sources for further study.

Worthington, Ian, ed. *Alexander the Great: A Reader.* New York: Routledge, 2003. A collection of essays on all aspects of Alexander's life and career. One chapter addresses Alexander's campaigns in Asia, and another considers his generalship.

SEE ALSO: c. 700-330 B.C.E., Phalanx Is Developed as a Military Unit; 480-479 B.C.E., Persian Invasion of Greece; 359-336 B.C.E., Philip II Expands and Empowers Macedonia; August 2, 338 B.C.E., Battle of Chaeronea; 336 B.C.E., Alexander the Great Begins Expansion of Macedonia; 332 B.C.E., Founding of Alexandria; 327-325 B.C.E., Alexander the Great Invades the Indian Subcontinent; 323 B.C.E., Founding of the Ptolemaic Dynasty and Seleucid Kingdom; c. 323-275 B.C.E., Diadochi Divide Alexander the Great's Empire.

RELATED ARTICLE in *Great Lives from History: The Ancient World*: Alexander the Great.

327-325 B.C.E.
ALEXANDER THE GREAT INVADES THE INDIAN SUBCONTINENT

After Alexander's army won several hard-fought battles in India, his soldiers refused to march farther eastward, and he was forced to order the army to return to Babylon.

LOCALE: The Indus Valley (in modern Pakistan and northwestern India)

CATEGORIES: Expansion and land acquisition; wars, uprisings, and civil unrest

KEY FIGURES

Alexander the Great (356-323 B.C.E.), king of Macedonia, r. 336-323 B.C.E.

Porus (d. c. 318 B.C.E.), ruler of a small kingdom in eastern Punjab

SUMMARY OF EVENT

When Alexander the Great ascended to the Macedonian throne in 336 B.C.E., he probably did not have the goal of becoming the greatest conqueror of history. After suppressing insurrections in Greek states, however, he relatively quickly took over the imperial governments of Asia Minor, Egypt, Mesopotamia, and Persia. Each victory increased his appetite for additional conquests. When conquering a community, Alexander brutally crushed all opposition, sold many of the local people into slavery, and insisted on the payment of taxes. He appointed a satrap (or local administrator) that he could trust and attempted to involve as many local personnel as possible. Increasingly, he recognized the importance of respecting local customs. In his new capital Babylon, therefore, he introduced Asian court ceremonies, causing discomfort among some of his Greek and Macedonian officers.

By early 327 B.C.E., Alexander had secured the northern frontiers of Mesopotamia and Persia. By then, he had the goal of expanding his empire farther eastward than the Persians had controlled under Darius III, which was beyond the Indus River. Although his knowledge of India was limited, he knew that the historian Herodotus had written that the country had great riches and gold. Perhaps he was also motivated by stories about his mythological ancestors Dionysus and Heracles visiting India. His commanders argued that the project was impractical, but Alexander was stubborn.

In the summer of 327 B.C.E., Alexander began his Indian campaign by establishing bases and colonies in present-day Afghanistan, along the Kabul River and its northern tributaries. Many communities avoided bloodshed by agreeing to pay taxes to the invaders. One such town was renamed Nysa, where Alexander's scholars interpreted the local Hindu deity, probably Indira, to be the same as Dionysus. When communities resisted, Alexander's soldiers slaughtered numerous people as examples. The Assaceni Kingdom in the Swat Valley, with its thirty thousand soldiers and large fortress at Massaga, put up an especially bloody struggle. The Assaceni, even after their defeat, continued to rebel against Macedonian rule.

When Alexander crossed the Indus River in the spring of 326 B.C.E., he was welcomed by Omphis, the ruler of the small kingdom of Taxila. Omphis was happy to make an alliance with Alexander in hopes of defeating his archenemy, Porus, ruler of Paurava, which was located east of the large and turbulent Hydaspes (modern Jhelum) River. When Alexander proposed negotiations, Porus rejected the offer, for he was confident that Alexander would be unable to cross the swelling Hydaspes during the monsoon rains.

Alexander the Great (mounted, top center) leads his troops. (Library of Congress)

In May, 326 B.C.E., Alexander's soldiers managed to bridge the river with rafts north of Porus's camp. The exact location of the resulting Battle of the Hydaspes is unknown. Although Porus's army had more soldiers (estimated at 34,000 to 15,000), Alexander had the advantages of a large mobile cavalry, many more archers, the phalanx formation, and capable commanders such as Craterus, Ptolemy, and Coenus. Porus's army had two hundred elephants, but the invaders made them panic and stampede. After eight hours, the invaders were victorious. Alexander was nevertheless impressed with Porus's courage, so he allowed him to remain the ruler of Paurava. Near the battlefield, Alexander founded two cities, Nicaea (meaning victory town) and Bucephala (in honor of his horse killed in the battle).

In June, Alexander's forces crossed the Chenab and Ravi Rivers, capturing Sangala (near modern Amritsar) and other communities. They campaigned as far as the Beas River. Alexander wanted to push on to the powerful kingdom of Magadha in the Ganges Valley, but his commanders, faced with monsoon rains and uncertain dangers, refused to march farther eastward. Alexander was so furious that he stayed in his tent for three days. After sacrificing to the gods, Alexander finally conceded that the omens were unfavorable for more eastern battles. However, even when he ordered the troops to return to Babylon, he remained angry with his officers.

Rather than returning the way he came, Alexander insisted that the return trip would be an occasion for additional conquests. As the army rode down the Hydaspes and Indus Rivers on rafts, they raided and subdued numerous villages along the way. During an assault on a village of the Malli tribe, Alexander almost died when an arrow entered his chest, barely missing his heart, but he soon recovered. In July, 325 B.C.E., the army reached the mouth of the Indus. About half of the soldiers boarded ships for the Persian Gulf. Alexander and the other soldiers began their disastrous march of fifteen hundred miles across the Gedrosian desert and mountainous terrain.

SIGNIFICANCE

Alexander's invasion allowed Europeans to learn more about India and its culture, including its agricultural products and its mathematical and scientific developments. The resulting fusion of European and Indian culture contributed to the great scientific advances in the period known as the Hellenistic age. However, the Indian campaign was not a military success. Within twenty years after Alexander's departures, no Greek colonies remained in India. While Alexander's army was in this distant country, moreover, his empire tended to break apart, and the disastrous march to Babylon resulted in the deaths of thousands of soldiers. If Alexander had not invaded the lands east of Persia, it is possible that his empire might have been more unified at the time of his death.

Alexander's invasion had very little impact on India. As soon as the invaders left, the local tribes and communities reasserted their independence. Although it is possible that Indians learned more about Greek science, philosophy, and military tactics as a result of the invasion, the Indians already had some access to Greek culture as a result of their commercial relations with Persia. The invasion did have the long-term consequence of promoting fear of European imperialism.

—Thomas Tandy Lewis

FURTHER READING

Arrian, Flavius. *The Campaigns of Alexander.* New York: Penguin Classics, 1977. Although writing four hundred years later, Arrian is considered the most dependable of the ancient historians.

Bosworth, A. Brian. *Alexander and the East: The Triumph of Tragedy.* Oxford, England: Oxford University Press, 1996. A scholarly and detailed account of Alexander's conquests, taking a moralistic and critical approach to the violent conquests.

Fuller, John F. C. *The Generalship of Alexander.* New Brunswick, Vt.: Rutgers University Press, 1961. Considered the best treatment of the military techniques and strategies of Alexander.

Hammond, Nicholas. *The Genius of Alexander the Great.* Durham: University of North Carolina Press, 1997. A very readable biography by an outstanding scholar who takes a balanced but generally favorable view of Alexander.

Wood, Michael. *In the Footsteps of Alexander the Great.* Berkeley: University of California Press, 1997. The companion work for a television series, the volume has beautiful illustrations and interesting discussions of the places that Alexander visited.

SEE ALSO: 359-336 B.C.E., Philip II Expands and Empowers Macedonia; August 2, 338 B.C.E., Battle of Chaeronea; 336 B.C.E., Alexander the Great Begins Expansion of Macedonia; 333 B.C.E., Battle of Issus; 332 B.C.E., Founding of Alexandria; October 1, 331 B.C.E., Battle of Gaugamela; c. 323-275 B.C.E., Diadochi Divide Alexander the Great's Empire.

RELATED ARTICLE in *Great Lives from History: The Ancient World*: Alexander the Great.

325-323 B.C.E.
ARISTOTLE ISOLATES SCIENCE AS A DISCIPLINE

Aristotle was the first philosopher to approach the study of nature in a systematic way, establishing science as a discipline and providing a starting place for natural philosophers into the Middle Ages.

LOCALE: Athens
CATEGORIES: Cultural and intellectual history; science and technology

KEY FIGURE

Aristotle (384-322 B.C.E.), founder and head of the Lyceum

SUMMARY OF EVENT

Born in Stagira in northern Greece and the son of the physician to Amyntas II of Macedonia (r. c. 393-370/369), Aristotle came to Athens when he was seventeen years old and studied at Plato's Academy for twenty years. When Plato died in 347 B.C.E., Aristotle left the academy and traveled for twelve years, visiting various centers of learning in Asia Minor and Macedonia. During this period of travel, he developed his interest in the natural sciences, to which he applied his method of inquiry. He returned to Athens in 335 B.C.E. after a brief period of tutoring Alexander the Great (356-323 B.C.E.), Amyntas's grandson, and established the Lyceum, a school that became a center of learning. He taught there until a year before his death.

The range of topics discussed and developed by Aristotle at the Lyceum is overwhelming: natural philosophy with its considerations of space, time, and motion; the heavenly bodies; life and psychic activities; ethical and political problems; animals and biological matters; and rhetoric and poetics. Further, he is sometimes credited with creating new fields of research, such as terrestrial dynamics and optics. He also taxonomized plants and animals and organized earlier Greeks' ideas about planetary astronomy in *Peri ouranou* (c. 350 B.C.E.; *On the Heavens*, 1939).

Perhaps the most significant aspect of Aristotle's work is his development of a "scientific" approach to these studies. This "scientific" approach recognizes the existence of independent disciplines, each employing its own principles and hypotheses. Such an approach also works out a methodology or procedure for each field of study, aiming at true and certain knowledge.

The Greek term that Aristotle uses for "scientific knowledge" is *episteme*, which can best be translated as "true knowledge" or the "most certain knowledge." This knowledge includes the awareness of an object, of its causes, and that it can be no other way. Medieval scholars translated the Greek *episteme* as the Latin *scientia*, which came into English as "science."

In recognizing independent fields of study, Aristotle showed a significant departure from Plato's philosophy. Plato had envisioned one single science. For him, true knowledge was the contemplation of the Forms: Virtue, Justice, Beauty, and Goodness. All other disciplines were subordinate to knowledge of the Forms. Aristotle, on the other hand, did not advocate a hierarchical structure of knowledge. Each study locates its own particular subject matter and defines its principles from which conclusions are to be drawn. Almost all his treatises begin with the same format: "Our task here concerns demonstrative science," that is, logic; or "Human conduct belongs to political science."

Aristotle's insistence on the division of sciences, each using special principles, is indicative of his rejection of any absolute master plan of knowledge. He does, however, recognize "common principles," or principles shared by more than one science. For example, the "equals from equals" principle of mathematics can be used in geometry to deduce a conclusion about a line. Aristotle warns the geometrician, however, that this can be done "if he assumes the truth not universally, but only of magnitudes." Aristotle never intends the same common principles to be universally applied in exactly the same way throughout all the sciences. If this were the case, there would not be "sciences," but rather "Science."

The second important feature of Aristotle's scientific approach concerns methodology. In the *Analytica posterioria* (335-323 B.C.E.; *Posterior Analytics*, 1812), he develops the general technique that the particular disciplines are to employ in order to achieve scientific knowledge. First, an investigation must always begin with what is "better known" to humans. They must begin with observable data and facts, and not construct wild hypotheses. Second, human beings must proceed to a knowledge of the cause of the facts; mere observation is not enough. Observing something only indicates that something is the case; it does not explain why it is the case. Learning the cause tells people why, and this involves a logical demonstration. Third, the cause or reason of the fact must be of "that fact and no other." This criterion is the basis for a scientific law because it demands a universal connection between the subject and its attributes.

The second and third criteria require a deductive system of demonstration that is expressed in the universal positive form of the syllogism that Aristotle developed in the *Analytica priora* (335-323 B.C.E.; *Prior Analytics*, 1812). There is also what might be called an "inductive" approach to his method of science. Aristotle raises the question of how humans know the universal principles from which demonstration is to proceed. He answers that human knowledge of such principles begins with many sense perceptions of similar events. Human memory unifies these perceptions into a single experience. The human intellect or mind then understands the universal import of the experience. From many similar experiences, humans recognize a universal pattern.

Aristotle's method of science combines the theoretical and the practical. The theoretical aspect includes logical demonstrations and universal principles. The practical includes the necessary role of sense perception as it relates to particular objects. In the *Metaphysica* (335-323 B.C.E.; *Metaphysics*, 1801), he warns that physicians do not cure men-in-general in a universal sense; rather they cure Socrates or Callias, a particular man. He adds that one who knows medical theory dealing with universals without experience with particulars will fail to effect a cure. Instead, he advises the use of procedures grounded in common sense that have proven their validity in practice.

Aristotle. (Library of Congress)

One application of this method is in Aristotle's writings on biology. He makes theoretical interpretations based on his dissection of marine animals and empirical observations, although he does also rely on other writers' descriptions of some animals. Based on these researches, he arranges a "ladder of nature." Because he can see changes in the realm of plants and animals, he affirms the reality of nature and the value of its study. He is optimistic that he could use natural history to find causal explanations of physiology.

Significance

For Aristotle, scientific knowledge included the observation of concrete data, the formulation of universal principles, and the construction of logical proofs. Greek "science" prior to Aristotle, largely a melange of philosophical and quasimythological assumptions, blossomed after his investigations into the specialized work of Theophrastus (c. 372-c. 287 B.C.E.) in botany, Herophilus (c. 335-c. 280 B.C.E.) in medicine, and Aristarchus of Samos (c. 310-c. 230 B.C.E.) in astronomy.

Aristotle also pioneered the notion that there are many, distinct disciplines of knowledge rather than a single, unified science; that there are multiple structuring principles for these disciplines rather than one, overarching set of concepts applicable to them all; that standards of scientific rigor vary among disciplines; and that there is no single, universal scientific method. At the same time, he believed in systematic, empirical investigation of natural phenomena, from which general theories might arise, as opposed to creating a theoretical structure and then fitting the data into it. His identification of many of the scientific disciplines and his methodology for studying them remain valid today.

—*Joseph J. Romano, updated by Amy Ackerberg-Hastings*

Further Reading

Barnes, Jonathan, ed. *The Cambridge Companion to Aristotle*. New York: Cambridge University Press, 1995. A straightforward, readable introduction to Aristotle's thought for nonspecialists and students. Essays offer a clear exposition of his central philosophical concerns.

Bolton, Robert, and Robin Smith, eds. *Logic, Dialectic, and Science in Aristotle*. Special issue of *Ancient Philosophy* 14 (1994). Seven scholars of ancient Greek philosophy try to resolve puzzling sections in Aristotle's works on these subjects.

Byrne, Patrick H. *Analysis and Science in Aristotle.* Albany: State University of New York Press, 1997. Offers a new interpretation of Aristotle's *Prior* and *Posterior Analytics* as a unified whole, arguing that a nondeductive form of ancient mathematical analysis influenced Aristotle's thinking. Reading the *Analytics* with this perspective in mind sheds new light on Aristotle's theories of the syllogism, demonstration, and the principles of science.

Ferejohn, Michael. *The Origins of Aristotelian Science.* New Haven, Conn.: Yale University Press, 1991. An in-depth discussion of the theoretical structure of Aristotle's scientific method.

Golthelf, Allan, and James G. Lennox, eds. *Philosophical Issues in Aristotle's Biology.* Cambridge: Cambridge University Press, 1987. Noted Aristotelian scholars focus on the relationship between Aristotle's biological researches and writings and the methods he proposed in works such as the *Analytics*.

Lindberg, David C. *The Beginnings of Western Science.* Chicago: University of Chicago Press, 1992. An introductory-level, award-winning book which aims clear and thorough explanations of ancient and medieval scientific ideas to a diverse audience.

McKeon, Richard. *Introduction to Aristotle.* Reprint. New York: Modern Library, 1992. A general introduction to Aristotle which mainly includes selections from a number of his works, with some discussion of his scientific method.

Sfendoni-Mentzou, Demetra, et al., eds. *Aristotle and Contemporary Science.* 2 vols. New York: P. Lang, 2000-2001. A collection of essays from a symposium held in 1997 assessing Aristotle's continuing influence on science in fields such as Newtonian and quantum mechanics, relativity theory, mathematics, cosmology, biology, psychology, philosophy of mind, logic, ethics, politics, poetics, and economics.

SEE ALSO: 600-500 B.C.E., Greek Philosophers Formulate Theories of the Cosmos; c. 500-400 B.C.E., Greek Physicians Begin Scientific Practice of Medicine; c. 380 B.C.E., Plato Develops His Theory of Ideas; c. 335-323 B.C.E., Aristotle Writes the *Politics*; c. 300 B.C.E., Euclid Compiles a Treatise on Geometry; c. 275 B.C.E., Greeks Advance Hellenistic Astronomy; c. 250 B.C.E., Discoveries of Archimedes; c. 157-201 C.E., Galen Synthesizes Ancient Medical Knowledge; 415 C.E., Mathematician and Philosopher Hypatia Is Killed in Alexandria.

RELATED ARTICLES in *Great Lives from History: The Ancient World*: Anaximander; Anaximenes of Miletus; Apollonius of Perga; Archimedes; Aristotle; Empedocles; Eudoxus of Cnidus; Hero of Alexandria; Hypatia; Plato; Pliny the Elder; Thales of Miletus.

323 B.C.E.

FOUNDING OF THE PTOLEMAIC DYNASTY AND SELEUCID KINGDOM

When Alexander the Great's generals divided his empire, Ptolemy Soter and Seleucus I Nicator acquired major realms, which their successors ruled for nearly three centuries.

LOCALE: Egypt and western Asia from the Mediterranean to India

CATEGORIES: Government and politics; wars, uprisings, and civil unrest

KEY FIGURES

Perdiccas (365-321 B.C.E.), regent for Philip III and Alexander IV, 323-321 B.C.E.

Ptolemy Soter (367/366-283/282 B.C.E.), ruler of Egypt, r. 305-285 B.C.E.

Seleucus I Nicator (358/354-281 B.C.E.), founder and ruler of the Seleucid Empire, r. 305-281 B.C.E.

Antigonus I Monophthalmos (382-301 B.C.E.), founder king of the Antigonid Dynasty, r. 306-301 B.C.E.

Demetrius Poliorcetes (336-283 B.C.E.), son of Antigonus I and king of Macedonia, r. c. 294-c. 288 B.C.E.

SUMMARY OF EVENT

Alexander the Great left no heir or obvious successor to rule an empire that extended from the Balkans to India when he died at Babylon on June 13, 323 B.C.E. On his deathbed, Alexander gave his signet ring to Perdiccas, his second-in-command. After rancorous debate, the generals present in Babylon accepted Perdiccas as regent for two members of Macedonia's royal dynasty—Alexander's mentally retarded half brother, who took the title Philip III Arrhidaeus, and Alexander's posthumous son, Alexander IV. First-rank generals were assigned to govern various provinces of the empire as satraps under the direction of the regent. Ptolemy received Egypt as his territory. Seleucus, a second-rank officer, did not receive a satrapy in 323 B.C.E. but was promoted to command of the Companion Cavalry, the position previously held by Perdiccas.

Ptolemy, one of the first satraps to conclude that Alexander's empire could not be held together, rapidly established his rule in Egypt. Ptolemy arrested the previous satrap, who had grown wealthy through corruption. After executing the offender, Ptolemy appropriated his fortune for himself. He sent forces to occupy Cyrenaica (modern-day Libya), asserting it was part of his territory. Perdiccas had arranged to send Alexander's embalmed corpse to Macedonia for burial in the ancient royal tombs. Ptolemy, however, intercepted the funeral cortege and brought it to Egypt, where he planned to build an elaborate mausoleum in which Alexander's remains would be exhibited.

Perdiccas, who wanted to keep Alexander's empire together and may have hoped to become king himself, found Ptolemy's independence infuriating. In 320 B.C.E., he set out with the royal army to attack Ptolemy but was unable to penetrate the Nile Delta and lost many men in the attempt. Perdiccas's officers revolted against his leadership and assassinated him. At a second division of the empire later that year, Seleucus, who had joined the revolt against Perdiccas, received the satrapy of Babylon, Ptolemy was confirmed as satrap of Egypt, and Antigonus replaced Perdiccas as commander of the royal army in Asia.

While still calling himself satrap, Ptolemy began behaving as though he were king. He chose Alexandria for his capital and erected a magnificent palace. Ptolemy desired to have Alexandria replace Athens as the cultural center of the Greek world. Near the palace he established his Museum (House of the Muses), to which he attracted outstanding artists, poets, scholars, and scientists, whose creative work the Ptolemies supported. Ptolemy and his son attempted to obtain copies of every known book for the adjoining library, assembling a collection that ultimately contained some half million papyrus rolls. To attract commerce, Ptolemy improved the city's harbor and started construction of an enormous lighthouse, the Pharos, which rose more than 350 feet (108 meters) and was celebrated as one of the Seven Wonders of the Ancient World.

Ptolemy began a religious policy designed to build support for his dynasty. During his satrapy, he carried out the religious duties that came with the office of pharaoh, rebuilding temples and carrying out the requisite sacri-

Ptolemy Soter. (Hulton|Archive)

fices. It was not until his actual coronation, at Memphis in 304 B.C.E., that the Egyptian priests sacrificed to him as pharaoh, the living god who maintained the divine order on earth and who would join the immortal deities after death. Ptolemy also built temples to the Greek gods, especially Dionysus, whom he claimed as an ancestor. When the citizens of Rhodes established a cult of Ptolemy the Savior to honor him for his help in defeating a siege by Demetrius Poliorcetes, he accepted their deification and the appellation of Soter (savior). However, Ptolemy Soter was not worshiped as a god by Greeks and Macedonians in Egypt until after his death. Ptolemy also sponsored the invention of a new god, Serapis, who formed a divine pair with Isis, uniting Greek and Egyptian religious symbols for the polyglot population within his kingdom.

Seleucus did not establish his independence as easily as Ptolemy had. Babylon was a wealthy province but could not provide its ruler with effective manpower. Seleucus, therefore, depended on mercenary soldiers to defend his rule. When Antigonus, commanding an overwhelming army, arrived in Babylon in 316 B.C.E. and called on Seleucus to account for his administration, Seleucus fled to Egypt. Ptolemy, who suspected that Antigonus hoped to establish himself as ruler of Alexan-

RULERS OF THE PTOLEMAIC DYNASTY, 323-30 B.C.E.

Ruler	*Reign*
Philip III Arrhidaeus	323-317
Alexander IV	323-311
Ptolemy Soter	305-285
Ptolemy II Philadelphus	288-246
Ptolemy III Euergetes	246-221
Ptolemy IV Philopator	221-205
Ptolemy V Epiphanes	205-180
Ptolemy VI Philometor	180-145
Ptolemy VII Neos Philopator	145
Ptolemy VIII Euergetes II	170-116
Ptolemy IX Soter II	116-107
Ptolemy X Alexander I	107-88
Ptolemy IX Soter II (restored)	88-80
Ptolemy XI Alexander II	80
Ptolemy XII Neos Dionysos	80-51
Cleopatra VII	51-30
Ptolemy XIII	51-47
Ptolemy XIV	47-44
Ptolemy XV Caesarion	44-30

der's entire domain, welcomed Seleucus and put him in charge of his fleet. Seleucus proved an effective commander at sea and on land. After operating successfully in the Aegean, he joined Ptolemy in defeating Demetrius at the Battle of Gaza in 312 B.C.E.

Seleucus I Nicator celebrated the victory by recruiting four thousand of Demetrius's vanquished mercenaries and returned to Babylon. His successors dated the establishment of the Seleucid Dynasty as 312 B.C.E. Seleucus's smaller force defeated two large armies Antigonus sent against him, and both times Seleucus added routed mercenaries to his army. He felt free to move east, where he took control of Media, Susa, Persis, Parthia, and Bactria. Unlike Alexander's other officers, Seleucus did not repudiate the Persian wife he had married at Alexander's command. He effectively used his wife and half-Persian son to portray his dynasty as legitimate rulers of his Asian, as well as his Greek and Macedonian, subjects. Seleucus earned the appellation Nicator (victorious) during his campaigns, being defeated only in India, where the winning general granted him many elephants (perhaps five hundred) when agreeing to a peace treaty.

Antigonus I Monophthalmos assumed the title of king in 306 B.C.E. after defeating Ptolemy's fleet at the Battle of Salamis (both Philip III and Alexander IV had already been killed); he then made his son Demetrius co-king. The next year Ptolemy and Seleucus also proclaimed themselves kings—Seleucus had been acting as a king since 312 B.C.E. and Ptolemy since 323 B.C.E. The three major Hellenistic dynasties were now openly established: the Antigonid in Europe, the Ptolemaic in Egypt, and the Seleucid in Asia.

SIGNIFICANCE

Ptolemy, unique among Alexander's successors in dying a natural death, created a compact kingdom, protected by the outlying territories of Cyrenaica, Cyprus, and Palestine. It outlasted all other Hellenistic monarchies until the death of Cleopatra VII and the Roman conquest in 30 b.c.e. His great city of Alexandria protected and expanded the Greek cultural and scientific heritage and then bequeathed it to medieval Europe and the Islamic world.

Of the various contenders, Seleucus came closest to reconstituting Alexander's empire. When he was assassinated in 281 B.C.E., he held (except for Egypt) most of the Persian Empire that Alexander had conquered and was poised to invade Europe, hoping to add Macedonia and Greece to his dominions. His realm stretched from the Mediterranean Sea almost to the Indus Valley and included much of present-day Turkey, plus Syria, Lebanon, Iraq, Iran, Afghanistan, and parts of Turkmenistan, Uzbekistan, Tajikistan, and Pakistan.

The Ptolemaic and Seleucid Dynasties influenced later religious and political ideas. The Ptolemaic cult of Isis and Serapis proved popular throughout the Greek-speaking world and spread across the Roman Empire. The worship of Isis, a gentle goddess and queen of Heaven, made it easy for believers to accept Christianity, with its cult of the Virgin Mary, mother of God. The Hellenistic principle of divine monarchs informed medieval and Renaissance theories of monarchy. Although Christian kings were not worshiped as gods, they considered themselves divinely chosen leaders whose acts could not be challenged by mortals.

—Milton Berman

FURTHER READING

Ellis, Walter M. *Ptolemy of Egypt*. New York: Routledge, 1994. Informative, favorable brief biography of Ptolemy.

Grainger, John D. *Seleukos Nicator: Constructing a Hellenistic Kingdom*. New York: Routledge, 1990. Detailed scholarly biography of the founder of the Seleucid kingdom.

Green, Peter. *Alexander to Actium: The Historical Evolution of the Hellenistic Age*. Berkeley: University of

California Press, 1990. Provides an excellent overview of the Hellenistic world in which Ptolemy and Seleucus flourished. Includes a detailed chronology from 323 to 30 B.C.E. and genealogies of the Hellenistic dynasties.

Hölbl, Günther. *A History of the Ptolemaic Empire*. Translated by Tina Saavedra. New York: Routledge, 2001. Stresses the political significance of the Ptolemaic treatment of Egyptian and Greek religion. Provides a useful chronology of Ptolemaic Egypt.

Sherwin-White, Susan M., and Amélie Kuhrt. *From Samarkhand to Sardis: A New Approach to the Seleucid Empire*. Berkeley: University of California Press, 1993. Contends that the Seleucid Empire was based on a partnership with many cultures, not just on Macedonian and Greek domination.

See also: 336 B.C.E., Alexander the Great Begins Expansion of Macedonia; 333 B.C.E., Battle of Issus; 332 B.C.E., Founding of Alexandria; October 1, 331 B.C.E., Battle of Gaugamela; 327-325 B.C.E., Alexander the Great Invades the Indian Subcontinent; c. 323-275 B.C.E., Diadochi Divide Alexander the Great's Empire.

Related articles in *Great Lives from History: The Ancient World*: Alexander the Great; Antigonus I Monophthalmos; Ptolemy Soter; Seleucus I Nicator.

c. 323-275 B.C.E.
Diadochi Divide Alexander the Great's Empire

After Alexander the Great's death, his empire, extending from Macedonia to India, was divided through warfare between his generals into three major kingdoms, continuing the spread of Greek culture eastward.

Locale: Macedonia (now northern Greece), Asia Minor (now Turkey), Syria, and Egypt

Categories: Expansion and land acquisition; government and politics; wars, uprisings, and civil unrest

Key Figures

Alexander the Great (356-323 B.C.E.), king of Macedonia, r. 336-323 B.C.E.

Perdiccas (365-321 B.C.E.), Macedonian general and territorial ruler

Antipater (397-319 B.C.E.), Macedonian statesman, regent of Macedonia, r. 321-319 B.C.E.

Antigonus I Monophthalmos (382-301 B.C.E.), Macedonian general and local ruler; king of Macedonia, r. 306-301 B.C.E.

Ptolemy Soter (367/366-283/282 B.C.E.), Macedonian general; governor of Egypt, 323-305 B.C.E.; king of Egypt, r. 305-285 B.C.E.

Seleucus I Nicator (358/354-281 B.C.E.), Macedonian general; satrap of Babylonia, 321-305 B.C.E.; king of Babylonia and surrounding territories, r. 305-281 B.C.E.

Summary of Event

The Macedonian king Alexander the Great, who had conquered Egypt and the entire Middle East extending into India, died in 323 B.C.E. without clearly designating a successor; his generals temporarily designated as corulers Alexander IV (r. 323-311 B.C.E.), Alexander's posthumous son by the Bactrian princess Roxana, and Philip III Arrhidaeus (r. 323-317 B.C.E.), Alexander's half brother who suffered from some kind of dysfunction, possibly mental retardation or epilepsy. Neither exercised power, and both were murdered on the orders of Alexander's warring generals within a few years. From 323 to 301 B.C.E., a series of civil wars resulted in the final division of the empire between three of Alexander's generals, known as the Diadochi (Greek for "successors"), after the battle of Ipsus in 301. At first Perdiccas, commander of the cavalry, was made regent and effectively controlled the Asiatic part of the empire, while Antipater, governor of Macedonia while Alexander was absent on campaign, was in command of the European part; shortly thereafter, the general Ptolemy was put in command of Egypt. In western Asia Minor (modern Turkey) Antigonus was made satrap (governor) of Phrygia, and in north Greece Lysimachus (c. 361-281 B.C.E.) was made satrap of Thrace. In 321 B.C.E., Antigonus, Antipater, and Ptolemy, accusing Perdiccas of trying to usurp the throne, made war with him; he was killed that year. Antipater was made regent by the victors but died in 319. Antigonus I Monophthalmos conquered all of Asia Minor except the area ruled by Eumenes (362-316 B.C.E.), formerly Alexander's secretary and a Greek.

The new Macedonian regent, Polyperchon (394-c. 303 B.C.E.), allied with Eumenes and fought Antigonus, who allied with Ptolemy and Antipater's son Cas-

THE DEATHS OF THE DIADOCHI, 321-281 B.C.E.	
Perdiccas	321, slain by mutineers who were bribed by Ptolemy
Craterus	320, killed by Eumenes while invading Cappadocia
Antipater	319, died
Eumenes	316, slain by own men who were bribed by Antigonus
Polysperchon	303, died
Antigonus	301, killed in battle with Seleucus and Lysimachus, allies of Cassander
Cassander	300, died after being recognized as king of Macedonia
Demetrius	283, died in prison
Ptolemy	283, died
Lysimachus	281, killed in hand-to-hand combat by Seleucus at Battle of Corupedion
Seleucus	280, murdered by Ptolemy Keraunos, disinherited son of Ptolemy

sander (c. 358-297 B.C.E.). In 316, Cassander took total control of the European part of the empire, ordering the deaths of Philip III and Olympias (c. 375-316 B.C.E.), Alexander's mother. In the same year, Eumenes, in Asia, was betrayed by his own troops and executed by order of Antigonus. Seleucus, who governed to Babylon (near modern Baghdad, Iraq), escaped to Egypt; Ptolemy, Cassander, and Lysimachus became allies against Antigonus in 315, restoring Seleucus to power in 312. In 311, a peace treaty gave Antigonus rule of most of the Asiatic part of the empire except the area from Babylon eastward, which was ruled by Seleucus I Nicator, although Seleucus had to give up India to local rulers. After 310, the empire was permanently divided into independent kingdoms.

Antigonus and his son Demetrius Poliorcetes (336-283 B.C.E.) tried to conquer the whole empire, succeeding only in Greece. In 301, at the battle of Ipsus in Phrygia (modern Turkey), the combined forces of Cassander, Lysimachus. Ptolemy Soter, and Seleucus decisively defeated Antigonus's army, and Antigonus was killed. Demetrius continued to hold parts of Greece and some cities in Asia Minor and Syria. Cassander's death in 297 enabled Demetrius to seize the Macedonian throne, but by 285, he was defeated and captured by the allied armies of Lysimachus and Pyrrhus of Epirus (319-272 B.C.E.), dying in captivity two years later. Lysimachus now ruled most of European Greece and Macedeonia and part of Asia Minor, turning against and defeating Pyrrhus, but defeated in his turn and killed by Seleucus's forces at the Battle of Corupedion in Lydia (modern Asiatic Turkey) in 281.

That same year, Seleucus was assassinated; warfare between the kingdoms set up by Alexander's generals continued until Antigonius's Macedonian kingdom and Antiochus's Asiatic kingdom were forced to ally in the face of an invasion by Gauls from the Danube valley in 279. Finally, after 275, the former empire of Alexander was divided into three major kingdoms, that of the Ptolemies in Egypt, with its capital at Alexandria; the revived Macedonian kingdom of the Antigonids (descendants of Antigonus), whose capital was Pella in Macedonia; and the Seleucid (descendants of Seleucus) empire centering on Syria and at first including the Asiatic part of the empire, with its capital at Antiochus (modern Antalya, in southeastern Turkey near the Mediterranean Sea).

SIGNIFICANCE

Subsequently there were wars between these kingdoms in southern Syria (modern Israel, Jordan, and southern Lebanon), and contests for the allegiance of the Greek city-states. In 224 B.C.E., Persia fought successfully for independence from the Seleucid Empire, which was driven back to the Euphrates River (in modern Iraq). In the following century, the Seleucids lost more and more territory, notably as a result of the Jewish revolt of 164, while in western Asia Minor (modern Turkey), a fourth kingdom, much smaller than the other three, was set up by Attalus (269-197 B.C.E.) at Pergamum (modern Bergama) in about 280. After four wars with the rising power of Rome, beginning in 229 B.C.E., the Antigonid state finally lost its independence to Rome in 146; Rome also conquered Greece. In 133 B.C.E., the last Attalid king of Pergamum died and bequeathed his kingdom to Rome, while what was left of the Seleucid kingdom, now reduced to Syria, was conquered in 64 B.C.E. by the Roman general Pompey (106-48 B.C.E.). The last of the Diadochi kingdoms to survive, the Ptolemaic state of Egypt, lost its independence to Rome at the Battle of Actium in 31 B.C.E.; its last ruler was the famous Cleopatra VII (69-30 B.C.E.).

The Hellenistic kingdoms of the Diadochi presided over Greek expansion into Asia and Africa, establishing large, multicultural cities, such as Alexandria and Antioch. The period was marked by a rise of syncretism in religion and the construction of elaborate artistic monuments such as the lighthouse of Alexandria, the Colossus of Rhodes, and the enormous Altar of Pergamum. It was also a time of great scholarship and scientific investigation, much of it promoted by the existence of the library of Alexandria.

—*Stephen A. Stertz*

Further Reading

Billows, Richard A. *Antigonos the One-Eyed and the Creation of the Hellenistic State*. Berkeley: University of California Press, 1995. A biography of Antigonus that synthesizes much research.

_______. *Kings and Colonists: Aspects of Macedonian Imperialism*. New York: E. J. Brill, 1995. A good general account of the jostling for power in the post-Alexander era. Index.

Bosworth, A. B. *The Legacy of Alexander: Politics, Warfare, and Propaganda Under the Successors*. New York: Oxford University Press, 2002. Discusses developments in Iran, India, Babylon, and Greece during the period 323-311 B.C.E. Includes a useful chronology.

Rostovzeff, Mikhail. *The Social and Economic History of the Hellenistic World*. 3 vols. 1941. Reprint. New York: Oxford University Press, 1993. A massive, standard general work. Bibliography and indexes.

Shipley, Graham. *The Greek World After Alexander, 323-30 B.C.* New York: Routledge, 2000. Discusses political changes in the Hellenistic world as well as developments in religion, literature, science, philosophy, and political thought. Bibliographies, indexes, and timeline.

Will, E. L. "The Formation of the Hellenistic Kingdoms" and "The Succession to Alexander." In *The Hellenistic World*. Vol. 7, part 1, of *Cambridge Ancient History*, edited by F. W. Walbank et al. 2d ed. New York: Cambridge University Press, 1984. Essential for the English reader.

See also: 359-336 B.C.E., Philip II Expands and Empowers Macedonia; 336 B.C.E., Alexander the Great Begins Expansion of Macedonia; 332 B.C.E., Founding of Alexandria; 327-325 B.C.E., Alexander the Great Invades the Indian Subcontinent; 323 B.C.E., Founding of the Ptolemaic Dynasty and Seleucid Kingdom.

Related articles in *Great Lives from History: The Ancient World*: Alexander the Great; Antigonus I Monophthalmos; Antiochus the Great; Cleopatra VII; Olympias; Philip II of Macedonia; Ptolemy Soter; Seleucus I Nicator.

c. 321 B.C.E.
Mauryan Empire Rises in India

The Mauryan Empire was the first indigenous centralized state in India: politically united, economically prosperous, militarily strong, and culturally vibrant.

Locale: India

Categories: Government and politics; wars, uprisings, and civil unrest; expansion and land acquisition

Key Figures

Chandragupta Maurya (c. 346-298 B.C.E.), Indian emperor, r. c. 321-301 B.C.E.

Dhanananda (d. c. 321 B.C.E.), Nanda king

Kauṭilya (fl. 300 B.C.E.), Indian philosopher, scholar, and adviser to Chandragupta Maurya

Alexander the Great (356-323 B.C.E.), king of Macedonia, r. 336-323 B.C.E.

Seleucus I Nicator (358/354-281 B.C.E.), Macedonian general, king of Babylonia and other territories, r. 305-281 B.C.E.

Summary of Event

The social origin and early life of Chandragupta Maurya, the founder of the Mauryan Dynasty, are obscure. Hindu literary tradition, notably the *Purāṇas* (anthologies of Hindu thought compiled in the fourth-sixth century C.E.) and Viśākhadatta's play *Mudrārākṣasa* (possibly fourth century C.E. or later; *Mudraraksasam*, 1900), describe him as the eldest son of Maurya, a prince of the Nanda Dynasty, who was the son of King Sarvarthasiddhi by his a mistress named Mura, most probably the daughter of a Persian resident of Pataliputra. However, two Buddhist texts based on earlier traditions—the *Mahāvamsatīkā* (compiled c. seventh-tenth centuries C.E.) and Upatissa's *Mahābodhivamsa* (c. tenth century)—describe Chandragupta as a Kṣatriya (member of the caste of nobles and warriors) hailing from the clan of the Moriyas, kinsmen of the Śakyas. According to these accounts, his father, the clan chief, died in a border fracas and left his family destitute. His widow, helped by her brothers, escaped to Pushpapura (Pataliputra), where she gave birth to a son, Chandragupta. The fatherless boy was taken by his maternal uncles to a cowherd's home to be raised in safe anonymity. At the age of seven or eight, the boy was sold by his foster father to a hunter to work at the latter's cattle ranch. As the story goes, once when the little boy was playing a "king-game" (*rajakilam*) at the village common with his companions, he was spotted by Kauṭilya, a wise, ambitious Brahman from Taxila and a former officer of the Magadhan court.

The Nanda kings, reputed to be base born, ruled the empire of Magadha (343-321 B.C.E.) with an iron hand. Kauṭilya had visited the Pataliputra court of Dhanananda (probably a nickname, literally meaning "opulent" Nanda; also known as Chandramas Nanda and as Agrammes or Xandramas in Greek accounts), the youngest of the five Nanda brothers. He had been placed in charge of the royal alms office but had lost the job because of his homely visage and arrogant manners. Deeply incensed at this insult, Kauṭilya had vowed to end Nanda rule and had escaped from Pataliputra in the guise of an Ājīvika ascetic. It was during his wanderings as an ascetic that he chanced on Chandragupta and noticed in the boy's speech and demeanor a potential for a royal career.

Following his education at Taxila, Chandragupta worked with Kauṭilya to begin assembling a coalition of forces to address the Greek domination of parts of northern India and then the Nandas of Magadha. Alexander the Great had crossed the Khyber Pass, entered the region of what is modern-day Pakistan, and defeated the Indian prince Porus at the Battle of Hydaspes (326 B.C.E.). However, the Greek conqueror faced multiple problems in holding on to his Indian conquests. The republican peoples (*arattas*, or *arastrakas*, kingless peoples) of the Punjab region had proved especially intractable. Moreover, Alexander was never sure of the areas that he had conquered, which were threatened by rebellions among both the Greeks and Indians. Sometime before 323, Alexander divided his Indian possessions into six satrapies, three on the west of the Indus, which he placed under Greek governors, and three on the east of the Indus, which he placed under Indian governors.

In the 1990's, these Mauryan period stupas were discovered near Sanchi. (AP/Wide World Photos)

The Greek biographer Plutarch (c. 46-after 120 C.E.) states in his account of Alexander that the young Chandragupta visited Alexander with the intention of inducing the Macedonian emperor to attack Magadha and depose the tyrant Dhanananda. Reportedly, Alexander was upset at the young Indian leader's proposal and ordered that he be killed. Under Kauṭilya's mentorship, Chandragupta began recruiting followers with a view to creating a coalition of powerful Indian rulers against the foreign rule of the Macedonian Greeks and subsequently ousting the Nandas from the throne of Magadha. Though the details of this Kauṭiya-Chandragupta enterprise are not available, doubtless Chandragupta found his ardent followers from among the *arastraka* peoples of the Punjab, who had opposed the Greek pres-

THE KINGS OF THE MAURYAN DYNASTY, C. 321-185 B.C.E.

Ruler	*Reign*
Chandragupta Maurya	c. 321-298
Bindusāra	298-273
Aśoka	273/265-238
Kunala	232-225
Daśaratha	232-225
Samprati	225-215
Salisuka	215-202
Devavarman	202-195
Satadhanvan	195-187
Bṛhadratha	187-185

ence in their land. In 326 B.C.E., when Alexander was busy with his military advance into the interior of the Indian subcontinent, Qandahār raised the standard of rebellion under an Indian chief known as Samaxus in the Greek accounts, and the Ashvayana people killed the Greek governor Nicanor. His replacement, Philip, an experienced army commander, was also assassinated. The Greek position was weakened further with Alexander's untimely death in Babylon in 323. By 321, the Greeks withdrew from Indian territories, and as the historian Justin (second century C.E.) reports, Chandragupta liberated the Greek-occupied regions of India.

Chandragupta's next mission, battle with the Nandas, began in earnest but ended in failure because of his strategic blunder of trying to take over the interior of the country without first conquering the frontiers. After this failure, he completed the conquest of the frontier regions, stationing garrisons to protect them against rebellions. He then led his vast force toward Magadha, besieged Pataliputra, and following a grim, pitched battle with the Magadhan commander, Bhaddasala, either deposed or killed the incumbent ruler Dhanananda in 321 B.C.E.

Having conquered Magadha and extended his sway over the Punjab region up to the Indus, Chandragupta dealt with Seleucus I Nicator, Alexander's famous general who had become the ruler of Babylon by about 305 B.C.E. Intending to recover the Indian regions from Chandragupta's control, Seleucus crossed the Indus around 305-304. His expedition, however, led to a settlement with Chandragupta in which the Greeks ceded the satrapies of Qandahār, Kabul, Herāt, and Bluchistan to the Indians and Chandragupta presented five hundred war elephants to Seleucus. A diplomatic relation between the two former adversaries was established following the appointment of Megasthenes (c. 342-282 B.C.E.) by Seleucus as his official ambassador at the court of Magadha. Plutarch provides a vivid description of Chandragupta's further conquests south of the Vindhya range and writes that the emperor of Magadha subdued the whole of India.

Two sources—Megasthenes's celebrated account *Indica* (third century B.C.E.; original lost, fragments translated as *Ancient India as Described by Megasthenes and Arrian*, 1877) and Kauṭilya's *Arthaśāstra* (dates vary, c. fourth century B.C.E.-third century C.E.; *Treatise on the Good*, 1961)—provide detailed descriptions of the Mauryan administration and government as well as the social and economic condition of India under Chandragupta's reign. The Jain traditions speak of Chandragupta's conversion to Jainism and his abdication of his throne in his late middle age. He became a disciple of the Jain saint Yatindra Bhadrabahu of the Digambara sect, who, following a famine in Pataliputra, led a migration of the Digambara Jain residents of Magadha toward Mysore. The Mauryan emperor is believed to have ended his life at Sravana Belgola, following the Jain practice of fasting to death.

SIGNIFICANCE

The Mauryan Empire (c. 321-c. 185 B.C.E.) was the first united, centralized state in post-Buddhist India and was characterized by a sort of benevolent despotism that was efficient and effective. In his *Treatise on the Good*, Kauṭilya described the structure of government and administration during Chandragupta Maurya's reign, and Megasthenes commented on the prosperity, security, and all-round cultural fecundity of the land at the time.

—Narasingha P. Sil

FURTHER READING

Bhargava, Purushottam L. *Chandragupta Maurya: A Gem of Indian History*. New Delhi: D. K. Printworld, 1996. Straightforward, popular, but dependable biography.

Chattopadhyaya, C. D. "Early Life of Chandragupta Maurya." In Vol. 1 of *B.C. Law Volume*, edited by Devdatta R. Bhandarkar et al. Calcutta, India: Bhandarkar Oriental Research Institute, 1945. A deeply scholarly investigation by a renowned expert.

Dikshitar, V. R. Ramachandra. *Mauryan Polity*. Delhi: Motilal Banarasidass, 1993. A standard study of administration and government under the Mauryan Dynasty.

McCrindle, John W. *McCrincle's Ancient India: As De-*

scribed by Megasthenes and Arrian. 1877. Reprint. New Delhi: International Books and Periodicals Supply Service, 1984. Classic sourcebook of ancient accounts of the reign of Chandragupta Maurya.

Mookerji, Radha K. *Chandragupta Maurya and His Times*. 4th ed. Delhi: Motilal Banarasidass, 1999. A truly magisterial study, first published in 1943.

Pradhan, Sita N. *Chronology of Ancient India from the Times of the Rigvedic King Divodasa to Chandragupta Maurya with Glimpses into the Political History of the Period*. 1927. Reprint. Varanasi: Bharatiya Publishing House, 1979. Helpful political history of the period. A sound background of the history of the Mauryan regime.

Raychaudhuri, Hemchandra. *Political History of Ancient India from the Accession of Parikshit to the Extinction of the Gupta Dynasty*. Commentary by Bratindra N. Mukherjee. 7th ed. Delhi: Oxford University Press, 1996. A classic work, first published in 1923.

Sastri, K. A. Nilkanta, ed. *A Complete History of India*. Vol. 2. Bombay: Orient Longmans, 1957. Superb history by an acknowledged master. Especially good in respect to the history of Mauryan rule in the south.

Smith, Vincent A. *The Early History of India from 600 B.C. to the Muhammadan Conquest: Including the Invasion of Alexander*. 4th ed. Oxford: Clarendon Press, 1962. Standard scholarly account in spite of some criticism by postcolonial scholars of India.

SEE ALSO: c. 4th century B.C.E.-3d century C.E., Kauṭilya Compiles a Treatise on Practical Statecraft; 336 B.C.E., Alexander the Great Begins Expansion of Macedonia; 327-325 B.C.E., Alexander the Great Invades the Indian Subcontinent; c. 323-275 B.C.E., Diadochi Divide Alexander the Great's Empire.

RELATED ARTICLES in *Great Lives from History: The Ancient World*: Alexander the Great; Chandragupta Maurya; Seleucus I Nicator.

c. 320 B.C.E.
THEOPHRASTUS INITIATES THE STUDY OF BOTANY

The Greek scientist Theophrastus wrote The Causes of Plants *and* The History of Plants, *initiating the study of botany.*

LOCALE: Athens
CATEGORIES: Cultural and intellectual history; science and technology; philosophy

KEY FIGURE
Theophrastus (c. 372-c. 287 B.C.E.), Greek philosopher

SUMMARY OF EVENT
Peri phytikon historion (translated in *Enquiry into Plants and Minor Works on Odours and Weather Signs*, 1916; often designated by the Latin title, *De historia plantarum*) and *Peri phytikon aition* (partial translation in *De Causis Plantarum*, 1976) are the earliest substantial works of botany written in ancient Greek. They are most commonly referred to as *The History of Plants* and *The Causes of Plants*. Together they provide a full system of botany. Although earlier writers often focused only on the dietary or medicinal value of plants, Theophrastus was interested in plants as a form of knowledge. *The History of Plants* provides descriptions and contains nine books. In the first book, he considers general issues such as identification of the parts of plants and their division into tree, shrub, undershrub, and herb. The remaining books treat particular issues: the growth and care of domestic trees, wild plants, trees and plants of distant places, the timbers and their specific uses, shrubs, herbaceous plants, saps, and medicinal uses of plants. *The Causes of Plants* treats physiology and consists of six books: how plants come into being, including grafting and budding; how the environment affects plants; how culture affects plants; how cereals originated and became cultivated; unnatural influences, including disease and death; and the odor and taste of plants.

Discussion of around 550 plant species and varieties native to the regions between the Atlantic and India appears in these works. Theophrastus's sources include poets, philosophers, and especially Empedocles (c. 490-c. 430 B.C.E.) and Democritus (c. 460-c. 370 B.C.E.)—pre-Socratic philosophers who had written about plants. He also records the beliefs and practices of those native to the regions in which particular plants grew, such as farmers, physicians, and root-cutters. In addition, he includes oral reports, technical writings, and even the notes of companions of Alexander the Great who studied plants for their military significance. Although it might seem "unscientific" to present travelers' tales and even superstitions in a scientific work, such was the practice

Theophrastus, as portrayed on the cover of a seventeenth century botanical book. (Library of Congress)

even into the eighteenth century. Moreover, Theophrastus often cautions the reader that further investigation was necessary.

Originally named Tyrtamus, Theophrastus was born in Eresus on the island of Lesbos. According to Diogenes Laertius, he studied first with Alcippus, then with Plato, and finally with Aristotle, who renamed him Theophrastus (he of the godlike speech) because of the divine way in which he spoke. When Aristotle retired to Chalcis in 322 B.C.E., Theophrastus assumed leadership of the Lyceum, attracting two thousand students during the course of his long life.

Theophrastus in the main accepted Aristotle's metaphysical assumptions, though he did question their application. In particular he doubted Aristotle's reliance on teleology, or the idea that everything has a purpose. In the heavens, but more particularly on Earth, coincidence or necessity seems to characterize events, such as the birth and nutrition of animals. As phenomena vary in the degree to which they manifest order, Theophrastus argued that there must be different ways of knowing things. Reason knows first principles, for example, while the senses know the causes of natural objects, such as inanimate things, animals, and plants. On the other hand, Aristotle had employed the methods of observation, and Theophrastus's botanical works parallel Aristotle's *Ton peri ta zōa historiai* (c. 348-346 B.C.E.; *Zoology*, 1812) and *Peri zōōn moriōn* (c. 335-323 B.C.E.; *On the Parts of Animals*, 1882). The empirical aspect of Aristotle's thought appealed greatly to Theophrastus. Although Theophrastus did recognize analogies between plant and animal, he realized their limitations. Furthermore, he recognized the difficulties of generalizations about plants because, as a whole, they do not all share parts in common. Plants without roots, stem, flowers, or other parts exist. Thus, there is a method of knowledge unique to plants. The object of study was therefore not the universal but the particular, grounded in sense perceptions and not in reason.

Although Theophrastus is often called the "father of botany," he, like his teacher Aristotle, was interested in a wide range of subjects, both philosophical and scientific. Diogenes Laertius lists 224 titles authored by Theophrastus, including works on logic, metaphysics, ethics, law, medicine, religion, mathematics, the natural sciences, and earlier philosophers, totaling 232,850 lines. Other than the two botanical books, only a few short scientific treatises; an essay on metaphysics; the *Characteres ethikoi* (c. 319 B.C.E.; *The Moral Characters of Theophrastus*, 1702, best known as *Characters*), which illustrates Aristotle's moral types; and fragments or summaries of a few other works exist today.

SIGNIFICANCE

Theophrastus's observations led to many distinctions that form the foundation of the science of botany. Although he did not use the modern terms, he recognized the differences between parenchymatous and prosenchymatous tissues; between petalous and apetalous flowers; among hypogynous, perigynous, and epigynous insertions of the corolla, between angiosperms and gynmosperms; and between monocotyledons and dicotyledons. Some of his accounts, such as that of germinating seeds, reveal careful personal observation. Ideas from his botanical works may have found their way into Arabic commentaries, and in the late fifteenth century the first two Latin translations of these works appeared. The plant descriptions of Otto Brunfels (1488-1534) and Leonhard Fuchs (1501-1566) used word-for-word translations from the works of Theophrastus and other ancient botanists.

—*Kristen L. Zacharias*

FURTHER READING

Fortenbaugh, William W., Pamela M. Huby, and Anthony A. Long, eds. *Theophrastus of Eresus: Sources for His Life, Writings, Thought, and Influence*. 2 vols. Leiden, the Netherlands: E. J. Brill, 1993. The first scholarly effort in more than a century to collect all the historical documents—text, translations, and commentary—on the fragments of and testimonies about Theophrastus. A collection of articles on a wide variety of Theophrastus's works, including pieces on teleology and the transmission of his works into Arabic.

Greene, Edward Lee. *Landmarks of Botanical History.* Part 1. Edited by Frank N. Egerton. Stanford, Calif.: Stanford University Press, 1983. Written in the late nineteenth century, this reissued work presents a long chapter on the botany of Theophrastus arguing that his works were the basis of the botany of the sixteenth century.

Sharples, R. W. *Theophrastus of Eresus: Sources for His Life, Writings, Thought, and Influence*. New York: E. J. Brill, 1995. Presents a short overview of Theophrastus's botanical works and comments on the doxographical references to these works.

Theophrastus. *Metaphysics*. Translated, with an introduction and commentary, by Marlein Van Raalte. New York: E. J. Brill, 1993. A translation that includes an extensive analysis of its passages, especially Theophrastus's views on teleology.

SEE ALSO: 6th-4th century B.C.E. (traditionally, 1st millennium B.C.E.), Suśruta, Indian Physician, Writes Medical Compendium; c. 500-400 B.C.E., Greek Physicians Begin Scientific Practice of Medicine; 325-323 B.C.E., Aristotle Isolates Science as a Discipline; c. 300 B.C.E., Stoics Conceptualize Natural Law; c. 157-201 C.E., Galen Synthesizes Ancient Medical Knowledge.

RELATED ARTICLES in *Great Lives from History: The Ancient World*: Anaxagoras; Anaximander; Archimedes; Aristotle; Democritus; Empedocles; Pliny the Elder; Theophrastus.

312 B.C.E.
FIRST ROMAN AQUEDUCT IS BUILT

The first Roman aqueduct was built to transport water into cities to supply community baths and inaugurated an advance in hydraulic engineering and architecture that continued to operate in Europe for many centuries.

LOCALE: Rome (now in Italy) and numerous cities under its dominion

CATEGORY: Science and technology

KEY FIGURE

Sextus Julius Frontinus (c. 35-103 C.E.), appointed water commissioner by Nerva in 97 C.E.

SUMMARY OF EVENT

The engineering of aqueduct construction was complicated and based on a piecemeal evolution of techniques over five hundred years. The water, tapped from springs, streams, or reservoirs, was allowed to descend down a gently sloping channel until it reached a point of distribution. The main conduit was generally rather tall and narrow, approximately 5 feet by 2 feet (1.5 meters by 0.6 meter). Because of the gravitational flow of the water, aqueducts had to be laid out carefully. If their slope was too slight, the water became sluggish; if it was too steep, pressures would build up to cause overflowing and ruptures. Vitruvius (fl. first century B.C.E.), the celebrated architect of Augustus's time, recommended a fall of one in two hundred, an excellent gradient which could not, however, always be maintained. Because the velocity of the water needed to be controlled and hills and valleys had to be circumvented, an aqueduct was usually much longer than the straight distance between inlet and outlet. The aqueducts operated on the principle of constant offtake, so the outlets within the city were always open. Once an aqueduct was finished, it required constant maintenance to clean out deposits left by the hard Roman water.

An aqueduct could be constructed in three different ways. It could be led through a tunnel cut into the ground, laid in a ditch and covered over, or raised above the surface of the ground on a wall or series of arches. This last

A Roman aqueduct in Segovia, Spain. (PhotoDisc)

procedure generally recommended itself because its building materials were cheap while lead pipe for laying underground was expensive. Still, a long aqueduct often made use of all three methods. The first Roman aqueduct, the Aqua Appia of 312 B.C.E., ran its 10-mile (16-kilometer) course mostly underground, as did the Aqua Anio Vetus of 272 B.C.E. The third Roman aqueduct, however, the Aqua Marcia, built in 144-140 B.C.E., drew its waters from the Anio River behind Tivoli only 16 miles (26 kilometers) northeast of Rome and traveled 58 miles (93 kilometers) before it reached the city. It was a high-level type aqueduct that crossed the Roman campagna on a series of arches nearly 6 miles (10 kilometers) long and entered the city at a level of 195 feet (60 meters) above the Tiber River, high enough to supply the Capitoline, Caelian, and Aventine hills. When the Aqua Tepula of 125 B.C.E. and the Aqua Julia of 40 B.C.E. were built, their channels were superimposed upon those of the Marcian aqueduct near its approach to the city, making Tepula and Julia high-level types as well. The Aqua Virgo of 19 B.C.E., terminating in the Campus Martius, and the Aqua Alsietina of 2 B.C.E., supplying the Trastevere, were again underground. The famous Aqua Claudia was a very lofty structure reaching the highest hills of the city including the Palatine. The Aqua Traiana of 109 C.E., with its outlet on the Janiculum, had underground conduits, while the Aqua Alexandrina of 226 C.E. was carried on arches for most of its course.

The same methods of construction were used in the provinces. Occasionally refinements were made, as in the aqueducts of Lyons, where siphons were used to carry water down and then up the other side of a valley or ravine. Siphons were probably used more often than most scholars have yet recognized. Bridges of arches were utilized by Roman engineers only in valleys that were up to 164 feet (50 meters) deep. Deeper valleys were crossed by means of siphons, and the number of siphons also depended on the number of valleys traversed by the aqueduct. Among the more famous remains of provincial aqueducts is the magnificent Pont du Gard, the bridge of the aqueduct for the city of Nîmes in southern France. This aqueduct, 31 miles (50 kilometers) long, crossed the Gard on a triple row of arches 900 feet (274 meters) long and 162 feet (49 meters) above the river. Built during the reign of Augustus, it remains one of the finest extant examples of Roman engineering. Hardly less spectacular is the gray granite bridge of the aqueduct of Segovia in Spain. Still in use, it crosses the valley next to the city on a series of arches 2,530 feet (771 meters) in length and 94 feet (29 meters) at their greatest height. In this category belongs also the magnificent span of the Roman aqueduct at Cherchel in Algeria, which served ancient Caesarea. One of the most impressive sights in north Africa is the ruins of the aqueduct built by Hadrian to bring water from inland mountains to Carthage. It was 82 miles (132 kilometers) in length, and some of its arches, 341 of which are still standing, reached a height of 130 feet (40 meters).

Although it is impossible to say when Roman aqueduct construction reached its apogee, one might well hold that the building of the famous Aqua Claudia best represents that point in history. When this aqueduct was dedicated on August 1, 52 C.E., the birthday of the emperor whose name it bears, the famous Sextus Julius Frontinus (c. 35-c. 103 C.E.) was already seventeen. Frontinus was the man who, as *curator aquarum* from 97 C.E. until some time before 103, was to be the authority on Roman aqueducts through his celebrated work *De aquis urbis Romae* (n.d.; *Aqueducts*, 1925).

The Claudia, begun in 38 C.E. under Emperor Caligula, is often regarded as the highest sustained achievement in Roman aqueduct construction. As the last and in many ways the most impressive stone aqueduct, Frontinus considered it especially magnificent. Conceived on a greater scale than any before it, it stretched virtually across the campagna, drawing water from a spring near Tivoli to enter Rome by the now-famous *Porta Maggiore*, the eastern entrance into the city. Of its far-reaching line of arches, one section of 154 still stands intact together with many smaller groups of arches, one of which preserves the highest point of the aqueduct at more than 88 feet (27 meters). The enormous size of the undressed stones, laid dry, makes the work remarkable. Together with its associated aqueduct, the Aqua Anio Novus, it cost the Roman government fifty-five million sesterces.

SIGNIFICANCE

Beyond Frontinus, primary accounts of the aqueducts are limited. Strabo (64/63 B.C.E.-after 23 C.E.) praised the skills of the engineers in his geographical works, while Vitruvius included one chapter on aqueducts in his famous ten books on architecture. Frontinus himself appears to have been an administrative manager with no hydraulic experience, composing *De aquis urbis Romae* to show that he had mastered knowledge of the aqueducts. Yet enough has been learned of the aqueducts to know that Romans perceived them as the mark of civilized living, well worth the constant maintenance and expense they required. Successfully supplying millions of gallons of water to Rome's major cities, aqueducts were made to look beautiful to display them as the focus of civic pride that they were.

—M. Joseph Costelloe,
updated by Amy Ackerberg-Hastings

FURTHER READING

Aicher, Peter J. *Guide to the Aqueducts of Ancient Rome*. Wauconda, Ill.: Bolchazy-Carducci, 1995. Provides a history of the construction of the aqueducts, an in-depth discussion of each of the eleven aqueducts of Rome, and a field guide to the ruins. Appendices include an information chart on the ancient aqueducts, information on modern Roman aqueducts, and a summary of relevant inscriptions. Maps, figures, bibliography, and index.

Evans, Harry B. *Water Distribution in Ancient Rome: The Evidence of Frontinus*. Ann Arbor: University of Michigan Press, 1994. Evans, a historian of ancient engineering, includes a translation of *De Aquis* and analysis of Frontinus' descriptions of Roman aqueducts.

Hodge, A. Trevor. *Roman Aqueducts and Water Supply*. 2d ed. Newburyport, Mass.: Focus: 2002. A comprehensive study that covers all aspects of aqueduct construction and function. An unusually practical study of ancient water supply methods.

_______. "Siphons in Roman Aqueducts." *Scientific American* 252 (June, 1985): 114-119. Well-explained account of the technology involved in Roman aqueducts.

Landels, J. G. *Engineering in the Ancient World*. Rev. ed. Berkeley: University of California Press, 2000. Includes a substantial chapter on water engineering, as well as chapters on Vitruvius and Frontinus. The author is a rare combination of classicist and engineer.

O'Connor, Colin. *Roman Bridges*. New York: Cambridge University Press, 1993. O'Connor's explanation of Roman engineering in this area treats the aqueduct as a special bridge.

SEE ALSO: 447-438 B.C.E., Building of the Parthenon; 312-264 B.C.E., Building of the Appian Way.